THE GOLF COURSE

Geoffrey S. Cornish and Ronald E. Whitten

Foreword by Robert Trent Jones

Special Photography by Brian D. Morgan

The Rutledge Press
New York, New York

The authors gratefully acknowledge permission to quote from:

T. C. Simpson and others, *The Game of Golf* (London: The Lonsdale Library, Seeley Service and Co., Ltd., 1931).

Herbert Warren Wind, "Understanding Golf Course Architecture" from *Golf Digest Magazine*, November 1966. Copyright © 1981 by Golf Digest/Tennis Inc.

Bernard Darwin, *James Braid* (London: Hodder & Stoughton, 1952). Reprinted with the permission of A. P. Watt, Ltd.

Walter Travis, "Merits and Demerits of the Garden City Links" from *Country Life Magazine*, February 1906. Reprinted with the permission of Doubleday & Co., Garden City, New York.

Charles Blair Macdonald, *Scotland's Gift: Golf* (New York: Charles Scribner's Sons, 1928). Reprinted with the permission of Charles Scribner's Sons.

H. J. Whigham, "The Ideal Golf Links" from *Scribner's Magazine*, May 1909. Copyright © 1909 by Charles Scribner's Sons; copyright renewed. Reprinted with the permission of Charles Scribner's Sons.

W. C. Fownes, "Oakmont—Where You Must Play Every Shot" from *The Golf Journal*, May 1973. Reprinted with the permission of the United States Golf Association.

Robert Trent Jones, "The Common Interests of the Golf Architect and the Greenkeeper" from *The Greenkeeper's Reporter*, February 1935. Reprinted with the permission of the Golf Course Superintendents Association of America.

Horace G. Hutchinson, *Fifty Years of Golf* (New York: Charles Scribner's Sons, 1919). Reprinted with the permission of Charles Scribner's Sons.

William S. Flynn, "Golf Course Architecture and Construction—Analysis of Layout" from *Bulletin of the Green Section of the USGA*, October 1927. Reprinted with the permission of the United States Golf Association.

James Braid, *Advanced Golf* (London: Methuen and Co., Ltd., 1908).

Robert Trent Jones, "Design with Respect to Play" from *The Golf Journal*, June 1959. Reprinted with the permission of the United States Golf Association.

Revised edition, 1987

Published by The Rutledge Press
A Division of W. H. Smith Publishers Inc., 112 Madison Avenue, New York, New York 10016

Second Printing 1982; Revised 3rd Printing 1984
Printed in the United States of America
Designed by Allan Mogel

Library of Congress Cataloging in Publication Data

Cornish, Geoffrey S.,
    The golf course.

    Bibliography: p.
    Includes index.
    1. Golf Courses—History.   2. Golf courses—Designs and plans.   3. Architects—Biography.
4. Golf courses—Great Britain. 5. Golf courses—United States.   I. Whitten, Ronald E.   II. Title.
GV975.C65   796.352'068   81-10627
ISBN 0-8317-3943-6

Title Page: *Cape Cod, Massachusetts. As the ocean receded, sandy fields formed. Golf evolved over five centuries in Scotland, on these fields or links along the estuaries of the rivers Eden, Tay and Forth, endowing the game with a mystical link to sand.*

Contents

Foreword

Until now, the hundreds of books and the millions of words that have been written about the great game of golf have been conspicuously deficient in detailing the men who have been responsible for providing the very cornerstone of the game—the golf course architects.

With few exceptions they have suffered an undeserved anonymity. This despite the fact they have created an art form on one of the broadest canvases available to man and despite the fact their work has been admired and enjoyed for centuries. It has been their unwarranted fate to have left the mark of their genius without true recognition.

The Golf Course will right a wrong that has been more than 200 years in persisting. Geoffrey S. Cornish and Ronald E. Whitten finally have set the record straight. This book is a monumental achievement, one that adds a previously missing and vital chapter to the history of golf. It is an accomplishment I know was years in compiling and one for which golfers the world over and especially golf course architects ever will be indebted.

Besides serving to identify the practitioners of our profession from the past as well as those presently actively engaged, this book also gives credit to those who were responsible for innovations that not only changed the appearance of golf courses, but that materially affected the method of play. Golf today, in all honesty, is what the golf course architects have made it—a game of relaxed recreation and limitless enjoyment for millions and a demanding examination of exacting standards for those few who would seek to excel—depending on the requirements of the moment.

I found *The Golf Course* to be fascinating and, to a certain degree, not unlike viewing a long-forgotten movie on television. It revived memories of "giants" I had known in the past: Stanley Thompson, with whom I was associated early in my career; Albert W. Tillinghast, who told me of his work as we walked the fairways during the playing of the 1934 U.S. Open at Merion; and Donald Ross at Pinehurst during the founding of the American Society of Golf Course Architects in 1948.

One of the outstanding accomplishments of the book is the tracing of the "lineage" of many who started their careers as golf course construction workers or as assistants to other architects and who went on to become golf course architects in their own right. Also identified are the sons of architects who have continued and perpetuated the names of their fathers in the profession.

I would be remiss if I did not acknowledge the role credited to me and to my sons, Bob, Jr., and Rees, in the profession. It is most gratifying to know my work has been recognized and appreciated by my peers.

Geoff Cornish and Ron Whitten are to be complimented for a job well done. They have written a long-overdue book that has done a great service to the game and to the men who have made it possible.

Robert Trent Jones

P. 6–7: Links holes at Spyglass Hill GC, Ca., by Jones. The natural links of Scotland form the foundation for the practice of course architecture.

Preface

Golf is one of those few games played on a field with virtually no rigid dimensions. Why? Obviously, size has something to do with it. An eighteen-hole course typically requires well over a hundred acres, and such a large area is far more difficult to standardize than the relatively small space of a football field or a tennis court. Geographic variation is another factor. The game has been played in many different locales, on widely differing terrains. It has proved impossible, even if it were desirable, to create a standard playing field adaptable to all sites.

But these facts alone do not provide a complete explanation. Even courses of the same acreage, situated side by side on similar terrains, can look and play quite differently. So there must be a more fundamental reason for all the variety found on golf layouts. And, indeed, there is. The fact is that every individual who has ever laid out a course has had his own particular ideas as to how it should be done.

Golfers should cherish that fact, for the endless variety of golf layouts has added much to the charm and interest of the sport, and even more to the challenge of mastering it. Yet the men responsible for this endless variety, the golf course architects, have been largely forgotten by the golfing public. The aim of this book is to re-introduce them.

Not all golf architects were masters of the art, by any means. Some, indeed, were amazingly casual in the creation of their designs. Nevertheless, almost all of them influenced, to a greater or lesser degree, the development of the game. As a collective discipline, the practice of golf course architecture has had an impact reaching beyond golf itself, into such realms as concern for the environment and the aesthetics of our landscape.

Herb Graffis, longtime close observer of the golf scene, once compared the efforts of course designers with those of the artists who planned the gardens of the French chateaux and stately English country homes of earlier centuries. The comparison was apt. Golf architecture has indeed become an art, with each course a small collection of eighteen unique compositions.

This book is a history of the men who practiced the art of golf design. The subject has not been examined to any great degree before. Previous books on golf design, especially those by H. S. Colt, Alister Mackenzie, George C. Thomas, Jr., and Robert Hunter, were superior treatises on the philosophy of course architecture; but none documented the evolution of courses nor the persons contributing to it. In contrast, this book touches only briefly upon philosophy of design, for it is so comprehensive a topic as to warrant a separate volume of its own.

This book is not a history of the game itself, its championships or its great champions. Those topics have been covered elsewhere many times, and exceedingly well, by such writers as Bernard Darwin and Herbert Warren Wind. In addition, such events had only indirect bearing on course design.

Nor is the book a history of the implements and rules of the game. These have affected golf course architecture, but limitations of space have necessitated brevity in their treatment here.

Finally, this is not a book on the history of course maintenance. Certainly the course superintendent has been the single most important figure in maintaining and embellishing the designer's creation, and it was with difficulty that we refrained from devoting a major portion of the text to the development of turfgrass science and course maintenance. But, as with other topics, these are of collateral interest, and so discussion of them has been limited.

What is contained in this book is a comprehensive history of the men who practiced golf course architecture and the way in which their art evolved. The narrative portion of the text traces the development of the profession from its early days in Scotland to achievements of the very recent past. It focuses upon many of the architects who had an impact, favorable or otherwise, on golf courses through the years, and concludes with an analysis of their accomplishments.

The second portion of the book profiles several hundred men who made important contributions to the his-

8

P. 9: Hole #15, Cypress Point GC, California, by Mackenzie. Britishers carried links traditions around the world. Alister Mackenzie, the first international designer, established his reputation here. Of the architects active between the Wars, his philosophy most influenced post-War design.

tory of course design. A perusal of the profiles reveals some fascinating sidelights of this history. One is the fact that for many, many years, golf course architects came from other vocations. There were golf professionals, superintendents, engineers and agronomists, of course; but there were also bankers, lawyers, professors, physicians and even a socialist politician. Clearly the lure of golf design extended to men from all walks of life, at least until contemporary demand for specialization established landscape architecture as the preferred academic background.

Another significant fact revealed by the profiles is the striking continuity between generations of designers. Perhaps no other art has displayed it on quite such a scale. Dozens of father-and-son or designer-and-apprentice combinations are evident, reaching beyond a single generation and sometimes into several. Indeed, if all architects were plotted on a graph, very few would be unconnected with at least one other designer. The profile section also contains the most comprehensive listings of architects' works ever compiled, followed by an outline of miscellaneous matters related to this history. Another section contains a master list of golf courses cross referenced to their designers, both those profiled and others.

The major goals of this book are to provide an awareness to the golfing public of the many factors and influences that affect golf courses, and to promote a better understanding of the one that affects them most—the golf course architect. At one point in the text we have broadly categorized designers, but final judgment of their worth must rest with the individual golfer. It might be pointed out, however, that if one characteristic separated the successful from the unsuccessful designer, it was tenacity. Former USGA President Frank Tatum, Jr., put it best: "The ones whose work has survived are those who have had the wit and guts to get it right regardless." [1]

In the pages that follow, we believe you will discover that many tenacious golf architects did "get it right regardless." The world of golf is better because of them, and perhaps the world at large is a little better because of what they wrought.

[1] Paper presented to the American Society of Golf Course Architects, Pebble Beach, California, April 1976.

P. 10-11: *Hole #7, Shoal Creek GC, by Nicklaus. The challenge of golf course design has lured persons from all walks of life, including a number of the greatest golfers of all time.*

PART ONE

1.

Golf Evolves on the Links of Scotland

Games similar to golf have been played in Europe since the Middle Ages. But it was in Scotland that a pastime using a club, a ball and a hole developed, over a period of 500 years or more, into the game we know today as golf. In this same time span, the playing fields of the game evolved into what are today called golf courses. The earliest of these playing fields were found on the Scottish linksland. The location of linksland, often publicly owned, in a northern latitude where summer daylight hours extend from 3 A.M. to 11 P.M. made it possible for persons other than those of a leisure class to use them. Thus, golf established an early democratic tradition in Scotland.

It has been a widely held belief that the term "links" refers to Scottish courses located on sandy deposits left centuries ago along the seacoast by the receding ocean. From a golf architect's point of view this is only partially true. The North Sea may well have deposited rolling dunes of sand along the shoreline, but true linksland consisted of rich alluvial deposits of soil left upon sand dunes by a river as it flowed into the sea. True links, then, would be the golf courses formed by nature on or near river estuaries. Indeed, the game of golf was first played in Scotland along the estuaries of the rivers Eden, Tay and Forth.

The earliest Scottish links were designed entirely by nature. A typical links consisted of high, windswept sand dunes and of hollows where grass grew if the soil was reasonably substantial. The grass was predominantly bentgrass with a little fescue interspersed. Its stiff, erect blades, characteristic of turf growing in close proximity to salt water, were sufficient to support the leather-bound, feather-stuffed golf ball.

The terrain of a linksland usually dictated the route a player would follow. Golfers who batted their "featheries" about a links naturally aimed their shots for the playable sward. The dunes were to be avoided, for the only vegetation that grew there with any regularity was the dreaded whin, a prickly scrub also known as gorse or furze.

There were no trees or ponds on these ancient links,

but there were numerous natural hazards. Certain areas of grass would be grazed bare by livestock. Sheep seeking shelter in hollows or behind hillocks would wear down the turf. The nests and holes of small game would collapse into pits. Wind and water would then erode the topsoil from these areas, revealing the sandy base beneath. Such sandy wastelands, sand and pot bunkers dotted the landscape of a links and menaced many a golf shot.

There were no tees or fairways, as such, nor even putting greens. The putting areas were of the same bristly grass that grew everywhere else. It is speculated that the earliest golfers made rabbit holes their putting cups; and if this is the case, perhaps the putting areas were nibbled a little closer by rabbits. But since it was customary to tee one's ball within a club length of the previous cup, a well-manicured putting surface was not known on an early links.

Man had little to do even with maintaining the early courses. Bird droppings and periodic showers from the sea kept the turf healthy. The sandy base beneath the soil provided excellent drainage. Grazing sheep and wild game kept the grass clipped, and if it became too lush, the golfer simply abstained from playing. The sandy wastelands and bunkers went unraked, except when smoothed by random gusts of strong wind.

This then was the earliest form of the golf course. It is possible that the original links were single holes, played out and back to a starting point. But as the popularity of the game increased, and because most linksland was common public land unrestricted by boundaries, golfers would wander onward as far as they could find playable ground before turning back. Thus, there was no standard number of holes for a round of golf. The early links at Leith and Musselburgh had five holes each, North Berwick seven, Prestwick twelve, Gullane thirteen and Montrose twenty-five.

The preeminent course of this early period of golf in Scotland, and even today, was the old links at St. Andrews. Records indicate that it existed in a primitive form as early as 1414. While some argue that the Old Course is

16

P. 14-15: *Stone bridge, St. Andrews. Since the dawn of the profession, course designers have crossed this bridge on the Old Course, seeking the basic principles of their art. P. 17: Spyglass Hill GC, Ca., by Jones. The practice of course design on inland sites demanded major modifications to create the links conditions inherent in this hole on natural linksland.*

no longer a true links because of the rapid recession of the sea during the last century, it nevertheless began as a totally natural links. The playable areas of grass were bordered by thick patches of heather, and a majority of the natural sand bunkers were hidden from a player's view until he went searching for his ball.

The outline of the hole routing at St. Andrews resembled a shepherd's crook. The links had twelve putting areas, ten of which served the player both on his outward trek and again on the homeward one. This arrangement led to the adoption of the terms "out" and "in" to designate which of the common holes a golfer was playing. The remaining two holes were used only once apiece, as the eleventh and the home holes. A round of golf at St. Andrews, therefore, consisted of twenty-two holes, eleven out to the farthest point and eleven back.

Around the middle of the eighteenth century, two innovations to the existing game of golf were introduced. One of these was the creation of private golf clubs whose members continued to play on the ancient public links.

The three earliest clubs were The Honourable Company of Edinburgh Golfers (established in 1744 on the Links of Leith), The Society of St. Andrews Golfers (established in 1754) and The Honourable Company of Golfers at Blackheath (the first golf club outside Scotland, established in 1766). Continued growth of private golf clubs contributed significantly to the need for course planners after 1850.

The other important innovation of the eighteenth century occurred at St. Andrews. For the first time, man began changing some of nature's handiwork on the Old Course. Many of these changes would have an impact far in the future when designers began searching for basic principles of golf course architecture.

The first notable change was to the putting areas. Sometime in the 1700s, although it is not known precisely when, greens were instituted at St. Andrews and particular attention was focused on keeping these surfaces adequately turfed.

In 1764, feeling the first four holes were not sufficiently challenging, the Society of St. Andrews Golfers

P. 18: A man-made bunker at Muirfield GC in Scotland. The natural bunkers that peppered the landscape of the ancient links were later stabilized with sod or railway ties (sleepers).

P. 19: (Top) *Linksland far from the ocean in Nebraska.*
P. 19: (Bottom) *Machrie Hotel GC, Scotland,*
by Willie Campbell. Built around 1890 and remodeled
by Steel in the 1970s, Machrie is one of the scores
of true links scattered along the British and Irish coastlines.
Campbell, like many fellow Scots, emigrated to
America in the late nineteenth century, carrying the traditions
of his native links across the ocean to the New World.

P. 20: The earliest Scottish links were designed entirely by nature and consisted of high, windswept sand dunes and hollows where grass grew if the soil was reasonably substantial. P. 21: (Top) The routing outline at St. Andrews resembles a shepherd's crook. Finalized in the 19th century, it was primitively in existence in the 15th. P. 21:(bottom) Widening the Old Course around 1848 introduced strategy. Previously, play across hazards had been mandatory (above). Wider fairways (below) provided long, safe routes for the prudent, with direct routes available to reward success by more daring golfers. The Old Course thus exemplified, in different periods, two competing philosophies of design, namely penal and strategic.

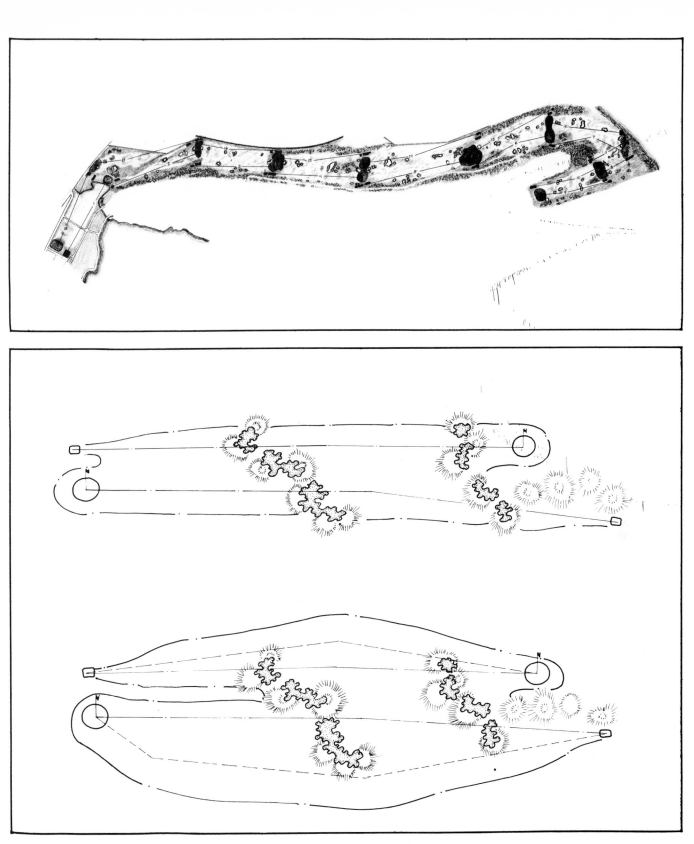

21

consolidated them into two long holes in order to maintain the integrity of the Old Course. This eliminated two greens and four holes, as each hole was played twice in a round, and thus reduced a round of golf at St. Andrews to eighteen holes. (Legend has a more romantic explanation for this change. A bottle of Scotch contained eighteen jiggers. The consumption rate was a jigger per hole. St. Andrews golfers felt the round should conclude with the bottle.)

In 1832 the practice began of cutting two cups into each of the common greens, creating eight "double greens" on which two matches, one heading out and one heading in, could be played at once.

Two years later King William IV was induced to recognize the St. Andrews links to be "Royal and Ancient." The Society of St. Andrews Golfers seized the opportunity to proclaim St. Andrews the official "Home of Golf" and the Society the foremost authority on the game. Prior to this, the Links of Leith had generally been considered the Home of Golf, but the Honourable Company of Edinburgh Golfers, the true patriarch of private clubs, had disbanded at Leith in 1831. (The Honourable Company reestablished at Musselburgh in 1836 and again at Muirfield in 1891.) Left without its strongest promoter and patron, the Links of Leith soon deteriorated and in 1834 could muster little to dispute St. Andrews's claim to its title.

St. Andrews thus became "The Royal and Ancient Golf Club of St. Andrews," and the golfing community afforded it the respect due royalty. Eighteen holes became the standard for any new course because St. Andrews had eighteen holes. Nearly every new course would be compared with St. Andrews to determine its merits and faults. Purists felt it near blasphemy to refer to anything but a linksland course, like St. Andrews, as a links. New terms were invented to describe inland and, by implication, inferior golfing grounds. The first term used was "green," which led to such derivatives as "greenkeeper," "green fee" and "green committee." Later, "golfing-course" became popular, and finally "golf course."

22

P. 22: Troia GC built in 1978 on true linksland in Portugal.
P. 23: (Top) The approach to the 17th green at St. Andrews, perhaps the first golf green planned by man.
P. 23: (Bottom) Turnberry, located on the western coast of Scotland, provided ideal links conditions.

Its lofty title, however, did not prevent the links at St. Andrews from being further altered. As a public course, in a town devoted to the game, St. Andrews had always seen considerable play. The narrow strip of playable grass was only some forty yards wide; and despite the use of double greens, play became increasingly congested and hazardous. Between 1848 and 1850, the course was widened by replacing the closest crops of heather with turf and by expanding the double greens into huge hundred-yard-wide surfaces. The widened course and huge double greens offered a unique feature: The holes could be played either as the "right-hand" course or in reverse as the "left-hand" course. During the same period of alteration, a new seventeenth green was also built. And in the first recorded instance of such a practice, some artificially created hazards were added to the Old Course.

An accidental but far-reaching result of the course widening was the introduction of the element of strategy into the game of golf. A player was no longer compelled to carry every hazard. He could, if he preferred, play a longer but safer route around a hazard at some sacrifice but without suffering an undue penalty. Previously, St. Andrews, like most links, not only required compulsory carries over most hazards but also penalized with whins, heather, sandy lies or lost balls any shot that strayed off line.

Thus, St. Andrews exemplified, in different periods, the two major, competing schools of thought in golf architecture. Originally it was an example of what in modern times is labeled "penal design." But after 1850 the Old Course, despite its blind hazards and fearsome bunkers with equally fearsome names, advanced the theory of "strategic design" by providing direct routes with substantial rewards to the bold player while offering safer but longer routes, at the cost of a stroke or part of one, to the less daring.

The original natural links of Scotland, especially St. Andrews, form the foundation for the practice of golf course architecture today. Their impressive settings and true golf values have exerted a profound influence on golf architecture to the present time and no doubt will do so forever. In the early development of the game of golf, its players, its rules and its implements all had to adapt to fit the existing conditions of nature as found on the links. As man began laying out and building golf courses, however, the opposite soon resulted. While the avowed purpose of course designers throughout history has been to imitate nature, the actual practice of golf architecture has demanded modifications of existing terrain and soil to create conditions resembling those found on the links.

24

SHOTS SUBSEQUENT TO THE TEE-SHOT
FURTHEST FROM THE HOLE
AS THE CROW FLIES
PLAYS FIRST
13TH

P. 24: A form of pot bunker by the Dyes peppers the landscape at La Quinta Hotel GC in Ca.
P. 25: (Top) Royal Dublin, opened in 1885, was one of Ireland's first formal courses.
P. 25: (Bottom) Courses at Killarney in Ireland were planned first by the Parks and later by Guy Campbell and F. W. Hawtree.

2.

Golf Spreads to England and Beyond

Wherever Scots went, they carried their national pastime and the lore of their links with them. The game of golf was introduced sporadically over a number of decades to distant outposts of the British Empire and other parts of the world, first by Scotsmen and later by Englishmen.

It had first spread to England, where a band of Scots played over a seven-hole course at Blackheath in 1608. By 1758 Molesey Hurst at Hampton was played regularly by the actor David Garrick and was praised as a "very good" golfing ground by a party of his Scottish friends. Another early formal layout was Old Manchester on Kersal Moor, opened around 1818.

Golf was known in America as early as 1779, and a golf club was founded in Charleston, South Carolina, in 1786. A club was formed in Calcutta, India, in 1829 and another at Bombay in 1842. Scottish officers convalescing near the Pyrenees introduced the game to France and built the Continent's oldest course, the Pau Golf Club, in 1856. It was also played in Hong Kong and on the Cape of Good Hope in South Africa by Scottish soldiers and engineers. By the 1870s courses had appeared in Australia and New Zealand, and by 1876 there were five in Canada: at Montreal, Quebec, Toronto, Brantford and Niagara-on-the-Lake.

Most of this early golf was played on rudimentary courses consisting of only a few holes. As golf spread far from Scotland, courses were laid out informally under widely different climatic conditions and on innumerable soil types and varying terrains. It was soon observed that blind shots, steep climbs, sharp drop offs, very flat terrain and a superabundance of natural problems including water and heavy underbrush did not contribute to pleasurable golf. Moreover, none of these early layouts achieved anything near the golfing satisfaction of the Scottish links, and few lasted beyond their initial season.

Despite its far-ranging introduction, golf was still not widely known or played as late as the first half of the nineteenth century, even in Scotland. But by the mid-1800s several events combined to capture the attention of the public in England and Scotland.

A number of widely publicized golf matches were held on the finest of the Scottish links, including St. Andrews and Musselburgh, in the 1840s. The expanding British railway system made it possible for large crowds to travel to and watch such exhibitions. The more venturesome of these spectators soon tried the links themselves.

Then, in 1848, the gutta-percha golf ball was invented. The introduction of this rubber-covered ball revolutionized golf. The cost of the old featherie was about four shillings; the new "gutty" cost only a single shilling. In addition, the gutty was much more durable. The featherie would more often than not split open when struck incorrectly; the new gutta-percha would merely dent under the same inexpert blow. Golf thus became a less frustrating and more affordable game.

The gutty led in turn to a revolution in golf club making, for its durability permitted far greater use of iron-headed clubs. Increasing use of irons resulted in the unintentional widening of fairways as the irons beat down the heather and bentgrass grew up in its place.

These several factors brought golf an increasing popularity through the last half of the nineteenth century. Yet its spread was not nearly as rapid as one might expect. By 1857 there were only seventeen golf clubs in Scotland, most of them playing over a handful of ancient, hallowed links. The growth of golf in other parts of Great Britain was even slower. By 1888 there were seventy-three golf courses in Scotland, fifty-seven in England, six in Ireland and two in Wales. More would come in the next decade. The first formal courses in England after the introduction of the gutty were Westward Ho! (1864), Wimbledon (1865) and Hoylake (1869). Early formal courses in Ireland included Royal Belfast (1881), Royal Dublin (1885), Portrush (1888), Lahinch (1892), Portmarnock (1894) and Sligo (1894).

The earliest records of golf course designers and their works date from this period of growth in the latter part of the nineteenth century. The first recognized designer was Allan Robertson, the long-time professional and clubmaker of St. Andrews, who died in 1859. Robertson is

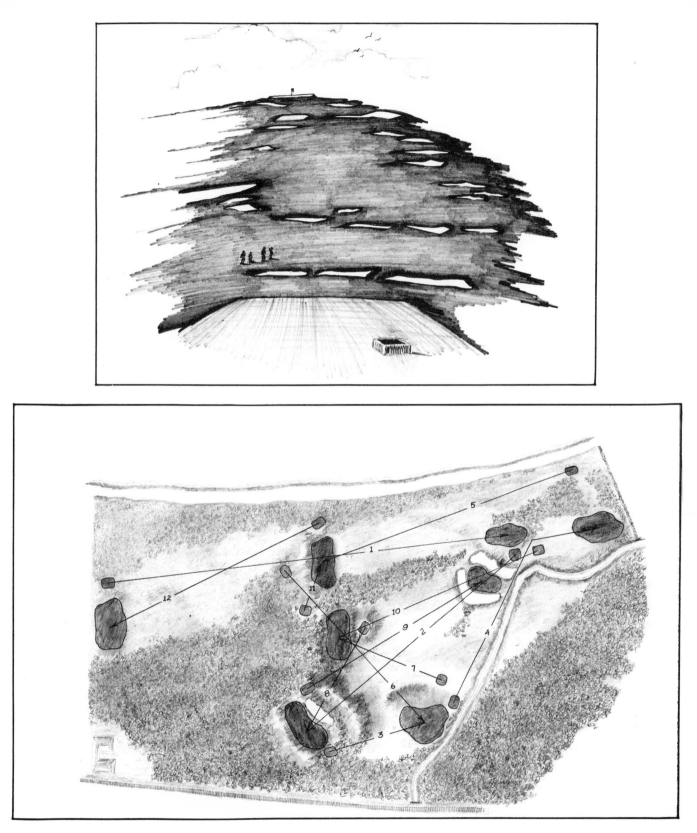

P. 26–27: *St. Georges (now Royal), Sandwich, by Purves (1877), one of many* 29
links laid out along English coasts in the half of the 19th century.
P. 29: (Top) *The geometric design of inland England, with square bunkers in*
procession down the fairway to square greens. P. 29: (Bottom) *Prestwick,*
site of the first Open in 1860, was cross routed from 1851 to 1882.

usually credited with supervising the widening of the Old Course and with creation of its seventeenth green. He also did a ten-hole course at Barry, Angus, Scotland, in 1842, which forms the basis for the present championship course known as Carnoustie; and he laid out links in other parts of Scotland.[1] Allan Robertson's brother, David, emigrated to Australia in 1848 and introduced golf to that continent. It is quite likely that in so doing he planned one or more of Australia's earliest courses.

Old records indicate that most people turned to professionals like Allan Robertson to provide them with new golfing grounds. It seemed natural that the men who taught the game, made the implements and were the most proficient players should also lay out the courses. In the 1850s several clubs hired individuals to maintain the turf of their existing links and greens. These "greenkeepers" were soon called upon to help establish new golf courses. More often than not, the professional and the greenkeeper at a course were one and the same person. This person sometimes took on a third hat as a course designer.

Among the greenkeepers and professionals who laid out courses in the British Isles during the last third of the nineteenth century were the twins Willie and Jamie Dunn (of Musselburgh and Royal Blackheath), Willie's son Tom (of Musselburgh and later Wimbledon), Charles Hunter (of Prestwick), George Lowe (of St. Anne's-on-the-Sea), the brothers Tom and George Morris (of St. Andrews), the brothers Willie and Mungo Park (of Musselburgh), Douglas Rolland (of Elie and later Malvern), Archie Simpson (of Royal Aberdeen) and David Strath (of North Berwick).

These early course planners did their work on the spot, never resorting to a drawing board, with most courses laid out in a few days or less. They selected natural greensites, plotted holes to these sites and then arranged the holes into a circuit. Little construction was undertaken, for the natural contours of the land were seldom altered. Existing hazards, including roads, hedgerows and even stone walls, were incorporated; and existing turf was utilized. Except for assuring that a supply of sand for top-dressing the putting greens was close at hand, these designers rarely considered future maintenance.

P. 30–31: A stabilized bunker on hole #4 at Royal St. Georges, Sandwich. The numerous courses established along the coasts of England in the latter part of the nineteenth century retained the styles of the Scottish links, in stark contrast to most inland courses of the same period with their artificially geometric features.

30

Most of these same men were active in modifying existing courses, both the famous links and rudimentary layouts where golf had been played informally for centuries. Modifications to the hallowed links became necessary for a variety of reasons. They could not accommodate the increasing crowds as golf gained in popularity and thus became dangerous. Alterations to many were required when the eighteen-hole course became standard. Greater length was also required, because the new gutty nearly always outflew the old featherie. The planning and execution of changes to the ancient links by particular individuals were important to the future of golf architecture, for they established a tradition whereby clubs sought out recognized designers.

Sometimes the professional acted as a consultant, recommending modifications to existing courses or changes and adjustments to new ones already thought out by club members. Despite the knowledge that these greenkeepers, professionals and others possessed, and the fact that most of them learned the game on the ancient Scottish links, some of their courses are at best termed "dismal." Tom Simpson, himself an architect and student of course architecture, was prompted to christen the years from 1885 to 1900 the "Dark Ages of Golf Architecture." Simpson wrote:

> They failed to reproduce any of the features of the courses on which they were bred and born, or to realize the principles on which they had been made. Their imagination took them no farther than the conception of flat gun-platform greens, invariably oblong, round or square, supported by railway embankment sides or batters. . . . The bunkers that were constructed on the fairways may be described as rectangular ramparts of a peculiarly obnoxious type, stretching at regular intervals across the course, and having no architectural value whatever . . .[2]

Even the work of Old Tom Morris, called "Old Tom" to distinguish him from his famous son "Young Tom," was sometimes disappointing. A native of St. Andrews, Old Tom apprenticed under Allan Robertson and then served as greenkeeper and professional at the Prestwick links before returning, after Robertson's death, to serve in the same capacity at the Old Course. The most prominent name in the world of golf in the late 1800s, Old Tom Morris was called upon to modify a number of the ancient links. He also created new courses on superb linksland. But his results were sometimes curious. For example, his layout at Westward Ho! (Royal North Devon) originally had twelve holes that crossed one another.

In defense of Old Tom, he probably did as much as was required of any golf course designer of that time; and

he produced layouts that were functional for the game he knew so well. The statement of Horace Hutchinson in 1898 that "the laying out of a golf course is a wonderfully easy business, needing very little special training . . ."[3] was not naive. It reflected the prevailing attitude of the time.

Old Tom Morris did make lasting contributions to the development of golf course architecture. He was apparently the first to ignore the traditional "loop" routing of nine holes out and nine back. For example, his routing of the course at Muirfield, which opened in 1891, utilized two nines with each starting and finishing at the clubhouse. Moreover, Muirfield's nines ran in different directions: the front nine clockwise, the back counter-clockwise. And only once did three successive holes play in the same direction. Such sophisticated routing took maximum advantage of wind conditions, forcing the player during a round to confront it from all angles. Morris's layout at Royal County Down in Northern Ireland, which opened about the same time as Muirfield, featured a similar routing plan.

It is quite possible that Old Tom has been blamed for changes that others made in his courses after they were opened for play. The "gun-platform" greens mentioned by Simpson may not have been Morris's creation; he was known to have utilized natural sites for his greens. The reputations of designers are plagued to this day by changes in their layouts made without their knowledge or consent, which upset strategy, balance and, in extreme cases, the continuity of the round.

Another of the early course designers, Tom Dunn, has been accused of lacking imagination. In retrospect, contemporary golf architects realize that Dunn strove for the functional in an age before funds and techniques were available for creating imaginative features. His great contribution was in designing inexpensive layouts for the multitudes who were taking up the game.

The latter half of the nineteenth century did see the introduction of a great many developments in turf maintenance. Foremost, of course, was the creation of the profession of greenkeeper, also called custodian or curator. The first turf cutter used to cut holes for putting cups was invented in 1849 at Royal Aberdeen. Lining the hole with a metal cup to prevent its being destroyed began about 1874 at the Crail Golf Club. The lawn mower was invented in 1830 but was not widely used on golf courses until decades later. Prior to its use, most inland courses in climates where bluegrasses predominated could only be played in autumn or winter, or during droughts, for at other times the turf was too lush. The practice of watering the putting surfaces originated in the 1880s, and by 1894

32

St. Andrews had sunk a well next to each of its massive greens to insure a steady source of water.

Despite the best efforts of greenkeepers, however, most of the inland golf courses created in this period suffered a common malady. Their turf was rock hard in summer and mushy in winter. Rolling of greens, a beneficial practice on the sandy links, proved disastrous on these clay soils. Except for those laid out in natural linksland, the courses of the late 1880s in the British Isles were built on land totally unsuited for playing the game of golf. And with agronomic knowledge, construction techniques and equipment so primitive, it was impossible to modify existing terrain and soil.

[1] Obituary, *Dundee Gazette*, September 1859, reprinted in an appendix in Clark, *Golf, A Royal and Ancient Game* (London: Macmillan, 1899).
[2] T. C. Simpson, *The Game of Golf*, IX New York: A. S. Barnes, (revised 1951), p. 162.
[3] Horace Hutchinson, "Concerning Golf Greens," *Harper's Weekly Magazine*, March 13, 1897, p. 274.

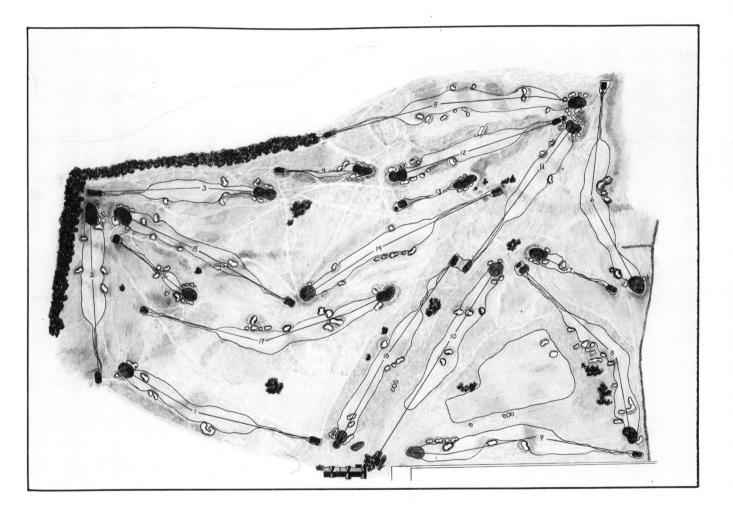

P. 33: *Outline of Muirfield GC, Scotland. Ignoring cross routing and the traditional single loop, Tom Morris, in 1891 produced a double loop of 2 nines with opposite rotations. Seldom did three successive holes play in the same direction and the wind was encountered in all quarters on early holes. Such sophisticated planning was a huge step in course design.*

3

3.

The Heathlands Era

Dozens of sorry inland courses built on impervious clay soils convinced most golf purists that only the ancient links could provide excellent golf. But a few golf course prospectors were unconvinced and kept searching for suitable inland terrain comparable to the best linksland. Their search was fruitful, for at the turn of the century they unearthed a mother lode of fine golfing land less than fifty miles south and west of London.

Here were the "heathlands," with well-drained, rock-free, sandy soil and a gently undulating terrain. This was true "golf country," and its discovery was a major step in the development of golf course architecture. Many of the world's greatest courses have since been created on land similar to that of the heaths, which, except for the presence of trees, is not unlike that of the links. The long delay in discovery of the heathlands, despite their proximity to London, is not difficult to understand. The heathlands were covered with undergrowth of heather, rhododendrons, Scotch fir and pines. Only a fool, it seemed, would spend time building a golf course in such a wasteland when vast meadows were available for the purpose.

The "fools" that did build courses in the heathlands became the most prominent golf architects of their day. Four names in particular stand out: Willie Park, Jr., J. F. Abercromby, H. S. Colt and W. Herbert Fowler. Their prominence was due in part to their vision in recognizing the true potential of this unlikely terrain and in part to their ability to shape the land into splendid golf holes.

And shape the land they did. Heather and other undergrowth had to be removed from most areas earmarked as playable. Many trees had to be felled, although all four architects integrated trees into their designs (a practice unknown before their time) and thus created a strategic and aesthetic asset not available to the old links. Earth had to be moved and contoured into green sites, tees and hazards. These men never moved earth when natural green sites and satisfactory contours could be found; but where nature was deficient, they were not reluctant to make alterations. The cleared areas had to be prepared

and seeded or sodded, and they took special interest in the types of grasses that would be planted.

All these tasks would seem to be modest undertakings in modern times, but in the early 1900s they called for new techniques in course construction. Considering the primitive state of available construction equipment, the results achieved by these designers and builders were extraordinary.

The first pioneering architect of this era was Willie Park, Jr. A superior golfer who won The Open twice, Park had been active in planning and modifying courses since 1890, first with his father, Willie Park, and then on his own. But it was not until 1901, when the original course at Sunningdale, Berkshire, England, in the heart of the heathlands, and the Huntercombe Golf Club, some fifteen miles northwest, were opened that Willie Park, Jr., demonstrated what revolutionary aspects of course design could be accomplished when new methods of course building were used. Here he proved what he had written in 1896:

> The laying out of a golf course is by no means a simple task . . . Great skill and judgement and a thorough acquaintance with the game are absolutely necessary to determine the best position for the respective holes and teeing grounds and the situation of the hazards.[1]

Sunningdale and Huntercombe stood in stark contrast to the countless geometric layouts with square greens, steep banks and stern cross bunkers previously built on whatever terrain existed. They featured tees and landing areas that were built up or lowered. Most of the greens were raised above the fairway level, had gentle shapes, were large and undulating. One green, the thirteenth at Huntercombe, was two-tiered. Both courses featured bold, manmade hazards, clearly visible to a golfer from the tee. Sunningdale even had an artificial pond.

The two courses made a reputation for Willie Park, Jr., and it has never diminished. Sir Guy Campbell, a fine mid-twentieth century designer, felt Park was the first really capable golf course architect, the man who set the

36

standard by which those who followed developed and amplified the art. Tom Simpson also gave Willie high marks, although he felt that Willie persisted throughout his career in placing bunkers only for the purpose of catching a poor shot. Herbert Warren Wind has written that Park had a sure touch for "devising golf holes that looked natural and played well." [2]

Park's later works continued to support his reputation. During his wide and active travels as a professional designer, Willie planned courses throughout the British Isles and Europe. He also laid out an estimated seventy courses in the United States and Canada, the best known being the North course at the Olympia Fields Country Club near Chicago, Woodway Country Club in Connecticut, and the Calgary Golf and Country Club in Alberta, Canada. Though at times ably assisted by his brothers, Willie was so busy as an architect that in the end, it is said, he literally worked himself to death. He died in 1925.

Willie Park, Jr., had done the preliminary routing on another early heathlands course, Worplesdon Golf Club in Surrey. But the course was completed by J. F. Abercromby, considered by mid-twentieth century course designer Frank Pennink and others to be one of the finest golf architects ever to practice in Britain. Like Park, Abercromby built his reputation on the heathlands. Unlike Park, "Aber" did very little work elsewhere.

Besides Worplesdon, Abercromby laid out several other courses in Surrey. Coombe Hill Golf Club, once considered "the finest and most artistic example of artificial construction work," [3] opened in 1908. He also did both the Old course and, after World War I, the New course at the Addington Golf Club. Abercromby spent most of his life as president of Addington and constantly sought to improve on his work there. He died just before World War II and, unfortunately, his New course was abandoned by the club just after the War. But Addington's Old course survived and has been highly regarded even in recent times.

H. S. Colt was the third of the revolutionaries who dared to carve golf courses out of the heather and pines of central England. Colt had his first design experience in 1894, when he laid out the Rye Golf Club on the southeast coast of England. But during the next half-dozen years, he was content to remain a solicitor and play a little competitive golf.

Upon the opening of Sunningdale in 1901, however, he became the club's secretary, and his interest in course design was soon renewed. Impressed with the basic design of Sunningdale, Colt supervised many changes during his twelve-year stint at the club. He replaced much of the heather that bounded the fairways with planted pines. He also altered and expanded the course to compensate for the greater distances golfers achieved with the rubber-cored golf ball. (This new ball was invented by Coburn Haskell of the United States in 1898 and gained acceptance in Great Britain in 1902 when Alex Herd used it in winning the Open. It flew some 15 to 20 percent farther than the gutty and thus necessitated lengthening and other alterations of existing courses.) In the process of expanding Sunningdale, Colt developed many of the exhilarating elevated tees that still exist on the older course today.

While serving at Sunningdale, Colt began planning courses in the surrounding heathlands for other clubs. Among them were Stoke Poges Golf Club (which opened in 1908), Swinley Forest Golf Club (1910) and thirty-six holes for St. George's Hill Golf Club (1913), of which eighteen survive. Swinley Forest, one of the first courses ever routed through a thick forest of trees, was considered by Colt himself to be his best design or, as he modestly put it, "the least bad course" he had ever done. He also experimented with the concept of integrating golf courses with housing and planned several such arrangements.

Colt was particularly adept at establishing turf in any environ. He could also be relied upon to make regular inspections of his work long after its completion to assist with the normal problems experienced by infant courses. He is said to have been the first to use a drawing board consistently to plan course designs, and he was apparently also the first to include tree-planting instructions. H. S. Colt was the first full-time golf course architect who had not previously been a professional golfer. He remained an amateur all his life, and he was a fine amateur competitor.

Colt, like Willie Park, Jr., did not always incorporate strategic concepts into his golf designs; but in his early British courses he did restore a strategic relationship between the placement of fairway and greenside bunkers, a "links" concept missing from most inland courses.

Colt also traveled far and wide to design courses. The majority of his work was done in the British Isles and Europe. Although the partners in his design firm, particularly Charles Alison, did most of the work that bears his name in North America, Colt did make at least two extended trips to the United States and Canada. He had a major part in planning courses for the Toronto Golf Club (1912) and the Hamilton Golf and Country Club (1914), both in Ontario, Canada; and the new course for the Country Club of Detroit, Michigan (1914). At home, his designs include a second eighteen, the New course, at Sunningdale; two courses for the Wentworth Golf Club;

and two remodeled courses for Royal Portrush in Northern Ireland. But perhaps a true measure of the respect in which he was held was his selection to design the third course, the Eden, at St. Andrews, which opened in 1912.

During this era, yet another Briton set out in the heathlands to build an ideal course. In 1902 W. Herbert Fowler, who had longed to design a golf course, was invited by his brother-in-law to do so on property at Tadsworth in Surrey. Fowler spent two years planning his course at a time when two days were still sufficient for many course builders, and initially rode through the heather on horseback, searching for proper greensites and then tracking each hole backward from there.

His creation, which opened in 1904, was called Walton Heath; it attracted even more attention than Park's Sunningdale had three years earlier. A special train brought dignitaries to the course; and the initial match was an exhibition by Vardon, Taylor and Braid, golf's "Great Triumvirate."

Fowler soon found his talents in sufficient demand to practice architecture full time. A somewhat despotic man, he quickly felt the need to put his hand to a traditional linksland course, and in 1908 his total redesign of the Royal North Devon Golf Club at Westward Ho! was completed. It, too, met with immediate acclaim.

Fowler remodeled the Saunton links, across the bay from North Devon, and laid out two more heathlands courses, the Red and the Blue, at the Berkshire Golf Club. All of these opened after the War, by which time Fowler was busy laying out courses on both coasts of the United States. One of his most impressive American works is Eastward Ho!, which one suspects he had a hand in naming, at Chatham, Massachusetts, on Cape Cod. Eastward Ho! combines the rolling terrain and ocean setting of a links with the tree-lined fairways and elevated greens of a heathlands course.

Herbert Fowler was perhaps the most naturally gifted architect of his time. "I never knew anyone who could more swiftly take in the possibilities of a piece of ground," Bernard Darwin once wrote, "and I think his clients thought, quite unjustly, that he had not taken sufficient pains, because he could see so clearly and work so fast." [4]

The original course at Walton Heath (Fowler built a second one there after the War) particularly impressed one of its first players, James Braid. Braid became the club's first professional upon its opening in 1904 and remained there the rest of his life. While Braid had no hand in changing the courses at Walton Heath, he was a five-time Open champion and thus received a great many requests to design courses. Though it was always an avocation with him, Braid took his designing seriously and stubbornly refused to change a design once it had been planned. He disliked even the suggestion that some hole be altered. In the beginning he did little more than stake out a rough layout and instruct a committee on how to properly construct and maintain the course. But he soon began conducting inspection trips to his courses, perhaps to insure that no one did change his designs. By the 1920s Braid was considered a most competent architect.

He was responsible for planning hundreds of courses, many of them on paper. His most prominent works, to which he paid personal attention, include the remodeled courses at Carnoustie Golf Club and Blairgowrie Golf Club, the East and West eighteens of Dalmahoy Golf Club, and the King's and Queen's courses at Gleneagles Hotel, all in Scotland.

Another of the Great Triumvirate, John Henry Taylor, also laid out a number of courses in the early 1900s. After the War, Taylor joined forces with Frederick G. Hawtree, a greenkeeper who had founded the British Golf Greenkeepers Association in 1912. The firm of Hawtree and Taylor designed some fifty-five courses in the British Isles and remodeled a similar number. They paid particular attention to the promotion of publicly owned courses, founding the Artisan Golfers Association and the National Association of Public Golf Courses, and they conceived and planned England's first municipal courses before World War I. Their most prominent work was the remodeling of the Royal Birkdale Golf Club into a championship course in 1931.

The third member of the Triumvirate, Harry Vardon, did a number of course designs but fewer than Braid or Taylor, partly because he spent many years before the War in ill health. Two other prominent architects, Alister Mackenzie and C. H. Alison, began their careers as assistants to H. S. Colt during the heathlands era. Their greatest creations would come after World War I.

Although this period lasted only fifteen years, from 1900 to 1914, it was a most important time in the history of golf course architecture. For the first time, golf architecture became a profession rather than simply a sideline for a club professional or greenkeeper.

Men like Park, Abercromby, Colt and Fowler proved on the heaths that exciting and pleasurable golf could be produced in any locale, so long as proper techniques in course building were used. These techniques included on-site study of the terrain, detailed plans developed on a drawing board, and on-site supervision or inspection once construction began.

They also realized that where a satisfactory natural

40

contour could be utilized in the design of a hole, it should be so used. But where none existed, natural-appearing sites for greens, tees, landing areas and even bunkers could be created by men.

The competent designers in this period recognized that aesthetics are an intrinsic part of the game of golf. When designing a course, these men subdued harsh natural features. They incorporated trees into the design of certain holes. They abhorred geometrically shaped greens and hazards and built theirs to blend into the surrounding terrain, although courses that were geometric and featured cross bunkers and artificial lines were still being created by others elsewhere in Britain.

Lastly, it was in this period that the strategic school of golf course design began to influence some people. Most of the courses built in the British Isles between 1900 and 1914, including those of Park, Abercromby, Colt and Fowler, were still of the penal variety. But particular holes on some of the more prominent courses could certainly have been classified as "strategic."

This is attributable in no small part to the enduring influence of the Old Course at St. Andrews. Park, Abercromby, Colt and Fowler all played much of their golf at the Old Course, as did many other designers in the British Isles. It was still the course to which every other course was compared. And its subtle strategies were only then beginning to be realized and appreciated.

The continuing significance of St. Andrews in this period was apparent in revisions of the golf course at Woking. One hole in particular, the fourth, had a considerable influence on at least one golf course architect and did a great deal to educate the golfing public in fundamental design principles.

The Woking Golf Club had been originally laid out by Tom Dunn in 1893 in Surrey, England. Ironically, it was right in the center of the heathlands; and had it shown any imaginative design at all, it would surely have attracted the attention that Sunningdale did years later. Instead, it was one of those functional but unexciting courses with square greens, giant cross bunkers bisecting many fairways and pot bunkers peppering the landscape.

P. 40: *Queen's* (top) *and King's* (lower right) *courses at Gleneagles show an English heathland influence in Scotland. P. 40: (Lower left) Possible playing routes on the Road Hole (#17) at St. Andrews. Principles of famous links holes were adapted to the heathlands by Colt and others. Paton and Low modeled their 4th at Woking near London after the 16th at St. Andrews.*

But in the early twentieth century, Woking was remodeled by two of the club's more domineering members, Stuart Paton and John L. Low. Neither had previously practiced architecture, but both were fine golfers, especially Low; both had a great interest in the game and were to write eloquently on it; and both had an abiding passion for St. Andrews. They set about to pattern Woking after the Old Course. They had sense enough not to try to imitate it but rather to recreate the playing strategies presented by the Old Course.

Paton paid particular attention to Woking's greens and over the years added various subtle slopes and mounds until finally not a single flat, square green remained. He and Low also did a great deal in rebunkering the course. It was one particular bunker, or pair of bunkers, that made such an impact upon club member Tom Simpson, who would later design many courses himself.

The fourth hole at Woking resembled the sixteenth at St. Andrews in that both were straightaway par-4s with a railline running along the right. Paton furthered the resemblance by placing a pair of bunkers in the center of the fourth fairway at the landing area in the manner of the "Principal's Nose" at the Old Course's sixteenth. Many years later Simpson recalled hearing the outrage and condemnation of the revised hole by his fellow members at Woking and wrote:

> . . . I went out, fully prepared to find myself in complete agreement with the views which had been so eloquently expressed. So far, however, from agreeing, I realised for the first time, as soon as I saw this much-maligned hazard, that the true line to the hole should not always be the centre of the fairway, and the placing of a bunker had a far more serious and useful purpose than merely the punishing of a bad shot. This led me to see the importance of golf architecture as an art as well as a science. . . .[5]

Paton and Low never designed or remodeled another course, although they spent years refining Woking. Yet they deserve mention in any history of golf course architecture, for they demonstrated, perhaps before anyone else, that it was possible on an inland course to challenge a golfer in more than one way, as did the links of Scotland.

[1] William Park, Jr., *The Game of Golf* (2nd ed.; 1896), p. 194.
[2] Herbert Warren Wind, "Understanding Golf Course Architecture," *Golf Digest Magazine,* November 1966, p. 25.
[3] T. C. Simpson, *The Game of Golf*, IX New York: A. S. Barnes (revised 1951), p. 170.
[4] Bernard Darwin, *James Braid*: London: Hodder and Stoughton (1952), p. 81.
[5] Simpson, *The Game of Golf*, p. 165.

4.

Golf Spreads to America

It is clear that golf found its way from Great Britain to North America, but when and by whom it was introduced to this continent is not certain. There were golf clubs in South Carolina and Georgia soon after the American Revolution, but there is no definitive evidence that golf was actually played at them despite their titles. The oldest authenticated golf clubs in North America were Canadian—the Royal Montreal formed in 1873 and the Royal Quebec in 1874. There were many hunt, field and polo clubs in America long before these, further complicating claims as "America's oldest golf club."

The title of Father of American Golf has generally been given to John Reid, a Scot who settled in Yonkers, New York. In 1888 Reid and several hardy friends staked out a rough three-hole golf course near his home, and they were hardy because it was early spring. Later that year they built a six-hole course in a nearby pasture and formed a golfing organization that they unabashedly named the St. Andrews Golf Club. Over the years, St. Andrews has persisted in calling itself the oldest golf club in the United States.

The claim of St. Andrews, however, is disputed by many. The Foxburg (Pennsylvania) Country Club maintains it was established on a nine-hole course laid out by Joseph M. Fox in 1887, while the Dorset (Vermont) Field Club was apparently in existence by 1886 and possessed a functional course. Andrew Bell of Burlington, Iowa, who was educated in Scotland, returned home in 1881 with golf clubs under each arm and proceeded to build a four-hole course on his father's property. In 1882 George Grant and his nephew, Lionel Torrin, both English tea merchants, laid out nine holes on the estate of Russell Montague in White Sulphur Springs, West Virginia, and called their creation the Oakhurst Golf Links.

J. Hamilton Gillespie, a transplanted Scot, batted a gutty about what is now downtown Sarasota, Florida, as early as 1883 and later laid out some of that state's first courses. English golf writer Horace Hutchinson claimed to have introduced the game to members of the Meadow Brook Hunt Club of Hempstead, New York, sometime

before 1887—to no avail, he added. At about the same time, Alex Findlay, still another Scot, introduced the game to Omaha, Nebraska.

Charles Blair Macdonald, who had studied as a youth at the University of St. Andrews, told of playing the game at a homemade course on deserted Douglas Field upon his return to Chicago as early as 1875. An avid promoter of the game, Macdonald built a small, seven-hole course at Lake Forest, Illinois, in 1892. He then constructed a nine-hole course for the Chicago Golf Club at Belmont, Illinois, which he rapidly expanded to a modest eighteen. Then, in 1895, he laid out the nation's premier first-rate eighteen-hole course, also for the Chicago Golf Club, at Wheaton, Illinois.

Once golf was introduced to America, its spread was swift and sure. By 1896 there were over eighty courses in the United States; and by 1900 there were 982, with at least one in each of the forty-five states. In fact, by the turn of the century courses in the United States outnumbered those in Britain, although none was comparable in quality to the famous links of Scotland nor to the heathland courses that would appear in England in the early years of the twentieth century.

The first professional imported to design a course in America was Willie Dunn, of the Musselburgh Dunns, called "Young Willie" to distinguish him from "Old Willie," his father. Young Willie, who had been trained by his famous and much older brother, Tom Dunn, was lured over by a rich syndicate to build a course for the newly organized Shinnecock Hills Golf Club. This course, at Southampton, New York, was completed in 1891 and was far from perfect; although considering the inexperience of Willie's crew and the primitive equipment he had, its creation was miraculous. It had only twelve holes at first; but Dunn, who remained at the club as pro-green-keeper, later added a nine-hole women's course and in 1895 integrated this with the main course to make a full eighteen holes. It included a number of blind shots and a railroad line that came into play. Unfortunately, Willie was never given an adequate budget to maintain it, but

44

P. 42-43: Hole #7 at Ekwanok GC, Vermont, by Dunn and Travis, one of the few first-rate American courses at the turn of the century. P. 45: Alex Findlay of Montrose, Scotland, introduced golf to Omaha around 1887. Later, under the auspices of the Florida East Coast RR and Wright & Ditson, he laid out hundreds of functional courses for a rapidly growing golf public.

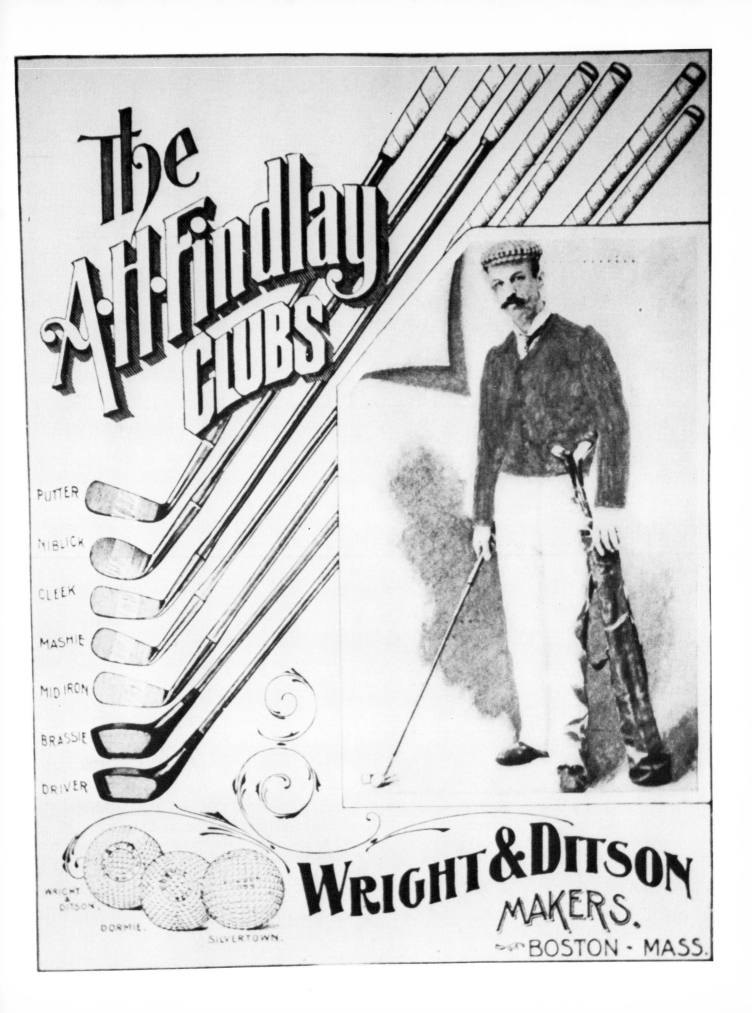

Memorandum.

From

THOMAS MORRIS
Golf Club and Ball Manufacturer

ST ANDREWS

To

July 1893

This is to certify that Robert Foulis has served his apprenticeship and for some time as journeyman with me as Golf Club and Ball Maker, to my entire satisfaction. He is also well acquainted with the game of Golf, and a good player. Of sober and industrious habits and trustworthy I have much pleasure in recommending him to any Club as greenkeeper &c

Tom Morris

P. 46: *Memorabilia of early course designers in the U.S. Robert Foulis from St. Andrews, John Duncan and Seymour of the famed Dunn family and "Bert" Way from England's Westward Ho! were all part of the great "Scottish Invasion" started by "Young Willie" Dunn.*

Shinnecock Hills was still a cut above the typical layout appearing on the American countryside. It was built on links-type land near the sea and was constructed only after Dunn had devised a well-conceived design. It should have served as a model for others wanting to build a course; but because it was inaccessible, located far out on Long Island, few golf developers spent the time or money to visit Shinnecock to see what a golf course should look like.

It was a shame they didn't, for woeful courses were appearing everywhere. People who could barely play the game and who knew nothing about building a golf course were doing just that to meet the demand. George Wright, for one, laid out a primitive course in Boston's Franklin Park. The owner of a Wright & Ditson Sporting Goods Store, he no doubt felt the availability of a course would increase sales of his newly imported clubs and balls. Henry Hewett, a railroad engineer from Paterson, New Jersey, designed a course for the new Tuxedo (New York) Golf Club; and polo fancier Lemuel Altemus built one for the Devon Golf Club in Philadelphia. In the process of laying it out, he rode around on a polo pony, in order, he said, to secure proper driving distances.

Perhaps because of the abundance of amateur "designers," Young Willie Dunn remained in America, teaching the game, making equipment and laying out several more courses for affluent clientele. He also spread the word back to the Old Country that the United States was a plum waiting to be picked.

Consequently, a good many of Willie's friends and acquaintances flocked to the United States. He even lent some of them the travel fare. Not all came to design golf courses, by any means. Some were club makers, some greenkeepers, some players and some considered themselves golf Renaissance men, able to do any task related to the game. Others, being novices to golf, could do none of these. But they came, for Young Willie Dunn became convinced that the real future of golf lay not in Scotland, nor Britain, nor Europe, but in America.

Among those he personally summoned were his two nephews, Seymour and John Duncan Dunn. After working with two sporting goods firms, J. D. landed the job of professional at Ardsley Country Club and later became golfer-in-chief for the Florida West Coast Railroad. In that capacity he designed and constructed several courses along the railroad's route in Florida, including the original course at what is now known as the Belleview Biltmore Hotel. J. D.'s chief rival at this time was Alex Findlay, the Scot from Omaha, who was now golfer-in-chief of the Florida East Coast Railroad. Findlay laid out re-

sort courses up and down his company's route, which stretched from St. Augustine to Palm Beach. Both men later designed numerous other courses across the nation.

Willie's second nephew, Seymour, arrived in New York at the age of twelve and became J. D.'s assistant at Ardsley. After schooling at Lawrenceville, New Jersey, he returned to Europe periodically to occupy professional berths and to plan and build courses with his father's help, among them layouts for the kings of Belgium and Italy. He subsequently built numerous courses in the northeastern United States, as well as Britain's and America's first indoor golf schools, the latter said to be the largest ever attempted. He eventually settled as professional at the Lake Placid Club in upstate New York.

Willie Dunn also sent for W. H. "Bert" Way, who had served with him on his brother Tom's construction crews in Europe. Way, a native of Westward Ho! in England, brought his brothers Ernest and Jack along. Bert ultimately settled in Ohio and built many Midwestern courses, including the original Detroit Golf Club and Country Club of Detroit courses, the original Firestone Country Club course in Akron Ohio and his home course, Mayfield Country Club in Cleveland, where he introduced John D. Rockefeller to the game. Ernest worked as a pro-greenkeeper in Detroit until after World War I, when he took up course design. He planned several courses in Michigan, including the Grosse Ile Country Club and the Pontiac Country Club. Jack, the youngest, worked as a pro-greenkeeper all his life, although he effected numerous design changes at Canterbury Country Club near Cleveland, where he served for many years.

William H. Tucker, another Englishman who had worked with the Dunns in Europe, also came at the behest of Willie. He soon landed jobs designing and building nine holes for the Maidstone Club on Long Island and remodeling the latest layout of the St. Andrews Golf Club. Before his death in 1954, Tucker designed or remodeled over 120 courses. His son, William H. Tucker, Jr., joined him in the business in later years; and the firm created courses in the Midwest, the Pacific Northwest and the Southwest. Tucker was also a turfgrass consultant of note.

Of course, not everyone agreed with Willie Dunn that the future of golf would be in America. Willie himself had more than once speculated that its future might rest in France, where his brother Tom devoted a good deal of effort. Alex Findlay's brother, Fred, went to Australia and designed several courses down under before moving to the United States. Willie Smith of the Carnoustie family came first to the United States but after winning the

1899 Open, settled in Mexico, where he built that country's earliest courses, beginning with San Pedro. Laurie Waters, a protégé of Old Tom Morris, left St. Andrews for South Africa, where, as an expert player, he was a pioneer designer.

But the destination of a majority of golfing emigrants from Britain at the turn of the century was the United States. Among others that came were:

• Charles Maud, an Englishman who relocated in California. With the assistance of Colonel W. E. Pedley, he designed and built that state's first course, the nine-hole Pedley Farms in Arlington, which ultimately became the Victoria Golf Club.

• Robert D. Pryde, a Scot who settled in Connecticut. Besides coaching the original Yale golf teams, Pryde designed the original New Haven Country Club, Race Brook Country Club and others.

• Robert White, a native of St. Andrews, who would lay out many a course across the United States during a fifty-year career. White originally came to America to study agronomy. He developed a reputation as a fine turfgrass consultant, and many clubs retained him in that capacity. He also served as the first president of the Professional Golfers Association of America when it was organized in 1916.

• H. J. Tweedie, a native of Hoylake, England, who landed a job along with his brother, L. P., running a Spalding sporting goods store in Chicago. Both men were fine amateur golfers; and Herbert James found time to lay out many early Chicago-area courses, including Midlothian, Flossmoor and Glenview country clubs.

• James and Robert Foulis, brothers who were born and raised in St. Andrews and who learned the game from Old Tom Morris. James came to America in 1895, and Robert joined him a year later. James, who won the 1896 U. S. Open, spent most of his time as pro-greenkeeper at a series of Chicago-area clubs. He also designed a number of courses around Chicago, including Hinsdale; and he consulted on Onwentsia. Robert eventually settled in St. Louis, where he designed many area courses, most notably the first version of the Bellerive Country Club where he served as professional for many years.

• Willie Watson, a Scot who arrived in 1898 to build the Minikahda Club course in Minneapolis to the plans of Robert Foulis. Watson remained at Minikahda as its summer professional, wintering in Pasadena, California. He became a well-known course designer in both regions, creating such courses as Interlachen in Minneapolis and Hillcrest in Los Angeles.

Two Scots who came to America to live and work,

P. 48: *Golf scenes from* Harper's Weekly, *circa 1890. Most early American golf was played on rudimentary courses, over stone walls, chasms and plowed fields, and around livestock. Man-made features looked artificial, with steep banks and sharp drop-offs, and mounds of soil-covered stone called "chocolate drops" were popular as obstructions. Yet these early courses were functional despite their shortcomings.*

Donald J. Ross and Tom Bendelow, deserve special mention. Ross, a one-time golf student of Old Tom Morris, hired on as professional of the Oakley Country Club in Boston in 1898, having been persuaded to emigrate by Professor Robert Wilson of Harvard who had met him while visiting Dornoch. James Tufts, of the American Soda Fountain Company, soon convinced Ross to work as winter professional at a new resort he was building in North Carolina. (Ross continued summer pro duties in the Boston area for several years.) The resort was named Pinehurst; once Ross arrived, he set about rebuilding and expanding the lackluster nine-hole layout that Tufts had installed. He subsequently built three additional courses at Pinehurst, #2 which opened in 1907, #3 (1910) and #4 (1919).

Despite their sand greens, the courses at Pinehurst impressed many affluent patrons from the north, and Donald Ross soon found his talents as a golf course designer in great demand. Ross is often said to have been the first full-time course designer in America, although he retained his position as professional and later golf manager at Pinehurst until his death in 1948. He was to become the most prominent golf architect of his day and one of the most respected.

Tom Bendelow, also from Scotland, quit a steady job with the *New York Herald* in 1895 to join the sporting goods firm of A. G. Spalding & Bros. as a "design consultant." In that capacity Bendelow claimed to have laid out hundreds of courses for clients who sought assistance from the huge sporting goods firm. He was, without doubt, the most prolific course builder in America in the early years of the century.

Tom was apparently a character, and quite a few colorful tales have developed concerning him. The most widely circulated but least embroidered concerned his method of design, which was dubbed "eighteen stakes on a Sunday afternoon." In fact, Bendelow did lay out a considerable number of courses somewhat in this manner, although he used more than eighteen stakes. He would stake out a first tee; pace off a hundred yards or so, stake out a cross bunker; pace on farther, stake out another bunker or some mounds; march on farther and stake out his green site. After doing this nine times, he would leave instructions with the club on how to properly build and maintain the course and then be on his way.

Golf historians have been aghast at such an operation, but it is an error to assume that Tom Bendelow was in any way a "con artist" in an era of otherwise competent, conscientious golf architects. In reality, Tom was widely respected as an architect in his later years, and

wrote and lectured on the subject at the University of Illinois. The fact is, in the late 1890s and very early 1900s, nearly all the golf courses in America were laid out in such a fashion. Designers of that time, like Alex Findlay, Robert White and even Donald Ross on occasion, practiced this method. It was all club members expected and all they were willing to pay for: The going rate was $25.00 per job, regardless of how long it took to stake the layout.

Few designers remained to supervise construction of their designs. The greenkeeper hired by the club, most often a Britisher, would actually build the course and over the years refine it, often changing even the designer's routing concept, which had been recorded only by stakes long since gone. Additional features were undoubtedly added to these courses by Scottish pro-greenkeepers after visits home to the links, for many an early northern professional spent a winter now and again in Scotland. Individual greenkeepers, therefore, had as much to do with this early American course design as did men credited with the "designing"; for if a designer was even brought in, he often did nothing more than route the layout with stakes.

Consequently, most American courses in this period were primitive compared with those in Britain and Scotland. Most were built quickly and inexpensively. In one of the numerous moves of the St. Andrews Golf Club, only two days were required to lay out and "build" a nine-hole course; and The Country Club (Brookline, Massachusetts) budgeted $50.00 to build its first six-hole course. Construction normally consisted of removing fences, clearing away surface stones and mowing the grass. The stones were often piled into mounds and when covered with dirt, were thought to make perfectly good hazards. These sharp mounds, nicknamed "chocolate drops," became the fashion for a time and were even added to courses which had no stones to cover. Little islands of unmowed vegetation were often left in the bunkers of these early courses. These "dragon's teeth" added nothing to the aesthetic values but did contribute to player frustration and to a high rate of lost balls.

Some early layouts had holes crossing one another. Nearly all greens were indistinguishable from fairways, and most natural obstructions were considered legitimate hazards. "Stone walls, trees, ploughed fields, fences, and chasms," wrote one golf enthusiast in 1895, "present excellent sporting requirements on a course, for variety is the spice of life."[1] In seeking the rationale for placement and style of manmade features and clearing lines at older clubs in the United States, golf architects of later eras were baffled. One explanation was provided by Elmer O. Cappers, historian at The Country Club (Brookline), who pointed out that the coexistence of golfers and horsemen in the early days at his club determined such matters.

For all their shortcomings, American courses at the turn of the century were functional. It is amazing that early greenkeepers were able to build and maintain their courses as well as they did with so little in the way of equipment, materials and skilled help available. These "sand lot" courses provided adequate training grounds for thousands of beginning golfers. But the expert golfers, or those who fancied themselves such, clamored for better courses on which to play their beloved game. It was this impetus that led to the advancement of course architecture in America in the early years of the twentieth century. Three courses created during that time—Myopia, north of Boston, the Garden City Golf Course on Long Island and the National Golf Links of America on Long Island—particularly influenced the state of the art.

[1] Henry E. Howland, "Golf," *Scribner's Magazine*, May 1895, p. 531.

P. 50: (Top) *Ekwanok GC, Vermont, Hole #10.* (Bottom) *CC of Lincoln, Nebraska, Hole #2 by W. H. Tucker, Sr., who came to the U.S. before the turn of the century at the behest of Willie Dunn and was active in course design until the 1950s.*

P. 50-51: Hole #12, Point Judith CC, Rhode Island.
*Clubs grew protective of their chocolate drops, steep
banks and sharp drop-offs. Acquiring a unique charm
as they mellowed into the landscape, such features
became traditional on some older courses in the East.*

5.

Landmark American Courses

Herbert C. Leeds was one of those dissatisfied with American golf courses at the turn of the century. But he was determined to do something about it. Well to do and a fine natural athlete, he had developed into a scratch player within two years of taking up the game and became one of the ruling fathers of the Myopia Hunt Club north of Boston shortly after joining in 1896. Leeds persuaded the membership to build a new course to replace the club's rudimentary nine holes; and soon after they consented, he was appointed to lay out the replacement.

Leeds took the task seriously. He visited Shinnecock Hills, which by then had a full eighteen holes, and came away convinced that he could build a comparable course. He started by locating his greensites in natural hollows and on natural plateaus, like those he had observed at Shinnecock. He then gave special attention to the construction of the greens. Not content to simply mow patches of grass, he had each green shaped into rolling surfaces; for he was determined that Myopia would not be cursed with a single flat, lifeless green.

Leeds routed his course to take advantage of the natural terrain. Stone walls, left over from the days when the land served as pastures and fields, were covered with soil and grassed to make them playable. Stone walls were not a legitimate golf hazard, Leeds felt, but mounds were. He later uncovered the walls, heaped the stones into mounds and re-covered them with soil to produce Myopia's giant "chocolate drops," still a feature of the course.

Finally, he had bunkers added: several on some short holes, almost none on the holes he felt to be challenging enough already. When his nine-hole layout was completed, it was selected to serve as the site for the 1898 U.S. Open.

The participants in that Open praised Leeds for his efforts and especially for the greens, which were unlike any in the country. But Leeds was not satisfied. He felt Myopia needed another nine to be a "proper links." The club soon purchased adjoining land, and Leeds laid out a second nine on decidedly hilly ground. Again paying particular attention to the greens, he took two years to con-

54

P. 52-53: Sea Island, Georgia, Hole #7, Plantation Course by W. J. Travis, a major contributor to the landmark American courses created after 1900.
P. 54: Hole #13, The Mid Ocean Club, Bermuda, by C. B. Macdonald.
P. 55: The Chicago GC. Huge, deeply-creased greens and steep banks appear often on layouts by Macdonald and by his proteges, Raynor and Banks.

struct the addition. When completed, Myopia's eighteen holes were termed as fine a test of golf as any in the United States, and the club hosted three National Opens in the next eight years.

Herbert Leeds savored his reputation as a golf course designer. He went abroad in 1902 to study the famous Scottish links. After his return, he laid out a number of courses, including the first Kebo Valley Course at Bar Harbor, Maine, and the original Palmetto Country Club in Aiken, South Carolina. But Myopia was his favorite, and he remained at the club until his death, nurturing and refining the course.

At about the time that Leeds was completing his initial nine at Myopia, another man of leisure, Devereux Emmet, began planning a course for his friends in Garden City, New York. His little nine-hole effort was called the Island Golf Links, and it lasted until 1899. By that time,

Emmet and his fellow golfing enthusiasts had decided to establish a more formal organization. They incorporated the Garden City Golf Club, bought the Island Golf Links and surrounding property, and Emmet proceeded to re-model his small course into a full eighteen.

For a neophyte, Emmet did a remarkably good job laying out the Garden City course on the flat, treeless, windswept terrain. He routed the holes so that a player faced differing wind conditions on every hole. There were few parallel holes, so shots drastically off line would end up in unfavorable lies. Several roads ran through the course, but Emmet utilized them as he would creeks, as hazards. He did build several cross bunkers in the fairways, which were popular in that day; but his bunkers were for the most part shallow and easy to recover from.

The finest feature of Garden City was its turf. The greens, although basically flat, were hardy and consistent.

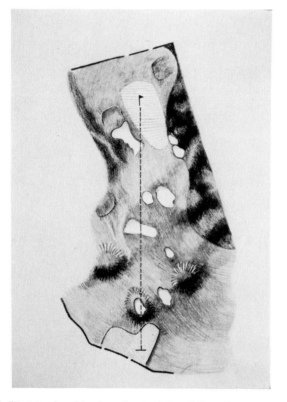

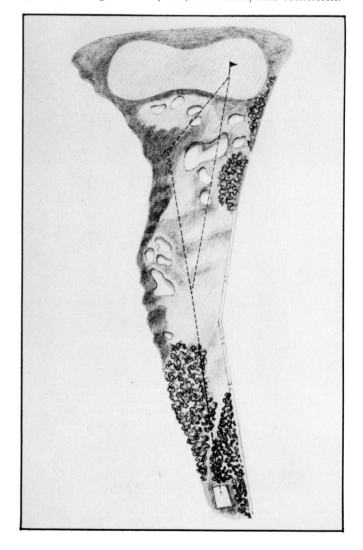

P. 56–57: *Macdonald adapted principles of British holes to the National Golf Links and later courses. Among his favorites were REDAN, #15 at North Berwick (P. 56, left); LONG, #14 (P. 56, right) and EDEN, #11 (P. 57, left), both at St. Andrews. Hole #3 at the National (P. 57, top right) is his version of ALPS, #17 at Prestwick. Originals like SHORT (P. 57, lower right) also appeared on subsequent layouts.*

The fairways were similar, and some felt that Garden City's fairways were superior to the greens on most other courses.

The turf was outstanding because Emmet had the good fortune to work on a piece of land ideally suited for the growing of grass—a large alluvial deposit of loam, like the Scottish linksland, resting on layers of gravel and sand. The fine soil and salt air nurtured erect, thin-bladed grasses and the underlying strata provided excellent drainage. When the 1902 U. S. Open was played on Garden City, the course was well-received by both Americans and Britons.

But as one writer has noted, while Garden City certainly made the reputation of Devereux Emmet as a course architect, it was also nearly his downfall. Emmet would spend the rest of his life designing and building courses all along the eastern seaboard. But he would expe-

rience several failures trying to duplicate what he had done at Garden City: build a respectable layout with superb turf for under two thousand dollars. He would never again find terrain so perfect for the playing of golf, not even at other nearby sites in Garden City.

Fortunately, once Emmet realized that each course site presented a unique situation, and once he convinced his clientele to provide him with adequate funds, he was able to create a number of notable courses. His list of later accomplishments includes the Wee Burn Club in Darien, Connecticut; the original Congressional Country Club course near Washington, D.C.; and Leather Stocking Country Club at the Otsega Hotel in Cooperstown, New York.

It may have been beneficial to Emmet that by 1908 people had forgotten that he had designed Garden City.

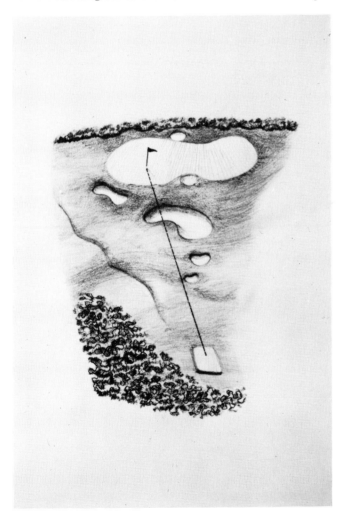

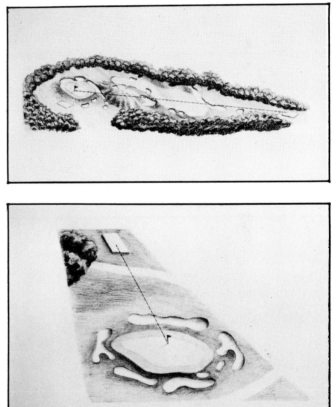

P. 58: *The Macdonald style as seen on Hole #7 (top) and bunkering on #15 (center) at the Mid Ocean Club. P. 58-59: Macdonald's greatest design first, the CAPE, #5 at Mid Ocean. P. 58: (Bottom) Planting love grass at Pinehurst. Upon arrival, Donald Ross set about to upgrade the resort's lackluster nine.*

By that time the Garden City Golf Club was being considered the work of Walter J. Travis, whose revisions were to make it a truly outstanding course. Travis had been born in Australia but was raised from an early age in the United States. He didn't take up golf until the age of thirty-five, but by his thirty-ninth birthday he was the top amateur in the country. By 1899 he was also dabbling in golf course design, working in collaboration with John Duncan Dunn on the Ekwanok Golf Club in Vermont and writing about the subject in various periodicals. Travis was also a member of the Garden City Golf Club and was runner-up in the 1902 Open on his home course.

In a 1906 magazine article, Travis analyzed the Garden City course and suggested several improvements. He felt the bunkers on several holes, especially those near the green, should be deepened, and cross bunkers filled in. He thought certain fairways should be narrowed, either by allowing the rough grass to grow or by the installation of "pot bunkers." And he suggested reworking the famous Garden City greens:

The dream of having at least a few greens resemble some of the well-known ones in Great Britain is easily capable of realization. All that is necessary is to denude the present greens of their surface of turf, by means of a turf-cutting machine which peels it off in continuous rolls of even, uniform depth, arrange the undulations as desired, replace the sod, and fill in the interstices with fine, screened loam mixed with seed.[1]

Travis was able to convince his club to allow him to institute his suggestions; being a three-time U. S. Amateur and British Amateur champion no doubt helped. Over the next two years he reworked every green, carefully preserving the hallowed turf as he did so. He also built some new tees to extend the length of some holes and, in certain cases, to reroute play. He rebunkered each hole, digging some as deep as a man's height so that their faces had to be built up with layers of sod stacked like bricks, as at Muirfield and other courses in Scotland. In all, he added fifty new bunkers.

Garden City, as revised by Travis, hosted the 1908 U. S. Amateur and, just as six years previously, the participants were enthusiastic about the course. "The fairway and the boldly undulating putting-greens were even as velvet," wrote one onlooker, "but those hazards! . . . bunkers, traps and pots lurk on either side of the straight and narrow path, awaiting the pull or the slice of the unwary!"[2]

The "Grand Old Man," as Travis had come to be known, would design or remodel a good many courses in the next twenty years, including the East and West courses at the Westchester Country Club, Rye, New York; Yahnundasis at Utica, New York; and the original nine holes at the Sea Island Golf Club in Georgia. His true love, however, was the first course he ever had a hand in creating, Ekwanok in Manchester, Vermont. Ekwanok may have been the country's best golf course in the early 1900s, but it did not receive the early public attention of Myopia or Garden City. Travis touted its merits often, and by 1914 it was selected as the site for the National Amateur. Travis added a second course, Equinox, adjoining Ekwanok in the early twenties. At his death, in accordance with his wishes, Travis was buried near his beloved Vermont courses.

Walter Travis had a certain set of principles that he tried to instill in each of his courses. Hazards should be placed in relation to greens, he believed, so as to require "thinking" golf. Certain holes should necessitate deliberate slices, while others should require deliberate draws. One or two tee shots per round should call for an exceptionally fine carry, as should one or two approach shots. And greens should always be undulating, never flat.

Often, perhaps too often, Travis tried to institute his principles by means of a most effective weapon: the small, deep pot trap. He used the pot trap to such excess that critics of later years would label him a follower of the penal school of golf design, a master of the "God-fearing approach," a flamboyant but unimaginative architect. Certainly some of the criticism is justified, but Travis never deliberately set out to build a penal course. He had spent his entire golfing career as a notoriously short hitter. He had kept himself alive in countless matches by keeping himself in play and by mastering a deadly putting stroke. That philosophy carried over into his designs. His pot bunkers never hurt players, he said, so long as they stayed out of them.

One last note about Travis's redesign of the Garden City Golf Club: He remodeled the eighteenth hole, a par-3 across water, by building a severely tilting green and fronting it with a huge, deep bunker on the left and a smaller, steepfaced bunker on the right. Knowledgeable golfers quickly recognized the hole for what it was: Travis's version of the Eden, the eleventh hole at the Old Course at St. Andrews. It was not an imitation, Travis would point out, but an adaptation of that highly respected and highly feared par-3.

That idea was intriguing, modeling a hole on an American course after one from a famous old British links. But it was not originally Walter Travis's. It belonged to Charles Blair Macdonald.

Macdonald was the man who had designed and built America's first eighteen-hole course. He was a wealthy, intelligent man, devoted to the game of golf. He had been one of the founding fathers of the United States Golf Association, and was its first Amateur champion. But he was also, in the minds of some, stubborn, egotistical and autocratic.

Certainly Macdonald had the perfect personality to try something different and daring. In 1901, after reading a British magazine survey on the "best holes" in the United Kingdom, Macdonald resolved to build a "classical golf course in America, one which would eventually compare favorably with the championship links abroad, and serve as an incentive to the elevation of the game in America."[3]

Macdonald established a number of rules for this project. First, the course must be a links. He would only build it near the sea, on land as nearly comparable to the old linksland as could be found. After years of searching from Cape Cod to Cape May, he found two such sites, both on Long Island, New York. He eventually chose a site near Southampton and, coincidentally, adjacent to the Shinnecock Hills Golf Club.

Second, Macdonald's ideal course must contain a full eighteen holes of an exemplary nature. Not even St. Andrews, he felt, had eighteen first-class holes, but his course would. To this end, he solicited the opinions of many prominent golfers as to the ingredients of great golf holes. He personally made at least three trips to Great Britain, observing the most famous and many lesser-known courses. He surveyed and sketched dozens of holes, concentrating only on the features he considered distinctive. "I only approve of the Maiden at Royal St. Georges," he later wrote, "as a bunker, not a hole."[4] He would not be afraid to combine two or three features from different holes into a single hole on his ideal course, and, in the

end, more than half would be composites.

Third, he would spare no expense in making his course the best in the world. He spent a great deal of his own money on the project and also solicited subscriptions from seventy enthusiastic friends at an initial thousand dollars per membership.

Fourth, where nature was deficient, it would have to be improved upon. This was perhaps the most revolutionary action in course building in its time. When he examined the site, Macdonald was delighted to locate natural settings for several of his proposed holes, especially for his versions of Prestwick's Alps and the Redan at North Berwick. But he had a great deal of soil moved around to create "natural" settings for other holes. He also had some 10,000 loads of topsoil hauled in and spread around. He created a turf nursery, one of the first of its kind, and experimented with numerous varieties of grasses to transplant on his course. Since the site was in need of artificial watering, he had a complete irrigation system for greens installed. The greens themselves were built "scientifically," with strata of seaweed, loam and top-dressing to preserve moisture.

Fifth, Macdonald would obtain the assistance of the best experts in their respective fields, for mediocre talent could never result in an ideal course. He sought out Professor C. V. Piper of the United States Department of Agriculture for agronomic help and enlisted the aid of a local surveyor, Seth J. Raynor, to serve as his construction engineer. Raynor was to prove so invaluable that he would construct all the courses later laid out by Macdonald, as well as designing many of his own. In addition, Macdonald invited the opinions of such experienced golfers as Walter Travis, Devereux Emmet and his own son-in-law, H. J. Whigham.

Finally, Macdonald intended that each hole should make a golfer think before he swung. Naturally, the features of the best holes that Macdonald adapted had, for the most part, always required the golfer to place the ball rather than swing aimlessly. But Macdonald went further. Each of his holes provided for an alternative line of play. On each tee the player was called upon to exercise his judgment: Could he carry the bunker in front of the pin, or should he play to the right? Does it accomplish anything to drive over these bunkers, or should he place the drive down the intended fairway? Macdonald wanted long hitters and short hitters on equal terms when they played a match on his course.

C. B. Macdonald completed his course in 1909, after eight years of planning and two years of actual construction. It was named, somewhat immodestly, The National Golf Links of America. But the course lived up to its name as well as to its advance billing. It was like no other course in the country, and every player, every writer, every course designer who viewed it marveled at it. British observers, too, were astonished at what an ideal links creation Charlie Macdonald had wrought. Horace Hutchinson, Bernard Darwin and Ben Sayers, professional at North Berwick, all wrote laudatory articles about The National Golf Links in British publications between 1910 and 1913, the ultimate tribute to an American course.

Macdonald, who coined the title "golf architect" in 1902, would design fifteen other courses before his death in 1939, adhering to the same principles that made The National Golf Links so successful. But his clients would find his projects expensive. His Yale Golf Club, for instance, cost nearly half a million dollars, and his Lido Golf Club cost three quarters of a million. Macdonald never personally accepted a fee for any of his architectural work, however, with the exception of a lifetime membership in the club for which he was working.

All of Macdonald's later designs featured the same sort of adaptation of famous holes. He invariably built a "Redan" on each of his courses, and an "Eden." He also built a "Cape" hole on each layout, patterned after his fourteenth at The National. That hole, a dogleg par-4 across a bay with the green perched precariously close to the water, was truly a design original by Macdonald. The same hole can be found at the Yale Golf Club (the third), the St. Louis Country Club (the eighth) and, most dramatically, at the Mid-Ocean Club in Bermuda where it appears as the fifth hole.

Macdonald spent the majority of his time at The National Golf Links in his later years and forever tinkered with the bunkering on some holes and the slope of the greens on others. He was uncharacteristically hesitant to join in the acclaim for his magnificent creation; even as late as 1928 he wrote, "I am not confident the course is perfect and beyond criticism to-day." [5]

But Macdonald was a perfectionist. For the rest of the golfing world, The National was a course without

peer. Its excellence would cause the rebuilding of many American golf courses, even some of the best, and would influence the quality of courses yet to be conceived.

Despite somewhat rigid classical lines, the work of Macdonald, as well as W. J. Travis and others, contributed great impressiveness to the style of American course architecture. Certainly Myopia and Garden City, and also Ekwanok, were fine American courses. At the same time, Sunningdale, Walton Heath and Woking, across the Atlantic, were also exceedingly well done. But The National was in a class by itself. It would be accurate to say that Charles Blair Macdonald and The National Golf Links of America revolutionized golf course architecture. Soon after it opened, H. J. Whigham wrote:

> There are many features about the National Links which will make the course famous; for example, the undulating putting greens, the absence of blind holes—nearly every tee commands a view of the entire length of the hole—and the size of the bunkers. But the main achievement is that a course has been produced where every hole is a good one and presents a new problem. That is something which has never yet been accomplished, even in Scotland; and in accomplishing it here, Mr. Macdonald has inaugurated a new era in golf.[6]

It is interesting to speculate on the influence that thoughts and trends from America may have had on British golf architecture in the years before World War I. America was preeminent in early earth-moving techniques, while turfgrass research was soon underway at a number of agricultural colleges. Several American architects were prolific writers, and many course planners from Britain and America were shuttling back and forth across the Atlantic. Doubtless an interchange of ideas among contemporaries occurred, and the highly laudatory articles describing The National Golf Links in British publications no doubt enhanced this influence.

[1] Walter J. Travis, "Merits and Demerits of the Garden City Links," *Country Life*, February 1906, p. 446.
[2] "The Amateur Golf Championship of 1908," *Harper's Weekly Magazine*, September 26, 1908, p. 10.
[3] C. B. Macdonald, *Scotland's Gift—Golf*, London: Charles Scribner's Sons, 1928, p. 173.
[4] Ibid., p. 182.
[5] Ibid., p. 193.
[6] H. J. Whigham, "The Ideal Golf Links," *Scribner's Magazine*, May 1909, p. 585.

6

6.

The Pennsylvanian Influence

Myopia in Massachusetts, Garden City and the National Golf Links on Long Island and Ekwanok in Vermont all contributed significantly to the advancement of American golf architecture in the early 1900s. By 1910 the scene of important activity had shifted to Pennsylvania. In the years before the first World War, that state was full of men who dreamed of building first-rate golf courses and did so. Their names are now familiar in golf design: Henry C. Fownes and his son, William C. Fownes; George C. Thomas, Jr.; A. W. Tillinghast; Hugh Wilson; William S. Flynn; and George Crump.

Henry C. Fownes's brainchild was the Oakmont Country Club. Fownes, son of a Pittsburgh steel tycoon, conceived the idea of building a links-type course on the plateau overlooking the Allegheny River northeast of the steel town. He organized a golf club in 1903 to fund his project, secured the property and drew the plans for his dream course. Then he set out with a crew of 150 men and two dozen mule teams and spent a year building it.

When Oakmont opened in 1904, it featured eight par-5's, one par-6 (the 560-yard twelfth hole) and a total par of 85 (this was bogey 85 corresponding to neither today's par nor today's bogey). It had no trees to speak of but did have huge, rolling greens; and its length reflected the acceptance of the Haskell ball.

Henry Fownes was satisfied with his course, but his son, William, was not. The younger Fownes, after he won the 1910 U. S. Amateur, appointed himself permanent course consultant to the Oakmont club and for the next thirty years continually made suggestions on how it could be improved. In summer he lived at the clubhouse and beginning in 1911, spent many an evening walking the course with its greenkeeper, deciding what changes were to be made.

Fownes was determined to make Oakmont the toughest course in the world. "A shot poorly played," he once remarked, "should be a shot irrevocably lost."[1] In order to implement this philosophy, Fownes sought the assistance of two greenkeepers, first John McGlynn and later Emil "Dutch" Loeffler. (Loeffler remained as green-keeper at Oakmont throughout his life, but during the 1920s, he and McGlynn maintained an active golf design and building practice on the side.)

The revisions made to the Oakmont course by Fownes and his assistants were numerous. Holes were lengthened and the par reduced. Ditches were dug in the rough to improve drainage and to create playing problems. The ditches were played as hazards and were, in fact, almost unplayable. Greens were canted in another effort to improve drainage, and kept cut very short. And a huge number of bunkers were added throughout the course.

Oakmont became the epitome of the penal style of golf course architecture. At one time, the course is said to have had 220 bunkers, an average of a dozen per hole. Since the heavy clay base upon which the course was built prevented the digging of all but a few deep bunkers, Fownes and Loeffler concocted a device to add to the difficulty of the otherwise flat, shallow bunkers. It was a special rake that, when dragged through the thick, brown river sand in Oakmont's bunkers, left deep grooves or furrows. Many felt it took two special talents to extract a ball from an Oakmont bunker—one if the ball sat on a ridge in the sand, another if it settled in a trough. Others believed that since a ball seldom stayed on the ridges in the sand, Oakmont's bunkers were easier to recover from than those raked in the conventional manner. Indeed, several neighboring courses adopted Oakmont's furrowed rake. In the 1960s, the river sand was replaced, the furrows eliminated and almost a quarter of the bunkers filled in. But that still left some 180 of them, which is sand enough for any challenge.

Oakmont's greens were always clipped exceedingly short, to approximately 3/32nds of an inch; and at Fownes's insistence, they were watered and rolled with a heavy roller before most golf events. Except for some modifications (most notably the relocation of number eight, an admittedly "awful" green), the club through the years has zealously preserved their greens basically as they were in the days of Fownes and Loeffler, and jealously protected their reputation as treacherous to putt.

P. 62-63: Merion GC, Hole #11, East Course by Hugh Wilson. In the years just before WWI, Pennsylvania was full of men who dreamed of building first-rate courses. Names like Fownes, Thomas, Tillinghast, Flynn, Crump and Wilson are now familiar. P. 65: Plantings in the bunkers at Merion leave the impression of British parkland and links courses.

William Fownes certainly achieved what he set out to accomplish. Oakmont has not been revered but feared. It is a decidedly homely course in appearance. Yet the club has wisely protected it from any massive facelifting. Oakmont remains as a classic example of the penal school of golf design.

At about the time Henry Fownes was opening Oakmont, George C. Thomas, Jr., was planning a course at the other end of Pennsylvania. Thomas was from one of the state's oldest and wealthiest families. He lived on the family estate, the Bloomfield Farm, in the Chestnut Hill area of Philadelphia. There he dabbled in landscaping and gardening, and even wrote a book about roses.

In 1905 a newly formed golf club offered to purchase the Bloomfield Farm as the site for their course. Thomas accepted, on condition that he be allowed to design the course. The club agreed, reasoning that Thomas had some previous course design experience, in Massachusetts and New Jersey; and, perhaps of greater importance, he didn't want to be paid for his services.

Thomas invited his close friend Samuel Heebner, then president of the Golf Association of Philadelphia, to assist him in the work. Together they routed the course, supervised its construction and refined it with the placement of traps and the planting of trees. The house in which Thomas was born and raised became the clubhouse, and in 1908 the Mount Airy Country Club was officially opened. Within a few years of its opening, the club changed its name to the Whitemarsh Valley Country Club. Ever since, the course has remained basically as Thomas and Heebner designed it, with small greens, liberal trapping and unusual balance. One of its par-3's was a monster at 235 yards. Another was a mere 125-yard pitch. Both were difficult to par.

Sam Heebner never designed another course; but Thomas, who moved to California after the War, did several more. To George Thomas, golf design was never really a profession, and often he did not accept a fee for his work. But he took his avocation seriously. He had very definite ideas about how a golf hole should challenge a golfer and how it should not, and he was not always tolerant of others' criticisms of his ideas.

Thomas was one of the few American golf course architects to record his philosophy in a book. That work, *Golf Architecture in America*, published in 1927, remains one of the finest in the literature of golf. In addition to his book, George C. Thomas, Jr., is best known for his marvelous work in California that includes the North and South courses for the Los Angeles Country Club (for

which Englishman Herbert Fowler did the preliminary plan), the Ojai Valley Golf Club, the Bel-Air Country Club and the Riviera Country Club.

Like Thomas, Albert W. Tillinghast was the son of a wealthy Philadelphian. The elder Tillinghast owned a rubber works, and for the first thirty years of his life Albert was a playboy. He was infatuated with the game of golf and made several trips to Scotland before the turn of the century, specifically to the shop of Old Tom Morris at St. Andrews, where he enjoyed discussions on design philosophy. Back home, "Tilly" belonged to Philadelphia's most fashionable clubs, and he competed in several national amateur championships.

In 1907 a close friend of the Tillinghast family, Charles Worthington (of pump fame and later to be the mower-equipment magnate), asked Albert to assist him in laying out a golf course. Worthington was building a resort on the Delaware River and reasoned that a "sporty links" would insure its success. Although he knew absolutely nothing about building a golf course, Tilly accepted the offer.

He soon took complete charge of the project, examining the site, drawing the plans and supervising the construction. The finished project, the Shawnee Country Club, was a remarkably fine first effort. Tilly had incorporated both the Delaware and Binnikill Rivers into his design and built some rather novel teeing areas on several holes. Shawnee quickly became the most popular resort in the Poconos. It remains in existence today, although the course has been radically redesigned and bears little resemblance to the original Tillinghast design.

Nevertheless, Albert Tillinghast, at the age of thirty-two, had discovered his calling. Tilly was determined to be the best in his new-found profession and with typical intensity, devoted all his energies to it. He established an office in Manhattan, gathered together a construction crew and advertised his availability. He was stubborn enough not to accept any design job unless his firm could also construct the course. This allowed him to insure that his plans would be carried out correctly. It also meant a bigger fee from each client.

There are those who say that, in his time, Albert W. Tillinghast was indeed the best. He was not as prolific as many of his contemporaries, they admit; nor did he ever build a breathtaking course on dramatic terrain. But, they argue, his courses have endured the test of time. A look at his list of accomplishments lends support to that view. Among his best-known works are the Upper and Lower courses at Baltusrol and the Ridgewood Country Club in

New Jersey, the East and West courses at Winged Foot and the Black course at Bethpage State Park in New York, the Five Farms course of the Baltimore Country Club in Maryland, the San Francisco Golf Club in California, the Brook Hollow Country Club in Texas and the Hermitage Country Club in Virginia. These courses, as well as most others Tilly designed, survived over the years, having been changed very little.

Sad to say, the memory of Albert Tillinghast did not last. By the late 1920s Tilly had made himself well over a million dollars. By the end of the Depression he had lost it all. And by 1937 Tilly had forsaken the game of golf entirely, and he spent his remaining years in obscurity running an antique shop in Beverly Hills, California. Indeed, so totally forgotten was Tilly that for years after his death, writers, when talking of his works, referred to him as "Arthur" or "Archie" Tillinghast. It was not until 1974, when someone noticed that four USGA championships were being held on courses of his design, that the public was reintroduced to Albert Tillinghast. That was accomplished by USGA official Frank Hannigan in a widely circulated magazine article that still stands as the most thorough profile of any American golf architect.

Another Philadelphian who entered golf course architecture by chance was Hugh Wilson. Wilson was a member of the Merion Cricket Club (renamed in 1942 the Merion Golf Club) and was on the committee appointed to plan a new course in 1909 when the club decided to move to new quarters. The committee decided a first-hand look at the famous courses of Britain was needed before any attempt to build a course was made. Hugh Wilson was given the honor of making the trip. It has been suggested that Wilson, who suffered with illness throughout his life, was sent to Britain in hopes it would restore his health. It's more likely that he was chosen because his business, insurance brokerage, allowed him an extended leave of absence, and because he was the best golfer of the group.

Before he left, Wilson paid a visit to the site of the National Golf Links of America in Southampton. He not only carefully examined the course under construction there but also discussed an itinerary with C. B. Macdonald, who had made many similar journeys years before.

Wilson spent seven months in England and Scotland, playing and studying courses and sketching the features that most impressed him. When he returned, the committee was content to let Hugh have at it. So, with the aid of committee member Richard Francis, who could read a

transit, Wilson plotted out an eighteen hole course on the L-shaped 127 acres Merion had purchased in Ardmore. C. B. Macdonald and H. J. Whigham both offered advice on the endeavor.

But when the new Merion course opened in 1912, it did not attract much public attention. Four of the holes, numbers 1, 10, 11 and 12, originally played across Ardmore Avenue. In the early 1920s Wilson redesigned these holes to eliminate the road crossings. Over the years, after the course was remodeled and refined, the golfing world came to recognize its virtues.

It started with two par-5's among the first four played and finished with three demanding holes routed around an abandoned stone quarry. There were no blind shots to any green. All its bunkers, which eventually numbered some 120, were also clearly visible. Legend has it that Joe Valentine, Merion's legendary greenkeeper, would spread bed sheets on the site of a proposed bunker while Wilson would assure himself, from some vantage point back down the fairway, that the hazard could be seen. Long ago these bunkers were dubbed the "White Faces of Merion."

It has been suggested that Hugh Wilson grasped the basic concepts of British golf design and conveyed them in his work, even better than Charles Blair Macdonald. It is not quite fair, however, to compare Merion and the National Golf Links. They are two fine courses born of different intentions. Hugh Wilson never meant to duplicate any British golf hole in his design of Merion. Rather, he had hoped to capture the flavor, beauty and playability of a British parkland course. Certain subtle touches at Merion, such as patches of Scotch broom in several bunkers, wicker-basket pins instead of the usual flagsticks and a wild swale in the seventeenth green reminiscent of the Valley of Sin at St. Andrews, leave that impression, as does the overall effect when playing the course. But Merion has always been an innovative, thoroughly American original.

Hugh Wilson was involved in the design of a few other courses. In 1914 he laid out a second course at Merion, the West Course located a few miles down the road, which has always suffered unduly by continual comparison with the original course. In 1925 he began a complete revision of the East Course's bunkering. But he died unexpectedly that year of pneumonia, at only forty-five years of age.

Another designer closely connected with Merion was William S. Flynn. Flynn had been lured from his home in Massachusetts to the construction site of Merion in 1911 with an offer to become its greenkeeper. He worked on

the construction crew and then did serve as greenkeeper for a very short time before leaving for war service. But Flynn made three enduring friendships in this short time at Merion. One was with Joe Valentine, the construction foreman who, on Flynn's recommendation, succeeded him as greenkeeper. Another was with Hugh Wilson himself. Flynn respected Wilson's knowledge, talent and experience in the British Isles and Wilson provided Flynn with practical suggestions that he was able to apply to his new courses.

Flynn's third friendship was with Howard C. Toomey, a civil engineer who worked on the construction of Merion East. When Flynn decided after the War to enter the profession of course architecture, he formed a partnership with Toomey. Howard handled bookkeeping and construction aspects; Bill took care of public relations and the actual designing.

The firm of Toomey and Flynn operated out of Philadelphia for over a dozen years. They created some magnificent layouts, including the Spring Mill course for the Philadelphia Country Club; the Cascades course for The Homestead in Hot Springs, Virginia; the James River

course for the Country Club of Virginia in Richmond; and the Cherry Hills Country Club in Denver. They were also chosen to finish revising the bunkering at Merion East after Hugh Wilson's death.

One final Pennsylvania contribution to golf architecture in this period was by George A. Crump, although the course he built is actually in New Jersey, some twenty miles southeast of Philadelphia. Crump was the founder of the Pine Valley Golf Club in Clementon, New Jersey, generally considered the most difficult course in the world. Crump, the millionaire owner of the Colonnades Hotel in Philadelphia, conceived his idea to build a dream course in the sandy pine forest of New Jersey in 1912. Although he had the financial backing of many enthusiastic club members, including George C. Thomas, Jr., Crump spent over a quarter of a million dollars of his own money on the project.

Crump literally moved to the site and walked every foot of the property in an attempt to devise a basic layout. Finally, in 1913, he secured the services of H. S. Colt, who was touring the eastern seaboard, to help him route his

P. 68: *Merion GC, Hole #9, East course.*
P. 69: *(Left) Merion's wicker basket pins enhance the sense of a British parkland course.* P. 69: *(Right) Wilson's "White Faces of Merion," created with the help of legendary superintendent Joe Valentine.*

course. When Colt visited the site, he surely was struck by its similarity to the land around Sunningdale, the architect's home course in Britain. Indeed, countless British visitors to Pine Valley have remarked on the uncanny resemblance of the two settings.

Together Crump and Colt routed a preliminary layout that proved to be so sound that it was altered only twice during construction. Colt, on a later visit, convinced Crump to make the par-3 fifth into a long-iron shot rather than the short pitch originally planned. The fifteenth hole was extended from a par-4 to a par-5 when finally constructed.

In 1914 Crump and his crew began a long, tedious term of construction. Thousands of trees were felled and the stumps removed; they stopped counting at 22,000 stumps. The area was replete with natural springs, which provided much needed water. But it also necessitated the creation of several concrete dams to form spring-fed lakes. Soil was hauled in for tees, fairways and greens, for the existing land was primarily sand, although with modern irrigation systems the sand would have been ideal.

By the end of 1914 Crump had eleven holes ready for play, the original nine plus the present tenth and eighteenth holes. By 1917 all but four holes, numbers 12 through 15, were complete. But then, in January of 1918, George Crump died. The club raised sufficient funds to finish the eighteen holes, and Hugh Wilson of Merion, and his brother Alan, spent the remainder of 1918 completing Pine Valley. The Wilsons made a few alterations to the plans of Crump and Colt, most notably the aforementioned extension of the fifteenth hole.

Even before it formally opened as an eighteen-hole course in 1919, Pine Valley had earned a phenomenal reputation, not only among golfers but among golf architects. Travis, Tillinghast and Flynn all visited the course and were enthusiastic about its possibilities. Donald Ross and Charles Blair Macdonald both pronounced it the greatest course in the country.

What garnered Pine Valley such high praise from designers who were normally partial to their own works was perhaps the unique concept of the course. No other American course was like Pine Valley. Its fairways and greens were islands of playable turf, surrounded by natural sandy wastelands. Nearly every hole featured a forced

carry over unmaintained sand and brush to the fairway and another such carry to the green. While a great many trees had been removed in building Pine Valley, a great many remained, and over the years more grew back. By mid-century, few other courses in America were as thickly forested. The artificial lakes Crump built also came into play. Certain greens were precariously close to the water, like those of numbers 14 and 18.

Because it required such precise placement of each golf shot, Pine Valley was punishing to even the finest of players. Its introduction marked the zenith of the penal school of golf course architecture in America. No course quite like it has been built since, and no course has ever been as demanding of every stroke. Pine Valley remains today just as it did when it opened, a monument to its creator, George Crump, who never lived to see its fruition.

Emphasis on the Pennsylvanian influence on this period of golf design history is not intended to imply that other designers were not busy doing impressive things

elsewhere. Among the designs of John Duncan Dunn in this period was the Quaker Ridge Country Club in Mamaroneck, New York. C. B. Macdonald tackled a new challenge in 1914, the construction of a links entirely upon land reclaimed from the sea. This course, the Lido Golf Club in Long Beach, New York, opened after the War.

By 1911 Donald Ross had embraced the profession almost full time, although he was still professional at Pinehurst, North Carolina. While he continued to operate from there, his reputation had become such that he was called upon to design courses in many parts of the country. Among the dozens of Donald Ross courses that opened in this period before World War I were the Brae Burn Country Club in Massachusetts, the Wannamoisett Country Club in Rhode Island, the Oakland Hills Country Club in Michigan, the Scioto Country Club in Ohio, the Bob O'Link Golf Club in Illinois, the Broadmoor Golf Club in Colorado and the Atlanta Athletic Club (now the East Lake Country Club) in Georgia.

The British invasion of golf talent into the United States also continued in this era. Foremost among the second wave of emigrants who would have an impact on American course architecture were Herbert Strong and Norman Macbeth.

Strong, a professional from St. George's Golf Club in England, came to the United States with his brother Leonard in 1905 to compete in several golf events. Strong remained in the States and while serving as professional at the Inwood Country Club in New York, redesigned and rebuilt that club's course. He soon devoted a majority of his time to course design, and by the 1930s Herbert Strong would be responsible for some of the finest courses in North America: the Canterbury Country Club in Cleveland, Ohio; the Metropolis Golf Club in New York; Ponte Vedra Golf Club in Florida; Club Laval Sur Le Lac in Montreal; and Manoir Richelieu in Quebec.

Norman Macbeth, a tall, quiet Scot, ventured to America in 1901 and subsequently settled in Los Angeles. A fine player, who would win both the Southern and Northern California Amateur titles, Macbeth had his first design experience assisting in the layout of a new eighteen holes for the Los Angeles Country Club in 1911. He designed several southern California courses, including the San Gabriel Country Club, the Annandale Golf Club and his home course, the Wilshire Country Club.

And there were others who came in the early 1900s: Leslie Brownlee, a Scot who introduced the game to Oklahoma and built that territory's first courses; Grange "Sandy" Alves, who worked primarily as a greenkeeper in Cleveland but also designed several Ohio-area courses; Albert Murray, who moved with his brother Charles from England to Canada at an early age, won the Canadian Open at twenty and eventually designed several Canadian layouts; William Kinnear, a Scot who settled in Saskatoon in 1910 and did several early courses including Riverside Country Club in Saskatchewan; and Robert Johnstone, who served as professional at the Seattle Golf Club for many years and did a number of fine courses on the West Coast, including his own club's course.

A disturbing but temporary postscript to this period arose in 1916 when golf architects accepting fees for their services were stripped of their amateur status under the Amateur Rule. It was restored in 1921, however, when it was decided that the true definition of professionalism lay in making a profit from skill in playing the game.

[1] The Golf Journal, U.S.G.A. May 1973, p. 8.

P. 70: *Before and after the First World War, earth was moved by horses or mules pulling scrapers.*
P. 71: *Months were sometimes required to move the necessary earth and rough grade in a single green. Architects took advantage of the leisurely pace to alter their plans and add subtle touches as their features were executed on the ground.*

7.

The Roaring Twenties:
The Golden Age of Course Design

When the Great War in Europe broke out in 1914, it found many Britons who relied upon golf for a livelihood in America. Some of those involved in golf course architecture returned to their native land, while others stayed on in their new homes. Around this time, Herbert Fowler set up offices in the United States; but by the early 1920s he moved back to Britain, where he designed, among other fine courses, thirty-six holes for The Berkshire. Willie Park, Jr., came to North America at about the same time Fowler did. But unlike Fowler, he remained in America until 1924, when he returned to Scotland because of serious illness. He died a year later.

Among other emigrants who, like Park, chose to stay in America after the War were:

· Wilfrid Reid, who had competed on several occasions in the United States. Reid settled as a club professional but designed over fifty courses and remodeled some forty others in a period of thirty years.

· Tom Winton, who came to America to work for Willie Park and then took a position with the Westchester County (New York) Park Commission. He built and maintained several public courses for that county.

· Harry Robb, of Montrose, Scotland, who built the Milburn Golf and Country Club in Kansas City, Kansas, and became its pro. He also laid out several other courses in Kansas.

· James Dalgleish, of Nairn, Scotland, who, like Robb, settled in Kansas City. Dalgleish designed courses all across the Midwest.

· David Hunter, the son of Charles Hunter of Prestwick, who did several courses in the New Jersey area while serving as professional at Baltusrol and Essex County (New Jersey) CC.

· David T. Millar, of Arbroath, Scotland, who settled in Detroit and was responsible for several courses in that area.

· Willard Wilkinson, who came from England and was associated with Tillinghast before starting a career that continued from the 1920s into the early 1960s.

H. S. Colt also practiced course architecture in America sporadically during the war years. Later he encouraged a new associate, Charles Hugh Alison, to join him. The two had met when Colt was laying out the Stoke Poges Golf Club in Britain where Alison was club secretary.

Perhaps because he had started in the same fashion, Colt was sympathetic to the young Alison's earnest desire to learn the trade. He gave Alison the chance to work with him, and Charles showed himself to be adept at supervising construction and equally talented at designing golf holes. By 1920 the two had formed a full partnership.

Alison was probably the first truly "worldwide" golf course architect. He was responsible for a majority of the work of the firm of Colt and Alison in the United States, including the North Shore and Knollwood Country Clubs near Chicago, Illinois; the Burning Tree Club near Washington, D.C.; and the complete rebuilding of nearby Chevy Chase. He also worked in Australia and Europe, and was the first architect to build first-rate courses in Japan. At the time of his death, in 1952, he was working on yet another course, this one in South Africa.

If Alison was not the first worldwide designer, then the title surely belongs to Alister Mackenzie. Mackenzie was a physician by profession; but he abandoned his medical practice in 1909 after assisting H. S. Colt with the design of his home club's course, Alwoodley, in Leeds. He worked with Colt on several other courses, most notably the Eden at St. Andrews, and for a time was a partner in the firm of Colt, Alison and Mackenzie. But by 1925 he was on his own and spent the remaining years of his life globetrotting, producing fine courses in such widespread locales as Ireland (where he remodeled the Lahinch Golf Club), Uruguay (the Golf Club de Uruguay), Australia (where he did several, including the West course of the Royal Melbourne Golf Club), Argentina (the Jockey Club at San Isidro) and Canada (the North course of the St. Charles Country Club in Winnipeg). Mackenzie finally settled in the United States where, as will be noted, he did perhaps his finest work.

P. 72–73: *Hole #17, Cypress Point by Mackenzie. Many of the fine American courses of the 1920s were planned by visiting or transplanted Britishers.*
P. 75: (Top) *Sea Island, Georgia, Seaside 9 was originally the work of Colt and Alison.* P. 75: (Bottom) *Longmeadow CC, Massachusetts, was planned in 1922 by Donald Ross, soon to become the top name in American course design.*

Tom Simpson, who had obtained a legal degree at Cambridge but found no need to practice law, joined Herbert Fowler's firm in 1910. After the War they were partners in a company that expanded in the 1920s to include J. F. Abercrombie and A. C. M. Croome.

Simpson was one of the great characters in the history of golf course architecture. He was a wealthy man and an accomplished writer and artist. He made a major contribution with *The Architectural Side of Golf*, which he authored in 1929 with H. N. Wethered. It featured numerous ink-and-wash sketches of golf holes, all by Simpson.

Simpson was, in fact, eccentric. He traveled from construction site to construction site in a silver, chauffeur-driven Rolls Royce, invariably dressed in cloak and beret with riding crop in hand. He once selected an assistant on the basis of the young man's suggestion as to how to mount a license plate attractively on a Rolls. Such an artistic eye, Simpson felt, would be valuable in course design. Eccentric or not, Tom Simpson's judgment was sound. The young assistant he hired was Philip Mackenzie Ross, who would prove himself after World War II to be one of Britain's finest designers.

Tom Simpson's abilities as a golf course architect were also sound. During the twenties in Britain, he did such fine work as the remodeled New Zealand Golf Club at Byfleet in England and the Cruden Bay course in Aberdeen. His finest efforts, however, were found on the Continent, at courses like Deauville (the New course), Chantilly and Morfontaine in France.

James Braid continued to produce fine layouts during the 1920s. He did, among others, a new course for Royal Musselburgh, and the East and West courses at Dalmahoy; and he remodeled the Carnoustie Golf Club into the severe test of golf we know today. His assistant at Carnoustie was John R. Stutt, a landscape contractor, who remained associated with Braid through the rest of the old man's design career and who became increasingly involved in the planning.

Another one-time Braid assistant was Cecil Hutchison, a former British Army officer and one of Scotland's finest amateurs. Hutchison learned a great deal from Braid and in the twenties began building courses of his own design. He worked on occasion with Guy Campbell, another ex-Army officer and a descendant of a golfing family.

Sir Guy Campbell was a successful amateur golfer and a superb writer. He worked with Bernard Darwin on the sports staff of the *London Times* until the mid-1920s when he resigned, unable to resist the lure of golf course design. His first work was the West Sussex Golf Club in England, done with the assistance of Hutchison. Guy Campbell maintained a steady design practice the rest of his life. Among his best works were the revisions of the Prince's Golf Club in England (with J. S. F. Morrison) and the Killarney Golf Club in Ireland. Sir Guy died in 1960 while laying out his only course in the United States, the Tides Inn in Virginia.

One other designer worked with Hutchison and Campbell at West Sussex. He was S. V. Hotchkin, also a former Army officer, who first became involved in course design in 1922 after purchasing and remodeling the Woodhall Spa Golf Club. For a time Hotchkin, Hutchison and Campbell were partners in an architectural firm. They later separated and Hotchkin moved to South Africa, ostensibly to retire. But he undertook to plan several of that country's finest courses, including the Humewood and Durban Country Clubs.

By the 1920s golf course architecture was also a full-time profession for a great many on the western side of the Atlantic. It was a special period of growing prosperity in America. Construction costs, real estate values and interest rates were low. Clients were willing and able to pay for the best and gave designers a free hand. Consequently, the twenties have been called the Golden Age of Golf Course Architecture in America, and these years saw the flair and style of golf courses enhanced immeasurably.

There had been some 742 courses in the United States in 1916. By 1923 there were 1,903. By 1929 there would be 5,648! That was an average increase of approximately 600 new courses per year from 1923 to 1929. Such a rapid growth rate would not be approached again until 1967.

It may seem impossible that a few dozen professional course architects could design so many courses in the United States and abroad, considering the fact that train rides between projects took days and boat trips required weeks. The truth is, professional designers did only a fraction of the courses built in the twenties. A good many courses, perhaps a majority, were still being laid out and built by locals or immigrants who remained indefinitely as pro-greenkeepers. Alex "Nipper" Campbell, for example, was a Scot who designed and built the Moraine Country Club in Dayton, Ohio, and then stayed on as its professional for decades. While men like this sometimes designed a few other courses in their locale, they never truly practiced course architecture.

There were also countless instances of "in-house" planning and design by a member or committee of a private club or by a city or county official for a new public layout. The Maidstone Golf Links, originally laid out by

William Tucker, was completely redesigned by club member C. Wheaton Vaughan.

Even in cases where a professional designer was hired, the architect sometimes provided the client with no more than one or two days at the actual site. In that time he would inspect the land, route the course, prepare an outline, sketches or diagrams of the holes and instruct the members on how to construct and maintain the course. This may have been a step above the practice of "eighteen stakes on a Sunday afternoon," but it was not a very big step. It left many clubs, or governing bodies in the case of public courses, to fend for themselves; and it is doubtful if such procedures ever produced a course as the architect had envisaged it. In some cases, the architect was not even present at the site. James Braid remodeled the St. Andrews Golf Club on Mt. Hope, New York, without ever setting foot on the property or even in the country. He recommended changes solely by examining topographical maps of the course at his home in England.

The preferable method involved an architect who, after inspecting the site and designing the basic course layout, would remain himself or leave an experienced superintendent to build the course, with the architect periodically visiting the site to inspect the evolution of his design and make adjustments and corrections as needed. A good number of these construction superintendents, men like Orrin Smith and James Harrison, later entered the field of golf course design.

Toomey and Flynn, Herbert Strong, Walter Travis, A. W. Tillinghast, Devereux Emmet, John D. Dunn and C. B. Macdonald were still very active along the east coast of the United States during the "Roaring Twenties." Macdonald was always assisted by his right-hand man, Seth Raynor, on the dozen or so courses he designed in these years.

Raynor not only constructed all of Macdonald's designs but did some sixty courses of his own. He had established his own practice in 1915 but was most prolific after the War. He played the main role in the remodeling of the Chicago Golf Club, which has been credited entirely, but incorrectly, to Macdonald. Other Raynor originals include the Country Club of Fairfield and the Greenwich Country Club, both in Connecticut, and the Yeaman's Hall Club in Charleston, South Carolina.

Raynor was responsible for luring two academicians into the field of golf design. The first was Charles H. Banks, an English professor at the Hotchkiss School of Salisbury, Connecticut, which hired Raynor to lay out its course. Banks served on the construction committee and worked closely with Raynor; when the latter moved on,

Banks resigned and went with him.

The other was Ralph M. Barton, a faculty member at the University of Minnesota. Raynor was hired to design a course for that institution, and Barton volunteered to supervise the construction. When this course was complete, Barton, like Banks, joined Raynor full time. (Ironically, at least one other math professor became a golf course architect, although in this case, Seth Raynor had nothing to do with the conversion. He was John Bredemus, a prominent Texas designer of the 1930s.)

The team of Raynor, Banks and Barton, along with C. B. Macdonald, went on to create another university course. In the mid-1920s they designed and built the excellent Yale University Golf Club. It was to be Raynor's last effort, for he died of pneumonia in 1926. Banks, who would die only five years later, finished several of Raynor's designs and did quite a few fine courses of his own in the East and Bermuda. Barton returned to his native New Hampshire and planned a number of courses in New England, including one nine of the Hanover Country Club owned by Dartmouth College. Macdonald did no more designing (except for endless tinkering with the National Golf Links), preferring to write his memoirs, which were published in 1928 as *Scotland's Gift—Golf.* This book contains several passages concerning his philosophy of golf course architecture.

Also active on the East Coast were: Maurice J. McCarthy, an Irish immigrant who is best known for the several courses he did at Hershey, Pennsylvania; Fred Findlay, Alexander's brother, who was hired from Australia by a Virginia seed firm and did most of his designing in that state; Orrin E. Smith, a former construction superintendent for both Donald Ross and Willie Park, Jr., who opened his own offices in Hartford, Connecticut, in 1924; Wayne E. Stiles, a landscape architect, and John R. Van Kleek, a landscape architect and civil engineer, who, as the Boston and Florida firm of Stiles and Van Kleek, did such notable courses as the Taconic Golf Club in Massachusetts; and Alfred H. Tull, a Walter Travis apprentice who became a partner of Devereux Emmet and his son in the firm of Emmet, Emmet and Tull.

In the Midwest, Chicago was a hotbed of golfing activity. Besides the old Scot Tom Bendelow, at least a dozen other full or part-time golf course architects could be found in that area. Among them were: Robert Bruce Harris, formally trained as a landscape architect; William B. Langford and Theodore Moreau, the firm of Langford and Moreau; C. D. Wagstaff; Leonard Macomber; Frank Macdonald and Charles Maddox, the firm of Macdonald and Maddox; Jack Daray; Harry Collis; Edward B. Dearie,

Jr.; Joseph A. Roseman; and George O'Neill. In Indianapolis, prominent amateur golfer William H. Diddel opened a practice.

On the West Coast, Willie Watson and William H. Tucker were busy during the 1920s. Tucker also had an active construction firm that built courses for a young Canadian designer, A. Vernon Macan. Macan laid out courses all along the West Coast, including the Broadmoor Country Club in Seattle, the Fircrest Country Club in Tacoma, the California Golf Club of San Francisco and a host of layouts in his home province of British Columbia.

Watson's construction superintendent for a time was William P. Bell, an easterner who came west in search of a fortune. Billy, who built most of the courses that George C. Thomas, Jr., designed in California in the 1920s, also had his own design firm. By the end of the decade, Billy Bell was one of the busiest architects of all. His early works include the Del Rio Golf and Country Club in Modesto, California, and the fine Stanford University Golf Club in Palo Alto.

Two nationally known amateur golfers became prominent golf designers in the Far West during the twenties. H. Chandler Egan, a two-time U.S. Amateur champion, moved from Chicago to Medford, Oregon, and laid out several courses in the Pacific Northwest, including the original Eugene Country Club in Oregon and the Indian Canyon Golf Course in Spokane, Washington. Max H. Behr, a U. S. Amateur runner-up, designed courses in southern California, including Rancho Santa Fe Golf Club and the Lakeside Golf Club of Hollywood.

One area on the West Coast, the Monterey Peninsula in California, was the location of two new courses that captured the attention of the golfing world in the 1920s. The courses, which were less than a mile apart, were the Pebble Beach Golf Links and the Cypress Point Club.

Pebble Beach opened for play in 1919. Its designers were two local men, Jack Neville and Douglas Grant. Neville was chosen because he was a fine golfer, several times a California Amateur champion, and because he was employed by the Pacific Improvement Company, the firm that owned the land and wisely chose to develop it into a golf course. Neville asked his friend, Douglas Grant, also a California Amateur champion, to assist him.

Neither man had any previous course design or construction experience. But like Hugh Wilson, George Crump and several other neophyte designers before them, Neville and Grant did an incredibly fine job. The course was adapted nicely into the existing terrain and very little

earth was moved. The greens were deliberately kept small and were liberally contoured. Most importantly, they managed to build seven holes on which the ocean came into play.

Pebble Beach was not a links, for it was located on bluffs overlooking Carmel Bay. But it had a distinctive links feel about it, strung out in loop fashion and subject to the strong ocean winds. It was a resort course from the very start and was available for everyone to play. In fact, its official title for years was the Del Monte Golf and Country Club after the Del Monte Lodge located there.

Although Pebble Beach has been modified on some occasions, including very minor changes by Alister Mackenzie in collaboration with Robert Hunter, and by H. Chandler Egan, who revised the bunkering on several holes in 1928, the course remains as Neville and Grant devised it, a dramatic combination of inland and seaside golf. Grant was content to play the game after that and never worked on another course design. Neville worked with several professional architects on other projects and also experienced the termination before construction of numerous projects of his own design. He remained at Pebble Beach all his life, and even in the 1970s USGA officials consulted with him before tampering with the course.

Ten years after the opening of Pebble Beach, Cypress Point, the work of the Britisher Alister Mackenzie, was unveiled. Cypress Point did not have a long, exciting stretch of ocean frontage like its neighbor, but its three dramatic ocean holes more than sufficed. The sixteenth hole was the most breathtaking. It was a long, long par-3 over a bay to a green set on a peninsula. The sixteenth has become, over the years, the most photographed and perhaps the most recognizable golf hole in the country. It also graphically demonstrates the strategic philosophy of golf design at its heroic extreme. On the sixteenth the bold player shoots directly to the green, 220 yards away, across pounding surf some 100 feet below. The cautious golfer plays short to dry land on the left, and then pitches to the green with hope of putting for a par. Without the alternate route, Cypress Point's sixteenth would have been a terribly penal hole, unreachable to all but a few strong golfers; with it, the sixteenth requires a player to choose his route before swinging. (Despite considerable evidence to the contrary, some claim the sixteenth was first planned as a par-4 with the tee farther back.)

The fifteenth, which is a par-3 as well, also borders an ocean bay, but it is a short pitch with the green much closer to the precipice. The seventeenth is a dogleg par-4, with the tee shot across the water and the fairway split

P. 78: (Top) *The Donald Ross bunker style, preserved through several remodelings on Course #2 at Pinehurst.*

P. 78: (Bottom) *Typical Ross bunkers at Monroe CC, Pittsford, New York. By the mid-1920s, Ross was receiving more requests for his services than he could accept. Some 3,000 men were employed annually building his courses.*

into two by a stand of cypress trees. The course has several other masterful holes.

Cypress Point was possibly Alister Mackenzie's best course to that time. Ironically, the founders of Cypress Point had not originally retained Mackenzie as their architect. They had hired Seth Raynor, who had done the nearby Monterey Peninsula Country Club course. But Raynor died and although he had left preliminary plans for the course, they were never used.

Two of Mackenzie's assistants at Cypress Point deserve mention. Robert Hunter, who assisted on several of Mackenzie's California designs, is best known for his dissertation on golf course architecture entitled *The Links,* which was published in 1925. Jack Fleming, who served as construction foreman on many of Mackenzie's designs, was later active as a course architect on his own in the 1950s and 60's. Mackenzie himself did other courses in California during the 1920s, including the Pasatiempo Golf Club in Santa Cruz and the Haggin Oaks Municipal Golf Course in Sacramento.

Mackenzie, Thomas, Bell, Tillinghast and many others made major contributions to course design in the 1920s. But the outstanding figures in course design in this period were probably the veteran Scot, Donald Ross, and a Scottish-born Canadian, Stanley Thompson.

Donald Ross had been designing courses in the United States since the early 1900s. By 1920 he was probably the most active architect in the country. He had a nationwide reputation and was hired to build courses from coast to coast. Indeed, six of the eight National Opens between 1919 and 1926 were played on courses of his design. Each new course gained him more attention, and it became a symbol of status to have a Donald Ross layout. The Northland Country Club in Duluth, Minnesota, turned down a fine Willie Watson design, even after Ross himself had urged them to accept it. They wanted a Donald Ross course, which he reluctantly gave them.

Many of Ross's designs were simply built to his plans and instructions, without his personal supervision; and the architect often commiserated over the fact that layouts credited to him were not as he had intended. But he himself continually worked on at least eight courses at a time during the twenties and had a loyal crew of construction supervisors over the years, including Walter B. Hatch, Walter Johnston, James B. McGovern, James Harrison and Henry T. Hughes, who carried out his designs at other sites. The courses he did in this era were of a uniformly high standard. Among them were the Plainfield

P. 80-81: *La Quinta Hotel GC., Ca., by Dye (1980), where lines of bunkers and mounds are in harmony with natural land forms. Principles of art were first applied to golf design in the 1920s by Stanley Thompson and others.*

P. 82–83: *Elaborate Ross bunkers at Plainfield CC. P. 83: (Right) Three of the five principles of art include harmony (Los Leones, Chile, top), emphasis (Pebble Beach GC, center) and proportion (Banff Springs, bottom).*

Country Club in New Jersey; the Salem and Winchester Country Clubs in Massachusetts; the East and West courses at the Oak Hill Country Club and the Monroe Country Club, both near Rochester, New York; the East and West courses at the Country Club of Birmingham in Alabama; the Essex Golf and Country Club and Rosedale in Ontario; the Belle Meade Country Club in Tennessee; and the River Oaks Country Club in Texas.

In the late 1920s, Donald Ross, the architect with more offers than he could ever fulfill, actually pursued a contract to design a course. It is likely this was the only time in his long career that he did so, but he had seen the site for the intended course and was intrigued by its possibilities. Ross's proposal won. Perhaps because it had required an extra effort to get the job, he gave an unusual amount of personal attention to the course.

The result was the Seminole Golf Club in North Palm Beach, Florida, possibly Ross's finest creation. Laid out along two small ridges just off the Atlantic, Seminole was an exquisite job. It was heavily bunkered, 187 in all; but the bunkers were positioned and constructed to convey a sense of the nearby rolling surf.

The course was built to provide a challenge for every level of handicap. Each hole had multiple tees and alternate routes to the green, for by this time Ross was a confirmed advocate of strategic golf design. One hole, the fifteenth, featured alternate fairways: a shorter route with tempting water carries, and a longer but drier route for those content to play the par-5 in par. Seminole exists today with but one exception, just as it did when Donald Ross first opened it in 1929.

Another major force in the twenties was Stanley Thompson. One of a clan of Canadian tournament golfers, Thompson entered the design field following his return from France after the War. He soon became the most conspicuous course architect in Canada, and his reputation spilled over the border to the United States, into the Caribbean and on to South America. Part of his fame was certainly attributable to the magnificent Banff and Jasper courses he constructed in the rugged Rockies of Alberta. Built in high country devoid of topsoil along a rushing mountain river, Banff had the dubious distinction of being the first course in history to cost a million dollars to construct.

Thompson was most vocal in the 1920s in expounding the merits of strategic design, and his works reflected his philosophy. Besides Banff and Jasper, other impressive courses he did in those years included the Royal York Golf and Country Club in Ontario (now known as St.

84

About GOLF COURSES
Their Construction and Up-Keep

◆

Stanley Thompson & Co.
Limited
Toronto   Montreal
Cleveland

George's) and the Ladies Golf Club of Toronto (probably the single "ladies only" golf club still in existence).

Stanley Thompson also launched the careers of several prominent contemporary designers. At one time or another, Geoffrey S. Cornish, Robert Moote, C. E. Robinson, Howard Watson and Norman Woods all worked for and with Thompson. And Robert Trent Jones, who, fresh out of Cornell, began assisting in the refining of Banff after it had opened, became Thompson's partner in 1930 and remained a lifelong friend even after he began his own illustrious career.

Important articles by American golf architects were appearing in periodicals of the twenties. Max Behr was a prolific writer, as were Walter Travis, founder and editor of *American Golfer*, and A. W. Tillinghast, who wrote for and later edited *Golf Illustrated*. The first years of the 1920s had also seen the publication in Great Britain of a book on course architecture by H. S. Colt assisted by C. H. Alison and A. Mackenzie, and another by Mackenzie on his own.

P. 84–85: *Memorabilia.* (Upper left) *Mackenzie in one of his own bunkers at Cypress Point. Resemblance of bunker shapes to the outline of nearby trees is in keeping with the art principle of harmony.* (Upper right) *Title page of Thompson's brochure.* (Lower left) *Evans was a strong advocate of formal training in golf design.* (Lower right) *Wee Burn CC., Conn. (1923) is a Dev Emmet masterpiece.*

8.

Golf Architecture in Depression and War

With readily available capital and an abundance of golf design talent, it seemed that the Golden Age of Golf Course Architecture would last forever. In reality, the era lasted only a scant ten years. The stock market crash of 1929, the bank closings of the early 1930s and the Great Depression brought an abrupt halt to course development in the United States.

The bank closings were especially harmful. Without financing, planned projects were shelved and existing projects abandoned. It was the rare club that had no members who lost fortunes.

Long-established clubs were able to weather the financial storm by implementing austerity measures. But the newer clubs, those born of the boom of the 1920s and patronized by younger men of new-found wealth, were vulnerable because they were overextended financially. Liberal lifetime or single-fee memberships had been handed out as promotional gimmicks. The remaining regular members could not meet the periodic dues. Such new clubs had operation and maintenance expenses to meet, as well as fees to course architects, contractors and sub-contractors. With insufficient revenues, they were forced to disband.

In New York, the Midvale Golf and Country Club filed for bankruptcy soon after its new golf course was finished. Midvale was the first professional design of architect Robert Trent Jones, and it marked an inauspicious debut to what would be an illustrious career. In California, the Lake Norconian Club collapsed, taking with it the finely designed course of John Duncan Dunn, who had been promoting it as his masterpiece. Real estate development courses, like Norman Macbeth's Midwick Club near Pasadena and George C. Thomas, Jr.'s El Caballero in Tarzana, also closed and the land was sold.

Most public and municipal courses managed to stay open, but they were poorly funded and maintained. The feast of the 1920s and the famine that followed in the 1930s clearly demonstrated to architects that the most magnificently designed and built course would not remain magnificent for very long when adequate funds were not available for upkeep.

Golf course architecture did not become a lost art during the American thirties and the war that followed, but it did become a highly neglected one. In the twenty years between 1932 and 1952, a total of only 200 new courses opened for play. In the same span of time, some 600 courses closed forever.

Times were hard for men in the golf design profession. Full-time architects, especially those who also contracted the construction, were severely affected. With clients defaulting on huge sums of money, many of these architects lost fortunes while trying to settle their accounts honorably from their own resources. Mackenzie, Tillinghast and Strong, among others, were never able to recoup their losses, and all three died in straitened circumstances.

Part-time architects fared somewhat better. Some, like Fred Findlay and Edward Dearie, were able to make a living working as greenkeepers or club managers. Others, like Wilf Reid, Jack Daray and Harry Collis, served as club professionals. Some, like Alfred Tull, entered the maintenance equipment business; and many others practiced professions unrelated to golf, like Norman Macbeth, who operated a cement firm.

A number of America's most prominent architects would die during the thirties. Tom Bendelow, Charles Banks, H. Chandler Egan, Devereux Emmet, Charles Blair Macdonald, Alister Mackenzie, Maurice McCarthy and George C. Thomas, Jr., were among them.

But there were some bright spots on the bleak American landscape of the Depression. In 1932 the long-awaited "dream course" of golfing phenomenon Robert Tyre "Bobby" Jones, Jr., opened in Augusta, Georgia. Jones called it the Augusta National Golf Club, and from its beginning the course was something very special. Jones had asked the renowned Alister Mackenzie to help design his course, and together they routed a stunning layout through the grounds of an old arboretum.

Augusta National was specifically designed with spectator golf in mind. Several greens were situated to provide vantage points from nearby hillsides. Several mounds were created to serve as seats for viewers, and over the

P. 86-87: *The Augusta National GC, Georgia, by Mackenzie. Although the Depression was worldwide, course construction outside the U.S. continued at a steady pace. Nationally there were a few bright spots, including "Bobby" Jones, Jr.'s "Dream course" at Augusta. P. 89: Prairie Dunes CC, Kansas, by Perry Maxwell, another bright spot on the bleak Depression landscape.*

years many more would be added. But Augusta National was also a player's course. The fairways were broad, and little rough existed. Instead, Mackenzie and Jones utilized natural hazards of trees (there were thousands of tall Georgia pines lining the fairways) and water (two streams and a pond came into play on five holes on the front nine). The greens were large, with flowing contours. And the very few bunkers, only twenty-two at the beginning, were expertly placed.

Soon after Augusta opened, its nines were reversed, for it was felt that the water holes, including the now-famous Amen corner of eleven through thirteen, should be tackled later in the round. Augusta National was in some ways the first uniquely American golf course. It was a model of strategic design, reflecting the principles of Mackenzie and Jones. Mackenzie had codified his principles in his book, *Golf Architecture*, in 1920; and he was able to express all those "essentials of an ideal course" at Augusta National.

Jones, who, like Mackenzie, was a devout admirer of St. Andrews, strongly felt alternative routes should be provided for players of lesser ability. But he also felt there should be rewards, especially on par-5 holes, for those who took a chance and succeeded.

At Augusta every hole looked deceptively simple; and, indeed, a high handicap golfer could keep the ball in play for an enjoyable round. But every hole had a preferred target, a spot from which it was most advantageous to play the next stroke. Augusta National could yield low rounds, but only to a golfer who thought his way around the course.

By the fifties Augusta National emerged as a standard for American golf course architecture. This was due in no small part to those progressive ideas of Alister Mackenzie and Bobby Jones.

Alister Mackenzie was responsible for other courses in the States during the 1930s, most of which were completed after his death. His associate on several projects was a former Oklahoma banker turned course designer, Perry Maxwell. Maxwell was probably the most prolific golf architect in America during the Depression.

This was ironic, for Maxwell did the bulk of his work in the so-called Dust Bowl area of Kansas, Oklahoma and Texas. But those very areas contained industries unaffected by the generally depressed economy of the United States. Oil interests in Tulsa hired Maxwell to build them a course, and in 1935 he gave them Southern Hills Country Club. The Carey Salt people of Hutchinson, Kansas, also hired Maxwell, and in 1937 he built the Prairie Dunes Country Club.

90

P. 90-91:
(Upper left and
bottom) *Scenes at
Augusta National.*
(Upper Right)
*Free-form style
of post-war architect
E.L. Packard was
probably influenced
by Mackenzie's.*

Prairie Dunes, featuring striking linkslike qualities, was originally planned as an eighteen-hole course. Only nine were built, however, and for twenty years the course had the reputation of being the best nine-hole course in the country. Perry's son, J. Press Maxwell, added nine more holes in 1957, following his father's routing plan and adding some touches of his own.

In 1936 Perry Maxwell lost the bid to lay out the Colonial Country Club for oilman Marvin Leonard in Fort Worth, Texas (architect John Bredemus was hired), but he was later retained to build three new holes at the course in preparation for the 1941 U. S. Open. Those holes are now perhaps the best at Colonial, the third, the fourth and the infamous fifth.

Perry Maxwell was especially noted for his severely contoured greens, which long ago were dubbed "the Maxwell Rolls." The most prominent example of the Maxwell Rolls is at Augusta National, which hired Perry in the late 1930s to rebuild some of its holes. Greens like the first, the tenth and the fourteenth are the result of Maxwell's handiwork. Among other very prominent courses on which Maxwell rebuilt the greens into rolling terrors were the Saucon Valley Country Club, the Pine Valley Golf Club (George Crump's masterpiece) and the Gulph Mills Golf Club, all three in the vicinity of Philadelphia.

The latter course was another of Donald Ross's great creations. Ross was still active in the 1930s, although the Depression curtailed his travels and he stayed closer to his home in Pinehurst, North Carolina. This allowed him to concentrate on his pet project, the Pinehurst courses.

By 1936 Ross had successfully converted the old sand greens of the three courses there to Bermuda grass and had sculptured them into visible, raised putting surfaces with undulating approaches, a style by that time widely recognized as his trademark. (Conversion to grass had been delayed because the high degree of perfection of the sand greens was felt to be superior to seeded Bermuda grass.)

Ross then set about rearranging the courses, re-bunkering nearly every hole and adding strategic mounds and hollows. The result when he finished, although truthfully he was never finished with Pinehurst and was forever refining the courses, was two pleasant resort courses, Pinehurst Numbers 1 and 3, and one long, deceptive, top-flight layout, Pinehurst Number 2, which was good enough to host the National PGA Championship a year after it opened.

At Pinehurst Number 2, Donald Ross demonstrated a brilliantly deceptive form of strategic design. The course appeared to be straightforward. Its fairways were not par-ticularly wide, but there was little rough. The greens were small and undulating, but very few of them were protected by more than a single bunker.

But the illusions soon vanished once a round at Pinehurst Number 2 was begun. A ball off the fairway was either in the pines on a mat of pine needles or on the soft, sandy soil cluttered with clumps of wiry "love" grass. An errant driver at Pinehurst seldom found a good lie.

And the tiny greens required a great deal of concentration. Some bunkers were well forward of the green, and the careless player could find his approach land over the bunker but short of the putting surface. Many holes had only one bunker at the corner or side of the green. Yet to follow one's natural inclination and play away from the bunker was often a mistake. Ross counterbalanced most bunkers with greenside mounds and hollows, most of which posed more difficult recovery problems than the sand.

Donald Ross considered his Pinehurst Number 2, with all its subtleties, to be his finest achievement.

Strangely enough, although the Great Depression was worldwide, golf course construction outside the United States continued at a steady pace. In the British Isles an average of forty new courses opened every year in the thirties, and professional architects were kept busy remodeling other British layouts into exciting tests of golf. In this period, Taylor and Hawtree rebuilt the Royal Birkdale Golf Club into such a fine course that it was proposed as the permanent site of The Open; C. K. Hutchison planned major changes to the thirty-six holes at the Turnberry Hotel to bring play closer to the nearby ocean; Guy Campbell revised the Killarney Golf Club of Ireland into a lovely lake-front course; and Tom Simpson remodeled the Ballybunion Golf Club into a dramatic oceanside test that was probably the best in Ireland.

New layouts were also appearing in other parts of the British Empire. In Canada the firm of Thompson and Jones kept busy, producing such solid courses as Digby Pines and Cape Breton Highlands (known also as the Keltic Lodge) in Nova Scotia, the Green Gables Golf Club on Prince Edward Island and Capilano in British Columbia. In Australia Alex Russell, who had assisted Alister Mackenzie in designing the Royal Melbourne course, laid out a second eighteen, the East course, for that club as well as many others throughout the country.

In Japan Kinya Fujita, who had attended college in America and had studied golf course architecture under Alison, was creating many fine layouts: the East and West courses at Kasumigaseki, the King's and Queen's courses at Narashino and the Nasu Golf Club. Hugh Alison was

also busy in Japan, creating such courses as Hirona and a new Tokyo Golf Club; and he inspected his pupil Fujita's work at Kasumigaseki. The deep bunkers he installed at those courses, including Kasumigaseki, with Fujita's blessing, so awed Japanese golfers that they derived from his name a word for them, "Arisons."

By the mid-1930s it appeared that golf course construction, both in the United States and abroad, might be on the rise again. In America, the federal WPA program allowed many municipalities to hire course architects to design and build public courses. Men like Robert Trent Jones, who had established a U. S. practice separate from Thompson's by the mid-1930s, Robert Bruce Harris, Perry Maxwell and Donald Ross took advantage of this program. Since the purpose of the WPA and similar programs in the United States and Canada was to create jobs, each course employed two hundred or more men during construction. Use of earth-moving equipment was limited, and these WPA courses were literally hand-built by men using only hand tools and wheelbarrows in most cases.

Actually, this method of construction was not entirely alien to the practices of the time. Although the bulldozer, which appeared in the 1920s, and the steam shovel,

P. 93: *Hole #2, Prairie Dunes CC, Hutchinson, Kansas, by Perry Maxwell. Natural plum thicket abounds in the rough at Prairie Dunes, enhancing the seaside impression of the course. Despite its location, far from the ocean deep in the American heartland, Prairie Dunes possesses striking links-like qualities.*

93

which was developed much earlier, had become major earth-moving tools, many architects before World War II preferred older methods, using horses, mules and scrapers for green and bunker construction, feeling that more natural lines could be achieved in this manner.

American architects also began to find employment remodeling existing courses. Many of the courses created in the boom of the 1920s were slapdash jobs, especially those laid out and built by organizations without professional design help. Little attention had been paid to strategy, balance and bunker placement. Some had pretentious features. Dozens of courses boasted a green with two large, symmetrical mounds, invariably dubbed "Mae West." Competent architects were hired to rectify the problems and eliminate such features.

Albert Tillinghast, who was hired in the 1930s by the PGA to advise member clubs on alterations, claimed to have eliminated some 7,427 useless bunkers in a two-year period. Many of these were penal fairway bunkers and others were obnoxious cross hazards. The effects of their elimination were dramatic, both in money saved and in enhanced player enjoyment.

But just as the profession seemed on the road to recovery, the second World War erupted in Europe in 1939. It abruptly altered the plans of those who thought a second golf boom was on the horizon. World War II put a great many men and women back to work, but it curtailed the golfing industry to an even greater degree than had the Great Depression.

Petroleum products became precious commodities. Courses outside metropolitan areas found themselves isolated and, without sufficient revenues, soon closed. The Maidstone Club on the far point of Long Island, summer playground of the very rich, and the Boca Raton Club near Palm Beach, Florida, winter playground of the same group, both folded for lack of patronage, closing four courses in the process. But so did Olympia Fields near Chicago with its self-contained community, including its own schools and fire department, and its four courses.

Even clubs without financial difficulties found it hard to maintain their courses without oil, fertilizer and manpower. Clubs like Augusta National, and Interlachen in Minneapolis, which was to have held the 1942 U. S. Open, closed for the duration and their fairways became pastures.

But the fate of North American courses was minor compared to the physical destruction inflicted upon European and Far Eastern countrysides. Some seaside courses, like Turnberry, were deliberately paved over and used as airfields, while others in Britain became training grounds for the British and the millions of American, Canadian, continental and overseas troops pouring into England. Other courses, from Prince's in England to Biarritz in France, from Oahu in Hawaii to Kawana Fuji in Japan, became pockmarked battlefields or bombed-out rubble. In a life-or-death struggle, the preservation of golfing grounds was of no importance.

The War would end, of course, and reconstruction begin once more. And by the late 1940s golf would again become one of the preferred pastimes of millions, and golf course design would reemerge as a vigorous profession. Among the prominent architects who would not live to see that day were Herbert Fowler, Cecil Hutchison, Norman Macbeth, William S. Flynn, Herbert Strong and Albert Tillinghast. And as was the case in the first World War, a number of promising but unknown associate architects would not survive combat and would never have the chance to prove their talents.

P. 94: *Waterville CC, Maine. Rigid lines testify to Orrin Smith's early use of steam shovels for final grading of greens and bunkers.* P. 95: (Top and bottom) *Undulations in greens dubbed "Maxwell Rolls," pot bunkers and other features at Prairie Dunes enhance the impression of Scottish links in the sand hills of Kansas.*

9

9.

The Age of Robert Trent Jones: Part I

A flurry of course reconstruction followed the second World War. In North America courses that had been left idle for as long as five years required extensive reconditioning before they could be reopened. Many clubs used this opportunity to remodel their layouts; and as a result, architectural business was fairly brisk. A brief recession in 1949-50 and the outbreak of the Korean Conflict slowed this activity for a time. But by 1953 course architecture was once again a healthy profession in the United States, with an average of one hundred new courses opened yearly in the last eight years of the decade, in addition to numerous remodeled or reconditioned layouts. By the 1960s, over 400 new courses were opening annually.

Up until the early sixties there were still many non-architect designed courses coming into play. But with more sophistication required in planning and construction, new clubs and course promoters turned to professional course designers. By the late 1960s, except for modest layouts, the majority of new courses in the United States were architect designed.

The era after World War II was one of transition. Golf course construction was revolutionized by modern earth-moving equipment. Where once it took up to 200 men, with horse-drawn scrapers, wheelbarrows and hand tools, two or three years to build an eighteen-hole course, by 1960 a dozen workers with modern equipment could construct a more elaborate eighteen in a few months.

The decade of the 1920s had seen the introduction of new techniques for the preparation and maintenance of golf courses. The practice of cultivating and carefully smoothing fairway seed beds became common. Prior to that time, pastures had often simply been mowed for use as fairways, and areas previously in other crops or cleared from forests were seeded with a minimum of fine grading. The greenkeeper then had to level these rough areas over a period of decades to achieve "billiard table" fairways. In the early twenties, gang units for mowing fairways had been developed, and horses to pull them were replaced by the golf course tractor. A mower with extra blades was used for putting greens, while quick coupling green, tee

P. 96–97: *Dorado Beach, Hole #13, West Course by Jones. P. 98: Ailsa Course, Turnberry Hotel, Scotland, by Fernie, revised by Hutchison, and restored after WWII by Mackenzie Ross. P. 99: Hole 10 (above), Green 12 (below), Ailsa.*

and fairway irrigation systems were introduced by the latter part of the decade.

Greater technical and scientific developments occurred in the 1950s and 60s. The production of improved grasses, such as hybrid Bermudas and ryegrasses, bluegrass cultivars and bentgrasses, did much to advance the state of course maintenance, as did new fertilizers and chemicals. Research into turfgrass propagation and management led to a better understanding of how grass grows. It was not until the 1950s, in fact, that soil scientists really understood how water moved through turfgrass soils and how such soils became compacted. The California method for building greens was developed by the University of California. In 1960 the USGA method for putting green construction was introduced, and in 1966 Dr. W. Daniel introduced a method for holding water above a plastic layer. In the 1950s the men who maintained golf courses had adopted the title "course superintendent," and turfgrass management became increasingly scientific as an increasing array of quality materials and equipment became available to the superintendent.

By the 1950s automatic irrigation of courses had been introduced. It was continually improved over the years to replace hose and sprinklers as well as snap valves. Universal adoption of fairway irrigation also occurred in the 1950s, adding to golfing enjoyment and playing uniformity over an entire season.

But the transition was greatest in the profession of golf course architecture itself. The decade following World War II saw the deaths of nearly all the pioneer golf course designers. Foremost, of course, was the "grand master," Donald J. Ross, who died at Pinehurst in 1948. In 1950 the great James Braid passed away; and in 1951, H. S. Colt, John Duncan Dunn and Robert Pryde. In 1952 Colt's partner, C. H. Alison, Willie Dunn, Jr., and Perry Maxwell all died, as did the other giant designer of his time, Canadian Stanley Thompson. They were followed a year later by Wayne Stiles and Billy Bell. William H. Tucker died in 1954 and the Briton Frederick G. Hawtree in 1955. With few exceptions, all had courses on their drawing boards at the time of their deaths.

But there were course architects to carry on the traditions established by these and other pioneer designers. Preeminent among the new wave of designers in the fifties was Robert Trent Jones, and in the next quarter century he was to exert an influence on golf architecture unparalleled in its history.

Of course, Trent Jones's was not a new face in the golf world. He had been an assistant, and later partner, to Stanley Thompson. In the mid-thirties Jones established

his own practice, building a series of municipal courses with WPA labor in upstate New York. He managed a few jobs during the War but, of greater significance, made several contacts with influential people and important organizations so that by the end of the War, Jones was busy preparing courses for the IBM Corporation and the West Point Military Academy. A great deal of what he did in the forties and fifties attracted nationwide attention, and by 1960 his name was known worldwide by golfers. Astonishingly, it was also recognized by nongolfers.

In 1946 Jones was hired by the Augusta National Golf Club to recondition its course and to remodel several holes. He altered greens numbers 8, 11, 12, and 13, and affected drastic changes to the entire eleventh hole. Originally a slight left-to-right dogleg with the teeing area to the right of the tenth green, number 11 played a maximum of 375 yards. Jones made it straightaway by cutting a slot deep in the trees to the left of the tenth green to increase the hole's yardage to 445. He also dammed Rae's Creek, which meandered alongside the left side and in back of the green. This formed a pond that embraced the entire left side of the green. It also elevated the water level to make it visible from the fairway.

Jones also reshaped one other hole, number 16. Instead of the short par-3 over a creek, Jones dammed the creek, rotated the direction of the hole ninety degrees and created the present sixteenth, a mid-to-long iron shot over the pine-lined pond to a kidney-shaped green. Both 11 and 16 attracted much attention at the annual Masters Tournament, but the sixteenth drew the most praise. Over the years the hole has been featured in nearly every golf publication. It also captured the fancy of one American president, Dwight D. Eisenhower, who painted an oil view from the tee.

In 1948 Trent Jones collaborated with Robert Tyre Jones, Jr. (the immortal "Bobby" Jones, who, with Alister Mackenzie, had laid out Augusta National) on a new course in Bobby's hometown of Atlanta. The course was named Peachtree, and while it was perhaps intended to be another expression of Robert Tyre Jones's golfing philosophy, it in fact became an expression of Robert Trent Jones's design philosophy. Peachtree's features were unprecedented. Its tees were huge, some the size of normal greens and one a long, serpentine eighty yards. Such tees, Jones reasoned, permitted exceptional flexibility, allowing the course to play from under 6,000 yards to over 7,400 by the simple readjustment of the tee markers. Broad tees also spread out wear, Jones felt, thus easing the demands on maintenance men. Peachtree's greens were also enormous. They averaged some 8,000 square feet, twice the size of the typical green of the day; and one in particular, number 10, was considered the largest in the country at over 10,000 square feet.

Trent Jones deliberately created five or six definite pin positions on each green. These smaller areas were intended to be the true targets of the approach shot, but each large green surface spread out the play and the wear. Peachtree's greens have always been its most controversial feature, with some players terming the undulating surfaces "elephant burial grounds." Yet the club is protective of its greens; and in the 1970s, when all eighteen were converted from Bermuda to bentgrass, each green was mapped on a grid and reconstructed to preserve every hump and hollow.

Other aspects of Peachtree were also unique. The second hole had a pond splitting the fairway. Some holes were severely bunkered; others featured mounds and hollows rather than traps. Peachtree was what Trent Jones called "modern golf course architecture." It was a broad, sweeping layout that, depending on the pin and tee marker locations, could be played an infinite number of ways. Peachtree had its promoters and its critics, but all agreed it was a uniquely American product and would probably be a standard for future courses.

In 1949 Robert Trent Jones was retained by the Oakland Hills Country Club to revise their Donald Ross layout for the 1951 United States Open Championship. Jones followed the routing of the old layout, but he altered every hole and modified mounds and side slopes at most greens while retaining the Ross putting surfaces. Jones practiced what he dubbed "target golf," establishing specific targets for tee shots. He did the same for approaches by using multiple and multilevel pin positions. A number of fairways were pinched by bunkers at both sides, and the greens were severely bunkered. When the 1951 Open was conducted, not a single golfer was able to crack its par-70 until the final round, when only two did so. Ben Hogan, the champion of that Open (with a closing 67), termed Oakland Hills "a monster" and apparently had a few choice words off the record for its architect. Some astute observers realized the condition of the course for the Open, with its ankle-deep rough and closely mowed greens, was responsible in part for the high tournament scores. But in the mind of the public at large, Robert Trent Jones was the villain, or the hero, depending on one's philosophy.

The eminent writer Herbert Warren Wind did a lengthy article on Robert Trent Jones in *The New Yorker Magazine* at about this time, and he definitely came off as a hero in that piece. Publicity of this type was particularly beneficial for an American golf architect, for although both Travis and Tillinghast had been associated with leading American golf magazines of their day, British publications generally gave more attention to course architects and architecture than did American periodicals. Some notable exceptions to this rule were articles by Herb Graffis, author of several books and founder and longtime editor of *Golfdom*. Two books written in the late forties did have chapters devoted to golf architecture, and these helped spotlight the profession in both Britain and America. The *History of Golf in Britain* was coauthored by architect Sir Guy Campbell, and Herbert Warren Wind's *The Story of American Golf* appeared first in 1948 with subsequent editions in 1956 and 1975.

In the 1950s and 60s, articles by Wind dealing with the role of the golf course architect appeared in several publications, including *The New Yorker*. A further elaboration on the subject appeared later in his widely read two-part series in *Golf Digest*. Wind's articles did much to kindle the interest of the American golfing public in course architecture; and probably as a result, many golfers became interested in knowing who planned the course on which they played.

But it took more than a few isolated incidents of national publicity to create the enormous force in golf course architecture that Robert Trent Jones became. Trent Jones was a talented, artistic man, a good administrator able to seek out and surround himself with capable assistants, and apparently a master salesman who could attract men like Laurance Rockefeller for backing. But his most significant attribute was that, throughout his career, Robert Trent Jones was a student of golf architecture.

He was the first architect who expressly entered the field without having first trained in another profession or been involved in another golf-related business. He had been a fine amateur golfer (as good as one could expect with the name Bobby Jones in the twenties), but he was never a professional golfer with preconceived notions on how to punish the fade, the draw or some such shot. Nor was he a superintendent, concerned primarily with laying out eighteen holes that could be mowed entirely with gang mowers. Yet he was keenly aware of the interaction of the three professions.

Trent Jones was a student. He literally created his own major, golf architecture, while at Cornell University, taking classes he recognized would be imperative for his profession. He took not only the obvious courses, like landscape architecture, surveying, hydraulics, horticulture, agronomy and turfgrass science, but also audited

P. 102: *Turnberry Hotel, Ailsa Course, Short 15th (top) and 17th (bottom) Holes.*
P. 103: *Innovations of the 1950s which revolutionized golf course construction and design included modern earth moving equipment (top), golf cars (center) and irrigation of fairways (bottom) in addition to greens.*

102

courses in philosophy, history and the classics.

He also inspected as many golf courses as he could and sought out experts in the field. Even the great Tillinghast, after he had apparently lost much of his zest for golf architecture, found himself on more than one occasion confronted by the eager young Jones seeking an explanation or, some say, an argument. And Jones landed a position in 1929 working for Stanley Thompson on the refining of the magnificent Banff course in the Canadian Rockies.

As early as 1935 Trent Jones was writing about a third school of golf architecture. Besides the penal and strategic schools, Jones said, there existed a "heroic school" of course design. The heroic was a blend of the best of the penal and strategic schools. He explained:

> The trapping (in the heroic) is not as profuse as in the penal, nor as scarce as in the strategic. Traps vary from ugly, treacherous-looking ones to small, insignificant pot-bunkers. The line of flight is usually blocked by some formidable looking hazard placed at a diagonal and involving a carry of from 170 to 220 yards in which the player is allowed to bite off as much as he feels he can chew. If his game . . . is not equal to the task, a safe alternate route to play round it is provided. The same principle is used in the green design, in which the green is placed at an angle to the line of flight with an opening allowed for the cautious.[1]

In other words, as in strategic design, a heroic hole gives the golfer a choice of routes; but as in penal design, the player is punished if he gambles and fails by playing a poor shot. At first, the most common "diagonal hazard" Jones utilized for such purposes was the deep bunker, so steep-faced that a shot had to be wasted to get out. He was very fond of Tillinghast's bunkering at Winged Foot, two courses that the young designer cited as examples of heroic architecture. Over the years, Jones increasingly utilized water as the heroic hazard; and nearly every Trent Jones course would feature one or more greens perched ominously over a pond or creek, as well as other holes with similar water hazards.

But Jones was never an advocate of a strictly heroic or strategic or penal course. The trend, he felt, was to courses that featured all three philosophies blended into an appropriate combination depending on whether the course was intended as a municipal operation, a resort or a private layout to host tournaments. The course Jones always felt best reflected this trend was Jasper Park in Alberta, which was designed by Stanley Thompson and opened in 1925. In the forties and fifties, when Jones was on his own, he continued to popularize this blend or style

of architecture; and he felt Peachtree boasted holes of all three philosophies.

Jones has maintained that he absorbed much of his feeling for contemporary design from Thompson; but there is evidence, as well as the belief of other Thompson associates, that Trent Jones also exerted considerable influence on Thompson.

Robert Trent Jones produced in the 1950s such renowned courses as The Dunes in South Carolina (with its par-5 thirteenth that horseshoes around a lake as the ultimate heroic hole); Old Warson Country Club and Bellerive Country Club, both in St. Louis; Coral Ridge Country Club in Florida; Shady Oaks Golf Club and Houston Country Club, both in Texas; and Point O' Woods Golf and Country Club in Michigan. Abroad he created the Cotton Bay Club in the Bahamas, the original Dorado Beach course in Puerto Rico and the Brasilia Country Club for the new capital of Brazil.

Trent Jones's chief "rival" in the fifties, at least in terms of publicity, was Louis S. "Dick" Wilson, an associate of Toomey and Flynn in the late twenties and early thirties. Like many others, Dick Wilson abandoned design work during the Depression and managed a course in Florida until after the War. Then he formed his own firm and designed the West Palm Beach Country Club in 1949. This course, one of the first of what would be an explosion of courses in Florida, garnered fine reviews, and Wilson soon located other clients.

By the late 1950s Dick Wilson had created a small empire of courses in Florida, laying out such notable clubs as DeSoto Lakes, Tequesta and Cypress Lake. In the early sixties he created some of his best work in that state with the original thirty-six holes at Doral, the Bay Hill Club and Pine Tree. Wilson also presided over development of major golfing resorts in the Bahamas, at Arawak (now Paradise Island), Princess Hotel and Lucayan. Among his other clients was National Cash Register of Dayton, Ohio, for whom Wilson laid out two courses, the North and South, in the early fifties. Wilson also designed courses at new sites for the very old Meadow Brook Club and Deepdale Club, both on Long Island. Meadow Brook attracted special attention since its old course, forced to move due to rising taxes and encroaching suburbs, was so well respected. Wilson's Meadow Brook was greeted with immediate acclaim, and some went so far as to declare it the best course in the United States at the time.

Dick Wilson was not the student of classics and Cornell-trained designer that Robert Trent Jones was, but he was certainly talented. Having learned his craft through on-the-job training, Wilson was proud of the fact that he could personally build the courses he designed. Whether Jones and Wilson ever had a personal rivalry is conjecture now, although it was rumored that the very busy and selective Wilson accepted the commission to design Royal Montreal's forty-five new holes in 1958 partly because he had heard that Trent Jones was after it. In the fifties, countless comparisons were made of the two architects and their works. One article written during these years said they were producing the best courses ever built.

As it turned out, Dick Wilson shared the spotlight with Trent Jones for only fifteen years, for he died in 1965 at age sixty-one. Wilson died with half a dozen courses under construction and plans for many more at his office. He wrote very little about his profession and so left very little concerning his philosophy of design, except for his magnificent courses. They remain outstanding examples of the art. With the exceptions of Donald Ross and Robert Trent Jones, no architect has such an impressive list of consensus top-flight courses to his credit.

With Wilson's death, his associate, Joseph Lee, whom Wilson had recruited back in the National Cash Register days in Dayton, assumed the firm's practice. Two other Wilson-trained designers, Robert von Hagge and Robert A. Simmons, had already gone out on their own, with Wilson's blessing, before 1965.

Robert Trent Jones and Dick Wilson were not the only architects active in the fifties, of course. There were a great many others, and many of them created courses of substantial merit.

Besides Trent Jones, Stanley Thompson's stable turned out the following:

• Clinton E. Robinson, who established his practice in Canada after the War. Robinson designed the eighteen-hole addition for the Sunningdale Country Club in Ontario, the Brudenell Golf and Country Club on Prince Edward Island and the Upper Canada Village course in Ontario, among other magnificent layouts.

• Howard Watson, who began working for Thompson the very day that Clinton Robinson did. Watson started on his own in 1950, and much of his early solo work was in the Caribbean at courses like Caymanas Golf and Country Club in Jamaica and the Country Club de Medellin in Colombia. But Watson soon had excellent work in Canada to his credit, too, like the Pinegrove Country Club and Carling Lake Golf Club in Quebec, the Board of Trade Country Club in Ontario and many others. He also trained his son, John, who started his own practice in the 1970s.

• Geoffrey S. Cornish, who, after a stint as an instruc-

tor at the University of Massachusetts, set up a practice in the early fifties. By the late sixties Cornish, with his associate, William G. Robinson, a graduate landscape architect who joined him in 1964, had designed more courses in New England than any other person. Crestview Country Club in Massachusetts, two courses for Quechee Lakes Country Club in Vermont, the Eastman Lakes Golf Course in New Hampshire, the Stratton Mountain Club in Vermont, York Downs in Toronto, Cranberry Valley on Cape Cod, the new Ashburn Golf Club in Nova Scotia, the Porto Carras Links in Greece and two courses for the Summerlea Golf and Country Club near Montreal were among the 170 new courses designed by Cornish and Robinson and in play by the late seventies.

• Norman H. Woods, who based his practice in western Canada after Thompson's death. Woods designed many fine courses, including Kokanee Springs Golf Club in British Columbia, Rossmere Golf and Country Club in Manitoba, Lords Valley Country Club in Pennsylvania and the fine nine-hole Hilands Country Club in Montana.

Dick Wilson, of course, began with the old Pennsylvania firm of Toomey and Flynn. Among other assistants of that firm who established their own practices after the War were:

• William F. Gordon, who formed his company in 1941 to seed military installations and was very busy by the late 1940s. His son, David, a pilot in the War, finished college at Penn State and then joined the firm. By the fifties the two were full partners, and together they were responsible for such superior layouts as the Grace course at Saucon Valley Country Club in Pennsylvania, the Stanwich Club in Connecticut, Buena Vista Country Club in New Jersey and the Indian Spring Country Club in Maryland. William Gordon died in 1973 at age eighty, and David Gordon continued the work of the firm. Before entering the firm of Toomey and Flynn, Bill Gordon had supervised golf course construction for Willie Park, Jr., Leonard Macomber, Donald Ross and others. Probably no other architect in history received such broad practical experience before setting up his own practice, nor was any more imbued with the history of the art.

• Robert F. Lawrence, who had also worked for Walter Travis and who, like Dick Wilson, had settled as a course manager in Florida during the War. Lawrence produced such works as the Plantation Golf Club and the South course of the Fort Lauderdale Country Club while in that state but did his best-known designs after moving to the Southwest in the early sixties. There he did Desert Forest Golf Club and Camelback Country Club in Arizona, and

P. 106: (Top) *Timed automatic irrigation of courses led to uniform greenness throughout the golf season.* (Center) *R. B. Harris' bunkers are in proportion to one another and in harmony with the landscape.* (Bottom) *The Harris style as seen on the Brute Course at the Playboy CC, Wisconsin.*

P. 106-107: *Manchester CC, Vermont, by Cornish and Robinson, where style was dictated by rugged terrain.*

Paradise Hills and the South course of the University of New Mexico in Albuquerque. "Red" Lawrence died in 1976, and associates Jeff Hardin and Greg Nash continued the practice in the Southwest.

Many designers trained under Donald Ross. Those active in the fifties included:

· The Hughes brothers, Lawrence, Frank and Henry. Lawrence and Frank originally worked on Ross construction crews supervised by their father, Henry T. Hughes, while young Henry herded the sheep used to clip long grass along fairway edges. The three brothers worked as a team in the late forties, producing as one of their first works the magnificent Club de Golf de Mexico in Mexico City. Henry B. Hughes eventually located in Denver, Colorado, where he created many of that state's fine courses, including Columbine Country Club, Bookcliff Country Club and the Country Club of Fort Collins. Lawrence preferred the rapidly developing southern California area; and with Frank supervising the construction, he built beautiful layouts in wasteland areas, like Thunderbird Country Club and Eldorado Country Club in Palm Springs, and the Desert Inn Golf Club in Las Vegas. At the time of his death in 1975, Lawrence Hughes was busy again in Mexico, where he had completed, among others, the Santa Anita and San Isidro Golf Clubs.

· Eugene "Skip" Wogan, one of Massachusetts's most revered professional golfers. Although he maintained the professional's position at Essex Country Club in Manchester, Massachusetts, he laid out several fine courses in New England. His son, Philip, later became prominent in course design.

· Ellis Maples, who had the good fortune to be the son of a close friend of Donald Ross. Ellis's father, Frank, was the longtime superintendent of the Pinehurst Country Club courses and a sometime course architect himself. Young Maples worked on construction crews for Ross and was supervising construction of the Raleigh (North Carolina) Country Club at the time of the architect's death. Maples finished that course and spent the next few years debating whether to become a touring professional, a pro-superintendent or a course designer. By 1954 he had decided on the last; and by the mid-1960s he was the most prolific architect in the Carolinas since Ross. Maples created the Number 5 course at Pinehurst, the Grandfather Golf and Country Club near Linville, and both the Country Club of North Carolina and the Country Club of South Carolina. He also started Edwin B. Seay in the business, as well as his own son, Dan Maples, who became his partner.

· Orrin Smith, who had served as a construction superintendent for Willie Park and Donald Ross, and later established his own firm in the twenties. He resumed his practice in the late forties. Smith died in 1958, but he left his own group of protégés who continued the practice. That group included:

· William F. Mitchell, of the prominent Mitchell greenkeeping family of New England. Mitchell, who passed away in 1974, did such courses as Old Westbury Golf and Country Club in New York; the Country Club of New Seabury on Cape Cod; the Longboat Key Club and the President Country Club, both in Florida; Tanglewood Golf Club in Ohio; and the Mount Pleasant Country Club in Massachusetts. Mitchell's brother, Sam, was associated with him for several years in the 1950s.

· Albert Zikorus, who finished Smith's works after his death. On his own, Zikorus designed, among many others, Glastonbury Hills Country Club and Tunxis Plantations in Connecticut, Twin Hills Golf Club and Walpole Country Club in Massachusetts and the fine Punta Borinquen Golf Club in Puerto Rico.

· James Gilmore Harrison, who organized his own business just after the War. Harrison hired a Penn State agronomy student named Ferdinand Garbin as one of his first associates. Garbin later became Harrison's son-in-law, and then his partner. In the late sixties Garbin went out on his own, but in the fifties and sixties the two produced such courses as Sewickley Heights Country Club in Pennsylvania and Lakeview Country Club in West Virginia.

Departed pioneer designers William H. Tucker, Perry Maxwell and Billy Bell all left sons to carry on their work. William H. Tucker, Jr., was fifty-nine years old at the time of his father's death, but he had assisted the elder Tucker in course design and construction all his adult life. Tucker Jr. died in 1962 after a relatively short period of practice on his own.

J. Press Maxwell had done all of his father's construction work from the late forties on due to Perry's failing health. After his father's death, Press Maxwell designed many fine layouts of his own in the Southwest, including Oak Cliff in Dallas; East Ridge in Shreveport; Farmington in Memphis; and the Hiwan Golf Club, Boulder Country Club and Kissing Camels, all in Colorado.

William P. Bell's son was William F. Bell, who built a practice in the fifties and sixties that was even larger than his productive father's. William F. Bell worked mainly in southern California on courses like Torrey Pines, Saticoy Country Club, Industry Hills and the Sandpiper Links, and in Hawaii on courses like the Makaha Inn complex. Other associates of the elder Bell also went to work for themselves in California. They included Robert E. Baldock (the Shore course of the Monterey Peninsula Country Club and the San Joaquin Country Club) and William H. Johnson (Pala Mesa Golf Club and Knollwood Country Club).

Some of the "old-time" architects reactivated their practices after the War; and men like Jack Daray, William H. Diddel, Jack Fleming, William B. Langford, Charles Maddox, Sr., Harold Paddock, Alfred Tull and C. D. Wagstaff, all of whom had been active in the 1920s, were busier than ever. They all had young protégés eager to try their own skills, but none had more than Robert Bruce Harris. From Harris's Chicago office came David Gill, Edward Lawrence Packard (whose son, Roger, a graduate landscape architect, joined him in 1971), Kenneth Killian, Richard Nugent, William Spear and Richard Phelps, each of whom formed his own business in the fifties or sixties.

R. B. Harris himself was very productive in this period and created such courses as Signal Point in Michigan, Hillcrest in Illinois and the Country Club of Florida, which he personally considered his best effort. Harris died in 1976 after a fifty-year career as a golf course architect and sometime landscape designer.

In Mexico famed Mexican Amateur champion Percy Clifford started a course design practice in the 1950s. Clifford, who had worked closely with the Hughes brothers in the creation of the Club de Golf Mexico, established himself as the premier course architect of his country with such works as Bellavista in Mexico City, Pierre Marques in Acapulco and the links-type Baja Mar Country Club in Baja. By the mid-1970s almost half the courses in Mexico were Clifford designed.

The list of designers who began in the 50s is too long to give adequate justice. For each man named, a dozen or more have had to be omitted. Here it must suffice to note that in North America for the twenty years following the second World War, the golf boom was such that over one hundred full or part-time course architects could remain busy and productive, and still not satisfy the demand.

The same could be said for Britain and the Continent. Activity after the War included reconditioning old courses and creating new ones from the ruins of many abandoned golfing grounds. Sir Guy Campbell continued to practice in this period until his death in 1960. A major project of Campbell's at this time was the complete remodeling of Prince's in Sandwich.

John S. F. Morrison, the former associate of Colt and Alison, worked with Campbell at Prince's and then built his own business on the Continent, designing such

P. 109: *Hole #10, West Course, The Broadmoor Hotel, Colorado. An architect's style evolves and changes over the course of his career, and often his work can be identified and classified in distinct periods. This hole is illustrative of the Trent Jones bunker style of the early 1960s.*

courses as Le Biella and La Mandria in Italy. His assistant, John Hamilton Stutt, the son of John R. Stutt, continued the practice in Europe after Morrison's death in 1961.

Scottish architect Philip Mackenzie Ross, who had worked for Tom Simpson before going out on his own in the 1930s, also practiced in this era until his death in 1974. He developed his most prominent reputation in the late forties by rebuilding the Ailsa course at Turnberry into a dramatic oceanside layout after it had been paved over as a wartime airport.

Frederick W. Hawtree assumed his father's business upon the death of F. G. Hawtree in 1955. A talented designer who had learned the trade well from his father, Hawtree designed the superb courses at Royal Waterloo in Belgium and Saint Nom la Breteche in France, as well as many others.

Also active on the Continent in this era were Britons John D. Harris, who worked extensively in the Caribbean and Far East, as well; Donald Harradine; Henry Cotton; and the firm of Cotton, Pennink and Lawrie, composed of C. K. Cotton, J. J. F. Pennink and C. D. Lawrie. D. M. A. Steel, golf correspondent for the *London Sunday Telegraph,* joined this firm as a partner in 1971 after a six-year "trainee" period.

Native European designers were rare, but two of the more successful were German Bernard von Limburger, who did the Bremen, Lindau and Dusseldorf courses; and Spaniard Javier Arana, who did the El Prat, Rio Real and Guadalmina courses. Irish designers by the mid 1960s included Eddie Hackett (Eire) and Tom McAuley (Ulster).

The dominant influence on British and European golf course architecture in this period was American course design. F. W. Hawtree attributed a "panache and style" to American courses previously unknown on the eastern side of the Atlantic. Some felt the influence began as early as the twenties, at a time when American competitive golf began to dominate the world golf scene. Others felt it was a natural result of the post-war use of more inland "American-type" terrain and American construction methods in Britain and Europe. Still others attributed it to the worldwide fame of Robert Trent Jones. Whatever the source, the influence was real, and by the early 1970s the transition was complete. Such far-flung courses as Woburn in Britain, Tobago in the Caribbean and Mt. Mitchell in North Carolina all featured broad, sweeping fairways, large, undulating greens, long tees, yawning bunkers of glistening white sand and finely manicured playing areas. Unknowing observers would be hard pressed to believe the courses were not the works of major American golf course architects. But, in fact, they were all the creations of Britons. Woburn was done by C. D. Lawrie, Tobago by John D. Harris and Mt. Mitchell by F. W. Hawtree, the self-proclaimed admirer of American golf course design.

¹ Robert Trent Jones, "The Common Interests of the Golf Architect and the Greenkeeper," *The Greenkeeper's Reporter,* February 1935, p. 12.

P. 110-111: *Vastly different design styles can be seen in Robert Trent Jones' Cerromar Beach GC, Puerto Rico (lower left)* and his *Four Seasons GC, Missouri (lower right), both done in the 1970s, as compared with Pete Dye's 1980 course, La Quinta Hotel GC, Ca. (upper left and right). Jones' different styles, from the early 1950s on, were adopted and modified by so many American and British architects that they came to constitute "contemporary style." Dye's novel features attracted widespread attention, perhaps because they were so unlike others of the period and so completely in contrast to those of Trent Jones.*

110

111

10

10.
The Age of Robert Trent Jones: Part II

The history of golf course architecture since 1965 is difficult to discuss, for the events are so recent that any analysis of them can be fraught with misinterpretation. A few points, however, can be stated with some certainty.

Until the late 1960s, real estate, construction and financing costs were favorable, and golf course design and development was a thriving worldwide enterprise. But by the mid-1970s costs had skyrocketed and the picture changed.

Inflation took its toll, and the costs of building and maintaining a golf course multiplied drastically in a decade's time. New laws, including environmental regulations in America and land-use policies in Japan, further increased the expense; and quite often planned projects could not meet the regulations. High quality construction, including fully automated irrigation systems, special drainage systems and new formulas for building greens, also increased costs.

The price of an average course in this period came to at least a half million dollars for construction alone, with-

out any consideration for other development costs. Unfortunately, many golfers were unable or unwilling to pay fees commensurate with these higher costs. By 1974 tight money had greatly curtailed construction and forced a number of shakily financed golf developments into bankruptcy. But by the late seventies American course development had picked up somewhat, particularly in the Sun Belt. British architects, with their far-flung practices sometimes stretching over several continents, remained busy. In Canada golf construction kept a steady pace, particularly in the oil-rich west. It was also fairly brisk in Europe and the Far East.

But while many an American course architect found himself as busy as ever planning courses and preparing specifications, an astonishing number of projects fell victim to raging inflation or unyielding regulations. As a result, the number of courses actually built and opened for play in the United States annually was less than a quarter of what it had been in the sixties. Development of new, strictly private country clubs all but ceased, although

P. 112–113: Green #16, Eagle Vail GC by Von Hagge and Devlin. P. 114:
Mount Mitchell GC, by F. W. Hawtree. P. 115: (Top) Beau Desert GC, England,
by W. H. Fowler. American style became the dominant influence on course
design after World War II. P. 115: (Bottom) The Connecticut GC. Architects,
builders and superintendents dealt with increasingly difficult properties.

some existing clubs remodeled their layouts or added nines. But few courses could generate enough cash to cover expenses, let alone a profit, especially in regions with short playing seasons. Consequently, the majority of new courses in the late sixties and seventies were built either as municipally owned courses or as part of larger integrated real estate or resort developments. Courses at year-round resorts like Stratton Mountain in Vermont, which caters to golfers in summer and skiers in winter, became especially popular with investors.

Private clubs still in existence were sometimes forced by high taxes and reduced membership to move to new sites. Fortunately, sale of their valuable in-town land would normally pay for the development of a more elaborate facility on less expensive land farther out. The old Colonial Country Club in Memphis, Tennessee, for example, whose tight, 6,400-yard course had been the site of many tournaments, sold its prime location to developers. In exchange, it obtained sufficient land out in the country to build two courses. These were designed by Joseph Finger, a fine Houston, Texas-based architect who also did the Concord in New York and Pleasant Valley in Arkansas.

The ever-increasing value of land also affected the development of golf course architecture. Not only would dramatic, oceanfront courses become the exception in this period, but so too would courses on gently rolling, tree-lined terrains. Designers were increasingly confronted with the worst possible property, often the "left-over" land of a developer, on which to build their courses. Herbert Warren Wind once observed that had Pebble Beach been built in the contemporary era, there would be no holes on those magnificent seaside cliffs. Obviously, such land would be reserved by the developers for home sites, to be sectioned in parcels as narrow as possible to maximize profits. No doubt the less-expensive home sites would be those fronting the course. It should be noted, of course, that several homes do border the actual Pebble Beach Golf Links, but they share with the course the tremendous ocean views.

Yet any number of course architects rose to the challenge of less-than-desirable sites. Courses in this period were constructed on sanitary landfills (Mangrove Bay Municipal Golf Course, St. Petersburg, Florida, by William Amick, where marsh gas is piped off for city lighting), rocky, cactus-covered land (Baja Mar Country Club, Baja California, Mexico, by Percy Clifford), reclaimed lakes (the North course of the Firestone Country Club, by Robert Trent Jones), marsh lands (Hilton Head Golf Club by George W. Cobb), and in gravel pits and strip mines

(Laurel Green Country Club in western Pennsylvania, by Xen Hassenplug), slag heaps (Blyth Golf Club in England, by J. H. Stutt), and even on ledge rock (The Connecticut Golf Club, by Cornish and Robinson). Of all the traits necessary and desirable in a first-rate course architect, perhaps none was more important in this period than imagination. The ability to hew silken courses from sow's pens surely separated the poor designer from the successful one in the seventies.

The ranks of golf course designers had continued to expand in the late 1950s as more men felt the need to express themselves through molding of the landscape. Some new designers came directly from related professions, like Robert Muir Graves, a landscape architect; Ted G. Robinson, a land planner; Jack Kidwell, a pro-superintendent; and Jack Snyder, a landscape architect and second-generation superintendent. But most had worked for established architects, as had Francis J. Duane, who was with Robert Trent Jones from 1945 until 1963.

Prior to hiring Duane, Jones had worked almost alone; but from then on his office gradually expanded. In 1961 Yale engineering graduate Roger Rulewich entered the firm, taking over after Duane's departure as a major figure in the eastern office. Robert Trent Jones, Jr., joined his father in 1962 and was responsible for setting up a Pacific branch of the business, based in California. Jones's younger son, Rees, signed on with the organization in 1965. In 1968 graduate landscape architect Cabell Robinson started in the New Jersey office, establishing a permanent Jones branch in Spain in 1970 after Ronald Kirby (who had represented Jones in Europe from 1965 to 1969) formed his own design firm with touring professional Gary Player as a consultant.

By 1980 there were over 400 Trent Jones courses located in forty-two states and twenty-three countries. Robert Trent Jones, Jr., established his own practice in 1972 with ties to his father's. Rees Jones started his own entirely separate practice in 1974 and in the same year wrote an influential book on golf course developments, in collaboration with landscape architect Guy L. Rando. Both Robert Jr. and Rees developed individual styles unique from their famous father's, and each was the architect of top-flight layouts.

Although the fame of Robert Trent Jones had not abated nationally or internationally, other architects began to influence the field of course design. Three men in particular, Desmond Muirhead, Pete Dye and George Fazio, deserve special note because of their impact on course architecture and the national attention they have drawn to it in recent years.

Desmond Muirhead, a Scot who trained in Britain as a land planner, moved to the United States via Canada, where he attended the University of British Columbia and planned a golf course in Vancouver. In the early sixties he assisted in the development of the Sun City retirement village in Arizona and became intrigued with the relationship of its golf course to the housing plan.

By 1963 Muirhead had formed his own course design and construction firm, and the courses he developed attracted immediate attention. His distinctive style resembled that of few other architects. It could almost be said that Muirhead sculpted his courses from the terrain. His tees were parabolic, serpentine or pronged, and nearly always dozens of yards in length. Some of his greens appeared to flow into the horizon; others were so severely contoured as to resemble rolling surf. His water hazards, which were numerous, were free form in design; and he routed his holes around them in unique fashions. On one hole a green would be located on an island and on another, a fairway would be. Sometimes a tee, and sometimes a landing area, would be perched on a peninsula. Muirhead's bunkers resembled jigsaw pieces from a totally white puzzle.

Muirhead also prided himself on combining his courses into pleasing arrangements with the surrounding environment, be it a housing development or a desert wasteland. He abhorred architects who deliberately routed several holes in one direction so as to maximize the available frontage land for housing developers. He has also crusaded for more rational routing of courses to protect players from one another and adjoining landowners from errant shots.

Muirhead's critics argued that his style was really nothing more than contemporary landscape architecture and had been demonstrated in the mid-fifties by course architect Edward Lawrence Packard. They also claimed Muirhead's designs were sterile, well-manicured lawns devoid of any true golfing values. But the architect maintained his courses followed modern-day principles of strategic design and maximum flexibility. Among his creations are Mission Hills Golf and Country Club in Palm Springs, California; Baymeadows Country Club in Jacksonville, Florida; McCormick Ranch Golf Club in Scottsdale, Arizona; and Bent Tree Club in Dallas, Texas.

Paul "Pete" Dye entered the profession about the same time as Muirhead. An insurance salesman turned golf architect, Dye spent the first few years of his design career without conspicuous success. But in the mid-1960s,

after he made a tour of the grand old courses of Scotland, he began to develop his own style of design, a style as unique as Muirhead's but diametrically opposed to it.

Dye felt that graceful mounds and undulations on a golf course were artificial. True natural features, he observed, were characterized by abrupt change. These were the features that most impressed him on the Scottish links: the swales and hollows and pits around fairways and greens, the jagged sand hills and especially the steep bunker faces shored up by railroad "sleepers."

Respectful, too, of the works of many of the great early American architects, like Ross, Tillinghast and Macdonald, Pete Dye began to develop a philosophy that disdained the typical features of modern American golf courses, the same features, ironically, that British designers at this time were wholeheartedly embracing.

Dye's new courses sported tight, undulating fairways with small, wildly undulating greens surrounded by mounds, swales, hollows or pot bunkers, and roughs maintained in indigenous vegetation. Many of his tees, bunkers and even water hazards were lined with upright railroad ties, so many that the railroad tie came to be known as Dye's trademark. One Dye course, Oak Tree Golf Club near Edmond, Oklahoma, has some 8,000 ties running about it!

His courses were also shorter than most, often less than 6,200 yards from the regular tees and not over 6,500 from the back. Pete Dye prided himself on designing each hole with women players in mind, perhaps because his wife, Alice, was one of the country's premier amateur golfers. His placement of front tees was not an afterthought but rather the deliberate attempt to provide women with the opportunity to play each hole as designed but within their capabilities.

Dye's most prominent works include The Golf Club near Columbus, Ohio; Crooked Stick near Indianapolis, Indiana; the Harbour Town Golf Links on Hilton Head Island, South Carolina; and Cajuiles, a dramatic seaside layout in the Dominican Republic.

Dye's critics most often complained that his designs were exceedingly difficult to maintain. His severely contoured greens, small deep bunkers, huge wasteland bunkers and other novel features were not suited for modern maintenance equipment, they said. An elevated tee surrounded by a bank of railroad ties was charming, but it required daily hand mowing and the lifting and lowering of the mower at that.

In reality, few features on a Pete Dye layout were truly revolutionary, even in America. C. B. Macdonald, for instance, lined several of his bunkers with railway ties

at the National Golf Links. Perry Maxwell was notorious for his small, treacherous greens. Devereux Emmet had long experimented with mounds and hollows as substitutes for greenside bunkers, and Donald Ross did much the same at times. But in the late 1960s and early 1970s, no other golf course architect had the courage and the tenacity to try such different approaches to course design; his results caused immediate and widespread attention, probably because they were so opposite to the style ushered in by Robert Trent Jones in the 1950s and adopted and modified by nearly all contemporary American and British architects.

By the early seventies Pete's brother, Roy Dye, had joined him in the business and had been responsible for such typical "Dye designs" as the revised Country Club of Montreal and Waterwood National Golf Club in Texas. As contradictory as it might seem, the multitalented Jack Nicklaus worked at separate times with both Pete Dye and Desmond Muirhead. With Dye, he collaborated on Harbour Town; and with Muirhead, he assisted on several courses including Mayacoo Lakes in Florida. In the mid-1970s, Nicklaus formed a course design firm that planned,

P. 118: (Top) *Hole #14, Stratton Mountain GC in Vermont ski country, by Cornish and Robinson.*
P. 118: (Bottom) *Hole #18, Wild Dunes GC on the coast of South Carolina, by George and Tom Fazio.*
P. 119: *Hole #3, Eagle Vail GC high in the Colorado Rockies, by Von Hagge and Devlin. Many new courses built after the late 1960s were integrated with housing, resorts or other forms of recreation.*

among others, Muirfield Village in Ohio (with the advice and counsel of Muirhead), Glen Abbey in Toronto and Shoal Creek in Birmingham, Alabama.

George Fazio had been a successful club professional and competitive golfer in the 1940s and 50s. When he retired, he intended to operate a car dealership and a few daily fee golf courses in Pennsylvania; but friends lured him into designing a course. By the time he had completed it—the Atlantis Country Club in Tuckertown, New Jersey—Fazio was hooked on course design as a new career. His early works, like the Jackrabbit Road course of the Champions Golf Club in Texas and Moselem Springs Country Club in Pennsylvania, were warmly received. But it was not until the late 1960s that George Fazio was recognized as a major force in American course design.

By then it was apparent that Fazio had steadily, through a progression of works, developed into a fine classical course architect. His designs were not modernistic like Muirhead's, nor rugged like Dye's. They were, instead, reminiscent of the grand old courses of the Golden Era. Fazio's courses had a graceful and appealing appearance that belied their youthfulness. And they were challenging without being repetitive in the process. One Fazio hole might feature a huge bunker in the inside corner of a dogleg and a tightly bunkered green. The next might feature a trap on the outside of a dogleg and a green devoid of sand.

George Fazio certainly had a wealth of experience and observation upon which to draw. He learned the game in Philadelphia, amidst the bright collection of courses by Hugh Wilson, Donald Ross, William Flynn, William Gordon and others. Merion was a particular favorite of Fazio, and he nearly won a U. S. Open there. He also served as head professional for several years at Pine Valley, and he not only played the course on countless occasions but absorbed its nuances. With this background, Fazio was able to instill in his own works the distinctive qualities of many of the great American courses.

The works of George Fazio include Jupiter Hills in Florida, which contains a series of holes seemingly appropriated from Pine Valley; Butler National Golf Club in Chicago; Devil's Elbow Golf Club at Moss Creek; and the National Golf Club in Toronto.

Fazio also became a favorite architect of clubs hosting major tournaments in the seventies. In this capacity he made major revisions, including creation of several new holes at such hallowed courses as Oak Hill in New York and Inverness in Ohio. Fazio's nephew, Tom Fazio, ably assisted him on most of his works almost from the beginning, and became his partner in 1973.

P. 120–121: *Arrowhead GC, Colorado, by Robert Trent Jones, Jr. In the 1970s Robert Trent Jones' sons, Robert, Jr. and Rees, developed unique design philosophies and established private practices of their own. Bob Jr.'s dramatic Arrowhead GC illustrates his personal concept of the golf course as a work of art within the context of the surrounding environment.*

Muirhead, Dye and Fazio all left individual impressions on the history of golf course architecture in the sixties and seventies. Other designers may not have had the same impact but still produced impressive works. All too often, however, their creations have not been known outside their immediate communities, because they never hosted a major tournament; because their owners did not seek, or even shunned, publicity; or because prominent nearby courses overshadowed them. Such situations have never been conducive to widespread awareness of any course architect; and only time will determine whether a particular course, or a particular designer, attains the recognition deserved.

It is interesting to reflect upon the many decades of architects and their courses and to wonder which men will still be well regarded in fifty or one hundred years. Willie Park, Jr., and H. S. Colt certainly are two "pioneer" professional architects worth remembering. Donald Ross and Stanley Thompson did so many, many fine courses in the twenties and thirties that their reputations will surely not fade. Alister Mackenzie, one of the first to codify his aims and one of the few able to demonstrate them in layouts all over the globe, has had perhaps greater influence among newer generations of course architects than he had among his peers.

But the man who had the greatest impact on the profession of golf course architecture, and upon the game of golf itself, was Robert Trent Jones. This may seem a brash assertion, but an objective review of course design history supports it. It is possible that if the name of any golf course architect of the past or present is still well known in a hundred years, it will be that of Robert Trent Jones.

It is equally interesting to speculate on which contemporary courses will be highly considered in another century's time. Indeed, one must wonder whether any course will endure the test of time that the Old Course at St. Andrews has withstood.

But such speculation raises ominous thoughts. Will golf course architecture, and even golf courses themselves, still exist in fifty or one hundred years? The eloquent Alistair Cooke raised that point in his foreword to *The World Atlas of Golf,* and he was not optimistic. Cooke feared the last quarter of the twentieth century would be the twilight of golf design. Voracious governmental taxation and regulation, he felt, would eventually swallow up the glorious playing fields of the game.

The thought is sobering. It would be very sad for a marvelous layout to open one day and survive for only a short time because of active hostility or submissive apathy. And it would be tragic indeed should the day ever come when Merion is plowed under or St. Andrews paved over.

Let us hope such fears are groundless and that the powers that be will recognize the values, whether artistic, historical, ecological or simply recreational, of the golf courses within their domain. Surely the game that has been played for over half a millennium on the links of Scotland, and for a century in North America, is too durable to simply disappear.

P. 122-123: *Wild Dunes GC established Tom Fazio's reputation as a first-rate designer.* P. 124: (Top) *Double green, Eagle Vail GC by Von Hagge and Devlin.* P. 124: (Bottom) and 125: *Keystone Ranch GC by R. T. Jones, Jr., where design is related to environment.*

124

11.
Evolution of Golf Course Features

Nature and golf architects have shared in the evolution of course design. Each has influenced the style, shape, size and placement of greens, tees, fairways and hazards, although the dominance of each influence has varied in different periods. Thus, this evolution was not in a straight line. The trends have tended to proceed in a circular manner, in the form of an upward spiral.

P. 126–127: *Quechee Lakes, Vermont, #17, Highland Course. Holes which are initially controversial often achieve fame.* P. 128: (Top) *Form follows function. Shape, size and bunkers at green vary with type and length of approach shot.* (Bottom) *Forced carry over two hazards is penal and unfair.*

GEOFFREY S. CORNISH · WILLIAM G. ROBINSON
AMERICAN SOCIETY OF GOLF COURSE ARCHITECTS

WITCH CREEK

SALT
MARSH

A TIDAL RIVER

14

P. 129: (Top) *Good strategic holes encourage advanced planning. Here, the tee shot must clear the fairway bunker or the second shot carry traps near the green. (Bottom) A "Cape"-type hole entices the player to cut as much corner as he dares. Such heroic holes bring out the gambler in a golfer.*

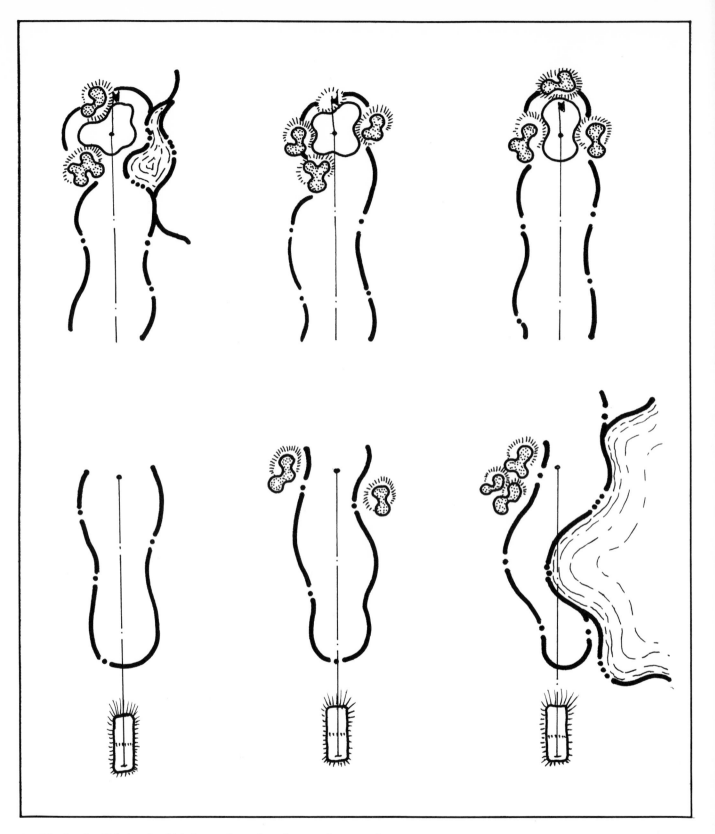

P. 130: *Good golf holes should balance shot values from stroke to stroke. Thus, combining the upper left approach with the lower right drive places too much pressure on a player, while the lower left drive and upper right green lacks challenge. Appropriate combinations of shot values are crucial to integrity and playing interest of a layout.*

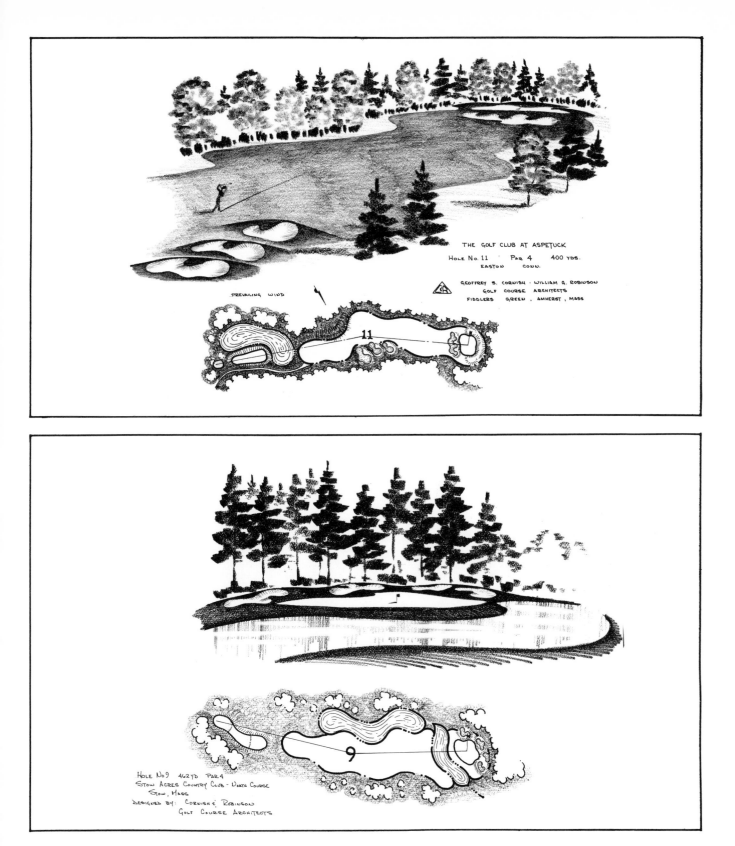

THE GOLF CLUB AT ASPETUCK
HOLE No. 11   PAR 4   400 YDS.
EASTON   CONN.

GEOFFREY S. CORNISH · WILLIAM G. ROBINSON
GOLF COURSE ARCHITECTS
FIDDLERS GREEN , AMHERST , MASS

PREVAILING WIND

11

HOLE No 9   462 YD   PAR 4
STOW ACRES COUNTRY CLUB - NORTH COURSE
STOW, MASS
DESIGNED BY: CORNISH & ROBINSON
GOLF COURSE ARCHITECTS

9

P. 131: *Tee shot values are similar on these par-4's, but approach shot
values are not. (Top) The second shot must carry the deep front bunker,
but with no trouble beyond the green, the shot value for a long or medium
iron is fair. (Bottom) The shallow green is surrounded by trouble and is
so severe for the long iron or fairway wood second that it may be unfair.*

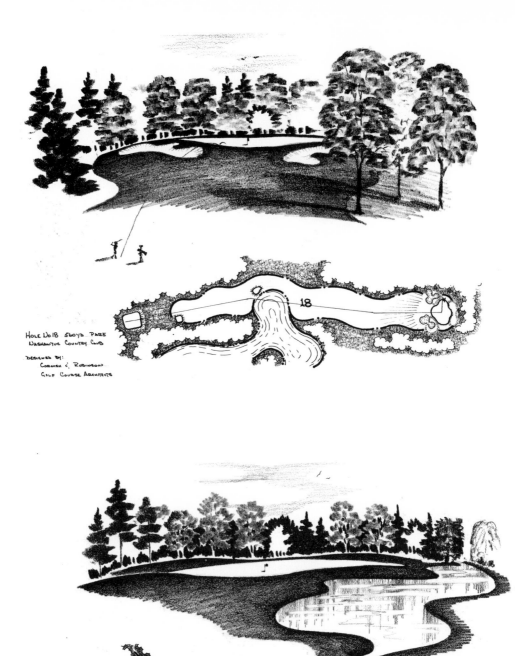

HOLE No.18 560yd PAR5
NASHAWTUC COUNTRY CLUB

DESIGNED BY:
CORNISH & ROBINSON
GOLF COURSE ARCHITECTS

P. 132: (Top) *This hole was considered unfair because a long hitter might reach the pond with his drive; yet the tee shot emphasizes accuracy while the second shot stresses length. The approach to the elevated green tests depth perception. (Bottom) Shot values increase as the golfer nears the green, but never become unfair. Both controversial par-5's were accepted.*

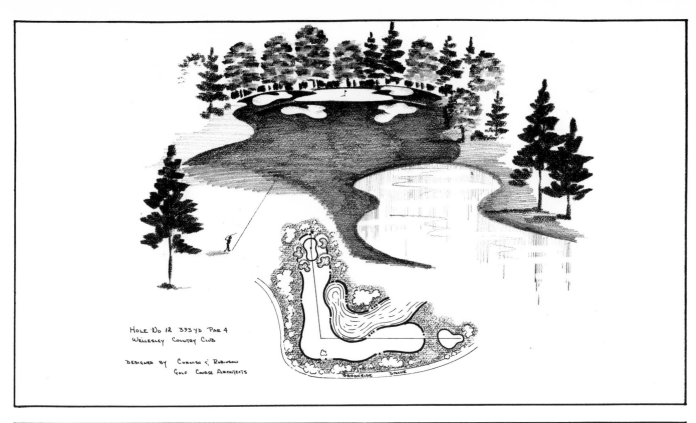

HOLE No 12 393 YD PAR 4
WELLESLEY COUNTRY CLUB

DESIGNED BY CORNISH & ROBINSON
GOLF COURSE ARCHITECTS

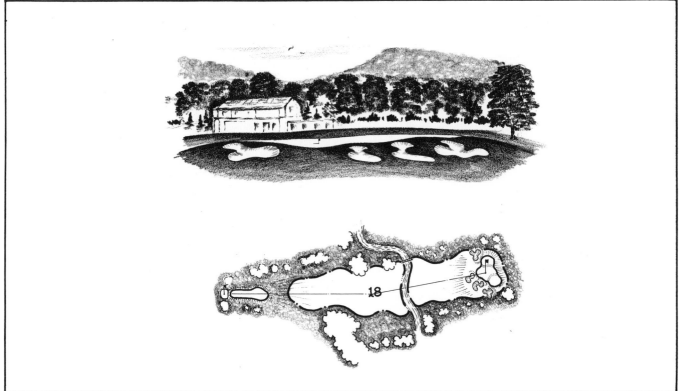

P. 133: *These par-4's have severe shot values for all but long, accurate hitters. (Top) The shot values of the tee and approach shots are determined by how close the golfer dares play to the pond. (Bottom) The value of a long, straight drive is great, because four deep bunkers guard the raised green.*

133

P. 134: *The par-5 fourth at Oakmont CC is a penal hole on a course that celebrates the penal philosophy. Yet the shot values are fair for all classes of players. The most timid golfer can reach the green in three adequate strokes, without encountering huge risk. The numerous bunkers are primarily a psychological hazard, although they will catch errant shots.*

P. 135: *In contrast, the par-5 thirteenth at Dorado Beach East has unfair shot values for the average golfer, though it is a sterling example of the heroic philosophy of Robert Trent Jones. A cautious player, driving clear of the first lake, must then hit a long, accurate wood or face a third over more water, palms and a trap. But the hole is a thriller for the daring.*

P. 136–137: *The par-5 fifteenth at Eastman GC
tests golfers of all abilities on their own levels.
At 480 yards, it can be reached in two long shots, or
in three by short hitters. The average drive will
find a level lie in the valley and an easy second to
a landing area short of the green. The long hitter
runs the risk of being caught by fairway and
greenside bunkers.*

138

P. 138: (Top) "Greens" were born at St. Andrews in the 1700s when attention was focused on keeping some areas turfed. (Center) Following this example, other courses nestled greens in hollows, sheltered from the wind. (Bottom) By the late 1800s, greens were made by leveling tops off natural plateaus. P. 139: (Top) At Sunningdale in 1901, Willie Park first moved earth to create raised, contoured putting surfaces. (Bottom) This developed into the sculptured green of contemporary design.

P. 140: (Top) *Until 1875 a player teed his ball on the green. Then level areas were provided off the green, though often too small to support grass.* (Center) *Artificial surfaces were tried, as were multiple tees. After WWII huge tees evolved, but their raised, square appearance proved monotonous.* (Bottom) *Free forms, introduced by Lawrence Packard, solved this problem.*

P. 141: (Top) *"Bunkers" were originally scars on the links, resulting from livestock sheltering behind hills or gardeners quarrying sea shells, and later from golf balls rolling into hollows. (Center) Greenkeepers began to modify and stabilize these scars, sometimes changing their shapes. (Bottom) This practice led to the dramatic bunkering of today.*

141

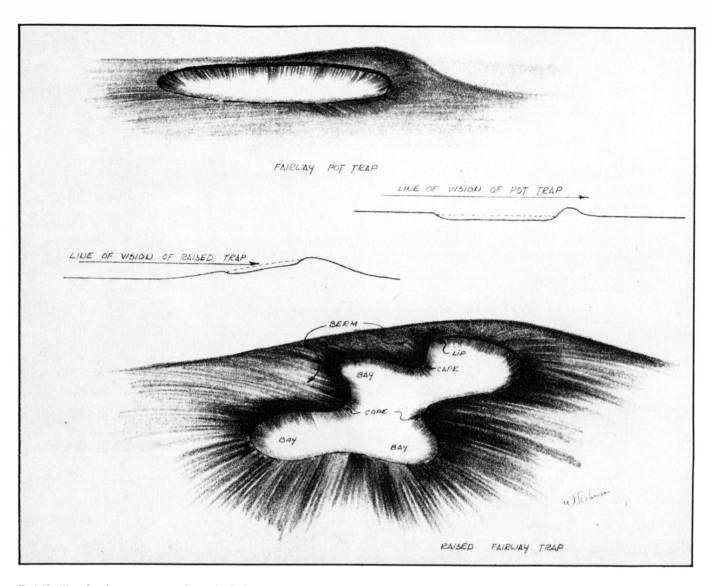

FAIRWAY POT TRAP

LINE OF VISION OF POT TRAP

LINE OF VISION OF RAISED TRAP

BERM

LIP

CAPE

BAY

CAPE

BAY

BAY

RAISED FAIRWAY TRAP

P. 142: *Two bunker types arose from the links model,*
the pit or pot (above) and the raised trap (below).
P. 143: *Theories of bunker placement changed through*
history. (Top) At first most were penal cross traps.
Later they became lateral and strategic. A modern
formula states that the further one hits, the more
accurate he must be; thus (far right) axes of bunkers
converge. (Bottom) Before WWII many bunkers adjoined
putting surfaces. Later placed far out, they caught
only high handicappers. A compromise was the result.

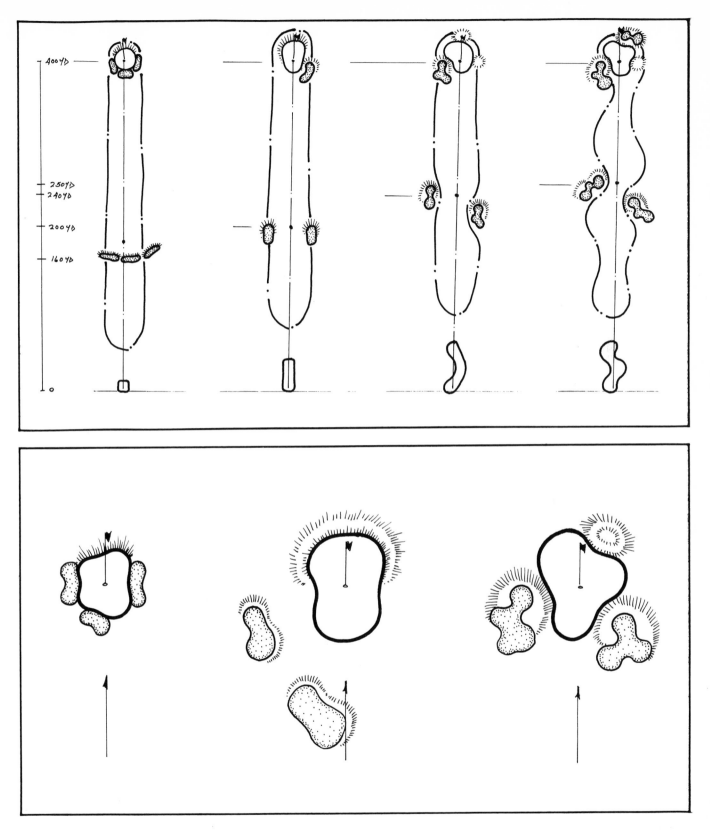

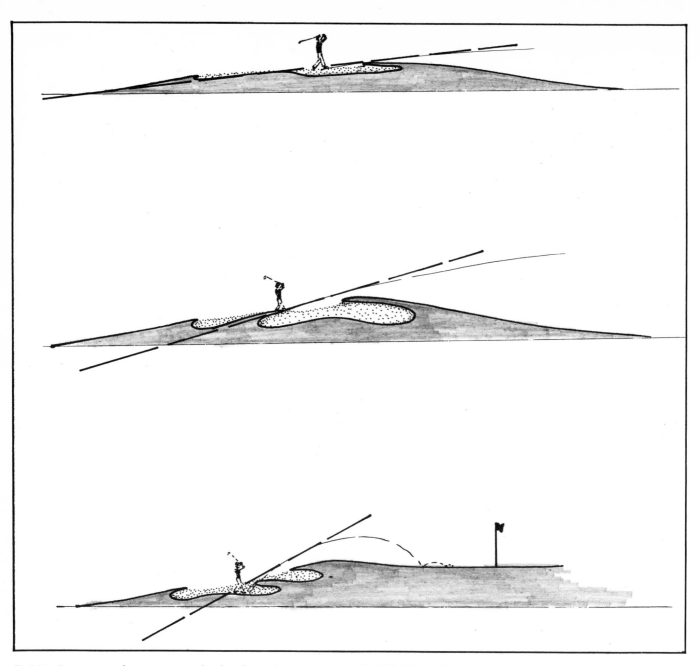

P. 144: *One aspect of contemporary bunker design is embodied in the concept that the closer a bunker is to the green, the greater should be its depth and the steeper its face. Thus, the distant trap (top) is shallow, while the one at greenside (bottom) is deep.*

P. 145: *(Top) Concentric mowing patterns around greens add the art principle of rhythm or radiation. (Bottom) Boundaries between fairway and rough can be straight or contoured. Wavy lines enhance target golf and eye appeal and help combat energy shortages.*

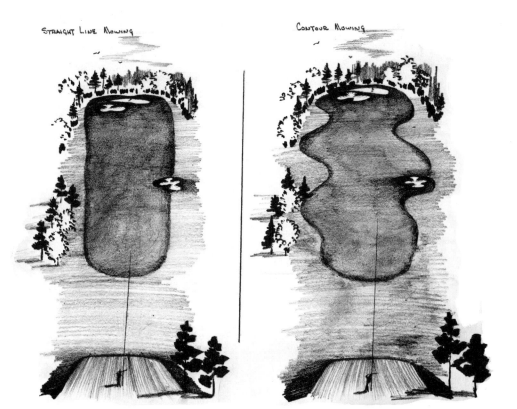

STRAIGHT LINE MOWING

CONTOUR MOWING

145

P. 146: *Golf architects have experimented endlessly, with varying degrees of success. One experiment which ended favorably was the introduction by Alister Mackenzie of a green with enormous undulations at Sitwell Park in England. The green first met with a storm of protest from the golfing public and was eventually accepted and later copied worldwide. A similar cycle of initial opposition, gradual acceptance and final endorsement has greeted many innovations in course design throughout its history.*

P. 147: *Not all experiments have been as successful as Mackenzie's, however. Some novel ideas have been tried and found wanting. Among the failures were (top) target areas requiring short irons from tees on dogleg par-four or -five holes; (lower left) extremely sharp doglegs; and (lower right) bunkers extending into putting surfaces, requiring putts around them. Innovations like these, which met with undiminished disfavor, have tended to be dropped or modified out of existence.*

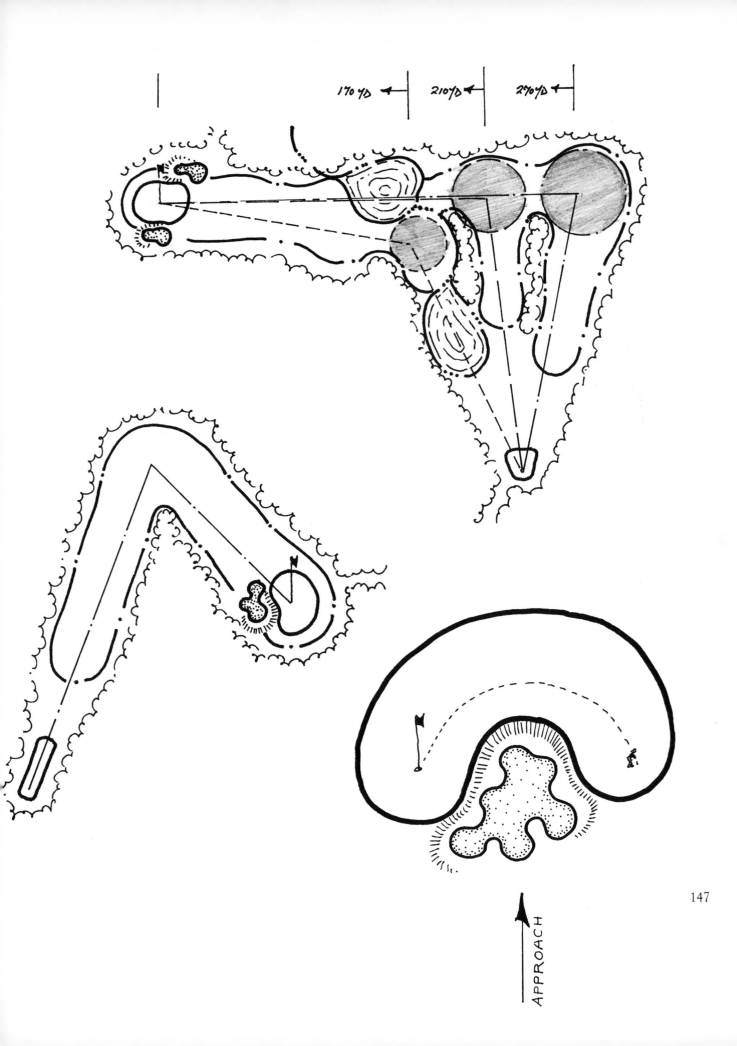

APPROACH

147

12

12.

Developments in Allied Fields

An evolutionary process parallel to the upward spiral of design is apparent in the increasing perfection of the greensward and conditioning of golf courses. This process was advanced by course superintendents and was supported by scientists, manufacturers and dealers. Superior conditioning in turn affected course design, as did improvements in playing equipment and the mechanics of the game. A chronological list of the highlights of these collateral developments includes:

· As golf evolved on the links, it was played on natural turf, around and over numerous scars known as "bunkers" to Scottish farmers. Most bunkers were caused by livestock sheltering from gale-force winds on the lee side of hills, while a few of the deepest were excavations from which sea shells had been quarried. More scars developed as divots accumulated in hollows or at the foot of slopes where balls stopped rolling. Soon greenkeepers modified the configurations of these scars.

· Ball makers, such as the Gourlays of Leith and Musselburgh and Allan Robertson of St. Andrews, made the earliest golf balls from leather and feathers. These were replaced by the gutta-percha after 1846. By that time, drivers, spoons, irons, and putters were all in use. Club heads were made from hard thorn wood.

· As golf spread in the British Isles and course designers resorted to penal cross bunkers and geometric features, greenkeepers saw to it that some of their greens were nestled among hillocks, sheltered from drying winds. These greens followed the natural contours of their locations, although some lost their contours by decades of top-dressing with sand. Before the last quarter of the nineteenth century, green areas were not cultivated. They were merely turf converted to "putting surfaces" and maintained by grazing, sanding and foot traffic.

· By the later 1800s greenkeepers were experimenting with different grasses and with methods for maintaining the turf. The pioneer in grass studies was seedsman Martin H. Sutton, who established Sutton's Grass Station in 1863 at Reading, England.

· The gutta-percha ball proved too hard for the hard thorn club heads of the time. These hard woods were replaced by fruitwoods (apple, pear and beech) and iron heads. The ash shaft was superseded by hickory. A simple golf bag came into use for carrying the increasing number of clubs.

· As greens and other features became more natural and linkslike in the heathlands era in England, course conditioning improved. Greens were mowed. Fairways were still kept short by grazing sheep, but gasoline- and steam-propelled mowers (invented in England in 1896) were in evidence on golf courses by the early 1900s. British seed companies continued research and advisory services, and expanded availability of their products and services to other parts of the British Empire and to the United States.

· With the universal adoption of the hard-core ball in the early 1900s, persimmon replaced fruitwoods in club heads.

· In America turfgrass research was initiated before the turn of the century in Connecticut, Michigan and Rhode Island. About the same time, the great "Scottish invasion" of greenkeepers and professionals into North America introduced techniques for course construction and maintenance.

· The rubber-cored "Haskell" ball was invented in the United States around 1900 and was soon adopted universally.

· In 1904 the center-shafted putter, another American invention, was introduced. It ushered in an age of invention that resulted in a decline of the skill needed to play golf. Further deterioration of the game was soon halted by regulations issued by the ruling bodies of golf. Actions in the field of course architecture also helped maintain the integrity of the game with features previously overlooked on the ancient links used as models.

· As American architects began to embellish natural features and artificially create others, greenkeepers also advanced the state of their art. Scientists became increas-

P. 148–149: *A swan glides peacefully over a pond at Mountain Shadows GC, Arizona. Golf courses offer a number of ecological benefits, not the least of these being a refuge for many forms of life crowded out of urban and suburban areas. P. 151: (Top) An alligator takes the air at Harbour Town, South Carolina. (Bottom) A deer roams the rough at Cypress Point GC.*

ingly helpful. C. V. Piper, agrostologist of the United States Department of Agriculture, was consulted on establishment of grass at the National Golf Links of America, perhaps the first time such a professional scientist contributed to the creation of a golf course.

• By the 1900s golf professionals insisted on separate practice fairways. "Maniac Hill" at Pinehurst, featuring a fairway, tee and bunker, was one of the first.

• By 1910 the practice of mowing fairways using horses with leather boots pulling single mowers became common in America. In 1914 Charles Worthington introduced a horse-drawn three-unit mower, and in 1919 designed and built a golf course tractor. By the end of World War I the use of multibladed reel mowers on greens became universal.

• British greenkeepers formed an association in 1912.

• Francis Ouimet's victory in the 1913 U.S. Open at The Country Club (Brookline, Massachusetts) inspired a new wave of interest in the game in America. This in turn led to a new demand for courses by Americans, a demand left unsatisfied until the boom that followed the War.

• Size and weight of the golf ball were regulated in 1915 although standards differed on each side of the Atlantic.

• In 1916 American professionals formed the Professional Golfers Association.

• C. V. Piper and R. A. Oakley published *Turf for Golf Courses* in 1917, the first American book devoted to the subject.

• The Green Section of the United States Golf Association was established in 1920 to advise on turf problems of member courses. After World War II it was headed successively by Fred V. Grau and Alexander M. Radko who was assisted by Carl H. Schwartzkopf after 1979.

• Matched sets of numbered clubs were introduced in the 1920s, and steel shafts were legalized.

• In 1926 greenkeepers in the United States and Canada formed a continent-wide professional society, The National Greenkeepers Association, which became The Golf Course Superintendents Association of America after World War II.

• In 1927 Lawrence S. Dickinson established a school for greenkeepers at the Stockbridge School of Massachusetts Agricultural College. In the mid-1950s the school was headed by Dr. Eliot C. Roberts and in 1959 by Dr. Joseph Troll, who presided over its expansion into the largest program of its type in the world.

• In 1929 the British Board of Greenkeeping Research established a research station at Bingley, Yorkshire, England. This became the center for turfgrass research in Great Britain.

• During the Depression years professional Gene Sarazen developed a straight-faced sand wedge, which provided still another challenge for course architects. In an opposing move, the R & A and the USGA placed a limit of fourteen clubs for a round, and ball velocity was limited.

• H. Burton Musser and Fred V. Grau established a turfgrass extension and research team in the 1930s at Pennsylvania State College. It was continued into the seventies at Penn State by the team of Joseph Duich, Donald Waddington and John C. Harper II.

• In 1936 the National Golf Foundation, a nonprofit organization dedicated to the advancement of golf, was established by Herb and Joe Graffis, publishers of *Golfdom* magazine. Executive directors of the NGF since then have included Glen Morris, Rex McMorris, Harry Eckhoff, William Pack and Don A. Rossi, appointed in 1970, who greatly expanded the Foundation's activities.

• During the 1950s, the National Golf Foundation rescued American golf architects from a precarious situation. Prior to that time, owners turned to their architects for initial advice on the economic feasibility of a new course. The architect often found himself involved in a conflict of interest. But Harry Eckhoff, East Coast representative of the NGF, developed a procedure whereby the Foundation provided feasibility data for groups contemplating new courses. If the project was deemed feasible, the Foundation recommended hiring a course architect. The Eckhoff plan rapidly became standard. While the architect continued to give his client the benefit of his own economic observations, he was relieved of the ultimate responsibility of determining whether the project would ultimately be profitable.

• With the advent of scientific turf management and power golf in the quarter century after 1955, many hazards became antiquated, requiring their relocation.

• For better or worse, the powered golf cart was universally accepted in North America by the late 1950s. In providing for its use, the architect sometimes found that modifications required in his plans could result in the classic dilemma of "the tail waggin' the dog."

• The Golf Development Council was established in Britain in 1965 with roles similar to those of the National Golf Foundation in the United States. Secretaries until 1980 included W. B. J. Armstrong, G. A. McPartlin and W. D. Hughes.

• By the 1960s a growing number of contractors were specializing in golf course construction on both sides of the Atlantic, making it possible for architects and owners to bid their work competitively to skilled firms. In 1970

American contractors formed the Golf Course Builders of America.

· Computers became involved to a limited extent in course planning in the 1970s. One firm experimented with forecasting course capacity from plans and advising where congestion could occur. Computers were also involved in estimating cuts and fills, planning irrigation and drainage, and in correlating the latter with surrounding developments.

· By the mid-1960s landscape architecture became the preferred academic background for the aspiring golf architect, with additional studies in soil, plant and turfgrass science together with civil engineering. Although formal courses in course architecture were seldom, if ever, avail-

able at the university level, golf architects were frequently invited to lecture and conduct seminars for students in landscape architecture.

· The inventors remained busy in the 1970s, which saw the introduction of graphite shafts, Surlyn-covered balls, balls with new dimpled patterns and golf club heads weighted heel and toe. Once again, technology threatened the traditional parameters of the game and of golf course design.

Professional golfer Walter Hagen once remarked, in the early 1920s, that golf architecture had outstripped advances in equipment. From a designer's point of view, Hagen was perhaps too optimistic. Still, as Hagen also pointed out, as courses improved so did the quality of golfers, and there is no doubt that courses, and golfers, have improved tremendously since the early days of golf.

But credit for this fact must be shared by all the allied professions. Golf architects have created ever more challenging and interesting courses. Course superintendents and turfgrass experts have made immense strides in course conditioning. Inventors and manufacturers have continually improved the implements, while teachers of the game have refined their techniques to make the golf swing simpler to comprehend.

Despite healthy differences of opinion among professions over the merit of their respective contributions, all have advanced the state of the game because of an overriding common interest, their love of golf.

P. 153: (Top) *First meeting, ASGCA, Pinehurst, 1948. From left, W. P. Bell, R. White, W. Langford, D. Ross, R. B. Harris, S. Thompson, W. Gordon, R. T. Jones, W. Diddell, J. B. McGovern. Absent: Daray, Lawrence, Maxwell. (Bottom) Ross Award Presentation, Scotland, 1980. From left: J. Kidwell, R. Phelps, G. H. Micklem, J. Snyder, R. T. Jones, R. Nugent.*

13.

Perspective

In reviewing the history of golf course architecture, it is possible to divide those who practiced it into three groups: those who provided the functional, inexpensive layouts demanded by their times; those who constructed attractive, enjoyable golf courses that advanced the state of the art; and those who created superior designs, often pioneering trends in the process.

Little credit has been given to the first group, the functional designers; yet the world of golf owes them a great debt. These are the planners—men like Tom Dunn of Britain and Tom Bendelow of America, who provided scores of courses that enabled legions of newcomers to play the game. They did what their times and locales required of them, building "sand-lot" layouts for communities that could afford nothing more. Occasionally one of their layouts developed into a well-regarded course, but for the most part the functional designers dealt in quantity and economy rather than quality. Functional designers had a profound effect on the game of golf itself, but not upon the practice of architecture. Yet, as Horace Hutchinson once said of Tom Dunn, "A man is not to be criticized because he is not in advance of his times." [1]

The second group consists of the accomplished designers, men like Wayne Stiles and Seth Raynor. They were masters of their craft, creating above-average courses and an occasional outstanding layout. It could well be said that a majority of the 500 or so men throughout history who practiced golf course design as a profession or devoted avocation attained this position. The early accomplished architects established a very high standard for golf design, and succeeding generations maintained and improved upon it. Because of their sheer numbers, many such architects never achieved widespread recognition, although their works often did.

The final group is the smallest. It comprises the virtuosos of golf course architecture, the perfectionists who designed and built outstanding courses, and often masterpieces of design. Some, like George Crump, did but a single layout; others, like Willie Park, Jr., H. S. Colt, Donald Ross and Robert Trent Jones, were among the most prolific in history. Nearly all the virtuosos received the accolades due them in their lifetimes, although even then they were usually overshadowed by their own works. Their superior works were ahead of their times, and perhaps every virtuoso was ahead of his time in one aspect or another of golf design and construction.

What has distinguished one group from another, the functional from the accomplished and the latter from the virtuosos, has been, of course, their golf courses and the extent to which they embodied the three basic considerations of golf design—namely, the game itself, aesthetics and future maintainability. One good way to evaluate the respective works of each group is to use the concept of shot values.

This concept is most easily explained in terms of objectives and problems. Even the functional architects planned their layouts to feature these for players. But the accomplished architects went further. They deliberately planned each hole on their courses to pose an objective to be reached by the golfer and problems to be avoided. The objectives and problems, and the correct way to reach the former and avoid the latter, were not always readily apparent, for the goal was to challenge not only the player's game but also his mind. William S. Flynn once defined this goal perfectly:

> The principal consideration of the architect is to design his course in such a way as to hold the interest of the player from the first tee to the last green and to present the problems of the various holes in such a way that they register in the player's mind as he stands on the tee or on the fairway for the shot to the green. [2]

These individual challenges to a golfer's mental and physical abilities are the shot values, or playing values, of a golf hole. The measure of shot values is based on how attainable the objective is and how difficult the problems are. Holes with weak shot values have easily reachable objectives and relatively few problems, and are therefore mediocre. But holes with shot values too great have nearly

P. 154–155: *La Quinta Hotel GC. An avowed aim of architects has been to use natural contours, but the actual practice of architecture often requires alteration of terrain and soil to create the enjoyable golf found on the links.*

unreachable objectives and abound with problems, and are therefore unfair. Those with honest shot values balance the severity of the problems with the attainability of the objectives. The challenge to a golfer when confronted with these honest holes is to decide what type of shot is required in each situation (high or low, maneuvered from right to left or left to right, etc.) and then to execute this shot.

The distinction, then, between a functional architect and an accomplished architect is that courses of the former rarely contained well-conceived shot values, while designs of the latter nearly always did. The difference between the design of an accomplished architect and that of a virtuoso is more subtle. The accomplished architect normally thought of each golf hole as a unit, with the green as the ultimate objective and bunkers, trees, streams, lakes, mounds, rough, prevailing winds and the like as the problems. The accomplished architect would attempt to design a hole with honest shot values by balancing a number of these problems with factors affecting how attainable the green was, including its size and location, and the length and width of the hole.

The virtuoso, however, being a perfectionist, strove to create each golf hole so that every single shot presented an objective and one or more problems. The goal of the virtuoso was to achieve holes with honest shot values on every required shot, whether it was the drive to the landing area, the approach shot to the green or the second stroke on a par-5. This is precisely the point of William S. Flynn in his aforementioned definition of shot values.

Indeed, the shot values of the green itself were examined by the virtuoso. James Braid wrote with some foresight in 1908:

> The greens should be large when they are expected to be reached in good play by a long shot and correspondingly small when it is generally an iron club that will be used to get to them. It will be noted that the size of the green is not at all dependent on the length of the hole. . . . As to the undulations, they may be of all kinds, and a pronounced knob, not in the very centre of the green but a few yards to one side, is generally an excellent thing; but the hole should never be cut either on the knob or very close behind it, because that would make it next to impossible to hole out from the other side. The purpose of the knob is to make the player avoid it or to play his approach to the side on which the hole is; and if he fails to do that and gets the knob in between his ball and the hole, he will have an unusually difficult putting problem to think out.[3]

Among virtuosos themselves, and among accomplished architects, too, differences have always existed in the manner of presentation of the objectives and problems of golf holes. This is the classic schism of competing philosophies—penal versus strategic. While it is a certainty that most contemporary golf course architects adhere to the strategic school, many of the best early designers, accomplished and virtuosos, practiced essentially penal design.

But even a penal golf hole can contain honest shot values, just as a strategic golf hole can have unfair values. For example, compare the fourth at Oakmont Country Club with the thirteenth at Dorado Beach's East course in Puerto Rico. Both are double dogleg par-5's, and both are about 540 yards from the back tees. Oakmont's fourth features no less than eighteen bunkers, including the famous "church pews" to the left of the tee shot landing area. The hole turns slightly right at that bunker, with a cluster of bunkers opposite it in the right rough. Two more clusters of bunkers frame the landing area for the second shot, and the fairway swings farther right at that point and slightly downhill to the green. The putting surface has a huge, deep bunker to its front left and two more bunkers to the right rear. The hole has few trees.

To the average golfer, the fourth is a true three-shot hole. The objectives on the first two shots are quite clear: to stay in the approximate center of the fairway. However, the less accurate can play short of the first fairway bunkers, and short again of the second set. A long approach is then required, but the green does have an unobstructed entrance on its right and is so situated as to permit a draw to remain on the green. With so many traps, the fourth at Oakmont is unforgiving of the errant shot. But when analyzed for its playing values, it is a fair hole for all. Perhaps the one criticism that can be made of it is that its shot values themselves are not balanced. That is, each stroke on the hole must be played with the same amount of concern. A more reasonable balance of the shot values would permit a more relaxed second shot after tangling with the gargantuan "church pews" bunker on the tee shot.

In contrast, the thirteenth at Dorado Beach East has only a few bunkers but features three water hazards. The first is to the left of the tee shot area, and the fairway swings to the left after passing it. In the vicinity of the second shot landing area there is a small drainage ditch in the left rough and a second large lake to the right. Perched on the far side of the lake is the green, fronted by one bunker and backed by two more. To compound the problems, many trees are scattered along the hole.

This is a prime example of the work of the hole's designer, Robert Trent Jones, and of his strategic/heroic philosophy. A drive over the left lake is rewarded with the opportunity to carry the second lake and reach the green in two strokes. For the more conventional, the fairway is wide and deep to the right of the first lake, and there are no fairway bunkers. But the problem lies with the conventional second shot. It depends too heavily upon length. If the objective of the second shot is to get past the lake on the right and provide an unobstructed approach shot to the green, it is unattainable for many golfers who drove to the right to avoid the first lake. The lake on the right also garners many a sliced second shot. Many players must play the approach to the green not only over the second lake but also over, around or between palm trees that border it. The shot values at the thirteenth at Dorado Beach East therefore verge on being too severe, even though, strategically, the hole provides several avenues to avoid flirting with the lakes.

The latter hole also raises another point. Nearly every architect who ever consciously worked on creating varying shot values in his designs was careful not to base those values on the expert player's game alone. Robert Trent Jones said it himself:

> As far as possible, there should be problems for each class of golfer to solve according to his mechanical skill and mental keenness. These problems should be interesting; there should always be something for each golfer to do, and that something should lie within the realm of his particular repertoire.[4]

But as the thirteenth at Dorado Beach East demonstrates, what may be honest shot values for the expert are unfair for the less talented. The converse is also true. Fair shot values for high handicap golfers are usually dull and weak for better players.

Perhaps the hardest task for golf course architects has been to build courses that challenge all levels of golfers within each golfer's respective capabilities. A series of successively shorter tees has not been the answer, although that step, promoted by H. S. Colt as early as 1910, was one in the right direction. The use of bunkers and water hazards as the main challenges to golfers in recent times has also been misguided on some occasions. Water hazards are often necessary, as large quantities of water are needed for irrigation, and excavations for lakes often produce fill for other uses. But water is the most unforgiving of problems, even for top players; and in the late seventies Mark Cox of the PGA of America urged designers to limit water hazards to two per nine holes.

A shot from a sand bunker, especially a fairway bunker, has always been the most difficult to consistently execute for the average golfer. In the course of golf design history, great strides have been made in the construction and appearance of sand bunkers. The hideous square cross bunkers of the late nineteenth century were replaced by attractive, natural-looking bunkers, in multifarious shapes and sizes. In the thirties Stanley Thompson, with his young associate Robert Trent Jones, created "flash traps" that featured graceful but pronounced mounds with sand flashed in irregular configurations upon their faces. In the post-World War II boom, most architects had their own bunkering styles as trademarks, from long, serpentine bunkers to absolutely flat sand surfaces lined with railroad ties. But regardless of style, bunkers remain bunkers. Their use, too, has been overdone on occasions. Heavy bunkering on a few holes to challenge the average golfer is appropriate. But heavy bunkering on every hole can destroy the playing value for the majority of golfers.

The key is that advice offered by Robert Trent Jones. The problems should lie within the particular realm of the golfer. To the average player, a grassy hollow, a downhill lie or even a single tree can be challenging enough. Therefore, in recent decades there has been a trend toward utilizing fewer bunkers but substituting natural problems in their place. The concern then arises whether interests and challenges for the expert player are being sacrificed.

If they are, it may not always be an altogether bad result. Contemporary concepts have led to the creation or rebuilding of courses with playing values geared to the challenge and enjoyment of the average player, and with a sincere effort made to keep them interesting for the low handicapper.

An offshoot of this trend has been the emergence in the 1960s of the "Executive course," with golf architect William Amick as the staunchest advocate. Executive courses, comprised of more par-3 than par-4 and -5 holes, were so named by William F. Mitchell because business executives could play them in a couple of hours. With a total par of between 60 and 66, executive layouts have never been considered championship courses under popular definitions. Yet the courses themselves have been popular, not only because they can be played rather quickly but also because they take up less land, are less costly to construct and maintain, and are encouraging to beginning players. Such courses, if well designed, can truly challenge all aspects of a golfer's game, including the tee shot, as indeed can a well-designed par-3 layout.

When considering the classes of golfers that a course should challenge, one must not forget women. That was precisely what was done for many decades by functional, accomplished and virtuoso designers. In the earliest days, short, modest ladies' nines adjoining a main course were established. But first in Britain and later in America, women refused to be relegated to what were usually inferior courses. An attempt was then made to adapt regular courses for women, usually by the addition of shorter tees. But very little consideration was given by their designers to whether the shot values were too great or too weak for the various female abilities from these "women's tees."

It was not until after World War II that serious studies were undertaken to create golf holes with appropriate playing values for women as well as men. Ironically, some architects felt it couldn't be done and again suggested the only rational solution was separate courses for female golfers, designed and built for their various abilities. For social and economic reasons, it is unlikely that will ever happen (although the Ladies Golf Club in Toronto, opened in the mid-twenties, is still active). Therefore, another of the challenges in the decades ahead will be planning courses to serve the games of men and women, expert and high handicapper alike.

Another challenge that has continued to face golf course architects over the years deserves discussion. That is the challenge to the planner to assure that his plan is implemented the way he envisaged it.

Obviously this has not been a problem to every architect on every course. Functional architects hardly ever thought about it. Even virtuoso designers like Donald Ross occasionally prepared and staked a layout for an owner of modest means with little concern as to what would be the ultimate result. In Ross's case, he did such jobs because he believed that golf should be as widely available as possible; and if funds did not permit him to supervise construction or even make periodic visits, that was still no reason not to set the owner on the right road.

On the majority of course design and construction operations, where time was taken to create and implement shot values on every hole, only the one-time architects were entirely confident and strictly in control of the results. Almost every professional golf architect had to rely on any number of other people. If construction was done by "lump sum" contract, the owner hired the course contractor; and while the architect still had supervision or inspection authority, he was in a way at the mercy of an often unfamiliar group of construction men. This was also true, but to a lesser extent, when the work was done by "force account," that is by the owner acting as his own contractor, hiring personnel and equipment on his own payroll and purchasing materials directly.

As an alternative, several architects provided their own contract services for construction. That allowed them to maintain a pool of skilled construction men who were experienced in executing their plans. Firms like Toomey and Flynn, Macdonald and Maddox, A. W. Tillinghast, and W. F. and David Gordon were design and construction businesses.

One other method was to subcontract particular parts of the work to specialized contractors. One company might do clearing and general grading, another the building of greens and tees, another the irrigation system and still another the preparation of seed beds and seeding. Specialists were prominent in the twenties. Some, like irrigation genius Wendell P. Miller, who designed and installed irrigation systems for courses like Augusta National and Southern Hills, and the Wood Brothers, who hand-molded the green designs of Perry Maxwell to the latter's satisfaction, were as well known in their day as the golf architects themselves. In Britain, James Braid and John R. Stutt formed an enduring architect–contractor relationship. In more recent times, subcontracting to specialists has been a common method of golf course construction in the United States, particularly in the South.

Regardless of the method used, the architect often faced the choice of supervising the construction himself day by day, or leaving a trusted employee in charge while making periodic visits of inspection to check on the progress. Few architects opted for the former, since very few could afford to devote all their time to a single project. But a few, like Herbert Strong and Dick Wilson (in his early days after World War II), did so.

Many appointed a construction foreman, sometimes an apprentice designer but more often the future greenkeeping superintendent. If the architect left sufficient sketch plans or diagrams and made lengthy follow-up visits, the results would usually satisfy him. The more trustworthy the foreman, the more artistic license the designer allowed him.

The inspection visits were especially important. All too often, difficulties would arise in attempting to duplicate in actual soil and terrain what the architect envisaged on paper. This was especially true in creating greens and placing hazards. Sometimes the architect would therefore provide only preliminary plans for them and come back to personally supervise their actual construction.

Golf architects soon recognized that there was no substitute for the combination of drawing-board and on-site designing, because the characteristics of terrain most needed for planning and estimating costs were not always apparent on topographic maps or aerial photographs. For

159

example, they didn't depict spectacular backdrops, the prevailing wind and perhaps subtle contours.

Whatever the method of design and construction, great layouts arose as the talented designer recognized his diamonds in the rough, translated them onto paper and then returned during construction to assure their proper development and sometimes their modification. Sadly, the flexibility to make modifications became more difficult as permit requirements became more rigid in the 1970s and as more courses were integrated with housing or other forms of recreation.

Construction implements also hampered many an architect's dreams. In the early days, courses were built by hand or with teams of horses or mules pulling "Fresno" scrapers, which slowly peeled away the earth and deposited it elsewhere. It was a tedious process but ideal for the artistic designer with the understanding client, for every nuance of every feature envisaged could be painstakingly perfected.

It was not until after World War II, when tilt blades and other equipment were introduced, that bulldozers could produce flowing lines that satisfied the designers.

Once the course was completed and opened, the architect always found his work at the mercy of a new group of individuals. There was the superintendent, of course, and the club owner or owners. Various club committees and elected officials, as well as local golf associations that utilized it, exercised differing controls over the course. If they respected his work and understood the shot values of each hole and the purpose of each feature that he created, and if they were cognizant of the many factors, like weather and the economy, that could affect the playability of the course beyond the architect's anticipation or control, then his finished product was safe and would endure as he had imagined it. The course superintendent and his ability to understand the designer's philosophy was most often the key.

When those in day-to-day contact with the golf course ignored shot values and features of the holes, the designer's efforts were negated. The man who set the cups could turn a well-planned green into a nightmare by thoughtless positioning of the hole; and the man who placed the tee markers could do the same on the tee shot by carelessly placing them to the back when a wind was gusting into the tee.

In-house redesigning of a course often caused additional harm. A club chairman might remove a feature he found offensive, and the next year his successor restore it and remove other features. The waste of money and player inconvenience were unnecessary, and if the features were trees, streams or other natural objects, the harm was irreparable.

An attempt to obviate such results occurred by the 1960s. Some golf architects, with William G. Robinson pioneering the practice, developed long-range planning for the course. The architect, with input from the club professional, the course superintendent and a committee from the club, would create a long-range plan outlining what changes, if any, were needed. When finalized, it was submitted to the membership and, if approved, became part of the club's by-laws and could not be altered except in accordance with them. This ingenious method maintained the course as envisaged by the original designer while allowing an organized updating of the layout.

Despite the best-conceived designs of any architect, nearly every course sooner or later requires updating. Time physically erodes and changes the course. Time also erodes the shot values of the holes. Changes and improvements in equipment, as well as refinement of players' talents, compromise once-admirable objectives and once-fearsome problems. More often, though, the task of updating an architect's work will fall upon a generation of subsequent designers. Revisions to their predecessor's works can be done sympathetically, even if totally new holes are required, but only if the new architect understands and respects the philosophy and aims of his predecessor.

That respect can be developed by the study of the history of golf course architecture and should be developed, not only by future golf architects, but by anyone who ever played and enjoyed the game of golf. Even if the designer was merely functional, his motives and contributions to the spread of the game itself should be realized. If the designer was an accomplished architect, his unique talents and characteristic features should be identifiable to anyone who takes the time to evaluate his compositions. And if the designer was a virtuoso, then an understanding and appreciation of his work is of even greater importance, for only then will his masterworks be preserved.

---

[1] Horace Hutchinson, *Fifty Years of Golf*, p. 168.
[2] William S. Flynn, "Golf Course Architecture and Construction—Analysis of Layout," *Bulletin of Green Section of the U.S.G.A.*, October 1927, p. 194.
[3] James Braid, *Advanced Golf*, London: Methuen, pp. 256 and 258.
[4] Robert Trent Jones, "Design with Respect to Play," *U.S.G.A. Journal*, June 1959, p. 25.

PART TWO

PROFILES

These biographical profiles of golf course-designers and others who've made an impact on the history of golf design were prepared using a multitude of sources and records.

The course lists following each architect's profile contain only works verified by the authors. None of the lists is intended to represent the complete work of any particular designer. In many cases, architects (especially the pioneers) did many more courses than are listed, but the names of some of those courses are yet to be determined. As this book goes to press, many present-day designers have designs on their drawing boards which, for a variety of reasons, are not listed.

Abbreviations used include:

ASGCA for the American Society of Golf Course
    Architects
BAGCA for the British Association of Golf Course
    Architects
GCSAA for the Golf Course Superintendents Association of
    America
CGCSA for the Canadian Golf Course Superintendents
    Association
ASLA for the American Society of Landscape Architects
CSLA for the Canadian Society of Landscape Architects
USGA for the United States Golf Association
LPGA for the Ladies Professional Golfers Association
PGA for the Professional Golfers Association
A for added holes. Example: A 9 indicates added 9 holes.
R for remodeled holes. (Remodeling runs the gamet from
    minor revisions to total creation of a new layout.)
NLE for No longer exists
GC for Golf Club
CC for Country Club
RC for Racquet Club
TC for Tennis Club
YC for Yacht Club
TPC for Tournament Players Club
Univ for University
Precision indicates a precision course, those shorter courses
    consisting mainly of par 3 and par 4 holes, commonly
    called Executive Courses.
The number of holes is indicated within parentheses. E.g.
    (9), (27), etc. If no number is given, it is presumed the
    course or project consisted of 18 holes.

John Frederick Abercromby (1861 - 1935)
Born: Felixstowe, Suffolk, England. Died: Addington, Surrey, England at age 74.

J.F. Abercromby, a doctor's son, took up golf in his youth and eventually became a scratch player, competing successfully in matches around London. At the turn of the century he was hired as private secretary to a financier at Bridley Manor, southwest of London. Impressed with three new golf courses in the area (Sunningdale, Walton Heath and Woking), his employer instructed Abercromby to provide him with a course.

Somewhat audaciously, "Aber" decided to lay out the course himself. He consulted with Willie Park Jr. and Jack White during the initial stages, but the final product, Worplesdon GC, was basically Abercromby's design. Choosing to pursue a career in golf architecture, he soon landed the commission for Coombe Hill GC and then laid out a course for Addington GC, built just before WWI. Abercromby settled at Addington, serving as its secretary and "benevolent despot" for the remainder of his life. He eventually built a second course there, and was constantly refining both.

In the 1920s Abercromby joined Herbert Fowler, Tom Simpson and Arthur Croome in the design firm of Fowler, Abercromby, Simpson and Croome. Most of his work for the firm, done primarily in collaboration with Fowler, was in the London heathlands area. Abercromby was considered a totally free-hand artist, never measuring distances nor sketching designs, but laying out golf holes on site and supervising their creation. Contemporary critics felt he made the most natural-looking hazards of any architect of the day, and some considered him the finest British designer of the era before World War I.

Courses by: J.F. Abercromby
England: Addington GC (New Course), Surrey (1933); Addington GC (Old Course), Surrey (1914); Coombe Hill GC (1909), with Willie Park Jr; Cowdray Park GC, with Herbert Fowler; Knole Park GC, Kent (1924), with Herbert Fowler; Liphook GC (1922), with A.C.M. Croome; Manor House Hotel GC (1930), with Herbert Fowler; West Kent GC, Kent (1916), with Herbert Fowler; Worplesdon GC,

Surrey (1908).
Courses Remodeled & Added to by: J.F. Abercromby
England: Worplesdon GC, Surrey (R.), with Willie Park Jr.
Netherlands: Haagsche GC (NLE, A.9).

Charles Henry "Chic" Adams
Chic Adams began his golf career working for his father, who for many years held the position of course superintendent at Cherokee (Iowa) CC. Turning professional in the 1940s, Adams served as pro-superintendent at Sioux City (Iowa) CC for over a decade. A member of both the PGA of America and the GCSAA, he began designing courses as a sideline in the early 1950s, and eventually resigned his club job to devote full time to golf architecture. In the late 1950s he moved his design and construction business to Atlanta and concentrated on building courses in the Southeast. He retired in the early 1970s, moving first to Southern Florida and then to the Myrtle Beach area of South Carolina.
Courses by: Chic Adams
Alabama: Skyline CC, Mobile (1962).
Florida: Airco GC, Tampa (1962); Bay West Lodge & CC (1968); Diamond Hills G&CC (1959); Portage Y&CC, Treasure Lake (1959); Scenic Hills G&CC, Pensacola (1959); Seminole Lake G&CC (1962); Top of the World GC, Clearwater (Precision, 27, 1971); Turf and Surf GC (9, 1956); Yacht GC (1965).
Georgia: Castle View T&CC, Atlanta (1960); Dobbins AFB GC (9, 1959); Golfland GC (Par 3, 9, 1959); Monroe CC (9, 1958); Pinetree CC, Marietta (1961); Riverside G&CC, Macon (1961).
Iowa: American Legion GC (9, 1956).
Kansas: Brookridge G&CC, Overland Park (27, 1963).
Kentucky: Hurstborne CC, Louisville (R.27, 1967).
Maine: Fairlawn CC, East Poland (1960).
Missouri: North Shore CC, St. Louis (27, 1959), with Homer Herpel; St. James Muni (9, 1966).
Tennessee: Fox Meadows CC, Memphis (1957); Valleybrook G&CC, Hixson (1957).
Courses Remodeled & Added to by: Chic Adams
Georgia: East Lake CC (Course No. 2), Atlanta (R.).
Iowa: Ottumwa G&CC (A.9, 1959).

Rokuro and Shiro Akaboshi
Rokuro and Shiro Akaboshi took up golf in their native Japan and were later educated in the U.S. at Princeton University where Rokuro served as captain of the golf team. Returning to Japan after college, the brothers became pioneers of the game in that country. Rokuro was an accomplished competitor, winning the inaugural Japanese Open in 1927, and Shiro was highly regarded as a teacher.

The Akaboshi brothers collaborated on the design of many courses in the 1920s and '30s and are generally considered Japan's first native golf architects. It is estimated that they planned over sixty of the country's early courses, including Hodogaya CC, Naruo CC and Abiko GC. They also laid out courses in other parts of Asia, including Taiwan G&CC in Taipei.
Courses by: Shiro Akaboshi
Japan: Abiko CC (1930), with Rokuro Akaboshi; Hakone CC, Kanagawa (18, 1954); Naruo CC, with Rokuro Akaboshi.
Taiwan: Taiwan G&CC, Taipei (1914), with Rokuro Akaboshi.
Courses Remodeled & Added to by: Shiro Akaboshi
Japan: Hodogayo CC, Yokohama (R.), with Rokuro Akaboshi.

James Alexander
James Alexander, superintendent of British Transport Hotels, assisted golf architect Philip Mackenzie Ross with the replanning of the Ailsa course at Turnberry, Scotland, after World War II. He then replanned the Arran course at Turnberry himself. He also planned major changes to the Queen's course at Gleneagles in the 1950s (in order to make it more equal to the King's course as a test of golf) and collaborated on the Prince's course at Gleneagles with I. Marchbanks and T. Telford. In addition, Alexander made extensive changes at Manor House Hotel Course in Devonshire, England.

Charles Hugh Alison (1882 - 1952)
Born: Preston, Lancashire, England. Died: Johannesburg, South Africa at age 70.

Hugh Alison was educated at Malvern and Oxford University where he was an outstanding cricket player and golfer. He was the youngest member of the Oxford and Cambridge Golfing Society team that toured the U.S. in 1903. He won every match he played during that tour.

After college Alison worked for a time as a journalist and then served as club secretary for the newly formed Stoke Poges GC near London. There he met H.S. Colt, who was laying out the course. Intrigued by course design since his early golfing days, Alison assisted Colt with the completion of Stoke Poges and then worked for Colt in the construction of several other London-area courses.

After service with the British Army during World War I, Major Alison rejoined Colt. They formed a partnership that lasted twenty years and included, at different times, J.S.F. Morrison and Alister Mackenzie. While Colt handled most of the design work in Britain and on the Continent, Alison worked extensively in North America and the Far East. Nearly all the courses built by the firm of Colt and Alison in the United States during the 1920s and '30s were designed by Hugh Alison.

Alison was coauthor (with Colt) of *Some Essays on Golf Course Architecture* (1920) and contributed to *Golf Courses: Design, Construction and Upkeep*, edited by M.A.F. Sutton (1933; revised 1950).
Courses by: C.H. Alison
Georgia: Sea Island GC (Seaside 9), St. Simons Island (1928), with H.S. Colt.

Illinois: Briarwood CC {formerly Briergate CC}, Deerfield (1921), with H.S. Colt; Knollwood C, Lake Forest (1923), with H.S. Colt; North Shore CC, Glenview (1924), with H.S. Colt.
Iowa: Davenport CC (1924), with H.S. Colt.
Maryland: Burning Tree C, Bethesda (1924), with H.S. Colt.
Michigan: Orchard Lake CC (1926), with H.S. Colt.
New Jersey: Canoe Brook CC (North Course), Millburn (NLE, 1924), with H.S. Colt.
New York: Century GC, White Plains (1926), with H.S. Colt; Colony CC, Algonac (1923), with H.S. Colt; Fresh Meadow CC {formerly Lakeville CC}, Great Neck (1925), with H.S. Colt; Old Oaks CC, Purchase (1927), with H.S. Colt; Park CC, Buffalo (1928), with H.S. Colt; Timber Point GC, Great River (1927), with H.S. Colt.
Ohio: Kirtland CC, Willoughby (1921), with H.S. Colt; Westwood CC, Rocky River (1924), with H.S. Colt.
Wisconsin: Milwaukee CC (1929), with H.S. Colt.
Ontario: York Downs GC, Toronto (NLE, 1921), with H.S. Colt.
Australia: Huntingdale GC, Victoria (1941), with S. Berriman.
Belgium: Royal Waterloo GC (NLE, 36, 1923), with H.S. Colt.
England: Brancepeth Castle GC, Durham (1924), with H.S. Colt and Alister Mackenzie; Cuddington GC (1929), with H.S. Colt and J.S.F. Morrison; Effingham GC (1927), with H.S. Colt; Ham Manor GC, Sussex (1936), with H.S. Colt and J.S.F. Morrison; Leckford GC (9, 1929), with H.S. Colt and J.S.F. Morrison; Moor Park GC (West Course), Hertfordshire (1923), with H.S. Colt and Alister Mackenzie; Sunningdale GC (New Course), Berkshire (1922), with H.S. Colt; Teignmouth GC (1924), with H.S. Colt and Alister Mackenzie; Trevose G&CC (27, 1926), with H.S. Colt and J.S.F. Morrison; Wentworth GC (East Course), Surrey (1924), with H.S. Colt and J.S.F. Morrison; Wentworth GC (West Course), Surrey (1924), with H.S. Colt and J.S.F. Morrison.
France: Golf Club de Touquet (Sea Course) (1930), with H.S. Colt and J.S.F. Morrison.
Ireland: County Sligo GC (1922), with H.S. Colt and Alister Mackenzie.
Japan: Fuji CC (1932); Hirona CC (1932); Kawana GC (Fuji Course), Shizuoka (1936); Tokyo CC (1932).
Netherlands: Eindhoven GC (1930), with H.S. Colt and J.S.F. Morrison; Haagsche G&CC (1939), with H.S. Colt and J.S.F. Morrison; Kennemer G&CC (1929), with H.S. Colt and J.S.F. Morrison; Utrecht GC (1929), with H.S. Colt and J.S.F. Morrison.
Scotland: Longniddry GC (1921), with H.S. Colt.
South Africa: Bryanston CC (1950); Vereeniging CC, Transvaal (1938).
Spain: Real C de la Puerta de Hierro (Old), Madrid (1932), with J.S.F. Morrison and H.S. Colt; Real G de Pedrena (1928), with J.S.F. Morrison and H.S. Colt.
Sweden: Stockholm GC (1932), with H.S. Colt and J.S.F. Morrison.
Wales: Pyle and Kenfig GC (1922), with H.S. Colt.
West Germany: Falkenstein GC (1930), with H.S. Colt and J.S.F. Morrison; Frankfurter GC (1928), with H.S. Colt and J.S.F. Morrison; Hamburger Land und GC (1935), with H.S. Colt and J.S.F. Morrison.

Courses Remodeled & Added to by: C.H. Alison
Georgia: Sea Island GC (Plantation 9), St. Simons Island (R., 1928), with H.S. Colt.
Illinois: Bob O'Link CC, Highland Park (R., 1924), with H.S. Colt.
Maryland: Chevy Chase CC (R., 1924), with H.S. Colt.
Michigan: CC of Detroit, Grosse Pointe Farms (R., 1927), with H.S. Colt; Lochmoor C, Grosse Pointe Woods (R., 1920), with H.S. Colt.
Pennsylvania: Baederwood GC (R., 1927), with H.S. Colt.
England: Northumberland GC (R., 1924), with H.S. Colt and Alister Mackenzie; Royal Lytham & St. Annes GC, Lancashire (R., 1930), with H.S. Colt; Sunningdale GC (Old Course), Berkshire (R., 1922), with H.S. Colt.
Ireland: Royal Dublin GC (R., 1921), with H.S. Colt.
Japan: Kasumigaseki GC (East Course), Saitama (R., 1930); Kasumigaseki GC (West Course), Saitama (R., 1930); Kawana GC (Oshima Course), Shizuoka (R., 1936).
Malaysia: Royal Selangor GC (Old Course) (R., 1931), with H.S. Colt.
Northern Ireland: Belvoir Park GC, Belfast (R., 1927), with H.S. Colt.
Scotland: Muirfield GC, East Lothian (R., 1925), with H.S. Colt.

Peter Alliss (1931 -   )
Born: Berlin, Germany.
Peter Alliss, the son of famed British professional golfer Percy Alliss, won numerous tournaments after turning professional in 1946. He was an eight-time member of the British Ryder Cup team and wrote several books on golf, including one novel.
In the 1970s Alliss began regular commentating on televised golf broadcasts both in Britain and the U.S. He also teamed with David Thomas in a design-and-build firm that handled several projects in the UK and the Continent, most notably 36 holes at The Belfry, which became the new home of the British PGA and a Ryder Cup site. A sour economy at the end of the decade convinced Alliss and Thomas to concentrate their energies on the construction end of the business and let others handle the design. They continued to build courses for other architects well into the 1980s, but did not engage in further architecture on their own.

Courses by: Peter Alliss
England: Belfry GC (Brabazon Course) (1979), with David Thomas; Belfry GC (Derby Course) (1979), with David Thomas; Dewsbury District GC, with David Thomas; Hessle GC, with David Thomas; Hill Valley G&CC (27, 1975), with David Thomas; King's Lynn GC (1975), with David Thomas; Thorpe Wood GC (1975), with David Thomas.
Northern Ireland: Clandeboye GC (New Course), County Down (1973), with David Thomas and T.J.A.McAuley.
Scotland: Blairgowrie GC (Lansdowne Course), Perthshire (9, 1974), with David Thomas.

Courses Remodeled & Added to by: Peter Alliss
France: Golf de La Baule (R., 1977), with David Thomas.
Ireland: Dundalk GC (R., 1975), with David Thomas; Dundalk GC (A.9, 1975), with David Thomas.

Northern Ireland: Ballyclare GC (R.9, 1973), with David Thomas and T.J.A.McAuley.
Scotland: Blairgowrie GC (Rosemount Course) (R., 1974), with David Thomas; Haggs Castle GC (R.), with David Thomas; Turnberry GC (Ailsa Course), Ayrshire (R., 1976), with David Thomas.

Grange Gordon "Sandy" Alves (1885 - 1939)
Born: Aberdeen, Scotland. Died: Cleveland, Ohio at age 54.
Grange Alves, called "Sandy" after his hair color, learned golf from his father and was a successful amateur player before emigrating to the United States at age nineteen. He worked as a stonemason's apprentice in Barre, Vt. until 1909 when he landed a position as pro-greenkeeper at French Lick Springs, Indiana. While there, a flood ravaged the course and Alves supervised its reconstruction, redesigning several holes in the process.
Donald Ross was hired soon afterward to design a second course and Alves constructed it. Impressed with his work, Ross recommended Alves to Shaker Heights CC of Cleveland, Ohio. He was hired to supervise construction of its Donald Ross course, and stayed on in 1915 as the club's first professional. Eight years later he was chosen by fellow Masons to design and build a course for the Masonic organization in Cleveland. With Ross' help he created the Acacia CC which opened in 1923. Alves remained there as pro-greenkeeper until his death.
While at Acacia, Alves designed a number of Cleveland-area courses on the side. He was highly regarded as a golf instructor and continued to be a good player, winning the Ohio Open in 1922 and 1925. In addition, he served as vice president of both the GCSAA and the PGA of America.

Courses by: Sandy Alves
Ohio: Acacia CC, South Euclid (1921), with Donald Ross; Highland Meadows CC, Sylvania (1928); Highland Park GC (Blue Course) (1929); Highland Park GC (Red Course) (1927); Lyndhurst GC (1925); Madison CC (27, 1926); Meadowlands GC, Willoughby (9, 1930); Middle Bass Island GC, Sandusky (1930); Ridgewood Muni, Cleveland (1924); Twin Lakes CC, Kent (1925); University Heights GC, Cleveland (9, 1929).

Courses Remodeled & Added to by: Sandy Alves
Indiana: French Lick GC (Valley Course) (R., 1911).
Ohio: East Liverpool CC (A.9, 1928); Oakwood C, Cleveland (A.6, 1928); Sylvania CC, Toledo (R.6, 1929).

William Walker Amick (1932 -   ) ASGCA, President, 1977.
Born: Scipio, Indiana.
Bill Amick received his B.A. Degree from Ohio Wesleyan University (where he played on the golf team) and was then employed as a graduate assistant in Turfgrass Management at Purdue University. After two years as an officer in the U.S. Air Force, Amick returned to Indiana to train under golf architect William H. Diddel.
After stints with Diddel and designer Chic Adams, Amick formed his own practice in Ohio in 1959. Within a few years he moved to northern Florida.
A low handicap golfer and thoughtful architect, Bill Amick established himself in several facets of the profession. His residential development layouts helped establish standards of integrating housing with golf. He did considerable research on conversion of sanitary landfills into golf courses, and designed several model landfill course projects. He helped popularize shorter courses consisting of par three and four holes, the so-called "executive" or "precision" layouts that Amick preferred to call "challenge courses."
In the 1980s Amick was at the forefront of a movement to reintroduce a shorter golf ball, an idea his mentor Bill Diddel had promoted some forty years earlier. Amick served as first president of the American Modified Golf Association, an organization dedicated to the experimentation and evaluation of "modified" golf balls, those that travel only half the distance of normal compression balls. In 1986, Amick laid out Eagle Landing CC in Hanrahan, S.C., the first course designed solely for use of such modified golf balls.

Courses by: Bill Amick
Alabama: Chattahoochee CC, Abbeville (9, 1964); Cumberland Lake CC, Birmingham (1968).
Florida: A.C. Read GC (Seaside Course), Pensacola (1962); Alhambra G&CC, Orlando (1970); Beacon Woods CC, New Port Richey (1974); Crestview CC (9, 1961); Fairgreen CC, New Smyrna Beach (Precision, 1978); Fairway GC, Orlando (1972); Fort Walton Beach Muni (1962); Havana CC (9, 1963); Hollywood GC, Fort Walton Beach (1966); Island GC, Fort Walton Beach (1985); Jefferson CC, Monticello (9, 1965); Killearn G&CC (1967); Mangrove Bay GC, St. Petersburg (1977); Meadow Oaks G&CC, Hudson (Precision, 1985); Monsanto Employees GC, Pensacola (1961); Ocean G Links, Daytona Beach (Par 3, 10, 1982); Palm Harbor GC, Flager Beach (1973); Panama City Beach GC (1968); Pelican Bay G&CC, Daytona Beach (1979); Perdido Bay CC, Pensacola (1963); Pineview G&CC (1968); Rocky Bayou CC, Niceville (1973); Sawgrass GC (Oakbridge Course), Ponte Vedra Beach (1972); Seminole Valley GC, Chattahoochee (1986); Serrento Valley CC, Laurel (1987); Seven Rivers G&CC, Crystal River (1968); Shalimar Pointe CC {formerly Lake Lorraine GC}, Shalimar (1968); Sherwood G&CC, Titusville (9, 1968); Sorrento Valley CC, Laurel (1985); Spruce Creek GC, Daytona Beach (1974); St. Joseph's Bay CC (1962); Tiger Point G&CC (East Course), Gulf Breeze (9, 1979); Tiger Point G&CC (West Course), Gulf Breeze (1965); Vineyards GC, Naples (1987).
Georgia: Briar Creek CC, Sylvania (9, 1963); Donalsonville CC (9, 1970); Green Meadows CC, Augusta (1962); Pineknoll CC, Sylvester (9, 1968).
Illinois: Chester CC (9, 1969).
New Hampshire: Sky Meadow GC, Nashua (1987).
North Carolina: Highlands Falls CC, Highlands (9, 1962).
Ohio: Homestead GC, Tipp City (1973).
South Carolina: Eagle Landing GC, Hanahan (1987); Three Pines CC, Woodruff (1969).
Tennessee: Chestuee G&CC, Etawah (1971); Windyke CC (West Course), Germantown (1963).

Courses Remodeled & Added to by: Bill Amick
Florida: A.C. Read GC (Mainside Course), Pensacola (R., 1970); Eglin AFB GC, Niceville (A.9, 1976); Harbor City Muni, Eau Gaullie (R., 1970); Magnolia Valley

G&CC, New Port Richey (R., 1986); Magnolia Valley G&CC, New Port Richey (A.4, 1986); Melbourne G&CC (R., 1977); Patrick AFB GC, Cocoa Beach (R.); Seminole GC, Tallahassee (A.9, 1969).
Georgia: Monroe CC (A.9, 1971); Rivermont G&CC, Alpharetta (R., 1983).
Kentucky: Pine Valley GC, Elizabethtown (A.9, 1986).
Louisiana: City Park GC (Course No. 1), New Orleans (R.3, 1983).
Missouri: Hillcrest CC, Kansas City (R.1, 1984).
New Hampshire: Wentworth-by-the-Sea GC, Portsmouth (R., 1987).

Roy Albert Anderson (1918 -   )
Born: Hot Springs, Arkansas.
R. Albert Anderson, the son of a club professional and nephew of two golf course superintendents, was raised and educated in Racine, Wisconsin. He took up golf architecture following the Second World War, operating from a summer residence in Racine and a winter home in Sarasota, Florida. Among numerous courses he designed and built were six that he owned and operated.
Courses by: R.Albert Anderson
Alabama: Rolling Green CC, Prattville (1967).
Florida: Clewiston CC; CC of Brevard (1959); Englewood G&CC (1966); Forest Lakes CC, Sarasota (1964); Futurama GC, Sarasota (Par 3, 1963); Golden Tee GC, Sarasota (Par 3, 1970); Green Valley CC, Clermont (9, 1966); Harbor City Muni, Eau Gaullie (1963); Heather Hills GC (1963); Lehigh CC (1960); Little Cypress G&CC, Wauchulla (9, 1965); Red Lake CC, Venice (1959); Rolling Green G&CC, Sarasota (1968); Santa Rosa G&CC, Brandenton (1970); Seminole GC, Tallahassee (9, 1959); Sorrento Par 3 GC (Par 3, 9, 1975); Starke G&CC (9, 1959); Sunnybreeze Palms GC (27, 1971); Sunrise National CC, Sarasota (1971); Venice East GC (Precision, 1961); Woodcrest Par 3 GC, Sarasota (Par 3, 1970).
Georgia: Cairo CC (1962); Four Seasons CC, Wrens (9).
Illinois: Shady Lawn GC, Beecher (1971).
Indiana: Broadmoor CC, Shareville; Cary CC; Cedar Lake GC (1957); Hollow Acres GC, Delphi (9); Pheasant Valley GC, Crown Point.
Missouri: Terre du Lac CC, Bonne Terre (1969); Tower Tee GC, St. Louis (Par 3, 1969).
Ohio: Copeland Hills CC, Columbiana; Golden Tee GC, Sharonville (Par 3, 3, 1966); Orchard Hills CC, Bryan (9, 1955); Puckerbrush GC, Willoughby; Southern Hills GC, Youngstown.
Tennessee: Carrol Lake CC, McKenzie; Four Seasons CC, Smithville; Shelbyville CC.
Wisconsin: Oak Hill GC, Oak Creek (1962); Spring Valley GC, Union Center (9, 1959).
Courses Remodeled & Added to by: R.Albert Anderson
Florida: Bobby Jones Muni (American Course), Sarasota (R., 1963); Capital City CC, Tallahassee (R., 1960); Keystone G&CC (R., 1959); Palm-Aire West CC (Champions Course), Sarasota (R., 1969); Palma Sola GC, Bradenton (R., 1968); Punta Gorda CC (R., 1966).
Minnesota: Wilmar CC (A.9, 1960).

Charles F. Ankrom (1936 -   ) ASGCA
Born: West Virginia.
Charles Ankrom attended West Virginia University and took additional courses in golf course turf and real estate at the University of Florida. In the 1960s he was employed as Director of Golf and in-house golf architect with the General Development Corporation in Florida.
Ankrom served as National Director of Golf Operations for the Boise Cascade Recreation Communities Group for two years. In 1972 he founded his own course design firm based in southern Florida.
Courses by: Chuck Ankrom
Florida: Big Cypress at Royal Palm CC (1982); Boca Raton Muni (27, 1982); Crystal Lakes GC, Okeechobee (9, 1977); Indian River Plantation GC (Precision, 1978); Martin Downs CC (Crane Creek Course) (1976), with Arthur Young; Martin Downs CC (Tower Course) (1982); Port Malabar GC (9, 1967); Sandpiper Bay GC (Family Course) (9, 1981); Savanna C, Port St. Lucie (Precision, 1985); Sebastian Muni (1982); Tidewater Beach GC, Destin (1987); TPC at Monte Carlo, Fort Pierce (1982).
Courses Remodeled & Added to by: Chuck Ankrom
Florida: Heritage Ridge GC, Hobe Sound (A.9, 1981); Heritage Ridge GC, Hobe Sound (R.9, 1981); Port Charlotte CC (R., 1970); Sandpiper Bay CC (Sinners Course), Port St. lucie (R., 1982).

Javier Arana (1904 - 1974)
Born: Bilbao, Vizcaya, Spain. Died: Marbella, Spain at age 70.
Renowned golfer Javier Arana began designing courses in 1936. Although he confined his work to his native Spain, he was recognized as a leading contemporary golf course architect. His characteristic trademark was an isolated tree found in one or more fairways of nearly every course he built.
Courses by: Javier Arana
Spain: Aloha Golf (1976); Campo de G El Saler (1967); Club de G Cerdana (27, 1945); Club de G Los Monteros; Club de G Ulzama; Club de G Ulzama (9, 1965); Golf Guadalamina (North Course) (1959); Golf Guadalamina (South Course) (1959); Golf Rio Real (1965); Real Automovil C de Espana (1967); Real C de G El Prat (1954); Real Sociedad de G Neguri La Galea (1960); Real Sociedad Hipica Espanola (27, 1956); Reina Cristina GC.

Brian T. Ault (1947 -   ) ASGCA
Born: Washington D.C.
Brian Ault earned an associate degree in Civil Engineering and for a short time served as an inspector for the Washington, D.C. Highway Department. In 1973 he became an associate architect in the firm of Edmund B. Ault, Ltd. where he had been personally tutored by his father. In 1984 he became a full partner with his father and Tom Clark in Ault, Clark & Associates, Ltd.

Courses by: Brian Ault
Arkansas: Mountain Ranch GC, Fairfield Bay (1984), with Tom Clark and Edmund B. Ault.
Indiana: West Boggs Muni, Lakeview (9, 1978), with Edmund B. Ault.
Iowa: Sundown GC, Burlington (Par 3, 9, 1978), with Tom Clark and Edmund B. Ault.
Louisiana: Eden Isles CC, Slidell (1976), with Edmund B. Ault.
Maryland: Heritage Harbour GC (9, 1982), with Tom Clark and Edmund B. Ault; TPC at Avenel, Potomac (1986), with Edmund B. Ault, Tom Clark and Bill Love.
Missouri: Paradise Pointe GC, Smithville (1983), with Tom Clark; Poplar Bluff Muni (1980), with Tom Clark and Edmund B. Ault.
New Jersey: Concordia GC (1986), with Bill Love; Quail Brook Park GC (1982), with Tom Clark and Edmund B. Ault.
Pennsylvania: Clinton CC, Lockhaven , with Edmund B. Ault; Mountain View GC (1987), with Edmund B. Ault and Tom Clark.
Virginia: Hollows GC (1984), with Tom Clark; Penderbrook GC (1979), with Edmund B. Ault.
West Virginia: Lakeview Inn & CC (North Course), Morgantown (1984), with Tom Clark.
Courses Remodeled & Added to by: Brian Ault
Connecticut: Rolling Hills CC, Wilton (R.5, 1984), with Tom Clark; Woodbridge CC (R.1, 1986).
Delaware: Brandywine CC, Wilmington (R.7, 1987), with Bill Love.
Maryland: Manor CC, Rockville (R.4, 1986), with Edmund B. Ault and Bill Love; Sherwood Forest GC, Annapolis (R.4, 1986).
Massachusetts: Pleasant Valley CC, Sutton (R.3, 1984), with Tom Clark.
Mississippi: Columbus CC (R.9, 1985); Mississippi State Univ GC (R.9, 1986); Northwood CC, Meridian (R.2, 1985).
Nevada: Tropicana CC, Las Vegas (R., 1984), with Tom Clark.
New Jersey: Greenacres CC, Lawrence (R.2, 1983), with Tom Clark and Bill Love.
New York: Ridgemont CC (R.2, 1984).
North Carolina: Duck Woods GC, Kitty Hawk (R.7, 1986), with Tom Clark; Paradise Point GC (Gold Course), Camp LeJeune (R.7, 1979), with Tom Clark.
Pennsylvania: Chambersburg CC (A.9, 1977), with Edmund B. Ault; Oak Tree GC (R.2, 1983), with Bill Love.
Tennessee: Woodmont CC (A.9, 1977), with Edmund B. Ault.
Virginia: Army-Navy CC (Fairfax Course), Fairfax (R.2, 1984), with Edmund B. Ault and Bill Love; Kingsmill GC (River Course), Williamsburg (R.5, 1982), with Tom Clark and Edmund B. Ault; Westwood CC, Vienna (R., 1984), with Edmund B. Ault.

Edmund B. Ault (1908 -) ASGCA
Born: Washington, D.C.
Edmund Ault studied Construction Engineering at Columbia (Md.) Technical Institute and for a time was employed in that field. He trained for several seasons with golf architect Fred Findlay and entered private practice as a course designer in 1946. For several years in the late 1950s he partnered with professional golfer Al Jamison.
A one-time scratch golfer, Ault played in the National Amateur on several occasions. He served in the Green Section of the USGA, was a past president of the District of Columbia Golf Association, and chaired the Design Standards Committee of the ASGCA. Long an advocate of flexibility in courses, Ault pioneered the systematic coordination of pin placements with tee marker locations.
A most prolific designer, Ed Ault once estimated that he had designed or remodeled one fourth of all the courses in the Maryland and Virginia suburbs around Washington, D.C.
Courses by: Edmund B. Ault
Arkansas: Balboa GC, Hot Springs Village (1987), with Tom Clark; Berksdale GC, Bella Vista (1977); Branchwood GC, Bella Vista (Par 3, 9, 1983), with Tom Clark; Cherokee Village CC (North Course) (1973); Cherokee Village CC (South Course) (1962); Coronado GC, Hot Springs Village (Precision, 1983), with Tom Clark; Cortez GC, Hot Springs Village (1977); DeSoto GC, Hot Springs Village (1972); Kingswood GC, Bella Vista (1977); Maumelle G&CC (1969); Metfield GC, Bella Vista (Precision, 1983), with Tom Clark; Mountain Ranch GC, Fairfield Bay (1984), with Brian Ault and Tom Clark; Scotsdale GC, Bella Vista (1987), with Tom Clark.
Delaware: Delcastle Farms GC (1971); Dover AFB GC (9, 1961), with Al Jamison; Garrison's Lake GC (1965); Pike Creek Valley GC (1972); Shawnee CC (9, 1964); Sussex Pines CC (1966).
Florida: Carrollwood Village G&TC (27, 1971); CC of Coral Springs (1969).
Indiana: Christmas Lake G&CC, Santa Claus (9, 1970); Wesselman Park GC (9, 1970); West Boggs Muni, Lakeview (9, 1978), with Brian Ault.
Iowa: Sundown GC, Burlington (Par 3, 9, 1978), with Tom Clark and Brian Ault.
Louisiana: Eden Isles CC, Slidell (1976), with Brian Ault.
Maryland: Aberdeen Proving Grounds GC (9, 1965); All-View GC (1968); Aviation Y&CC (1962); Baltimore CC (West Course) (1962); Bay Hills GC (1968); Bretton Woods GC, Germantown (1968); Caroline CC (9, 1963); Chartwell G&CC (1961), with Al Jamison; Crofton GC (1963); Diamond Ridge GC (1968); Dwight D. Eisenhower GC, Annapolis (1969); Falls Road Muni (1960), with Al Jamison; Generals GC, Crownsville (1969); Hawthorne CC (9, 1960), with Al Jamison; Henson Creek GC (Precision, 1963); Heritage Harbour GC (9, 1982), with Tom Clark and Brian Ault; Hobbit's Glen GC, Columbia (1965); Hunt Valley Inn & CC (1970); Lakewood CC (1960), with Al Jamison; Montgomery Village CC (1966); Northwest Park GC, Wheaton (27, 1964); Oakcrest CC (1969), with Al Jamison; Oakland CC (9, 1965); Paint Branch GC (1965); Piney Branch G&CC (1969); Poolesville GC (1959), with Al Jamison; Ralph G. Cover Estate GC (1962); Sligo Park GC (9, 1956), with Al Jamison; Turf Valley CC (North Course) (1959), with Al Jamison; Turf Valley CC (South Course) (1963); TPC at Avenel, Potomac (1986), with Brian Ault, Tom Clark and Bill Love; Western Maryland GC (1968).
Missouri: Meadow Lake Acres CC (1961), with Al Jamison; Pointe Royale G&CC (1986), with Tom Clark; Poplar Bluff Muni (1980), with Brian Ault and Tom Clark.
Nevada: Las Vegas CC (1965).
New Jersey: Quail Brook Park GC (1982), with Brian Ault and Tom Clark;

Ramblewood CC (27, 1961); Spooky Brook GC (1969).
New York: McGuire AFB GC (9, 1967); Riverton GC, Henrietta (1974).
North Carolina: Etowah Valley CC (1967); Wedgewood CC.
Ohio: Country Club Villages of America; Lakeside GC (9, 1963); Mayfair CC (1968); Ravenna CC (1972); Town & Country GC (1970); Windmill Lakes GC, Cleveland (1972).
Pennsylvania: Belles Springs GC (1969); Center Square GC (1963); Charnita CC (1967); Clinton CC, Lockhaven , with Brian Ault; Corry Muni; Great Cove GC (1967); Hidden Valley CC, Pittsburgh (1964); Honey Run G&CC (1971); Iron Masters CC (1965); Juniata GC, Philadelphia (Precision, 1965); Lewistown CC (1973); Middleburg GC (1969); Monroe Creek GC (1967); Mountain View GC (1987), with Brian Ault and Tom Clark; North Hills Muni (1964); Northampton Valley CC (1964); Oak Tree GC (1967); Olde Hickory GC (9, 1966); Olmstead AFB GC; Outdoor CC; Pennsylvania National G&CC (1967); Pleasant View GC (1960), with Al Jamison; Sinking Valley CC (1962); Summit CC (9, 1967); Toftrees CC, State College (1971); Tyoga CC, Wellsboro; Tyrone CC; Waynesboro CC (9, 1971).
South Carolina: Cane Patch Par 3 GC, Myrtle Beach (Par 3, 27, 1982); Midway GC (Par 3, 27, 1984), with Bill Love; Myrtlewood CC (Palmetto Course), Myrtle Beach (1972).
Tennessee: Blue Lake GC; Toqua GC (1987), with Tom Clark.
Virginia: Bolling AFB GC (1960), with Al Jamison; Broad Bay Point G&CC, Virginia Beach (1986), with Tom Clark; Bryce Mountain GC (1972); Bushfield CC (9, 1962), with Al Jamison; Chantilly National G&CC (1960), with Al Jamison; Cypress Point GC, Virginia Beach (1986), with Tom Clark; CC of Petersburg (1968); CC of Virginia (Tuckahoe Course), Richmond (9, 1972); Deer Run Muni, Newport News (27, 1969); Edwin R.Carr Estate GC (1959), with Al Jamison; Herndon Centennial Muni (1979); Hidden Creek CC (1969); Holston Hills CC, Marion (9, 1968); Lake Fairfax GC (1959), with Al Jamison; Langley AFB GC (1965); Leesburg G&CC (1969); Loudoun G&CC (1959), with Al Jamison; Mill Quarter Plantation GC (1979); Penderbrook GC (1979), with Brian Ault; Reston South GC (1969); River Bend G&CC {formerly Forest Lake CC} (1960), with Al Jamison; Shannon Green GC, Fredericksburg (1971); Sigwick G&CC; South Wales G&RC (1957); Spotswood CC, Harrisburg (9, 1960); Springfield G&CC (1960), with Al Jamison; Sterling Park GC (1963); Stonehenge GC, Bon Air (1969); Summit GC (9, 1987), with Tom Clark; Winton CC (1972).
West Virginia: Green Hills CC (1962); Pines CC (1968); Preston CC (9, 1965); Sandy Brae G&CC (1969).
Wisconsin: Brightondale Muni (27, 1971).
Montserrat: Belham River Valley GC (9, 1968).

Courses Remodeled & Added to by: Edmund B. Ault
Arkansas: Bella Vista CC (R., 1977); CC of Little Rock (R., 1968); Indian Hills GC, Fairfield Bay (R., 1981); Newport CC (A.9, 1978).
Delaware: Dover CC (R.9, 1969); Green Hill Muni (R., 1971); Shawnee CC (A.9, 1960), with Al Jamison; Shawnee CC (A.9, 1984), with Bill Love.
Florida: Bardmoor CC (East Course), Largo (R., 1986); Broken Woods G&RC, Coral Springs (R., 1973); Miles Grant CC, Stuart (R., 1975); Sawgrass GC (Oceanside Course), Ponte Vedra Beach (R., 1985).
Indiana: Fendrich GC, Evansville (R., 1968).
Kentucky: Highland CC, Fort Thomas (R., 1961).
Maryland: Argyle CC, Chevy Chase (R., 1960), with Al Jamison; Bethesda CC (R.9, 1966); Bethesda CC (A.9, 1966); Bethesda Naval Hospital GC (R.9, 1961); Bonnie View CC (R., 1961); Burning Tree C, Bethesda (R., 1963); Chester River Y&CC, Chestertown (R., 1972); Congressional CC (Blue Course), Bethesda (R.2, 1981), with Tom Clark and Bill Love; Elkridge CC, Baltimore (R., 1974); Fountain Head CC, Hagerstown (R., 1968); Hillendale CC, Phoenix (R., 1962); Indian Head GC (R.9, 1966); Kenwood CC (R., 1962); Longview Muni (R.3, 1981), with Bill Love; Manor CC, Rockville (R.4, 1986), with Brian Ault and Bill Love; Norbeck CC, Rockville (R., 1965); Silver Springs GC (R., 1958), with Al Jamison; Suburban CC (R., 1964); Suburban CC (R.4, 1982), with Bill Love; U.S. Navy Medical Center GC (R.); Woodholme CC, Pikesville (R., 1964).
Missouri: Hickory Hills CC, Springfield (R., 1974).
New York: Blue Hill GC (R., 1963); Hampshire CC, Mamaroneck (R., 1962).
Ohio: Marietta CC (R., 1970); Oak Tree CC (R., 1969).
Pennsylvania: Bucknell University GC (A.9, 1963); Butler CC (R., 1963); Chambersburg CC (A.9, 1977), with Brian Ault; Conewango Valley CC (R., 1972); Indiana CC (R., 1969); Nottingham CC (R., 1962); South Hills GC, Hanover (R., 1973); VFW GC, Indiana (A.9, 1969).
Tennessee: Woodmont CC (A.9, 1977), with Brian Ault.
Virginia: Army-Navy CC (Arlington Course), Arlington (R.3, 1985); Army-Navy CC (Arlington Course), Arlington (R.5, 1986), with Tom Clark and Bill Love; Army-Navy CC (Fairfax Course), Fairfax (R., 1962); Army-Navy CC (Fairfax Course), Fairfax (R.2, 1984), with Brian Ault and Bill Love; Belle Haven CC, Alexandria (R., 1969); Eastern Shore Y&CC, Onancock (R., 1962); Fort Belvoir GC (R.9, 1975); Fort Belvoir GC (A.9, 1975); Hampton GC (R., 1972); Hermitage CC, Richmond (A.9, 1971); Hermitage CC, Richmond (R., 1971); International Town & CC (R., 1975); Kingsmill GC (River Course), Williamsburg (R.5, 1982), with Brian Ault and Tom Clark; Meadowbrook CC, Richmond (R., 1975); Salisbury CC (R., 1967); Shenvallee Lodge & GC (A.9, 1961); Shenvallee Lodge & GC (R.9, 1961); Spotswood CC, Harrisburg (A.9, 1964); Westwood CC, Vienna (R., 1984), with Brian Ault; Winchester G&CC (R., 1966).
West Virginia: Clarksburg CC (A.9, 1964); Clarksburg CC (R.9, 1964); Parkersburg CC (R., 1965).
Puerto Rico: Dorado del Mar GC, Dorado (R., 1973).
Switzerland: Caslano GC (R., 1966).

Gary Roger Baird (1941 -) ASGCA
Born: Glendale, California.
Gary Baird received a B.Sc. degree in Landscape Architecture from California Polytechnic Institute in Pomona. In 1969 he joined the firm of Robert Trent Jones Inc. as a design associate, remaining until 1977 when he formed his own firm. After several remodeling jobs along the Pacific coast, Baird relocated to Nashville, Tennessee.
In the mid-1980s Baird designed a novel course in Japan that utilized common fairways with tees and greens at each end. This "two-way" system allowed the course to be played both ways.

Courses by: Gary Roger Baird
Arizona: Rio Rico G&CC (1975), with Robert Trent Jones Jr.
California: Bodega Harbour GC (9, 1977), with Robert Trent Jones Jr; Lake Shastina G&CC, Weed (1972), with Robert Trent Jones and Robert Trent Jones Jr; Mountain Shadows GC (North Course), Rohnert Park (1974); Murrieta GC (1970), with Robert Trent Jones and Robert Trent Jones Jr; Spring Valley Lake CC, Victorville (1971), with Robert Trent Jones and Robert Trent Jones Jr.
Colorado: Arrowhead GC, Littleton (1974), with Robert Trent Jones Jr; Steamboat Village CC, Steamboat Springs (1974), with Robert Trent Jones Jr.
Hawaii: Princeville Makai GC, Kauai (27, 1971), with Robert Trent Jones Jr; Waikoloa Village GC, Kamuela (1972), with Robert Trent Jones Jr.
Nevada: Incline Green GC, Incline Village (Precision, 1971), with Robert Trent Jones and Robert Trent Jones Jr.
North Dakota: Oxbow CC, Hickson (1974), with Robert Trent Jones Jr.
Oregon: West Delta Park GC, Portland (1971), with Robert Trent Jones and Robert Trent Jones Jr.
Tennessee: Fountaingate CC, Ooltewah (1987); Hermitage GC, Old Hickory (1986); Shaftsbury GC, Fairfield Glade (1987).
Texas: El Dorado CC, McKinney (1982); Horseshoe Bay CC (Slick Rock Course), Marble Falls (1973), with Robert Trent Jones and Robert Trent Jones Jr; Las Colinas Sports C, Irving (1983), with Robert Trent Jones Jr.
Fiji: Pacific Harbour G&CC (1977), with Robert Trent Jones Jr.
Indonesia: Pondok Indah GC (1977), with Robert Trent Jones Jr.
Japan: Shishido Kokusai GC (Shizu Course), Ibaraki (1986).
Mexico: Isla de la Piedra GC, Mazatlan (9, 1972), with Robert Trent Jones Jr; Palma Real GC, Ixtapa (1977), with Robert Trent Jones Jr; Pok-Ta-Pok GC, Cancun (1978), with Robert Trent Jones Jr.
Thailand: Navatanee CC (1975), with Robert Trent Jones Jr.

Courses Remodeled & Added to by: Gary Roger Baird
California: Bel-Air CC, Los Angeles (R.1, 1975), with Robert Trent Jones Jr; Birnam Wood GC, Santa Barbara (R., 1977), with Robert Trent Jones Jr; Corral De Tierra CC, Salinas (R., 1983); Del Paso CC (R., 1983); Glendora CC (R., 1970), with Robert Trent Jones and Robert Trent Jones Jr; Green Hills CC, Millbrae (R., 1983); Menlo CC, Redwood City (R., 1970), with Robert Trent Jones and Robert Trent Jones Jr; Palo Alto Hills G&CC, Palo Alto (R., 1982); Palo Alto Muni (R., 1980), with Robert Trent Jones Jr; Pasatiempo GC, Santa Cruz (R., 1984); Petaluma G&CC (R., 1983).
Hawaii: Mauna Kea Beach Hotel GC, Kameula (R., 1976), with Robert Trent Jones Jr.
Oregon: Eugene CC (R., 1983); Roseburg CC (A.9, 1980); Roseburg CC (R.9, 1980).
Tennessee: Belle Meade CC, Nashville (R., 1981); Chattanooga G&CC (R., 1983).

Robert Earl Baldock (1908 -)
Born: Omaha, Nebraska.
California-based golf architect Bob Baldock planned more than 350 courses in his career. A former Class A PGA golfer, he worked at one time for golf architect William P. Bell. His career spanned from the 1950s into the 1980s. In 1984, Baldock was honored with an Outstanding Service Award by the NGF in recognition for the many occasions that he donated architectural services to Veterans Administration Hospitals, Air Force bases and small communities that could not afford professional assistance in building their courses.

Courses by: Bob Baldock
Alabama: Huntsville Muni (1968); Skycenter GC, Huntsville , with Robert L. Baldock.
Arizona: Elden Hills GC, Flagstaff (1960); General Blanchard GC, Davis Monthan AFB.
California: Alta Sierra CC, Grass Valley (1965), with Robert L. Baldock; Antioch Muni; Azuza Green GC (1965); Baywood G&CC, Arcata (1958); Beale AFB CC; Bear Valley GC (1962); Bethel Island GC (1966), with Robert L. Baldock; Blue Lake Springs GC, Arnold (1966); Butte Creek G&CC (1965), with Robert L. Baldock; Castle AFB GC (9, 1955); Chimney Rock GC, Napa (1966), with Robert L. Baldock; College of the Sequoias GC, Fresno (4, 1953); Comstock CC, Davis (1965); Corral De Tierra CC, Salinas (1959); Diablo Creek GC, Concord (1963); El Macero CC (1961); Eureka Muni (9, 1957), with Robert L. Baldock; Exeter Muni (9, 1963); Fairway Glen GC, Santa Clara (9, 1961); Fresno West G&CC (1966), with Robert L. Baldock; Gold Hills CC, Redding (1979), with Robert L. Baldock; Hacienda Hotel Par 3 GC, Bakersfield (1957); Heather Farms GC, Walnut Creek (1966); Horse Thief G&CC, Tehachapi (1974), with Robert L. Baldock; Irwindale Muni (1965), with Robert L. Baldock; JFK Memorial GC, Napa (1958), with Jack Fleming and Ben Harmon; King City GC (Precision, 9, 1953); Lazy H GC (9); Leland Meadows Par 3 GC, Long Bain (1962); Lemore Muni (9, 1963); Lew Galbraith Muni, Oakland (1966); Lindale Greens GC, Sacremento (1965), with Robert L. Baldock; Lindsay Muni (9, 1963); Livermore VA Hospital GC (Par 3, 9); Los Banos CC (9, 1963); Los Robles Greens GC, Thousand Oaks (9, 1964); Madera CC (9, 1955); Mariposa Pines GC (1973), with Robert L. Baldock; Merced G&CC, Slater (1961); Moffett Field GC (9, 1956); Monterey Peninsula CC (Shore Course), Pebble Beach (1961), with Jack Neville; Mount Whitney CC, Lone Pine (9, 1959); Mountain Shadows GC (South Course), Rohnert Park (1963); Oakdale G&CC (9, 1963); Palo Alto VA Hospital GC (Par 3, 9); Pariso Springs CC, Soledad (9, 1955); Peach Tree CC, Marysville (1960); Ponderosa Muni (9); Rancho del Ray GC (9, 1963); River Island GC, Porterville (1963); Selma Valley CC (1958); Sherwood Forest GC, Sanger (1968), with Robert L. Baldock; Sierra Sky Ranch GC, Oakhurst (9, 1954); Skywest Public GC, Hayward (1964); Swallow's Nest GC, Sacremento (Par 3, 1964); Tall Pines GC (9, 1972), with Robert L. Baldock; Teaford Lake GC, Bass Lake (1972); Tracy CC (9, 1956); Tulare CC (1956); Turlock G&CC, with Jack Fleming; Valley Gardens CC, Santa Cruz (1971), with Robert L. Baldock; West Winds GC, George AFB (9, 1965); Westside GC, Firebaugh (Par 3, 9, 1947); Willow Park GC, Castro Valley (1966), with Robert L. Baldock; Yolo Fliers C, Woodland (9, 1950); Yosemite Lakes GC, Coarse Gold (1965), with Robert L. Baldock.
Colorado: Lowry AFB GC (1961).

Florida: Tyndall AFB GC, Panama City Beach (9, 1964).

Hawaii: Hickman AFB GC, Oahu (1966), with Robert L. Baldock; Mililani GC (1966), with Robert L. Baldock; Olomana G Links, Waimanolo (1969), with Robert L. Baldock; Pukalani CC (1979), with Robert L. Baldock; Ted Makalena GC, Waipahu (1971), with Robert L. Baldock.

Idaho: Cascade GC (9); Cherry Lane GC, Meridian (9, 1979), with Robert L. Baldock; Crane Creek CC, Boise (1962); Kimberland Meadows GC, New Meadows (9, 1985), with Robert L. Baldock; Lewiston CC (1974), with Robert L. Baldock; Nampa Muni (9, 1985), with Robert L. Baldock; Silver Sage GC, Mountain Home (9, 1956).

Kansas: Forbes GC, Topeka (9, 1962).

Kentucky: Lexington VA Hospital GC (Par 3, 9); Warren Meadows CC, Bowling Green (9, 1983), with Robert L. Baldock.

Maine: Tagus VA Hospital GC (Par 3, 9).

Massachusetts: Otis AFB GC (1972).

Michigan: Kincheloe Memorial GC, Kinross (9); Sawyer AFB GC (1968).

Missouri: Belton Muni (1965).

Montana: Glacier View GC, West Glacier (1972), with Robert L. Baldock; Glasgow AFB GC (9, 1983), with Robert L. Baldock.

Nevada: Alladin Hotel GC, Las Vegas (NLE, Par 3, 9); Black Mountain G&CC, Henderson (1959); Brookside GC, Reno (1964); Carson City Muni (9, 1956); Casa de Mar G&CC (9); Hacienda Hotel Par 3 GC, Las Vegas (NLE, Par 3, 9, 1956); Stead AFB GC (1965); White Pines GC, Ely (9, 1957); Winnemucca Muni.

New Mexico: Four Hills CC, Albuquerque (1961); Los Altos Muni, Albuquerque (1960).

Oregon: Emerald Valley GC, Creswell (1966), with Robert L. Baldock; Illinois Valley GC, Cave Junction (9, 1977), with Robert L. Baldock; Ontario Muni GC (1965), with Robert L. Baldock; White City VA Hospital GC (Par 3, 9).

Pennsylvania: Hideout GC, Lake Ariel (9).

Washington: Hangman Valley Muni, Spokane (1968), with Robert L. Baldock; Pasco Muni (NLE,); Swallow's Nest GC, Clarkston (9, 1964); Whispering Firs GC, McChord AFB (9, 1961).

Wyoming: Jackson Hole G&TC (1961); Olive Glenn GC, Cody (1970), with Robert L. Baldock.

Mexico: San Antonio Shores GC (1970), with Robert L. Baldock.

Philippines: Manila G&CC, Makati (1961); Phillipines CC (1961).

Tahiti: Golf D'Atimaona CC, Papeete (1967), with Robert L. Baldock.

Courses Remodeled & Added to by: Bob Baldock

California: Antioch Muni (A.9, 1957); Belmont CC, Fresno (R., 1956); Eureka Muni (A.6, 1966), with Robert L. Baldock; Fort Washington G&CC, Pinedale (R., 1956); Indian Hills CC, Riverside (R., 1968), with Robert L. Baldock; Kings River G&CC, Kingsbury (R., 1961); Plumas Lake G&CC, Marysville (A.9, 1962); Plumas Lake G&CC, Marysville (R.9, 1962); Polvadero CC, Coalinga (R.9); San Joaquin GC (R., 1961); Santa Maria GC (R., 1965), with Robert L. Baldock; Shorecliffs CC, San Clemente (R., 1985), with Robert L. Baldock; Sierra View CC, Visalia (A.9, 1966), with Robert L. Baldock; Soule Park GC, Ojai (A.9, 1970), with Robert L. Baldock; 1001 Ranch GC (R., 1972), with Robert L. Baldock.

Hawaii: Ala Wai GC, Waikiki (R., 1962); Mid-Pacific CC, Honolulu (R., 1968), with Robert L. Baldock; Waialae GC, Honolulu (R., 1966).

Idaho: Eagle Hills GC (A.9, 1975), with Robert L. Baldock; University of Idaho GC, Moscow (R.9); University of Idaho GC, Moscow (A.9).

Oregon: Bend G&CC (A.9, 1972), with Robert L. Baldock; Grant's Pass CC (A.14), with Robert L. Baldock; Grant's Pass CC (R.), with Robert L. Baldock; Reames G&CC, Klamath Falls (A.9, 1966), with Robert L. Baldock.

Wyoming: Casper CC (R.9, 1960); Casper CC (A.9, 1960).

Robert Lee Baldock (1945 -)
Born: Avalon, California.

As a student at Fresno State College in California, young Bob Baldock assisted his golf architect father, Robert E. Baldock, on weekends and during summers. He became a partner with his father in the business in 1968.

Courses by: Robert L. Baldock

Alabama: Skycenter GC, Huntsville , with Bob Baldock.

California: Alta Sierra CC, Grass Valley (1965), with Bob Baldock; Bethel Island GC (1966), with Bob Baldock; Butte Creek G&CC (1965), with Bob Baldock; Chimney Rock GC, Napa (1966), with Bob Baldock; Eureka Muni (9, 1957), with Bob Baldock; Fresno West G&CC (1966), with Bob Baldock; Gold Hills CC, Redding (1979), with Bob Baldock; Horse Thief G&CC, Tehachapi (1974), with Bob Baldock; Irwindale Muni (1965), with Bob Baldock; Lindale Greens GC, Sacramento (1965), with Bob Baldock; Mariposa Pines GC (1973), with Bob Baldock; Sherwood Forest GC, Sanger (1968), with Bob Baldock; Tall Pines GC (9, 1972), with Bob Baldock; Valley Gardens CC, Santa Cruz (1971), with Bob Baldock; Vineyards GC, St. Helena (1985), with Bob Baldock; Willow Park GC, Castro Valley (1966), with Bob Baldock; Yosemite Lakes GC, Coarse Gold (1965), with Bob Baldock.

Hawaii: Hickman AFB GC, Oahu (1966), with Bob Baldock; Mililani GC (1966), with Bob Baldock; Olomana G Links, Waimanolo (1969), with Bob Baldock; Pukalani CC (1979), with Bob Baldock; Ted Makalena GC, Waipahu (1971), with Bob Baldock.

Idaho: Cherry Lane GC, Meridian (9, 1979), with Bob Baldock; Kimberland Meadows GC, New Meadows (9, 1985), with Bob Baldock; Lewiston CC (1974), with Bob Baldock; Nampa Muni (9, 1985), with Bob Baldock.

Kentucky: Warren Meadows CC, Bowling Green (9, 1983), with Bob Baldock.

Montana: Glacier View GC, West Glacier (1972), with Bob Baldock; Red Lodge CC (9, 1983), with Bob Baldock.

Oregon: Emerald Valley GC, Creswell (1966), with Bob Baldock; Illinois Valley GC, Cave Junction (9, 1977), with Bob Baldock; Ontario Muni GC (1965), with Bob Baldock.

Washington: Hangman Valley Muni, Spokane (1968), with Bob Baldock.

Wyoming: Olive Glenn GC, Cody (1970), with Bob Baldock.

Mexico: San Antonio Shores GC (1970), with Bob Baldock.

Tahiti: Golf D'Atimaona CC, Papeete (1967), with Bob Baldock.

Courses Remodeled & Added to by: Robert L. Baldock

California: Bermuda Dunes CC (A.9, 1986); Eureka Muni (A.6, 1966), with Bob Baldock; Indian Hills CC, Riverside (R., 1968), with Bob Baldock; Santa Maria GC (R., 1965), with Bob Baldock; Shorecliffs CC, San Clemente (R., 1985), with Bob Baldock; Sierra View CC, Visalia (A.9, 1966), with Bob Baldock; Soule Park GC, Ojai (A.9, 1970), with Bob Baldock; 1001 Ranch GC (R., 1972), with Bob Baldock.

Hawaii: Mid-Pacific CC, Honolulu (R., 1968), with Bob Baldock.

Idaho: Eagle Hills GC (A.9, 1975), with Bob Baldock.

Nevada: Black Mountain G&CC, Henderson (A.18, 1987).

Oregon: Bend G&CC (A.9, 1972), with Bob Baldock; Grant's Pass CC (A.14), with Bob Baldock; Grant's Pass CC (R.), with Bob Baldock; Reames G&CC, Klamath Falls (A.9, 1966), with Bob Baldock.

Charles Henry Banks (1883 - 1931)
Born: Amenia, New York. Died: New York City, New York at age 48. Interred: Salisbury, Connecticut.

Charles Banks graduated from Yale University in 1906. He then returned to his preparatory school, Hotchkiss in Salisbury, Conn. where he served as English instructor and track coach for fifteen years. While a member of the school's construction committee, he met Seth J. Raynor, who had been hired to design and build a new golf course at Hotchkiss. He worked closely with Raynor on the job, and in 1921 resigned his teaching position to join Raynor's firm. "Josh" Banks stayed with Raynor until the latter's death in 1926, assisting him (and, on a few projects, C. B. Macdonald) in the design and construction of such courses as Fox Chapel in Pennsylvania and Yale University GC in Connecticut.

Banks finished ten of Raynor's projects and designed or remodeled over thirty other courses in the late 1920s. Nicknamed "Steam Shovel" Banks by his colleagues, he was an enthusiastic believer in massive earth moving to create huge elevated greens and deep bunkers. Legend has it that at Whippoorwill Club in Armonk, N.Y. (a Ross course he completely redid, and claimed by many to be Bank's masterpiece), this enthusiasm for depth was dampened when a steam shovel excavating an exceptionally deep pond disappeared in the ooze. Fortunately the operator was rescued, but the steam shovel is said to still lie deep beneath the sixth fairway a half century later.

Banks also carried on the Macdonald/Raynor tradition of including adaptations of famous golf holes in each design. Invariably an "Eden," "Redan," "Alps," or other renowned hole can be found on a Banks layout.

Charles Banks died of a heart attack in 1931. His last project was Castle Harbour GC in Bermuda, which abutted the famous Mid Ocean Club, a course he had helped to construct a decade earlier.

Courses by: Charles Banks

California: Monterey Peninsula CC (Dunes Course), Pebble Beach (1926), with Seth Raynor.

Connecticut: Yale University GC, New Haven (1926), with Charles Blair Macdonald and Seth Raynor.

Georgia: Lookout Mountain GC {formerly Fairyland CC} (1925), with Seth Raynor.

Hawaii: Mid-Pacific CC, Honolulu (9, 1927), with Seth Raynor; Waialae CC, Honolulu (1925), with Seth Raynor.

Maryland: Annapolis Roads GC (9).

New Jersey: Essex County CC (West Course), West Orange (1930); Forsgate CC (East Course) (1931); Hackensack (27, 1930); Knoll GC (1929); Rock Spring CC (1927).

New York: Knollwood CC, Elmsford (1927), with Seth Raynor; Southampton GC (1927), with Seth Raynor; Tamarack CC, Portchester (1929); Westhampton CC (Oneck Course) (NLE, 1929).

Virginia: Cavalier G&YC (1930).

Bermuda: Castle Harbour GC, Tuckerstown (1932); Mid-Ocean C, Tuckerstown (1924), with Charles Blair Macdonald and Seth Raynor.

Colombia: CC of Bogota.

Venezuela: Junko CC.

Courses Remodeled & Added to by: Charles Banks

Connecticut: Hotchkiss School GC, Lakeville (R., 1930).

Massachusetts: Wyantenuck GC, Great Barrington (R.3).

New Jersey: Forest Hill Field C, Bloomfield (R., 1927); Montclair GC, Verona (A.9).

New York: Knollwood CC, Elmsford (R., 1927); Whippoorwill CC, Armonk (R., 1930).

Cecil Barcroft

Secretary of Royal Dublin GC in Ireland at the beginning of the Twentieth Century, Cecil Barcroft laid out many Irish golf courses. His contemporaries admired the expert manner in which he routed courses around hilly sites, but Barcroft himself preferred his works on natural linksland.

Courses by: Cecil Barcroft

Ireland: Castle GC, Dublin (1913), with Tom Hood and W.C. Pickeman; Howth GC (9, 1914).

Courses Remodeled & Added to by: Cecil Barcroft

Ireland: Bray GC (R.9, 1914); County Louth GC, Baltray (R.), with N. Halligan; Waterford GC, County Waterford (A.9).

Herbert H. Barker

Herbert Barker served as head professional at Garden City GC, N.Y. from 1900 to 1911. He later held a similar position with Roebuck CC in Alabama. During the first two decades of the 20th Century, he laid out many courses in the Northeast and South.

Courses by: Herbert Barker

Georgia: Brookhaven CC (NLE, 1911); Capital City C; Druid Hills CC, Atlanta (1912).

Maryland: Columbia CC (1910).

Ohio: Mayfield CC, South Euclid (1911), with William "Bert" Way.

Virginia: CC of Virginia (Westhampton Course) (1908).

Ralph Martin Barton (1875 - 1941)
Born: Newport, New Hampshire. Died: New Hampshire at age 66.

Ralph Barton attended Phillips Exeter Academy and Dartmouth College and also took courses at Harvard and the University of Chicago. From 1904 until the early 1920s he pursued a career in the academic world, teaching mathematics and holding administrative posts at Dartmouth College, the University of New Mexico, Lombard College and the University of Minnesota. While at Minnesota he undertook supervision of the University's golf course, designed by Seth Raynor.

This experience left Barton permanently enamored with golf architecture, and he subsequently trained under Raynor and C.B. Macdonald during the design and construction of Yale Golf Club in Connecticut. In 1923 he entered private practice, establishing a golf course architecture and engineering firm in New Hampshire which he maintained until his death. For a few months in 1941 Barton worked with the bridge division of the New Hampshire State Highway Department.

Ralph Barton was a member of the American Mathematical Society and was listed in *Who's Who in America*.

Courses by: Ralph Barton

Connecticut: Sleeping Giant GC (9).

Maine: Bridgton Highlands GC (9).

Massachusetts: Greenfield CC; Magnolia GC.

New Hampshire: Ammonoosuc Inn & GC (9, 1929); Concord CC (1927); Hanover CC, Dartmouth College (9); Laconia CC (9, 1921); Lakeport CC; Lancaster CC; Mackenzie's GC (9); Mountain View GC (9, 1929); Newport CC; North Conway CC; Peckets CC; Plymouth CC; Profile C (9, 1930); Sugar Hill CC; Waumbek Village GC.

Vermont: Newport CC (9); Wilmington CC (NLE,).

Courses Remodeled & Added to by: Ralph Barton

Massachusetts: Greenfield CC (R., 1931).

Robert D. Beard (1914 -)

A native of Indiana, Robert Beard established a design and build firm in Fort Wayne in 1959. His course design work, done over a 25 year period, was mainly in Indiana, Michigan and Ohio.

Courses by: Robert Beard

Indiana: Big Pine GC, Attica; Canterbury Green GC, Fort Wayne (Precision, 1971); Cedar Creek GC, Leo; Crestview GC, Muncie (9); Havenhurst GC, New Haven (1967); Lake James CC, Angola; Lakeside GC, Fort Wayne (27); Pond A River GC, Woodburn (9); Tri-County GC, Muncie; Zollner GC, Tri-State University (1971).

Michigan: Case Leasing GC, Celina (9); Cedar Creek GC, Battle Creek; Coldwater CC; Evergreen CC, Hudson (9); Katke GC, Ferris State Univ. (1974); Katke-Cousins GC, Oakland Univ.; Manley's GC, Albion; Maple Hill GC, Augusta (9); Stony Creek GC, Rochester (1978); Tomac Woods GC, Albion.

Ohio: Marvin Rupp GC, Stryker.

Max Howell Behr (1884 - 1955)
Born: New York City, New York. Died: Los Angeles, California at age 71.

Max Behr attended the Lawrenceville School in New Jersey and graduated in 1905 from Yale University, where he had been a member of the golf team coached by pioneer golf designer Robert Pryde. He had learned golf at Morris County CC in New Jersey, and as a youth had competed in several father-son tournaments with his father Herman.

Behr was a perennial bridesmaid in competition, losing the 1907 and 1908 New Jersey Amateurs and the 1908 U.S. Amateur, all to the same golfer, Jerome Travers. He finally won the New Jersey title in 1909 and successfully defended it in 1910, gaining his only victory over Travers in the final of the latter event.

In 1914 Behr became the first editor of the New York-based Golf Illustrated magazine. He resigned from the publication after the death of his first wife in 1918 and moved to California, where he continued to write on golf, especially on the design and construction of courses. He remained active as an author well into his sixties. In the early 1920s Behr also began designing and remodeling courses, but his business was curtailed during the Depression, and after World War II, when others resumed course design careers, Behr had lost interest.

Max Behr was something of a radical. In golf he was a strong advocate of the "floater" golf ball, petitioning the USGA for over fifteen years to adopt it. He didn't believe in rough on his course designs, preferring instead to defend his greens from every conceivable approach shot. He was outspoken on politics and religion, and late in his life developed his own religion based on his interpretation of numbers, although he disavowed any connection with Numerology, to which he was opposed.

Courses by: Max Behr

California: Hacienda CC, La Habra (1922); Lakeside GC of Hollywood, North Hollywood (1924); Montebello GC; Montecito CC, Santa Barbara (1922); Oakmont CC, Glendale (1924); Pasadena GC (NLE, 1920); Rancho CC, Los Angeles (NLE, 1922); Rancho Santa Fe CC (1927).

Courses Remodeled & Added to by: Max Behr

California: Brentwood CC (R.); California CC, Culver City (A.9); California CC, Culver City (R.9); Victoria GC, Riverside (A.9, 1923); Victoria GC, Riverside (R.9, 1923).

Alex Bell

A native of Scotland who trained under Ben Sayers at North Berwick, Alex Bell settled in Hawaii around the turn of the century. He designed several of Hawaii's earliest golf courses, including Oahu CC (1912) and Maui CC. Bell's son Art was a distinguished competitive golfer and club pro, having served at several California clubs, including famed Pebble Beach Golf Links.

Courses by: Alex Bell

Hawaii: Maui CC (9, 1927), with William McEwan; Oahu CC (1912); Palolo Muni (NLE, 9, 1931).

Earl Lee "Smiley" Bell (1899 - 1955)
Born: Lenexa, Kansas. Died: Kansas City, Missouri at age 56.

Smiley Bell began his career in golf running horse-drawn mowers for his father, Henry Bell, greenkeeper at Mission Hills CC in Kansas City, Kansas. He later worked as caddymaster at the club, and in the mid-twenties formed a course construction and management firm in Kansas City.

Bell opened his first commercial driving range, "Smiley's Sportland" (the first operation of its kind in the Midwest) in 1928. He also worked on several Kansas and Missouri-area courses reconstructing greens, often converting them from sand to grass. In the mid-thirties he built Armour Fields GC, a daily fee course that he operated until it was subdivided in the early fifties. This led to other course design projects and until his death Bell was busy planning and constructing Midwestern courses with the avowed intent of bringing golf to as many communities as possible.

Courses by: Smiley Bell

Kansas: Coffeyville CC (9, 1954); El Dorado CC (9, 1950); Hillcrest Muni, Coffeyville (9, 1923); Manhattan CC (1949); Smiley's Sportland GC, Kansas City (NLE, Par 3, 1930).

Missouri: Armour Fields GC, Kansas City (NLE, 1937); Camp Crowder GC; Columbia Muni (9, 1954); Twin Hills CC, Joplin (9).

Courses Remodeled & Added to by: Smiley Bell

Arkansas: Hot Springs G&CC (Arlington course) (R.); Hot Springs G&CC (Majestic Course) (R., 1949).

Kansas: Garden City CC (R.); Independence CC (R.); Park Hills CC (R., 1953).

Missouri: Columbia CC (R.); Excelsior Springs CC (R., 1951); Shifferdecker CC (R.9); Shifferdecker CC (A.9).

William Francis Bell (1918 - 1984) ASGCA, President, 1957.
Born: Pasadena, California. Died: Pasadena, California at age 66.

William F. Bell, son of golf architect Billy Bell, trained and worked with his father after graduating from the University of Southern California. He took over the practice upon his father's death in 1953, and retained the firm name of William P. Bell and Son in his honor.

Bell, often called Billy Bell Jr., laid out over 200 courses in his lifetime, most of them along the Pacific coast and Hawaii. Ironically, he'd died in the same manner as his father, of a heart attack in Pasadena, at almost the same age.

Courses by: William F. Bell

Arizona: Forty Niners CC, Tuscon (1961); Maryvale GC, Phoenix (Precision, 1961); Mesa CC (1950), with William P. Bell; Papago Park GC, Phoenix (27, 1963); Pima GC, Scottsdale (1959); Randolph Park GC (South Course), Tucson (1961); Rolling Hills CC, Tucson (Precision, 1962); Tucson CC (1949), with William P. Bell; Wickenburg CC (1950), with William P. Bell; Yuma G&CC (1951), with William P. Bell.

California: Alameda Muni (Jack Clark Course) (1957); Alhambra Muni (1955); Alisal GC (1955); Americana Canyon Hotel GC {formerly Canyon GC} (1962); Ancil Hoffman GC, Sacremento (1965); Antelope Valley CC, Palmdale (1957); Apple Valley CC (9, 1951), with William P. Bell; Bakersfield CC (1949), with William P. Bell; Banning Muni; Bermuda Dunes CC; Blue Skies CC, Yucca Valley (1957); Blythe Muni (1969); Bonita GC (1958); California CC, Whittier (1957); Calimesa G&CC (1958); Canyon CC, Palm Springs (1962); Chevy Chase CC, Glendale , with William P. Bell; China Lake GC (1956); Costa Mesa G&CC (Los Lagos Course) (1968); Costa Mesa G&CC (Mesa Linda Course) (1968); Crystalaire CC (1958); DeBell GC, Burbank (1958), with William H. Johnson; Diamond Bar GC (1964); Dryden Park Muni (1961); Eaton Canyon GC (6, 1959); Fullerton G&CC (27, 1963); Green Tree GC (27, 1963); Heartwell GC, Long Beach (Par 3, 1962); Hesperia G&CC (1957); Hidden Valley Lake CC (1970); Industry Hills GC (Eisenhower Course) (1979); Industry Hills GC (Zaharias Course) (1980); Irvine Coast CC (1954), with William P. Bell; Jurupa Hills CC, Riverside (1960); Kern River CC, Bakersfield (1953), with William P. Bell; Kern Valley GC (9); Knollwood CC, Granada Hills (1957), with William H. Johnson; La Mirada GC (1963); Lake Arrowhead CC (1963); Lake Don Pedro GC (1971); Lake Wildwood GC, Grass Valley (1971); Lomas Santa Fe GC, Solana Beach (1964); Los Coyotes CC (27, 1958); Los Verdes G&CC (1965); Marina GC (1963); Mesa Verde CC, Costa Mesa (1959); Monterey Hills GC (Par 3, 9, 1949), with William P. Bell; Mountain View CC, Thousand Palms (1985); Newport Beach CC (1954), with William P. Bell; Newporter Inn GC, Newport Beach (Par 3, 9, 1962); North Kern CC (1959); North Ridge CC (1954), with William P. Bell; Olivas Park Muni, Ventura (1967); P L Malibu CC (1980); Palm City CC, Palm Desert (1962); Palm Meadows GC; Palo Alto Muni (1954), with William P. Bell; Pico Rivera Muni (9, 1969); Pine Mountain Lake CC (9, 1971); Rancho Bernardo Inn & CC (West Course) (1962); Rancho Duarte GC (9, 1982); Rancho Los Penasquitos GC, Poway (1964); Rancho San Joaquin CC, Irvine (1969); Recreation Park GC, Long Beach; River Ridge GC, Oxnard (1986); Riviera Marin GC, San Rafael; Rolling Hills GC, with William P. Bell; Salton City CC (1963); San Luis Rey GC (1965); Sandpiper G Links, Goleta (1972); Saticoy CC (1964); Sepulveda GC (Balboa Course) (1953), with William P. Bell and William H. Johnson; Sepulveda GC (Encino Course) (1953), with William P. Bell and William H. Johnson; Shoal Canyon GC, Glendale (Precision, 9, 1979); Silver K GC, Oxnard (9, 1975); Singing Hills CC (Willow Glen Course), El Cajon (1953), with William P. Bell and William H. Johnson; Skylinks GC, Long Beach (1959); South Hills CC, West Covina (1954), with William P. Bell; Sunset Oaks CC, Rocklin (1963); Tamarisk CC, Rancho Mirage (1953), with William P. Bell; Tony Lema Memorial GC, San Leandro (1983); Torrey Pines Muni (North Course), La Jolla (1957); Torrey Pines Muni (South Course), La Jolla (1957); Valle Grande GC, Bakersfield (9, 1954), with William P. Bell; Valley Hi CC, Sacremento (1961); Victoria Muni, Carson (1962); Whittier Narrows GC (27, 1960).

Colorado: Valley CC, Aurora (1960).

Hawaii: Hawaii Kai CC (Championship Course), Honolulu (1973); Keauhou Kona CC, Kailua-Kona (1971); Makaha Inn & CC (East Course), Oahu (1968); Makaha Inn & CC (West Course), Oahu (1969).

Idaho: Idaho Falls CC (1970); Sand Creek Muni, Idaho Falls (1974).

Montana: Bitterroot River CC (1974).

Nevada: Calvada Valley G&CC, Pahrump (1979); Dunes Hotel CC, Las Vegas (1964); Hidden Valley CC, Reno (1958).

Oregon: Forest Hills GC (1953), with William P. Bell; Illahee Hills CC (1961).

Utah: Bonneville Muni, Salt Lake City (9, 1952), with William P. Bell; Dugway GC; Glendale Park Muni, Salt Lake City (1973); Hidden Valley CC, Draper (27,

1960); Hobble Creek GC, Springville (1973); Mountain Dell GC, Salt Lake City (1960), with William H. Neff; Oakridge CC (1957), with William H. Neff; Riverside CC, Provo (1960), with William H. Neff.

Guam: Windward Hills G&CC.

Courses Remodeled & Added to by: William F. Bell

Arizona: Encanto Muni, Phoenix (A.9, 1952), with William P. Bell.

California: Apple Valley CC (A.9, 1963); Bel-Air CC, Los Angeles (R., 1968); Coronado GC (R., 1968); Del Paso CC (R., 1958); DeBell GC, Burbank (R., 1966); Furnace Creek GC (A.9, 1967); Hillcrest CC, Los Angeles (Par 3, A.9, 1950), with William P. Bell; Irvine Coast CC (R., 1966); La Cumbre G&CC, Santa Barbara (R., 1957); Lake Arrowhead CC (R.2, 1977); Lake Tahoe CC (A.9, 1965); Los Alamitos GC (R., 1960); Los Alamitos GC (A.12, 1960); Montebello GC (R.5, 1962); Oakmont CC, Glendale (R., 1967); Ojai Valley Inn & CC, Ojai (R., 1948), with William P. Bell; Riverside G&CC, Coyote (A.9); San Clemente Muni (A.9, 1957); San Clemente Muni (R.9, 1957); San Gabriel CC (R., 1958); Valle Grande GC, Bakersfield (A.9, 1964).

Colorado: Overland Park Muni, Denver (A.9, 1956).

Hawaii: Hawaii Kai CC (Executive Course), Honolulu (R., 1973); Keauhou Kona CC, Kailua-Kona (A.9, 1986), with Robin Nelson.

Nevada: Las Vegas GC (A.9, 1955).

New Jersey: Point Pleasant GC (9, 1910).

Oregon: Columbia-Edgewater CC, Portland (R., 1970); Riverside G&CC, Portland (R., 1970); Rogue Valley CC, Medford (R.9, 1949), with William P. Bell; Rogue Valley CC, Medford (A.9, 1949), with William P. Bell.

Utah: Bonneville Muni, Salt Lake City (A.9, 1956), with William H. Neff; Rose Park GC, Salt Lake City (A.9, 1960), with William H. Neff; The Country Club, Salt Lake City (R., 1952), with William P. Bell.

William Park Bell (1866 - 1953) ASGCA, Charter Member; President, 1952.
Born: Canonsburg, Pennsylvania. Died: Pasadena, California at age 67.

Billy Bell studied agriculture at Duff's Business College in Pittsburgh, Pennsylvania. In 1911 he moved to California where he became caddymaster at Annandale GC in Pasadena and then greenkeeper at Pasadena Golf Club.

Bell served as construction superintendent for golf architect Willie Watson on a number of Southern California courses before going into private practice as a course designer in 1920. In his early years he often collaborated with architect George C. Thomas Jr., and while Thomas is listed as architect of record (and Bell as construction superintendent) for these courses, Billy made major contributions.

By the 1930s Bell had earned a reputation as the most prolific architect in the West. During World War II he served as a turf consultant to the U.S. Army Corps of Engineers, and in 1946 was awarded a commendation by the Southern California chapter of the PGA for his efforts in creating courses for wounded servicemen. After the war, Billy was joined in practice by his son William F. Bell.

Billy Bell died of a heart attack at age 67 in Pasadena, the town where he'd begun his career.

Courses by: William P. Bell

Arizona: Arizona Biltmore GC (Adobe Course), Phoenix (1928); El Rio GC, Tucson; Encanto Muni, Phoenix (1936); Mesa CC (1950), with William F. Bell; Randolph Park GC (North Course), Tucson (1930); Tucson CC (1949), with William F. Bell; Wickenburg CC (1950), with William F. Bell; Yuma G&CC (1951), with William F. Bell.

California: Alameda Muni (Earl Fry Course) (1927); Alondra Park GC (Course No. 1), Lawndale (1947), with William H. Johnson; Altadena GC (9, 1939); Apple Valley CC (9, 1951), with William F. Bell; Bakersfield CC (1949), with William F. Bell; Balboa Park GC, San Diego (1921); Baldwin Hills GC, Los Angeles (NLE, 1926), with George C. Thomas Jr; Bayside CC, San Diego; Bel-Air CC, Los Angeles (1927), with George C. Thomas Jr and Jack Neville; Birmingham VA Hospital GC (Par 3, 9); Brookside Muni (Course No.1), Pasadena (1928); Brookside Muni (Course No.2), Pasadena (1928); Castlewood CC (Hill Course), Pleasanton (1923); Castlewood CC (Valley Course), Pleasanton (1923); Chevy Chase CC, Glendale , with William F. Bell; Circle J GC, Newhall (1954); Del Rio G&CC, Brawley (1926); El Caballero CC, Tarzana (NLE, 1926), with George C. Thomas Jr; Fox Hills GC (NLE, 1926), with George C. Thomas Jr; Furnace Creek GC (9, 1939); Irvine Coast CC (1954), with William F. Bell; Kern River CC, Bakersfield (1953), with William F. Bell; La Jolla CC (1927); Laguna CC; Lakewood GC (1933); Los Angeles National GC; Marine Memorial GC, Santa Ana; Marine Memorial GC, Camp Pendleton; Meadowlark CC, Huntington Beach (1922); Monterey Hills GC (Par 3, 9, 1949), with William F. Bell; Mountain Meadows G&CC (NLE, 1922); Navajo Canyon CC; Newport Beach CC (1954), with William F. Bell; North Ridge CC (1954), with William F. Bell; Ojai Valley Inn & CC, Ojai (1925), with George C. Thomas Jr; Palo Alto Muni (1954), with William F. Bell; Palos Verdes CC (1924), with George C. Thomas Jr; Rancho Park GC, Los Angeles (1947), with William H. Johnson; Riviera CC (1927), with George C. Thomas Jr; Rolling Hills GC, with William F. Bell; San Clemente Muni (9, 1928); San Diego CC, Chula Vista (1921); San Pedro Community Hotel GC (Par 3, 9); San Pedro CC; Santa Susana CC; Sepulveda GC (Balboa Course) (1953), with William F. Bell and William H. Johnson; Sepulveda GC (Encino Course) (1953), with William F. Bell and William H. Johnson; Singing Hills CC (Willow Glen Course), El Cajon (1953), with William F. Bell and William H. Johnson; South Hills CC, West Covina (1954), with William F. Bell; Stanford University GC, Palo Alto (1930); Sunnyside CC, Fresno; Sunset Fields GC (NLE,); Tamarisk CC, Rancho Mirage (1953), with William F. Bell; Tilden Park GC, Berkeley (1937); Valle Grande GC, Bakersfield (9, 1954), with William F. Bell; Ventura Muni, Montalvo (1930); Virginia CC (1939); Western Avenue GC, Los Angeles (1950); Willowick GC, Santa Ana (1928); Woodland Hills CC (1925).

Hawaii: Kanehoe Marine GC (1947); Navy-Marine GC, Pearl Harbor (1947).

Idaho: Sun Valley GC (9, 1947).

Nevada: Las Vegas GC (9, 1938).

Oregon: Forest Hills GC (1953), with William F. Bell.

Utah: Bonneville Muni, Salt Lake City (9, 1952), with William F. Bell; Hidden Valley CC, Salt Lake City (NLE, 1928).

Wisconsin: Wrigley Estate GC, Lake Geneva.

Mexico: Tijuana CC {formerly Aqua Caliente GC} (1928).

Courses Remodeled & Added to by: William P. Bell

Arizona: Encanto Muni, Phoenix (A.9, 1952), with William F. Bell.

California: Annandale CC (A.2, 1947); Annandale CC (R.2, 1948); Crystal Springs GC (R.); Hacienda CC, La Habra (R., 1947); Hillcrest CC, Los Angeles (Par 3, A.9, 1950), with William F. Bell; Indian Hill GC, Riverside (R.); La Cumbre G&CC, Santa Barbara (A.9, 1920), with George C. Thomas Jr; La Cumbre G&CC, Santa Barbara (R.9, 1920), with George C. Thomas Jr; Los Angeles CC (North Course) (R., 1928); Oakmont CC, Glendale (R., 1934); Ojai Valley Inn & CC, Ojai (R., 1948), with William F. Bell; Pasadena GC (NLE, R., 1926); Red Hill CC, Cucamonga (A.9, 1947); Riverside GC, Herndon (R.9, 1939); Riverside GC, Herndon (A.9, 1939); San Francisco GC (R., 1947); Valley C of Montecito, Santa Barbara (R., 1946); Victoria GC, Riverside (R., 1949).

Idaho: Sun Valley GC (A.9, 1947).

Oregon: Rogue Valley CC, Medford (R.9, 1949), with William F. Bell; Rogue Valley CC, Medford (A.9, 1949), with William F. Bell.

Utah: The Country Club, Salt Lake City (R., 1952), with William F. Bell.

Thomas M. Bendelow (1872 - 1936)
Born: Aberdeen, Scotland. Died: River Forest, Illinois at age 64.

Tom Bendelow, one of America's pioneer golf course architects, learned the game as a youngster in Scotland, and made several trips as a teenager to St. Andrews. He became a good enough player to join Harry Vardon in an exhibition match in 1900, shortly before Vardon won the U.S. Open.

Bendelow moved to the United States in 1885 and went to work as a typesetter for the New York Herald newspaper. In 1895, he noticed an advertisement in the classified section seeking a young golfer willing to teach the game to a family. He answered the ad and was hired by the Platt family, whose patriarch was a co-founder of Standard Oil. As part of his duties, Bendelow laid out a short golf course on the grounds of the Platt estate on Long Island. It was the first of over 400 layouts Bendelow planned in his career.

Bendelow soon was laying out many rudimentary courses in the New York area. He also became manager at the nation's first municipal golf course, Van Cortlandt Park in the Bronx. In that capacity, he remodeled its nine hole course and added a second nine, organized America's first public golfers association and instituted the first system of reserved starting times during peak periods.

Later, as a salaried employee of A.G. Spalding sporting goods concern, Bendelow staked out modest layouts through the country, as far south as Florida and as far west as California.

He was transferred by Spalding to Chicago after World War I, and in 1920 left the company to become chief golf architect for the American Park Builders, taking over for designer William B. Langford, who had formed a partnership with Theodore Moreau.

Principally a functional architect, Bendelow refined his procedures in Chicago, producing elaborate detailed plans and molding plaster scale models to demonstrate proposed green contours. He lectured about golf architecture at the University of Illinois and wrote about it for national publications.

Despite such credentials, Bendelow's reputation after his death centered on the primitive staking method Bendelow (as well as many of his contemporaries) utilized around the turn of the century. This simple method was labelled pejoratively "eighteen-stakes-on-a-Sunday afternoon." Ironically, Bendelow, a deeply religious man, never laid out a course on a Sunday. He refused to even play golf on a Sunday, so strict was his personal doctrine. He never drank alcohol, never swore and never told off-color jokes. His only apparent weakness was for the huge cigars he constantly smoked. None of his relatives could recall if he smoked them on Sundays.

Courses by: Tom Bendelow

California: Griffith Park GC (Wilson Course), Los Angeles (1914); Paso Robles GC (NLE, 9); Point Loma GC (1912); Redondo Beach GC (9); Santa Barbara CC (NLE,); Santa Cruz G&CC (9).

Colorado: Boulder CC (NLE, 9, 1918); City Park GC, Pueblo (1914); Greeley CC (9); Lakewood CC, Denver (1908).

Connecticut: Manchester CC (9); Ridgefield GC (NLE,); Stonybrook GC, Litchfield (9).

Florida: Dubsdread CC, Orlando (1923); Palma Ceia G&CC, Tampa (1917); Temple Terrace G&CC (1921); West Orange CC, Oakland (NLE,).

Georgia: CC of Savannah (NLE,); East Lake CC {formerly Atlanta Athletic C (Course No. 1)}, Atlanta (1910).

Illinois: Abingdon CC (9); Aurora CC (1914); Automobile C of Peoria (NLE, 9); Bel-Mar GC (9, 1919); Bloomington CC (9, 1912); Champaign CC (1904); Chevy Chase CC, Wheeling (1925); Columbus Park GC, Chicago (9, 1921); Crawford County GC, Robinson (9, 1919); Cross Roads CC, Lawrenceville (9, 1915); CC of Decatur (9); Dempster GC, Chicago (NLE, 9); Diversey GC, Chicago (NLE, 9, 1916); Dixon CC (9); Edgewood GC, Polo (9); Elgin Wing Park GC (9); Garfield Muni, Chicago (9, 1911); Glen Oak CC, Glen Ellyn (1911); Glendale CC, Bloomingdale (NLE,); Greenview GC, Centralia (1922); Harlem GC, Forest Park (NLE,); Hillsdale GC, Bellwood (9); Hillside Muni (NLE,); Illini CC, Springfield (9); Ingersoll Muni (1920); Jacksonville CC (9, 1925); Joliet CC (9, 1905); Kankakee CC (9, 1915); Kishwaukee CC, DeKalb (9, 1923); La Grange CC (1913); Lake Shore CC, Glencoe (1909); Lake Waneawega GC (9); Leroy CC (9); Lincoln CC (9); Lincolnshire CC (Course No. 1), Crete (1929); Lincolnshire CC (Course No. 2), Crete (1929); Madison Park Muni; Maywood CC, Hillside (NLE,); Medinah CC (Course No. 1) (1924); Medinah CC (Course No. 2) (1926); Medinah CC (Course No. 3) (1928); Midland CC, Kewanee (9, 1911); Monmouth CC (9); Mount Carroll GC (9); Naperville CC (1920); Nelson Park GC, Decatur (1917); North Shore GC, Kenilworth (NLE, 9, 1905); Olympia Fields CC (Course No. 2) (NLE, 1920); Olympia Fields CC (South Course) (1916); Ottawa CC (9, 1923); Peoria North Shore CC (NLE, 9); Peter Jans GC, Evanston (1916); Rock Island CC, Blue Island (NLE, 9, 1926); Rock Springs CC, Alton (9, 1912); Roselawn GC, Danville (9); Sinnissippi Park GC, Rockford (NLE, 1914); Skokie CC, Glencoe (1904); Soangetaha CC, Galesburg; South Shore CC, Chicago (9, 1906); Sportsman G&CC, Northbrook; St. Charles CC (1928); Sunnyside GC, Decatur (1921); Urbana CC (1922); Villa Olivia CC, Bartlett (9, 1926); Woodlawn CC, Farmer City (9); Woodstock GC, Indianapolis (9, 1916).

Indiana: Boonville GC (9); CC of Connersville (9); CC of Terre Haute (9); French

Lick GC (Valley Course) (1907); Garrett CC (9); Hammond CC (9); Hazelden CC (9, 1915); Helfrich Muni (1923); Highland G&CC, Indianapolis (NLE, 1906); Huntington CC (9); Kendalville CC (9); Kentland CC (9); Kokomo CC (9, 1906); Lafayette CC (9); Mississinewa CC, Peru (9); Potowatomi, Michigan City (9); Tolliston GC, Gary (9); Wawasee GC, Syracuse (9); Wicker Park GC, Hammond.

Iowa: Cedar Rapids CC (NLE, 1904); Centerville G&CC (9); Clinton CC (1920); Dubuque G&CC (1923); Ellis Park Muni, Cedar Rapids (NLE, 9, 1920); Elmwood G&CC, Marshalltown (9); Fort Dodge CC; Geneva G&CC, Muscatine (NLE, 9); Hyperion Field C, Grimes (1901); Iowa City CC (NLE,); Keokuk CC (9); Mason City CC (9, 1918); Oelwein CC (9); Oskaloosa CC (9); Ottumwa G&CC (9); Sioux City CC (9); Sunnyside CC, Waterloo (NLE,); Wapsipinicon GC, Independence (9); Waveland GC, Des Moines (9, 1910).

Kansas: Hutchinson CC (NLE,); Leavenworth CC (1922); Mission Hills CC, Fairway (1915); Topeka CC (9, 1906).

Kentucky: Audubon CC, Louisville (NLE, 1908); Cherokee C, Louisville (1903); CC of Paducah (NLE, 9); Fort Mitchell CC, Covington (9); Highland CC, Fort Thomas (NLE, 9, 1914); Lexington CC (1906).

Louisiana: Aurora CC; Baton Rouge Muni (NLE, 9); West End CC, New Orleans (1921).

Maryland: Elkridge CC, Baltimore (9).

Michigan: Atlas Valley GC {formerly Flint GC}; Birmingham CC (9, 1916); Bloomfield Hills CC (1909); Charlotte CC (9); Duck Lake GC, Albion (9, 1922); Escanaba CC (9); Grand Beach CC (9, 1912); Green Ridge CC, Grand Rapids (1922); Highland Park GC, Grand Rapids (1929); Hillsdale G&CC (9, 1909); Huron Hills CC, Ann Arbor (9, 1922); Kalamazoo CC (9, 1909); Ludington Hills GC, Ludington (9, 1920); Manistee G&CC (9, 1901); Marshall CC (NLE, 9); Meadow Heights CC, Jackson (9); Mullet Lake G&CC (9); Northport Point G&CC (9); Owosso CC (9); Palisades Park GC (NLE, 9); Plymouth Park GC, Niles (9); Riverside CC, Menominee (9); Rochester GC; Saginaw CC (9); South Haven GC (9); Spring Lake G&CC; Stag Island GC, Port Huron (9); Traverse City CC (9); Wawonowin GC, Ishpeming (9).

Minnesota: Detroit CC, Detroit Lakes (9, 1917); Lafayette C, Minnetonka Beach (9, 1915); Minneapolis GC (1917).

Mississippi: Alexandria G&CC (9); Biloxi CC (NLE, 9, 1918); CC of Jackson (NLE, 9); Pass Christian CC (9).

Missouri: Carthage Muni (9); Columbia CC (9, 1921); Evanston GC, Kansas City (NLE, 1903); Excelsior Springs CC (1915); Hannibal CC (NLE, 9, 1909); Joplin CC (NLE, 1922); Kansas City CC (NLE,); Oakwood CC, Kansas City (9, 1912); Westborough CC, Kirkwood (1908).

Montana: Billings G&CC (9).

Nebraska: Beatrice CC (9); Elmwood Park Muni (1916); Fremont GC (9, 1930).

New Jersey: Colonia CC; East Orange Muni (9, 1926); Essex County CC (East Course) (1898); Forest Hill GC, Bloomfield; Glen Ridge GC, (NLE, 9, 1900); Hackensack CC (NLE, 9, 1900); Hillside G&TC, Plainfield (NLE, 1898); Hollywood GC, Deal (NLE, 9, 1898); Montclair CC (NLE, 9, 1898); Morris County GC, Morristown (1897); Plainfield GC (NLE, 1901); Point Pleasant GC (9, 1910); Somerset Hills CC, Bernardsville (NLE, 9); Suburban GC, Elizabeth (NLE, 9, 1896); Yountakah CC, Delawanna (NLE, 9, 1899).

New Mexico: Santa Fe CC.

New York: Auburn CC (9); Chappaqua CC (NLE,); Dyker Beach GC, Brooklyn (9, 1897); Dyker Meadow GC, Brooklyn (NLE, 9, 1899); Eagle's Nest CC, Blue Mountain Lake (9, 1900); Flushing GC (NLE, 9); Forest Park GC, Bronx (1910); Fort Erie GC (9); Fox Hills GC (1899); Huntington GC (NLE, 9, 1899); Mahopac GC, Lake Mahopac (NLE, 9, 1900); Mohawk GC, Schenectady (NLE, 1900); Oakland GC, Bayside (NLE, 9, 1896); Onondaga G&CC (NLE,); Oswego CC (NLE, 9); Pelham Manor GC (NLE, 9, 1898); Pratt Estate GC, Glen Cove (9, 1895); Sunset Park GC (NLE,); Yahnundasis GC, Utica (NLE, 9).

North Carolina: Tryon CC (9).

Ohio: Butler County GC (9); Coshocton T&CC (9); Hamilton County CC (1911); Hyde Park CC, Cincinnati (NLE, 1903); Kettenring CC, Defiance (9, 1919); Lorain CC (9); Losantiville CC, Cincinnati (1906); Moundbuilders CC, Newark (1927); Mount Vernon CC (9); Plum Brook GC, Sandusky (9, 1914); Rosemont GC, Akron; Shawnee CC, Lima (9); St. Marys CC; Union CC, Dover (NLE, 9); Western Hills GC, Cincinnati; Wyoming CC, Cincinnati (9).

Pennsylvania: Allegheny CC, Sewickley (1902); Butler CC (9, 1906); Greensburg CC (9, 1904); Grove City CC (1917); Lake Shore GC, Erie; Monongahela Valley CC (9); Sharon CC; St. Clair CC, Pittsburgh (1916); Stanton Heights CC, Pittsburgh (1909); The Country Club, Donora (9); Union City GC (1915); Wanango CC, Reno (1914).

South Carolina: Anderson CC; CC of Charleston (NLE, 1901).

South Dakota: Minnehaha CC, Sioux Falls (NLE, 9).

Texas: Breckenridge CC (9); Corpus Christi CC (NLE, 9); Dallas CC (1908); El Paso CC (1910); Fort Worth CC (NLE, 1911); Lakewood CC, Dallas (1912); River Crest CC, Fort Worth (1911); Sherman GC (9, 1907).

Washington: Jefferson Park Muni (1917).

West Virginia: Huntington CC (9, 1919).

Wisconsin: Big Foot CC, Fontana; Blue Mound G&CC, Milwaukee (NLE, 1903); Chenequa GC, Hartland (9); CC of Beloit (NLE, 9, 1909); Fox River CC, Green Bay (9, 1917); Lake Lawn GC, Delaran; Lincoln Park GC, Milwaukee (9, 1922); Manitowoc GC; Nakoma CC, Madison (1920); Northernaire CC, Three Lakes (9); Old Hickory GC, Beaver Dam (9, 1920); Oshkosh CC (9, 1916); Quit-Qui-Oc GC, Elkhart Lake (9); Racine CC (9, 1909); Sheboygan Town & CC (9, 1905); Town & Country C, Fond du Lac (9); Tripoli CC, Milwaukee (1922); Tuscumbia CC, Green Lake; Washington Park Muni, Racine (9, 1917).

Wyoming: Casper CC (NLE, 9); Cheyenne CC (NLE,).

Alberta: Calgary Muni; Lethbridge GC (9); Medicine Hat GC (9).

British Columbia: Vernon G&CC.

Manitoba: Birds Hill GC; St. Charles CC (West Nine), Winnipeg (NLE, 9, 1904).

Ontario: Caledonia Springs GC (9); Thunder Bay CC (9).

Quebec: Royal Ottawa C, Hull (1917).

Courses Remodeled & Added to by: Tom Bendelow
Illinois: Elgin CC (A.9); Elgin CC (NLE, R.9).
Indiana: West Baden GC (R.9); West Baden GC (A.18).
Michigan: Birmingham CC (A.9, 1920).

Minnesota: Northland CC, Duluth (NLE, R.9, 1912); Northland CC, Duluth (NLE, A.9, 1912).

New York: Apawamis C, Rye (A.9, 1896); Nassau CC, Glen Cove (NLE, A.9, 1900); Nassau CC, Glen Cove (NLE, R.9, 1900); Rockaway Hunting C, Cedarhurst (NLE, A.9, 1900); Van Cortlandt Park GC, Bronx (A.9, 1899).

Ohio: Oakwood C, Cleveland (A.9, 1915).

Tennessee: Memphis CC (NLE, A.).

Wisconsin: Geneva Lake Y&GC, Lake Geneva (R.); Milwaukee CC (NLE, A.9).

David W. Bennett (1935 -) ASGCA
Born: Dallas, Texas.

A graduate of Texas Tech, Dave Bennett was employed as a landscape architect with the Texas Highway Department for seven years. In 1965 he joined the staff of golf architect Leon Howard, leaving in 1970 to form his own practice. At different times in the 1970s, Bennett utilized PGA Tour golfers Terry Dill and Lee Trevino as consultants.

Courses by: Dave Bennett
Arizona: Arthur Pack GC, Tucson (1977); Canoa Hills GC, Green Valley (1979); Desert Hills CC, Tucson (1978).
Colorado: Peaceful Valley CC, Colorado Springs.
Florida: Hurlburt Field GC (1975).
Illinois: West Village GC, Aurora (1979).
Kentucky: Woodson Bend CC, Burnside (9, 1975), with John F. Robinson.
Montana: Point North GC, Billings (1978), with Theodore Wirth.
New Mexico: Santa Teresa CC (Spanish Dagger Course), Sunland Park (1976); Santa Teresa CC (Yucca Course), Sunland Park (1976).
Texas: Cimarron CC, McAllen (1984); Grover Keaton Muni, Dallas (1978); Lost Creek GC (1973); Maxwell Muni (New Course) (1979); Prestonwood CC (Hills Course), Dallas (1986).
Mexico: Taboada GC.
Venezuela: Club de G de Caracas (1979).

Courses Remodeled & Added to by: Dave Bennett
Arizona: Oro Valley G&CC, Tucson (R., 1983).
Mississippi: Castlewood CC (A.9, 1982).
Oklahoma: Arrowhead State Park GC, Eufaula (A.9, 1981).
Texas: Pecan Valley Muni, Fort Worth (A.9, 1981).

Bradford L. Benz (1946 -) ASGCA
Born: Oelwein, Iowa.

Bradford Benz attended Iowa State University, receiving a bachelor's degree in 1968 and a master degree in 1970, both in Landscape Architecture. After college he joined golf architect Dick Phelps, becoming his partner in 1973. In 1980, Benz struck up a friendship with Mike Poellot while the two, along with many fellow ASGCA members, toured several classic Scottish links. Poellot soon joined Phelps and Benz in their Colorado operation, and two years later Benz and Poellot formed their own design partnership based in California.

Drawing on Poellot's contacts in the Far East, Benz and Poellot laid out several courses in the Pacific Basin in the 1980s. Perhaps their most significant work was Beijing Golf Club, the first private golf club ever built in the Peoples Republic of China.

Courses by: Brad Benz
Arizona: Fred Enke Muni, Tucson (1983), with Mike Poellot and Mark Rathert; Gainey Ranch GC, Scottsdale (27, 1985), with Mike Poellot and Mark Rathert.
California: Spring Valley GC, Milpitas (1987), with Mike Poellot.
Colorado: Copper Mountain GC (NLE, Precision, 1980), with Dick Phelps; Englewood Muni (1982), with Dick Phelps and Mike Poellot; Raccoon Creek GC, Littleton (1984), with Dick Phelps and Mike Poellot; Rifle Creek GC (9), with Dick Phelps and Mike Poellot; Springhill GC, Aurora (Precision, 1977), with Dick Phelps; West Meadows GC, Englewood (1984), with Dick Phelps and Mike Poellot.
Missouri: Longview Lake GC, Lee's Summit (27, 1986), with Mike Poellot and Mark Rathert.
Montana: Briarwood CC (1985), with Mike Poellot.
Nebraska: Heritage Hills GC, McCook (1981), with Dick Phelps.
Nevada: Northgate CC, Reno (27, 1987), with Mike Poellot; Wildcreek GC, Sparks (1980), with Dick Phelps.
New Mexico: Elephant Butte G&CC, Truth or Consequence (9, 1975), with Dick Phelps; Ladera GC, Albuquerque (27, 1980), with Dick Phelps.
North Dakota: Prairiewood GC, Fargo (Precision, 9, 1976), with Dick Phelps.
South Dakota: Southern Hills CC, Hot Springs (1979), with Dick Phelps.
Texas: Firewheel Muni (Course No. 1), Garland (1983), with Dick Phelps and Mike Poellot; Indian Creek GC (Course No. 1), Carrollton (1983), with Dick Phelps and Mike Poellot.
China: Beijing GC (North Course) (1987), with Mike Poellot and Mark Rathert; Beijing GC (South Course) (1988), with Mike Poellot and Mark Rathert.
Hong Kong: Clearwater Bay CC (1984), with Mike Poellot.
Japan: Glenoaks CC (1983), with Mike Poellot; Kannami Springs G&CC (1982), with Mike Poellot; Oak Meadows CC (1984), with Mike Poellot.
Taiwan: Lai Lai International G&CC, Kaohsiung (1985), with Mike Poellot.

Courses Remodeled & Added to by: Brad Benz
Colorado: Dos Rios CC, Gunnison (A.9, 1982), with Dick Phelps and Mike Poellot; Grand Lake GC (R.9, 1978), with Dick Phelps; Grand Lake GC (A.9, 1978), with Dick Phelps; Meadow Hills GC, Denver (R., 1983), with Dick Phelps and Mike Poellot.
Montana: Riverside CC, Bozeman (A.9, 1981), with Dick Phelps.
New Mexico: Riverside CC, Carlsbad (A.9, 1984), with Mike Poellot and Mark Rathert; Riverside CC, Carlsbad (R.9, 1984), with Mike Poellot and Mark Rathert.
North Dakota: Heart River GC, Dickinson (A.9, 1984), with Dick Phelps and Mike Poellot; Heart River GC, Dickinson (R.9, 1984), with Dick Phelps and Mike Poellot.
South Dakota: Huron CC (A.9, 1975), with Dick Phelps; Huron CC (R.9, 1975), with Dick Phelps.
Wyoming: Riverton CC, Riverton (A.9, 1982), with Dick Phelps and Mike Poellot; Riverton CC, Riverton (R.9, 1982), with Dick Phelps and Mike Poellot.

169

Robert Berthet (1952 -) BAGCA
Born: France.

A former junior and university golf champion, Robert Berthet graduated as a professional golf teacher in 1973. Two years later he obtained an "Ecole Speciale d'Architecture" degree from the University of Paris. In 1976 Berthet formed his own golf design firm called Archigolf, which handled projects on the Continent and Northern Africa.

Berthet served as editor of the French golf magazine Golf Pro, as a technical consultant to the French Golf Association and has honorary secretary for the French P.G.A.

Courses by: Robert Berthet
France: Bois le Roe GC (9, 1983); Flaine GC (1984); L'Isle d'Abeau GC (1983); Olhain GC (9, 1983); Royan GC (1983).
Courses Remodeled & Added to by: Robert Berthet
France: Cannes CC (R., 1981); Royal G d'Evian, Evian (R., 1976).

Richard A. Bigler
Born: Utah.

As a teenager Richard Bigler worked on several course construction projects in Utah for architect William H. Neff. After a stint in the U.S. Navy and a mission for his Mormon Church, Bigler obtained a Landscape Architecture degree from the University of California at Berkeley in 1959. Bigler then worked for several years as an irrigation specialist and then as a draftsman on several Southern California projects for course designer Larry Hughes. In the mid '60s Bigler opened his own landscape design office in Southern California, handling city and county parks as well as some public golf courses.

Courses by: Richard Bigler
California: Anaheim Hills GC (1972); La Contenta CC, Valley Springs (1973); Oceanside Muni GC (1973); Palm Lakes GC, Fresno (Precision, 1986); Ridgemark G&CC, Hollister.
Nevada: Meadow Valley GC, Caliente (9, 1986).
Courses Remodeled & Added to by: Richard Bigler
California: DeBell GC, Burbank (R., 1984); Hillsview GC (A.9); Visalia Plaza GC (R., 1984).

Charles R. "Buck" Blankenship (1906 -)

Buck Blankenship operated a dairy farm in Kentucky until retiring in the early 1950s. A fine golfer, he became a member of the PGA of America in 1955 and served as pro-superintendent at several Kentucky courses. He also began designing and constructing golf courses on a part-time basis in the 1960s, and by the early 1970s had designed or remodeled some thirty-five layouts.

Courses by: Buck Blankenship
Kansas: Village Greens GC, Ozaukie (9, 1968).
Kentucky: Bright Leaf GC, Harrodsburg (1963); Burlington GC (1960); Hickory Hills CC, Liberty (9); Juniper Hills GC, Frankfort; Lakeshore CC, Madisonville (9, 1971); Lone Oak CC, Nicholasville (1969); New GC, Versailles (1969); Park Mammoth GC, Park City (1964); Spring Lake CC, Lexington (1949); Taylorsville Lake GC (9).
Courses Remodeled & Added to by: Buck Blankenship
Indiana: Valley View GC, New Albany (A.9, 1968).
West Virginia: Riviera CC, Huntington (A.9, 1960).

Bruce E. Borland (1958 -) ASGCA
Born: Peoria, Illinois.

A 1981 graduate of the University of Illinois in Landscape Architecture, Bruce Borland worked in succession for golf architect David Gill, the golf design firm of Killian and Nugent and the Hitchcock Landscape Architecture Design firm. In early 1984 Borland rejoined Dick Nugent, who had formed his own design business the previous year.

Borland was among the first golf architects to utilize a computer in the actual design of a golf course. In the mid-1980s he adapted a computer program in order to analyze golf designs in terms of optimum shot values, club selection sequence and balance.

K. Warner Bowen (1935 -)
Born: Crystal, Michigan.

Following military service during the Korean War, Warner Bowen received an A.A. degree from Ferris State College and a B.A. degree from Michigan State University. He later did graduate work under Dr. James Beard, then head of Turfgrass Science at Michigan State. At his father's urging, Bowen entered private practice in Sheridan, Michigan as a course architect and builder in 1964. He involved himself in all phases of the design and construction of a golf course, including personally sculpting tees, greens and other features with his own bulldozer.

Courses by: Warner Bowen
Arizona: Yuma East GC.
Florida: Reservation GC {formerly Jekyll-Hyde GC}, Lakeland (Precision, 9).
Michigan: Benona Shores GC, Shelby (1979); Centennial Acres GC, Sunfield (9, 1979); Highland Burne GC (NLE, 9, 1971); Holland Lake GC, Sheridan (9); North Kent GC, Rockford (1979); Rogue River GC, Rolling Hills GC, Ionia; Schuss Mountain GC, Mancelona (1977); Spring Valley GC, Reed City (9); Twin Oaks GC, St. John (9); Walnut Woods CC; Western Woods GC (1971).

James Braid (1870 - 1950)
Born: Earlsferry, Fife, Scotland. Died: London, England at age 80.

James Braid, who learned golf at age 4 and won his first tournament at age 8, played his early golf with such prodigies as Jack and Archie Simpson and his cousin Douglas Rolland. He left school as a teenager, obtained work as an apprentice carpenter at St. Andrews and honed his golfing skills on the side. He played in his first professional tournament in 1894. In 1896 Braid became professional at Romford GC in England and in 1904 moved to the newly opened Walton Heath GC, where he

served as its professional for the rest of his life.

Braid, along with John Henry Taylor and Harry Vardon (the "Great Triumvirate"), dominated competitive golf during the first two decades of the twentieth century. He won most of his prestigious titles within a span of ten years: the British Open in 1901, 1905, 1906, 1908 and 1910, the News-of-the-World Matchplay Championship in 1903, 1905, 1907 and 1911, and the French Open in 1910.

Braid had worked on the design of a course or two as a young professional at Romford. He was called upon to design several courses soon after his initial victory in the British Open, and he wrote knowledgeable articles about course design as early as 1908. But it was not until after his active competitive days were over that Braid devoted much of his time to golf course architecture.

Fearing the ocean, he seldom ventured even as far as the Continent, thus most of his work was done in the British Isles. He did design one course in America and one in Singapore, but both were done solely from topographic maps. Braid was greatly respected for accurate and detailed working drawings of the courses he laid out.

Many of Braid's designs were constructed by contractor John R. Stutt, and a nearly perfect accord was reached between the two. Often subject to motion sickness, Braid dreaded travel by car, so Stutt's on-site work was invaluable to him. Braid also started C.K. Hutchison in design and collaborated with him on several projects.

Shortly before his death, James Braid was granted membership in the Royal and Ancient Golf Club, making him one of the first professional golfers ever to be so honored.

Courses by: James Braid
England: Arcot Hall GC, Northumberland , with John R.Stutt; Barnehurst GC, Kent; Basingstoke GC; Bognor Regis GC, Sussex; Bridport and West Dorset GC; Budock Vean Hotel GC (9, 1922); Charnwood Forest GC, Leicester (9); Church Stretton GC, Shropshire; Clitheroe GC, Lancashire , with John R.Stutt; Colchester GC, Essex (1909); Copthorne GC, Sussex; Croham Hurst GC, Surrey (1912), with F.G. Hawtree; Dorking GC, Surrey (9, 1897); Drayton Park GC, Birmingham , with John R.Stutt; Dunstable Downs GC, Bedfordshire; Eaglescliffe GC, County Durham , with John R.Stutt; Exeter G&CC, Countess Wear, Devon , with John R.Stutt; Finchley GC, London , with John R.Stutt; Fulford Heath GC (1934), with John R.Stutt; Henley GC (1908); Home Park GC, Surrey; Hoylake Muni GC; Ipswich GC, Suffolk (NLE, 1927); Kingswood GC, Surrey , with John R.Stutt; Luffenham Heath GC (1911); Mere G&CC, Surrey (1934), with John R.Stutt and George Duncan; Middlesborough GC, with John R.Stutt; Newton Abbot GC, Devonshire (1930); North Hants GC, Hampshire (1904); North Shore GC (1910); North Worcestershire GC (1906); Orsett GC, Essex , with John R.Stutt; Oswestry GC, Shropshire , with John R.Stutt; Perranporth GC (1927), with John R.Stutt; Petersborough Milton GC, Northamptonshire , with John R.Stutt; Romford GC; Royal Blackheath GC (1923), with John R.Stutt; Royal Cromer GC, Norfolk; Scarborough North Cliff GC, Yorkshire (1927), with John R.Stutt; Sherborne GC; Southport and Ainsdale GC (1923); St. Austell GC (1912); St. Enodoc GC, Cornwall; Stinchcombe Hill GC; Theydon Bois GC, Essex (9, 1897); Thorpeness GC, Suffolk; Tiverton GC, Devon , with John R.Stutt; Torquay GC, Devonshire , with John R.Stutt; Truro GC, Cornwall , with John R.Stutt; Tyrrells Wood GC, Devonshire; West Park GC, Devonshire; West Hove GC, Sussex (1910); Wilderness GC, Kent; Workington GC, Cumbria (1922).
Ireland: Dundalk GC (1905); Limerick GC (9, 1920); Mullingar GC, County Westmeath (1932), with John R.Stutt; Newlands GC, County Dublin (1926).
Isle of Man: Peel GC; Ramsey GC, Cambridgeshire (1935), with John R.Stutt.
Northern Ireland: Carnalea GC (1927), with John R.Stutt; Kirkistown Castle GC (1902).
Scotland: Airdrie GC, Lanarkshire; Balmore GC, Glasgow; Belleisle GC, Ayrshire (1927), with John R.Stutt; Blairgowrie GC (Wee Course), Perthshire , with John R.Stutt; Blairmore and Strone GC, Argyll; Boat-of-Garten GC, Invernesshire , with John R.Stutt; Brechin GC, Angus; Brora GC, Sutherland; Buchanan Castle GC, Stirlingshire (1936), with John R.Stutt; Carnoustie GC (Burnside Course), Angus (1926); Cawder GC (Cawder Course) (1933), with John R.Stutt; Cawder GC (Keir Course) (1933), with John R.Stutt; Colville Park GC (1922); Cowal GC, Argyll; Crow Wood GC, Glasgow (1925), with John R.Stutt; Dalmahoy GC (East Course), Midlothian (1926), with John R.Stutt; Dalmahoy GC (West Course), Midlothian (1926), with John R.Stutt; Deaconsbank GC, Glasgow (1922); Downfield GC, Dundee (1932); Dullatur GC, Glasgow; Forfar GC, Angus; Fort Augustus GC, Invernesshire (9, 1930); Fortrose and Rosemarkie, Invernesshire; Glenbervie GC, Stirlingshire; Glencruitten GC, Argyll (1905); Gleneagles Hotel GC (Kings Course), Perthshire (1919), with C.K. Hutchison; Gleneagles Hotel GC (Queen's Course), Perthshire (1919), with C.K. Hutchison; Greenock GC, Renfrewshire (27); Hamilton GC, Lanarkshire , with John R.Stutt; Hayston GC, Glasgow (1926), with John R.Stutt; Hilton Park GC (Allender Course), Dunbarton , with John R.Stutt; Ingliston GC, with John R.Stutt; Kelso GC, Roxboroughshire; Kingsknowe GC, Edinburgh (1908); Kirriemuir GC, Perthshire; Musselburgh GC (1937), with John R.Stutt; Powfoot GC (1903); Ratho Park GC, Edinburgh (1928), with John R.Stutt; Ravelston GC (9, 1912); Rothesay GC, Island of Bute; Routenburn GC, Ayrshire (1920); Royal Musselburgh GC, East Lothian (1925), with John R.Stutt; Seafield GC (1930), with John R.Stutt; Stranraer GC, Wigtownshire (1906); Turnhouse GC, Edinburgh (1909); Williamwood GC, Glasgow; Wishaw GC, Lanarkshire.
Singapore: Singapore Island GC (Bukit Course) (1924).
Wales: Flint GC; Holyhead GC (1912); Machynlleth GC, Powys (1905); Monmouthshire GC; Portmadoc GC; Rhyl GC (9); St. Deiniol GC (1905); Welshpool GC, Powys (1929), with John R.Stutt.
Courses Remodeled & Added to by: James Braid
New York: St. Andrews GC, Hastings-on-Hudson (R., 1930).
Channel Islands: La Moye GC (R., 1938).
England: Berkhampsted GC, Hertfordshire (R.12, 1927); Berkhampsted GC, Hertfordshire (A.6, 1927); Berwick-upon-Tweed GC, Northumberland (R., 1925); Bramley GC (R.); Brighton and Hove GC, Sussex (A.9, 1910); Bush Hill Park GC (R.); Cockermouth GC (R.2); Denham GC (R.); Enfield GC (R.); Ganton GC (R., 1919); Hankley Common GC, Surrey (A.9, 1922); Hankley Common GC, Surrey (R.9, 1922); Hunstanton GC, Norfolk (A.9, 1910); Hunstanton GC, Norfolk (R.9, 1910); Leamington and County GC, with John R.Stutt; Littlestone GC, Kent (R.); Northamptonshire County GC (R.), 1920); Northumberland GC (R., 1911); Parkstone GC, Dorset (R., 1927), with John R.Stutt; Queens Park GC, Bourne-

mouth (R.); Sherwood Forest GC, Nottinghamshire (R., 1935), with John R.Stutt; Thetford GC (R.); Verulam GC (R., 1910); Wallasey GC, Cheshire (R., 1929), with John R.Stutt.

Ireland: Ballybunion GC (Old Course) (A.9, 1927); Ballybunion GC (Old Course) (R.9, 1927); Howth GC (R.9, 1929), with John R.Stutt; Howth GC (A.9, 1929), with John R.Stutt; Limerick GC (A.9, 1928); Rosapenna GC, County Donegal (R.); Tullamore GC, County Offaly (R., 1938); Waterford GC, County Waterford (A.9, 1934), with John R.Stutt; Waterford GC, County Waterford (R.9, 1934), with John R.Stutt.

Northern Ireland: Bangor GC, County Donegal (R., 1932), with John R.Stutt.

Scotland: Alyth GC (R.); Blairgowrie GC (Rosemount Course) (R.10, 1934), with John R.Stutt; Blairgowrie GC (Rosemount Course) (A.8, 1934), with John R.Stutt; Broomie Knowe GC, Midlothian (R.); Bruntsfield Links, Davidson's Main (R.); Carnoustie GC, Angus (R., 1926), with John R.Stutt; Cochrane Castle GC, Renfrewshire (A.10, 1949), with John R.Stutt; Cochrane Castle GC, Renfrewshire (R., 1949), with John R.Stutt; Crieff GC, Perthshire (R.); Edzell GC (R., 1934), with John R.Stutt; Elie Golf House C, Fife (R., 1921); Forres GC, Morayshire (R.); Murcar GC, Aberdeen (R.); Nairn GC, Nairnshire (R., 1938); Newtonmore GC, Invernesshire (R.); Prestwick GC, Ayrshire (R., 1918); Prestwick GC, Ayrshire (A.4, 1918); Prestwick GC, Ayrshire (R., 1930), with John R.Stutt; Royal Burgess G Society of Edinburgh (R., 1932); Royal Troon GC, Ayrshire (R., 1923).

Wales: Aberdovey GC (R.); Pwllheli GC (A.9, 1909); Pwllheli GC (R.9, 1909); Royal Porthcawl GC, Mid Glamorgan (R., 1910).

Jeffrey D. Brauer (1955 -   ) ASGCA
Born: Albany, New York.

Jeff Brauer graduated from the University of Illinois in 1977 with a Bachelor's Degree in Landscape Architecture. He immediately went to work for the design firm of Killian and Nugent, working on the design of such prominent layouts as Kemper Lakes GC near Chicago. Brauer's largest involvement during that period was the design and construction supervision of Lake Arrowhead GC, Nekoosa, Wisconsin.

When the Killian and Nugent firm dissolved in 1983, Brauer remained with Ken Killian for a year. He then formed his own design company, Golfscapes, based in Arlington, Texas.

On several of his early solo projects, Brauer worked with PGA Tour veteran Jim Colbert. Many of those jobs were related to Colbert's daily fee course lease/ management business.

Courses by: Jeff Brauer

Illinois: Robert A.Black GC, Chicago (Precision, 9, 1979), with Ken Killian and Dick Nugent.

Texas: Chester W. Ditto Muni, Arlington (1982), with Ken Killian and Dick Nugent; Mission CC, Odessa (1983), with Ken Killian and Dick Nugent.

Wisconsin: Lake Arrowhead GC, Nekoosa (1984), with Ken Killian and Dick Nugent.

Courses Remodeled & Added to by: Jeff Brauer

California: San Bernardino CC (A.1, 1986), with Jim Colbert.

Kansas: Manhattan CC (R.1, 1985).

Louisiana: Northwood CC, Shreveport (A.9, 1986).

Nebraska: Fairbury CC (R.1, 1984); Holdrege CC (A.9, 1985); Oak Hills CC, Omaha (R.2, 1984).

Nevada: Desert Rose GC, Las Vegas (R., 1984), with Jim Colbert; Las Vegas GC (R., 1986), with Jim Colbert.

Texas: Great Southwest GC, Arlington (R., 1983), with Ken Killian and Dick Nugent; Plano Muni (R., 1986), with Jim Colbert; Weeks Park GC, Wichita Falls (R.10, 1986); Wichita Falls GC (R.2, 1986).

John Bredemus (1890 - 1946)
Born: St. Louis, Missouri. Died: Guadalajara, Mexico at age 56.

John Bredemus attended Harvard University and he established himself as a fine athlete as a participant in the 1904 Olympic Games. For a short time he taught college mathematics in the east before moving to Texas after the first World War. There he turned professional and played, without much success, in several professional tournaments. In 1922 he designed and built the Hermann Park GC for the City of Houston and remained as its professional.

Bredemus is one of several rather obscure figures in golf course architecture. Legend has it that he was an eccentric, hating shoes, refusing to play with new golf balls, and considering the tops of tall trees to be ideal vantage points for golf course planning. It is nevertheless a fact that he did some of the finest layouts in the state of Texas during the 1920s and '30s. Towards the end of his Texas career he was assisted by Ralph Plummer, a young professional golfer who went on to make a name for himself as a course architect following World War II.

In the late 1930s Bredemus moved to Mexico following a dispute with the U.S. Government over income taxes. He continued to design golf courses and at his death had over a half dozen fine Mexican layouts to his credit.

Courses by: John Bredemus

Texas: Brae Burn CC, Bellaire; Colonial CC, Fort Worth (1935); Edinburg CC (9, 1927); Galveston CC (1932); Galveston Muni (NLE, 1931); Harlingen Muni (NLE, 1930); Hermann Park GC, Houston (1923); McCloskey Hospital GC, Fort Worth (Par 3, 9); Memorial Park GC, Houston (1935); Mercedes CC (9, 1929); Oso Beach GC, Corpus Christi (1939); Pine Forest CC, Houston (NLE,); Ridglea CC (North Course), Fort Worth; Rockwood Muni, Fort Worth (1933); Seguin CC (9); Tenison Muni (West Course), Dallas (1924); Z. Boaz GC, Fort Worth.

Mexico: Acapulco CC; Churubusco CC, Mexico City; Club de G Hermosillo (NLE,); Guadalajara CC (9, 1942); Monterrey CC; Tampico CC (9, 1970).

Courses Remodeled & Added to by: John Bredemus

Texas: Cedar Crest GC, Dallas (R., 1926); Glen Garden CC (R.9); Glen Garden CC (A.9).

Mexico: Guadalajara CC (A.9, 1948); Mexico City CC (R., 1939).

Russell F. Breeden (1917 -   )
Born: Alvamar County, Virginia.

Russell Breeden entered private practice as a golf course designer in 1961 after training under golf architect Fred Findlay. By 1980 he had designed over seventy courses, supervising construction of many of them. He was joined in his work during the 1980s by his son Dan Breeden.

Courses by: Russell Breeden

North Carolina: Beechwood CC, Ahoskie; Ocean Isle Beach GC (1978), with Dan Breeden; Pawtuckett GC, Charlotte (1973); Pine Tree GC, Asheboro; Pinewood CC; Raintree CC (North Course), Charlotte (1971); Raintree CC (South Course), Charlotte (1971); Rock Barn GC, Conover (1969); Sapphire Lakes CC, Sapphire (9, 1984), with Dan Breeden; Scotch Meadows CC, Morganton (1968).

South Carolina: Bay Tree Golf Plantation (Gold Course) (1972), with George Fazio and Tom Fazio; Bay Tree Golf Plantation (Green Course) (1972), with George Fazio and Tom Fazio; Bay Tree Golf Plantation (Silver Course) (1972), with George Fazio and Tom Fazio; Bear Creek GC, Spartanburg (1980), with Dan Breeden; Bonnie Brae GC (1961); Chester GC, Greenville (1971); Chickasaw Point GC, Fair Play (1973); Cypress Bay GC, North Myrtle Beach (1972); Huntington Hills GC, Spartanburg; Kings Grant GC, Charleston; Lan-Yair GC, Spartanburg; Linrick GC, Columbia (1972); Mid Carolina CC, Prosperity; Pawpaw CC, Bamberg (1981); Pine Ridge CC, Edgefield (1969); Pineland Plantation G&CC, Mayesville (1974); Pleasant Point Plantation CC, Beaufort; Possum Trot GC, North Myrtle Beach (1968); Ramsgate GC, Inman (1983), with Dan Breeden; Robber's Roost GC, North Myrtle Beach (1968); Shadowmoss G&TC, Charleston (1971); Village Greens CC (1983), with Dan Breeden; Widow Maker GC, Spartanburg (1979), with Dan Breeden; Wildewood CC, Columbia (1974).

Virginia: Jordan Point CC, Hopewell (9, 1974); Sleepy Hole Muni, Portsmouth (1972); Suffolk CC.

Courses Remodeled & Added to by: Russell Breeden

North Carolina: Kinston CC (R., 1983), with Dan Breeden.

South Carolina: Greenville CC (Riverside Course) (R., 1971); Lancaster CC (R., 1969); Woodlands CC (R., 1980), with Dan Breeden.

Virginia: Halloud Muni (A.9).

William H. Brinkworth
Bill Brinkworth served as pro-greenkeeper and manager at Jasper Park GC in Alberta, Canada, from 1920 until his retirement in 1959. He designed several western Canada courses during that time.

Courses by: William Brinkworth

Alberta: Derrick C, Edmonton (1959); Edmonton G&CC; Elk Island National Park GC; Highlands GC, Edmonton; Prince Rupert GC, Edmonton; Sherwood Park GC, Edmonton.

Saskatchewan: Elmwood G&CC; Regina GC; Wascana G&CC.

Courses Remodeled & Added to by: William Brinkworth

Alberta: Jasper Park GC, Jasper (R., 1948).

Ernest Brown
Canadian designer Ernie Brown planned several courses in his home province of British Columbia in the 1960s and '70s. His projects emphasized the family aspect of the country club by providing some form of outdoor activity for every member of the family. On a couple of his courses, Brown experimented with the covering of a portion of each tee for play on rainy days.

Courses by: Ernest Brown

British Columbia: Chilliwack G&CC (18, 1958); McCleery GC, Vancouver; Prince George CC; Shuswap Lake Estates G&CC, Blind Bay (9); Sparwood GC (9, 1984); Sunshine Coast G&CC, Roberts Creek (9, 1970), with Roy Taylor; Sunshore GC, Chase (Precision, 9, 1968).

Courses Remodeled & Added to by: Ernest Brown

British Columbia: Vernon G&CC (R.5, 1968).

Leslie Brownlee
A native of Scotland, Leslie Brownlee emigrated to America where he served for several years as professional at the Fort Smith (Ark.) CC. He designed the first golf courses in Oklahoma, including the nine-hole Muskogee CC (1907) and Lakeview CC in Oklahoma City (9, 1907). Brownlee's stepbrother, Arthur Jackson, was also a pioneer golf architect in Oklahoma.

John G. Bulla (1914 -   )
Born: Newell, West Virginia.

Veteran PGA touring pro Johnny Bulla was best known as the "Po-Do pro," as a result of his long running contract with a cut-rate golf ball manufacturer. Twice a runner-up in the British Open and once a second-place finisher at the Masters, Bulla dabbled in course design in the late 1940s and early 1950s. After retiring from active competition and taking a club pro job, Bulla laid out several courses as a sideline in the Southwest.

Courses by: Johnny Bulla

Arizona: Leisure World GC, Mesa (Precision, 9); Orange Tree CC, Scottsdale (1958), with Lawrence Hughes; Thunderbird CC, Phoenix (1957), with Clarence Suggs.

Colorado: Pagosa Pines GC (1980).

Courses Remodeled & Added to by: Johnny Bulla

Arizona: Arizona CC, Phoenix (R., 1962).

Cuthbert Strachan Butchart (1876 - 1955)
Born: Carnoustie, Scotland. Died: Ossining, New York at age 79.

Cuthbert Butchart, one of twin sons of golf club maker John Butchart, became a professional golfer in his teens and at age twenty-three took a position as professional at Royal County Down in Northern Ireland. He remained there for several years, staking out or reconstructing a number of Irish courses before returning to Scotland in 1904.

After working as a professional and laying out a few courses in Scotland, Butchart moved on to Germany. There he designed and built Berlin GC, served as its professional and became golf teacher to German royalty. A fine golfer, he also won the 1913 German PGA championship. Several courses of his design were under construction in Germany when World War I broke out. Butchart was interned and spent the next two years in a German prisoner-of-war camp.

Upon his release, Butchart returned to Scotland but soon moved to the United States where he became head professional at the newly opened Westchester Biltmore CC in New York. He lived in America for the remainder of his life, spending summers in New York and winters in Florida. As an avocation, he began marketing handmade woods bearing his famous club-making family name. He also designed and remodeled several American courses, many of them in Florida during the boom of the 1920s.

Courses by: C.S. Butchart
Florida: Eustis CC (NLE,); Mayfair CC, Sanford (1927).
East Germany: Berlin G&CC (1911); Opperdorf Estate GC, Berlin.
England: North Middlesex GC; Porters Park GC, Hertfordshire (1899).
Ireland: Bundoran GC, County Donegal.
Northern Ireland: Belvoir Park GC, Belfast; Fortwilliam GC, Belfast; Royal County Down GC (Course No. 2), Newcastle; Whitehead GC, County Antrim (1904).
West Germany: Bad Kissengen GC.
Courses Remodeled & Added to by: C.S. Butchart
England: Highgate GC, London (R., 1904).
Northern Ireland: Royal County Down GC, Newcastle (R.).

Willard C. Byrd (1919 -) ASGCA
Born: Whiteville, North Carolina.
Following military service in the U.S. Navy during World War II, Willard Byrd attended North Carolina State, receiving a B.S. degree in Landscape Architecture in 1948. He worked first in recreational site planning with the U.S. Army Corps of Engineers and later as a land planning consultant in North Carolina and Florida. He then served as assistant manager and designer in the Southeastern office of a large landscape architecture and city planning firm.

In 1956 he founded Willard C. Byrd and Associates, Landscape Architects, Town Planners and Golf Course Architects. By 1979 Byrd's Atlanta, Ga. based firm had completed some 720 projects, including work on seventy-five golf courses.
Courses by: Willard Byrd
Alabama: Indian Oaks CC, Phoenix City (1976).
Florida: Bay Point Y&CC (Club Meadows Course), Panama City (1972); Breakers GC (West Course), West Palm Beach (1970); Lake City CC (1970); Longboat Key C (Harborside Course), Sarasota (1983), with Clyde Johnston; Oaks CC (Blue Heron Course), Sarasota (1984); Oaks CC (Eagle Course), Sarasota (1984).
Georgia: Atlanta CC, Marietta (1965), with Joseph S. Finger; Cherokee Town & CC (Riverside Course), Dunwoody (9, 1977); Dunwoody CC (1966); Fairfield Plantation CC, Carrollton (1973); Francis Lake GC, Valdosta (1973); Landings at Skidaway Island (Plantation) (1984), with Clyde Johnston; Northwood G&CC, Lawrenceville; Spring Hill CC, Tifton; Thomas County GC, Thomasville; Thomaston CC (9); White Path CC, Ellijay; Wilson CC.
North Carolina: Beech Mountain GC, Banner Elk (1969); Carolina Sands GC, White Lake; CC of North Carolina (Cardinal Course), Pinehurst (9, 1970); CC of North Carolina (Dogwood Course), Pinehurst (1963), with Ellis Maples; Gates Four G&CC, Fayetteville (1974); Happy Valley CC, Wilson (1973); Lake Hickory CC (27, 1968); MacGregor Downs CC, Cary (1967); Willow Creek CC, High Point (1964).
South Carolina: Heather Glen GC, Little River (1987), with Clyde Johnston; Indigo Run GC, Hilton Head Island (27, 1987), with Clyde Johnston; Litchfield CC (1966); Patriots Point G Links, Charleston (1984), with Clyde Johnston; Port Royal GC (Planters Row Course), Hilton Head Island (1984), with Clyde Johnston; River Hills CC, Lake Wylie (1969); Seabrook Island GC (Ocean Winds Course) (1973); Shipyard GC (Brigantine Nine), Hilton Head Island (9, 1982), with Clyde Johnston; Wexford CC, Hilton Head Island (1984), with Clyde Johnston.
Tennessee: Fox Den CC, Knoxville (1969).
Courses Remodeled & Added to by: Willard Byrd
Alabama: CC of Mobile (R.), with Clyde Johnston.
Florida: Deerwood CC, Jacksonville (R., 1977); Longboat Key C (Islandside Course), Sarasota (R., 1984), with Clyde Johnston; Ponce de Leon CC, St. Augustine (A.2, 1977), with Clyde Johnston; Ponce de Leon CC, St. Augustine (R.2, 1977), with Clyde Johnston.
Georgia: Cherokee Town & CC (Hillside Course), Dunwoody (R.); Griffin CC (A.9), with Clyde Johnston; Idle Hour CC (R.); Savannah Inn & CC (R., 1966).
Kentucky: Highland CC, Fort Thomas (R.).
North Carolina: Alamance CC, Burlington (R.), with Clyde Johnston; Emorywood CC, High Point (R., 1980); Forsyth CC, Winston-Salem (R.); Sedgefield CC, Greensboro (R., 1977).
South Carolina: Port Royal GC (Barony Course), Hilton Head Island (R., 1984), with Clyde Johnston; Port Royal GC (Robbers Row Course), Hilton Head Island (R., 1984), with Clyde Johnston.
Tennessee: Green Meadow CC, Marysville (R., 1984).

Charles Raymond Calhoun
While attending Iowa State University studying horticulture, Charles Calhoun opened a landscape contracting business. He continued in that business for nearly 20 years, specializing in grounds management. After obtaining a Masters in Agronomy and Plant Physiology from Iowa State in 1964, Calhoun began designing golf courses in small central Iowa communities. Stressing the importance of properly constructed greens, Calhoun converted many small sand green courses to grass.
Courses by: Charles Calhoun
Iowa: Gowrie G&CC (9, 1965); Jesup G&CC (9, 1967); River Bend GC, Story City (9, 1970); Waukon G&CC (1975).
Courses Remodeled & Added to by: Charles Calhoun
Iowa: Appanoose G&CC (R., 1973); Colfax GC (R., 1973); Kalona GC (R.9); Oak Leaf CC (R.); Pella G&CC (R., 1976); Silvercrest G&CC (R.); Wildwood Muni GC,

Charles City (R., 1976).

Alexander "Nipper" Campbell (1880 - 1942)
Born: Troon, Scotland. Died: Dayton, Ohio at age 62.
The oldest of seven golfing brothers, Alec Campbell came to the U.S. in 1896. A fine competitive player, he became club professional at The Country Club in Brookline, Mass. in 1899, a position he maintained until World War I. Campbell was generally credited with discovering Francis Ouimet, a youngster who lived along the 12th fairway of The Country Club and who stunned the golfing world by defeating veterans Harry Vardon and Ted Ray for the 1913 U.S. Open title at that very course.

While at Brookline, Campbell laid out and remodeled several Eastern courses. During that time, he also earned the nickname "Nipper" for his habit of often taking a nip or two of Scotch to get himself started.

Ohio Governor John Cox lured Nipper to Dayton to serve as pro at Miami Valley CC. While there, Campbell designed and built Morraine CC, where he served as head professional until his death.

While at Morraine, Nipper taught extensively constructed clubs and continued to design golf courses. He did over thirty original designs in his lifetime.

Sir Guy Colin Campbell (1885 - 1960)
Born: England. Died: Irvington, Virginia at age 75. Interred: St. Andrews, Scotland.
Sir Guy Campbell, great-grandson of Robert Chambers (an early British golf historian and codesigner of the original nine-hole course at Hoylake), was educated at Eton and at the University of St. Andrews. He was a fine oarsman and cricket player. As a golfer, he won several medals in competition at St. Andrews, and was a semifinalist in the 1907 British Amateur Championship.

During World War I, Campbell served in the infantry and was wounded in action. He also served in World War II as a member of the Royal Rifle Corps, even though he was in his late fifties at the time.

Campbell joined the staff of the London Times in 1920 as a special correspondent and later as editor of sports under the legendary Bernard Darwin. He also wrote countless magazine articles on golf and several books. Most notable was his contribution to *A History of Golf in Britain* (1952) edited by Darwin, in which Campbell outlined the history of course architecture in Britain.

Campbell began designing golf courses in the late 1920s, working in conjunction with Cecil K. Hutchison and S.V. Hotchkin on a series of layouts. He maintained a steady practice during the 1930s and resumed it after the second World War. He assumed the hereditary rank of baronet upon the death of his father, Sir Guy T. Campbell, in 1931.
Courses by: Sir Guy Campbell
Virginia: Tides Inn & CC (Tartan Course), Irvington (9, 1960).
England: Ashridge GC, Hertfordshire (1932), with C.K. Hutchison and S.V. Hotchkin; Beamish Park GC (1950), with Henry Cotton; Kington GC, Herefordshire (1926), with C.K. Hutchison and S.V. Hotchkin; Leeds Castle GC, with C.K. Hutchison and S.V. Hotchkin; Prince's GC (Red Course), Kent (9, 1951), with J.S.F. Morrison; Seascale GC, Cumbria (9, 1892); Shoreham GC, Southdown, with C.K. Hutchison and S.V. Hotchkin; Warsash GC, with C.K. Hutchison and S.V. Hotchkin; West Sussex GC, Sussex (1930), with C.K. Hutchison and S.V. Hotchkin.
Ireland: Killarney G & Fishing C (Killeen), County Kerry (6, 1939); Killarney G & Fishing C (Mahony's Point), County Kerry (12, 1939).
Courses Remodeled & Added to by: Sir Guy Campbell
England: Felixstowe Ferry GC, Suffolk (R., 1949), with Henry Cotton; Prince's GC (Blue Course), Kent (R., 1951), with J.S.F. Morrison; Royal Cinque Ports GC, Deal (R., 1946), with Henry Cotton; Royal West Norfolk GC, Norfolk (R., 1928), with C.K. Hutchison and S.V. Hotchkin; Rye GC, Deal (R.); Seacroft GC, Lincolnshire (R.); Sundridge Park GC (East Course), Kent (R., 1927), with C.K. Hutchison; Trevose G&CC (R.); Trevose G&CC (A.9); Woodhall Spa GC, Lincolnshire (R., 1926), with C.K. Hutchison and S.V. Hotchkin.
Ireland: Royal Dublin GC (R.).
Netherlands: Haagsche G&CC (R., 1947).
Scotland: Machrihanish GC, Argyllshire (R.); North Berwick GC, East Lothian (R., 1930), with C.K. Hutchison and S.V. Hotchkin.

Willie Campbell
Born in Musselburgh, Scotland, Willie Campbell planned courses in the British Isles before emigrating to the United States in the early 1890s. In 1894 he became the first professional at The Country Club, Brookline, Mass. where he presided over one of its expansions. Later, while serving as summer pro at Essex CC in Manchester, Mass., he planned other courses in the Northeast.
Courses by: Willie Campbell
Massachusetts: Oakley CC (NLE, 9, 1898); Tatnuck CC, Worcester (NLE, 9, 1899); The Country Club, Brookline (9, 1893).
Pennsylvania: Torresdale-Frankford CC, Philadelphia (9, 1895).
Rhode Island: Wannamoisett CC, Rumford (NLE, 1899).
England: Seascale GC (9).
Scotland: Machrie Hotel GC (9, 1891).
Courses Remodeled & Added to by: Willie Campbell
Massachusetts: Franklin Park GC, Boston (R., 1900); The Country Club, Brookline (A.3, 1895).

Warren David Cantrell (1905 - 1967)
Born: Hillsboro, Texas. Died: Irving, Texas at age 61.
Warren Cantrell attended Armour Institute of Technology in Chicago and Texas A & M, earning degrees in engineering and architecture. Following graduation he formed a contracting business in Texas. It evolved into a large operation, headed by his brother, which handled such major projects as the roof for the Houston Astrodome.

Cantrell himself left the firm in 1940 because of ill health. A fine golfer, he turned professional and became a club pro in Lubbock, Texas. He soon became involved in local and sectional PGA activities and was eventually elected treasurer and later president (1964 - 1965) of the PGA of America. He also served as the golf coach at Texas Tech University from 1953 to 1958.

Cantrell designed his first course after World War II and by the 1950s was busy planning on a part-time basis throughout West Texas and New Mexico. He designed some thirty courses in his career. His son William, a Texas Tech graduate, finished several Cantrell designs after Warren's death, and later tried his hand at some designs of his own in Texas.

Courses by: Warren Cantrell

New Mexico: Colonial Park CC, Clovis (9); Farmington CC (9); Lovington Muni (9, 1954); Ocotillo Park GC, Hobbs (9, 1955); Zuni Mountain GC, Grants (9, 1961).

Texas: Andrews County GC (1955); Big Springs CC (1960); Caprock G&CC, Lubbock; Farwell CC (9); Lake Oaks CC (Course No. 1), Waco (1960); Lake Oaks CC (Course No. 2), Waco (1960); Old Elm GC, Abilene; Robstown CC (1960); San Angelo CC; Tascosa GC, Amarillo; Treasure Island GC, Lubbock (1964).

Courses Remodeled & Added to by: Warren Cantrell

New Mexico: Albuquerque CC (R., 1959); Hobbs CC (R.9, 1957); Hobbs CC (A.9, 1957).

Texas: Amarillo CC (R., 1960); Lubbock CC (R.9); Lubbock CC (A.9); Meadowbrook Muni, Ft. Worth (R.27, 1955).

Thomas E. Clark (1948 -) ASGCA
Born: Pennsylvania.

Tom Clark attended Penn State University, receiving a B.S. degree in Landscape Architecture in 1971. He joined the Maryland-based firm of Edmund B. Ault, Ltd. that same year. Over the next dozen years Clark had primary responsibility on over fifty design projects along the Eastern Seaboard, Southeast and Midwest.

In 1984 Clark became a full partner with Edmund and Brian Ault in the reorganized company called Ault, Clark and Associates.

Courses by: Tom Clark

Arkansas: Balboa GC, Hot Springs Village (1987), with Edmund B. Ault; Branchwood GC, Bella Vista (Par 3, 9, 1983), with Edmund B. Ault; Coronado GC, Hot Springs Village (Precision, 1983), with Edmund B. Ault; Metfield GC, Bella Vista (Precision, 1983), with Edmund B. Ault; Mountain Ranch GC, Fairfield Bay (1984), with Brian Ault and Edmund B. Ault; Scotsdale GC, Bella Vista (1987), with Edmund B. Ault.

Georgia: Statham's Landing GC (1987), with Bill Love.

Iowa: Sundown GC, Burlington (Par 3, 9, 1978), with Brian Ault and Edmund B. Ault.

Maryland: Heritage Harbour GC (9, 1982), with Brian Ault and Edmund B. Ault; TPC at Avenel, Potomac (1986), with Edmund B. Ault, Brian Ault and Bill Love.

Missouri: Paradise Pointe GC, Smithville (1983), with Brian Ault; Pointe Royale G&CC (1986), with Edmund B. Ault; Poplar Bluff Muni (1980), with Brian Ault and Edmund B. Ault.

New Jersey: Quail Brook Park GC (1982), with Brian Ault and Edmund B. Ault.

Pennsylvania: Mountain View GC (1987), with Edmund B. Ault and Brian Ault.

Tennessee: Toqua GC (1987), with Edmund B. Ault.

Virginia: Broad Bay Point G&CC, Virginia Beach (1986), with Edmund B. Ault; Cypress Point, Virginia Beach (1986), with Edmund B. Ault; Hollows GC (1984), with Brian Ault; Summit GC (9, 1987), with Edmund B. Ault.

West Virginia: Lakeview Inn & CC (North Course), Morgantown (1984), with Brian Ault.

Courses Remodeled & Added to by: Tom Clark

Arizona: Arizona CC, Phoenix (R., 1986), with Bill Love.

Arkansas: CC of Little Rock (R., 1980).

Connecticut: Rolling Hills CC, Wilton (R.5, 1984), with Brian Ault.

Kansas: Mission Hills CC, Fairway (R.7, 1984).

Louisiana: Eden Isles CC, Slidell (R.1, 1983).

Maryland: Congressional CC (Blue Course), Bethesda (R.2, 1981), with Edmund B. Ault and Bill Love; Swan Creek CC, Belair (R.9, 1978).

Massachusetts: Pleasant Valley CC, Sutton (R.3, 1984), with Brian Ault.

Mississippi: CC of Jackson (R.9, 1979); Gulf Hills GC (R., 1985).

Nevada: Tropicana CC, Las Vegas (R., 1984), with Brian Ault.

New Jersey: Greenacres CC, Lawrence (R.2, 1983), with Brian Ault and Bill Love.

North Carolina: Duck Woods GC, Kitty Hawk (R.7, 1986), with Brian Ault; Paradise Point GC (Gold Course), Camp LeJeune (R.7, 1979), with Brian Ault.

Oklahoma: Walnut Creek CC, Oklahoma City (R.9, 1983).

Pennsylvania: Tyoga CC (A.9, 1979).

Virginia: Army-Navy CC (Arlington Course), Arlington (R.5, 1986), with Edmund B. Ault and Bill Love; Cedar Point C, Norfolk (R., 1986); Kingsmill GC (River Course), Williamsburg (R.5, 1982), with Brian Ault and Edmund B. Ault; Roanoke CC (R.5, 1985); Sewells Point GC (R., 1986).

Percy Clifford (1907 - 1984) ASGCA
Born: Mexico City, Mexico. Died: Chicago, Illinois at age 77.

Percy Clifford, the son of British citizens, was born and reared in Mexico City but attended college in England. Clifford was an outstanding amateur golfer, winning six Mexican Amateur and three Mexico Open titles. His first experience in course design came in the late 1940s when he assisted golf architect Lawrence Hughes in planning Club de Golf de Mexico. Envisioning a top-flight course, Clifford did much to organize the club and spent months personally selecting the site and reviewing the plans. After that experience, Clifford felt confident that he could handle design projects on his own.

By 1980 Clifford had designed nearly half of Mexico's golf courses. His layouts, comparable to some of the best in Britain and America, contributed significantly to the advance of golf in his native country. Most were done on relatively modest budgets, for throughout his career Percy deplored the extravagance in both construction and maintenance of North American courses.

Clifford's daughter Sandra Fullmer was a former Women's Amateur Champion of Mexico, Spain and Germany. His son-in-law Paul Fullmer served as the first Executive Secretary of the ASGCA.

The first Mexican citizen admitted to the ASGCA, Clifford was granted Fellow status in that Society in 1977. He spent his last years in retirement at Rancho Santa Fe, Calif. where he routinely shot his age. In late 1984, Percy Clifford succumbed to cancer.

Courses by: Percy Clifford

Colombia: Club de G Baru (1973).

Mexico: Bahia de Banderas (1974); Bajamar GC (1974); Campestre de Lagunero (1957); Centro Deportivo GC, Acapulco (9, 1947); Chihuahua CC (1956); Club de G de Mexico (1949), with Lawrence Hughes; Club de G Avandara (1950); Club de G Bellavista, Mexico City (1955); Club de G Bugambillian, Guadalajera (1964); Club de G Cerro Alto (9, 1963); Club de G Dos Mares, Ensenada (1962); Club de G Erandeni (1975); Club de G Hacienda, Mexico City (1956); Club de G La Canada, Mexico City (36, 1972); Club de G La Villa Rica, Vera Cruz (9, 1971); Club de G Laguna (36, 1969); Club de G Monte Castillo (1963); Club de G Morelia (9, 1960); Club de G Obregon, Sonora (1953); Club de G Piramides (36, 1966); Club de G Ranchitos, Morales (1967); Club de G Rio Seco, Valles (9, 1961); Club de G San Carlos, Toluca (1968); Club de G San Gasper; Club de G San Luis (1958); Club de G Tabashines, Morales (1973); Club de G Vallescondido, Mexico City (1974); Club Campestre de Queretaro (9, 1951); Club Campestre Agunero (1951); Club Campestre Torreon (1974); Del Bosque CC (9); Del Lago GC (1970); El Bosque CC (1960); Las Huertas CC (1965); Los Flamingos CC, Puerto Vallarta (1975); Pierre Marques GC, Acapulco (27, 1969); Queretaro CC (1955); Torreon GC.

Courses Remodeled & Added to by: Percy Clifford

Mexico: Acapulco CC (R.9); Acapulco CC (A.9); Chapultepec CC (R., 1972).

Lloyd Clifton
Course superintendent at a series of Florida clubs during the 1950s and 1960s, Lloyd Clifton served as President of the Florida Turfgrass Association in 1954. In the mid-sixties Clifton began designing and building golf courses. His work, all of it done in Florida, continued well into the 1980s.

Courses by: Lloyd Clifton

Florida: Cypress Creek CC, Orlando (1970); Highland Lakes GC, Palm Harbor (Precision, 27, 1980); Hunter's Creek CC, Kissimmee (1986); Indigo Lakes CC, Daytona Beach (1976); Plantation Bay GC (1986); Rosemont G&CC, Winter Park (1973); Silver Pines GC (NLE, Precision, 9, 1980); Sweetwater Oaks CC, Longwood (1976); West Orange GC (1967); Willow Lakes G&CC (Troon Course), Jacksonville (1974); Winter Pines GC, Winter Park.

Courses Remodeled & Added to by: Lloyd Clifton

Florida: Casselberry G&CC (R.9, 1973); Casselberry G&CC (A.9, 1973); Deer Run CC (R., 1982); Dubsdread GC, Orlando (R.); Ocean Palm CC, Flagler Beach (R., 1974); Riviera CC, Ormand Beach (R.); Sherwood G&CC, Titusville (A.9, 1985).

Paul N. Coates Jr.
For over thirty years, Ramsey (Minn.) county engineer Paul Coates maintained a part-time golf design practice laying out public layouts in Minnesota and neighboring states.

Courses by: Paul Coates

Minnesota: Bloomington CC; Cedarholm Muni (9); Gem Lake GC (9, 1955); Hastings CC; Hyland Greens CC; Keller GC, St. Paul (1929); Mendota Heights GC (1929); Northfield GC; Stillwater CC (1957).

Courses Remodeled & Added to by: Paul Coates

Iowa: Waveland GC, Des Moines (R., 1937).

Minnesota: Midland Hills CC, St. Paul (R.).

George W. Cobb (1914 - 1986) ASGCA
Born: Savannah, Georgia. Died: Greenville, South Carolina at age 71.

George Cobb attended the University of Georgia, graduating in 1937 with a degree in Landscape Architecture. He was employed by the National Park Service as a landscape architect until 1941, when he entered the U.S. Marine Corps as an engineering officer.

The Marine Corps recognized in Cobb, a landscape architect and scratch golfer, the makings of a golf course architect. So he was assigned to design and build a golf course for Camp LeJeune, North Carolina. Unsure of his abilities, Cobb asked and got permission to retain Fred Findlay as course architect, for, as he later put it, "I didn't want to be court-martialed if it turned out bad." Cobb acted as construction superintendent on this and a second layout built by Findlay at Camp LeJeune.

Cobb's first solo project was at the Cherry Point (N.C.) Marine Corps Air Station in 1946. He entered private practice as a golf architect in 1947 but was recalled to active duty in 1951. Following his second tour in the Marines, Cobb reentered private practice as a golf architect and land planner, opening an office in Greenville, S.C. in 1956. In the 1950s and 1960s he has served as design consultant to Augusta National GC, and developed a close friendship with Bobby Jones. When the club decided to install a nine-hole par 3 course, Cobb was asked to design it. When Jones authored an autobiography (*Golf is My Game*) in 1959, Cobb drafted the attractive hole-by-hole diagrams of Augusta National used as illustrations.

Though several of his designs were used as professional tournament sites, Cobb prided himself in providing attractive, playable layouts that resort players found enjoyable, not frustrating.

Courses by: George W. Cobb

Alabama: Burningtree CC, Decatur (1966); Fort McClellan GC (9, 1971); Goosepond Colony GC, Scottsboro (1971); Inverness CC, Birmingham (1973); Pine Tree CC, Birmingham (1969); Still Waters CC, Dadeville (1972).

Florida: Deerwood CC, Jacksonville (1961); Gainesville G&CC (1963).

Georgia: Augusta National GC, Augusta (Par 3, 9, 1960), with Robert Tyre "Bobby" Jones Jr; Brookfield West G&CC, Atlanta (1972); Browns Mill GC, Atlanta (1970); Doublegate Plantation CC, Albany (1964); Forest Heights CC, Statesboro (1966); Green Island CC, Columbus (1960); Lakeside CC, Atlanta (1960); Mary Calder GC, Savannah (9, 1967); Milledgeville CC (1961); Sea Palms G&CC, St. Simons Island (18, 1967); Waynesboro CC (9, 1963); Windsor Forest CC, Savannah (9, 1962).

Maryland: Fort Eustis GC (1956); Fort Meade GC (Parks Course) (1956); Laurel

CC (1957); Laurel Pines CC; Prospect Hill CC, Bowie (1956); University of Maryland GC, College Park (1956).

New York: Eisenhower College GC, Seneca (Precision, 9, 1972).

North Carolina: Bald Head Island CC (1972); Bryan Park GC (Course No.1), Greensboro (1973), with John LaFoy; Cabarrus CC, Concord (1966); Carmel CC (North Course), Charlotte (1950); Cherry Point GC (1946); Cleghorn Plantation G&CC, Rutherfordton (1972); Connestee Falls CC, Brevard (1972); Croasdaile CC, Durham (1965); CC of Sapphire (1958); Finley GC, Univ of N Carolina (1951); Green Valley GC, Greensboro (1947); High Meadows GC, Roaring Gap (1964); Hound Ear CC, Blowing Rock (1963); Jacksonville CC (1951); Linville Ridge CC, Linville (1983), with John LaFoy; Mountain Glen GC, Newland (1963); Mountain Valley GC, Waynesville (Par 3, 9, 1961); North Hills CC, Raleigh (1967); Oak Island CC, Southport (1962); Paradise Point GC (Gold Course), Camp LeJeune (1945); Pope AFB GC, Fayetteville (9, 1970); Quail Hollow CC, Charlotte (1961); Raleigh Golf Assoc GC (9, 1958); Rolling Hills CC, Monroe (1964); Wildcat Cliffs CC, Highlands (1962); Willow Haven CC, Durham (1958).

Ohio: Sharon C, Sharon Center (1965).

South Carolina: Adventure Inn GC, Hilton Head Island (NLE, 9, 1965); Berkeley CC, Moncks Corner (1961); Botany Woods GC, Greenville (Par 3, 9, 1963); Cat Island CC, Fripp Island (1985), with Byron Comstock; Charleston AFB GC (9, 1966); Clemson University GC (1976), with John LaFoy; Cobb's Glen CC, Anderson (1975), with John LaFoy; Fort Jackson GC, Columbia (1949); Fripp Island CC (1964); Green Valley CC, Greenville (1958); Greenwood CC (9, 1950); Holly Tree CC, Greenville (1973), with John LaFoy; J.C. Long Estate GC, Mt. Pleasant (9, 1957); Keowee Key CC, Seneca (1977), with John LaFoy; Myrtlewood GC (Pines Course), Myrtle Beach (1966); Port Royal GC (Barony Course), Hilton Head Island (1964); Port Royal GC (Robbers Row Course), Hilton Head Island (9, 1965); Santee-Cooper CC (1968); Sea Pines Plantation GC (Ocean Course), Hilton Head Island (1967); Sea Pines Plantation GC (Sea Marsh Crs), Hilton Head Island (1961); Shipyard GC (Clipper and Galleon Nines), Hilton Head Island (1970); Snee Farm CC, Charleston (1970); Spanish Wells CC, Hilton Head Island (9, 1970); Spring Valley CC, Columbia (1961); Star Fort National GC, Ninety-Six (1969); Surf GC, Myrtle Beach (1960); Woodlands CC (1975), with John LaFoy.

Tennessee: Clarksville CC (1966); Frank G Clement GC, Dickson; Stonebridge GC, Memphis (1974); Warriors Path State Park GC, Kingsport (1970).

Virginia: New Quarter Park GC (1977), with John LaFoy; Pohick Bay GC (1978), with John LaFoy; Red Wing Lake GC, Virginia Beach (1971); Tides Inn & CC (Golden Eagle Course), Irvington (1976), with John LaFoy.

West Virginia: CC of Charleston (1969); Glade Springs CC, Beckley (1973); Mountwood Park GC (1977), with John LaFoy.

Bahamas: Andros Island CC (NLE, 9, 1965).

Courses Remodeled & Added to by: George W. Cobb

Alabama: CC of Birmingham (East Course) (R., 1964); Green Valley CC, Birmingham (A.9, 1963); Green Valley CC, Birmingham (R.9, 1963); Mountain Brook C, Birmingham (R., 1968); Vestavia CC (R., 1962).

Florida: Beauclerc CC, Jacksonville (A.9, 1961); Indian Lakes CC (R.9, 1974); Indian Lakes CC (A.9, 1974); Timuquana CC, Jacksonville (R., 1963).

Georgia: Athens CC (A.9, 1985), with John LaFoy; Augusta National GC, Augusta (R., 1967); Capital City C (R., 1962); Coosa CC (R., 1973); Dublin CC (R.9); Dublin CC (A.9); East Lake CC, Atlanta (R., 1960); Fort McPherson GC (R., 1965); Savannah GC (R., 1963); Waynesboro CC (A.9, 1984), with John LaFoy.

Maryland: Aviation Y&CC (R., 1967).

Minnesota: Somerset CC, St. Paul (R., 1976), with John LaFoy.

North Carolina: Chapel Hill CC (R., 1957); Greensboro CC (Irving Park Course) (R., 1968); High Hampton Inn GC (R., 1958); Hillandale CC, Durham (R., 1957); Pope AFB GC, Fayetteville (A.9, 1975), with John LaFoy; Rolling Hills CC, Monroe (A., 1967), with John LaFoy; Starmount Forest CC, Greensboro (R., 1972).

South Carolina: CC of Spartanburg (R.9, 1959); CC of Spartanburg (A.9, 1959); Fripp Island CC (R., 1976), with John LaFoy; Greenville CC (Riverside Course) (R., 1960); Greenwood CC (A.9, 1958); Port Royal GC (Robbers Row Course), Hilton Head Island (A.9, 1974), with John LaFoy; Springs Mill CC, Fort Mill (A.9, 1960).

Virginia: Army-Navy CC (Fairfax Course), Fairfax (R., 1959); Belle Haven CC, Alexandria (R., 1959); Tides Inn & CC (Tartan Course), Irvington (A.9, 1968).

West Virginia: Rainelle CC (R., 1976), with John LaFoy; Twin Falls State Park GC, Mullens (A.9, 1981), with John LaFoy.

John N. Cochran (1913 - 1985)

Born: Mississippi. Died: Denver, Colorado at age 72.

John Cochran received his undergraduate degree in engineering and did graduate study on turfgrasses at Abraham Baldwin College in Georgia and Penn State University. He turned professional in 1937 and played the Tour for ten years, winning the 1939 Mississippi Open and 1940 Southeastern PGA. He also laid out his first course around that time, though it was over twenty years before he did another. Cochran was a club pro in Georgia and Mississippi until 1957, when he became professional at Columbine CC near Denver, Colo. and later at Denver CC.

In 1962 Cochran resigned to found Golf Club Operations Inc., a turnkey organization that designed, built and operated country clubs. Press Maxwell served as the firm's golf architect and Cochran worked with him on the design and construction of Hiwan GC and Boulder CC. When Maxwell resigned in the late 1960s, Cochran continued the business by taking on the full responsibilities of golf course architect.

In the last years of his life, Cochran worked on building what he considered his best design, Fox Acres CC. Cochran died of a heart attack at his home in Denver.

Courses by: John Cochran

Colorado: Dos Rios CC, Gunnison (9, 1966); Fox Acres CC, Red Feather Lake (1983).

Iowa: Crow Valley CC, Bettendorf (1970).

Courses Remodeled & Added to by: John Cochran

Colorado: City Park GC, Pueblo (R., 1966); CC of Fort Collins (R.); Denver CC (R.3, 1966); Snowmass GC, Snowmass-at-Aspen (A.9, 1973).

Louisiana: Bayou De Siard CC, Monroe (R., 1973).

Milton Coggins (1902 -) ASGCA

Born: Arizona.

Milt Coggins studied economics at the University of Redlands in California, receiving a B.A. degree in 1926. Having played basketball, baseball, tennis and golf, he sought a sports-oriented profession. He operated a sporting goods store in the 1930s, then played professional tennis for eleven years, and in 1950 became sports director at Camelback Inn in Phoenix. Coggins then served as golf professional at Encanto Municipal GC where he remained until 1961. While at Encanto, he designed his first course in 1956. After 1961, Coggins practiced golf architecture on a full-time basis until his retirement in the mid-1970s.

Courses by: Milt Coggins

Arizona: Camelot CC, Mesa (1967); Christown G&CC, Phoenix (9, 1962); Fort Huachuca GC (9, 1970); Glen Lakes GC, Glendale (9, 1968); Kingman GC (9, 1973); Lakes West GC, Sun City (1968), with James Winans, John W. Meeker and Jeff Hardin; Overgaard GC (9, 1970); Paradise Valley Park GC, Phoenix (NLE, 9, 1972); Pinetop CC (1961); Pinetop Lakes G&CC (1973); Prescott CC (1972); Rio Verde CC (Quail Run Course), Scottsdale (9, 1973), with Fred Bolton; Rio Verde CC (White Wing Course) (9, 1973), with Fred Bolton; Rolling Hills GC, Tempe (NLE, Precision, 1961); Sun City CC, with Jeff Hardin and Greg Nash; Sun City Lakes West GC (1968), with James Winans; Sun City North GC (1960); Sun City South GC (1962); Sunland Village GC, Mesa (1975), with Jeff Hardin and Greg Nash; Villa Monterey CC, Scottsdale (NLE, 9, 1965).

California: Cherry Hills GC, Sun City (1963).

Colorado: Ranch at Roaring Fork GC, Carbondale (Precision, 9, 1973).

Florida: Sun City Center G&CC (North Course) (9, 1961).

New Mexico: Alto Lakes G&CC (9, 1968).

Texas: Clear Lake CC (Routing), Houston (1963).

Courses Remodeled & Added to by: Milt Coggins

Arizona: Apache Wells CC, Mesa (A.9, 1966); Camelot CC, Mesa (A.9, 1974); Coronado GC, Scottsdale (A.9, 1976); Fort Huachuca GC (A.9, 1971), with Gary Panks.

Neil Coles (1934 -)

Born: London, England.

Neil Coles turned professional in 1950 and played successfully on the British and European tours for over twenty years. A three-time British PGA Match Play champion, Coles was a member of eight Ryder Cup teams.

In the late 1970s Coles teamed with fellow touring pros Brian Huggett and Roger Dyers in a golf design partnership.

Courses by: Neil Coles

England: Hickleton GC, Yorkshire , with Brian Huggett and Roger Dyer; Tilgate Forest GC, Crawley (1982), with Brian Huggett and Roger Dyer.

Scotland: Hazelhead Muni (Course No. 2), Aberdeen (1975), with Brian Huggett.

Courses Remodeled & Added to by: Neil Coles

England: West Wiltshire GC (R., 1972), with Brian Huggett and Roger Dyer.

Harry J. Collis (1877 - 1938)

Born: England. Died: Flossmoor, Illinois at age 60.

Harry Collis emigrated to America in the late 1890s and became greenkeeper at Indianapolis CC. In 1906 he moved to the Chicago area to work as pro-greenkeeper for Flossmoor CC. While at Flossmoor, Collis remodeled the course into a popular tournament site, developed a turf cutter that was eventually patented and created a strain of bentgrass named after the club.

The remodeling at Flossmoor led to other course design jobs, and after World War I Collis worked steadily on a part-time basis planning courses all across the United States. On occasion he collaborated with his friend Jack Daray, professional at nearby Olympia Fields CC. Collis also operated the Flossmoor Turf Nurseries of Chicago, specializing in Flossmoor bentgrass.

In the late 1920s Collis resigned from Flossmoor to pursue his own activities full time. But the Depression intervened, and he was never able to develop a prosperous business. He struggled through the 1930s to maintain his turf farm and other Chicago-area properties before ultimately losing them to bankers and tax men. Flossmoor CC then offered Collis the position of greenkeeper but he died in 1938 just before his scheduled return to the club.

Courses by: Harry Collis

Arizona: La Palma CC (NLE, 1919); Phoenix CC (1919); San Marcos Hotel & C, Chandler (1922).

Florida: Homosassa CC (NLE,).

Illinois: Cherry Hills CC, Flossmoor (1932), with Jack Daray; Dundee CC, with Jack Croke; Freeport CC; Glenwoodie GC, Chicago Heights (1923), with Jack Daray; Harlem Hills CC, Rockford; Indian Wood G&CC, Matteson; Laramie CC, Chicago (NLE,); Navajo Fields CC, Worth (NLE,); Normandy CC, Flossmoor; Park Forest GC; Pistakee Hills CC, McHenry; Richton Park GC.

Indiana: Longwood CC, Dyer.

Iowa: Newton CC (9).

Maryland: Manor CC, Rockville (1923).

Michigan: Chickaming GC; Walled Lake CC (NLE,).

Mississippi: Rainbow Bay GC {formerly Edgewater GC}, Biloxi , with Jack Daray.

Courses Remodeled & Added to by: Harry Collis

Illinois: Flossmoor CC (R.); Medinah CC (Course No. 3) (A.5, 1932); Medinah CC (Course No. 3) (R., 1932).

Michigan: Meadowbrook CC, Detroit (A.12, 1921), with Jack Daray; Meadowbrook CC, Detroit (R.6, 1921), with Jack Daray.

Wisconsin: Rhinelander CC (A.9).

Harry Shapland Colt (1869 - 1951)

Born: St. Amands, England. Died: St. Amands, England at age 82.

H.S. Colt studied law at Cambridge University where he became captain of the golf team. After admission to the bar, Colt practiced for several years as a solicitor in Hastings. But his first love was golf. He was a member of the Royal and Ancient Golf Club of St. Andrews and won the Jubilee Vase on the Old Course in 1891 and 1893.

In 1894 he assisted golf professional Douglas Rolland in the design of a new course for Rye GC. He served from 1901 to 1913 as the first club Secretary for the newly opened Sunningdale GC.

Colt was a fine golfer all his life. He was a semi-finalist in the 1906 British Amateur and played for the English team against the Scottish two years later. His skills and previous design experience led to an invitation to lay out a course near London in the early 1900s. Other contracts soon followed, and Colt ultimately abandoned the practice of law for the practice of course architecture. By World War I he had established himself as one of the world's leading designers.

Colt trained a number of men who later developed into first rate golf architects themselves, including C.H. Alison (his partner for over twenty years), Alister Mackenzie (a partner for a short time), J.S.F. Morrison (who worked with him during the last thirty years of his career) and John Harris (son of Charles Harris, one of his construction supervisors).

Several firsts in golf course design are generally attributed to H.S. Colt. He was the first designer not to have been a professional golfer. He was the first to consistently use a drawing board in preparing his course designs. He was the first to prepare tree-planting plans for his layouts.

H.S. Colt outlined his philosophy of architecture in *Golf Course Architecture*, which he co-authored with Alison in 1920. He also contributed to *The Book of the Links* edited by Martin H.F. Sutton (1919) and *Golf Courses: Design, Construction and Upkeep*, edited by Martin A.F. Sutton (1933).

Courses by: H.S. Colt
  Georgia: Sea Island GC (Seaside 9), St. Simons Island (1928), with C.H. Alison.
  Illinois: Briarwood CC {formerly Briergate CC}, Deerfield (1921), with C.H. Alison; Knollwood C, Lake Forest (1923), with C.H. Alison; North Shore CC, Glenview (1924), with C.H. Alison; Old Elm C, Fort Sheridan (1913), with Donald Ross.
  Iowa: Davenport CC (1924), with C.H. Alison.
  Maryland: Burning Tree C, Bethesda (1924), with C.H. Alison.
  Michigan: CC of Detroit, Grosse Pointe Farms (1914); Orchard Lake CC (1926), with C.H. Alison.
  New Jersey: Canoe Brook CC (North Course), Millburn (NLE, 1924), with C.H. Alison; Pine Valley GC, Clementon (1919), with George Crump.
  New York: Century GC, White Plains (1926), with C.H. Alison; Colony CC, Algonac (1923), with C.H. Alison; Fresh Meadow CC {formerly Lakeville CC}, Great Neck (1925), with C.H. Alison; Old Oaks CC, Purchase (1927), with C.H. Alison; Park CC, Buffalo (1928), with C.H. Alison; Timber Point GC, Great River (1927), with C.H. Alison.
  Ohio: Kirtland CC, Willoughby (1921), with C.H. Alison; Westwood CC, Rocky River (1924), with C.H. Alison.
  Wisconsin: Milwaukee CC (1929), with C.H. Alison.
  Manitoba: Pine Ridge G&CC (NLE,).
  Ontario: Hamilton G&CC, Ancaster (1914); Hamilton G&CC (Ladies 9), Ancaster (1915); St. George's G&CC, Islington (NLE, 1920); Toronto GC (1912); York Downs CC, Toronto (NLE, 1921), with C.H. Alison.
  Belgium: Royal Waterloo GC (NLE, 36, 1923), with C.H. Alison.
  England: Alwoodley GC, Leeds (1907), with Alister Mackenzie; Barton-on-Sea GC; Beaconsfield GC (1914); Blackmoor GC (1913); Brancepeth Castle GC, Durham (1924), with C.H. Alison and Alister Mackenzie; Brockenhurst Manor GC (1919); Calcot Park GC (1930); Camberley Heath GC, Surrey (1913); Copt Heath GC, Warwickshire (1910); Cuddington GC (1929), with J.S.F. Morrison and C.H. Alison; Denham GC (1910); Edgbaston GC, Warwickshire (1909); Effingham GC (1927), with C.H. Alison; Ham Manor GC, Sussex (1936), with C.H. Alison and J.S.F. Morrison; Hopewood GC; Isle of Purbeck GC (Purbeck Course), Dorset; Kingsthorpe GC (1908); Leamington and County GC (1908); Leckford GC (9, 1929), with J.S.F. Morrison and C.H. Alison; Lilleshall Hall GC (1935), with J.S.F. Morrison; Manchester GC, Lancashire; Moor Park GC (High Course), Hertfordshire (1911); Moor Park GC (West Course), Hertfordshire (1923), with C.H. Alison and Alister Mackenzie; Newquay GC; Northamptonshire County GC (1909); Prestbury GC (1920), with J.S.F. Morrison; Rowlands Castle GC (1902); Royal Wimbledon GC, Surrey (1908); Rye GC, Deal (1894), with Douglas Rolland; Sandy Lodge GC (1910), with Harry Vardon; Southfield GC; St. George's Hill GC, Surrey (36, 1913); Stoke Poges GC (1908); Sunningdale GC (New Course), Berkshire (1922), with C.H. Alison; Swinley Forest GC (1910); Tandridge GC (1925); Teignmouth GC (1924), with C.H. Alison and Alister Mackenzie; Trevose G&CC (27, 1926), with C.H. Alison and J.S.F. Morrison; Tyneside GC; Wentworth GC (East Course), Surrey (1924), with C.H. Alison and J.S.F. Morrison; Wentworth GC (West Course), Surrey (1924), with C.H. Alison and J.S.F. Morrison; Worthing GC (Lower Course) (1906); Worthing GC (Upper Course) (1906).
  France: Golf Club de St. Cloud (Green Course) (1913); Golf Club de St. Cloud (Yellow Course) (1946), with J.S.F. Morrison; Golf Club de Touquet (Forest Course) (1908); Golf Club de Touquet (Sea Course) (1930), with J.S.F. Morrison and C.H. Alison.
  Ireland: County Sligo GC (1922), with C.H. Alison and Alister Mackenzie; Dun Laoghaire GC, Dublin (1910).
  Netherlands: Eindhoven GC (1930), with C.H. Alison and J.S.F. Morrison; Haagsche G&CC (1939), with C.H. Alison and J.S.F. Morrison; Kennemer G&CC (1929), with C.H. Alison and J.S.F. Morrison; Utrecht GC (1929), with C.H. Alison and J.S.F. Morrison.
  Northern Ireland: Royal Belfast GC.
  Scotland: Longniddry GC (1921), with C.H. Alison; St. Andrews (Eden Course), Fife (1913), with Alister Mackenzie.
  Spain: Real C de la Puerto de Hierro (Old), Madrid (1932), with J.S.F. Morrison and C.H. Alison; Real G de Pedrena (1928), with J.S.F. Morrison and C.H. Alison.
  Sweden: Stockholm GC (1932), with C.H. Alison and J.S.F. Morrison.
  Trinidad and Tobago: St. Andrews GC, Moka (NLE, 1940), with J.S.F. Morrison.
  Wales: Clyne GC (1920), with C.H. Alison; Pyle and Kenfig GC (1922), with C.H. Alison; St. Mellons GC (1937), with J.S.F. Morrison and Henry Cotton.
  West Germany: Falkenstein GC (1930), with C.H. Alison and J.S.F. Morrison; Frankfurter GC (1928), with C.H. Alison and J.S.F. Morrison; Hamburger Land und GC (1935), with C.H. Alison and J.S.F. Morrison.

Courses Remodeled & Added to by: H.S. Colt
  California: Mosely GC (R., 1913).
  Georgia: Sea Island GC (Plantation 9), St. Simons Island (R., 1928), with C.H. Alison.
  Illinois: Bob O'Link CC, Highland Park (R., 1924), with C.H. Alison.
  Maryland: Chevy Chase CC (R., 1924), with C.H. Alison.
  Michigan: CC of Detroit, Grosse Pointe Farms (R., 1927), with C.H. Alison; Lochmoor C, Grosse Pointe Woods (R., 1920), with C.H. Alison.
  Pennsylvania: Baederwood GC (R., 1927), with C.H. Alison.
  Quebec: Royal Montreal GC (South Course), Dixie (R., 1913).
  England: Abercrombie CC (R.); Broadstone GC, Dorset (A.8); Broadstone GC, Dorset (R., 1920); Burhill GC, Surrey (A.9, 1913); Churston GC (R., 1918); Formby GC (R., 1937); Ganton GC (R., 1930); Handsworth GC (R.); Harborne GC (R.); Hendon GC, Middlesex (R., 1926); Little Aston GC, Staffordshire (R., 1925); Moseley GC, Worcestershire (R., 1918); Northumberland GC (R., 1924), with C.H. Alison and Alister Mackenzie; Robin Hood GC (R., 1930); Royal Liverpool GC, Hoylake (R., 1920); Royal Lytham & St. Annes GC, Lancashire (R., 1930), with C.H. Alison; Royal Lytham & St. Annes GC, Lancashire (R., 1936), with J.S.F. Morrison and J.S.F. Morrison; Royal Worlington and Newmarket GC, Suffolk (R.9, 1906); Sandiway GC, Cheshire (R., 1938); Sunningdale GC (Old Course), Berkshire (R., 1922), with C.H. Alison; Ulverston GC, Cumbria (R., 1910); Woodhall Spa GC, Lincolnshire (R., 1912); Worplesdon GC, Surrey (R., 1932).
  France: Golf de Biarritz (R.).
  Ireland: Castle GC, Dublin (R., 1918); Rosapenna GC, County Donegal (R., 1916); Royal Dublin GC (R., 1921), with C.H. Alison.
  Malaysia: Royal Selangor GC (Old Course) (R., 1931), with C.H. Alison.
  Northern Ireland: Belvoir Park GC, Belfast (R., 1927), with C.H. Alison; Royal Portrush GC (Dunluce Course) (R., 1933); Royal Portrush GC (Dunluce Course) (R., 1946), with J.S.F. Morrison; Royal Portrush GC (Valley Course) (R., 1933); Royal Portrush GC (Valley Course) (R., 1946), with J.S.F. Morrison.
  Scotland: Muirfield GC, East Lothian (R., 1925), with C.H. Alison.
  Wales: Aberdovey GC, Merioneth (R.); Borth and Ynyslas GC (R.); Royal Porthcawl GC, Mid Glamorgan (R., 1913); Southerndown GC, Glamorgan (R., 1919).

William Connellan
  William Connellan, a former construction foreman for architect Donald Ross, was associated with Wilfrid Reid in the golf design firm of Reid and Connellan during the Twenties and Thirties.
Courses by: William Connellan
  Michigan: Bald Mountain GC, Detroit , with Wilfrid Reid; Bob O'Link CC, Novi , with Wilfrid Reid; Brae Burn GC, Plymouth , with Wilfrid Reid; Harsens Island GC, with Wilfrid Reid; Indian River GC (9), with Wilfrid Reid; Indianwood G&CC (Old Course), Lake Orion (1928), with Wilfrid Reid; Plum Hollow G&CC, Southfield , with Wilfrid Reid; Port Huron CC, with Wilfrid Reid; Tam O'Shanter CC, Orchard Lake , with Wilfrid Reid.
Courses Remodeled & Added to by: William Connellan
  Michigan: Birmingham CC (R., 1928), with Wilfrid Reid; Black River CC (A.9), with Wilfrid Reid; Grosse Ile G&CC (R.), with Wilfrid Reid; Orchard Lake CC (R., 1928), with Wilfrid Reid.

Graham Cooke (1949 -   )
Born: Toronto, Ontario, Canada.
  Graham Cooke attended Michigan State University, receiving a degree in Landscape Architecture in 1971. Returning to Canada, he trained under Quebec golf architect Howard Watson for the next six years.
  Cooke entered private practice in the late 1970s and by 1980 had completed the 36 hole Dorval Muni as well as numerous alterations to existing courses. A fine competitive golfer, he was runner-up in the 1979 Canadian Amateur Championship.

William Coore (1946 -   )
Born: North Carolina.
  Bill Coore grew up in the Pinehurst area of North Carolina and played for Wake Forest University, which he attended on an academic, not an athletic, scholarship. After graduating in 1968 he decided to pursue a career in golf design, so he worked on construction crews of several Pete Dye projects in the Southeast.
  In the mid Seventies Coore helped build Waterwood National GC in Texas (a Roy Dye design) and then worked as assistant to its course superintendent Gary Grandstaff. When Grandstaff joined Dye on a Mexican project, Coore took over as superintendent, and over the next several years rebuilt and modified most holes at Waterwood. In the early 1980s Bill Coore spent two years designing and building his first solo layout. The result, Rockport (Texas) CC, so impressed popular PGA Tour golfer (and avid course design historian) Ben Crenshaw that Crenshaw asked Coore to join him in a golf design partnership.
Courses by: Bill Coore
  Texas: Kings Crossing G&CC, Corpus Christi (1986); Rockport CC (1985).
Courses Remodeled & Added to by: Bill Coore
  Texas: Waterwood National GC, Huntsville (R., 1981).

Geoffrey St. John Cornish (1914 -   ) ASGCA, President, 1975; BAGCA (Honorary Member).
Born: Winnipeg, Manitoba, Canada.
  Geoffrey S. Cornish received a Bachelor's Degree from the University of British Columbia and a Masters from the University of Massachusetts, both in Agronomy. His interest in golf course architecture developed after his graduation in 1935 when he was hired to evaluate soils for Capilano GC, then under construction by architect Stanley Thompson in West Vancouver. Cornish joined Thompson and trained under him for four years before becoming greenkeeper at St. Charles CC in Winnipeg.
  During World War II Cornish served with the Canadian Army overseas, then

175

returned to become an associate of Thompson in 1946. This was followed by a five-year association with pioneer turfgrass scientist Lawrence S. Dickson at the University of Massachusetts. In 1952 Cornish entered private practice as a golf architect.

During his first years as a designer, Cornish specialized in par three layouts, and was assisted in artwork and drafting by his wife, the former Carol Burr Gawthrop. He later established himself as a competent designer of full sized layouts too, and in 1964 took on a partner, young Penn State graduate William G. Robinson.

Robinson moved to the Pacific Northwest in 1977, and in 1983 Cornish was joined in the business by Brian M. Silva, a graduate landscape architect and agronomist.

By 1980 Geoffrey Cornish had planned more courses in the New England area than any other architect in history. He had also designed or remodeled layouts in many other parts of the U.S., Canada and Europe.

Cornish authored numerous articles on course design and turfgrass as well as two books. The first, *Golf Course Design - An Introduction* was prepared with William G. Robinson in 1971 and was widely distributed by the National Golf Foundation. The other was *The Golf Course*, co-authored with Ronald E. Whitten and first published in 1981.

Numerous awards were bestowed upon Geoffrey Cornish during his career. He received a Distinguished Service Award from the GCSAA in 1981, the Donald Ross Award from the ASGCA in 1982 and an Outstanding Service Award by the National Golf Foundation in 1984.

Courses by: Geoffrey S. Cornish

Connecticut: Blackledge CC, Hebron (1966), with William G. Robinson; Cedar Knob CC, Somers (1963); Century Hills CC, Rocky Hill (1974), with William G. Robinson; Cliffside CC, Simsbury (1959); Clinton CC (1967), with William G. Robinson; Connecticut GC {formerly Golf Club at Aspetuck}, Easton (1966), with William G. Robinson; Crestbrook CC, Watertown (9, 1962); Ellington Ridge CC (1959); Farms CC, Wallingford (1961); Hop Meadow CC, Simsbury (1961); Laurel View Muni, Hamden (1969), with William G. Robinson; Millbrook C, Greenwich (9, 1963); Minnechaug GC, Glastonbury (9, 1959); Neipsic Par 3 GC, Glastonbury (1974), with William G. Robinson; Oak Lane CC, Woodbridge (1961); Patton Brook GC, Southington (Precision, 1967), with William G. Robinson; Pautipaug CC, Norwich (1960); Portland GC (1974), with William G. Robinson; Simsbury Farms Muni (1971), with William G. Robinson; South Pine Creek GC, Fairfield (Par 3, 9, 1968), with William G. Robinson; Sterling Farms Muni, Stamford (1971), with William G. Robinson; Westwoods CC, Farmington (Precision, 1964).

Maine: Bangor Muni (1963); Running Hills CC, Frye Island , with William G. Robinson.

Maryland: Towson G&CC (1971), with William G. Robinson.

Massachusetts: Allendale CC, New Bedford (1961); Blue Rock GC, South Yarmouth (1961); Captains GC, Brewster (1985), with Brian Silva; Chicopee Muni (1964); Cranberry Valley GC, Harwich (1974), with William G. Robinson; Crestview CC, Agawam (1957); Crestwood CC, Rehoboth (1959); Crystal Springs GC, Haverhill (1960); Dunfey's GC, Hyannis (Par 3, 1966), with William G. Robinson; Edgewood CC, Southwick (1963); Far Corner Farm GC, West Boxford (1967), with William G. Robinson; Farm Neck GC, Martha's Vineyard (9, 1976), with William G. Robinson; Foxborough CC (9, 1955); Grasmere GC, Falmouth (Par 3, 9), with William G. Robinson; Greylock Glen CC, Adams (1973), with William G. Robinson; Heritage Hills GC, Lakeville (Par 3, 1970), with William G. Robinson; Hickory Ridge CC, Amherst (1969), with William G. Robinson; Holly Ridge GC, South Sandwich (Par 3, 1966), with William G. Robinson; Indian Meadow CC, Westboro (1960); Indian Ridge CC, Andover (1961); International GC, Bolton (1956); Iyanough Hills GC, Hyannis (1975), with William G. Robinson; Kingsway GC (1986), with Brian Silva; Little St. Andrews GC, Springfield (Par 3, 9, 1961); Middleton GC (Par 3, 1965), with William G. Robinson; Midway GC, Groton (Par 3, 9, 1953); Nashawtuc CC, Concord (1961); Oak n' Spruce GC, South Lee (9, 1954); Ocean Edge GC, Brewster (1986), with Brian Silva; Pine Oaks GC, Easton (9, 1966), with William G. Robinson; Poquoy Brook GC, Lakeville (1963); Powder Horn GC, Lexington (Par 3, 1964); Quashnet Valley CC (9, 1976), with William G. Robinson; Rehoboth GC (1966), with William G. Robinson; Sea View Village GC (Par 3, 9, 1953); Shaker Farms CC, Westfield (1954); Spring Valley CC, Sharon (1960), with Samuel Mitchell; Stow Acres CC (North Course), Stow (1965), with William G. Robinson; Sun Valley GC, Rehobeth (1956); Swansea GC (1962); Thomson C, North Reading (1963); Thunderbird GC, Tyngsboro (Par 3, 1963); Trull Brook GC, North Tewksbury (1962); Veterans Memorial GC, Springfield (1960); Wampatuck CC, Canton (9, 1957); Wareham GC (1963); White Cliffs GC, Plymouth (NLE, 9, 1961).

New Hampshire: Bretwood GC, Keene (1967), with William G. Robinson; Cold Spring GC (1976), with William G. Robinson; Eastman Lake CC, Grantham (1975), with William G. Robinson; Sunningdale GC, Dover (9, 1961).

New Jersey: Bowling Green GC, Milton (1966), with William G. Robinson; Hillman's GC (Par 3, 9, 1962).

New York: Addison Pinnacle CC (9, 1969), with William G. Robinson; Colonie CC, Albany (1963); CC of Ithaca (1958); Endwell Greens GC, Johnson City (1965), with William G. Robinson; Grassy Brook GC, Alder Creek (9, 1974), with William G. Robinson; Heritage Hills of Westchester, Somers (9, 1974), with William G. Robinson; Higby Hills CC, Utica (1966), with William G. Robinson; Honey Hill CC, Newport (1967), with William G. Robinson; Vesper Hills CC, Otisco , with William G. Robinson; Vestal Hills CC, Binghampton (1957).

Ohio: Dayton CC (1965), with William G. Robinson; Westfield CC (North Course) (1974), with William G. Robinson; Zoar Village GC (1974), with William G. Robinson.

Pennsylvania: Hershey Pocono GC, White Haven (1970), with William G. Robinson; Host Farms GC (Executive Course), Lancaster (Precision, 9, 1967), with William G. Robinson; Mill Race GC, Benton (9, 1973), with William G. Robinson; River Valley CC, Westfield (9, 1962); Standing Stone GC, Huntingdon (1972), with William G. Robinson; Sugarloaf GC (1966), with William G. Robinson; Wilkes-Barre Muni (1967), with William G. Robinson.

Rhode Island: Alpine CC, Granston (1960); Cranston CC (1974), with William G. Robinson; Exeter CC (1964); Hillsgrove GC (Par 3, 9, 1954); Kirkbrae CC, Lincoln (1961); Quidnesset CC, East Greenwich (9, 1959); Warwick Neck GC (1954); Woodland CC, North Kingston (9, 1963).

Vermont: Farms Motel GC (Par 3, 1970), with William G. Robinson; Killington GC (1983); Manchester CC (1969), with William G. Robinson; Mount Snow GC (1970), with William G. Robinson; Quechee Lakes CC (Highland Course) (1970), with William G. Robinson; Quechee Lakes CC (Lakeland Course) (1975), with William G. Robinson; Stratton Mountain Golf Academy (1972), with William G. Robinson; Stratton Mountain GC (1969), with William G. Robinson.

West Virginia: Canaan Valley State Park GC (1966), with William G. Robinson; Pipestem State Park GC (1966), with William G. Robinson; Twin Falls State Park GC, Mullens (9, 1966), with William G. Robinson.

New Brunswick: Campobello Provincial Park GC (9), with William G. Robinson.

Nova Scotia: Halifax G&CC (New Ashburn) (1969), with William G. Robinson.

Ontario: York Downs G&CC, Toronto (27, 1970), with William G. Robinson.

Quebec: Summerlea G&CC (Cascades Course), Montreal (1960); Summerlea G&CC (Dorion Course), Montreal (1960).

Greece: Links at Porto Carras, New Marmoras (1975), with William G. Robinson.

Courses Remodeled & Added to by: Geoffrey S. Cornish

Arizona: Paradise Valley CC, Scottsdale (R., 1984), with Gary Panks.

Connecticut: Avon CC (A.9, 1966), with William G. Robinson; Avon CC (R.18, 1966), with William G. Robinson; CC of Darien (R.3, 1983); CC of Fairfield (R.2, 1963); CC of Farmington (R.1, 1960); Glastonbury Hills CC (R.4, 1973), with William G. Robinson; Hartford GC, West Hartford (R.2, 1972), with William G. Robinson; Innis Arden GC, Old Greenwich (R.3, 1983), with Brian Silva; Keney Park GC, Hartford (R.3), with William G. Robinson; Madison CC (R., 1985), with Brian Silva; New London CC (R.5), with William G. Robinson; Orange Hills GC (A.9, 1957); Pequabuc CC (A.3), with William G. Robinson; Quinnatisset CC (A.9, 1967), with William G. Robinson; Stanley GC, New Britain (R.27, 1975), with William G. Robinson; Stanwich C, Greenwich (R.3, 1985), with Brian Silva; Watertown CC (A.9, 1970), with William G. Robinson; Wee Burn CC, Darien (R.4, 1978), with William G. Robinson; Wethersfield CC (R.1, 1978), with William G. Robinson; Wethersfield CC (R., 1983), with Brian Silva; Woodway CC, Darien (R.4), with William G. Robinson.

Delaware: DuPont CC (DuPont Course), Wilmington (R., 1980), with William G. Robinson; DuPont CC (Louviers Course), Wilmington (R., 1980), with William G. Robinson; DuPont CC (Montchanin Course), Newark (R., 1980), with William G. Robinson; DuPont CC (Nemours Course), Wilmington (R., 1980), with William G. Robinson.

Maine: Biddeford and Saco CC (A.9, 1986), with Brian Silva; Brunswick GC (A.9, 1964), with William G. Robinson; Prouts Neck GC (R., 1959); Purpoodock C (R.2, 1985), with Brian Silva; Riverside Muni, Portland (A.9, 1967), with William G. Robinson; Treadway-Samoset GC, Rockport (R.), with William G. Robinson; Waterville CC (A.9, 1966), with William G. Robinson; Webhannett GC, Kennebunkport (R.4, 1970), with William G. Robinson.

Massachusetts: Bedford AFB GC (R., 1985), with Brian Silva; Berkshire Hills CC, Pittsfield (R.4), with William G. Robinson; Blue Hill CC, Canton (R., 1985), with Brian Silva; Brae Burn CC, West Newton (R.2, 1970), with William G. Robinson; Brewster Green GC (NLE, A.2, 1979), with William G. Robinson; Dedham Hunt & Polo C (R.2), with William G. Robinson; Duxbury YC (A.9, 1969), with William G. Robinson; Ellinwood CC, Athol (A.9, 1969), with William G. Robinson; Fall River CC (A.9, 1975), with William G. Robinson; Foxborough CC (A.9, 1970), with William G. Robinson; Framingham CC (A.2), with William G. Robinson; Franconia Muni, Springfield (R.7, 1973), with William G. Robinson; Fresh Pond Muni, Cambridge (A.9, 1967), with William G. Robinson; Hopedale CC (R.); Juniper Hills GC (A.9, 1952); Longmeadow CC, Springfield (R.1, 1960); Marlborough CC, Marlboro (A.9, 1969), with William G. Robinson; Meadow Brook GC, Reading (R.9, 1964); Myopia Hunt C, Hamilton (R., 1962); Myopia Hunt C, Hamilton (R., 1985), with Brian Silva; Oak Hill CC, Fitchburg (R.5, 1966), with William G. Robinson; Pine Brook CC, Weston (R., 1985), with Brian Silva; Quabog GC (R.2), with William G. Robinson; Ridder's GC (A.9, 1963); Segregansett CC (A.9, 1976), with William G. Robinson; Springfield CC (A.7, 1985), with Brian Silva; Stow Acres CC (South Course), Stow (R.9, 1965), with William G. Robinson; Stow Acres CC (South Course), Stow (A.9, 1965), with William G. Robinson; Tatnuck CC, Worcester (R.5), with William G. Robinson; The Country Club, Brookline (R.2, 1960); The Country Club, Brookline (R.2, 1969), with William G. Robinson; Wahconah CC, Dalton (A.9, 1959), with Rowland Armacost; Wellesley CC (A.9, 1961); Weston GC (R.2, 1982); Woodland CC, Newton (R., 1964); Worcester CC (R.2).

Michigan: Crystal Downs CC, Frankfort (R., 1985), with Brian Silva; CC of Detroit, Grosse Pointe Farms (R., 1986), with Brian Silva.

Minnesota: Interlachen CC, Edina (R., 1985), with Brian Silva; Minneapolis GC (R., 1985), with Brian Silva; Somerset CC, St. Paul (R., 1979), with William G. Robinson; Wayzata CC (R., 1985), with Brian Silva; Woodhill CC, Wayzata (R., 1979), with William G. Robinson.

Missouri: Algonquin CC, Glendale (R., 1986), with Brian Silva.

New Hampshire: Abenaqui C (R.), with William G. Robinson; Beaver Meadows Muni (A.9, 1968), with William G. Robinson; Hanover CC, Dartmouth College (R., 1970), with William G. Robinson; Province Lake CC (A.9, 1986), with Brian Silva; Wentworth-by-the-Sea GC, Portsmouth (A.9, 1965), with William G. Robinson.

New Jersey: Echo Lake CC, Westfield (A.3, 1968), with William G. Robinson; Echo Lake CC, Westfield (R.3, 1968), with William G. Robinson; Howell Park GC, Farmingdale (R., 1985), with Brian Silva; Knickerbocker CC, Tenafly (R.6, 1973), with William G. Robinson; Navesink CC, Red Bank (R., 1986), with Brian Silva; Packanack Lake CC (A.9, 1963); Preakness Hills CC, Paterson (R., 1984), with Brian Silva.

New York: Bedford G&TC (R.9); CC of Buffalo, Williamsville (R., 1965), with William G. Robinson; Heritage Hills of Westchester, Somers (A.9, 1967); Highland Park CC (A.9, 1973), with William G. Robinson; Ives Hill CC, Watertown (A.9, 1974), with William G. Robinson; Monroe CC (R.2, 1965), with William G. Robinson; Nassau CC, Glen Cove (R., 1984), with Brian Silva; Oswego CC (A.9, 1977), with William G. Robinson; Powelton C, Newburgh (R.4, 1985), with Brian Silva; Rockaway Hunting C, Cedarhurst (R., 1985), with Brian Silva; Schuyler Meadows C, Loudonville (R., 1985), with Brian Silva; Shepard Hill CC (A.9, 1970), with William G. Robinson; Siwanoy CC, Bronxville (R.), with William G. Robinson; Sodus Point GC (A.9, 1966), with William G. Robinson; Sodus Point GC (R.9, 1966); St. Lawrence Univ, Canton (A.12, 1971), with William G. Robinson; Thendara CC, Old Forge (R.1, 1968), with William G. Robinson; Twin Hills GC, Spencerport (Precision, A., 1967), with William G. Robinson; Westwood CC, Williamsville (R., 1959); Whippoorwill CC, Armonk (R., 1984), with Brian Silva; Wildwood GC, Rush (R.,

1985), with Brian Silva.

Ohio: Avon Oaks CC (R.6, 1978), with William G. Robinson; Canterbury CC, Shaker Heights (R., 1978), with William G. Robinson; CC of Hudson (R., 1982); Miami Valley CC, Dayton (R., 1965), with William G. Robinson; Portage CC, Akron (R.), with William G. Robinson; Salem GC (R., 1981); Shaker Heights CC (R., 1982); Sharon C, Sharon Center (R., 1986), with Brian Silva; Tippecanoe CC, Canfield (R., 1983); Westfield CC (South Course) (R.9, 1967), with William G. Robinson; Westfield CC (South Course) (A.9, 1967), with William G. Robinson; Worthington Hills CC (R.2, 1985), with Brian Silva; Youngstown CC (R., 1984).

Pennsylvania: Concordville CC (A.4, 1974), with William G. Robinson; CC of Scranton (R., 1983), with Brian Silva; Mill Race CC, Benton (A.9, 1977), with William G. Robinson.

Rhode Island: Agawam Hunt C, Providence (R., 1963); Metacomet CC, East Providence (R.2, 1957); Point Judith CC (R.9, 1964), with William G. Robinson; Quidnesset CC, East Greenwich (A.9, 1974), with William G. Robinson; Rhode Island CC, West Barrington (R.), 1960); Valley Ledgemont CC (A.9, 1963); Warwick CC (A.9, 1953); Woonsocket CC (A.9, 1961), with Samuel Mitchell.

Vermont: Basin Harbor C (R.); Ekwanok CC, Manchester (R.8, 1957); Killington GC (A.9, 1985), with Brian Silva; Montague GC (A.3), with William G. Robinson; Stratton Mountain GC (A.9, 1984), with Brian Silva.

British Columbia: Point Grey G&CC (R., 1973), with William G. Robinson; Quilchena G&CC (R.6, 1979), with William G. Robinson.

Manitoba: Breezy Bend CC (R., 1973), with William G. Robinson; Elm Ridge CC (Course No. 1) (R., 1978), with William G. Robinson; Elmhurst G Links, Winnepeg (R.2), with William G. Robinson; St. Charles CC (North Nine), Winnipeg (R.), with William G. Robinson; St. Charles CC (West Nine), Winnipeg (R.), with William G. Robinson; St. Charles CC (West Nine), Winnipeg (R.), with William G. Robinson.

New Brunswick: Fredericton GC (R.2, 1967), with William G. Robinson.

Charles Kenneth Cotton (1887 - 1974) BAGCA, Founding Member; President, 1974.

Born: Sonning-on-Thames, England. Died: Reading, England at age 86.

C.K. Cotton, a graduate of Cambridge University, took up the game of golf after college and quickly developed into a fine player. He was a scratch golfer for over thirty years.

Cotton worked for nearly twenty years as Club Secretary at a series of British golf clubs. After World War II he decided to assist in reconstruction of the many war-torn layouts in Britain and the Continent. He soon began planning original designs too.

Through the years, C.K. Cotton started a number of aspiring designers in the business, including J.J.F. Pennink, Charles Lawrie and Donald Steel.

Courses by: C.K. Cotton

Denmark: Randers GC (9, 1958); St. Knuds GC (1954), with J.J.F. Pennink.

England: Brickendon Grange G&CC (1964), with J.J.F. Pennink; Lamberhurst GC, with J.J.F. Pennink; Lee Park GC, Liverpool (1954), with J.J.F. Pennink; Marsden Park GC, Lancashire (9, 1969); Ross on Wye GC (1967), with J.J.F. Pennink; Stressholme GC, with J.J.F. Pennink; Tunbridge Wells GC (9); Wentworth GC (Short Nine), Surrey (9, 1948), with J.J.F. Pennink.

Ireland: Courtown GC, County Wexford , with John Harris.

Italy: Olgiata CC (27, 1961), with J.J.F. Pennink.

Wales: St. Pierre G&CC (Old Course), Gwent (1962), with J.J.F. Pennink; Tenby GC, Dyfed.

Courses Remodeled & Added to by: C.K. Cotton

England: Army GC (R., 1965), with J.J.F. Pennink; Frilford Heath GC (Green Course) (R.9, 1968), with J.J.F. Pennink; Frilford Heath GC (Green Course) (A.9, 1968), with J.J.F. Pennink; Frilford Heath GC (Red Course) (A.9, 1968), with J.J.F. Pennink; Frilford Heath GC (Red Course) (R.9, 1968), with J.J.F. Pennink; Ganton GC (R., 1948); Hexham GC (R., 1956), with J.J.F. Pennink; Louth GC, Lincolnshire (R.), with J.J.F. Pennink; Mendip GC, Avon (A.9, 1965), with J.J.F. Pennink; Royal Lytham & St. Annes GC, Lancashire (R., 1952), with J.J.F. Pennink; Saunton GC (East Course), Devonshire (R.), 1952), with J.J.F. Pennink; West Lancashire GC, Lancashire (R.).

Ireland: Athlone GC (R.); Cork GC, County Cork (R., 1975), with J.J.F. Pennink and C.D. Lawrie.

Italy: Circolo G Lido di Venezia (A.9, 1958), with John Harris; Venice GC (A.9, 1958).

Scotland: Downfield GC, Dundee (R., 1964).

Singapore: Singapore Island CC (Island Course) (R., 1965), with J.J.F. Pennink.

Wales: Ashburnham GC (A.1, 1947); Ashburnham GC (R., 1947); Brynhill GC, Glamorganshire (R.); Royal Porthcawl GC, Mid Glamorgan (R., 1950).

Thomas Henry Cotton (1907 -   ) BAGCA (Honorary Member).

Born: Holmes Chapel, Cheshire, England.

Henry Cotton has been described as the greatest British golfer of his day. He won three British Opens and half a dozen other national titles. He trained as a golf architect under Sir Guy Campbell, initially providing war damage appraisals following World War II. He later worked with J. Hamilton Stutt before establishing his own business in the late 1950s. Cotton designed many layouts in Britain and the Continent, working in a variety of terrains ranging from swamps and rice fields to pine forests. His layout at Penina in Portugal, which involved the planting of tens of thousands of trees, was his particular favorite, and he lived on the course for years.

In the course of his 60 career, Cotton wrote ten books and contributed to countless golf journals and newspapers. He claimed never to have counted the number of courses he designed nor tournaments he won but could remember each vividly.

Courses by: Henry Cotton

England: Abridge GC (1964); Ampfield Par 3 GC (Par 3, 1963); Beamish Park GC (1950), with Sir Guy Campbell; Canons Brook GC (1962); Ely City GC (1961); Farnham Park GC, Folly Hill (Par 3, 1966); Sene Valley, Folkstone and Hythe GC (1960); Windmill Hill GC (1972).

France: Mont D'Arbois GC (1968).

Italy: Bergamo L'Albenza GC (1959); Bologna GC (1959); Tirrenia CC (1968); Torino GC, Turin (1956), with John Harris.

Madeira Islands: Santo da Serra GC (9).

Portugal: Monte Gordo GC; Penina GC (1964); Vale do Lobo GC (1969).

Scotland: Gourock GC; Moray GC (New Course), Morayshire (1970); Windyhill GC.

Wales: St. Mellons GC (1937), with H.S. Colt and J.S.F. Morrison.

Courses Remodeled & Added to by: Henry Cotton

Channel Islands: La Moye GC (R., 1966).

England: Castle Eden and Peterlee GC (R.); Eaglescliffe GC, County Durham (R.); Felixstowe Ferry GC, Suffolk (R., 1949), with Sir Guy Campbell; Royal Cinque Ports GC, Deal (R., 1946), with Sir Guy Campbell; Temple GC, Berkshire (R.).

France: New GC, Deauville (A.9).

Italy: Campo Carlo Magno GC (R.); Lido Di Venezia GC, Venice (R.).

Portugal: Penina GC (A.9, 1975); Vale do Lobo GC (A.9, 1975).

Scotland: Stirling GC, Stirlingshire (R.).

Spain: Real C de la Puerto de Hierro (New), Madrid (R., 1964).

Archibald "Pete" Craig

Pete Craig served as pro-superintendent at Penfield CC in New York until the late 1950s when he resigned to design and build golf courses on a full-time basis.

Courses by: Pete Craig

New York: Clifton Springs CC (9, 1962); College GC, Delhi (9); Deerfield CC (27, 1966); Francourt Farms GC, Elmira (1963); Green Hills CC, Rochester , with Joseph Demino; Island Valley GC, Rochester (1961); Janley Hills GC (9); Northway Heights G&CC, Ballston Lake; Penfield CC; Salmon Creek CC, Rochester; Shadow Lake G&RC, Rochester (27); Sunnycrest CC, Rochester (27); Thunder Ridge CC, Rush (1973), with Joseph Demino; Twin Hills GC, Spencerport (1970); Victor Hills GC (9); Whispering Hills GC, Conesis; Wildwood GC, Rush (Precision, 1973); Winged Pheasant GC, Farmington (1963).

Courses Remodeled & Added to by: Pete Craig

New York: Ballston Spa & CC (R.9, 1965); Ballston Spa & CC (A.9, 1965).

Arthur Capel Molyneux Croome (1866 - 1930)

Born: Stroud, Gloucestershire, England. Died: Maidenhead, Berkshire, England at age 64.

Educated at Wellington and Oxford, A.C.M. Croome was one of Britain's great sportsmen, playing cricket, rugby and track at school, and golf, curling and billiards later. Following graduation, he accepted a post as schoolmaster, athletic coach and house parent at the Radley school, where he remained until 1910. It was during this period that Croome took up golf, and he was soon competing in the British Amateur and other championships.

At the turn of the century, Croome founded the Oxford and Cambridge Golfing Society with his friends John L. Low and R.H. DeMontmorency. The group played exhibition matches on both sides of the Atlantic and numbered C.H. Alison among its early members. "Crumbo," as Croome was called by his friends, served as captain and later president of the Society.

Croome supplemented his income at Radley by writing articles on golf for London newspapers, notably the Evening Standard and Morning Post. Following his retirement from Radley, he turned to journalism full time, covering cricket for the London Times as well as continuing his golf columns.

While a newspaperman, Croome met and formed a lasting friendship with golf architect J.F. Abercromby. Fascinated by the design aspect of the sport, Croome assisted 'Aber' on the design of several British courses and after World War I became a partner in the architectural firm of Fowler, Abercromby, Simpson and Croome. His role was primarily that of business manager and publicist for the company, but he was entirely responsible for the design of at least one course, Liphook GC in the heathlands. The excellence of this course caused it to be considered a design milestone, but Croome was prevented from further participation in course designs by the ill health that plagued the last years of his life.

George Arthur Crump (1871 - 1918)

Born: Philadelphia, Pennsylvania. Died: Merchantville, New Jersey at age 46. Interred: Philadelphia.

George Crump, the wealthy owner of the Hotel Colonnades in Philadelphia, was an avid hunter, fisherman and golfer, finishing as runner-up in the 1912 Philadelphia Amateur. He was among the founders of Philadelphia CC before the turn of the century and played most of his golf there. But he harbored a dream of building his own golf course in the sand hills of New Jersey and in 1912 convinced a syndicate of friends to invest in the project.

Crump sold his hotel, purchased 184 acres of sand hills near Clementon, New Jersey, and moved to the site to create his dream. His Pine Valley GC became one of the world's toughest courses and certainly the most ferociously penal golf course of its time. Crump spent the last six years of his life and over a quarter million of his own dollars developing it. Many professional golf architects examined the work in progress, but only Britisher H.S. Colt, who had assisted Crump in the original routing, was allowed to make recommendations. Colt, impressed by Crump's carefully planned holes, suggested few modifications.

George Crump died suddenly in January, 1918. Fourteen holes at Pine Valley were completed at the time, but numbers 12 through 15 had only been roughed out. It took time to raise the necessary funds and four more years to complete construction, but under the guidance of Hugh Wilson, aided by his brother Alan and Britisher C.H. Alison, the full eighteen holes of Pine Valley finally opened in 1922. George Crump's creation has long been considered a landmark in course architecture, and generally acknowledged to be among the world's finest. In 1985, Pine Valley was ranked the Top Course in both the country and the world in separate polls conducted by *Golf Digest* and *Golf* magazines.

George Cumming (1879 - 1949)

Born: Bridge of Weir, Scotland. Died: Toronto, Ontario, Canada at age 70.

George Cumming emigrated to Canada as a young man, and soon landed a position as club professional at Toronto GC. It was a job he would retain the rest of his life.

A fine golfer, Cumming won the 1908 Canadian Open and was a runner-up in the event four times. Generally regarded as the dean of Canadian golf professionals, Cumming helped found the Canadian PGA and served as its president on five occasions.

Aside from his teaching and club-making duties, Cumming found time to design dozens of golf courses throughout Canada.

Courses by: George Cumming
Ontario: Brantford G&CC (1920), with Nicol Thompson; Mississauga G&CC, Port Credit (1906), with Percy Barrett; Sarnia GC (9, 1915); Windemere House GC (9, 1920).
Quebec: Green Valley GC.

Robert E. Cupp (1939 -)
Born: Lewistown, Pennsylvania.

After graduating in 1961 from the University of Miami with a degree in Art, Bob Cupp served in the military. During that stint, he obtained a Masters in Fine Arts from the University of Alaska. After discharge, Cupp returned to Florida, worked for a short time in advertising, then took a job as a pro shop manager at a daily fee operation near Miami. He soon found himself assisting the rebuilding of portions of the golf course. When other clubs in the area requested his services, Cupp returned to school and obtained an Associate Degree in Agronomy from Broward Jr. College. In 1968 he received his first contract as a course architect - the revision of one nine and addition of a second nine to Homestead AFB GC. In the next four years Cupp designed and constructed several South Florida courses. In 1973 a friend introduced him to golfer Jack Nicklaus, who was at the time forming his own design firm. Cupp accepted Nicklaus' offer to work as a senior designer in the firm. Cupp worked on all Nicklaus projects in the East and in Europe for over a decade. He and another Nicklaus employee, Jay Morrish, collaborated on other designs under the corporate name Golforce, Inc.

In 1985 Bob Cupp left the Nicklaus organization and established his own design firm in South Florida.

Courses by: Bob Cupp
Alabama: Shoal Creek, Birmingham (1977), with Jack Nicklaus and Jay Morrish.
Arizona: Continental Foothills GC, Cave Creek (1987); Desert Highlands GC, Scottsdale (1984), with Jack Nicklaus, Jay Morrish and Scott Miller; TPC at Star Pass, Tuscon (1987).
California: Bear Creek GC, Wildomar (1982), with Jack Nicklaus, Jay Morrish and Scott Miller; Club at Morningside, Rancho Mirage (1983), with Jack Nicklaus, Jay Morrish and Scott Miller.
Colorado: Breckenridge GC (1985), with Jack Nicklaus; Castle Pines GC, Castle Rock (1981), with Jack Nicklaus, Jay Morrish and Scott Miller; CC of the Rockies, Avon (1984), with Jack Nicklaus and Jay Morrish; Meridian GC, Englewood (1984), with Jack Nicklaus and Scott Miller; Singletree GC, Edwards (1981), with Jay Morrish.
Florida: Bear Lakes CC, West Palm Beach (1984), with Jack Nicklaus; Bear's Paw CC, Naples (1980), with Jack Nicklaus, Jay Morrish and Scott Miller; Boca Pointe CC, Boca Raton (1982), with Jay Morrish; Cheeca Lodge GC (Par 3, 1981), with Jay Morrish; Costa Del Sol G&RC (1971); Grand Cypress Golf Academy, Orlando (3, 1985), with Jack Nicklaus; Grand Cypress GC, Orlando (1984), with Jack Nicklaus; Hidden Valley GC, Miami (Precision, 1972); Loxahatchee C, Jupiter (1985), with Jack Nicklaus and Tom Pearson; Sailfish Point CC, Stuart (1981), with Jack Nicklaus and Jay Morrish; Walden Lake CC, Plant City (1978), with Jay Morrish.
Georgia: Port Armor CC, Lake Oconee (1987).
Michigan: Grand Traverse GC (The Bear Course), Acme (1985), with Jack Nicklaus; Indianwood G&CC (New Course), Lake Orion, with Jerry Pate.
Mississippi: Annandale GC, Jackson (1981), with Jack Nicklaus, Jay Morrish and Scott Miller.
North Carolina: Elk River GC, Banner Elk (1984), with Jack Nicklaus; Horseshoe GC, Cummings Cove (1986); Laurel Ridge CC, Waynesville (1986).
Ohio: CC at Muirfield Village, Dublin (1982), with Jack Nicklaus and Jay Morrish.
South Carolina: Turtle Point G Links, Kiawah Island (1981), with Jack Nicklaus and Jay Morrish.
Texas: Hills of Lakeway Golf Academy, Lakeway (3, 1985), with Jack Nicklaus, Jay Morrish and Scott Miller; Hills of Lakeway GC, Lakeway (1980), with Jack Nicklaus, Jay Morrish and Scott Miller; Lochinvar GC, Houston (1980), with Jack Nicklaus and Jay Morrish.
Utah: Park Meadows GC, Park City (1983), with Jack Nicklaus and Jay Morrish.
Ontario: Glen Abbey GC, Oakville (1976), with Jack Nicklaus and Jay Morrish.
Cayman Islands: Britannia GC (Precision, 9, 1985), with Jack Nicklaus.
Japan: New St. Andrews GC, Ontawara City (1976), with Jack Nicklaus and Jay Morrish.

Courses Remodeled & Added to by: Bob Cupp
Florida: Crooked Creek G&CC, Miami (R., 1970); Frenchman's Creek GC (North Course), North Palm Beach (R., 1983), with Jay Morrish; Frenchman's Creek GC (South Course), North Palm Beach (R., 1983), with Jay Morrish; Grand Cypress GC, Orlando (A.9, 1986), with Jack Nicklaus; Homestead AFB GC (R.9, 1969); Homestead AFB GC (A.9, 1969); Lost Tree C, Singer Island (R., 1980), with Jay Morrish.
Georgia: Atlanta CC, Marietta (R., 1980), with Jay Morrish; Augusta CC (R., 1983); Augusta National GC, Augusta (R., 1984), with Jay Morrish and Scott Miller; Augusta National GC, Augusta (R., 1985), with Jack Nicklaus.
Illinois: Bryn Mawr GC, Lincolnwood (R., 1982), with Jay Morrish; Evanston GC, Skokie (R., 1982).
Massachusetts: Weston GC (R., 1986).
Michigan: Grand Traverse GC (Newcombe Course), Acme (R., 1983).
New York: Brooklea CC, Rochester (R., 1984); St. Andrews GC, Hastings-on-Hudson (R., 1985), with Jack Nicklaus; Wanakah CC (R., 1983), with Jay Morrish.
Ohio: Scioto CC, Columbus (R., 1983).
Tennessee: Colonial CC (South Course), Cordova (R., 1984).
Texas: Colonial CC, Fort Worth (R., 1982), with Jay Morrish; Preston Trail GC, Dallas (R., 1982), with Jay Morrish.
West Virginia: Greenbrier GC (Greenbrier Course), White Sulphur Spgs (R.,

1978), with Jack Nicklaus and Jay Morrish.
Australia: Australian GC, Kensington (R., 1977), with Jack Nicklaus and Jay Morrish.
Japan: Atsugi International CC (East Course), Kanagawa (R., 1983), with Jay Morrish; Atsugi International CC (West Course), Kanagawa (R., 1985), with Jay Morrish.

George C. Curtis
After decades as head professional and course superintendent at various Tennessee country clubs, George Curtis took up golf architecture in 1960. For over ten years Curtis divided his time between laying out courses throughout the Southeast and running a cattle ranch in Jackson, Tennessee.

Courses by: George C. Curtis
Louisiana: Pine Hills GC, West Monroe (1974).
Mississippi: Fernwood CC, McComb (1969); Liveoaks CC, Jackson; Pine Hills CC, Calhoun City (1969); Rolling Hills CC, Crystal Springs (1969).
Tennessee: Houston Levee CC, Germantown (1971); Milan CC (9, 1960).

James Dalgleish (1865 - 1935)
Born: Berkshire, England. Died: Kansas City, Missouri at age 70.

James Dalgleish was one of many young British golfers who moved to America in the late 1890s. He landed a job managing the golf department for the A.G. Spalding & Bros. Sporting Goods Store in New York City, where he remained for five years. After brief stints at clubs in New York and Vermont, Dalgleish moved to Kansas City, Mo., where he laid out and built Evanston GC and remained as its pro/greenkeeper.

Dalgleish became the dean of golf professionals in the Kansas City area and in 1927 was a charter member of the organization now known as the GCSAA. He laid out a number of courses across the Midwest, but much of his work, done in the early days of American golf development, was later replaced or abandoned.

Courses by: James Dalgleish
Kansas: Chevy Chase CC, Kansas City (NLE, 1931); Homestead CC, Prairie Village (NLE,); Macdonald Park Muni, Wichita (1911); Victory Hills CC, Kansas City (1927).
Minnesota: Pine Beach East GC, Madden Beach (1926).
Missouri: Automobile C, Grandview (NLE,); St. Andrews GC, Kansas City (NLE,); Swope Park GC, Kansas City (1917).
Nebraska: Valley View GC, Omaha (NLE, 1926).

Courses Remodeled & Added to by: James Dalgleish
Missouri: Evanston GC, Kansas City (R.); Log Cabin C, Clayton (R.).

Jack L. Daray Sr. (1881 - 1958) ASGCA, Charter Member.
Born: Louisiana. Died: Coronado, California at age 76.

Jack Daray turned professional in 1901, served briefly as club pro at Highland CC, Grand Rapids, Mich. and then at Olympia Fields CC for many years. He also worked winters as teaching pro at clubs along the Mississippi Gulf Coast. Among Daray's students were Princeton University President Woodrow Wilson (later President of the United States) and baseball great Ty Cobb.

Daray was one of a number of Chicago professionals who designed courses on the side during the 1920s. He kept active in the Thirties and resumed his design work after World War II. Although ill health necessitated his move to southern California in the early 1950s, he was still designing courses at the time of his death.

Jack Daray was a charter member of the PGA of America in 1916. His elder son, Captain Jack Daray Jr., took up the practice of course architecture in the late 1970s after retiring from a naval career.

Courses by: Jack Daray
Alabama: Don Hawkins Muni, Birmingham (1923); Old Spanish Fort CC, Mobile.
California: Circle R Ranch GC, Escondido (1956); Coronado GC (1957); Navy GC (North Course), San Diego (1956); Sail Ho GC, San Diego (Par 3, 9, 1957); Sea 'N Air GC (Precision, 1959); SeaBees GC, Port Hueneme (Precision, 9, 1958).
Illinois: Cherry Hills CC, Flossmoor (1932), with Harry Collis; Glenwoodie GC, Chicago Heights (1923), with Harry Collis; Illenwick Fields GC, Bensenville; Mellody Farm CC, Lake Forest (NLE, 1928), with George O'Neill and Jack Croke; White Pines CC (East Course), Bensonville (1930); White Pines CC (West Course), Bensonville (1930).
Louisiana: Metairie CC (1925); Tchefuncta GC, Covington (1925).
Michigan: Big Rapids CC (1921); Cascade Hills CC, Grand Rapids (1927); Hastings CC (9, 1922); Hy Pointe CC, Grand Rapids (1928).
Mississippi: Gulf Hills CC (1922); Oak Shore CC; Rainbow Bay GC {formerly Edgewater GC}, Biloxi, with Harry Collis.

Courses Remodeled & Added to by: Jack Daray
Illinois: Olympia Fields CC (North Course) (R., 1946); Olympia Fields CC (South Course) (R., 1946).
Michigan: Meadowbrook CC, Detroit (A.12, 1921), with Harry Collis; Meadowbrook CC, Detroit (R.6, 1921), with Harry Collis.

John R. Darrah (1903 - 1971) ASGCA
Born: Chicago, Illinois. Died: Matteson, Illinois at age 68.

John Darrah received a degree in Engineering from Crane College in Chicago, worked as an engineer for a coal firm in Wyoming and then returned to Illinois to work for the Union Fuel Company. Darrah resigned in 1931 due to ill health. After his recovery he took a position as greenkeeper at Beverly CC near Chicago, where he remained until 1947. He then moved to Olympia Fields CC and restored the two remaining courses after the complex had been nearly abandoned during the war.

In 1949 Darrah left Olympia Fields to form a golf course construction business. After rebuilding and renovating many Chicago-area courses, he began designing as well as building. In the 1960s he planned several dozen courses in the Midwest.

Courses by: John Darrah
Illinois: Arispie Lake GC, Princeton (9, 1968); Morris CC (1970); Wyaton Hills GC (9, 1968).
Indiana: Arrowbrook CC, Chesterfield.

Kentucky: Hopkinsville G&CC (1971); London GC (1969).
Courses Remodeled & Added to by: John Darrah
Illinois: Kankakee CC (A.10, 1963); Kankakee CC (R.8, 1963).
Indiana: Valparaiso CC (R.9, 1962); Valparaiso CC (A.9, 1962); Youche CC, Crown Point (A.9, 1963); Youche CC, Crown Point (R.9, 1963).
Mississippi: Back Acres CC (R.9, 1967); Back Acres CC (A.9, 1967).

Robert Michael Dasher (1951 -   ) ASGCA
Born: Atlanta, Georgia.
Mike Dasher attended Georgia Tech University, receiving a Bachelor's Degree in Civil Engineering in 1973 and a Masters in Civil Engineering in 1980. From 1973 to 1979 Dasher was employed as a project superintendent for The Wadsworth Company, one of the largest golf course contractors in the United States. In 1980 he joined the golf design firm of Arthur Hills and Associates, running the Orlando, Fla. branch of the company.
Courses by: Mike Dasher
Florida: Bonita Bay C, Bonita Springs (1985), with Arthur Hills and Steve Forrest; Cape Coral Muni (1986), with Arthur Hills and Steve Forrest; Cross Creek CC, Fort Myers (Precision, 1985), with Arthur Hills and Steve Forrest; Foxfire CC, Naples (1985), with Arthur Hills and Steve Forrest; Gator Trace GC, Ft. Pierce (1986), with Arthur Hills and Steve Forrest; Ironhorse GC, West Palm Beach (1987), with Arthur Hills and Steve Forrest; TPC at Eagle Trace, Coral Springs (1984), with Arthur Hills and Steve Forrest; Tampa Palms CC, Tampa (1987), with Arthur Hills and Steve Forrest; Vista Plantation GC, Vero Beach (Precision, 1985), with Arthur Hills and Steve Forrest.
Georgia: Landings at Skidaway Island (Palmetto) (1985), with Arthur Hills and Steve Forrest; Standard C, Norcross (1986), with Arthur Hills and Steve Forrest; Windward CC, Atlanta (1987), with Arthur Hills and Steve Forrest.
Louisiana: Southern Trace CC, Shreveport (1986), with Arthur Hills and Steve Forrest.
Michigan: Honors C, Brighton (1987), with Arthur Hills and Steve Forrest.
South Carolina: Palmetto Dunes CC (Hills Course), Hilton Head Island (1986), with Arthur Hills and Steve Forrest.
Courses Remodeled & Added to by: Mike Dasher
Florida: Vista Royale GC, Vero Beach (A.9, 1981), with Arthur Hills and Steve Forrest.
Georgia: Capital City C (R., 1985), with Arthur Hills; Druid Hills CC, Atlanta (R., 1985), with Arthur Hills.
Kentucky: Highland CC, Fort Thomas (A.9, 1985), with Arthur Hills and Steve Forrest; Summit Hills CC, Ft. Mitchell (R., 1985), with Arthur Hills and Steve Forrest.
Michigan: Orchard Lake CC (R., 1984), with Arthur Hills and Steve Forrest.
Ohio: Fremont CC (R., 1985), with Arthur Hills; Terrace Park CC, Cincinnati (R., 1984), with Arthur Hills.

Arthur L. Davis (1939 -   ) ASGCA
Born: Georgia.
Arthur Davis attended Abraham Baldwin College in Tifton, Ga. where he worked part-time for Southern Turf Nurseries, which specialized in newly-developed hybrid Bermudagrasses. In the course of his work, Davis met golf architects Robert Trent Jones, George Cobb, Dick Wilson, William Mitchell, Alfred Tull and others. The experience convinced him to change his major from Agronomy to Landscape Architecture, and he received the B.L.A. degree from the University of Georgia in 1963.
Following graduation, Davis was employed with the firm of Willard C. Byrd and Associates until 1967, when he established his own practice in Atlanta. In 1970 he was joined by Ron Kirby and professional golfer Gary Player in the firm of Davis, Kirby and Player Inc.
A few years later the firm dissolved, and Davis established his own course design business based in Rome, Georgia.
Courses by: Arthur Davis
Alabama: Heatherwood GC, Birmingham (1987).
Florida: Summertree GC, New Port Richey (9, 1983).
Georgia: Arrowhead GC, Jasper (1968); Berkeley Hills CC, Norcross (1971), with Ron Kirby and Gary Player; Cross Creek C, Atlanta (1967), with James T. Shirley; Green Acres C, Dexter (9, 1969); Old Town C, Zebulon (9, 1968); Pebble Brook CC, Manchester (9, 1970), with Ron Kirby; Pine Isle CC, Lake Lanier (1972), with Ron Kirby and Gary Player; River North G&CC, Macon (1973), with Ron Kirby and Gary Player; Royal Oaks GC, Cartersville (9, 1971), with Ron Kirby and Gary Player; Twin Creek CC, Dahlonega (1970); West Oak GC, Marietta.
Illinois: Holiday Inn GC, Crete (9, 1970), with Ron Kirby.
Maryland: Swan Point GC, Issue (1987).
South Carolina: Dolphin Head GC, Hilton Head Island (1973), with Ron Kirby and Gary Player.
Tennessee: Bent Creek Mountain Inn CC {formerly Cobbly Nob G Links}, Gatlinburg (1972), with Ron Kirby and Gary Player; Centennial CC, Chattanooga (1977); Concord GC (1977).
Ivory Coast: Riviera Africaine GC (9, 1972), with Ron Kirby and Gary Player.
Japan: Odawara CC (1973), with Ron Kirby and Gary Player.
Puerto Rico: Palmas del Mar GC, Humacao (1973), with Ron Kirby and Gary Player.
Spain: El Paraiso GC (1974), with Ron Kirby and Gary Player.
Courses Remodeled & Added to by: Arthur Davis
Georgia: Cartersville CC (R.9, 1972), with Ron Kirby and Gary Player; Cartersville CC (A.9, 1972), with Ron Kirby and Gary Player; Coosa CC (R., 1979); Evan Heights GC (R.9, 1977); Little Mountain CC (R., 1970), with Ron Kirby; Sandy Run GC (R., 1970), with Ron Kirby; Standard C, Atlanta (NLE, R.1), with Ron Kirby and Gary Player; Warner Robins AFB GC, Macon (R., 1970), with Ron Kirby.
New Mexico: Alto Lakes G&CC (A.9, 1973), with Ron Kirby and Gary Player.
Tennessee: Chattanooga G&CC (R.4, 1975); Lawrenceburg CC (A.9, 1967); Lawrenceburg CC (R.4, 1976); Montclair CC, Chattanooga (R.9); Montclair CC, Chattanooga (A.9); Stones River CC (R.9, 1977).

Texas: Royal Oaks CC, Dallas (R., 1982); Stevens Park GC (R., 1983); Tenison Muni (East Course), Dallas (R., 1983); Tenison Muni (West Course), Dallas (R., 1983).

William F. Davis (1863 - 1902)
Born: Scotland. Died: New York at age 39.
William Davis left Hoylake, England, to take up duties as pro-greenkeeper at Royal Montreal around 1881. After a few years he moved on to the U.S., where he designed Newport CC in Rhode Island. He planned several other courses in New York and New England while serving as professional at Apawamis CC. Because he was too busy to do so himself, he recommended the Canadian engineer Henry Hewett to plan Tuxedo (N.Y.) CC.
Around 1889, Davis returned to Montreal for a few years and laid out several courses in eastern Canada. He then returned to the States and settled as professional at Newport CC.
Courses Remodeled & Added to by: William F. Davis
New York: Apawamis C, Rye (9); Shinnecock Hills GC (NLE, 12, 1895).
Rhode Island: Newport CC (9, 1894).
Ontario: Ottawa GC (NLE, 1897).

Edward B. Dearie Jr. (1888 - 1952)
Born: Philadelphia, Pennsylvania. Died: Evanston, Illinois at age 64.
Ed Dearie was a noted authority on golf course construction and maintenance. He began his career as greenkeeper at Wanango CC in Reno, Penn. and later spent several years building courses for golf architect Donald Ross in Pennsylvania and Illinois.
In 1921 Dearie settled at Ridgemoor CC in Chicago. Ten years later he moved to Oak Park CC, where he served as course superintendent until his retirement in 1951. During the 1920s and '30s he built a dozen new courses and remodeled an equal number in the greater Chicago area.
Dearie was a charter member of both the GCSAA and the Midwest Association of Greenkeepers. He wrote extensively on the construction and upkeep of golf courses for national periodicals in the 1920s and '30s.
Courses by: Edward B. Dearie Jr
Illinois: Big Oaks GC; Fort Sheridan GC (Par 3, 9); Rob Roy GC; St. Andrews G&CC (Course No. 1), West Chicago (1928); St. Andrews G&CC (Course No. 2), West Chicago (1929).
Courses Remodeled & Added to by: Edward B. Dearie Jr
Illinois: La Grange CC (R., 1926); Oak Park CC (R., 1916); Ridgemoor CC, Harwood Heights (R., 1933); Waveland GC, Chicago (R.9, 1932).

James Newton Demaret (1910 - 1983)
Born: Fort Worth, Texas. Died: Houston, Texas at age 73.
Three-time Masters champion Jimmy Demaret was co-owner with Jack Burke of Champions GC in Houston, Texas. He and Burke collaborated with Ralph Plummer on creation of its Cypress Creek course and with George Fazio on its Jackrabbit eighteen. The pair also worked with Joe Finger in designing The Concord in New York. On his own, Demaret designed Onion Creek CC in Austin, Texas a few years before his death.

Bruce Devlin (1937 -   )
Born: Armidale, New South Wales, Australia.
Bruce Devlin took up golf at the age of thirteen. While receiving training as a plumber by his father (and eventually attaining the rank of master plumber) Devlin also played a great deal of amateur golf. After winning the 1959 Australian Amateur and the 1960 Australian Open he turned professional, moved to the U.S. and over the next dozen years won nine tournaments on the PGA Tour as well as many events around the world.
In 1966 Devlin was asked by members of The Lakes GC in New South Wales to recommend an architect to redesign their course. He had always admired the work of American Dick Wilson, who had died the previous year, so he suggested a Wilson trainee, Robert von Hagge. Devlin worked closely with Hagge on remodeling of The Lakes, and the two soon formed a partnership in Australia. In 1969 they expanded into the United States as the firm of von Hagge and Devlin.
From the beginning Devlin took an active role in the construction supervision of the firm's courses. As his professional career slowed, he assumed increased design responsibilities.
Courses by: Bruce Devlin
California: Blackhawk CC, Danville (1981), with Robert von Hagge; Tierra Del Sol GC, California City (1978), with Robert von Hagge.
Colorado: Eagle Vail CC, Avon (1975), with Robert von Hagge.
Florida: Bay Point Y&CC (Lagoon Legend Course), Panama City (1986), with Robert von Hagge; Bayshore Muni, Miami Beach (1969), with Robert von Hagge; Boca Del Mar G&TC, Boca Raton (1972), with Robert von Hagge; Boca Lago G&CC (East Course), Boca Raton (1975), with Robert von Hagge; Boca Lago G&CC (West Course), Boca Raton (1975), with Robert von Hagge; Boca West CC (Course No. 3), Boca Raton (1974), with Robert von Hagge; Boynton Beach Muni (27, 1984), with Robert von Hagge; Briar Bay GC, Miami (Precision, 9, 1975), with Robert von Hagge; Card Sound GC, North Key Largo (1976), with Robert von Hagge; Colony West GC, Tamarac (1970), with Robert von Hagge; Colony West GC (Course No. 2), Tamarac (Precision, 1974), with Robert von Hagge; Doral CC (Gold Course), Miami (1969), with Robert von Hagge; Doral Park CC (Silver Course), Miami (1984), with Robert von Hagge; East Lake Woodlands G&CC (North Course), Oldsmar (1979), with Robert von Hagge; Eastwood Muni, Ft. Myers (1978), with Robert von Hagge; Emerald Hills CC, Hollywood (1969), with Robert von Hagge; Fountains G&RC (North Course), Lake Worth (1970), with Robert von Hagge; Fountains G&RC (South Course), Lake Worth (1972), with Robert von Hagge; Fountains G&RC (West Course), Lake Worth (1981), with Robert von Hagge; Holiday Springs CC, Margate (1975), with Robert von Hagge; Hunters Run GC (East Course), Boynton Beach (1979), with Robert von Hagge; Hunters Run GC (North Course), Boynton Beach (1979), with Robert von Hagge; Hunters Run

GC (South Course), Boynton Beach (1979), with Robert von Hagge; Indian Spring CC (East Course), Boynton Beach (1975), with Robert von Hagge; Indian Spring CC (West Course), Boynton Beach (1980), with Robert von Hagge; Key Biscayne GC (1972), with Robert von Hagge; Marco Shores CC, Marco Island (1974), with Robert von Hagge; Ocean Reef C (Harbor Course), North Key Largo (1976), with Robert von Hagge; Palm-Aire CC (Palms Course), Pompano Beach (1969), with Robert von Hagge; Palm-Aire CC (Sabals Course), Pompano Beach (Precision, 1969), with Robert von Hagge; Poinciana G&RC, Kissimmee (1973), with Robert von Hagge; Sandalfoot Cove G&CC, Margate (27, 1970), with Robert von Hagge; Sherbrooke G&CC, Lake Worth (1979), with Robert von Hagge; TPC at Prestancia (Course No. 1) {formerly CC of Sarasota}, Sarasota (1976), with Robert von Hagge; Winter Springs GC {formerly Big Cypress GC} (1973), with Robert von Hagge; Woodlands CC (East Course), Tamarac (1969), with Robert von Hagge; Woodlands CC (West Course), Tamarac (1969), with Robert von Hagge; Woodmont CC (Cypress Course), Tamarac (1976), with Robert von Hagge; Woodmont CC (Pines Course), Tamarac (1976), with Robert von Hagge.

Idaho: Shamanah GC, Boise (1983), with Robert von Hagge.

Missouri: Oaks GC, Osage Beach (1980), with Robert von Hagge.

New Mexico: Tanoan GC, Albuquerque (27, 1978), with Robert von Hagge.

North Carolina: Brandywine Bay GC, Morehead City (1983), with Robert von Hagge.

Ohio: Quail Hollow Inn & CC, Painesville (1975), with Robert von Hagge.

Tennessee: Nashville G&AC {formerly Crockett Springs National G&CC}, Brentwood (1972), with Robert von Hagge.

Texas: Chase Oaks GC (Blackjack Course), Plano (1986), with Robert von Hagge; Chase Oaks GC (Sawtooth Course), Plano (9, 1986), with Robert von Hagge; Club at Falcon Point, Katy (1985), with Robert von Hagge; Club at Sonterra (North Course), San Antonio , with Robert von Hagge; Crown Colony CC, Lufkin (1979), with Robert von Hagge; Gleneagles CC (King's Course), Plano (1985), with Robert von Hagge; Gleneagles CC (Queen's Course) (1919), with Robert von Hagge; Hollytree CC, Tyler (1982), with Robert von Hagge; Northgate CC, Houston (1985), with Robert von Hagge; Northshore CC, Portland (1985), with Robert von Hagge; Raveneaux CC (Gold Course), Spring (1980), with Robert von Hagge; Raveneaux CC (Orange Course), Spring (1986), with Robert von Hagge; Rayburn G&CC (Green Nine), Jasper (9, 1984), with Robert von Hagge; TPC at The Woodlands {formerly Woodlands Inn & CC (East Course)} (1982), with Robert von Hagge; Vista Hills CC, El Paso (1975), with Robert von Hagge; Walden on Lake Conroe CC, Montgomery (1976), with Robert von Hagge; Walden on Lake Houston GC (1985), with Robert von Hagge; Willow Creek GC, Spring (1982), with Robert von Hagge; Woodlands Inn & CC (South Course) (1983), with Robert von Hagge.

Wisconsin: Brookfield Hills GC (Precision, 1971), with Robert von Hagge.

Australia: Campbelltown GC, Sydney (1976), with Robert von Hagge; Lakes GC, Sydney (1970), with Robert von Hagge; Magnolia Hills CC, Suncoast (1975), with Robert von Hagge; Ocean Shores GC, Brunswick , with Robert von Hagge.

Bahamas: Cape Eleuthera GC (1971), with Robert von Hagge.

France: Golf Les Bordes (1987), with Robert von Hagge.

Japan: Daisifu Central CC, Fukoka (1971), with Robert von Hagge; Kawaguchiko GC, Mt. Fuji (1979), with Robert von Hagge.

Tahiti: Travelodge GC, Papeete (9), with Robert von Hagge.

Courses Remodeled & Added to by: Bruce Devlin

Arizona: Tucson National GC, Tucson (R., 1979), with Robert von Hagge; Tucson National GC, Tucson (A.9, 1979), with Robert von Hagge.

Florida: Doral CC (Blue Course), Miami (R., 1971), with Robert von Hagge; Doral CC (Gold Course), Miami (R., 1982), with Robert von Hagge; Doral CC (Red Course), Miami (R., 1985), with Robert von Hagge; Ocean Reef C (Dolphin Course), Key Largo (R., 1969), with Robert von Hagge.

Texas: Ranchland Hills GC, Midland (R., 1983), with Robert von Hagge.

Mark DeVries (1927 -)

Mark DeVries attended Michigan State University, receiving a B.A. degree in Landscape Architecture in 1949. He was employed as a landscape architect with the Grand Rapids (Mich.) Department of Parks until 1963, when he entered private practice. His company handled the design of many golf courses in the Sixties and Seventies.

Courses by: Mark DeVries

Michigan: Alpine CC, Comstock Park (1965); Chase Hammond Muni, Muskegon (1969); Courtland Hills GC, Rockford (1979); English Hills GC, Walker (Precision, 9, 1973); Hickory Hills CC, Grand Rapids (1980); Meadowood GC, Cascade (9, 1973); Mount Pleasant CC (9, 1975); Saskatoon GC, Alto (27, 1973); Springfield Oaks GC, Davisburg (1974); Tyler's Creek GC, Alto (1973); Western Greens GC, Wright (1963); Whispering Willows GC, Livonia (1968).

Courses Remodeled & Added to by: Mark DeVries

Michigan: Broadmoor GC (A., 1963); Forest Hills GC (R.8, 1986); Forest Hills GC (A.10, 1986); Meadowood GC, Cascade (A.9, 1986).

William Hickman Diddel (1884 - 1985) ASGCA, Charter Member; President, 1954, 1965.

Born: Indianapolis, Indiana. Died: Zionsville, Indiana at age 100.

A graduate of Wabash College in Indiana, Bill Diddel lettered in baseball, basketball, football and track. He was a member of a national collegiate championship basketball team and later coached basketball for one season at Wabash.

Diddel was also an excellent golfer, but unfortunately Wabash never fielded a golf team. Still, Diddel achieved individual success, winning the Indiana Amateur in 1905, 1906, 1907, 1910 and 1912. He retained his golfing skills throughout his life, and shot his age more times (over 1,000 rounds in all) than any golfer in history.

His first design experience occurred in 1921 when, as a member of Highland G&CC in Indianapolis, Diddel finished a new course routed by Willie Park Jr.

Buoyed by the experience, Diddel began full-time practice as a golf course architect in 1922. He did over seventy-five courses in a career that spanned over fifty years.

Bill Diddel loved to experiment. He built one course, Woodland CC in Carmel, Ind. (where he and his wife lived for years in a log cabin) without any sand bunkers. Instead Diddel used numerous mounds and grass traps. In the late Thirties he developed and patented a "short" golf ball, one that traveled about half the distance of a regular ball. It took over thirty years before others realized the potential of such an invention.

Bill Diddel was confined to a wheelchair during the last decade of his life. He died in a nursing home in his native Indiana just a few months short of his 101st birthday.

Courses by: William H. Diddel

Arkansas: Hot Springs G&CC (Arlington course) (1932).

Florida: Bardmoor CC (East Course), Largo (1968); Bardmoor CC (North Course), Largo (1974); Bardmoor CC (South Course), Largo (1974); CC of Naples (1963); Jupiter Island C, Jupiter (1958); Melbourne G&CC (1926); Sunset G&CC, St. Petersburg (1926); Sunset Hills CC, Tarpon Springs (1926).

Illinois: Carbondale CC (9, 1929); Danville CC (9, 1928); Edgewood Valley CC, LaGrange (1926); Rolling Green CC, Arlington Heights (1930); Sunset Ridge CC, Northbrook (1924).

Indiana: Beechwood GC, LaPorte (1930); Beeson Park GC, Winchester (9, 1932); Benton CC (9, 1941); Brookshire GC, Carmel (1971); Coffin Muni, Indianapolis (1931); Columbus CC (9, 1946); Crawfordsville Muni (1931); CC of Indianapolis (1923); Danville CC (1927); Elcona CC, Elkhart (1955); Elks CC, West Lafayette (1928); Elks CC, Marion (18, 1961); Erskine Muni, South Bend (1934); Evansville CC; Fendrich GC, Evansville (1945); Forest Hills CC, Richmond (1931); Forest Park GC, Brazil (9, 1935); Fort Harrison GC (1970); Fox Cliff CC, Martinsville (1970); Green Hills G&CC, Selma (1925); Greentree CC, Carmel (1959); Hamilton Muni, Evansville (1951); Hawthorne Hills CC, Indianapolis (27, 1963); Highland G&CC, Indianapolis (1921), with Willie Park Jr; Hillcrest CC, Indianapolis (1924); Honeywell GC, Wabash (9); Kilbuck GC, Anderson (1965); Marion CC (9, 1927); Martinsville CC (1925); Meridian Hills CC, Indianapolis (1923); Mineral Springs GC, Martinsville (1953); Minnestrista GC, Muncie (9, 1930); Oak Hill GC, Middlebury (1962); Oak Lawn GC, Elkhart (1962); Purdue University GC (South Course), West Lafayette (1934); Riverside Muni, Indianapolis (1935); Rockville Lake GC (9, 1959); Rolling Hills CC, Newburgh; Rozella Ford GC, Warsaw; Rushville Elks CC (9, 1950); Shady Hills GC, Marion (1957); Shelbyville Elks CC (9, 1930); Speedway 500 GC, Indianapolis (1928); Sun Blest GC, Noblesville (1940); Tipton Muni (9, 1963); Ulen CC, Lebanon (1924); Valley View GC, New Albany (1962); Walnut Grove GC, New Albany (1969); Woodland GC, Carmel (1951).

Kansas: Wichita CC (1950).

Kentucky: Frankfort CC (1949); Highland CC, Fort Thomas (9, 1954); Wildwood CC, Louisville (1952).

Michigan: Echo Lake CC, Detroit (1927); Forest Lake CC, Bloomfield Hills (1926); Hidden Valley C, Gaylord (1957); Lake St Clair CC, Detroit (1929); Shanty Creek GC (Deskin course), Bellaire (1968).

Missouri: Crystal Lake CC, St. Louis (1929).

Montana: Lewiston Elks CC (9, 1948); Meadow Lark CC, Great Falls (1949).

Ohio: California GC, Cincinnati (1936); Fairborn CC (1961); Greene CC, Yellow Springs; Hamilton Muni (1958); Indian Valley GC, Cincinnati; Kenwood CC (Kendale Course), Cincinnati (1930); Kenwood CC (Kenview Course), Cincinnati (1930); Meadowbrook CC, Dayton (9, 1956); Miami View GC, Miamitown (1961); Reeves Memorial GC, Cincinnati (9, 1965); Sharon Woods CC, Sharon Center (1935); Swaim Fields GC, Cincinnati (9, 1933); Twin Run GC, Cincinnati (1965); Walnut Grove CC, Dayton (9, 1962); Western Row GC, Mason (1965); Wright-Patterson AFB GC, Dayton (1953).

Oklahoma: Mohawk Park Muni (Woodbine Course), Tulsa (1934).

Texas: Northwood C, Dallas (1948).

Wisconsin: Brynwood CC, Milwaukee (1954); Lakeside CC, Manitowoc (1956).

Courses Remodeled & Added to by: William H. Diddel

Arkansas: CC of Little Rock (R., 1929); Hot Springs G&CC (Majestic Course) (R., 1932).

Colorado: Denver CC (R., 1957).

Florida: Mountain Lake C, Lake Wales (R., 1961); Oceanside G&CC, Ormond Beach (A.9); Oceanside G&CC, Ormond Beach (R.9); Ponce de Leon CC, St. Augustine (R., 1955).

Illinois: Oak Park CC (R., 1955); Westmoreland CC, Wilmette (R., 1963).

Indiana: Anderson CC (R.9, 1935); Anderson CC (A.9, 1935); Coffin Muni, Indianapolis (R., 1954); CC of Terre Haute (R.9, 1928); CC of Terre Haute (A.9, 1928); Fort Wayne CC (R., 1950); Green Hills G&CC, Selma (R., 1951); Hillcrest G&CC, Batesville (R.9, 1933); Kokomo CC (A.9, 1925); Kokomo CC (R.9, 1925); Lafayette CC (R.9, 1924); Marion CC (R., 1955); North Shore CC, Syracuse (R.9, 1927); North Shore CC, Syracuse (A.9, 1927); Sarah Shank Muni, Indianapolis (R.9, 1941); Sarah Shank Muni, Indianapolis (A.9, 1941); Speedway 500 GC, Indianapolis (A.9, 1956); Tipton Muni (A.9, 1967); Wawasee GC, Syracuse (A.9, 1927); Wawasee GC, Syracuse (R.9, 1927); Woodmar CC, Hammond (R.9, 1967).

Kansas: Macdonald Park Muni, Wichita (R., 1950); Mission Hills CC, Fairway (R., 1957).

Kentucky: Big Spring CC, Louisville (R., 1951); Louisville CC (R., 1955).

Michigan: Barton Hills CC, Ann Arbor (R., 1952); Birmingham CC (R., 1930); Black River CC (A.9, 1956); Black River CC (R.9, 1956); Forest Lake CC, Bloomfield Hills (A.4, 1959); Forest Lake CC, Bloomfield Hills (R., 1959); Orchard Lake CC (R., 1954).

Missouri: Midland Valley CC, St. Louis (R., 1928); Oakwood CC, Kansas City (R., 1961); Westwood CC, St. Louis (R., 1961).

Montana: Harve Elks CC (R., 1950).

Nebraska: Happy Hollow C, Omaha (R., 1946).

Ohio: Avon Fields GC, Cincinnati (R., 1933); Clovernook CC, Cincinnati (R., 1962); Kenwood CC (Kendale Course), Cincinnati (R., 1966); Kenwood CC (Kenview Course), Cincinnati (R., 1966); Still Meadow CC (R., 1956); Swaim Fields GC, Cincinnati (A.9, 1955); Western Hills GC, Cincinnati (R., 1931).

Pennsylvania: Shawnee CC, Shawnee-on-Delaware (R., 1953); Shawnee CC, Shawnee-on-Delaware (A.9, 1963); Shawnee CC, Shawnee-on-Delaware (R.18, 1963).

Tennessee: Millington NAS GC, Memphis (R., 1966).

Ontario: Hamilton G&CC, Ancaster (R., 1966).

William H. Dietsch Jr. (1928 -)
Born: Atlanta, Georgia.

Bill Dietsch graduated from Staunton Military Academy in 1946 and attended the University of Pennsylvania where he majored in Mechanical Engineering. He then served with the U.S. Army and was a witness to the first test of the hydrogen bomb in the South Pacific.

Following military duty, Dietsch started in course maintenance in 1955 under superintendent Scott Tuppen. Shortly thereafter, Tuppen was hired to build courses for Robert Trent Jones, and he took his assistant with him. Dietsch worked for the Jones organization for twelve years, and for a time was closely associated with Jones' chief assistant Francis Duane.

In 1967 Dietsch entered private practice as a course architect based in Florida.

Courses by: Bill Dietsch

Florida: CC of Miami (South Course), Hialeah (1968); Golf Club of Delray (Precision, 1983); Lakeview GC, Delray Beach (Precision,); Oriole G&TC, Margate (27, 1982); Springtree GC, Sunrise (Precision, 1972); Sunrise Lakes Phase 3 GC, Sunrise (Precision, 9, 1981).

Courses Remodeled & Added to by: Bill Dietsch

Florida: Miami Springs GC (R.10, 1982); Pasadena GC, St. Petersburg (R.); Rolling Green G&CC (A.9); Rolling Hills CC, Ft. Lauderdale (A.9, 1983).

Francis J. Duane (1921 -) ASGCA, President, 1972.
Born: Bronx, New York.

Frank Duane studied Landscape Architecture at the State University of New York, graduating in 1944. He was employed for a short time as a landscape architect with the New Hampshire Department of Forestry and Recreation, then in 1945 went to work for golf architect Robert Trent Jones. He became chief assistant to Jones and remained with him until 1963, when he went out on his own. In 1965 Duane was stricken with myelitus, a debilitating disease that confined him to a wheelchair. Undaunted, Duane continued his design practice. For a period in the early 1970s he worked in partnership with legendary golfer Arnold Palmer.

Courses by: Frank Duane

Alabama: Turtle Point Y&CC, Florence (1964), with Robert Trent Jones.

California: El Dorado Hills GC (Precision, 1964), with Robert Trent Jones; Half Moon Bay CC (1973), with Arnold Palmer.

Colorado: Eisenhower GC (Blue Course), US Air Force Academy (1959), with Robert Trent Jones and Robert Trent Jones.

Florida: Apollo Beach G & Sea C (9, 1962), with Robert Trent Jones; CC of Miami (East Course), Hialeah (1962), with Robert Trent Jones; CC of Miami (North Course), Hialeah (NLE, Par 3, 1962), with Robert Trent Jones; CC of Miami (West Course), Hialeah (1962), with Robert Trent Jones; Mariner Sands GC (Green Course), Stuart (1973), with Arnold Palmer; Meadows CC (Highlands Course), Sarasota (9, 1976); Meadows CC (Meadows Course), Sarasota (9, 1976); Patrick AFB GC, Cocoa Beach (9, 1961), with Robert Trent Jones; Ponte Vedra C (Lagoon Course), Ponte Vedra Beach (9, 1962), with Robert Trent Jones; Royal Palm Y&CC, Boca Raton (1960), with Robert Trent Jones; Spring Lake G&CC, Sebring (1979).

Georgia: Chattahoochee GC, Gainesville (1959), with Robert Trent Jones; Landings at Skidaway Island (Magnolia) (1973), with Arnold Palmer.

Hawaii: Honolulu International CC (1976), with Arnold Palmer; Kapalua GC (Bay Course), Maui (1974), with Arnold Palmer.

Louisiana: Timberlane CC, Gretna (1959), with Robert Trent Jones.

Michigan: Point O'Woods G&CC, Benton Harbor (1958), with Robert Trent Jones.

Missouri: Bellerive CC, Creve Coeur (1959), with Robert Trent Jones.

Montana: Big Sky GC (1974), with Arnold Palmer; Yellowstone G&CC, Billings (1959), with Robert Trent Jones.

New Hampshire: Portsmouth G&CC (1957), with Robert Trent Jones.

New Jersey: Goldman Hotel GC, East Orange (9); Howell Park GC, Farmingdale (1971); Montammy CC, Alpine (1966); Preakness Valley Park GC; Tamcrest CC, Alpine (9, 1970); Tammy Brook CC, Cresskill (1962), with Robert Trent Jones.

New York: Brae Burn CC, Purchase (1964); Fallsview Hotel GC, Ellenville (9, 1962), with Robert Trent Jones; Glimmerglass State Park GC, East Springfield; Golf Hill G&CC, Fatogue (1966); Hampstead GC at Lido, Long Beach (1956), with Robert Trent Jones; Hampton GC; Merrick Park GC (9, 1967); North Hills CC, Manhasset (1961), with Robert Trent Jones; North Shore Towers GC, Little Neck (1976); Osiris CC, Walden (9, 1965); Pines Hotel GC, South Fallsburg (9, 1960), with Robert Trent Jones; Pleasant View Lodge GC, Freehold (9, 1968); Rock Hill G&CC, Manorville (1966); Seven Oaks GC, Colgage Univ. (9, 1955), with Robert Trent Jones; Sound Shore GC, Greenport; Spook Rock GC, Ramapo (1969); Sycamore GC, Rarenna (1973); Tall Timbers CC, Slingerlands (1967); Tuxedo Park C, Tuxedo Park (1947), with Robert Trent Jones; Wildwood CC, Riverhead (1964).

North Carolina: Duke University GC, Durham (1957), with Robert Trent Jones; Sugar Hollow GC, Banner Elk (Precision, 1974); Tanglewood GC (West Course), Clemmons (1957), with Robert Trent Jones.

South Carolina: Myrtle Beach National GC (North Course) (1973), with Arnold Palmer; Myrtle Beach National GC (South Course) (1973), with Arnold Palmer; Myrtle Beach National GC (West Course) (1973), with Arnold Palmer; Sea Pines Plantation GC (Club Course), Hilton Head Island (1976), with Arnold Palmer.

Tennessee: Scona Lodge GC, Alcoa (9, 1957), with Robert Trent Jones.

Texas: Corpus Christi CC (1965), with Robert Trent Jones.

Vermont: Fox Run GC, Ludlow (9, 1968); Sugarbush GC, Warren (1963), with Robert Trent Jones.

Virginia: Stumpy Lake GC, Norfolk (1957), with Robert Trent Jones.

Ontario: London Hunt & CC, London (1960), with Robert Trent Jones.

Colombia: El Rincon C, Bogota (1963), with Robert Trent Jones.

Jamaica: Half Moon-Rose Hall GC, Montego Bay (1961), with Robert Trent Jones.

Puerto Rico: Dorado Beach GC (East Course), Dorado (9, 1958), with Robert Trent Jones; Dorado Beach GC (West Course), Dorado (9, 1958), with Robert Trent Jones.

Courses Remodeled & Added to by: Frank Duane

Connecticut: CC of New Canaan (R., 1960), with Robert Trent Jones; Innis Arden GC, Old Greenwich (R., 1964); Millbrook C, Greenwich (R.3, 1964); Patterson C, Fairfield (R.1, 1965); Ridgewood CC, Danbury (R., 1959), with Robert Trent Jones.

Florida: CC of Orlando (R., 1959), with Robert Trent Jones.

New Jersey: Arcola CC, Paramus (R., 1960), with Robert Trent Jones; Blue Hill GC (R., 1970); Cherry Valley CC (R.12, 1978); Colonia CC (R., 1970); Crestmont CC, West Orange (R.3, 1963); Essex County CC (West Course), West Orange (R.9, 1967).

New York: Bartlett CC, Olean (R., 1960), with Robert Trent Jones; Bellevue CC, Syracuse (A.4, 1972); Bellevue CC, Syracuse (R.14, 1972); Bethpage State Park GC (Blue Course), Farmingdale (R.); Bethpage State Park GC (Green Course), Farmingdale (R.); Bethpage State Park GC (Red Course), Farmingdale (R.); Bethpage State Park GC (Yellow Course), Farmingdale (R.); Century GC, White Plains (R., 1959), with Robert Trent Jones; Cherry Valley CC, Garden City (R., 1962), with Robert Trent Jones; Douglaston Park GC, Douglaston (R.5, 1964); Elmwood CC, White Plains (R.1, 1977); Engineers GC, Roslyn (R.3, 1970); Engineers GC, Roslyn (R.18, 1977); Garden City CC (R.6, 1970); Garden City GC (R., 1958), with Robert Trent Jones; Hampshire CC, Mamaroneck (R.4, 1964); Huntington CC (R., 1960), with Robert Trent Jones; Inwood CC (R., 1972); IBM CC (R.1, 1978); La Tourette Muni, Staten Island (R.4, 1964); Mill River CC (R.4, 1971); Moonbrook CC, Jamestown (R., 1959), with Robert Trent Jones; Muttontown G&CC, East Norwich (R.1, 1964); Nassau CC, Glen Cove (R., 1970); Old Oaks CC, Purchase (R.6, 1968); Old Westbury G&CC (R.2, 1972); Plandome CC (R.); Pleasant View Lodge GC, Freehold (A.9, 1978); Quaker Ridge CC, Scarsdale (R., 1964); Richmond County CC, Staten Island (R.4, 1970); Ridgeway CC (R.9, 1976); Rockville CC (R.1, 1965); Sands Point CC, Port Washington (R., 1961), with Robert Trent Jones; Sands Point CC, Port Washington (R., 1964); Scarsdale GC, Hartsdale (R.4, 1965); Seawane C, Hewlitt Harbor (R., 1964); South Fork CC (R.3, 1974); Woodcrest CC (R., 1976).

Pennsylvania: Westmoreland CC, Export (R., 1958), with Robert Trent Jones.

Vermont: Marble Island G&YC, Essex Junction (R.9, 1964).

Colombia: El Rincon C, Bogota (Par 3, A., 1964), with Robert Trent Jones.

Puerto Rico: Dorado Beach GC (East Course), Dorado (A.9, 1961), with Robert Trent Jones; Dorado Beach GC (West Course), Dorado (A.9, 1966), with Robert Trent Jones.

Joan Frederik Dudok Van Heel (1925 -) BAGCA
Born: Naarden, The Netherlands.

After obtaining a Masters at Law from Leiden University, J.F. Dudok Van Heel worked as an apprentice banker, and then in the oil, petrochemical, pharmaceutical and real estate industries.

A noted Continental golfer, Dudok van Heel won 14 national titles, and represented The Netherlands in international competition for 25 years.

After handling the financing and management of several European golf projects, he founded Golf Development International, based in Belgium, in the mid-1970s. Dudok van Heel served as course architect for several GDI projects.

Courses by: J.F. Dudok Van Heel

Netherlands: De Dommel GC, Hertogenbosch; Golf Club de Schoot, Sint Oedenrode (9, 1973); Sluispolder GC (9, 1985).

West Germany: Kohlerhof GC, Bonn; Olching GC, Munich .

Courses Remodeled & Added to by: J.F. Dudok Van Heel

Austria: Murhof GC, Frohnleiten (A.9, 1963).

West Germany: Chiemsee GC, Prien (A.9).

George Duncan (1893 - 1964)
Born: Aberdeen, Scotland. Died: Scotland at age 70.

George Duncan won the British Open in 1920 and was runner-up in 1927. A member of several Ryder Cup teams, he served as its captain in 1929.

Duncan laid out several courses on his own and in collaboration with his friends James Braid and Abe Mitchell. He was primarily responsible for restoring the course at Royal Dornoch to eighteen holes after World War II. Duncan added four new holes to replace four lost to the R.A.F. The four "lost" holes were later returned to Royal Dornoch and made into the short, nine-hole Struie course.

Courses by: George Duncan

England: Hallowes GC, Yorkshire; Harrogate GC, Yorkshire (1897), with Sandy Herd; Mere G&CC, Surrey (1934), with James Braid and John R.Stutt; Tapton Park GC, Derby (1936).

Scotland: Stonehaven GC.

Courses Remodeled & Added to by: George Duncan

England: Harrogate GC, Yorkshire (R.); Wheatley GC, Yorkshire (R.).

Scotland: Royal Dornoch GC, Sutherland (R., 1947); Royal Dornoch GC, Sutherland (A.4, 1947).

John Duncan Dunn (1874 - 1951)
Born: North Berwick, Scotland. Died: Los Angeles, California at age 67.

John Duncan Dunn trained as a professional greenkeeper and course builder under his father Tom Dunn. After laying out a few courses in Britain and on the Continent, he followed his uncle Young Willie, only nine years his senior, to the U.S. in 1894. He worked briefly with sporting goods firms Slazengers and Bridgeport Arms and then acquired the post of professional at the newly opened Ardsley-on-Hudson CC.

By 1900 J.D. was in charge of planning, building and operating golf courses for the Florida West Coast Railroad. Around the same time, he collaborated with Walter Travis on the design of several courses in the Northeast. Throughout these years he made numerous trips back to Britain and the Continent, often in the company of his brother Seymour, who had joined him in America.

J.D. settled in California after World War I, where he was hired as professional at Los Angeles CC. He continued to reside in that state until his death. An excellent teacher of golf, John Duncan Dunn was also a competent landscape artist and the author of numerous magazine articles and books on golf instruction.

Courses by: John Duncan Dunn

California: Atascadero CC (NLE, 1927); Brockway GC, Kings Beach (9, 1927); Catalina GC, Avalon (1925); Idyllwild CC; Lake Elsinore GC (NLE,); Lake Norconian C (NLE, 1928); Los Serranos Lakes CC (North Course), Chino (1925); Parkridge CC; Peter Pan CC (NLE,); Rio Hondo CC, Downey; Santa Ana CC (1924).

Florida: Belleview-Biltmore Hotel & C (West) (9, 1899); El Merrie Del CC (NLE,); Fairmede CC (NLE,); Gables GC (NLE, 9, 1898); Ocala GC (NLE, 9); Winter Park GC (NLE, 1900).

Maine: Cape Arundel GC, Kennebunkport (1900), with Walter J. Travis.

New York: Catskills Village GC (NLE, 1900); Interstate Park GC (NLE, 9, 1900); Long Beach Hotel GC (NLE, 1900); Muirfield Golf Links (NLE, 1931); Quaker Ridge CC, Scarsdale (9, 1915).

Ohio: Elks CC, Hamilton.

Vermont: Ekwanok CC, Manchester (1900), with Walter J. Travis.

England: Lee-on-the-Solent GC (1905).

France: Golf de Dinard, with Tom Dunn; Golf de Hardelot; Hendaye GC.

Netherlands: Clingendael GC; Doornsche GC, Utrecht (NLE, 1894); Hilversum GC (1910); Noord Nederlandse G&CC; Rosendaelsche GC, Arnhem (1896).

Courses Remodeled & Added to by: John Duncan Dunn

Massachusetts: Essex CC, Manchester (R.), with Walter J. Travis.

Seymour Dunn (1882 - 1959)

Born: Prestwick, Scotland. Died: Lake Placid, New York at age 77.

Seymour Dunn traveled to America at age 12 to work as assistant to his brother John Duncan Dunn at Ardsley-on-Hudson. He later held numerous professional and golf teaching positions on both sides of the Atlantic, among them at the Griswold Hotel and Stevens Hotel in America, Ealing in England, in France, and Royal County Down in Northern Ireland. Seymour finally settled down in 1906 at Lake Placid CC in New York to raise a family, but by the 1930s was on the move again.

Throughout his career, Seymour traveled back and forth to Great Britain on a number of business ventures, sometimes accompanied by J.D. The brothers established in 1900 the first indoor golf school at Bournemouth, England, and later founded a similar school in New York City, which became the world's largest.

Seymour Dunn ranked among the great teachers of golfing fundamentals, numbering Jim Barnes, Walter Hagen, Gene Sarazen and Joe Kirkwood among his students. He was the author of *Golf Fundamentals, Elementary Golf Instruction, Standardized Golf Instruction* and *Golf Jokes.* Seymour designed numerous courses as an avocation, both in Europe and America.

Courses by: Seymour Dunn

Florida: Lake Placid C, Sebring (NLE,); Silver Spring GC, Ocala (NLE,); Tampa Bay Hotel GC (NLE, 9, 1899).

Mississippi: CC of Laurel.

New Jersey: Fort Monmouth GC.

New York: Ausable C; Cazenovia CC (9); Chautauqua GC (9); Craig Wood CC (9); Fawn C; Indole G&CC (9); Lafayette CC, Syracuse; Lake Placid C (Lower Course) (1909); Lake Placid C (Practice Course) (9, 1909); Locust Hill CC, Rochester (9, 1928); Paul Smith's Adirondack C (9); Raquette Lake GC (9); Saranac Inn G&CC; Schroon Lake GC (9, 1923); Ticonderoga CC; Tuscarora CC.

Belgium: Antwerp GC; King Leopold Private Course; Royal GC de Belgique, Brussels (1906); Royal Zoute GC (1908).

France: Chemay Estate GC; D'Allegre Estate GC (9); Rothschild Estate GC.

Italy: King Emmanual Private Course; Ugolino GC, Florence.

Courses Remodeled & Added to by: Seymour Dunn

New Jersey: Red Bank G&CC (R.).

France: Racing C de France (Valley), La Boulie (R.).

Northern Ireland: Royal County Down GC, Newcastle (R., 1905).

Tom Dunn (1849 - 1902)

Born: Royal Blackheath, England. Died: Blagdon, England at age 52.

Tom Dunn became professional at Wimbledon (London Scottish) in 1870. Its course had originally been laid out by his father, Old Willie Dunn, with eighteen holes, but over the years it had been reduced to seven. In his first year, Tom extended it again to eighteen holes. He later held posts of professional at North Berwick, Tooting Bec near London, Meyrick Park in Bournemouth and other courses.

Tom Dunn was the most prolific course designer of his day. He produced layouts that were inexpensive and serviceable, making it possible for increasing numbers of golfers from all social classes to take up the game. A great salesman, he was quoted as telling each of his clients, "God meant this site to be a golf course." The first designer to work on inland rather than links sites, Tom Dunn was a firm believer in a cross bunker requiring a forced carry from the tee, another for the approach and an even third on a three-shot hole. Dunn himself considered Broadstone in England, where he was "not stinted for men, money or materials," to be his best effort. He always felt Meyrick Park to be his greatest challenge because of its dense cover of heather, furze and pine forest.

Tom was married to Isabel Gourlay, "the greatest woman golfer of her day" and descendant of the Gourlays of Musselburgh (renowned golf instructors to the Kings of Scotland and ball makers to the Royal Family of Great Britain). Tom traveled to America on several occasions, visiting brother Young Willie, sons John Duncan and Seymour, and daughter May, who was a pioneer woman professional golfer.

Despite his presence in the U.S., it is doubtful that Tom ever laid out an American golf course. While many a club in the United States claimed to have a Tom Dunn course, those layouts were all designed by one of the other Dunns. Tom's work in Great Britain and on the Continent, however, was extensive, and he claimed to have some 137 courses to his credit.

Courses by: Tom Dunn

Canary Islands: Ralara GC.

England: Ashley Wood GC, Dorset (9, 1893); Bath GC (1880); Beckenham Place Park GC (1907); Bramshaw GC (Manor Course) (1880); Brighton and Hove GC, Sussex (9, 1887); Broadstone GC, Dorset (1898); Bromley GC; Bude and North Cornwall GC (1890); Bulwell Forest GC (1902); Burhill GC, Surrey (9, 1907); Buscot Park GC; Chiselhurst GC, Kent (1894); Eltham Warren GC (1890); Enfield GC (1893); Erewash Valley GC, Derbyshire (1905); Felixstowe Ferry GC, Suffolk (NLE, 9, 1880); Frinton GC, Frinton-on-Sea (1896); Ganton GC (1891); Hampstead GC (9, 1894); Hastings and St. Leonards GC (1893); Hastings GC, Sussex (NLE, 1893); Huddersfield GC, Yorkshire (1891); Kinsdown GC (1880); Lansdown GC (1894);

Lindrick GC (1891); Maidenhead GC (1898); Meyrick Park GC, Hampshire (1894); North Oxford GC (1908); Northwood GC (1891); Nottingham City GC; Penwortham GC (1908); Richmond GC (1891); Royal Cinque Ports GC, Deal (9, 1892); Royal Mid-Surrey GC, Surrey (1892); Royal Worlington and Newmarket GC, Suffolk (9, 1892); Royston GC (1893); Saunton GC (1897); Seacroft GC, Lincolnshire (1892); Seaford GC, Sussex (1887); Sheringham GC (9); Sherwood Forest GC, Nottinghamshire (1904); Surbiton GC (1895); Tooting Bec C (1890); Ventnor GC (9, 1892); Weston-Super-Mare GC, Somerset (1892); Whickham GC (1911); Woking GC (1893).

France: Coubert GC; Golf de Biarritz (1888), with Willie Dunn Jr; Golf de Dinard, with John Duncan Dunn.

Netherlands: Haagsche GC (NLE, 1893).

Scotland: Blairgowrie GC (Rosemount Course) (9, 1889).

Courses Remodeled & Added to by: Tom Dunn

England: Littlestone GC, Kent (R.); London Scottish GC (A.9, 1870); London Scottish GC (R., 1901).

Ireland: Cork GC, County Cork (R.9, 1880).

Scotland: North Berwick GC, East Lothian (R., 1883).

Willie Dunn Sr. (1821 - 1878)

Born: Musselburgh, Scotland. Died: North Berwick, Scotland at age 57.

Old Willie Dunn was the patriarch of a distinguished line of professional golfers and course designers. He was born into a golfing family, although his father was a plasterer by trade. Legend has it that a Dunn was partly responsible for the interest of King James I in golf at Leith. Whether or not this is true, the name of Dunn has been renowned in the world of golf for centuries.

Old Willie was partnered with his twin brother Jamie in a famous challenge match played over St. Andrews, Musselburgh and North Berwick for the then-huge purse of 400 pounds. The twin Dunns were losers to the pair of Allan Robertson and Old Tom Morris.

In 1850 Willie undertook the duties of greenkeeper and professional at Royal Blackheath in England, where he was joined two years later by Jamie. After twenty years they returned to Scotland, working first at Leith, later at Musselburgh, and finally at North Berwick. Old Willie is known to have rebuilt several holes at Royal Blackheath, to have designed the first Wimbledon course for the London Scottish Regiment in 1865 and to have planned a number of three-hole layouts.

Four golf course designers who became famous on both sides of the Atlantic were sons and grandsons of Old Willie: Tom Dunn, Young Willie Dunn, John Duncan Dunn and Seymour Dunn. Several of Willie's other descendants became well-known professional or amateur golfers in Great Britain and the United States. Cameron and Robert Dunn, both sons of Seymour, became prominent American professionals, while Norman "Dick" Dunn, Young Willie's son, returned to England, served in the British Army during World War I and later became a well known amateur golfer in Great Britain.

Courses by: Willie Dunn

England: London Scottish GC (NLE, 9, 1865).

France: Pau GC (1856).

Courses Remodeled & Added to by: Willie Dunn

England: Royal Blackheath GC (NLE, R.).

Willie Dunn Jr. (1865 - 1952)

Born: Musselburgh, Scotland. Died: London, England at age 87.

Young Willie Dunn trained as a professional, greenkeeper and course builder under his brother Tom, sixteen years his senior and well-established in England. Young Willie served as professional at Westward Ho! for a few months in 1886, then laid out the Chingford course near London before moving to Biarritz in France. While working as professional at Biarritz, which he had helped his brother build, Willie met American W.K. Vanderbilt and was persuaded to try his hand at an American course.

Willie was the first Dunn to relocate to the U.S., and the course he created for the Vanderbilt syndicate, Shinnecock Hills on Long Island, opened with twelve holes in 1891. To build it, he had employed a crew of 150 Indians, none of whom had ever seen a golf course, golf ball or club. Willie remained at Shinnecock for several years as pro-greenkeeper and won an unofficial U.S. Open in 1894. As a golfer, he was among the first to experiment with steel shafts and cardboard tees.

As a designer, Young Willie was ahead of the heathlands architects in utilizing an occasional lateral bunker in place of the traditional cross bunker. He was also the first of a group of colorful designers in America of fluctuating fortune. He experienced periods of great wealth followed by periods of near penury. During lean times his family would be dispatched home to England to await improved circumstances. Young Willie numbered John D. Rockefeller, John L. Sullivan, Buffalo Bill Cody and Zane Grey among his close friends.

Until 1910 Willie remained on the Eastern Seaboard, laying out courses and working as a pro-greenkeeper, making only occasional trips back to Britain and the Continent. He was then employed as a club designer with the firm of Crawford, MacGregor and Canby Co. of Dayton, Ohio. In the early 1920s Willie moved to St. Louis and later to Menlo Park, California. He returned to England in 1940 and remained there until his death in 1952.

Courses by: Willie Dunn Jr

Georgia: Jekyll Island GC (NLE, 9, 1894).

Iowa: Algona CC (9, 1920).

Maryland: Baltimore CC (Roland Park Course) (NLE, 1898).

New Jersey: Lakewood GC (9, 1892); Lawrence Harbour CC.

New York: Apawamis C, Rye (1898), with Maturin Ballou; Ardsley CC, Ardsley-on-Hudson (1895); Elmira CC (9); Rockaway Hunting C, Cedarhurst (NLE, 9, 1894); Scarsdale GC, Hartsdale (9, 1898); Shinnecock Hills GC (Ladies Course) (NLE,); Westbrook CC, Great River (1893).

Pennsylvania: Philadelphia CC (NLE, 9, 1893).

Quebec: Royal Montreal GC (South Course), Dixie (1900).

England: Chingford GC (1888); John O'Gaunt GC (Carthagena Course), Bedfordshire.

France: Golf de Biarritz (1888), with Tom Dunn.

Courses Remodeled & Added to by: Willie Dunn Jr
New York: Shinnecock Hills GC (NLE, R.12, 1892); Shinnecock Hills GC (NLE, A.8, 1892).

Robert Charles Dunning (1901 - 1979)
Born: Kansas City, Kansas. Died: Emporia, Kansas at age 78.
Bob Dunning attended military academies, where he excelled at all sports, and for a time played semi-pro baseball. He then attended Kansas University and Emporia State College, receiving a B.A. degree in 1921.

Following college, he became a professional golfer and after apprenticing under Art Hall of Kansas City became pro-greenkeeper at McAlester (Okla.) CC. He worked on several course remodeling jobs while at McAlester and in the Mid-Thirties attended the Massachusetts Turfgrass School, where he met Dr. John Monteith. He joined Monteith as an assistant in 1940.

Dunning spent World War II with the Army Corps of Engineers developing Bermudagrass runways in Texas. After the War he assisted Ralph Plummer in establishing several veterans hospital courses in the South and then formed a successful turf equipment business in Tulsa, Oklahoma. During the 1950s, Dunning was highly regarded as a turfgrass expert and greens consultant. His Texas experience had convinced him that golf greens could be built on bases consisting almost entirely of sand, and he converted several sand green courses in Oklahoma to sand-base grass greens with great success.

Dunning retired from his equipment business in 1960 and, with the assistance of his wife Inez, devoted the next fifteen years to the full-time design and construction of golf courses. The death of his wife and his own health forced him to retire in 1978.
Courses by: Bob Dunning
Kansas: Alvamar GC, Lawrence (1968); Dubs Dread GC, Piper (1963); Happy Hunting C, Lenexa (9); Leawood South CC, Leawood (1969); Pawnee Prairie Muni, Wichita (1970).
Louisiana: New Orleans VA Hospital GC (Par 3, 9, 1946), with Ralph Plummer.
Missouri: Blue Hills CC, Kansas City (1964); Holiday Hills CC, Branson.
Oklahoma: Elk City G&CC (9, 1953); Falconhead GC, Burneyville (1953), with Waco Turner; Hobart CC (9, 1965); Pauls Valley G&CC; Pauls Valley Muni GC (9, 1951); Sunset CC, Bartesville; Sunset Hills GC, Guymon; Woodward Muni (9, 1954).
Texas: McKinney Muni GC (9, 1946), with Ralph Plummer.
Courses Remodeled & Added to by: Bob Dunning
Kansas: Coffeyville CC (R., 1965); Indian Hills CC, Prairie Village (R., 1965); Kansas City CC, Shawnee Mission (R., 1964); Macdonald Park Muni, Wichita (R., 1963); Meadowbrook CC, Prairie Village (R., 1966); Mission Hills CC, Fairway (R., 1964); Sim Park Muni, Wichita (R., 1963).
Missouri: Excelsior Springs CC (Par 3, A.9, 1963); Hickory Hills CC, Springfield (R., 1962); St. Joseph CC (R.1, 1973).
Oklahoma: McAlester CC (R.9, 1960).

Alice O'Neal Dye (1927 -) ASGCA
Born: Indianapolis, Indiana.
Alice O'Neal met her future husband, Pete Dye, while both were students at Rollins College in Winter Park, Florida. They married in 1950 and moved to her hometown of Indianapolis, where both became insurance salespersons. They both also worked on their golf games. Pete had some competitive success, but never came close to matching his wife's impressive record. Over the years, Alice Dye won seven Indiana Women's Amateur titles (including three prior to their marriage), three Florida State Women's Amateur titles, five Women's Western Senior Championships and two USGA Women's Senior Amateur Championships. She was named to the 1970 Curtis Cup team at age 42, was selected as Florida Senior Woman Golfer of the Year five years in succession, and was voted to the Indiana Hall of Fame.

Alice left the insurance business after the birth of their first son in 1952, but Pete continued until 1959, when he quit to pursue a career in golf design. Pete and Alice formed a company and began designing and building small-town layouts around central Indiana. It was an extremely low budget operation in the beginning; for one project, Alice propagated a stand of bentgrass in their front yard and transported it to the course site in the trunk of their Oldsmobile.

In those early days, Alice handled all the drafting for Pete. "Pete couldn't read a contour map. I had to teach him," she later recalled. "And he never did learn to draw." While their sons were young, Alice handled projects close to home while Pete went out on the road, and for a time mainly handled the paperwork of the business. Once the boys reached their teens, she again took a more active role in the design aspect of their projects.

Alice Dye considered her most valuable contribution to golf architecture to be the expert attention she devoted to the planning and placement of tees and hazards to create proper challenges for female golfers. For years she spoke and wrote extensively on the need for more than a single set of tees for women. The wide variance in womens' skills at any course, she contended, dictated forward and back (and sometimes even middle) tees for women, just as had been provided for years for men.

In 1982 Alice Dye became the first woman member of the ASGCA.
Courses by: Alice Dye
California: La Quinta Hotel GC (Mountain Course), La Quinta (1981), with Pete Dye and Lee Schmidt; PGA West GC (Stadium Course), La Quinta (1986), with Pete Dye and Lee Schmidt.
Florida: TPC at Sawgrass, Ponte Vedra Beach (1980), with Pete Dye.
Indiana: El Dorado CC, Greenwood (9, 1959), with Pete Dye; Heather Hills CC, Indianapolis (1961), with Pete Dye; Monticello CC (1963), with Pete Dye; William S. Sahm Muni, Indianapolis (1963), with Pete Dye.
South Carolina: Harbour Town G Links, Hilton Head Island (1969), with Pete Dye and Jack Nicklaus.
Texas: Austin CC (1984), with Pete Dye.
Dominican Republic: Casa de Campo (Links Course), La Ramona (1976), with Pete Dye and Lee Schmidt.

Kenneth E. Dye Jr. (1953 -) ASGCA
Born: San Antonio, Texas.
No relation to the Pete Dye clan, Ken Dye received a Landscape Architecture Degree from North Carolina State University in 1976, after lettering on the golf team (and often playing as number one man) for four years. Dye joined the Houston-based golf design firm of Joseph S. Finger and Associates in 1976. In 1984 he became a full partner with Finger in the firm, and the company's name was changed to Finger, Dye and Associates to reflect the partnership.
Courses by: Ken Dye
Colorado: Battlement Mesa CC, Parachute (1987), with Joseph S. Finger.
Mississippi: Deerfield CC, Madison (1980), with Joseph S. Finger.
Texas: Cottonwood Creek Muni, Waco (1985), with Joseph S. Finger; Deerwood GC, Kingwood (1983), with Joseph S. Finger; Grapevine Muni (1980), with Joseph S. Finger and Byron Nelson; Hackberry Creek CC, Irving (1986), with Joseph S. Finger; Kingwood CC (Forest Course) (1982), with Joseph S. Finger; Stonebriar CC, Dallas (1987), with Joseph S. Finger.
Courses Remodeled & Added to by: Ken Dye
Florida: Shalimar Pointe CC, Shalimar (R., 1986), with Joseph S. Finger.
Louisiana: Oakbourne CC, Lafayette (R., 1985), with Joseph S. Finger.
Texas: Lubbock CC (R.), with Joseph S. Finger; Panorama CC, Conroe (R., 1985), with Joseph S. Finger; Preston Trail GC, Dallas (R., 1985), with Joseph S. Finger; Prestonwood CC (Creek Course), Dallas (R., 1979), with Joseph S. Finger.

Paul Burke Dye (1955 -) ASGCA
Born: Indianapolis, Indiana.
P.B. Dye attended the University of Tampa (Fla.) for several years, but his career choice was always golf course design. As the younger son of golf architect Pete and Alice Dye, he learned more about the subject at home and working on various family projects than he did at any school. Resembling his father in voice and mannerisms and his mother in physical appearance, P.B. Dye developed a golf game, and a creativity in course design, that rivaled both of them.

Some of his earliest collaborations with his father attracted immediate national attention. Long Cove Club, on Hilton Head Island, S.C., was named one of America's 100 Greatest Courses by Golf Digest magazine only two years after it opened. Their creation at The Honors Course, near Chattanooga, Tenn. was named the Best New Private Course of 1984 by the same publication. By the mid-1980s P.B. Dye was handling course designs entirely on his own.
Courses by: P.B. Dye
Georgia: Links GC, Savannah (1987).
Pennsylvania: Montour Heights CC, Pittsburgh (1987).
South Carolina: Debordieu Colony CC, Pawley's Island (1987), with Pete Dye; Long Cove C, Hilton Head Island (1982), with Pete Dye; Secession GC, Beaufort (1988).
Tennessee: Honors Course, Ooltewah (1983), with Pete Dye.
Courses Remodeled & Added to by: P.B. Dye
Alabama: CC of Birmingham (West Course) (R., 1986), with Pete Dye.

Perry O'Neal Dye (1952 -)
Born: Indianapolis, Indiana.
Perry Dye, Pete and Alice Dye's older son, first accompanied his golf architect parents to course construction sites at age 12. While still a teenager, he absorbed enough knowledge to be heavily involved in the initial routing of the first course at Johns Island, Fla. During college, he served as project manager for a number of his father's designs, including Harbour Trees near Indianapolis. After graduating from the University of Denver with a Degree in Real Estate Marketing, Perry Dye left the family business to pursue a career in housing development and construction. The recession of the late 1970s caused him to abandon his plans, and he rejoined his father in the course design business. In 1982 Perry Dye formed his own course design company, Dye Designs Inc. Based in Colorado, and later in Arizona, the firm concentrated on real estate development courses. Dye continued to occasionally collaborate with his father on certain designs well into the 1980s. Their most notable joint effort was TPC of Plum Creek near Castle Rock, Colorado.
Courses by: Perry Dye
Arizona: Red Mountain Ranch GC, Mesa (1987).
Colorado: Copper Creek GC, Copper Mountain (1987); Riverdale GC (Dunes Course), Brighton (1986); TPC at Plum Creek, Castle Rock (1984), with Pete Dye.

Pete Dye, born Paul Dye (1925 -) ASGCA
Born: Urbana, Ohio.
After attending Rollins College and Stetson University in Florida, Pete Dye was employed as a life insurance salesman in Indianapolis. A fine amateur golfer, he won the Indiana Amateur in 1958 after being runner-up in 1954 and 1955. He also served as chairman of the Green Committee at CC of Indianapolis, where he guided the club through a major replanting of its course. In 1959 Dye left the insurance business after becoming one of the youngest members of the "Million Dollar Round Table" in his company. With his wife Alice, he laid out his first course that same year and soon embarked on a career in course design.

Dye had done a series of low-budget courses in the Midwest by 1963, when he and Alice toured the great courses of Scotland. When they returned, Pete began to incorporate into his designs several of the features and principles they had observed in Scotland, including small greens, undulating fairways, pot bunkers, railroad tie bulkheads and deep native roughs. The characteristic Pete Dye style that evolved had considerable impact on late-twentieth century course architecture.

Dye created some of the world's top courses, including Teeth of the Dog in the Dominican Republic, The Golf Club near Columbus, Ohio, Harbour Town Golf Links on Hilton Head Island, S.C. and the original Tournament Players Club at Ponte Vedra, Florida. The latter ushered in an era of "stadium courses" designed with massive spectator mounds.
Courses by: Pete Dye
California: Carmel Valley Ranch GC, Carmel (1980), with David Pfaff; La Quinta Hotel GC (Citrus Course), La Quinta (1987), with Lee Schmidt; La Quinta Hotel GC (Dunes Course), La Quinta (1983), with Lee Schmidt; La Quinta Hotel GC

(Mountain Course), La Quinta (1981), with Lee Schmidt and Alice Dye; Mission Hills G&CC (Resort Course), Rancho Mirage (1987), with Lee Schmidt; PGA West GC (Stadium Course), La Quinta (1986), with Alice Dye and Lee Schmidt.

Colorado: CC of Colorado, Colorado Springs (1973), with Roy Dye; Glenmoor CC, Englewood (1985); TPC at Plum Creek, Castle Rock (1984), with Perry Dye.

Florida: Amelia Island Plantation GC, Fernadina Beach (27, 1973); Delray Dunes G&CC, Delray Beach (1969), with Jack Cabler; John's Island C (North Course), Vero Beach (1973); John's Island C (South Course), Vero Beach (1970), with Jack Nicklaus; Moorings GC, Vero Beach (Precision, 1972); Old Marsh GC, West Palm Beach (1987); TPC at Sawgrass, Ponte Vedra Beach (1980), with Alice Dye.

Illinois: Oakwood CC, Coal Valley (1964); Plainfield Elks GC (9, 1961); Yorktown GC, Belleville (Par 3, 1963).

Indiana: Crooked Stick GC, Carmel (1966); Eagle Creek Muni, Indianapolis (27, 1974), with David Pfaff; El Dorado CC, Greenwood (9, 1959), with Alice Dye; Harbour Trees GC, Noblesville (1973), with David Pfaff; Heather Hills CC, Indianapolis (1961), with Alice Dye; Monticello CC (1963), with Alice Dye; William S. Sahm Muni, Indianapolis (1963), with Alice Dye.

Iowa: Des Moines G&CC (Blue Course), West Des Moines (1968); Des Moines G&CC (Red Course), West Des Moines (1967).

Maryland: Martingham G&TC, St. Michaels (1971), with Roy Dye.

Michigan: Radrick Farms GC, Ann Arbor (1966); Wabeek CC, Bloomfield Hills (1971), with Roy Dye and Jack Nicklaus.

Mississippi: Pine Island GC, Ocean Springs (1974), with David Pfaff.

Nebraska: Firethorn GC, Lincoln (1984).

North Carolina: Cardinal GC, Greensboro (1976); Oak Hollow GC, High Point (1972), with David Pfaff.

Ohio: Avalon Lakes GC, Warren (1967), with William Newcomb; Little Turtle C, Columbus (1971), with Roy Dye; The Golf Club, New Albany (1967); TRW GC, Chesterfield (1972), with Roy Dye.

Oklahoma: Oak Tree CC (East Course), Edmond (1985); Oak Tree CC (West Course), Edmond (1981); Oak Tree GC, Edmond (1976).

South Carolina: Debordieu Colony CC, Pawley's Island (1987), with P.B. Dye; Harbour Town G Links, Hilton Head Island (1969), with Alice Dye and Jack Nicklaus; Long Cove C, Hilton Head Island (1982), with P.B. Dye.

Tennessee: Honors Course, Ooltewah (1983), with P.B. Dye.

Texas: Austin CC (1984), with Alice Dye.

Virginia: Kingsmill GC (River Course), Williamsburg (1976).

West Virginia: Coal Ridge CC (9, 1985).

Wisconsin: Americana Lake Geneva GC (Briarpatch) (1971), with Jack Nicklaus; River Run GC, Kohler (1987).

Dominican Republic: Casa de Campo (Links Course), La Ramona (1976), with Alice Dye and Lee Schmidt; Casa de Campo (Teeth of the Dog Course), La Romana (1971).

Courses Remodeled & Added to by: Pete Dye

Alabama: CC of Birmingham (West Course) (R., 1986), with P.B. Dye.

Arizona: Randolph Park GC (North Course), Tucson (R.4, 1980), with David Postlethwaite.

Connecticut: TPC of Connecticut, Cromwell (R., 1984), with David Postlethwaite.

Florida: Delray Dunes G&CC, Delray Beach (R., 1978); Marco Island CC (R., 1979); TPC at Sawgrass, Ponte Vedra Beach (R., 1983).

Indiana: Crooked Stick GC, Carmel (R., 1978); Crooked Stick GC, Carmel (R., 1986); CC of Indianapolis (R., 1957).

Nebraska: CC of Lincoln (R.3, 1963).

New York: En-Joie CC, Endicott (R.2, 1984), with David Postlethwaite; Piping Rock C, Locust Valley (R., 1985).

Ohio: Kirtland CC, Willoughby (R., 1961).

South Carolina: Harbour Town G Links, Hilton Head Island (R., 1984).

Texas: Preston Trail GC, Dallas (R.1, 1981), with David Postlethwaite.

Roy A. Dye (1929 -) ASGCA
Born: Springfield, Ohio.

Roy Dye graduated from Yale University with a bachelor's degree in Chemical Engineering. After a career in that profession for almost twenty years, Roy joined his brother Pete Dye in the practice of golf course design in 1969. After working with Pete on several projects, Roy handled several designs on his own, though many of them — including Waterwood National in Texas and Country Club of Colorado — were still credited as Pete Dye designs. Much of his later work was done in the Southwest and in Mexico.

Courses by: Roy Dye

Arizona: Anasazi GC, Phoenix (1983), with Gary Grandstaff; Gambel G Links, Carefree (NLE, 9, 1983), with Gary Grandstaff.

Colorado: CC of Colorado, Colorado Springs (1973), with Pete Dye.

Maryland: Martingham G&TC, St. Michaels (1971), with Pete Dye.

Michigan: Wabeek CC, Bloomfield Hills (1971), with Pete Dye and Jack Nicklaus.

Ohio: Little Turtle C, Columbus (1971), with Pete Dye; TRW GC, Chesterfield (1972), with Pete Dye.

Texas: Waterwood National GC, Huntsville (1976).

Mexico: La Mantarraya GC, Las Hadras (9, 1974), with Gary Grandstaff; San Carlos G&CC, Sonora (1980), with Gary Grandstaff; San Gil GC, San Juan El Rio (1977).

Courses Remodeled & Added to by: Roy Dye

Quebec: CC of Montreal, St. Laurent (R., 1975).

Mexico: La Mantarraya GC, Las Hadras (A.9, 1984).

Henry Chandler Egan (1884 - 1936)
Born: Chicago, Illinois. Died: Everett, Washington at age 51. Interred: Medford, Oregon.

H. Chandler Egan graduated from Harvard in 1905. He was one of the top early college amateur golfers in America, winning the NCAA in 1902, the U.S. Amateur in 1904 and 1905 (and finished as runner-up in 1909), and the Western Amateur in 1902, 1904, 1905 and 1907.

In the early 1910s Egan retired from national competition and moved to an ap-

ple farm in Medford, Oregon. From there he introduced golf to southwestern Oregon and competed successfully along the West Coast, winning the Pacific Northwest Amateur title in 1915, 1920, 1923, 1925 and 1932. He is perhaps best known for his 1929 "comeback" on the national level, when he reached the semi-finals of the U.S. Amateur at the age of forty-five. He was subsequently selected as a member of the 1930 and 1934 Walker Cup teams.

Egan became involved in golf course design shortly after his move to Medford. He laid out his first course there in 1911 and over the next twenty years designed and built several other Pacific Northwest courses. He revised the Pebble Beach Golf Links specifically for the 1929 Amateur, where he played such outstanding golf. Egan was constructing a course in Washington at the time of his unexpected death from pneumonia.

Courses by: H. Chandler Egan

California: Bayside Muni, Eureka (1933); Green Hills CC, Millbrae (1930), with Alister Mackenzie and Robert Hunter; Pacific Grove G Links (9, 1932).

Georgia: North Fulton Muni, Atlanta (1935).

Oregon: Bend G&CC (9, 1926); Coos CC, Coos Bay (9); Eastmoreland GC, Portland (1921); Eugene CC, Springfield (NLE, 1926); Hood River GC (1922), with Hugh Junor; Oswego Lake CC, Lake Oswego (1926); Reames G&CC, Klamath Falls (9, 1924); Riverside G&CC, Portland (1926); Rogue Valley CC, Medford (1911); Seaside CC (9); Tualatin CC (1912), with George Junor; West Hills Muni, Portland (NLE, 1924).

Washington: Indian Canyon GC, Spokane (1935); Legion Memorial GC, Everett (1937); West Seattle GC, Seattle (1939).

Courses Remodeled & Added to by: H. Chandler Egan

California: Pebble Beach G Links (R., 1928).

Oregon: Waverley CC, Portland (R., 1930).

Devereux Emmet (1861 - 1934)
Born: New York, New York. Died: Garden City, New York at age 73.

Devereux Emmet was the son of a judge and a descendant of Thomas Addison Emmet, a founder of Tammany Hall. The Emmet family was listed in Ward McAllister's *First Forty Families in America.* Dev and prominent architect Stanford White married sisters who were nieces of financier A.T. Steward.

Emmet was a golfer and huntsman. For two decades he routinely bought hunting dogs in the south in the spring, trained them on Long Island through the summer, sold them in Ireland in the autumn and spent the winter hunting and golfing in the British Isles. One such winter was devoted to measuring British golf holes for his friend C.B. Macdonald, who was then planning The National Golf Links of America. Emmet was a founding member of The National.

Emmet's earliest design work, including Island Golf Links, Cherry Valley (built on property belonging to his father-in-law) and a few other layouts, was donated at no charge. Later he turned professional and received a fee for his work. In 1930 he formed the partnership of Emmet, Emmet and Tull with his son, Devereux Emmet Jr., and Alfred Tull, and continued with it until his death in 1934.

Courses by: Devereux Emmet

Connecticut: Fulton Estate GC, Salisbury (1933), with Alfred H. Tull; Hob Nob Hill GC, Salisbury (NLE, 1934), with Alfred H. Tull; Keney Park GC, Hartford (1927), with Alfred H. Tull; Kent Fulton Estate GC; Wee Burn CC, Darien (1923).

Maryland: Congressional CC (Blue Course), Bethesda (9, 1924); Congressional CC (Gold Course), Bethesda (9, 1924).

Massachusetts: Cape Cod CC, North Falmouth (9, 1929), with Alfred H. Tull.

New Jersey: Cooper River GC, Camden (NLE, 1929), with Alfred H. Tull; Greenacres CC, Lawrence (1932), with Alfred H. Tull.

New York: Briar Hall GC, Briarcliff Manor (1923); Briarcliff Lodge GC (1923); Broadmoor CC, New Rochelle (NLE, 1929), with Alfred H. Tull; Cherry Valley CC, Garden City (1916); Coldstream GC, East Hempstead (1925); Edison CC, Rexford (1926); Eisenhower Park GC (Red Course), East Meadow (1914); Garden City GC (1901); Glen Head CC {formerly Women's National G&CC} (1923); Glenwood CC, Farmingdale; Hampshire CC, Mamaroneck (1927), with Alfred H. Tull; Harrison Williams Private Course, Bayville (3, 1932), with Alfred H. Tull; Huntington Crescent CC, Huntington (1931), with Alfred H. Tull; Huntington Crescent CC (West Course), Huntington (NLE, 1931), with Alfred H. Tull; Huntington CC (1911); Intercollegiate GC (NLE, 9, 1926); Island G Links, Garden City (NLE, 9, 1899); Laurelton GC (North Course) (NLE, 1925); Laurelton GC (South Course) (NLE, 1924); Lawrence GC (1924); Leatherstocking CC, Cooperstown (1909); Leewood GC, Eastchester (1926); Mahopac GC; Manhattan CC, Freeport (1917); Mayflower GC, New York (NLE, 1930), with Alfred H. Tull; McGregor GC, Saratoga Spa (1921); Meadow Brook C, Westbury (NLE, 1914); Mohawk GC, Schenectady; Nassau CC, Glen Cove (1927), with Alfred H. Tull; Northport CC (1921); Pelham CC (1921); Pomonok CC, Flushing (NLE, 1921); Queensboro Links, Astoria (1917); Rockaway Hunting C, Cedarhurst (1919); Rockville CC (1924); Rockwood Hall CC, Tarrytown (1929), with Alfred H. Tull; Schenectady CC; Schuyler Meadows C, Loudonville (1928), with Alfred H. Tull; Seawane C, Hewlitt Harbor (1927), with Alfred H. Tull; St. George's G&CC, Stony Brook; St. Lawrence Univ, Canton (9, 1900); Vanderbilt Estate GC, Manhasset (NLE, 9, 1929), with Alfred H. Tull; Vernon Hills CC, Mt. Vernon (1928), with Alfred H. Tull.

North Carolina: Hog Back Mountain C, Tryon (NLE, 9, 1931), with Alfred H. Tull.

West Virginia: Crispin Center GC, Wheeling; Oglebay Park GC, Wheeling.

Bahamas: Cable Beach Hotel & GC, Nassau (1928), with Alfred H. Tull.

Bermuda: Belmont Hotel & C, Warwick (9, 1924); Castle Inn GC (NLE, Par 3, 9); Hotel Frascati GC (NLE, Par 3, 9, 1930); Riddell's Bay G&CC, Warwick (1922).

Courses Remodeled & Added to by: Devereux Emmet

Delaware: Henry F. DuPont Private Course, Wilmington (R., 1929), with Alfred H. Tull.

New York: Bedford G&TC (R.9); Bedford G&TC (A.9); Bonnie Briar CC, Larchmont (R., 1928), with Alfred H. Tull; Engineers GC, Roslyn (R., 1921); Huntington CC (R., 1928), with Alfred H. Tull; Old Country Club, Flushing (NLE, R., 1928), with Alfred H. Tull; Powelton C, Newburgh (R.6, 1921); Powelton C, Newburgh (A.12, 1921); Wheatley Hills GC, East Williston (R., 1929), with Alfred H. Tull.

Bermuda: Belmont Hotel & C, Warwick (A.9, 1928); St. George Hotel GC, Warwick (R., 1928), with Alfred H. Tull.

Paul E. Erath (1905 -)

Paul Erath became a member of PGA in 1933 and served as pro-superintendent at several Pennsylvania clubs before joining the construction staff of golf architect Dick Wilson in the 1950s. After supervising Wilson's reconstruction of Dunedin CC in Florida, Erath returned to Pennsylvania to build Laurel Valley CC to Wilson's plans. He remained at Laurel Valley as its course superintendent, designing a number of local golf courses as a sideline.

Courses by: Paul E. Erath

Pennsylvania: Champion Lakes GC, Bolivar (1965); Pleasant View CC, Norvelt (1967); Port Cherry Hills CC, McDonald (1966); Saranac GC, Stahistown (9, 1964); Venango Valley GC, Venango (1973).

Courses Remodeled & Added to by: Paul E. Erath

Pennsylvania: Fox Chapel GC, Pittsburgh (R., 1968); Laurel Valley CC, Ligonier (R., 1965).

Lindsay B. Ervin (1942 -) ASGCA

Born: Brownwood, Texas.

Lindsay Ervin, a graduate landscape architect, trained under golf architect David Gill and then joined a landscape architecture firm. In 1976 he designed his first solo course, Hog Neck GC in Easton, Maryland. In 1979 he established his own practice based in Maryland.

Courses by: Lindsay Ervin

Maryland: Cove Creek CC, Stevensville (1980); Hog Neck GC, Easton (27, 1976); Needwood GC, Rockville (Precision, 9, 1981); Prospect Bay CC, Graysonville (1984).

New York: Villa Roma CC, Calakoon (1987).

Virginia: Birdwood GC, Charlottesville (1984).

Courses Remodeled & Added to by: Lindsay Ervin

New York: Forest Park GC, Bronx (R., 1986).

Charles "Chick" Evans (1890 - 1979)

Born: Indianapolis, Indiana. Died: Chicago, Illinois at age 89.

Chick Evans, winner of the 1916 U.S. Open and Amateur, wrote extensively about golf architecture for periodicals in the 1920s. For a short period in the 1920s he was associated with Tom Bendelow who instructed him in course design. His best-known creation was Cutten Fields CC in Guelph, Ontario, Canada, designed and built in the late 1920s. He set up a design office in Chicago, but his output was severely curtailed by the Depression. In 1927 Evans was hired by the Cook County (Ill.) Board of Parks to "dot the forest preserves with golf."

Keith E. Evans (1944 -) ASGCA

Born: Plymouth, Michigan.

Keith Evans graduated from Michigan State University with a B.A. degree in Business Administration in 1966. Following military service, during which he was a member of the U.S. Army European Rifle Team, he was employed by Lever Brothers and later with Capital Irrigation.

In 1973 Evans returned to Michigan State to study Landscape Architecture, receiving his degree in 1976. He was associated in course design with golf architects Joseph S. Finger in 1977 and Dick Watson in 1978 before joining the staff of Rees Jones in 1979.

Courses by: Keith Evans

Georgia: Jones Creek GC, Augusta (1986), with Rees Jones.

Kansas: Rolling Meadows GC, Junction City (1981), with Richard Watson.

Nebraska: Tara Hills GC, Papillion (Precision, 9, 1978), with Richard Watson.

New Jersey: Pinch Brook GC, Florham Park (Precision, 1984), with Rees Jones.

North Carolina: Harbour Pointe GC, New Bern (1986), with Rees Jones; Pinehurst CC (Course No. 7) (1986), with Rees Jones.

Virginia: Hell's Point GC, Virginia Beach (1982), with Rees Jones; Stoney Creek GC, Wintergreen (1986), with Rees Jones.

Courses Remodeled & Added to by: Keith Evans

Florida: Crystal Lago CC, Pompano Beach (R., 1981), with Rees Jones.

Illinois: Skokie GC, Glencoe (R., 1981), with Rees Jones.

New Jersey: Flanders Valley GC (A.9, 1982), with Rees Jones; Ridgewood CC (R., 1981), with Rees Jones.

New York: Westchester CC (South Course), Rye (R., 1983), with Rees Jones; Westchester CC (West Course), Rye (R., 1982), with Rees Jones.

Floyd Farley (1907 -) ASGCA, President, 1966.

Born: Kansas City, Missouri.

Floyd Farley began his career in golf as a caddy in 1919. He was later employed as professional at Crestwood CC, in Kansas City, Ks., Dundee GC, and Twin Hills GC in Oklahoma City. He designed and built Woodlawn GC in Oklahoma City and then operated it from 1932 to 1947. During that period Farley won the Oklahoma PGA Championship (in 1936 and 1942) and the Oklahoma Match Play Open in 1937. In 1947 he designed and built Meridian GC in Oklahoma City, which he owned until 1961.

Prior to 1947, Farley had helped many small Oklahoma communities construct golf courses. He then devoted himself full-time to golf course architecture and developed a decided preference for par 70 layouts, with three par-3 and two par-5 holes per nine. Farley felt his own style to have been most influenced by golf architects William P. Bell and Perry Maxwell.

In the early Eighties Farley and his wife Betty retired to Sedona, Arizona.

Courses by: Floyd Farley

Kansas: Clay Center GC (9, 1964); Hidden Lakes CC, Derby (1958); Lake Forest GC (NLE, 9); Leroy King Private Course, Hesston (3, 1956); McConnell AFB GC, Wichita (9, 1959); Overland Park Muni (27, 1971); Salina Muni (1970).

Missouri: A.L. Gustin Jr. Memo. GC, Columbia (1957); Ava G&CC (9, 1966); Cabool-Mountain Grove GC, Cabool (9, 1969); Current River CC, Doniphan (9, 1970); Fort Leonard Wood GC (1958); Green Hills CC, Willard (9, 1969); Jamestown CC, St. James (9, 1969); Lake Valley G&CC, Camdenton (1969); Marceline CC (9, 1970); Salem G&CC (9, 1969); Sedalia CC (1970); Twin Oaks CC, Spring-

field (1956), with Horton Smith; Wedgewood CC (9); Willow Springs CC (9, 1970).

Nebraska: Holmes Park Muni, Lincoln (1964); James H. Ager Jr GC, Lincoln (Par 3, 9, 1964); Knolls GC, Lincoln (Par 3, 9, 1962); Mahoney GC, Lincoln (1975); Meadowbrook GC, Omaha (Par 3, 9, 1963); Miracle Hill GC, Omaha (1963).

New Mexico: New Mexico Military Institute GC, Roswell (1957); New Mexico State Univ GC, Las Cruces (1962).

Oklahoma: Adams Park Muni, Bartlesville (1962); Alva G&CC (9, 1950); Arrowhead State Park GC, Eufaula (9, 1960); Atoka Muni (9, 1964); Beavers Bend State Park GC, Broken Bow (9, 1976); Broadmoore CC, Moore (1962); Brookside GC, Oklahoma City (9, 1956); Cedar Valley GC, Guthrie (27, 1974); Earlywine Park GC, Oklahoma City (1976); El Reno CC (9, 1948); Fort Cobb Lake State Park GC, Lake Cobb (1965); Fountainhead State Park GC (1965); Hook & Slice GC, Oklahoma City (Par 3, 9, 1972); John Conrad GC, Midwest City (Precision, 1971); Kickingbird GC, Edmond (1971); Kingfisher GC (9); La Fortune Park Muni, Tulsa (1961); Lake Hefner GC (South Course), Oklahoma City (1962); Lake Texoma State Park GC, Kingston (1958); McAlester CC (9, 1956); Meridian GC, Oklahoma City (1947); Midwest City Muni (Precision, 9, 1957); Mohawk Park Muni (Pecan Valley Course), Tulsa (1957); Nemaha G&CC (NLE, 1957); Norman GC (9, 1949); Quail Creek G&CC, Oklahoma (1961); Recreation GC, Healdton (9, 1961); Roman Nose State Park GC, Watonga (9, 1960); Sand Springs Muni (1958); Sequoyah State Park GC, Hulbert (1959); Seth Hughes GC, Tulsa (NLE, Par 3, 9, 1958); Shattuck GC (9, 1970); Sulphur Hills CC (9, 1960); Tinker AFB GC (9, 1961); Walnut Hills CC, Oklahoma City (1954); Western Village GC, Tulsa (NLE, Par 3, 9, 1954); Westwood Muni; Westwood Park Muni, Norman (1968); Wewoka Muni (9, 1949); Woodlawn GC, Oklahoma City (1932).

Courses Remodeled & Added to by: Floyd Farley

Kansas: Crestwood CC, Pittsburgh (A.9, 1978); Crestwood CC, Pittsburgh (R.3, 1978); Four Oaks GC, Pittsburg (A.9, 1980); Indian Hills CC, Prairie Village (R., 1958); Kansas City CC, Shawnee Mission (R.2, 1959); Lake Quivira CC, Kansas City (R., 1958); Milburn G&CC, Overland Park (R., 1957); Mission Hills CC, Fairway (R.2, 1959); Rolling Hills CC, Wichita (R., 1963).

Missouri: Metro GC, Kansas City (NLE, R., 1958).

Nebraska: Norfolk CC (A.5); Norfolk GC (R.13).

Oklahoma: Altus GC (A.9); Cedar Valley GC, Guthrie (A.9, 1979); Cedar Valley GC, Guthrie (A.9, 1986); Elks CC, Duncan (A.9, 1950); Hillcrest CC, Bartlesville (R.9, 1960); La Fortune Park Muni, Tulsa (Par 3, A.18, 1965); Lake Hefner GC (North Course), Oklahoma City (R.); Lawton CC (A.9, 1957); Lew Wentz Memorial GC, Ponca City (R.9); Lew Wentz Memorial GC, Ponca City (A.9); Lincoln Park Muni (East Course), Oklahoma City (R., 1965); Lincoln Park Muni (West Course), Oklahoma City (R., 1965); Mohawk Park Muni (Woodbine Course), Tulsa (R.); Mohawk Park Muni (Woodbine Course), Tulsa (R., 1957); Oklahoma City G&CC (R.10); Rolling Hills CC, Tulsa (R., 1957); Tulsa CC (A.3, 1968); Tulsa CC (R., 1968); Twin Hills G&CC, Oklahoma City (R.1).

George Fazio (1912 - 1986) ASGCA

Born: Norristown, Pennsylvania. Died: Jupiter, Florida at age 75.

George Fazio played on the professional golf tour, winning the 1946 Canadian Open, tying Hogan and Mangrum in the 1950 U.S. Open (losing to Hogan in the playoff), and placing fifth and fourth respectively in the 1952 and 1953 Opens. During the same years, he also served as resident professional at several clubs, including famed Pine Valley in New Jersey.

Fazio entered private practice as a course architect in 1959 and advanced rapidly in the profession to become one of the nation's leading designers. In 1962 he was joined by his nephew Tom. The Fazios were consulting architects for a number of major golf tournaments, including the Masters and several U.S. Opens. In the early 1980s, George designed several courses with another nephew, Jim (Tom's brother).

Among the best known George Fazio designs were Moselem Springs CC in Pennsylvania, Edgewood Tahoe GC in Nevada, Butler National GC in Illinois and Jupiter Hills GC in Florida.

Courses by: George Fazio

Arizona: Willowbrook GC, Sun City (1973), with Tom Fazio, James Winans and John W. Meeker; Willowcreek GC, Sun City (1973), with Tom Fazio, John W. Meeker and Greg Nash.

Connecticut: Ridgefield Muni (1974), with Tom Fazio.

Florida: East Lakes GC, Palm Beach Gardens (1981), with Tom Fazio; Eastpointe CC, Palm Beach Gardens (1976), with Tom Fazio; Hawk's Nest G&CC, Vero Beach (1987), with Jim Fazio; Jonathan's Landing GC, Jupiter (1978), with Tom Fazio; Jupiter Hills C (Hills Course), Jupiter (1970), with Tom Fazio; Jupiter Hills C (Village Course), Jupiter (1979), with Tom Fazio; Palm Beach Polo & CC (North Course), West Palm Beach (1979), with Tom Fazio; Palm-Aire CC (Cypress Course), Pompano Beach (1974), with Tom Fazio; Palm-Aire CC (Oaks Course), Pompano Beach (1973), with Tom Fazio; Reserve G&CC, Fort Pierce (1984), with Jim Fazio; Riverbend CC, Tequesta (Precision, 1978), with Tom Fazio.

Hawaii: Turtle Bay GC (Old Course), Oahu (1971), with Tom Fazio, James Winans and John W. Meeker.

Illinois: Butler National GC, Oak Brook (1974), with Tom Fazio; Marriott Lincolnshire GC (1975), with Tom Fazio.

Massachusetts: Oak Ridge GC, Agawam , with Tom Fazio; Presidents GC, North Quincy (Precision, 1976), with Tom Fazio; Wollaston CC, Milton (1976), with Tom Fazio.

Nevada: Edgewood Tahoe CC, Stateline (1968), with Tom Fazio.

New Jersey: Americana Great Gorge GC, McAfee (27, 1971), with Tom Fazio; Atlantis GC, Tuckerton (1961).

North Carolina: Pinehurst CC (Course No. 6) (1978), with Tom Fazio.

Ohio: Sawmill Creek GC, Huron (1973), with Tom Fazio.

Oklahoma: Indian Springs CC (River Course), Broken Arrow (1968).

Pennsylvania: Bristolwood GC, Bristol (Par 3, 1963); Downingtown Inn GC (1967); Hershey CC (East Course) (1970); Kimberton GC (1962); Moselem Springs CC, Fleetwood (1964); Pocono Manor GC (West Course) (1965); Silver Spring GC, Mechanicsburg (Precision, 1969); Squires GC, Ambler (1963); Tanglewood GC, Stroudsburg (1965); Waynesborough CC, Paoli (1965).

South Carolina: Bay Tree Golf Plantation (Gold Course) (1972), with Russell Breeden and Tom Fazio; Bay Tree Golf Plantation (Green Course) (1972), with Russell Breeden and Tom Fazio; Bay Tree Golf Plantation (Silver Course) (1972), with Russell Breeden and Tom Fazio; Moss Creek Plantation GC (South Course), Hilton Head Island (1975), with Tom Fazio; Palmetto Dunes CC (Fazio Course), Hilton Head Island (1974), with Tom Fazio.

Texas: Champions GC (Jackrabbit Course), Houston (1964); El Dorado GC, Humble (1964).

Ontario: National GC, Woodbridge (1976), with Tom Fazio.

Bahamas: Coral Harbour GC, Nassau (NLE, 1965).

Costa Rica: Cariari International CC, San Jose (1973), with Tom Fazio.

Panama: Coronado Beach GC, Panama City (1974), with Tom Fazio.

Puerto Rico: Rio Mar GC, Palmer (1976), with Tom Fazio.

Virgin Islands: Mahogany Run GC, St. Thomas (1980), with Tom Fazio.

Courses Remodeled & Added to by: George Fazio

California: Bel-Air CC, Los Angeles (R.1, 1967).

Connecticut: Tumble Brook CC, Bloomfield (A.9, 1975), with Tom Fazio.

Florida: Everglades C, Palm Beach (R., 1979), with Tom Fazio; Jupiter Hills C (Hills Course), Jupiter (R., 1974), with Tom Fazio; Jupiter Hills C (Hills Course), Jupiter (A.3, 1974), with Tom Fazio; Jupiter Island C, Jupiter (R.), with Tom Fazio.

Georgia: Atlanta Athletic C (Highlands Course), Duluth (R., 1975), with Tom Fazio; Augusta National GC, Augusta (R., 1972).

Indiana: Meridian Hills CC, Indianapolis (R., 1980), with Tom Fazio.

Maryland: Columbia CC (R.), with Tom Fazio; Congressional CC (Gold Course), Bethesda (A.9, 1977), with Tom Fazio; Hillendale CC, Phoenix (R., 1968).

New York: Apawamis C, Rye (R., 1977), with Tom Fazio; Nevele GC, Ellenville (R.), with Tom Fazio; Oak Hill CC (East Course), Rochester (R., 1979), with Tom Fazio; Oak Hill CC (East Course), Rochester (A.3, 1979), with Tom Fazio; Winged Foot GC (West Course), Mamaroneck (R.), with Tom Fazio.

Ohio: Inverness C, Toledo (R., 1978), with Tom Fazio; Inverness C, Toledo (A.4, 1978), with Tom Fazio.

Oklahoma: Southern Hills CC, Tulsa (R., 1976), with Tom Fazio.

Pennsylvania: Aronimink GC, Newton Square (R., 1978), with Tom Fazio; Chester Valley CC (R., 1964); Langhorne GC (R., 1958).

Tom Fazio (1945 -   ) ASGCA

Born: Norristown, Pennsylvania.

Tom Fazio entered the business of golf course architecture as a teenager in 1962, assisting his uncle George Fazio in course construction. His on-the-job training and experience gave him intimate knowledge in engineering, landscape design, soils, accounting and business. By the early Seventies he became a full partner with George and the partnership became one of the nation's leading course design firms. Tom gradually took over the business from his uncle and in the early 1980s formed his own firm. While participating in many of his uncle's finest designs, Tom gained national attention on his own with such designs as Wild Dunes in South Carolina, The Vintage Club in California, Barton Creek in Texas and Wade Hampton in North Carolina.

Courses by: Tom Fazio

Arizona: Ventana Canyon G&RC, Tucson (27, 1985); Willowbrook GC, Sun City (1973), with George Fazio, James Winans and John W. Meeker; Willowcreek GC, Sun City (1973), with George Fazio, John W. Meeker and Greg Nash.

California: Vintage C (Desert Course), Indian Wells (1984); Vintage C (Mountain Course), Indian Wells (1981).

Connecticut: Ridgefield Muni (1974), with George Fazio.

Florida: Bluewater Bay GC, Niceville (1981); East Lakes GC, Palm Beach Gardens (1981), with George Fazio; Eastpointe CC, Palm Beach Gardens (1976), with George Fazio; Golden Eagle GC, Tallahassee (1986); John's Island C (West Course), Vero Beach (1987); Jonathan's Landing GC, Jupiter (1978), with George Fazio; Jupiter Hills C (Village Course), Jupiter (1979), with George Fazio; Lake Nona GC, Orlando (1986); Long Point GC, Amelia Island (1987); Mariner SandS CC (Gold Course), Stuart (1982); Old Trail GC, Jupiter (1986); Palm Beach Polo & CC (North Course), West Palm Beach (1979), with George Fazio; Palm-Aire CC (Cypress Course), Pompano Beach (1974), with George Fazio; Palm-Aire CC (Oaks Course), Pompano Beach (1973), with George Fazio; Pelican's Nest GC, Bonita Springs (1986); PGA National GC (Champion Course), Palm Beach Gardens (1981); PGA National GC (Haig Course), Palm Beach Gardens (1980); PGA National GC (Squire Course), Palm Beach Gardens (1981); Riverbend CC, Tequesta (Precision, 1978), with George Fazio; Windstar C, Naples (1983).

Hawaii: Turtle Bay GC (Old Course), Oahu (1971), with George Fazio, James Winans and John W. Meeker.

Illinois: Butler National GC, Oak Brook (1974), with George Fazio; Marriott Lincolnshire GC (1975), with George Fazio.

Massachusetts: Oak Ridge GC, Agawam , with George Fazio; Presidents GC, North Quincy (Precision, 1976), with George Fazio; Wollaston CC, Milton (1976), with George Fazio.

Nevada: Edgewood Tahoe CC, Stateline (1968), with George Fazio.

New Jersey: Americana Great Gorge GC, McAfee (27, 1971), with George Fazio.

North Carolina: Pinehurst CC (Course No. 6) (1978), with George Fazio; Wade Hampton GC, Cashiers (1987).

Ohio: Sawmill Creek GC, Huron (1973), with George Fazio.

Oklahoma: Golf Club of Oklahoma, Broken Arrow (1982).

South Carolina: Bay Tree Golf Plantation (Gold Course) (1972), with Russell Breeden and George Fazio; Bay Tree Golf Plantation (Green Course) (1972), with Russell Breeden and George Fazio; Bay Tree Golf Plantation (Silver Course) (1972), with Russell Breeden and George Fazio; Cotton Dike GC, Dataw Island (1985); CC of Callawassie, Callawassie Island (1986); Moss Creek Plantation GC (North Course), Hilton Head Island (1979); Moss Creek Plantation GC (South Course), Hilton Head Island (1975), with George Fazio; Osprey Point G Links, Kiawah Island (1987); Palmetto Dunes CC (Fazio Course), Hilton Head Island (1974), with George Fazio; Wachesaw Plantation GC, Pawley's Island (1986); Wild Dunes G Links (Links Course), Isle of Palms (1980); Wild Dunes G Links (Yacht Harbor Course), Isle of Palms (1986).

Texas: Barton Creek C, Austin (1986).

Ontario: National GC, Woodbridge (1976), with George Fazio.

Costa Rica: Cariari International CC, San Jose (1973), with George Fazio.

Panama: Coronado Beach GC, Panama City (1974), with George Fazio.

Puerto Rico: Rio Mar GC, Palmer (1976), with George Fazio.

Virgin Islands: Mahogany Run GC, St. Thomas (1980), with George Fazio.

Courses Remodeled & Added to by: Tom Fazio

Arizona: McCormick Ranch GC (Palm Course), Scottsdale (R., 1981); McCormick Ranch GC (Pine Course), Scottsdale (R., 1981).

Connecticut: Tumble Brook CC, Bloomfield (A.9, 1975), with George Fazio.

Florida: Bardmoor CC (East Course), Largo (R., 1984); Bluewater Bay GC, Niceville (A.9, 1986); Everglades C, Palm Beach (R., 1979), with George Fazio; Jupiter Hills C (Hills Course), Jupiter (R., 1974), with George Fazio; Jupiter Hills C (Hills Course), Jupiter (A.3, 1974), with George Fazio; Jupiter Island C, Jupiter (R.), with George Fazio.

Georgia: Atlanta Athletic C (Highlands Course), Duluth (R., 1975), with George Fazio; Atlanta Athletic C (Highlands Course), Duluth (R., 1980); Augusta National GC, Augusta (A.2, 1986).

Indiana: Meridian Hills CC, Indianapolis (R., 1980), with George Fazio.

Maryland: Columbia CC (R.), with George Fazio; Congressional CC (Gold Course), Bethesda (A.9, 1977), with George Fazio.

New York: Apawamis C, Rye (R., 1977), with George Fazio; Nevele GC, Ellenville (R.), with George Fazio; Oak Hill CC (East Course), Rochester (A.3, 1979), with George Fazio; Oak Hill CC (East Course), Rochester (R., 1979), with George Fazio; Winged Foot GC (West Course), Mamaroneck (R., 1973), with George Fazio.

Ohio: Inverness C, Toledo (R., 1978), with George Fazio; Inverness C, Toledo (A.4, 1978), with George Fazio.

Oklahoma: Southern Hills CC, Tulsa (R., 1976), with George Fazio.

Pennsylvania: Aronimink GC, Newton Square (R., 1978), with George Fazio.

Texas: Columbia Lakes CC, West Columbia (R., 1981); Tennwood C, Hockley (R.18, 1979).

Fred Federspiel

Fred Federspiel served for many years as superintendent of several courses, including Oswego Lake CC in Oregon. He laid out a number of courses in the Pacific Northwest in the 1950s and '60s.

Courses by: Fred Federspiel

Oregon: Marysville GC, Corvallis (9, 1958); McNary GC, Salem (1962), with Fred Sparks; Meriwether National GC, Hillsboro (1962); Pineway GC, Lebanon (Precision, 9, 1958); Rhodo Dunes GC, Florence (9, 1960); Salishan G Links, Gleneden Beach (1965); Santiam GC, Salem (1957); Spring Hill CC, Albany (1960); Sunriver CC (South Course) (1969).

Washington: Briarcliff G&CC, Rainier (1969); Royal Oaks CC, Vancouver (1952).

Courses Remodeled & Added to by: Fred Federspiel

Oregon: Agate Beach GC, Newport (R.9, 1965); Corvallis CC (A.9, 1957).

Washington: Olympia G&CC (A.9, 1959).

Michael George Fenn (1915 - 1982) BAGCA

Born: England. Died: Lyon, France at age 67.

Except for schooling in England and service with the Royal Naval Commandos during World War II, Fenn spent most of his life in France. At the end of the war he restored a war-torn 9 hole course in Leckford, England and then returned to France where he participated in restoration of courses in that country and Belgium. Following training with golf architect F.W. Hawtree, he added course design to his services.

Courses by: Michael G. Fenn

France: Assoc. Sportive du G de Meribel (9); Club de Palmola, Toulouse; Club de Toulouse; Golf de Besancon; Golf de Bourgogne, Dijon (9); Golf de Claris; Golf de Clermont-Ferrand; Golf de Lann-Rohou, Brest; Golf de St. Laurent; Golf de Touraine, Tours; Golf du Clair Vallon, Clairis; Golf Club de Brotel, Hieres-sur-Amby; Golf Club de Quiberon; Golf Club de Reims; Golf Club de Reims; Golf Club de Villette-D'Anthon; Golf Puy de Dome.

Courses Remodeled & Added to by: Michael G. Fenn

France: Club de Lyon (A.9); Golf de Nancy-Aingeray (R.).

Marvin H. Ferguson (1918 - 1985) ASGCA

Born: Texas. Died: Bryan, Texas at age 66.

Dr. Marvin Ferguson graduated from Texas A & M University and received a Ph.D. degree from the University of Maryland. From 1940 until 1969 he was engaged in turfgrass research with the USGA Green Section and Texas A & M. Ferguson played a major role in developing the USGA method of green construction. In 1973 he was presented the USGA's Green Section Award for his extended turfgrass research.

In 1969 Ferguson began to design golf courses. While he did relatively few courses in his career, they were characterized by well-thought-out strategic holes and excellent turfgrass conditions.

Courses by: Marvin Ferguson

Arkansas: Ben Geren GC, Ft. Smith (1970).

Kansas: Wolf Creek GC, Olathe (1972).

Louisiana: Les Vieux Chenes GC, Youngsville (1977).

Missouri: Bahnfyre GC, St. Louis (1981); CC of Missouri, Columbia (1974); West Plains CC (1977).

Tennessee: Holly Hills CC, Cordova (1972).

Texas: Briarcrest CC, Bryan (1971); Cielo Vista GC, El Paso (1977).

Courses Remodeled & Added to by: Marvin Ferguson

Arkansas: Hardscrabble CC, Fort Smith (R., 1970).

Missouri: Hillcrest CC, Kansas City (R.4, 1975); Westwood CC, St. Louis (R.1, 1969).

New Mexico: Ocotillo Park GC, Hobbs (A.9, 1969).

Pennsylvania: Carrollton CC (R.9, 1969).

Texas: Abilene CC (R.1, 1975); Brae Burn CC, Bellaire (R.4, 1969); Bryan Muni (R.6, 1971); Coronado G&CC, El Paso (R., 1972); Eastern Hills CC, Garland (R.5, 1986); Northwood C, Dallas (R.5, 1974).

Willie Fernie (1851 - 1924)
Born: St. Andrews, Scotland. Died: Troon, Scotland at age 73.

Willie Fernie was one of five golfing brothers who grew up at St. Andrews. His siblings were George (a long-time pro-greenkeeper at Dumfries who laid out Hunstanton in 1898), Tom, Harry and Eddie.

Willie was the best golfer of the lot, winning the 1883 British Open in a playoff after finishing second the year before. In all he had five runner-up finishes in The Open.

Fernie served as pro-greenkeeper at several Scottish clubs, ultimately settling at Troon (which he laid out) in 1887. He remained there the rest of his life, staking out many courses on the side. Among his best known are the Ailsa and Arran courses at Turnberry.

Courses by: Willie Fernie
England: Aldeburgh GC, Suffolk (1894); Whitsand Bay Hotel GC, Cornwall (1909).
Scotland: Cardross GC, Dumbartonshire (1895); Pitlochry GC, Perthshire (1908); Troon Portland GC, Ayrshire (1905); Turnberry GC (Ailsa Course), Ayrshire (1909); Turnberry GC (Arran Course), Ayrshire (1909); Whitecraigs GC, Glasgow (1905).
Wales: Southerndown GC, Glamorgan (1905).

Courses Remodeled & Added to by: Willie Fernie
England: Felixstowe Ferry GC, Suffolk (NLE, R.).
Scotland: Cochrane Castle GC, Renfrewshire (R., 1921); Royal Troon GC, Ayrshire (R., 1900).

Leo J. Feser (1900 - 1976)
Born: Minnesota. Died: Mesa, Arizona at age 76.

Leo Feser served as superintendent at Woodhill CC, Wayzata, Minn. for 30 years. He was a charter member of the GCSAA and served as a national director and vice president in the mid-1930s. He also edited the association's trade journal, and after his retirement an annual golf writing award was established by the GCSAA in his honor.

Feser's first experience in course design was in 1924, when he laid out Minnesota's first privately owned daily-fee course at Orono. He did no other design work until after leaving Woodhill in 1951. He and his sons then began purchasing and operating daily fee layouts, which Feser remodeled. During this period Feser also designed a couple of new small layouts.

Courses by: Leo J. Feser
Minnesota: Hudson CC; Medina Public GC (1956); Orono Public GC, Wayzata (1927).

Homer D. Fieldhouse
Based in Wisconsin, Homer Fieldhouse designed courses throughout the Midwestern states from the mid-1950s through the 1970s.

Courses by: Homer Fieldhouse
Illinois: Braidwood GC (9, 1965); Gibson Woods Muni, Monmouth (1966).
Iowa: Lake Creek CC, Storm Lake (1972).
Minnesota: Valley High GC, Houston (9, 1970).
Ohio: Candywood GC, Vienna (1966); Ponderosa CC, Warren (1966).
Wisconsin: Camelot CC, Lomira (1966); Cedar Springs GC, Waupacas; Clifton Highlands GC, Prescott (1972); Dodge Point GC, Dodgeville (9); Eagle Bluff CC, Hurley (1967); Golden Sands GC, Cecil (1970); Golf Village GC, Neenah (Precision, 9); Rock River Hills GC, Horizon (1965).

Courses Remodeled & Added to by: Homer Fieldhouse
South Dakota: Hillcrest G&CC, Yankton (A.9, 1972).
Wisconsin: Fox Lake CC (A.9, 1965).

Alexander H. Findlay (1865 - 1942)
Born: Scotland. Died: Philadelphia, Pennsylvania at age 76.

Alex Findlay emigrated to the United States in the early 1880s to manage a ranch in Nebraska. There he introduced the game of golf and laid out a golf course in 1885. Findlay was later in charge of planning, constructing and operating courses for the Florida East Coast Railroad, the same position as that held by John Duncan Dunn with the rival Florida West Coast Railroad.

Findlay was for a time associated in course development with Wright and Ditson and later with Wanamakers, both prominent East Coast sporting goods firms. In addition, he continued to plan courses on his own, doing over 100 layouts in his design career, many of them constructed by his sons Norman, Ronald and Richard.

Alex Findlay was one of the genuine pioneers in the game. He played a series of American exhibitions with the great Harry Vardon, played some 2,400 courses during his lifetime and established dozens of course records. In 1926 he visited the Vatican where he tried unsuccessfully to establish a 6-hole golf course.

Courses by: Alex Findlay
Arkansas: Fort Smith CC (9).
Florida: Breakers GC (Ocean Course), Palm Beach (9, 1905); Miami G Links, Miami (NLE, 9); Oceanside G&CC, Ormond Beach (9, 1911); St. Augustine CC (NLE, 9, 1908).
Maine: Belgrade Hotel GC, Belgrade Lakes (9); Grindstone Inn GC, Winter Harbor (9); Megunticook GC, Rockport (9); Summit Springs GC, Poland (9); Tarratine C of Dark Harbor, Islesboro (9, 1914).
Maryland: Chester River Y&CC, Chestertown (1924); Royal Swan CC, Betterton (1924).
Massachusetts: Bear Hill GC, Wakefield (9); Brockton CC, Brockton (9); Dedham Hunt & Polo C; Great Island GC; Greenfield CC (9, 1896); Long Meadow GC, Lowell (9); Meadow Brook GC, Reading (9); Miacomet G Links, Nantucket; Northfield CC, East Northfield (9, 1912); Siasconset GC, Nantucket (9); Vesper CC, Tyngsboro (9).
Montana: Butte CC (1909).
New Hampshire: Ferncliffe CC; Granliden Hotel GC, Lake Sunapee (9); Intervale GC, Manchester (9, 1899); Maplewood GC; Mount Pleasant House GC; Mount Vernon GC; Russell Cottage GC, Kearsarge (9); Twin Mountain GC (9).
New Jersey: Blackwood CC, Gloucester Township (1929); Cohanzick CC, Bridge-

ton (1971); Medford Lakes CC (1930); Moorestown Field C (9); Newark Athletic C (NLE, 1900); Pennbrook GC, Basking Ridge (1927); Pitman GC (1929); Tavistock CC, Haddonfield; Woodbury CC (9).
New York: CC of Rochester (NLE,); Lake George C; Lake Placid C (Upper Course) (1910); Saranac Lake GC (9, 1919).
North Carolina: Eseeola Lodge GC (NLE, 1912).
Oklahoma: Guthrie GC (9).
Pennsylvania: Aronimink GC, Philadelphia (NLE, 1913); Centre Hills CC, State College (9); Clearfield-Curwensville CC (1924); Clinton CC, Lockhaven (NLE, 9, 1910); Coatesville CC (1921); Galen Hall GC, Wernersville (1910); Green Pond CC, Bethlehem (1931); Langhorne GC; Lebanon CC (NLE,); Llanerch CC, Havertown; Luden Riverside CC (1930); Manor CC, Sinking Springs; Phillipsburg CC (1924); Reading CC (1923); Roseneath Farms GC (Par 3, 9, 1936); Shamokin Valley CC (9); Tredyffrin, Paoli; Tyrone CC (1925); Walnut Lane GC, Philadelphia (1935).
Tennessee: CC of Bristol (NLE, 9); Tate Springs GC.
Texas: Beaumont CC (1907); San Antonio CC (1908).
Virginia: Roanoke CC (NLE, 1907).
West Virginia: Greenbrier GC (Lakeside Course), White Sulphur Spgs (NLE, 9).
Bahamas: Nassau G Links (NLE, 6).

Courses Remodeled & Added to by: Alex Findlay
New Jersey: Essex County CC (East Course) (NLE, A.9, 1900).
Pennsylvania: Pittsburgh Field C (NLE, R.5).

Frederick A. Findlay (1872 - 1966)
Born: Scotland. Died: Charlottesville, Virginia at age 94.

Fred Findlay, the son of a British Army officer, joined the Army at the age of fourteen and served for twenty-one years, most of them as a bandmaster. Upon retiring from the service he moved to Australia, where he spent thirteen years as a club professional and did his first golf design work.

After the first World War, Findlay moved to the United States, following older brother Alex who had emigrated there as a young man and became a pioneer golf promoter and course designer. Fred settled in Virginia, where he served as professional and superintendent at various clubs and designed a number of courses over the next thirty years. In his later years he was partnered with his son-in-law, Raymond "Ben" Loving Sr., in a course design and construction firm later maintained by his grandson, Raymond "Buddy" Loving Jr.

Findlay remained active as a golf architect into the early 1960s. A fine landscape artist and poet as well as golfer, he consistently shot his age during the last twenty years of his life. Although an artist, he detested blueprints and claimed the land was his drawing board.

Courses by: Fred Findlay
Maryland: Bethesda CC (9, 1927).
North Carolina: Chapel Hill CC (1940); Paradise Point GC (Green Course), Camp LeJeune (1939).
Pennsylvania: Yardley CC (1929).
South Carolina: Parris Island GC (1941).
Virginia: Appomattox CC, with Ben Loving; Augusta CC, Staunton (1927); Bide-A-Wee CC, Portsmouth (1955), with Ben Loving; Boonsboro CC, Lynchburg (1927); Carper Valley GC; Crater CC (1934); CC of Culpepper (9, 1960), with Ben Loving; Farmington CC, Charlottesville (1928); Glenwood CC, Richmond (1925); Hopewell CC (1940); Hunting Hills CC, Roanoke (1965), with Ben Loving and Buddy Loving; Ingleside Augusta CC, Saunton (1926); Keswick C of Virginia (1938); Lakeview CC, with Ben Loving and Buddy Loving; Laurel GC (1926); Lawrenceville CC (1960), with Ben Loving; Luray GC (NLE, 1934); McIntire Park GC, Charlottesville (9, 1952), with Ben Loving; Meadowbrook CC, Richmond (1959), with Ben Loving; Ole Monterey CC, Roanoke (1934); Shenandoah CC; South Boston CC (Old Course) (1942); South Hill CC; Spotswood CC, Harrisonburg (NLE, 1935); Swannanoa GC, Waynesboro (1926); Tides Inn & CC (Short Nine), Irvington (Precision, 9); Williamsburg CC (NLE, 1935); Williamsburg Inn GC (NLE, Par 3, 9, 1946); Winchester G&CC (1960), with Ben Loving; Wytheville CC (9).

Courses Remodeled & Added to by: Fred Findlay
Virginia: CC of Virginia (James River Course), Richmond (R., 1931); CC of Virginia (Westhampton Course) (R., 1931); Washington G&CC, Arlington (R.).

Joseph S. Finger (1918 -) ASGCA
Born: Houston, Texas.

Joseph Finger received a Bachelor's degree in Engineering in 1939 from Rice University, where he had been captain of the golf team under coach Jimmy Demaret. He continued his education at the Massachusetts Institute of Technology, receiving his Master's degree in 1941.

Finger was employed for five years in oil refining and then became president of a plastics manufacturing company where he developed a corrugated plastic building panel. During these years he also operated a dairy farm.

In 1956 Finger planned his first golf course, a nine-hole addition to a course near Houston. His early work included a number of courses for the U.S. Air Force as well as several jobs where he had received leads from former coach Demaret. Finger wrote the first publication examining golf design as a business, *The Business End of Building or Rebuilding a Golf Course*, distributed by the National Golf Foundation in 1973.

Courses by: Joseph S. Finger
Arkansas: Bella Vista CC (1966); Burns Park Muni, North Little Rock (1961); Meadowbrook CC, West Memphis; Pleasant Valley CC, Little Rock (27, 1969).
California: Cypress Lakes GC, Travis AFB (1960).
Colorado: Battlement Mesa CC, Parachute (1987), with Ken Dye.
Georgia: Atlanta CC, Marietta (1965), with Willard Byrd; Moody AFB GC, Valdosta (9, 1968).
Louisiana: Ellendale CC, Houma (1967).
Mississippi: Deerfield CC, Madison (1980), with Ken Dye; Keesler AFB GC, Gulfport (9, 1964).
New Mexico: Picacho Hills CC, Las Cruces (1979).
New York: Concord Hotel GC (Championship Course), Kiamesha Lake (1964);

Glen Oak C, Old Westbury (27, 1971).
Oklahoma: Cedar Ridge CC, Broken Arrow (1969).
Tennessee: Colonial CC (North Course), Cordova (1971); Colonial CC (South Course), Cordova (1971).
Texas: Amarillo Muni (1962); Bayou GC, Texas City (1973); Baywood CC, Houston (NLE,); Blue Lake Estates GC, Marble Falls (Par 3, 9, 1962); Cottonwood Creek Muni, Waco (1985), with Ken Dye; Deerwood GC, Kingwood (1983), with Ken Dye; Golfcrest CC, Houston (1970); Grapevine Muni (1980), with Ken Dye and Byron Nelson; Hackberry Creek CC, Irving (1986), with Ken Dye; Kingwood CC (Forest Course) (1982), with Ken Dye; Kingwood CC (Island Course) (1974); Laredo CC (1985), with Baxter Spann; Las Colinas CC, Dallas (1964); Laughlin AFB GC (9); Perrin AFB GC, Sherman (9, 1962); Piney Point GC, Houston (Par 3, 9, 1961); Riverhill C, Kerrville (1974), with Byron Nelson; San Felipe CC, Del Rio (9, 1960); Starr Hollow GC, Fort Worth (Par 3, 9, 1967); Stonebriar CC, Dallas (1987), with Ken Dye; Tejas GC, Houston (1966); Valley International CC, Brownsville (1966); World Houston GC.
Mexico: Bosques Del Lago CC (East Course), Mexico City (1974); Bosques Del Lago CC (West Course), Mexico City (1974); Club de G Tequisquiapan, Queretaro (1985); Club Atlas Campo de Golf, Guadalajara (1970); Hacienda San Gaspar GC, Cuernavaca (1984); Marina Vallarta GC, Puerto Vallarta (1986); Pulgas Pandas GC, Aguacaliente (9, 1985).

Courses Remodeled & Added to by: Joseph S. Finger
Arizona: Arizona CC, Phoenix (R.4, 1960).
Arkansas: Blytheville CC (R.9, 1968); Blytheville CC (A.9, 1968); Burns Park Muni, North Little Rock (A.9, 1965); CC of Little Rock (R.3, 1965); Pine Bluff CC (A.9, 1968); Pine Bluff CC (R.9, 1968).
Florida: Shalimar Pointe CC, Shalimar (R., 1986), with Ken Dye.
Georgia: Atlanta Athletic C (Highlands Course), Duluth (A.9, 1971); Augusta National GC, Augusta (R.1, 1979), with Byron Nelson; Bacon Park GC, Savannah (R., 1973); Highland CC, LaGrange (A.9, 1972); Peachtree GC, Atlanta (R., 1973).
Louisiana: Baton Rouge CC (R., 1973); Oakbourne CC, Lafayette (R., 1985), with Ken Dye; Shreveport CC (A.3, 1960); Shreveport CC (R.15, 1960).
New Jersey: Montammy CC, Alpine (R.4, 1971).
New York: Grossinger's GC (A.9, 1970); Grossinger's GC (R., 1970); Lawrence Park Village (R., 1970); Muttontown G&CC, East Norwich (R., 1971); Westchester CC (West Course), Rye (R., 1971).
Pennsylvania: Westmoreland CC, Export (R., 1967); Westmoreland CC, Export (A.12, 1967).
Tennessee: Richland CC, Nashville (R.9, 1967).
Texas: Brae Burn CC, Bellaire (R.4, 1966); Columbian C, Carrollton (R.6, 1971); Galveston CC (R.6, 1972); Lackland AFB GC (R.); Lakeside CC, Houston (R.14, 1968); Lubbock CC (R.), with Ken Dye; Oak Hill CC, San Antonio (R.6, 1961); Oak Hill CC, San Antonio (A.3, 1961); Panorama CC, Conroe (R., 1985), with Ken Dye; Preston Trail GC, Dallas (R., 1985), with Ken Dye; Prestonwood CC (Creek Course), Dallas (R., 1979), with Ken Dye; Randolph Field GC, San Antonio (R.3, 1958); Randolph Field GC, San Antonio (A.9, 1958); River Oaks CC, Houston (R., 1969); San Antonio CC (R.15, 1959); Victoria CC (R., 1985), with Baxter Spann; Westwood CC, Houston (R.3, 1970); Westwood CC, Houston (A.15, 1970); Willow Brook CC, Tyler (R.9, 1953); Willow Brook CC, Tyler (R., 1980).
Mexico: Club Campestre de Leon (A.9, 1985).

John Francis "Jack" Fleming (1896 -)
Born: Tuam, County Galway, Ireland.

Jack Fleming left his native Ireland at the age of 18 bound for Manchester, England, in search of a position as a gardener to some wealthy Briton. After classes in agriculture and a stint tending a soccer grounds, he landed a job as a "pick and shovel" man at a golf course being built by Dr. Alister Mackenzie.

Working his way through the ranks, Fleming became a construction foreman for Mackenzie in 1920. In 1926 he was sent to Marin County, Calif. where he supervised the building of Meadow CC to a design by Mackenzie and Robert Hunter.

Mackenzie, who also moved to California, designed a number of layouts built by Fleming, among them the dramatic Cypress Point Club. When the Depression hit, at his mentor's urging Fleming accepted a position as superintendent of grounds for the San Francisco Parks Department. Fleming stayed there until his retirement in 1962.

Following Mackenzie's death in 1934, Fleming completed some of his unfinished courses and then built a few of his own. In the late 1940s he designed and built a number of par-3 and precision courses in the San Francisco area, and by the late 1950s had developed a flourishing practice. He continued, until his retirement in 1975, to be an active course architect in northern California.

Courses by: Jack Fleming
California: Adam Springs G&CC, Cobb (9); Almaden G&CC, San Jose (1955); Baymeadows GC, San Francisco (Precision, 9, 1960); Blue Rock Springs GC, Vallejo (9, 1961); Boulder Creek GC (Precision, 9); Buchanan Fields GC, Concord (Precision, 9, 1962); Calero Hills CC, San Jose; Cypress Hills GC, Colma (27, 1963); Dry Creek GC, Galt (1963); Glenhaven G&CC, Milpitas (1961); Golden Gate Fields GC, Albany (Precision, 9, 1954); Golden Gate GC, San Francisco (Par 3, 9, 1950); Harding Park GC (Fleming Nine), San Francisco (9, 1962); IBM GC, San Jose (Par 3, 9); JFK Memorial GC, Napa (1958), with Bob Baldock and Ben Harmon; Lake Chabot Vallejo GC, Vallejo (Precision, 1955); Mace Meadows GC, Jackson (9); Manteca GC (9, 1966); Mather AFB GC, Sacramento (1963); McLaren Park GC, Daly City (9, 1962); Meadowwood CC, St. Helena (9, 1965); Mount St. Helena GC, Calistoga (9); Newark GC (1959); Pruneridge Farms GC, Santa Clara (Precision, 9, 1967); Riverbend G&CC, Broderick (1967); Riverside G&CC, Coyote (9); Roseville Rolling Green GC (Par 3,); Salinas Fairways GC (1957); Santa Rosa G&CC (1958), with Ben Harmon; Sharon Heights G&CC, Menlo Park (1962); Sierra View CC, Visalia (9, 1956); Spring Creek G&CC, Ripon (9); Swenson Park Muni, Stockton (1952); Tanforan GC (Precision,); Turlock G&CC, with Bob Baldock; Warm Springs GC, Fremont (9).
Colorado: Centennial GC, Littleton (NLE, Par 3, 9).

Courses Remodeled & Added to by: Jack Fleming
California: Harding Park GC, San Francisco (R., 1934); Lincoln Park GC, San Francisco (R.); Olympic C (Ocean Course), San Francisco (R.).

William S. Flynn (1890 - 1945)
Born: Milton, Massachusetts. Died: Philadelphia, Pennsylvania at age 54.

William Flynn graduated from Milton High School, where he had played interscholastic golf and competed against his friend Francis Quimet. He laid out his first course at Hartwellville, Vt. in 1909 and was then hired to assist Hugh Wilson with completion of the East course at Merion GC in Pennsylvania.

Flynn found his services as a course architect much in demand as a result of his work at Merion. He and Wilson had hoped to form a design partnership, but Wilson's failing health prevented it. Instead, Flynn joined forces after World War I with Wilson's friend Howard Toomey, a prominent civil engineer. Flynn was responsible for design and construction, Toomey handled business and financial matters and Hugh Wilson continued to collaborate on courses until his death in 1925. William Gordon, Robert Lawrence and Dick Wilson all started out as assistants with the firm of Toomey and Flynn and all later became prominent designers in their own right.

Flynn's second love was the art of greenkeeping. He lectured at Penn State and he wrote many articles and pamphlets on the subject. He also started a number of men in the profession, including the great Joe Valentine, long-time superintendent at Merion, whom he met when he himself was serving as greenkeeper at Merion prior to World War I.

Courses by: William S. Flynn
Colorado: Cherry Hills CC, Englewood (1923).
Florida: Boca Raton Hotel & C (1928), with Howard Toomey; Boca Raton Hotel & C (North Course) (NLE, 1928), with Howard Toomey; Cleveland Heights G&CC, Lakeland (1925), with Howard Toomey; Indian Creek CC, Miami Beach (1930), with Howard Toomey; Normandy Shores GC, Miami Beach (1916), with Howard Toomey.
Illinois: Mill Road Farm GC, Lake Forest (NLE, 1927), with Howard Toomey.
New Jersey: Atlantic City CC, Northfield (1923); Seaview GC (Pines Course), Absecon (9, 1931), with Howard Toomey; Springdale CC, Princeton (1928), with Howard Toomey; Woodcrest CC, Cherry Hill , with Howard Toomey.
New York: Pocantico Hills GC, Tarrytown; Shinnecock Hills GC, Southampton (1931), with Howard Toomey.
North Carolina: Plymouth CC (9, 1937).
Ohio: Elyria CC; Pepper Pike C; The Country Club, Cleveland (1931), with Howard Toomey.
Pennsylvania: CC of Harrisburg (1916); Doylestown CC (1916); Green Valley CC, Lafayette Hills (1924), with Howard Toomey; Huntingdon Valley CC, Abington (1927), with Howard Toomey; Lancaster CC (1920); Lehigh CC, Emmaus (1926), with Howard Toomey; Manufacturers G&CC, Oreland; Philadelphia CC, Gladwyne (1927), with Howard Toomey; Philmont CC (North Course), Philadelphia (1924), with Howard Toomey; Rolling Green CC, Springfield (1926), with Howard Toomey.
Vermont: Hartwellville CC (NLE, 1911).
Virginia: Cascades GC, Virginia Hot Springs (1923); CC of Virginia (James River Course), Richmond (1928), with Howard Toomey.

Courses Remodeled & Added to by: William S. Flynn
Colorado: Denver CC (R., 1923).
Delaware: Hercules Powder C, Wilmington (R.).
Florida: Miami Beach Polo C (NLE, R.).
Illinois: Glen View GC, Golf (R.).
Maryland: Burning Tree C, Bethesda (R.); Columbia CC (R.); US Naval Academy GC, Annapolis (R.); Woodmont CC, Rockville (R.).
Massachusetts: The Country Club, Brookline (A.9, 1927), with Howard Toomey.
New Jersey: Pine Valley GC, Clementon (R., 1929); Springdale CC, Princeton (R., 1938).
New York: Creek C, Locust Valley (R.); Glen Head CC (R.); Tuxedo Park C (NLE, R.); Westchester CC (South Course), Rye (R.); Westchester CC (West Course), Rye (R.).
Pennsylvania: Bala CC, Philadelphia (R.9); Bala CC, Philadelphia (A.9); CC of York (R.); Eaglesmere CC (R.); Gulph Mills GC, King of Prussia (R., 1932); Manor CC, Sinking Springs (R.); Merion GC (East Course), Ardmore (R., 1925), with Howard Toomey; Philadelphia CC, Gladwyne (R., 1938), with Perry Maxwell; Plymouth CC, Norristown (R.); Springhaven C, Wallingford (R.); Whitemarsh Valley CC, Chestnut Hill (R.).
Virginia: Norfolk CC (R.); Washington G&CC, Arlington (R., 1919); Yorktown CC (R.).
Washington, D.C.: East Potomac Park GC (R.); Rock Creek Park GC (R.).

Steven P. Forrest (1956 -) ASGCA
Born: Marion, Virginia.

Steve Forrest graduated from Virgina Tech in 1979, earning a Bachelor of Landscape Architecture Degree. He immediately became a Design Associate of golf architect Arthur Hills, for whom he had worked during college. Forrest worked out of the Toledo, Ohio branch of Arthur Hills and Associates.

Courses by: Steve Forrest
Florida: Bonita Bay C, Bonita Springs (1985), with Arthur Hills and Mike Dasher; Cape Coral Muni (1986), with Arthur Hills and Mike Dasher; Club at Pelican Bay, Naples (1980), with Arthur Hills; Cross Creek CC, Fort Myers (Precision, 1985), with Arthur Hills and Mike Dasher; Foxfire CC, Naples (1985), with Arthur Hills and Mike Dasher; Gator Trace GC, Ft. Pierce (1986), with Arthur Hills and Mike Dasher; Ironhorse GC, West Palm Beach (1987), with Arthur Hills and Mike Dasher; Lakewood GC, Naples (Precision, 1979), with Arthur Hills; Quail Creek CC (Creek Course), Naples (1982), with Arthur Hills; Quail Creek CC (Quail Course), Naples (1981), with Arthur Hills; Tampa Palms CC, Tampa (1987), with Arthur Hills and Mike Dasher; TPC at Eagle Trace, Coral Springs (1984), with Arthur Hills and Mike Dasher; Vista Plantation GC, Vero Beach (Precision, 1985), with Arthur Hills and Mike Dasher; Wyndemere G&CC, Naples (27, 1980), with Arthur Hills.
Georgia: Kings Bay Naval Sub Base GC, St. Marys (1986), with Arthur Hills; Landings at Skidaway Island (Palmetto) (1985), with Arthur Hills and Mike Dasher; Standard C, Norcross (1986), with Arthur Hills and Mike Dasher; Windward CC, Atlanta (1987), with Arthur Hills and Mike Dasher.
Louisiana: Southern Trace CC, Shreveport (1986), with Arthur Hills and Mike

Dasher.
Michigan: Honors C, Brighton (1987), with Arthur Hills and Mike Dasher.
South Carolina: Palmetto Dunes CC (Hills Course), Hilton Head Island (1986), with Arthur Hills and Mike Dasher.
Texas: Trophy C (Creek Course), Roanoke (9, 1984), with Arthur Hills.
Courses Remodeled & Added to by: Steve Forrest
Florida: Cypress Lake CC, Ft. Myers (R., 1982), with Arthur Hills; Hole-in-the-Wall GC, Naples (R., 1984), with Arthur Hills; Vista Royale GC, Vero Beach (A.9, 1981), with Arthur Hills and Mike Dasher.
Indiana: Honeywell GC, Wabash (A.9, 1980).
Kentucky: Big Spring CC, Louisville (R., 1982), with Arthur Hills; Fort Mitchell CC, Covington (R., 1982), with Arthur Hills; Highland CC, Fort Thomas (A.9, 1985), with Arthur Hills and Mike Dasher; Summit Hills CC, Ft. Mitchell (R., 1985), with Arthur Hills and Mike Dasher.
Michigan: Barton Hills CC, Ann Arbor (R., 1983), with Arthur Hills; Birmingham CC (R., 1985), with Arthur Hills; Bloomfield Hills CC (R., 1981), with Arthur Hills; Chemung Hills CC (R., 1986), with Arthur Hills; CC of Detroit, Grosse Pointe Farms (R., 1981), with Arthur Hills; Forest Lake CC, Bloomfield Hills (R., 1981), with Arthur Hills; Grosse Ile G&CC (R., 1981), with Arthur Hills; Indianwood G&CC (Old Course), Lake Orion (R., 1984), with Arthur Hills; Lochmoor C, Grosse Pointe Woods (R., 1981), with Arthur Hills; Orchard Lake CC (R., 1984), with Arthur Hills and Mike Dasher; Plum Hollow G&CC, Southfield (R., 1984), with Arthur Hills; Riverview Highlands GC, Riverview (A.9, 1980), with Arthur Hills; Western G&CC, Redford (R., 1984), with Arthur Hills.
New Jersey: Pennbrook GC, Basking Ridge (R., 1984), with Arthur Hills.
New York: CC of Rochester (R., 1982), with Arthur Hills; Monroe CC (R., 1984), with Arthur Hills; Park CC, Buffalo (R., 1983), with Arthur Hills.
Ohio: Clovernook CC, Cincinnati (R., 1984), with Arthur Hills; Hyde Park CC, Cincinnati (R., 1984), with Arthur Hills; Inverness C, Toledo (R., 1983), with Arthur Hills; Sylvania CC, Toledo (R., 1983), with Arthur Hills.

James Foulis Jr. (1870 - 1928)
Born: St. Andrews, Scotland. Died: Chicago, Illinois at age 58. Interred: Wheaton, Illinois.
James Foulis and his brothers David, Robert, John and Simpson all grew up on the links at St. Andrews. Their father, James Sr., was foreman of Old Tom Morris's golf shop for some 35 years. Old Tom taught the game to each of the boys, and the three eldest helped him in constructing courses. All of the brothers except John were avid golfers, but James was was the best, eventually winning the second U.S. Open in 1896.
Foulis emigrated to the United States in 1895 to serve as the first professional at C.B. Macdonald's Chicago GC. He remained as club maker and professional until 1905, routing a number of midwestern courses during the period. His brother David joined him in the early 1900s and together they developed the first mashie-niblick club, which they patented in 1905. Marketing this and other clubs under the name J & D Foulis Company, they operated a highly successful club manufacturing firm until the 1920s.
After working at several clubs in Chicago and St. Louis, Foulis became pro-greenkeeper at Olympia Fields CC in 1917. He supervised construction of the four courses laid out there, then left in 1922 to pursue a golf design career. He worked part time as an architect until 1927, when he and engineer Ralph Wymer formed the short-lived Pioneer Golf and Landscape Company, which disbanded when Foulis died the following year.
Courses by: James Foulis
Colorado: Denver CC (1902).
Illinois: Bonnie Brook CC, Waukegan; Edgebrook GC (NLE, 1921); Hickory Hills CC, Palos Park (1923); Onwentsia C, Lake Forest (9, 1896), with Robert Foulis; Pipe O'Peace GC, Blue Island (1927).
Minnesota: Meadowbrook GC, Hopkins.
Missouri: Glen Echo CC, Normandy (1901), with Robert Foulis; St. Louis CC (NLE, 9, 1898); Sunset CC, St. Louis (1910), with Robert Foulis.
Tennessee: Memphis CC (NLE, 9, 1905).
Wisconsin: Burlington CC; Hillmoor CC, Lake Geneva (1924); Milwaukee CC (NLE, 9); Nippersink Manor CC, Genoa City.
Courses Remodeled & Added to by: James Foulis
Illinois: Calumet CC (NLE, R., 1911); Onwentsia C, Lake Forest (A.9, 1898), with Robert Foulis, H.J. Tweedie and H.J. Whigham.
Michigan: Kent CC, Grand Rapids (R.9, 1900).

Robert Foulis (1873 - 1945)
Born: St. Andrews, Scotland. Died: Orlando, Florida at age 71. Interred: Wheaton, Illinois.
Robert Foulis worked from an early age in Old Tom Morris' golf shop at St. Andrews, and assisted in the construction of a few courses designed by Morris. Though he had learned the game from Old Tom, Foulis never played much competitive golf because of poor eyesight, the result of two childhood accidents.
In 1895 Robert's brother James accepted a position in the United States. Following him to the States in 1896, Robert assisted James in laying out and building Onwentsia Club in Lake Forest, Ill. and stayed on as its first professional. Soon after the turn of the century, the remaining Foulis brothers, their sister and parents all moved to America and settled in Wheaton, Illinois. By this time James was a renowned competitive golfer and course designer. Robert was well known, too, having toured the small towns of the Midwest teaching golf and staking out courses.
In 1902, James and Robert designed and built Glen Echo CC in St. Louis, and Robert again stayed on as professional. He then created a number of St. Louis-area golf courses, including Bellerive CC in 1910. Becoming Bellerive's first pro-greenkeeper upon its completion, Foulis remained there until his retirement in late 1942. He continued to practice course architecture on a part-time basis. Robert Foulis was an early member of both the PGA of America and the GCSAA.
Courses by: Robert Foulis
Illinois: Onwentsia C, Lake Forest (9, 1896), with James Foulis.
Minnesota: Minikahda C, Minneapolis (9, 1906), with William Watson.

Missouri: Algonquin CC, Glendale (1904); Bellerive CC, Normandy (NLE, 1910); Bogey CC, St. Louis (1910); Forest Park Muni, St. Louis (1913); Glen Echo CC, Normandy (1901), with James Foulis; Jefferson City CC (9, 1922); Log Cabin C, Clayton (1909); Meadow Brook CC, St. Louis (NLE, 1911); Midland Valley CC, St. Louis (1911); Normandie GC, St. Louis (1901); North Shore CC, St. Louis (NLE,.); Riverview CC; Sunset CC, St. Louis (1910), with James Foulis.
Wisconsin: Lake Geneva CC (9, 1897).
Courses Remodeled & Added to by: Robert Foulis
Illinois: Onwentsia C, Lake Forest (A.9, 1898), with James Foulis, H.J. Tweedie and H.J. Whigham.
Minnesota: Town & Country C, St. Paul (R.).
Missouri: Glen Echo CC, Normandy (R., 1904); Log Cabin C, Clayton (R., 1935); Triple A CC, Forest Park (R.).

William Herbert Fowler (1856 - 1941)
Born: Edmonton, England. Died: London, England at age 85.
Herbert Fowler, born into an affluent family, was educated at Rottingdean and at Grove House School, Tottenham. He was an excellent cricket player in his youth, his size and stature making him an intimidating opponent.
Fowler took up golf at the age of 35 and was soon a successful scratch amateur. He was a member of both the Royal and Ancient Golf Club of St. Andrews and the Honourable Company of Edinburgh Golfers. His first course design opportunity came when a group headed by his brother-in-law agreed to finance construction of Walton Heath Golf Club in the early 1900s.
Walton Heath opened to critical acclaim, and while Fowler remained a lifelong director of the club, he was soon busy with other courses. In the early 1920s he partnered with Tom Simpson in the firm of Fowler and Simpson. Simpson did most of the firm's work on the Continent, while Folwer concentrated on British courses. He also spent a considerable amount of time in the United States during World War I and designed several American courses. The firm later expanded to include J.F. Abercromby and Arthur Croome, with the latter partners acting primarily as consultants.
Courses by: Herbert Fowler
California: Ambassador Hotel GC, Los Angeles (NLE, 1920); Lake Merced G&CC, Daly City (NLE, 1922); Los Angeles CC (South Course) (1911).
Massachusetts: Eastward Ho! CC, Chatham (1922).
England: Abbeydale GC, Yorkshire (1922); Beau Desert GC, Staffordshire (1921); Berkshire GC (Blue Course), Surrey (1928), with Tom Simpson; Berkshire GC (Red Course) (1928), with Tom Simpson; Blackwell GC, Worcestershire; Bradford GC, Yorkshire; Cowdray Park GC, with J.F. Abercromby; Delamere Forest GC, Cheshire (1910); Knole Park GC, Kent (1924), with J.F. Abercromby; Lord Mountbatten Estate GC, with Tom Simpson; Manor House Hotel GC (1930), with J.F. Abercromby; Mortimer Singer Estate GC; North Foreland GC, Kingsgate (1919), with Tom Simpson; Saunton GC (New Course), Devonshire (NLE, 1935); Walton Heath GC (New Course), Surrey (1915); Walton Heath GC (Old Course), Surrey (1904); West Kent GC, Kent (1916), with J.F. Abercromby; West Surrey GC, Surrey (NLE, 1909); Woodcote Park GC, Surrey (1912); Yelverton GC, Devon (1905).
Scotland: Cruden Bay G&CC, Aberdeen (27, 1926), with Tom Simpson.
Wales: Bull Bay GC, Gwynedd (1913).
Courses Remodeled & Added to by: Herbert Fowler
California: Del Paso CC (R., 1921); Old Del Monte G&CC, Monterey (R.9, 1912); Old Del Monte G&CC, Monterey (A.9, 1912).
Pennsylvania: Allegheny CC, Sewickley (R., 1922); Allegheny CC, Sewickley (A.3, 1922).
England: Broadstone GC, Dorset (R.); Cowdray Park GC (R.2); Ganton GC (R.); Huddersfield GC, Yorkshire (R.); Royal Lytham & St. Annes GC, Lancashire (R.); Royal North Devon GC, Westward Ho! (R., 1908).
Wales: Aberdovey GC, Merioneth (R.); Southerndown GC, Glamorgan (R.).

Henry Clay Fownes (1856 - 1935)
Born: Pittsburgh, Pennsylvania. Died: Pittsburgh, Pennsylvania at age 79.
H.C. Fownes began working in the iron manufacturing business with his brother-in-law, William Clark. He later formed the Carrie Furnace Company with his own brother, William C. Fownes, operating it until 1896, when it was bought out by the Carnegie Steel Corporation. By then Fownes was a wealthy man and was content to serve as director of several steel firms and two banks, and to play a great deal of golf. He was an accomplished golfer, qualifying at age 45 for the 1901 U.S. Open with a score one stroke less than that of his son.
In 1903 Fownes formed Oakmont CC in a Pittsburgh suburb and laid out its course. He participated actively in the refinements of the course in its early years, but Oakmont remained in its basic routing just as he planned it. H.C. Fownes served as president of Oakmont for over twenty years until his death from pneumonia in 1935.

William Clarke Fownes Jr. (1878 - 1950)
Born: Chicago, Illinois. Died: Oakmont, Pennsylvania at age 72.
William C. Fownes Jr. was the son of Henry Clay Fownes, but was named after his uncle. He followed in his father's footsteps in both business and pleasure, working in the steel business, taking up golf and assisting H.C. with the original design of Oakmont CC. William became a premier golfer in the early 1900s, winning four Pennsylvania Amateurs and the 1910 U.S. Amateur. He was also selected as captain of the first American Walker Cup team in 1922 and served as president of the USGA in 1925 and '26.
William Fownes served for many years as chairman of the Green Committee at Oakmont, and in that capacity worked closely with legendary greenkeeper Emil "Dutch" Loeffler in turning Oakmont into an increasingly fearsome course. Together, they created countless bunkers and a special rake to groom them. They also experimented with the greens until they were lightning fast. Fownes tinkered, groomed and promoted the course all his life, becoming a leading turfgrass authority in the process. He was made an honorary member of the GCSAA in 1932 for his efforts at Oakmont, but he never showed an inclination to work on any other course.

Manuel L. Francis (1903 -)

Born aboard a Brazilian steamship bound for Portugal, Manny Francis came to America at age 16. Francis worked on construction crews building courses on Long Island for Donald Ross and other architects in the 1920s, and was promoted to construction foreman when it was discovered that he was the only man who could start the tractors. When the Depression made construction work scarce, Francis became greenkeeper at South Portland (Maine) CC and later at Haverhill (Mass.) CC.

Francis then moved on to Vesper CC in Lowell, Mass., where he served as superintendent from 1950 through 1974. During his tenure there, he developed "Vespers," a velvet bentgrass with special putting qualities, and became widely known in the United States and Mexico as a turfgrass consultant. He also designed or redesigned a number of golf courses on the side, including Green Harbor CC at Marshfield, Mass., which he operated (after his retirement) with his son Manny Jr. In 1980 Francis was presented with a Distinguished Service Award by the GCSAA in recognition of his contributions to golf and turfgrass development.

Courses by: Manny Francis

Massachusetts: Bedford AFB GC (9, 1957); Dun Roamin GC, Gilbertsville (9); Green Harbor CC, Marshfield; Hickory Hill GC, Lawrence; Westminster GC, Fitchburg (9, 1955).

New Hampshire: Whip-poor-will CC, Hudson (9, 1959).

Courses Remodeled & Added to by: Manny Francis

Massachusetts: Blue Hill CC, Canton (R.6, 1956); Framingham CC (R.); Ould Newberry CC, Newburyport (R., 1955); Vesper CC, Tyngsboro (R.).

New Hampshire: Abenaqui CC, Rye (R.3, 1954); Exeter CC (R.); Keene CC (R., 1957); Rochester CC (R.).

Mexico: Churubusco CC, Mexico City (R.); Club de G Bellavista, Mexico City (R.).

Ronald W. Fream

Ronald Fream received a B.S. degree in Ornamental Horticulture from California Polytechnic Institute at Pomona, in 1964. He also did graduate work in turfgrass management at Washington State University. Fream was employed by Robert Trent Jones Inc. from 1966 to 1969, worked as construction superintendent for Robert F. Lawrence in Arizona in 1970, and was then associated for two years with golf architect Robert Muir Graves. He then became a partner in a golf design firm with Commander John Harris and professional golfer Peter Thomson.

Fream had primary responsibility for projects of the firm in the U.S., Africa, Europe and the Caribbean. In 1980 he left the Harris firm to operate his own company, Ronald Fream Design Group, based in California.

Courses by: Ronald Fream

California: Bixby GC, Long Beach (Precision, 9, 1980), with Peter Thomson and Michael Wolveridge; Carmel Mountain Ranch GC, Rancho Bernardo (1986); Desert Falls CC, Palm Desert (1985).

Washington: Canyon Lakes G&CC, Kennewick (1981), with Peter Thomson, Michael Wolveridge and John Steidel; Kayak Point GC, Stanwood (1974), with Peter Thomson, Michael Wolveridge and Terry Storm; Mint Valley Muni, Longview (1976), with Terry Storm; Tapps Island GC, Sumner (9, 1981), with Peter Thomson and Michael Wolveridge.

Brunei: Pantai Mentiri GC, Bandar Seri (1984); Royal Brunei Polo C, Jerudong Park (1986).

China: Guilin-Lijiang G&CC (36, 1987).

Fiji: Fijian Hotel GC (Precision, 9, 1973), with Peter Thomson and Michael Wolveridge.

Indonesia: Bali Handara CC, Pancasari (1975), with John Harris, Peter Thomson and Michael Wolveridge; Jagorawi G&CC, Chibinong (1978), with Peter Thomson and Michael Wolveridge; National GC, Jakarta Pusat , with Peter Thomson and Michael Wolveridge; Nongsa Indah CC.

Malaysia: Kalab Golf di Raja Darul Ehsan, Ampang Jay (9, 1984); Pilmoor Estate GC, Kaula Lumpur; Rantau Petronas GC (Links Course), Kertah (9, 1984); Saujana G&CC (Orchid Course), Subang (1986); Saujana G&CC (Palm Course), Subang (1985); Taman Tun Abdul Razak GC, Ampangjaya (9, 1984).

Portugal: Estoril Sol GC, Estoril (Precision, 9, 1976), with John Harris, Peter Thomson and Michael Wolveridge.

Singapore: Sentosa Island GC (Serapong Course) (1983), with Peter Thomson and Michael Wolveridge; Tanah Merah CC (1983).

South Korea: Dragon Valley GC, Yongpyeong (27).

St. Kitts: Royal St. Kitts GC (1977), with John Harris, Peter Thomson and Michael Wolveridge.

Sweden: Askersunds GC, Ammeberg (1987); Molndals GC, Goteborg; Soderkoping GC.

Trinidad and Tobago: Balandra Beach GC (1982), with Peter Thomson and Michael Wolveridge; St. Andrews GC, Maraval (1975), with John Harris, Peter Thomson and Michael Wolveridge.

Tunisia: El Kantaoui GC, Soussenord (1977), with John Harris, Peter Thomson and Michael Wolveridge; Monastir International GC (36, 1987); Montaza Tabarka G Resort, Tabarka (1987).

Courses Remodeled & Added to by: Ronald Fream

California: Almaden G&CC, San Jose (R., 1979), with Peter Thomson and Michael Wolveridge; Brentwood CC (R.3, 1983); DeLaveaga CC, Santa Cruz (R.2, 1983); Hacienda CC, La Habra (R., 1978), with Peter Thomson and Michael Wolveridge; Marine Memorial GC, Santa Ana (R., 1980), with Peter Thomson and Michael Wolveridge; Miramar Memorial GC, San Diego (R., 1981), with Peter Thomson and Michael Wolveridge; Napa Valley CC, Napa (A.9, 1987); Napa Valley CC, Napa (R.9, 1987); San Juan Hills CC, San Juan Capistrano (R., 1981), with Peter Thomson and Michael Wolveridge; Santa Ana CC (R., 1983); Seacliff CC, Huntington Beach (R., 1985); Shadow Mountain GC, Palm Desert (R., 1981); Tamarisk CC, Rancho Mirage (R., 1981).

Montana: Glacier View GC, West Glacier (R., 1975), with Terry Storm.

Nevada: Edgewood Tahoe CC, Stateline (R., 1980), with Peter Thomson and Michael Wolveridge.

Oregon: Sunriver CC (South Course) (R., 1978), with Peter Thomson and Michael Wolveridge.

Texas: El Paso CC (R., 1986).

Washington: Broadmoor GC, Seattle (R.2, 1982), with Peter Thomson and Michael Wolveridge; Cedarcrest GC, Marysville (R., 1982), with Peter Thomson and Michael Wolveridge; Manito G&CC, Spokane (R., 1979), with Peter Thomson and Michael Wolveridge; Seattle GC (R.2, 1981), with Peter Thomson and Michael Wolveridge; West Seattle GC, Seattle (R., 1979), with Peter Thomson and Michael Wolveridge.

Alberta: Glendale CC, Edmonton (R.3, 1981), with Peter Thomson and Michael Wolveridge.

Argentina: Jockey C (Blue Course), San Isidro (R., 1983); Jockey C (Red Course), San Isidro (R., 1983); Marayui G&CC (R., 1985); San Isidro GC (R.3, 1983).

Indonesia: Kebayoran GC, Jajarta (R., 1980), with Peter Thomson and Michael Wolveridge.

Malaysia: Gentling Highlands GC (R., 1984), with Peter Thomson and Michael Wolveridge; Royal Selangor GC (New Course), Kuala Lumpur (R., 1983); Royal Selangor GC (Old Course) (R., 1983).

New Zealand: Willunga GC (R.3, 1983).

Singapore: Jurong CC (R., 1982); Keppel C (R.18, 1983); Singapore Island GC (Sime Course) (R., 1982); Warren C (A.12, 1983); Warren C (R.6, 1983).

Sweden: Ljunghusens GC, Hoellviksnaes (R.); Skelleftea GC (R.).

Kinya Fujita (1889 - 1969)

Born: Tokyo, Japan. Died: Kasumigaseki, Japan at age 80.

Kinya Fujita, son of a wealthy Japanese banking family, was educated at Waseda University, where he excelled at several sports. He worked for three years in his family's bank and then traveled to the United States for graduate studies. He attended the University of Chicago, Miami of Ohio and Columbia University. For a time he worked for a silk importing firm in New York City before returning to Tokyo to organize and operate an import-export firm with American backing.

Fujita's interest in golf course design was roused when he met C.H. Alison, who was laying out Tokyo GC in 1914. Fujita traveled to Britain in 1919 to meet again with Alison and to study his techniques. Returning to his own country, he organized Kasumigaseki CC in the 1920s and built its first course, the East eighteen. He also served as the club's captain, its secretary and the Chairman of its board of directors. For good measure Fujita was the club champion in 1929, 1933 and 1935. After laying out a second course at Kasumigaseki, Fujita invited Alison to inspect both courses and recommend changes. Alison made only slight alterations to both courses, mainly adding its now-famous deep bunkers.

Fujita designed several courses before World War II, and his services were in demand during the reconstruction period after the war. He remained a lifelong patriarch at Kasumigaseki and died on its grounds while making plans to remodel its highly respected East Course.

Courses by: Kinya Fujita

Japan: Chiba CC; Higashi Matsuyama GC, Saitama; Ito International GC, Shizuoko; Kasumigaseki GC (East Course), Saitama (1929); Kasumigaseki GC (West Course), Saitama (1932); Narashino CC (Kings Course), Chiba; Narashino CC (Queens Course); Nasu GC, Tochiga; Oarai GC, Ibaraki; Sanrizuka GC; Shiun CC, Nugata; Shizuoka CC; Yahata CC.

Courses Remodeled & Added to by: Kinya Fujita

Japan: Kawana GC (Fuji Course), Shizuoka (R.).

Paul Fullmer (1934 -) ASGCA

Born: Evanston, Illinois.

Paul Fullmer received his Bachelor's Degree in Journalism from Notre Dame University in 1955. He worked for two years as a sports columnist with the Aurora (Ill.) Beacon News and then began a career in public relations with the Chicago firm of Selz, Seabolt and Associates. He became president of the firm in 1979.

Fullmer became the first Executive Secretary of the ASGCA when it retained Selz, Seabolt in 1970. He assisted in executing numerous changes in Society policies. His wife Sandra (daughter of golf architect Percy Clifford) was a former Women's Amateur Champion of Mexico, Spain and Germany (winning all three in one year) as well as a four-time Chicago District Champion.

Jose "Pepe" Gancedo (1938 -)

Spanish businessman Pepe Gancedo won the Spanish Amateur five times and was six times a member of Spain's World team. He entered the field of golf course architecture in 1971, concentrating his efforts in his native country.

Courses by: Pepe Gancedo

Spain: Club de G Costalita, Malaga (1977); Santa Ponsa GC, Majorca (1975); Torrequebrada GC, Malaga (1977).

Ferdinand Garbin (1928 -) ASGCA, President, 1968.

Born: Pennsylvania.

Ferdinand Garbin studied agronomy under H. Burton Musser at Penn State University, receiving a B.S. degree in Turfgrass Science in 1959. He was associated for a number of years with golf architect James G. Harrison, and married Harrison's daughter Joan. In the mid-1960s Garbin entered private practice on his own, based near Pittsburgh.

Courses by: Ferdinand Garbin

Michigan: Warwick Hills G&CC, Grand Blanc (1957), with James Gilmore Harrison.

New Jersey: Knob Hill CC, with James Gilmore Harrison.

New York: Cragie Brae GC, Leroy (1962), with James Gilmore Harrison; Happy Acres CC, Webster (1958), with James Gilmore Harrison; Peek 'n Peak GC, Clymer (1973).

Ohio: Chippewa CC, Barberton (9, 1964), with James Gilmore Harrison; Hidden Valley GC, New Philadelphia (1960), with James Gilmore Harrison; Pleasant Vue GC, Paris (9, 1964), with James Gilmore Harrison; Spring Hill CC, Richmond (1963), with James Gilmore Harrison; Tannenhauf GC, Alliance (1957), with James Gilmore Harrison.

Pennsylvania: Beaver Lakes CC, Aliquippa (1974); Blairsville CC (1963), with James Gilmore Harrison; Blue Knob Resort GC, Claysburg (9, 1974); Blueberry

Hill GC, Warren (9, 1961), with James Gilmore Harrison; Bradford GC (1964), with James Gilmore Harrison; Carradam CC, Irwin (1962), with James Gilmore Harrison; Cedarbrook GC, Smithton (1963), with James Gilmore Harrison; Chestnut Ridge CC, Indiana (1963), with James Gilmore Harrison; Cumberland CC, Carlisle (1961), with James Gilmore Harrison; Downing Muni, Erie (1962), with James Gilmore Harrison; Folmont Resort GC, Somerset (1975); Four Seasons GC, Jennerstown (Precision, 1974); Glen Oak CC, Waverly (1961), with James Gilmore Harrison; Hidden Valley GC, Pottstown , with James Gilmore Harrison; Highland Springs GC, Wellsburg (1960), with James Gilmore Harrison; Indiana CC (1963), with James Gilmore Harrison; Lake Lawn GC, Irwin (Precision, 1971); Lakeview CC, North East (1957), with James Gilmore Harrison; Lenape Heights GC, Ford City (9, 1966); Logo de Vita GC, Greensburg (9, 1980); Meadowwink GC, Murraysville (1970); Mount Cobb Muni, Scranton (1958), with James Gilmore Harrison; Mulberry Hill GC, East Huntington (1984); Penn State Univ GC (White Course), State College (1965), with James Gilmore Harrison; Pine Ridge GC, Meadville (9, 1960), with James Gilmore Harrison; Rolling Acres CC, Beaver Falls (1960), with James Gilmore Harrison; Rolling Hills CC, Pittsburgh (1961), with James Gilmore Harrison; Sewickley Heights CC, Sewickley (1960), with James Gilmore Harrison; Shamrock GC, Ligonier (9, 1980); Silver Lake School GC, Pittsburg (1975); Sportsman's GC, Harrisburg (1964), with James Gilmore Harrison; Valley Brook CC, McMurray (27, 1966); Windber CC (1961), with James Gilmore Harrison.

Virginia: Beaver Hill CC, Martinsville (1972); Blacksburg CC (Valley Course); Castle Rock GC, Pembroke (1971).

West Virginia: Bridgeport CC (1957), with James Gilmore Harrison; Lakeview Inn & CC (South Course), Morgantown (1955), with James Gilmore Harrison.

Puerto Rico: Dorado del Mar GC, Dorado (1962), with James Gilmore Harrison; Punta Borinquen CC (1960).

Courses Remodeled & Added to by: Ferdinand Garbin

Kentucky: Bellefonte CC, Ashland (R., 1960), with James Gilmore Harrison.

New Jersey: Tavistock CC, Haddonfield (R., 1954), with James Gilmore Harrison.

New York: Elmira CC (A.7, 1968).

Ohio: Alliance CC (R., 1983); Birchwood GC, Sharon (R.9, 1974); Birchwood GC, Sharon (A.9, 1974); Chippewa CC, Barberton (A.9, 1967); Hilltop GC, Coshocton (R., 1986); Pleasant Vue GC, Paris (A.9, 1967); Steubenville CC (R.9, 1970); Steubenville CC (A.9, 1970); Sunnyhill GC, Mogador (R., 1967); Sunnyhill GC, Mogador (A.9, 1967).

Pennsylvania: Alcoma CC (R., 1984); Beaver Valley CC, Beaver Falls (R.9, 1958), with James Gilmore Harrison; Beaver Valley CC, Beaver Falls (A.9, 1958), with James Gilmore Harrison; Blue Ridge CC, Harrisburg (R., 1964), with James Gilmore Harrison; Blueberry Hill GC, Warren (A.9, 1969); Brookside CC, Pottstown (R.9, 1959), with James Gilmore Harrison; Brookside CC, Pottstown (A.9, 1959), with James Gilmore Harrison; Butler CC (R., 1986); Chippewa CC, Bentlyville (R.9, 1964), with James Gilmore Harrison; Chippewa CC, Bentlyville (A.9, 1964), with James Gilmore Harrison; Chippewa CC, Bentlyville (A.9, 1964); Churchill Valley CC, Churchill (R., 1960), with James Gilmore Harrison; Conestoga CC, Lancaster (R., 1986); Cross Creek GC, Titusville (A.9, 1971); Cross Creek GC, Titusville (R.9, 1971); Duquesne GC (R., 1985); Edgewood CC, Pittsburgh (R., 1960), with James Gilmore Harrison; Emporium CC (A.9, 1970); Emporium CC (R.9, 1970); Four Seasons GC, Jennerstown (Par 3, A.18, 1976); Frosty Valley CC, Danville (R., 1986); Greenville CC (R.9, 1970); Greenville CC (A.9, 1970); Hanover CC, Abbottstown (R., 1986); Hidden Valley CC, Pottstown (R.9, 1958), with James Gilmore Harrison; Hidden Valley CC, Pottstown (A.9, 1958), with James Gilmore Harrison; Highland CC, New Kensington (R., 1975); Highland CC, Pittsburgh (A.3, 1986); Highland CC, Pittsburgh (R., 1986); Latrobe CC (A.9, 1963), with James Gilmore Harrison; Lebanon CC (R., 1986); Longue Vue C, Verona (R., 1980); Meadia Heights CC, Lancaster (R., 1985); Meadville CC (R., 1978); Montour Heights CC, Coraopolis (A.9, 1962), with James Gilmore Harrison; Montour Heights CC, Coraopolis (R.9, 1962), with James Gilmore Harrison; Oak Lake GC, Merwin (A.9, 1985); Oakmont CC (R., 1983); Penn State Univ GC (Blue Course), State College (R., 1965), with James Gilmore Harrison; Rolling Acres CC, Beaver Falls (A.9, 1986); Seven Springs GC, Champion (R.9, 1980); Sewickley Heights CC, Sewickley (R., 1986); Shannopin CC, Ben Avon Heights (R., 1986); Somerset CC (A.9, 1986); St. Clair CC, Pittsburgh (R., 1960), with James Gilmore Harrison; St. Jude CC, Chicora (A.4, 1985); Suncrest GC, Butler (R.); Sunnehanna CC, Johnstown (R., 1980); Valley Heights CC, Oakmont (R., 1962), with James Gilmore Harrison; Wanango CC, Reno (R., 1986); Youghiogheny CC, McKeesport (R.3, 1985).

West Virginia: Black Knight CC, Beckley (R., 1986); Skyline GC (A.9); Skyline GC (R.); Tygarts Valley CC, Elkins (R., 1957), with James Gilmore Harrison.

Ronald M. Garl (1945 -)

A native of Alabama, Ronald Garl attended the University of Florida on the first scholarship ever granted by the Florida State Golf Association. He graduated in 1967 with a B.S.A. degree in Turfgrass Science and shortly thereafter entered private practice as a golf course architect based in Lakeland. Garl served as President of the Florida State Golf Association in 1979.

Courses by: Ron Garl

Alabama: Ozark G&CC (9).

Florida: Avila G&CC, Tampa (1979); Babe Zaharias GC, Tampa (1972); Bird Bay G&CC, Venice (Precision, 1974); Bloomingdale Golfers C, Valrico (1984); Buffalo Creek GC, Manatee (1987); Burnt Store Marina GC, Punta Gorda (Precision, 1981); Clearwater G Park (Precision, 1971); Continental CC, Wildwood (1972); Cypress Greens CC, Sun City Center (9, 1981); Cypresswood G&RC, Winter Haven (1974); CC at Heathrow, Lake Mary (1986); Del Tura CC, North Fort Myers (Precision, 1983); Disney World CC (Wee Links), Lake Buena Vista (6, 1982); Fiddlesticks CC (Long Mean Course), Fort Myers (1982); Fiddlesticks CC (Wee Friendly Course), Fort Myers (1982); Golden Ocala G&CC, Ocala (1986); Golf Hammock CC, Sebring (1976); Grenelefe G&RC (South Course), Haines City (1983); Hideaway CC, Fort Myers (Precision, 1984); Imperialakes CC, Mulberry (1976); Kingsway CC, Lake Suzy (1978); La Cita G&CC, Titusville (1982); Lake Fairways GC, North Fort Myers (Precision, 1981); Macdill AFB GC (New Course), Tampa (1985); Northdale G&CC, Tampa (1978); Palm Beach Polo & CC (South Course), West Palm Beach (1985), with Jerry Pate; Plantation G&CC (East Course), Venice (1980); Plantation G&CC (West Course), Venice (Precision, 1984); Prairie Oaks G&CC, Sebring (1985); River's Edge Y&CC, Fort Myers (1986); Rocky Point GC, Tampa (1983); St. Andrews South GC, Punta Gorda (1981); Sugarmill Woods G&CC, Homosassa (1975); Tall Pines at River Ridge GC, New Port Richey (Precision, 1985); Timber Pines GC, New Port Richey (Precision, 1982); TPC at Prestancia (Course No. 2), Sarasota (1987); Valle Oaks GC, Zephyr Hills (1979).

New Mexico: Angel Fire GC, Eagle Nest (9, 1980).

North Carolina: Holly Forest GC, Sapphire (1982).

Texas: Fairway Oaks G&CC, Abilene (1980).

Alberta: Hidden Valley GC, Edmonton.

Courses Remodeled & Added to by: Ron Garl

Alabama: Lakewood GC (Azalea Course), Point Clear (A.9, 1986).

Florida: Cleveland Heights G&CC, Lakeland (R.3, 1982); Cleveland Heights G&CC, Lakeland (A.9, 1982); Macdill AFB GC (Old Course), Tampa (R., 1984); Martin County G&CC (R.18, 1982); Naples Beach Hotel GC (R., 1979); Nine Eagles GC, Odessa (R.9, 1985); Nine Eagles GC, Odessa (A.3, 1985); Rogers Park GC, Tampa (R.); Seven Springs G&CC, New Port Richey (A.18, 1978); Seven Springs G&CC, New Port Richey (R.18, 1981); Tiger Point G&CC (East Course), Gulf Breeze (A.9, 1984), with Jerry Pate; Tiger Point G&CC (East Course), Gulf Breeze (R.9, 1984), with Jerry Pate; University of Florida GC, Gainesville (R.); Walden Lake CC, Plant City (A.9, 1986); Wedgewood G&CC, Lakeland (R., 1984).

Nevada: Las Vegas CC (R., 1981).

J. Porter Gibson (1931 -) ASGCA

Born: Charlotte, North Carolina.

J. Porter Gibson attended Carlisle Military School in South Carolina and received B.S. and Civil Engineering degrees from Belmont Abbey College in North Carolina. He later earned an additional C.E. from Clemson University. From 1958 to 1960 Gibson designed golf courses for the Sam Snead Golf and Motor Lodge franchise. The following several years he planned courses for the R & G Construction Company.

Between 1971 and 1974, Gibson was a partner in the firm of Tait-Toski-Gibson Inc., involved in golf course and community planning and construction. This firm, which included well-known golf teacher Bob Toski, was a pioneer in the use of waste water for irrigation. In the late 1970s Gibson practiced course design in North and South Carolina on his own.

Courses by: J. Porter Gibson

Florida: Palm Beach National G&CC, West Palm Beach (1962); Tomoka Oaks G&CC, Ormand Beach (1964).

Georgia: Toccoa G&CC, Toccoa (9).

Maryland: Breton Bay CC, Leonardtown; White Plains GC, LaPlata (1974).

North Carolina: Elizabeth City GC (1965); Flagtree CC, Fairmont (1982); Gastonia National GC, Gaston; Mallard Head CC, Mooresville (1980); Mooresville GC; Northgreen Village GC, Rocky Mount (1974); Piney Point CC, Norwood (1964); Riverside CC, Robbins (1983); Westport GC, Denver (1968); Woodbridge CC, Kings Mountain (1971).

South Carolina: Cherokee National G&CC, Gaffney (1967); Deer Track CC (North Course), Myrtle Beach (1974); Deer Track CC (South Course), Myrtle Beach (1982); Stone Creek Cove GC, Anderson (9, 1975); Wedgefield Plantation GC, North Georgetown (1974).

Virginia: Ivy Hill CC, Forrest; Round Meadow CC, Christiansburg (9).

Courses Remodeled & Added to by: J. Porter Gibson

Georgia: Bacon Park GC, Savannah (R.9, 1971); Bacon Park GC, Savannah (A.3, 1971).

North Carolina: Pine Lake CC, Charlotte (R.9, 1965); Pine Lake CC, Charlotte (A.9, 1965).

South Carolina: Rock Hill CC (A.9, 1974).

David Arthur Gill (1919 -) ASGCA

Born: Keokuk, Iowa.

David Gill attended Iowa State University and obtained a degree in Landscape Architecture in 1942 from the University of Illinois. After service in the U.S. Army during World War II, he obtained a license as a civil engineer in Illinois. He then went to work for golf architect Robert Bruce Harris, assisting in the design and construction of several Midwestern courses.

Gill opened his own office in Illinois in the early 1950s. Although struck with polio in 1953, he made a remarkable recovery and was able to resume the practice of golf architecture on a full-time basis. Dave Gill went to extraordinary lengths to train and assist young people interested in entering the profession. He was one of the most learned students of old British architects and link courses among his brethren.

Courses by: David Gill

Arizona: Royal Palms Inn & C, Mesa (Precision, 9, 1970); Valley CC, Scottsdale (NLE, 1957).

Florida: Tides GC, St. Petersburg (1972); Vinoy Park C, St. Petersburg (9, 1962).

Georgia: Cherokee Town & CC (Hillside Course), Dunwoody (1957).

Illinois: Arlington GC, Arlington Heights (NLE, 1966); Arlington Lakes GC, Arlington Heights (Precision, 1979), with Garrett Gill; Arlington Park GC, Arlington Heights (Precision, 1963); Cress Creek CC, Naperville (1961); Hillcrest Acres GC, Barrington (1964); Kenloch G Links, Lombard (Precision, 9, 1963); Links at Nichols Park, Jacksonville (1979), with Garrett Gill; Village Links of Glen Ellyn (27, 1966).

Indiana: Hulman Links of Terre Haute (1977), with Garrett Gill.

Iowa: Geneva G&CC, Muscatine (1980), with Garrett Gill; Green Valley Muni, Sioux City (1960); Highland Park GC, Mason City (9, 1965); Spencer G&CC (1966).

Minnesota: Bunker Hills Muni, Coon Rapids (1968); Dwan GC, Bloomington (1970).

Missouri: Mosswood Meadows GC, Monroe City (9, 1984), with Garrett Gill.

Nebraska: Lochland CC, Hastings (1964).

North Dakota: Tom O'Leary GC, Bismarck (9, 1983), with Garrett Gill.

South Dakota: Meadowbrook GC, Rapid City (1976), with Garrett Gill.

Wisconsin: Cherokee CC, Madison (1964); Ives Groves GC, Racine (1971); North Shore CC, Mequon (27, 1965); Villa Du Parc CC, Mequon (1963).

Courses Remodeled & Added to by: David Gill
Alabama: Decatur CC (A.9); Decatur CC (R.9, 1959).
Illinois: Apple Orchard CC, Bartlett (R.4, 1960); Arrowhead GC, Wheaton (A.9, 1969); Cherry Hills CC, Flossmoor (A.9, 1966); Downers Grove GC, Belmont (R.3, 1976); Glen Oak CC, Glen Ellyn (R.4, 1965); Jackson CC, Carbondale (A.9, 1967); Kishwaukee CC, DeKalb (A.9, 1964); Naperville CC (R.5, 1969); Park Ridge CC (R.4, 1964); Rochelle CC (R.9, 1965); Rochelle CC (A.9, 1965); Rock Island Arsenal C (R., 1966); Rolling Green CC, Arlington Heights (R.6, 1968); Sandy Hollow Muni, Rockford (R., 1973); St. Charles CC (R., 1967); Sunset CC, Mt. Morris (R.4, 1963).
Iowa: Lakeshore CC, Council Bluffs (A.9, 1969); Westwood GC, Newton (A.9, 1967).
Michigan: Cascade Hills CC, Grand Rapids (R.); Harbor Point GC, Harbor Springs (R.15, 1972); Harbor Point GC, Harbor Springs (A.3, 1972); Marquette G&CC (A.9, 1967).
Minnesota: Green Haven GC, Anoka (R.3, 1971).
Missouri: Cape Girardeau CC (A.9, 1969); Cape Girardeau CC (R.9, 1969).
Nebraska: Fremont GC (R.7, 1961); Fremont GC (A.11, 1961); Happy Hollow C, Omaha (R., 1964); Highland CC, Omaha (R., 1973).
Wisconsin: Blue Mound G&CC, Wauwautosa (R.3, 1960); Brown's Lake GC, Burlington (R.2, 1963); Brynwood CC, Milwaukee (R.6, 1964); Meadowbrook Town & CC, Racine (R., 1962); Ozaukee CC, Mequon (R.3, 1968); Racine CC (R.); West Bend CC (A.9, 1959); Westmoor GC, Brookfield (R.9, 1973).

Garrett D. Gill (1953 -   ) ASGCA
Born: Chicago, Illinois.
Garrett Gill received a Bachelor's Degree in Landscape Architecture from the University of Wisconsin, and earned a Master's Degree in the subject at Texas A & M. During his school years, he trained under his father, golf architect David Gill, and in the late 1970s joined the Gill firm full-time. While at Texas A & M, he wrote a forty-page thesis, *Golf Course Design and Construction Standards*, which soon entered selected golf course bibliographies.

Courses by: Garrett Gill
Illinois: Arlington Lakes GC, Arlington Heights (Precision, 1979), with David Gill; Links at Nichols Park, Jacksonville (1979), with David Gill.
Indiana: Hulman Links of Terre Haute (1977), with David Gill.
Iowa: Geneva G&CC, Muscatine (1980), with David Gill.
Missouri: Mosswood Meadows GC, Monroe City (9, 1984), with David Gill.
North Dakota: Tom O'Leary GC, Bismarck (9, 1983), with David Gill.
South Dakota: Meadowbrook GC, Rapid City (1976), with David Gill.

John Hamilton Gillespie (1852 - 1923)
Born: Dumfrieshire, Scotland. Died: Sarasota, Florida at age 72.
Colonel J. Hamilton Gillespie, a transplanted Scot, was hitting golf balls around what is now downtown Sarasota, Fla. as early as 1885. Gillespie, who became Mayor of Sarasota in the 1920s, laid out a nine hole course, later known as Sarasota Municipal, in 1886. It is generally considered to be Florida's earliest course. After it opened, Gillespie was called to prepare courses in Florida and other Southern states.

Frank Clark Glasson (1913 -   )
Born: San Jose, California.
The superintendent at Los Altos G&CC (Calif.) after World War II, Clark Glasson worked with retired professional Tom Nicoll in restoring the course. In 1950 Glasson formed a course construction firm and by the mid Fifties was designing courses, several of which he owned and operated. He continued his work well into the Eighties.

Courses Remodeled & Added to by: Clark Glasson
California: Deep Cliff GC, Cupertino (1961); Emerald Hills Elks GC, Redwood City (Precision, 9, 1959); Fall River Valley G&CC, Fall River Mills (1980); Indian Pines G&TC, Mi-Wuk Village (9); Little Wuk GC, Napa (9); Los Gatos G&CC, San Jose (Precision, 9, 1959); Palo Alto Hills G&CC, Palo Alto (1957); San Ramon CC (1962); Shasta Valley CC, Montague (9); Sunken Gardens Muni, Sunnyvale (9); Sunnyvale Muni; Sunol Valley GC (Cypress Course), Sunol (1967); Sunol Valley GC (Palm Course), Sunol (1967); Twain Harte GC (Precision, 9, 1961); Wikiup G&TC, Santa Rosa (Precision, 9, 1964).
Colorado: Lake Arbor GC, Arvada.
Nevada: Showboat CC, Las Vegas (1959).

Courses Remodeled & Added to by: Clark Glasson
California: Los Altos G&CC (R., 1978); Pasatiempo GC, Santa Cruz (R., 1977); Peninsula G&CC, San Mateo (R.); Rio del Mar GC, Aptos (R.).

Harold W. Glissmann (1909 -   )
Born: Douglas County, Nebraska.
Harold Glissmann began his career in golf in the 1930s helping his father Henry and brother Hans construct and operate three daily-fee courses near Omaha, Nebraska. When these courses closed during World War II, Glissmann became grounds superintendent at the famed Boys Town community near Omaha.
In the 1950s Glissmann formed a golf design and construction firm and built many small-town courses in Nebraska and Iowa. He also owned and operated several daily-fee layouts in Omaha, including Miracle Hills GC. He retired from his design work in 1965 but continued to serve as a turfgrass consultant for clubs and businesses during the 1970s.

Courses by: Harold Glissmann
Iowa: Emmettsburg G&CC (9, 1951), with Henry C. Glissmann; Five-by 80 GC, Menlo (9, 1965); Ida Grove G&CC (9); Lakeview GC, Ralston (9, 1966).
Nebraska: Cedar Hills GC, Omaha (Precision, 9, 1959); Dundee GC, Omaha (NLE,), with Henry C. Glissmann; Harrison Heights GC, Omaha (NLE, 1933), with Henry C. Glissmann; Indian Hills GC, Omaha (NLE, 1934), with Henry C. Gliss-

mann; Lakeview GC, Ralston (9, 1968); Maple Village GC, Omaha (Par 3, 9, 1962); Ralston GC (NLE,), with Henry C. Glissmann; Ryan Hill GC, Osceola (9, 1969); Seward CC (9, 1964); Valley View GC, Central City (9); Valley View GC, Fremont (9); Westwood Heights GC, Omaha (Par 3, 9, 1964).

Courses Remodeled & Added to by: Harold Glissmann
Iowa: Council Bluffs CC (NLE, R., 1935), with Henry C. Glissmann.
Nebraska: Fremont GC (R.); Kearney CC (R.).

Joel Goldstrand (1939 -   )
Born: St. Paul, Minnesota.
A member of two University of Houston NCAA Championship teams, Joel Goldstrand played on the PGA Tour during the Sixties and then served as head professional at Minneapolis (Minn.) Golf Club.
As a sidelight to his club professional duties, Goldstrand laid out a series of fine low budget courses in rural Iowa and Minnesota. Among the most respected was Double Eagle GC, a nine hole reversible layout Goldstrand designed to be played both forwards and backwards.

Courses by: Joel Goldstrand
Minnesota: Benson GC (9); Double Eagle GC, Eagle Bend (9, 1984); Hidden Greens GC, Hastings (1986); Ortonville Muni; Tipsinah Mounds GC, Grant (9, 1982).

David W. Gordon: (1922 -   ) ASGCA, President, 1959.
Born: Mt. Vernon, New York.
Son of golf architect William F. Gordon, David Gordon served as a pilot with the U.S. Army Air Force in World War II. He then completed his education at Penn State University, receiving a B.S. degree in Agronomy. From 1947 to 1952 he worked in the field as a construction superintendent for his father's firm.
David became a partner in the Gordon firm in 1952 and was involved in all aspects of the business. He continued to maintain the practice after his father's death in 1974, retiring from active work in the mid 1980s.

Courses by: David Gordon
Connecticut: East Mountain Muni, Waterbury (1955), with William Gordon; Stanwich C, Greenwich (1963), with William Gordon; Western Hills GC, Waterbury (1960), with William Gordon.
Delaware: DuPont CC (Louviers Course), Wilmington (1955), with William Gordon; DuPont CC (Montchanin Course), Newark (Precision, 1955), with William Gordon.
Florida: Hidden Hills CC, Jacksonville (1967).
Maryland: Hillendale CC, Phoenix (1954), with William Gordon; Indian Spring C (Chief Course), Silver Spring (1955), with William Gordon; Indian Spring C (Valley Course), Silver Spring (1955), with William Gordon; Ocean City G&YC, Berlin (1958), with William Gordon; Sparrows Point CC, Baltimore (1954), with William Gordon; Willow Brook GC, Moorestown (1969), with William Gordon.
New Jersey: Buena Vista CC, Buena (1957), with William Gordon; Green Knoll GC, Somerset (27, 1960), with William Gordon; Lake Lackawanna GC, Byram (Precision, 9, 1955), with William Gordon; Medford Village CC {formerly Sunny Jim GC}, Medford (1964), with William Gordon; Oak Hill GC, Milford , with William Gordon; Princeton CC (1964), with William Gordon; Rockleigh GC (Bergen Course), Hackensack (9, 1963), with William Gordon; Tall Pines GC, Sewell , with William Gordon.
New York: Bay Park GC, East Rockaway (9); Bethlehem Steel C, Hellertown (27, 1956), with William Gordon; Finger Lakes GC , Ithaca; North Woodmere GC (9); Rockland Lake GC (North Course), Congers; Rockland Lake GC (South Course), Congers (Precision,).
Ohio: Browns Run CC, Middleton (1958), with William Gordon.
Pennsylvania: Bethlehem Muni (1955), with William Gordon; Blackwood CC, Douglasville (1970), with William Gordon; Blue Mountain GC, Linglestown; Bon Air CC, Glen Rock (1954), with William Gordon; Bucks County GC, Jamison , with William Gordon; Colonial CC, Harrisburg (1956), with William Gordon; Colonial GC, Uniontown (1973), with William Gordon; Cornwells CC, Cornwells Heights (1960), with William Gordon; Danville CC, with William Gordon; Edgewood in the Pines GC, Hazilton; Fairways GC, Warrington (1958), with William Gordon; Frosty Valley CC, Danville (1960), with William Gordon; Glenhardie CC, Wayne (9); Hawk Valley GC, Bowmansville (1971), with William Gordon; Hershey's Mill GC, Malvern; Indian Valley CC, Telford (1954), with William Gordon; Locust Valley CC, Coopersburg (1963), with William Gordon; Mahoning Valley CC, Leighton (1962), with William Gordon; Manada GC, Lebanon (9); Saucon Valley CC (Grace Course), Bethlehem (1957), with William Gordon; Saucon Valley CC (Junior Course), Bethlehem (6, 1955), with William Gordon; Saucon Valley CC (Weyhill Course), Bethlehem , with William Gordon; South Hills GC, Hanover (1960), with William Gordon; St. Clair CC, Pittsburgh (1954), with William Gordon; Sunnybrook GC, Plymouth Meeting (1956), with William Gordon; Upper Main Line CC, Philadelphia (1962), with William Gordon; Warrington CC (1958), with William Gordon; Wedgewood GC, Allentown (1963), with William Gordon; White Manor CC, Malvern (1963), with William Gordon; Whitford CC, Downington (1958), with William Gordon.
Virginia: Ethelwood CC, Richmond (1957), with William Gordon; Warwick CC, with William Gordon; Williamsburg CC (1960), with William Gordon; Willow Oaks CC, Richmond (1959), with William Gordon.
West Virginia: Clinton Springs CC, Wheeling (1959), with William Gordon.
Quebec: Elm Ridge CC (Course No. 1), Ile Bizard (1958), with William Gordon; Elm Ridge CC (Course No. 2), Ile Bizard (1958), with William Gordon; Richelieu Valley CC (Blue Course), Montreal (1963), with William Gordon; Richelieu Valley CC (Red Course), Montreal (1963), with William Gordon.
Bermuda: Queens Park GC (Precision, 9, 1958).

Courses Remodeled & Added to by: David Gordon
Connecticut: Hartford GC, West Hartford (R., 1965), with William Gordon.
Delaware: DuPont CC (DuPont Course), Wilmington (R., 1955), with William Gordon; DuPont CC (Nemours Course), Wilmington (R., 1955), with William Gordon.
Florida: Timuquana CC, Jacksonville (R., 1969).
Maryland: Newton CC (A.9), with William Gordon.

New Jersey: Canoe Brook CC (North Course), Millburn (R., 1955), with William Gordon; Canoe Brook CC (South Course), Summit (R., 1955), with William Gordon; Greenacres CC, Lawrence (R., 1955), with William Gordon; Lawrenceville School GC (R., 1954), with William Gordon; Little Mill CC, Marlton (A.9); Raritan Arsenal CC, Somerville (R.); Rockleigh GC (Rockleigh Course), Hackensack (R., 1963), with William Gordon; Seaview GC (Bay Course), Absecon (R., 1957), with William Gordon; Seaview GC (Pines Course), Absecon (A.9, 1957), with William Gordon.

New York: Binghampton CC, Endwell (R., 1958), with William Gordon; Engineers GC, Roslyn (R., 1958), with William Gordon; Hyde Park Muni (North Course), Niagara Falls (R., 1962), with William Gordon; Hyde Park Muni (South Course), Niagara Falls (A.9, 1962), with William Gordon; Hyde Park Muni (South Course), Niagara Falls (R.9, 1962), with William Gordon; Moonbrook CC, Jamestown (R., 1958), with William Gordon; Yahnundasis GC, Utica (R.5, 1960), with William Gordon.

Ohio: Lancaster CC (A.9, 1961), with William Gordon.

Pennsylvania: Bethlehem Steel Club (R.), with William Gordon; Bethlehem Steel Club (A.9), with William Gordon; Brookside CC, Pottstown (R.9, 1955), with William Gordon; Brookside CC, Pottstown (A.9, 1955), with William Gordon; Buck Hill Inn & CC, Buck Hill Falls (R., 1956), with William Gordon; Chambersburg CC (R., 1955), with William Gordon; CC of Northampton County, Easton (A.6); CC of Northampton County, Easton (R.12); Galen Hall GC, Wernersville (R., 1955), with William Gordon; Gulph Mills GC, King of Prussia (R.7, 1958), with William Gordon; Lancaster CC (R.12, 1959), with William Gordon; Lancaster CC (A.6, 1959), with William Gordon; Lehigh CC, Emmaus (R., 1959), with William Gordon; Manufacturers G&CC, Oreland (A.9, 1963), with William Gordon; Meadowlands CC, Blue Ball (R., 1958), with William Gordon; Northampton GC (R.12); Northampton GC (A.6); Philmont CC (North Course), Philadelphia (R., 1956), with William Gordon; Radnor Valley CC, Villanova (R.4, 1968), with William Gordon; Radnor Valley CC, Villanova (A.14, 1968), with William Gordon; Saucon Valley CC (Saucon Course), Bethlehem (R., 1956), with William Gordon; Susquehanna Valley CC, Hummels Wharf (R., 1955), with William Gordon; Twin Lakes GC, Souderton (A.9); Twin Lakes GC, Mainland (A.9); Wildwood GC, Allison Park (R., 1955), with William Gordon; Williamsport CC (R., 1964).

Virginia: Hermitage CC, Richmond (R., 1963).

West Virginia: Oglebay Park GC, Wheeling (Par 3, A., 1957), with William Gordon.

William F. Gordon (1893 - 1974) ASGCA, Charter Member; President, 1953, 1967.

Born: Rhode Island. Died: Abington, Pennsylvania at age 80.

William Gordon was an outstanding track star in his youth and served as an athletic instructor with the U.S. Navy during World War I. Upon discharge he took a job as salesman with the Peterson Seed Company and in 1920 joined the Carter's Tested Seed Company as superintendent of its golf course construction division. In this capacity he constructed courses for such well-known golf architects as Willie Park Jr., Leonard Macomber, Donald Ross and Devereux Emmet.

In 1923 Gordon joined the firm of Toomey and Flynn, where he remained until 1941. During the Depression, he was also part owner and manager of Marble Hall GC in Philadelphia. Gordon founded the Pennsylvania Public Golfers Association and served as its first president from 1936 to 1940, and was also a member and president (in 1940) of the Philadelphia Public Golfers Association.

In 1941 Gordon formed his own corporation, which was involved until 1945 in the seeding of military installations. For the next five years the firm constructed golf courses for Donald Ross and J.B. McGovern. From 1950 to 1973 Gordon designed and built courses on his own under the incorporated name of William F. Gordon Co. Most of his layouts planned after 1953 were done in collaboration with his son David. Bill Gordon served as first chairman of the ASGCA's Historical Committee.

Courses by: William Gordon

Connecticut: East Mountain Muni, Waterbury (1955), with David Gordon; Stanwich C, Greenwich (1963), with David Gordon; Western Hills GC, Waterbury (1960), with David Gordon.

Delaware: DuPont CC (Louviers Course), Wilmington (1955), with David Gordon; DuPont CC (Montchanin Course), Newark (Precision, 1955), with David Gordon.

Florida: Ocala Muni (Course No. 1) (1947).

Maryland: Hillendale CC, Phoenix (1954), with David Gordon; Indian Spring C (Chief Course), Silver Spring (1955), with David Gordon; Indian Spring C (Valley Course), Silver Spring (1955), with David Gordon; Ocean City G&YC, Berlin (1958), with David Gordon; Sparrows Point CC, Baltimore (1954), with David Gordon; Willow Brook GC, Moorestown (1969), with David Gordon.

New Jersey: Buena Vista CC, Buena (1957), with David Gordon; Green Knoll GC, Somerset (27, 1960), with David Gordon; Lake Lackawanna GC, Byram (Precision, 9, 1955), with David Gordon; Medford Village CC {formerly Sunny Jim GC}, Medford (1964), with David Gordon; Oak Hill GC, Milford , with David Gordon; Princeton CC (1964), with David Gordon; Rockleigh GC (Bergen Course), Hackensack (9, 1963), with David Gordon; Tall Pines GC, Sewell , with David Gordon.

New York: Bethlehem Steel C, Hellertown (27, 1956), with David Gordon.

Ohio: Browns Run CC, Middleton (1958), with David Gordon.

Pennsylvania: Bethlehem Muni (1955), with David Gordon; Blackwood CC, Douglasville (1970), with David Gordon; Bon Air CC, Glen Rock (1954), with David Gordon; Bucks County GC, Jamison , with David Gordon; Colonial CC, Harrisburg (1956), with David Gordon; Colonial GC, Uniontown (1973), with David Gordon; Conestoga CC, Lancaster; Cornwells CC, Cornwells Heights (1960), with David Gordon; Danville CC, with David Gordon; Fairways GC, Warrington (1958), with David Gordon; Frosty Valley CC, Danville (1960), with David Gordon; Hawk Valley GC, Bowmansville (1971), with David Gordon; Indian Valley CC, Telford (1954), with David Gordon; Locust Valley CC, Coopersburg (1963), with David Gordon; Mahoning Valley CC, Leighton (1962), with David Gordon; Saucon Valley CC (Grace Course), Bethlehem (1957), with David Gordon; Saucon Valley CC (Junior Course), Bethlehem (6, 1955), with David Gordon; Saucon Valley CC (Weyhill Course), Bethlehem , with David Gordon; South Hills GC, Hanover (1960), with David Gordon; St. Clair CC, Pittsburgh (1954), with David Gordon; Sunnybrook CC, Plymouth Meeting (1956), with David Gordon; Upper Main Line CC, Philadelphia (1962), with David Gordon; Warrington CC (1958), with David Gordon; Wedgewood GC, Allentown (1963), with David Gordon; White Manor CC, Malvern (1963), with David Gordon; Whitford CC, Downington (1958), with David Gordon.

Virginia: CC of Fairfax (9, 1946); Ethelwood CC, Richmond (1957), with David Gordon; Goose Creek CC, Leesburg (1953); Warwick CC, with David Gordon; Williamsburg CC (1960), with David Gordon; Willow Oaks CC, Richmond (1959), with David Gordon.

West Virginia: Berry Hills CC, Charleston (1952); Clinton Springs CC, Wheeling (1959), with David Gordon.

Quebec: Elm Ridge CC (Course No. 1), Ile Bizard (1958), with David Gordon; Elm Ridge CC (Course No. 2), Ile Bizard (1958), with David Gordon; Richelieu Valley CC (Blue Course), Montreal (1963), with David Gordon; Richelieu Valley CC (Red Course), Montreal (1963), with David Gordon.

Washington, D.C.: Fort DuPont Muni (9, 1948).

Courses Remodeled & Added to by: William Gordon

Connecticut: Hartford GC, West Hartford (R., 1965), with David Gordon.

Delaware: DuPont CC (DuPont Course), Wilmington (R., 1955), with David Gordon; DuPont CC (Nemours Course), Wilmington (R., 1955), with David Gordon.

Maryland: Newton CC (A.9), with David Gordon.

New Jersey: Alpine CC (R., 1953); Canoe Brook CC (North Course), Millburn (R., 1955), with David Gordon; Canoe Brook CC (South Course), Summit (R., 1955), with David Gordon; Greenacres CC, Lawrence (R., 1955), with David Gordon; Lawrenceville School GC (R., 1954), with David Gordon; Rockleigh GC (Rockleigh Course), Hackensack (R., 1963), with David Gordon; Seaview GC (Bay Course), Absecon (R., 1957), with David Gordon; Seaview GC (Pines Course), Absecon (A.9, 1957), with David Gordon.

New York: Binghampton CC, Endwell (R., 1958), with David Gordon; Engineers GC, Roslyn (R., 1958), with David Gordon; Hyde Park Muni (North Course), Niagara Falls (R., 1962), with David Gordon; Hyde Park Muni (South Course), Niagara Falls (R.9, 1962), with David Gordon; Hyde Park Muni (South Course), Niagara Falls (A.9, 1962), with David Gordon; Moonbrook CC, Jamestown (R., 1958), with David Gordon; Yahnundasis GC, Utica (R.5, 1960), with David Gordon.

Ohio: Lancaster CC (A.9, 1961), with David Gordon.

Pennsylvania: Bethlehem Steel Club (A.9), with David Gordon; Bethlehem Steel Club (R.), with David Gordon; Brookside CC, Pottstown (R.9, 1955), with David Gordon; Brookside CC, Pottstown (A.9, 1955), with David Gordon; Buck Hill Inn & CC, Buck Hill Falls (R., 1956), with David Gordon; Chambersburg CC (R., 1955), with David Gordon; Galen Hall GC, Wernersville (R., 1955), with David Gordon; Gulph Mills GC, King of Prussia (R.7, 1958), with David Gordon; Hanover CC, Abbottstown (R.); Lancaster CC (R.12, 1959), with David Gordon; Lancaster CC (A.6, 1959), with David Gordon; Lehigh CC, Emmaus (R., 1959), with David Gordon; Manufacturers G&CC, Oreland (R.1, 1952); Manufacturers G&CC, Oreland (A.9, 1963), with David Gordon; Meadowlands CC, Blue Ball (R., 1958), with David Gordon; Philmont CC (North Course), Philadelphia (R., 1956), with David Gordon; Radnor Valley CC, Villanova (A.14, 1968), with David Gordon; Radnor Valley CC, Villanova (R.4, 1968), with David Gordon; Saucon Valley CC (Saucon Course), Bethlehem (R., 1951); Saucon Valley CC (Saucon Course), Bethlehem (R., 1956), with David Gordon; Susquehanna Valley CC, Hummels Wharf (R., 1955), with David Gordon; Wildwood GC, Allison Park (R., 1955), with David Gordon.

West Virginia: Oglebay Park GC, Wheeling (Par 3, A., 1957), with David Gordon; Southmore CC, Charleston (R., 1952).

Washington, D.C.: Langston GC (A.9, 1953).

Roy L. Goss

Dr. Roy Goss, a Washington State University turfgrass specialist, was best known for turfgrass research and assistance he gave course superintendents. He also designed several courses in the 1970s with course superintendent Glen Proctor.

Courses by: Roy L. Goss

Washington: Alderbrook G&CC, Union (1970), with Glen Proctor; Hi Cedars GC, Orting (1971), with Glen Proctor; Lake Padden Muni, Bellingham (1970), with Glen Proctor; Tumwater Valley GC, Olympia (1970), with Glen Proctor.

Mary Perceval "Molly" Gourlay (1898 -)

Born: Basingstoke, Hampshire, England.

Molly Gourlay, a member of the 1932 and 1934 Curtis Cup teams for Great Britain, won two English Ladies Championships, three French Ladies Opens, three Swedish Ladies Opens and two Belgian Ladies Opens.

During the height of her competitive career, Gourlay assisted golf architect Tom Simpson on the design and redesign of several courses, including County Louth, Carlow and Ballybunion, all in Ireland.

Gary James Grandstaff (1948 -)

After graduating from Penn State University with a degree in Agronomy and Turf Management, Gary Grandstaff worked as a golf course superintendent at various Ohio courses for five years.

In 1971, Grandstaff joined the construction crew at Wabeek CC in Michigan, being built by Roy Dye. Grandstaff worked on several Dye projects, then served for a time as course superintendent at Waterwood National in Texas after it opened in 1975.

In 1977, Grandstaff left Waterwood and rejoined Roy Dye in Mexico. The two constructed layouts in the Southwest during the next five years. By 1983 ill health had curtailed Roy Dye's activities, and Grandstaff formed his own course design business, Golf West Inc., based in Phoenix.

Courses by: Gary Grandstaff

Arizona: Anasazi GC, Phoenix (1983), with Roy Dye; Brookview CC, Surprise (1985); Gambel G Links, Carefree (NLE, 9, 1983), with Roy Dye.

Ohio: Catawba Island C, Port Clinton (1987).

Mexico: La Mantarraya GC, Las Hadras (9, 1974), with Roy Dye; San Carlos G&CC, Sonora (1980), with Roy Dye.

Courses Remodeled & Added to by: Gary Grandstaff
Arizona: Pinnacle Peak CC, Scottsdale (R., 1985).

Douglas S. Grant (1887 - 1981)
Born: Irvington, New York. Died: England at age 95.
California amateur champion Douglas Grant was invited by his friend Jack Neville to help design the course that became the famous Pebble Beach Golf Links. Although he did no other design work, Grant was consulted on changes at Pebble Beach.

Charles M. Graves (1905 -   )
Born: Topeka, Kansas.
Born in the Midwest, Charles Graves moved with his family to Birmingham, Ala. at age 5. Graves was one of the first to specialize in parks and recreation planning, having studied it in college and graduate school at Birmingham Southern University, the University of Birmingham and Georgia Tech. He opened his own landscape design company in 1933. Over the years Graves planned hundreds of city, county and state parks. In the '60s he began to incorporate golf courses into certain park complexes, and handled the design and construction supervision himself. Graves retired in 1979.
Courses by: Charles M. Graves
Alabama: Lagoon Park GC, Montgomery (1978); Point Mallard Park GC, Decatur (1969).
Georgia: Westwood GC, Marietta (1971).
Tennessee: Buford Ellington GC, Horton State Park (1963); McKellar GC, Memphis (1972).

Robert Muir Graves (1930 -   ) ASGCA, President, 1974.
Born: Trenton, Michigan.
Robert Muir Graves attended Michigan State University and received a B.Sc. degree in Landscape Architecture from the University of California in 1953. He entered private practice as a licensed landscape architect in 1955 and gradually concentrated on golf design within the next four years. After 1959 he was involved in designing, remodeling or consulting on some 300 golf courses throughout the United States and abroad, working in all major vegetative and climate zones.
Although he was not the first landscape architect to become a golf course planner, Graves was generally felt to have ushered in the era of landscape architecture as the preferred academic background for course designers. He wrote extensively on a number of topics relating to golf course architecture and lectured on the subject at University of California, Utah State University and Harvard Graduate School of Design.
Courses by: Robert Muir Graves
California: Big Canyon CC, Newport Beach (1971); Blackberry Farm GC, Cupertino (Par 3, 9, 1962); Boundary Oaks GC (1969); Carmel Valley G&CC, Carmel (1964); Chalk Mountain Muni, Atascadero (1980); Diablo Hills GC, Walnut Creek (Precision, 9, 1974); El Cariso GC, Sylmar (Precision, 1977); Franklin Canyon GC, Rodeo (1968); La Purisima GC, Lompoc (1986), with Damian Pascuzzo; Lake Merced G&CC, Daly City (1965); Las Positas Muni, Livermore (1967); Moraga CC (Precision, 9, 1974); Navy Postgraduate School GC, Monterey (9, 1961); Northstar at Tahoe GC, Truckee (1979); Rio Bravo GC, Bakersfield (1982); Rossmoor CC (North Course), Walnut Creek (Precision, 9, 1974); Royal Oaks GC, Clayton (NLE, Par 3, 9, 1961); San Jose Muni (1968); Santa Clara Muni (1986), with Damian Pascuzzo; Sea Ranch GC (9, 1973); Villages G&CC, San Jose (27, 1970); Walnut Creek Muni (1968).
Idaho: Bigwood GC, Sun Valley (9, 1971); McCall Muni (1983).
Montana: Bill Roberts Muni, Helena (9, 1978).
Nevada: Jackpot GC (9, 1970).
Oregon: Black Butte Ranch GC (Big Meadows), Sisters (1972); Paradise Inn Ranch GC, Grants Pass (1987), with Damian Pascuzzo.
Utah: Murray Muni (1983).
Washington: Centerwood GC, Gig Harbor (1986), with Damian Pascuzzo; Pasco Muni (1982); Port Ludlow GC (1975); Spokane County GC, Spokane (1987), with Damian Pascuzzo; Three Rivers GC, Kelso (1982); Washington State Univ GC, Pullman (9, 1971).
Japan: Kurabone GC (1978).
Malaysia: Labuan GC (9, 1975); Mount Kinabalu GC, Kundasang (1973); Sabah G&CC, Kota Kinbalu .
Courses Remodeled & Added to by: Robert Muir Graves
California: Alameda Muni (Jack Clark Course) (R., 1978); Almaden G&CC, San Jose (R.1, 1968); Baywood G&CC, Arcata (R., 1980); Contra Costa CC, Pleasant Hill (R., 1976); Del Paso CC (R., 1985), with Damian Pascuzzo; Diablo Creek GC, Concord (R.5, 1974); Diablo G&CC (R.2, 1964); El Cerrito G&CC (R.); El Macero CC (R., 1985), with Damian Pascuzzo; Gleneagles International GC, San Francisco (R., 1982); Green Hills CC, Millbrae (R., 1965); Green Valley CC, Suisun (R., 1965); Hillcrest CC, Los Angeles (R.6, 1974); Laguna Hills GC (R.); Lakeside GC of Hollywood, North Hollywood (R., 1972); Leisure Town GC, Vacaville (R., 1979); Lew Galbraith Muni, Oakland (R., 1980); Los Altos G&CC (R.9, 1973); McLaren Park GC, Daly City (R., 1979); Meadow C, Fairfax (R., 1964); Merced G&CC, Slater (R., 1977); Mira Vista G&CC, Berkeley (R.1, 1967); Moffett Field GC (A.9, 1968); Navy Postgraduate School GC, Monterey (R.4, 1968); Navy Postgraduate School GC, Monterey (A.9, 1972); North Ridge CC, Sacramento (R., 1986), with Damian Pascuzzo; Oceana CC, Oceanside (R., 1979); Orinda CC (R., 1977); Pajaro Valley CC, Watsonville (R., 1965); Palo Alto Hills G&CC, Palo Alto (R.5, 1968); Presidio GC, San Francisco (R., 1964); Rancho San Joaquin CC, Irvine (R., 1972); River Island GC, Porterville (R., 1975); Round Hill G&CC, Alamo (R., 1975); San Jose CC (R., 1968); San Luis Bay Inn & CC, Avila Beach (R., 1984); San Mateo Muni (R.); Sandpiper G Links, Goleta (R., 1986), with Damian Pascuzzo; Saratoga GC (R., 1966); Sequoyah CC, Stockton (R.13, 1968); Stockdale CC, Bakersfield (A.9, 1975); Stockdale CC, Bakersfield (R.9, 1975); Stockton G&CC (R.); Swenson Park Muni, Stockton (A.9, 1970); Twin Lakes GC, Goleta (R., 1985), with Damian Pascuzzo; Van Buskirk Muni, Stockton (A.9, 1970); Woodbridge G&CC, Lodi (R., 1985), with Damian Pascuzzo.

Idaho: Bigwood GC, Sun Valley (R., 1979); Crane Creek CC, Boise (R.2, 1982); Hillcrest CC, Boise (R.6, 1968); Plantation GC, Boise (R., 1975).
Montana: Buffalo Hill GC, Kalispell (R., 1977); Buffalo Hill GC, Kalispell (A.9, 1977); Laurel G&RC (R., 1979); Marias Valley G&CC, Shelby (R., 1976); Miles City Town & CC (R., 1976); Missoula CC (R., 1977); Yellowstone G&CC, Billings (R., 1980).
Nevada: Glenbrook CC, Lake Tahoe (R.).
Oregon: Columbia-Edgewater CC, Portland (R., 1966); Michelbook CC, McMinnville (A.9, 1984), with Damian Pascuzzo; Oswego Lake CC, Lake Oswego (R., 1973); Portland GC (R., 1985); Salishan G Links, Gleneden Beach (R.); Santiam GC, Salem (R., 1978); Springfield CC (R., 1979); Waverley CC, Portland (R.1, 1978).
Washington: Artondale G&CC, Gig Harbor (R., 1979); Kelso Elks GC (NLE, R.); Lake Wilderness CC, Maple Valley (R., 1986), with Damian Pascuzzo; Meadow Springs GC, Richland (R.9, 1973); Meadow Springs GC, Richland (A.9, 1973); Overlake G&CC, Medina (R., 1986), with Damian Pascuzzo; Royal Oaks CC, Vancouver (R., 1982); Sahalee CC, Redmond (R.); Sands Point CC, Seattle (R., 1981).
Wyoming: Casper CC (R., 1973); Casper Muni (R., 1973).

Denis Griffiths (1947 -   ) ASGCA
Born: Marshalltown, Iowa.
Denis Griffiths received a Bachelor's degree in Landscape Architecture in 1970, then immediately went to work for the Atlanta, Ga. golf design firm of Davis, Kirby, Player and Associates.
In 1980 Griffiths became a full partner with Ron Kirby in Kirby, Griffiths and Associates. One of Griffiths' designs, Pole Creek GC in Winter Park, Colo., was selected by Golf Digest magazine as the Best New Public Course in 1984.
Courses by: Denis Griffiths
Alabama: CC of Alabama, Eufaula (1986), with Ron Kirby; North River GC, Tuscaloosa (NLE, 1978), with Ron Kirby and Gary Player.
Colorado: Pole Creek GC, Tabernash (1983), with Ron Kirby.
Georgia: Grimball GC, Savannah (5, 1986), with Ron Kirby; Nob North GC, Dalton (1978), with Ron Kirby.
North Carolina: Twin Valley CC, Wadesboro (9), with Ron Kirby.
South Carolina: Marsh Point GC, Kiawah Island (1976), with Ron Kirby and Gary Player.
Texas: Fair Oaks Ranch G&CC, Boerne (1979), with Ron Kirby and Gary Player.
Virginia: Brandermill CC, Midlothian (1976), with Ron Kirby and Gary Player.
West Virginia: Shawnee GC, Institute (9, 1979), with Ron Kirby.
Bophutatswana: Gary Player CC, Sun City (1979), with Ron Kirby and Gary Player.
Canary Islands: Maspalomas GC (North Course) (1974), with Ron Kirby and Gary Player.
Japan: Niigata Forest GC, Toyoura Village (36, 1975), with Ron Kirby; Nishi Nihon GC, Nogata (1975), with Ron Kirby; Sun Lake CC, Utsunomiya (1986), with Ron Kirby.
Philippines: Kamirag GC, Cebu Island (36, 1982), with Ron Kirby; Lake Paoay GC, Ilocos Norte (1979), with Ron Kirby; Puerto Azul GC, Pasay City (1980), with Ron Kirby.
South Africa: Roodepoort Muni (1985), with Ron Kirby and Gary Player; Welkom Muni (1987), with Ron Kirby and Gary Player.
Spain: Almerimar GC, Almeria (1975), with Ron Kirby and Gary Player; Escorpion GC, Valencia (1975), with Ron Kirby and Gary Player.
Courses Remodeled & Added to by: Denis Griffiths
Alabama: Huntsville Muni (R., 1984), with Ron Kirby.
Florida: Everglades C, Palm Beach (R., 1984), with Ron Kirby.
Georgia: Bacon Park GC, Savannah (R., 1985), with Ron Kirby; Bacon Park GC, Savannah (A.9, 1986), with Ron Kirby; Dalton CC (R., 1977), with Ron Kirby; Savannah GC (A.9, 1984), with Ron Kirby.
Louisiana: New Orleans CC (R., 1985), with Ron Kirby.
Missouri: Bellerive CC, Creve Coeur (R.1, 1985), with Ron Kirby.
Texas: Fair Oaks Ranch G&CC, Boerne (A.9, 1985), with Ron Kirby; Hogan Park GC, Midland (A.9, 1978), with Ron Kirby; Midland CC (R., 1979), with Ron Kirby; Oak Hill CC, San Antonio (R.2, 1978), with Ron Kirby.
Virginia: Deer Run Muni, Newport News (R.27, 1986), with Ron Kirby; Deer Run Muni, Newport News (A.9, 1986), with Ron Kirby.
Philippines: Wack Wack G&CC (East Course), Manila (R., 1979), with Ron Kirby.
South Africa: Kensington GC, Johannesburg (R., 1980), with Ron Kirby; Royal Johannesburg GC (West Course) (R., 1985), with Ron Kirby.

Robert G. Grimsdell
Born: Amersham, England.
A fine competitive golfer in his youth and a devotee of H.S. Colt, Bob Grimsdell moved to South Africa in the late Twenties to establish himself in a year round golf career.
He became pro-greenkeeper at several South African clubs, including Royal Johannesburg, whose East Course he laid out in the mid-1930s.
After World War II, Grimsdell became a full-time golf course architect. Over the next thirty years he established himself as the leading designer in South Africa and surrounding nations.
Courses by: Robert G. Grimsdell
South Africa: Defence GC, Bloemfontein (9); King David CC, Cape Town (1956); Royal Johannesburg CC (East Course) (1933); Swartkop CC, Pretoria (1948).
Zimbabwe: Bancroft GC (1954); Sherwood GC, Salisbury (1959); Warren Hills GC, Salisbury (1957).
Courses Remodeled & Added to by: Robert G. Grimsdell
South Africa: Durban CC (R., 1959); Pretoria GC (R., 1948); Scottburgh GC, Natal (R.).

194

Edwin DeWitt "Sonny" Guy (1910 - 1981)
Born: Mississippi. Died: Brandon, Mississippi at age 70.

Long-time Mississippi club professional Sonny Guy served as a director of the Southern Turfgrass Association in the 1950s and helped organize the Mississippi Chapter of the PGA. Over the years the "Dean of Mississippi Golf," as he was known, designed over twenty golf courses within his home state. Shortly after his death, the city of Jackson renamed Livingston Park GC, one of his last designs, in his honor.

Courses by: Sonny Guy

Mississippi: Grove Park GC, Jackson (9); Lakeside GC, Miss. State Univ.; Robbinhead Lakes GC, Brandon (1977); Sonny Guy Muni, Jackson (1949); University of Mississippi GC, Oxford; University of Southern Mississippi GC, Hattiesburg (1959).

Herman C. Hackbarth (1883 - 1974)
Born: Oconomowoc, Wisconsin. Died: Little Rock, Arkansas at age 91.

Herman "Hack" Hackbarth began his nearly fifty year golf career as professional and greenkeeper at Little Rock CC, Ark. in 1907. At that time the club had only a six-hole sand greens course, but over the years Hackbarth enlarged and remodeled it into one of the best in the state. He was a well-respected golf teacher, and although never successful competitively himself, several of his pupils won state titles.

Hackbarth was also prominent as a golf architect in Arkansas, planning over forty courses including such fine layouts as Hardscrabble CC and Pine Bluff CC. A turfgrass expert, he introduced bentgrass greens to Arkansas in 1939 when he installed them at Little Rock CC. He was also instrumental in organizing a state greenkeepers association.

Hackbarth remained at Little Rock CC until 1956 and even after retirement lived on the course and played it almost every day.

Courses by: Herman Hackbarth

Arkansas: Belvedere CC, Hot Springs (1949); Carroll County GC, Berryville (9, 1965); CC of Little Rock (1910); Hardscrabble CC, Fort Smith (1926); Kiwanis Muni, Little Rock; Magnolia CC (9, 1953); Pine Bluff CC (9, 1936); Pla-Mor GC, Fort Smith (1933); Rebsamen Park Muni, Little Rock (27, 1953); Riverdale GC, Little Rock (1932); Western Hills CC, Little Rock (1961).

Missouri: Dogwood Hills GC, Osage Beach (1963).

Eddie Hackett (1910 -) BAGCA
Born: Dublin, Ireland.

Eddie Hackett attended the Catholic University School in Dublin, Ireland, and then worked as a golf professional for nearly fifty years, beginning as an assistant at Royal Dublin. He also worked at Johannesburg CC in South Africa, and at Elm Park and Portmarnock in Ireland. During these years, he also worked closely with Henry Cotton in England and Belgium and with F.W. Hawtree, who was designing the second course at Killarney GC and the Westport course.

Hackett designed his first golf course in 1964, and over the next twenty years designed and remodeled scores of Irish layouts. He was also consulting golf architect to the Golfing Union of Ireland, Bord Failte and Great Southern Hotels.

Courses by: Eddie Hackett

Ireland: Ashford Castle GC, County Galway (9, 1984); Bantry GC, County Cork (9, 1974); Beaverstown GC (1985); Beech Park Rathcoole GC, County Dublin; Blacklion GC, County Levon (9); Bodenstown GC, County Kildare (1973); Boyle GC, County Roscommon (9); Cahir Park GC, County Tipperary (9, 1968); Ceann Sibeal GC, County Kerry (9); Clongowes Wood College GC, County Kildare (9, 1966); Connemara GC, County Galway (1973); Donegal Town GC, County Donegal; Dublin and County GC (1972); Dublin Sports C, County Dublin (9, 1977); Dungarvan GC, County Waterford (9); Enniscrone GC, County Sligo (9); Killarney Racetrack GC (Precision, 1986); Letterkenny GC, County Donegal; Lismore GC, County Waterford (9); Mahon Muni, County Cork; Rockwell College GC (9); Stepaside GC, Dublin (9, 1981); Trabolgan GC (9); Tuam GC, County Galway (9); Waterville G Links, County Kerry (1972).

Courses Remodeled & Added to by: Eddie Hackett

Ireland: Abbey Leix GC, County Loais (R.); Ardee GC, County Louth (R.); Ardee GC (A.9, 1985); Arklow GC, County Wicklow (A.9); Balbriggan GC, County Dublin (R.); Ballina GC, County Mayo (R.); Ballinasloe GC, County Galway (R.); Ballinrobe GC, County Mayo (R.); Ballybofey & Stranorlar GC, County Donegal (A.9); Ballybunion GC (Old Course), County Kerry (R., 1964); Ballyliffin GC, County Donegal (R.); Baltinglass GC, County Wexford (R.); Bandon GC, County Cork (R.); Birr GC, County Offaly (R.); Blacklion GC, County Levon (R.); Borris GC, County Carlow (R.); Brandon GC (R.); Callan GC, County Kilkenay (R.); Carlow GC, County Carlow (R.); Carrick-on-Shannon GC, County Leitrim (R.); Carrick-on-Suir GC, County Tipperary (R.); Castle GC, Dublin (R.); Castlebar GC, County Mayo (A.9); Castlebar GC, County Mayo (R.9); Castlerea GC, County Roscommon (R.); Castletroy GC, County Limerick (R.); Charleville GC, County Cork (R.); Claremorris GC, County Mayo (R.); Clonmel GC, County Tipperary (A.9); Clontarf GC, Dublin (R.); Coollattin GC, County Wicklow (R.); Corballis GC, County Dublin (R.); County Caven GC (A.9); County Longford GC (A.9); County Sligo GC (R., 1983); Courtown GC, County Wexford (R.); Donabate GC, County Dublin (R.); Dooks GC, County Kerry (R.); Douglas GC, County Cork (R.); Dun Laoghaire GC, Dublin (R.); Dungarvan GC, County Waterford (R.); East Cork GC, County Cork (R.); Edmondstown GC, Dublin (R.); Elm Park G & Sports C, Dublin (R.); Ennis GC, County Clare (R.); Enniscorthy GC, County Wexford (R.); Fermoy GC, County Cork (R.); Forest Little GC, County Dublin (R.); Foxrock GC, County Dublin (R.); Gort GC, County Galway (R.); Greenore GC, County Louth (R.); Greystones GC, County Wexford (R.); Gweedore GC, County Donegal (R.); Heath GC, County Loais (R.); Hermitage GC, County Dublin (R.); Island GC, County Dublin (R.); Killiney GC, County Dublin (R.); Limerick GC (R.); Lismore GC, County Waterford (R., 1965); Loughrea GC, County Galway (R.); Lucan GC, County Dublin (R.); Malahide GC, County Dublin (R.); Milltown GC, Dublin (R.); Mitchelstown GC, County Cork (R.); Monkstown GC, County Cork (R.); Mountrath GC, County Loais (R.); Mullingar GC, County Westmeath (R.); Mulrany GC, County Mayo (R.); Muskerry GC, County Cork (R.); Nenagh GC, County Tipperary (A.9, 1970); New Ross GC, County Wexford (R.); Newcastle West GC, County Limerick (R.); Newlands GC, County Dublin (R.); North West GC, County Donegal (A.9); North West GC, County Donegal (R.); Nuremore GC, County Monaghan (R.); Oughterard GC, County Galway (A.9); Parknasilla GC, County Kerry (R.); Portmarnock GC, Dublin (R.1); Portumna GC, County Galway (R.); Rathfarnham GC, County Dublin (R.); Roscommon GC, County Roscommon (R.); Roscrea GC, County Tipperary (R.); Rossmore GC, County Monaghan (R.); Royal Dublin GC (R.2, 1984); Royal Tara GC, County Meath (R.); Rush GC, Dublin (R.); Skerries GC, County Dublin (A.9); Slade Valley GC, County Dublin (R.); St. Anne's GC, Dublin (R.9); St. Anne's GC, Dublin (A.9); Strandhill GC, County Sligo (R.); Swinford GC, County Mayo (R.); Thurles GC, County Tipperary (R.); Tralee GC, County Kerry (NLE, R.); Trim GC, County Meath (R., 1970); Tullamore GC, County Offaly (R.); Waterford GC, County Waterford (R.); Westport GC, County Mayo (R.); Wicklow GC, County Wicklow (R.).

Northern Ireland: Cairndnu GC, County Antrim (R.); Castlerock GC, County Londonderry (R.); City of Derry GC, Londonderry (A.9); Enniskillen GC, County Fermanagh (R.); Massereene GC, County Antrim (R.); Omagh GC, County Tyrone (R.); Strabane GC, County Tyrone (A.9).

Walter Charles Hagen (1892 - 1969)
Born: Rochester, New York. Died: Traverse City, Michigan at age 76.

Famed professional golfer Walter Hagen, who won two U.S. Opens, four British Opens and five PGA championships, worked as a consultant to the design team of Stiles and Van Kleek. "The Haig" also laid out a couple of courses on his own in the 1930s.

Courses by: Walter Hagen

Florida: Pasadena GC, St. Petersburg (1923), with Wayne Stiles and John Van Kleek.

Michigan: Dearborn Hills CC, Dearborn , with Mike Brady.

Japan: Koganei CC, Tokyo (1937).

Robert von Hagge, born Robert Bernhardt Hagge (1930 -)
Born: Texas.

Robert von Hagge, the adopted son of Indiana superintendent Bernhardt F. "Ben" Hagge, literally grew up on a golf course. Ben Hagge had constructed courses in the 1920s for such architects as William Diddel, Donald Ross and George O'Neil, and also tried a few designs himself.

After two years at Annapolis, young Bob Hagge transferred to Purdue University where he graduated with a degree in Agricultural Engineering in 1951. He then spent a few years on the PGA Tour, worked as a club professional in the Catskill Mountains of New York, and tried his hand at acting in Hollywood. During that time he was involved in successive (unsuccessful) marriages to golfing sisters Alice and Marlene Bauer. In 1957 he joined the golf architectural firm of Dick Wilson Inc. in Florida. Training under Wilson, he quickly proved adept at course design and building.

Hagge established his own practice in Delray Beach, Fla. in 1963, and soon gained a reputation as an elaborate showman. He changed his surname to von Hagge and toured golf course sites in a gold lame cape. Some of his early works, particularly Boca Rio GC in Florida, were equally spectacular and attracted widespread attention.

In the mid-1960s von Hagge was hired to redesign The Lakes GC in Australia at the recommendation of professional golfer Bruce Devlin. Von Hagge and Devlin became friends and colleagues, forming a course design partnership in Australia in 1968. The following year, the firm of von Hagge and Devlin was established in the United States. They practiced together for over fifteen years, based first in Florida and later in Texas.

Courses by: Robert von Hagge

California: Blackhawk CC, Danville (1981), with Bruce Devlin; Tierra Del Sol GC, California City (1978), with Bruce Devlin.

Colorado: Eagle Vail CC, Avon (1975), with Bruce Devlin.

Florida: Bay Hill C, Orlando (1961), with Dick Wilson, Joe Lee and Bob Simmons; Bay Point Y&CC (Lagoon Legend Course), Panama City (1986), with Bruce Devlin; Bayshore Muni, Miami Beach (1969), with Bruce Devlin; Boca Del Mar G&TC, Boca Raton (1972), with Bruce Devlin; Boca Lago G&CC (East Course), Boca Raton (1975), with Bruce Devlin; Boca Lago G&CC (West Course), Boca Raton (1975), with Bruce Devlin; Boca Rio GC, Boca Raton (1967); Boca West CC (Course No. 3), Boca Raton (1974), with Bruce Devlin; Boynton Beach Muni (27, 1984), with Bruce Devlin; Briar Bay GC, Miami (Precision, 9, 1975), with Bruce Devlin; Cape Coral CC (1963), with Dick Wilson; Card Sound GC, North Key Largo (1976), with Bruce Devlin; Colony West GC, Tamarac (1970), with Bruce Devlin; Colony West GC (Course No. 2), Tamarac (Precision, 1974), with Bruce Devlin; Cypress Creek CC, Boynton Beach (1964); Cypress Lake CC, Ft. Myers (1960), with Dick Wilson; Doral CC (Blue Course), Miami (1962), with Dick Wilson; Doral CC (Gold Course), Miami (1969), with Bruce Devlin; Doral CC (Green Course), Miami (Par 3, 9, 1967); Doral CC (Red Course), Miami (1962), with Dick Wilson; Doral CC (White Course), Miami (1967); Doral Park CC (Silver Course), Miami (1984), with Bruce Devlin; East Lake Woodlands G&CC (North Course), Oldsmar (1979), with Bruce Devlin; Eastwood Muni, Ft. Myers (1978), with Bruce Devlin; Emerald Hills CC, Hollywood (1969), with Bruce Devlin; Fountains G&RC (North Course), Lake Worth (1970), with Bruce Devlin; Fountains G&RC (South Course), Lake Worth (1972), with Bruce Devlin; Fountains G&RC (West Course), Lake Worth (1981), with Bruce Devlin; Golden Gate CC, Naples (1965), with Dick Wilson; Hillcrest G&CC, Hollywood (1966); Holiday Springs CC, Margate (1975), with Bruce Devlin; Hunters Run GC (East Course), Boynton Beach (1979), with Bruce Devlin; Hunters Run GC (North Course), Boynton Beach (1979), with Bruce Devlin; Hunters Run GC (South Course), Boynton Beach (1979), with Bruce Devlin; Indian Spring CC (East Course), Boynton Beach (1975), with Bruce Devlin; Indian Spring CC (West Course), Boynton Beach (1980), with Bruce Devlin; Key Biscayne GC (1972), with Bruce Devlin; Marco Shores CC, Marco Island (1974), with Bruce Devlin; Ocean Reef C (Harbor Course), North Key Largo (1976), with Bruce Devlin; Palm-Aire CC (Palms Course), Pompano Beach (1969), with Bruce Devlin; Palm-Aire CC (Sabals Course), Pompano Beach (Precision, 1969), with Bruce Devlin; Pine Tree CC, Delray Beach (1962), with Dick Wilson and Joe Lee;

Poinciana G&RC, Kissimmee (1973), with Bruce Devlin; Pompano Beach CC (Pines Course) (1967); Royal Oak G&CC, Titusville (1964), with Dick Wilson; Sandalfoot Cove G&CC, Margate (27, 1970), with Bruce Devlin; Sherbrooke G&CC, Lake Worth (1979), with Bruce Devlin; Tamarac CC, Ft. Lauderdale (1961), with Dick Wilson; TPC at Prestancia (Course No. 1) {formerly CC of Sarasota}, Sarasota (1976), with Bruce Devlin; Winter Springs GC {formerly Big Cypress GC} (1973), with Bruce Devlin; Woodlands CC (East Course), Tamarac (1969), with Bruce Devlin; Woodlands CC (West Course), Tamarac (1969), with Bruce Devlin; Woodmont CC (Cypress Course), Tamarac (1976), with Bruce Devlin; Woodmont CC (Pines Course), Tamarac (1976), with Bruce Devlin.

Idaho: Shamanah GC, Boise (1983), with Bruce Devlin.

Kentucky: Boone Aire GC, Florence (1968).

Mississippi: CC of Jackson (27, 1963), with Dick Wilson.

Missouri: Hidden Lake GC, Osage Beach (9, 1969); Oaks GC, Osage Beach (1980), with Bruce Devlin.

New Mexico: Tanoan GC, Albuquerque (27, 1978), with Bruce Devlin.

North Carolina: Brandywine Bay GC, Morehead City (1983), with Bruce Devlin.

Ohio: Carolina Trace GC, Harrison (9, 1969); Coldstream CC, Cincinnati (1960), with Dick Wilson, Joe Lee and Bob Simmons; Quail Hollow Inn & CC, Painesville (1975), with Bruce Devlin.

Tennessee: Nashville G&AC {formerly Crockett Springs National G&CC}, Brentwood (1972), with Bruce Devlin.

Texas: Chase Oaks GC (Blackjack Course), Plano (1986), with Bruce Devlin; Chase Oaks GC (Sawtooth Course), Plano (9, 1986), with Bruce Devlin; Club at Falcon Point, Katy (1985), with Bruce Devlin; Club at Sonterra (North Course), San Antonio , with Bruce Devlin; Crown Colony CC, Lufkin (1979), with Bruce Devlin; Gleneagles CC (King's Course), Plano (1985), with Bruce Devlin; Gleneagles CC (Queen's Course) (1919), with Bruce Devlin; Hollytree CC, Tyler (1982), with Bruce Devlin; Northgate CC, Houston (1985), with Bruce Devlin; Northshore CC, Portland (1985), with Bruce Devlin; Raveneaux CC (Gold Course), Spring (1980), with Bruce Devlin; Raveneaux CC (Orange Course), Spring (1986), with Bruce Devlin; Rayburn G&CC (Green Nine), Jasper (9, 1984), with Bruce Devlin; TPC at The Woodlands {formerly Woodlands Inn & CC (East Course)} (1982), with Bruce Devlin; Vista Hills CC, El Paso (1975), with Bruce Devlin; Walden on Lake Conroe CC, Montgomery (1976), with Bruce Devlin; Walden on Lake Houston GC (1985), with Bruce Devlin; Willow Creek GC, Spring (1982), with Bruce Devlin; Woodlands Inn & CC (South Course) (1983), with Bruce Devlin.

Wisconsin: Brookfield Hills GC (Precision, 1971), with Bruce Devlin.

Australia: Campbelltown GC, Sydney (1976), with Bruce Devlin; Lakes GC, Sydney (1970), with Bruce Devlin; Magnolia Hills CC, Suncoast (1975), with Bruce Devlin; Ocean Shores GC, Brunswick , with Bruce Devlin.

Bahamas: Cape Eleuthera GC (1971), with Bruce Devlin.

France: Golf Les Bordes (1987), with Bruce Devlin.

Japan: Daisifu Central CC, Fukoka (1971), with Bruce Devlin; Kawaguchi-ko GC, Mt. Fuji (1979), with Bruce Devlin.

Puerto Rico: El Conquistador Hotel & C, Fujardo (NLE, 1967).

Tahiti: Travelodge GC, Papeete (9), with Bruce Devlin.

Courses Remodeled & Added to by: Robert von Hagge

Arizona: Tucson National GC, Tucson (R., 1979), with Bruce Devlin; Tucson National GC, Tucson (A.9, 1979), with Bruce Devlin.

Florida: Doral CC (Blue Course), Miami (R., 1971), with Bruce Devlin; Doral CC (Gold Course), Miami (R., 1982), with Bruce Devlin; Doral CC (Red Course), Miami (R., 1985), with Bruce Devlin; Ocean Reef C (Dolphin Course), Key Largo (R., 1969), with Bruce Devlin; Pompano Beach CC (Palms Course) (R., 1967).

Ohio: Camargo C, Cincinnati (R., 1963); Scioto CC, Columbus (R., 1963), with Dick Wilson and Joe Lee.

Texas: Ranchland Hills GC, Midland (R., 1983), with Bruce Devlin.

Eugene Hamm (1923 -) ASGCA

Born: North Carolina

After service in the U.S. Navy during World War II, Gene Hamm trained in golf management at Pinehurst, N.C. under the GI Bill. Following admission to the PGA, he became assistant to club pro Ellis Maples (who later became a golf course architect himself). In the mid-1950s Hamm left a head professional job to supervise construction of Duke University GC in Durham, N.C. to the design of Robert Trent Jones.

In 1959, after assisting on a second Jones project, Hamm opened his own course design firm and was active in the Carolinas and Virginia for more than twenty years. Always a fine competitive golfer, he won both the 1978 and 1979 Carolinas Seniors on courses of his own design.

Courses by: Gene Hamm

North Carolina: Burlington GC, Greensboro (Par 3, 1961); Cape G&CC, Wilmington (1984); Cheviot Hills GC, Raleigh (1968); Colonial CC, Thomasville (1973); Echo Farms G&CC, Wilmington (1974); Falling Creek GC, Kinston (1970); Foxfire CC (Course No. 1), Pinehurst (1968); Foxfire CC (Course No. 2), Pinehurst (9, 1973); Lochmere GC, Cary (1985); North Ridge CC (Lakes Course), Raleigh (1968); North Ridge CC (Oaks Course), Raleigh (1972); Pilot Knob Park GC, Pilot Mountain (1962); Pine Lake CC, Charlotte (9, 1963); Pine Tree GC, Kernersville (1972); Pinewild CC (Holly Course), Pinehurst (1987); Pinewild CC (Magnolia Course), Pinehurst (1987); River Bend GC, New Bern (1975); Royal Oaks CC, Chapel Hill (1971); Wake Forest CC (1967); Wildwood CC, Raleigh (1961); Williamston CC (9, 1974); Yadkin CC, Yadkinville (1962).

South Carolina: Azalea Sands GC, North Myrtle Beach (1972); Beachwood GC, North Myrtle Beach (1968); Burning Ridge GC (East Course), Myrtle Beach (1986); Burning Ridge GC (West Course), Myrtle Beach (1979); Eagle Nest GC, North Myrtle Beach (1972); Indian Wells GC, Myrtle Beach (1984); Pineland CC, Nichols (1971); Quail Creek GC, Myrtle Beach (1970); Raccoon Run GC, Myrtle Beach (1976); River Oaks GC, Myrtle Beach (1987); Rose Hill GC, Hilton Head Island (27, 1982); Sea Gull GC, Pawley's Island (1970).

Virginia: Chatham CC (1958); Floyd CC (9, 1969); Gay Hill CC, Galax (9, 1963); Lynwood G&CC, Martinsville; South Boston CC (New Course) (1963); Spooncreek GC, Stuart (9, 1962); Tuscarora CC, Danville (1960).

Courses Remodeled & Added to by: Gene Hamm

North Carolina: Belvedere Plantation CC, Hampstead (A.9, 1983); Carolina Pines G&CC (R., 1985); Chapel Hill CC (R., 1973); Chicora CC, Dunn (R., 1963); Danville CC (R., 1958); Foxfire CC (Course No. 2), Pinehurst (A.9, 1980); Green Valley G&CC, Fayetteville (R., 1960); Henderson CC (A.9, 1970); Henderson CC (R.9, 1970); Sedgefield CC, Greensboro (R., 1961); Sippihaw CC, Fuquay-Varina (A.9, 1968); Washington Y&CC (A.9, 1973).

Tennessee: Cleveland CC (R., 1968).

Virginia: Danville CC (R.); DuPont GC, Martinsville (R.9, 1965); DuPont GC, Martinsville (A.9, 1965); Forest Park CC, Martinsville (A.9, 1964); Forest Park CC, Martinsville (R.9, 1964); South Boston CC (Old Course) (R.9, 1963).

George Hansen (1891 - 1951)

Born: Milwaukee, Wisconsin. Died: Milwaukee, Wisconsin at age 60.

George Hansen was superintendent of the Milwaukee (Wis.) Parks Department for over thirty years. He literally built the public golf system in that city. Starting with one nine hole course in 1920, which he remodeled, Hansen designed and constructed five new layouts for Milwaukee, including the highly regarded Brown Deer Park GC. Largely because of his efforts, Brown Deer hosted the USGA Publinks championship in 1951. Sadly, Hansen died shortly before the event.

Courses by: George Hansen

Wisconsin: Brown Deer Park GC, Milwaukee (1929); Currie Park GC, Wauwautosa (1927); Grant Park GC, Milwaukee (1920); Greenfield Park GC, West Allis (1923); Whitnall GC, Hales Corner (1932).

Walter S. Harban (1857 - 1938)

Died: Washington, D.C. at age 89.

Dr. Walter S. Harban was a dentist to several Presidents of the United States. In his spare time, he planned the first version of Columbia CC in Maryland and collaborated with golf architect William H. Tucker on the design of Bannockburn Club in Glen Echo, Maryland. Harban, while serving as a club official at Columbia, sought professional assistance on turfgrass problems from the U.S. Department of Agriculture. That effort led Harban and others to propose to the USGA that a formal turfgrass consulting body be created. The USGA's Green Section was formed in 1920, and Harban served as a member until his death. After retiring from dentistry, Harban dabbled in course design and experimented in developing new putting grass strains.

Courses by: Dr. Walter S. Harban

Maryland: Argyle CC, Chevy Chase , with William H. Tucker; Bannockburn G&CC, Glen Echo (NLE,), with William H. Tucker.

Washington, D.C.: West Potomac Park GC (9, 1920), with Walter J. Travis.

Jeff D. Hardin (1933 -) ASGCA

Born: Tolleson, Arizona.

Jeff Hardin received a B.Sc. degree in Civil Engineering from the University of Arizona in 1959 and was employed for eleven years as a civil engineer, construction manager and golf course designer with the Del E. Webb Corporation in Arizona and California. In this capacity he collaborated on projects in Arizona, California, Hawaii and Spain with such well-known golf architects as Robert Lawrence, George and Tom Fazio, and Milt Coggins.

In 1972 Hardin formed his own course design and engineering management company. Hardin used an engineering approach to integrate golf and housing, providing detailed drainage plans of course and subdivision, grading plans, cost estimates and quantities all checked by computer. Greg Nash partnered for a time with Hardin shortly after the firm's establishment.

Courses by: Jeff Hardin

Arizona: Aspen Valley GC, Flagstaff (9, 1973), with Greg Nash; Bellaire GC, Phoenix (Precision, 1973), with Red Lawrence and Greg Nash; Briarwood GC, Sun City West (1979), with Greg Nash, John W. Meeker and Tom Ryan; Canada Hills CC (Course No. 1), Tucson (1982), with Greg Nash; Canada Hills CC (Course No. 2), Tuscon (1985); Continental GC, Scottsdale (Precision, 1978), with Greg Nash; Cottonwood CC, Sunlakes (1983), with Greg Nash; Country Meadows GC, Peoria (Precision, 9, 1978), with Greg Nash; Dobson Ranch GC, Mesa (Precision, 1974), with Red Lawrence and Greg Nash; El Conquistador Hotel GC, Tucson (Precision, 9, 1982), with Greg Nash; Gold Canyon Ranch GC, Apache Junction (1982), with Greg Nash; Goodyear G&CC (West Course), Litchfield Park (1974), with Red Lawrence and Greg Nash; Hillcrest GC, Sun City West (1978), with Greg Nash, John W. Meeker and Tom Ryan; Lake East GC, Sun City (Precision, 1970), with James Winans and John W. Meeker; Lakes West GC, Sun City (1968), with Milt Coggins, James Winans and John W. Meeker; Leisure World GC, Mesa (Par 3, 36, 1980), with Greg Nash; Los Caballeros GC, Wickenburg (1981), with Greg Nash; Palmbrook CC, Sun City (1972), with James Winans and John W. Meeker; Paradise Valley Park GC, Phoenix (Precision, 9, 1986); Pebblebrook GC, Sun City West (1979), with Greg Nash, John W. Meeker and Tom Ryan; Quail Run GC, Sun City (Precision, 9, 1977), with Greg Nash; Riverview GC, Sun City (1972), with James Winans and John W. Meeker; Stardust GC, Sun City West (Precision, 1979), with Greg Nash and Tom Ryan; Sun City CC, with Milt Coggins and Greg Nash; Sun City CC (1966), with James Winans and John W. Meeker; Sun Lakes GC (1973), with James Winans and Greg Nash; Sunland Village GC, Mesa (1975), with Milt Coggins and Greg Nash; Union Hills CC, Sun City (1974), with Greg Nash; Villa de Paz CC, Phoenix , with Greg Nash.

Nevada: Los Prados GC, Las Vegas (1987).

Colombia: La Colina CC, Bogota (1984), with Greg Nash.

Courses Remodeled & Added to by: Jeff Hardin

Arizona: Aspen Valley GC, Flagstaff (A.9, 1981), with Greg Nash; Rio Verde CC (Quail Run Course), Scottsdale (A.9, 1981), with Greg Nash; Rio Verde CC (White Wing Course) (A.9, 1983), with Greg Nash; Sun Lakes GC (A.9, 1979), with Greg Nash; Villa de Paz CC, Phoenix (A.9, 1976), with Greg Nash.

Thomas Benjamin Harmon (- 1974)

Ben Harmon earned a degree in engineering at Washington State University and in 1952 was hired by Patrick Markovich to serve as his assistant professional at Richmond (Calif.) CC. A few years later, Markovich bought a large ranch and invited Harmon to lay out and construct a golf course on it. The result was the original Silverado CC. Harmon later constructed a few courses for golf architect Lawrence Hughes and designed several projects of his own in California in the 1960s before his death in a fishing accident at sea.

Courses by: Ben Harmon

California: Bennett Valley GC, Santa Rosa (1970); Glenn G&CC, Willows (9, 1960); JFK Memorial GC, Napa (1958), with Bob Baldock and Jack Fleming; Santa Rosa G&CC (1958), with Jack Fleming; Silverado CC (North Course), Napa (1955), with Johnny Dawson; Watsonville CC (1963); Wilcox Oaks CC, Red Bluff (1956).

Donald Harradine (1911 -) BAGCA, Founding Member; Chairman, 1980. ASGCA (corresponding member).
Born: Enfield, England.

Donald Harradine was educated at Woolwich Polytechnic and trained as a golf professional, greenkeeper and clubmaker under his stepfather J.A. Hockey, who had himself designed three courses. Harradine's first golf design experience came in 1930, when he remodeled a course at Ragaz Spa, Switzerland. He then worked for and with British golf architects John Morrison, Sir Guy Campbell, C.K. Cotton and Fred Hawtree.

In his career, Harradine worked on some 300 courses in Angola, Austria, Cyprus, France, Germany, Greece, Italy, Liechtenstein, Poland, Portugal, Rumania, Spain, Canary Islands, Switzerland and Yugoslavia. He also wrote numerous articles on course maintenance, and with the assistance of his wife founded the International Greenkeepers Association. In the 1980s his son Peter Harradine joined him in the golf design business.

Courses by: Donald Harradine

Austria: Linz GC, Tillyburg (1960); Seefeld-Wildmoos GC, Seefeld (1968).
France: Club de Strasbourg; Golf de Chaumont en Vexin, Paris (1963); Golf de Valbonne (1966); Golf Club de Campagne, Nimes; Le G du Rhin, Mulhouse (9).
Greece: Corfu G&CC, Corfu (1972); Glyfada GC, Athens (1964); Island of Rhodes GC, Rhodes (1966).
Italy: Arenzano G&TC (1959); Barlassina CC, Milano (1957); Cervino GC, Cervinia (9, 1955); Lanzo Intelvi GC (9, 1962).
Romania: Diplomatic C, Bucharest (9).
Switzerland: Breitenloo GC, Zurich (1964); Interlaken-Unterseen GC (1965); Ostschweizischer GC, Niederburen (1948); Schoenenberg G&CC (1969).
West Germany: Bad Worishoffen GC (1980); Bayerwald G und Land C, Waldkirchen (9, 1970); Bielefelder GC, Bielefeld (9); Chiemsee GC, Prien (9); Erding-Grunbach GC (9); Goettingen GC (9); Hohenstauffen GC, Goppingen (9); Klingenburg-Gunzberg GC; Oberau GC, Gut Buchwies (1974); Pyrrmonter GC, Bad Byrmont (9); Regensburg G und Land C (1966); St Eurach Land und GC, Iffeldorf (1973); Tegernseer GC, Bad Wiessee (9, 1960); Vestischer GC, Recklinghausen .
Yugoslavia: Bled GC (1972).

Courses Remodeled & Added to by: Donald Harradine

Austria: Schloss Pichlarn GC, Irdning (A.9, 1978).
France: Montreux GC (R.).
Italy: Varese GC (R.).
Switzerland: Bad Raqaz GC (NLE, R., 1930); Davos GC (A.9); Davos GC (R.9); Geneva G&CC (NLE, R.); Lugano GC (R.); Villars GC (R.9); Zumikon G&CC, Zurich-Zumikon (R.).
West Germany: Augsburg GC (R., 1982), with Peter Harradine; Garmish-Partnekirchen GC (R.); Heidelberg G & Sports C (R.); Kassel-Wilhelmhohe GC (A.9, 1980), with Peter Harradine; Oberschwaben-Bad Waldsee GC (R.); Schloss Myllendonk GC, Monchengladbach (A.9).

William E. Harries

Between the wars, William Harries operated the landscape design firm of Harries and Hall based in Buffalo, New York. After World War II Harries was associated with the firm of Tryon and Schwartz & Associates Inc. of East Aurora, New York.

Courses by: William Harries

New York: Amherst Audubon GC, Williamsville; Beaver Island GC, Grand Island (1963), with A.Russell Tryon; Brighton Park GC, Tonawanda (1962), with A.Russell Tryon; Brookfield GC, Clarence (1927); Byrncliff CC, Varysborg; Byron Meadows CC, Batavia; Elma Meadows GC, Elma (1959), with A.Russell Tryon; Hyde Park Muni (North Course), Niagara Falls (1928); Hyde Park Muni (South Course), Niagara Falls (9, 1928); Normanside CC, Elsmere (1927); Oneonta CC; Sheridan Park GC, Kenmore (1933); Shorewood CC, Dunkirk (9); Turin Highlands GC, Turin; Westwood CC, Williamsville (1954).

Courses Remodeled & Added to by: William Harries

New York: Brooklea CC, Rochester (R.); East Aurora CC (R.9), with A.Russell Tryon; East Aurora CC (A.9), with A.Russell Tryon; Moonbrook CC, Jamestown (A.9, 1928); Orchard Park CC, Buffalo (R., 1950); Thendara CC, Old Forge (A.9, 1959), with A.Russell Tryon.

John Dering Harris (1912 - 1977)
Born: Chobham, Surrey, England. Died: Puttenham, Surrey, England at age 64.

John Harris, a low-handicap golfer nearly all his life, was educated in civil engineering at Nautical College in Berkshire, England. His father Frank and uncle operated a construction firm specializing in golf courses. Joining the firm after college, Harris had the opportunity to work with most of the leading British golf architects. He became director of the business after his father's death in the 1930s but discontinued operations when war broke out.

Harris served with the Royal Navy during World War II, attaining the rank of Commander. He returned to golf design in the late 1940s, working with architect C.K. Cotton, with whom he formed a partnership in the early 1950s. In 1960 Harris left to establish his own firm and began worldwide operation. By the 1970s his associates included Bryan Griffiths and Michael Wolveridge of Great Britain, Peter Thomson (five times British Open champ) of Australia and Ronald Fream of the United States.

Although many of the courses bearing Harris's name were designed and built by members of his staff, most were his own designs, and he traveled the globe to supervise their construction. It was noted after his death that he may have been better known abroad than in Great Britain, for he did relatively little work in his native land. Harris himself once estimated that he had participated in the design, remodeling and construction of over 450 courses.

Courses by: John Harris

Australia: Royal Canberra GC, Yarralumia (1960); Southport GC, Queensland .
Austria: Enzesfeld G&CC (1972).
Barbados: Barbados G&CC, Christchurch (1974).
Canary Islands: Costa Teguise GC, Lanzarote (27, 1978).
Denmark: Copenhagen GC.
England: Chelmsford GC, Essex; Cirencester GC, Gloucestershire; Cranbrook GC, Kent (1969); Gatton Manor Hotel & GC, Surrey (1969); Panshanger GC, Hertfordshire (1975); Southwood GC, Hampshire (9, 1977), with Michael Wolveridge; Staverton Park GC, Northamptonshire (1977); Telford Hotel G&CC, Great Hay (1979), with Peter Thomson and Michael Wolveridge; Washington GC, Dunham (1979), with Michael Wolveridge.
France: Club de Valescure; Golf d'Ormesson (1968); Golf des Chateaux de Villarceaux.
Hong Kong: Royal Hong Kong GC (Eden Course), Fanling (1968), with Peter Thomson and Michael Wolveridge.
Indonesia: Bali Handara CC, Pancasari (1975), with Peter Thomson, Michael Wolveridge and Ronald Fream.
Ireland: Courtown GC, County Wexford , with C.K. Cotton; East Cork GC, County Cork (9, 1971); Fermoy GC, County Cork; Lahinch GC (Castle Course), County Clare (Precision, 9, 1971); Shannon GC, County Clare (1966).
Italy: Alassio GC; Albarella GC, Rovigo (1975), with M. Croze; Garlenda GC (1965); Le Fronde GC, Avigliana (1975); Margara GC, Allessandria (1975); Menaggio E. Cadenabbia GC, Milan (1972); Padova GC (1966); Piandiscole GC, Premeno (1964); Torino GC, Turin (1956), with Henry Cotton; Verona GC (1963); Villa Condulmer GC (1961), with M. Croze.
Jamaica: Runaway Bay CC, St. Annes (1961).
Japan: Nambu Fuji GC, Kwate (1974), with Peter Thomson and Michael Wolveridge.
New Zealand: Flaxmere GC, Hastings (1966); Harewood GC, Christchurch (1967), with Peter Thomson and Michael Wolveridge; Karori GC, Wellington (1968), with Peter Thomson and Michael Wolveridge; Maramarua GC, Pokeno (1969), with Peter Thomson and Michael Wolveridge; Taieri GC, Mosgiel (1967), with Peter Thomson and Michael Wolveridge; Wairakei International GC, Taupo (1975), with Peter Thomson and Michael Wolveridge.
Northern Ireland: Bushfoot GC (9).
Portugal: Estoril Sol GC, Estoril (Precision, 9, 1976), with Peter Thomson, Michael Wolveridge and Ronald Fream.
Scotland: Dougalston GC, Glasgow (1977), with Michael Wolveridge; Inverness GC, Invernesshire (1968), with Peter Thomson and Michael Wolveridge; Renfrew GC, Renfrewshire .
Singapore: Singapore Island GC (New Course) (1963), with J.J.F. Pennink.
Spain: Campo de G Somosaguas, Madrid (1971); Club de G Poniente Magaluf, Mallorca (1978); Penas Rojas GC, Alicante (1973); Playa Granada GC, Granada (9, 1974); Real C de la Puerto de Hierro (New), Madrid (1962); Real C de G de Menorca, Shangri-La (9, 1976); Son Servera GC, Mallorca (9, 1967); Vista Hermosa GC, Cadiz (9, 1975).
St. Kitts: Royal St. Kitts GC (1977), with Peter Thomson, Michael Wolveridge and Ronald Fream.
Trinidad and Tobago: St. Andrews GC, Maraval (1975), with Peter Thomson, Michael Wolveridge and Ronald Fream; Tobago GC, Mount Irvine (1969).
Tunisia: El Kantaoui GC, Soussenord (1977), with Peter Thomson, Michael Wolveridge and Ronald Fream.
West Germany: Bonn-Godesberg GC (1960).

Courses Remodeled & Added to by: John Harris

Denmark: Aalborg GC (A.9).
Fiji: Nadi GC (A.9).
Ireland: Elm Park G & Sports C, Dublin (R., 1963); Mallow GC, County Cork (R.9); Mallow GC, County Cork (A.9); Royal Tara GC, County Meath (A.9); Royal Tara GC, County Meath (R.9); Tramore GC, County Waterford (R.); Youghal GC, County Cork (R.9); Youghal GC, County Cork (A.9).
Italy: Barlassina CC, Milano (R.); Circolo G Lido di Venezia (R.9, 1958); Circolo G Lido di Venezia (A.9, 1958), with C.K. Cotton; La Mandria GC, Turin (A.9, 1966); Le Betulle GC, Biella (R.); Villa D'este GC, Como (R.).
Netherlands: Rotterdamsche GC, Rotterdam (R.).
New Zealand: Hutt GC, Wellington (R., 1966); Nelson GC (R., 1967), with Peter Thomson and Michael Wolveridge; North Shore GC (R., 1969), with Peter Thomson and Michael Wolveridge; Russley GC (R., 1967), with Peter Thomson and Michael Wolveridge; Timaru GC (R., 1968), with Peter Thomson and Michael Wolveridge.
Spain: Real C de la Puerto de Hierro (Old), Madrid (R., 1962); Real Sociedad Hipica Espanola (R.), with Michael Wolveridge.

Robert Bruce Harris (1896 - 1976) ASGCA, Charter Member; President, 1947, 1948.
Born: Gillman, Illinois. Died: Chicago, Illinois at age 80.

Following service in the U.S. Navy during World War I, Robert Bruce Harris attended the University of Illinois, earning a degree in Landscape Architecture. In 1919 he opened a landscape design business in Chicago and planned a number of school grounds and parks. An avid golfer, he laid out his first course, Old Channel Trail GC in Michigan, in 1926. Although his firm continued to specialize in landscape design in the 1930s, he did design and build several more courses during that period.

Harris had faith in the future of golf even during the Depression and the post-war years, and successfully renovated several abandoned courses and operated them as daily-fee facilities. His first-hand experiences as a course operator during the Depression and the Second World War, coping with labor and material shortages, were responsible for his emphasis on economical maintenance requirements in his designs. According to his detractors, he emphasized maintenance almost to a fault, resulting in oval bunkering placed too far from putting surfaces.

Following World War II, Harris devoted virtually full time to golf architecture and rapidly became a leader in the profession. By the 1950s he was busy designing courses throughout the Midwest and the South, and estimated that he planned or remodeled over 150 during his career. He was also responsible for training a number of men who became successful course architects, including Edward Lawrence Packard, David Gill, Dick Nugent, Ken Killian, Dick Phelps and William James Spear.

Harris was the first to conceive a professional society for golf architects, patterned after the ASLA. Together with Stanley Thompson, Harris organized such an association. He was a charter member and the first president of the group, called the American Society of Golf Course Architects. Harris was coauthor with Robert Trent Jones of an influential chapter on course design that appeared in the first edition (1950) of H. Burton Musser's *Turf Management*. He spent his final years in retirement at CC of Florida, his personal favorite design.

Courses by: Robert Bruce Harris

Alabama: Azalea City GC, Mobile (1957).

Arizona: Oro Valley G&CC, Tucson (1958); Tucson National GC, Tucson (1963).

Colorado: Flatirons CC, Boulder (1933).

Florida: CC of Florida, Delray Beach (1957).

Illinois: Benton CC (9, 1961); Eagle Point Park GC, Clinton (9); Flora GC (9); Glenbard GC, Glen Ellyn (NLE, 1930); Hillcrest CC, Long Grove (1964); Illinois State Univ. GC, Normal (1963); Indian Lakes CC (Iroquois Trail Course), Bloomingdale (1965); Indian Lakes CC (Sioux Trail Course), Bloomingdale (1965); Lake of the Woods GC, Mahomet (1954); Lincoln Greens GC, Springfield (1957); Lockhaven CC, Alton (1955); Maplecrest GC, Downers Grove (NLE, 9, 1958); Midlane CC, Wadsworth (1964); Orchard Hills G&CC, Waukegan (1930); Sullivan CC (1954); Timber Trails CC, LaGrange (1931); Timberlake GC, Sullivan (9); Valley Green CC, Aurora (9, 1962); Village Greens of Woodridge (1959); Virginia CC (9); Western Illinois Univ GC, Macomb (NLE, 9, 1942).

Indiana: Clearcrest CC, Evansville (NLE, 9, 1955); Decatur GC (9).

Iowa: Finkbine GC, Iowa City (1953); Gates Park GC, Waterloo (1949); Valley Oaks GC, Clinton (1965).

Kentucky: Iroquois GC, Louisville (9, 1949); Standard CC, Louisville (9, 1950).

Louisiana: Lakewood CC, New Orleans (1962).

Michigan: Heather Highlands GC, Holly (27, 1966); Old Channel Trail GC, Montague (9, 1926); Signal Point C, Niles (9, 1964).

Minnesota: Breckenridge GC; Wayzata CC (1958).

Missouri: Meadowbrook CC, Ballwin (1961); Ruth Park GC, University City (9, 1931).

North Dakota: Apple Creek G&CC, Bismarck; Bois de Sioux GC, Wahpeton; Grand Forks CC (1964); Jamestown CC (9).

Ohio: Belmont CC, Perrysburg (1968); Kittyhawk Muni (Eagle Course), Dayton (1962); Kittyhawk Muni (Hawk Course), Dayton (1961); Kittyhawk Muni (Kitty Course), Dayton (Precision, 1961); Riverbend GC, Miamiburg (1962).

South Dakota: Chamberlain CC (9, 1952).

Tennessee: Bluegrass CC, Hendersonville (1961).

Wisconsin: Americana Lake Geneva GC (Brute), Lake Geneva (1968); Gateway GC, Land O'Lakes (9); Riverside Muni, Janesville (1946); Village Green GC, Green Bay (9).

Courses Remodeled & Added to by: Robert Bruce Harris

California: Monterey Peninsula CC (Shore Course), Pebble Beach (R., 1962).

Florida: Delray Beach G&CC (R., 1962); Sanlando G&CC, Altamonte Springs (NLE, R.).

Illinois: Acacia CC, Harlem (NLE, R., 1951); Briarwood CC, Deerfield (R., 1958); Freeport CC (R.2); Illini CC, Springfield (A.9, 1950); Illini CC, Springfield (R.9, 1962); Itasca CC (R., 1953); Macomb CC (R.); Midwest CC (East Course), Oakbrook (R.); Midwest CC (West Course), Oakbrook (R.9, 1954); Midwest CC (West Course), Oakbrook (A.9, 1954); Parkview Muni, Pekin (A.9, 1956); Parkview Muni, Pekin (R.9, 1956); South Side CC, Decatur (R.); Thorngate CC, Deerfield (R., 1951); Timber Trails CC, LaGrange (R., 1966).

Indiana: La Fontaine GC, Huntington (R., 1946).

Iowa: Duck Creek Park GC, Davenport (R., 1957); Sunnyside CC, Waterloo (NLE, R., 1938).

Maine: Bay City CC (NLE, R.9, 1951); Bay City CC (NLE, A.9, 1951).

Minnesota: Somerset CC, St. Paul (R., 1958).

New York: North Hills CC (R.1, 1949).

North Dakota: Edgewood Muni, Fargo (R., 1951); Fargo CC (A.9); Riverbend GC, Grand Forks (R., 1951).

Ohio: Columbus CC (R.2, 1960); Inverness C, Toledo (A.9, 1957); Inverness C, Toledo (R.9, 1957); Toledo CC (R., 1960).

Tennessee: Bluegrass CC, Hendersonville (A.2, 1966); Bluegrass CC, Hendersonville (R., 1966).

James Gilmore Harrison (1900 -   ) ASGCA, President, 1955, 1969.
Born: Pennsylvania.

Jim Harrison worked for golf architect Donald Ross, first as a teamster and later as a foreman, between 1921 and 1927. He was then associated for a short time with Hartford-based architect Orrin Smith. In the late 1920s Harrison entered private practice, planning and building his own course, Pennhurst at Turtle Creek, Pennsylvania. Between 1955 and 1964 he was joined in practice by his son-in-law, Ferdinand Garbin.

Courses by: James Gilmore Harrison

Kentucky: Cedar Knoll CC, Ashland (9).

Maryland: Maplehurst CC, Frostburg (9, 1955).

Michigan: Warwick Hills G&CC, Grand Blanc (1957), with Ferdinand Garbin.

New Jersey: Battleground CC (Routing), Freehold (1963); Knob Hill CC, with Ferdinand Garbin.

New York: Cragie Brae GC, Leroy (1962), with Ferdinand Garbin; Happy Acres CC, Webster (1958), with Ferdinand Garbin.

Ohio: Chippewa CC, Barberton (9, 1964), with Ferdinand Garbin; Geneva-on-the-Lake GC (9, 1954); Hidden Valley GC, New Philadelphia (1960), with Ferdinand Garbin; Pleasant Vue GC, Paris (9, 1964), with Ferdinand Garbin; Spring Hill CC, Richmond (1963), with Ferdinand Garbin; Springvale CC, North Olmstead (1950); Tannenhauf GC, Alliance (1957), with Ferdinand Garbin; Walnut Hill CC, Columbus (1955).

Pennsylvania: Beaumont CC, Hollidayburg (1967); Blairsville CC (1963), with Ferdinand Garbin; Blueberry Hill GC, Warren (9, 1961), with Ferdinand Garbin; Bradford GC (1964), with Ferdinand Garbin; Carradam CC, Irwin (1962), with Ferdinand Garbin; Cedarbrook GC, Smithton (1963), with Ferdinand Garbin; Chestnut Ridge CC, Indiana (1963), with Ferdinand Garbin; Cumberland CC, Carlisle (1961), with Ferdinand Garbin; Downing Muni, Erie (1962), with Ferdinand Garbin; Erie MacCaune CC, Erie (1964); Foxbury CC (1968); Glen Oak CC, Waverly (1961), with Ferdinand Garbin; Greenville CC (9); Hidden Valley CC, Reading; Hidden Valley GC, Pottstown , with Ferdinand Garbin; Highland Springs GC, Wellsburg (1960), with Ferdinand Garbin; Indiana CC (1963), with Ferdinand Garbin; Johnstown Elks CC; Lakeview CC, North East (1957), with Ferdinand Garbin; Mount Cobb Muni, Scranton (1958), with Ferdinand Garbin; Mount Lebanon CC (1947); North Fork CC, Johnstown (1948); Park Hills CC, Altoona (1966); Penn State Univ GC (White Course), State College (1965), with Ferdinand Garbin; Pine Acres CC, Bradford (1970); Pine Ridge GC, Meadville (9, 1960), with Ferdinand Garbin; Punxsutawney CC (1969); Range End GC, Dillsburgh (1955); Rittwood CC, Butler (1966); Rolling Acres CC, Beaver Falls (1960), with Ferdinand Garbin; Rolling Hills CC, Pittsburgh (1961), with Ferdinand Garbin; Scotch Valley GC, Holidaysburg; Sewickley Heights CC, Sewickley (1960), with Ferdinand Garbin; Sportsman's GC, Harrisburg (1964), with Ferdinand Garbin; Suncrest GC, Butler (9, 1948); Tamarack CC, Mt. Lebanon (1966); Venango Trails GC, Pittsburgh (1955); VFW GC, Indiana (9, 1963); Wave Oak CC, Waverly (1954); Willowbrook CC, Belle Vernon (1949); Windber CC (1961), with Ferdinand Garbin.

West Virginia: Bridgeport CC (1957), with Ferdinand Garbin; Cheat Lake GC, Morgantown (1954); Lakeview Inn & CC (South Course), Morgantown (1955), with Ferdinand Garbin; Sleepy Hollow GC, Hurricane (1955).

Puerto Rico: Dorado del Mar GC, Dorado (1962), with Ferdinand Garbin.

Courses Remodeled & Added to by: James Gilmore Harrison

Kansas: Milburn G&CC, Overland Park (R., 1925), with Orrin Smith.

Kentucky: Bellefonte CC, Ashland (R., 1960), with Ferdinand Garbin.

Missouri: Blue Hills CC, Kansas City (NLE, R., 1926), with Orrin Smith; Oakwood CC, Kansas City (A.9, 1925), with Orrin Smith.

New Jersey: Tavistock CC, Haddonfield (R., 1954), with Ferdinand Garbin.

Ohio: Geneva-on-the-Lake GC (A.9, 1966); Lake Forest CC, Hudson (R., 1965).

Pennsylvania: Beaver Valley CC, Beaver Falls (R.9, 1958), with Ferdinand Garbin; Beaver Valley CC, Beaver Falls (A.9, 1958), with Ferdinand Garbin; Bedford Springs C0 (R., 1966); Bloomsburg CC (R., 1948); Blue Ridge CC, Harrisburg (R., 1964), with Ferdinand Garbin; Brookside CC, Pottstown (R.9, 1959), with Ferdinand Garbin; Brookside CC, Pottstown (A.9, 1959), with Ferdinand Garbin; Centre Hills CC, State College (R., 1948); Chippewa CC, Bentlyville (A.9, 1964), with Ferdinand Garbin; Chippewa CC, Bentlyville (R.9, 1964), with Ferdinand Garbin; Churchill Valley CC, Churchill (R., 1960), with Ferdinand Garbin; Edgewood CC, Pittsburgh (R., 1960), with Ferdinand Garbin; Fox Chapel GC, Pittsburgh (R.); Grandview GC, Curwensville (R., 1979); Hidden Valley CC, Pottstown (R.9, 1958), with Ferdinand Garbin; Hidden Valley CC, Pottstown (A.9, 1958), with Ferdinand Garbin; Highland CC, Pittsburgh (R., 1954); Hill Crest CC, New Kensington (A.9, 1950); Hillcrest CC (A.9); Irwin CC (R., 1950); Latrobe CC (A.9, 1963), with Ferdinand Garbin; Montour Heights CC, Coraopolis (A.9, 1962), with Ferdinand Garbin; Montour Heights CC, Coraopolis (R.9, 1962), with Ferdinand Garbin; Penn State Univ GC (Blue Course), State College (R., 1965), with Ferdinand Garbin; Pike Run CC, Donegal (R., 1955); St. Clair CC, Pittsburgh (R., 1960), with Ferdinand Garbin; Suncrest GC, Butler (A.9, 1966); Valley Heights CC, Oakmont (R., 1962), with Ferdinand Garbin.

Virginia: Fredericksburg CC (A.9); Fredericksburg CC (A.9).

West Virginia: Tygarts Valley CC, Elkins (R., 1957), with Ferdinand Garbin; Woodland CC, Weston (R., 1953).

Xenophon G. Hassenplug (1908 -   ) ASGCA
Born: Bellevue, Ohio.

Xen Hassenplug attended Ohio Wesleyan University and Toledo University, majoring in Civil Engineering. His first experience in golf course construction came in 1946, when he was involved in planning irrigation and seeding of an eighteen hole course planned by J.B. McGovern at Overbrook CC near Philadelphia. McGovern died during construction of the course, and Hassenplug went on to complete the eighteen holes and then to collaborate with golf architect Dick Wilson on two other Pennsylvania projects, Radnor Valley near Philadelphia and Westmoreland CC near Pittsburgh. Upon completion of these layouts, Hassenplug entered private practice, combining golf course design, land planning, irrigation and civil engineering.

Courses by: X.G. Hassenplug

New York: Chautauqua GC (Course No. 2); Shelridge CC, Medina (1974).

Ohio: Brookside Park GC, Ashland (9, 1969); Buckeye Hills CC, Washington Court Hou (1971); Fairway Pines GC, Painesville (1987); Glenwood Muni, Ashland (9).

Pennsylvania: Alanwood GC, Sarver (Precision, 1980); Laurel Greens GC, Latrobe (Precision, 1979); Lone Pine GC, Washington (1969); Lucky Hills CC, Franklin (9, 1979); Mayfield CC, Clarion (1968); Overbrook CC, Radnor (1947), with J.B. McGovern; Radnor Valley CC, Villanova (1953), with Dick Wilson; Rivers Bend GC, Everett (1966); Seven Oaks GC, Beaver (1977); Seven Springs GC, Champion (1968); Sheraton Inn GC, Greensburg (Precision, 9, 1981); Silver Springs Resort GC; Timberlink GC, Ligonier (1964); Valley Green GC, Greensburg (1964); Westmoreland CC, Export (1948), with Dick Wilson.

West Virginia: Brooke Hills Park GC, Wellsburg (1977); Coonskin Park GC, Charleston (Par 3, 1973); Esquire CC, Huntington (1973); Huntington Elks CC, Martha (1975); Marshall Park GC, Moundsville (Par 3, 1974); St. Marys GC (9, 1968); Waterford Park GC, Chester (9, 1968).

Courses Remodeled & Added to by: X.G. Hassenplug

Maryland: Cumberland CC (R.11, 1966).
New Jersey: Lone Pine GC (R., 1986).
New York: Chautauqua GC (R., 1980).
Ohio: Bowling Green University GC (R.9, 1972).
Pennsylvania: Chartiers CC, Pittsburgh (R., 1969); DuBois CC (R.9, 1968); Elk County CC, Ridgway (R.9, 1966); Indian Lake GC, Central City (A.9, 1968), with Arnold Palmer; Ligonier CC (R.9, 1965); Mount Odin Muni, Greensburg (R.9, 1967); North Park GC, Pittsburgh (R., 1969); Pittsburgh Field C (R., 1962); Pittsburgh Field C (R., 1970); Pleasant Valley CC, Mt. Pleasant (R.9, 1968); South Hills GC, Pittsburgh (R., 1979); South Park GC, Pittsburgh (R., 1969).
West Virginia: Guyen G&CC, Huntington (R.3, 1974).

Walter B. Hatch (1884 - 1960)
Born: Brockton, Massachusetts. Died: Amherst, Massachusetts at age 75.

Walter Hatch graduated from the Massachusetts Agricultural College in 1905 and went to work for Donald Ross, eventually becoming his associate. He is said to have introduced Ross to the use of topographical plans in course design. Hatch traveled widely in the United States and Canada, supervising construction for Ross and sometimes entering into construction contracts. He also planned a number of layouts, although Ross was the architect of record for all except two: Amherst GC and Thomas Memorial GC at Turners Falls. Both were in the vicinity of Amherst, Mass. where Hatch maintained an office in the Ross name.

Walter Hatch left the field of golf architecture during the Depression as a result of financial difficulties. He became collector of taxes in Amherst and a researcher for a local attorney, Bruce Brown.

Courses by: Walter Hatch

Colorado: Broadmoor GC (East Course), Colorado Springs (9, 1918), with Donald Ross; Broadmoor GC (West Course), Colorado Springs (9, 1918), with Donald Ross; Wellshire GC, Englewood (1926), with Donald Ross.
Connecticut: Wampanoag CC, West Hartford (1926), with Donald Ross.
Maryland: Fountain Head CC, Hagerstown (1925), with Donald Ross.
Massachusetts: Amherst GC; Ellinwood CC, Athol (9), with Donald Ross; Greenock CC, Lee (9, 1927), with Donald Ross; Thomas Memorial GC, Turners Falls; Toy Town Tavern GC, Winchendon (NLE, 9), with Donald Ross; Whitinsville CC (9, 1925), with Donald Ross.
New Hampshire: Kingswood CC, Wolfeboro , with Donald Ross.
Ohio: Hawthorne Valley CC, Cleveland , with Donald Ross; Springfield CC, with Donald Ross.
Rhode Island: Warwick CC (9, 1924), with Donald Ross.
Tennessee: Brainerd Muni, Chattanooga (1925), with Donald Ross.
Nova Scotia: White Point Beach GC, Hunts Point , with Donald Ross.

Frederick George Hawtree (1883 - 1955)
Born: Ealing, Middlesex, England. Died: Hayes, Kent, England at age 72.

F.G. Hawtree, the first of three generations of British golf course architects, started out as a greenkeeper. He began designing courses around 1912. Following service with the British Army during World War I, he practiced on his own until 1922, when he formed the partnership of Hawtree and Taylor with J.H. Taylor, one of British golf's "Great Triumvirate." The firm continued until World War II, when it was voluntarily liquidated.

As managing director of the firm, Hawtree was responsible for the day-to-day details and design work, while Taylor handled early interviews with clients and appeared at official openings. At one time, Hawtree had four highly regarded Irish foremen (Regan, Ryan, Brick and Ward) working under him. Each had a special flair for shaping golf courses, and they were widely known throughout the British Isles and on the Continent.

Hawtree and Taylor created some fifty new courses and remodeled another fifty, including the famous Royal Birkdale Golf Club. They also produced one of the world's first all-weather driving ranges in London. In 1931 Hawtree built 27 holes for himself at Addington, and thus established Britain's first privately owned daily-fee course.

F.G. Hawtree was instrumental in founding the British Golf Greenkeepers Association and the National Association of Public Golf Courses, and served as president of both. He was also on the board of the Sports Turf Research Institute and on the council of the English Golf Union.

Courses by: F.G. Hawtree

England: Addington Court GC (Lower Course), Surrey (1931), with J.H. Taylor; Addington Court GC (Old Course), Surrey (1931), with J.H. Taylor; Addington Palace GC, Surrey (1923), with J.H. Taylor; Batchwood Hall GC, St. Albans (1936), with J.H. Taylor; Bigbury GC (1923), with J.H. Taylor; Chigwell GC, Essex (1925), with J.H. Taylor; Cock Moor Woods GC, Birmingham (1926), with J.H. Taylor; Croham Hurst GC, Surrey (1912), with James Braid; Easingwold GC, North Yorkshire (1930), with J.H. Taylor; Elfordleigh GC, Devon (1932), with J.H. Taylor; Gorleston GC, Suffolk (1926), with J.H. Taylor; Harborne Church Farm GC, Birmingham (1926), with J.H. Taylor; Harpenden GC, Hertfordshire (1931), with J.H. Taylor; Hartsbourne CC, Hertfordshire (1946), with Fred W. Hawtree; Heysham GC, Lancashire (1910), with Sandy Herd; High Post GC, Wiltshire (1922), with J.H. Taylor; Highwoods GC, Bexhill-on-Sea (1925), with J.H. Taylor; Hill Barn GC, Sussex (1935), with J.H. Taylor; Hollingbury Park GC, Sussex (1922), with J.H. Taylor; Ifield G&CC, Sussex (1927), with J.H. Taylor; Ipswich GC, Purdis Heath (1921), with J.H. Taylor; Knowle GC, Gloucestershire , with J.H. Taylor; Lickey Hills GC, Birmingham , with J.H. Taylor; Marston Green Muni, Birmingham (NLE,), with J.H. Taylor; Maxstoke Park GC, Birmingham (1948), with Fred W. Hawtree; Norwich Muni, with J.H. Taylor; Pinner Hill GC, Middlesex (1929), with J.H. Taylor; Pype Hayes Muni, Warwickshire (1932), with J.H. Taylor; Richmond Park GC (Dukes Course), London (1923), with J.H. Taylor; Richmond Park GC (Princes Course), London (1923), with J.H. Taylor; Rickmansworth GC, Hertfordshire (1937), with J.H. Taylor; Ruislip GC, Middlesex (1938), with J.H. Taylor; Selsdon Park Hotel GC, Surrey (1929), with J.H. Taylor; Southampton GC, Hampshire (27, 1935), with J.H. Taylor; Southcliffe and Canwick GC, Lincolnshire , with J.H. Taylor; Swinton Park GC, Lancashire (1926), with J.H. Taylor; Tinsley Park GC, Yorkshire , with J.H. Taylor; Warren GC, Cheshire (9, 1911), with J.H. Taylor; Wells GC, Gloucestershire (9); Wells-by-the-Sea GC (Par 3, 9), with J.H. Taylor; Welwyn Garden City GC, Hertfordshire (1922), with J.H. Taylor; White Webbs Muni, Enfield, Middlesex (1932), with J.H. Taylor; Woodlands Manor GC, Sevenoaks (1928), with J.H. Taylor; Woolacombe Bay Hotel GC (Par 3, 9), with J.H. Taylor; Wyke Green GC, Middlesex (1928), with J.H. Taylor.
Ireland: Arklow GC, County Wicklow (1926), with J.H. Taylor.
Italy: Pallanza GC, Lake Maggiore .
Portugal: Lisbon Sports C (9, 1922).
Scotland: Hilton Park GC (Hilton Course) (1922), with J.H. Taylor.
Sweden: Bastad GC (1928), with J.H. Taylor.
Wales: Abergele and Pensare GC, Clwyd , with Fred W. Hawtree; Holywell GC, Clywed (9), with J.H. Taylor; Rhuddlan GC, Clwyd (1930), with J.H. Taylor.

Courses Remodeled & Added to by: F.G. Hawtree

England: Boyce Hill GC, Essex (R.9); Dyke GC, Brighton, Sussex (R., 1947), with Fred W. Hawtree; Filton GC (R.9), with J.H. Taylor; Filton GC (A.9), with J.H. Taylor; Freshwater Bay GC, Isle of Wright (R.); Hainault Forest GC (Course No. 1), Essex (A.9), with J.H. Taylor; Henbury GC, Gloucestershire (R.); Hull GC, Yorkshire (R.), with J.H. Taylor; Littlehampton GC, Sussex (R.9), with J.H. Taylor; Littlehampton GC, Sussex (A.9), with J.H. Taylor; Rochford Hundred GC, Essex (R.); Royal Birkdale GC, Southport (R., 1932), with J.H. Taylor; Sonning GC, Berkshire (A.9), with J.H. Taylor; Sonning GC, Berkshire (R.9), with J.H. Taylor; West Middlesex GC, Middlesex (A.9), with J.H. Taylor.
Monaco: Monte Carlo CC (R.).
Scotland: Williamwood GC, Glasgow (R.), with J.H. Taylor.
Wales: Ashburnham GC (R., 1914), with J.H. Taylor; Royal Porthcawl GC, Mid Glamorgan (R., 1925), with J.H. Taylor; Royal Porthcawl GC, Mid Glamorgan (A.4, 1925), with J.H. Taylor.

Frederick William Hawtree (1916 -) BAGCA, Founding Member; Chairman, 1974, President, 1975. ASGCA (corresponding member).
Born: Bromley, Kent England.

F.W. Hawtree joined his father's firm, Hawtree & Taylor, upon graduation from Oxford in 1938. During World War 11, he served with the Royal Artillery in the Far East, where he was captured as a Japanese P.O.W. On his return to England he re-entered private practice with his father in the course architecture firm of Hawtree & Son.

After his father's death in 1955, Hawtree continued the firm and completed some 70 courses over the next 25 years. He was joined in 1969 by A.H.F. Jiggens and in 1974 by his son, Martin, the third generation of Hawtree golf architects. Hawtree & Son created courses in Britain, Ireland, France, Italy, Spain, Belgium, Holland, Germany, Switzerland, Iran, South Africa, El Salvador, Morocco and the U.S.

F.W. Hawtree remained active in the golfing organizations founded by his father and was himself influential in forming the BAGCA in 1970. He also participated from its beginnings in the Golf Development Council, for whom he wrote *Elements of Golf Course Layout and Design*.

Hawtree summed up his own design philosophy in *The Golf Course: Planning, Designing Construction and Maintenance*, published in 1983.

Courses by: Fred W. Hawtree

North Carolina: Mount Mitchell GC, Burnsville (1973).
Belgium: Limburg GC, Hasselt (1966); Royal Waterloo GC (Course No. 1), Ohain (1961); Royal Waterloo GC (Course No. 2), Ohain (Precision, 1961).
El Salvador: Casino C, San Salvador; CC of Cuzcatlan (9).
England: Addington Court GC (New Course), Surrey; Bedwell Park GC (1983), with Martin Hawtree; Bowring Park GC, Liverpool; Brackenwood Muni, Cheshire; Braintree GC, Essex; Broome Manor GC, Wiltshire (1976), with Martin Hawtree; Chester GC (1973), with A.H.F. Jiggens; Chestnut Park GC, Herts; Chipping Sodbury GC, Avon (27, 1971); Chorley GC (18), with A.H.F. Jiggens; Cold Ashby GC, Northamptonshire (1974); Cold Norton GC; Congleton GC, with A.H.F. Jiggens; Deangate Ridge GC, Kent (1972); Downshire GC, Berkshire (1973); Duxbury Park GC, Lancashire (1975), with Martin Hawtree and A.H.F. Jiggens; Eastham Lodge GC, Cheshire (9, 1975), with Martin Hawtree and A.H.F. Jiggens; Easthampstead Park GC, Wokingham (1973); Eaton GC, Cheshire (1965); Enmore Park GC, Somerset (1975), with A.H.F. Jiggens; Foxhills GC (Chertsey Course), Surrey (1973); Foxhills GC (Longcross Course), Surrey (1973); Hartsbourne CC, Hertfordshire (1946), with F.G. Hawtree; Hatchford Brook Muni, Birmingham; High Elms GC, Kent (1969), with Martin Hawtree; Hilltop & Manwood Farm GC, Birmingham (1979), with Martin Hawtree; Humberstone Heights GC, Leicestershire (1977), with Martin Hawtree; Ingestre GC, Staffordshire (1977), with Martin Hawtree; Kings Norton GC, Worcestershire (27), with Martin Hawtree; Little Hay GC, Hertfordshire (1977), with Martin Hawtree; Lullingstone Park GC, Kent (27, 1967); Malkins Bank GC, Cheshire (1980), with A.H.F. Jiggens; Maxstoke Park GC, Birmingham (1948), with F.G. Hawtree; Minchinhampton GC (New Course), Gloucestershire (1975); Mowsbury Muni, Bedfordshire (1975), with Martin Hawtree; Newcastle-under-Lyme GC, Staffordshire , with Martin Hawtree; Normanby Hall GC, Lincolnshire (1978), with A.H.F. Jiggens; Normanby Park GC, Scunthorpe (1979), with Martin Hawtree; P L London CC (1976), with Martin Hawtree; Port Sunlight GC (9); Portsdown Hill GC; Poult Wood GC, Kent (1974); Risebridge GC, Essex (1972); Scunthorpe GC, Lincolnshire , with A.H.F. Jiggens; St. Michael Jubilee GC (9); Stockgrove GC (9); Tamworth Muni, Staffordshire (1975), with Martin Hawtree and A.H.F. Jiggens; Wellingborough GC, Northhamptonshire , with A.H.F. Jiggens; Western Park GC, Leicester (1973); Widnes Muni, Lancashire (9, 1977), with A.H.F. Jiggens; Woodbridge GC, Suffolk; Worsley GC, Lancashire , with A.H.F. Jiggens.
France: Club de Lyon (27); Golf de Bondues, Roubaix; Golf de Cornouaille, Quimper (9, 1959); Golf de Domont, Paris; Golf de Lyon; Golf de Metz Cherisey, Metz (9); Golf de Rochefort en Yvelines, Paris (1964); Golf de Seraincourt, Meulan; Golf de St. Samson, Pleumeur-Bodou; Golf de Valcros; Golf de Vaudreuil; Golf du Prieure (East Course), Sailly; Golf du Prieure (West Course), Sailly; La Herliere CC, Arras (1973); St. Nom La Breteche GC (Blue Course) (1959); St. Nom La Breteche GC (Red Course) (1959).
Iran: Imperial Sports C, Tehran .
Ireland: Brainroe GC, County Wicklow (1978), with Martin Hawtree; Corballis

GC, County Dublin , with A.H.F. Jiggens; Forest Little GC, County Dublin (1972), with A.H.F. Jiggens; Howth Castle GC, County Dublin (36); Westport GC, County Mayo , with Martin Hawtree and A.H.F. Jiggens.

Morocco: Golf de Cabo Negro (9).

Netherlands: Wittem G&CC (9).

Northern Ireland: Killymoon GC, County Tyrone; Lisburn GC, Belfast; Malone GC, Belfast (27).

Scotland: Balnagask GC, Aberdeen , with Martin Hawtree; East Kilbride GC, Lanarkshire; Grangemouth Muni, Shirlingshire (1973); Torrance House GC, Lanarkshire (1979), with Martin Hawtree.

South Africa: Plettenberg Bay CC, Cape Province; The Country Club, Johannesburg (27).

Spain: Bendinat GC (9), with Martin Hawtree; Golf Club de Pals, Gerona (9, 1966); La Penaza GC, Zaragoza (1972); Roca Llisa GC, Ibiza (9, 1971); Son Vida GC, Mallorca (1964); Vallromanas GC, Barcelona (1969).

Switzerland: Bad Ragaz GC.

Wales: Abergele and Pensare GC, Clwyd , with F.G. Hawtree; Anglesey GC (1982), with Martin Hawtree; Fairwood Park GC, Swansea; Glynhir GC, Llandeilo (1967); Penrhos GC, Gwynedd (9, 1986), with Martin Hawtree.

West Germany: Dusseldorfer GC; Land und GC Dusseldorf (East Course), Hubbelrath (1961); Land und GC Dusseldorf (West Course), Hubbelrath (Precision, 1972).

Courses Remodeled & Added to by: Fred W. Hawtree

Belgium: Les Buttes Blanches GC (R.); Royal GC Les Buttes Blanches, Ghent (R.3, 1953).

England: Ashton-in-Makerfield GC, Lancashire (A.9); Bebington GC (A.9); Berwick-upon-Tweed GC, Northumberland (A.9); Bromborough GC (R.), with A.H.F. Jiggens; Burnham and Berrow GC, Somerset (A.9, 1973); Delamere Forest GC, Cheshire (R., 1962); Doncaster GC, Yorkshire (R.7, 1979), with Martin Hawtree; Dyke GC, Brighton, Sussex (R., 1947), with F.G. Hawtree; Enmore Park GC, Somerset (A.9, 1979), with A.H.F. Jiggens; Farnham Park GC, Stoke Poges (A.9, 1983), with Martin Hawtree; Finham Park GC, Coventry (R.3); Gog Magog GC, Cambridgeshire (A.9); Grimsby GC, Lincolnshire (R., 1973); Hillside GC, Lancashire (A.9, 1967); Hillside GC, Lancashire (R.9, 1967); Huyton & Prescot GC (R.), with A.H.F. Jiggens; Immingham GC, Lincolnshire (A.9, 1981), with Martin Hawtree; Ipswich GC, Purdis Heath (Precision, A.9), with A.H.F. Jiggens; John O'Gaunt GC (Carthagena Course), Bedfordshire (R.); Lindrick GC (R.); Lutterworth GC, Leicestershire (A.9); Malton & Norton GC, Yorkshire (A.9), with Martin Hawtree; Malvern GC, Worcestershire (A.9); Marsden Park GC, Lancashire (A.9); Nelson GC, Lancashire (A.9), with A.H.F. Jiggens; Oakdale GC, Yorkshire (R.7, 1977), with A.H.F. Jiggens; Prenton GC, Cheshire (R.); Pyecombe GC, Sussex (R.4, 1980), with Martin Hawtree; Royal Birkdale GC, Southport (R., 1967); Royal Birkdale GC, Southport (R., 1974); Royal Liverpool GC, Hoylake (R., 1967); Royal Mid-Surrey GC, Surrey (R.3, 1982), with Martin Hawtree; Salisbury & South Wilts GC, Wiltshire (R.6, 1983), with Martin Hawtree; Sandiway GC, Cheshire (R.3, 1959); Theydon Bois GC, Essex (A.2, 1976), with Martin Hawtree; Wellingborough GC, Northhamptonshire (A.9), with Martin Hawtree; Wellingborough GC, Northhamptonshire (R., 1983), with A.H.F. Jiggens; Welwyn Garden City GC, Hertfordshire (R.), with Martin Hawtree; West Lancashire GC, Lancashire (R.); Woodbridge GC, Suffolk (A.9); Worcestershire GC (A.9), with A.H.F. Jiggens; Worsley GC, Lancashire (A.9), with A.H.F. Jiggens.

France: Club de la Barouge, Mazamet (A.9, 1985), with Martin Hawtree; Fontainbleau GC (R., 1965); Fontainbleau GC (A.4, 1965); Golf de Toulouse (A.9, 1981).

Ireland: Killarney G & Fishing C (Killeen), County Kerry (R.6, 1971); Killarney G & Fishing C (Killeen), County Kerry (A.12, 1971); Killarney G & Fishing C (Mahony's Point), County Kerry (R.12, 1971); Killarney G & Fishing C (Mahony's Point), County Kerry (A.6, 1971); Portmarnock GC, Dublin (A.9, 1964); Portmarnock GC, Dublin (R., 1964); Woodbrook GC, County Dublin (A.2), with A.H.F. Jiggens and Martin Hawtree; Woodbrook GC, County Dublin (R.), with Martin Hawtree and A.H.F. Jiggens.

Italy: Cervino GC, Cervinia (A.9).

Monaco: Monte Carlo CC (R.); Monte Carlo CC (A.2).

Northern Ireland: Massereene GC, County Antrim (A.9); Tandragee GC, County Armaugh (A.9), with Martin Hawtree.

Portugal: Lisbon Sports C (A.9).

Scotland: Bruntsfield Links, Davidson's Main (R., 1972); Bruntsfield Links, Davidson's Main (A.7, 1972); Morton Hall GC (R.5); Morton Hall GC (A.9); Nortonhall GC, Edinburgh (R.5, 1979), with Martin Hawtree; Nortonhall GC, Edinburgh (A.9, 1979), with Martin Hawtree; Western Gailes GC, Ayrshire (R.4, 1975).

Spain: Club de G Llavaneras, Barcelona (R.); Club de G San Andres de Llavaneras, Barcelona (R.); Club de G Terramar, Sitges (A.9); Golf Club de Pals, Gerona (A.9, 1970).

Switzerland: Lenzerheide Valbella GC, Lenzerheide (A.9).

Wales: Nefyn and District GC, Gwynedd (R.), with A.H.F. Jiggens; Royal St. Davids GC, Harlech (R., 1960); Swansea Bay GC, West Glamorgan (R.6, 1984), with Martin Hawtree.

Zimbabwe: Royal Salisbury GC (A.2, 1968); Royal Salisbury GC (R., 1968).

Martin Hawtree (1947 -) BAGCA

Born: Beckenham, Kent, England.

After receiving an Arts Degree at the University of Liverpool, Martin Hawtree remained at Liverpool for three years doing research in the history of modern town planning for his doctorate. He joined his father's firm, Hawtree & Son, in 1973. The following year the firm hired scratch golfer John Davis as another partner.

While families such as the Dunns and the Maples may have worked longer in the business world of golf in general, the Hawtree dynasty - F.G., F.W. and Martin - were probably involved in the longest continuous practice of golf course architecture on record, dating from 1912.

Courses by: Martin Hawtree

England: Bedwell Park GC (1983), with Fred W. Hawtree; Broome Manor GC, Wiltshire (1976), with Fred W. Hawtree; Duxbury Park GC, Lancashire (1975), with Fred W. Hawtree and A.H.F. Jiggens; Eastham Lodge GC, Cheshire (9, 1975), with Fred W. Hawtree and A.H.F. Jiggens; High Elms GC, Kent (1969), with Fred W. Hawtree; Hilltop & Manwood Farm GC, Birmingham (1979), with Fred W. Hawtree; Humberstone Heights GC, Leicestershire (1977), with Fred W. Hawtree; Ingestre GC, Staffordshire (1977), with Fred W. Hawtree; Kings Norton GC, Worcestershire (27), with Fred W. Hawtree; Little Hay GC, Hertfordshire (1977), with Fred W. Hawtree; Mowsbury Muni, Bedfordshire (1975), with Fred W. Hawtree; Newcastle-under-Lyme GC, Staffordshire , with Fred W. Hawtree; Normanby Park GC, Scunthorpe (1979), with Fred W. Hawtree; P L London CC (1976), with Fred W. Hawtree; Tamworth Muni, Staffordshire (1975), with Fred W. Hawtree and A.H.F. Jiggens.

Ireland: Brainroe GC, County Wicklow (1978), with Fred W. Hawtree; Westport GC, County Mayo , with Fred W. Hawtree and A.H.F. Jiggens.

Scotland: Balnagask GC, Aberdeen , with Fred W. Hawtree; Torrance House GC, Lanarkshire (1979), with Fred W. Hawtree.

Spain: Bendinat GC (9), with Fred W. Hawtree.

Wales: Anglesey GC (1982), with Fred W. Hawtree; Penrhos GC, Gwynedd (9, 1986), with Fred W. Hawtree.

Courses Remodeled & Added to by: Martin Hawtree

England: Doncaster GC, Yorkshire (R.7, 1979), with Fred W. Hawtree; Farnham Park GC, Stoke Poges (A.9, 1983), with Fred W. Hawtree; Immingham GC, Lincolnshire (A.9, 1981), with Fred W. Hawtree; Malton & Norton GC, Yorkshire (A.9), with Fred W. Hawtree; Pyecombe GC, Sussex (R.4, 1980), with Fred W. Hawtree; Royal Mid-Surrey GC, Surrey (R.3, 1982), with Fred W. Hawtree; Salisbury & South Wilts GC, Wiltshire (R.6, 1983), with Fred W. Hawtree; Theydon Bois GC, Essex (A.2, 1976), with Fred W. Hawtree; Wellingborough GC, Northhamptonshire (A.9), with Fred W. Hawtree; Welwyn Garden City GC, Hertfordshire (R.), with Fred W. Hawtree.

France: Club de la Barouge, Mazamet (A.9, 1985), with Fred W. Hawtree.

Ireland: Woodbrook GC, County Dublin (A.2), with Fred W. Hawtree and A.H.F. Jiggens; Woodbrook GC, County Dublin (R.), with Fred W. Hawtree and A.H.F. Jiggens.

Northern Ireland: Tandragee GC, County Armaugh (A.9), with Fred W. Hawtree.

Scotland: Nortonhall GC, Edinburgh (A.9, 1979), with Fred W. Hawtree; Nortonhall GC, Edinburgh (R.5, 1979), with Fred W. Hawtree.

Wales: Swansea Bay GC, West Glamorgan (R.6, 1984), with Fred W. Hawtree.

Alexander "Sandy" Herd (1868 - 1944)

Born: St. Andrews, Scotland. Died: London, England at age 76.

Sandy Herd won numerous major golf tournaments, including the 1902 British Open in which he used the new rubber-core Haskell ball, and the British Professional Matchplay at age 58. He served as head professional for years at Coombe Hill, where he garnered 13 of his 19 lifetime holes-in-one. During his golf career, Sandy Herd participated in the design of several courses.

Courses by: Sandy Herd

England: Aspley Guise & Woburn Sands GC, Buckinghamshire , with Charles Willmott; Harrogate GC, Yorkshire (1897), with George Duncan; Heysham GC, Lancashire (1910), with F.G. Hawtree; Lees Hall GC, Yorkshire (1909); Malden GC, Surrey (1926), with H. Bailey; Pannal GC, Yorkshire (1906); Ulverston GC, Cumbria (1894); Wakefield GC (1912).

Donald Herfort Jr. ASGCA

Don Herfort was employed as senior accountant with the 3-M Corporation in St. Paul, Minn. when he was appointed to a committee in charge of building the company's golf course. After consulting with two professional architects, the committee elected to design its own course, and Herfort was chosen to lay it out and supervise its construction. About the same time, Herfort was involved in the conversion of Lisbon Bissel GC in nearby North Dakota from sand to grass greens. With these experiences behind him and several prospective projects awaiting him, Herfort left 3-M to devote full time to course architecture.

Courses by: Don Herfort

Minnesota: Baker Park GC (9, 1986); Birnamwood GC, Burnsville (Par 3, 9, 1969); Chromonix CC, Hugo (9, 1970); Cimarron GC, East Oakdale (Par 3, 9, 1971); Como Muni (Course No. 2), St. Paul (1986); Country View GC, St. Paul (Par 3, 9, 1970); Dellwood National GC, White Bear Lake (1970); Indian Hills CC, North St. Paul (1971); Little Crow CC, Spicer (1969); Oak Glen GC, Stillwater (27, 1983); Purple Hawk CC, Cambridge (1969); Tartan Park GC, St. Paul (1965).

South Dakota: Kuehn Park GC, Sioux Falls (9, 1975).

Wisconsin: Royal Scot CC, Green Bay (1970).

Courses Remodeled & Added to by: Don Herfort

Iowa: Oneota CC, Decorah (R.9); Oneota CC, Decorah (A.9).

Michigan: Pine Grove CC, Iron Mountain (R., 1982).

Minnesota: Cleary Lake GC, Hennepin (R., 1986); Cuyuna CC, Deerfield (R.9); Cuyuna CC, Deerfield (A.9); Detroit CC, Detroit Lakes (A.9, 1969); Edenvale GC (R., 1972); Galls GC (R.); Hastings CC (R., 1986); Interlaken GC, Fairmount (A.9, 1968); Interlaken GC, Fairmount (R.9, 1968); Keller GC, St. Paul (R.1, 1970); Manitou Ridge GC, White Bear Lake (R., 1978); Minnetonka CC, Excelsior (R.3, 1968); New Prague GC (A.9, 1967); New Ulm GC (A.9, 1966); Northfield GC (R.9, 1976); Northfield GC (A.9, 1976); Northland CC, Duluth (R., 1968); Phalen Park GC, St. Paul (R., 1976); Pine Beach East GC, Madden Beach (R., 1981); Red Wing CC (R.9, 1967); Wadena GC (R.9, 1977); White Bear G&YC (R.1, 1971); Whitefish GC, Pequot Lakes (A.9, 1981).

North Dakota: Enderlin GC (R.9, 1968); Lisbon Bissell GC, Lisbon (R.9, 1965).

South Dakota: Elmwood Park GC, Sioux Falls (R., 1977).

Wisconsin: Amery GC (R.9, 1968); Eagle River CC (A.9, 1986); Eagle River CC (R.3, 1986); Hudson CC (A.9, 1969); Hudson CC (R.9, 1969); Nemadji Muni, Superior (A.9, 1984); New Richmond GC (A.9, 1982); New Richmond GC (R.5, 1982).

Homer G. Herpel (1906 - 1977)

Born: St. Louis, Missouri. Died: University City, Missouri at age 71.

After working as a newspaper cartoonist in his youth, Homer Herpel turned to golf as a career. He became a member of the PGA of America in 1937 and served as professional at several St. Louis clubs. After retiring as a club professional in 1955, he began designing and supervising construction of courses in the St. Louis area. Herpel worked first in association with golf architect/contractor Chic Adams and later did over a dozen layouts of his own in greater St. Louis and other sections of Missouri.

Courses by: Homer Herpel
Missouri: Ballwin Muni GC (9); Fox Creek CC, Ballwin; Lodge of the Four Seasons GC, Lake Ozark (Precision, 9, 1957); North Shore CC, St. Louis (27, 1959), with Chic Adams; Paddock CC, Florissant (1964); Teamsters GC (9).

Arthur Wright Hills (1930 -   ) ASGCA
Born: Toledo, Ohio.
   Art Hills first became interested in golf as a youngster when he worked on the maintenance crew at Meadowbrook CC near Detroit. He later studied agronomy at Michigan State University, where he played on the golf team, and then earned a master's degree in Landscape Architecture at the University of Michigan. Hills was employed with a landscape design firm in Los Angeles for a short time before entering private practice as a golf course architect in 1967, based in Toledo. He later concentrated his efforts in Florida and the Southeast.
Courses by: Arthur Hills
Colorado: Tamarron CC, Durango (1975).
Florida: Bonita Bay C, Bonita Springs (1985), with Steve Forrest and Mike Dasher; Cape Coral Muni (1986), with Steve Forrest and Mike Dasher; Club at Pelican Bay, Naples (1980), with Steve Forrest; Cross Creek CC, Fort Myers (Precision, 1985), with Steve Forrest and Mike Dasher; Foxfire CC, Naples (1985), with Steve Forrest and Mike Dasher; Gator Trace GC, Ft. Pierce (1986), with Steve Forrest and Mike Dasher; Imperial GC (East Course), Naples (1973); Ironhorse GC, West Palm Beach (1987), with Steve Forrest and Mike Dasher; Lakewood GC, Naples (Precision, 1979), with Steve Forrest; Myerlee CC, Fort Myers (Precision, 1972); Palmetto Pine CC, Cape Coral (1970); Quail Creek CC (Creek Course), Naples (1982), with Steve Forrest; Quail Creek CC (Quail Course), Naples (1981), with Steve Forrest; Tampa Palms CC, Tampa (1987), with Steve Forrest and Mike Dasher; TPC at Eagle Trace, Coral Springs (1984), with Steve Forrest and Mike Dasher; Vista Plantation GC, Vero Beach (Precision, 1985), with Steve Forrest and Mike Dasher; Vista Royale GC, Vero Beach (1974); Wilderness CC, Naples (1974); Wyndemere G&CC, Naples (27, 1980), with Steve Forrest.
Georgia: Kings Bay Naval Sub Base GC, St. Marys (1986), with Steve Forrest; Landings at Skidaway Island (Palmetto) (1985), with Steve Forrest and Mike Dasher; Standard C, Norcross (1986), with Steve Forrest and Mike Dasher; Windward CC, Atlanta (1987), with Steve Forrest and Mike Dasher.
Kansas: Tallgrass C, Wichita (1983).
Louisiana: Southern Trace CC, Shreveport (1986), with Steve Forrest and Mike Dasher.
Michigan: Giant Oak CC, Temperance (1971); Honors C, Brighton (1987), with Steve Forrest and Mike Dasher; Millrace CC, Jonesville (9, 1970); Moors of Portage GC, Portage (1979); Wyndwyck CC, St. Joseph (1968).
Ohio: Detwiler GC, Toledo (1969); Dunham Muni, Cincinnati (Precision, 9, 1977); Glenview Muni, Cincinnati (1974); Shaker Run GC, Middletown (1979); Weatherwax GC, Middletown (36, 1971).
South Carolina: Palmetto Dunes CC (Hills Course), Hilton Head Island (1986), with Steve Forrest and Mike Dasher.
Texas: Trophy C (Creek Course), Roanoke (9, 1984), with Steve Forrest.
Japan: Higashi Ibaragi CC, Ibaragi (36, 1974).
Courses Remodeled & Added to by: Arthur Hills
Florida: Cypress Lake CC, Ft. Myers (R., 1982), with Steve Forrest; Dunedin CC (R., 1971); Hole-in-the-Wall GC, Naples (R., 1984), with Steve Forrest; Vista Royale GC, Vero Beach (A.9, 1981), with Steve Forrest and Mike Dasher.
Georgia: Capital City C (R., 1985), with Mike Dasher; Druid Hills CC, Atlanta (R., 1985), with Mike Dasher.
Kentucky: Big Spring CC, Louisville (R., 1982), with Steve Forrest; Fort Mitchell CC, Covington (R., 1971); Fort Mitchell CC, Covington (R., 1982), with Steve Forrest; Highland CC, Fort Thomas (A.9, 1985), with Steve Forrest and Mike Dasher; Summit Hills CC, Ft. Mitchell (R., 1985), with Steve Forrest and Mike Dasher.
Michigan: Barton Hills CC, Ann Arbor (R., 1983), with Steve Forrest; Birmingham CC (R., 1985), with Steve Forrest; Bloomfield Hills CC (R., 1981), with Steve Forrest; Chemung Hills CC (R., 1986), with Steve Forrest; CC of Detroit, Grosse Pointe Farms (R., 1981), with Steve Forrest; Detroit GC (North Course) (R., 1978); Forest Lake CC, Bloomfield Hills (R., 1981), with Steve Forrest; Grosse Ile G&CC (R., 1981), with Steve Forrest; Indianwood G&CC (Old Course), Lake Orion (R., 1984), with Steve Forrest; Lochmoor C, Grosse Pointe Woods (R., 1981), with Steve Forrest; Meadowbrook CC, Detroit (R., 1974); Orchard Lake CC (R., 1984), with Steve Forrest and Mike Dasher; Plum Hollow G&CC, Southfield (R., 1984), with Steve Forrest; Riverview Highlands GC, Riverview (A.9, 1980), with Steve Forrest; Western GC, Redford (R., 1984), with Steve Forrest.
New Jersey: Pennbrook GC, Basking Ridge (R., 1984), with Steve Forrest.
New York: CC of Rochester (R., 1982), with Steve Forrest; Monroe CC (R., 1984), with Steve Forrest; Park CC, Buffalo (R., 1983), with Steve Forrest.
Ohio: Belmont CC, Perrysburg (R., 1974); Bowling Green University GC (R., 1968); Clovernook CC, Cincinnati (R., 1984), with Steve Forrest; Fairlawn CC, Akron (R., 1973); Fremont CC (R., 1984), with Mike Dasher; Highland Meadows CC, Sylvania (R., 1974); Hyde Park CC, Cincinnati (R., 1984), with Steve Forrest; Inverness C, Toledo (R., 1970); Inverness C, Toledo (R., 1983), with Steve Forrest; Orchard Hills CC, Bryan (R.9, 1967); Orchard Hills CC, Bryan (A.9, 1967); Ottawa Park GC, Toledo (R., 1974); Sycamore Creek CC (R., 1969); Sylvania CC, Toledo (R., 1983), with Steve Forrest; Terrace Park CC, Cincinnati (R., 1977); Terrace Park CC, Cincinnati (R., 1984), with Mike Dasher; Toledo CC (R., 1974); Wildwood CC, Middletown (R., 1970).
Ontario: Board of Trade CC (West Course), Woodbridge (R.9, 1975); Board of Trade CC (West Course), Woodbridge (A.9, 1975); Essex G&CC, LaSalle (R., 1969).

Reuben P. Hines Sr. (- 1964)
   Reuben Hines, a golf course superintendent for most of his life, was a member of the GCSAA. In the late 1940s and early 1950s he held the post of Superintendent of

Parks in Washington, D.C., and was in charge of five golf courses as well as numerous parklands. He also served as a turf consultant to several area golf clubs.
   Hines owned and operated a turf nursery in Maryland during the 1950s, and his close contact with golf course contractors and builders led to several remodeling jobs. By the late 1950s he had also designed a half-dozen courses.
Courses by: Reuben Hines
Maryland: Beaver Creek CC, Hagerstown (1956).
Virginia: Courthouse CC, Fairfax (1955); Oak Hills CC, Richmond (1959); Warrentown CC (1959).
Washington, D.C.: Oxon Run GC (9, 1956).
Courses Remodeled & Added to by: Reuben Hines
Maryland: Manor CC, Rockville (R., 1958).

Donald Hoenig
   Donald Hoenig planned several courses in New England in the 1960s, both on his own and in collaboration with his father. Among them were the widely known Pleasant Valley CC at Sutton, Mass., his own course, Raceway at Thompson, Conn., and a floodlit eighteen-hole precision course, the Firefly GC in Seekonk, Mass., for LPGA golfer Joanne Gunderson Carner and her husband Don.

George A. Hoffman (1892 - 1977)
Born: Hackensack, New Jersey. Died: Big Springs, Texas at age 84.
   George Hoffman moved with his parents to a ranch in west Texas at the turn of the century. He gained experience in golf course construction by helping build a course in the Dominican Republic in 1919.
   Returning to Texas in the 1920s, Hoffman entered private practice as a golf architect and designed numerous courses in the western part of the state. With a working knowledge of Spanish, he also landed jobs in Mexico, Central and South America. He remained active until his retirement in the 1970s.
Courses by: George Hoffman
Texas: Ascarte Park Muni, El Paso (27, 1955); Lady Bird Johnson Muni, Fredericksburg (9, 1969); Olmos Basin GC, San Antonio (1963); Riverside GC, San Antonio (Precision, 20, 1962); Riverside Park, San Antonio (NLE,); Victoria CC; Windcrest GC, San Antonio (9, 1964).
Mexico: Club Campestre de Saltillo (9); Juarez CC.

Karl Hoffmann
   Educated as an architect and engineer, Karl Hoffmann was involved in building reconstruction and renovation in his native Berlin, Germany after World War I. An avid golfer, he also assisted golf architect Tom Simpson in the design of Bad Ems, which became Germany's main championship layout during the 1930s.
   The experience led Hoffmann to pursue many golf design projects. In the mid-1930s he took young Bernard von Limburger as a partner. World War II forced von Limburger to flee the country, but Hoffmann remained in Germany and after the war restored many courses, including Bad Ems.
   For a short time before his death in the Fifties, Hoffmann worked in partnership with Herbert E. Gaertner, a former club secretary who also dabbled in course architecture.
Courses by: Karl Hoffmann
East Germany: Chemnitzer GC, Slauv-Floeha , with Bernhard von Limburger; Gaschwitz GC, Leipzig , with Bernhard von Limburger; Neustadt GC (9), with Bernhard von Limburger; Wittenberg GC (9), with Bernhard von Limburger.
Switzerland: Basel G&CC (1928), with Bernhard von Limburger; Neuchatel GC (9, 1928), with Bernhard von Limburger.
West Germany: Bad Driburger GC (9), with Bernhard von Limburger; Breslau GC (9); Donaveschingen GC; Essener GC Haus Oefte, Essen (11), with Bernhard von Limburger; Feldafing GC (1926), with Bernhard von Limburger; Garmish-Partnekirchen GC, with Bernhard von Limburger; Golf und Land C Cologne, with Bernhard von Limburger; Konstaz GC, with Bernhard von Limburger; Krefelder GC, Krefeld (1930), with Bernhard von Limburger; Mannheim-Viernheim GC, Mannheim (9), with Bernhard von Limburger; Mittelrheinscher GC, Bad Ems; Stuttgarter GC, Monsheim (1927), with Bernhard von Limburger.
Courses Remodeled & Added to by: Karl Hoffmann
West Germany: Hanover GC, Garbson (R.), with Bernhard von Limburger.

William Benjamin Hogan (1912 -   )
Born: Dublin, Texas.
   Ben Hogan, winner of all four major professional golf championships and four U.S. Opens, was a perceptive golf course critic throughout his career. He especially admired the works of Dick Wilson, and shortly before the architect's death had talked of doing a course with him. Ten years later, Hogan finally did consult on the design of a layout, the Trophy Club near Fort Worth, Texas, designed by a Wilson protege Joe Lee. Except for suggesting changes at Colonial and Shady Oaks in Fort Worth, Hogan did no other course design work.

Cecil B. Hollingsworth
   A high school football and golf star in Los Angeles, Cecil Hollingsworth attended UCLA and was employed as assistant football coach and physical education instructor there in the early 1930s. He then purchased and operated a daily-fee golf course in the 1940s, and in the '50s began a large golf complex in El Cajon, Singing Hills CC. Hollingsworth designed most of the courses he owned.
Courses by: Cecil B. Hollingsworth
Arkansas: Twin Lakes GC, Mountain Home (1978).
California: Alondra Park GC (Course No. 2), Lawndale (Par 3, 1950); Singing Hills CC (Oak Glen Course), El Cajon (1967); Singing Hills CC (Pine Glen Course), El Cajon (Precision, 1967).

Frederic Clark Hood (1886 - 1942)
Born: Chelsea, Massachusetts. Died: Boston, Massachusetts at age 76.

Although A.C.M. Croome (Liphook), H.C. Leeds (Myopia) and Hugh Wilson (Merion) are often referred to as "one-time architects," the truth is that each was active in the design of several layouts. In contrast, Frederick C. Hood of Kittanset was truly a "one-timer."

Founder and President of the Hood Rubber Company, F.C. Hood was responsible for planning The Kittansett Club at Marion, Mass., built in 1923. While credit for the design is sometimes given to William S. Flynn and his friend Hugh Wilson, and while club records indicate that several experts, including Donald Ross, were consulted, no construction contract was ever awarded to any architect. Instead, Hood, working from preliminary plans prepared by Flynn, completed specifications and acted as construction superintendent of a crew of local men with Kittansett's future greenkeeper, Elliot "Mike" Pierce, as foreman. Most of Flynn's plans were changed by Hood, but he did give credit to Wilson and Flynn for creation of the famous third hole that plays over a beach and ocean cove.

F.C. Hood should not be confused with F.G. Hood, who designed several courses in New Zealand.

Charles "Gus" Hook

Gus Hook was the Director of Parks and Recreation for Baltimore, Md. for several decades. In this capacity he designed three new municipal courses and remodeled two others.
Courses by: Gus Hook
Maryland: Carroll Park Muni, Baltimore; Mount Pleasant Muni, Baltimore (1933); Pine Ridge Muni, Lutherville (1959).
Courses Remodeled & Added to by: Gus Hook
Maryland: Clifton Park Muni, Baltimore (R.); Forest Park Muni, Baltimore (R.).

Stafford Vere Hotchkin (1876 - 1953)
Born: Woodhall Spa, Lincolnshire, England. Died: Woodhall Spa, Lincolnshire, England at age 77.

S.V. Hotchkin served in the Leicestershire Yeomanry during World War I. An officer in the 17th Lancers, he attained the rank of Colonel by the time of his retirement from the military. In 1922-23 he served as a Conservative Member of Parliament and for many years held the post of alderman in the Lincolnshire County Council.

Hotchkin's first golf design experience was the remodeling of his home course, Woodhall Spa, which he purchased in 1920. He then formed Ferigna Ltd., a firm that dealt with all phases of the golf course business, including design, construction, maintenance, equipment and seed. In the mid-1920s he made an extended tour of South Africa, designing or remodeling a number of the nation's top courses, and many considered him the best architect to have worked there.

In 1930 Hotchkin was joined by fellow military officers Cecil Hutchison and Guy Campbell in a golf design partnership. After a few years, Hutchison and Campbell went into business for themselves, and Hotchkin continued designing on his own until World War II. He then retired to serve as secretary at Woodhall Spa, a position that was later held by his son Neil.
Courses by: S.V. Hotchkin
England: Ashridge GC, Hertfordshire (1932), with Sir Guy Campbell and C.K. Hutchison; Grimsby GC, Lincolnshire (1923); Kington GC, Herefordshire (1926), with C.K. Hutchison and Sir Guy Campbell; Leeds Castle GC, with Sir Guy Campbell and C.K. Hutchison; Links GC, Newmarket; Purley Downs GC, Surrey; RAF Cranwell GC; Sandilands GC, Sutton-on-Sea; Shoreham GC, Southdown , with Sir Guy Campbell and C.K. Hutchison; Stoke Rochford GC, Lincolnshire (1924); Warsash GC, with Sir Guy Campbell and C.K. Hutchison; West Sussex GC, Sussex (1930), with Sir Guy Campbell and C.K. Hutchison.
South Africa: Humewood CC, Port Elizabeth (1929); Maccauvlei CC, Transvaal (1926); Mobray CC, Cape Province (1923); Port Elizabeth GC.
Courses Remodeled & Added to by: S.V. Hotchkin
England: Royal West Norfolk GC, Norfolk (R., 1928), with C.K. Hutchison and Sir Guy Campbell; Woodhall Spa GC, Lincolnshire (R., 1922); Woodhall Spa GC, Lincolnshire (R., 1926), with Sir Guy Campbell and C.K. Hutchison.
Scotland: North Berwick GC, East Lothian (R., 1930), with Sir Guy Campbell and C.K. Hutchison.
South Africa: Durban CC (R., 1928); East London CC, Cape Province (R.); Mowbray CC (R.); Royal Port Alfred GC, Port Elizabeth (R.).

Hugh Leon Howard (1928 -   )
Born: Graham, Texas.

Leon Howard studied agronomy at Texas A & M University, receiving a Bachelor's Degree in 1954 and a Master's Degree in 1959. While in school, he worked part-time remodeling greens on local golf courses. The experience formed the basis for his Master's thesis, *Compaction Problems in Putting Green Soils*, which was later referred to by the USGA Green Section Committee in preparing their specifications for greens construction.

Howard designed and built his first original layout in 1958. The next year he formed a Texas-based landscape architecture firm, concentrating on the design and construction of golf courses in the southwestern United States. Until 1965 he was assisted by David Bennett. In the mid-1970s was joined by his brother, Charles Howard.
Courses by: Leon Howard
Alabama: Willowbrook CC, Huntsville (1966).
Arkansas: Hindman Park GC, Little Rock (1967); Indian Hills GC, Fairfield Bay (1976), with Charles Howard; Lake DeGray State Park GC, Bismarck (1976), with Charles Howard; Red Apple Inn GC, Heber Springs (9, 1969).
Colorado: Eagle CC, Broomfield (9, 1961).
Kansas: Schilling AFB GC, Salina (NLE, 1965).
Mississippi: Greenville Muni (1968); Mississippi Valley State Univ GC, Greenwood (1973).
Nebraska: Applewood Muni, Omaha (1970).
New Mexico: Conchos Lake GC, Conchos (9, 1967); Gallup Muni (9, 1965); Sierra

Vista GC, White Sands .
Oklahoma: Durant CC; Page Belcher Muni (Course No. 1), Tulsa (1977); Trails GC, Moore (1979), with Charles Howard.
Tennessee: Druid Hills GC, Fairfield Glade (1971); Mill Creek GC, Nashville (1973); Temple Hills CC, Columbia (1973); Two Rivers Muni, Nashville (1974), with Charles Howard.
Texas: Bar-K GC, Lago Vista (Par 3, 9); Brownwood CC (1970); Casa Blanca GC, Laredo (1967); Casaview CC, Dallas (NLE,); Castro CC (9); Chaparral CC, Sequin (1970); Clear Creek GC, Killeen (1970); Cleburne Muni; Corpus Christi G Center (27, 1965); Deer Trail CC, Woodville (9); DeCordova Bend CC, Granbury; Diboll Muni (9, 1968); Dyess AFB GC, Abilene (9); Freestone CC, Teague (9); Granbury GC (9); Harker Heights Muni (1966); Harlingen CC (1968); Hempstead CC (9); Highland Lakes GC, Kingsland (1967); Holly Lake Ranch GC, Hawkins (1971); Hurricane Creek CC, Anna (1970); Kaufman GC; L.B. Houston Muni, Dallas (1969); Lago Vista CC, Lake Travis (1971); Lake Bastrop GC; Lakeway GC (Live Oak Course), Lake Travis (1966); Lakeway GC (Yaupon Course), Lake Travis (1971); Lakewood Village GC; Landa Park GC, New Braufels (1969); Lost Pines GC, Bastrop (9, 1973); M & W GC, Winnsboro (1970); Meadowlakes G&CC, Marble Falls (NLE, 9, 1972); Mesquite Muni (1965); Morris Williams Muni, Austin (1965); Nocona Hills CC (1974), with Charles Howard; Nolan River CC; Oak Ridge CC, Madisonville (9); Olney G&CC; Pecan Plantation GC, Granbury (1971); Pedernales CC, Spicewood (9, 1967); Pinewood GC, Beaumont (1961); Red Oaks GC; River Hills CC, Robstown (1965); Riverview CC, Cleburne (1964); Rockdale CC (9, 1965); Rolling Hills CC, Moody; Ross Rogers Muni (Course No. 1), Amarillo (1968); Ross Rogers Muni (Course No. 2), Amarillo (1977), with Charles Howard; Shady Oaks GC, Baird (1967); Sherill Park Muni (East Course), Richardson (1973); Sherill Park Muni (West Course), Richardson (1980), with Charles Howard; Sinton Muni (1968); Sotogrande G&TC, Fort Worth (Par 3, 1969); Spring Lake CC, Rosebud (1967); Sun Country Resort GC, Lake Whitney (1969); Van Zandt CC, Canton (1966); Webb Hill CC, Wolfe City (1968); Western Hills CC, Ft. Worth (1969); Wildflower CC, Temple (1987), with Charles Howard; Wildwood CC, Beaumont (1966); Woodcreek CC (Cypress Creek Course), Wimberley (NLE, 1977); Woodhaven CC, Ft. Worth (1969); World of Resorts GC, Lago Vista (1976), with Charles Howard.
Virginia: Burke Lake Park GC, Annandale (Par 3, 1970); Greendale Muni, Alexandria (1977), with Charles Howard; Ross Hill Muni, Annadale (1973).
Courses Remodeled & Added to by: Leon Howard
Arkansas: Texarkana CC (R.).
Louisiana: Shreveport C (R.9, 1958).
New Mexico: Albuquerque CC (R., 1964).
Texas: Columbian C, Carrollton (A.9, 1960); Hilltop Lakes GC, Normangee (A.9, 1970); Lakewood CC, Dallas (R., 1964); Point Venture Y&CC, Jonestown (A.9, 1974), with Charles Howard.

Melvin A. "Curley" Hueston (1895 - 1978)
Died: Seattle, Washington at age 83.

A PGA professional for over 50 years, Mel "Curley" Hueston served at a succession of courses in the State of Washington, including 15 years at Indian Canyon GC in Spokane. Curley also designed a number of golf courses in the Pacific Northwest.
Courses by: Mel "Curley" Hueston
Idaho: Avondale-on-Hayden GC, Hayden Lake (1968); Coeur D'Alene GC (1956).
Washington: Liberty Lake GC, Spokane; Moses Lake GC (1956); Othello G&CC (9); Sham-Na-Pum GC, Richland .

Henry Barry Hughes (1908 -   )
Born: Chillicothe, Missouri.

Henry B. Hughes was the son of Henry T. Hughes, a construction superintendent for Donald Ross at The Broadmoor in Colorado. While Henry was too young to join father's Lawrence and Frank on their father's construction crew, he did herd the sheep used in those days to clip grass around the fairways.

In 1924 the senior Hughes moved his family to Denver, where he constructed Cherry Hills CC for William S. Flynn and remained as its greenkeeper. While Lawrence and Frank went to work for Ross, Henry served on his father's crew until 1933, when he took over the head greenkeeper position.

Hughes remained at Cherry Hills until 1947, then traveled to Mexico City to construct Club de Golf de Mexico for his brother Lawrence. He returned to Denver in 1950 and for the next thirteen years served as superintendent at Green Gables GC and designed courses in the Rocky Mountain area. By the mid-1960s he was devoting full time to golf architecture, retaining an associate, Richard Watson.

Hughes retired from design work in 1970 but remained active in golf, operating a course in Denver that catered to senior play.
Courses by: Henry B. Hughes
Colorado: Aurora Hills GC, Aurora (1969); Bookcliff CC, Grand Junction (9, 1958); Columbine CC, Littleton (1955); CC of Fort Collins (9, 1960); Estes Park GC (1958); Glenwood Springs GC (9, 1953); Hyland Hills CC, Bloomfield (27, 1959); John F. Kennedy Muni, Denver (27, 1968); Lake Estes GC, Estes Park (Precision, 9); Limon GC (9, 1967); Loveland GC (9, 1960); Meadow Hills GC, Denver (1957); Meeker CC (9, 1971); Montrose CC (9, 1961); Paradise Valley CC, Englewood (27, 1961); Riverdale GC (Knolls Course), Brighton (1965); Sterling CC (1956); Twilight GC, Denver (Par 3, 9, 1960); Valley Hi GC, Colorado Springs (1958); Windsor Gardens GC, Denver (Precision, 9, 1963).
Kansas: Belleville CC (9, 1968), with Richard Watson; Scott County GC, Scott City (9, 1968), with Richard Watson.
Nebraska: Ashland CC (9, 1968), with Richard Watson; Atkinson-Stuart GC (9, 1969), with Richard Watson; Bloomfield-Wausa GC (9, 1969), with Richard Watson; Colonial GC, Lincoln (NLE, Par 3, 9, 1964), with Richard Watson; Friend CC (9, 1967), with Richard Watson; Mid-County CC, Arapahoe (9, 1968), with Richard Watson; Wayne CC (9, 1969), with Richard Watson.
Texas: Hunsley Hills CC, Canyon (1962).
Utah: Willow Creek CC, Sandy (1959).
Wyoming: Midway GC, Greybull (9, 1970), with Richard Watson; Old Baldy C,

Saratoga (1964); Paradise Valley CC, Casper (1958); Rolling Green CC, Green River (9, 1967).

Courses Remodeled & Added to by: Henry B. Hughes

Colorado: Columbine CC, Littleton (R., 1966); CC of Fort Collins (A.9, 1969); Fort Morgan Muni (R.9); Fort Morgan Muni (A.9); Hillcrest CC, Durango (R.9, 1954); Hillcrest CC, Durango (R.9, 1969); Overland Park Muni, Denver (R., 1966); Pueblo CC (A.9); Pueblo CC (R.9).

Lawrence Marion Hughes (1897 - 1975) ASGCA

Born: Chillicothe, Missouri. Died: San Diego, California at age 78.

Lawrence Hughes's father, Henry T. Hughes, was employed as construction supervisor for Donald Ross, and in their late teens Larry and brother Frank went to work for him on The Broadmoor. After discharge from the Army following World War I, Hughes returned to work for Ross, building a number of courses for him before settling down upon completion of Holston Hills CC in Knoxville, Tenn. to serve as its manager and greenkeeper.

During the Depression, Hughes operated a garage in Denver, Colo. and did a little course design work on the side. But it was not until after World War II that he was offered the opportunity to establish a full-time business. In 1946 he met Johnny Dawson, prominent amateur golfer, member of a golfing family and avid real estate promoter. Dawson was sure of the value of development in Southern California and convinced Hughes that there were sufficient underground springs to support golf courses on its desertlike terrain. With Dawson raising the financial backing, Hughes began designing. In 1947 his first course, Mission Valley CC in San Diego (later renamed Stardust CC) opened for play. For the next two decades he continued to create courses in the Southwest and in Mexico, beginning with Club de Golf de Mexico, done with the help of Mexican golfer Percy Clifford in 1950. Hughes was assisted on many of his jobs by his brothers Frank and Henry and apprentice Harry Rainville. Henry Hughes and Harry Rainville both went on to form successful golf design businesses of their own.

Courses by: Lawrence Hughes

Arizona: Antelope Hills GC, Prescott (1956); London Bridge GC, Lake Havasu City (1970); Orange Tree CC, Scottsdale (1958), with Johnny Bulla; Paradise Valley CC, Scottsdale (1957); Pinewood CC, Munds Park (1958); Scottsdale CC (1954).

California: Corona National GC, Corona (1964); DeAnza Desert CC, Borrego Springs (1959); Eldorado CC, Palm Desert (1958); Green River CC (Orange Course), Corona (1959); Indio Muni (Par 3, 18, 1964); La Canada-Flintridge CC (1962); La Quinta CC (1959); Las Posas CC, Camarillo (1958); Marin GC, Novato (1957); Marine Corps GC, Nebo (Par 3, 1952); Roadrunner Dunes GC, Borrego Springs (Par 3, 1964); Round Hill G&CC, Alamo (1960); Santa Barbara Community GC (1955); Stardust CC, San Diego (1947); Thunderbird CC, Cathedral City (1951); Twentynine Palms Muni; Via Verde CC, San Dimas .

Nevada: Desert Inn & CC, Las Vegas (1952); Reno CC (1958).

South Dakota: Tomahawk Lake GC {formerly Homestead Mine GC}, Deadwood (9).

Texas: Coronado G&CC, El Paso (1961); Shady Oaks CC, Fort Worth (1959), with Robert Trent Jones and Ralph Plummer.

Mexico: Bosques De San Isidro GC, Guadalajara (1973); Club de G de Mexico (1949), with Percy Clifford; Club de G Acozac (1973); Club de G Santa Anita (1969); Club Campestre de Hermosillo, San Buenaventura (27, 1949); Club Santiago Manzanillo (1975); El Campestre Chiluca, Mexico City (1975); Mexicali G&CC (1960); Valle Alto GC, Monterrey (1955).

Courses Remodeled & Added to by: Lawrence Hughes

California: Barbara Worth GC, Holtville (R.).

Mexico: El Cid G&CC, Mazatlan (A.9, 1971); Guadalajara CC (R., 1974).

T. Frank Hummel (1926 -)

Born: La Junta, Colorado.

Frank Hummel attended Willamette University and Colorado University, receiving a B.S. Degree in Engineering in 1948. During the early 1950s, he won many regional amateur golf titles while working as a combustion engineer in Pueblo, Colorado. Turning professional in 1956, he served as club pro in Fort Morgan and later in Greeley.

In the early 1960s Hummel designed and built a second nine at Highland Hills Muni in Greeley. After a few additional projects, he resigned his professional position in 1968 to form a course design firm with Theodore Rupel, superintendent of famed Cherry Hills CC in Denver. In 1970 Hummel formed his own golf design and construction business with offices in Colorado and Arizona. A licensed pilot, he was active through the 1970s creating courses in some of the more remote areas of the Great Plains.

Courses by: Frank Hummel

Colorado: Aspen Muni (1970); Bunker Hill CC, Brush (9); Cedar Ridges GC, Rangley (9, 1986); Collindale GC, Fort Collins (1970); Durango Muni (9); Eisenhower GC (Silver Course), US Air Force Academy (1977); Foxhill CC, Longmont (1973); Gleneagle CC, Colorado Springs (1973); Riverview Muni, Sterling (9, 1972); South Ridge Greens GC, Fort Collins (1984); Twin Peaks Muni, Longmont (1978); Wray CC (9, 1970).

Kansas: Buffalo Dunes Muni, Garden City; Emporia Muni (1970); Hesston Muni (1976); Mariah Hills Muni, Dodge City (1974); Prairie Dog GC, Norton (9, 1969).

Montana: Jawbone Creek GC, Harlowton (9, 1980); Madison Meadows GC, Ennis (9, 1982); Pine Ridge G&CC, Roundup (9, 1982); Powder River CC, Broadus (1982).

Nebraska: Chadron CC (9); Chappell CC (9, 1973); Grand Island Muni (1977); Scottsbluff CC (1976).

Wyoming: Buffalo Muni (9); Gillette CC; Lusk GC (9); Niobrara GC (9); Red Butte CC, Gillette (9, 1981); Westview Park GC, DuBois (9); Wheatland CC (9).

Courses Remodeled & Added to by: Frank Hummel

Colorado: Highland Hills Muni, Greeley (A.9, 1963); Hyland Hills CC, Bloomfield (A.9, 1984); Loveland GC (A.9, 1977).

Wyoming: Kendrick Muni, Sheridan (A.9, 1984).

Charles Hunter (1836 - 1921)

Charles Hunter succeeded Old Tom Morris as greenkeeper and professional at Prestwick. He planned several Scottish courses, including the original Macrihanish, St. Nicholas Prestwick and the original five holes at Troon. His son David emigrated to the United States, where he became professional at Baltusrol and laid out several New Jersey courses.

Wiles Robert Hunter (1874 - 1942)

Born: Terre Haute, Indiana. Died Santa Barbara, California at age 68.

Robert Hunter attended Indiana University, receiving a B.A. Degree in 1896. He was a world-renowned sociologist and author, writing such works as *Poverty* (1904), *Labor in Politics* (1915), *Why We Fail As Christians* (1919) and *Revolution* (1940). He spent his life addressing and attempting to solve serious social problems, was among the organizers of the Chicago Bureau of Charities in the late 1890s, and lived for a time at Jane Addams' Hull House and later at Toynbee Hall in England.

In the early 1900s Hunter served as chairman of the New York Commission for the Abolition of Child Labor. He also participated in a campaign against tuberculosis. In 1910 he ran unsuccessfully for Governor of Connecticut on the Socialist ticket. He later resigned from the party and in 1917 moved to California, where he taught and wrote for years at the University of California at Berkeley.

Ironically, Robert Hunter was also an avid enthusiast of golf, in those days considered an elitist sport. During his stays in Great Britain, he studied the great courses. He had also frequent contact in America with prominent course designers. Hunter wrote one of the classic books in the literature of course architecture, *The Links* (1926), still considered one of the finest essays on the subject and containing some remarkable illustrations of genuine links.

Hunter was instrumental in luring Alister Mackenzie to California and, shortly after publication of *The Links*, began assisting the talented Britisher with most of the courses he did in that state. Although there is little evidence of a formal partnership, most club records list "Mackenzie and Hunter" as the architects of Cypress Point Club (1927), Meadow GC (1928), Northwood CC (1928), and Valley Club of Montecito (1928), and with remodeling of Monterey Peninsula CC and Pebble Beach.

Courses by: Robert Hunter

California: Cypress Point C, Pebble Beach (1928), with Alister Mackenzie; Green Hills CC, Millbrae (1930), with Alister Mackenzie and H. Chandler Egan; Meadow C, Fairfax (1927), with Alister Mackenzie; Mira Vista G&CC {formerly Berkeley CC}, Berkeley (1921), with William Watson; Northwood GC, Guernerville (9, 1928), with Alister Mackenzie; Pittsburg GC (9), with Alister Mackenzie; Valley C of Montecito, Santa Barbara (1928), with Alister Mackenzie.

Courses Remodeled & Added to by: Robert Hunter

California: Monterey Peninsula CC (Dunes Course), Pebble Beach (R., 1928), with Alister Mackenzie; Pebble Beach G Links (R., 1927), with Alister Mackenzie.

May Dunn Hupfel (1880 - 1948)

Born: Wimbledon, England. Died: California at age 68.

May Dunn was the daughter of Tom and Isabella Gourlay Dunn. "Queenie," as she was called throughout her life, learned golf at an early age and competed against her brothers John Duncan and Seymour on makeshift golfing grounds.

Sent to Germany to work as a governess, May married at age 18. The marriage lasted only a short time, but produced a daughter. May returned to Britain to raise her child, and played only social golf for a period of 17 years.

When World War I erupted, May traveled to the United States in hopes of making a living teaching golf to wealthy women. Almost immediately she landed a job writing an instruction series for the New York Herald. Her subsequent efforts at promoting women's golf in America caused many to consider May Dunn as America's first women professional, though in truth she was not.

As a Dunn, it was inevitable that sooner or later she would design a course or two. In 1916, she visited Nevada and laid out both Reno GC and Tahoe Tavern GC. She also served as pro/manager at both.

Both her design and golf professional careers ended in 1920 when she married Californian Adolf Hupfel, but her short foray into golf architecture made her the first woman to actively engage in the golf design business.

Michael John Hurdzan (1943 -) ASGCA, President, 1984.

Born: Wheeling, West Virginia.

Dr. Michael Hurdzan graduated from Ohio State University in 1966 and earned an M.S. in Turfgrass Physiology and a Ph.D. in Environmental Plant Physiology at the University of Vermont. From 1957 to 1966 Hurdzan worked occasionally for golf architect Jack Kidwell of Columbus, Ohio, and in the early 1970s began practicing with him on a full-time basis. In 1976 they formed the partnership of Kidwell and Hurdzan Inc.

Although Hurdzan once stated that the chances of becoming a golf course architect were about equal to that of being struck by lightning, the progress of his own career proved it could be done. During his years at the University of Vermont, he operated a ski and sports shop. He also established the University Tree Service, which engaged in course construction as well as other landscape services. The firm added new nines to Barre (Vt.) CC and Newport (Vt.) CC, and had twenty-eight employees by the time Hurdzan sold it to return to Ohio.

By the late 1970s Kidwell and Hurdzan was one of the most active course design firms in the nation. In addition to his practice, Hurdzan completed a B. Sc. Degree in Landscape Architecture at Ohio State University and taught an advanced turfgrass course there, became a Major in the Special Forces Reserves and wrote monthly columns for Weeds, Trees and Turf and Golf Business magazines. He also found time to work on a book on a history of golf course architecture and to establish an extensive library of golf books and large collection of clubs and balls from past eras.

Courses by: Michael Hurdzan

Indiana: Hidden Valley GC, Lawrenceburg (1976), with Jack Kidwell.

Kentucky: Frances Miller Memorial GC, Murray State Univ. (1982), with Jack Kidwell.

Massachusetts: Dennis Highlands GC, Dennis (1984), with Jack Kidwell.

Ohio: Beckett Ridge G&CC, Cincinnati (1974), with Jack Kidwell; Blue Ash GC (1979), with Jack Kidwell; Buttermilk Falls GC, Georgetown (1981), with Jack Kidwell; Deer Creek State Park GC, Mt. Sterling (1979), with Jack Kidwell; Hickory Hills CC, Georgesville (1979), with Jack Kidwell; Oxbow G&CC, Belpre (1974), with Jack Kidwell; Ridenoor Park GC, Gahanna (Precision, 9, 1976), with Jack Kidwell; San Dar Acres GC, Bellville (Precision, 1976), with Jack Kidwell; Shawnee Lookout GC, Cincinnati (1976), with Jack Kidwell; Shawnee State Park GC, Portsmouth (1979), with Jack Kidwell; Vineyards GC, Cininnati (1986), with Jack Kidwell.

Texas: Oak Ridge CC, Richardson , with Jack Kidwell.

Courses Remodeled & Added to by: Michael Hurdzan
Indiana: Hillcrest G&CC, Batesville (R.9, 1984), with Jack Kidwell.
Kentucky: Kenton County CC, Independence (R.9, 1974), with Jack Kidwell; Kenton County CC, Independence (A, 1981), with Jack Kidwell; Summit Hills CC (A.1, 1980), with Jack Kidwell; Summit Hills CC (R.10, 1980), with Jack Kidwell; World of Golf (R., 1979), with Jack Kidwell; World of Golf (A.10, 1979), with Jack Kidwell.
New York: Troy CC (R.9, 1975), with Jack Kidwell; Troy CC (A.9, 1975), with Jack Kidwell.
Ohio: Brookside CC, Columbus (R.2, 1977), with Jack Kidwell; Brookside Park GC, Ashland (A.9, 1977), with Jack Kidwell; California GC, Cincinnati (A.5, 1975), with Jack Kidwell; Elyria CC (R.2, 1975), with Jack Kidwell; Foxfire GC (A.9, 1984), with Jack Kidwell; Groveport GC (R., 1977), with Jack Kidwell; Kenwood CC (Kendale Course), Cincinnati (R., 1981), with Jack Kidwell; Kenwood CC (Kenview Course), Cincinnati (R., 1977), with Jack Kidwell; Lakewood CC, Westlake (R.1, 1975), with Jack Kidwell; Marion CC (R., 1977), with Jack Kidwell; Miami Shores GC, Troy (R.9, 1977), with Jack Kidwell; Miami Valley CC, Dayton (R., 1980), with Jack Kidwell; Mohican Hills GC, Wooster (A.9, 1975), with Jack Kidwell; Mount Vernon CC (R., 1977), with Jack Kidwell; Neumann Park GC, Cincinnati (A.9, 1975), with Jack Kidwell; Shawnee CC, Lima (R., 1978), with Jack Kidwell; Table Rock GC, Centerburg (A.9, 1976), with Jack Kidwell; Westwood CC, Rocky River (R., 1984), with Jack Kidwell; Wildwood GC, Fairfield (R.3, 1977), with Jack Kidwell; Xenia GC, Xenia (A.9, 1982), with Jack Kidwell; York Temple CC, Columbus (R.1, 1975), with Jack Kidwell; Zanesville CC (R.5, 1981), with Jack Kidwell.
West Virginia: Deerfield CC, Weston (R.9, 1978), with Jack Kidwell; Deerfield CC, Weston (A.9, 1978), with Jack Kidwell.

Horace G. Hutchinson (1859 - 1932)
Born: London, England. Died: London, England at age 73.

Horace Hutchinson, renowned British golfer, won the first two British Amateur championships in 1886 and 1887. He was a prolific golf writer whose numerous publications included the first instruction book on the game, *Hints on Golf* (1886), the *Badminton Book of Golf* (1886) and *Fifty Years of Golf* (1919). Passages in his books provide insight into the development of golf course design during the years when the game was spreading from Scotland to England, throughout the British Empire and to the United States. His references to The National Golf Links of America and Myopia Hunt Club were especially laudatory and helped establish those courses as landmarks in course architecture.

Around 1886 Hutchinson assisted the owner of Royal Eastbourne GC in planning the course. This was the site of the notorious "Paradise Green," with contours so severe that if a player missed the hole on his first putt he might putt forever. Hutchinson was also the designer of Royal West Norfolk in England and the nine-hole Isles of Scilly GC.

Cecil Key Hutchison (1877 - 1941)
Born: East Lothian, Scotland. Died: London, England at age 64.

C.K. Hutchison was educated at Eton College, Windsor, where he excelled at all sports. He played on the cricket team, won the school mile and competed in golf and skating. The son of a locally prominent golfer, he learned the game on the links at Muirfield. By the turn of the century he was one of the top amateurs in Britain, winning the St. George's Challenge Cup in 1903 and 1910, and the Golf Illustrated Gold Vase in 1909. Hutchison represented Scotland in the annual England-Scotland matches each year from 1904 to 1912. He was also runner-up in the 1909 British Amateur Championship, where he tragically bogied the home hole at his own home course, Muirfield, to lose one down.

Hutchison joined the Coldstream Guards, fought in the Boer War and later joined the Royal Scots, attaining the rank of Major. Captured by Germans during World War I, he was confined to a P.O.W. Camp for several years.

After the war, his competitive game having suffered, Hutchison turned instead to golf course design. He served as assistant to James Braid during the construction of Gleneagles and the reconstruction of Carnoustie. In the mid-1920s he formed a firm with Colonel S.V. Hotchkin, who had assisted him with remodeling of Woodhall Spa. Guy Campbell, a former Times sports writer whose background was remarkably similar to Hutchison's, also joined the firm. Together the three designed and built many impressive courses in Great Britain during the period from the late twenties to mid-thirties, when golf development was at a near standstill in the United States.

Hutchison was highly regarded in his time for his refreshing approach to golf design and his eagerness to incorporate innovations in his works.

Courses by: C.K. Hutchison
England: Ashridge GC, Hertfordshire (1932), with Sir Guy Campbell and S.V. Hotchkin; Kington GC, Herefordshire (1926), with Sir Guy Campbell and S.V. Hotchkin; Leeds Castle GC, with Sir Guy Campbell and S.V. Hotchkin; Shoreham GC, Southdown , with Sir Guy Campbell and S.V. Hotchkin; Warsash GC, with Sir Guy Campbell and S.V. Hotchkin; West Sussex GC, Sussex (1930), with Sir Guy Campbell and S.V. Hotchkin.
Scotland: Gleneagles Hotel GC (Kings Course), Perthshire (1919), with James Braid; Gleneagles Hotel GC (Queen's Course), Perthshire (1919), with James Braid.
Courses Remodeled & Added to by: C.K. Hutchison
England: Ganton GC (R.); Prince's GC (Blue Course), Kent (R.); Royal West Norfolk GC, Norfolk (R., 1928), with Sir Guy Campbell and S.V. Hotchkin; Sundridge Park GC (East Course), Kent (R., 1927), with Sir Guy Campbell; Tadmarton Heath

GC, Banbury (A.9, 1923); Woodhall Spa GC, Lincolnshire (R., 1926), with Sir Guy Campbell and S.V. Hotchkin.
Scotland: North Berwick GC, East Lothian (R., 1930), with Sir Guy Campbell and S.V. Hotchkin; Pitlochry GC, Perthshire (R.); Turnberry GC (Ailsa Course), Ayrshire (R., 1938).

Seichi Inouye (1905 -   )
One of Japan's leading golf course architects, Seichi Inouye worked under Kinya Fujita for many years before going out on his own. Inouye designed over thirty-five courses in the Far East during his career.
Courses by: Seichi Inouye
Japan: Kasugai CC (East Course), Nagoya; Kasugai CC (West Course), Nagoya; Kyushu Shima CC (1964); Musashi CC (Sasai Course), Saitama (1959); Musashi CC (Toyoka Course), Saitama (1959); Takanodai CC, Chiba (1954); Totsuka CC (West Course), Kanagawa (1961); Yomiuri CC, Tokyo (1964); Yomiuri CC (Blue Course), Osaka; Yomiuri CC (Red Course), Osaka .

Arthur J. Jackson (1894 - 1981)
Born: Scotland. Died: Oklahoma City, Oklahoma at age 87.

Born in Scotland, Arthur Jackson traveled to America in the early 1900s to join his stepbrother Leslie Brownlee in the Oklahoma Territory. After constructing the first golf courses in Oklahoma to Brownlee's designs, Jackson served as professional at a succession of clubs. While at Tulsa CC just before World War I, he laid out his first course on the Ponca City estate of E.W. Marland, oil magnate and later Governor of Oklahoma.

In 1920 Jackson designed and built Lincoln Park Municipal in Oklahoma City. He remained as its pro until his retirement in 1952. He continued to design courses throughout his tenure at Lincoln Park and even did a few in the Oklahoma City area after retirement.

Jackson organized the Oklahoma section of the PGA of America. He was an outstanding teacher and trainer of young professional golfers, and among his assistants at Lincoln Park were U.C. Ferguson (who succeeded him at the course), Ralph Hutchinson (who served for many years at Saucon Valley) and Ralph's brother, Willard.

Courses by: Arthur Jackson
Oklahoma: Airport GC, Oklahoma City (NLE,); Lew Wentz Memorial GC, Ponca City (9, 1951); Lincoln Park Muni (East Course), Oklahoma City (1932); Lincoln Park Muni (West Course), Oklahoma City (1921); Marland Estate GC, Ponca City (NLE, 9, 1915); McAlester CC (NLE,); Northwest Park Muni, Oklahoma City (NLE, 1933); Southwest Park Muni, Oklahoma City (NLE, 1932); Trosper Park GC, Oklahoma City (1958); Woodson Park GC, Oklahoma City (NLE,).
Courses Remodeled & Added to by: Arthur Jackson
Oklahoma: Frederick GC (R.), 1949).

Thomas Ridgeway Jackson Jr. (1941 -   )
Born: Kennett Square, Pennsylvania.

Tom Jackson trained under and worked for golf architect Robert Trent Jones from 1965 to 1968. After a five-year stint as an assistant to designer George Cobb, he entered private practice in 1973.

Over the next dozen years, Jackson designed over thirty courses in the Southeast.
Courses by: Tom Jackson
Alabama: Terri Pines CC, Culman (1984).
Florida: East Lake Woodlands G&CC (South Course), Oldsmar (1974); Sandestin GC (Baytowne Course), Destin (1985); Sandestin GC (Links Course), Destin (1976).
North Carolina: Carolina Shores GC, Calabash (1975); Granada Farms CC, Granite; High Vista CC, Arden (1978); Hyland Hills GC, Southern Pines (1974); Ine's Lodge GC, Laurinburg (1984); Land Harbour GC, Blowing Rock (Precision, 1982); Links O'Tryon, Tryon (1987); Midland Farms CC, Pinehurst; Willow Creek GC, Blowing Rock (Precision, 9).
South Carolina: Fairfield Ocean Ridge GC {formerly Oristo G&RC}, Edisto Island (1973); Hickory Knob State Park GC, McCormack (1982); Pebble Creek CC, Taylors (1976); River C, Pawley's Island (1985); Spartanburg GC, Roebuck (1984).
Courses Remodeled & Added to by: Tom Jackson
Georgia: Sea Palms G&CC, St. Simons Island (A.9, 1974).
North Carolina: Hound Ear CC, Blowing Rock (R.); Oakwoods CC, North Wilkesboro (R.); Quail Hollow CC, Charlotte (R., 1974); Sapphire Lakes CC, Sapphire (A.9, 1985).
South Carolina: Summersett CC, Travelers Rest (R., 1979).

Francis L. James (- 1952)
Died: Moscow, Idaho.

Frank James served as Western States Representative for William H. Tucker & Son in the Pacific Northwest during the 1910s and early 1920s. In that capacity, James supervised construction of many Tucker layouts as well as the designs of other architects built by Tucker's company.

By 1924 James had formed his own design-and-build company. When the economy curtailed course construction in the early Thirties, James worked as pro-manager of a series of clubs, laying out courses on the side during those years. He returned to full-time course design after World War II, and remained active until his death in 1952.
Courses by: Frank James
Idaho: Pinecrest Muni, Idaho Falls; Rolling Hills GC, Weisner (9, 1947); University of Idaho GC, Moscow (9, 1937).
Montana: Missoula CC (9, 1949).
Oregon: Pendleton CC (9, 1957).
Washington: Jackson Park Muni, Seattle , with William H. Tucker; Linden G&CC, Puyallup (9), with William H. Tucker and Gregor MacMillan; Mapleview G&CC, Renton (1933); Olympia G&CC (9), with William H. Tucker; Roche Harbor GC, San Juan , with William H. Tucker and Gregor MacMillan; Sands Point CC, Seattle (1928), with William H. Tucker; Veterans Memorial GC, Walla Walla .

Courses Remodeled & Added to by: Frank James
Washington: Walla Walla CC (A.9, 1947).

Alfred Jamison (1908 -   )
Born: Wilmington, Delaware.
   Following a long career as a professional, Al Jamison was associated with golf architect Edward B. Ault in the 1950s. After the firm of Ault and Jamison was dissolved in the latter part of the decade, Jamison designed a few courses on his own before his retirement.
Courses by: Al Jamison
Delaware: Dover AFB GC (9, 1961), with Edmund B. Ault.
Maryland: Chartwell G&CC (1961), with Edmund B. Ault; Falls Road Muni (1960), with Edmund B. Ault; Hawthorne CC (9, 1960), with Edmund B. Ault; Lakewood CC (1960), with Edmund B. Ault; Oakcrest CC (1969), with Edmund B. Ault; Poolesville GC (1959), with Edmund B. Ault; Sligo Park GC (9, 1956), with Edmund B. Ault; Turf Valley CC (North Course) (1959), with Edmund B. Ault.
Missouri: Meadow Lake Acres CC (1961), with Edmund B. Ault.
Pennsylvania: Pleasant View GC (1960), with Edmund B. Ault.
Virginia: Bolling AFB GC (1960), with Edmund B. Ault; Bushfield CC (9, 1962), with Edmund B. Ault; Chantilly National G&CC (1960), with Edmund B. Ault; Edwin R.Carr Estate GC (1959), with Edmund B. Ault; Gordon Trent GC, Martinsville (1962), with Claude Bingham; Lake Fairfax GC (1959), with Edmund B. Ault; Lake Wright GC, Norfolk (1966); Loudoun G&CC (1959), with Edmund B. Ault; Pinecrest CC (Course No. 2), Fairfax; River Bend G&CC {formerly Forest Lake CC} (1960), with Edmund B. Ault; Springfield G&CC (1960), with Edmund B. Ault.
Courses Remodeled & Added to by: Al Jamison
Delaware: Shawnee CC (A.9, 1960), with Edmund B. Ault.
Maryland: Argyle CC, Chevy Chase (R., 1960), with Edmund B. Ault; Silver Springs GC (R., 1958), with Edmund B. Ault.
Virginia: Washington G&CC, Arlington (R.).

Donald Ray January (1929 -   )
Born: Plainfield, Texas.
   Well-known touring professional Don January collaborated with Billy Martindale on the planning of several courses in the southwest during the mid-1970s.
Courses by: Don January
Oklahoma: Walnut Creek CC, Oklahoma City (1976), with Billy Martindale.
Texas: Great Hills GC, Austin , with Billy Martindale; Los Rios CC, Plano (1974), with Billy Martindale; Plano Muni, with Billy Martindale; Royal Oaks CC, Dallas (1970), with Billy Martindale; Walnut Creek GC, Mansfield , with Billy Martindale; Woodcrest CC, Grand Prairie , with Billy Martindale; Woodland Hills GC, Nacogdoches , with Billy Martindale.
Courses Remodeled & Added to by: Don January
Texas: Lake Country Estates GC, Ft. Worth (A.9, 1975), with Billy Martindale.

Alfred Harry French Jiggens (1908 - 1985) BAGCA
Born: England. Died: Chester, England at age 76.
   A chartered surveyor and civil engineer, A.H.F. Jiggens served in local governments for over fifty years. Retiring in 1968, "Jigg" joined the golf design firm of F.W. Hawtree. Concentrating primarily on the business aspects of the firm and engineering problems of courses, Jigg did personally handle the designs of several layouts in the late 1970s.
   Jiggens was a founding member of the BAGCA and had been inducted as a Senior Member shortly before his death.
Courses by: A.H.F. Jiggens
England: Chester GC (1973), with Fred W. Hawtree; Chorley GC (18), with Fred W. Hawtree; Congleton GC, with Fred W. Hawtree; Duxbury Park GC, Lancashire (1975), with Fred W. Hawtree and Martin Hawtree; Eastham Lodge GC, Cheshire (9, 1975), with Fred W. Hawtree and Martin Hawtree; Enmore Park GC, Somerset (1975), with Fred W. Hawtree; Malkins Bank GC, Cheshire (1980), with Fred W. Hawtree; Normanby Hall GC, Lincolnshire (1978), with Fred W. Hawtree; Scunthorpe GC, Lincolnshire , with Fred W. Hawtree; Tamworth Muni, Staffordshire (1975), with Fred W. Hawtree and Martin Hawtree; Wellingborough GC, Northhamptonshire , with Fred W. Hawtree; Widnes Muni, Lancashire (9, 1977), with Fred W. Hawtree; Worsley GC, Lancashire , with Fred W. Hawtree.
Ireland: Corballis GC, County Dublin , with Fred W. Hawtree; Forest Little GC, County Dublin (1972), with Fred W. Hawtree; Westport GC, County Mayo , with Fred W. Hawtree and Martin Hawtree.
Courses Remodeled & Added to by: A.H.F. Jiggens
England: Bromborough GC (R.), with Fred W. Hawtree; Enmore Park GC, Somerset (A.9, 1979), with Fred W. Hawtree; Huyton & Prescot GC (R.), with Fred W. Hawtree; Ipswich GC, Purdis Heath (Precision, A.9), with Fred W. Hawtree; Nelson GC, Lancashire (A.9), with Fred W. Hawtree; Oakdale GC, Yorkshire (R.7, 1977), with Fred W. Hawtree; Wellingborough GC, Northhamptonshire (R., 1983), with Fred W. Hawtree; Worcestershire GC (A.9), with Fred W. Hawtree; Worsley GC, Lancashire (A.9), with Fred W. Hawtree.
Ireland: Woodbrook GC, County Dublin (R.), with Fred W. Hawtree and Martin Hawtree; Woodbrook GC, County Dublin (A.2), with Fred W. Hawtree and Martin Hawtree.
Wales: Nefyn and District GC, Gwynedd (R.), with Fred W. Hawtree.

Leo I. Johnson (1918 -   )
Born: Homer, Nebraska.
   In 1935 Leo Johnson began working at Sioux City (Iowa) CC, where he eventually became course superintendent. He designed, built, owned and operated a nine-hole par-3 course, Sun Valley GC, in Sioux City in the 1950s. Johnson left Sioux City in 1958 to pursue a career in course design and was still active in the 1970s based in the Phoenix-Tucson area.

Courses by: Leo Johnson
Iowa: Ankeny G&CC (9); Brookside GC, Kingsley (1965); Emerald Hills GC, Arnolds Park (1973); Quail Creek GC, North Liberty (1970); Sun Valley CC, Sioux City (Par 3, 9, 1961); Van Buren GC, Keosauqua (1970).
Kansas: Lakewood CC {formerly Paganica CC}, Hutchinson (1972).
Minnesota: Brightwood Hills GC, New Brighton (1969); Worthington CC.
Montana: Cottonwood CC, Glendive (9, 1962).
North Dakota: Cando GC (1968); Riverwood Muni, Bismarck (1969).
Courses Remodeled & Added to by: Leo Johnson
Kansas: Council Grove CC (R.9, 1970); Elkhart GC (R.9, 1969); Eureka GC (R.9, 1969).
Nebraska: Kearney CC (R.9, 1972); Kearney CC (A.9, 1972).

Walter Irving Johnson Jr.
   Walter Johnson was associated with golf architect Donald Ross until Ross's death. He then established his own practice on a part-time basis.
Courses by: Walter I. Johnson
Florida: Palma Sola GC, Bradenton (1924), with Donald Ross.
Massachusetts: Fresh Pond Muni, Cambridge (9, 1932); Sun Valley GC (Routing).
Rhode Island: North Kingstown Muni (1944).
Courses Remodeled & Added to by: Walter I. Johnson
North Carolina: CC of Salisbury (R.), with Donald Ross.
Rhode Island: Potowomat CC, Warwick (A.9, 1928).

William H. Johnson (1898 - 1979) ASGCA
Born: Pittsburg, Kansas. Died: Los Angeles, California at age 80.
   Bill Johnson, who had worked on a number of railroad crews as a youth, joined Willie Watson's construction crew at Lake Arrowhead, Calif. in 1924. After working on other course construction projects for Watson and William P. Bell, Johnson became greenkeeper of the Los Angeles County Parks System in 1931. He remained in that position until 1958, gaining a wide reputation as a turfgrass expert. Johnson designed his first golf course, a new nine-hole "Roosevelt" layout at Griffith Park, when the original course had been taken over by an expansion of the nearby zoo.
   Johnson began designing courses steadily after World War II, working first on a series of collaborations with William P. Bell and later on his own. An honorary member of the Southern California PGA, Johnson belonged to the GCSAA and served as its President in 1951.
Courses by: William H. Johnson
California: Alondra Park GC (Course No. 1), Lawndale (1947), with William P. Bell; Arroyo Seco GC, Banning (Par 3, 1960); Big Tee GC, Buena Park (Par 3, 9, 1947); Compton GC, Los Angeles (Par 3, 9, 1952); Devonshire GC, Chatsworth (Par 3, 27, 1959); DeBell GC, Burbank (1958), with William F. Bell; Donneybrook GC, San Bernardino (NLE, Par 3, 1961); El Caballero CC, Tarzana (1957); El Camino CC, Oceanside (1953); Glen Avon GC (Par 3, 1959); Griffith Park GC (Coolidge Course), Los Angeles (Par 3, 9, 1941); Griffith Park GC (Los Feliz Course), Los Angeles (Par 3, 9, 1944); Griffith Park GC (Roosevelt Course), Los Angeles (9, 1933); Harbor Park GC, Wilmington (9, 1957); Knollwood CC, Granada Hills (1957), with William F. Bell; Massacre Canyon Inn & CC (River), Gilman Hot Springs (NLE, 9, 1958); Oceanside GC (1957); Pala Mesa G&TC, Fallbrook (1961); Pedley Par 3 GC, Los Angeles (Par 3,); Rancho Park GC, Los Angeles (1947), with William P. Bell; Roy Rogers GC, Chatsworth (Par 3, 9, 1956); San Fernando VA Hospital GC (Par 3, 9); San Gorgonio GC, Banning (Par 3, 9, 1962); Sepulveda GC (Balboa Course) (1953), with William F. Bell and William P. Bell; Sepulveda GC (Encino Course) (1953), with William F. Bell and William P. Bell; Sepulveda VA Hospital GC, Encino (Par 3, 9); Silver Creek GC, San Bernardino (9, 1960); Singing Hills CC (Willow Glen Course), El Cajon (1953), with William F. Bell and William P. Bell; South Gate GC (Par 3, 9, 1948); Squires GC, Fallbrook (Par 3, 9, 1961); Twin Lakes GC, El Monte (Par 3, 1954).
Courses Remodeled & Added to by: William H. Johnson
California: Bel-Air CC, Los Angeles (R.3, 1958); Glendora CC (R.9); Griffith Park GC (Harding Course) (R.9, 1948); Griffith Park GC (Wilson Course), Los Angeles (R., 1948); Victoria GC, Riverside (R.3, 1958).

Clement B. "Johnny" Johnston (1922 - 1982)
Born: North Carolina. Died: Enfield, North Carolina at age 60. Interred: Wake Forest, North Carolina.
   A longtime PGA professional, Johnny Johnston served as golf coach for Wake Forest in the late 1940s and early 1950s for teams that included young Arnold Palmer. Johnston later served as head professional at several North Carolina clubs, including Sea Scape GC in Kitty Hawk and Echo Farms G&CC in Wilmington.
   A former officer in the Carolinas PGA, and its "Pro of the Year" in 1975, Johnston became a Quarter Century member of the PGA of America shortly before his death in 1982.
   Johnston dabbled in golf course design throughout his professional life. His first design was at Reidsville, N.C., done after leaving Wake Forest. Over the years he handled several low-budget layouts around North Carolina. In his last years he was assisted by his son Clyde, who subsequently pursued a full-time career in golf architecture.
Courses by: Clement B. "Johnny" Johnston
North Carolina: Sumner Hills GC, with Clyde Johnston; Tamarac GC, Reidville (1956).
Courses Remodeled & Added to by: Clement B. "Johnny" Johnston
North Carolina: Echo Farms G&CC, Wilmington (R., 1978), with Clyde Johnston; Scotfield CC, Enfield (R.), with Clyde Johnston.

Clyde B. Johnston (1952 -   ) ASGCA
Born: Houston, Texas.
   The son of one-time Wake Forest coach Johnny Johnston, Clyde Johnston learned the game at an early age. As a teenager he assisted his father both in pro shop operations and in several course-remodeling projects.
   Johnston obtained a Bachelor of Landscape Architecture degree from North

Carolina State University in 1973. He then worked for two years as a landscape architect for Willard Byrd and Associates in Atlanta. After a year with the golf design firm of Kirby, Player and Associates, Johnston rejoined Willard Byrd in 1977, this time serving as both a landscape and golf course architect. Johnston operated a branch of the firm from the South Carolina coast, where he supervised several golf design projects on Hilton Head Island and the Charleston area in the 1980s.

Johnston became a member of the ASLA in 1977, and later became a member of the ASGCA.

Courses by: Clyde Johnston
Florida: Longboat Key C (Harborside Course), Sarasota (1983), with Willard Byrd.
Georgia: Landings at Skidaway Island (Plantation) (1984), with Willard Byrd.
North Carolina: Sumner Hills GC, with Clement B. "Johnny" Johnston.
South Carolina: Heather Glen GC, Little River (1987), with Willard Byrd; Indigo Run GC, Hilton Head Island (27, 1987), with Willard Byrd; Patriots Point G Links, Charleston (1984), with Willard Byrd; Port Royal GC (Planters Row Course), Hilton Head Island (1984), with Willard Byrd; Shipyard GC (Brigantine Nine), Hilton Head Island (9, 1982), with Willard Byrd; Wexford GC, Hilton Head Island (1984), with Willard Byrd.

Courses Remodeled & Added to by: Clyde Johnston
Alabama: CC of Mobile (R.), with Willard Byrd.
Florida: Longboat Key C (Islandside Course), Sarasota (R., 1984), with Willard Byrd; Ponce de Leon CC, St. Augustine (A.2, 1977), with Willard Byrd; Ponce de Leon CC, St. Augustine (R.2, 1977), with Willard Byrd.
Georgia: Griffin CC (A.9, 1979).
North Carolina: Alamance CC, Burlington (R.), with Willard Byrd; Echo Farms G&CC, Wilmington (R., 1978), with Clement B. "Johnny" Johnston; Emorywood CC, High Point (R., 1980), with Willard Byrd; Scotfield CC, Enfield (R.), with Clement B. "Johnny" Johnston.
South Carolina: Port Royal GC (Barony Course), Hilton Head Island (R., 1984), with Willard Byrd; Port Royal GC (Robbers Row Course), Hilton Head Island (R., 1984), with Willard Byrd.

William Johnston (1925 -)
Born: Donora, Pennsylvania.
Bill Johnston grew up in Ogden, Utah. After service in the Navy during World War II, he attended the University of Utah, where he played on the golf team. Upon his graduation in 1950, Johnston became a professional golfer, and that same year also participated in his first golf course design.
Johnston spent fifteen years on the PGA Tour, during which he won the Utah Open. He then served as head professional at a series of Arizona golf clubs. He also resumed designing golf courses.
When he turned fifty, Johnston divided his time between golf design and competition on the newly formed PGA Senior Tour.

Courses by: William Johnston
Arizona: Arizona Biltmore GC (Links Course), Phoenix (1978).
Texas: Dominion CC, San Antonio (1985); Tapatio Springs CC, Boerne (1981).
Utah: Vernal CC (9, 1950).

Courses Remodeled & Added to by: William Johnston
Arizona: Elden Hills GC, Flagstaff (R., 1979).

Robert Johnstone (- 1937)
Born: North Berwick, Scotland. Died: Seattle, Washington.
In 1905 Robert Johnstone became professional at Seattle GC, a position he held for the rest of his life. He laid out a new course for the club in 1907. He later designed several other courses in the Pacific Northwest.

Courses by: Robert Johnstone
California: Ingleside GC, San Francisco (NLE, 1925); Mountaindale CC (NLE,); Potrero G&CC, Inglewood (NLE, 1909); Presidio GC, San Francisco (1914).
Washington: Inglewood CC, Kenmore (1923), with A.Vernon Macan; Lake Ridge GC, Seattle (1930); Mercer Island G&CC; Seattle GC (1907).

Alexander H. Jolly (1882 - 1948)
Born: St. Andrews, Scotland. Died: Michigan at age 66.
A.H. Jolly was one of six brothers who were active in the business world of golf in the U.S. and Canada between 1901 and 1965. Jolly designed several courses in the States, and at each stayed on for a time as full-time summer or winter professional.

Courses by: A.H. Jolly
Arizona: Douglas CC (1947).
Michigan: Gladestone CC (9, 1936); North Shore GC, Menominee (1928); Riverside CC, Menominee (1923).
Wisconsin: Oconto GC (9, 1929).

Courses Remodeled & Added to by: A.H. Jolly
Arizona: Nogales CC (NLE, R., 1945).

Rees Lee Jones (1941 -) ASGCA, President, 1978.
Born: Montclair, New Jersey.
Rees Jones graduated from Yale University with a Degree in History in 1963 and went on to study Landscape Architecture at Harvard University's Graduate School of Design. In 1964 he joined his father's firm, Robert Trent Jones Inc., where he was involved in the design or supervision of over fifty golf courses. Rees Jones entered private practice in golf course design in 1974, and subsequently planned a number of notable layouts on his own.
In 1974 Jones coauthored the influential Urban Land Institute publication *Golf Course Developments* with landscape architect Guy L. Rando. Jones himself designed, collaborated on the design or supervised the construction of each of the developments described in the book.
By 1985, Rees Jones had designed or remodeled over fifty golf courses, including a seventh course for Pinehurst CC in North Carolina. He also restored The Country Club, Brookline, Mass. in preparation for the 1988 U.S. Open.

Courses by: Rees Jones
Alabama: Alpine Bay Y&CC, Alpine (1973), with Robert Trent Jones.
Connecticut: Fairview CC, Greenwich (1969), with Robert Trent Jones.
Florida: Inverrary CC (East Course), Lauderhill (1970), with Robert Trent Jones; Inverrary CC (South Course), Lauderhill (Precision, 1970), with Robert Trent Jones; Inverrary CC (West Course), Lauderhill (1970), with Robert Trent Jones; Key West Resort GC, Key West (1983); Kings Point G&CC, Sun City Center (Precision, 1974), with Robert Trent Jones; Kings Point G&CC (Course No. 1), Delray Beach (Precision, 1972), with Robert Trent Jones; Kings Point G&CC (Course No. 2), Delray Beach (Par 3, 1973), with Robert Trent Jones; Turnberry Isle G&CC (North Course), North Miami (1974), with Robert Trent Jones; Turnberry Isle G&CC (South Course), North Miami (1971), with Robert Trent Jones.
Georgia: Gordon Lakes GC, Fort Gordon (1975), with Robert Trent Jones; Jones Creek GC, Augusta (1986), with Keith Evans; Metropolitan G&TC {formerly Fairington G&TC}, Decatur (1969).
Illinois: Rail GC, Springfield (1974), with Robert Trent Jones.
Kentucky: Griffin Gate GC, Lexington (1981).
Maryland: Ocean Pines G&CC, Ocean City (1972), with Robert Trent Jones.
Massachusetts: Tara Ferncroft CC, Danvers (1970), with Robert Trent Jones.
New Jersey: Panther Valley CC, Allamuchy (1969), with Robert Trent Jones; Pinch Brook GC, Florham Park (Precision, 1984), with Keith Evans.
New York: Bristol Harbor Village GC, Canandaigua (1974), with Robert Trent Jones; Crag Burn C, Elma (1971), with Robert Trent Jones; Montauk G&RC, Montauk Point (1968), with Robert Trent Jones; Ransom Oaks CC, Amherst (1971), with Robert Trent Jones.
North Carolina: Bryan Park GC (Course No. 2), Greensboro (1986); Greenbrier GC, New Bern (1987); Harbour Pointe GC, New Bern (1986), with Keith Evans; Pinehurst CC (Course No. 7) (1986), with Keith Evans.
Pennsylvania: Eagle Lodge GC, Lafayette Hill (1982).
South Carolina: Arcadian Shores G&RC, Myrtle Beach (1974); Bear Creek GC, Hilton Head Island (1979); CC of Hilton Head, Hilton Head Island (1986); Gator Hole GC, North Myrtle Beach (1980); Haig Point GC, Daufuskie Island (1986); Oyster Reef GC, Hilton Head Island (1981); Waterway Hills GC, Myrtle Beach (27, 1975).
Tennessee: Graysburg Hills GC, Chuckey (1979).
Texas: Rayburn G&CC (Blue Nine), Jasper (9, 1973); Sugar Creek CC, Sugarland (27, 1970), with Robert Trent Jones.
Virginia: Glenwood GC, Virginia Beach (1985); Greenbrier GC, Chesapeake (1985); Hell's Point GC, Virginia Beach (1982), with Keith Evans; Stoney Creek GC, Wintergreen (1986), with Keith Evans.
Wisconsin: Springs GC, Spring Green (1974), with Robert Trent Jones.
Namibia: Swakopmund GC (9, 1977).

Courses Remodeled & Added to by: Rees Jones
California: La Jolla CC (R., 1983).
Connecticut: Redding CC (A.9, 1980).
Florida: Crystal Lago CC, Pompano Beach (R., 1981), with Keith Evans.
Illinois: Skokie GC, Glencoe (R., 1981), with Keith Evans.
Indiana: Fort Wayne CC (R., 1978).
Kansas: Kansas City CC, Shawnee Mission (R., 1978).
Massachusetts: CC of New Seabury (Blue Course), South Mashpee (R., 1985); CC of New Seabury (Green Course), South Mashpee (R., 1985); The Country Club, Brookline (R., 1986).
Michigan: Leland CC (R.9, 1979); Leland CC (A.9, 1979).
New Jersey: Canoe Brook CC (North Course), Millburn (R., 1973), with Robert Trent Jones; Canoe Brook CC (South Course), Summit (R., 1978); Flanders Valley GC (A.9, 1982), with Keith Evans; Forest Hill Field C, Bloomfield (R., 1986); Montclair CC, Verona (R., 1977); Ridgewood CC (R., 1981), with Keith Evans; Woodcrest CC, Cherry Hill (R.1, 1983).
New York: Cold Spring G&CC, Cold Spring Harbor (R., 1968), with Robert Trent Jones; Muttontown G&CC, East Norwich (R., 1968), with Robert Trent Jones; Rye GC (R., 1982); Tam O'Shanter GC, Brookville (R., 1967), with Robert Trent Jones; Westchester CC (South Course), Rye (R., 1983), with Keith Evans; Westchester CC (West Course), Rye (R., 1982), with Keith Evans.
North Carolina: Carmel CC (North Course), Charlotte (R., 1984); Carmel CC (South Course), Charlotte (R., 1984); CC of North Carolina (Dogwood Course), Pinehurst (R., 1979); Myers Park CC, Charlotte (R., 1978); Pinehurst CC (Course No. 4) (R., 1982).
Tennessee: Meadowview GC, Kingsport (R., 1978).
Virginia: Boonsboro CC, Lynchburg (R., 1981); Salisbury CC (R., 1986); Shenandoah Valley CC, Middleburg (R., 1986).
Ontario: Hamilton G&CC, Ancaster (R., 1982).

Robert Trent Jones (1906 -) ASGCA, Charter Member; President, 1950.
Born: Ince, England.
Robert Trent Jones moved with his parents to the United States in 1911. He became a scratch golfer while still a teenager and set a course record at the age of sixteen while playing in the Rochester City Golf Championship. He was low amateur in the 1927 Canadian Open. Jones attended Cornell University, where he followed a course of studies personally selected to prepare himself for a career in golf course architecture. Completing this program in 1930, he undertook additional courses in art. While still at Cornell, he had designed several greens at the Sodus Bay Heights GC in New York. While the course was subsequently remodeled, two of his greens were retained by the club as the earliest examples of Jones's work.
In 1930 Jones became a partner with Canadian golf architect Stanley Thompson in the firm of Thompson, Jones & Co., with offices in Toronto and New York. These two architects were profoundly influential in the nearly universal acceptance of strategic design in North America. Jones's oft-quoted philosophy was that every hole should be a hard par but easy bogey.
By the mid-1960s Robert Trent Jones had become the most widely known and probably the most influential course architect in history. Robert Trent Jones served as architectural consultant to numerous courses hosting major championship tournaments, many of them courses of his own design. By 1980 he had planned over 400 courses in play in forty-two states and twenty-three countries, and had remo-

deled many others, logging an estimated 300,000 miles by air annually in the process. In 1974, Jones was selected to design a course near Moscow, the first to be done in Russia since those of the British Colony of Czarist days. Sadly, the course was never built.

Jones was the author of many essays on golf course architecture, including contributions to Herbert Warren Wind's *The Complete Golfer* (1954), Will Grimsley's *Golf - Its History, Events and People* (1966) and Martin Sutton's *Golf Courses - Design, Construction and Upkeep* (2nd ed., 1950). The Sutton work featured several of Jones's freehand sketches of golf holes. Jones was also the subject of countless articles. The most significant of these to the profession of golf course architecture was Herbert Warren Wind's profile in New Yorker magazine.

Robert Trent Jones was the first recipient of the ASGCA's Donald Ross Award for outstanding contributions to golf course architecture. He became an advisory member of the National Institute of Social Science, a member of the American Academy of Achievement and recipient of its 1972 Golden Plate Award, and was granted membership to the Royal and Ancient Golf Club of St. Andrew. In 1981 Jones was given the William D. Richardson Award by the GWAA in recognition of his consistent outstanding contributions.

That same year the Metropolitan Golf Association presented him with its Distinguished Service Award. In 1987 the GCSAA honored him with its Old Tom Morris Award. He and his wife, the former lone Tefft Davis of Montclair, New Jersey, raised two sons, Robert Jr. and Rees, both of whom followed their father in the practice of golf architecture.

Courses by: Robert Trent Jones

Alabama: Alpine Bay Y&CC, Alpine (1973), with Rees Jones; Turtle Point Y&CC, Florence (1964), with Frank Duane.

Alaska: Eagle Glen GC, Elmendorf AFB (1972), with Robert Trent Jones Jr.

Arizona: Goodyear G&CC (Blue Course), Litchfield Park (1965); Goodyear G&CC (Gold Course), Litchfield Park (1966); Village of Oak Creek CC (1972), with Robert Trent Jones Jr.

California: Birnam Wood GC, Santa Barbara (1968), with Robert Trent Jones Jr; Calabasas Park CC (1968), with Robert Trent Jones Jr; El Dorado Hills GC (Precision, 1964), with Frank Duane; Laguna Seca G Ranch (1970), with Robert Trent Jones Jr; Lake Shastina G&CC, Weed (1972), with Robert Trent Jones Jr and Gary Roger Baird; Mission Viejo CC (1966); Murrieta GC (1970), with Robert Trent Jones Jr and Gary Roger Baird; Pauma Valley CC (1960); Silverado CC (South Course), Napa (1967), with Robert Trent Jones Jr; Spring Valley Lake CC, Victorville (1971), with Robert Trent Jones Jr and Gary Roger Baird; Spyglass Hill G Links, Pebble Beach (1966); Sunset Dunes GC, Colton (Par 3, 1963); Tecolote Canyon GC, San Diego (Precision, 1964); Valencia GC (1965).

Colorado: Eisenhower GC (Blue Course), US Air Force Academy (1959), with Robert Trent Jones and Frank Duane; Eisenhower GC (Blue Course), US Air Force Academy (1959), with Robert Trent Jones and Frank Duane.

Connecticut: Black Hall C, Old Lyme (1968), with Roger Rulewich; Bruce Memorial GC, Greenwich (1964); Fairview CC, Greenwich (1969), with Rees Jones; Lyman Meadow GC, Middlefield (1969), with Roger Rulewich; Patterson C, Fairfield (1946); Rockrimmon CC, Stamford (9, 1949).

Delaware: Wilmington CC (South Course), Greenville (1960).

Florida: All-American GC, Sharpes (Par 3, 1963); American Golfers C, Fort Lauderdale (Precision, 1957); Apollo Beach G & Sea C (9, 1962), with Frank Duane; Beauclerc CC, Jacksonville (9, 1955); Coral Ridge CC, Fort Lauderdale (1956); CC of Miami (East Course), Hialeah (1962), with Frank Duane; CC of Miami (North Course), Hialeah (NLE, Par 3, 1962), with Frank Duane; CC of Miami (West Course), Hialeah (1962), with Frank Duane; Grenelefe G&RC (West Course-)(Routing), Haines City (1971); Inverrary CC (East Course), Lauderhill (1970), with Rees Jones; Inverrary CC (South Course), Lauderhill (Precision, 1970), with Rees Jones; Inverrary CC (West Course), Lauderhill (1970), with Rees Jones; Kings Point G&CC, Sun City Center (Precision, 1974), with Rees Jones; Kings Point G&CC (Course No. 1), Delray Beach (Precision, 1972), with Rees Jones; Kings Point G&CC (Course No. 2), Delray Beach (Par 3, 1973), with Rees Jones; MacDonald Estate GC, Bal Harbour (2, 1955); Patrick AFB GC, Cocoa Beach (9, 1961), with Frank Duane; Ponte Vedra C (Lagoon Course), Ponte Vedra Beach (9, 1962), with Frank Duane; Royal Palm Y&CC, Boca Raton (1960), with Frank Duane; Turnberry Isle G&CC (North Course), North Miami (1974), with Rees Jones; Turnberry Isle G&CC (South Course), North Miami (1971), with Rees Jones.

Georgia: Atlanta Athletic C (Highlands Course), Duluth (9, 1967); Atlanta Athletic C (Riverside Course), Duluth (1967); Chattahoochee GC, Gainesville (1959), with Frank Duane; Gordon Lakes GC, Fort Gordon (1975), with Rees Jones; Peachtree GC, Atlanta (1948), with Robert Tyre "Bobby" Jones Jr; Standard C, Atlanta (NLE, 1951); Stone Mountain GC (1971), with Roger Rulewich; Sunset Hills CC, Carrollton (9, 1949); University of Georgia GC, Athens (1968), with Roger Rulewich.

Hawaii: Hawaii Kai CC (Executive Course), Honolulu (Precision, 1962); Mauna Kea Beach Hotel GC, Kameula (1965); Royal Kaanapali GC (North Course), Maui (1963).

Idaho: Elkhorn GC, Sun Valley (1975), with Robert Trent Jones Jr.

Illinois: Hilldale GC, Hoffman Estates (1972), with Roger Rulewich; Norris Estate GC, St. Charles (9, 1935); Pottawatomie Park GC, St. Charles (9, 1936); Rail GC, Springfield (1974), with Rees Jones.

Indiana: Otter Creek GC, Columbus (1964).

Kansas: Crestview CC (North Course), Wichita (1969), with Robert Trent Jones Jr; Crestview CC (South Course), Wichita (9, 1969), with Robert Trent Jones Jr; Custer Hill GC, Fort Riley (9, 1960).

Kentucky: CC of Paducah (9, 1965).

Louisiana: Santa Maria GC, Baton Rouge (1987), with Roger Rulewich; Timberlane CC, Gretna (1959), with Frank Duane.

Maryland: Camp David GC (1, 1954); Golden Triangle GC, Beltville (9, 1971), with Roger Rulewich; Ocean Pines G&CC, Ocean City (1972), with Rees Jones.

Massachusetts: Crumpin Fox C, Bernardston (9, 1978), with Roger Rulewich; Tara Ferncroft CC, Danvers (1970), with Rees Jones.

Michigan: Boyne Highlands GC (Heather Course), Harbor Springs (9, 1968); Boyne Highlands GC (Moor Course), Harbor Springs (9, 1968); Point O'Woods G&CC, Benton Harbor (1958), with Frank Duane; Treetops GC, Gaylord (1987), with Roger Rulewich.

Minnesota: Hazeltine National GC, Chaska (1962); Jonathan Par 30 GC, Chaska (Precision, 9, 1974).

Missouri: Bellerive CC, Creve Coeur (1959), with Frank Duane; Four Seasons G&CC, Lake Ozark (1974), with Roger Rulewich; Old Warson CC, Ladue (1955).

Montana: Yellowstone G&CC, Billings (1959), with Frank Duane.

Nebraska: Capehart GC, Bellevue (1964).

Nevada: Incline Green GC, Incline Village (Precision, 1971), with Robert Trent Jones Jr and Gary Roger Baird; Incline Village GC (1964); Lakeridge CC, Reno (1971), with Robert Trent Jones Jr.

New Hampshire: Portsmouth G&CC (1957), with Frank Duane.

New Jersey: Duke Estate GC, Somerville (NLE, 9, 1940); Lyons VA Hospital GC (9, 1947); Panther Valley CC, Allamuchy (1969), with Rees Jones; Tammy Brook CC, Cresskill (1962), with Frank Duane; Upper Montclair CC, Clifton (27, 1956); Wayne CC (NLE, 1951); Willingboro CC (1966).

New York: Albany CC (1963); Amsterdam Muni (1938); Baiting Hollow CC, Riverhead (1966); Bristol Harbor Village GC, Canandaigua (1974), with Rees Jones; Carlton Island GC (NLE,), with Stanley Thompson; Cornell University GC, Ithaca (9, 1940); Crag Burn C, Elma (1971), with Rees Jones; Durand-Eastman Park GC, Rochester (1934); Eisenhower Park GC (Blue Course), East Meadow (1951); Eisenhower Park GC (White Course), East Meadow (1950); Fallsview Hotel GC, Ellenville (9, 1962), with Frank Duane; Frear Park GC, Troy (9, 1931); Green Lakes State Park GC, Fayetteville (1935); Hampstead GC at Lido, Long Beach (1956), with Frank Duane; Hancock Muni (NLE, 9, 1947); Hominy Hill GC, Colts Neck (1965); IBM CC, Poughkeepsie (1945); James Baird State Park GC, Pleasant Valley (1948); Marine Park GC, Brooklyn (1963); Midvale G&CC, Penfield (1931), with Stanley Thompson; Montauk G&RC, Montauk Point (1968), with Rees Jones; North Hills CC, Manhasset (1961), with Frank Duane; Pines Hotel GC, South Fallsburg (9, 1960), with Frank Duane; Quaker Hill GC, Pawling (9, 1935); Radisson Greens GC, Baldwinsville (1977), with Roger Rulewich; Ransom Oaks CC, Amherst (1971), with Rees Jones; Seven Oaks GC, Colgage Univ. (9, 1955), with Frank Duane; Sodus Point GC (9, 1926); Tuxedo Park C, Tuxedo Park (1947), with Frank Duane; West Point GC, US Military Academy (1950); Wiltwyck CC, Kingston (1955).

North Carolina: Carolina Trace G&CC, Sanford (27, 1973), with Roger Rulewich; Duke University GC, Durham (1957), with Frank Duane; Tanglewood GC (East Course), Clemmons (9, 1965); Tanglewood GC (West Course), Clemmons (1957), with Frank Duane.

Ohio: Arthur Raymond GC, Columbus (1955); Firestone CC (North Course), Akron (1969), with Roger Rulewich; Winding Hollow CC, Columbus (1952).

Oregon: Eugene CC (1967), with Robert Trent Jones Jr; West Delta Park GC, Portland (1971), with Robert Trent Jones Jr and Gary Roger Baird.

Pennsylvania: Tamiment CC (1947).

South Carolina: Dunes G&BC, Myrtle Beach (1949); Greenville CC (Chanticleer Course) (1970); Palmetto Dunes CC (Jones Course), Hilton Head Island (1969); Seabrook Island GC (Crooked Oaks Course) (1981), with Roger Rulewich.

Tennessee: Link Hills CC, Greenville (1947); Scona Lodge GC, Alcoa (9, 1957), with Frank Duane.

Texas: Corpus Christi CC (1965), with Frank Duane; Horseshoe Bay CC (Apple Rock Course), Marble Falls (1985), with Roger Rulewich; Horseshoe Bay CC (Ram Rock Course), Marble Falls (1981), with Roger Rulewich; Horseshoe Bay CC (Slick Rock Course), Marble Falls (1973), with Robert Trent Jones Jr and Gary Roger Baird; Houston CC (1957); Shady Oaks CC, Fort Worth (1959), with Lawrence Hughes and Ralph Plummer; Sugar Creek CC, Sugarland (27, 1970), with Rees Jones.

Vermont: Sugarbush GC, Warren (1963), with Frank Duane; Woodstock CC (1963).

Virginia: Fort Belvoir GC (9, 1949); Golden Horseshoe GC, Williamsburg (1964); Golden Horseshoe GC (Spotswood 9), Williamsburg (Precision, 9, 1965); Lower Cascades GC, Virginia Hot Springs (1963); Stumpy Lake GC, Norfolk (1957), with Frank Duane.

West Virginia: Bel-Meadow G&CC, Mount Clare (1967); Cacapon Springs GC, Berkeley Springs (1973); Speidel GC, Wheeling (1972), with Roger Rulewich.

Wisconsin: Madeline Island G Links (1967), with Robert Trent Jones Jr; Springs GC, Spring Green (1974), with Rees Jones.

Alberta: Kananaskis Country GC (Mount Kidd) (1984), with Roger Rulewich; Kananaskis Country GC (Mount Loretta) (1983), with Roger Rulewich.

British Columbia: Rivershore GC, Kamloops (1981), with Roger Rulewich.

Ontario: London Hunt & CC, London (1960), with Frank Duane.

Bahamas: Cotton Bay C, Eleuthera (1955).

Belgium: Golf de Bercuit, Grez Doiceau (1968).

Bermuda: Port Royal GC, Southampton (1970), with Roger Rulewich; St. George's GC (Precision, 1986), with Roger Rulewich.

Brazil: Brasilia GC (1958).

Colombia: El Rincon C, Bogota (1963), with Frank Duane.

Dominican Republic: Playa Dorada GC, Playa Dorado (1979), with Roger Rulewich.

England: Moor Allerton GC, Yorkshire (27, 1971), with Cabell Robinson.

Guadeloupe: Golf de St. Francois (1977), with Roger Rulewich.

Ireland: Ballybunion GC (New Course), County Kerry (1985), with Roger Rulewich and Cabell Robinson.

Italy: I Roveri GC, Turin (27, 1976), with Cabell Robinson.

Jamaica: Half Moon-Rose Hall GC, Montego Bay (1961), with Frank Duane.

Japan: Golf 72 (Higashi Course) (1972), with Robert Trent Jones Jr; Golf 72 (Kita Course) (1972), with Robert Trent Jones Jr; Golf 72 (Minami Course) (1972), with Robert Trent Jones Jr; Golf 72 (Nishi Course) (1972), with Robert Trent Jones Jr.

Martinique: Empress Josephine GC (1976), with Roger Rulewich.

Mexico: Tres Vidas en la Playa (East Course) (NLE, 1969); Tres Vidas en la Playa (West Course) (NLE, 1969).

Morocco: Royal G Dar Es Salaam (Blue Course), Rabat (1974), with Cabell Robinson; Royal G Dar Es Salaam (Green Course), Rabat (9, 1974), with Cabell Robinson; Royal G Dar Es Salaam (Red Course), Rabat (1971), with Cabell Robinson.

Philippines: Luisita GC, Tarlac (1968).

Portugal: Quinta da Marinha GC, Faro (1985), with Cabell Robinson; Troia GC, Setubal (1980), with Cabell Robinson.

Puerto Rico: Cerromar Beach GC (North Course), Dorado Beach (1972), with Roger Rulewich; Cerromar Beach GC (South Course), Dorado Beach (1972), with Roger Rulewich; Dorado Beach GC (East Course), Dorado (9, 1958), with Frank Duane; Dorado Beach GC (West Course), Dorado (9, 1958), with Frank Duane.

Sardinia: Pevero GC, Costa Smeralda (1972), with Cabell Robinson.

Spain: Club de G Mijas (Los Lagos Course), Fuengirola, Malaga (1976), with Cabell Robinson; Club de G Mijas (Los Olivos Course), Fuengirola, Malaga (1984), with Cabell Robinson; El Bosque GC, Valencia (1975), with Cabell Robinson; Los Lagos GC, Mijas (1976), with Cabell Robinson; Nueva Andalucia GC (Las Brisas Course), Marbella, Malaga (1968); Nueva Andalucia GC (Par 3 Course), Marbella, Malaga (Par 3, 1968); Nueva Andulucia GC (Los Naranjos Course), Marbella, Malaga (1977), with Cabell Robinson; Sotogrande GC (New Course), Cadiz (1975), with Cabell Robinson; Sotogrande GC (Old Course), Cadiz (1964); Sotogrande GC (Short Course), Cadiz (Par 3, 9, 1964).

Switzerland: Geneva G&CC (1973), with Cabell Robinson.

Virgin Islands: Carambola Beach GC {formerly Fountain Valley GC}, Frederiksted (1966).

Courses Remodeled & Added to by: Robert Trent Jones

Alabama: CC of Birmingham (West Course) (R., 1959); Lakewood GC (Dogwood Course), Point Clear (R., 1949).

Arkansas: North Hills CC, North Little Rock (R., 1979), with Roger Rulewich.

California: Annandale CC (R., 1970), with Robert Trent Jones Jr; California GC of San Francisco (R., 1968), with Robert Trent Jones Jr; Cypress Point C, Pebble Beach (R.1, 1966); El Caballero CC, Tarzana (R., 1964); Glendora CC (R., 1970), with Robert Trent Jones Jr and Gary Roger Baird; Hacienda CC, La Habra (R., 1971), with Robert Trent Jones Jr; Menlo CC, Redwood City (R., 1970), with Robert Trent Jones Jr and Gary Roger Baird; Olympic C (Lake Course), San Francisco (R., 1954); San Gabriel CC (R., 1972), with Robert Trent Jones Jr; Silverado CC (North Course), Napa (R., 1967), with Robert Trent Jones Jr; Stanford University GC, Palo Alto (R., 1968), with Robert Trent Jones Jr.

Colorado: Broadmoor GC (East Course), Colorado Springs (A.9, 1954); Broadmoor GC (West Course), Colorado Springs (A.9, 1965).

Connecticut: CC of New Canaan (R., 1960), with Frank Duane; Greenwich CC (R., 1963); Hartford GC, West Hartford (R., 1966); Innis Arden GC, Old Greenwich (R., 1960); Ridgewood CC, Danbury (R., 1959), with Frank Duane; Round Hill C, Greenwich (R., 1952).

Florida: Apollo Beach G & Sea C (A.9, 1971), with Roger Rulewich; Boca Raton Hotel & C (R., 1963); CC of Orlando (R., 1959), with Frank Duane; La Gorce CC, Miami (R., 1953); Melreese GC, Miami (A.4, 1966); Melreese GC, Miami (R., 1966); Ponte Vedra C (Ocean Course), Ponte Vedra Beach (R., 1954).

Georgia: Augusta National GC, Augusta (R.3, 1950); Fort Benning GC (Pineside Course) (A.9, 1950); Sea Island GC (Plantation 9), St. Simons Island (R.9, 1949); Sea Island GC (Seaside 9), St. Simons Island (R., 1949).

Illinois: St. Charles CC (R., 1936).

Kentucky: CC of Paducah (A.9, 1979), with Roger Rulewich.

Maine: Portland CC, Falmouth (R., 1951).

Maryland: Burning Tree C, Bethesda (R., 1963); Chevy Chase CC (R., 1948); Congressional CC (Blue Course), Bethesda (A.9, 1957); Congressional CC (Blue Course), Bethesda (R.9, 1962); Congressional CC (Blue Course), Bethesda (R., 1969), with Roger Rulewich; Elkridge CC, Baltimore (R., 1956); Golden Triangle GC, Beltville (A.9, 1976), with Roger Rulewich; Green Spring Valley Hunt C, Garrison (A.9, 1958); Green Spring Valley Hunt C, Garrison (R.9, 1958); Suburban CC (R., 1949).

Massachusetts: International GC, Bolton (R., 1969).

Michigan: Bloomfield Hills CC (R., 1968); Bloomfield Hills CC (R., 1978), with Roger Rulewich; CC of Detroit, Grosse Pointe Farms (R., 1950); CC of Detroit, Grosse Pointe Farms (Precision, A.9, 1968); Detroit GC (North Course) (R., 1953); Detroit GC (South Course) (R., 1953); Oakland Hills CC (North Course), Birmingham (R., 1969), with Roger Rulewich; Oakland Hills CC (South Course), Birmingham (R., 1950); Oakland Hills CC (South Course), Birmingham (R., 1972), with Roger Rulewich; Oakland Hills CC (South Course), Birmingham (R., 1984), with Roger Rulewich.

Minnesota: Hazeltine National GC, Chaska (R., 1978), with Roger Rulewich; Interlachen CC, Edina (R., 1962).

Missouri: St. Louis CC, Clayton (R., 1952).

New Jersey: Arcola CC, Paramus (R., 1960), with Frank Duane; Baltusrol GC (Lower Course), Springfield (R., 1952); Canoe Brook CC (North Course), Millburn (R., 1973), with Rees Jones; Crestmont CC, West Orange (R., 1978), with Roger Rulewich; Essex County CC (East Course) (R., 1960); Galloping Hills GC, Union (R., 1949); Galloping Hills GC, Union (R., 1955); Glen Ridge CC (R., 1949); Glen Ridge CC (R., 1978), with Roger Rulewich; Green Brook CC, Caldwell (R., 1948); Montclair GC, Verona (R., 1935); Montclair GC, Verona (R., 1959); North Jersey CC, Wayne (R., 1979), with Roger Rulewich; Rockleigh GC (Bergen Course) (R., 1964); Tavistock CC, Haddonfield (R., 1959).

New York: Bartlett CC, Olean (R., 1960), with Frank Duane; Bellport GC (R., 1965); Bonnie Briar CC, Larchmont (R., 1936), with Stanley Thompson; Century GC, White Plains (R., 1959), with Frank Duane; Cherry Valley CC, Garden City (R., 1962), with Frank Duane; Cold Spring G&CC, Cold Spring Harbor (R., 1968), with Rees Jones; Colonie Muni (A.9, 1980), with Roger Rulewich; CC of Buffalo, Williamsville (R., 1954); CC of Ithaca (NLE, R., 1939); CC of Rochester (A.3, 1960); CC of Rochester (R., 1960); Dellwood CC, New City (R., 1956); Garden City GC (R., 1935); Garden City GC (R., 1958), with Frank Duane; Huntington CC (R., 1960), with Frank Duane; IBM CC, Poughkeepsie (A.9, 1948); IBM CC, Poughkeepsie (R.9, 1948); IBM CC, Port Washington (R., 1954); IBM CC, Poughkeepsie (R., 1985), with Roger Rulewich; Locust Hill CC, Rochester (R., 1931); Moonbrook CC, Jamestown (R., 1959), with Frank Duane; Muttontown G&CC, East Norwich (R., 1968), with Rees Jones; National G Links of America, Southampton (R., 1948); National G Links of America, Southampton (R., 1969); New York Hospital GC, White Plains (R., 1960); Niagara Falls CC, Lewiston (R., 1938); North Hempstead CC, Port Washington (R., 1960); Oak Hill CC (East Course), Rochester (R., 1956); Oak Hill CC (East Course), Rochester (R., 1967); Pelham CC (R., 1977), with Roger Rulewich; Powelton C, Newburgh (R., 1953); Quaker Ridge CC, Scarsdale (R., 1962); Rockland CC, Sparkill (R.); Sands Point CC, Port Washington (R., 1961), with Frank Duane; Scarsdale GC, Hartsdale (R., 1962); Seven Oaks GC, Colgage Univ. (A.9, 1965); Siwanoy CC, Bronxville (R., 1953); Sleepy Hollow GC, Scarboro-on-Hudson (R., 1966); Stafford CC (R., 1931), with Stanley Thompson; Tam O'Shanter GC, Brookville (R., 1967), with Rees Jones; Valley View GC, Utica (R., 1940); Valley View Muni (R., 1938); Vestal Hills CC, Binghampton (NLE, R., 1938); Winged Foot GC (West Course), Mamaroneck (R., 1958); Woodmere C, Great Neck (R., 1952).

North Carolina: Charlotte CC (R., 1962); Charlotte CC (R., 1984); CC of North Carolina (Cardinal Course), Pinehurst (A.9, 1980); CC of North Carolina (Dogwood Course), Pinehurst (R., 1977); Pinehurst CC (Course No. 4) (R., 1973), with Roger Rulewich; Pinehurst CC (Course No. 5) (R., 1974), with Roger Rulewich; Tanglewood GC (East Course), Clemmons (A.9, 1970), with Roger Rulewich; Tanglewood GC (West Course), Clemmons (R., 1973).

Ohio: Firestone CC (South Course), Akron (R., 1959).

Oklahoma: Southern Hills CC, Tulsa (R., 1957).

Oregon: Portland GC (R., 1950).

Pennsylvania: Centre Hills CC, State College (A.9, 1967); Gulph Mills GC, King of Prussia (R.4, 1966); Oakmont CC (R., 1964); Pittsburgh Field C (R., 1952); Valley Brook CC, McMurray (R., 1978), with Roger Rulewich; Westmoreland CC, Export (R., 1958), with Frank Duane.

South Carolina: Dunes G&BC, Myrtle Beach (R., 1979), with Roger Rulewich.

Tennessee: Belle Meade CC, Nashville (R., 1957).

Texas: Colonial CC, Fort Worth (R., 1960).

Vermont: Woodstock CC (R., 1969); Woodstock CC (R., 1975), with Roger Rulewich.

Virginia: Cascades GC, Virginia Hot Springs (R., 1961); CC of Fairfax (A.9, 1952).

Wisconsin: Milwaukee CC (R., 1975), with Roger Rulewich.

Wyoming: Jackson Hole G&TC (R., 1966), with Robert Trent Jones Jr.

Bermuda: Mid-Ocean C, Tuckerstown (R., 1953).

Brazil: Itanhanga GC, Tijuca (R., 1958).

Colombia: El Rincon C, Bogota (Par 3, A., 1964), with Frank Duane.

France: Chamonix GC (R., 1980), with Cabell Robinson; Golf de Bondues, Roubaix (R.18, 1968); Golf de Bondues, Roubaix (A.9, 1968).

Greece: Glyfada GC, Athens (R., 1978), with Cabell Robinson.

Italy: Olgiata CC (R., 1984).

Japan: Sobhu CC, Chiba (R., 1971).

Mexico: Pierre Marques GC, Acapulco (R., 1982).

Puerto Rico: Dorado Beach GC (East Course), Dorado (A.9, 1961), with Frank Duane; Dorado Beach GC (West Course), Dorado (A.9, 1966), with Frank Duane.

West Germany: Hamburg-Ahrensburg GC, Hamburg (R., 1978), with Cabell Robinson.

Robert Trent Jones Jr. (1939 -) ASGCA

Born: Montclair, New Jersey.

After receiving a B.A. Degree from Yale University, Robert Trent Jones Jr. joined his father's golf design firm in 1960. Eventually he took over the California office and acquired full responsibility for the firm's Western and Pacific Basin practice. In 1972, "Bobby" left his father's firm and formed Robert Trent Jones II Group, based in California.

Bobby Jones long advocated the concept of golf courses as a works of art blended within the environment, and built specific examples of that philosophy, such as Sentryworld in Wisconsin, where he designed a widely-photographed "flower" hole, a par-3 surrounded by formal flower beds. By 1985 he had designed over seventy-five courses and remodeled many others, in addition to those he worked on with his father.

Courses by: Robert Trent Jones Jr

Alaska: Eagle Glen GC, Elmendorf AFB (1972), with Robert Trent Jones.

Arizona: Rio Rico G&CC (1975), with Gary Roger Baird; Village of Oak Creek CC (1972), with Robert Trent Jones.

California: Birnam Wood GC, Santa Barbara (1968), with Robert Trent Jones; Bodega Harbour GC (9, 1977), with Gary Roger Baird; Calabasas Park CC (1968), with Robert Trent Jones; Coto de Caza GC (1987), with Don Knott; Forest Meadows GC (Precision, 1980); Laguna Seca G Ranch (1970), with Robert Trent Jones; Lake Shastina G&CC, Weed (1972), with Robert Trent Jones and Gary Roger Baird; Links at Monarch Beach, Laguna Niguel (1984), with Gary Linn; Murrieta GC (1970), with Robert Trent Jones and Gary Roger Baird; Poppy Hills GC, Pebble Beach (1986), with Don Knott; Shoreline Park Muni GC (1983), with Gary Linn; Silverado CC (South Course), Napa (1967), with Robert Trent Jones; Spanish Bay G Links, Pebble Beach (1987), with Don Knott, Frank "Sandy" Tatum and Tom Watson; Spring Valley Lake CC, Victorville (1971), with Robert Trent Jones and Gary Roger Baird.

Colorado: Arrowhead GC, Littleton (1974), with Gary Roger Baird; Beaver Creek GC, Avon (1982), with Don Knott; Keystone Ranch GC, Dillon (1980), with Don Knott; Skyland GC, Crested Butte (1984), with Gary Linn; Steamboat Village CC, Steamboat Springs (1974), with Gary Roger Baird.

Hawaii: Kiahuna Plantation GC, Poipu Beach (1983), with Don Knott; Makena GC (New Course), Maui (1987), with Don Knott; Makena GC (Old Course), Maui (1981), with Don Knott; Princeville Makai GC, Kauai (27, 1971), with Gary Roger Baird; Waikoloa Beach GC, Kamuela (1981); Waikoloa Village GC, Kamuela (1972), with Gary Roger Baird.

Idaho: Elkhorn GC, Sun Valley (1975), with Robert Trent Jones.

Kansas: Crestview CC (North Course), Wichita (1969), with Robert Trent Jones; Crestview CC (South Course), Wichita (9, 1969), with Robert Trent Jones.

Louisiana: Le Triomphe GC, Lafayette (1986), with Gary Linn.

Maine: Sugarloaf GC, Carrabassett Valley (1986), with Don Knott.

Nevada: Incline Green GC, Incline Village (Precision, 1971), with Robert Trent Jones and Gary Roger Baird; Lakeridge CC, Reno (1971), with Robert Trent Jones; Spanish Trail G&CC, Las Vegas (1985), with Don Knott.

New Mexico: Cochiti Lake GC (1980).

North Dakota: Oxbow CC, Hickson (1974), with Gary Roger Baird.

Oregon: Eugene CC (1967), with Robert Trent Jones; Sunriver GC (North Course) (1980), with Don Knott; West Delta Park GC, Portland (1971), with Robert Trent Jones and Gary Roger Baird.

Texas: Horseshoe Bay CC (Slick Rock Course), Marble Falls (1973), with Robert Trent Jones and Gary Roger Baird; Las Colinas Sports C, Irving (1983), with Gary Roger Baird.

Wisconsin: Madeline Island G Links (1967), with Robert Trent Jones; Sentry-World GC, Stevens Point (1982).

Alberta: Glencoe G & CC (Forest Course), Calgary (1984), with Don Knott and Gary Linn; Glencoe G & CC (Meadow Course), Calgary (1985), with Don Knott and Gary Linn.

Australia: Joondalup GC (1985), with Don Knott; Mandurah Resort GC (1986), with Don Knott; National GC of Australia (1986), with Don Knott.

Fiji: Pacific Harbour G&CC (1977), with Gary Roger Baird.

France: Les Terrasses de Geneve G&CC, Bossey (1985), with Don Knott.

Indonesia: Pondok Indah GC (1977), with Gary Roger Baird.

Japan: Golden Valley GC (1986), with Gary Linn; Golf 72 (Higashi Course) (1972), with Robert Trent Jones; Golf 72 (Karuizawa Course) (1976); Golf 72 (Kita Course) (1972); Golf 72 (Minami Course) (1972), with Robert Trent Jones; Golf 72 (Nishi Course) (1972), with Robert Trent Jones; Hokkaido CC (Ohnuma Course) (1981); Oak Hills CC (1982); Pine Lake GC (1984), with Don Knott and Gary Linn; Sapporo CC (36, 1976); Shizukuishi GC (1984), with Don Knott; Springfield GC (1986), with Don Knott and Gary Linn.

Malaysia: Bukit Jambul CC (1983); Desaru Resort GC (1982).

Mexico: Isla de la Piedra GC, Mazatlan (9, 1972), with Gary Roger Baird; Palma Real GC, Ixtapa (1977), with Gary Roger Baird; Pok-Ta-Pok GC, Cancun (1978), with Gary Roger Baird.

Philippines: Alabang G&CC (1969); Calatagan GC (1983), with Don Knott; Canlubang GC (1978).

Singapore: Tuas GC (36, 1986), with Don Knott.

South Africa: Wild Coast Holiday Inn GC (1983), with Don Knott.

Thailand: Navatanee CC (1975), with Gary Roger Baird.

Courses Remodeled & Added to by: Robert Trent Jones Jr

California: Annandale CC (R., 1970), with Robert Trent Jones; Bel-Air CC, Los Angeles (R.1, 1975), with Gary Roger Baird; Birnam Wood GC, Santa Barbara (R., 1977), with Gary Roger Baird; California GC of San Francisco (R., 1968), with Robert Trent Jones; Glendora CC (R., 1970), with Robert Trent Jones and Gary Roger Baird; Hacienda CC, La Habra (R., 1971), with Robert Trent Jones; Menlo CC, Redwood City (R., 1970), with Robert Trent Jones and Gary Roger Baird; Palo Alto Muni (R., 1980), with Gary Roger Baird; Pruneridge Farms GC, Santa Clara (R.); San Gabriel CC (R., 1972), with Robert Trent Jones; Santa Rosa G&CC (R., 1979); Silverado CC (North Course), Napa (R., 1967), with Robert Trent Jones; Stanford University GC, Palo Alto (R., 1968), with Robert Trent Jones.

Hawaii: Mauna Kea Beach Hotel GC, Kameula (R., 1976), with Gary Roger Baird; Princeville Makai GC, Kauai (A.18, 1987), with Don Knott; Turtle Bay GC (Old Course), Oahu (R., 1978); Waikoloa Village GC, Kamuela (R., 1981).

Idaho: Sun Valley GC (A.4, 1979), with Don Knott; Sun Valley GC (R., 1979), with Don Knott.

Kansas: Crestview CC (South Course), Wichita (A.9, 1977).

Texas: Mill Creek G&CC, Salado (R.5, 1981); Mill Creek G&CC, Salado (A.13, 1981).

Wyoming: Jackson Hole G&TC (R., 1966), with Robert Trent Jones.

Mexico: Churubusco CC, Mexico City (R.); Isla de la Piedra GC, Mazatlan (A.9, 1987).

Robert Tyre "Bobby" Jones Jr. (1902 - 1971)
Born: Atlanta, Georgia. Died: Atlanta, Georgia at age 69.

Bobby Jones was one of the greatest golfers of all time, winning fifteen major titles in the world of golf during an amateur career. While he never practiced course architecture himself, he consulted with Alister Mackenzie on Augusta National in the early 1930s, with Robert Trent Jones on Peachtree in the early 1950s and with George Cobb on the par-3 course at Augusta National in 1959. All three courses were originally conceptualized by Jones. The first two exerted a profound influence on the golf design profession throughout North America, and Augusta's par-3 started a modest nation-wide boom in par-3 courses.

Stephen Kay (1951 -)
Born: New York City, New York.

A member of the Flushing (N.Y.) High School golf team in the mid-1960s, Stephen Kay became enamored with golf architecture when reading a definitive article on the subject by Herbert Warren Wind. After obtaining a Bachelor of Landscape Architecture Degree from the State University of New York's College of Environmental Sciences and Forestry at Syracuse, Kay attended the graduate Turfgrass Management Program at Michigan State University, completing the normal two year program in one year.

While at Michigan State, he met golf architect William Newcomb, and joined his firm in 1977. He was made a full partner in 1980. In the fall of 1983 Kay returned to the metropolitan New York area where he established his own golf architectural practice. Among his earliest solo projects was a nine hole course in the tiny Kingdom of Bhutan in the Himalayan Mountains.

Courses by: Stephen Kay

Illinois: Fox Run GC, Elk Grove (1983), with William Newcomb.

Michigan: Boyne Mountain GC (Monument Course), Boyne Falls (1986), with William Newcomb; Grand Traverse GC (Newcombe Course), Acme (1979), with William Newcomb; Holiday Greens GC (Precision, 1982), with William Newcomb; Partridge Point GC, Ludington (9, 1985), with William Newcomb.

New York: Leonard Litwin Private Course (1, 1987); Stan Peschel Estate GC, Boston Corners (9, 1987).

Bhutan: Royal Bhutan GC, Thimphu (9, 1986).

Courses Remodeled & Added to by: Stephen Kay

Connecticut: Millbrook C, Greenwich (R., 1984).

Michigan: Chemung Hills GC, Howell (A.9, 1983), with William Newcomb; Holiday Inn GC, Mt. Pleasant (R., 1980), with William Newcomb; Port Huron CC (R., 1982), with William Newcomb; Schuss Mountain GC, Mancelona (R., 1980), with William Newcomb; Traverse City CC (R., 1982), with William Newcomb.

New Jersey: Tamcrest CC, Alpine (R., 1984).

New York: Ardsley CC, Ardsley-on-Hudson (R., 1986); Blue Hill GC (R., 1986); Crab Meadow GC, Northport (R.3, 1986); Dix Hills GC (R., 1986); Glen Head CC (R., 1985); Huntington Crescent CC, Huntington (R.2, 1986); Knollwood CC, Elmsford (R., 1984); Lawrence GC (R., 1982); Middle Bay CC, Oceanside (R., 1984); Old Oaks CC, Purchase (R., 1981), with William Newcomb; Quoque Field C (R.2, 1987); Seawane C, Hewlitt Harbor (R., 1984).

Gary Kern (1937 -) ASGCA
Born: Indianapolis, Indiana.

Gary Kern studied engineering at Texas A & M and Purdue Universities, then became a licensed land surveyor in Indiana, Ohio and Kentucky. He was employed for a time with a civil engineering firm specializing in land planning for single and multi-family developments.

Kern was encouraged by golf architect William Diddel to enter the field in 1969. After assisting on the design of one course, Kern went on to plan a number of layouts on his own and after 1974 devoted full time to golf architecture.

Courses by: Gary Kern

Indiana: Acres of Fun GC, Greenfield (Par 3, 9, 1974); Brook Hill GC, Brookville (9, 1975); Mohawk Hills GC, Carmel (9, 1972); Nappanee Muni (9, 1979); Royal Hylands GC, Knightstown (1977); Sky Valley GC, Hillsboro (9, 1972); Tomahawk Hills GC, Jamestown (9, 1971); Turkey Run GC, Waveland (1973).

Missouri: Casey GC, Pacific (3); South County GC, St. Louis (1987).

Courses Remodeled & Added to by: Gary Kern

Illinois: Cardinal Creek GC, Scott AFB (R.); Cherry Hills CC, Flossmoor (R., 1985); Green Hills CC, Mount Vernon (A.9, 1979); Mount Vernon GC (A.9); Rolling Hills GC, Godfrey (R.); Sunset Hills CC, Edwardsville (A.2); Sunset Hills CC, Edwardsville (R.); Sycamore Hills GC, Paris (A.10, 1976); Sycamore Hills GC, Paris (R.8, 1976).

Indiana: Delaware GC, Muncie (R.); El Dorado CC, Greenwood (R.9, 1976); El Dorado CC, Greenwood (A.9, 1976); Greenfield CC (A.9, 1976); Greenfield CC (R.9, 1976); Jasper Muni (A.9, 1987); Maplecrest CC, Goshen (R.); Milligan Park GC, Crawfordsville (A.9, 1977); Plymouth CC (R.); Tippecanoe Lake CC, Leesburg (R.); Woodland GC, Carmel (R., 1983).

Missouri: Lake Forest G&CC, Lake St. Louis (A.9, 1986); Lake Forest G&CC, Lake St. Louis (R.9, 1986).

William H. Kidd Sr. (1886 - 1967)
Born: Monteith, Scotland. Died: Minneapolis, Minnesota at age 81.

Willy Kidd emigrated to the United States in the early 1900s, becoming professional at Algonquin CC in St. Louis. He later moved to Interlachen CC in Minneapolis, remaining until his retirement in 1958, when he was succeeded by his son, Willy Jr. The senior Kidd was runner-up in the 1914 Western Open. He took up golf design upon his retirement from Interlachen.

Courses by: Willie Kidd

Minnesota: Elk River CC (1962); Faribault CC (1956); Island View GC, Winona (Par 3, 9); Princeton GC (9, 1956).

Courses Remodeled & Added to by: Willie Kidd

Minnesota: Albany CC (A.9, 1960).

Jack Kidwell (1918 -) ASGCA, President, 1979.
Born: Ohio.

Jack Kidwell graduated from Columbus (Ohio) Central High School and studied at Utah State Agriculture College. In 1938 he and his father purchased Beacon Light GC, a nine-hole layout in west Columbus, and Jack served as its pro-superintendent for 28 years. Kidwell became a Class A PGA professional and a Class A golf superintendent during that time. He also rebuilt all the greens at Beacon Light, an experience that led him to accept an offer to design a full eighteen in 1957.

Kidwell left Beacon Light and entered the field of course architecture on a full-time basis in 1959. He built many public layouts and gained a reputation for designing courses that were both playable and maintainable. In 1976 he and Dr. Michael Hurdzan founded the firm of Kidwell and Hurdzan, Inc.

A low handicap golfer all his life, Jack Kidwell was made Director of Golf at Hickory Hills CC, a course he considered among his finest designs. In 1984, the Golf Course Association presented him with an Award of Merit.

Courses by: Jack Kidwell

Florida: River Greens GC, Avon Park (1969).

Indiana: Hidden Valley GC, Lawrenceburg (1976), with Michael Hurdzan.

Kentucky: Frances Miller Memorial GC, Murray State Univ. (1982), with Michael Hurdzan.

Massachusetts: Dennis Highlands GC, Dennis (1984), with Michael Hurdzan.

Ohio: Bash Recreation GC, Dublin (NLE, Precision, 1965); Beckett Ridge G&CC, Cincinnati (1974), with Michael Hurdzan; Blackhawk GC, Galena (1964); Blacklick Woods Metro Park GC (No. 1), Reynoldsburg (1964); Blacklick Woods Metro Park GC (No.2), Reynoldsburg (Precision, 1972); Blue Ash GC (1979), with Michael Hurdzan; Bolton Field GC, Columbus (1969); Broadview GC, Pataskala (9, 1968); Buttermilk Falls GC, Georgetown (1981), with Michael Hurdzan; Deer Creek State Park GC, Mt. Sterling (1979), with Michael Hurdzan; Hiawatha GC, Mt. Vernon (9, 1961); Hickory Flat GC, West Lafayette (1968); Hickory Hills CC, Georgesville (1979), with Michael Hurdzan; Hueston Woods State Park, Oxford (1969); HV-JAC GC, Delaware (Precision, 9, 1968); Kings Mill GC, Waldo (9, 1960); Larch Tree CC, Trotwood (1971); Lee Win GC, Salem (1967); Licking Springs G & Trout C, Newark (1963); Mohican Hills GC, Wooster (9, 1972); Oakhurst CC, Grove City (1958); Oxbow G&CC, Belpre (1974), with Michael Hurdzan; Pickaway CC, Circleville; Pine Hills GC, Carrol (1962); Pleasant Hill GC, Monroe (1970); Pleasant Valley GC, Medina (1969); Port Columbus GC, Columbus (1968); Punderson Lake GC, Cleveland (1969); Reeves GC, Cincinnati (Par 3, 9, 1973); Reid Park GC (North Course), Springfield (1965); Reid Park GC (South Course), Springfield (1966); Ridenoor Park GC, Gahanna (Precision, 9, 1976), with Michael Hurdzan; River Greens GC, West Lafayette (1967); Salt Fork State Park GC, Cambridge (1972); San Dar Acres GC, Bellville (Precision, 1976), with Michael Hurdzan; Shawnee Lookout

GC, Cincinnati (1976), with Michael Hurdzan; Shawnee State Park GC, Portsmouth (1979), with Michael Hurdzan; Sugar Isle GC, New Carlisle (9, 1972); Table Rock GC, Centerburg (9, 1973); Tanglewood GC, Delaware (1968); Thornapple CC, Columbus (1966); Twin Lakes GC, Mansfield (1959); Upper Landsdowne CC, Asheville (9, 1962); Vineyards GC, Cininnati (1986), with Michael Hurdzan; Vista View Village GC, Zanesville (1973); Willow Run GC, Alexander (1963); Wilson GC, Columbus (Precision, 9, 1972).

Texas: Oak Ridge CC, Richardson , with Michael Hurdzan.

Courses Remodeled & Added to by: Jack Kidwell

Indiana: Hillcrest G&CC, Batesville (R.9, 1984), with Michael Hurdzan.

Kentucky: Kenton County CC, Independence (R.9, 1974), with Michael Hurdzan; Kenton County CC, Independence (A.9, 1981), with Michael Hurdzan; Summit Hills CC (A.1, 1980), with Michael Hurdzan; Summit Hills CC (R.10, 1980), with Michael Hurdzan; World of Golf (A.10, 1979), with Michael Hurdzan; World of Golf (R., 1979), with Michael Hurdzan.

New York: Troy CC (R.9, 1975), with Michael Hurdzan; Troy CC (A.9, 1975), with Michael Hurdzan.

Ohio: Blacklick Woods Metro Park GC (No. 1), Reynoldsburg (A.13, 1972); Brookside CC, Columbus (R.2, 1977), with Michael Hurdzan; Brookside Park GC, Ashland (A.9, 1977), with Michael Hurdzan; California GC, Cincinnati (A.5, 1975), with Michael Hurdzan; Camargo C, Cincinnati (R.1, 1965); Elyria CC (R.2, 1975), with Michael Hurdzan; Fostoria CC (A.10, 1972); Fostoria CC (R., 1972); Foxfire GC (A.6, 1984); Foxfire GC (A.9, 1984), with Michael Hurdzan; Galion CC (A.9, 1967); Groveport GC (A.9, 1973); Groveport GC (R., 1977), with Michael Hurdzan; Kenwood CC (Kendale Course), Cincinnati (R., 1981), with Michael Hurdzan; Kenwood CC (Kenview Course), Cincinnati (R., 1977), with Michael Hurdzan; Lakewood CC, Westlake (R.1, 1975), with Michael Hurdzan; Lakota Hills CC, West Chester (A.9, 1971); Lakota Hills CC, West Chester (R.9, 1971); Marion CC (R., 1977), with Michael Hurdzan; Miami Shores GC, Troy (R.9, 1977), with Michael Hurdzan; Miami Valley CC, Dayton (R., 1980), with Michael Hurdzan; Mohican Hills GC, Wooster (A.9, 1975), with Michael Hurdzan; Mount Vernon CC (R., 1977), with Michael Hurdzan; Neumann Park GC, Cincinnati (A.9, 1975), with Michael Hurdzan; Ohio Univ GC, Athens (A.9, 1963); Piqua CC (A.9, 1974); Shawnee CC, Lima (R., 1978), with Michael Hurdzan; Snyder Park CC, Springfield (R.4, 1962); Table Rock GC, Centerburg (A.9, 1976), with Michael Hurdzan; Table Rock GC, Centerburg (A.9, 1978); Wildwood GC, Fairfield (R.3, 1977), with Michael Hurdzan; Woodland GC, Cable (A.9, 1976); Wright-Patterson AFB GC, Dayton (R.4, 1971); Xenia GC, Xenia (A.9, 1982), with Michael Hurdzan; York Temple CC, Columbus (R.1, 1975), with Michael Hurdzan; Zanesville CC (R.5, 1981), with Michael Hurdzan.

West Virginia: Deerfield CC, Weston (A.9, 1978), with Michael Hurdzan; Deerfield CC, Weston (R.9, 1978), with Michael Hurdzan.

Kenneth K. Killian (1931 -   ) ASGCA, President, 1986.
Born: Chicago, Illinois.

Ken Killian graduated in 1957 from the University of Illinois with a B.S. degree in Landscape Architecture. From 1957 to 1964 he was employed with golf architect Robert Bruce Harris. In 1964 he formed the partnership of Killian and Nugent Inc. with Dick Nugent, another Harris assistant. The two worked together for nearly twenty years, collaborating on such designs as Kemper Lakes, site of the 1989 PGA.

In 1983, Killian and Nugent formed individual firms. While remaining based in the Chicago area, Killian handled projects in the Southeast and Southwest as well as the Midwest.

Courses by: Ken Killian

Arizona: Pueblo El Mirage CC, El Mirage (1985).

Illinois: Buffalo Grove GC (1968), with Dick Nugent; Concord Green GC, Libertyville (Par 3, 9, 1964), with Dick Nugent; Edgebrook GC, Sandwich (1967), with Dick Nugent; Forest Preserve National GC, Oak Forest (1981), with Dick Nugent and Bob Lohmann; Greenshire GC, Waukegan (1964), with Dick Nugent; Kemper Lakes GC, Hawthorne Woods (1979), with Dick Nugent; Moon Lake GC, Hoffman Estates (1973), with Dick Nugent; River Oaks GC, Calumet City (1971), with Dick Nugent; Robert A.Black GC, Chicago (Precision, 9, 1979), with Dick Nugent and Jeff Brauer; Tally Ho GC, Vernon Hills (9, 1979), with Dick Nugent; Warren Park GC (Precision,), with Dick Nugent; Weber Park GC, Skokie (Par 3, 9, 1973), with Dick Nugent; Western Illinois Univ GC, Macomb (9, 1971), with Dick Nugent.

Indiana: Oak Meadow G&TC, Evansville (1972), with Dick Nugent; Sand Creek C, Chesterton (1979), with Dick Nugent and Bob Lohmann; Woodmar CC, Hammond (1982), with Dick Nugent.

Ohio: Shelby Oaks GC, Sidney (1964), with Dick Nugent; Sugar Creek G&CC, with Dick Nugent.

Texas: Chester W. Ditto Muni, Arlington (1982), with Dick Nugent and Jeff Brauer; Mission CC, Odessa (1983), with Dick Nugent and Jeff Brauer.

Virginia: Poplar Forest GC, Lynchberg (9, 1980), with Dick Nugent.

Wisconsin: Abbey Springs GC, Fontana (1972), with Dick Nugent; Evergreen GC, Elkhorn (1973), with Dick Nugent; Lake Arrowhead GC, Nekoosa (1984), with Dick Nugent and Jeff Brauer; Tuckaway CC, Franklin (1967), with Dick Nugent.

Courses Remodeled & Added to by: Ken Killian

Illinois: Bartlett Hills G&CC, Bartlett (R.1, 1985); Bob O'Link CC, Highland Park (R., 1968), with Dick Nugent; Butterfield CC, Hinsdale (R., 1969), with Dick Nugent; Chevy Chase CC, Wheeling (R.), with Dick Nugent; Countryside GC (R., 1978), with Dick Nugent; Crystal Lake CC (R., 1980), with Dick Nugent; Deerpath Park GC, Lake Forest (R., 1971), with Dick Nugent; Deerpath Park GC, Lake Forest (R., 1981), with Dick Nugent; Elgin CC (R., 1978), with Dick Nugent; Evanston CC, Skokie (R., 1972), with Dick Nugent; Exmoor CC, Highland Park (R., 1969), with Dick Nugent; Fox Lake CC (R., 1973), with Dick Nugent; Glen Oak CC, Glen Ellyn (R., 1983); Glencoe GC (R., 1964), with Dick Nugent; Glencoe GC (R., 1982), with Dick Nugent and Bob Lohmann; Glenview Park GC, Glenview (R., 1985); Great Lakes NTC GC, North Chicago (A.9, 1971), with Dick Nugent; Green Acres CC, Northbrook (R.1, 1982), with Dick Nugent; Highland Park GC (R.5, 1977), with Dick Nugent; Hillcrest CC, Long Grove (R., 1979), with Dick Nugent; Kemper Lakes GC, Hawthorne Woods (R., 1987); Lake Shore CC, Glencoe (R., 1971), with Dick Nugent; Lansing Sportsman's C, Lansing (A.9, 1976), with Dick Nugent; Lincolnshire CC (Course No. 1), Crete (R., 1964), with Dick Nugent; Lincolnshire CC (Course No. 2), Crete (R.), with Dick Nugent; Marriott Lincolnshire GC (R.2, 1981), with Dick Nugent; McHenry GC (R.1, 1970), with Dick Nugent; Medinah CC (Course No. 3) (R., 1970), with Dick Nugent; Midlothian CC (R.), with Dick Nugent; North Shore CC, Glenview (R.), with Dick Nugent; Onwentsia C, Lake Forest (R., 1969), with Dick Nugent; Park Ridge CC (R.3, 1966), with Dick Nugent; Pinecrest G&CC, Huntley (R., 1979), with Dick Nugent; Ravinia Green CC, Deerfield (R., 1973), with Dick Nugent; Ridge CC, Chicago (R., 1972), with Dick Nugent; Ruth Lake CC, Hinsdale (R., 1980), with Dick Nugent; Silver Lake GC (North Course), Orland Park (R.1, 1978), with Dick Nugent; Skokie CC, Glencoe (R., 1973), with Dick Nugent; Sportsman G&CC, Northbrook (R.), with Dick Nugent; Spring Creek GC, Spring Valley (A.9, 1966), with Dick Nugent; Spring Creek GC, Spring Valley (R.9, 1966), with Dick Nugent; Sunset Valley GC, Highland Park (R., 1977), with Dick Nugent; Twin Orchards CC (Red Course), Long Grove (R.), with Dick Nugent; Villa Olivia CC, Bartlett (R., 1975), with Dick Nugent; Westmoreland CC, Wilmette (R.), with Dick Nugent; White Pines CC (East Course), Bensonville (R., 1982), with Dick Nugent; White Pines CC (West Course), Bensonville (R., 1982), with Dick Nugent; Wilmette Park GC, Glenview (R., 1979), with Dick Nugent.

Indiana: Chain O'Lakes GC, South Bend (R., 1966), with Dick Nugent.

Michigan: Berrien Hills CC, Benton Harbor (R., 1965), with Dick Nugent; Lost Lake Woods GC, Ypsilanti (A.9, 1974), with Dick Nugent.

Minnesota: Meadowbrook GC, Hopkins (A.9, 1966), with Dick Nugent.

Ohio: Lancaster CC (R., 1986).

South Dakota: Minnehaha CC, Sious Falls (R.6, 1976), with Dick Nugent.

Texas: Great Southwest GC, Arlington (R., 1983), with Dick Nugent and Jeff Brauer.

Wisconsin: Blackhawk CC, Madison (R., 1982), with Dick Nugent; Blue Mound G&CC, Wauwautosa (R., 1980), with Dick Nugent; Brynwood CC, Milwaukee (R., 1968), with Dick Nugent; Hartford CC (R.9, 1969), with Dick Nugent; Hartford CC (A.9, 1969), with Dick Nugent; Maple Bluff CC, Madison (R., 1973), with Dick Nugent; Reedsburg CC (A.9, 1978), with Dick Nugent and Bob Lohmann.

William Kinnear (- 1945)
Born: Leven, Scotland.

A professional golfer from Scotland, William Kinnear designed several courses and revised a number of established layouts in western Canada between the wars while serving as professional at Riverside CC in Saskatoon. His designs included Saskatoon CC and Riverside CC.

Ronald Kirby (1932 -   )
Born: Beverly, Massachusetts.

Ron Kirby, a member of the 1949 Massachusetts State High School Championship Golf Team, studied at the Boston Museum School of Fine Arts in 1946 and '47. He then attended the University of Massachusetts Stockbridge School of Agriculture on a Francis Ouimet Scholarship, receiving an Associate Degree in Agronomy in 1953.

Kirby served as superintendent on a number of golf courses, including one in the Bahamas designed by Dick Wilson. In the mid-1960s he was employed by Robert Trent Jones Inc., building courses in the U.S. and England. In 1970 he formed an association with golf architect Arthur Davis, based in Georgia. PGA professional Gary Player served for a time as a consulting partner in the firm.

In the late Seventies, Davis and Player left the firm, and associate Denis Griffiths became Kirby's partner.

Courses by: Ron Kirby

Alabama: CC of Alabama, Eufaula (1986), with Denis Griffiths; North River GC, Tuscaloosa (NLE, 1978), with Gary Player and Denis Griffiths.

Colorado: Pole Creek GC, Tabernash (1983), with Denis Griffiths.

Georgia: Alpine Valley GC; Berkeley Hills CC, Norcross (1971), with Arthur Davis and Gary Player; Grimball GC, Savannah (5, 1986), with Denis Griffiths; Little Course, Norcross (3); Nob North GC, Dalton (1978), with Denis Griffiths; Pebble Brook CC, Manchester (9, 1970), with Arthur Davis; Pine Isle CC, Lake Lanier (1972), with Arthur Davis and Gary Player; River North G&CC, Macon (1973), with Arthur Davis and Gary Player; Royal Oaks GC, Cartersville (9, 1971), with Arthur Davis and Gary Player.

Illinois: Holiday Inn GC, Crete (9, 1970), with Arthur Davis.

North Carolina: Twin Valley CC, Wadesboro (9), with Denis Griffiths.

South Carolina: Dolphin Head GC, Hilton Head Island (1973), with Arthur Davis and Gary Player; Marsh Point GC, Kiawah Island (1976), with Gary Player and Denis Griffiths.

Tennessee: Bent Creek Mountain Inn CC {formerly Cobbly Nob G Links}, Gatlinburg (1972), with Arthur Davis and Gary Player.

Texas: Fair Oaks Ranch G&CC, Boerne (1979), with Gary Player and Denis Griffiths.

Virginia: Brandermill CC, Midlothian (1976), with Gary Player and Denis Griffiths.

West Virginia: Shawnee GC, Institute (9, 1979), with Denis Griffiths.

Bophutatswana: Gary Player CC, Sun City (1979), with Gary Player and Denis Griffiths.

Canary Islands: Maspalomas GC (North Course) (1974), with Gary Player and Denis Griffiths.

Ivory Coast: Riviera Africaine GC (9, 1972), with Arthur Davis and Gary Player.

Japan: Niigata Forest GC, Toyoura Village (36, 1975), with Denis Griffiths; Nishi Nihon GC, Nogata (1975), with Denis Griffiths; Odawara CC (1973), with Arthur Davis and Gary Player; Sun Lake CC, Utsunomiya (1986), with Denis Griffiths.

Philippines: Kamirag GC, Cebu Island (36, 1982), with Denis Griffiths; Lake Paoay GC, Ilocos Norte (1979), with Denis Griffiths; Puerto Azul GC, Pasay City (1980), with Denis Griffiths.

Puerto Rico: Palmas del Mar GC, Humacao (1973), with Arthur Davis and Gary Player.

South Africa: Roodepoort Muni (1985), with Gary Player and Denis Griffiths; Welkom Muni (1987), with Gary Player and Denis Griffiths.

Spain: Almerimar GC, Almeria (1975), with Gary Player and Denis Griffiths; El Paraiso GC (1974), with Arthur Davis and Gary Player; Escorpion GC, Valencia (1975), with Gary Player and Denis Griffiths.

Courses Remodeled & Added to by: Ron Kirby

Alabama: Huntsville Muni (R., 1984), with Denis Griffiths.
Florida: Everglades C, Palm Beach (R., 1984), with Denis Griffiths.
Georgia: Bacon Park GC, Savannah (R., 1985), with Denis Griffiths; Bacon Park GC, Savannah (A.9, 1986), with Denis Griffiths; Cartersville CC (R.9, 1972), with Arthur Davis and Gary Player; Cartersville CC (A.9, 1972), with Arthur Davis and Gary Player; Dalton CC (R., 1977), with Denis Griffiths; Druid Hills CC, Atlanta (R.); Little Mountain CC (R., 1970), with Arthur Davis; Sandy Run GC (R., 1970), with Arthur Davis; Savannah GC (A.9, 1984), with Denis Griffiths; Standard C, Atlanta (NLE, R.1), with Arthur Davis and Gary Player; Standard C, Atlanta (NLE, A.1, 1971); Warner Robins AFB GC, Macon (R., 1970), with Arthur Davis.
Louisiana: New Orleans CC (R., 1985), with Denis Griffiths.
Missouri: Bellerive CC, Creve Coeur (R.1, 1985), with Denis Griffiths.
New Mexico: Alto Lakes G&CC (A.9, 1973), with Arthur Davis and Gary Player.
Texas: Fair Oaks Ranch G&CC, Boerne (A.9, 1985), with Denis Griffiths; Hogan Park GC, Midland (A.9, 1978), with Denis Griffiths; Midland CC (R., 1979), with Denis Griffiths; Oak Hill CC, San Antonio (R.2, 1978), with Denis Griffiths.
Virginia: Deer Run Muni, Newport News (R.27, 1986), with Denis Griffiths; Deer Run Muni, Newport News (A.9, 1986), with Denis Griffiths.
Philippines: Wack Wack G&CC (East Course), Manila (R., 1979), with Denis Griffiths.
South Africa: Kensington GC, Johannesburg (R., 1980), with Denis Griffiths; Royal Johannesburg GC (West Course) (R., 1985), with Denis Griffiths.

Ben Knight (1889 -   )

Ben Knight emigrated from Scotland to Minnesota in 1909. In 1919 he laid out Winona GC in Minnesota, remaining as its professional until his retirement in 1952. He also laid out courses as a sideline, designing thirty-two courses in Wisconsin and Minnesota during his career.

Courses by: Ben Knight

Iowa: Burlington GC (9).
Minnesota: Winona CC (9, 1919).

Donald Joseph Knott ASGCA

Don Knott attended the University of California at Berkeley, receiving a Bachelor of Landscape Architecture Degree in 1969 and a Master of Architecture Degree in 1973. He immediately went to work for Robert Trent Jones Inc., and worked closely for a year with Robert Trent Jones Jr. After three years with Trent Jones Sr. in Malaga, Spain, Knott rejoined Bobby Jones, who had formed his own company, in 1977. In 1979 he married Victoria Susan Graves, eldest daughter of golf architect Robert Muir Graves.

Courses by: Don Knott

California: Coto de Caza GC (1987), with Robert Trent Jones Jr; Poppy Hills GC, Pebble Beach (1986), with Robert Trent Jones Jr; Spanish Bay G Links, Pebble Beach (1987), with Robert Trent Jones Jr, Frank "Sandy" Tatum and Tom Watson.
Colorado: Beaver Creek GC, Avon (1982), with Robert Trent Jones Jr; Keystone Ranch GC, Dillon (1980), with Robert Trent Jones Jr.
Hawaii: Kiahuna Plantation GC, Poipu Beach (1983), with Robert Trent Jones Jr; Makena GC (New Course), Maui (1987), with Robert Trent Jones Jr; Makena GC (Old Course), Maui (1981), with Robert Trent Jones Jr.
Maine: Sugarloaf GC, Carrabassett Valley (1986), with Robert Trent Jones Jr.
Nevada: Spanish Trail G&CC, Las Vegas (1985), with Robert Trent Jones Jr.
Oregon: Sunriver GC (North Course) (1980), with Robert Trent Jones Jr.
Alberta: Glencoe G & CC (Forest Course), Calgary (1984), with Robert Trent Jones Jr and Gary Linn; Glencoe G & CC (Meadow Course), Calgary (1985), with Robert Trent Jones Jr and Gary Linn.
Australia: Joondalup GC (1985), with Robert Trent Jones Jr; Mandurah Resort GC (1986), with Robert Trent Jones Jr; National GC of Australia (1986), with Robert Trent Jones Jr.
France: Les Terrasses de Geneve G&CC, Bossey (1985), with Robert Trent Jones Jr.
Japan: Pine Lake GC (1984), with Robert Trent Jones Jr and Gary Linn; Shizukuishi GC (1984), with Robert Trent Jones Jr; Springfield GC (1986), with Robert Trent Jones Jr and Gary Linn.
Philippines: Calatagan GC (1983), with Robert Trent Jones Jr.
Singapore: Tuas GC (36, 1986), with Robert Trent Jones Jr.
South Africa: Wild Coast Holiday Inn GC (1983), with Robert Trent Jones Jr.

Courses Remodeled & Added to by: Don Knott

Hawaii: Princeville Makai GC, Kauai (A.18, 1987), with Robert Trent Jones Jr.
Idaho: Sun Valley GC (R., 1979), with Robert Trent Jones Jr; Sun Valley GC (A.4, 1979), with Robert Trent Jones Jr.

Harold B. Lamb

A professional golfer based in Salt Lake City, Utah, Hal Lamb won the 1922 Utah Open. He designed several of his home state's earliest courses, including The Country Club, Salt Lake City.

William Boice Langford (1887 - 1977) ASGCA, Charter Member; President, 1951, 1963.

Born: Austin, Illinois. Died: Sarasota, Florida at age 89.

William B. Langford suffered from polio as a child and took up golf as part of a rehabilitation program. He developed into a fine amateur player and was a member of three Yale University NCAA Championship teams from 1906 to 1908.

After earning a Master's Degree in Mining Engineering at Columbia University, Langford returned to Chicago and worked as course architect for the American Park Builders. He formed his own course design firm in 1918 in partnership with engineer Theodore J. Moreau.

Langford and Moreau were active in course design and construction throughout

the Midwest from the 1920s to World War II. They produced detailed engineering drawings and balanced cuts and fills for construction as early as the 1920s. Late in his career, Langford estimated that he had designed some 250 courses and had at one time employed eighty men, including three survey crews to prepare topographic maps and set grading stakes.

Langford also owned and operated several daily-fee courses in the Chicago area and was a strong promoter of public courses. He served for many years on the USGA Public Links Committee, as well as on local and regional public golf associations. During and after the Depression, he wrote several articles advocating six-hole courses with multiple tees to speed play and accommodate play for the average working man.

The Langford and Moreau firm dissolved in the early 1940s, but after World War II Langford again developed a golf design business. In the 1960s, in semiretirement, he served as consulting golf architect to the landscape architecture firm of McFadzean and Everly of Winnetka, Illinois.

Bill Langford retired to Florida in the late 1960s. He died there in 1977, just a few weeks short of his ninetieth birthday.

Courses by: William B. Langford

Arkansas: Al Amin Temple CC, Little Rock , with Theodore J. Moreau; Texarkana CC (1927), with Theodore J. Moreau.
Florida: Eglin AFB GC, Niceville (1925), with Theodore J. Moreau; Granada GC, Coral Gables (9, 1925), with Theodore J. Moreau; Kelsey City GC, West Palm Beach (NLE, 1924), with Theodore J. Moreau; Key West GC (NLE, 1923), with Theodore J. Moreau; Lake Worth Muni (1924), with Theodore J. Moreau; Parkhurst CC, Boynton Beach (NLE, 1925), with Theodore J. Moreau; St. Lucie River CC, Port Sewall (NLE, 1924), with Theodore J. Moreau; Valparaiso CC (NLE, 1927), with Theodore J. Moreau; West Palm Beach CC (NLE, 1921), with Theodore J. Moreau.
Illinois: Acacia CC, Harlem (1924), with Theodore J. Moreau; Aroma Park GC, Kankakee; Bryn Mawr GC, Lincolnwood (1921), with Theodore J. Moreau; Butterfield CC, Hinsdale (1922), with Theodore J. Moreau; Doering Estate GC, Chicago (6, 1931), with Theodore J. Moreau; Franklin County CC, West Frankfort (9, 1922), with Theodore J. Moreau; Golden Acres CC, Schaumberg (27, 1928), with Theodore J. Moreau; Kankakee Elks CC, St. Anne (1936), with Theodore J. Moreau; Maple Crest GC, LaGrange (Par 3, 9, 1951); Marquette Park GC, Chicago (1917), with Theodore J. Moreau; Mid City GC, Chicago (NLE, 1924), with Theodore J. Moreau; Morris CC (NLE, 9, 1925), with Theodore J. Moreau; Oaklawn GC, Chicago (Par 3, 9, 1952); Ridgemoor CC, Harwood Heights (1921); Riverside CC, North Riverside (1917); Ruth Lake CC, Hinsdale (1926), with Theodore J. Moreau; Skokie Playfield GC, Winnetka (NLE, Par 3, 9), with Theodore J. Moreau; South Bluff CC, Peru (9); St. Clair CC, Belleville (1927), with Theodore J. Moreau; Twin Orchard CC, Bensenville (NLE, 1924), with Theodore J. Moreau; Village Green CC, Mundelein (1955).
Indiana: Buena Vista CC, Vincennes (9, 1921); Christiana CC, Elkhart (9, 1925), with Theodore J. Moreau; Culver Military Academy GC (1920), with Theodore J. Moreau; Dykeman Park Muni, Logansport (9), with Theodore J. Moreau; East Shore GC, Culver (1922), with Theodore J. Moreau; Gary CC, Merrillville (1921), with Theodore J. Moreau; Harrison Hills CC, Attica (9, 1923), with Theodore J. Moreau; La Porte CC, Pine Lake (9); Maxwelton GC, Syracuse; Oakland City GC (9, 1946).
Iowa: Credit Island GC, Davenport (1925), with Theodore J. Moreau; Duck Creek Park GC, Davenport (1927); Ellis Park Muni, Cedar Rapids (1949); Oneota CC, Decorah (9, 1921); Wakonda C, Des Moines (1922), with Theodore J. Moreau.
Kansas: Meadow Lake CC, Kansas City (NLE, 1917); Milburn G&CC, Overland Park (1917).
Kentucky: Audubon CC, Louisville (1921), with Theodore J. Moreau; Bowling Green CC, with Theodore J. Moreau; Henderson G&CC, with Theodore J. Moreau; Indian Hills CC, Bowling Green .
Michigan: Blythefield CC, Belmont (1927), with Theodore J. Moreau; CC of Lansing (1919), with Theodore J. Moreau; Iron River CC (1932), with Theodore J. Moreau; Marquette G&CC (9, 1927), with Theodore J. Moreau; Portage Park GC, Houghton (NLE, 9, 1916).
Minnesota: Mankato GC, with Theodore J. Moreau.
Mississippi: Clarksdale CC (1921), with Theodore J. Moreau.
Nebraska: Happy Hollow C, Omaha (1926), with Theodore J. Moreau; Highland CC, Omaha (1924), with Theodore J. Moreau; Omaha CC (1927), with Theodore J. Moreau.
North Dakota: Town & Country C, Devil's Lake (9, 1920), with Theodore J. Moreau.
Ohio: Avon Fields GC, Cincinnati (1924), with Theodore J. Moreau; Clovernook CC, Cincinnati (1924), with Theodore J. Moreau; Fairlawn CC, Akron (1917), with Theodore J. Moreau; Hillcrest CC, Cincinnati (NLE, 1925), with Theodore J. Moreau; Portage CC, Akron (1918).
South Carolina: Greenville CC (Riverside Course) (1919).
South Dakota: Minnehaha CC, Sious Falls (1922), with Theodore J. Moreau.
Tennessee: Chickasaw CC, Memphis (1922); Colonial CC, Memphis (NLE, 1916); CC of Morristown (1957); Gatlinburg G&CC (1956); Green Meadow CC, Marysville (1958); Ridgeway CC, Memphis (NLE, 9, 1919).
Texas: State Line GC, Texarkana (1930), with Theodore J. Moreau.
Wisconsin: Lawsonia Links, Green Lake (1929), with Theodore J. Moreau; Leathem Smith Lodge GC, Sturgeon Bay (9, 1930), with Theodore J. Moreau; North Shore Acres CC, Kenosha (1927,); Our CC, Salem (1927), with Theodore J. Moreau; Ozaukee CC, Mequon (1922), with Theodore J. Moreau; Spring Valley CC, Salem (1927), with Theodore J. Moreau; West Bend CC (9), with Theodore J. Moreau.
Jamaica: St. James GC, Montego Bay (NLE, 9).

Courses Remodeled & Added to by: William B. Langford

Florida: Breakers GC (Ocean Course), Palm Beach (A.9, 1926); Breakers GC (Ocean Course), Palm Beach (R.9, 1926), with Theodore J. Moreau; Coral Gables Biltmore GC, Coral Gables (R.); Everglades C, Palm Beach (R., 1937), with Theodore J. Moreau; Martin County G&CC (R.9); Martin County G&CC (A.9, 1951).
Illinois: Barrington Hills CC, Barrington (R.1, 1946); Beverly CC, Chicago (R.4); Biltmore CC, Barrington (R., 1957); Bloomington CC (A.9, 1917); Bryn Mawr GC, Lincolnwood (R., 1951); Fresh Meadow G&CC, Hillside (R., 1956); Glen Oak CC, Glen Ellyn (R., 1922), with Theodore J. Moreau; Hickory Hills CC, Palos Park (Par

211

3, A.9, 1954); Highland Park GC (R.3, 1939), with Theodore J. Moreau; Idlewild CC, Flossmoor (R.); Mid City GC, Chicago (NLE, R., 1931), with Theodore J. Moreau; Park Ridge CC (R., 1949); Ravisloe CC, Homewood (R.), with Theodore J. Moreau; Ridgemoor CC, Harwood Heights (R., 1927), with Theodore J. Moreau; Riverside GC, North Riverside (R., 1951); Skokie CC, Glencoe (R., 1938), with Theodore J. Moreau; Tam O'Shanter CC, Niles (NLE, R., 1948); Westmoreland CC, Wilmette (R.); Winnetka Park GC (Par 3, A.9, 1960).

Indiana: Christiana CC, Elkhart (A.9, 1945).
Iowa: Keokuk CC (R., 1951).
Kentucky: Louisville CC (R., 1921), with Theodore J. Moreau.
Minnesota: Mankato GC (A.9, 1954).
Tennessee: Ridgeway CC, Memphis (NLE, A.9, 1950).
Wisconsin: Westmoor GC, Brookfield (R.5, 1955).

Robert F. "Red" Lawrence (1893 - 1976) ASGCA, Charter Member; President, 1956, 1964.
Born: White Plains, New York. Died: Tucson, Arizona at age 83.
Red Lawrence (so-called because of his hair color) got his first golf design experience working for Walter Travis on the construction of two courses at Westchester Biltmore CC in 1919. From 1921 to 1932 Red was employed by the design firm of Toomey and Flynn.
In the late 1920s Lawrence constructed several Toomey and Flynn designs in Florida, including thirty-six holes at the Boca Raton Hotel. When the design firm dissolved during the Depression, Lawrence became course superintendent at Boca Raton, where he remained for twenty years. While there, he became friends with the club's teaching professional, Tommy Armour. As a joke, Lawrence persuaded Armour to instruct a wealthy patron while sitting under a beach umbrella with drink in hand. Armour did it not once, but often, and this unorthodox teaching arrangement quickly became Armour's trademark!
In the late 1930s Lawrence designed a few courses in the Miami area, but most were not built until after World War II. As business improved after the War, Lawrence resigned from Boca Raton to devote full time to golf course architecture. He worked primarily in Florida until 1958, when he moved to Tucson, Arizona. Continuing his practice in the Southwest, Lawrence did some of his finest work, including Desert Forest CC and University of New Mexico GC. In the 1970s he was assisted by civil engineer Jeff Hardin.
Courses by: Red Lawrence
Arizona: Bellaire GC, Phoenix (Precision, 1973), with Jeff Hardin and Greg Nash; Boulders GC, Carefree (9, 1969); Camelback GC (Padre Course), Scottsdale (1970); CC of Green Valley (1971); Desert Forest GC, Carefree (1962); Dobson Ranch GC, Mesa (Precision, 1974), with Jeff Hardin and Greg Nash; Fountain of the Sun GC, Mesa (Precision, 1971); Goodyear G&CC (West Course), Litchfield Park (1974), with Jeff Hardin and Greg Nash; Meadow Hills CC, Nogales (1963); Nautical Inn GC, Lake Havasu City (Precision, 10, 1974); Santa Cruz CC, Nogales (1974); Sierra Estrella GC, Goodyear (9, 1962); Tubac Valley CC (1960); Tucson Estates GC (East Course) (Precision, 9, 1972); Tucson Estates GC (West Course) (Par 3, 9, 1960).
Florida: Dania CC (9, 1951); Diplomat CC, Hollywood (1957); Fort Lauderdale CC (South Course) (1951); Miami Beach Par 3 GC (1961); Miami Shores CC (1937); Plantation GC, Ft. Lauderdale (1951); Pompano Beach CC (Palms Course) (1954); Redland G&CC, Homestead (1947); Sunset GC, Hollywood (9, 1952).
New Mexico: Horizon CC, Belen (9, 1972); Paradise Hills G&CC, Albuquerque (1960); Sunport CC, Albuquerque (Par 3, 1970); University of New Mexico GC (South Crs.), Albuquerque (1966).
Courses Remodeled & Added to by: Red Lawrence
Arizona: San Marcos Hotel & C, Chandler (R., 1963); Sierra Estrella GC, Goodyear (A.9, 1967); Tucson CC (R.3, 1963); Tucson National GC, Tucson (R.6, 1966).
Florida: Bayshore GC, Miami Beach (NLE, R.); Boca Raton Hotel & C (R., 1947); Delray Beach G&CC (A.9, 1962); Fort Lauderdale CC (North Course) (R., 1951); Orange Brook CC (East Course), Hollywood (R., 1961); Orange Brook CC (West Course), Hollywood (R.9, 1955); Orange Brook CC (West Course), Hollywood (A.9, 1961).

Charles Dundas Lawrie (1923 - 1976) BAGCA
Born: Edinburgh, Scotland. Died: Edinburgh, Scotland at age 53.
C.D. Lawrie was educated at Fettes and at Oxford, where he was a cricket star. After service with the Coldstream Guards during World War II, he was involved in sports administration and amateur golf. He reached the semi-finals of the 1955 Scottish Amateur and won thirty-two consecutive matches with partner Donald Steel in the annual Halford Hewitt tournament. He also served as honorary captain of the 1961 and 1963 Walker Cup teams.
Lawrie, specializing in the administration of golf events, coordinated the activities of many British Open tournaments. His last was in 1972 at Muirfield. He also served as chairman of the Royal and Ancient Selection Committee, and chose Walker Cup participants from 1963 to 1967. In the late 1960s Lawrie became a partner in the golf design firm of Cotton (C.K.) Pennink, Lawrie and Partners Ltd., but had completed only a handful of courses before his untimely death in 1976.
Courses by: C.D. Lawrie
England: Abbey Hill GC, Buckinghamshire (1975), with J.J.F. Pennink; Fakenham GC, Norfolk (9, 1973), with J.J.F. Pennink; Rookery Park GC, Suffolk, with J.J.F. Pennink; Royal Lytham & St. Annes GC (Short Crs), Lancashire (Precision,), with J.J.F. Pennink; Southwick Park GC (HMS Dryad), Hampshire (1977), with J.J.F. Pennink; Twickenham GC, Middlesex (9, 1976), with J.J.F. Pennink; Winter Hill GC, Berkshire (1976), with J.J.F. Pennink; Woburn G&CC (Duchess Course), Buckinghamshire (1976), with J.J.F. Pennink and D.M.A.Steel; Woburn G&CC (Duke Course), Buckinghamshire (1974), with J.J.F. Pennink.
Scotland: Livingston G&CC, Edinburgh (1978), with J.J.F. Pennink; Westhill GC, Aberdeenshire (1977), with J.J.F. Pennink.
Courses Remodeled & Added to by: C.D. Lawrie
England: Corhampton GC, Hampshire (R.9), with J.J.F. Pennink; Romsey GC, Hampshire (R.), with J.J.F. Pennink; Royal Wimbledon GC, Surrey (R.), with J.J.F. Pennink.

Ireland: Cork GC, County Cork (R., 1975), with C.K. Cotton and J.J.F. Pennink.

Richard William LaConte (1931 -) ASGCA
After working for years as a golf course superintendent, Richard LaConte was associated with golf architect William F. Mitchell for a short time before Mitchell's death in 1974. He then practiced on his own and, for one year, in partnership with Ted McAnlis. In the 1980s LaConte left course design to concentrate on housing developments. On two such developments, he worked with McAnlis on the layouts.
Courses by: Richard W. LaConte
Florida: Lone Pine GC, West Palm Beach (Precision, 1981), with Ted McAnlis; Suntree CC (North Course), Melbourne (1976).
Ohio: Briardale Greens Muni, Euclid (1977), with Ted McAnlis; Chapel Hills GC, Ashtabula; Dorlon Park GC, Columbiana (1972); Duck Creek GC, Ravenna (1972); Leaning Tree GC, West Richfield (Precision, 1972), with Ted McAnlis; Parkview Heights GC, Mayfield Heights (Precision, 1971); Rolling Green GC, Huntsburg (1967); Whetstone CC, Marion (1972), with William F. Mitchell.
Courses Remodeled & Added to by: Richard W. LaConte
Louisiana: Brechtel Memorial Park GC, New Orleans (A.9, 1978), with Ted McAnlis; Brechtel Memorial Park GC, New Orleans (R.9, 1978), with Ted McAnlis.
Ohio: Grandview CC, Middlefield (R.), with Ted McAnlis; Willard CC (A.9, 1971), with Ted McAnlis.

John B. LaFoy (1946 -) ASGCA
Born: Forest Hills, New York.
A native of New York, John LaFoy was raised in Greenville, S.C., where he was a schoolmate with George Cobb Jr., son of prominent golf architect George Cobb. After receiving a B.A. degree in Architecture from Clemson University in 1968, LaFoy went to work for Cobb. His early duties included accompanying Cobb on frequent consultations at Augusta National, an experience much envied by other course architects.
A three-year stint in the U.S. Marine Corps interrupted LaFoy's employment with Cobb. When he returned, he soon became a full partner in the business.
LaFoy assumed much of the design responsibilities when illness slowed Cobb in the early Eighties. Several courses credited to George Cobb, including the dramatic mountaintop Linville Ridge GC in North Carolina, were done almost entirely by LaFoy.
LaFoy maintained the design business in Greenville after Cobb's death in 1986.
Courses by: John LaFoy
Alabama: Mountain Brook C, Birmingham (1985).
Georgia: Foxcreek GC, Atlanta (Precision, 1986).
North Carolina: Bryan Park GC (Course No.1), Greensboro (1973), with George W. Cobb; Linville Ridge CC, Linville (1983), with George W. Cobb.
South Carolina: Clemson University GC (1976), with George W. Cobb; Cobb's Glen CC, Anderson (1975), with George W. Cobb; Holly Tree CC, Greenville (1973), with George W. Cobb; Keowee Key CC, Seneca (1977), with George W. Cobb; Woodlands CC (1975), with George W. Cobb.
Virginia: New Quarter Park GC (1977), with George W. Cobb; Pohick Bay GC (1978), with George W. Cobb; Tides Inn & CC (Golden Eagle Course), Irvington (1976), with George W. Cobb.
West Virginia: Mountwood Park GC (1977), with George W. Cobb.
Courses Remodeled & Added to by: John LaFoy
Alabama: Grayson Valley CC, Birmingham (R.); Mountain Brook C, Birmingham (R., 1985); Valley Hill CC (R.27, 1985).
Florida: Palma Ceia G&CC, Tampa (R.4, 1986).
Georgia: Athens CC (A.9, 1985), with George W. Cobb; Stone Mountain GC (R.9, 1986); Waynesboro CC (A.9, 1984), with George W. Cobb.
Minnesota: Somerset CC, St. Paul (R., 1976), with George W. Cobb.
North Carolina: Cape Fear CC, Wilmington (R., 1986); Cleveland CC, Shelby (R., 1986); CC of Sapphire (R.1, 1985); Greensboro CC (Carlson Farms Course) (R.1, 1985); High Meadows GC, Roaring Gap (R., 1985); Pine Lake CC, Charlotte (R., 1986); Pope AFB GC, Fayetteville (A.9, 1975), with George W. Cobb; Rolling Hills CC, Monroe (A., 1967), with George W. Cobb; Rolling Hills CC, Monroe (R., 1986).
South Carolina: CC of Spartanburg (R., 1985); Florence CC (R., 1986); Fort Jackson GC, Columbia (R.4, 1986); Fripp Island CC (R., 1976), with George W. Cobb; Port Royal GC (Robbers Row Course), Hilton Head Island (A.9, 1974), with George W. Cobb.
Tennessee: Ridgefields CC, Kingsport (R., 1986).
Virginia: Tides Inn & CC (Tartan Course), Irvington (A.3, 1984); Tides Inn & CC (Tartan Course), Irvington (R., 1986).
West Virginia: Fincastle CC, Bluefield (R.); Rainelle CC (R., 1976), with George W. Cobb; Twin Falls State Park GC, Mullens (A.9, 1981), with George W. Cobb.

Joseph L. Lee (1922 -)
Born: Oviedo, Florida.
Joe Lee, an outstanding high school and college athlete, graduated from the University of Miami with a degree in education. He took up golf while still in college and after teaching math for a year at Delray Beach Junior High School in Florida, decided instead to pursue a professional golf career. Golf architect Dick Wilson, a Delray Beach acquaintance, helped Lee to land the job of assistant pro at Moraine CC in Dayton, Ohio, which Wilson was remodeling at the time.
Lee spent two years at Moraine and while Wilson was working on the neighboring NCR CC courses, Lee lived with Wilson's family. In 1952 Lee left Moraine to assist the completion of NCR. He went on to supervise construction of several Wilson designs and in the mid-1950s was given major responsibility for design and construction of Villa Real GC in Havana, Cuba.
By 1959 Lee was a full partner with Wilson. He finished four courses Wilson had been building at the time of his death in 1965 and then established his own practice with the assistance of many of the same crew that had been with Wilson for a decade or more. Concentrating mainly in the Sunbelt, Lee created some of America's top courses as well as outstanding resort layouts in the Caribbean.

Courses by: Joe Lee

Alabama: Lakewood GC (Azalea Course), Point Clear (9, 1967); Riverchase CC, Birmingham (1975); Wynlakes CC, Montgomery (1987), with Rocky Roquemore.

California: La Costa CC (Gold Course), Carlsbad (1964), with Dick Wilson; La Costa CC (Orange Course), Carlsbad (9, 1973); Sunnylands GC, Rancho Mirage (9, 1962), with Dick Wilson.

Delaware: Bidermann GC, Wilmington , with Dick Wilson.

Florida: Banyan GC, West Palm Beach (1973), with Rocky Roquemore; Barefoot Bay G&CC, Sebastian (Precision, 1972); Bay Hill C, Orlando (1961), with Dick Wilson, Robert von Hagge and Bob Simmons; Bent Pine GC, Vero Beach (1979); Boca G&TC, Boca Raton (1986); Boca Greens GC, Boca Raton (1979); Boca West C (Course No. 4), Boca Raton (1982); Boca Woods CC (South Course), Boca Raton (1981); Bocaire CC, Boca Raton (1985), with Rocky Roquemore; Bonaventure CC (East Course), Fort Lauderdale (1970); Broken Sound CC, Boca Raton (1987); Broken Sound GC, Boca Raton (1976); Camino Del Mar CC, Boca Raton (1975); Canongate GC, Orlando (Precision, 1968); Century GC, West Palm Beach (Precision, 1968); Century Village GC, Deerfield Beach (Precision, 1976); Del-Aire CC, Delray Beach (27, 1978); Disney World GC (Magnolia Course), Lake Buena Vista (1970), with Rocky Roquemore; Disney World GC (Palm Course), Lake Buena Vista (1970), with Rocky Roquemore; Errol Estates Inn & CC, Apopka (27, 1972); Feather Sound CC, St. Petersburg (1975); Gadsden CC, Quincy (1975); Gator Creek GC, Sarasota (1976); Halie Plantation GC, Gainesville (1986); Hamlet of Delray Beach GC (1973), with Rocky Roquemore; Harbour Ridge CC (Golden Marsh Course), Stuart (1985); Harder Hall Hotel GC, Sebring (1958), with Dick Wilson; High Ridge CC, Boynton Beach (1982); Hole-in-the-Wall GC, Naples (1958), with Dick Wilson; Interlachen CC, Winter Park (1986); International G&CC, Orlando (1986); Island Dunes GC, Jensen Beach (Precision, 9, 1983); JDM CC (East Course), Palm Beach Gardens (1964), with Dick Wilson; JDM CC (North Course), Palm Springs Gardens (9, 1964), with Dick Wilson; JDM CC (South Course), Palm Springs Gardens (9, 1964), with Dick Wilson; Lacuna CC, Lantana (1985); Lake Buena Vista C (1972), with Rocky Roquemore; Little C, Delray Beach (Par 3, 1969); Lone Palm GC, Lakeland (1965), with Dick Wilson; Marriott Orlando World GC, Orlando (1986); Melreese GC, Miami (1962), with Dick Wilson; Orange Lake CC, Kissimmee (27, 1982); Palm-Aire West CC (Lakes Course), Sarasota (1982); Pine Tree CC, Delray Beach (1962), with Dick Wilson and Robert von Hagge; Piper's Landing G&CC, Stuart (1981); Quail Ridge CC (North Course), Delray Beach (1974); Quail Ridge CC (South Course), Delray Beach (1977); Rainbow's End G&CC, Dunellon (1979); River Ranch GC, Lake Wales (9, 1977); Sugar Mill CC, New Smyrna Beach (1970); Suwannee River Valley CC, Jasper (9); Tequesta CC, Jupiter (1958), with Dick Wilson; Turtle Creek C, Jupiter (1969); Tuscawilla CC, Winter Springs (1973).

Georgia: Bent Tree CC, Jasper (1973); Big Canoe GC, Lake Sconti (1974), with Rocky Roquemore; Bull Creek GC, Columbus (1971); Callaway Gardens GC (Gardensview Crs), Pine Mountain (1969); Callaway Gardens GC (Mountainview Crs), Pine Mountain (1963), with Dick Wilson; Callaway Gardens GC (Skyview Course), Pine Mountain (1969); Canongate GC, Palmetto (1965), with Dick Wilson; Canongate-on Lanier GC, Cumming (1970), with Rocky Roquemore; Flat Creek GC, Peachtree City (1970); Hidden Hills CC, Stone Mountain (1974), with Rocky Roquemore; Horseshoe Bend CC, Roswell (1975), with Rocky Roquemore; Indian Hills CC, Marietta (1970), with Rocky Roquemore; Island C, St. Simons Island (1975), with Rocky Roquemore; Jekyll Island GC (Indian Mounds Course) (1975); Jekyll Island GC (Oleander Course) (1961), with Dick Wilson; Jekyll Island GC (Pine Lakes Course) (1967); Mystery Valley CC, Lithonia (1965), with Dick Wilson; Okefenokee GC, Waycross (1983), with Rocky Roquemore; Rivermont G&CC, Alpharetta (1970), with Rocky Roquemore; Sea Island GC (Marshside 9), St. Simons Island (1973), with Rocky Roquemore; Sea Island GC (Retreat 9) (9, 1959), with Dick Wilson; Snapfinger Woods GC, Decatur (27, 1974), with Rocky Roquemore; Tally Mountain C, Tallapoosa (1974); Valdosta CC (27, 1981), with Rocky Roquemore; White Oak GC, Newnan (1987), with Rocky Roquemore.

Illinois: Cog Hill GC (Course No. 3), Lemont (1964), with Dick Wilson; Cog Hill GC (Course No. 4), Lemont (1964), with Dick Wilson; Pine Meadow GC, Mundelein (1985), with Rocky Roquemore; Plum Tree National GC, Harvard (1970).

Louisiana: Beau Chene G&RC (Magnolia Course), Mandeville (9, 1983), with Rocky Roquemore; Beau Chene G&RC (Oak Course), Mandeville (1974), with Rocky Roquemore; Eastover CC, New Orleans (1987), with Rocky Roquemore; Squirrel Run GC, New Iberia (1987).

Nevada: Desert Rose GC, Las Vegas (1964), with Dick Wilson.

New Jersey: Bedens Brook C, Skillman , with Dick Wilson.

New York: Cavalry C, Manlius (1966), with Dick Wilson.

North Carolina: Cross Creek CC, Mount Airy (1982), with Rocky Roquemore; Kenmure GC, Flat Rocks (1983), with Rocky Roquemore.

Ohio: Coldstream CC, Cincinnati (1960), with Dick Wilson, Robert von Hagge and Bob Simmons.

South Carolina: Houndslake CC, Aiken (1976), with Rocky Roquemore.

Tennessee: Fall Creek Falls State Park GC, Pikesville (1972), with Rocky Roquemore; Montclair CC, Chattanooga (Precision, 9); Stonehenge GC, Fairfield Glade (1984), with Rocky Roquemore.

Texas: Trophy C (Oaks Course), Roanoke (1976), with Ben Hogan; Woodlands Inn & CC (West Course) (1973).

Virginia: Crossings G&CC {formerly Half Sinke GC}, Richmond (1977).

Bahamas: Bahamas Princess Hotel & CC (Emerald), Freeport (1965), with Dick Wilson and Bob Simmons; Bahamas Princess Hotel & CC (Ruby), Freeport (1967); Fortune Hills GC, Freeport (9, 1972); Great Harbour Cay CC, Berry Island (1969); Lucaya Park G&CC, Freeport (1964), with Dick Wilson and Bob Simmons; Lyford Cay C, New Providence (1960), with Dick Wilson and Bob Simmons; Paradise Island G&CC, Nassau (1962), with Dick Wilson and Bob Simmons; Shannon G&CC, Freeport (1970); South Ocean Beach Hotel GC, New Providence Is. (1971); Treasure Cay GC, Abaco (1966), with Dick Wilson.

Colombia: Club Lagos De Caujarel, Barranquilla (1972).

Cuba: Villa Real GC, Havana (1957), with Dick Wilson.

Guam: Anderson AFB GC (1968).

Portugal: Quintado de Lago GC (Course No. 2), Faro (27, 1987), with Rocky Roquemore.

St. Marten: Mullet Bay GC (1974).

Venezuela: Barquisimeto CC (1979); Guataparo GC, Valencia (1982), with Rocky Roquemore; Izcaragua CC, Caracas (1982), with Rocky Roquemore.

Courses Remodeled & Added to by: Joe Lee

Florida: Breakers GC (Ocean Course), Palm Beach (R., 1966); Clearwater CC (R., 1966); Clearwater CC (R., 1967); Fernadina Beach GC (A.9, 1975); Gulfstream GC, Delray Beach (R., 1958), with Dick Wilson; Indian Creek CC, Miami Beach (R.), with Dick Wilson; John's Island C (South Course), Vero Beach (R., 1984); JDM CC (North Course), Palm Springs Gardens (A.9, 1969); JDM CC (South Course), Palm Springs Gardens (A.9, 1970); Orange Tree CC, Orlando (R.1, 1983); Palm Beach National G&CC West Palm Beach (R., 1980); Ponte Vedra C (Lagoon Course), Ponte Vedra Beach (A.9, 1981); Sara Bay CC, Sarasota (R., 1980); Seascape G&RC, Destin (A.9, 1980); Seascape G&RC, Destin (R., 1980); Sugar Mill CC, New Smyrna Beach (A.9, 1983), with Rocky Roquemore; Tyndall AFB GC, Panama City Beach (A.9, 1975), with Rocky Roquemore.

Georgia: Callaway Gardens GC (Lakeview Course) , Pine Mountain (A.9, 1963), with Dick Wilson; Cherokee Town & CC (Riverside Course), Dunwoody (A.9, 1986), with Rocky Roquemore; Flat Creek GC, Peachtree City (A.9, 1983), with Rocky Roquemore; Green Island CC, Columbus (R., 1978), with Rocky Roquemore.

Illinois: Cog Hill CC (Course No. 1), Lemont (R., 1963), with Dick Wilson; Cog Hill GC (Course No. 2), Lemont (R., 1963), with Dick Wilson; Cog Hill GC (Course No. 4), Lemont (R., 1977); Glenwoodie GC, Chicago Heights (R., 1978); St. Andrews G&CC (Course No. 1), West Chicago (R., 1968); St. Andrews G&CC (Course No. 2), West Chicago (R., 1968).

Kentucky: Owensboro CC (R., 1978).

Louisiana: Baton Rouge CC (R., 1967); Beau Chene G&RC (Magnolia Course), Mandeville (A.9, 1985); New Orleans CC (R.9, 1982); Tchefuncta GC, Covington (A.9).

Michigan: Warwick Hills G&CC, Grand Blanc (R., 1967).

North Carolina: Highlands Falls CC, Highlands (R.5, 1985), with Rocky Roquemore; Highlands Falls CC, Highlands (A.13, 1985), with Rocky Roquemore.

Ohio: Scioto CC, Columbus (R., 1963), with Dick Wilson and Robert von Hagge.

Pennsylvania: Hidden Valley CC, Pittsburgh (R., 1968); St. Clair CC, Pittsburgh (A.9, 1971).

Virginia: CC of Virginia (Tuckahoe Course), Richmond (A.9, 1986), with Rocky Roquemore.

Wisconsin: Lawsonia Links, Green Lake (A.9, 1983), with Rocky Roquemore.

Herbert Corey Leeds (1855 - 1930)

Born: Boston, Massachusetts. Died: Hamilton, Massachusetts at age 75.

Herbert Leeds graduated from Harvard College in 1877 and was awarded a B.A. Degree in 1891. A lifelong sportsman, he was an excellent baseball and football player while in college. He was also a yachting enthusiast and spent three years sailing in the Far East and West Indies. As late as the turn of the century, Leeds was a crew member in several International Cup Races and his book *Log of the Columbia* (1899) related his experiences aboard a racing yacht. He was also an expert card player and wrote *The Laws of Bridge* and *The Laws of Euchre*.

Leeds took up golf when he was nearly forty but within two years was playing at scratch. Though beyond his prime when national amateur tournaments became prominent, he did win several club championships and invitation tournaments. He was a member of the USGA Executive Committee in 1905.

Leeds' first golf design experience was the creation of a new eighteen-hole course for Myopia Hunt Club, replacing its rudimentary nine-hole layout, which had been built by R.M. Appleton, master of the club's fox hounds. Leeds, who remained at Myopia all his life and served as Captain of its Green Committee, built the front nine in 1896 and the back nine in 1901. The course exists today, with only minor changes, just as he created and refined it.

Leeds' efforts at Myopia created a landmark course, the scene of many early matches, including four U.S. Opens. It was praised by leading American and British golfers and written about in publications on both sides of the Atlantic. Myopia's historian, Edward Weeks, once observed about Leeds:

He never ceased digging new traps. It was his habit to carry small white chips in his pocket . . . . When the drive of a long hitter was sliced or hooked Leeds would place a marker on the spot and a new trap filled with soft white Ipswich sand would appear. This resulted in some holes being praised by British professionals as the most skillfully trapped in the United States. After a tour of the great links of Britain in 1902, Leeds returned to the United States to build several other courses. Although club champion at The Country Club, Brookline, Mass., there is no evidence that he participated in any of its expansions. He did however create the original course at Essex CC in Manchester, as well as Bass Rocks GC in Gloucester. He also worked outside his native state, as far north as Maine (the original nine at Kebo Valley Club in Bar Harbor) and as far south as South Carolina (the original nine at Palmetto CC in Aiken).

Peter W. Lees (1868 - 1923)

Peter Lees, greenkeeper at Royal Mid Surrey, emigrated to the United States around 1910 to construct and maintain Lido GC on Long Island for architect Charles Blair Macdonald. He had been recommended for the job by J.H. Taylor, one of the "Great Triumvirate" of British golf.

Lees was described in obituaries as a noted golf architect and is known to have designed the original nine at Hempstead CC on Long Island and to have revised Ives Hill CC at Watertown, New York. He was better known, however, as a constructor of courses for such architects as Macdonald, Tillinghast and others.

Stanley Leonard

A well-known professional golfer from Vancouver, British Columbia, Stan Leonard won many tournaments in the U.S. and Canada. In 1974 he was appointed Director of Golf at Desert Island CC in California.

Leonard assisted a number of golf architects in planning courses in the 1960s, and later did design work on his own and in collaboration with Philip Tattersfield of Tattersfield Associates Ltd. Land Design Group, Vancouver, B.C.

Courses by: Stan Leonard
Alberta: Red Wood Meadows GC, Bragg Creek , with Philip Tattersfield.
British Columbia: Tall Timber GC, Langley (1979), with Wayne Lindberg and Philip Tattersfield; 108 Mile Resort GC, Cariboo (1970), with Philip Tattersfield.
Courses Remodeled & Added to by: Stan Leonard
California: Desert Island CC, Rancho Mirage (R.), with Philip Tattersfield.
British Columbia: Peace Portal GC, Douglas (R.), with Philip Tattersfield.

Gordon G. Lewis (1950 -)
Born: Paola, Kansas.
   A 1974 graduate of Kansas State University, Gordon Lewis worked summers on course construction crews for Floyd Farley. After working for architect David Gill and park-planner Charles Graves, Lewis formed his own business based on the west coast of Florida in late 1979.
Courses by: Gordon G. Lewis
Florida: Alden Pines GC, Pineland (1981); Deer Run GC, Lehigh (Precision, 1983); Eagle Ridge CC, Ft. Myers (1983); Forest CC (Bobcat Course), Fort Myers (1980); Forest CC (Deer Course), Fort Myers (9, 1980); Kelly Greens GC, Ft. Myers Beach (1987); Royal Tee CC, Cape Coral (27, 1986); Spanish Wells CC, Bonita Springs (1980); Vintage G&CC, Fort Myers (1985).
Courses Remodeled & Added to by: Gordon G. Lewis
Florida: Forest CC (Deer Course), Fort Myers (A.9, 1986); Harder Hall Hotel GC, Sebring (R., 1985).

William B. Lewis Jr.
   Based in North Carolina in the 1970s, William Lewis planned numerous courses in the Southeast.
Courses by: William B. Lewis
Florida: Bent Tree G&RC, Sarasota (1975); Village Green GC, Sarasota (Precision, 1969); Village Green GC, Bradenton (Precision, 1971); Village Green GC, Tavares (Precision, 1976); Whiskey Creek GC, Ft. Myers (Precision, 1972).
North Carolina: Fairfield Mountains GC, Lake Lure (1973); Glen Cannon GC, Brevard (1966); Great Smokies Hilton GC, Asheville (1975); Wolf Laurel GC, Mars Hill (1969).
South Carolina: Tega Cay CC (Cross Keys Course), Fort Mill (1971); Tega Cay CC (South Winds Course), Fort Mill (1973).

Bernhard von Limburger (1901 - 1981)
Born: Leipzig, Germany. Died: Stuttgart, West Germany at age 80.
   Bernhard von Limburger learned golf in Scotland at age thirteen and won the German Amateur in 1921, '22 and '25. He represented Germany thirty-five times in international golf competition. He earned a degree in law but never practiced, choosing instead to publish a German golf magazine that he edited until the mid-1930s. During this period, he laid out a few courses which were, by his own admission, terrible designs.
   In the 1930s Limburger formed a partnership with Berlin golf professional Karl Hoffmann, already an accomplished designer. Hoffmann and Limburger created several top courses in Germany before World War II and also operated a number of them. But their business was terminated by the war, and Limburger returned to his native Leipzig to work as a club manager. In 1943 he fled to south Germany and never returned to Leipzig, which became part of the Communist zone after the war.
   Hoffmann and Limburger tried to resume their practice at the close of the war, but Hoffmann died shortly thereafter. Limburger was successful in landing several commissions to build courses for American military bases in the newly created West Germany in the late 1940s, and by the 1950s he was designing full time. In the 1960s and '70s he was busy designing and constructing courses in many parts of Europe.
   Always a strong advocate of strategic design and a strong opponent of water hazards and over-bunkering (especially with what he termed "jigsaw-puzzle pieces"), Limburger developed a distinctly European style of golf architecture. All German Open tournaments after World War II through 1978 were played on courses he had designed or revised. Limburger was also the author of three golf books published in West Germany.
Courses by: Bernhard von Limburger
Austria: Badgastein GC (9, 1962); Bellach GC; Murhof GC, Frohnleiten (9, 1962); Schloss Fuschl G&CC (Par 3, 9); Schloss Pichlarn GC, Irdning (9, 1972).
East Germany: Chemnitzer GC, Slauv-Floeha , with Karl Hoffmann; Gaschwitz GC, Leipzig , with Karl Hoffmann; Neustadt GC (9), with Karl Hoffmann; Wittenberg GC (9), with Karl Hoffmann.
Northern Ireland: Clandeboye GC (Old Course), County Down , with T.J.A.McAuley and William Rennick Robinson.
Spain: Atalaya Park Hotel G&CC (1976).
Switzerland: Basel G&CC (1928), with Karl Hoffmann; Blumisberg G&CC, Bern (1959); Neuchatel GC (9, 1928), with Karl Hoffmann; Zurich-Hittnau G&CC (1964).
West Germany: Augsburg GC (1959); Bad Driburger GC (9), with Karl Hoffmann; Bad Waldsee GC (9); Bayreuth GC; Delkenheim GC (1982); Dortmunder GC, Dortmund (1956); Duren GC, Bad Duren (9, 1965); Dusseldorf Land und GC (East Course) (1961); Dusseldorf Land und GC (West Course) (Precision, 1963); Essener GC Haus Oefte, Essen (11), with Karl Hoffmann; Feldafing GC (1926), with Karl Hoffmann; Freiburger GC, Freiburg (1970); Furth GC; Garmisch-Partnekirchen GC, with Karl Hoffmann; Golf und Land C Cologne, with Karl Hoffmann; Golf und Landclub Oswestfallen, Lippe (9); Gut Steinberg GC; Hamburg-Ahrensburg GC, Hamburg; Hamburg-Waldorfer GC, Hoisbuettel; Harz GC, Bad Harzburg (9, 1972); Heidelberg G & Sports C; Herrenalb-Bernbach GC (9); Intercontinental GC (9); Kassel-Wilhelmhohe GC (9); Konstaz GC, with Karl Hoffmann; Kornwestheim GC; Krefelder GC, Krefeld (1930), with Karl Hoffmann; Lindau-Bad Schachen GC, Lindau (1954); Lohersand GC, Rendsburg (9); Mannheim-Viernheim GC, Mannheim (9), with Karl Hoffmann; Marienburger GC, Cologne; Morsum-Sylt GC, Sylt (9); Munchener GC, Munich; Neckartal GC, Stuttgart; Oberfranken GC, Bayreuth (9); Oberschwaben-Bad Waldsee GC; Oldenburgischer GC (9); Ostwestfalen-Lippe GC, Bad Salzuflen (9); Pfalz GC, Neustadt (9, 1971);

Reichswald GC, Nuremburg; Saarbrucken GC (1961); Sauerland GC, Neheim-Husten (9); Schloss Anholt GC (9); Schloss Braunfels GC (9, 1970); Schloss Myllendonk GC, Monchengladbach (9, 1964); Schloss Rheden GC (9); Siegen-Olpe GC, Seigen (9); Spangdahlem GC (9); Stuttgarter GC, Monsheim (1927), with Karl Hoffmann; Timmendorfer Strand GC (Course No. 1); Timmendorfer Strand GC (Course No. 2) (Precision); Ulm-Do GC (9, 1964); Ulm-Do GC (9); Weidenbruck - Gutersloh GC; Westfaelischer GC, Gutersloh; Wuppertal GC (9); Zur Vahr GC (Garlstedt Course), Bremen (1966).
Courses Remodeled & Added to by: Bernhard von Limburger
Austria: Murhof GC, Frohnleiten (A.9, 1972).
Czechoslovakia: Marienbad GC (R.).
Northern Ireland: Clandeboye GC (Old Course), County Down (R., 1969), with T.J.A.McAuley.
West Germany: Bergisch Land und GC, Wuppertal (R.); Falkenstein GC (R.); Frankfurter GC (R.); Hamburg-Falkenstein GC (R.); Hamburg-Waldorfer GC, Hoisbuettel (R., 1973); Hanover GC, Garbson (R.), with Karl Hoffmann; Kiel GC (R.); Kitzenberg GC, Kiel (R.); Kronberg GC (R.).

Albert Anthony Linkogel (1907 - 1982)
Born: St. Louis, Missouri. Died: Marthasville, Missouri at age 74.
   Al Linkogel served as superintendent at Westwood CC, St. Louis, Mo. from the 1930s until 1953, when he resigned to operate a turf nursery, lawn and garden supply business. In the 1950s he began converting sand green courses in Missouri and Illinois to grass. He also designed several original courses in those states.
Courses by: Al Linkogel
Illinois: Columbia GC (1960); Hillcrest GC, Washington (Par 3,).
Missouri: Cape Girardeau CC (9, 1955); St. Ann GC, St. Louis (9, 1950); St. Charles GC (1956).

Gary D. Linn (1955 -) ASGCA
Born: Wichita, Kansas.
   An early interest in golf was practically unavoidable for Gary Linn, whose parents and siblings were all avid amateur golfers. Linn attended Kansas State University and received a Bachelor of Landscape Architecture degree in 1978. After a short stint with a large architectural/planning firm in his hometown of Wichita, Linn joined Robert Trent Jones Jr.'s California organization in late 1978 as a design associate.
Courses by: Gary Linn
California: Links at Monarch Beach, Laguna Niguel (1984), with Robert Trent Jones Jr; Shoreline Park Muni GC (1983), with Robert Trent Jones Jr.
Colorado: Skyland GC, Crested Butte (1984), with Robert Trent Jones Jr.
Louisiana: Le Triomphe GC, Lafayette (1986), with Robert Trent Jones Jr.
Alberta: Glencoe G & CC (Forest Course), Calgary (1984), with Robert Trent Jones Jr and Don Knott; Glencoe G & CC (Meadow Course), Calgary (1985), with Robert Trent Jones Jr and Don Knott.
Japan: Golden Valley GC (1986), with Robert Trent Jones Jr; Pine Lake GC (1984), with Robert Trent Jones Jr and Don Knott; Springfield GC (1986), with Robert Trent Jones Jr and Don Knott.

Bruce A. Littell
   Raised in Houston, Texas, Bruce Littell obtained a B.S. Degree in Landscape Architecture from Texas A & M in 1961. He joined the course design firm of Jay Riviere in 1965, and formed his own business two years later.
Courses by: Bruce Littell
Texas: Bear Creek Golf World (Executive Crs.), Houston (1978); Bear Creek Golf World (Presidents Crs.), Houston (1979); Cape Royale CC; Clay County CC, Henrietta (9, 1970); Goose Island Lake GC; Houston Golf Academy (Par 3, 9); Kingwood CC (Lake Course) (1977); Kirbywood CC, Cleveland (9); Padre Isle GC (1971); Point Venture Y&CC, Jonestown (1972); Royale Green GC, Coldspring; Sunnyside CC; Woodcreek CC (Brook Hollow Course), Wimberly (1973).
Courses Remodeled & Added to by: Bruce Littell
Texas: Texas A&M Univ GC, College Station (R., 1973).

Karl V. Litten (1933 -)
Born: Braxton County, West Virginia.
   After studying architecture and engineering at Steubenville College and Ohio University, Karl Litten worked as a civil engineer for twelve years, first in Ohio and then in Florida. In 1968 he joined golf architect Robert von Hagge and eventually became Vice President of the firm of von Hagge and Devlin. In 1979 Litten formed his own golf design firm based in Florida. In the mid-1980s, professional golfer Gary Player served as a consulting partner in his firm.
Courses by: Karl Litten
Florida: Alaqua CC (1987), with Gary Player; Belle Glade Muni (9, 1987), with Gary Player; Boca Delray G&CC, Delray Beach (Precision, 1983); Boca Grove Plantation CC, Boca Raton (1982); Boca Woods CC (North Course), Boca Raton (1984); Cheval Polo & CC, Tampa (1986); Gleneagles CC (East Course), Delray Beach (1985); Gleneagles CC (West Course), Delray Beach (1985); Ironwood CC, Longwood (1987), with Gary Player; Lake Worth Park GC (Par 3, 9, 1985); Overoaks CC, Kissimmee (1986), with Gary Player; Polo C, Boca Raton (1986); Stonebridge G&CC, Boca Raton (1985); Stonewal SC, Lake Park (1984).
Massachusetts: White Cliffs of Plymouth GC (Precision, 1986), with Gary Player.
Tennessee: Southern Hills CC, Murfreesboro .
Texas: Piney Woods CC, Nacagdoches (1982).
United Arab Emirates: Emerates GC, Dubai (1987).
Courses Remodeled & Added to by: Karl Litten
Texas: Sleepy Hollow G&CC (Lake Course), Dallas (R., 1983); Sleepy Hollow G&CC (River Course), Dallas (R., 1983).

Edward G. "Ted" Lockie (1908 -)

A longtime PGA professional in East Moline, Ill., Ted Lockie designed several courses in the Quad-Cities area in the 1960s and '70s before his retirement to Palm Beach Gardens, Fla. in 1976.

Courses by: Ted Lockie

Illinois: Golfmohr GC, East Moline (1967); Pinecrest G&CC, Huntley (1972); Short Hills CC, East Moline .

Wisconsin: Grandview GC, Hortonville (1969).

Courses Remodeled & Added to by: Ted Lockie

Iowa: Davenport CC (R.2, 1965).

Emil F. "Dutch" Loeffler (1894 - 1948)

Born: Pittsburgh, Pennsylvania. Died: Oakmont, Pennsylvania at age 54.

Dutch Loeffler's entire career was spent at Oakmont CC. He began as a caddy at the age of ten, became caddymaster in 1912, greenkeeper in 1913 (when John McGlynn vacated the position) and head professional in 1930. He was a fine golfer, winning the 1920 and 1922 Pennsylvania Opens and qualifying for the 1920 and 1921 U.S. Opens. He was also a member of the GCSAA and served as its national treasurer in 1929.

Loeffler was best known for his work at Oakmont as course superintendent, a position he held, even while serving as club professional, until his retirement in 1947. He instituted the changes and maintenance practices suggested by William C. Fownes Jr. to make Oakmont the world's toughest golf course. He had several ideas of his own, including the weighted rake that formed the furrows in Oakmont's bunkers.

In the 1920s Loeffler was associated with John McGlynn in the design and build firm of Loeffler-McGlynn Co. The firm constructed courses of its own design, did reconstructions at established layouts and also contracted to execute the work of other architects.

Courses by: Emil Loeffler

Pennsylvania: Alcoma CC (1923), with John McGlynn; Ambridge CC, with John McGlynn; Beaver Valley CC, Beaver Falls (9), with John McGlynn; Cedar Rocks CC, Wheeling , with John McGlynn; Del Mar CC, Ellwood City (9), with John McGlynn; Greene County GC, Waynesburg , with John McGlynn; Hannastown CC, Greensburg , with John McGlynn; Highland CC, Pittsburgh (1920), with John McGlynn; Hillcrest CC (9), with John McGlynn; Kittanning CC (1922), with John McGlynn; Latrobe CC (9), with John McGlynn; Montour Heights CC, Coraopolis (9), with John McGlynn; Nemacolin CC, Beallsville , with John McGlynn; Oakmont East GC, Oakmont , with John McGlynn; Pleasant Valley CC, Mt. Pleasant , with John McGlynn; Shannopin CC, Ben Avon Heights (1920), with John McGlynn; St. Jude CC, Chicora , with John McGlynn; Titusville CC, with John McGlynn; Uniontown CC, with John McGlynn; Westmoreland CC, Verona (NLE,), with John McGlynn; Wildwood GC, Allison Park , with John McGlynn.

Courses Remodeled & Added to by: Emil Loeffler

Michigan: Red Run GC, Royal Oak (R.), with John McGlynn.

Pennsylvania: Butler CC (R.), with John McGlynn; Chartiers CC, Pittsburgh (R.), with John McGlynn; Edgewood CC, Pittsburgh (R.); Huntingdon Valley CC, Abington (NLE, R.); Monongahela Valley CC (R.9), with John McGlynn; Monongahela Valley CC (A.9), with John McGlynn; Oakmont CC (R., 1920), with William C. Fownes Jr; Pittsburgh Field C (R.).

Robert M. Lohmann (1952 -) ASGCA

Bob Lohmann graduated in 1974 from the University of Wisconsin with a B.S. Degree in Landscape Architecture. The following year he joined the design firm of Killian and Nugent, handling principal design responsibility for several new courses including Forest Preserve National in Oak Forest, Ill., a layout selected as one of the nation's Top Public Courses in 1984.

Lohmann remained for a time as a partner with Dick Nugent when Killian and Nugent disbanded, but in 1985 Lohmann struck out on his own. His firm, Lohmann Golf Designs Inc., was based in Crystal Lake, Illinois.

Bob Lohmann was a member of both the ASGCA and the ASLA.

Courses by: Bob Lohmann

Illinois: Canterbury Place GC, Crystal Lake (1987); Forest Preserve National GC, Oak Forest (1981), with Ken Killian and Dick Nugent.

Indiana: Sand Creek C, Chesterton (1979), with Ken Killian and Dick Nugent.

Wisconsin: Fox Hills CC, Mishicot (1987).

Courses Remodeled & Added to by: Bob Lohmann

Illinois: Countryside GC (R., 1985); Crystal Lake CC (R., 1985); Glencoe GC (R., 1982), with Ken Killian and Dick Nugent; Pinecrest G&CC, Huntley (R., 1985); Villa Olivia GC, Bartlett (R.).

Wisconsin: Ozaukee CC, Mequon (R., 1984); Reedsburg CC (A.9, 1978), with Ken Killian and Dick Nugent; Rock River Hills GC, Horizon (A.9, 1987).

William Robert Love (1952 -) ASGCA

Born: Cookeville, Tennessee.

Bill Love obtained an A.A. Degree in Graphic Arts from Prince George's Community College, Largo, Md. in 1972, and then attended Catholic University of America in Washington, D.C., where he obtained a Bachelor of Science Degree in Architecture. After practicing in the field of architecture for a time, Love enrolled at the University of Virginia and became the school's first graduate student to base a masters thesis on golf course design. He received his Master's Degree in Landscape Architecture from Virginia in 1978, and promptly joined the Wheaton, Md. firm of Edmund B. Ault, for whom he had previously worked on a part-time basis.

A member of the ASGCA, Love was also a member of the ASLA.

Courses by: Bill Love

Georgia: Statham's Landing GC (1987), with Tom Clark.

Maryland: TPC at Avenel, Potomac (1986), with Edmund B. Ault, Brian Ault and Tom Clark.

New Jersey: Concordia GC (1986), with Brian Ault.

North Carolina: Charles T. Myers GC (9, 1986).

South Carolina: Midway GC (Par 3, 27, 1984), with Edmund B. Ault.

Virginia: Ivy Creek Farm GC (9, 1985).

Courses Remodeled & Added to by: Bill Love

Arizona: Arizona CC, Phoenix (R., 1986), with Tom Clark.

Delaware: Brandywine CC, Wilmington (R.7, 1987), with Brian Ault; Shawnee CC (A.9, 1984), with Edmund B. Ault.

Kansas: Lake Quivira CC, Kansas City (R.4, 1984); Milburn G&CC, Overland Park (R.6, 1985).

Maryland: Congressional CC (Blue Course), Bethesda (R.2, 1981), with Edmund B. Ault and Tom Clark; Longview Muni (R.3, 1981), with Edmund B. Ault; Manor CC, Rockville (R.4, 1986), with Edmund B. Ault and Brian Ault; Suburban CC (R.4, 1982), with Edmund B. Ault.

New Jersey: Greenacres CC, Lawrence (R.2, 1983), with Brian Ault and Tom Clark.

Pennsylvania: North Hills Muni (R.10, 1984); Oak Tree GC (R.2, 1983), with Brian Ault.

Virginia: Army-Navy CC (Arlington Course), Arlington (R.5, 1986), with Edmund B. Ault and Tom Clark; Army-Navy CC (Fairfax Course), Fairfax (R.2, 1984), with Edmund B. Ault and Brian Ault; Fredericksburg CC (R.1, 1985).

Raymond F. "Buddy" Loving Jr. (1926 -) ASGCA

Born: Richmond, Virginia.

Buddy Loving received a B.A. Degree from the University of Virginia and an additional degree from Phillips College. He also took courses in landscape architecture, turfgrass science and financial management at Virginia Polytechnic Institute. He was trained in golf course architecture by his grandfather Fred Findlay, for whom he began working part time in 1946, and by his father Raymond Sr. (known as Ben), who also did some design work.

For a period in the late 1960s, Loving worked in partnership with fellow architect Algie Pulley in a company that handled both original designs and constructed layouts designed by others. That company, GolfAmerica, disbanded in the mid-1970s and Loving resumed solo practice of golf architecture.

Courses by: Buddy Loving

Maryland: Winters Run GC, Bel Air (1973).

Virginia: Boar's Head Inn GC, Charlottesville (Par 3, 9, 1967); Confederate Hills CC, Highland Springs (1972), with Algie Pulley; Country Club Lake, Dumfries (Precision, 1971), with Algie Pulley; Evergreen CC, Haymarket (1968), with Algie Pulley; Greene Hills C, Stanardsville (1970); Hunting Hills CC, Roanoke (1965), with Fred Findlay and Ben Loving; Lake Monticello GC, Palmyra (1972), with Algie Pulley; Lakeview CC, with Fred Findlay and Ben Loving; Lakeview Motor Inn GC, Roanoke (Precision, 9, 1972); Pen Park GC, Charlottesville (9, 1974); Retreat G&CC, Berryville (1973); Shenandoah Valley CC, Middleburg (27, 1974); Virginia Tech GC, Blacksburg (1973); Waters Edge GC, Penhook (1987); Williamsburg Colony Inn GC (Par 3, 9, 1973).

Courses Remodeled & Added to by: Buddy Loving

Virginia: Army-Navy CC (Arlington Course), Arlington (R.5, 1970), with Algie Pulley; Army-Navy CC (Fairfax Course), Fairfax (R.2, 1970), with Algie Pulley; CC of Fairfax (R., 1969), with Algie Pulley; CC of Virginia (James River Course), Richmond (R.3, 1974); Farmington CC, Charlottesville (A.9, 1965), with Ben Loving; Farmington CC, Charlottesville (R., 1986); Hunting Hills CC, Roanoke (R., 1987); Patuxent NAS GC (R.); Staunton CC (R., 1986); Tides Inn & CC (Golden Eagle Course), Irvington (R., 1987); Washington G&CC, Arlington (R.5, 1969), with Algie Pulley.

George Low Sr. (1874 - 1950)

Born: Carnoustie, Scotland. Died: Clearwater, Florida at age 76.

Pioneer American golfer George Low was joint runner-up in the 1899 United States Open and before World War I had worked as professional at Baltusrol in New Jersey, Ekwanok in Vermont, and Huntington Valley in Pennsylvania. He also served as golf instructor to two U.S. Presidents, William Howard Taft and Warren G. Harding.

Low designed several courses in the Northeast. In the 1920s he formed a short-lived partnership with golf architect Herbert Strong before moving to Clearwater, Florida. There he served as professional at Belleview-Biltmore until poor health necessitated his retirement in 1940. Low's son George Jr. was long associated with the PGA Tour and was a respected putting expert.

Courses by: George Low Sr

Maryland: Rodgers Forge CC, Baltimore (1923), with Herbert Strong.

New Jersey: Echo Lake CC, Westfield (1913), with Donald Ross; Weequahic GC, Newark (9, 1914).

New York: Blind Brook CC, Portchester; Hotel Champlain GC, Lake Bluff (1917).

Vermont: Rutland CC (9, 1902).

Courses Remodeled & Added to by: George Low Sr

Florida: Clearwater CC (R.).

New Jersey: Rockaway River CC, Denville (A.9, 1916).

New York: Bluff Point CC, Lake Champlain (R., 1920); Nassau CC, Glen Cove (R., 1924), with Herbert Strong; Nassau CC, Glen Cove (A.3, 1924), with Herbert Strong.

John Laing Low (1869 - 1929)

Born: Fife, Scotland. Died: Woking, England at age 59.

John Low learned golf at St. Andrews and was an avid competitor all his life. He reached the semi-finals at the British Amateur in 1897 and 1898 and was runner-up in 1901. He also won many tournaments at St. Andrews, including the Silver Cross in 1900 and 1909.

A graduate of Cambridge University, Low assisted in the creation of the Oxford and Cambridge Golfing Society in 1897 and served as its captain for twenty years. He organized the Society's first matches in America in 1903 and captained the team that included C.H. Alison. Low was also a respected authority on the rules of golf, serving as chairman of the Rules Committee of the Royal and Ancient until 1921.

John Low was on the staff of the Pall Mall Gazette and later the Athletic News, and wrote extensively about golf in those and other newspapers. He also wrote several books on golf, including *Concerning Golf* (1903), the first to codify the principles of golf course architecture.

In the early 1900s Low and fellow club member Stuart Paton worked together in remodeling Woking GC. Their efforts turned a staid Tom Dunn layout into a remarkably strategic course. Although they did no other design work, the discussion, publicity and controversy arising from their changes at Woking contributed greatly to the development of golf course architecture.

John Low's principles of golf course architecture, which were widely circulated and followed during his lifetime, included these points:

1. A gclf course should provide entertainment for the high and medium handicapper while at the same time present a searching and difficult test for the accomplished golfer.
2. The one aim of inventors is to reduce the skill required for golf. Golf architects must wage a battle against inventors by designing courses that emphasize golfing skills over equipment.
3. The shortest, most direct line to the hole, even if it be the center of the fairway, should be fraught with danger.
4. The architect must allow the ground to dictate play. The good architect sees that there is a special interest for the accomplished golfer in each stroke, just as the billard player always has in mind the next stroke or strokes.
5. The fairway must be oriented to both the tee and the green, thereby stressing the importance of placing the tee shot in a position from which the green can be approached with safety.
6. Bunkers should be used sparingly by the architect. Except on one-shot holes, they should never be placed within 200 yards of the tee. Ridges and depressions are the best way of controlling the entrance to the green. The best hazard on a course is a fairway bunker 200 to 235 yards from the tee, placed five to ten yards off the accomplished player's most favorable line to the green.
7. Whenever possible, putting greens should be of the low, narrow plateau type, with the plateau tilting away, not toward, the player. No green should be higher at the back than it is in front, for that gives a player confidence. Only half the flagstick should be seen from where the approach shot should be played.
8. A course should never pretend to be, nor is it intended to be, an infallible tribunal of skill alone. The element of chance is the very essence of the game, part of the fun of the game.
9. All really great golf holes involve a contest of wits and risks. No one should attempt to copy a great hole because so much may depend on its surroundings as well as some features miles away in the background which influence and affect the play of the hole. If the terrain is suitable, some of the character of the original might be incorporated elsewhere.
10. Inequalities of putting green surfaces should not be exaggerated. A tilt from front to back, or left to right or vice versa is sufficient. There should always be a special position for the flagstick on important days.
11. Committees should leave well enough alone, especially when they have a really fine course.

George Lowe

Originally from Carnoustie, George Lowe moved to England where he became greenkeeper at St. Annes in the early 1890s. In England he planned several layouts including a new course for his home club, Royal Lytham and St. Annes, when it changed locations in 1896.

Courses by: George Lowe

England: Ripon City GC, Yorkshire (9, 1905); Royal Birkdale GC, Southport (1889), with Charles Hawtree; Royal Lytham & St. Annes GC, Lancashire (1897); Windermere GC, Cumbria (1892).

Courses Remodeled & Added to by: George Lowe

England: Seascale GC, Cumbria (A.9, 1902).

A. Vernon Macan (1882 - 1964) ASGCA

Born: Dublin, Ireland. Died: Victoria, British Columbia at age 82.

Vernon Macan attended Trinity College in Dublin and earned a degree in law at the University of London. He then emigrated to Vancouver, British Columbia where he established a law practice and became one of the area's top amateur golfers. He won a number of regional events in Canada and, across the border, was victorious in both the Washington State Amateur and the Pacific Northwest Amateur in 1913.

After World War I, Macan decided to pursue a career in golf design. His fame as a player led to several projects, and by the 1920s he was the busiest architect in the Pacific Northwest. He continued to design courses until his death, assisted on his last projects by civil engineer Donald Hogan.

Courses by: A.Vernon Macan

California: California GC of San Francisco (1926); San Geronimo National GC (1965).

Idaho: Hillcrest CC, Boise (9, 1940); Purple Sage Muni, Caldwell (1963).

Oregon: Alderwood CC, Portland (NLE,); Columbia-Edgewater CC, Portland (1925); Colwood National GC, Portland (1929).

Washington: Broadmoor GC, Seattle (1927); Edgewater Muni, Pasco (1954); Fircrest GC, Tacoma (1925); Inglewood CC, Kenmore (1923), with Robert Johnstone; Manito G&CC, Spokane (1922); Overlake G&CC, Medina (1953); Sunland CC, Sequim (9, 1964); Yakima CC (1956).

British Columbia: Cowichan G&CC (9, 1947); Marine Drive GC, Vancouver (1923); Nanaimo G&CC (1961); Penticton G&CC; Richmond CC; Royal Colwood G&CC, Victoria; Shaughnessy G&CC, Vancouver (1960); Shaughnessy Heights C, Vancouver (NLE,).

Courses Remodeled & Added to by: A.Vernon Macan

Idaho: Hillcrest CC, Boise (A.9, 1957).

Oregon: Alderwood CC, Portland (R., 1949); Waverley CC, Portland (R.).

Washington: Seattle GC (R., 1950); Wenawatchee CC (A.9, 1958).

British Columbia: Victoria GC, Oak Bay (R., 1930).

Norman Macbeth (1879 - 1940)

Born: Bolton, England. Died: Los Angeles, California at age 61.

Norman Macbeth learned his golf at Lytham and St. Annes and as a teenager lowered his handicap from 18 to 2 in the space of three season. He won Amateur titles in England and India before moving to the United States in 1903. He settled in Los Angeles in 1908. A businessman all his life, including many years as Vice President of the Riverside Cement Company, Macbeth remained active in amateur golf, winning the Southern California Amateur on two occasions and the Northern California Amateur once.

In 1910 Macbeth assisted in the design of the old Los Angeles CC course. Following service with the American Red Cross in Europe during World War I, he designed and built a number of southern California courses, many of which (like the highly regarded Midwick CC and St. Andrews GC of Laguna Niguel) succumbed to the Depression.

Courses by: Norman Macbeth

California: Midwick CC, Monterey Park (NLE,); San Gabriel CC; St. Andrews GC, Laguna Niguel (NLE,); Wilshire CC, Los Angeles (1919).

Courses Remodeled & Added to by: Norman Macbeth

California: Annandale GC, Pasadena (R., 1921).

Charles Blair Macdonald (1856 - 1939)

Born: Niagara Falls, Ontario, Canada. Died: Southampton, New York at age 83.

Charles Blair Macdonald was the son of a Scottish father and a Canadian mother. Macdonald himself grew up in Chicago but returned to his father's homeland in 1872 to attend the University of St. Andrews. There he learned the game of golf under the tutelage of his grandfather and was able to watch matches involving Old and Young Tom Morris, David Strath, Robert Clark (author of *Golf, A Royal and Ancient Game*), D.D. Whigham (whose son, H.J. later married Macdonald's daughter, Frances) and many other renowned golfers.

The game, the Old Course, the town of St. Andrews and Old Tom made deep and lasting impressions on Macdonald. Returning to Chicago in 1875, he described the next few years as the "dark ages" because of the virtual impossibility of playing golf. He ended up knocking balls around a deserted Civil War training camp. Then in 1892 he laid out the nine-hole Chicago GC at Belmont. This was expanded to eighteen holes the next year, making it the first eighteen-hole course in the United States. In 1895 the club moved to Wheaton, where Macdonald laid out a new eighteen holes.

Throughout his life, golf course design was an avocation for Macdonald, and he never accepted a fee for his services. During his years in Illinois he was with the Chicago Board of Trade. In 1884 he married Frances Porter of Chicago. They had two daughters, Janet and Frances. The family moved to New York in 1900, where Macdonald became a partner in the firm of C.D. Barney & Co., Stockbrokers.

Golf and golf design were C.B.'s abiding passions. Macdonald won the first U.S. Amateur Championship in 1895. He was a founder of the Amateur Golf Association of the United States, which evolved into the USGA. He conceived the Walker Cup Series, coined the title "golf architect" in 1902 and was considered by golf historiansas the "Father of American Golf Course Architecture." His proteges in golf design included Seth Raynor, Charles Banks and Ralph Barton.

Macdonald's reminiscences, *Scotland's Gift—Golf*, provided a detailed discussion of his principles of golf architecture. He also wrote extensively about course architecture in other publications. One of his most widely circulated pieces dealt with Macdonald's ingredients for an ideal golf course. Among the points he listed were:

1. There can be no really first-class golf course without good material to work with. The best material is a sandy loam in gentle undulations, breaking into hillocks in a few places. Securing such land is really more than half the battle. Having such material at hand to work upon, the completion of an ideal course becomes a matter of experience, gardening and mathematics.
2. The courses of Great Britain abound in classic and notable holes, and one has only to study them and adopt their best and boldest features. Yet in most of their best holes there is always room for improvement.
3. Nothing induces more to the charm of the game than perfect putting greens. Some should be large, but the majority should be of moderate size; some flat, some hillocky, one or two at an angle, but the great majority should have natural undulations, some more and others less undulating. It is absolutely essential that the turf should be very fine so the ball will run perfectly true.
4. Whether this or that bunker is well-placed has caused more intensely heated arguments (outside of the realms of religion) than has ever been my lot to listen to. Rest assured, however, when a controversy is hotly contested over several years as to whether this or that hazard is fair, it is the kind of hazard you want and it has real merit. When there is unanimous opinion that such and such a hazard is perfect, one usually finds it commonplace. I know of no classic hole that doesn't have its decriers.
5. To my mind, an ideal course should have at least six bold bunkers, at the end of two-shot holes or very long carries from the tee. Further, I believe such holes would be improved by opening the fair green to one side or the other, giving short or timid players an opportunity to play around the hazards if so desired, but of course properly penalized by loss of distance for so playing. Other than these bold bunkers, no other hazards should stretch directly across a hole.
6. What a golfer most desires is variety in the one, two and three shot holes, calling for accuracy in placing the ball, not alone in the approach but also from the tee. Let the first shot be played in relation to the second shot in accordance with the run of the ground and the wind. Holes so designed permit the player to, if he so wishes, take risks commensurate to the gravity of the situation.
7. Tees should be in close proximity to previous greens. This walking fifty to one hundred fifty yards to the next tee mars the course and delays the game. Between hole and next teeing ground people sometimes forget and commence playing some other game.
8. Hills on a golf course are a detriment. Mountain climbing is a sport in itself and has no place on a golf course. Trees in the course are also a serious defect, and even when in close proximity prove a detriment.
9. Glaring artificiality of any kind detracts from the fascination of the game.

Courses by: Charles Blair Macdonald

Connecticut: Yale University GC, New Haven (1926), with Seth Raynor and Charles Banks.

Illinois: Chicago GC, Wheaton (1895); Downers Grove GC {formerly Chicago GC}, Belmont (1893).

Maryland: Gibson Island GC (1922), with Seth Raynor.

Missouri: St. Louis CC, Clayton (1914), with Seth Raynor.

New York: Creek C, Locust Valley (1925), with Seth Raynor; Deepdale GC, Great Neck (NLE, 1925), with Seth Raynor; H.P. Whitney Estate GC, Manhasset , with Seth Raynor; Lido GC, Long Beach (NLE, 1917), with Seth Raynor; Links GC, Roslyn (NLE, 1919), with Seth Raynor; Moore Estate GC, Roslyn , with Seth Raynor; National G Links of America, Southampton (1911); Otto Kahn Estate GC, Manhasset (NLE, 1925), with Seth Raynor; Piping Rock C, Locust Valley (1913), with Seth Raynor; Sleepy Hollow GC, Scarboro-on-Hudson (1914), with Seth Raynor.

West Virginia: Greenbrier GC (Old White Course), White Sulphur Spgs (1915), with Seth Raynor.

Bermuda: Mid-Ocean C, Tuckerstown (1924), with Seth Raynor and Charles Banks.

Alister Mackenzie (1870 - 1934)
Born: Normanton, Yorkshire, England. Died: Santa Cruz, California at age 63.

Dr. Alister Mackenzie, the son of Highland parents, graduated from Cambridge University with degrees in Medicine, Natural Science and Chemistry. In the South African War he served as a surgeon with the Somerset Light Infantry, where he closely observed and analyzed the ability of Boer soldiers to hide effectively on treeless veldts. After the war he returned to Britain to practice medicine in the city of Leeds.

In 1907 golf architect H.S. Colt, on a visit to Alwoodley GC near Leeds, stayed overnight at Mackenzie's home. Impressed with Mackenzie's models of greens and bunkers, Colt invited his collaboration on the revision of Alwoodley. Over the next few years Mackenzie gradually gave up his medical practice to devote full time to golf course architecture. In 1914 he won first prize in C.B. Macdonald's *Country Life* magazine competition for the best two-shot hole for the proposed Lido GC on Long Island, New York. This competition, judged by Bernard Darwin, Horace Hutchinson and Herbert Fowler, brought Mackenzie considerable publicity on both sides of the Atlantic.

With the outbreak of war in Europe, Mackenzie returned to medicine as an army surgeon but soon transferred to the Royal Engineers to develop camouflage techniques based on the knowledge he had gained in South Africa. The art and science of camouflage as developed by Mackenzie was credited with saving thousands of lives. Years later, Mackenzie observed that successful course design, like camouflage, depended on utilizing natural features to their fullest extent and creating artificial features that closely imitated nature.

Shortly after the Armistice in 1918, Mackenzie made his first trip to the United States, where he collaborated with Colt and Alison on the revision of Chevy Chase near Washington, D.C. He later designed a number of courses in the U.S. and Canada on his own or in collaboration with others. Cypress Point in California finally established his reputation as a golf course architect. During the 1920s he also planned courses in the British Isles, Australia, New Zealand and South America.

Of all the course architects of the Golden Age of Golf Design, Mackenzie probably exerted the greatest influence on contemporary design. Features he listed in 1920 as essential for an ideal golf course became standards for course architecture after World War II.

Alister Mackenzie was the author of *Golf Architecture*, published in 1920. In it, he codified thirteen essential features of an ideal golf course. They were:

1. The course, where possible, should be arranged in two loops of nine holes.
2. There should be a large proportion of good two-shot holes, two or three drive-and-pitch holes, and at least four one-shot holes.
3. There should be little walking between greens and tees, and the course should be arranged so that in the first instance there is always a slight walk forwards from the green to the next tee; then the holes are sufficiently elastic to be lengthened in the future if necessary.
4. The greens and fairways should be sufficiently undulating, but there should be no hill climbing.
5. Every hole should have a different character.
6. There should be a minimum of blindness for the approach shots.
7. The course should have beautiful surroundings, and all the artificial features should have so natural an appearance that a stranger is unable to distinguish them from nature itself.
8. There should be a sufficient number of heroic carries from the tee, but the course should be arranged so that the weaker player with the loss of a stroke or portion of a stroke shall always have an alternate route open to him.
9. There should be infinite variety in the strokes required to play the various holes—interesting brassy shots, iron shots, pitch and run-up shots.
10. There should be a complete absence of the annoyance and irritation caused by the necessity of searching for lost balls.
11. The course should be so interesting that even the plus man is constantly stimulated to improve his game in attempting shots he has hitherto been unable to play.
12. The course should be so arranged so that the long handicap player, or even the absolute beginner, should be able to enjoy his round in spite of the fact that he is piling up a big score.
13. The course should be equally good during winter and summer, the texture of greens and fairways should be perfect, and the approaches should have the same consistency as the greens.

Courses by: Alister Mackenzie
California: Charlie Chaplin Estate GC, Beverly Hills (Par 3, 9); Cypress Point C, Pebble Beach (1928), with Robert Hunter; Green Hills CC, Millbrae (1930), with Robert Hunter and H. Chandler Egan; Haggin Oaks Muni (South Course), Sacramento (1932); Harold Lloyd Estate GC, Beverly Hills (NLE, Par 3, 9); Meadow C, Fairfax (1927), with Robert Hunter; Northwood GC, Guerneville (9, 1928), with Robert Hunter; Pasatiempo GC, Santa Cruz (1929), with Robert Hunter; Pittsburg GC (9), with Robert Hunter; Sharp Park GC, Pacifica (1931); Stockton G&CC; Valley C of Montecito, Santa Barbara (1928), with Robert Hunter.
Georgia: Augusta National GC, Augusta (1933), with Robert Tyre "Bobby" Jones Jr.
Michigan: University of Michigan GC, Ann Arbor (1931), with Perry Maxwell.
New York: Adirondacks C, Lake Placid (NLE,).
Ohio: Ohio State Univ GC (Gray Course), Columbus (1939), with Perry Maxwell;

Ohio State Univ GC (Scarlet Course), Columbus (1939), with Perry Maxwell.
Manitoba: St. Charles CC (North Nine), Winnipeg (9, 1930).
Argentina: Jockey C (Blue Course), San Isidro (1935); Jockey C (Red Course), San Isidro (1935).
Australia: Australian GC, Kensington (27, 1926); Flinders GC, Victoria; Lake Karrinyup CC, Perth (1927), with Alex Russell; New South Wales GC, Sydney (1928), with Alex Russell; Royal Melbourne GC (West Course), Black Rock (1926), with Alex Russell; Sandringham GC, Melbourne; Victoria GC, Cheltenham (1927); Yarra Yarra GC, Melbourne (1929), with Alex Russell.
England: Alwoodley GC, Leeds (1907), with H.S. Colt; Blackpool Park GC, Lancashire (1925); Brancepeth Castle GC, Durham (1924), with H.S. Colt and C.H. Alison; Cavendish GC, Derbyshire (1925); Darlington GC, Durham (1909); Felixstowe Ferry GC, Suffolk (1919); Fulford GC, Yorkshire (1909); Grange-over-Sands GC, Cumbria (1919); Hadley Wood GC, Hertfordshire (1922); Ilkley GC, Yorkshire; Moor Allerton GC, Yorkshire (NLE, 1922); Moor Park GC (West Course), Hertfordshire (1923), with H.S. Colt and C.H. Alison; Moortown GC, Yorkshire (1909); Oakdale GC, Yorkshire (1914); Reddish Vale GC, Cheshire (1912); Scarborough Southcliff GC; Sitwell Park GC, Yorkshire (1913); Teignmouth GC (1924), with H.S. Colt and C.H. Alison; Walsall GC, Staffordshire (1909); Wheatley GC, Yorkshire (1913).
Ireland: County Sligo GC (1922), with H.S. Colt and C.H. Alison; Douglas GC, County Cork; Galway GC, County Galway; Muskerry GC, County Cork .
Isle of Man: Douglas Muni (1927).
New Zealand: Heretaunga GC, Wellington .
Scotland: Duff House Royal GC, Banff (1909); Hazelhead Muni (Course No. 1), Aberdeen (1927); Pitreavie GC, Fife (1923); St. Andrews (Eden Course), Fife (1913), with H.S. Colt.
Uruguay: Golf Club de Uruguay, Montevideo; Punta del Este GC, Canteril .

Courses Remodeled & Added to by: Alister Mackenzie
California: California GC of San Francisco (R.); Claremont CC, Oakland (R.); Lake Merced G&CC, Daly City (R., 1929); Monterey Peninsula CC (Dunes Course), Pebble Beach (R., 1928), with Robert Hunter; Pebble Beach G Links (R., 1927), with Robert Hunter; Redlands CC (R.).
Michigan: Crystal Downs CC, Frankfort (A.9, 1933), with Perry Maxwell; Crystal Downs CC, Frankfort (R.9, 1933), with Perry Maxwell.
New York: Bayside Links, Queens (R., 1932); Lake Placid C (Upper Course) (R., 1931).
South Carolina: Palmetto GC, Aiken (R., 1931).
Argentina: Mar de Plata GC (R., 1930).
Australia: Kingston Heath GC, Cheltenham (R., 1928); Royal Adelaide GC, Seaton (R., 1926); Royal Queensland GC, Hamilton (R., 1927); Royal Sydney GC, Sydney (R.).
England: Buxton and High Peak GC, Derbyshire (R.); City of Newcastle GC, Northumberland (R.); Harrogate GC, Yorkshire (R.); Headingley GC, Leeds (R.); Manchester GC, Lancashire (R.); Northumberland GC, (R., 1924), with H.S. Colt and C.H. Alison; Royal St. George's GC, Kent (R.); Sandmoor GC, Leeds (R.); West Herts GC, Hertfordshire (R.), 1922); Weston-Super-Mare GC, Somerset (R.); Willingdon GC, Sussex (R.); Worcester G&CC, Worcestershire (R.); Worcestershire GC (R.).
Ireland: Cork GC, County Cork (A.9, 1927); Cork GC, County Cork (R.9, 1927); Lahinch GC (Old Course), County Clare (A.11, 1927); Lahinch GC (Old Course), County Clare (R., 1927).
Isle of Man: Castletown GC (R.).
New Zealand: Titirangi GC (R., 1926).
Scotland: Blairgowrie GC (Rosemount Course) (A.9, 1927); Blairgowrie GC (Rosemount Course) (R.9, 1927); Duff House Royal GC, Banff (R., 1926), with Charles A.Mackenzie; Newtonmore GC, Invernesshire (R.); Royal Troon GC, Ayrshire (R.); St. Andrews (Old Course), Fife (R.).

Leonard Macomber (1885 - 1954)
Born: Brookline, Massachusetts. Died: Washington, D.C. at age 69.

Trained as a civil engineer, Leonard Macomber planned courses from New York to Wisconsin while based in Chicago during the 1920s. In 1937 he traveled to Russia hoping to interest that country in golf, but was unsuccessful. His last course, Belle Haven CC in Alexandria, Va. was finished shortly before his death.

Courses by: Leonard Macomber
Florida: National Town & CC, Lake Wales (NLE,).
Illinois: Biltmore CC, Barrington; Breakers Beach CC, Northbrook (NLE,); Cedardell GC, Plano; Libertyville CC; Mission Hills CC, Northbrook (NLE, 1926); Silver Lake GC (North Course) {formerly Euclid Hill CC}, Orland Park (1928); Waukegan Willow GC, Techny (NLE,).
Indiana: Curtis Creek CC (1928).
New York: Drumlins C, Syracuse .
Ohio: National Town & CC (NLE,); Poland CC, Youngstown; Tam O'Shanter CC (Dales Course), Canton (1928); Tam O'Shanter CC (Hills Course), Canton (1928); West Hills CC, Canton .
Virginia: Belle Haven CC, Alexandria (1954).
Wisconsin: Bulls Eye CC, Wisconsin Rapids (9); Maple Crest CC, Kenosha .

Courses Remodeled & Added to by: Leonard Macomber
Pennsylvania: Butler CC (A.9, 1928); Butler CC (R.9, 1928).

Gregor MacLeod MacMillan
Born: Montana.

Following graduation in the early Twenties from the University of Washington with a degree in Civil Engineering, Greg MacMillan worked as a surveyor for the Balcom Canal Lumber Company of Seattle. When Balcom headed a group of businessmen organizing the Olympic G&CC, MacMillan was assigned to oversee the golf course construction. His knowledge impressed Frank James, the Western States Representative of the course's contractor, William H. Tucker & Son, and after Olympic opened, James hired MacMillan to help design and supervise Tucker projects along the West Coast.

James soon resigned to pursue his own golf design career, and MacMillan took his place in the Tucker organization. In the next 8 years, he designed and built courses with William H. Tucker in nine Great Plains and Western states. The Depression forced Tucker to close his Western office in 1931, and MacMillan moved to California, where he built miniature golf layouts and ran a landscaping service catering to wealthy patrons in Beverly Hills. On Tucker's recommendation, MacMillan was hired to design and build a nine hole course for the El Mirador Hotel in Palm Springs. It became one of the first golf courses in that exclusive community, but after one successful season the hotel closed, the course was abandoned and MacMillan found himself unpaid and in debt.

In 1934 MacMillan and wife moved to Montana, where he obtained a position with the U.S. Army Corps of Engineers. He later became Director of Operations of federal WPA projects in Montana, and in that capacity helped organize several golf course projects that put countless numbers back to work and brought the game to small Montana communities. MacMillan prepared the architectural plans for these nine hole layouts.

Several promotions led to transfers to Colorado and then California, but MacMillan returned to Montana after World War II. He served as Secretary of the Helena Chamber of Commerce and then as Training Officer for the Seriously Disabled in the Veterans Administration.

During this time, MacMillan's interest in golf course design continued. Though limited mainly to weekends, he designed and supervised the construction of several Montana courses in the Forties and Fifties. On most of the projects he accepted no fee.

Courses by: Gregor MacMillan
California: El Mirador Hotel GC, Palm Springs (NLE, 9, 1932).
Montana: Anaconda CC (9); Cabinet View CC, Libby (9); Green Meadow CC, Helena (9, 1946); Hamilton CC (9); Hilands GC (9, 1950), with Norman H. Woods; Kalispell G&CC (9, 1963); Polson G&CC (9); University of Montana GC, Missoula (9, 1959); Whitefish Lake GC (9, 1937).
Nebraska: CC of Lincoln (1923), with William H. Tucker; Hillcrest CC, Lincoln (1925), with William H. Tucker; Pioneer Park GC, Lincoln (1932), with William H. Tucker.
Washington: Linden G&CC, Puyallup (9), with William H. Tucker and Frank James; Roche Harbor GC, San Juan , with William H. Tucker and Frank James.
Courses Remodeled & Added to by: Gregor MacMillan
Montana: Green Meadow CC, Helena (R., 1960); Whitefish Lake GC (R.9, 1960); Whitefish Lake GC (A.9, 1960).

Charles Eugene Maddox Sr. (1898 -   )
Born: Centralia, Illinois.
Chuck Maddox spent his early days honing his golf game on Chicago-area courses and working for his father in the Maddox Construction Company. The company had been formed in 1870 as a road grading firm by Asa Maddox, Chuck's grandfather. Chuck's father, Eugene Maddox, branched out into golf course construction when he took command of the firm in the early 1900s.

After the first World War Maddox became head of the company and concentrated its efforts on golf development. In 1923 he joined forces with Frank Macdonald, a native Scot who had served as a club manager and course superintendent in Chicago. The firm of Macdonald and Maddox created a number of impressive Chicago-area courses, several of them owned and operated by Maddox. They also constructed courses for other prominent architects in the Twenties, including Langford and Moreau, Robert Bruce Harris and C.D. Wagstaff.

During the Depression, Maddox lost most of his course holdings. His construction company abandoned golf and worked instead on oil rigs and government projects. Following World War II, Maddox reorganized the construction outfit and soon found plenty of work restoring and reconstructing courses for other architects. In the 1950s, joined by sons Charles Jr. and William, he began designing courses again as well as building them.

While constructing some of the best works of architects like Edward Lawrence Packard and Robert Bruce Harris, Maddox has also created some notable layouts of his own, including one of America's few true linksland courses on Dauphin Island, Alabama.

Courses by: Charles Maddox
Alabama: Isle Dauphine CC (1962).
Illinois: Atwood GC, Rockford (1971); Bartlett Hills G&CC, Bartlett , with Frank P. MacDonald; Blackhorse GC, Downers Grove (Par 3, 9, 1966); Chicago G & Saddle C, Chicago (NLE,), with Frank P. MacDonald; Danville VA Hospital GC (9, 1951); Downey VA Hospital GC, Chicago (1978); DuWayne Motel GC, Chicago (Par 3, 9, 1960); Edgewood CC, Virden (9, 1962); Ellwood Greens CC, DeKalb (1972); Forest Hills CC, Rockford (1976); Gleneagles GC (Red Course), Lemont (1924), with Frank P. MacDonald; Gleneagles GC (White Course), Lemont (1924), with Frank P. MacDonald; Lakeview CC, Lodi (9, 1957); Menard GC, Petersburg (9, 1964); Nordic Hills GC, Itasca , with Frank P. MacDonald; Old Wayne GC, Chicago (1960); Palos CC, Palos Park (1925), with Frank P. MacDonald; Parkview Muni, Pekin (9, 1930), with Frank P. MacDonald; Prestwick CC, Orland Park (NLE, 1929), with Frank P. MacDonald; River Forest CC, Elmhurst , with Frank P. MacDonald; Shambolee GC, Petersburg (9, 1964); Silver Lake GC (South Course), Orland Park , with Frank P. MacDonald; Stonehenge GC, Barrington (1970); Sun and Fun Par 3 GC; Terrace Hills GC, Algonquin (1985); Waukegan GC, with Frank P. MacDonald.
Indiana: Beverly Shores CC (1930), with Frank P. MacDonald; Frankfort GC (9, 1965); Golf Club of Indiana, Lebanon (1973); Hoosier Links, New Palestine (1973); Lake Hills G&CC, St. John (27), with Frank P. MacDonald; Old Oakland GC, Oaklandon (1964), with William Maddox; Turkey Creek CC, Gary , with Frank P. MacDonald; Vincennes GC (9, 1974).
Michigan: Elks CC, Benton Harbor (1967); Georgetown GC, Ann Arbor (Par 3, 9), with Charles Maddox Jr; Raisin River CC, Monroe (1963).
Minnesota: Brookview CC, Minneapolis (27, 1968); Majestic Oaks GC, Blaine (27, 1971); Olympic Hills GC, Eden Prairie (1971); Rolling Green CC, Hamel (1969).
Missouri: Crackerneck CC, Blue Springs (1964), with William Maddox.
North Dakota: Larrimore CC (9, 1963).
South Dakota: Hillsview GC, Pierre (9, 1966); Moccasin Creek GC, Aberdeen (1969).

Wisconsin: Crandon GC (9), with Frank P. MacDonald; Rhinelander CC (9), with Frank P. MacDonald; Spring Brook CC, Antigo (9), with Frank P. MacDonald; Trout Lake CC, with Frank P. MacDonald.
Courses Remodeled & Added to by: Charles Maddox
Illinois: Brookridge CC, Park Ridge (R., 1929), with Frank P. MacDonald.
Indiana: Orchard Ridge CC, Fort Wayne (R., 1929), with Frank P. MacDonald.
South Dakota: Elmwood Park GC, Sioux Falls (A.9, 1966).

William Eugene Maddox (1925 -   )
Born: Chicago, Illinois.
The son of golf architect and contractor Chuck Maddox, Bill Maddox was associated for many years with his father and brother Charles Jr. He then took to the drawing board on his own and had to his credit several courses in Florida.
Courses by: William Maddox
Florida: Bonita Springs G&CC (1977); Zellwood Station CC, Zephyrhills (1974).
Illinois: Pheasant Run Lodge GC, St. Charles (1961).
Indiana: Old Oakland GC, Oaklandon (1964), with Charles Maddox.
Missouri: Crackerneck CC, Blue Springs (1964), with Charles Maddox.

Charles Mark Mahannah Jr. (1941 -   ) ASGCA
Born: Miami, Florida.
Charles Mahannah, son of golf architect Mark Mahannah, was practically reared on a golf course, and followed much the same route as his father in becoming a golf course architect. He served for a time as course superintendent at Kings Bay in Miami (a course his father designed and built), where he helped develop a special self-tolerant Bermudagrass blend for greens that are in close proximity to the ocean.

Charles then worked for his father in course design, eventually becoming his partner. In the late 1970s, when his father reduced his active involvement, Charles Mahannah formed his own design company.
Courses by: Charles Mahannah
Florida: Bonaventure CC (West Course), Fort Lauderdale (1974); Caloosa CC, Sun City Center (1981), with Mark Mahannah; Fontainebleau Park CC (West Course), Miami (1979), with Mark Mahannah; Isla del Sol GC, St. Petersburg (1977), with Mark Mahannah; Jacaranda CC (West Course), Plantation (1975), with Mark Mahannah; Jacaranda West CC, Venice (1976), with Mark Mahannah; Kendale Lakes G&CC, Miami; Kendale Lakes West CC, Miami (Precision,); Miles Grant CC, Stuart (Precision, 1972), with Mark Mahannah; Raintree GC, Pembroke Pines (1984); Ventura CC, Orlando (Precision, 1980), with Mark Mahannah.
Courses Remodeled & Added to by: Charles Mahannah
Florida: Palma Ceia G&CC, Tampa (R., 1979), with Mark Mahannah; Sun City Center G&CC (North Course) (A.9, 1972), with Mark Mahannah.

Charles Mark Mahannah Sr. (1906 -   ) ASGCA
Born: Miami, Florida.
Mark Mahannah's first job on a golf course was on the construction crew for William S. Flynn at Boca Raton Hotel & C, north of Miami. He later was a member of the course maintenance crew at Miami Biltmore CC and in the early 1940s became its head greenkeeper. The club was closed during World War II, and Mahannah spent the duration as a technical advisor on turf problems at an Army post in Pinellas County, Florida.

After the War, Mahannah renovated one eighteen at Miami Biltmore. It reopened under the name Riviera CC, and Mahannah served as its superintendent.

His experience at restoring the course led to other contracts, which he handled part-time until the early Fifties, when Mahannah resigned to practice course design full-time.

Preferring local jobs, Mahannah did few designs outside Florida and the Caribbean.
Courses by: Mark Mahannah
Florida: Boca Teeca CC, Boca Raton (27, 1968); Caloosa CC, Sun City Center (1981), with Charles Mahannah; Calusa CC, Miami (1969); Cocoa Beach Muni (1968); El Conquistador CC, Bradenton (1973); Fontainebleau Park CC (East Course), Miami (1971); Fontainebleau Park CC (West Course), Miami (1979), with Charles Mahannah; Greynold Park GC, Miami Beach (9, 1964); Haulover Beach GC, Miami (Par 3, 1964); Hillcrest East GC (Precision), Homestead AFB GC (9, 1961); Indian Trail CC, Palm Beach; Isla del Sol GC, St. Petersburg (1977), with Charles Mahannah; Jacaranda CC (East Course), Plantation (1970); Jacaranda CC (West Course), Plantation (1975), with Charles Mahannah; Jacaranda West CC, Venice (1976), with Charles Mahannah; Key Biscayne Hotel GC, Miami Beach (Par 3, 1954); Key Colony CC, Key Biscayne (NLE, Par 3, 1962); Kings Bay Y&CC, Miami (1959); Lake Venice CC, Venice (1959); Lost Tree C, Singer Island (1960); Miles Grant CC, Stuart (Precision, 1972), with Charles Mahannah; Mirror Lakes CC, Lehigh Acres (1970); Ocean Reef C (Dolphin Course), Key Largo (1951); Okeechobee G&CC (1966); Plantation Hotel GC, Crystal River (1958); Presidential CC, North Miami Beach (1962); Rio Pinar CC, Orlando (1958); Royal Palm Beach G&CC, Palm Beach (1960); Sandpiper Bay CC (Sinners Course), Port St. lucie (1961); Sun City Center G&CC (South Course) (1967); Ventura CC, Orlando (Precision, 1980), with Charles Mahannah.
Bahamas: Grand Bahama Hotel & CC, Freeport (27, 1961).
Chile: Club Campestre de Bucaramanga, with Jaime Saenz.
Colombia: Macarena GC; Santa Marta GC (1972).
Courses Remodeled & Added to by: Mark Mahannah
Florida: Coral Gables Biltmore GC, Coral Gables (R.); Crystal River CC (R., 1958); Everglades C, Palm Beach (R., 1958); Gulfstream GC, Delray Beach (R.3, 1960); Hollywood Beach Hotel CC (R., 1955); Naples Beach Hotel GC (R., 1953); Normandy Shores CC, Miami Beach (R.); Palma Ceia G&CC, Tampa (R., 1979), with Charles Mahannah; Port Charlotte CC (R.9); Port Charlotte CC (A.9); Riviera CC, Ormand Beach (R., 1954); Sun City Center G&CC (North Course) (A.9, 1972), with Charles Mahannah; Tarpon Springs CC (R., 1957); Westview CC, Miami (A.9, 1955).
Cuba: Havana Biltmore GC (R., 1957).

Pier Luigi Mancinelli (1920 -)
Born: Treviso, Italy.

Educated at Cambridge University in England and the University of Rome, Pier Mancinelli was studying orchestral conducting at the outbreak of World War II. He enlisted in the Italian Air Force and became one of its youngest squadron commanders. After the Allies invaded Italy, Mancinelli defected and turned himself over to advancing British forces.

After VE Day, he returned to the University of Rome and did graduate work in Civil Engineering. Following a stint as music critic for an Italian newspaper, Mancinelli spent eight years supervising the construction of roads in East Africa. There, urged on by fellow employees and golf enthusiasts, he constructed a makeshift golf course in the shadow of Mt. Kilimanjaro.

In the late Fifties, Mancinelli returned to Italy and took a job with a corporation involved with constructing Olgiata CC near Rome to the design of British golf architect C.K. Cotton. Working as site manager at Olgiata, Mancinelli studied golf design under Cotton, and upon completion of the course followed his mentor's advice and entered the field on a part-time basis.

In the early '70s Mancinelli, after brief employment with the World Bank, founded an Italian golf magazine and his own course design firm, both based in Rome. His designs were more successful than his magazine. One of his most notable works, Is Molas GC on the Island of Sardinia, was selected as the site for the Italian Open soon after it opened in 1976.

Courses by: Pier Mancinelli
Brazil: Quinta de Arambepe GC, Bahia (1978).
France: Gassin GC, St. Tropez (1985); Lyon-Charbonniere GC (1985); Sporting C de Beauvallon (9).
Iran: Mehr Shahr GC (1978).
Italy: Carimate Parco GC (1963); Castlefalfi GC (1985); Contea di Gradella GC, Milan (1986); Elba GC (9, 1968); San Vito de Normanni GC, Brindisi (9, 1972).
Ivory Coast: Abidjan GC (9, 1983); Yamoussoukro GC (1981).
Sardinia: Is Molas GC (1975).
Courses Remodeled & Added to by: Pier Mancinelli
France: St. Nom La Breteche GC (Blue Course) (R., 1979); St. Nom La Breteche GC (Red Course) (R., 1979).
Italy: Carimate Parco GC (R.); Ugolino GC, Florence (R., 1980).
Switzerland: Lugano GC (R.3, 1984).

Dan Frank Maples (1947 -) ASGCA
Born: Pinehurst, North Carolina.

Dan Maples received an Associate of Science degree from Wingate Junior College in North Carolina and a Bachelor's Degree in Landscape Architecture from the University of Georgia in 1972. During his summers from 1964 to 1972, he worked in golf course construction and maintenance for his father, golf architect Ellis Maples.

In 1972 Maples joined his father's firm and became a full partner two years later. In the early 1980s he went into business for himself, retaining offices in Pinehurst while working throughout the Southeast. One of his first solo designs, Oyster Bay Golf Links, was selected by Golf Digest magazine as the Best New Resort Course of 1983. As a hobby, Dan Maples researched the history of course construction at Pinehurst.

Courses by: Dan Maples
Alabama: Sehoy Plantation GC, Huntsboro (9, 1973), with Ellis Maples.
North Carolina: Apple Valley GC, Lake Lure (1986), with Ellis Maples; Cramer Mountain CC, Cramerton (1986); CC of Whispering Pines (South Course) (1974), with Ellis Maples; Green Valley GC, Kings Mountain (9, 1974), with Ellis Maples; Keith Hills CC, Buies Creek (1975), with Ellis Maples; Marsh Harbour G Links, Calabash (1980); Mountain Springs G&CC, Linville (Precision, 1978), with Ellis Maples; Oyster Bay G Links, Sunset Beach (1983); Pearl GC, Sunset Beach (1987); Pit G Links, Aberdeen (1984); Sea Trail G Links, Sunset Beach (1986); Seven Lakes West GC, West End (1987).
South Carolina: Heritage GC, Pawley's Island (1986).
Tennessee: Roan Valley CC, Mountain City (1983), with Ellis Maples.
Virginia: Devil's Knob GC, Wintergreen (1977), with Ellis Maples; Ford's Colony CC, Williamsburg (1986), with Ellis Maples; Olde Mill GC, Hillsville (1974), with Ellis Maples; Tazewell County CC, Pounding Mill (9, 1978), with Ellis Maples.
Courses Remodeled & Added to by: Dan Maples
North Carolina: Bermuda Run G&CC, Clemmons (A.9, 1986); Deep Springs CC, Madison (A.9, 1978), with Ellis Maples; Hope Valley CC, Durham (R., 1986); Woodlake CC, Vass (A.9, 1986).
Tennessee: Cherokee CC, Knoxville (R., 1985); Gatlinburg G&CC (R., 1974), with Ellis Maples.

Ellis Maples (1909 - 1984) ASGCA, President, 1973.
Born: Pinehurst, North Carolina. Died: Pinehurst, North Carolina at age 75.

Beginning at age fourteen, Ellis Maples worked during the summer months for his father Frank Maples, a longtime construction superintendent for Donald Ross and greenkeeper at Pinehurst CC. Ellis attended Lenoir Rhyne College in North Carolina, then worked as an assistant in the Pinehurst golf shop for a year before spending seven seasons as assistant greenkeeper to his father at two other Pinehurst-area courses, Mid Pines and Pine Needles.

In 1937 Maples assisted William S. Flynn and Dick Wilson in the construction of a nine-hole layout in Plymouth, North Carolina. He remained at Plymouth as its pro-greenkeeper until 1942, when he entered war service as an Army Engineer agronomist and technical advisor.

In 1947, while working as pro-manager at New Bern (N.C.) CC, Maples redesigned the course. He soon remodeled two other local layouts and planned a third. In 1948 he supervised construction of the last design done by Donald Ross, Raleigh (N.C.) CC. Maples worked as pro-superintendent at Raleigh until 1953 when, deciding against a career as a touring pro, he entered private practice as a golf course architect.

His firm handled over 70 course design projects in the Southeast over the next thirty years, including such perennial Top 100 layouts as CC of North Carolina and

Grandfather G&CC. The firm included Edwin B. Seay for eight years, and then one of his sons, Dan. Another son, Joe, served as longtime head pro at Boone (N.C.) GC, one of Ellis' first designs, and a third son, David, was a golf course builder.

Ellis Maples was a life member of the PGA of America.

Courses by: Ellis Maples
Alabama: Sehoy Plantation GC, Huntsboro (9, 1973), with Dan Maples.
Georgia: Goshen Plantation CC, Augusta (1968), with Ed Seay; West Lake CC, Augusta (1968), with Ed Seay.
North Carolina: Apple Valley GC, Lake Lure (1986), with Dan Maples; Bermuda Run G&CC, Clemmons (1971), with Ed Seay; Boone CC (1959); Brook Valley G&CC, Greenville (1967), with Ed Seay; Carmel CC (South Course), Charlotte (9, 1962); Cedar Brook GC, Elkin (1965), with Ed Seay; Cedar Rock CC, Lenoir (1965); Cedarwood CC, Matthews (1963); Chockoyette CC, Roanoke Rapids (1972), with Ed Seay; Coherie CC, Clinton (9, 1950); CC of Johnston County, Smithfield (1967), with Ed Seay; CC of North Carolina (Dogwood Course), Pinehurst (1963), with Willard Byrd; CC of Whispering Pines (East Course) (1959); CC of Whispering Pines (South Course) (1974), with Dan Maples; CC of Whispering Pines (West Course) (1970), with Ed Seay; Deep Springs CC, Madison (9, 1971), with Ed Seay; Duck Woods GC, Kitty Hawk (1968), with Ed Seay; Forest Oaks CC, Greensboro (1962); Gaston CC, Gastonia (1959); Grandfather G&CC, Linville (1986), with Ed Seay; Green Valley GC, Kings Mountain (9, 1974), with Dan Maples; Greensboro CC (Carlson Farms Course) (1963); Indian Valley CC, Burlington (1974), with Ed Seay; Keith Hills CC, Buies Creek (1975), with Dan Maples; Meadow Greens CC, Eden (1962); Mountain Springs G&CC, Linville (Precision, 1978), with Dan Maples; Pine Brook GC, Winston-Salem (1955); Pinehurst CC (Course No. 5) (1961), with Richard S. Tufts; Quarry Hills CC {formerly Piedmont Crescent CC}, Burlington , with Ed Seay; Red Fox CC, Tryon (1965), with Ed Seay; Roanoke CC, Williamston (1955); Sapona CC, Lexington (1967), with Ed Seay; Siler City CC (9, 1959); Twin Oaks GC, Greensboro (Par 3, 1957); Walnut Creek CC, Goldsboro (1968), with Ed Seay; Winston Lake Park GC, Winston-Salem (1964); Woodlake CC {formerly Lake Surf CC}, Vass , with Ed Seay.
South Carolina: Calhoun C, St. Matthews (9, 1959); Columbia CC (27, 1962); CC of Orangeburg (1960); CC of South Carolina, Florence (1969), with Ed Seay; Midland Valley CC, Aiken (1961); Wellman CC, Johnsonville (1970), with Ed Seay.
Tennessee: Ridgeway CC, Collierville (1972), with Ed Seay; Roan Valley CC, Mountain City (1983), with Dan Maples.
Virginia: Chatmoss CC, Martinsville (1960); Countryside CC, Roanoke (1967), with Ed Seay; Devil's Knob GC, Wintergreen (1977), with Dan Maples; Ford's Colony CC, Williamsburg (1986), with Dan Maples; Kempsville Meadows G&CC, Norfolk (1954); Lexington GC (1971), with Ed Seay; Olde Mill GC, Hillsville (1974), with Dan Maples; Tazewell County CC, Pounding Mill (9, 1978), with Dan Maples.
Courses Remodeled & Added to by: Ellis Maples
North Carolina: Carmel CC (South Course), Charlotte (A.9, 1970), with Ed Seay; Deep Springs CC, Madison (A.9, 1978), with Dan Maples; Emorywood CC, High Point (R.9, 1962); Kinston CC (R., 1954); Myers Park CC, Charlotte (R., 1962); New Bern G&CC (A.9, 1954); New Bern G&CC (R.9, 1954); Reynolds Park GC, Winston Salem (R., 1966), with Ed Seay; Roxboro CC (A.9, 1969), with Ed Seay; Smithfield CC (A.9, 1963); Smithfield CC (R.9, 1963); Stanly County CC, Badin (R., 1966), with Ed Seay.
Tennessee: Gatlinburg G&CC (R., 1974), with Dan Maples.

Lane Lee Marshall (1937 -) ASGCA
Born: Rochester, New York.

A graduate landscape architect, Lane Marshall served as President of the ASLA in 1977 and 1978. In addition to his landscape practice, he designed a number of golf courses in Florida. In the early 1980s, Marshall curtailed his design activities and joined the Department of Landscape Architecture at Texas A & M University.
Courses by: Lane Marshall
Florida: Bobby Jones Muni (Executive Course), Sarasota (Precision, 1977); Capri Isles GC, Venice (1973); Foxfire CC, Sarasota (9, 1975); Manatee County GC, Bradenton (1977); Myakka Pines GC, Englewood (27, 1978); Tarpon Lake Village GC, Palm Harbor (1975); Tarpon Woods GC, Palm Harbor (1975); Wildflower CC, Grove City (Precision, 1972).
North Dakota: Williston Muni, with Carl Thuesen.

Jerry Martin (1939 -) ASGCA
Born: Phoenix, Arizona.

Jerry Martin grew up in Tucson, Arizona but attended high school in Morocco. He returned to the U.S. to study fine arts at the University of Arizona. Following military service, he worked for a year on a surveying crew before returning to the University of Arizona, where he earned a degree in City Planning in 1967.

Martin was employed for five years with a civil engineering firm and was then associated with the the west coast branch of Robert Trent Jones Inc. for another five. He then became in-house golf architect and manager of recreational planning with Jack G. Robb Engineering of Costa Mesa, California. In 1980 Martin formed his own golf design practice based in Tucson.

William Martindale

Texas A & M graduate and one-time PGA Tour player Billy Martindale designed several courses in partnership with Don January during the early 1970s. January rejoined the PGA Tour in 1976, but Martindale continued design work in Texas for several years before turning to a career in the oil business.
Courses by: Billy Martindale
Oklahoma: Walnut Creek CC, Oklahoma City (1976), with Don January.
Texas: Bentwood CC, San Angelo (1980); Great Hills GC, Austin , with Don January; Los Rios CC, Plano (1974), with Don January; Oak Forest CC, Longview; Pecan Hollow GC; Pine Forest GC, Bastrop (1982); Plano Muni, with Don January; Royal Oaks CC, Dallas (1970), with Don January; Walnut Creek GC, Mansfield , with Don January; Woodcrest CC, Grand Prairie , with Don January; Woodland Hills GC, Nacogdoches , with Don January.

Courses Remodeled & Added to by: Billy Martindale
Texas: Lake Country Estates GC, Ft. Worth (A.9, 1975), with Don January.

Wallace Bruce Matthews (1904 -) ASGCA
Born: Hastings, Michigan.
Bruce Matthews received a Landscape Architecture degree from Michigan State College in 1925. His first course design experience was with the golf architecture firm of Stiles and Van Kleek of Boston, Massachusetts and St. Petersburg, Florida. In 1929 he entered private practice in Michigan. His first original design was a second nine at Manistee CC.
When the Depression curtailed course construction Matthews became manager/greenkeeper at Green Ridge CC in Grand Rapids. He remained in that position until 1959 but continued to design golf courses on the side. In 1960 he re-entered golf architecture on a full-time basis with his son Jerry as his partner. He also owned and operated a course of his own design, Grand Haven CC, that was perennially selected as one of the Top Public Courses in America.
Courses by: Bruce Matthews
Indiana: Summertree GC, Crown Point (1974), with Jerry Matthews.
Michigan: Antrim Dells GC, Atwood (9, 1971), with Jerry Matthews; Birchwood Farm G&CC, Harbor Springs (1974), with Jerry Matthews; Blossom Trails GC, Benton Harbor (1952); Brookshire CC, Wiliamston (9, 1955); Candlestone GC, Belding (1978), with Jerry Matthews; Crystal Lake GC, Beulah (9, 1970), with Jerry Matthews; Dun Rovin CC, Northville (1956); Eldorado GC, Mason (9, 1966), with Jerry Matthews; Fellows Creek GC, Wayne (1961), with Jerry Matthews; Flint Elks CC, Flint (9, 1960), with Jerry Matthews; Forest Akers GC (West Course), East Lansing (1958); Godwin Glen GC, South Lyon (27, 1972), with Jerry Matthews; Grand Blanc GC (1967), with Jerry Matthews; Grand Haven GC (1965), with Jerry Matthews; Highland Hills GC, Dewitt (1963), with Jerry Matthews; Independence Green GC, Farmington (Precision, 1965), with Jerry Matthews; Kaufman GC, Wyoming (1963), with Jerry Matthews; Lake of the Hills GC, Haslett (Par 3, 9, 1968), with Jerry Matthews; Lake of the North GC, Mancelona (9, 1971), with Jerry Matthews; Lake Isabella GC, Weidman (1970), with Jerry Matthews; Lakewood Shores G&CC, Oscoda (1969), with Jerry Matthews; Lincoln Hills GC, Birmingham (9, 1963), with Jerry Matthews; McGuires Evergreen GC, Cadillac (27, 1954); Mitchell Creek GC, Mitchell (1982), with Jerry Matthews; Riverside CC, Battle Creek (9, 1964), with Jerry Matthews; Royal Oak GC (9, 1960), with Jerry Matthews; Salem Hills GC (1961), with Jerry Matthews; San Marino GC, Farmington (9, 1965), with Jerry Matthews; Sandy Ridge GC, Midland (1966), with Jerry Matthews; Scott Lake CC, Comstock Park (1961), with Jerry Matthews; Shenandoah G&CC, Walled Lake (1964), with Jerry Matthews; Southmoor GC, Flint (1965), with Jerry Matthews; St. Clair Shores CC (1974), with Jerry Matthews; Sugar Springs GC, Gladwin (1978), with Jerry Matthews; Sunnybrook CC, Grandville (1955); Tyrone Hills CC, Livingston (1958); University Park GC, Muskegon (9, 1966), with Jerry Matthews; Wellington Hills GC, Gaylord (9, 1980), with Jerry Matthews; West Ottawa GC, Holland (1964), with Jerry Matthews; White Birch Hills GC, Bay City (1953); Wilderness Valley GC, Gaylord (1980), with Jerry Matthews; Willowood CC, Flint (1960); Winding Creek GC, Zeeland (1967), with Jerry Matthews; Wolverine GC, Mt. Clemens (1965), with Jerry Matthews.
Courses Remodeled & Added to by: Bruce Matthews
Indiana: Elcona CC, Elkhart (R., 1969), with Jerry Matthews; Fort Wayne CC (R.3, 1968), with Jerry Matthews.
Michigan: Birmingham CC (R.3, 1963), with Jerry Matthews; Blythefield CC, Belmont (R.5, 1973), with Jerry Matthews; Bonnie View GC, Eaton (R.4, 1978), with Jerry Matthews; Bonnie View GC, Eaton (A.2, 1978), with Jerry Matthews; Cadillac CC (R.1, 1977), with Jerry Matthews; Cascade Hills CC, Grand Rapids (R., 1980), with Jerry Matthews; Crockery Hills GC, Nuncia (A.9, 1976), with Jerry Matthews; Crockery Hills GC, Nuncia (R.5, 1976), with Jerry Matthews; CC of Detroit, Grosse Pointe Farms (R., 1962), with Jerry Matthews; Eldorado GC, Mason (A.9, 1978), with Jerry Matthews; Farmington CC (R., 1962), with Jerry Matthews; Green Ridge CC, Grand Rapids (R., 1930); Green Ridge CC, Grand Rapids (R., 1950); Indian Hills GC, Okemos (R., 1968), with Jerry Matthews; Indian Lake GC, Manistique (R.3, 1980), with Jerry Matthews; Indian Run GC, Scotts (A.9, 1972), with Jerry Matthews; Kalamazoo Elks CC, Kalamzoo (R.2, 1976), with Jerry Matthews; Knollwood CC, Birmingham (A.1, 1969), with Jerry Matthews; Knollwood CC, Birmingham (R.1, 1969), with Jerry Matthews; Lakepointe CC, St. Clair Shores (NLE, A.6, 1964), with Jerry Matthews; Ludington Hills GC, Ludington (R.4, 1975), with Jerry Matthews; Ludington Hills GC, Ludington (A.9, 1975), with Jerry Matthews; Manistee G&CC (A.9, 1930); Manistee G&CC (R.9, 1930); Meadowbrook CC, Detroit (R.1), with Jerry Matthews; Midland CC (R.), with Jerry Matthews; Mount Pleasant CC (A.9, 1981), with Jerry Matthews; Muskegon CC (R.3, 1979), with Jerry Matthews; Old Channel Trail GC, Montague (A.9, 1966), with Jerry Matthews; Old Channel Trail GC, Montague (R.11, 1966), with Jerry Matthews; Pine Lake CC, Orchard Lake (R.1, 1972), with Jerry Matthews; Pine River CC, Alma (A.9, 1961), with Jerry Matthews; Plum Hollow G&CC, Southfield (R.1, 1966), with Jerry Matthews; Saginaw CC (R.2, 1979), with Jerry Matthews; Spring Lake G&CC (R.1, 1978), with Jerry Matthews; Stonycroft Hills CC, Bloomfield Hills (R.5, 1979), with Jerry Matthews; Traverse City CC (R.), with Jerry Matthews; Walnut Hills CC, East Lansing (R.2, 1963), with Jerry Matthews; Washtenaw CC, Ypsilanti (R.1, 1962), with Jerry Matthews; White Lake GC, Whitehall (R., 1965), with Jerry Matthews; Winters Creek GC, Big Rapids (R.9, 1980), with Jerry Matthews.
Wisconsin: Brynwood CC, Milwaukee (A.2, 1979), with Jerry Matthews; Brynwood CC, Milwaukee (R.1, 1979), with Jerry Matthews.
Ontario: Essex G&CC, LaSalle (A.2, 1976), with Jerry Matthews.

Gerald Herbert Matthews (1934 -) ASGCA
Born: Grand Rapids, Michigan.
Jerry Matthews attended Michigan State University, receiving a B.S. Degree in Landscape Architecture as well as B.S. and M.S. Degrees in Urban Planning. During his schooling, he worked for ten summers in golf course maintenance and also supervised the construction of one course designed by his father, architect Bruce Matthews.
In 1960 Matthews and his father established the golf architectural partnership. Over the years, Jerry took on the active design work of the firm with his father acting as consultant. Eventually he formed a separate design group based in Lansing, Michigan which was involved in golf course and landscape architecture as well as land planning.
Courses by: Jerry Matthews
Indiana: Summertree GC, Crown Point (1974), with Bruce Matthews.
Michigan: Antrim Dells GC, Atwood (9, 1971), with Bruce Matthews; Birchwood Farm G&CC, Harbor Springs (1974), with Bruce Matthews; Candlestone GC, Belding (1978), with Bruce Matthews; Crystal Lake GC, Beulah (9, 1970), with Bruce Matthews; Eldorado GC, Mason (9, 1966), with Bruce Matthews; Fellows Creek GC, Wayne (1961), with Bruce Matthews; Flint Elks CC, Flint (9, 1960), with Bruce Matthews; Godwin Glen GC, South Lyon (27, 1972), with Bruce Matthews; Grand Blanc GC (1967), with Bruce Matthews; Grand Haven GC (1965), with Bruce Matthews; Highland Hills GC, Dewitt (1963), with Bruce Matthews; Independence Green GC, Farmington (Precision, 1965), with Bruce Matthews; Kaufman GC, Wyoming (1963), with Bruce Matthews; Lake of the Hills GC, Haslett (Par 3, 9, 1968), with Bruce Matthews; Lake of the North GC, Mancelona (9, 1971), with Bruce Matthews; Lake Isabella GC, Weidman (1970), with Bruce Matthews; Lakewood Shores G&CC, Oscoda (1969), with Bruce Matthews; Lincoln Hills GC, Birmingham (9, 1963), with Bruce Matthews; Mitchell Creek GC, Mitchell (1982), with Bruce Matthews; Riverside CC, Battle Creek (9, 1964), with Bruce Matthews; Royal Oak GC (9, 1960), with Bruce Matthews; Salem Hills GC (1961), with Bruce Matthews; San Marino GC, Farmington (9, 1965), with Bruce Matthews; Sandy Ridge GC, Midland (1966), with Bruce Matthews; Scott Lake CC, Comstock Park (1961), with Bruce Matthews; Shenandoah G&CC, Walled Lake (1964), with Bruce Matthews; Southmoor GC, Flint (1965), with Bruce Matthews; St. Clair Shores CC (1974), with Bruce Matthews; Sugar Springs GC, Gladwin (1978), with Bruce Matthews; University Park GC, Muskegon (9, 1966), with Bruce Matthews; Wellington Hills GC, Gaylord (9, 1980), with Bruce Matthews; West Ottawa GC, Holland (1964), with Bruce Matthews; Wilderness Valley GC, Gaylord (1980), with Bruce Matthews; Winding Creek GC, Zeeland (1967), with Bruce Matthews; Wolverine GC, Mt. Clemens (1965), with Bruce Matthews.
Courses Remodeled & Added to by: Jerry Matthews
Indiana: Elcona CC, Elkhart (R., 1969), with Bruce Matthews; Fort Wayne CC (R.3, 1968), with Bruce Matthews.
Michigan: Birmingham CC (R.3, 1963), with Bruce Matthews; Blythefield CC, Belmont (R.5, 1973), with Bruce Matthews; Blythefield CC, Belmont (R.1, 1985); Bonnie View GC, Eaton (R.4, 1978), with Bruce Matthews; Bonnie View GC, Eaton (A.2, 1978), with Bruce Matthews; Cadillac CC (R.1, 1977), with Bruce Matthews; Cascade Hills CC, Grand Rapids (R., 1980), with Bruce Matthews; Cascade Hills CC, Grand Rapids (R.9, 1984); Crockery Hills GC, Nuncia (A.9, 1976), with Bruce Matthews; Crockery Hills GC, Nuncia (R.5, 1976), with Bruce Matthews; CC of Detroit, Grosse Pointe Farms (R., 1962), with Bruce Matthews; CC of Lansing (R.1, 1984); Dearborn CC (R.1, 1985); Eldorado GC, Mason (A.9, 1978), with Bruce Matthews; Elmbrook GC, Traverse City (R.3, 1985); English Hills GC, Walker (A.9, 1985); Farmington CC (R., 1962), with Bruce Matthews; Fellows Creek GC, Wayne (A.9, 1986); Forest Hills GC (R.1, 1984); Frankenmuth GC (R.2); Frankenmuth GC (A.1); Grand Hotel GC, Mackinac Island (R.4, 1985); Holland Lake GC, Sheridan (A.9); Holland Lake GC, Sheridan (R.1, 1986); Indian Hills GC, Okemos (R., 1968), with Bruce Matthews; Indian Lake GC, Manistique (R.3, 1980), with Bruce Matthews; Indian Run GC, Scotts (A.9, 1972), with Bruce Matthews; Kalamazoo Elks CC, Kalamzoo (R.2, 1976), with Bruce Matthews; Kent CC, Grand Rapids (R.1, 1985); Knollwood CC, Birmingham (R.1, 1969), with Bruce Matthews; Knollwood CC, Birmingham (A.1, 1969), with Bruce Matthews; Lakepointe CC, St. Clair Shores (NLE, A.6, 1964), with Bruce Matthews; Lakeview Hills CC, Lexington (R.1, 1983); Lincoln GC, Muskegon (A.2, 1986); Lincoln Hills GC, Birmingham (R.1, 1984); Ludington Hills GC, Ludington (R.4, 1975), with Bruce Matthews; Ludington Hills GC, Ludington (A.9, 1975), with Bruce Matthews; Maple Hill GC, Hemlock (R.1, 1984); Meadowbrook CC, Detroit (R.1), with Bruce Matthews; Meadowbrook CC, Detroit (R.2, 1985); Midland CC (R.), with Bruce Matthews; Mission Hills GC, Plymouth (A.9, 1986); Mount Pleasant CC (A.9, 1981), with Bruce Matthews; Muskegon CC (R.3, 1979), with Bruce Matthews; Old Channel Trail GC, Montague (R.11, 1966), with Bruce Matthews; Old Channel Trail GC, Montague (A.9, 1966), with Bruce Matthews; Pine Lake CC, Orchard Lake (R.1, 1972), with Bruce Matthews; Pine Lake CC, Orchard Lake (A.2, 1985); Pine River CC, Alma (A.9, 1961), with Bruce Matthews; Plum Hollow G&CC, Southfield (R.1, 1966), with Bruce Matthews; Rackham Park Muni, Huntington (R.9, 1985); Ramshorn CC, Fremont (A.9, 1986); Saginaw CC (R.2, 1979), with Bruce Matthews; Saginaw CC (R.2, 1985); Sault St. Marie Muni (NLE, A.9, 1985); Spring Lake G&CC (R.1, 1978), with Bruce Matthews; Spring Lake G&CC (R.2, 1985); Stonycroft Hills CC, Bloomfield Hills (R.5, 1979), with Bruce Matthews; Traverse City CC (R.), with Bruce Matthews; Walnut Hills CC, East Lansing (R.2, 1963), with Bruce Matthews; Walnut Hills CC, East Lansing (R.4, 1984); Washtenaw CC, Ypsilanti (R.1, 1962), with Bruce Matthews; White Lake GC, Whitehall (R., 1965), with Bruce Matthews; Winters Creek GC, Big Rapids (R.9, 1980), with Bruce Matthews; Wolverine GC, Mt. Clemens (A.27, 1986).
Pennsylvania: Sunnehanna CC, Johnstown (R.1, 1985).
Wisconsin: Brynwood CC, Milwaukee (A.2, 1979), with Bruce Matthews; Brynwood CC, Milwaukee (R.1, 1979), with Bruce Matthews.
Ontario: Essex G&CC, LaSalle (A.2, 1976), with Bruce Matthews.

Charles E. Maud
Englishman Charles Maud emigrated to California where he laid out the state's first golf course in 1892. Known as Pedley Farms GC (later Arlington GC and then Victoria GC), it was owned by Colonel W.E. Pedley, who assisted Maud in laying out several other early California courses. Although Max Behr revised the original nine and added an additional nine, Victoria GC retained several of Maud's holes.
Charles Maud was the winner of the first California Amateur in 1899 and served as the first President of the Southern California Golf Association in 1900.
Courses by: Charles Maud
California: Delmar CC (NLE, 9); Old Del Monte G&CC, Monterey (9, 1897); Victoria GC, Riverside (9, 1892), with Col. W.E. Pedley.

Perry Duke Maxwell (1879 - 1952) ASGCA, Charter Member.
Born: Princeton, Kentucky. Died: Tulsa, Oklahoma at age 73.

Perry Maxwell, of Scottish descent, was educated at the University of Kentucky. In 1897 he moved to the Ardmore Indian Territory to recover from an attack of tuberculosis and settled in what would become, in 1907, the State of Oklahoma. He was employed as a cashier and later as Vice-President of the Ardmore National Bank, becoming one of the town's leading citizens. Around 1909 he took up the game of golf after reading an article by H.J. Whigham, and in 1913, with his wife's assistance, he laid out a rudimentary nine-hole course on their farm north of Ardmore. This course became Dornick Hills G&CC.

Maxwell retired from banking soon after his wife's death in 1919 and spent the next several years touring American's most prominent southern and eastern golf courses. He added a second nine to Dornick Hills in 1923 and installed the first grass greens in the State of Oklahoma at the same time. Shortly thereafter he was hired to build courses in Tulsa and Oklahoma City and by 1925 was working full time as a golf architect. He worked for three years in the early Thirties with Alister Mackenzie and supervised completion of some of Mackenzie's work after his death.

Maxwell was best known for his wildly undulating greens, and his reputation was of such stature that he was hired to rebuild greens at Augusta National, Pine Valley, The National Golf Links and others. His last designs, following the amputation of his right leg in 1946, were supervised by his son J. Press Maxwell, who later became a golf architect himself. It is estimated that during his career Perry Maxwell designed some seventy courses and remodeled fifty others.

Courses by: Perry Maxwell
Alabama: Lakewood GC (Dogwood Course), Point Clear (1947), with Press Maxwell.
Illinois: Rochelle CC (9, 1930).
Iowa: Veenker Memorial GC, Iowa State Univ. (1934).
Kansas: Arkansas City CC (9, 1937); Prairie Dunes CC, Hutchinson (9, 1937).
Louisiana: Bayou De Siard CC, Monroe (1949), with Press Maxwell; Palmetto CC, Benton (1950), with Press Maxwell.
Michigan: University of Michigan GC, Ann Arbor (1931), with Alister Mackenzie.
Missouri: Grandview Muni, Springfield (1947), with Press Maxwell.
North Carolina: Old Town C, Winston-Salem (1928); Reynolds Park GC, Winston Salem (1941); Starmount Forest CC, Greensboro (1929).
Ohio: Ohio State Univ GC (Gray Course), Columbus (1939), with Alister Mackenzie; Ohio State Univ GC (Scarlet Course), Columbus (1939), with Alister Mackenzie.
Oklahoma: Dornick Hills G&CC, Ardmore (9, 1913); Elks CC, Duncan (9); Hillcrest CC, Bartlesville; Lake Hefner GC (North Course), Oklahoma City (1951), with Press Maxwell; Lawton CC (9, 1948), with Press Maxwell; Muskogee CC (1924); Oakwood CC, Enid (1947), with Press Maxwell; Oklahoma City G&CC (1930); Ponca City CC (9); Rolling Hills CC, Tulsa (1926); Shawnee Elks CC, Shawnee; Southern Hills CC, Tulsa (1936); Twin Hills G&CC, Oklahoma City (1926); University of Oklahoma GC, Norman (1950), with Press Maxwell.
Pennsylvania: Chester Valley CC (1928); Eugene Grace Estate GC, Bethlehem; Melrose CC, Cheltenham (1927).
Texas: Anderson GC, Killeen (9, 1948), with Press Maxwell; Knollwood GC, Irving (NLE, 1952), with Press Maxwell; Randolph Field GC, San Antonio (9, 1948), with Press Maxwell; Riverside CC {formerly CC of Austin}, Austin (1950), with Press Maxwell; Walnut Hills CC, Ft. Worth (NLE,).

Courses Remodeled & Added to by: Perry Maxwell
Florida: Clearwater CC (R.).
Georgia: Augusta National GC, Augusta (R., 1937).
Kansas: Topeka CC (A.9, 1938); Topeka CC (R.9, 1938).
Michigan: Crystal Downs CC, Frankfort (R.9, 1933), with Alister Mackenzie; Crystal Downs CC, Frankfort (A.9, 1933), with Alister Mackenzie.
Missouri: Excelsior Springs CC (NLE, Par 3, A.9).
Nebraska: Omaha CC (R.).
New Jersey: Pine Valley GC, Clementon (R., 1933).
New York: Links GC, Roslyn (R.); Maidstone C, East Hampton (R.); National G Links of America, Southampton (R.1); Rockaway Hunting C, Cedarhurst (R., 1946); Westchester CC (South Course), Rye (R.).
North Carolina: Hope Valley CC, Durham (R.).
Oklahoma: Dornick Hills G&CC, Ardmore (R.9, 1923); Dornick Hills G&CC, Ardmore (A.9, 1923); Lincoln Park Muni (East Course), Oklahoma City (R.); Lincoln Park Muni (West Course), Oklahoma City (R.); Mohawk Park Muni (Woodbine Course), Tulsa (R., 1934); Oaks CC, Tulsa (R.); Ponca City CC (A.9).
Pennsylvania: Flourtown CC, Philadelphia (NLE, R., 1939); Gulph Mills GC, King of Prussia (R., 1937); Merion GC (East Course), Ardmore (R.); Merion GC (West Course), Ardmore (R., 1939); Philadelphia CC, Gladwyne (R., 1938), with William S. Flynn; Saucon Valley CC (Saucon Course), Bethlehem (R., 1947).
Texas: Colonial CC, Fort Worth (A.3, 1940).

James Press Maxwell (1916 -   ) ASGCA, President, 1960.
Born: Ardmore, Oklahoma.

The son of golf architect Perry Maxwell, Press Maxwell started in the business upon graduation from high school. His father put him to work running mule teams and fresno scrapers at such sites as Southern Hills and Augusta National.

After service as a pilot with the U.S. Air Force during World War II, Maxwell returned to his father's firm. By this time Perry Maxwell had lost a leg, so Press handled most of the on-site supervision of new courses.

Continuing the firm after his father's death in 1952, Maxwell designed and built many courses along the Gulf Coast, flying from course to course in his own Cessna. In the early 1960s he moved his base to Colorado and in the early 1970s retired from full-time practice to maintain a ranch.

Courses by: Press Maxwell
Alabama: Lakewood GC (Dogwood Course), Point Clear (1947), with Perry Maxwell.
California: Seacliff CC {formerly Huntington Seacliff CC}, Huntington Beach (1965).
Colorado: Applewood GC, Golden (18, 1961); Boulder CC (1965); Cimarron Hills GC, Colorado Springs (1974); Cortez Muni (9, 1964); Hiwan GC, Evergreen

(1965); Inverness GC, Englewood (1974); Kissing Camels GC, Colorado Springs (1961); Lake Valley GC, Boulder (1964); Pinehurst CC, Denver (27, 1960); Rolling Hills CC, Golden (1968); Snowmass GC, Snowmass-at-Aspen (9, 1967); Vail GC (1966); Woodmoor CC, Monument (1965).
Louisiana: Bayou De Siard CC, Monroe (1949), with Perry Maxwell; East Ridge CC, Shreveport (1957); Palmetto CC, Benton (1950), with Perry Maxwell.
Mississippi: Hattiesburg CC (1962).
Missouri: Fremont Hills CC, Nixa (9, 1971); Grandview Muni, Springfield (1947), with Perry Maxwell; Tri-way GC, Republic (9, 1971).
Oklahoma: Lake Hefner GC (North Course), Oklahoma City (1951), with Perry Maxwell; Lawton CC (9, 1948), with Perry Maxwell; Meadowbrook CC, Tulsa (9, 1954); Oakwood CC, Enid (1947), with Perry Maxwell; University of Oklahoma GC, Norman (1950), with Perry Maxwell.
Tennessee: Edmund Orgill GC, Millington (1970); Farmington CC, Germantown (1968).
Texas: Anderson GC, Killeen (9, 1948), with Perry Maxwell; Brookhaven CC (Championship Course), Dallas (1959); Brookhaven CC (Masters Course), Dallas (1959); Brookhaven CC (Presidents Course), Dallas (1959); Club at Sonterra (South Course) {formerly Canyon Creek CC} (1960); Irving CC (NLE, 9, 1957); Knollwood GC, Irving (NLE, 1952), with Perry Maxwell; Oak Cliff CC, Dallas (1955); Pecan Valley CC, San Antonio (1963); Randolph Field GC, San Antonio (9, 1948), with Perry Maxwell; Riverbend CC, Sugarland (1958); Riverside GC {formerly CC of Austin}, Austin (1950), with Perry Maxwell; Sleepy Hollow G&CC (Lake Course), Dallas (1957); Sleepy Hollow G&CC (River Course), Dallas (1957); Village CC, Dallas (1969).

Courses Remodeled & Added to by: Press Maxwell
Colorado: Bookcliff CC, Grand Junction (A.5, 1967); Cherry Hills CC, Englewood (R., 1959); Cherry Hills CC, Englewood (Par 3, A.9, 1961); Columbine CC, Littleton (R., 1958); Cortez Muni (A.9, 1974); Denver CC (R., 1964); Greeley CC (R.9, 1962); Greeley CC (A.9, 1962); Lakewood CC, Denver (R., 1962); Patty Jewett GC, Colorado Springs (A.18, 1968).
Kansas: Prairie Dunes CC, Hutchinson (A.9, 1956).
New York: Rockaway Hunting C, Cedarhurst (R., 1955).
Oklahoma: Oklahoma City G&CC (R., 1952).
Texas: Pinecrest CC, Longview (R.9, 1959); Pinecrest CC, Longview (A.9, 1959).
Utah: Park City GC (R.9, 1972); Park City GC (A.9, 1972).

Theodore McAnlis
Civil engineer Ted McAnlis entered the golf business by forming a group to finance Briarwood GC in Cleveland, Ohio, a daily-fee layout that he designed and constructed. While serving as Briarwood's manager for 8 years, McAnlis designed several courses in Ohio. Following this he worked as design engineer with George and Tom Fazio from 1973 through 1975. In 1976, McAnlis teamed with Dick LaConte in a design-and-build business in Florida. LaConte/McAnlis Associates lasted only one year, then McAnlis practiced course design by himself. On a couple of projects in the early Eighties, LaConte consulted with McAnlis.

Courses by: Ted McAnlis
Florida: Greenview Cove GC, West Palm Beach (1980); Heritage Ridge GC, Stuart (9, 1979); Imperial Lakes GC, Palmetto (1987); Indianwood G&CC, Indiantown (Precision, 9, 1982); Lakes GC, Parrish (1986); Lone Pine GC, West Palm Beach (Precision, 1981), with Richard W. LaConte; Misty Creek CC, Sarasota (1985); Palms of Terra Ceia GC, Palmetto (1986); River Wilderness Y&CC, Parrish (1984); St. Andrews CC (East Course), Boca Raton (1982); St. Andrews CC (West Course), Boca Raton (1985); Wellington GC, West Palm Beach (1984).
Ohio: Briardale Greens Muni, Euclid (1977), with Richard W. LaConte; Briarwood GC, Broadview Heights (18, 1967); Leaning Tree GC, West Richfield (Precision, 1972), with Richard W. LaConte; Midway GC, Amherst (9, 1971); Wildwood CC, Fairfield (9, 1969).

Courses Remodeled & Added to by: Ted McAnlis
Florida: Palm Beach Polo & CC (North Course), West Palm Beach (R., 1981).
Louisiana: Brechtel Memorial Park GC, New Orleans (R.9, 1978), with Richard W. LaConte; Brechtel Memorial Park GC, New Orleans (A.9, 1978), with Richard W. LaConte.
Ohio: Briarwood GC, Broadview Heights (A.9, 1973); Grandview CC, Middlefield (R.), with Richard W. LaConte; Oakwood C, Cleveland (R.2, 1971); Pine Valley GC, Grafton (A.9, 1971); Pine Valley GC, Grafton (R.9, 1971); Willard CC (A.9, 1971), with Richard W. LaConte.

Thomas John Andrew McAuley (1930 -   ) BAGCA
A graduate of Queens University of Ulster, Northern Ireland, and fellow of the Institution of Civil Engineers and the Institution of Structural Engineers, T.J.A. McAuley worked as an assistant to German golf architect Dr. Bernhard von Limburger from 1969 to 1973. During those years, he also collaborated with Peter Alliss and David Thomas in course design. He later combined his practice as a golf architect with partnership in a firm of consulting, civil and structural engineers located in Belfast, Northern Ireland.

Courses by: T.J.A.McAuley
England: Birchwood GC, Cheshire (1979); Shaw Hill G&CC, Lancashire (1983); Welcombe Hotel GC, Stratford-on-Avon (1979).
Northern Ireland: Clandeboye GC (New Course), County Down (1973), with Peter Alliss and David Thomas; Clandeboye GC (Old Course), County Down , with Bernhard von Limburger and William Rennick Robinson; Dunmurry GC (1982); Enniskillen GC, County Fermanagh; Fort Royal GC, County Donegal (9, 1974).
Scotland: Gleneagles Hotel GC (Glendevon Course), Perthshire (1985).

Courses Remodeled & Added to by: T.J.A.McAuley
England: Grange GC, Coventry (R., 1983).
Isle of Man: Howstrake GC (R.).
Northern Ireland: Ballyclare GC (R.9, 1973), with Peter Alliss and David Thomas; Bangor GC, County Donegal (R.1, 1977); Castlecoole GC (A.1, 1982); Clandeboye GC (Old Course), County Down (R., 1969), with Bernhard von Limburger.

Maurice J. McCarthy Sr. (1875 - 1938)
Born: County Cork, Ireland. Died: Flushing, New York at age 63.

Maurice McCarthy came to the United States at the age of fifteen and obtained a job as a teaching professional in Pittsfield, Massachusetts. A few years later he laid out his first course, Jefferson County GC (now Ives Hill GC) in Watertown, New York. Throughout his life, course design remained a part-time endeavor for McCarthy. He was proudest of his accomplishments as a teacher. His son, Maurice Jr., was the 1928 NCAA Champion and a top-flight amateur in the 1930s.

McCarthy served as professional at several New York-area clubs but in his later years was employed exclusively by A.G. Spalding Sporting Goods Co. in New York City, where he gave lessons to all purchasers of golf clubs.

It is estimated that Maurice McCarthy designed or remodeled about 125 courses during his lifetime, most of them in the Eastern and Middle Atlantic states. His most famous works are at Hershey, Pennsylvania where he laid out four different courses over the years for his friend Milton Hershey. These range from a short beginner's course, Spring Creek GC, to a nationally recognized championship course, Hershey CC's West Course.

Courses by: Maurice McCarthy
Connecticut: E. Gaynor Brennan GC {formerly Hubbard Heights CC}, Stamford .
Michigan: Marywood CC, Battle Creek .
New Jersey: Knickerbocker CC, Tenafly (NLE,).
New York: Ives Hill CC, Watertown (9, 1899); Old Flatbush CC, Brooklyn (NLE, 9, 1925); Peninsula GC, Amityville; Willow Ridge CC {formerly Green Meadow CC}, Port Chester (1916).
Pennsylvania: Hershey CC (West Course) (1930); Hotel Hershey GC, Hershey (9, 1928); Kingsport CC; Mahoning Valley CC, Lansford (NLE,); Parkview Manor GC, Hershey (1927); Spring Creek GC, Hershey (9, 1933).
South Carolina: Forest Lakes C, Columbia .
Courses Remodeled & Added to by: Maurice McCarthy
Connecticut: Woodway CC, Darien (R.).
New Jersey: Green Brook CC, Caldwell (R., 1925); White Beeches G&CC, Haworth (R.).

Mark R. McCumber (1952 -)
Born: Jacksonville, Florida.

Mark McCumber grew up on Hyde Park GC in Jacksonville, Fla., where he and his brothers dug crabgrass for free green fees. After high school, he attended Brooklyn Bethel College in Brooklyn Heights, New York, studying for the ministry. Ultimately, he opted for a golf career, and after several attempts, McCumber gained his PGA Tour card in 1978. He experienced success as a competitive player, winning two Doral Open titles as well as the Western Open.

In the late 1970s, McCumber became involved with his brothers Jim, Gary and Tim in the golf course construction business. Mark laid out a course near Jacksonville called The Ravines, which his brothers constructed to serve as a showcase for their talents. The family business soon gained other course design-and-build contracts, and by the mid-1980s Mark divided his time between the PGA Tour and golf course design. His firm also took on two design associates, Christopher Commins and Michael Beebe.

Courses by: Mark McCumber
Florida: Cutter Sound CC, Stuart (1985); Deep Creek GC, Port Charlotte (1985); Dunes CC, Sanibel Island (Precision, 1983); Magnolia Point G&CC, Green Cove Springs (1986); Ravines GC, Middleburg (1979).
Mississippi: Windance G&CC, Gulfport (1986).

Michael J. McDonagh
Born: Ireland.

Michael McDonagh, a cousin of Jack Fleming, came to America in the late 1920s. When McDonagh moved to California, Fleming put him in charge of building Haggin Oaks GC in Sacramento to the design of Alister Mackenzie. After completion of the course, McDonagh remained in Sacramento, and eventually became course superintendent for all municipal courses in the city. While in that capacity, McDonagh tried his hand at golf course design on several occasions.

Courses by: Michael J. McDonagh
California: Bing Mahoney GC, Sacramento (1952); Haggin Oaks GC (North Course), Sacramento (1956).
Courses Remodeled & Added to by: Michael J. McDonagh
California: Yolo Fliers C, Woodland (A.9, 1955).

James Bernard McGovern (- 1951) ASGCA, Charter Member.

J.B. McGovern spent most of his design career as an associate of Donald Ross, running his office in Wynnewood, Pennsylvania. The two had met when Ross was hired to build a new course for McGovern's home course, Aronimink. For a short period following Ross' death in 1948, McGovern planned several courses on his own.

Courses by: J.B. McGovern
Georgia: CC of Columbus, with Donald Ross.
Kentucky: Idle Hour CC, Lexington , with Donald Ross.
Ohio: Lancaster CC (1926), with Donald Ross.
Pennsylvania: Overbrook CC, Radnor (1947), with X.G. Hassenplug.
Courses Remodeled & Added to by: J.B. McGovern
New York: Irondequoit CC, Rochester (A.9, 1948).
Pennsylvania: Green Valley CC, Lafayette Hills (R., 1946); Gulph Mills GC, King of Prussia (R., 1946); Llanerch CC, Havertown (R., 1949).

Alexander G. McKay (1893 - 1964)
Born: Aberdeen, Scotland. Died: Nashville, Tennessee at age 71.

Alex McKay learned golf at Cruden Bay GC in Aberdeen and turned professional at a young age. After spending three years in Egypt, he moved to America following World War I. He worked at odd jobs before landing the position of supervisor of the Louisville (Ky.) city parks in 1926. He remained for ten years as professional and greenkeeper for the city's golf courses and in that capacity remodeled two existing courses and designed and built three new ones, including the popular Shawnee GC.

In the mid-1930s McKay designed Meadowbrook CC in West Virginia and became its first pro-superintendent. Following World War II, he took a similar position at Holston Hills in Tennessee. In the late 1940s he began experimenting at Holston Hills with bentgrass greens, then a rarity in the South. His success resulted in commissions to convert other clubs from Bermuda to bent greens, and in the process he often recommended changes to the course layout.

In the early 1950s McKay resigned from Holston Hills to work full time as a course architect, contractor and turf consultant. He supervised the construction of several courses for other golf architects, notably William B. Langford, and also designed a number of courses himself.

Courses by: Alex McKay
Kentucky: Benton G&CC (9); Greenville CC (9); Hillcrest Muni, Owensboro; Indian Springs CC, Barbourville (9, 1963); L & N GC, Brooks; Seneca Muni, Louisville (1928); Shawnee Muni, Louisville (1927).
Maryland: Chestnut Ridge CC, Lutherville (9, 1956).
New York: Commack Hills G&CC (1955).
North Carolina: Statesville CC (1962).
Tennessee: CC of Bristol (1959); Lake View GC, Johnson City (Precision, 9, 1963); Nubbins Ridge CC, Knoxville; Pine Oaks Muni, Johnson City (1963); Smoky Mountain CC, Newport; Southwest Point G&CC, Kingston .
Virginia: Glenrochie CC, Abington (9, 1958); Lake Bonaventure CC, St. Paul (9, 1957).
West Virginia: Edgewood CC, Charleston; Meadowbrook CC, Charleston (1937).
Courses Remodeled & Added to by: Alex McKay
Kentucky: Cherokee GC, Louisville (R., 1927); Crescent Hill GC, Louisville (R., 1926).
Ohio: Wright-Patterson AFB GC, Dayton (A.9, 1960); Wright-Patterson AFB GC, Dayton (R.9, 1960).
Tennessee: Chattanooga G&CC (R., 1953); Cherokee CC, Knoxville (R., 1950); Holston Hills CC, Knoxville (R.3, 1953); Moccasin Bend GC, Chattanooga (R.).
Virginia: Spotswood CC, Harrisonburg (A.9, 1965).

Chester Mendenhall (1895 -)
Born: Montgomery County, Kansas.

Raised on a farm in Oklahoma, Chet Mendenhall was hired in 1921 to construct Sims Park Municipal GC in Wichita, Kansas. He remained there as greenkeeper until 1929, when he took a similar position with Wichita CC. In 1934 he moved to Mission Hills CC in Kansas City, serving as superintendent until his retirement in 1965. He began designing and remodeling courses as a "second career" after retirement.

Mendenhall was a charter member of the GCSAA and served as its President in 1948. He was also a member for several years of the USGA Green Section Committee.

Courses by: Chet Mendenhall
Missouri: California CC (9); Centralia CC; Claycrest CC, Liberty (1969); Linn CC; Shirkey GC, Richmond (1968); Tarkio CC.
Courses Remodeled & Added to by: Chet Mendenhall
Kansas: Fort Hays CC, Hays (R.9); Lake Quivira CC, Kansas City (R., 1968); Medicine Lodge Muni (R.9); Osawatomie Muni (A.9, 1972); Shawnee CC, Topeka (R.); Topeka CC (R.1).
Missouri: Excelsior Springs CC (R., 1965).

Fraser M. Middleton BAGCA
Based in Scotland, golf architect Fraser Middleton was involved in the design and construction of golf courses for over 40 years. He built courses for several leading British architects after World War II, including P.M. Ross, C.K. Cotton and J.H. Stutt. In the Seventies, Middleton began designing courses himself. Fraser Middleton was a charter member of the BAGCA, and was installed as a Senior Member of the group in 1980.

Courses by: Fraser Middleton
England: Cambridgeshire Hotel GC (1974); Davenport GC, Cheshire; Hounslow Heath GC, Middlesex .
Scotland: Annanhill GC, Ayrshire (1957); Balbirnie Park GC (1983); Camperdown GC (1960); Dale GC, Shetland; Dalmilling GC, Ayrshire (1960); Dunnikier Park GC, Fife (1963); Glenrothes GC, Fife (1958), with J. Hamilton Stutt.
Courses Remodeled & Added to by: Fraser Middleton
Northern Ireland: Greenisland GC (R., 1985); Greenisland GC (A.9, 1985).
Scotland: Aberdour GC (A.3, 1981); Ballochmyle GC (A.9); Invergordon GC, Highland (A.9); Nairn Dunbar GC, Nairnshire (A.9); Strathaven GC, Lanarkshire (A.9); West Lothian GC, Bo'ness (A.9).
Wales: Creigiau GC, Cardiff (A.9, 1982).

Scott R. Miller (1956 -)
Born: Wichita, Kansas.

While a student at Colorado State University, Scott Miller spent two summers working on the construction crew at Shoal Creek in Alabama, a Jack Nicklaus design. After graduating with a Landscape Architecture degree in 1978, Miller worked briefly for a golf course contractor in Florida before joining the staff of Jack Nicklaus and Associates. Miller worked closely with Senior Designer Jay Morrish (with whom he'd developed a friendship at Shoal Creek) out of the company's western office in Tulsa, Oklahoma. For five years, nearly all the Nicklaus projects west of the Mississippi, as well as those in Japan, were handled by Morrish and Miller. When Morrish left the company in 1983 for his own practice, Miller assumed the vacated position in the Nicklaus organization. He soon moved the base of Western operations to Scottsdale, Arizona.

Courses by: Scott Miller
Arizona: Desert Highlands GC, Scottsdale (1984), with Jack Nicklaus, Jay Morrish and Bob Cupp; Desert Mountain GC (Cochise Course), Carefree (1988), with Jack Nicklaus; Desert Mountain GC (Geronimo Course), Carefree (1988), with Jack Nicklaus; Desert Mountain GC (Renegade Course), Carefree (1987), with Jack Nicklaus; La Paloma GC, Tucson (27, 1985), with Jack Nicklaus.

California: Bear Creek GC, Wildomar (1982), with Jack Nicklaus, Jay Morrish and Bob Cupp; Club at Morningside, Rancho Mirage (1983), with Jack Nicklaus, Jay Morrish and Bob Cupp.

Colorado: Castle Pines GC, Castle Rock (1981), with Jack Nicklaus, Jay Morrish and Bob Cupp; CC of Castle Pines, Castle Rock (1986), with Jack Nicklaus; Meridian GC, Englewood (1984), with Jack Nicklaus and Bob Cupp.

Florida: Bear's Paw CC, Naples (1980), with Jack Nicklaus, Jay Morrish and Bob Cupp.

Mississippi: Annandale GC, Jackson (1981), with Jack Nicklaus, Jay Morrish and Bob Cupp.

Texas: Hills of Lakeway Golf Academy, Lakeway (3, 1985), with Jack Nicklaus, Jay Morrish and Bob Cupp; Hills of Lakeway GC, Lakeway (1980), with Jack Nicklaus, Jay Morrish and Bob Cupp.

Japan: Kazusa GC, Tokyo (1985), with Jack Nicklaus and Jay Morrish; Mito International GC, Tokyo (1987), with Jack Nicklaus; Sunnyfield GC, Gozenyama (1986), with Jack Nicklaus and Jay Morrish.

Courses Remodeled & Added to by: Scott Miller

Georgia: Augusta National GC, Augusta (R., 1984), with Jay Morrish and Bob Cupp.

Texas: Dallas Athletic C (Blue Course), Mesquite (R., 1986), with Jack Nicklaus.

Harrison G. Minchew (1956 -) ASGCA

Born: Augusta, Georgia.

Harrison Minchew took up the game on an old Donald Ross course at Forest Hills GC in Augusta, Georgia. While in high school, he worked on its course maintenance crew. His interest in golf course architecture developed as he listened to old-timers at Forest Hills describe how the course had been built and altered over the years.

Minchew attended the University of Georgia, and worked part-time during his senior year for golf architects Ron Kirby and Denis Griffiths. Upon graduating with a Landscape Architecture degree in 1979, Minchew went to work on the west coast for designer Ron Fream.

In 1982, Minchew moved back east and became an associate of Ed Seay in the Palmer Course Design Company. He handled major resopnsibility for a number of the firm's projects, including the remodeling of his beloved Forest Hills GC in Augusta.

Courses by: Harrison Minchew

Arizona: Arrowhead CC (North Course), Glendale (1985), with Arnold Palmer and Ed Seay; Arrowhead CC (South Course), Glendale (1986), with Arnold Palmer and Ed Seay.

California: PGA West GC (Palmer Course), La Quinta (1986), with Arnold Palmer and Ed Seay.

Florida: Marsh Landing CC, Ponte Vedra (1986), with Arnold Palmer and Ed Seay; Monarch CC (1987), with Arnold Palmer and Ed Seay; Plantation at Ponte Vedra GC (1987), with Arnold Palmer and Ed Seay.

Louisiana: Bluffs CC (1987), with Arnold Palmer and Ed Seay.

North Carolina: TPC at Piper Glen, Charlotte (1987), with Arnold Palmer and Ed Seay.

Washington: Semiahmoo GC, Everett (1986), with Arnold Palmer and Ed Seay.

Courses Remodeled & Added to by: Harrison Minchew

Florida: Sawgrass GC (Oceanside Course), Ponte Vedra Beach (A.9, 1985), with Arnold Palmer, Ed Seay and Bob Walker.

Georgia: Forest Hill GC, Augusta (R., 1986), with Arnold Palmer and Ed Seay.

Samuel S. Mitchell (1909 - 1986) ASGCA

Born: Manchester, Massachusetts. Died: Canton, Massachusetts at age 76.

Sam Mitchell was the second of four sons (Robert, Sam, Henry and William) of Robert A. Mitchell, longtime greenkeeper at Kernwood CC in Salem, Massachusetts. His uncle Enoch Crombie was one of Donald Ross' first construction superintendents. Not surprisingly, he and his brothers all became active in golf course design, construction and maintenance.

Mitchell graduated from the Stockbridge School of Agriculture of the University of Massachusetts in 1928. He worked for a time for the firm of Langford and Moreau, and was later employed with the Metropolitan District Commission of Boston as greenkeeper at Ponkapoag GC. While in Ponkapoag, he constructed a third nine to the design of Donald Ross.

In the 1950s Mitchell was involved in a design-and-build partnership with brothers William and Henry. He entered private practice as a golf architect in 1958.

Mitchell also operated an extensive sod business and managed a course of his own design, Easton (Mass.) GC. Two sons, Samuel Jr. and Phillip, became golf course superintendents.

A past President of the New England Golf Course Superintendents Association, Mitchell was awarded lifetime Fellow status by the ASGCA in 1984. He died in 1986 after suffering a heart attack in his home.

Courses by: Samuel Mitchell

Massachusetts: Brookmeadow GC, Canton (1968); Chestnut Hill CC, Newton (9, 1962); CC of Norwood (1975); Dighton GC (Par 3, 9, 1963); Easton CC (9, 1961); Little Harbor GC, Wareham (Par 3, 1963); Lost Brook GC, Norwood (Par 3, 9); Norwood CC; Spring Valley CC, Sharon (1960), with Geoffrey S. Cornish.

Rhode Island: Melody Hill GC, Harmony (9, 1965).

Courses Remodeled & Added to by: Samuel Mitchell

Massachusetts: Braintree Muni (R.); Braintree Muni (A.11); D.W. Field Muni, Brockton (A.2, 1972); Easton CC (A.9, 1967); Gardner Muni (R.2, 1968); Hatherly CC, North Scituate (A.3, 1968); Hatherly CC, North Scituate (R.2, 1976); Hollis Memorial GC, Braintree (A.11, 1971); Hollis Memorial GC, Braintree (R., 1971); Martin Memorial GC, Weston (A.9, 1963); Natick CC (R.4, 1960); Natick CC (A.9, 1960); Whaling City CC, New Bedford (A.9, 1964).

New York: Onondaga G&CC, Fayetteville (R.2, 1982), with Phil Wogan.

Rhode Island: Kirkbrae CC, Lincoln (R.3, 1969); Melody Hill GC, Harmony (A.9, 1975); Woonsocket CC (A.9, 1961), with Geoffrey S. Cornish.

William Follet Mitchell (1912 - 1974) ASGCA

Born: Salem, Massachusetts. Died: West Palm Beach, Florida at age 62.

William F. Mitchell was involved with golf courses from an early age. A son of Robert A. Mitchell, respected course superintendent who taught at the Essex County (Mass.) Agricultural School in the 1920s and later became superintendent at Kernwood CC, Bill Mitchell obtained his first greenkeeper's job at the age of nineteen. A few years later, while working as greenkeeper at Lake Sunapee GC in North Sutton, N.H., he established a turf farm specializing in Velvet bentgrass for greens. He operated the business successfully for decades. Through his turf business Bill gained first-hand experience in golf course construction and in the late 1930s assisted golf architect Orrin Smith in the construction or reconstruction of several New England layouts.

After serving as a Navy pilot during World War II, Mitchell became superintendent at Charles River CC near Boston. In the late 1940s he and two of his brothers, Samuel and Henry, formed a golf design and construction firm, Mitchell Brothers, which continued until the mid-fifties. Sam then left to do designing and consulting on his own. Henry returned to a superintendent's position and did a little design work on the side (notably Dennis Pines and the second nine of Cummaquid, both on Cape Cod). Bill continued in design full-time.

By the 1960s Mitchell had planned courses as far south as Florida and as far west as Michigan. By the early 1970s he had done some 150 original designs and 200 remodeling jobs. He was an early advocate of separate courses designed specifically for women golfers, and shortly before his death had been retained by the LPGA to build such a course. He is also credited with having coined the title "executive course" to describe shorter precision courses consisting of only par three and par four holes. Such courses, he said, could be quickly and enjoyably played by business executives at the tail end of a hectic workday.

Courses by: William F. Mitchell

Connecticut: Tumblebrook CC, Bloomfield (9, 1948), with Orrin Smith.

Florida: Atlantis GC (1960); Brooksville G&CC (1972); Deerfield CC, Deerfield Beach (Precision, 1964); East Bay CC, Largo (1962); Hollybrook G&CC, Hollywood (1968); Lockmoor GC, North Ft. Myers (1972); Longboat Key C (Islandside Course), Sarasota (1961); Palm Beach Lakes CC, West Palm Beach (Precision, 1966); Palm-Aire CC (Palms Course), Pompano Beach (1960); President CC (North Course), West Palm Beach (1970); President CC (South Course), West Palm Beach (1972); Rolling Hills CC, Ft. Lauderdale (1961); Southern Manor CC, Boca Raton (NLE, 1962); Tavares Cove GC, West Palm Beach (Precision, 1971); University of South Florida GC, Tampa (1967).

Maine: Loring AFB GC, Limestone (1959).

Maryland: Eaglehead G&CC, New Market (1971).

Massachusetts: Billerica GC (Par 3, 9, 1952), with Al Zikorus; CC of New Seabury (Blue Course), South Mashpee (1964); CC of New Seabury (Green Course), South Mashpee (1965); Green Hill Muni, Worcester (1968); Hillview CC, North Reading; Martin Memorial GC, Weston (9, 1952); Mount Pleasant CC, Boylston (1959); North Hill CC; Saddle Hill CC, Hopkinton (1962); Webb Brook GC, Burlington (1952).

Michigan: Bedford Valley CC, Battle Creek (1965); Gull Lake CC, Richland (1967).

New Hampshire: Amherst CC (1962); Goffstown CC (1962); Plausawa Valley CC, Concord (1965).

New Jersey: Fairview GC (1954).

New York: Bergen Point Muni, Babylon (1972); Colonie Muni (1969); Crab Meadow GC, Northport (1963); Emerald Green GC, Rock Hill (1970); Glen Cove Muni (1970); Hammersley Hill GC, Pawling (9, 1951); Indian Island Park GC, Riverhead (1973); Kutshers Hotel GC, Monticello (1962); Lido Springs GC, Lido Beach (Par 3, 1963); McCann Memorial GC, Poughkeepsie (1973); Noyac G&CC, Sag Harbor (1964); Old Westbury G&CC (27, 1962); Otterkill G&CC, Newburgh (1957); Park District GC, Fallsburgh (1959); Pine Hollow CC, East Norwich (1954); Putnam CC, Lake Mahopac; Stevensville Lake G&CC, Swan Lake (1966); Tarry Brae GC, South Fallsburgh (1958); Waldemere Hotel GC, Livingston Manor (1959); West Sayville GC (1970); Willows GC, Rexford (1967); Woodcrest C, Syosset (1963).

Ohio: Pebble Creek GC, Lexington (1974); Shady Hollow CC, Massillon; Tanglewood CC, Chagrin Falls (1966); Walden G&TC, Aurora (1974); Whetstone CC, Marion (1972), with Richard W. LaConte.

Pennsylvania: Cedarbrook CC, Blue Bell (1962); General Washington CC, Audubon (1962).

Vermont: Crown Point CC, Springfield (9, 1953); Stowe CC (1962).

New Brunswick: Mactaquac Provincial Park GC (1970).

Ontario: Maple Downs G&CC (1954).

Quebec: Fort Preval GC, Preval (9, 1961); Golf du Parc Carleton (9, 1963).

Portugal: Quintado de Lago GC (Course No. 1), Algarve (27, 1973).

Courses Remodeled & Added to by: William F. Mitchell

California: Americana Canyon Hotel GC (R., 1965); Canyon CC, Palm Springs (R., 1965).

Connecticut: Birchwood CC, Westport (R., 1946); Glastonbury Hills CC (R., 1952); Hartford GC, West Hartford (R., 1946), with Orrin Smith; High Ridge CC, Stamford (R.2, 1951), with Al Zikorus; High Ridge GC, Norwalk (R., 1946); Meadowbrook CC, Hamden (R., 1947); Milford CC (R., 1948); Minnechaug GC, Glastonbury (R.9, 1951), with Al Zikorus; Old Lyme GC (R., 1949); Racebrook CC, Orange (R., 1947), with Orrin Smith; Rockledge CC, West Hartford (R., 1947); Sleeping Giant GC (R., 1951); Tumble Brook CC, Bloomfield (A.9, 1948), with Orrin Smith; Wampanoag CC, West Hartford (R., 1949); Watertown CC (R., 1950).

Maine: Augusta CC, Augusta (R., 1939), with Orrin Smith; Bridgeton GC (R., 1939), with Orrin Smith; Mount Kineo GC, Kineo (R., 1940), with Orrin Smith; Portland CC, Falmouth (R., 1940), with Orrin Smith; Riverside Muni, Portland (R., 1948).

Maryland: Rocky Point GC, Essex (R., 1939), with Orrin Smith.

Massachusetts: Bear Hill GC, Wakefield (R., 1950); Cedar Glen GC, Saugus (R., 1931), with Orrin Smith; Charles River CC, Newton Centre (R., 1946); Colonial GC, Lynnfield (R.5, 1954), with Al Zikorus; Colonial GC, Lynnfield (A.9, 1963); Concord CC (A.9, 1967); Duxbury YC (R., 1951); Framingham CC (A.9, 1960); Franklin CC (A.2, 1949); Franklin CC (R., 1949); Franklin CC (R., 1956); Furnace Brook CC (R., 1947); Holden GC (R., 1957); Kernwood CC, Salem (R., 1950); Leicester Hill CC (R., 1950); Longmeadow CC, Springfield (R., 1956); Lynnfield Center GC (R., 1949); Needham GC (R., 1935), with Orrin Smith; North Adams

GC (R., 1939), with Orrin Smith; North Andover CC (R., 1947); Oak Hill CC, Fitchburg (R., 1938), with Orrin Smith; Ould Newberry CC, Newburyport (R., 1939), with Orrin Smith; Ponkapoag GC, Canton (A.9, 1955); Red Hill CC, Reading (A.9, 1951), with Al Zikorus; Red Hill CC, Reading (R.9, 1951), with Al Zikorus; Springfield CC (R., 1948); Unicorn CC, Stoneham (R., 1937), with Orrin Smith; Vesper CC, Tyngsboro (R., 1939), with Orrin Smith; Wayland CC (R., 1952); Wenham GC (R., 1938), with Orrin Smith; Whaling City CC, New Bedford (R.9, 1958); Winthrop GC (R., 1950), with Al Zikorus; Wollaston CC (R., 1956).

New Hampshire: Claremont CC (R., 1936), with Orrin Smith; CC of New Hampshire, North Conway (A.9, 1963); CC of New Hampshire, North Conway (R.9, 1963); Dover CC (R., 1940), with Orrin Smith; Hanover CC, Dartmouth College (R., 1937), with Orrin Smith; Laconia CC (R., 1938), with Orrin Smith; Lake Sunapee CC, New London (R., 1934), with Orrin Smith; Lebanon CC (R., 1937), with Orrin Smith; Nashua CC (R., 1949); Newport CC (R., 1937), with Orrin Smith; Rochester CC (R., 1939), with Orrin Smith.

New Jersey: White Beeches G&CC, Haworth (R., 1953).

New York: College Hill GC (R.); Dellwood CC, New City (R., 1951); En-Joie CC, Endicott (R.); Fresh Meadow CC, Great Neck (R., 1938), with Orrin Smith; Gardiner's Bay CC (R., 1954); Glen Head CC (R., 1949); Green Lakes State Park GC, Fayetteville (R., 1948); Grossinger's GC (R., 1959); Hiawatha CC, Syracuse (R., 1948); Huntington Crescent CC, Huntington (R., 1939), with Orrin Smith; Huntington Crescent CC (West Course), Huntington (R., 1939), with Orrin Smith; Huntington CC (R., 1967); Island Hills CC, Sayville (R., 1967); IBM CC, Endicott (R., 1948); Old Oaks CC, Purchase (R., 1949); Poughkeepsie Muni (R., 1953); Sadaquada GC, Utica (R., 1969); Saratoga Spa GC (R.); Saratoga Spa GC (A.9); Shinnecock Hills GC, Southampton (R., 1967); Southampton GC (R., 1965); Teugega CC, Rome (R., 1948); Van Cortlandt Park GC, Bronx (R., 1947).

North Carolina: Southern Pines CC (R., 1947).

Pennsylvania: Blue Ridge CC, Harrisburg (R., 1965).

Rhode Island: Newport CC (R., 1939), with Orrin Smith.

Vermont: Basin Harbor C (R., 1952); Brattleboro CC (R., 1948); Crown Point CC, Springfield (A.9, 1959); Equinox G Links, Manchester (R., 1967).

Quebec: Madge Lake GC, Magog, Quebec (R., 1960).

Theodore Moone

A British golf writer of the 1930s, Theodore Moone's best-known publication was *Golf From A New Angle*, which contained a discussion on golf design. He designed or remodeled at least four courses in the British Isles.

Courses by: Theodore Moone

England: Carlisle GC, Cumberland (1938).

Scotland: Eastwood GC, Renfrewshire .

Courses Remodeled & Added to by: Theodore Moone

Scotland: Dumfries and Galloway GC (R.); Kilmarnock GC, Barassie (R.).

Hugh C. Moore Sr. (1895 - 1972)

Born: Onley, Virginia. Died: Albany, Georgia at age 76.

After helping to construct Sea Island GC and Jekyll Island GC to plans of Walter Travis, Hugh Moore became superintendent at Sea Island and later constructed a second nine designed by Colt and Alison. He resigned in 1933 to work as a baseball umpire in Southern semi-pro leagues but returned to golf in 1942, remodeling and operating a course in Georgia. He later designed Bowden Muni in Macon, Ga. and remained as its superintendent until 1953, when he was hired to renovate the Dunedin (Fla.) CC into the national headquarters of the PGA of America. Moore also designed and remodeled several other courses in the Southeast.

Courses by: Hugh Moore

Alabama: Dothan CC (1960).

Georgia: Blakely CC (9, 1959); Bowden Muni, Macon (1949); Dawson CC; Sunset CC, Moultrie (1944); Turner AFB GC, Albany (9, 1953); Warner Robins AFB GC, Macon (9, 1951).

Courses Remodeled & Added to by: Hugh Moore

Florida: Lake Region Y&CC, Winter Haven (R., 1964).

Georgia: American Legion GC, Albany (R., 1954); Athens CC (R.); Augusta CC (R.); Glen Arven CC, Thomasville (R.4, 1942); Jekyll Island GC (Oceanside Course) (R.3, 1952); Pelham CC (R., 1939); Radium CC, Albany (R.).

North Carolina: Charlotte CC (R., 1955).

Robert Frederick Moote (1924 -   ) ASGCA

Born: Dunville, Ontario, Canada.

Bob Moote received a B.S. Degree in Agriculture and Ornamental Horticulture from Ontario Agricultural College in 1948. His first job was for golf architect Stanley Thompson, supervising projects in Canada, Jamaica and the U.S. In 1951 he became assistant landscape supervisor with Central Mortgage and Housing Corporation, where he remained for five years. In his spare time, Moote worked on a series of modest golf projects in Quebec, Ontario and the Maritimes Provinces.

In 1957 Moote became construction supervisor of a third nine at Oakdale G&CC near Toronto, then stayed on as its course superintendent for some twenty years. During those years he did part-time work with golf architect C.E. Robinson and served as a greens consultant to the Royal Canadian Golf Association. He also practiced course design with his brother David S. Moote, who served as President of the GCSAA in 1964. In 1976 he entered private practice as a full-time architect under the name R.F. Moote and Associates Ltd. In the early Eighties Moote's eldest son, David L. Moote, joined him in the design business.

Moote was a member of ASGCA as well as both the ASLA and CSLA.

Courses by: Robert Moote

New Brunswick: Gowan Brae GC, Bathurst , with Clinton E. Robinson.

Nova Scotia: Dundee Resort GC, Cape Breton (9, 1983); Le Portage GC, Cheticamp (1984).

Ontario: Barrie GC (1965), with David Moote; Beverly GC, Copetown , with Clinton E. Robinson; Blair Hampton GC, Minden (1964), with David Moote; Cedar Brook GC, London (Par 3, 1985); Craig Gowan GC, Woodstock , with Clinton E. Robinson; Deep River GC (9, 1952), with Howard Watson; Doon Valley GC, Kitchener , with Clinton E. Robinson; Downsview G&CC, Toronto (27, 1955), with Howard Watson; Dryden G&CC, with Clinton E. Robinson; Galt G & Curling C (1965), with David Moote; Georgetown GC, with Clinton E. Robinson; Hawthorne Valley G&CC, Mississauga (Par 3, 1961), with Clinton E. Robinson; Hornby Towers GC (1964), with David Moote; Lynwood GC, London (9, 1962), with David Moote; Maple City G&CC, Chatham , with Clinton E. Robinson; Maples of Ballantrae GC, Whitchurch (1983); Mount Hope G&CC, with Clinton E. Robinson; North Halton GC, Georgetown (1967), with David Moote; Orilla GC (1975), with David Moote; Pleasure Park GC, Concord (Par 3, 1961); Richmond Hill G&CC, Richmond , with Clinton E. Robinson; Scotch Settlement GC, Bradford (1984); Streetsville Glen GC (1967), with David Moote; Trafalgar G&CC, Milton , with Clinton E. Robinson; Twenty Valley G&CC, Beamsville , with Clinton E. Robinson; Wildcat Run GC, Cobourg (1985).

Quebec: Club de G Baie Comeau, Hauterire , with Clinton E. Robinson.

Colombia: CC de Manizales, Calais (1953), with Howard Watson; CC El Rodeo, Mendellin (1953), with Howard Watson.

Jamaica: Ironshore CC, Montego Bay (1971), with David Moote.

Martinique: La Pointe du Diamant GC (Par 3, 9, 1967), with David Moote.

Courses Remodeled & Added to by: Robert Moote

New York: Westwood CC, Williamsville (R., 1986).

Alberta: Shawnee Slopes GC, Calgary (R., 1979).

New Brunswick: Grand Falls GC (R., 1984).

Nova Scotia: Brightwood G&CC, Dartmouth (R., 1983); Dundee Resort GC, Cape Breton (A.9, 1983); Seaview GC, North Sydney (A.9, 1985).

Ontario: Bay of Quinte GC, Bellville (A.9), with Clinton E. Robinson; Bayview G&CC, Thornhill (R., 1986); Beechwood GC, Niagara Falls (A.9, 1985); Beechwood GC, Niagara Falls (R.9, 1985); Brantford G&CC (R.), with Clinton E. Robinson; Brooklea GC, Cambridge (R., 1985); Burlington GC (R., 1985); Credit Valley G&CC, Toronto (R.3, 1964), with David Moote; Goderich GC (R., 1976); Huntington GC, Nashville (R., 1961), with Clinton E. Robinson; Idylwylde GC, Sudbury (R.1, 1985); Kenora G&CC (R.7, 1986); Kenora G&CC (A.11, 1986); Kingsville GC (A.9, 1973), with David Moote; Listowel GC (R.8, 1982); Listowel GC (A.10, 1982); Lively GC, Sudbury (A.9, 1982); Lively GC, Sudbury (R.9, 1982); North Halton GC, Georgetown (R., 1984); Oakdale G&CC, Downsview (A.9), with Clinton E. Robinson; Oakdale G&CC, Downsview (R., 1986); Owen Sound GC (A.9, 1964), with David Moote; Owen Sound GC (R.9, 1964), with David Moote; Peel Village GC, Brampton (R., 1986); Port Colbourne GC (R., 1966), with David Moote; Port Colbourne GC (R., 1985); Puslinch Lake GC, Cambridge (R., 1984); St. Catharines G&CC (R.), with Clinton E. Robinson; Thornhill GC (R., 1985); Trehaven GC, Lake Simcoe (R., 1977); Westmount GC, Kitchener (A.4), with Clinton E. Robinson; Westmount GC, Kitchener (R.), with Clinton E. Robinson; Westmount GC, Kitchener (R.3, 1970), with David Moote; Westview GC, Aurora (R.9, 1964), with David Moote; Westview GC, Aurora (A.9, 1964), with David Moote; Westview GC, Aurora (R., 1984).

Quebec: Club de G Ile Perrot (R., 1980).

Jamaica: Paradise Park GC, Savanna-La-Mar (R., 1969), with David Moote.

Theodore J. Moreau (1890 - 1942)

Died: Wilmette, Illinois at age 51.

Civil engineer Theodore J. Moreau teamed with William B. Langford after World War I in a golf design and construction business based in Chicago. The firm of Langford & Moreau was among the busiest in the Midwest and South during the 1920s and '30s. While Moreau primarily handled the construction aspects of their projects, he also handled a few designs.

Courses by: Theodore J. Moreau

Arkansas: Al Amin Temple CC, Little Rock , with William B. Langford; Texarkana CC (1927), with William B. Langford.

Florida: Eglin AFB GC, Niceville (1925), with William B. Langford; Granada GC, Coral Gables (9, 1925), with William B. Langford; Kelsey City GC, West Palm Beach (NLE, 1924), with William B. Langford; Key West GC (NLE, 1923), with William B. Langford; Lake Worth Muni (1924), with William B. Langford; Parkhurst CC, Boynton Beach (NLE, 1925), with William B. Langford; St. Lucie River CC, Port Sewall (NLE, 1924), with William B. Langford; Valparaiso CC (NLE, 1927), with William B. Langford; West Palm Beach CC (NLE, 1921), with William B. Langford.

Illinois: Acacia CC, Harlem (1924), with William B. Langford; Bryn Mawr GC, Lincolnwood (1921), with William B. Langford; Butterfield CC, Hinsdale (1922), with William B. Langford; Doering Estate GC, Chicago (6, 1931), with William B. Langford; Franklin County CC, West Frankfort (9, 1922), with William B. Langford; Golden Acres CC, Schaumberg (27, 1928), with William B. Langford; Kankakee Elks CC, St. Anne (1936), with William B. Langford; Mid City GC, Chicago (NLE, 1924), with William B. Langford; Morris CC (NLE, 9, 1925), with William B. Langford; Ruth Lake CC, Hinsdale (1926), with William B. Langford; Skokie Playfield GC, Winnetka (NLE, Par 3, 9), with William B. Langford; St. Clair CC, Belleville (1927), with William B. Langford; Twin Orchard CC, Bensenville (NLE, 1924), with William B. Langford.

Indiana: Christiana CC, Elkhart (9, 1925), with William B. Langford; Dykeman Park Muni, Logansport (9), with William B. Langford; East Shore CC, Culver (1922), with William B. Langford; Gary CC, Merrillville (1921), with William B. Langford; Harrison Hills CC, Attica (9, 1923), with William B. Langford.

Iowa: Credit Island GC, Davenport (1925), with William B. Langford; Wakonda C, Des Moines (1922), with William B. Langford.

Kentucky: Audubon CC, Louisville (1921), with William B. Langford; Bowling Green CC, with William B. Langford; Henderson G&CC, with William B. Langford.

Michigan: Blythefield CC, Belmont (1927), with William B. Langford; CC of Lansing (1919), with William B. Langford; Iron River CC (1932), with William B. Langford; Marquette G&CC (9, 1927), with William B. Langford.

Minnesota: Mankato GC, with William B. Langford.

Mississippi: Clarkesdale CC (1921), with William B. Langford.

Nebraska: Happy Hollow C, Omaha (1926), with William B. Langford; Highland CC, Omaha (1924), with William B. Langford; Omaha CC (1927), with William B. Langford.

North Dakota: Town & Country C, Devil's Lake (9, 1920), with William B.

Langford.
Ohio: Avon Fields GC, Cincinnati (1924), with William B. Langford; Clovernook CC, Cincinnati (1924), with William B. Langford; Fairlawn CC, Akron (1917), with William B. Langford; Hillcrest CC, Cincinnati (NLE, 1925), with William B. Langford.
South Dakota: Minnehaha CC, Sious Falls (1922), with William B. Langford.
Texas: State Line GC, Texarkana (1930), with William B. Langford.
Wisconsin: Lawsonia Links, Green Lake (1929), with William B. Langford; Leathem Smith Lodge GC, Sturgeon Bay (9, 1930), with William B. Langford; Our CC, Salem (1927), with William B. Langford; Ozaukee CC, Mequon (1922), with William B. Langford; Spring Valley CC, Salem (1927), with William B. Langford; West Bend CC (9), with William B. Langford.
Courses Remodeled & Added to by: Theodore J. Moreau
Florida: Breakers GC (Ocean Course), Palm Beach (R.9, 1926), with William B. Langford; Everglades C, Palm Beach (R., 1937), with William B. Langford.
Illinois: Glen Oak CC, Glen Ellyn (R., 1922), with William B. Langford; Highland Park GC (R.3, 1939), with William B. Langford; Mid City GC, Chicago (NLE, R., 1931), with William B. Langford; Ravisloe CC, Homewood (R.), with William B. Langford; Ridgemoor CC, Harwood Heights (R., 1927), with William B. Langford; Skokie CC, Glencoe (R., 1938), with William B. Langford.
Kentucky: Louisville CC (R., 1921), with William B. Langford.

Sloan Morpeth
Noted Australian amateur golfer Sloan Morpeth won the New Zealand Open in 1928 and the New Zealand Amateur in 1920, '27, and '28. After his playing days were over, Morpeth turned to golf course architecture, designing and remodeling many courses in Australia and New Zealand.
Courses by: Sloan Morpeth
Australia: Surfer's Paradise GC, Queensland (1969).
Courses Remodeled & Added to by: Sloan Morpeth
Australia: Australian GC, Kensington (R., 1967).

Tom Morris Sr. (1821 - 1908)
Born: St. Andrews, Scotland. Died: St. Andrews, Scotland at age 87.
"Old Tom" Morris apprenticed under Allan Robertson at the Old Course at St. Andrews from 1839 to 1851. Following a bitter disagreement with Robertson concerning use of the gutta-percha ball (of which Robertson disapproved), Morris moved to Prestwick, where he held the position of pro/greenkeeper until 1865. He then returned to similar duties at St. Andrews, where he remained until his retirement in 1904. Morris won the British Open in 1861, '62, '64 and '67, and his son Tom Jr. won the Open four times by the age of twenty-two. Together, Old Tom and Young Tom Morris rank among the greatest golfers of all time. Old Tom's life was saddened by his son's sudden death in 1875 at the age of 25.
Those who knew him described Old Tom as a man it was impossible to dislike. Throughout his productive life he refused to play golf on Sundays and kept the Old Course closed on that day, feeling it needed a rest even if golfers didn't. His philosophy in regard to putting surface maintenance embraced "sand and more sand" as top-dressing.
Morris ranked at the top of recognized links designers in the last half of the nineteenth century. He practiced the art in an age when it was virtually impossible to alter existing contours in laying out a new course. A native of the linksland with an eye for every shot in golf, Old Tom developed a skill for utilizing every feature of natural terrain, a talent he passed on to an apprentice, Donald Ross.
Old Tom was the first to plan double-loop routings to take maximum advantage of the wind.
Courses by: Old Tom Morris
England: City of Newcastle GC, Northumberland (1980); Northampton GC, Northamptonshire (1894); Royal North Devon GC, Westward Ho! (1874); Wallasey GC, Cheshire (1891); West Herts GC, Hertfordshire (1897).
Ireland: Lahinch GC (Old Course), County Clare (1893); Rosapenna GC, County Donegal (1893).
Isle of Man: Castletown GC (1892).
Northern Ireland: Royal County Down GC, Newcastle (1891).
Scotland: Alyth GC, Tayside (1894); Askernish GC, Western Isles (1891); Callander GC, Stirlingshire; Crail GC, Fife (1892); Dunbar GC, East Lothian; Dunblane GC, Perthshire (1891); Elie Golf House C, Fife (1895); Glasgow GC (1904); Helensburgh GC; King James VI GC, Perth (1896); Kinghorn GC, Fife (1904); Ladybank GC, Fife (1879); Lanark GC, Lanarkshire; Luffness New GC, East Lothian (1894); Moray GC (Old Course), Morayshire (1889); Muirfield GC, East Lothian (1891); Perth GC, Perthshire (12, 1864); Prestwick GC, Ayrshire (12, 1851); Royal Burgess G Society of Edinburgh (1895); Royal Dornoch GC, Sutherland (9, 1887); St. Andrews (New Course), Fife (1894); St. Leonard's School for Girls GC, Fife (9, 1873); St. Michaels G Links, Fife (9, 1903); Stirling GC, Stirlingshire (1892); Tain GC, Rossshire (1890).
Wales: Pwllheli GC (9, 1900).
Courses Remodeled & Added to by: Old Tom Morris
England: Bradford GC, Yorkshire (A.13); Cleveland G Links, Yorkshire (R.); Cleveland G Links, Yorkshire (A.9, 1898).
Scotland: Carnoustie GC, Angus (R., 1867); Carnoustie GC, Angus (A.6, 1867); Cullen GC, Banffshire (R., 1892); Machrihanish GC, Argyllshire (R.); Machrihanish GC, Argyllshire (A.6, 1879); Nairn GC, Nairnshire (R., 1889); Newtonmore GC, Highland (R., 1897); Prestwick GC, Ayrshire (A.6, 1883); Saltcoats GC, Luffness (R., 1894); St. Andrews (Old Course), Fife (R.).

Jay Morrish (1936 -)
Born: Grand Junction Colorado.
Under a Trans-Mississippi Golf Association scholarship, Jay Morrish obtained a liberal arts education at Mesa Jr. College and the Universities of New Mexico and Colorado. He later received a Landscaping and Turf Management degree from Colorado State University. After teaching horticulture at Colorado State, Morrish joined a construction crew in California building the Spyglass Hill Golf Links to the design of Robert Trent Jones. He then moved to Phoenix to assist in construction of another Jones project, Goodyear G&CC. In 1967 Morrish joined the firm of George Fazio, aiding in layout and construction of several courses including Jupiter Hills. He then joined architect Desmond Muirhead, working on such jobs as Mayacoo Lakes. When Jack Nicklaus and Muirhead dissolved their relationship in 1973, Morrish accepted Nicklaus' offer to work as a designer in Nicklaus' new firm. He worked on most Nicklaus designs over the next ten years, operating a branch office in Tulsa, Oklahoma. Morrish also collaborated with another Nicklaus in-house designer, Bob Cupp, on certain courses under the corporate name of Golforce, Inc.
In 1983 Morrish left Nicklaus to pursue a golf design business of his own. Many of his works were done with PGA Tour player Tom Weiskopf serving as consultant. One of the earliest Morrish/Weiskopf collaborations, Troon G&CC in Arizona, was selected as the Best New Private Course of 1986 by Golf Digest magazine.
Courses by: Jay Morrish
Alabama: Shoal Creek, Birmingham (1977), with Jack Nicklaus and Bob Cupp.
Arizona: Desert Highlands GC, Scottsdale (1984), with Jack Nicklaus, Bob Cupp and Scott Miller; Forest Highlands GC, Flagstaff (1987), with Tom Weiskopf; Troon G&CC, Scottsdale (1985), with Tom Weiskopf; TPC of Scottsdale (1986), with Tom Weiskopf.
California: Bear Creek GC, Wildomar (1982), with Jack Nicklaus, Bob Cupp and Scott Miller; Club at Morningside, Rancho Mirage (1983), with Jack Nicklaus, Bob Cupp and Scott Miller.
Colorado: Castle Pines GC, Castle Rock (1981), with Jack Nicklaus, Bob Cupp and Scott Miller; CC of the Rockies, Avon (1984), with Jack Nicklaus and Bob Cupp; Singletree GC, Edwards (1981), with Bob Cupp.
Florida: Bear's Paw CC, Naples (1980), with Jack Nicklaus, Bob Cupp and Scott Miller; Boca Pointe CC, Boca Raton (1982), with Bob Cupp; Cheeca Lodge GC (Par 3, 1981), with Bob Cupp; Sailfish Point CC, Stuart (1981), with Jack Nicklaus and Bob Cupp; Walden Lake CC, Plant City (1978), with Bob Cupp.
Kansas: Willowbend GC, Wichita (1987), with Tom Weiskopf.
Mississippi: Annandale GC, Jackson (1981), with Jack Nicklaus, Bob Cupp and Scott Miller.
Ohio: CC at Muirfield Village, Dublin (1982), with Jack Nicklaus and Bob Cupp.
Oklahoma: Coves At Bird Island GC, Afton (Precision, 9, 1984).
South Carolina: Turtle Point G Links, Kiawah Island (1981), with Jack Nicklaus and Bob Cupp.
Texas: Hills of Lakeway Golf Academy, Lakeway (3, 1985), with Jack Nicklaus, Bob Cupp and Scott Miller; Hills of Lakeway GC, Lakeway (1980), with Jack Nicklaus, Bob Cupp and Scott Miller; Las Colinas Sports C (TPC Course), Irving (1986); Lochinvar GC, Houston (1980), with Jack Nicklaus and Bob Cupp; River Place CC, Austin (1986), with Tom Kite.
Utah: Park Meadows GC, Park City (1983), with Jack Nicklaus and Bob Cupp.
Ontario: Glen Abbey GC, Oakville (1976), with Jack Nicklaus and Bob Cupp.
Japan: Kazusa GC, Tokyo (1985), with Jack Nicklaus and Scott Miller; New St. Andrews GC, Ontawara City (1976), with Jack Nicklaus and Bob Cupp; Sunnyfield GC, Gozenyama (1986), with Jack Nicklaus and Scott Miller.
Courses Remodeled & Added to by: Jay Morrish
Arizona: Boulders GC (R., 1984); Boulders GC (A.9, 1986).
Florida: Frenchman's Creek GC (North Course), North Palm Beach (R., 1983), with Bob Cupp; Frenchman's Creek GC (South Course), North Palm Beach (R., 1983), with Bob Cupp; Lost Tree C, Singer Island (R., 1980), with Bob Cupp.
Georgia: Atlanta CC, Marietta (R., 1980), with Bob Cupp; Augusta National GC, Augusta (R., 1984), with Bob Cupp and Scott Miller.
Illinois: Bryn Mawr GC, Lincolnwood (R., 1982), with Bob Cupp.
New York: Wanakah CC (R., 1983), with Bob Cupp.
Oklahoma: Tulsa CC (R.5, 1984).
Texas: Colonial CC, Fort Worth (R., 1982), with Bob Cupp; Dallas CC (R., 1985); Las Colinas Sports C, Irving (A.9, 1986); Oak Hill CC, San Antonio (R., 1984); Onion Creek CC, Austin (R.7, 1985); Preston Trail GC, Dallas (R., 1982), with Bob Cupp.
West Virginia: Greenbrier GC (Greenbrier Course), White Sulphur Spgs (R., 1978), with Jack Nicklaus and Bob Cupp.
Australia: Australian GC, Kensington (R., 1977), with Jack Nicklaus and Bob Cupp.
Japan: Atsugi International CC (East Course), Kanagawa (R., 1983), with Bob Cupp; Atsugi International CC (West Course), Kanagawa (R., 1985), with Bob Cupp.

John Stanton Fleming Morrison (1892 - 1961)
Born: Deal, England. Died: Farnham, England at age 68. Interred: Woking, England.
J.S.F. Morrison attended Trinity College, Cambridge, where he won blues in cricket and soccer before World War I. After service in the Royal Flying Corps, he returned to Cambridge and won another blue in golf. He later won the 1929 Belgian Amateur. Morrison was especially fond of partners play and won the Worplesdon Foursomes in 1928 with Joyce Wethered and the Halford-Hewitt Cup five times with Henry Longhurst, the renowned British golf writer and Member of Parliament.
Morrison joined the golf design firm of Colt and Alison in the 1920s and by the early 1930s was made a partner and director of the firm of Colt, Alison and Morrison. He worked closely with H.S. Colt on a number of courses on the Continent and in Britain. Following World War II, he was involved in several restoration projects, including Prince's GC in collaboration with Sir Guy Campbell. Morrison was active well into the 1950s, assisted by J. Hamilton Stutt.
Courses by: J.S.F. Morrison
England: Cuddington GC (1929), with H.S. Colt and C.H. Alison; Fulwell GC, Middlesex; Ham Manor GC, Sussex (1936), with H.S. Colt and C.H. Alison; Kedleston Park GC, Derbyshire (1947), with John R.Stutt; Leckford GC (9, 1929), with H.S. Colt and C.H. Alison; Lilleshall Hall GC (1935), with H.S. Colt; Prestbury GC (1920), with H.S. Colt; Prince's GC (Red Course), Kent (9, 1951), with Sir Guy Campbell; Trevose G&CC (27, 1926), with H.S. Colt and C.H. Alison; Wentworth GC (East Course), Surrey (1924), with H.S. Colt and C.H. Alison; Wentworth GC (West Course), Surrey (1924), with H.S. Colt and C.H. Alison.
France: Golf Club de St. Cloud (Yellow Course) (1946), with H.S. Colt; Golf Club

de Touquet (Sea Course) (1930), with H.S. Colt and C.H. Alison.
Italy: La Mandria GC, Turin (9, 1956); Le Betulle GC, Biella (1958).
Netherlands: Eindhoven GC (1930), with H.S. Colt and C.H. Alison; Haagsche G&CC (1939), with H.S. Colt and C.H. Alison; Kennemer G&CC (1929), with H.S. Colt and C.H. Alison; Utrecht GC (1929), with H.S. Colt and C.H. Alison.
Spain: Real C de la Puerto de Hierro (Old), Madrid (1932), with H.S. Colt and C.H. Alison; Real G de Pedrena (1928), with H.S. Colt and C.H. Alison.
Sweden: Stockholm GC (1932), with H.S. Colt and C.H. Alison.
Trinidad and Tobago: St. Andrews GC, Moka (NLE, 1940), with H.S. Colt.
Wales: St. Mellons GC (1937), with H.S. Colt and Henry Cotton.
West Germany: Falkenstein GC (1930), with H.S. Colt and C.H. Alison; Frankfurter GC (1928), with H.S. Colt and C.H. Alison; Hamburger Land und GC (1935), with H.S. Colt and C.H. Alison.
Courses Remodeled & Added to by: J.S.F. Morrison:
England: Liphook GC (A.2, 1946); Liphook GC (R., 1946); North Foreland GC, Kingsgate (R.), with Tom Simpson; North Foreland GC, Kingsgate (R.); Prince's GC (Blue Course), Kent (R., 1951), with Sir Guy Campbell; Royal Lytham & St. Annes GC, Lancashire (R., 1936), with H.S. Colt and J.S.F. Morrison; Royal Lytham & St. Annes GC, Lancashire (R., 1936), with H.S. Colt and J.S.F. Morrison; Seaford GC, Sussex (R.); Sunningdale GC (New Course), Berkshire (R.).
Northern Ireland: Royal Portrush GC (Dunluce Course) (R., 1946), with H.S. Colt; Royal Portrush GC (Valley Course) (R., 1946), with H.S. Colt.
West Germany: Frankfurter GC (R., 1952), with J. Hamilton Stutt.

Desmond Muirhead (1924 -)
Born: England.
Desmond Muirhead studied architecture and engineering at Cambridge and horticulture at the University of British Columbia and Oregon University. He worked for several years as a landscape planner in British Columbia before moving to the United States in the late 1950s to work on retirement villages. He planned one course during his years in British Columbia.
Muirhead's interest in golf course design grew while working on the Sun City, Arizona developments. The son of a Scottish golfer, Muirhead claimed never to have been more than a high handicapper himself, but he recognized the need to make golf courses and housing developments compatible with one another. While he took no part in the routing of the courses at Sun City, he offered many suggestions, and jumped at the opportunity to lay out his own design within a real estate project in California in 1962.
By that time Muirhead had made a whirlwind tour of the great courses of America and Britain and came away convinced that he could offer some new ideas in the field of golf design. "Those courses have no mystique whatsoever," Muirhead once said in his outspoken style. "I owe very little allegiance to St. Andrews." Much of his early work involved the remodeling of existing West Coast courses, but as his designs gained national attention, the demand for his services increased. By the early 1970s Muirhead was busy laying out radical designs on both coasts.
Two tournament golfers lent their names to various Muirhead projects. Initially Gene Sarazen was listed as his partner, though he did little more than offer endorsements. Later Jack Nicklaus worked with Muirhead on several projects. Pundits called the pairing "The Bear and the Beard." The two dissolved their association during construction of Muirfield Village GC in Ohio.
In the mid-Seventies, Muirhead left the poor economy of America to handle several design projects in Australia. A decade later he returned to The States and resumed his design practice in Florida.
Courses by: Desmond Muirhead
Arizona: McCormick Ranch GC (Palm Course), Scottsdale (1972); McCormick Ranch GC (Pine Course), Scottsdale (1973).
California: Desert Island CC, Rancho Mirage (1970); Disneyland Hotel GC, Anaheim (NLE, Par 3, 9, 1963); Ironwood CC (South Course), Palm Desert (1974); Mission Hills G&CC (Old Course), Rancho Mirage (1970); Quail Lake CC, Moreno (1968); Rossmoor Leisure World GC, Rossmoor (1965); San Luis Bay Inn & CC, Avila Beach (9, 1968); Soboba Springs CC, San Jacinto (1967); Springs C, Rancho Mirage (1975).
Connecticut: Farmington Woods CC, Farmington (1970); Oronoque Village GC, Stratford (1971).
Florida: Aberdeen G&CC, Boynton Beach (1986); Baymeadows GC, Jacksonville (1969); Boca West C (Course No. 1), Boca Raton (1969); Boca West C (Course No. 2), Boca Raton (1971); Mayacoo Lakes CC, West Palm Beach (1973), with Jack Nicklaus; Silver Spring Shores G&CC, Ocala (1970).
Maryland: Rossmoor Leisure World GC, Silver Spring (Precision, 1966).
Michigan: Bay Valley GC, Bay City (1973), with Jack Nicklaus.
New Jersey: Rossmoor GC, Jamesburg (1967).
New Mexico: Rio Rancho G&CC, Albuquerque (1970).
New York: River Oaks CC, Grand Island (1972).
Ohio: Jack Nicklaus Sports Center (Bruin), Mason (Precision, 1972), with Jack Nicklaus; Jack Nicklaus Sports Center (Grizzly), Mason (1972), with Jack Nicklaus; Muirfield Village GC, Dublin (1974), with Jack Nicklaus.
Texas: Bent Tree GC, Dallas (1974); Woodlake CC, San Antonio (1972).
Vermont: Haystack CC, Wilmington (NLE, 1972).
British Columbia: Quilchena G&CC, British Columbia (1956).
Spain: La Moraleja GC, Madrid (1976), with Jack Nicklaus.
Courses Remodeled & Added to by: Desmond Muirhead
California: Alameda Muni (Jack Clark Course) (R., 1967); Brookside Muni (Course No.2), Pasadena (R., 1966); Fort Irwin GC, Barstow (R.); Presidio GC, San Francisco (R., 1973); Santa Ana CC (R.); South Hills CC, West Covina (R., 1968); Visalia CC (R., 1964).
Florida: Boca West C (Course No. 1), Boca Raton (R., 1985).
Maryland: All-View GC (R.).
Washington: Overlake G&CC, Medina (R., 1964).

Albert H. Murray (1888 - 1974)
Born: Nottingham, England. Died: Montreal, Canada at age 85.
Albert Murray emigrated to Canada in 1902, where he joined his older brother

Charlie at the Toronto GC. Charlie, who dabbled in course design during his career, took over the head professional job at Royal Montreal GC in 1905, and became a legend in that position before his death in 1930. Albert served as professional at a succession of Montreal-area courses while competing successfully in national events. He won many tournaments, including the Canadian Open in 1908 and 1913 and the Canadian PGA in 1924.
Albert Murray also laid out a number of courses in eastern Canada and upstate New York during his professional career.
Courses by: Albert Murray
New York: Massena GC (1958).
Quebec: CC of Montreal, St. Laurent (1910); Kanawaki GC (1912), with Charles Murray; Montreal Muni (Yellow Course); Royal Quebec CC (Kent Course), Montgomery Falls (NLE, 1914).
Courses Remodeled & Added to by: Albert Murray
New York: Malone GC (A.9, 1958).
New Brunswick: Edmunston GC (R.); Edmunston GC (A.11, 1947).

Frank Murray
In the late 1940s Frank Murray served as green committee chairman at Congressional CC in Maryland. He became interested in golf course construction at this time while helping build several courses designed by golf architect Alfred Tull. Murray then decided to build one for himself, and Brooke Manor Farms CC, constructed by Murray to Tull's design, was completed in 1955. Murray was so fascinated with golf course design by this time that he formed a design and construction firm with Russell Roberts, who had been in charge of maintenance at Brooke Manor Farms.
Murray soon sold his club in order to devote full time to his practice with Roberts. The two designed and built a number of courses along the eastern seaboard in the late 1950s. In 1959 the partnership was terminated and Murray moved to Florida, where he did several resort courses in the 1960s.
Courses by: Frank Murray
Delaware: Cavaliers CC, New Castle (1959), with Russell Roberts; Old Landing GC, Rehobeth (9), with Russell Roberts; Rehobeth Beach CC (1962), with Russell Roberts.
Florida: Crooked Creek G&CC, Miami (1968); Placid Lakes Inn & CC, Lake Placid (1966); Pompano Park GC, Pompano Beach (Precision, 1970); Sabal Palm CC, Tamarac (1968); Tierre Verde GC, Tierre Verde Island (1965); University Park CC, Boca Raton (1960); Vizcaya GC, Miami (1961).
Maryland: Andrews AFB GC (East Course) (1956), with Russell Roberts; Andrews AFB GC (West Course) (1961); Bel Aire G&CC, Bowie (27, 1959), with Russell Roberts; Hagerstown Muni (1957), with Russell Roberts; Maryland G&CC, Belair , with Russell Roberts; Swan Creek CC, Belair (1956), with Russell Roberts; Washingtonian CC (Country Club Course), Gaithersburg (1960), with Russell Roberts; Washingtonian CC (National Course), Gaithersburg (1962), with Russell Roberts.
Pennsylvania: Fairview G&CC, Quentin (1959), with Russell Roberts; Lebanon CC, with Russell Roberts; Penn Oaks CC, West Chester (1966), with Russell Roberts.
Puerto Rico: Berwind CC, Rio Grande (1966).
Courses Remodeled & Added to by: Frank Murray
Delaware: Newark CC (A.9, 1956), with Russell Roberts.

Renee V. Muylaert
Based near Toronto, brothers Renee and Charles Muylaert laid out numerous courses in the 1960s and 1970s, working almost entirely in the Canadian province of Ontario. Both were graduates of the Winter School for Turfgrass Managers of the University of Massachusetts and had been well-known course superintendents.
Renee began designing courses on a part-time basis in 1960 and entered the field full time in 1966. When Charles joined him in 1967, they set up the design-and-build firm of Green-Par Golf Construction Ltd. In addition to courses of their own design, the brothers made major or minor modifications to many established layouts. They also operated an extensive sod business.
Courses by: Renee Muylaert
Ontario: Aurora Highlands GC, Aurora (1980), with Charles Muylaert; Binbrook GC, Hamilton (1963); Brookside GC, Agincourt (27, 1967); Buttonville GC (9, 1980), with Charles Muylaert; Chinguacousy CC, Brampton (27, 1960); Derrydale GC, Brampton (Precision, 1968); Glen Cedars GC, Markham (1967); Glen Eagles GC, Bolton (1961); Gormley Green GC (1972); Greenhills CC, Lambeth (27, 1977), with Charles Muylaert; Horseshoe Valley GC, Barrie (1972), with Charles Muylaert; Indian Wells GC, Burlington (1972); Nanticoke GC, Simcoe (1977), with Charles Muylaert; Nobleton Lakes GC (1974); Pheasant Run CC, Newmarket (1979), with Charles Muylaert; Royal Downs GC, Thornhill (Precision, 1966); Spring Lakes GC (Course No. 1), Stouffville (1976), with Charles Muylaert; Spring Lakes GC (Course No. 2), Stouffville (1980), with Charles Muylaert; St. Catherines Muni (Precision, 1973); Steed and Evans GC, Fonthill (9, 1971); Strathroy CC (9, 1975); Sunset G Centre, Fort Erie (Par 3, 1973); Thistledown GC, Owen Sound (9, 1974); Trent GC, Bolsouer (9, 1974); Unionville Fairways (Par 3, 1962); Vaughan Valley GC (Precision, 1969); Victoria Park GC (Course No. 1), Guelph (1967); Victoria Park GC (Course No. 2), Guelph (1972).
Courses Remodeled & Added to by: Renee Muylaert
Ontario: Gormley Green GC (R.9, 1974), with Charles Muylaert.

Torakichi "Pete" Nakamura (1915 -)
Born: Kanagawa Prefecture, Japan.
Prominent Japanese golfer Torakichi Nakamura, a three-time winner of the Japanese Open, was individual champion of the 1957 Canada Cup Match held at Kasumigaseki GC. It was during this event that he acquired the nickname "Pete" through mutual agreement with his American competitors who found Torakichi difficult to pronounce.
Nakamura's victory at Kasumigaseki was credited with initiating a golf boom in Japan. In 1963 he began designing courses to accommodate that boom. Nakamura maintained his golfing skills well into the 1980s, winning the 1981 Japanese Seniors while shooting his age in the process.

Greg Nash (1949 -   ) ASGCA
Born: Hays, Kansas.

Greg Nash attended the University of Arizona, earning a Bachelor's degree in Landscape Architecture in 1972. He worked for two years as a golf course designer and construction supervisor with the Del E. Webb Corp., then joined Jeff Hardin in a golf architecture firm. In 1981 Nash formed his own business based in Phoenix.

Courses by: Greg Nash

Arizona: Aspen Valley GC, Flagstaff (9, 1973), with Jeff Hardin; Bellaire GC, Phoenix (Precision, 1973), with Red Lawrence and Jeff Hardin; Briarwood GC, Sun City West (1979), with Jeff Hardin, John W. Meeker and Tom Ryan; Canada Hills CC (Course No. 1), Tucson (1982), with Jeff Hardin; Continental GC, Scottsdale (Precision, 1978), with Jeff Hardin; Cottonwood CC, Sunlakes (1983), with Jeff Hardin; Country Meadows GC, Peoria (Precision, 9, 1978), with Jeff Hardin; Dobson Ranch GC, Mesa (Precision, 1974), with Red Lawrence and Jeff Hardin; Echo Mesa GC, Sun City West (Precision, 1985); El Conquistador Hotel GC, Tucson (Precision, 9, 1982), with Jeff Hardin; Gold Canyon Ranch GC, Apache Junction (1982), with Jeff Hardin; Goodyear G&CC (West Course), Litchfield Park (1974), with Red Lawrence and Jeff Hardin; Grandview GC, Sun City West (Precision, 1984); Hillcrest GC, Sun City West (1978), with Jeff Hardin, John W. Meeker and Tom Ryan; Leisure World GC, Mesa (Par 3, 36, 1980), with Jeff Hardin; Los Caballeros GC, Wickenburg (1981), with Jeff Hardin; Mesa Verde GC, Mesa (1986); Pebblebrook GC, Sun City West (1979), with Jeff Hardin, John W. Meeker and Tom Ryan; Quail Run GC, Sun City (Precision, 9, 1977), with Jeff Hardin; Roadhaven GC, Bullhead City (Precision, 9, 1984); Stardust GC, Sun City West (Precision, 1979), with Jeff Hardin and Tom Ryan; Sun City CC, with Milt Coggins and Jeff Hardin; Sun City Vistoso GC, Tucson (1986); Sun Lakes GC (1973), with James Winans and Jeff Hardin; Sunland Village GC, Mesa (1975), with Milt Coggins and Jeff Hardin; Union Hills GC, Sun City (1974), with Jeff Hardin; Villa de Paz CC, Phoenix , with Jeff Hardin; Willowcreek GC, Sun City (1973), with George Fazio, Tom Fazio and John W. Meeker.

Colombia: La Colina CC, Bogota (1984), with Jeff Hardin.

Thailand: Mahachia GC, Bangkok (27, 1981).

Courses Remodeled & Added to by: Greg Nash

Arizona: Anasazi GC, Phoenix (R.18, 1984); Aspen Valley GC, Flagstaff (A.9, 1981), with Jeff Hardin; Rio Verde CC (Quail Run Course), Scottsdale (A.9, 1981), with Jeff Hardin; Rio Verde CC (White Wing Course) (A.9, 1983), with Jeff Hardin; Sun Lakes GC (A.9, 1979), with Jeff Hardin; Villa de Paz CC, Phoenix (A.9, 1976), with Jeff Hardin.

Kansas: Smoky Hill CC, Hays (A.9, 1982).

Nevada: Boulder City GC (A.9, 1986).

William Henrichsen Neff (1905 -   ) ASGCA
Born: Holladay, Utah.

William H. Neff attended the University of Utah and graduated from the American Landscape School in Des Moines, Iowa. He practiced landscape architecture in Utah and Arizona for over twenty years.

A member of The Country Club in Salt Lake City, Neff was appointed to a committee in charge of remodeling the course in 1952. He hired Californian William P. Bell to design the changes and worked with the architect on the reconstruction. After Bell's death, Neff was hired by the architect's son, William F. Bell, to supervise construction of Riverside CC in Provo, Utah. Neff served as construction boss on three other Bell projects in Salt Lake City and then in 1956 decided to try his own hand at golf design. Over the next twenty years he created a number of Utah's top courses.

Courses by: William H. Neff

Colorado: Yampa Valley GC, Craig (9, 1983), with William Howard Neff.

Utah: Alpine CC, American Fork (1960); Bloomington CC, St. George (1972); Bountiful Muni (1976), with William Howard Neff; Cascade Fairways GC, Orem (1968); Davis Park GC, Kaysville (1968); Fore Lakes GC, Salt Lake City (Precision, 9, 1973), with William Howard Neff; Glenmore G&CC, Jordan (1967); Majestic Oaks GC, Salt Lake City (Par 3, 9, 1973); Mountain Dell GC, Salt Lake City (1960), with William F. Bell; Mountain View GC, Jordan (1968); Oakridge CC (1957), with William F. Bell; Park City GC (9, 1962); Riverside CC, Provo (1960), with William F. Bell; Stansbury Park CC, Tooele (1972); Sweetwater GC, Bear Lake (9, 1974), with William Howard Neff; Wasatch Mountain GC, Midway (1966); Westland Hills GC, Jordan (9).

Wyoming: Little America GC, Cheyenne (Precision, 9, 1974).

Courses Remodeled & Added to by: William H. Neff

Utah: Bonneville Muni, Salt Lake City (A.9, 1956), with William F. Bell; Cottonwood C, Salt Lake City (R.9, 1963); Cottonwood C, Salt Lake City (A.9, 1963); Hidden Valley CC, Draper (A.9, 1978), with William Howard Neff; Rose Park GC, Salt Lake City (A.9, 1960), with William F. Bell; The Country Club, Salt Lake City (R.9, 1954); Wasatch Mountain GC, Midway (A.9, 1972), with William Howard Neff.

William Howard Neff (1933 -   ) ASGCA
Born: Limon, Colorado.

William Howard Neff received a Bachelor's degree in Architecture from the University of Utah in 1958. During the next eight years, he worked as a draftsman for a land planning firm in Denver, for the Salt Lake City and County Planning Commission, and as a planning consultant/graphic designer in Salt Lake City. In 1966 he embarked on a career as a golf course architect, joining the practice of William Henrichsen Neff (who was no relation) of Salt Lake City. In the early Eighties Bill Neff established his own design business.

Courses by: William Howard Neff

Colorado: Yampa Valley GC, Craig (9, 1983), with William H. Neff.

Utah: Bountiful Muni (1976), with William H. Neff; East Bay GC, Provo (27, 1986); Fore Lakes GC, Salt Lake City (Precision, 9, 1973), with William H. Neff; Mount Ogden GC, Ogden (1984); Payson GC (1987); Sweetwater GC, Bear Lake (9, 1974), with William H. Neff.

Courses Remodeled & Added to by: William Howard Neff

Utah: Bloomington Hills CC (R., 1986); Brigham City G&CC (A.9, 1987); Davis Park GC, Kaysville (R., 1985); Forest Dale GC, Salt Lake City (R., 1987); Hidden Valley CC, Draper (A.9, 1978), with William H. Neff; Ogden G&CC (R., 1984); Park City GC (R., 1985); Southgate GC, St. George (R., 1986); Wasatch Mountain GC, Midway (A.9, 1972), with William H. Neff; Willow Creek CC, Sandy (R., 1981).

John Byron Nelson Jr. (1912 -   )
Born: Fort Worth, Texas.

Legendary professional golfer Byron Nelson, a contemporary of Ben Hogan, Sam Snead and Jimmy Demaret, won one U.S. Open, two PGA Championships and three Masters during a relatively short playing career.

In the 1960s Nelson served as a consultant to golf architect Ralph Plummer on several designs, notably Preston Trail GC near Dallas, which for years hosted a PGA Tour event named in Nelson's honor. After Plummer's death, Nelson served as consultant to another prominent Texan golf architect, Joe Finger. Among their collaborations was restoration of several holes at Augusta National.

Courses by: Byron Nelson

Texas: Grapevine Muni (1980), with Joseph S. Finger and Ken Dye; Great Southwest GC, Arlington (1965), with Ralph Plummer; Riverhill C, Kerrville (1974), with Joseph S. Finger.

Courses Remodeled & Added to by: Byron Nelson

Georgia: Augusta National GC, Augusta (R.1, 1979), with Joseph S. Finger.

Robert David "Robin" Nelson (1951 -   ) ASGCA
Born: Kentfield, California.

Robin Nelson attended the University of California at Berkeley, the University of Oregon and Chaminade University in Honolulu. Upon graduation from Berkeley, Nelson obtained his Landscape Architecture license in California and soon joined the golf design firm of Robert Muir Graves. After three years, Nelson joined the Ronald Fream Design Group and supervised construction of several layouts in the Far East.

In 1983 Nelson became Director of Golf Design for Belt, Collins and Associates, a large landscape design firm based in Hawaii.

Courses by: Robin Nelson

Hawaii: Francis Ii Brown GC, Mauna Lani Resort (1981), with Homer Flint and Raymond F. Cain; Kona International CC, Kailua-Kona (1987).

Australia: Burswood Island GC, Perth (1987); Meadows GC, Surfer's Paradise (1987).

Courses Remodeled & Added to by: Robin Nelson

Hawaii: Ala Wai GC, Waikiki (R., 1986); Hana Ranch G Park, Maui (R.3); Hickman AFB GC, Oahu (R., 1987); Kapalua GC (Bay Course), Maui (R., 1986); Kapalua GC (Village Course), Maui (R., 1987); Keauhou Kona CC, Kailua-Kona (A.9, 1986), with William F. Bell; Makaha Inn & CC (East Course), Oahu (R., 1987); Oahu CC (R., 1986); Pearl CC, Kaonohi (R.1, 1985); Waialae CC, Honolulu (R., 1984).

Malaysia: Kelab Golf Diraja Terengganu, Kuala Terengganu (R.9, 1986).

John Francis "Jack" Neville (1895 - 1978)
Born: St. Louis, Missouri. Died: Chino, California at age 83.

Jack Neville moved to Oakland, Calif. as a young boy and learned golf from Macdonald Smith and Jim Barnes. He was an excellent competitive golfer, winning the California State Amateur Championship in 1912, 1913, 1919, 1922 and 1929, and defeating H. Chandler Egan for the Pacific Northwest title in 1914. He was also a member of the 1923 Walker Cup team.

In 1915 Neville became a real estate salesman with the Pacific Improvement Company of Monterey, California. Company President S.F.B. Morse soon gave him the assignment of building a golf course on ocean frontage along Seventeen Mile Drive. The result was Pebble Beach Golf Links, which opened in 1919. Neville did the preliminary routing of the course and then called upon his friend Douglas Grant, another former California Amateur champion, to help with the bunkering. Pebble Beach remained as originally laid out except for some alteration of bunkering and natural erosion of the shore line.

Neville designed several other courses in the later 1920s but these were never built. He did assist George C. Thomas Jr., with the design of Bel-Air CC in Los Angeles in 1926 and Bob Baldock with the layout of the Shore course for Monterey Peninsula CC in 1961. He also laid out a second nine on dunes for Pacific Grove Municipal GC in 1959. Neville remained a real estate salesman all his life and never practiced golf course architecture as a vocation. His influence at Pebble Beach, nevertheless, remained so strong that officials continued to consult him throughout his life before making even modest changes to the course.

Courses by: Jack Neville

California: Bel-Air CC, Los Angeles (1927), with George C. Thomas Jr and William P. Bell; Monterey Peninsula CC (Shore Course), Pebble Beach (1961), with Bob Baldock; Pebble Beach G Links (1919), with Douglas S. Grant.

Courses Remodeled & Added to by: Jack Neville

California: Old Del Monte G&CC, Monterey (R.); Pacific Grove G Links (A.9, 1960).

William K. Newcomb Jr. (1940 -   )
Born: Logansport, Indiana.

Bill Newcomb, who won the Indiana Open as an amateur in 1961, attended the University of Michigan, receiving a Bachelor of Architecture degree in 1963 and a Master's in Landscape Architecture in 1965. From 1965 to 1967 he worked for golf architect Pete Dye, during which time he won the 1967 Michigan Amateur. In 1968 he formed William Newcomb Associates, based in Ann Arbor. His firm included several associates over the years, including John Robinson, Stephen Kay and James Lipe. Newcomb served for years as a lecturer at the University of Michigan's Department of Natural Resources and Michigan State University's Department of Agricultural Technology. He also coached the golf team at the University of Michigan in the 1970s.

Courses by: William Newcomb

Alaska: Anchorage Muni (1986).

Illinois: Fox Run GC, Elk Grove (1983), with Stephen Kay.

Indiana: Forest Park Muni, Noblesville (1970); Jasper Muni (9, 1970).

Kentucky: Greenbrier G&CC, Lexington (1971); Maysville CC (9).

Michigan: Boyne Highlands GC (Ross Memorial Crs), Harbor Springs (1987); Boyne Mountain GC (Alpine Course), Boyne Falls (1971); Boyne Mountain GC (Executive Course), Boyne Falls (Precision, 9, 1973); Boyne Mountain GC (Monument Course), Boyne Falls (1986), with Stephen Kay; Brookwood CC, Rochester (9); Crystal Mountain GC, Thomasville (1977); Grand Traverse GC (Newcombe Course), Acme (1979), with Stephen Kay; Great Oaks CC, Rochester; Green Hills GC, Linwood; Hampton Muni GC, Rochester (9); Holiday Greens GC (Precision, 1982), with Stephen Kay; Indianfield G&CC, Caro (1976), with Jim Lipe; Klinger Lake CC; Oasis GC, Plymouth (Precision,); Partridge Point GC, Ludington (9, 1985), with Stephen Kay; Portage Lake GC, Houghton (1972); Prairie Creek GC, DeWitt (9, 1978); Riverview Highlands GC, Riverview; Travis Pointe CC, Ann Arbor (1976), with Jim Lipe; Vassar G&CC; West Branch GC; Westland Muni (9); Willow Metro GC, New Boston (1978).

Ohio: Apple Valley GC, Howard (1972); Avalon Lakes GC, Warren (1967), with Pete Dye; Seven Hills GC, Hartville (1971); Union CC, New Philadelphia .

Courses Remodeled & Added to by: William Newcomb

Michigan: Barton Hills CC, Ann Arbor (R.); Battle Creek CC (R.); Boyne Highlands GC (Heather Course), Harbor Springs (A.9, 1975); Boyne Highlands GC (Moor Course), Harbor Springs (A.9, 1975); Chemung Hills GC, Howell (A.9, 1983), with Stephen Kay; Farmington CC (R.); Green Ridge CC, Grand Rapids (R.); Hickory Hills GC, Jackson (R.9, 1977); Hickory Hills GC, Jackson (A.9, 1977); Holiday Inn GC, Mt. Pleasant (R., 1980), with Stephen Kay; Kalamazoo CC (R.); Lake of the North GC, Mancelona (A.18, 1985); Pine Mountain GC, Iron Mountain (A.9, 1986); Plum Hollow G&CC, Southfield (R.); Port Huron CC (R., 1982), with Stephen Kay; Saginaw CC (R.); Schuss Mountain GC, Mancelona (R., 1980), with Stephen Kay; Spring Lake G&CC (R.); Traverse City CC (R., 1982), with Stephen Kay.

New York: Niagara Falls CC, Lewiston (R.); Old Oaks CC, Purchase (R., 1981), with Stephen Kay.

Ohio: Cincinnati CC (R.); Cincinnati CC (A.4, 1969); Congress Lake C, Hartville (R.); Fonderlac CC, Poland (A.9); Mayfield CC, South Euclid (R.); Trumbull CC, Warren (R.); Wooster CC (A.9, 1974).

Jack William Nicklaus (1940 -)

Born: Columbus, Ohio.

Jack Nicklaus was one of the truly great golfers of all time, winning twenty major championships: six Masters, five PGAs, four U.S. Opens, three British Opens and two U.S. Amateurs. He took an interest in golf course design early in his professional career, and started consulting on designs while still in his 20s.

Nicklaus worked first with designer Pete Dye on several projects and later with Desmond Muirhead. In 1974 Nicklaus formed his own golf architecture practice, which included Bob Cupp and Jay Morrish as full-time designers. Nicklaus allowed his assistants to prepare plans and then reviewed them in detail, making suggestions on changes to enhance playability and strategy. Something of a workaholic, Nicklaus continued to play the PGA Tour while personally inspecting his course projects during and after construction.

Cupp and Morrish eventually left to form their own design companies, and Nicklaus brought aboard new talent to serve as design associates, including Scott Miller, Tom Pearson, Jim Lipe and, for a short time, Paul Clute.

A stickler for high design and maintenance standards, Nicklaus was sometimes criticized for catering only to deep-pocket clients who built big-budget layouts. His courses, however expensive, attracted large spread attention and admiration. One, Shoal Creek, hosted the PGA Championship soon after it opened. Several became perennial sites on the PGA Tour. His Grand Cypress GC was a co-selection of the Best New Resort Course of 1984, and his Loxahatchee GC was named Best New Private Course in 1985, both by Golf Digest magazine.

Courses by: Jack Nicklaus

Alabama: Shoal Creek, Birmingham (1977), with Jay Morrish and Bob Cupp.

Arizona: Desert Highlands GC, Scottsdale (1984), with Jay Morrish, Bob Cupp and Scott Miller; Desert Mountain GC (Cochise Course), Carefree (1988), with Scott Miller; Desert Mountain GC (Geronimo Course), Carefree (1988), with Scott Miller; Desert Mountain GC (Renegade Course), Carefree (1987), with Scott Miller; La Paloma GC, Tucson (27, 1985), with Scott Miller.

California: Bear Creek GC, Wildomar (1982), with Jay Morrish, Bob Cupp and Scott Miller; Club at Morningside, Rancho Mirage (1983), with Jay Morrish, Bob Cupp and Scott Miller.

Colorado: Breckenridge GC (1985), with Bob Cupp; Castle Pines GC, Castle Rock (1981), with Jay Morrish, Bob Cupp and Scott Miller; CC of the Rockies, Avon (1984), with Jay Morrish and Bob Cupp; CC of Castle Pines, Castle Rock (1986), with Scott Miller; Meridian GC, Englewood (1984), with Bob Cupp and Scott Miller.

Florida: Bear Lakes CC, West Palm Beach (1984), with Bob Cupp; Bear's Paw CC, Naples (1980), with Jay Morrish, Bob Cupp and Scott Miller; Grand Cypress Golf Academy, Orlando (3, 1985), with Bob Cupp; Grand Cypress GC, Orlando (1984), with Bob Cupp; John's Island C (South Course), Vero Beach (1970), with Pete Dye; Loxahatchee C, Jupiter (1985), with Bob Cupp and Tom Pearson; Mayacoo Lakes CC, West Palm Beach (1973), with Desmond Muirhead; Sailfish Point CC, Stuart (1981), with Jay Morrish and Bob Cupp.

Georgia: CC of the South, Alpharetta (1986), with Tom Pearson.

Kentucky: Valhalla CC, Louisville (1987), with Tom Pearson.

Louisiana: CC of Louisiana, Baton Rouge (1986), with Tom Pearson; English Turn CC, Gretna (1987), with Tom Pearson.

Michigan: Bay Valley GC, Bay City (1973), with Desmond Muirhead; Grand Traverse GC (The Bear Course), Acme (1985), with Bob Cupp; Wabeek CC, Bloomfield Hills (1971), with Pete Dye and Roy Dye.

Mississippi: Annandale GC, Jackson (1981), with Jay Morrish, Bob Cupp and Scott Miller.

North Carolina: Elk River GC, Banner Elk (1984), with Bob Cupp.

Ohio: CC at Muirfield Village, Dublin (1982), with Jay Morrish and Bob Cupp; Jack Nicklaus Sports Center (Bruin), Mason (Precision, 1972), with Desmond Muirhead; Jack Nicklaus Sports Center (Grizzly), Mason (1972), with Desmond Muirhead; Muirfield Village GC, Dublin (1974), with Desmond Muirhead.

South Carolina: Harbour Town G Links, Hilton Head Island (1969), with Pete Dye and Alice Dye; Long Bay C, North Myrtle Beach (1987), with Tom Pearson; Melrose GC, Daufuskie Island (1987), with Tom Pearson; Turtle Point G Links, Kiawah Island (1981), with Jay Morrish and Bob Cupp.

Texas: Hills of Lakeway Golf Academy, Lakeway (3, 1985), with Jay Morrish, Bob Cupp and Scott Miller; Hills of Lakeway GC, Lakeway (1980), with Jay Morrish, Bob Cupp and Scott Miller; Lochinvar GC, Houston (1980), with Jay Morrish and Bob Cupp.

Utah: Park Meadows GC, Park City (1983), with Jay Morrish and Bob Cupp.

Wisconsin: Americana Lake Geneva GC (Briarpatch) (1971), with Pete Dye.

Ontario: Glen Abbey GC, Oakville (1976), with Jay Morrish and Bob Cupp.

Cayman Islands: Britannia GC (Precision, 9, 1985), with Bob Cupp.

Japan: Kazusa GC, Tokyo (1985), with Jay Morrish and Scott Miller; Mito International GC, Tokyo (1987), with Scott Miller; New St. Andrews GC, Ontawara City (1976), with Jay Morrish and Bob Cupp; Sunnyfield GC, Gozenyama (1986), with Jay Morrish and Scott Miller.

Spain: La Moraleja GC, Madrid (1976), with Desmond Muirhead.

Courses Remodeled & Added to by: Jack Nicklaus

Florida: Grand Cypress GC, Orlando (A.9, 1986), with Bob Cupp.

Georgia: Augusta National GC, Augusta (R., 1985), with Bob Cupp.

New York: St. Andrews GC, Hastings-on-Hudson (R., 1985), with Bob Cupp.

Ohio: Firestone CC (South Course), Akron (R., 1986), with Tom Pearson.

Texas: Dallas Athletic C (Blue Course), Mesquite (R., 1986), with Scott Miller.

West Virginia: Greenbrier GC (Greenbrier Course), White Sulphur Spgs (R., 1978), with Jay Morrish and Bob Cupp.

Australia: Australian GC, Kensington (R., 1977), with Jay Morrish and Bob Cupp.

Tom Nicoll

Scottish-born professional Tom Nicoll designed and built a number of courses in California before and after spending several years in Asia. In 1917 he moved to Manila to build and operate a course there for the United States government. In Manila, he taught a group of Japanese golfers who persuaded him to become the professional at Komazawa GC in Tokyo. As such, he was one of, if not the first, teaching professional in Japan.

Tom Nicoll should not be confused with Thomas H. Nicol, a civil engineer who planned several courses in Alabama in the 1960s.

Courses by: Tom Nicoll

California: Burlingame CC, Hillsborough; Los Altos G&CC; Menlo CC, Redwood City; San Jose CC (1912).

Ward W. Northrup (1932 -)

Born: Cedar Rapids, Iowa.

After attending Iowa State as an agricultural major, Northrup moved to Florida and became involved in course maintenance at Delray Beach CC. Following work on construction crews for architects Red Lawrence and Mark Mahannah, Northrup worked for Dick Wilson as a construction superintendent. In 1964 he became general manager at Bedens Brook Club in New Jersey, but three years later joined architect Joe Lee as an assistant. In the summer of 1972 Northrup formed his own course design firm, based in Florida.

Courses by: Ward Northrup

Alabama: Saugahatchee CC, Opelika (1976).

Florida: Buenaventura Lakes CC, Kissimmee (Precision, 9, 1983); Eaglewood CC, Hobe Sound (Precision, 1983); Imperial GC (West Course), Naples (1979); Jupiter West GC, Jupiter (1980); Lake Ajay GC (Par 3,); Maple Leaf Estates CC, Port Charlotte (Precision, 1982); Moorings of Manatee GC, Rustin (1985); Orlando NTC GC, Orlando (9, 1982); River Run G Links, Bradenton (1987); Sabal Point CC, Longwood (1981); Turkey Creek G&RC, Alachua (1977); Wekiva GC, Longwood (1974); Windermere CC (1987).

Georgia: Ansley GC, Atlanta (1979); Lands West GC, Douglasville (1974); Summit Chase G&CC, Snellville (1975).

Mississippi: Highland Lake Estates GC, Jackson (9, 1975).

Colombia: Barranquilla CC (1981); Club Campestre Cartagena (1981).

Courses Remodeled & Added to by: Ward Northrup

Florida: Jupiter Dunes GC, Jupiter (R.).

Georgia: Bowden Muni, Macon (A.9, 1974); Sunset Hills CC, Carrollton (A.9, 1975).

Richard P. Nugent (1931 -) ASGCA, President, 1981.

Born: Highland Park, Illinois.

Dick Nugent received a Bachelor's in Landscape Architecture degree in 1958 from the University of Illinois and then worked for six years with golf architect Robert Bruce Harris. In 1964 he and Kenneth Killian, another Harris assistant, formed a course design partnership that actively experimented with such design techniques as computer planning of automatic irrigation and the use of waste water in turf maintenance. In the early Eighties, the two dissolved their partnership and Nugent founded his own practice based in Long Grove, Illinois.

Courses by: Dick Nugent

Illinois: Buffalo Grove GC (1968), with Ken Killian; Concord Green GC, Libertyville (Par 3, 9, 1964), with Ken Killian; Edgebrook GC, Sandwich (1967), with Ken Killian; Forest Preserve National GC, Oak Forest (1981), with Ken Killian and Bob Lohmann; Glendale Lakes GC, Glendale Heights (1987); Golf Club of Illinois, Algonquin (1987); Greenshire GC, Waukegan (1964), with Ken Killian; Kemper Lakes GC, Hawthorne Woods (1979), with Ken Killian; Moon Lake GC, Hoffman Estates (1973), with Ken Killian; Oak Brook Hills CC, Oak Brook (1987), with Bruce Borland; River Oaks GC, Calumet City (1971), with Ken Killian; Robert A.Black GC, Chicago (Precision, 9, 1979), with Ken Killian and Jeff Brauer; Shewani CC, Watseka (1986); Tally Ho GC, Vernon Hills (9, 1979), with Ken Killian;

Warren Park GC (Precision,), with Ken Killian; Weber Park GC, Skokie (Par 3, 9, 1973), with Ken Killian; Western Illinois Univ GC, Macomb (9, 1971), with Ken Killian.

Indiana: Oak Meadow G&TC, Evansville (1972), with Ken Killian; Sand Creek C, Chesterton (1979), with Ken Killian and Bob Lohmann; Woodmar CC, Hammond (1982), with Ken Killian.

Ohio: Shelby Oaks GC, Sidney (1964), with Ken Killian; Sugar Creek G&CC, with Ken Killian.

Texas: Chester W. Ditto Muni, Arlington (1982), with Ken Killian and Jeff Brauer; Mission CC, Odessa (1983), with Ken Killian and Jeff Brauer.

Virginia: Poplar Forest GC, Lynchberg (9, 1980), with Ken Killian.

Wisconsin: Abbey Springs GC, Fontana (1972), with Ken Killian; Evergreen GC, Elkhorn (1973), with Ken Killian; Lake Arrowhead GC, Nekoosa (1984), with Ken Killian and Jeff Brauer; Tuckaway CC, Franklin (1967), with Ken Killian.

Courses Remodeled & Added to by: Dick Nugent

Illinois: Bob O'Link CC, Highland Park (R., 1968), with Ken Killian; Butterfield CC, Hinsdale (R., 1969), with Ken Killian; Chevy Chase CC, Wheeling (R.), with Ken Killian; Countryside GC (R., 1978), with Ken Killian; Crystal Lake CC (R., 1980), with Ken Killian; Deerpath Park GC, Lake Forest (R., 1971), with Ken Killian; Deerpath Park GC, Lake Forest (R., 1981), with Ken Killian; Deerpath Park GC (R., 1984); Elgin CC (R., 1978), with Ken Killian; Evanston GC, Skokie (R., 1972), with Ken Killian; Exmoor CC, Highland Park (R., 1969), with Ken Killian; Fox Lake CC (R., 1973), with Ken Killian; Glencoe GC (R., 1964), with Ken Killian; Glencoe GC (R., 1982), with Ken Killian and Bob Lohmann; Great Lakes NTC GC, North Chicago (A.9, 1971), with Ken Killian; Green Acres CC, Northbrook (R.1, 1982), with Ken Killian; Highland Park GC (R.5, 1977), with Ken Killian; Hillcrest CC, Long Grove (R., 1979), with Ken Killian; Lake Shore CC, Glencoe (R., 1971), with Ken Killian; Lansing Sportsman's C, Lansing (A.9, 1976), with Ken Killian; Lincolnshire CC (Course No. 1), Crete (R., 1964), with Ken Killian; Lincolnshire CC (Course No. 2), Crete (R.), with Ken Killian; Marriott Lincolnshire GC (R.2, 1981), with Ken Killian; McHenry GC (R.1, 1970), with Ken Killian; Medinah CC (Course No. 3) (R., 1970), with Ken Killian; Midlothian CC (R.), with Ken Killian; North Shore CC, Glenview (R.), with Ken Killian; Onwentsia C, Lake Forest (R., 1969), with Ken Killian; Park Ridge CC (R.3, 1966), with Ken Killian; Pinecrest G&CC, Huntley (R., 1979), with Ken Killian; Pipe O'Peace GC, Blue Island (R., 1987); Ravinia Green CC, Deerfield (R., 1973), with Ken Killian; Ridge CC, Chicago (R., 1972), with Ken Killian; Ruth Lake CC, Hinsdale (R., 1980), with Ken Killian; Ruth Lake CC, Hinsdale (R.1, 1984); Silver Lake GC (North Course), Orland Park (R.1, 1978), with Ken Killian; Skokie CC, Glencoe (R., 1973), with Ken Killian; Sportsman G&CC, Northbrook (R.), with Ken Killian; Spring Creek GC, Spring Valley (A.9, 1966), with Ken Killian; Spring Creek GC, Spring Valley (R.9, 1966), with Ken Killian; Sunset Valley GC, Highland Park (R., 1977), with Ken Killian; Twin Orchards CC (Red Course), Long Grove (R.), with Ken Killian; Villa Olivia CC, Bartlett (R., 1975), with Ken Killian; Westmoreland CC, Wilmette (R.), with Ken Killian; White Pines CC (East Course), Bensonville (R., 1982), with Ken Killian; White Pines CC (West Course), Bensonville (R., 1982), with Ken Killian; Wilmette Park GC, Glenview (R., 1979), with Ken Killian.

Indiana: Chain O'Lakes GC, South Bend (R., 1966), with Ken Killian.

Iowa: Wakonda C, Des Moines (R., 1987), with Bruce Borland.

Michigan: Berrien Hills CC, Benton Harbor (R., 1965), with Ken Killian; Lost Lake Woods GC, Ypsilanti (A.9, 1974), with Ken Killian.

Minnesota: Meadowbrook GC, Hopkins (A.9, 1966), with Ken Killian; Tartan Park GC, St. Paul (R.16, 1986); Town & Country C, St. Paul (R., 1986).

Oklahoma: Dornick Hills G&CC, Ardmore (R., 1985).

South Dakota: Minnehaha CC, Sious Falls (R.6, 1976), with Ken Killian; Westward Ho CC, Sioux Falls (R.1, 1985), with Bruce Borland.

Texas: Great Southwest GC, Arlington (R., 1983), with Ken Killian and Jeff Brauer; Harlingen CC (R., 1985); Midland CC (R., 1985).

Wisconsin: Big Foot CC, Fontana (R., 1986); Blackhawk CC, Madison (R., 1982), with Ken Killian; Blue Mound G&CC, Wauwautosa (R., 1980), with Ken Killian; Brynwood CC, Milwaukee (R., 1968), with Ken Killian; Hartford CC (A.9, 1969), with Ken Killian; Hartford CC (R.9, 1969), with Ken Killian; Lacrosse CC (R., 1985); Maple Bluff CC, Madison (R., 1973), with Ken Killian; North Shore CC, Mequon (R., 1985); Reedsburg CC (A.9, 1978), with Ken Killian and Bob Lohmann.

William Ogg (1889 - 1960)

Born: Carnoustie, Scotland. Died: Tampa, Florida at age 71.

Willie Ogg emigrated to the United States in 1914 and became professional/greenkeeper at Dedham (Mass.) Polo and Hunt Club, remaining there until 1921 when he took a similar position at Worcester CC. Ogg was an early graduate of the Massachusetts Agricultural College's Winter School for greenkeepers and a founding member of the PGA of America. An excellent player, he won several state Opens and the New England PGA title. Best known for the carefully balanced golf clubs he handmade and marketed, Willie Ogg also designed and remodeled several golf courses during his career.

Courses by: Willie Ogg

Georgia: James L. Key Muni, Atlanta (9, 1921).

Massachusetts: Green Hill Muni, Worcester (NLE, 1930); Wilbraham CC (1927).

Courses Remodeled & Added to by: Willie Ogg

Florida: Whispering Oaks CC, Ridge Manor (R.9, 1958); Whispering Oaks CC, Ridge Manor (A.9, 1959).

Massachusetts: Dedham Hunt & Polo C (R.).

New York: Albany CC (NLE, R.).

George O'Neil (1883 - 1955)

Born: Philadelphia, Pennsylvania. Died: Miami, Florida at age 72.

George O'Neil, one of the early American golf professionals, was employed with several Chicago-area clubs, including Midlothian, Beverly, Lake Shore and Edgewater. He was a fine teacher and helped develop the skills of young Chick Evans.

O'Neil practiced golf architecture as a sideline for several years and at one time or another worked with Chicago club professional/course designers Jack Daray, Joseph Roseman and Jack Croke. He formed his own full-time practice with offices in Chicago and Cleveland in the 1920s, but closed them in the height of the Depression. Undaunted, O'Neil then became active in the promotion of professional football and was part owner of a team for a time.

The last twenty years of O'Neil's life were spent battling serious illnesses. His medical expenses were covered by friend and former pupil Albert D. Lasker, the Chicago advertising magnate for whom O'Neil had built Melody Farms GC.

Courses by: George O'Neill

Florida: El Conquistador GC, Valparaiso (NLE, 1918).

Illinois: Barrington Hills CC, Barrington (1920), with Jack Croke and Joseph A.Roseman; Cedar Crest GC, Antioch; Crystal Lake CC, with Joseph A.Roseman and Jack Croke; Green Acres CC, Northbrook; Mellody Farm CC, Lake Forest (NLE, 1928), with Jack Croke and Jack Daray; Robin Hood CC (NLE,).

Indiana: South Bend CC.

Michigan: Erskine Park GC, with Chick Evans.

West Virginia: Greenbrier GC (Greenbrier Course), White Sulphur Spgs (1925).

Wisconsin: Maxwelton Braes GC, Bailey Harbor , with Joseph A.Roseman.

Courses Remodeled & Added to by: George O'Neill

California: Pasadena GC (NLE, R., 1920), with Jack Croke.

Illinois: Glen View GC, Golf (R.), with Joseph A.Roseman.

Virginia: CC of Virginia (James River Course), Richmond (R., 1938).

Edward Lawrence Packard (1912 -) ASGCA, President, 1970.

Born: Northampton, Massachusetts.

Larry Packard received a degree in Landscape Architecture from Massachusetts State College in 1935 and worked as a landscape architect with the National Park Service in Maine, the U.S. Corps of Engineers in Massachusetts and the Chicago Park District.

In 1946 Packard joined the staff of golf architect Robert Bruce Harris, where he remained until 1954, when he formed the design firm of Packard and Wadsworth with Brent Wadsworth. This association later divided into two separate organizations, the design firm of Packard Inc. and the construction firm of The Wadsworth Company.

Packard exerted a powerful influence on design trends, professional policy and innovations in the field of course architecture. He hastened the trend toward gentler sculpturing and pioneered free forms in shaping of course features. He played an important role in establishing his profession's outlook on American society and environmental concerns, and was among the earliest advocates of the use of waste water for golf course irrigation.

Packard was joined in his practice by his son Roger in the early Seventies. He retired from the business in 1986 to Innisbrook in Florida, whose Top 100 courses were considered by many to be his finest works and classic examples of integration of golf holes with clusters of condominiums.

Courses by: Edward Lawrence Packard

California: Leisure Village GC, Laguna Hills (Par 3, 9, 1977).

Florida: Countryside CC, Clearwater (27, 1973), with Roger Packard; Cypress Run CC, Tarpon Springs (1982); Eagle Creek G&TC, Naples (1982); Hilaman Park GC, Tallahassee (1972), with Roger Packard; Innisbrook GC (Copperhead Course), Tarpon Springs (27, 1974), with Roger Packard; Innisbrook GC (Island Course), Tarpon Springs (1970); Innisbrook GC (Sandpiper Course), Tarpon Springs (1972), with Roger Packard.

Illinois: Apple Valley CC, Bartlett (Par 3, 9, 1959); Belk Park GC, Wood River (9, 1957), with Brent Wadsworth; Brookhill GC, Rantoul (9, 1971); Carlinville GC (9, 1960); Chanute AFB GC, Rantoul (9, 1959); Coal Creek CC, Atkinson (9, 1958), with Brent Wadsworth; Countryside West GC, DeKalb (9, 1966); Crestwicke CC, Bloomington (1972), with Roger Packard; Da-De-Co GC, Ottawa (Par 3, 9, 1960); Deer Creek GC, Park Forest (1974), with Roger Packard; Deerfield Park GC, Riverswood (1963); Earl F. Elliot Park GC, Rockford (1965); Elgin CC (1968); Faries Park GC, Decatur (1964); Granite City GC (9, 1958), with Brent Wadsworth; Hickory Point GC, Decatur (1970); Hinsdale Par 3 GC (Par 3, 9, 1962); Jerseyville CC (9, 1958), with Brent Wadsworth; Kellogg GC, Peoria (27, 1974), with Roger Packard; Ledges CC, Roscoe; Lick Creek GC, Pekin (1972), with Roger Packard; Lincolnshire Fields GC, Champaign (1969); Milford GC; Mission Hills CC, Northbrook (1975), with Roger Packard; Oak Hills CC, Palos Heights (9, 1975); Palatine Hills GC (1965); Pekin CC (1963); Prestwick CC, Frankfort (1963); Ravinia Green CC, Deerfield (1962); Rend Lake GC, Benton (27, 1974), with Roger Packard; Shiloh Park GC, Zion (9, 1963); Spartan Meadows GC, Elgin (1972); Springbrook GC, Naperville (1973), with Roger Packard; Turnberry CC, Crystal Lake (1972), with Roger Packard; Urban GC, Chicago Heights (Par 3, 9, 1962); Urban Hills CC, Richton Park (1962); Vermillion Hills CC, Danville (9, 1959), with Brent Wadsworth; Wagon Wheel GC, Rockton (Par 3, 9, 1961); Wedgewood GC, Joliet (1970); Wildwood Park GC, Decatur (Par 3, 9, 1965).

Indiana: Indian Village CC, Lafayette (9, 1962).

Iowa: A.H. Blank GC, Des Moines (9, 1971); Beaver Hills CC, Cedar Falls (1971); Echo Valley G&CC, Des Moines (1970); Sunnyside CC, Waterloo (1968).

Kentucky: Audubon State Park GC, Henderson (9, 1965); Boots Randolph GC, Cadiz (1972); Lake Barkley State Park GC; Midland Trail GC, Middletown (1965); Pennyrile Forest State Park GC, Dawson Springs (9, 1963).

Michigan: Bay City CC (1965); Hampshire CC, Dowagiac (1961); L'Anse GC (9, 1962); Leslie Park GC, Ann Arbor (1967); Spring Meadows CC, Linden (1965), with Brent Wadsworth.

Missouri: Westmoreland G&CC, Sedalia (9, 1967); Whiteman AFB GC, Sedalia (9, 1958), with Brent Wadsworth.

Nebraska: Benson Park GC, Omaha (1964); Platteview CC, Omaha (1968).

New Jersey: Leisure Village GC, Woodlake (Par 3, 9, 1969); Woodlake CC, Lakewood (1972).

New York: Riverside CC, Syracuse (Par 3, 9, 1964); Wayne CC, Lyons (9, 1957), with Brent Wadsworth.

North Dakota: Maple River GC, West Fargo (9, 1966).

Ohio: Burning Tree GC, White Oak (Par 3, 9); Rawiga CC, Seville (9, 1959); Silver Lake CC, Akron (1959), with Brent Wadsworth.

South Dakota: Elmwood Park GC, Sioux Falls (1960); Westward Ho CC, Sioux Falls (27, 1958).

Tennessee: McMinnville CC (1969).

Wisconsin: Antigo & Bass Lake CC, Antigo (1961); Baraboo CC (9, 1961); Black River Falls GC (9, 1956), with Brent Wadsworth; Brown County GC, Green Bay (1966); Chaska GC, Greenville (1975), with Roger Packard; Iola Community GC (9, 1966); Lincoln Hills CC, Marshfield (9); Mascoutin GC, Berlin (1973), with Roger Packard; Naga-Waukee Park GC, Pewaukee (1966); Oakwood Park GC; Peninsula State Park GC, Fish Creek (1963); Rib Mountain Lodge GC, Wausau (Par 3, 9, 1961); River Island GC, Oconto Falls (9, 1961); Stevens Point CC (1968); Tumblebrook GC, Pewaukee (1963); Wausau GC (1965); Westview CC, Marshfield (1966).

South Korea: Bomun Lake GC, Kyongju (1978), with Roger Packard.

Venezuela: El Morro GC, Puerto La Cruz (1984), with Roger Packard.

Courses Remodeled & Added to by: Edward Lawrence Packard

Florida: Seven Lakes CC, Fort Myers (R., 1977).

Illinois: Barrington Hills CC, Barrington (R., 1964); Belk Park GC, Wood River (A.9, 1970); Bergen Park GC (R., 1962); Biltmore CC, Barrington (R., 1972); Bloomington CC (R., 1970); Bob O'Link CC, Highland Park (R., 1964); Brookwood CC, Addison (R., 1976), with Roger Packard; Bryn Mawr GC, Lincolnwood (R., 1964); Bunn Park GC, Springfield (R., 1967); Butterfield CC, Hinsdale (R., 1962); Calumet CC, Homewood (R.12, 1957), with Brent Wadsworth; Champaign CC (R., 1960); Chanute AFB GC, Rantoul (A.9, 1959); CC of Decatur (R., 1964); CC of Decatur (R., 1970); CC of Decatur (R., 1982), with Roger Packard; Danville CC (A.9, 1958), with Brent Wadsworth; Deerpath Park GC, Lake Forest (R., 1966); Glenview Park GC, Glenview (R., 1961); Greenville CC (R., 1958), with Brent Wadsworth; Hillsboro CC (R.9, 1974); Hillsboro CC (A.9, 1974); Hinsdale GC (R., 1975), with Roger Packard; Illini CC, Springfield (R., 1977); Indian Spring GC, Saybrook (A.9, 1971); Inverness GC, Palatine (R., 1967); Inwood GC, Joliet (R., 1970); Jacksonville CC (A.9, 1964); Knollwood C, Lake Forest (R., 1975), with Roger Packard; La Grange CC (R., 1976); Mattoon G&CC, 10590 (A.9, 1971), with Roger Packard; Medinah CC (Course No. 1) (R., 1969); Mount Hawley CC, Peoria (R., 1981), with Roger Packard; Naperville CC (R., 1982); North Shore CC, Glenview (R., 1969); Northmoor CC, Highland Park (R., 1965); Olympia Fields CC (North Course) (R., 1982); Olympia Fields CC (South Course) (R., 1982); Pontiac Elks GC (A.9); Ridgemoor CC, Harwood Heights (R., 1967); Ridgemoor CC, Harwood Heights (R., 1976), with Roger Packard; River Forest CC, Elmhurst (R., 1968); Riverside GC, North Riverside (R., 1977); Ruth Lake CC, Hinsdale (R., 1961); Ruth Lake CC, Hinsdale (R., 1975), with Roger Packard; Spring Lake CC, Quincy (A.9, 1966); Sunset Hills CC (A.9); Sunset Hills CC, Edwardsville (A.9, 1957), with Brent Wadsworth; Twin Orchards CC (White Course), Long Grove (R., 1966); Woodridge CC, Lisle (R., 1962); Woodruff GC, Joliet (R., 1966).

Indiana: Gary CC, Merrillville (R., 1958), with Brent Wadsworth; Purdue University GC (South Course), West Lafayette (R., 1968).

Iowa: A.H. Blank GC, Des Moines (A.9, 1980), with Roger Packard; Burlington GC (R.9, 1969); Burlington GC (A.9, 1969); Fort Dodge CC (R.9, 1958), with Brent Wadsworth; Waveland GC, Des Moines (R., 1965).

Kentucky: Big Spring CC, Louisville (R., 1964); Cherokee GC, Louisville (R., 1962); Cole Park GC, Campbell (R., 1970); Iroquois GC, Louisville (A.9, 1963); Seneca Muni, Louisville (R., 1962); Standard CC, Louisville (A.9, 1964).

Michigan: Cascade Hills CC, Grand Rapids (R., 1967); CC of Lansing (R., 1968); CC of Lansing (R., 1977), with Roger Packard; Lochmoor C, Grosse Pointe Woods (R., 1960); Midland CC (R., 1965); Midland CC (R., 1970); Pine Grove CC, Iron Mountain (A.9, 1962); Western G&CC, Redford (R., 1961).

Minnesota: Columbia Park Muni, Minneapolis (R., 1965); Theodore Wirth GC, Minneapolis (A.9, 1970); Westfield CC, Winona (R., 1960), with Brent Wadsworth.

Missouri: Cape Girardeau CC (A.2, 1957), with Brent Wadsworth; Cape Girardeau CC (R.2, 1957), with Brent Wadsworth; Columbia CC (R., 1970); Jefferson City CC (A.9, 1964); Jefferson City CC (R., 1968); Sunset CC, St. Louis (R., 1962).

New York: Wayne CC, Lyons (A.9, 1965).

Ohio: Canton Park District GC, Canton (A.9, 1975); Fairlawn CC, Akron (R., 1960); Fremont CC (R., 1960); Rosemont GC, Akron (A.9, 1959); Wright-Patterson AFB GC, Dayton (R.9, 1958), with Brent Wadsworth; Wright-Patterson AFB GC, Dayton (A.9, 1958), with Brent Wadsworth.

South Dakota: Minnehaha CC, Sioux Falls (R., 1961).

Wisconsin: Bulls Eye CC, Wisconsin Rapids (A.9, 1963); Chenequa GC, Hartland (A.9, 1963); Lacrosse CC (R., 1970); Merrill Hills CC, Waukesha (R., 1972); Minocqua CC (A.9, 1964); Minocqua CC (R.9, 1964); Muskego Lakes CC, Hales Corner (R., 1980), with Roger Packard; Racine CC (R., 1977), with Roger Packard; Stevens Point CC (R., 1975); Watertown CC (A.9, 1961), with Brent Wadsworth.

Roger Bruce Packard (1947 -) ASGCA

Born: Chicago, Illinois.

Roger Packard graduated from Colorado State University with a degree in Landscape Architecture. As an undergraduate, he worked summers in course construction for The Wadsworth Company of Plainfield, Ill., and upon graduation joined his father's golf course design firm. He took an active role in all Packard's designs and gradually took over major responsibility for the firm. After his father went into semi-retirement, Roger designed several notable layouts, including Sweetwater CC in Texas (the first championship layout designed primarily for women and home of the LPGA) and Eagle Ridge South in Galena, Ill., a co-recipient of Golf Digest's Best New Resort Course Award in 1984.

Courses by: Roger Packard

Florida: Countryside CC, Clearwater (27, 1973), with Edward Lawrence Packard; Hilaman Park GC, Tallahassee (1972), with Edward Lawrence Packard; Innisbrook GC (Copperhead Course), Tarpon Springs (27, 1974), with Edward Lawrence Packard; Innisbrook GC (Sandpiper Course), Tarpon Springs (1972), with Edward Lawrence Packard.

Illinois: Boughton Ridge GC, Bollingbrook (Precision, 9, 1981); Cantigny GC, Wheaton (27, 1987); Crestwicke CC, Bloomington (1972), with Edward Lawrence Packard; Deer Creek GC, Park Forest (1974), with Edward Lawrence Packard; Eagle Ridge GC (North Course), Galena (1977); Eagle Ridge GC (South Course), Galena (1984); Kellogg GC, Peoria (27, 1974), with Edward Lawrence Packard; Lake Barrington Shores GC, Barrington (1977); Lick Creek GC, Pekin (1972), with Edward Lawrence Packard; Mission Hills CC, Northbrook (1975), with Edward Lawrence Packard; Oak Brook GC (1982); Rend Lake GC, Benton (27, 1974), with Edward Lawrence Packard; Springbrook GC, Naperville (1973), with Edward Lawrence Packard; Turnberry CC, Crystal Lake (1972), with Edward Lawrence Packard.

Indiana: Briar Ridge CC, Dyer (1981); Crooked Creek CC (1980).

Kansas: Sunflower Hills GC, Bonner Springs (1977).

Missouri: Crescent CC (1979).

Texas: Oakmont CC, Corinth (1987); Riverside C, Grand Prairie (1984); Sweetwater CC, Sugarland (27, 1983).

Wisconsin: Chaska GC, Greenville (1975), with Edward Lawrence Packard; Mascoutin GC, Berlin (1973), with Edward Lawrence Packard; Rivers Bend GC, Germantown (Precision, 9, 1983); Timber Ridge CC, Minocquo (1976).

South Korea: Bomun Lake GC, Kyongju (1978), with Edward Lawrence Packard.

Venezuela: El Morro GC, Puerto La Cruz (1984), with Edward Lawrence Packard.

Courses Remodeled & Added to by: Roger Packard

Illinois: Barrington Hills CC, Barrington (R., 1982); Brookhill GC, Rantoul (A.9, 1977); Brookwood CC, Addison (R., 1976), with Edward Lawrence Packard; Bryn Mawr GC, Lincolnwood (A., 1985); CC of Decatur (R., 1982), with Edward Lawrence Packard; Hinsdale GC (R., 1975), with Edward Lawrence Packard; Knollwood C, Lake Forest (R., 1975), with Edward Lawrence Packard; Knollwood C, Lake Forest (R., 1982); La Grange CC (R., 1980); Mattoon G&CC, 10590 (A.9, 1971), with Edward Lawrence Packard; Medinah CC (Course No. 3) (A.2, 1986); Mount Hawley CC, Peoria (R., 1981), with Edward Lawrence Packard; North Shore CC, Glenview (R., 1982); Olympia Fields CC (North Course) (R.3, 1984); Ridgemoor CC, Harwood Heights (R., 1976), with Edward Lawrence Packard; Ruth Lake CC, Hinsdale (R., 1975), with Edward Lawrence Packard; Shady Lawn GC, Beecher (R., 1979); Short Hills CC, East Moline (R., 1982).

Indiana: Clearcrest CC, Evansville (A.9, 1982).

Iowa: A.H. Blank GC, Des Moines (A.9, 1980), with Edward Lawrence Packard; Dubuque G&CC (R.9, 1979); Hyperion Field C, Grimes (R., 1976).

Michigan: CC of Lansing (R., 1977), with Edward Lawrence Packard; Riverside CC, Menominee (R.9, 1982); Riverside CC, Menominee (A.9, 1982).

Missouri: Columbia CC (A.9, 1986).

Wisconsin: Big Foot CC, Fontana (R., 1981); Muskego Lakes CC, Hales Corner (R., 1980), with Edward Lawrence Packard; Racine CC (R., 1977), with Edward Lawrence Packard; West Bend CC (R., 1981).

Harold D. Paddock Sr. (1888 - 1969)

Born: San Diego, California. Died: Aurora, Ohio at age 81.

Professional golfer Harold Paddock owned and operated Moreland Hills CC and Aurora CC in Cleveland, Ohio. He began designing courses in the 1920s and reactivated his practice in the 1950s, doing a number of courses in the Cleveland area. Paddock's son, Harold Jr., was a fine amateur golfer and later served as professional at Moreland Hills.

Courses by: Harold Paddock

Michigan: Demor Hills CC, Morenci (1963).

Missouri: Westwood CC, St. Louis (1928).

Ohio: Astorhurst CC, Bedford; Avon Oaks CC; Breathnach CC, Akron; Bryan CC; Butternut Ridge CC, North Olmstead (1929); Cherry Ridge GC, Elyria; Chestnut Hill CC, Ravenna (9); Chuckie Creek CC, Bowling Green (1959); Columbia Hills CC, Columbia Station (1928); CC of Hudson; Grantwood CC, Solon; Griffiths Park GC, Akron; Hawthorne Hills CC, Lima (27, 1963); Highland Springs CC; Hinckley Hills GC, Hinckley (1964); Homelinks GC, Olmstead Falls; Ironton CC (9, 1951); Mercer County Elks CC, Celina (1960); Par Three GC, North Olmstead (Par 3,); Pine Hills GC, Cleveland (27, 1958); Pine Ridge CC, Cleveland; Spring Valley CC, Elyria (1928); Sugarbush CC, Garrettsville (1965); Valleaire GC, Hinckley; Valley View GC, Lancaster (1956); Willard CC (1959).

Courses Remodeled & Added to by: Harold Paddock

Florida: Mount Dora GC (R.9, 1959); Mount Dora GC (A.9, 1959).

Michigan: Hillsdale G&CC (A.9, 1927); Hillsdale G&CC (R.9, 1927).

Arnold Daniel Palmer (1929 -)

Born: Latrobe, Pennsylvania.

Arnold Palmer, son of the pro/greenkeeper at Latrobe CC, won four Masters, two British Opens, one U.S. Open and one U.S. Amateur as well as the hearts of millions of fans. He also became the first golfer to win a million dollars on the PGA Tour. He was generally credited with being a major force in the golf boom of the 1960s through his charismatic appearance and dashing devil-may-care style of play.

In the late Sixties, Palmer purchased Bay Hill CC in Orlando, Fla., and over the years remodeled many of its holes. Palmer worked as a design consultant with golf architect Francis Duane from 1969 to 1974. He then became associated with architect Edwin Seay, founding the Palmer Course Design Co. with offices in Florida and Ohio. While continuing to play on the PGA Tour and later the PGA Senior Tour, Palmer left most design activities to the professional architects in his firm.

In 1984 Palmer's company built the first golf course ever opened in Communist China.

Courses by: Arnold Palmer

Arizona: Arrowhead CC (North Course), Glendale (1985), with Ed Seay and Harrison Minchew; Arrowhead CC (South Course), Glendale (1986), with Ed Seay and Harrison Minchew; Mesa Del Sol CC (Blue Course), Yuma (1982), with Ed Seay; Mesa Del Sol CC (White Course), Yuma (1982), with Ed Seay.

California: Half Moon Bay CC (1973), with Frank Duane; Ironwood CC (Short Course), Palm Desert (Par 3, 9, 1975), with Ed Seay; Mission Hills G&CC (New Course), Rancho Mirage (1979), with Ed Seay; Pacific Rim GC (1987), with Ed Seay; PGA West GC (Palmer Course), La Quinta (1986), with Ed Seay and Harrison Minchew.

Colorado: Bear Creek GC, Golden (1986), with Ed Seay; Broadmoor GC (South Course), Colorado Springs (1976), with Ed Seay; Lone Tree GC, Littleton (1986), with Ed Seay.

Florida: Adios CC, Deerfield Beach (1985), with Ed Seay; Grenelefe G&RC (East Course), Haines City (1977), with Ed Seay and Bob Walker; Isleworth G&CC, Windermere (1986), with Ed Seay; Mariner Sands GC (Green Course), Stuart (1973), with Frank Duane; Marsh Landing CC, Ponte Vedra (1986), with Ed Seay and

Harrison Minchew; Matanzas Woods GC, Palm Coast (1986), with Ed Seay and Bob Walker; Monarch CC (1987), with Ed Seay and Harrison Minchew; Pine Lakes GC, Palm Coast (1980), with Ed Seay and Bob Walker; Plantation at Ponte Vedra GC (1987), with Ed Seay and Harrison Minchew; PGA National GC (The General Course), Palm Beach Gardens (1985), with Ed Seay; Saddlebrook G&TC (Palmer Course) (1986), with Ed Seay and Bob Walker; Spessard Holland GC, Melbourne (Precision, 1977), with Ed Seay; Suntree CC (South Course), Melbourne (1987), with Ed Seay; Wildcat Run CC, Estero (1985), with Ed Seay.

Georgia: Landings at Skidaway Island (Magnolia) (1973), with Frank Duane; Landings at Skidaway Island (Marshwood) (1979), with Ed Seay; Whitewater Creek CC (1987), with Ed Seay.

Hawaii: Honolulu International CC (1976), with Frank Duane; Kapalua GC (Bay Course), Maui (1976), with Frank Duane; Kapalua GC (Village Course) (1980), with Ed Seay; Turtle Bay GC (New Course), Kahuku, Oahu (1987), with Ed Seay.

Louisiana: Bluffs CC (1987), with Ed Seay and Harrison Minchew; Frenchman's Bend CC (1987), with Ed Seay.

Maryland: Prince Georges G&CC, Mitchellville (1981), with Ed Seay and Bob Walker.

Michigan: Shanty Creek GC (Legend Course) (1985), with Ed Seay and Bob Walker.

Montana: Big Sky GC (1974), with Frank Duane.

North Carolina: TPC at Piper Glen, Charlotte (1987), with Ed Seay and Harrison Minchew.

Ohio: Winberie GC, Port Clinton (1987), with Ed Seay.

South Carolina: Myrtle Beach National GC (North Course) (1973), with Frank Duane; Myrtle Beach National GC (South Course) (1973), with Frank Duane; Myrtle Beach National GC (West Course) (1973), with Frank Duane; Sea Pines Plantation GC (Club Course), Hilton Head Island (1976), with Frank Duane.

Texas: Golf Club at Fossil Creek, Fort Worth (1986), with Ed Seay; Hidden Hills GC, Austin (1986), with Ed Seay.

Utah: Jeremy Ranch GC, Park City (1980), with Ed Seay.

Virginia: Albermarle Farms GC (1986), with Ed Seay; Kingsmill GC (Plantation Course), Williamsburg (1986), with Ed Seay.

Washington: Semiahmoo GC, Everett (1986), with Ed Seay and Harrison Minchew.

Wyoming: Teton Pines GC (1986), with Ed Seay.

British Columbia: Whistler Village GC (1980), with Ed Seay and Bob Walker.

China: Chung-Shan GC (1985), with Ed Seay and Bob Walker.

Ireland: Tralee GC, County Kerry (1985), with Ed Seay.

Italy: Ca' Della Nave GC (1987), with Ed Seay.

Japan: Furano CC (1975), with Ed Seay; Iga Ueno CC (1974), with Ed Seay; Manago CC (1974), with Ed Seay; Minakami Kogen GC (Lower Course) (1986), with Ed Seay and Bob Walker; Minakami Kogen GC (Upper Course) (1986), with Ed Seay and Bob Walker; Niseko GC, Sapporo (1986), with Ed Seay and Bob Walker; Niseko Kogen GC, Sapporo (1986), with Ed Seay and Bob Walker; Nishi Biwako GC, with Ed Seay; Shimotsuke CC (1975), with Ed Seay; Tsugaru Kogen GC, Amori (1986), with Ed Seay and Bob Walker.

Mexico: Nuevo Vallarta GC (27, 1980), with Ed Seay and Bob Walker.

New Zealand: Walter Peak Resort GC (1987), with Ed Seay.

Taiwan: Formosa G&CC (1987), with Ed Seay.

Thailand: Bangpoo GC (1981), with Ed Seay.

Courses Remodeled & Added to by: Arnold Palmer

Arizona: Scottsdale CC (R., 1986), with Ed Seay and Bob Walker; Scottsdale CC (A.9, 1986).

Colorado: Cherry Hills CC, Englewood (R., 1977), with Ed Seay; Snowmass GC, Snowmass-at-Aspen (R., 1982), with Ed Seay.

Florida: Bay Hill C, Orlando (R.); Hidden Hills CC, Jacksonville (R., 1986), with Ed Seay and Bob Walker; Sawgrass GC (Oceanside Course), Ponte Vedra Beach (A.9, 1985), with Ed Seay, Bob Walker and Harrison Minchew; TPC at Monte Carlo, Fort Pierce (R., 1987), with Ed Seay.

Georgia: Forest Hill GC, Augusta (R., 1986), with Ed Seay and Harrison Minchew.

North Carolina: Quail Hollow CC, Charlotte (R., 1985), with Ed Seay.

Pennsylvania: Indian Lake GC, Central City (A.9, 1968), with X.G. Hassenplug; Oakmont CC (R., 1978), with Ed Seay.

Virginia: Keswick C of Virginia (R., 1987), with Ed Seay.

Gary A. Panks (1941 -)
Born: Flint, Michigan.

Gary Panks was the son of a golf professional at Sault St. Marie CC. In 1964 he received a B.S. Degree in Landscape Architecture from Michigan State University, where he played on the golf team and served as its captain in 1963. By 1980 he had won sixteen amateur tournaments.

Panks worked for a short time as assistant superintendent at Michigan State University GC and then held successive positions as a landscape architect or planning consultant with New York State Roadside Development, the Maricopa County (Ariz.) Park Department, the Bureau of Indian Affairs, rhw Department of the Interior and the City of Phoenix Parks Department. In 1971 he entered private practice as a golf course and landscape architect under the firm name of Gary Panks Associates. Among his early works was a clever 18 hole putting course for Desert Highlands GC, patterned after the huge practice putting surface at St. Andrews.

Courses by: Gary Panks

Arizona: Ahwatukee Lakes CC, Phoenix (Precision, 1980); Dave White Muni, Casa Grande (9); Ridge GC, Sedona (1986); Riverview GC, Mesa; Rolling Hills GC, Tempe (Precision, 1985); Silver Creek GC, White Mountain Lakes (1985); Sunbird GC, Chandler (1987); Tonto Vista CC, Rio Verde (Precision,).

New Mexico: Tierra del Sol GC.

Courses Remodeled & Added to by: Gary Panks

Arizona: Arizona CC, Phoenix (R.); Encanto Muni, Phoenix (R.); Fort Huachuca GC (A.9, 1971), with Milt Coggins; Orange Tree GC, Scottsdale (R.); Paradise Valley CC, Scottsdale (R., 1984), with Geoffrey S. Cornish; Phoenix CC (R.14, 1982); Pinetop CC (R., 1983); Rolling Hills GC, Tempe (A.9, 1985).

Arkansas: Red Apple Inn GC, Heber Springs (R.9, 1981); Red Apple Inn GC, Heber Springs (A.9, 1981).

British Columbia: Victoria GC, Oak Bay (R., 1981).

Mungo Park (1835 - 1904)
Born: Musselburgh, Scotland. Died: Silloth, England at age 69.

One of five sons and brother of Old Willie Park, Mungo Park learned golf at an early age but abandoned it for a period of twenty years while he worked as a seaman. Returning to Musselburgh in the early 1870s, he found his golfing skills were unaffected by the long layoff, and he won the 1874 British Open on the course where he'd been taught the game.

Mungo Park spent the remainder of his life serving as a clubmaker and teacher at various British clubs. He laid out several golf courses during this time, including Alnmouth, where he remained after its opening as its first professional.

Courses by: Mungo Park

England: Alnmouth GC, Northumberland (1896).

Courses Remodeled & Added to by: Mungo Park

Scotland: Bruntsfield Links, Davidson's Main (NLE, R., 1898), with Willie Park.

Willie Park Sr. (1833 - 1903)
Born: Musselburgh, Scotland. Died: Musselburgh, Scotland at age 70.

Old Willie Park won the first British Open at Prestwick in 1860 as well as three subsequent Opens. Old Willie Sr. was involved in laying out golf courses on his own, with his brother Mungo, and with son Willie Jr. It was difficult to distinguish between the work of Willie Park Sr. and the earliest courses of his son.

Courses by: Willie Park

England: Berwick-upon-Tweed GC, Northumberland (1892); Headingley GC, Leeds (1892); Hendon GC, Middlesex (1900), with Willie Park Jr; Muswell Hill GC, London (1893); Newbiggin-by-the-Sea GC, Northumberland (1885); Silloth-on-Solway GC, Cumbria (1894), with Willie Park Jr; Sundridge Park GC (East Course), Kent (1901), with Willie Park Jr; Sundridge Park GC (West Course), Kent (1901), with Willie Park Jr; West Middlesex GC, Middlesex (1891).

Ireland: Killarney GC, County Kerry (NLE, 9, 1883); Tramore GC, County Waterford (1894), with Willie Park Jr.

Northern Ireland: Larne GC, County Antrim (9, 1894); Portstewart GC, County Londonderry (1889).

Scotland: Baberton GC, Edinburgh (1893); Bathgate GC, East Lothian (1892); Biggar GC, Lanarkshire (1895); Crieff GC, Perthshire (1891); Duddington GC, Edinburgh (1897), with Willie Park Jr; Glencorse GC, Midlothian (1890); Grantown GC, Morayshire (1890); Gullane GC (Course No. 1), East Lothian (1882); Innellan GC, Argyllshire (9, 1895), with Willie Park Jr; Innerleithen GC, Peebleshire (9, 1886); Jedburgh GC, Roxburghshire (9, 1892); Lauder GC, Berwickshire (1896), with Willie Park Jr; Melrose GC, Roxburghshire (9, 1889); Murrayfield GC, Edinburgh (1896), with Willie Park Jr; Selkirk GC, Selkirkshire (9, 1883); Shiskine GC, Isle of Arran (12, 1896); St. Boswells GC, Roxburghshire (9, 1890); Torwoodlee GC, Selkirkshire (9, 1895), with Willie Park Jr; West Lothian GC, Bo'ness (1892); Western Gailes GC, Ayrshire (1897), with Willie Park Jr.

Courses Remodeled & Added to by: Willie Park

England: Berkhampsted GC, Hertfordshire (R., 1900), with Willie Park Jr; Broadstone GC, Dorset (R., 1898), with Willie Park Jr; Frinton GC, Frinton-on-Sea (R.), with Willie Park Jr.

Scotland: Bruntsfield Links, Davidson's Main (NLE, R., 1898), with Mungo Park; Forres GC, Morayshire (R.).

John A. "Jack" Park (1879 - 1935)
Born: Musselburgh, Scotland. Died: East Hampton, New York at age 56.

Jack Park supervised construction at the Maidstone (N.Y.) CC in 1898 and then worked with his brother Willie Jr. in Britain and another brother Mungo II in Argentina before returning to Maidstone to become its professional in 1915. He also assisted Willie in building courses following the latter's return to North America in 1916.

Mungo Park II (1877 - 1960)
Born: Musselburgh, Scotland. Died: Musselburgh, Scotland at age 83.

Mungo Park II, son of Old Willie Park and named for his uncle, served as professional at Dyker Meadow GC in New York and Galveston CC in Texas around the turn of the century. Between 1901 and 1904 he returned to England and worked as director of the Chiltern Estates, where his brother Willie was managing director.

From 1904 to 1913 Mungo was employed as a club professional in Argentina, where he planned several golf courses. Following service with the British Army during World War I, he returned to Argentina and laid out more layouts, including Adolfo Siro GC for the Swift family of meat packing fame. Altogether, he claimed some fifty-nine courses of his own design in that country.

Mungo moved to the United States from Argentina in 1924 to escort his brother Willie Jr., then fatally ill, home to Scotland. In 1925 he returned to the United States, completed Willie's unfinished courses and laid out a couple of his own. After that, Mungo filled a number of professional berths in the East and in the Southwest. He returned to Scotland permanently in the 1930s and planned several changes at Musselburgh.

Courses by: Mungo Park II

New York: Hollow Brook G&CC, Peekskill; Port-Au-Peck GC.

Argentina: Adolfo Siro GC; San Andres GC, San Martin .

Courses Remodeled & Added to by: Mungo Park II

Scotland: Royal Musselburgh GC, East Lothian (R., 1933).

Willie Park Jr. (1864 - 1925)
Born: Musselburgh, Scotland. Died: Edinburgh, Scotland at age 61.

The name of Willie Park Jr. is one of the most respected in the history of golf. He was a multi-faceted personality, a talented and prolific golf architect, one of the greatest golfers of his day, an entrepreneur and businessman, a club maker, inventor and author. A big man physically, his influence of the game of golf was equally imposing.

As a boy, Willie often played golf at Musselburgh with Young Willie Dunn, who was also destined to make his mark on the history of course architecture. From 1880 to 1894 Park served as assistant pro/greenkeeper under his uncle Mungo at Ryton in England. He then returned to Musselburgh, joining his father in the club and ballmaking firm of W. Park and Son. Continuing to refine his golf game, he won the British Open in 1887 and 1889, and was runner-up in 1898.

Willie was a perfectionist. He believed that matches were settled by putting and would spend twelve hours without a break on a practice green. He brought the same intensity to his design work. He laid out links and courses with his father and uncle, and later on his own with construction assistance from brothers Mungo II and Jack. Two of Park's courses, Sunningdale GC and Huntercombe GC, became landmarks in the history of course architecture. Huntercombe, of which Willie was a major stockholder and promoter, was among the first golf courses planned specifically for integration with housing, though the housing scheme was never executed and the project turned out to be a financial problem for Willie for many years.

Willie first traveled to the United States in 1895 and worked there until 1898, promoting golf and laying out some courses. When he returned to North America in 1916 (where he remained, except for a few visits home, until 1924), he was inundated with requests to design and redesign courses. He undertook a prodigious number, claiming seventy courses in North America in the years following World War I. He maintained several offices in the U.S. and Canada, was assisted by a loyal crew of construction bosses and personally visited nearly all of his courses periodically during construction.

In the course of his indefatigable career, Willie also found time to write two books; *The Game of Golf* (1896) and *The Art of Putting* (1920). Part of each was autobiographical. He was stricken with a fatal illness in 1924 and made one last journey home to Scotland, where he died in 1925. But his brilliant legacy survived. Sir Guy Campbell called him the "doyen" of course architects and credited him with setting the standards adhered to by the countless designers who followed. Willie Park Jr. was surely one of the virtuoso golf architects.

Courses by: Willie Park Jr
Arkansas: Hot Springs G&CC (Majestic Course) (1920).
Connecticut: CC of Farmington; CC of New Canaan (9); Madison CC (1909); New Haven CC; Shuttle Meadow CC, New Britain (1916); Tumble Brook CC, Bloomfield (9); Woodway CC, Darien (1916).
Florida: Alton Beach GC, Miami (NLE,).
Illinois: Olympia Fields CC (North Course) (1932).
Indiana: Highland G&CC, Indianapolis (1921), with William H. Diddel.
Maine: Castine GC.
Maryland: Rolling Road GC, Baltimore (1921).
Massachusetts: CC of New Bedford (1902); Fall River CC (9); Milton-Hoosic GC, Canton .
Michigan: Battle Creek CC; Flint GC (1917); Grand Rapids CC; Meadowbrook CC, Detroit; Pine Lake CC, Orchard Lake; Red Run GC, Royal Oak .
New Jersey: Glen Ridge GC; Ocean City CC (NLE,).
New York: Moonbrook CC, Jamestown (9, 1919); St. Albans CC.
North Carolina: Grove Park Inn CC, Asheville (1909).
Ohio: Congress Lake C, Hartville; CC of Ashland; East Liverpool CC (9, 1920); Sylvania CC, Toledo (1917); Toledo CC.
Pennsylvania: Berkshire CC, Reading; Chartiers CC, Pittsburgh (1919); Green Valley CC, Roxborough (NLE,); Indiana CC (NLE, 1919); Penn State Univ GC (Blue Course), State College (1921); Philmont CC (South Course), Philadelphia (1907); Youghiogheny CC, McKeesport .
Rhode Island: Agawam Hunt C, Providence; Pawtucket GC.
Vermont: St. Johnsbury CC (9, 1923).
Alberta: Bowness GC, Calgary; Calgary G&CC (1911); Calgary St. Andrews GC; St. Andrews GC, Calgary .
Manitoba: Winnepeg GC; Winnepeg Hunt C.
Nova Scotia: Brightwood G&CC, Dartmouth; Kentville GC.
Ontario: Abitibi GC, Iroquois Falls; Ottawa Hunt & GC; Toronto Hunt C; Weston G&CC, Toronto (1920).
Quebec: Beaconsfield G&CC, Montreal; Islesmere G&CC; Mount Bruno GC, Montreal (1918); Royal Montreal GC (North Course), Dixie (NLE, 1922); Royal Quebec CC (Royal Course), Boischatel (9, 1925); Senneville CC, Montreal (1919); Summerlea GC, Montreal (NLE, 27); Whitlock G&CC, Hudson Heights (1912).
Austria: Vienna GC; Wien GC, Vienna (1901).
Belgium: Koninklijke GC, Ostend; Royal Antwerp GC, Kapellenbos (1910).
England: Acton GC; Alton GC, Hampshire (1908); Barnton GC; Cooden Beach GC, Sussex (1912); Coombe Hill GC (1909), with J.F. Abercromby; Formby GC; Gog Magog GC, Cambridgeshire (1901); Hartepool CC, Durham (1906); Hendon GC, Middlesex (1900), with Willie Park; Huntercombe GC, Oxfordshire (1901); Knebworth GC, Hertfordshire (1908); Mid Kent GC, Gravesend (1909); Notts GC, Nottinghamshire (1900); Parkstone GC, Dorset (1910); Richmond Park GC, London (NLE.); Sheerness GC, Kent (9, 1906); Shooter's Hill GC, London (1903); Silloth-on-Solway GC, Cumbria (1894), with Willie Park; South Herts GC, London (1899); Stoneham GC, Hampshire (1908); Sudbury GC, Middlesex (1920); Sundridge Park GC (East Course), Kent (1901), with Willie Park; Sundridge Park GC (West Course), Kent (1901), with Willie Park; Sunningdale GC (Old Course), Berkshire (1901); Temple GC, Berkshire (1909), with J. Hepburn; Tynemouth GC, Northumberland (1913); Wembley GC; Wimbledon Common GC, London (1908).
France: Club de Rouen; Costebelle Golf Links, Hyeres; Golf de Dieppe; Royal G d'Evian, Evian (1905).
Ireland: Tramore GC, County Waterford (1894), with Willie Park; Waterford GC, County Waterford (9, 1912).
Monaco: Monte Carlo CC (1910).
Northern Ireland: City of Derry GC, Londonderry (1913).
Scotland: Ashludie GC, Angus; Bruntsfield Links, Davidson's Main (1923); Duddington GC, Edinburgh (1897), with Willie Park; Gullane GC (Course No. 2), East Lothian; Gullane GC (Course No. 3), East Lothian; Innellan GC, Argyllshire (9, 1895), with Willie Park; Lauder GC, Berwickshire (1896), with Willie Park; Murrayfield GC, Edinburgh (1896), with Willie Park; Old Ranfurly GC, Renfrewshire (1905); Torwoodlee GC, Selkirkshire (9, 1895), with Willie Park; Totteridge GC;

Western Gailes GC, Ayrshire (1897), with Willie Park.
Wales: Brynhill GC, Glamorganshire (1920); Glamorganshire GC.

Courses Remodeled & Added to by: Willie Park Jr
New Jersey: Atlantic City CC (NLE, A.13); Atlantic City CC (NLE, R.); Cherry Valley CC (R.).
New York: Maidstone C, East Hampton (A.9, 1899), with John A.Park; Maidstone C, East Hampton (R.11, 1925), with John A.Park.
Pennsylvania: Pittsburgh Field C (NLE, A.2, 1923); Pittsburgh Field C (NLE, R., 1923).
Quebec: Royal Montreal GC (South Course), Dixie (NLE, R., 1922).
England: Aldeburgh GC, Suffolk (R.); Berkhampsted GC, Hertfordshire (R., 1900), with Willie Park; Brighton and Hove GC, Sussex (R.); Broadstone GC, Dorset (R., 1898), with Willie Park; Burhill GC, Surrey (R.9); Chiselhurst GC, Kent (R., 1894); Frinton GC, Frinton-on-Sea (R.), with Willie Park; Maidenhead GC (R.); Northampton GC, Northamptonshire (R.); Nottingham City GC (R., 1910); Richmond GC (R.); Seaford GC, Sussex (R., 1906); Tooting Bec C (R.); Worplesdon GC, Surrey (R.), with J.F. Abercromby.
France: Dinard GC (R.); Racing C de France (Valley), La Boulie (R.).
Scotland: Burntisland Golf House C , Fife (R.); Carnoustie GC, Angus (R.); Glasgow Killermont GC, Glasgow (R.); Gullane GC (Course No. 1), East Lothian (R.); Kilspindle GC, East Lothian (R.); Luffness New GC, East Lothian (R.); Monifieth GC, Angus (R.); Montrose GC (Bloomfield Course), Angus (R.); Montrose GC (Medal Course), Angus (R.); Royal Burgess G Society of Edinburgh (R., 1905); Turnhouse GC, Edinburgh (R.).
Wales: Brynhill GC, Glamorganshire (R.); Southerndown GC, Glamorgan (R.).

Damian Pascuzzo (1959 -) ASGCA
Born: Pottsville, Pennsylvania.
Damian Pascuzzo graduated from California Polytechnic State University in San Luis Obispo in 1981, receiving a Bachelor's degree in Landscape Architecture. Upon graduation, he joined the golf design firm of Robert Muir Graves of Walnut Creek, California.

Courses by: Damian Pascuzzo
California: La Purisima GC, Lompoc (1986), with Robert Muir Graves; Santa Clara Muni (1986), with Robert Muir Graves.
Oregon: Paradise Inn Ranch GC, Grants Pass (1987), with Robert Muir Graves.
Washington: Centerwood CC, Gig Harbor (1986), with Robert Muir Graves; Spokane County GC, Spokane (1987), with Robert Muir Graves.

Courses Remodeled & Added to by: Damian Pascuzzo
California: Del Paso CC (R., 1985), with Robert Muir Graves; El Macero CC (R., 1985), with Robert Muir Graves; North Ridge CC, Sacremento (R., 1986), with Robert Muir Graves; Sandpiper G Links, Goleta (R., 1986), with Robert Muir Graves; Twin Lakes GC, Goleta (R., 1985), with Robert Muir Graves; Woodbridge G&CC, Lodi (R., 1985), with Robert Muir Graves.
Oregon: Michelbook CC, McMinnville (A.9, 1984), with Robert Muir Graves.
Washington: Lake Wilderness CC, Maple Valley (R., 1986), with Robert Muir Graves; Overlake G&CC, Medina (R., 1986), with Robert Muir Graves.

George A. "Pat" Pattison Jr.
Pat Pattison worked as pro/superintendent at Buckhannon (W.Va.) CC in the early 1950s. Upon moving to Florida at the end of the decade, he supervised construction of several courses and went on to form his own design and construction firm in Fort Lauderdale.

Courses by: Pat Pattison
Florida: Cooper Colony CC, Hollywood (Precision, 1959); Crystal Lake CC, Pompano Beach (1969); Hidden Valley GC, Boca Raton (Par 3, 1957); Whispering Lakes GC, Pompano Beach (Par 3, 1963).

Stanley F. Pelchar
Stanley Pelchar was active as a course designer in the 1920s, forming the Chicago firm of United States Architects Inc. with landscape architect Otto Clauss and engineer James Prendergast. In the 1950s Pelchar served as club manager at Biltmore CC in Barrington, Illinois.

Courses by: Stanley Pelchar
Illinois: Arrowhead GC {formerly Antlers CC}, Wheaton; Burnham Woods GC (1923); Garden of Eden GC, Momence (9); Lake Anna CC, Palos Park (NLE,); Walnut Hills GC, Chicago (9); Women's CC, Waukegan (NLE,).
Indiana: Indian Ridge GC, Hobart (1926); Surprise Park GC, Cedar Lake (9).
Wisconsin: Beloit CC; Four Seasons GC, Pembine (9); Krueger Muni, Beloit; Oneida G & Riding C, Green Bay (1928); Turtle Lake GC, Winchester .

John Jacob Frank Pennink (1913 - 1983) BAGCA
Born: Delft, The Netherlands. Died: Reading, England at age 70.
Frank Pennink attended Tonbridge School and Magdalen College of Oxford University. An excellent golfer, he won the English Amateur in 1937 and '38, the Royal St. Georges Challenge Cup in 1938, the Boy's International in 1930 and many other amateur tournaments. He was also a member of the 1938 Walker Cup team and was on English international teams for several years, first as a player and later as a nonplaying captain. He authored three books, *Home of Sports - Golf, Golfer's Companion* and *Frank Pennink's Choice of Golf Courses*.
In 1954 Pennink joined the established course design practice of C.K. Cotton. He eventually headed the firm that came to be known as Cotton (C.K.), Pennink, Lawrie and Partners Ltd. He was the most active designer in the firm, handling courses in Britain, the Continent, Africa and even the Far East. He was a founding member of the BAGCA and served for a time as its President.

Courses by: J.J.F. Pennink
Bangladesh: Dacca GC.
Channel Islands: Alderney GC (1970).
Czechoslovakia: Sklo Bohemia Podebrady GC (9, 1967).
Denmark: Kokkedal GC, Rungsted (1971); St. Knuds GC (1954), with C.K. Cotton.

England: Abbey Hill GC, Buckinghamshire (1975), with C.D. Lawrie; Barnham Broom GC, Norwich (1977); Basildon GC, Essex (1967); Bedlingtonshire GC, Northumberland (1972); Billingham GC, Durham (1968); Blackhill Wood GC, Staffordshire , with D.M.A.Steel; Brandon Wood GC, Coventry (1977); Brickendon Grange G&CC (1964), with C.K. Cotton; Broome Park GC, Kent (1981), with D.M.A.Steel; Bushey G & Squash C, Hertfordshire (9, 1980), with D.M.A.Steel; Crookhill Park GC, Yorkshire (1973); Edwalton GC, Nottinghamshire (27, 1981); Eton College GC, Windsor (Precision, 9, 1973); Fakenham GC, Norfolk (9, 1973), with C.D. Lawrie; Farnham Park GC, Stoke Poges (9, 1974), with D.M.A.Steel; Fleming Park GC, Hampshire (Precision, 1973); Halifax Bradley Hall GC, Yorkshire , with D.M.A.Steel; Harrow School GC, Middlesex (Precision, 9, 1978), with D.M.A.Steel; Hastings GC, Sussex; Hawkhurst G & CC, Kent (Precision, 9, 1968); Immingham GC, Lincolnshire (1975); Ingol G &Squash C, Lancashire (1984), with D.M.A.Steel; Lamberhurst GC, with C.K. Cotton; Lee Park GC, Liverpool (1954), with C.K. Cotton; Lowestoft GC; Oxton GC, Nottinghamshire (1973); Pastures GC, Derbyshire (Precision, 9, 1969); Rookery Park GC, Suffolk , with C.D. Lawrie; Ross on Wye GC (1967), with C.K. Cotton; Royal Lytham & St. Annes GC (Short Crs), Lancashire (Precision,), with C.D. Lawrie; Saunton GC (West Course), Devon (1975); Southwick Park GC (HMS Dryad), Hampshire (1977), with C.D. Lawrie; Stockwood Park GC, Bedfordshire (1973); Stoneyholme GC, Cumbria (1974); Stowe School GC; Stressholme GC, with C.K. Cotton; Tewkesbury Park GC, Gloucestershire (1976); Twickenham GC, Middlesex (9, 1976), with C.D. Lawrie; Walton Hall GC, Cheshire; Warrington GC, Cheshire; Wentworth GC (Short Nine), Surrey (9, 1948), with C.K. Cotton; Winter Hill GC, Berkshire (1976), with C.D. Lawrie; Woburn G&CC (Duchess Course), Buckinghamshire (1976), with C.D. Lawrie and D.M.A.Steel; Woburn G&CC (Duke Course), Buckinghamshire (1974), with C.D. Lawrie.

France: Club du Mans Mulsanne, Le Mans; Golf de Nantes.

Indonesia: Palembang GC, Sumatra .

Italy: Olgiata CC (27, 1961), with C.K. Cotton.

Lebanon: Golf Club of Lebanon, Beirut (9).

Libya: Benghazi GC; Tripoli GC.

Malaysia: Royal Selangor GC (New Course), Kuala Lumpur (1972); Sibu GC, Sarawak .

Morocco: Royal CC de Tangier.

Netherlands: Gelpenberg GC, Zweeloo (9, 1972); Geysteren G&CC, Eindhoven (13, 1974); Golf Club Broekpolder, Vlaardingen (1983); Kleiburg GC, Brielle (9, 1974); Sallandsche GC "De Hock"; Spaarwoude GC, Velsen (1977).

Poland: Jablonna GC, Warsaw (9).

Portugal: Dom Pedro Vilamoura GC (1975); Lisbon CC, Aroeira; Palmares GC, Algarve (1976); Vilamoura GC (1969).

Scotland: Livingston G&CC, Edinburgh (1978), with C.D. Lawrie; Royal Aberdeen GC (Ladies Course) (9); Westhill GC, Aberdeenshire (1977), with C.D. Lawrie.

Singapore: Sentosa Island GC (Sentosa Course); Singapore Island GC (New Course) (1963), with John Harris; Singapore Island GC (Sime Course).

Sweden: Kungsbacka GC (13, 1971); Stannum GC, Grabo .

Wales: Cradoc GC, Powys (1967); Langland Bay GC, West Glamorgan (1982); St. Pierre G&CC (Old Course), Gwent (1962), with C.K. Cotton.

West Germany: Golf Club Nordsec-Kurhof, Wik-Auf-Fuhr (9).

Zambia: Lusaka GC.

Courses Remodeled & Added to by: J.J.F. Pennink

Belgium: Keerbergen GC (R.).

England: Army GC (R., 1965), with C.K. Cotton; Ashbourne GC, Debryshire (R.); Bedale GC, Yorkshire (R.); Blackwell Grange GC, Durham (R.); Bury St. Edmonds GC (R.); Carlisle GC, Cumberland (R.); Chippenham GC, Wiltshire (R.); Corhampton GC, Hampshire (R.9), with C.D. Lawrie; Corhampton GC, Hampshire (A.9); Darlington GC, Durham (R.); Dartford GC, Kent (R.); Doncaster GC, Yorkshire (R.); Ellesmere GC, Lancashire (R.); Frilford Heath GC (Green Course) (R.9, 1968), with C.K. Cotton; Frilford Heath GC (Green Course) (A.9, 1968), with C.K. Cotton; Frilford Heath GC (Red Course) (A.9, 1968), with C.K. Cotton; Frilford Heath GC (Red Course) (R.9, 1968), with C.K. Cotton; Hexham GC (R., 1956), with C.K. Cotton; Louth GC, Lincolnshire (R.), with C.K. Cotton; Mendip GC, Avon (A.9, 1965); North Downs GC, Surrey (R.); Radcliffe on Trent GC, Nottinghamshire (R.); Rochdale GC, Lancashire (R.); Romsey GC, Hampshire (R.), with C.D. Lawrie; Royal Liverpool GC, Hoylake (R., 1966); Royal Lytham & St. Annes GC, Lancashire (R., 1952), with C.K. Cotton; Royal St. George's GC, Kent (R., 1975); Royal Wimbledon GC, Surrey (R.), with C.D. Lawrie; Rushcliffe GC, Nottinghamshire (R.); Rye GC, Deal (A.9); Saunton GC (East Course), Devonshire (R., 1952), with C.K. Cotton; Shifnal GC, Shropshire (R.); Shrewsbury GC, Shropshire (R.); Stocksfield GC, Northumberland (R.); Warrington GC, Cheshire (R.); Wigan GC, Lancashire (R.).

France: Borden G&CC, Amiens (R.9); Borden G&CC, Amiens (R.); Calais GC (R.).

Ireland: Bandon GC, County Cork (R.); Cork GC, County Cork (R., 1975), with C.K. Cotton and C.D. Lawrie.

Italy: Menaggio E. Cadenabbia GC, Milan (A.5); Menaggio E. Cadenabbia GC, Milan (R.).

Netherlands: Lurgan GC, County Armagh (R.); Noordwijkse GC (R.); Rosendaelsche GC, Arnhem (A.9); Rosendaelsche GC, Arnhem (R.9); Sallandsche GC, Diepenveen (R.); Utrecht GC (R.).

Northern Ireland: Castlerock GC, County Londonderry (A.9, 1985); Dunmurry GC (R.); Newtonstewart GC, County Tyrone (R.).

Scotland: Stornoway GC, Isle of Lewis (R.).

Singapore: Singapore Island CC (Island Course) (R., 1965), with C.K. Cotton; Singapore Island GC (Bukit Course) (R.).

Sweden: Halmstad GC (R.); Halmstad GC (A.9).

Switzerland: Breitenloo GC, Zurich (R.).

Wales: Caernarvonshire GC, Conway (R.).

West Germany: Duren GC, Bad Duren (A.9, 1975).

David Pfaff (1939 -   )
Born: Urbana, Ohio.

Son of a high school golf coach, David Pfaff was a fine arts major at Ohio University. He was working as an industrial designer for an aircraft industry when he got word that an old family friend—golf architect Pete Dye—was looking for a draftsman. Pfaff caught up with Dye on Hilton Head Island, S.C. (where Harbour Town was being built), who promptly put him to work drawing plans for several projects.

After working with Pete and his brother Roy for several years, Pfaff was placed in charge of Eagle Creek, a municipal course in Indianapolis. He designed and supervised construction of the layout, which was billed as a Pete Dye design even though Dye had little involvement.

Following work with Pete on the construction of Oak Tree in Oklahoma, the first Landmark Land project, Pfaff joined Landmark as an in-house course architect in the late 1970s. While continuing to work with Dye on some Landmark projects, Pfaff also designed and built several of that company's courses. Those, too, were generally advertised as Pete Dye designs, mainly because Pfaff's works closely resembled that of his mentor.

In the 1980s Pfaff left Landmark and formed his own design business based in Palm Desert, California.

Courses by: David Pfaff
California: Carmel Valley Ranch GC, Carmel (1980), with Pete Dye.

Indiana: Eagle Creek Muni, Indianapolis (27, 1974), with Pete Dye; Harbour Trees GC, Noblesville (1973), with Pete Dye.

Louisiana: Belle Terre CC, LaPlace (1982).

Mississippi: Pine Island GC, Ocean Springs (1974), with Pete Dye.

North Carolina: Oak Hollow, High Point (1972), with Pete Dye.

Richard Morgan Phelps (1937 -   ) ASGCA, President, 1980.
Born: Colorado Springs, Colorado.

Dick Phelps received a Master's in Landscape Architecture from Iowa State University prior to training under golf architect Robert Bruce Harris. In the mid-1960s he entered private practice as a course designer and after a short partnership with landscape architect Donald Brauer of Minnesota, established his own Colorado-based golf design firm. In the mid-1970s he made Brad Benz a partner, and in 1980 Mike Poellot joined the firm. Benz and Poellot left a few years later to form their own company in California, while Phelps remained in Colorado, headquartered in the Denver suburb of Evergreen.

Courses by: Dick Phelps
Arizona: Alta Mesa CC, Mesa (1985).

Colorado: Centennial Downs GC, Littleton (Precision, 9, 1986); Copper Mountain GC (NLE, Precision, 1980), with Brad Benz; Douglas Highlands GC (1987); Eagles Nest GC, Silverthorne (1986); Englewood Muni (1982), with Brad Benz and Mike Poellot; Foothills GC, Lakewood (27, 1971); Greenway Park GC, Broomfield (Par 3, 9, 1972); Heather Gardens CC, Aurora (Precision, 1973); Heather Ridge CC, Aurora (1973); Indian Tree GC, Arvada (27, 1971); Links GC, Highlands Ranch (Precision, 1986); Mechaneer GC, Fort Carson (1971); Perry Park CC, Larkspur (1972); Peterson Field GC, Colorado Springs (9, 1965); Pine Creek CC, Colorado Springs (1987); Raccoon Creek GC, Littleton (1984), with Brad Benz and Mike Poellot; Ranch CC, Westminster (1974); Rifle Creek GC (9), with Brad Benz and Mike Poellot; South Suburban GC, Littleton (27, 1974); Springhill GC, Aurora (Precision, 1977), with Brad Benz; West Meadows GC, Englewood (1984), with Brad Benz and Mike Poellot.

Iowa: Charles City CC (1964); Dysart G&CC (9, 1964); Glenhaven CC, Oelwein (9, 1965), with Emile Perret and Donald G. Brauer; Jester Park GC, Granger (1968).

Kansas: Smoky Hill CC, Hays (9, 1962).

Minnesota: Braemar GC, Edina (27, 1963); Honeywell CC, Orchard Gardens (27, 1963); Minnreg GC, Minneapolis (27, 1965).

Nebraska: Elks CC, Columbus (1965); Heritage Hills GC, McCook (1981), with Brad Benz.

Nevada: Wildcreek GC, Sparks (1980), with Brad Benz.

New Mexico: Elephant Butte G&CC, Truth or Consequence (9, 1975), with Brad Benz; Ladera GC, Albuquerque (27, 1980), with Brad Benz.

North Dakota: Prairiewood GC, Fargo (Precision, 9, 1976), with Brad Benz.

South Dakota: Southern Hills CC, Hot Springs (1979), with Brad Benz.

Texas: Firewheel Muni (Course No. 1), Garland (1983), with Brad Benz and Mike Poellot; Firewheel Muni (Course No. 2), Garland (1987); Indian Creek GC (Course No. 1), Carrollton (1983), with Brad Benz and Mike Poellot; Indian Creek GC (Course No. 2), Carrollton (1987).

Alberta: Maple Ridge GC, Calgary (9, 1968), with Claude Muret; Silver Springs G&CC, Calgary (1970), with Claude Muret.

Courses Remodeled & Added to by: Dick Phelps
Colorado: Colorado Springs CC (A.9, 1965); Copper Mountain GC (NLE, A.9, 1984); Dos Rios CC, Gunnison (A.9, 1982), with Brad Benz and Mike Poellot; Eagle CC, Broomfield (R.9, 1984); Eagle CC, Broomfield (A.9, 1984); Grand Lake GC (A.9, 1978), with Brad Benz; Grand Lake GC (R.9, 1978), with Brad Benz; Loveland GC (R.); Meadow Hills GC, Denver (R., 1983), with Brad Benz and Mike Poellot; Peterson Field GC, Colorado Springs (A.9, 1965); Tiara Rado GC, Grand Junction (R., 1986); Valley CC, Aurora (R., 1986); Valley Hi GC, Colorado Springs (R.9, 1983).

Iowa: Waverley GC (A.9, 1966); Waverley GC (R.9, 1966); Willow Creek GC, Des Moines (A.9, 1964).

Minnesota: Brookview CC, Minneapolis (R., 1965); Southview CC, West St. Paul (R.7, 1966).

Missouri: Windbrook GC, Parkville (R.7); Windbrook GC, Parkville (A.9).

Montana: Meadow Lake CC, Columbia Falls (A.9, 1984); Meadow Lake CC, Columbia Falls (R.9, 1984); Riverside CC, Bozeman (A.9, 1981), with Brad Benz.

North Dakota: Heart River GC, Dickinson (A.9, 1984), with Brad Benz and Mike Poellot; Heart River GC, Dickinson (R.9, 1984), with Brad Benz and Mike Poellot.

South Dakota: Huron CC (R.9, 1975), with Brad Benz; Huron CC (A.9, 1975), with Brad Benz.

Wyoming: Riverton CC, Riverton (R.9, 1982), with Brad Benz and Mike Poellot; Riverton CC, Riverton (A.9, 1982), with Brad Benz and Mike Poellot.

Gary Jim Player (1935 -   )
Born: Johannesburg, South Africa.

Gary Player turned professional in 1953 and won scores of tournaments throughout the world. One of only four men to complete golf's Grand Slam, he won three British Opens, three Masters, two PGA Championships and one U.S. Open. With Jack Nicklaus and Arnold Palmer, Player was considered one of golf's Big Three in the 1960s. At the height of his playing career, Player planned several courses in South Africa and Zimbabwe (Rhodesia) in collaboration with professional golfer Sidney F. Brews and Dr. Van Vincent. In the early Seventies, he was associated with American designers Ron Kirby and Art Davis. After nearly a decade as a consultant with Kirby, Player teamed with another golf architect, Floridian Karl Litten.

Courses by: Gary Player

Alabama: North River GC, Tuscaloosa (NLE, 1978), with Ron Kirby and Denis Griffiths.

Florida: Alaqua CC (1987), with Karl Litten; Belle Glade Muni (9, 1987), with Karl Litten; Ironwood CC, Longwood (1987), with Karl Litten; Overoaks CC, Kissimmee (1986), with Karl Litten.

Georgia: Berkeley Hills CC, Norcross (1971), with Arthur Davis and Ron Kirby; Pine Isle CC, Lake Lanier (1972), with Arthur Davis and Ron Kirby; River North G&CC, Macon (1973), with Arthur Davis and Ron Kirby; Royal Oaks GC, Cartersville (9, 1971), with Arthur Davis and Ron Kirby.

Massachusetts: White Cliffs of Plymouth GC (Precision, 1986), with Karl Litten.

South Carolina: Dolphin Head GC, Hilton Head Island (1973), with Arthur Davis and Ron Kirby; Marsh Point GC, Kiawah Island (1976), with Ron Kirby and Denis Griffiths.

Tennessee: Bent Creek Mountain Inn CC {formerly Cobbly Nob G Links}, Gatlinburg (1972), with Arthur Davis and Ron Kirby.

Texas: Fair Oaks Ranch G&CC, Boerne (1979), with Ron Kirby and Denis Griffiths.

Virginia: Brandermill CC, Midlothian (1976), with Ron Kirby and Denis Griffiths.

Bophutatswana: Gary Player CC, Sun City (1979), with Ron Kirby and Denis Griffiths.

Canary Islands: Maspalomas GC (North Course) (1974), with Ron Kirby and Denis Griffiths.

Ivory Coast: Riviera Africaine GC (9, 1972), with Arthur Davis and Ron Kirby.

Japan: Odawara CC (1973), with Arthur Davis and Ron Kirby.

Puerto Rico: Palmas del Mar GC, Humacao (1973), with Arthur Davis and Ron Kirby.

South Africa: Four Ways GC, Johannesburg , with Sidney Brews and Dr. Van Vincent; Roodepoort Muni (1985), with Ron Kirby and Denis Griffiths; Welkom Muni (1987), with Ron Kirby and Denis Griffiths.

Spain: Almerimar GC, Almeria (1975), with Ron Kirby and Denis Griffiths; El Paraiso GC (1974), with Arthur Davis and Ron Kirby; Escorpion GC, Valencia (1975), with Ron Kirby and Denis Griffiths.

Zimbabwe: Elephant Hills GC, Victoria Falls , with Sidney Brews and Dr. Van Vincent.

Courses Remodeled & Added to by: Gary Player

Georgia: Cartersville CC (A.9, 1972), with Arthur Davis and Ron Kirby; Cartersville CC (R.9, 1972), with Arthur Davis and Ron Kirby; Standard C, Atlanta (NLE, R.1), with Arthur Davis and Ron Kirby.

New Mexico: Alto Lakes G&CC (A.9, 1973), with Arthur Davis and Ron Kirby.

South Africa: Crown Mines GC, Johannesburg (R.), with Sidney Brews and Dr. Van Vincent.

Ralph M. Plummer (1900 - 1982) ASGCA, President, 1962.
Born: Smithfield, Texas. Died: Fort Worth, Texas at age 82.

A one time caddy at Glen Garden CC in Fort Worth, Ralph Plummer started his career as golf pro at a small South Texas club in the early 1920s. Several years later he was hired as professional for the new Galveston Municipal course being laid out by Houston pro-designer John Bredemus. Impressed with Plummer's interest in course design, Bredemus invited his assistance in laying out several area courses. Plummer resigned his job to work with Bredemus full time on courses in Texas, where the Depression had relatively little effect on golf development.

When Bredemus moved to Mexico, Plummer secured a position as professional at Greenville (Tx.) GC. After World War II, he designed and built several short courses at veteran's hospitals and then formed a firm specializing in the restoration of courses. By the 1950s he was once again designing golf courses.

In his most active years Plummer constructed all the courses he designed, but by the 1970s he was content to let other firms build them. He was still active as late as 1979, when he designed and supervised construction of a course near Fort Worth. Plummer was known for the attractiveness of his layouts and for his remarkable ability to estimate cuts and fills by eye and shape greens and bunkers without detailed plans.

Plummer designed or remodeled 86 courses during his career. He was involved in the design, construction or redesign of the three Texas courses that had hosted the U.S. Open—Colonial, Northwood and Champions.

Courses by: Ralph Plummer

Arizona: Francisco Grande CC, Casa Grande (1964).

Louisiana: Lake Charles G&CC (1956); New Orleans VA Hospital GC (Par 3, 9, 1946), with Bob Dunning; Sherwood Forest GC, Baton Rouge.

New Mexico: Altus CC (9, 1946); Artesia CC (9, 1946); Lincoln Hills CC, Riudoso.

Texas: Alice CC (1952); Atascocita CC, Humble (1956); Benbrook Muni, Ft. Worth (1962); Buckingham CC, Dallas (1960); Champions GC (Cypress Creek Course), Houston (1959); Columbian C, Carrollton (9, 1955); Dallas Athletic C (Blue Course), Mesquite (1954); Dallas Athletic C (Gold Course), Mesquite (1962); Denton CC; Eastern Hills CC, Garland (1956); Elkins Lake GC, Huntsville (1971); Gainesville Muni (1955); Golfcrest CC, Houston (NLE, 1951); Grand Prairie Muni (27, 1965); Great Southwest GC, Arlington (1965), with Byron Nelson; Hillcrest CC, Lubbock (1956); Hilltop Lakes GC, Normangee (9, 1963); Indian Creek CC, Abilene (1966); James Connally GC, Waco (1956); Lake Arlington GC, Arlington (1963); Lake Country Estates GC, Ft. Worth (9, 1973); Lakeside CC, Houston

(1952); Lakewood CC, Dallas (1947); Magnolia Ridge CC, Liberty (9, 1951); McKinney Muni GC (9, 1946), with Bob Dunning; Meadowbrook Muni, Ft. Worth (1960); Midland CC (1954); Mission CC (1959); Palm View Muni (1960); Palm View Muni, McAllen (1971); Pecan Valley Muni, Fort Worth (27, 1963); Pharoah's CC, Corpus Christi (1964); Port Arthur CC (1955); Preston Trail GC, Dallas (1965); Prestonwood CC (Creek Course), Dallas (1965); Ranchland Hills GC, Midland (1950); Ridglea CC (Championship Course), Ft. Worth (1966); Rio Grande Valley GC (1927); Riverside CC, Lake Jackson (1951); Riverside Muni, Victoria (9, 1951); Shady Oaks CC, Fort Worth (1959), with Robert Trent Jones and Lawrence Hughes; Sharpstown CC, Houston (1957); Shores CC, Lake Hubbard (1979); Squaw Creek CC, Ft. Worth (1977); Tanglewood-on-the-Texoma GC, Pottsboro (1964); Temple CC (9); Tenison Muni (East Course), Dallas (1960); Tennwood C, Hockley (1956); Terrell CC (1979); Texas A&M Univ GC, College Station (1950); Waco Muni; Westwood CC, Houston (1958).

Jamaica: Tryall G & Beach C (1958).

Courses Remodeled & Added to by: Ralph Plummer

Louisiana: City Park GC (Course No. 1), New Orleans (R.); Lafayette CC (R., 1960).

Minnesota: Minikahda C, Minneapolis (R., 1962).

Texas: Brae Burn CC, Bellaire (R.); Brook Hollow GC, Dallas (R., 1956); Club at Sonterra (South Course) (R., 1958); Dallas CC (R., 1947); Glen Lakes CC, Dallas (R., 1942); Hermann Park GC, Houston (R.9, 1952); Houston GC (R., 1957); Northwood C, Dallas (R., 1950); Pine Forest CC, Houston (NLE, R.9, 1956); Ridgewood CC, Waco (R., 1962); Ridglea CC (North Course), Fort Worth (R.6, 1959); River Crest CC, Fort Worth (R., 1946); River Oaks CC, Houston (R., 1957); Rockwood Muni, Fort Worth (R.18, 1964); Rockwood Muni, Fort Worth (A.9, 1964); Seguin CC (A.9, 1979); Tenison Muni (West Course), Dallas (R., 1960); Wichita Falls CC (R., 1964); Willow Brook CC, Tyler (R.9, 1953); Willow Brook CC, Tyler (A.9, 1953); Z. Boaz GC, Fort Worth (R., 1962).

Utah: The Country Club, Salt Lake City (R., 1963).

J. Michael Poellot (1943 -   ) ASGCA
Born: Pittsburgh, Pennsylvania.

Mike Poellot received a B.S. degree in Landscape Architecture from Iowa State University in 1966 after undergraduate work in Biological Sciences at West Virginia Wesleyan College.

A third generation golfer, Poellot took up the game at the age of twelve. While working in Thailand as a U.S. Army Intelligence officer in the early 1970s, he met Robert Trent Jones Jr., who was planning Navatanee GC in Bangkok. Jones hired Poellot to head his Asian office and direct work in Southeast Asia.

By 1980, as Senior Architect/Planner of the Robert Trent Jones II Group, Poellot had worked on the design and construction supervision of twenty Jones Jr. courses in both the U.S. and Far East. That year he met architect Brad Benz during an ASGCA sojourn to Scotland. The two found they shared many of the same ideas and Benz convinced Poellot to join him and partner Dick Phelps in Colorado. Phelps, Benz and Poellot Inc. worked the mountain states for three years. Benz and Poellot then left the company and formed their own partnership based in California. Drawing on Poellot's contacts they soon landed many contracts in the Far East, including the first private country club in Communist China, Beijing GC.

Courses by: Mike Poellot

Arizona: Fred Enke Muni, Tucson (1983), with Brad Benz and Mark Rathert; Gainey Ranch GC, Scottsdale (27, 1985), with Brad Benz and Mark Rathert.

California: Spring Valley GC, Milpitas (1987), with Brad Benz.

Colorado: Englewood Muni (1982), with Dick Phelps and Brad Benz; Raccoon Creek GC, Littleton (1984), with Dick Phelps and Brad Benz; Rifle Creek GC (9), with Dick Phelps and Brad Benz; West Meadows GC, Englewood (1984), with Dick Phelps and Brad Benz.

Missouri: Longview Lake GC, Lee's Summit (27, 1986), with Brad Benz and Mark Rathert.

Montana: Briarwood CC (1985), with Brad Benz.

Nevada: Northgate CC, Reno (27, 1987), with Brad Benz.

Texas: Firewheel Muni (Course No. 1), Garland (1983), with Dick Phelps and Brad Benz; Indian Creek GC (Course No. 1), Carrollton (1983), with Dick Phelps and Brad Benz.

China: Beijing GC (North Course) (1987), with Brad Benz and Mark Rathert; Beijing GC (South Course) (1988), with Brad Benz and Mark Rathert.

Hong Kong: Clearwater Bay CC (1984), with Brad Benz.

Japan: Glenoaks CC (1983), with Brad Benz; Kannami Springs G&CC (1982), with Brad Benz; Oak Meadows CC (1984), with Brad Benz.

Taiwan: Lai Lai International G&CC, Kaohsiung (1985), with Brad Benz.

Courses Remodeled & Added to by: Mike Poellot

Colorado: Dos Rios CC, Gunnison (A.9, 1982), with Dick Phelps and Brad Benz; Meadow Hills GC, Denver (R., 1983), with Dick Phelps and Brad Benz.

New Mexico: Riverside CC, Carlsbad (A.9, 1984), with Brad Benz and Mark Rathert; Riverside CC, Carlsbad (R.9, 1984), with Brad Benz and Mark Rathert.

North Dakota: Heart River GC, Dickinson (A.9, 1984), with Dick Phelps and Brad Benz; Heart River GC, Dickinson (R.9, 1984), with Dick Phelps and Brad Benz.

Wyoming: Riverton CC, Riverton (A.9, 1982), with Dick Phelps and Brad Benz; Riverton CC, Riverton (R.9, 1982), with Dick Phelps and Brad Benz.

Robert D. Pryde (1871 - 1951)
Born: Tayport, Fife, Scotland. Died: New Haven, Connecticut at age 79.

Robert Pryde grew up near St. Andrews, where he learned to play golf. He attended Harris Academy in Dundee and the Technical College of Glasgow. In 1892 he emigrated to the United States, became a cabinetmaker in New Haven, Connecticut and dabbled in the design of several buildings.

In 1895 Pryde was persuaded to build his first golf course, and from that point on his life was devoted to golf. He laid out a number of courses in Connecticut as well as a few in other states. Pryde was also an early golf coach at Yale University and from 1922 to 1946 served as secretary-treasurer of the Connecticut State Golf Association.

Courses by: Robert D. Pryde
Connecticut: Alling Memorial GC, New Haven; Meriden Park Muni; New Haven CC (NLE,); Pine Orchards CC, Brantford; Racebrook CC, Orange; Wethersfield CC.
Massachusetts: Wyantenuck GC, Great Barrington .

Nicholas T. Psiahas (1930 -   )
Born: Montclair, New Jersey.

Nicholas Psiahas began his career as an eleven-year-old caddie at Upper Montclair CC in New Jersey. After working on the maintenance crew at that course, he joined the golf construction firm of William Baldwin in 1955. Over the next eight years he served as construction superintendent for several Robert Trent Jones-designed courses built by Baldwin's company, including a new Upper Montclair CC, the Air Force Academy course in Colorado and Half Moon-Rose Hall in Jamaica.

In 1963 Psiahas formed his own business, Golf Construction Inc., and built courses for golf architects Frank Duane, David Gordon and Hal Purdy. In 1965 he began to design as well as construct courses.
Courses by: Nicholas Psiahas
New Jersey: Berkeley Township GC; Darlington County GC (1974); Overpeck County GC, Teaneack; Rolling Greens GC, Newton (1970); Two Bridges CC, Lincoln Park (Precision,); Wantage G Center (Par 3, 1972); Wayne G Centre.
Pennsylvania: Fernwood Resort GC (1968).
Courses Remodeled & Added to by: Nicholas Psiahas
New Jersey: Jumping Brook GC, Neptune (R.); North Jersey CC, Wayne (R.).

Algie Marshall Pulley Jr. (1940 -   ) ASGCA
Born: Petersburg, Virginia.

One-time course superintendent Algie Pulley worked for golf architect Ed Ault in the 1960s before forming a golf course construction firm with Buddy Loving and E.H. Coffey. In the early 1970s Pulley's GolfAmerica Inc., a firm based in California, designed, built and operated golf courses on both coasts. A poor economy led to disbandment of that corporation after a few years, and Pulley resumed designing layouts along the West Coast on his own.
Courses by: Algie Pulley
California: Chardonnay CC, Napa (27, 1987); Dixon Landing CC, Milpatas (NLE, 1979).
Delaware: Cripple Creek G&CC, Bethany Beach (1984).
Maryland: Century XXI Club, Germantown (1974); Jefferson Park GC, Fairfax (9, 1977); Marlboro CC {formerly Duke of Marlborough GC}, Upper Marlboro (1974).
Virginia: Confederate Hills CC, Highland Springs (1972), with Buddy Loving; Country Club Lake, Dumfries (Precision, 1971), with Buddy Loving; Evergreen CC, Haymarket (1968), with Buddy Loving; Lake Monticello GC, Palmyra (1972), with Buddy Loving; Montclair CC, Dumfries (1972).
West Virginia: Potomac C, Keyser (9, 1974).
Courses Remodeled & Added to by: Algie Pulley
California: Alhambra Muni (R.9, 1977); Alhambra Muni (A.9, 1977); Lake Arrowhead CC (R.2, 1976); San Bernardino CC (R.5, 1976).
Maryland: Hunt Valley Inn & CC (R.9, 1976).
Virginia: Army-Navy CC (Arlington Course), Arlington (R.5, 1970), with Buddy Loving; Army-Navy CC (Fairfax Course), Fairfax (R.2, 1970), with Buddy Loving; CC of Fairfax (R., 1969), with Buddy Loving; Washington G&CC, Arlington (R.5, 1969), with Buddy Loving.

Harold Chandler Purdy (1905 -   ) ASGCA
Born: Wabash, Indiana.

Hal Purdy graduated from high school in Wabash, Indiana and went to work as a surveyor for a local engineering firm. During the Depression, he served as manager at Lost Creek CC in Lima, Ohio before working for two years as a draftsman. He then purchased and operated Sidney (Ohio) CC until 1945, when he became executive vice-president of a construction firm.

In 1954 Purdy became a construction supervisor for architect William Gordon. He then entered private practice as a golf course architect in 1956. He was joined by his elder son, Dr. Mal Purdy, in the 1960s and was also assisted for a few years by his second son, Chandler.
Courses by: Hal Purdy
Connecticut: Aspetuck Valley CC, Weston (1966); Burning Tree CC, Greenwich (1962); H. Smith Richardson GC, with Malcolm Purdy; H. Smith Richardson Muni, Fairfield (1972), with Malcolm Purdy; Whitney Farms CC, Monroe (1979), with Malcolm Purdy.
Indiana: Elks CC, Elkhart (9, 1964); McMillen Park GC, Ft. Wayne (1971); Norwood GC, Huntington (1970); Shoaff Park GC, Ft. Wayne (9, 1966).
Kentucky: Carter Caves State Park GC, Olive Hill (9, 1963); General Butler State Park GC, Carrollton (9, 1964); Harmony Landing GC, Goshen (9, 1966); Jefferson High School GC, Jefferson (Par 3, 9, 1964); Jenny Wiley State Park GC, Pikeville (9, 1963); Kentucky Dam Village GC, Gilbertsville (1964).
Maryland: Lighthouse Sound GC, with Malcolm Purdy.
New Jersey: Apple Ridge CC, Mahwah (1966); Arrowbrook CC, Bordentown (1963); Atlantic City Electric Co. GC, Somers Point (Par 3, 9, 1964); B.L. England GC, Beesley Point (Par 3, 9, 1964); Bamm Hollow CC, Middletown (27, 1972), with Malcolm Purdy; Battleground CC, Freehold (1967); Bey-Lea GC, Toms River (1970); Clear Brook GC, Cranbury (1974), with Malcolm Purdy; Clearview GC, Lincoln Park (1966); Deer Park GC, Utica (Par 3, 9, 1966); Fairmount CC, Chatham (1961); Fiddler's Elbow CC, Bedminster (27, 1966); Flanders Valley GC (27, 1963); Florham Park GC (1974); Forsgate GC (West Course), Jamesburg (1974); Fox Hollow GC, Somerville (1962); Glenbrook CC, East Brunswick (1966); Glenwood CC; Hickman GC, Wayne (Par 3, 9, 1970); Knoll East GC, Boonton (1961); Mays Landing GC, Atlantic City (1964); Millburn GC (Par 3, 9, 1970); Morris County GC, Morristown (1968); Navesink GC, Red Bank (1964); Ocean Acres GC, Manahawkin (9, 1964); Old Tappan GC (9, 1970); Ramsey G&CC (9, 1965); Roxiticus CC, Mendham (1965); Summit GC (Par 3, 9, 1968); Sunset Valley GC, Pequannock (1974), with Malcolm Purdy; Tamarack GC, New Brunswick (27, 1973), with

Malcolm Purdy; Warrenbrook CC, Plainfield (1966).
New York: Catatonk GC, Candor (9, 1966); Central Valley GC (9, 1968); Chenango Valley GC, Binghampton (9, 1967); Columbia G&CC, Hudson (9, 1962); Dinsmore GC, Staatsburg (1957); Greenview GC, Central Square (1967); Hillandale GC, Huntington (9, 1961); Huguenot Manor GC, New Paltz (9, 1971); Kanon Valley GC, Oneida (1969); Locust Tree GC, New Paltz (1972); Monroe County GC, Churchville (9, 1968); Narrowsburg GC, Syracuse (9, 1959); Pompey Hills, Syracuse (1964); Rondout GC, Accord (9, 1969); Roxbury Run GC, Denver (9, 1974), with Malcolm Purdy; Sawyerkill GC, Saugerties (1965); Skaneatelas CC (9, 1966); Stony Ford GC, Goshen (1962); Sunny Hill GC, Greenville (Par 3, 9, 1967); Tioga GC, Nichols (1969); Village Green GC, Syracuse (1974), with Malcolm Purdy; West Hill CC, Camillus (1967); Windham CC (9, 1969).
Ohio: Sidney G&CC (9, 1945).
Pennsylvania: Mount Airy Lodge & CC, Mt.Pocono (1981), with Malcolm Purdy and Chandler Purdy.
Virginia: Luray Caverns CC, Luray (1976), with Malcolm Purdy.
Courses Remodeled & Added to by: Hal Purdy
California: Thunderbird CC, Cathedral City (R., 1973).
Connecticut: CC of Darien (R., 1974), with Malcolm Purdy.
Florida: Belleview-Biltmore Hotel & C (East), Clearwater (R., 1973), with Malcolm Purdy; Belleview-Biltmore Hotel & C (West) (R., 1973), with Malcolm Purdy.
Indiana: French Lick CC (Hill Course) (R., 1965); French Lick GC (Valley Course) (R., 1965).
New Jersey: Asbury Park GC (R., 1970); Braidburn CC (Lake Course), Florham Park (A.9, 1972), with Malcolm Purdy; Colonia CC (R., 1969); Covered Bridge GC, Englishtown (R., 1974), with Malcolm Purdy; Essex Fells CC (R., 1971), with Malcolm Purdy; Green Brook CC, Caldwell (R., 1979), with Malcolm Purdy; Medford Lakes CC (A.9, 1969); North Jersey CC, Wayne (R., 1965); Raritan Arsenal CC, Somerville (R.9, 1968); River Vale CC (R., 1968); Rock Spring CC (R., 1965); Rockaway River CC, Denville (R.), with Malcolm Purdy; Rutgers University, New Brunswick (A.9, 1963); Rutgers University, New Brunswick (R.9, 1963); Weequahic GC, Newark (A.9, 1969).
New York: Cazenovia CC (A.9, 1969); Inwood CC, Far Rockaway (R., 1959); IBM CC (R.9, 1961); Middle Bay CC, Oceanside (1963); Newburgh CC (R.9, 1965); Onondaga G&CC, Fayetteville (R., 1965); Wykagyl CC, New Rochelle (R., 1966).
Ohio: Losantiville CC, Cincinnati (R., 1961); Lost Creek CC, Lima (R., 1961); Middletown GC (R., 1962).

Malcolm Mills Purdy (1932 - 1983) ASGCA
Born: Lima, Ohio. Died: New Jersey at age 51.

Dr. Mal Purdy grew up on golf courses managed and operated by his father Hal Purdy. He earned a Doctorate in Industrial Psychology from Purdue University and worked in that field for fifteen years. In 1967 he joined his father's course design firm, which became known as The Purdys.

Mal Purdy was tragically killed in an automobile accident in late 1983.
Courses by: Malcolm Purdy
Connecticut: H. Smith Richardson GC, with Hal Purdy; H. Smith Richardson Muni, Fairfield (1972), with Hal Purdy; Whitney Farms CC, Monroe (1979), with Hal Purdy.
Maryland: Lighthouse Sound GC, with Hal Purdy.
New Jersey: Bamm Hollow CC, Middletown (27, 1972), with Hal Purdy; Clear Brook GC, Cranbury (1974), with Hal Purdy; Sunset Valley GC, Pequannock (1974), with Hal Purdy; Tamarack GC, New Brunswick (27, 1973), with Hal Purdy.
New York: Roxbury Run GC, Denver (9, 1974), with Hal Purdy; Village Green GC, Syracuse (1974), with Hal Purdy.
Pennsylvania: Mount Airy Lodge & CC, Mt.Pocono (1981), with Hal Purdy and Chandler Purdy.
Virginia: Luray Caverns CC, Luray (1976), with Hal Purdy.
Courses Remodeled & Added to by: Malcolm Purdy
Connecticut: CC of Darien (R., 1974), with Hal Purdy.
Florida: Belleview-Biltmore Hotel & C (East), Clearwater (R., 1973), with Hal Purdy; Belleview-Biltmore Hotel & C (West) (R., 1973), with Hal Purdy.
New Jersey: Braidburn CC (Lake Course), Florham Park (A.9, 1972), with Hal Purdy; Covered Bridge GC, Englishtown (R., 1974), with Hal Purdy; Essex Fells CC (R., 1971), with Hal Purdy; Green Brook CC, Caldwell (R., 1979), with Hal Purdy; Rockaway River CC, Denville (R.), with Hal Purdy.

Robert Dean Putnam

Bob Putnam worked as a commercial artist for years before joining golf architect Bob Baldock as a draftsman in the late Forties. In 1954 he established his own course design firm, based in Fresno, Calif. and carried on a modest steady practice for the next thirty years..
Courses by: Robert Dean Putnam
California: Rancho Canada GC (East Course), Carmel (1970); Rancho Canada GC (West Course), Carmel (1970); Visalia Plaza GC (1973).
New Mexico: Sandia Mountain GC, Albuquerque (Par 3, 1962); Tijeras Arroyo GC, Kirkland (1971).
Washington: Harrington G&CC (9, 1957).
Spain: La Manga Campo de G (North Course), Costa Blanca (1972); La Manga Campo de G (South Course) (1972); Las Lomas El Bosque GC, Madrid (1973).
Courses Remodeled & Added to by: Robert Dean Putnam
California: San Joaquin CC (R., 1972); Sunnyside CC, Fresno (R., 1973).

Everett J. Pyle

Everett Pyle worked under Donald Ross in the 1930s, building Twigg Memorial GC in Providence, R.I. for him, among others. From the 1940s through the 1960s Pyle served as Superintendent of Parks in Hartford, Connecticut. In that capacity he planned extensive changes at Keney Park and Goodwin Park golf courses. He also designed and revised several Connecticut courses on the side, including Pine Hill GC at Windsor.

David A. Rainville (1936 -) ASGCA
Born: Deadwood, South Dakota.

David Rainville received an A.A. Degree in Engineering from Fullerton Junior College in California in 1957. Beginning at age twelve, he worked at golf course maintenance or construction during the summers for his father, golf architect Harry Rainville.

In 1962, following military service, Rainville joined his father in the full-time practice of golf course design. Their California-based firm became known as David Rainville - Harry Rainville Golf Course Architects. After his father's death, Rainville continued the business, concentrating mainly on the greater Palm Springs area.

Courses by: David Rainville

California: Birch Hills GC, Brea (Precision, 1972), with Harry Rainville; Cathedral Canyon CC, Cathedral City (1975); Desert Princess CC, Cathedral City (1986); El Prado CC (Butterfield Stage Course), Chino (1976), with Harry Rainville; El Prado CC (Chino Creek Course), Chino (1970), with Harry Rainville; Escondido CC (1965), with Harry Rainville; Fountains GC, Escondido (Precision, 1986); Imperial GC, Brea (1974), with Harry Rainville; Laguna Hills GC (27), with Harry Rainville; Lake San Marcos Executive GC (Precision,); Lake San Marcos G&CC, with Harry Rainville; Lawrence Welk Village GC, Escondido (Precision, 1985); Mile Square GC, Fountain Valley (1969), with Harry Rainville; Needles Muni (1964), with Harry Rainville; Oasis CC, Palm Desert (1985); Ocean Meadows GC, Goleta (9, 1966), with Harry Rainville; Panorama Village GC (Par 3, 9), with Harry Rainville; Rossmoor CC (South Course), Walnut Creek (1964), with Harry Rainville; San Juan Hills CC, San Juan Capistrano (1966), with Harry Rainville; Seven Hills CC, Hemet (1973), with Harry Rainville; Shadowridge CC, Vista (1981); Upland Hills GC, Upland (1983); Warner Springs G Resort (1965), with Harry Rainville.

Nevada: Boulder City GC (9, 1973), with Harry Rainville.

Courses Remodeled & Added to by: David Rainville

California: Alta Vista CC, Placentia (A.9, 1973), with Harry Rainville; Cathedral Canyon CC, Cathedral City (A.9, 1986); Chevy Chase CC, Glendale (R.9, 1960), with Harry Rainville; Irvine Coast CC (R.), with Harry Rainville; Los Serranos Lakes CC (North Course), Chino (R., 1965), with Harry Rainville; Los Serranos Lakes G&CC (South Course), Chino (R., 1965), with Harry Rainville; Mesa Verde CC, Costa Mesa (R.); Newport Beach CC (R.), with Harry Rainville; Newport Beach CC (A.9, 1966), with Harry Rainville; Red Hill CC, Cucamonga (R.), with Harry Rainville; Santa Ana CC (R.), with Harry Rainville; Thunderbird CC, Cathedral City (R.), with Harry Rainville; Torrey Pines Muni (North Course), La Jolla (R., 1975); Torrey Pines Muni (South Course), La Jolla (R., 1975); Whispering Palms CC, Rancho Santa Fe (A.9, 1973), with Harry Rainville.

Harry M. Rainville (1905 - 1982)
Born: St. Onge, South Dakota. Died: Tustin, California at age 77.

Harry Rainville's early years were spent in a variety of occupations, including ranching, mining, general construction and merchandise sales. In the early 1940s he moved his family to California, where he worked at the Cal-Tech Rocket Assembly facility until 1944.

A friend of golf architect Lawrence Hughes, Rainville became construction superintendent on what became Stardust CC in San Diego in 1945. He went on to build five more courses for Hughes and was responsible for construction of several others, including Desert Inn CC in Las Vegas and Thunderbird CC in Palm Springs.

In 1952 Rainville entered private practice as a golf course designer. He was joined by his son David in 1962. For a short time professional golfer Billy Casper served as consultant to his firm. In the 1970s the firm began to operate, as well as design and build, golf facilities and by 1979 owned an interest in five successful courses.

Courses by: Harry Rainville

California: Alta Vista CC, Placentia (1961); Birch Hills GC, Brea (Precision, 1972), with David Rainville; Brea GC (Precision, 9); Candlewood CC, Whittier; Chula Vista Muni, Bonita (1961); El Prado CC (Butterfield Stage Course), Chino (1976), with David Rainville; El Prado CC (Chino Creek Course), Chino (1970), with David Rainville; El Rancho Verde CC, Rialto (1957); Escondido CC (1965), with David Rainville; Fallbrook CC (1962); Gene List Muni, Bellflower (Par 3, 9); Hemet West GC, Hemet (Par 3, 9); Imperial GC, Brea (1974), with David Rainville; Indian Wells CC (27, 1956); Laguna Hills GC (27), with David Rainville; Lake San Marcos G&CC, with David Rainville; Marina Del Ray GC, Venice (Precision, 9); Mile Square GC, Fountain Valley (1969), with David Rainville; National City GC (Precision, 1961); Needles Muni (1964), with David Rainville; Ocean Meadows GC, Goleta (9, 1966), with David Rainville; Panorama Village GC (Par 3, 9), with David Rainville; Pine Trees GC, Santa Ana (Par 3, 9); Rossmoor CC (South Course), Walnut Creek (1964), with David Rainville; San Juan Hills CC, San Juan Capistrano (1966), with David Rainville; Seven Hills CC, Hemet (1973), with David Rainville; Warner Springs G Resort (1965), with David Rainville; Western Hills G&CC, Chino (1963); Whispering Palms CC, Rancho Santa Fe (1965); Yorba Linda CC (1957).

Nevada: Boulder City GC (9, 1973), with David Rainville.

Courses Remodeled & Added to by: Harry Rainville

California: Alta Vista CC, Placentia (A.9, 1973), with David Rainville; Chevy Chase CC, Glendale (R.9, 1960), with David Rainville; Irvine Coast CC (R.), with David Rainville; Los Serranos Lakes CC (North Course), Chino (R., 1965), with David Rainville; Los Serranos Lakes G&CC (South Course), Chino (R., 1965), with David Rainville; Newport Beach CC (R.), with David Rainville; Newport Beach CC (A.9, 1966), with David Rainville; Rancho Santa Fe CC (R.); Red Hill CC, Cucamonga (R.), with David Rainville; San Diego CC, Chula Vista (R.1, 1962); Santa Ana CC (R.), with David Rainville; Thunderbird CC, Cathedral City (R.), with David Rainville; Whispering Palms CC, Rancho Santa Fe (A.9, 1973), with David Rainville.

Mark F. Rathert (1953 -) ASGCA
Born: Marion, Kansas.

Mark Rathert attended Butler County (Ks.) Community College on a golf scholarship, and later graduated with honors from Kansas State University, receiving a Bachelor's of Landscape Architecture degree. While in college, Rathert won an ASLA Distinguished Undergraduate Student Award in nationwide competition, and also redesigned his home town's 9 hole course when its greens were converted from sand to grass. After graduation he worked for Robert Trent Jones Jr. and then joined the California firm of Benz & Poellot in 1981.

Courses by: Mark Rathert

Arizona: Fred Enke Muni, Tucson (1983), with Brad Benz and Mike Poellot; Gainey Ranch GC, Scottsdale (27, 1985), with Brad Benz and Mike Poellot.

Missouri: Longview Lake GC, Lee's Summit (27, 1986), with Brad Benz and Mike Poellot.

China: Beijing GC (North Course) (1987), with Brad Benz and Mike Poellot; Beijing GC (South Course) (1988), with Brad Benz and Mike Poellot.

Courses Remodeled & Added to by: Mark Rathert

Kansas: Marion CC (R.).

New Mexico: Riverside CC, Carlsbad (R.9, 1984), with Brad Benz and Mike Poellot; Riverside CC, Carlsbad (A.9, 1984), with Brad Benz and Mike Poellot.

Seth J. Raynor (1874 - 1926)
Born: Manorville, New York. Died: West Palm Beach, Florida at age 51. Interred: Southampton, New York.

A Princeton graduate with a degree in Engineering, Seth Raynor operated a comfortable surveying and landscaping business in Southampton, N.Y. for many years. His introduction to golf design came quite by accident, when he was hired by Charles Blair Macdonald in 1908 to survey the property that would become The National Golf Links of America. Raynor so impressed Macdonald with his engineering knowledge that he was hired to supervise construction of The National. Once it was completed, Raynor went on to construct several more courses for Macdonald, including Piping Rock, Sleepy Hollow, The Greenbrier, and Lido.

In 1915 Raynor joined Macdonald as a partner and in the next ten years designed or remodeled nearly one hundred courses that appeared under his own name. C.B. Macdonald, by his own admission, concentrated on only a half dozen pet projects. In 1926 Seth Raynor died of pneumonia, leaving his assistants Charles Banks and Ralph Barton to complete his in-progress projects and to carry on the Macdonald tradition.

Courses by: Seth Raynor

California: Monterey Peninsula CC (Dunes Course), Pebble Beach (1926), with Charles Banks.

Connecticut: CC of Fairfield (1921); Greenwich CC; Hotchkiss School GC, Lakeville (9); Yale University GC, New Haven (1926), with Charles Blair Macdonald and Charles Banks.

Florida: Babson Park G&YC (NLE, 9, 1921); Everglades C, Palm Beach (9, 1919); Mountain Lake C, Lake Wales.

Georgia: Bon Air Vanderbilt Hotel GC (Lake Crs), Augusta; Lookout Mountain GC {formerly Fairyland CC} (1925), with Charles Banks.

Hawaii: Mid-Pacific CC, Honolulu (9, 1927), with Charles Banks; Waialae CC, Honolulu (1925), with Charles Banks.

Illinois: Shoreacres, Lake Bluff (1921).

Maryland: Gibson Island GC (1922), with Charles Blair Macdonald.

Minnesota: Midland Hills CC, St. Paul (1915); University of Minnesota GC, St. Paul (1921).

Missouri: St. Louis CC, Clayton (1914), with Charles Blair Macdonald.

New Jersey: Roselle CC.

New York: Blind Brook C (Routing), Portchester (1916); Cold Spring Harbor CC; Creek C, Locust Valley (1925), with Charles Blair Macdonald; Deepdale GC, Great Neck (NLE, 1925), with Charles Blair Macdonald; Fishers Island GC (1917); H.P. Whitney Estate GC, Manhasset , with Charles Blair Macdonald; Knollwood CC, Elmsford (1927), with Charles Banks; Lido GC, Long Beach (NLE, 1917), with Charles Blair Macdonald; Links GC, Roslyn (NLE, 1919), with Charles Blair Macdonald; Moore Estate GC, Roslyn , with Charles Blair Macdonald; Oakland GC, Bayside (NLE,); Otto Kahn Estate GC, Manhasset (NLE, 1925), with Charles Blair Macdonald; Piping Rock C , Locust Valley (1913), with Charles Blair Macdonald; Sleepy Hollow GC, Scarboro-on-Hudson (1914), with Charles Blair Macdonald; Southampton GC (1927), with Charles Banks; Suffolk County CC, East Islip (NLE,); Thousand Islands C, Alexandria Bay (1923); Westhampton CC (1914).

North Carolina: Green Park-Norwood GC, Blowing Rock (NLE,).

Ohio: Camargo C, Cincinnati (1921).

Pennsylvania: Fox Chapel GC, Pittsburgh (1925).

Rhode Island: Bayside CC (NLE, 9, 1923); Ocean Links, Newport (9, 1920); Wanumetonomy CC, Middletown (1922).

South Carolina: CC of Charleston; Yeaman's Hall C, Hanrahah (1925).

West Virginia: Greenbrier GC (Old White Course), White Sulphur Spgs (1915), with Charles Blair Macdonald.

Wisconsin: Blue Mound G&CC, Wauwautosa (1924).

Bermuda: Mid-Ocean C, Tuckerstown (1924), with Charles Blair Macdonald and Charles Banks.

Courses Remodeled & Added to by: Seth Raynor

Florida: Everglades C, Palm Beach (A.9, 1926).

Georgia: Augusta CC (R., 1926).

Illinois: Chicago GC, Wheaton (R., 1923).

New Jersey: Morris County GC, Morristown (R.6, 1917); Morris County GC, Morristown (A.12, 1917).

New York: Crawford CC (R.); Gardiner's Bay CC (R.9, 1915); Gardiner's Bay CC, Shelter Island (A.9, 1915); Nassau CC, Glen Cove (R.1).

Wilfrid Reid (1884 - 1973)
Born: Bulwell, Nottingham, England. Died: West Palm Beach, Florida at age 89.

Wilfrid Reid studied club and ball making under Tommy Armour's father, Willie, in Edinburgh, Scotland. A scratch golfer at 15, Wilf turned professional at 17 and was a protege of Harry Vardon, who helped him land a club professional job in Paris, France in the early 1900s. Reid was a fine competitive golfer despite his diminutive size, and he beat his mentor Vardon on several occasions.

Reid competed in the United States during several seasons before moving there at the behest of the DuPont family after the outbreak of World War I. He became a member of the PGA in 1917 and obtained U.S. citizenship in 1921. Wilf served as professional at several of America's top clubs, including CC of Detroit, Beverly CC,

The Broadmoor, and Seminole GC. He defeated Gene Sarazen in the 1924 Augusta Open, won the 1926 Michigan PGA and had 26 holes-in-one in his long playing career.

Reid began designing golf courses at an early age and had laid out courses in Europe and Britain before settling in the United States. He once estimated that he'd designed 58 courses and remodeled some 43 others during his design career. While based in Michigan during the 1920s, he partnered with another club professional, William Connellan. The firm of Reid and Connellan designed some 20 courses in that state alone. Wilfrid Reid retired to Florida in the early 1950s and consistently bettered his age in both social and competitive rounds.

Courses by: Wilfrid Reid
California: Olympic C (Lake Course), San Francisco (1917), with Walter Fovargue.

Delaware: DuPont CC, Wilmington (NLE, 1920); Green Hill Muni, Wilmington; Newark CC (9).

Michigan: Bald Mountain GC, Detroit , with William Connellan; Bob O'Link CC, Novi , with William Connellan; Brae Burn GC, Plymouth , with William Connellan; Flushing Valley CC, Flushing; Gaylord CC (1949); Harsens Island GC, with William Connellan; Indian River GC (9), with William Connellan; Indianwood G&CC (Old Course), Lake Orion (1928), with William Connellan; Plum Hollow G&CC, Southfield , with William Connellan; Port Huron CC, with William Connellan; Tam O'Shanter CC, Orchard Lake , with William Connellan.

England: Banstead Downs GC; Garrats Hall GC.

France: Cannes GC; Golf Club d'Aix-les-bains; Golf Ile de Berder; Pont St. Maxence GC; Racing C de France (Valley), La Boulie.

Courses Remodeled & Added to by: Wilfrid Reid
Michigan: Birmingham CC (R., 1928), with William Connellan; Black River CC (A.9), with William Connellan; Grosse Ile G&CC (R.), with William Connellan; Orchard Lake CC (R., 1928), with William Connellan.

Belgium: Royal Belgique GC, Brussels (R.).

England: Seacroft GC, Lincolnshire (R.9).

Robert A. Renaud
Born: Canada.

Robert Renaud became pro-manager at Pickens County CC in South Carolina in the early 1950s. After renovating the course (which had closed during World War II), he moved on to Thomson CC in Georgia and performed the same task. He later served as head professional at a number of Southern clubs and was twice voted South Carolina Golf Professional of the Year by his peers.

Renaud designed golf courses on a part-time basis during the 1950s and '60s In 1972 he resigned from his position as head professional at Hillwood CC in Nashville to pursue a full-time career in golf architecture. Renaud retired in 1979 to maintain and manage a course he had built in Crossville, Tennessee.

Courses by: Robert Renaud
Florida: Indian Pines GC, Rockledge (1974).

Indiana: Indian Lakes GC, Batesville (1986).

South Carolina: Fairfield CC, Winnsboro (1961).

Tennessee: Green River CC, Waynesboro (1972); Tansi Resort GC, Crossville (1973).

Courses Remodeled & Added to by: Robert Renaud
Georgia: Pickens County CC (R., 1953); Thomson CC (R.9, 1954).

South Carolina: Spring Lake CC, York (A.9, 1962).

Garrett J. Renn (1913 - 1968)
Born: Mt. Holly, New Jersey. Died: Camden, New Jersey at age 55.

Garry Renn held the position of superintendent of Philadelphia's municipal golf courses from 1950 until his death in an auto accident in 1968. A member of the PGA of America and the GCSAA, he designed several courses on a part-time basis.

Courses by: Garrett J. Renn
New Jersey: Little Mill CC, Marlton (1968).

Pennsylvania: Bryn Llawen GC, Ivyville (1969).

Joseph Michael "Mick" Riley (1905 - 1964)
Born: Burke, Idaho. Died: Salt Lake City, Utah at age 59.

Mick Riley competed against George Von Elm as a youngster and turned professional while still in his teens. In the 1920s he helped to construct Nibley Park GC in Salt Lake City and stayed on as its first professional. He served as pro at a series of Salt Lake City courses and in 1951 was awarded a citation of merit by the PGA of America for his efforts in promoting the game of golf. He was often called the "Father of Golf in Utah."

Riley was responsible for the design and construction of several Utah golf courses and was especially active in the years just after World War II. After his death, the Salt Lake County Commission named its newest course, Riley's last design, in his honor.

Courses by: Mick Riley
Utah: Brigham City G&CC; Copper GC (9); El Monte GC, Ogden (9, 1950); Empire G&CC, Vernal (9); Forest Dale GC, Salt Lake City (9, 1935); Fort Douglas VA Hospital GC (Par 3, 9, 1957); Logan G&CC (1949); Meadowbrook Muni, Salt Lake City (1950); Mick Riley GC, Murray (1965); Mt. Lomond G&CC, Ogden (1949); Oquirrh Hills Muni; Rose Park GC, Salt Lake City (9); Timpanogas Muni, Provo (1950); Tooele GC (9, 1949).

Wyoming: Purple Sage GC (9).

Courses Remodeled & Added to by: Mick Riley
Utah: Nibley Park GC, Salt Lake City (R., 1949).

Bertrand Jay Riviere (1933 -)
Born: Houston, Texas.

Jay Riviere was an outstanding high school and college athlete. While playing tackle on the Rice University football team, he was an All-Southwest Conference selection in 1954, '55 and '56. He also lettered on the Rice golf team. After college he worked as an assistant professional under Claude Harmon at Winged Foot GC in

New York.

Returning to Texas in 1962, Riviere became involved in golf course construction, working for George Fazio in the creation of the Jackrabbit Course of the Champions Golf Club. After work on other Fazio projects, Riviere struck out on his own as a golf course architect in 1965. Based in Houston, Riviere made professional golfer Dave Marr a partner in his design firm in 1980. Marr, a former PGA Champion, had also been an assistant to Claude Harmon in the late 1950s at Winged Foot.

Courses by: Jay Riviere
Missouri: Lakewood Oaks GC, Lees Summit (1980).

Texas: Bear Creek Golf World (Masters Course), Houston (1973); Bluebonnet CC, Navasota (1973); Clear Lake GC, Houston (1965); Club Del Lago, Conroe (1984), with Dave Marr; El Campo CC; Falls G&CC, New Ulm (1985), with Dave Marr; Frisch Auf Valley CC, LaGrange (9); Green Meadows CC, Katy; Hearthstone CC, Houston (1977); Killeen Muni; Lake Houston GC, Huffman; McAllen CC; Pasadena Ellington GC; Pine Forest CC, Houston (27); Pinecrest GC, Trinity; Point Aquarius CC, Conroe; Rayburn G&CC (Gold Nine), Jasper (9, 1968); River Plantation G&CC, Conroe (27, 1968); Roman Hills GC, Splendora; South Shore Harbour GC, League City (1983), with Dave Marr; Sun Meadow CC, Houston.

Panama: Club de G Panama.

Courses Remodeled & Added to by: Jay Riviere
Louisiana: Acadian Hills CC, Lafayette (R.); Bayou Bend CC, Crowley (R.); Lake Charles G&CC (R.); Oakbourne CC, Lafayette (R.); Pine Hills GC, Monroe (R.).

Michigan: Blythefield CC, Belmont (R., 1973).

Texas: Baywood CC, Houston (R.); Inwood Forest CC, Houston (A.9); Quail Valley CC, Missouri City (A.27); Riverbend CC, Sugarland (R.); Riverside Muni, Victoria (R.); Sharpstown CC, Houston (R.); Stephen F. Austin GC, San Felipe (R.); Temple CC (R.9); Temple CC (A.9).

Harry Robb Sr. (1894 - 1952)
Born: Montrose, Scotland. Died: Kansas City, Kansas at age 58.

Harry Robb apprenticed under pro James Winton (father of golf architect Tom Winton) on the links at Montrose. Besides learning club making from Winton, he also developed a fine competitive game and won several local Artisan tournaments. In 1912 he emigrated to America with his boyhood friend Tom Clark, who was also seeking work as a golf professional. After serving a short time as assistant pro at the Houston (Texas) CC, Robb moved to the Hutchinson (Ks.) GC, succeeding Clark as head professional. While in Hutchinson, he introduced the game to many small Kansas communities and laid out nine-hole courses in several of them.

In 1916 Robb moved to Kansas City, Ks., again at Clark's behest. There he supervised construction of Milburn G&CC to the plans of William B. Langford and stayed on as head professional. He remained at Milburn for the rest of his life, except for military service during World War I and a brief trip back to Scotland to marry his childhood sweetheart. He continued to design an occasional course while at Milburn and laid out several in the Kansas City area during the 1920s. Upon his retirement from Milburn in the early '50s, his son succeeded him as professional.

Courses by: Harry Robb
Kansas: Dodge City CC (9); Emporia CC (9); Iola CC (NLE, 9); Lake Barton GC, Great Bend; Newton CC (9); Old Mission G&CC, Kansas City (NLE, 27, 1930); Ottawa CC (9); Tomahawk Hills GC; White Lakes GC, Topeka (NLE,).

Russell Roberts (1922 -)
Born: Gaithersburg, Maryland.

Russell Roberts studied engineering while serving with the United States Navy during World War II. After the war he joined Frank Murray in the construction of several courses to the plans of golf architect Alfred Tull. Between 1955 and 1959 the partnership of Murray and Roberts was involved in designing and building courses of their own. After Murray relocated in Florida, Roberts continued to lay out courses on his own along the Atlantic seaboard.

Courses by: Russell Roberts
Delaware: Cavaliers CC, New Castle (1959), with Frank Murray; Mapledale CC, Dover; Old Landing GC, Rehobeth (9), with Frank Murray; Rehobeth Beach CC (1962), with Frank Murray.

Maryland: Andrews AFB GC (East Course) (1956), with Frank Murray; Bel Aire G&CC, Bowie (27, 1959), with Frank Murray; Chantilly Manor CC, Rising Sun (1969); Hagerstown Muni (1957), with Frank Murray; Holly Hill CC, Frederick (1974); Maryland G&CC, Belair , with Frank Murray; Nassawango CC, Snow Hill (1970); Newbridge CC, Largo; Northampton CC, Upper Marlboro (1972); Rocky Point GC, Essex (1971); Swan Creek GC, Belair (1956), with Frank Murray; Valley Springs GC, Oxen Hill (9); Washingtonian CC (Country Club Course), Gaithersburg (1960), with Frank Murray; Washingtonian CC (National Course), Gaithersburg (1962), with Frank Murray.

Pennsylvania: Fairview G&CC, Quentin (1959), with Frank Murray; Lebanon CC, with Frank Murray; Penn Oaks CC, West Chester (1966), with Frank Murray.

Virginia: Eastern Shore Y&CC, Onancock (9); Lakeview CC (27); Woodlawn CC, Mt. Vernon (9, 1969).

West Virginia: Moorefield Petersburg GC; Valley View CC, White Sulphur Spgs (9, 1963).

Courses Remodeled & Added to by: Russell Roberts
Delaware: Newark CC (A.9, 1956), with Frank Murray.

Maryland: Chestnut Ridge CC, Lutherville (R.9, 1966); Chestnut Ridge CC, Lutherville (A.9, 1966); Ocean City G&YC, Berlin (A.9).

Allan Robertson (1815 - 1859)
Born: St. Andrews, Scotland. Died: St. Andrews, Scotland at age 44.

Allan Robertson, a prominent St. Andrews ball maker and the greatest golfer of his day, is considered the first professional golfer in history. In 1858 he became the first person to break 80 at St. Andrews, an incredible feat at that time. He used a gutta-percha ball in his record round, even though as a maker of feathery balls, he had previously opposed the gutty.

At the urging of Sir Hugh Playfair, (who, as Provost of St. Andrews in 1842, had set about improving the town) Robertson exercised a general supervision of the St. Andrews links. He was credited with the 1848 modifications to the Old Course that widened the fairways and created the now-famous huge double greens. Robertson also built a new seventeenth green on the classic Road Hole. Apart from St. Andrews, Allan Robertson laid out links in various districts of Scotland, including a 10 hole course in Barry, Angus that ultimately became Carnoustie. He was certainly, if unofficially, the first greenkeeper and golf course designer in history as well as the first golf professional.

David Robertson

The elder brother of Allan Robertson, Davie Robertson was a ball maker and senior caddy at St. Andrews. In 1848 he emigrated to Australia, where he introduced golf and later helped to establish the Australian Golf Society. He laid out some of that country's first courses.

Cabell B. Robinson (1941 -) ASGCA
Born: Washington, D.C.
Cabell Robinson received a B.A. degree in History from Princeton University in 1963 and then studied design for a year at Harvard, where he was a classmate of Rees Jones, son of golf architect Robert Trent Jones. In 1967 he obtained a Bachelor's degree in Landscape Architecture from the University of California at Berkeley and in the autumn of that year went to work for Robert Trent Jones in New Jersey. In 1970 Robinson moved to Spain to organize a European office for Robert Trent Jones Inc. Over the next fifteen years, Robinson handled most of the Jones designs done in Britain, Europe and North Africa.
Courses by: Cabell Robinson
England: Moor Allerton GC, Yorkshire (27, 1971), with Robert Trent Jones.
Ireland: Ballybunion GC (New Course), County Kerry (1985), with Robert Trent Jones and Roger Rulewich.
Italy: I Roveri GC, Turin (27, 1976), with Robert Trent Jones.
Morocco: Royal G Dar Es Salaam (Blue Course), Rabat (1974), with Robert Trent Jones; Royal G Dar Es Salaam (Green Course), Rabat (9, 1974), with Robert Trent Jones; Royal G Dar Es Salaam (Red Course), Rabat (1971), with Robert Trent Jones.
Portugal: Quinta da Marinha GC, Faro (1985), with Robert Trent Jones; Troia GC, Setubal (1980), with Robert Trent Jones.
Sardinia: Pevero GC, Costa Smeralda (1972), with Robert Trent Jones.
Spain: Club de G Mijas (Los Lagos Course), Fuengirola, Malaga (1976), with Robert Trent Jones; Club de G Mijas (Los Olivos Course), Fuengirola, Malaga (1984), with Robert Trent Jones; El Bosque GC, Valencia (1975), with Robert Trent Jones; Los Lagos GC, Mijas (1976), with Robert Trent Jones; Nueva Andulucia GC (Los Naranjos Course), Marbella, Malaga (1977), with Robert Trent Jones; Sotogrande GC (New Course), Cadiz (1975), with Robert Trent Jones.
Switzerland: Geneva G&CC (1973), with Robert Trent Jones.
Courses Remodeled & Added to by: Cabell Robinson
France: Chamonix GC (R., 1980), with Robert Trent Jones.
Greece: Glyfada GC, Athens (R., 1978), with Robert Trent Jones.
West Germany: Hamburg-Ahrensburg GC, Hamburg (R., 1978), with Robert Trent Jones.

Clinton E. Robinson (1907 -) ASGCA, President, 1961, 1971.
Born: St. Amadee, Quebec, Canada.
C.E. "Robbie" Robinson received a B.S.A. Degree in 1929 from the University of Toronto's Agricultural College at Guelph, Ontario. He became interested in golf course architecture during his undergraduate years, when he updated and renovated the private course of Sir Joseph Flavelle (a Canadian magnate and prominent World War I statesman) at Fenelon Falls, Ontario. After graduation he embarked on an apprenticeship of several years duration with golf architect Stanley Thompson, who arranged a stint as course manager and superintendent at Sunningdale CC in London, Ontario for Robinson.
In 1936 Robinson returned to the Thompson firm and then served with the Royal Canadian Air Force during World War II. Following military service, he was employed in site selection and development of housing with the Canadian government's Central Mortgage and Housing Department.
Robinson entered full-time private practice as a course architect in 1961, having designed and remodeled several courses on a part-time basis prior to that. He became recognized as an authority on turfgrass culture and for several years was director of the Royal Canadian Golf Association's Green Section. Robinson exerted considerable influence on the policies of his architectural profession. The top names in Canadian golf architecture after the death of Stanley Thompson were generally considered to be those of Clinton Robinson and Howard Watson. Ironically, both had started work for Thompson on the same day in 1929. In addition to his native Canada, Robinson worked in the U.S., the Caribbean and South America.
Courses by: Clinton E. Robinson
Michigan: Lemontree GC, Belleville (9).
Pennsylvania: Warren GC.
Alberta: Windermere G&CC, Edmonton.
Manitoba: John Blumberg Muni, Winnipeg (27, 1970); Steinback Fly Inn GC (9).
New Brunswick: Gagetown GC, Oromocto (9); Gowan Brae GC, Bathurst , with Robert Moote; Sussex GC.
Newfoundland: Terra Nova National Park GC.
Nova Scotia: Northumberland G&CC, Pugwash; Oakfield CC, Grand Lake (1965).
Ontario: Antonio GC, Toronto (Precision,); Bayview G&CC, Thornhill; Beverly GC, Copetown , with Robert Moote; Blue Mountain G&CC, Collingwood (9); Bowmanville CC (9); Bridgeport Fairways, Connestoga (Precision, 1969); Cambridge GC; Cedar Brae G&CC, East Toronto; Chatham G&CC; Conestoga G&TC; Coral Creek G&CC, Fisherville (9); Craig Gowan GC, Woodstock , with Robert Moote; Craigowan G&CC, Woodstock; Dalewood G&Curling C, Port Hope; Dearhurst GC, Hidden Valley (Par 3,); Doon Valley GC, Kitchener , with Robert Moote; Dryden G&CC, with Robert Moote; East Park GC, London (Precision,); Elgin House GC, Port Carling (1969); Fort Frances GC; Galaglades G & CC, Cambridge; Georgetown GC, with Robert Moote; Hawthorne Valley G&CC, Mississauga (Par 3, 1961), with Robert Moote; Hidden Valley GC (Precision, 1968); Holiday Inn GC, Sarnia (Par 3, 9); Huron Pines G&CC, Blind River; Lido Golf Centre, Oakville; Maple City

G&CC, Chatham , with Robert Moote; Merry Hill G&CC; Mount Hope G&CC, with Robert Moote; Oxford G&CC, Woodstock; Parkview GC, Milliken; Richmond Hill G&CC, Richmond , with Robert Moote; Richview G&CC, Oakville; South Muskoka Curling & GC, Bracebridge (1973); Strathcona GC, Huntsville (Precision, 1970); Sturgeon Point GC; Sunningdale CC (New Course), London (1970); Trafalgar G&CC, Milton , with Robert Moote; Twenty Valley G&CC, Beamsville , with Robert Moote; Tyandaca Muni, Burlington; Upper Canada GC, Morrisburg (1966).
Prince Edward Island: Brudenell G&CC, Montague (1969); Mill River GC, O'Leary (1971); Stanhope G&CC.
Quebec: Club de G Baie Comeau, Hauterire , with Robert Moote.
Saskatchewan: Holiday Park GC, Saskatoon.
Colombia: Medellin GC, with Stanley Thompson.
Courses Remodeled & Added to by: Clinton E. Robinson
Michigan: Dearborn CC (R.); Monroe G&CC (R.); Red Run GC, Royal Oak (R.).
Pennsylvania: Melrose CC, Cheltenham (R.).
Alberta: Earl Grey GC (R.).
British Columbia: Burnaby Mountain GC (R.); University GC, Vancouver (R., 1985); Vancouver GC (R.).
Manitoba: Elmhurst G Links, Winnepeg (R.3); Pine Ridge G&CC, Winnipeg (R.); Portage La Prairie GC (R.9); Portage La Prairie GC (A.9); St. Charles CC (North Nine), Winnipeg (R.).
New Brunswick: Fredericton GC (R.1); Miramichi G&CC, Bushville (A.9); Moncton G&CC (R.); Restigouche G&CC, Campbellton (A.9); Riverside G&CC (R.); Westfield G&CC (R.9); Westfield G&CC (A.9).
Newfoundland: Ken-Wo G&CC, New Minas (A.9).
Nova Scotia: Abercrombie CC, New Glasgow (A.9); Lingan GC, Sydney (A.9); Oakville GC (R.); Seaview GC, North Sydney (A.9); Seaview GC, North Sydney (R.9); Truro GC (A.9); Truro GC (R.9).
Ontario: Barcoven GC (R.); Bay of Quinte GC, Bellville (A.9), with Robert Moote; Beach Grove G&CC, Walkerville (R.); Belleville G&CC, Marysville (A.9); Brantford G&CC (R.), with Robert Moote; Brantford G&CC (R.); Brockville CC (A.9); C.F.B. Borden GC (R.); Cherry Hill GC, Ontario (R.); Credit Valley G&CC, Toronto (R.); Dundas Valley GC (R.); Glen Lawrence G&CC, Kinston (R.); Glendale G&CC (R.); Golfland GC, Hamilton (Par 3, R.); Hamilton G&CC, Ancaster (A.9, 1975); Huntington GC, Nashville (R., 1961), with Robert Moote; Lake St. George G&CC (R.9); Lake St. George G&CC (A.9); Lambton G&CC, Toronto (R.); Manaki G&CC (R.); Muskoka Lakes G&CC, Port Carling (A.9); Oakdale G&CC, Downsview (A.9), with Robert Moote; Oakland Greens GC (A.9); Oshawa GC (R.6, 1981); Pine Lake GC (A.9); Rideau View CC, Manotick (A.9); Rosedale CC, Toronto (R.); Sarnia GC (R.); Spruce Needles GC, Timmins (R.9); Spruce Needles GC, Timmins (A.9); St. Catharines G&CC (R.), with Robert Moote; St. George's G&CC, Islington (R.4, 1967); St. Thomas G&CC (A.9); Thornhill GC (R.); Thunder Bay G&CC (R.); Westmount GC, Kitchener (R.), with Robert Moote; Westmount GC, Kitchener (A.4), with Robert Moote; Whirlpool GC, Niagara Falls (R.).
Prince Edward Island: Belvedere G & Winter C, Charlottetown (R.); Green Gables GC, Charlottetown (R.); Green Gables GC, Charlottetown (A.9).
Quebec: Beaconsfield G&CC, Montreal (R.); Elm Ridge CC (Course No. 1), Ile Bizard (R.); Kanawaki GC (R.); Ki-8-EB GC, Three Rivers (R.); Laval sur le Lac GC (R.); Royal Ottawa GC, Hull (R.).
Saskatchewan: Kenosee Lakes GC (A.9); Madge Lake GC (A.9); Madge Lake GC (R.9); Regina GC (R.); Wascana G&CC (R.); Waskesiu Lake GC (R.).

John F. Robinson (1947 -)
Born: Toronto, Ontario, Canada.
John Robinson, younger brother of golf architect William G. Robinson, attended the University of Michigan and received a Bachelor's degree in Landscape Architecture in 1970. During his college years, he worked summers for golf architect William Newcomb and upon graduation became his senior associate. Robinson assisted Newcomb in the design and construction of eight courses over a three-year period.
After a brief stint as a senior landscape architect with a large engineering firm in Toronto, Robinson laid out six courses of his own in Ontario, Kentucky and Antigua.
Robinson was then associated for a short period with golf architect Dave Bennett before collaborating on several projects with his brother Bill. In addition, he planned a housing development in Algeria and taught golf course architecture for Professor Jack Eggens at the University of Guelph.
Courses by: John F. Robinson
Kentucky: Woodson Bend CC, Burnside (9, 1975), with Dave Bennett.
Courses Remodeled & Added to by: John F. Robinson
New Brunswick: Rockwood Park GC (A.3), with William G. Robinson.
Ontario: Blue Mountain GC (A.9), with William G. Robinson; Cedar Glenn G&CC (A.9).

Theodore G. Robinson (1923 -) ASGCA, President, 1983.
Born: California.
Ted Robinson received an B.A. Degree in Naval Science from the University of California in 1944 and an Master's in Urban Planning and Landscape Architecture from the University of Southern California in 1948. Following graduation, he was employed with a general land planning and park design firm. In 1954 he established his own practice involved in land planning, subdivisions, and park design. He added golf course design to his business in the early Sixties after handling land plans on several residential development layouts.
Robinson had been introduced to golf by his father, who was active and well known in amateur golf circles and had long been involved with the game. Nevertheless, the transition from land planner to golf architect took Ted Robinson nearly ten years to accomplish. By the 1970s Robinson concentrated solely on course design and had worked extensively in the western United States, Mexico and the Pacific. Robinson also had planned two courses in Iran, but neither were ever built as a result of political unrest.
Courses by: Ted Robinson
Arizona: Dorado CC, Tucson (1972); Ocotillo CC, Chandler (27, 1987); Westbrook Village CC, Peoria (Precision, 1982).

California: Bernardo Heights CC, Rancho Bernardo (1983); Braemar CC (East Course), Tarzana (1963); Braemar CC (West Course), Tarzana (1963); Camarillo Springs CC (1971); Canyon Lake GC (1969); Canyon Lakes CC, Danville (1987); Casta del Sol GC, Mission Viejo (Precision, 1974); Cerritos Iron-Wood Nine GC, Cerritos (Precision, 9, 1976); Chaparral CC, Palm Desert (1980); Crow Canyon CC, Danville (1976); Desert Aire CC, Palmdale (1960); Desert Horizons CC, Indian Wells (1979); Desert Springs GC, Palm Desert (1986); DeAnza Palm Springs Mobile CC, Cathedral City (Precision, 1970); Diamond Oaks CC, Roseville (1964); Discovery Bay CC, Sacremento (1987); Fairbanks Ranch CC, Rancho Santa Fe (1984); Fountain Grove GC, Santa Rosa (1985); Indian Wells G Resort (East Course) (1986); Indian Wells G Resort (West Course) (1986); Inglewood GC (Par 3, 1965); Ironwood CC (North Course), Palm Desert (1978); Lake Lindero GC (Precision, 9); Lakes CC, Palm Desert (1983); Lomas Santa Fe Executive GC, Solana Beach (Precision, 1974); Marrakesh CC, Palm Desert (Precision, 1971); Meridian Valley CC, Kent (1967); Mission Bay GC, San Diego (Par 3, 1964); Mission Lakes CC, Desert Hot Springs (1972); Monterey CC, Palm Desert (27, 1979); Mountain Gate CC, Los Angeles (1975); Mountain Meadows GC, Pomona (1975); Navy GC (Cruiser Course), Cypress (9, 1970); North Ranch CC, Westlake (1975); Oak Tree CC, Tehachapi (1973); Oakmont CC (East Course), Santa Rosa (Precision, 1974); Oakmont CC (West Course), Santa Rosa (1964); Oaks North GC, Rancho Bernardo (Precision, 27, 1971); Old Ranch CC, Seal Beach (1968); Palm Desert Greens CC, Palm Desert (Precision, 1971); Palm Valley CC (North Course), Palm Desert (Precision, 1986); Palm Valley CC (South Course), Palm Desert (1984); Porter Valley CC, North Ridge (1968); Rams Hill CC, Borrego Springs (1982); Rancho Las Palmas CC, Rancho Mirage (27, 1977); Rancho Murieta CC (South Course), Sloughhouse (1979); Rancho Santa Ynez CC, Solvang (Par 3, 1984); Reflections GC, La Quinta (Par 3, 1986); Rolling Hills CC, Rolling Hills Estate (1969); San Vicente CC, Ramona (1972); Seven Lakes CC, Palm Springs (Precision, 1964); Silver Lakes CC, Helendale (27, 1975); Sun 'n Sky CC, Barstow (9); Sunrise CC, Rancho Mirage (Precision, 1974); Sunset Hills CC, Thousand Oaks (Precision, 1974); Vandenberg Village CC; Village CC, Lompoc (1962); Vista Valley CC, Vista (1979); Westlake Village GC (Precision, 1966); Wood Ranch GC, Simi Valley (1985).

Hawaii: Kalua Koi GC, Mauna Loa (1977); West Beach GC (1987).

Maryland: Tantallon CC (1961).

Nevada: Sunrise GC, Las Vegas (9, 1962).

New Mexico: Inn of the Mountain Gods GC, Mescalero (1976).

Oregon: Charbonneau GC, Wilsonville (Precision, 27, 1978); Summerfield G&CC, Tigard (Precision, 9, 1973); Tokatee GC, Blue River (1967).

Texas: Bear Creek G&RC (East Course), Dallas-Ft. Worth (1980); Bear Creek G&RC (West Course), Dallas-Ft. Worth (1981).

Washington: Everett G&CC (1969); Highland GC, Tacoma (Par 3, 9, 1968); Mill Creek CC, Bothell (1974); Sahalee CC, Redmond (27, 1969); Sudden Valley G&CC, Bellingham (1972).

Japan: Lakewood GC (East Course), Kanagawa (1973); Lakewood GC (West Course), Kanagawa (1970).

Mexico: Acapulco Princess CC (1972).

Courses Remodeled & Added to by: Ted Robinson

California: Alondra Park GC (Course No. 1), Lawndale (R., 1978); Candlewood CC, Whittier (R.6, 1971); El Dorado Park GC, Long Beach (R.12, 1962); Fullerton Muni (A.9); Hacienda CC, La Habra (R.2, 1965); Indian Wells CC (R., 1984); Ironwood CC (South Course), Palm Desert (R., 1978); La Jolla CC (R.3, 1973); Los Coyotes CC (R.6, 1970); Mountain Gate CC, Los Angeles (A.9, 1981); Navy GC (North Course), San Diego (R.6, 1970); Pala Mesa G&TC, Fallbrook (R., 1984); Palos Verdes CC (R., 1977); Pauma Valley CC (R.1, 1983); Rancho Bernardo Inn & CC (West Course) (R.3, 1984); Singing Hills CC (Oak Glen Course), El Cajon (R., 1981); Singing Hills CC (Pine Glen Course), El Cajon (R., 1982); Singing Hills CC (Willow Glen Course), El Cajon (R., 1981); Stardust CC, San Diego (R.6, 1976); Stoneridge CC, Poway (R.9, 1971); Stoneridge CC, Poway (A.9, 1971); Tamarisk CC, Rancho Mirage (R., 1972); Thunderbird CC, Cathedral City (R., 1986).

Nevada: Sunrise GC, Las Vegas (A.9, 1970).

Washington: Royal Oaks CC, Vancouver (R.2, 1970); Seattle GC (R., 1969); Yakima CC (R.5, 1974).

Bermuda: Southampton Princess GC (Par 3, R., 1972).

William Grieve Robinson (1941 -) ASGCA

Born: Ontario, Canada.

As a young man, Bill Robinson turned down an opportunity to play professional hockey, deciding instead for a career in golf design. He studied landscape architecture at Penn State University and graduated in 1964 after two summers' experience working for the firm of Robert Trent Jones. A scratch golfer, he was a member of the Penn State golf team.

Following graduation, Robinson joined the practice of golf architect Geoffrey S. Cornish. In 1977 he formed and became President of Cornish and Robinson Golf Course Designers Ltd. of Calgary, Alberta, and engaged in designing courses in oil rich Alberta and surrounding provinces. Robinson pioneered methods for modifying established layouts through long-range planning, and researched putting green design and bunker placement. A talented freehand artist, Robinson illustrated many magazine articles dealing with course design, and coauthored (with Cornish) the booklet, *Golf Course Design - An Introduction*, distributed by the National Golf Foundation in the early 1970s.

Courses by: William G. Robinson

Connecticut: Blackledge CC, Hebron (1966), with Geoffrey S. Cornish; Century Hills CC, Rocky Hill (1974), with Geoffrey S. Cornish; Clinton CC (1967), with Geoffrey S. Cornish; Connecticut GC {formerly Golf Club at Aspetuck}, Easton (1966), with Geoffrey S. Cornish; Laurel View Muni, Hamden (1969), with Geoffrey S. Cornish; Neipsic Par 3 GC, Glastonbury (1974), with Geoffrey S. Cornish; Patton Brook GC, Southington (Precision, 1967), with Geoffrey S. Cornish; Portland GC (1974), with Geoffrey S. Cornish; Simsbury Farms Muni (1971), with Geoffrey S. Cornish; South Pine Creek GC, Fairfield (Par 3, 9, 1968), with Geoffrey S. Cornish; Sterling Farms Muni, Stamford (1971), with Geoffrey S. Cornish.

Maine: Running Hills CC, Frye Island , with Geoffrey S. Cornish.

Maryland: Towson G&CC (1971), with Geoffrey S. Cornish.

Massachusetts: Cranberry Valley GC, Harwich (1974), with Geoffrey S. Cornish; Dunfey's GC, Hyannis (Par 3, 1966), with Geoffrey S. Cornish; Far Corner Farm GC, West Boxford (1967), with Geoffrey S. Cornish; Farm Neck GC, Martha's Vineyard (9, 1976), with Geoffrey S. Cornish; Grasmere GC, Falmouth (Par 3, 9), with Geoffrey S. Cornish; Greylock Glen CC, Adams (1973), with Geoffrey S. Cornish; Heritage Hills GC, Lakeville (Par 3, 1970), with Geoffrey S. Cornish; Hickory Ridge CC, Amherst (1969), with Geoffrey S. Cornish; Holly Ridge GC, South Sandwich (Par 3, 1966), with Geoffrey S. Cornish; Iyanough Hills GC, Hyannis (1975), with Geoffrey S. Cornish; Middleton GC (Par 3, 1965), with Geoffrey S. Cornish; Pine Oaks GC, Easton (9, 1966), with Geoffrey S. Cornish; Quashnet Valley CC (9, 1976), with Geoffrey S. Cornish; Rehoboth GC (1966), with Geoffrey S. Cornish; Stow Acres CC (North Course), Stow (1965), with Geoffrey S. Cornish.

New Hampshire: Bretwood GC, Keene (1967), with Geoffrey S. Cornish; Cold Spring GC (1976), with Geoffrey S. Cornish; Eastman Lake CC, Grantham (1975), with Geoffrey S. Cornish.

New Jersey: Bowling Green GC, Milton (1966), with Geoffrey S. Cornish.

New York: Addison Pinnacle CC (9, 1969), with Geoffrey S. Cornish; Endwell Greens GC, Johnson City (1965), with Geoffrey S. Cornish; Grassy Brook GC, Alder Creek (9, 1974), with Geoffrey S. Cornish; Heritage Hills of Westchester, Somers (9, 1974), with Geoffrey S. Cornish; Higby Hills CC, Utica (1966), with Geoffrey S. Cornish; Honey Hill CC, Newport (1967), with Geoffrey S. Cornish; Vesper Hills CC, Otisco , with Geoffrey S. Cornish.

Ohio: Dayton CC (1965), with Geoffrey S. Cornish; Westfield CC (North Course) (1974), with Geoffrey S. Cornish; Zoar Village GC (1974), with Geoffrey S. Cornish.

Pennsylvania: Hershey Pocono GC, White Haven (1970), with Geoffrey S. Cornish; Host Farms GC (Executive Course), Lancaster (Precision, 9, 1967), with Geoffrey S. Cornish; Mill Race GC, Benton (9, 1973), with Geoffrey S. Cornish; Standing Stone GC, Huntingdon (1972), with Geoffrey S. Cornish; Sugarloaf GC (1966), with Geoffrey S. Cornish; Wilkes-Barre Muni (1967), with Geoffrey S. Cornish.

Rhode Island: Cranston CC (1974), with Geoffrey S. Cornish.

Vermont: Farms Motel GC (Par 3, 1970), with Geoffrey S. Cornish; Manchester CC (1969), with Geoffrey S. Cornish; Mount Snow GC (1970), with Geoffrey S. Cornish; Quechee Lakes CC (Highland Course) (1970), with Geoffrey S. Cornish; Quechee Lakes CC (Lakeland Course) (1975), with Geoffrey S. Cornish; Stratton Mountain Golf Academy (1972), with Geoffrey S. Cornish; Stratton Mountain GC (1969), with Geoffrey S. Cornish.

Washington: Birch Bay GC (Par 3, 1982).

West Virginia: Canaan Valley State Park GC (1966), with Geoffrey S. Cornish; Pipestem State Park GC (1966), with Geoffrey S. Cornish; Twin Falls State Park GC, Mullens (9, 1966), with Geoffrey S. Cornish.

Alberta: Cardiff GC; Carstairs G&CC (9); Douglasdale Estates GC (Precision, 1985); Enoch Hills GC (36, 1987); Ponoka Community GC (1987); River Bend Muni, Red Deer (1986); Spruce Grove GC, Edmonton.

British Columbia: Gallaghers Canyon GC, Kelowna (1979); Hatch Point CC, Victoria (9, 1987); Okanagon Park GC, Kelowna (Par 3, 9, 1979); Poplar Hills G&CC, Fort Nelson (9, 1979).

New Brunswick: Campobello Provincial Park GC (9), with Geoffrey S. Cornish; Old Mill Pond GC (9, 1984).

Nova Scotia: Halifax G&CC (New Ashburn) (1969), with Geoffrey S. Cornish.

Ontario: Clairville GC, Toronto (1987); York Downs G&CC, Toronto (27, 1970), with Geoffrey S. Cornish.

Greece: Links at Porto Carras, New Marmoras (1975), with Geoffrey S. Cornish.

Courses Remodeled & Added to by: William G. Robinson

Connecticut: Avon CC (A.9, 1966), with Geoffrey S. Cornish; Avon CC (R.18, 1966), with Geoffrey S. Cornish; Glastonbury Hills CC (R.4, 1973), with Geoffrey S. Cornish; Hartford GC, West Hartford (R.2, 1972), with Geoffrey S. Cornish; Keney Park GC, Hartford (R.3), with Geoffrey S. Cornish; New London CC (R.5), with Geoffrey S. Cornish; Pequabuc CC (A.3), with Geoffrey S. Cornish; Quinnatisset CC (A.9, 1967), with Geoffrey S. Cornish; Stanley GC, New Britain (R.27, 1975), with Geoffrey S. Cornish; Watertown CC (A.9, 1970), with Geoffrey S. Cornish; Wee Burn CC, Darien (R.4, 1978), with Geoffrey S. Cornish; Wethersfield CC (R.1, 1978), with Geoffrey S. Cornish; Woodway CC, Darien (R.4), with Geoffrey S. Cornish.

Delaware: DuPont CC (DuPont Course), Wilmington (R., 1980), with Geoffrey S. Cornish; DuPont CC (Louviers Course), Wilmington (R., 1980), with Geoffrey S. Cornish; DuPont CC (Montchanin Course), Newark (R., 1980), with Geoffrey S. Cornish; DuPont CC (Nemours Course), Wilmington (R., 1980), with Geoffrey S. Cornish.

Maine: Brunswick GC (A.9, 1964), with Geoffrey S. Cornish; Riverside Muni, Portland (A.9, 1967), with Geoffrey S. Cornish; Treadway-Samoset GC, Rockport (R.), with Geoffrey S. Cornish; Waterville CC (A.9, 1966), with Geoffrey S. Cornish; Webhannett GC, Kennebunkport (R.4, 1970), with Geoffrey S. Cornish.

Massachusetts: Berkshire Hills CC, Pittsfield (R.4), with Geoffrey S. Cornish; Brae Burn CC, West Newton (R.2, 1970), with Geoffrey S. Cornish; Brewster Green GC (NLE, A.2, 1979), with Geoffrey S. Cornish; Dedham Hunt & Polo C (R.2), with Geoffrey S. Cornish; Duxbury YC (A.9, 1969), with Geoffrey S. Cornish; Ellinwood CC, Athol (A.9, 1969), with Geoffrey S. Cornish; Fall River CC (A.9, 1975), with Geoffrey S. Cornish; Foxborough CC (A.9, 1970), with Geoffrey S. Cornish; Framingham CC (A.2), with Geoffrey S. Cornish; Franconia Muni, Springfield (R.7, 1973), with Geoffrey S. Cornish; Fresh Pond Muni, Cambridge (A.9, 1967), with Geoffrey S. Cornish; Marlborough CC, Marlboro (A.9, 1969), with Geoffrey S. Cornish; Oak Hill CC, Fitchburg (R.5, 1966), with Geoffrey S. Cornish; Quabog GC (R.2), with Geoffrey S. Cornish; Segregansett CC (A.9, 1976), with Geoffrey S. Cornish; Stow Acres CC (South Course), Stow (R.9, 1965), with Geoffrey S. Cornish; Stow Acres CC (South Course), Stow (A.9, 1965), with Geoffrey S. Cornish; Tatnuck CC, Worcester (R.5), with Geoffrey S. Cornish; The Country Club, Brookline (R.2, 1969), with Geoffrey S. Cornish.

Minnesota: Somerset CC, St. Paul (R., 1979), with Geoffrey S. Cornish; Woodhill CC, Wayzata (R., 1979), with Geoffrey S. Cornish.

Montana: Crystal Lakes CC (A.9, 1986); Valley View GC (A.9, 1986); Valley View GC (R.9, 1986).

New Hampshire: Abenaqui C (R.), with Geoffrey S. Cornish; Beaver Meadows Muni (A.9, 1968), with Geoffrey S. Cornish; Hanover CC, Dartmouth College (R., 1970), with Geoffrey S. Cornish; Wentworth-by-the-Sea GC, Portsmouth (A.9,

1965), with Geoffrey S. Cornish.
New Jersey: Echo Lake CC, Westfield (A.3, 1968), with Geoffrey S. Cornish; Echo Lake CC, Westfield (R.3, 1968), with Geoffrey S. Cornish; Knickerbocker CC, Tenafly (R.6, 1973), with Geoffrey S. Cornish.
New York: CC of Buffalo, Williamsville (R., 1965), with Geoffrey S. Cornish; Highland Park CC (A.9, 1973), with Geoffrey S. Cornish; Ives Hill CC, Watertown (A.9, 1974), with Geoffrey S. Cornish; Monroe CC (R.2, 1965), with Geoffrey S. Cornish; Oswego CC (A.9, 1977), with Geoffrey S. Cornish; Shepard Hill CC (A.9, 1970), with Geoffrey S. Cornish; Siwanoy CC, Bronxville (R.), with Geoffrey S. Cornish; Sodus Point GC (A.9, 1966), with Geoffrey S. Cornish; St. Lawrence Univ, Canton (A.12, 1971), with Geoffrey S. Cornish; Thendara CC, Old Forge (R.1, 1968), with Geoffrey S. Cornish; Twin Hills GC, Spencerport (Precision, A., 1967), with Geoffrey S. Cornish.
Ohio: Avon Oaks CC (R.6, 1978), with Geoffrey S. Cornish; Canterbury CC, Shaker Heights (R., 1978), with Geoffrey S. Cornish; Miami Valley CC, Dayton (R., 1965), with Geoffrey S. Cornish; Portage CC, Akron (R.), with Geoffrey S. Cornish; Westfield CC (South Course) (R.9, 1967), with Geoffrey S. Cornish; Westfield CC (South Course) (A.9, 1967), with Geoffrey S. Cornish.
Pennsylvania: Concordville CC (A.4, 1974), with Geoffrey S. Cornish; Mill Race GC, Benton (A.9, 1977), with Geoffrey S. Cornish.
Rhode Island: Point Judith CC (R.9, 1964), with Geoffrey S. Cornish; Quidnesset CC, East Greenwich (A.9, 1974), with Geoffrey S. Cornish.
Vermont: Montague GC (A.3), with Geoffrey S. Cornish.
Alberta: Calgary G&CC (R., 1978); Canyon Meadows G&CC, Calgary (R., 1978); Edmonton G&CC (R., 1979); Inglewood Muni, Calgary (A.9, 1978); Innisfail G&CC (A.9, 1986); Lethbridge GC (A.9, 1982); Lethbridge GC (R., 1982); Red Deer G&CC (R., 1980); Sturgeon Valley G&CC, St. Alberts (A.12, 1979).
British Columbia: Point Grey G&CC (R., 1973), with Geoffrey S. Cornish; Quilchena G&CC (R.6, 1979), with Geoffrey S. Cornish; Vancouver GC (R.).
Manitoba: Breezy Bend CC (R., 1973), with Geoffrey S. Cornish; Dauphin G&CC (A.9, 1985); Elm Ridge CC (Course No. 1) (R., 1978), with Geoffrey S. Cornish; Elmhurst G Links, Winnepeg (R.2), with Geoffrey S. Cornish; St. Charles CC (North Nine), Winnipeg (R.), with Geoffrey S. Cornish; St. Charles CC (West Nine), Winnipeg (R.), with Geoffrey S. Cornish; St. Charles CC (West Nine), Winnipeg (R.), with Geoffrey S. Cornish.
New Brunswick: Fredericton GC (R.2, 1967), with Geoffrey S. Cornish; Rockwood Park GC (A.3), with John F. Robinson.
Nova Scotia: Northumberland G&CC, Pugwash (A.9, 1987).
Ontario: Blue Mountain GC (A.9), with John F. Robinson.
Saskatchewan: Riverside G&CC, Saskatoon (R., 1980).

William James Rockefeller (1864 - 1932)
Born: Binghampton, New York. Died: Toledo, Ohio at age 67.
W.J. Rockefeller grew up on his family's farm in New York, studied music for a time and worked as a hospital orderly before being hired as greenkeeper at the newly formed Inverness Club in Toledo, Ohio in 1903. He remained at Inverness for the rest of his life and in 1918 supervised construction of the remodeling and expansion of the course by Donald Ross. The experience led him to take on some design and reconstruction projects of his own in the Toledo area.
Rockefeller was also known as a fine turfman and teacher of course maintenance. Two of his students became outstanding course superintendents, Joe Mayo of Pebble Beach and Al Schardt of Buffalo.
Rockefeller's final project was the preparation of Inverness for the 1931 Open Championship, an exhaustive effort completed only a short time before his death in 1932.
Courses by: William J. Rockefeller
Ohio: Catawba Cliffs CC, Port Clinton; Lakemont CC; Mohawk CC, Tiffon; Napoleon CC.
Courses Remodeled & Added to by: William J. Rockefeller
Ohio: Kettenring CC, Defiance (A.9); Mohawk CC, Tiffon (A.9, 1967); Mohawk CC, Tiffon (R.18, 1967).

William A. "Rocky" Roquemore Jr. (1948 -)
Born: Lakeland, Georgia.
After attending the United States Air Force Academy and Georgia Tech, Rocky Roquemore joined his family in the business of building and operating daily-fee golf courses in the Atlanta area. His father had hired Floridian architect Joe Lee to lay out the first of their projects, and the design process so intrigued Roquemore that he begged Lee for a job. Lee made him a construction foreman in 1969, and stuck him in swamps and atop mountains on various projects. "After I saw he could take it," Lee was to recall some years later, "I brought him into the office."
Roquemore was made Lee's primary associate in 1971, and while remaining in the Atlanta area, he handled most of Lee's course design projects outside Florida. An experienced and talented designer, Roquemore received little public attention for his efforts, in much the same manner as Lee had been overshadowed by his mentor, the legendary Dick Wilson. One of his collaborations with Lee, Stonehenge GC in Fairfield Glade, Tenn. was selected as the Best New Resort Course of 1985 by Golf Digest Magazine and another, Pine Meadow GC near Chicago, was chosen the Best New Public Course of 1986.
Courses by: Rocky Roquemore
Alabama: Wynlakes CC, Montgomery (1987), with Joe Lee.
Florida: Banyan GC, West Palm Beach (1973), with Joe Lee; Bocaire CC, Boca Raton (1985), with Joe Lee; Disney World GC (Magnolia Course), Lake Buena Vista (1970), with Joe Lee; Disney World GC (Palm Course), Lake Buena Vista (1970), with Joe Lee; Hamlet of Delray Beach GC (1973), with Joe Lee; Lake Buena Vista C (1972), with Joe Lee.
Georgia: Big Canoe GC, Lake Sconti (1974), with Joe Lee; Canongate-on Lanier GC, Cumming (1970), with Joe Lee; Hidden Hills CC, Stone Mountain (1974), with Joe Lee; Horseshoe Bend CC, Roswell (1975), with Joe Lee; Indian Hills CC, Marietta (1970), with Joe Lee; Island C, St. Simons Island (1975), with Joe Lee; Okefenokee GC, Waycross (1983), with Joe Lee; Rivermont G&CC, Alpharetta (1970), with Joe Lee; Sea Island GC (Marshside 9), St. Simons Island (1973), with Joe Lee; Snapfinger Woods GC, Decatur (27, 1974), with Joe Lee; Valdosta CC (27, 1981), with Joe Lee; White Oak GC, Newnan (1987), with Joe Lee.
Illinois: Pine Meadow GC, Mundelein (1985), with Joe Lee.
Louisiana: Beau Chene G&RC (Magnolia Course), Mandeville (9, 1983), with Joe Lee; Beau Chene G&RC (Oak Course), Mandeville (1974), with Joe Lee; Eastover CC, New Orleans (1987), with Joe Lee.
North Carolina: Cross Creek CC, Mount Airy (1982), with Joe Lee; Kenmure GC, Flat Rocks (1983), with Joe Lee.
South Carolina: Houndslake CC, Aiken (1976), with Joe Lee.
Tennessee: Fall Creek Falls State Park GC, Pikesville (1972), with Joe Lee; Stonehenge GC, Fairfield Glade (1984), with Joe Lee.
Portugal: Quintado de Lago GC (Course No. 2), Faro (27, 1987), with Joe Lee.
Venezuela: Guataparo GC, Valencia (1982), with Joe Lee; Izcaragua CC, Caracas (1982), with Joe Lee.
Courses Remodeled & Added to by: Rocky Roquemore
Florida: Sugar Mill CC, New Smyrna Beach (A.9, 1983), with Joe Lee; Tyndall AFB GC, Panama City Beach (A.9, 1975), with Joe Lee.
Georgia: Cherokee Town & CC (Riverside Course), Dunwoody (A.9, 1986), with Joe Lee; Flat Creek GC, Peachtree City (A.9, 1983), with Joe Lee; Green Island CC, Columbus (R., 1978), with Joe Lee.
North Carolina: Highlands Falls CC, Highlands (R.5, 1985), with Joe Lee; Highlands Falls CC, Highlands (A.13, 1985), with Joe Lee.
Virginia: CC of Virginia (Tuckahoe Course), Richmond (A.9, 1986), with Joe Lee.
Wisconsin: Lawsonia Links, Green Lake (A.9, 1983), with Joe Lee.

Joseph A. Roseman Sr. (1888 - 1944)
Born: Philadelphia, Pennsylvania. Died: Chicago, Illinois at age 55.
Joseph Roseman began his golf career as a caddy at Philadelphia CC. In 1907 he was hired as professional for Des Moines (Iowa) G&CC and shortly after his arrival took on the additional duties of greenkeeper. Gifted as an inventor, he created a hitch for horses that could accommodate three gang mowers at once, later adopted a Model T Ford to serve as a tractor unit to pull his gang mowers and then invented a hollow mower roller to preserve the turf as it moved.
Following a brief stint as pro-greenkeeper in Racine, Wis., Roseman moved to the Chicago area in 1916. In neighboring Evanston, he founded the Roseman Tractor Mower Co. A short time later he laid out his first golf course, Westmoreland CC in Wilmette. He remained there as pro-superintendent until 1928, when he resigned to devote more time to his mower equipment company.
While course design was always a part-time endeavor, Roseman estimated that he had worked on more than fifty courses, many in collaboration with Jack Croke and George O'Neil. He also pioneered complete underground watering systems on several Chicago-area courses and built one of the first night-lighted par-3 courses in the country in 1933.
Courses by: Joseph A.Roseman
Florida: Fort Lauderdale CC (North Course) (1925).
Illinois: Barrington Hills CC, Barrington (1920), with George O'Neill and Jack Croke; Crystal Lake CC, with George O'Neill and Jack Croke; Glenview NAS GC (Course No. 2) (1927); Glenview NAS GC (Course No.1) (1927); Glenview Park GC {formerly Elmgate CC}, Glenview; Grand Marais GC, East St. Louis; Suburban CC, Waukegan; Waveland GC, Chicago (9, 1924); West Wilmette Illuminated GC, Wilmette (Par 3, 1933); Westmoreland CC, Wilmette (1917); Wilmette GC (1923); Wilmette Park GC, Glenview.
Indiana: Tippecanoe CC, Monticello (1920).
Michigan: Walnut Hills CC, East Lansing.
Wisconsin: Maxwelton Braes GC, Bailey Harbor , with George O'Neill; Petrifying Springs GC, Kenosha (1922); Racine CC.
Courses Remodeled & Added to by: Joseph A.Roseman
Illinois: Glen View CC, Golf (R.), with George O'Neill; Green Acres CC, Northbrook (R.); Tam O'Shanter CC, Niles (NLE, R., 1940).

Donald James Ross (1872 - 1948) ASGCA, Charter Member, Honorary President, 1947, 1948.
Born: Dornoch, Scotland. Died: Pinehurst, North Carolina at age 76.
Donald Ross, son of stonemason Mundo Ross, worked as an apprentice carpenter under Peter Murray of Dornoch. On the advice of John Sutherland, secretary of the Dornoch GC, Ross went to St. Andrews, where he learned club making at David Forgan's shop and studied golf with Old Tom Morris. In 1893 he returned to Dornoch GC and became its pro/greenkeeper. At Dornoch, he gained from Sutherland a lifelong interest in the propagation and maintenance of grass for golf and an understanding of the fundamental qualities of a good golf hole.
In 1898, at the urging of Harvard Astronomy Professor Robert Wilson, Ross emigrated to Boston, Massachusetts where he became pro/greenkeeper at Oakley CC, a rudimentarylayout that he quickly formalized. At Oakley he met members of the wealthy Tufts family of Medford. The Tufts persuaded Ross to become winter golf professional at the resort they were developing at Pinehurst, North Carolina. For several years he continued to spend summers at Oakley CC (and later Essex CC) in Massachusetts and winters at Pinehurst.
The planning and refining of courses at the Pinehurst golf complex brought Ross national fame. His services as a golf architect were soon in demand throughout North America, and from 1912 until his death in 1948, Ross was considered by many to be America's best known and most active course designer. By 1925, 3,000 men were employed annually in the construction of Ross courses. Donald J. Ross Associates Inc. had winter offices at Pinehurst, summer offices at Little Compton, R.I., and branch offices at North Amherst, Mass. (headed by Walter B. Hatch) and Wynnewood, Penn. (headed by J.B. McGovern). Despite his extensive practice, Ross continued as golf manager at Pinehurst until his death.
Ross's design style incorporated naturalness and a links touch derived from his Dornoch background and training with John Sutherland. He sculptured his greens with a characteristic style that molded putting surface contours into the existing terrain. His green sites nearly always put a premium on short recovery shots.
Donald Ross played a major role in forming the ASGCA and is considered the

Society's patron saint. Its official jacket is the Ross plaid, its annual award for contributions in furthering public understanding of golf architecture is named after him and it was no coincidence that the 1980 Annual Banquet and presentation of the Ross Award was held in Dornoch.

Courses by: Donald Ross

Alabama: CC of Birmingham (East Course) (1927); CC of Birmingham (West Course) (1929); CC of Mobile; Mountain Brook C, Birmingham.

California: Peninsula G&CC, San Mateo.

Colorado: Broadmoor GC (East Course), Colorado Springs (9, 1918), with Walter Hatch; Broadmoor GC (West Course), Colorado Springs (9, 1918), with Walter Hatch; Wellshire GC, Englewood (1926), with Walter Hatch.

Connecticut: CC of Waterbury (1922); Hartford GC, West Hartford (1925); Norwich Muni; Shennecossett GC, Groton; Wampanoag CC, West Hartford (1926), with Walter Hatch.

Florida: Belleview-Biltmore Hotel & C (East), Clearwater (1915); Bobby Jones Muni (American Course), Sarasota (1927); Bobby Jones Muni (British Course), Sarasota (1927); Brentwood GC, Jacksonville (1923); Coral Gables Biltmore GC {formerly Miami Biltmore GC (North Course)}, Coral Gables (1924); CC of Orlando (1918); Daytona Beach G&CC (South Course) (1924); Delray Beach G&CC (1927); Dunedin CC (1925); Florida CC, Jacksonville (NLE,); Fort Myers G&CC (1918); Gulfstream GC, Delray Beach (1923); Hyde Park GC, Jacksonville (1925); Keystone G&CC (9, 1927); Lake Wales CC (1923); Miami CC (NLE, 1919); New Smyrna GC (1922); Palm Beach CC (1917); Palma Sola GC, Bradenton (1924), with Walter I. Johnson; Panama CC, Lynn Haven (1927); Pelican GC, Clearwater (1926); Pinecrest on Lotela GC, Avon Park (1926); Ponce de Leon CC {formerly St. Augustine Links (North Course)}, St. Augustine (1916); Punta Gorda CC (1927); Riviera CC {formerly Miami Biltmore GC (South Course)}, Coral Gables; San Jose CC, Jacksonville (1935); Sara Bay CC, Sarasota (1925); Seminole GC, North Palm Beach (1929); St. Augustine Links (South Course) (NLE, 1915); Timuquana CC, Jacksonville (1923); University of Florida GC, Gainesville (1921).

Georgia: Athens CC (1926); Bacon Park GC, Savannah (1926); Brunswick CC (9, 1936); CC of Columbus, with J.B. McGovern; East Lake CC (Course No. 2) {formerly Atlanta Athletic C (Course No. 2)}, Atlanta (NLE, 1923); Forest Hill GC, Augusta (1927); Gainesville Muni (NLE, 9); Highland CC, LaGrange (9); Savannah GC; Savannah GC (Course No. 2) (NLE); Savannah Inn & CC (1927); Warm Springs GC (9).

Illinois: Beverly CC, Chicago (1907); Bob O'Link CC, Highland Park (1916); Calumet CC, Homewood (1920); Evanston GC, Skokie (1917); Hinsdale GC; Northmoor CC, Highland Park (1918); Oak Park CC (1916); Old Elm C, Fort Sheridan (1913), with H.S. Colt.

Indiana: Broadmoor CC, Indianapolis (1928); Fairview GC, Wayne (9); French Lick CC (Hill Course) (1916).

Iowa: Cedar Rapids CC (1928).

Kansas: Shawnee CC, Topeka (1921).

Kentucky: Idle Hour CC, Lexington , with J.B. McGovern; Tate Springs GC.

Maine: Augusta CC, Augusta (9, 1916); Biddeford and Saco CC (9); Cliff CC, Ogunquit; Lake Kezar C, Lovell (9); Penobscot Valley CC, Bangor (1924); Portland CC, Falmouth; York G&CC.

Maryland: Chevy Chase CC (1910); Fountain Head CC, Hagerstown (1925), with Walter Hatch; Hagerstown CC; Prince Georges G&CC, Landover (NLE, 1921); Silver Springs GC (1921).

Massachusetts: Belmont CC; Brae Burn CC, West Newton (1912); Charles River CC, Newton Centre (1921); Cohasset GC, Quincy; Concord CC (1914); CC of Pittsfield; Ellinwood CC, Athol (9), with Walter Hatch; Ellinwood CC, Athol (9); Essex CC, Manchester (1910); George Wright Muni, Boston (1931); Greenock CC, Lee (9, 1927), with Walter Hatch; Kernwood CC, Salem (1915); Longmeadow CC, Springfield (1921); Ludlow CC (1920); North Andover CC (9); Oak Hill CC, Fitchburg (1921); Oakley CC, Watertown (1899); Orchards GC, South Hadley; Oyster Harbors C, Osterville (1927); Plymouth CC; Pocasset GC (1916); Ponkapoag GC, Canton (1933); Salem CC, Peabody (1926); Sandy Burr CC, Wayland; Tatnuck CC, Worcester; Toy Town Tavern GC, Winchendon (NLE, 9), with Walter Hatch; Wachusett CC, West Boylston; Wellesley CC (9, 1910); Weston GC; Whaling City CC, New Bedford (9, 1920); Whitinsville CC (9, 1925), with Walter Hatch; Winchester CC (1903); Worcester CC (1914); Wyckoff Park GC, Holyoke.

Michigan: Barton Hills CC, Ann Arbor (1919); Brightmoor CC; Dearborn CC (1923); Detroit GC (North Course) (1916); Detroit GC (South Course) (1916); Franklin Hills CC, Franklin Woods (1930); Grosse Ile G&CC (1919); Highland GC, Grand Rapids; Monroe G&CC (1920); Muskegon CC (1910); Oakland Hills CC (North Course), Birmingham (1918); Oakland Hills CC (South Course), Birmingham (1917); Rackham Park Muni, Huntington (1925); Redford Muni, Detroit (1910); St. Clair CC; Warren Valley CC (East Course), Wayne; Warren Valley CC (West Course), Wayne; Western G&CC, Redford.

Minnesota: Northland CC, Duluth (1927); White Bear G&YC (1915); Woodhill CC, Wayzata (1916); Woodhill CC, Wayzata (1934).

Missouri: Hillcrest CC, Kansas City (1917).

New Hampshire: Bald Peak Colony C (1922); Balsams Hotel GC (Panorama Course), Dixville Notch; Bretton Woods GC, Mt. Washington Hotel (1915); Carter CC, Lebanon (1923); Kingswood CC, Wolfeboro , with Walter Hatch; Lake Sunapee CC, New London (1927); Lake Tarleton C, Pike (NLE); Manchester CC (1923); Maplewood CC, Bethlehem; Mount. Crotched CC, Francestown (NLE, 9, 1929); Wentworth-by-the-Sea GC, Portsmouth (9, 1910).

New Jersey: Crestmont CC, West Orange; Echo Lake CC, Westfield (1913), with George Low Sr; Essex Fells CC; Homestead CC, Spring Lake; Knickerbocker CC, Tenafly (1915); Lone Pine GC; Montclair GC, Verona (27); Plainfield CC (1920); Riverton CC; Seaview GC (Bay Course), Absecon (1915).

New York: Bellevue CC, Syracuse (1915); Brooklea CC, Rochester (1924); Chappequa CC, Mt. Kisco (1929); Cold Spring G&CC, Cold Spring Harbor; CC of Buffalo, Williamsville (1924); CC of Rochester (1914); Essex County Club, Hempstead; Fairview CC, Elmsford (NLE); Glen Falls CC (1928); Hudson River GC, Yonkers (NLE, 1916); Irondequoit CC, Rochester (9, 1916); Mark Twain GC, Elmira (1940); Monroe CC, Pittsford (1924); Oak Hill CC (East Course), Rochester (1926); Oak Hill CC (West Course), Rochester (1925); Rip Van Winkle GC, Palenville (9); Sagamore GC, Bolton Landing (1928); Siwanoy CC, Bronxville (1927); Teugega CC, Rome (1922); Thendara CC, Old Forge (9); Tupper Lake GC; Whippoorwill CC, Armonk (1925).

North Carolina: Alamance CC, Burlington (1948); Asheville CC {formerly Beaver Lake GC} (1924); Asheville Muni (1927); Benvenue CC, Rocky Mount (1931); Biltmore Forest GC, Asheville (1921); Cape Fear CC, Wilmington; Carolina G&CC, Charlotte (1928); Catawba CC, Newton (1946); Forsyth CC, Winston-Salem; Greensboro CC (Irving Park Course) (1911); Hendersonville CC (1936); Highland CC, Fayetteville (1947); Highlands CC (1926); Hillandale CC, Durham (1911); Hope Valley CC, Durham (1926); Lenoir CC (1945); Linville GC (1929); Mid Pines CC, Southern Pines (1921); Mimosa Hills CC, Morganton (1931); Monroe CC (9, 1943); Penrose Park GC, Reidsville; Pine Needles Lodge & CC, Southern Pines (1927); Pinehurst CC (Course No. 2) (9, 1901); Pinehurst CC (Course No. 3) (1910); Pinehurst CC (Course No. 4) (NLE, 1919); Pinehurst CC (Course No. 5) (NLE, 9); Raleigh CC (1949); Richmond Pines CC, Rockingham (1926); Roaring Gap G&CC (1914); Sedgefield CC, Greensboro (1925); Sedgefield CC (Red Course), Greensboro (NLE, 1925); Southern Pines CC (1912); Wilmington Muni (1927).

Ohio: Acacia CC, South Euclid (1921), with Sandy Alves; Athens CC (9); Brookside CC, Canton (1922); Columbus CC (9, 1907); Delaware CC (9); Elks CC, Columbus; Granville Inn GC, Granville (1924); Hamilton CC; Hawthorne Valley CC, Cleveland , with Walter Hatch; Hyde Park GC, Cincinnati; Lancaster CC (1926), with J.B. McGovern; Manakiki G&CC, Willoughby (1929); Miami Shores GC, Troy (1947); Miami Valley CC, Dayton (1919); Mill Creek GC (North Course), Youngstown (1928); Mill Creek GC (South Course), Youngstown (1928); Piqua CC (9); Portsmouth CC; Scioto CC, Columbus (1916); Shaker Heights CC (1915); Springfield CC, with Walter Hatch; Wyandot Muni, Worthington (1922).

Pennsylvania: Aronimink GC, Newton Square (1928); Buck Hill Inn & CC, Buck Hill Falls; Charles Schwab Estate GC, Loretto (9, 1917); CC of York (1925); Edgewood CC, Pittsburgh (1907); Flourtown CC, Philadelphia (NLE); Gulph Mills GC, King of Prussia (1919); Kahkwa C, Erie (1915); Lu Lu Temple CC, North Hills (1912); Philadelphia Cricket C; Pittsburgh Field C (1915); Pocono Manor GC (East Course); Rolling Rock GC, Ligonier; St. Davids GC, Philadelphia.

Rhode Island: Metacomet CC, East Providence (1921); Rhode Island CC, West Barrington (1911); Sakonnet GC, Little Compton (1921); Twiggs Muni, Providence (1932); Wannamoisett CC, Rumford (1916); Warwick CC (9, 1924), with Walter Hatch; Winnapaug GC, Westerly (9, 1928).

South Carolina: Camden CC (1934); Lancaster CC (9, 1940); Springs Mill CC, Fort Mill (9).

Tennessee: Belle Meade CC, Nashville (1921); Brainerd Muni, Chattanooga (1925), with Walter Hatch; Chattanooga G&CC; Holston Hills CC, Knoxville (1933); Memphis CC (1910); Richland CC, Nashville (1921); Ridgefields CC, Kingsport.

Texas: Galveston Muni (1948); Houston GC {formerly Houston CC}; Pinehurst CC, Orange; River Oaks CC, Houston (1924).

Vermont: Burlington CC.

Virginia: CC of Petersburg (NLE, 1928); Hampton GC {formerly Hampton Rhodes GC}; Jefferson-Lakeside CC, Richmond (1921); Washington G&CC, Arlington (1915).

Wisconsin: Kenosha CC.

Manitoba: Elmhurst G Links, Winnepeg; St. Charles CC (South Nine), Winnipeg (9).

New Brunswick: Algonquin Hotel GC, St. Andrews (27, 1927).

Nova Scotia: White Point Beach GC, Hunts Point , with Walter Hatch.

Ontario: Essex G&CC, LaSalle (1929); Roseland G&CC, Windsor (27).

Cuba: CC of Havana (1911); Havana Biltmore GC (1915).

Courses Remodeled & Added to by: Donald Ross

Colorado: Lakewood CC, Denver (R.).

Connecticut: Greenwich CC (R., 1946).

Florida: Belleview-Biltmore Hotel & C (West) (A.9, 1915); Belleview-Biltmore Hotel & C (West) (R.9, 1915); Palma Ceia G&CC, Tampa (R., 1923).

Georgia: Augusta CC (R.); Bon Air-Vanderbilt Hotel GC (Hill Crs), Augusta (R.); East Lake CC, Atlanta (R., 1915).

Illinois: Exmoor CC, Highland Park (R.); Indian Hill C, Winnetka (R., 1914); Ravisloe CC, Homewood (R.); Skokie CC, Glencoe (R., 1915).

Maine: Poland Springs GC (R.).

Maryland: Congressional CC (Blue Course), Bethesda (R., 1930).

Massachusetts: Bass River GC (R.); Brae Burn CC, West Newton (R., 1947); CC of New Bedford (R.); Hyannisport C (R.); Vesper CC, Lowell (R.9); Vesper CC, Lowell (A.9); Wianno CC (R.); Winchester CC (R., 1928); Woodland CC, Newton (R., 1927).

Michigan: Bloomfield Hills CC (R., 1936); Kent CC, Grand Rapids (A.9); Kent CC, Grand Rapids (R.9, 1898).

Minnesota: Interlachen CC, Edina (R., 1919); Minikahda C, Minneapolis (R., 1917).

New Jersey: Englewood CC (R., 1921); Essex County CC (East Course) (R., 1925); Plainfield CC (R., 1928); Plainfield CC (A.3, 1928); Ridgewood CC (NLE, R., 1916).

New York: Chautauqua GC (R.9, 1921); Chautauqua GC (A.9, 1921); Fox Hills GC (R.); Wykagyl CC, New Rochelle (R., 1920).

North Carolina: Charlotte CC (R., 1925); CC of Salisbury (R.), with Walter I. Johnson; Myers Park CC, Charlotte (R., 1947); Pinehurst CC (Course No. 1) (R.9, 1899); Pinehurst CC (Course No. 1) (A.9, 1899); Pinehurst CC (Course No. 1) (R., 1939); Pinehurst CC (Course No. 2) (A.9, 1903); Pinehurst CC (Course No. 2) (R., 1925); Pinehurst CC (Course No. 2) (R., 1935); Pinehurst CC (Course No. 3) (R., 1937).

Ohio: Columbus CC (A.9, 1914); Congress Lake C, Hartville (R.); Inverness C, Toledo (A.9, 1919); Inverness C, Toledo (R.9, 1919); Willowick CC, Cleveland (R., 1917); Youngstown CC (R.).

Pennsylvania: Allegheny CC, Sewickley (R.3, 1923); Bedford Springs C0 (R.); Cedarbrook CC, Philadelphia (NLE, R., 1921); Torresdale-Frankford CC, Philadelphia (R.9); Torresdale-Frankford CC, Philadelphia (A.9); Whitemarsh Valley CC, Chestnut Hill (R.).

Rhode Island: Agawam Hunt C, Providence (R.); Misquemicut GC, Watch Hill (R.); Newport CC (R.); Point Judith CC (A.9); Point Judith CC (R.9); Winnapaug GC, Westerly (A.9, 1928).

Vermont: Woodstock CC (R.).

Virginia: Hermitage CC, Richmond (R.).
Manitoba: Elmhurst G Links, Winnepeg (A.9).
New Brunswick: Riverside G&CC (R., 1937).
Nova Scotia: Brightwood G&CC, Dartmouth (R.).
Ontario: Rosedale CC, Toronto (R.).
Scotland: Royal Dornoch GC, Sutherland (R., 1922); Royal Dornoch GC, Sutherland (A.2, 1922).

Philip Mackenzie Ross (1890 - 1974) BAGCA, President, 1972.
Born: Edinburgh, Scotland. Died: London, England at age 83.
P.M. Ross learned golf at Royal Musselburgh and won several amateur medals as a youth. He served with the British Army during World War I and upon discharge looked for a golf-related job. By chance he met golf architect Tom Simpson, who hired him as a construction boss in 1920. By the mid-Twenties, Ross was a full partner in the firm of Simpson and Ross.
In the late 1930s Ross went to work on his own and developed a fine reputation as a designer in Great Britain and on the Continent. After World War II he demonstrated his talents to a new generation by reconstructing or restoring many war-ravaged courses.
In 1972 Ross was elected the first President of the BAGCA.
Courses by: P.M. Ross
Azores Islands: Furnas GC; San Miguel GC.
Belgium: Royal GC Des Fagnes, Balmoral Spa (1936), with Tom Simpson.
Canary Islands: Maspalomas GC (South Course) (1957).
Channel Islands: Royal Guernsey GC (1949).
England: Hythe Imperial GC, Kent (1950).
France: Borden G&CC, Amiens; Club d'Amiens (9); Club de la Barouge, Mazamet (9, 1935), with Tom Simpson; New GC, Deauville (1929), with Tom Simpson.
Northern Ireland: Balmoral GC, Belfast.
Portugal: Club de G Vidago.
Scotland: Southerness GC, Dumfrieshire (1949).
Spain: Club de Campo de Malaga, Torremolinos (1928), with Tom Simpson.
Courses Remodeled & Added to by: P.M. Ross
Belgium: Royal Antwerp GC, Kapellenbos (R.18, 1924); Royal Antwerp GC, Kapellenbos (A.9, 1924), with Tom Simpson.
England: Alnmouth GC, Northumberland (R.); Carlisle GC, Cumberland (R., 1948); Thetford GC (R.).
France: Golf de Hardelot (R.), with Tom Simpson; Golf Club de Touquet (Forest Course) (R., 1958).
Isle of Man: Castletown GC (R.).
Northern Ireland: Bangor GC, County Donegal (R.).
Portugal: Estoril GC (R.9, 1938); Estoril GC (A.9, 1938); Oporto GC, Espinto (R., 1958).
Scotland: Dumfries & County GC, Dumfriesshire (R., 1949); Glen GC, East Lothian (R.); Longniddry GC (R.); North Berwick Muni (Burgh Course), East Lothian (R.); Turnberry GC (Ailsa Course), Ayrshire (R., 1951), with James Alexander.
Wales: Pyle and Kenfig GC (A.9).

Robert Jack Ross
A civil engineer and prominent amateur golfer, Robert J. Ross served for years as City Engineer of Hartford, Connecticut. In his spare time, Ross designed several Connecticut courses in the 1920s and '30s. Decades later, most of his works were erroneously attributed to Donald Ross, an understandable if unfortunate consequence for any architect bearing the same name as a legend. The fact that some of his designs were considered those of the other Ross spoke well for the architectural abilities of Robert Ross.
Courses by: Robert J. Ross
Connecticut: Avon CC (9); Canton Public GC; Indian Hills CC, Newington; Stanley GC, New Britain; TPC of Connecticut {formerly Edgewood GC}, Cromwell (1928), with Maurice Kearney.
Courses Remodeled & Added to by: Robert J. Ross
Connecticut: Keney Park GC, Hartford (R.); Wethersfield CC (R.9, 1924); Wethersfield CC (A.9, 1924).

Roger G. Rulewich (1936 -   ) ASGCA, President, 1987.
Born: New Brunswick, New Jersey.
Roger Rulewich received a B.E. Degree in Civil Engineering from Yale University in 1958. Following graduation, he was employed for a time with a firm of consulting engineers and landscape architects. In 1961 he joined the firm of Robert Trent Jones Inc., where he quickly took an active role in the design and construction inspection of Jones courses in the United States and abroad.
By the 1970s Rulewich was Jones' chief associate, and though receiving little national attention, became a major force in the profession of golf architecture and was among the most active course architects in the world. In 1986, design of the Applerock Course of Horseshoe Bay CC in Texas, done in collaboration with Jones, was selected the year's Best New Resort Course by Golf Digest magazine.
Courses by: Roger Rulewich
Connecticut: Black Hall C, Old Lyme (1968), with Robert Trent Jones; Lyman Meadow GC, Middlefield (1969), with Robert Trent Jones.
Georgia: Stone Mountain GC (1971), with Robert Trent Jones; University of Georgia GC, Athens (1968), with Robert Trent Jones.
Illinois: Hilldale GC, Hoffman Estates (1972), with Robert Trent Jones.
Louisiana: Santa Maria GC, Baton Rouge (1987), with Robert Trent Jones.
Maryland: Golden Triangle GC, Beltville (9, 1971), with Robert Trent Jones.
Massachusetts: Crumpin Fox C, Bernardston (9, 1978), with Robert Trent Jones.
Michigan: Treetops GC, Gaylord (1987), with Robert Trent Jones.
Missouri: Four Seasons G&CC, Lake Ozark (1974), with Robert Trent Jones.
New York: Radisson Greens GC, Baldwinsville (1977), with Robert Trent Jones.
North Carolina: Carolina Trace G&CC, Sanford (27, 1973), with Robert Trent Jones.
Ohio: Firestone CC (North Course), Akron (1969), with Robert Trent Jones.

South Carolina: Seabrook Island GC (Crooked Oaks Course) (1981), with Robert Trent Jones.
Texas: Horseshoe Bay CC (Apple Rock Course), Marble Falls (1985), with Robert Trent Jones; Horseshoe Bay CC (Ram Rock Course), Marble Falls (1981), with Robert Trent Jones.
West Virginia: Speidel GC, Wheeling (1972), with Robert Trent Jones.
Alberta: Kananaskis Country GC (Mount Kidd) (1984), with Robert Trent Jones; Kananaskis Country GC (Mount Loretta) (1983), with Robert Trent Jones.
British Columbia: Rivershore GC, Kamloops (1981), with Robert Trent Jones.
Bermuda: Port Royal GC, Southampton (1970), with Robert Trent Jones; St. George's GC (Precision, 1986), with Robert Trent Jones.
Dominican Republic: Playa Dorada GC, Playa Dorado (1979), with Robert Trent Jones.
Guadeloupe: Golf de St. Francois (1977), with Robert Trent Jones.
Ireland: Ballybunion GC (New Course), County Kerry (1985), with Robert Trent Jones and Cabell Robinson.
Martinique: Empress Josephine GC (1976), with Robert Trent Jones.
Puerto Rico: Cerromar Beach GC (North Course), Dorado Beach (1972), with Robert Trent Jones; Cerromar Beach GC (South Course), Dorado Beach (1972), with Robert Trent Jones.
Courses Remodeled & Added to by: Roger Rulewich
Arkansas: North Hills CC, North Little Rock (R., 1979), with Robert Trent Jones.
Florida: Apollo Beach G & Sea C (A.9, 1971), with Robert Trent Jones.
Kentucky: CC of Paducah (A.9, 1979), with Robert Trent Jones.
Maryland: Congressional CC (Blue Course), Bethesda (R., 1969), with Robert Trent Jones; Golden Triangle GC, Beltville (A.9, 1976), with Robert Trent Jones.
Michigan: Bloomfield Hills CC (R., 1978), with Robert Trent Jones; Oakland Hills CC (North Course), Birmingham (R., 1969), with Robert Trent Jones; Oakland Hills CC (South Course), Birmingham (R., 1972), with Robert Trent Jones; Oakland Hills CC (South Course), Birmingham (R., 1984), with Robert Trent Jones.
Minnesota: Hazeltine National GC, Chaska (R., 1978), with Robert Trent Jones.
New Jersey: Crestmont CC, West Orange (R., 1978), with Robert Trent Jones; Glen Ridge CC (R., 1978), with Robert Trent Jones; North Jersey CC, Wayne (R., 1979), with Robert Trent Jones.
New York: Colonie Muni (A.9, 1980), with Robert Trent Jones; IBM CC, Poughkeepsie (R., 1985), with Robert Trent Jones; Pelham CC (R., 1977), with Robert Trent Jones.
North Carolina: Pinehurst CC (Course No. 4) (R., 1973), with Robert Trent Jones; Pinehurst CC (Course No. 5) (R., 1974), with Robert Trent Jones; Tanglewood GC (East Course), Clemmons (A.9, 1970), with Robert Trent Jones.
Pennsylvania: Valley Brook CC, McMurray (R., 1978), with Robert Trent Jones.
South Carolina: Dunes G&BC, Myrtle Beach (R., 1979), with Robert Trent Jones.
Vermont: Woodstock CC (R., 1975), with Robert Trent Jones.
Wisconsin: Milwaukee CC (R., 1975), with Robert Trent Jones.

Alex Russell
Australian amateur golfer Alex Russell counted the 1924 Australian Open among several victories in his career. In 1926 he assisted Alister Mackenzie in laying out the original course at Royal Melbourne GC and on several other Australian designs. Following Mackenzie's departure, Russell designed and built additional course at Royal Melbourne, as well as several others in Australia and New Zealand.
Courses by: Alex Russell
Australia: Lake Karrinyup CC, Perth (1927), with Alister Mackenzie; Royal Melbourne GC (East Course), Black Rock (1932); Royal Melbourne GC (West Course), Black Rock (1926), with Alister Mackenzie; Yarra Yarra GC, Melbourne (1929), with Alister Mackenzie.
New Zealand: Paraparaumu Beach GC (1949).

Edward Ryder
Ed Ryder attended Hofstra University, studying Landscape Architecture, Engineering and Business with the avowed intent of becoming a golf course architect. In 1960, on the advice of golf architect Geoffrey Cornish, Ryder joined the golf course contracting firm of C.B. Carlson & Sons. In that capacity he worked on construction sites of layouts designed by several prominent architects in the Northeast.
In the mid-1960s he began designing and remodeling courses in metropolitan New York in partnership with Val Carlson, one of C.B.'s sons. In 1970 Ryder moved to Florida where he opened his own golf design firm based in Coral Springs.
Courses by: Edward Ryder
Connecticut: Harry Brownson CC, Shelton (1964), with Val Carlson; Redding CC (9); Richter Park GC, Danbury.
Florida: Palm Gardens GC, Melbourne (Precision, 1979).
New York: Back O'Beyond GC, Brewster (9, 1964), with Val Carlson; Salem GC, North Salem , with Val Carlson.
Courses Remodeled & Added to by: Edward Ryder
New York: Banksville CC (Precision, A.).

Bernard "Ben" Sayers (1857 - 1924)
Born: Leith, Scotland. Died: North Berwick, Scotland at age 67.
A genuine character in golf history, five-foot three-inch Ben Sayers trained as an acrobat before deciding upon a career as a clubmaker and golf professional. Outspoken and flamboyant, Sayers thought nothing of turning a cartwheel on a green in celebration after sinking a putt.
After working as an assistant at Musselburgh, Sayers became professional at North Berwick, succeeding Davie Strath. He remained in that position for the remainder of his life.
A talented player, Sayers played in every British Open from 1880 to 1923, and although he never won it, he came close on several occasions.
Ben laid out several golf courses in the North Berwick area and elsewhere. He was best remembered, however, for the handmade clubs and golf balls which bore his name.

Courses by: Ben Sayers
Northern Ireland: Castlerock GC, County Londonderry (1901).
Scotland: Broomie Knowe GC, Midlothian (1906); Moffat GC (1904).

Mario D. Schjetnan

Mario Schjetnan, the son of a Norwegian settler in Mexico, became a club professional in that country. He began designing courses in Mexico in the late 1950s and by the Seventies was considered one of Mexico's top course architects.
Courses by: Mario D. Schjetnan
Mexico: Club Campestre de Leon (9, 1960); Club Lomas de Cocoyoc, Morales (1978).

Hans Carl Schmeisser (1892 - 1980)

Born: Ulm, Germany. Died: West Palm Beach, Florida at age 88.
Superintendent of Fort Lauderdale (Fla.) CC in the early 1950s and later superintendent of the Miami Beach Parks Department, Hans Schmeisser designed several Florida courses in the late 1950s and early '60s. One of his sons, John, was on the construction staff of Robert Trent Jones for a time, while a second, Otto, served as superintendent of Everglades Club at Palm Beach. Hans Schmeisser received a GC-SAA Distinguished Service Award in 1981.
Courses by: Hans Schmeisser
Florida: Forest Hill GC, West Palm Beach (Precision, 1966); Glen Oaks GC, Clearwater (Par 3, 9, 1960); Lakeland Par 3 GC (Par 3); Lauderdale Lakes CC, Ft. Lauderdale (Precision, 1960); Madison CC, Madison (9); Oak Ridge CC, Ft. Lauderdale (1962); Par Three GC, Lakeland (Par 3, 1960); Pines GC, Hollywood (Par 3, 1961); Sebring Shores GC (Par 3, 1964); Whispering Oaks CC, Ridge Manor (9, 1956).
Courses Remodeled & Added to by: Hans Schmeisser
Florida: Rocky Point GC, Tampa (R.); Sunset G&CC, St. Petersburg (R.); Temple Terrace G&CC (R., 1960).

Edwin B. Seay (1938 -   ) ASGCA, President, 1976.

Born: Dade City, Florida.
Ed Seay graduated from the University of Florida with a Bachelor's degree in Landscape Architecture, and was then commissioned as an officer in the U.S. Marine Corps. His architectural career began in 1964 as an associate of golf architect Ellis Maples. Under Maples, Seay was involved in the design and construction of 27 courses.
Seay entered private practice, based in Florida, in 1972. He later joined forces with legendary professional golfer Arnold Palmer. Their corporation became known as the Palmer Course Design Company. Seay handled designs throughout the world as Director of Design for the firm. In 1984, Palmer Course Design created the first golf course ever built in Communist China.
Courses by: Ed Seay
Arizona: Arrowhead CC (North Course), Glendale (1985), with Arnold Palmer and Harrison Minchew; Arrowhead CC (South Course), Glendale (1986), with Arnold Palmer and Harrison Minchew; Mesa Del Sol CC (Blue Course), Yuma (1982), with Arnold Palmer; Mesa Del Sol CC (White Course), Yuma (1982), with Arnold Palmer.
California: Ironwood CC (Short Course), Palm Desert (Par 3, 9, 1975), with Arnold Palmer; Mission Hills G&CC (New Course), Rancho Mirage (1979), with Arnold Palmer; Pacific Rim GC (1987), with Arnold Palmer; PGA West GC (Palmer Course), La Quinta (1986), with Arnold Palmer and Harrison Minchew.
Colorado: Bear Creek GC, Golden (1986), with Arnold Palmer; Broadmoor GC (South Course), Colorado Springs (1976), with Arnold Palmer; Lone Tree GC, Littleton (1986), with Arnold Palmer.
Florida: Adios CC, Deerfield Beach (1985), with Arnold Palmer; Grenelefe G&RC (East Course), Haines City (1977), with Arnold Palmer and Bob Walker; Isleworth G&CC, Windermere (1986), with Arnold Palmer; Marsh Landing CC, Ponte Vedra (1986), with Arnold Palmer and Harrison Minchew; Matanzas Woods GC, Palm Coast (1986), with Arnold Palmer and Bob Walker; Monarch CC (1987), with Arnold Palmer and Harrison Minchew; Pine Lakes GC, Palm Coast (1980), with Arnold Palmer and Bob Walker; Plantation at Ponte Vedra GC (1987), with Arnold Palmer and Harrison Minchew; PGA National GC (The General Course), Palm Beach Gardens (1985), with Arnold Palmer; Saddlebrook G&TC (Palmer Course) (1986), with Arnold Palmer and Bob Walker; Sawgrass GC (Oceanside Course), Ponte Vedra Beach (1974), with Arnold Palmer and Bob Walker; Spessard Holland GC, Melbourne (Precision, 1977), with Arnold Palmer and Bob Walker; Suntree CC (South Course), Melbourne (1987), with Arnold Palmer; Wildcat Run CC, Estero (1985), with Arnold Palmer.
Georgia: Goshen Plantation CC, Augusta (1968), with Ellis Maples; Landings at Skidaway Island (Marshwood) (1979), with Arnold Palmer; West Lake CC, Augusta (1968), with Ellis Maples; Whitewater Creek CC (1987), with Arnold Palmer.
Hawaii: Kapalua GC (Village Course) (1980), with Arnold Palmer; Turtle Bay GC (New Course), Kahuku, Oahu (1987), with Arnold Palmer.
Louisiana: Bluffs CC (1987), with Arnold Palmer and Harrison Minchew; Frenchman's Bend CC (1987), with Arnold Palmer.
Maryland: Prince Georges G&CC, Mitchellville (1981), with Arnold Palmer and Bob Walker.
Michigan: Shanty Creek GC (Legend Course) (1985), with Arnold Palmer and Bob Walker.
North Carolina: Bermuda Run G&CC, Clemmons (1971), with Ellis Maples; Brook Valley G&CC, Greenville (1967), with Ellis Maples; Cedar Brook CC, Elkin (1965), with Ellis Maples; Chockoyette CC, Roanoke Rapids (1972), with Ellis Maples; CC of Johnston County, Smithfield (1967), with Ellis Maples; CC of Whispering Pines (West Course) (1970), with Ellis Maples; Deep Springs CC, Madison (9, 1971), with Ellis Maples; Duck Woods GC, Kitty Hawk (1968), with Ellis Maples; Grandfather G&CC, Linville (1986), with Ellis Maples; Indian Valley CC, Burlington (1974), with Ellis Maples; Quarry Hills CC {formerly Piedmont Crescent CC}, Burlington , with Ellis Maples; Red Fox CC, Tryon (1965), with Ellis Maples; Sapona CC, Lexington (1967), with Ellis Maples; TPC at Piper Glen, Charlotte (1987), with Arnold Palmer and Harrison Minchew; Walnut Creek CC, Goldsboro (1968), with

Ellis Maples; Woodlake CC {formerly Lake Surf CC}, Vass , with Ellis Maples.
Ohio: Winberie GC, Port Clinton (1987), with Arnold Palmer.
South Carolina: CC of South Carolina, Florence (1969), with Ellis Maples; Wellman CC, Johnsonville (1970), with Ellis Maples.
Tennessee: Ridgeway CC, Collierville (1972), with Ellis Maples.
Texas: Golf Club at Fossil Creek, Fort Worth (1986), with Arnold Palmer; Hidden Hills GC, Austin (1986), with Arnold Palmer.
Utah: Jeremy Ranch GC, Park City (1980), with Arnold Palmer.
Virginia: Albermarle Farms GC (1986), with Arnold Palmer; Countryside CC, Roanoke (1967), with Ellis Maples; Kingsmill GC (Plantation Course), Williamsburg (1986), with Arnold Palmer; Lexington GC (1971), with Ellis Maples.
Washington: Semiahmoo GC, Everett (1986), with Arnold Palmer and Harrison Minchew.
Wyoming: Teton Pines GC (1986), with Arnold Palmer.
British Columbia: Whistler Village GC (1980), with Arnold Palmer and Bob Walker.
China: Chung-Shan GC (1985), with Arnold Palmer and Bob Walker.
Ireland: Tralee GC, County Kerry (1985), with Arnold Palmer.
Italy: Ca' Della Nave GC (1987), with Arnold Palmer.
Japan: Furano CC (1975), with Arnold Palmer; Iga Ueno CC (1974), with Arnold Palmer; Manago CC (1974), with Arnold Palmer; Minakami Kogen GC (Lower Course) (1986), with Arnold Palmer and Bob Walker; Minakami Kogen GC (Upper Course) (1986), with Arnold Palmer and Bob Walker; Niseko GC, Sapporo (1986), with Arnold Palmer and Bob Walker; Niseko Kogen GC, Sapporo (1986), with Arnold Palmer and Bob Walker; Nishi Biwako GC, with Arnold Palmer; Shimotsuke CC (1975), with Arnold Palmer; Tsugaru Kogen GC, Amori (1986), with Arnold Palmer and Bob Walker.
Mexico: Nuevo Vallarta GC (27, 1980), with Arnold Palmer and Bob Walker.
New Zealand: Walter Peak Resort GC (1987), with Arnold Palmer.
Taiwan: Formosa G&CC (1987), with Arnold Palmer.
Thailand: Bangpoo GC (1981), with Arnold Palmer.
Courses Remodeled & Added to by: Ed Seay
Alabama: Anniston CC (R., 1975).
Arizona: Scottsdale CC (R., 1986), with Arnold Palmer and Bob Walker.
California: San Jose CC (R., 1977).
Colorado: Cherry Hills CC, Englewood (R., 1977), with Arnold Palmer; Denver CC (R., 1975); Snowmass GC, Snowmass-at-Aspen (R., 1982), with Arnold Palmer.
Florida: Hidden Hills CC, Jacksonville (R., 1986), with Arnold Palmer and Bob Walker; Sawgrass GC (Oakbridge Course), Ponte Vedra Beach (R., 1982); Sawgrass GC (Oceanside Course), Ponte Vedra Beach (R., 1979); Sawgrass GC (Oceanside Course), Ponte Vedra Beach (A.9, 1985), with Arnold Palmer, Bob Walker and Harrison Minchew; TPC at Monte Carlo, Fort Pierce (R., 1987), with Arnold Palmer.
Georgia: Forest Hill GC, Augusta (R., 1986), with Arnold Palmer and Harrison Minchew.
North Carolina: Carmel CC (South Course), Charlotte (A.9, 1970), with Ellis Maples; Quail Hollow CC, Charlotte (R., 1985), with Arnold Palmer; Reynolds Park GC, Winston Salem (R., 1966), with Ellis Maples; Roxboro CC (A.9, 1969), with Ellis Maples; Stanly County CC, Badin (R., 1966), with Ellis Maples.
Pennsylvania: Allegheny CC, Sewickley (R., 1975); Oakmont CC (R., 1978), with Arnold Palmer.
Virginia: Keswick C of Virginia (R., 1987), with Arnold Palmer.

Donald R. Sechrest (1933 -   )

Born: St. Joseph, Missouri.
Don Sechrest received a B.S. degree in Business in 1956 from Oklahoma State University, where he had played on the golf team coached by Labron Harris Sr. Turning professional upon graduation, Sechrest worked with his former coach at Oklahoma State in Stillwater for 10 years, and during that time tried his hand at the PGA Tour. In 1966 he laid out and supervised the building of a course for Stillwater G&CC, and then served a short term as its club pro. In 1968 Sechrest entered private practice as a golf course architect based in Tulsa, Oklahoma.
Courses by: Don Sechrest
Iowa: Ames G&CC (1974).
Kansas: Southwind CC, Garden City (1980); Terradyne CC, Andover (1987).
Missouri: Loma Linda CC, Joplin (1978).
Oklahoma: Boiling Springs GC, Woodward; Greens G&RC, Oklahoma City (1973); Heritage Hills GC, Claremore (1977); Indian Springs CC (Windmill Course), Broken Arrow (1974); Page Belcher GC (Course No. 2), Tulsa (1987); Potowatomi Tribal GC, Shawnee; Shangri-La CC (Blue Course), Afton (1971); Shangri-La CC (Gold Course), Afton (1982); Stillwater G&CC (1966).
Texas: Brownsville CC (1977); Monte Cristo CC, Edinburg (1974).
Courses Remodeled & Added to by: Don Sechrest
Kansas: Dodge City CC (A.9, 1982).
Missouri: Carthage Muni (A.9, 1984); Carthage Muni (R.9, 1984); Greenbriar Hills CC, Kirkwood (R.); St. Joseph CC (R., 1984).
Oklahoma: Elk City G&CC (R.); Fort Cobb Lake State Park GC, Lake Cobb (A.9, 1986); Fort Sill GC (R.); Hillcrest CC, Bartlesville (R., 1985); Meadowbrook CC, Tulsa (A.9, 1970); Miami G&CC (A.9, 1985); Muskogee CC (R., 1970); Oklahoma City G&CC (R., 1977); Ponca City CC (R., 1980); Twin Hills G&CC, Oklahoma City (R., 1974).
Texas: Amarillo CC (R., 1983).

Jan Sederholm (1924 -   ) BAGCA

Born: Sweden.
Educated as an architect and land planner, Jan Sederholm planned residential developments and homes for over twenty years. An avid golfer eager to enter the field of golf course architecture, Sederholm was awarded a scholarship to do just that by the Swedish Golf Federation in 1972. He studied course design in England, Scotland and America, then made a survey of over two dozen of Sweden's best courses before laying out his first course in 1978.
Sederholm co-authored *Golf Course Planning*, a 1980 publication distributed by

the Swedish Golf Federation. He also served as President of the Golf Union of Scandinavia, and was presented an Award of Merit for his contributions to golf by the SGF in 1982.

Courses by: Jan Sederholm

Denmark: Hedeland GC (1980); Kalundborg GC (9, 1982); Odense GC (27, 1982); Roskilde GC (9, 1978); Viborg GC (9, 1978).

Finland: Aland GC (1978); Esbo GC (1982); Sarvik GC (1980).

Norway: Kjekstad GC (1980).

Sweden: Angelholm GC (1980); Fureso GC (1978); Himmerland GC (1981); Hulta GC (1981); Karlskoga GC (9, 1978); Loholm GC (1980); Malmo GC (1980); Nybro GC (9, 1980).

Courses Remodeled & Added to by: Jan Sederholm

Denmark: Hillerod GC, Nysogard (R.9, 1977); Hillerod GC, Nysogard (A.9, 1977); Kokkedal GC, Rungsted (R.); Kolding GC, Emerholtsuej (A.9, 1978); Odsherred GC, Hojdby (R.); Rungsted GC, Kyst (R., 1977); Sonderjyllands GC, Hedegard (A.9, 1978); Vejle GC (R.).

Sweden: Agesta GC (A.4, 1974); Agesta GC (A.13, 1976); Agesta GC (Precision, A.9, 1976); Boskogens GC (R.); Karlskrona GC (A.7, 1982); Korsloet GC, Koping (A.9, 1981); Ljunghusens GC, Malmo (R., 1977); Marks GC, Kinna (A.9, 1981); Motala GC (A.9, 1981); Straengnaes GC (R.9, 1979).

Brian M. Silva (1953 -) ASGCA
Born: Framingham, Massachusetts.

Brian Silva was introduced to golf course construction at an early age by his father John, a much sought-after bulldozer operator and shaper of golf course features. The elder Silva often permitted his son to operate a dozer at home, and Brian would push earth around for hours, experimenting with shapes. Silva also studied the plans and specifications of many golf architects, and watched as his father executed those plans on the ground.

Silva obtained an Associate Degree in Turf Management from the Stockbridge School of Agriculture of the University of Massachusetts in 1973. He then taught at the school under the renowned Dr. Joseph Troll while he worked on his Bachelor's in Landscape Architecture, which he obtained in 1976. Silva was an instructor of agronomy for three years at the Lake City (Fla.) Community College, and in 1981 received a Distinguished Service Award from the Florida Turfgrass Association. He then returned to Massachusetts to serve as an agronomist in the USGA Green Section's Northeast region.

In 1983 Silva joined veteran golf architect Geoffrey S. Cornish as a partner in the firm of Cornish and Silva Inc., and fulfilled his boyhood dream of becoming a golf course designer. His talents were soon recognized when his first original eighteen hole design, The Captains GC in Brewster, Mass., was selected by Golf Digest magazine as the Best New Public Course of 1985.

An unabashed fan of Donald Ross, Silva studied the architect's works extensively over the years and authored a comprehensive critique of the man.

Courses by: Brian Silva

Massachusetts: Captains GC, Brewster (1985), with Geoffrey S. Cornish; Kingsway GC (1986), with Geoffrey S. Cornish; Ocean Edge GC, Brewster (1986), with Geoffrey S. Cornish.

Courses Remodeled & Added to by: Brian Silva

Connecticut: Innis Arden GC, Old Greenwich (R.3, 1983), with Geoffrey S. Cornish; Madison CC (R., 1985), with Geoffrey S. Cornish; Stanwich C, Greenwich (R.3, 1985), with Geoffrey S. Cornish; Wethersfield CC (R., 1983), with Geoffrey S. Cornish.

Maine: Biddeford and Saco CC (A.9, 1986), with Geoffrey S. Cornish; Purpoodock C (R.2, 1985), with Geoffrey S. Cornish.

Massachusetts: Bedford AFB GC (R., 1985), with Geoffrey S. Cornish; Blue Hill CC, Canton (R., 1985), with Geoffrey S. Cornish; Myopia Hunt C, Hamilton (R., 1985), with Geoffrey S. Cornish; Pine Brook CC, Weston (R., 1985), with Geoffrey S. Cornish; Springfield CC (A.7, 1985), with Geoffrey S. Cornish.

Michigan: Crystal Downs CC, Frankfort (R., 1985), with Geoffrey S. Cornish; CC of Detroit, Grosse Pointe Farms (R., 1986), with Geoffrey S. Cornish.

Minnesota: Interlachen CC, Edina (R., 1985), with Geoffrey S. Cornish; Minneapolis GC (R., 1985), with Geoffrey S. Cornish; Wayzata CC (R., 1985), with Geoffrey S. Cornish.

Missouri: Algonquin CC, Glendale (R., 1986), with Geoffrey S. Cornish.

New Hampshire: Province Lake CC (A.9, 1986), with Geoffrey S. Cornish.

New Jersey: Howell Park GC, Farmingdale (R., 1985), with Geoffrey S. Cornish; Navesink CC, Red Bank (R., 1986), with Geoffrey S. Cornish; Preakness Hills CC, Paterson (R., 1984), with Geoffrey S. Cornish.

New York: Nassau CC, Glen Cove (R., 1984), with Geoffrey S. Cornish; Powelton C, Newburgh (R.4, 1985), with Geoffrey S. Cornish; Rockaway Hunting C, Cedarhurst (R., 1985), with Geoffrey S. Cornish; Schuyler Meadows C, Loudonville (R., 1985), with Geoffrey S. Cornish; Whippoorwill CC, Armonk (R., 1984), with Geoffrey S. Cornish; Wildwood GC, Rush (R., 1985), with Geoffrey S. Cornish.

Ohio: Sharon C, Sharon Center (R., 1986), with Geoffrey S. Cornish; Worthington Hills CC (R.2, 1985), with Geoffrey S. Cornish.

Pennsylvania: CC of Scranton (R., 1983), with Geoffrey S. Cornish.

Vermont: Killington GC (A.9, 1985), with Geoffrey S. Cornish; Stratton Mountain GC (A.9, 1984), with Geoffrey S. Cornish.

Robert A. Simmons (1908 -)
Born: Camden, Indiana.

Bob Simmons became a caddy at the age of 9 at Mississinewa CC in Indiana. He later became its caddymaster, assistant professional and finally head pro. While at Mississinewa, he made scale model greens of famous golf holes as a hobby, and laid out three courses in surrounding Indiana communities.

In 1956 Simmons became a construction supervisor for golf architect Dick Wilson, whom he'd met when the latter was building NCR CC in Dayton, Ohio. Simmons was responsible for constructing a number of outstanding Wilson designs including Moon Valley in Arizona, Bay Hill and Cypress Lakes in Florida, Coldstream in Ohio, Lyford Cay and Paradise Island in the Bahamas, and Royal Montreal in Canada. In 1961 Simmons formed his own practice as a golf course architect.

Courses by: Bob Simmons

Alabama: Olympia Spa & CC, Dothan (1968).

Arizona: Moon Valley CC, Phoenix (1958), with Dick Wilson.

Arkansas: Blytheville CC (9, 1957), with Dick Wilson.

Florida: Atlantis Inn & CC (1973); Bay Hill C, Orlando (1961), with Dick Wilson, Joe Lee and Robert von Hagge; Orange Tree CC, Orlando (1972); Palm Beach Par 3 GC (9, 1961), with Dick Wilson; Palmetto GC, South Miami (1960), with Dick Wilson.

Indiana: Arrowhead Park GC, Minster (1966); Carl E. Smock GC, Indianapolis; Club of Prestwick, Danville (1975); Green Acres CC, Kokomo (1967); Harrison Lake GC, Columbus; Highland Lake GC, Richmond (1971); Hillview CC; Lafayette City GC (1974); Lafayette CC (Battleground Course) (1968); Logansport CC (9); Pointe CC, Lake Monroe (1973); Quail Ridge G&TC, Bloomington; Valle Vista CC, Greenwood.

Kentucky: Bent Creek CC, Louisville; Glenwood Hall CC, Perry Park.

Louisiana: Oakbourne CC, Lafayette (1958), with Dick Wilson.

Missouri: Bent Oak GC, Oak Grove (1980).

Ohio: Coldstream CC, Cincinnati (1960), with Dick Wilson, Joe Lee and Robert von Hagge; Crest Hills CC, Cincinnati (1968).

Pennsylvania: Laurel Valley CC, Ligonier (1960), with Dick Wilson.

Tennessee: Town'N Country GC, Chattanooga (Par 3, 1963), with Dick Wilson.

Texas: Long Meadows CC, Jersey Village (NLE).

West Virginia: Fincastle CC, Bluefield (1963), with Dick Wilson; Greenbriar GC (Lakeside Course), Wht. Sulphur Springs (1962), with Dick Wilson.

Quebec: Royal Montreal GC (Black Course), Ile Bizard (9, 1959), with Dick Wilson; Royal Montreal GC (Blue Course), Ile Bizard (1959), with Dick Wilson; Royal Montreal GC (Red Course), Ile Bizard (1959), with Dick Wilson.

Bahamas: Bahamas Princess Hotel & CC (Emerald), Freeport (1965), with Dick Wilson and Joe Lee; Lucaya Park G&CC, Freeport (1964), with Dick Wilson and Joe Lee; Lyford Cay C, New Providence (1960), with Dick Wilson and Joe Lee; Paradise Island G&CC, Nassau (1962), with Dick Wilson and Joe Lee.

Venezuela: Lagunita CC, Caracas (1958), with Dick Wilson.

Courses Remodeled & Added to by: Bob Simmons

Florida: Atlantis GC (A.9, 1973); Bay Hill C, Orlando (A.9, 1969).

Indiana: CC of Connersville (A.9, 1962).

Kentucky: Idle Hour CC, Lexington (R., 1968).

Ohio: Salem GC (A.9, 1967).

Mexico: Club Campestre, Mexico City (R.), with Dick Wilson.

Thomas G. Simpson (1877 - 1964)
Born: Winkley Hall Estate, Lancashire, England. Died: Basingstoke, Hampshire, England at age 87.

Tom Simpson, who came from a wealthy family, studied law at Trinity Hall, Cambridge, and was admitted to the bar in 1905. A scratch golfer, he was a member of the Oxford and Cambridge Golfing Society and played a great deal at Woking. His interest in golf design developed as he observed the remodeling of Woking's course by club members John Low and Stuart Paton. On more than one occasion, Simpson defended their advanced designs in discussion with members of the club. As a result, Simpson began to develop particular ideas about course architecture himself, and by 1910 he had closed his legal practice and joined golf architect Herbert Fowler in the business.

After World War I, Simpson and Fowler were partners in a firm which for a short time included J.F. Abercromby and A.C.M. Croome. Simpson handled most of the firm's work on the Continent and some of his best designs were done in France. In the 1920s Simpson hired Philip Mackenzie Ross on a whim to assist him in the construction of courses. By the late '20s Fowler and Simpson had split up, and Simpson made the talented and enterprising Ross a partner. In the 1930s Simpson used famed golfer Molly Gourlay as a consultant, and thus was the first designer to solicit a woman's architectural suggestions.

Always a colorful figure, Tom Simpson toured the English countryside in a chauffer-driven silver Rolls Royce and often appeared for site inspections in an embroidered cloak and beret. Although he experimented with golf holes, he believed the Old Course at St. Andrews to be the only enduring text on course design. He was well-known for his excellent essays on the philosophy of golf architecture, and in addition to numerous articles wrote *The Architectural Side of Golf* with Herbert Newton Wethered (1929; 2nd edition entitled *Design for Golf*, 1952) and contributed to *The Game of Golf* (1931) and *Golf Courses: Design, Construction and Upkeep* (1933; 2nd edition, 1950). A consummate artist, Simpson illustrated his works with ink sketches and color washes, and also wrote and illustrated *Modern Etchings and Their Collectors* in 1919. He also practiced silk embroidery.

Simpson prided himself on supervising the construction of his designs, and as a result was not as prolific as some of his contemporaries. He retired from active course design with the outbreak of World War II. After the war he continued to write about the subject but did no further work in the field, and his final years were spent in seclusion at his estate in Hampshire.

Courses by: Tom Simpson

Austria: Schloss Mittersill GC (1936), with Molly Gourlay.

Belgium: Keerbergen GC; Royal GC du Sart Tilman, Liege; Royal GC Des Fagnes, Balmoral Spa (1936), with P.M. Ross.

England: Berkshire GC (Blue Course), Surrey (1928), with Herbert Fowler; Berkshire GC (Red Course) (1928), with Herbert Fowler; Bootle GC, Lancashire (1934); Clark Estate GC, Windlesham (Par 3); Heythrop College GC; James D. Rothchild Estate GC; Lord Mountbatten Estate GC, with Herbert Fowler; New Zealand GC, Surrey (1931); North Foreland GC, Kingsgate (1919), with Herbert Fowler; Rank Estate GC, Sussex (Par 3, 9); Roehampton GC, London; Sir Archibald Birkmyre Estate GC; Sir Mortimer Singer Estate GC; Sir Phillip Sassoon Estate GC.

France: Baron Edward de Rothchild Estate GC; Baron Henri de Rothchild Estate GC; Club de la Barouge, Mazamet (9, 1935), with P.M. Ross; Club de la Cordeliere, Chaource; Comte de Rougemont Estate GC; Duc de Gramont Estate GC; Golf de Chiberta, Biarritz (1925); Golf de Fountainbleau; Golf de Hossegor; Golf de Memillon; Golf de Morfontaine, Senlis (27, 1927); Golf de Valliere; Golf de Vaux de Cernay; Golf de Villard-de-Lans; Golf de Voisins; Golf Club d'Ozoir-la-Ferriere (27);

Gramont Estate GC (9); Hyde Estate GC (Par 3, 9); International C du Lys, Chantilly (27, 1927); New GC, Deauville (1929), with P.M. Ross.
Indonesia: Djakarta GC, Batavia; Sourabia GC.
Ireland: Kilkenny GC, County Kilkenny.
Scotland: Cruden Bay G&CC, Aberdeen (27, 1926), with Herbert Fowler.
Spain: Club de Campo de Malaga, Torremolinos (1928), with P.M. Ross; Club de G Terramar, Sitges (1922); Malaga GC (1925); Real C de San Sebastian.
Switzerland: Zumikon G&CC, Zurich-Zumikon (1931); Zurich G&CC (1935).
Courses Remodeled & Added to by: Tom Simpson
Belgium: Royal Antwerp GC, Kapellenbos (A.9, 1924), with P.M. Ross; Royal GC de Belgique, Brussels (R.).
England: Ashridge GC, Hertfordshire (R., 1934); Betchworth Park GC (R.); Camberley Heath GC, Surrey (R.); Felixstowe Ferry GC, Suffolk (R., 1936); Felixstowe Ferry GC, Suffolk (A.4, 1936); Hayling GC, Hampshire (R.); Huddersfield GC, Yorkshire (R.); Keighley GC, Yorkshire (R.); Knole Park GC, Kent (R.); Liphook GC (R.); North Foreland GC, Kingsgate (R.), with J.S.F. Morrison; North Hants GC, Hampshire (R.); Royal Lytham & St. Annes GC, Lancashire (R.); Rye GC, Deal (R.); Sunningdale GC (New Course), Berkshire (R., 1935); Wilmslow GC, Cheshire (R.).
France: Golf de Dieppe (R.); Golf de Hardelot (R.), with P.M. Ross.
Ireland: Ballybunion GC (Old Course), County Kerry (R., 1936), with Molly Gourlay; Carlow GC, County Carlow (R., 1937), with Molly Gourlay; County Louth GC, Baltray (R., 1938), with Molly Gourlay.
Scotland: Luffness New GC, East Lothian (R.); Muirfield GC, East Lothian (R., 1933); Royal Aberdeen GC (R.).
Spain: Real C de la Puerto de Hierro (Old), Madrid (R., 1938).
Wales: Glamorganshire GC (R.); Rhos-on-Sea GC, Gwynedd (R.), with Tom Simpson; Rhos-on-Sea GC, Gwynedd (R.); Royal Porthcawl GC, Mid Glamorgan (R., 1937).

Al Smith

Seattle-based golf course designer Al Smith constructed courses for several Pacific Northwest architects in the 1920s and 1930s. In the '50s Smith designed several courses on his own in the state of Washington.
Courses by: Al Smith
Washington: Brae Burn CC, Bellevue; Brookdale CC, Tacoma; Cross Roads GC, Seattle (Par 3); Everett Muni (1971); Glendale CC, Bellevue; Glendale G&CC, Bothel; Lake Samanish State Park GC, Issaquah (1958); Maplewood CC; North Shore CC, Tacoma (1962); Redmond G Links; Twin Lakes CC, Tacoma; Wayne Public GC, Bothel (Precision).

Ernest E. Smith (1901 -)
Born: Vestal, New York.
Ernie Smith began caddying at age 9 in Binghamton, New York. At age 20 he became an assistant professional at Binghamton and, became its professional at 25. His first design was Geneganslet GC in Greene, N.Y., completed in 1926. He then helped the Endicott-Johnson Shoe Co. route and construct a company course, En-Joie CC, which opened in 1927.
In the early 1930s Smith designed and constructed Ely Park GC in Binghamton and remained as its pro/superintendent. Although he did no further golf design work for some 25 years, he proved himself an able teacher and avid promoter of the game. He served as a Vice President of the PGA of America in 1941, and was on the executive board of the New York PGA for 28 years.
In the early 1950s Smith wintered in Florida where his interest in course design was renewed. He received commissions on a few Florida projects, and when he retired from Ely Park in 1963 Smith moved to that state to practice golf architecture full-time. He remained active through the late 1960s.
Courses by: Ernest E. Smith
Florida: Hobe Sound CC; Selva Marina CC, Atlantic Beach (1958); Seven Lakes CC, Fort Myers (Precision, 1971); Silver Lake G&CC, Leesburg (1962); South Seas Plantation GC, Captiva Island (9, 1969).
New York: Ely Park GC, Binghamton (1933); En-Joie CC, Endicott (1927); Geneganslet GC, Greene (1926).
Courses Remodeled & Added to by: Ernest E. Smith
Florida: Martin County G&CC (R., 1963); Rio Mar CC, Vero Beach (A.9, 1964).
New York: Ely Park GC, Binghamton (Par 3, A., 1962); Kass Inn & CC, Margaretville (Par 3, A., 1964).

Orrin Edward Smith (1883 - 1958)
Born: Southington, Connecticut. Died: New Britain, Connecticut at age 75.
Orrin Smith began his career as a construction superintendent for Willie Park Jr. on Shuttle Meadow CC in New Britain, Connecticut. He was later associated with Donald Ross on several projects, including Longmeadow (Mass.) CC.
Smith entered private practice as a course designer in 1925 and remained active through the mid-1950s, operating from his home in Hartford, Connecticut. He was influential in the early design career of James Gilmore Harrison and also trained golf architects William F. Mitchell and Albert Zikorus. The latter took over Smith's practice upon his retirement in 1955.
Courses by: Orrin Smith
Arkansas: Melbourne GC.
Connecticut: Birchwood CC, Westport (9); Deercrest CC, Greenwich (1957), with Al Zikorus; East Hartford GC (9); Longshore C Park, Westport; Louis Stoner Private Course, West Hartford (9); Suffield CC (9); Torrington CC; Tumblebrook CC, Bloomfield (9, 1948), with William F. Mitchell; Woodbridge CC.
Maine: Pine Valley GC, Southington (1950); Waterville CC (9, 1938).
Massachusetts: Brewster Green GC (NLE, 9, 1957); Duamyre CC, Enfield (NLE, 9); Framingham CC (9); Ludlow Muni, Chicopee (9), with Al Zikorus; Packachaug Hills CC, Worchester (9).
Missouri: J.J. Lynn Estate GC, Kansas City (NLE, 9).
Nebraska: East Ridge CC, Lincoln (NLE).
New Jersey: River Vale CC (1931).
New York: Embassy C, Armonk; Hilly Dale CC, Carmel; Plandome CC (1930);

Signal Hill CC, Armonk; Spring Rock CC, Central Valley (27, 1955).
Pennsylvania: Baldoc CC, Erwin; Pennhurst CC, Turtle Creek (NLE).
Courses Remodeled & Added to by: Orrin Smith
Connecticut: CC of Farmington (R.); East Hartford GC (A.9, 1956), with Al Zikorus; Hartford GC, West Hartford (R.), 1946), with William F. Mitchell; Hyfield CC, Middleburg (R.9, 1954), with Al Zikorus; Hyfield CC, Middleburg (A.9, 1954); Racebrook CC, Orange (R.), 1947), with William F. Mitchell; Rockledge CC, West Hartford (A.9, 1954); Rockledge CC, West Hartford (R.9, 1954), with Al Zikorus; Rockrimmon CC, Stamford (A.9, 1953), with Al Zikorus; Salmon Brook CC, Granby (NLE, R.); Stanley GC, New Britain (A.9, 1958), with Al Zikorus; Tumble Brook CC, Bloomfield (A.9, 1948), with William F. Mitchell; TPC of Connecticut, Cromwell (R., 1951).
Kansas: Macdonald Park Muni, Wichita (R., 1938); Milburn G&CC, Overland Park (R., 1925), with James Gilmore Harrison.
Maine: Augusta CC, Augusta (R., 1939), with William F. Mitchell; Bridgeton GC (R., 1939), with William F. Mitchell; Mount Kineo GC, Kineo (R., 1940), with William F. Mitchell; Portland CC, Falmouth (R., 1940), with William F. Mitchell.
Maryland: Rocky Point GC, Essex (R., 1939), with William F. Mitchell.
Massachusetts: Belmont CC (R.); Cedar Glen GC, Saugus (R., 1931), with William F. Mitchell; Framingham CC (A.5, 1954), with Al Zikorus; Needham GC (R., 1935), with William F. Mitchell; North Adams GC (R., 1939), with William F. Mitchell; Oak Hill CC, Fitchburg (R., 1938), with William F. Mitchell; Ould Newberry CC, Newburyport (R., 1939), with William F. Mitchell; Quincy CC (R.), with Al Zikorus; Unicorn CC, Stoneham (R., 1937), with William F. Mitchell; Vesper CC, Tyngsboro (R., 1939), with William F. Mitchell; Wenham GC (R., 1938), with William F. Mitchell.
Missouri: Blue Hills CC, Kansas City (NLE, R., 1926), with James Gilmore Harrison; Joplin CC (NLE, R.); Oakwood CC, Kansas City (A.9, 1925), with James Gilmore Harrison.
New Hampshire: Claremont CC (R., 1936), with William F. Mitchell; Dover CC (R., 1940), with William F. Mitchell; Hanover CC, Dartmouth College (R., 1937), with William F. Mitchell; Laconia CC (R., 1938), with William F. Mitchell; Lake Sunapee CC, New London (R., 1934), with William F. Mitchell; Lebanon CC (R., 1937), with William F. Mitchell; Newport CC (R., 1937), with William F. Mitchell; Rochester CC (R., 1939), with William F. Mitchell.
New York: Fresh Meadow CC, Great Neck (R., 1938), with William F. Mitchell; Huntington Crescent CC, Huntington (R., 1939), with William F. Mitchell; Huntington Crescent CC (West Course), Huntington (R., 1939), with William F. Mitchell; Lake Success GC (R.9, 1958), with Al Zikorus; Lake Success GC (A.9, 1958), with Al Zikorus.
Ohio: Columbus CC (R., 1937); Zanesville CC (R.).
Rhode Island: Newport CC (R., 1939), with William F. Mitchell.

Willie Smith (1872 - 1916)
Born: Carnoustie, Scotland. Died: Mexico City, Mexico at age 44.
Willie Smith, member of a famous Carnoustie golfing family, won the U.S. Open in 1899. Around that time he laid out Mexico's first golf course, the 9-hole San Pedro CC.
Smith eventually settled in Mexico, planning the first version of Mexico City CC and Chapultepec CC. After he died in the Revolution of 1916, his brother Alex completed construction of Chapultepec in 1921.
Courses by: Willie Smith
Mexico: Chapultepec CC (1921), with Alex Smith; Mexico City CC (1907); San Pedro GC (9, 1905).

Arthur Jack Snyder (1917 -) ASGCA, President, 1982.
Born: Rosedale, Pennsylvania.
Jack Snyder received a B.S. degree in Landscape Architecture from Pennsylvania State University in 1939. From 1939 to 1955 he owned two landscape architectural firms, Arthur J. Snyder Co. and Snyder Inc. During World War II he was involved in defense design and, for a brief period, in land surveying.
Snyder was one of three brothers, all of whom became course superintendents after training under their father Arthur Snyder. The senior Snyder had himself been trained by Emil Loeffler and John McGlynn at Oakmont. Jack served as superintendent at Oakmont in 1951-'52, and during that time rebuilt the 8th green. From 1956 to 1959 he was superintendent at White Mountain CC in Pinetop, Arizona.
Snyder entered private practice as a golf architect in 1958. Prior to that time he had been involved a few course remodeling projects and had designed a course at Jane Lew, West Virginia.
Courses by: Arthur Jack Snyder
Arizona: Apache Wells CC, Mesa (1963); Arizona City CC (1963); Beaver Creek CC, Lake Montezuma (1962); Black Canyon GC, Phoenix (NLE, Par 3, 9, 1961); Camelback GC (Indian Bend Course), Scottsdale (1978); Canon del Oro CC, Sedona (9, 1961); Canyon Mesa GC, Sedona (Precision, 9, 1985); Cave Creek Muni, Phoenix (1984); Concho Valley GC, St. John's (9, 1970); Coronado GC, Scottsdale (Precision, 9, 1965); Desert Sands G&CC, Mesa (Precision, 1969); Golden Hills Resort GC {formerly Apache CC}, Mesa (1960); Haven CC, Green Valley (1965); Hospitality Muni, Winslow (9, 1979); Ironwood GC (9); Ken McDonald Muni, Tempe (1974); Mountain Shadows CC, Scottsdale (Precision, 1962); Phoenician G&RC, Phoenix (1981); Poco Diablo GC, Sedona (Par 3, 9, 1966); Show Low CC (9, 1961); Silverbell Muni, Tucson (1979); Tierra Grande CC, Casa Grande; Villa Monterey CC, Scottsdale (Precision, 9, 1982).
California: Kern City GC, Bakersfield (9, 1961).
Hawaii: Kaanapali Kai GC, Lahaina (NLE, Precision, 1970); Royal Kaanapali GC (South Course), Maui (1976); Seamountain GC, Ka'u (1973); Wailea GC (Blue Course), Maui (1971); Wailea GC (Orange Course), Maui (1977).
Nevada: Eagle Valley Muni, Carson City (1977); Ruby View Muni, Elko (1969); Wells Muni (9, 1975).
New Mexico: Arroyo del Oso GC, Albuquerque (1965); Civitan Park Muni, Farmington (Par 3, 9, 1965); Puerto del Sol GC, Albuquerque (9, 1978); Quail Run GC, Santa Fe (Precision, 9, 1986); Scott Park Muni, Silver City (9, 1962).
Utah: San Juan GC, Monticello (9, 1964).

Virginia: Cedar Point C, Norfolk (1963).
West Virginia: Harmony Farm CC, Jane Lew (NLE, 9, 1940).
Courses Remodeled & Added to by: Arthur Jack Snyder
Arizona: Anasazi GC, Phoenix (R., 1983); Boulders GC, Carefree (A.9, 1974); Boulders GC, Carefree (R.2, 1978); Brookview CC, Surprise (R., 1986); Camelback GC (Padre Course), Scottsdale (R.2, 1980); Desert Forest GC, Carefree (R.2, 1978); Golden Hills Resort GC, Mesa (R., 1984); London Bridge GC, Lake Havasu City (A.9, 1984); Mesa CC (R., 1986); Orange Tree CC, Scottsdale (R.1, 1977); Papago Park GC, Phoenix (R.); Pinewood CC, Munds Park (R., 1965); Scottsdale CC (R.4, 1973); Tucson CC (R., 1972); White Mountain CC, Pinetop (A.9, 1959); Wickenburg CC (R.); Wigwam CC, Litchfield (NLE, A.9, 1961); Wigwam CC, Litchfield (NLE, R.9, 1961).
California: La Jolla CC (R.3, 1965).
Hawaii: Keauhou Kona CC, Kailua-Kona (R.3, 1981); Makaha Inn & CC (West Course), Oahu (R.); Volcano G&CC, Kilauea Volcano (A.9, 1969); Volcano G&CC, Kilauea Volcano (R.9, 1969); Waialae CC, Honolulu (R.3, 1969); Waiehu Muni (R.3, 1968).
Pennsylvania: Oakmont CC (R.1, 1952).
Utah: Rose Park GC, Salt Lake City (R.5, 1963).

Daniel Gordon "Des" Soutar (1882 - 1937)
Born: Carmyllie, Forfar, Scotland. Died: Sydney, Australia at age 55.
Des Soutar learned golf on the links of Carnoustie, where he watched and mimicked the swings of Freddie Tait, Archie Simpson and Willie Smith. He apprenticed as a carpenter at age 14, but decided early on that he wanted to be a golf professional.
In 1903 Soutar moved to Australia at the urging of his boyhood friend and golf rival Carnegie Clark (who would eventually also design many courses in that country). The two formed a club-making and teaching partnership and they soon were hired by Royal Sydney GC. They both became successful competitive golfers in their adopted homeland, and both won many tournaments. Somewhat pretentiously, Soutar wrote *The Australian Golfer* in 1906, which offered everything from basic instruction on how to play the game to critiques on Australia's most prominent layouts.
Soutar moved to Manly GC in 1911, where he taught, among others, Joe Kirkwood (who became a popular trick shot artist in America) and Jim Ferrier (a PGA Tour player for decades). He and Clark also formed the Australian PGA and Soutar won its first annual championship.
About the same time Soutar began laying out courses along the east coast of Australia and in nearby New Zealand.
In his later years, Soutar taught lessons in a downtown Sydney department store.
Courses by: Des Soutar
Australia: Elanora CC (1929); Glenora GC (1923); Kingston Heath GC, Cheltenham (1925).
New Zealand: Christchurch CC, Shirley.
Courses Remodeled & Added to by: Des Soutar
Australia: Royal Adelaide GC, Seaton (A.4); Royal Adelaide GC, Seaton (R.).

Robert Baxter Spann (1953 -)
Born: Baton Rouge, Louisiana.
Baxter Spann obtained a Bachelor of Landscape Architecture degree from Louisiana State University in 1979. During his college summers, Spann had worked in the field for the golf design firm of Joseph S. Finger and Associates. After graduation, Spann became a full-time associate in the Houston, Texas-based firm.
Courses by: Baxter Spann
Texas: Laredo CC (1985), with Joseph S. Finger.
Courses Remodeled & Added to by: Baxter Spann
Texas: Victoria CC (R., 1985), with Joseph S. Finger.

William James Spear (1929 -) ASGCA
Born: Iowa City, Iowa.
William James Spear trained under golf architect Robert Bruce Harris and entered private practice as a course designer in 1960. Over the next 25 years, he designed and remodeled over fifty courses in the upper Midwest.
Courses by: William James Spear
Georgia: Turtle Cove GC, Atlanta (9, 1971).
Illinois: Arrowhead CC, Chillicothe (9, 1960); Danville Elks C (1969); Hawthorn Ridge GC, Aledo (1977); Highland Springs CC, Rock Island (1968); Highland Woods GC, Hoffman Estates (1975); Lakeshore CC, Taylorsville (1970); Lakewood G&CC, Havana (9, 1966); Little Tam GC, Niles (Precision, 9, 1970); Marengo Ridge CC (9, 1964); Midland CC, Kewanee (1970); Park Place CC, DeKalb (9, 1965); Randall Oaks GC, Dundee (1965); Renwood CC, Gray's Lake (9, 1977); Rock River CC, Sterling (9, 1966); St. Elmo GC (9, 1969); Swan Hills GC, Avon (1971).
Indiana: Castlebrook G&CC, Lowell (1979); Elbel Park GC, South Bend (1964); Forest Park GC, Valparaiso (9, 1971); Grand Prairie GC, Kalamazoo (9, 1962); Playland Park G Center, South Bend (Par 3, 9, 1962).
Iowa: Amana Colonies GC, Amana (1987); Clinton Muni (1981); Palmer Hills GC, Bettendorf (1974).
Michigan: Brookwood GC, Buchanan (9, 1964).
Minnesota: Willow Creek GC, Rochester (1974).
North Dakota: Souris Valley GC, Minot (1967).
Ohio: Auglaize GC, Defiance (9, 1964); Edgecreek GC, Van Wert (1960).
Wisconsin: Hickory Grove CC, Fennimore (9, 1966); Voyager Village GC, Danbury (1971).
Courses Remodeled & Added to by: William James Spear
Illinois: Crawford County GC, Robinson (A.9, 1965); Effingham CC (A.9, 1968).

Bert Stamps (1911 -)
Born: Visalia, California.
Bert Stamps began as a caddy at the old Rancho CC in Los Angeles. An excellent golfer, he turned professional at age eighteen but soon applied for reinstatement as

an amateur, winning seven local tournaments in succession by one point. He again turned pro in 1932 and went to work in a pro shop. He was admitted to the PGA of America in 1938.
Stamps was stationed with the U.S. Army in the Far East during and after World War II. While there he won the Japanese Open in Osaka, an event instituted by occupation forces. Following military service, he became head professional at Cleveland (Tenn.) CC. Between 1945 and 1948, he competed sporadically on the PGA Tour and remodeled the Cleveland layout. He was soon hired to plan a new course in Baton Rouge, Louisiana. He continued to practice golf design on a part-time basis after returning to California in the 1950s.
Stamps was chosen Northern California PGA Professional of the Year in 1974. The same year he retired to become professional emeritus at Rancho Murieta CC near Sacramento, a course of his own design and construction.
Courses by: Bert Stamps
California: Airways GC, Fresno (1951); Belmont CC, Fresno (1956); Cameron Park CC, Shingle Springs (1965); Camino Heights GC (1966); DeLaveaga CC, Santa Cruz; Elkhorn GC, Lodi (1962); Feather River Park GC; Lawrence Links, North Highland (9); Mesquite CC, Palm Springs (1986); Oak Ridge GC, San Jose (1967); Paso Robles G&CC (1960); Rancho Murieta GC (North Course), Sloughhouse (1971); San Luis Obispo CC (1959).
Louisiana: Baton Rouge CC (1950).
Nevada: Sahara CC, Las Vegas (1962); Tropicana CC, Las Vegas (1961).
Courses Remodeled & Added to by: Bert Stamps
California: Cold Springs G&CC (A.9, 1981); Kings County CC, Hanford (A.9, 1961); Rio del Mar GC, Aptos (R., 1957); Woodbridge G&CC, Lodi (R., 1974).
Tennessee: Cleveland CC (R., 1947).

Donald M.A. Steel (1937 -) BAGCA
Born: Hillingdon, England.
Donald Steel attended Fettes College in Edinburgh and Cambridge University. Well-known as a rugby and cricket player, he also became a scratch amateur golfer and represented England in many international matches.
Within a few months after obtaining an Agricultural degree from Cambridge in 1961, Steel became the first golf correspondent for the London Sunday Telegram. Over the years he distinguished himself as a golf writer and historian. Among the golf books he edited were *The Golfer's Bedside Book, The Golf Course Guide, The Encyclopedia of Golf* (with Peter Ryde and Herbert Warren Wind) and *The Guiness Book of Golf Facts and Feats*, all of which were published in several editions.
In 1965, Steel joined the golf architectural firm of Cotton (C.K.), Pennink, Lawrie and Partners Ltd. as a trainee. He became a full partner in 1971. He handled an ever-increasing number of projects for the firm in the Seventies and Eighties. Steel also served for years as secretary/treasurer of the BAGCA.
Courses by: D.M.A. Steel
England: Beacon Park GC, West Lancashire (1982); Blackhill Wood GC, Staffordshire , with J.J.F. Pennink; Boothferry GC, Yorkshire (1981); Broome Park GC, Kent (1981), with J.J.F. Pennink; Bushey G & Squash C, Hertfordshire (9, 1980), with J.J.F. Pennink; Carlisle Race Track GC, Cumbria (1981); Farnham Park GC, Stoke Poges (9, 1974), with J.J.F. Pennink; Halifax Bradley Hall GC, Yorkshire , with J.J.F. Pennink; Harrow School GC, Middlesex (Precision, 9, 1978), with J.J.F. Pennink; Ingol G & Squash C, Lancashire (1984), with J.J.F. Pennink; Pitcheroak GC, Worchestershire (1973); Radley College GC (9); Woburn G&CC (Duchess Course), Buckinghamshire (1976), with J.J.F. Pennink and C.D. Lawrie.
Courses Remodeled & Added to by: D.M.A.Steel
Ireland: Lahinch GC (Castle Course), County Clare (R.); Lahinch GC (Castle Course), County Clare (A.9).
Scotland: Deeside GC, Aberdeen (A.9); Machrie Hotel GC (R.).

John Steidel (1950 -)
Born: Nyack, New York.
A graduate of the University of California at Berkeley with a degree in Landscape Architecture, John Steidel worked for 4 years for golf architect Robert Muir Graves. Then, after graduate studies in Urban Planning at Cal Poly-Pomona, he became an associate in the firm of Thomson, Wolveridge, Fream & Associates, working in the Pacific Northwest. In 1980, Steidel formed his own course design business based in Washington.
Courses by: John Steidel
Montana: Marian Hills CC, Maltz (9, 1983).
Washington: Canyon Lakes G&CC, Kennewick (1981), with Peter Thomson, Michael Wolveridge and Ronald Fream.
Courses Remodeled & Added to by: John Steidel
Montana: Missoula CC (R., 1985).
North Dakota: Minot CC (R., 1985).
Washington: Cedarcrest GC, Marysville (R.2, 1984); Everett G&CC (R.1, 1985); Liberty Lake GC, Spokane (R.1, 1984); Walla Walla CC (R., 1984).

Wayne E. Stiles (1884 - 1953) ASGCA, Charter Member.
Born: Boston, Massachusetts. Died: Wellesley, Massachusetts at age 68.
Wayne Stiles did not train formally for a career in landscape architecture. Instead he began working at age 18 as an office boy for landscape designer Franklin Brett. After being made a draftsman and finally a junior partner, Stiles opened his own landscape design and town planning office in Boston in 1915. He branched into golf design in the early 1920s.
Stiles formed a course design partnership with John R. Van Kleek in 1924. The firm of Stiles and Van Kleek had offices in Boston, New York City and St. Petersburg, and concentrated mainly on golf courses and their accompanying subdivisions. Over the years associates of the firm included professional golfer Walter Hagen (who was a consultant in course design), Thomas D. Church and Butler Sturdivant (both subsequent nationally known landscape architects), and Bruce Matthews (later a prominent course designer).
The firm dissolved before the Depression, when the real estate boom faded in Florida, but Stiles remained in practice almost exclusively as a golf course architect. During the Depression, he supervised CCC projects for the National Park Service.

After World War II he was active again.

Stiles served as President of the Boston Society of Landscape Architects for several years and was a member of the ASLA.

Courses by: Wayne Stiles
Alabama: Highland Park GC, Birmingham , with John Van Kleek.

Connecticut: Paul Block Private Course, Greenwich (9), with John Van Kleek.

Florida: Highland Park C, Lake Wales (1925), with John Van Kleek; Holly Hill G&CC, Davenport (NLE), with John Van Kleek; Kenilworth Lodge GC, Sebring (NLE), with John Van Kleek; Lake Jovita CC, with John Van Kleek; Palmetto G&CC, with John Van Kleek; Pasadena GC, St. Petersburg (1923), with John Van Kleek and Walter Hagen; Tarpon Springs CC (1927), with John Van Kleek.

Georgia: Glen Arven CC, Thomasville (1929), with John Van Kleek; Radium CC, Albany (1927), with John Van Kleek.

Maine: Boothbay Harbor CC (9), with John Van Kleek; Brunswick GC (9), with John Van Kleek; Riverside Muni, Portland; Wawenock GC, Damariscotta (9), with John Van Kleek; Wilson Lake CC (9), with John Van Kleek.

Massachusetts: Albemarle CC, West Newton (9); Berkshire Hunt & CC, Lenox (1930), with John Van Kleek; Cranwell School GC, Lenox , with John Van Kleek; D.W. Field Muni, Brockton (1927), with John Van Kleek; Duxbury YC (9); Franconia Muni, Springfield (1930), with John Van Kleek; Haverhill CC, with John Van Kleek; Larry Gannon Memorial GC, Lynn (1932); Marlborough CC, Marlboro (9), with John Van Kleek; Marshfield CC (9, 1922); Memorial Muni, Springfield (NLE), with John Van Kleek; Needham GC (9, 1923); Newton Commonwealth GC, Newton , with John Van Kleek; Pine Brook CC, Weston , with John Van Kleek; Putterham Meadows Muni, Brookline , with John Van Kleek; South Shore CC, Hingham (1923); Stony Brae GC, Quincy; Taconic GC, Williamstown (1927), with John Van Kleek; Thorny Lea GC, Brockton (1925), with John Van Kleek; Unicorn CC, Stoneham , with John Van Kleek; Wahconah CC, Dalton (9); Weld GC, with John Van Kleek; Woodland CC, Newton; Wyndhurst C, Lenox .

Missouri: Norwood Hills CC (East Course), St. Louis (1923); Norwood Hills CC (West Course), St. Louis (1922).

New Hampshire: Cochecho CC, Dover (9, 1921); CC of New Hampshire {formerly Kearsarge Valley CC}, North Conway (9, 1930), with John Van Kleek; Dover CC; Hooper GC, Walpole (9), with John Van Kleek; Mojalaki CC, Franklin (9), with John Van Kleek; Nashua CC (9, 1916), with John Van Kleek; Wentworth Hall GC, Jackson .

New Jersey: Brigantine CC (1927), with John Van Kleek; Wildwood G&CC, Cape May Court House (1923), with John Van Kleek.

New York: Woodstock CC.

North Carolina: Hamilton Lakes CC, Chimney Rock , with John Van Kleek.

South Carolina: Hartford Estate GC, Charleston .

Vermont: Barre CC (9, 1923); Brattleboro CC (9, 1916).

Courses Remodeled & Added to by: Wayne Stiles
Maine: Augusta CC, Augusta (A.9, 1926), with John Van Kleek; North Haven GC (R.), with John Van Kleek; Prouts Neck GC (A.9), with John Van Kleek; Prouts Neck GC (R.9), with John Van Kleek.

Massachusetts: CC of Pittsfield (R.); Franklin CC (R.); Marshfield CC (A.9, 1931); Monoosnock CC, Leominster (R.9), with John Van Kleek; Oak Hill CC, Fitchburg (A.9), with John Van Kleek; Sharon CC (R.9); Wellesley CC (R.9); Wollaston CC (R.); Woods Hole GC, Falmouth (R.).

New Hampshire: Bethlehem CC (R.); Crawford Notch CC (R.), with John Van Kleek; Laconia CC (A.9).

Pennsylvania: Gulph Mills GC, King of Prussia (R., 1941).

Vermont: Rutland CC (R.9), with John Van Kleek; Rutland CC (A.9), with John Van Kleek; Woodstock CC (9, 1924); Woodstock CC (R.9, 1924), with John Van Kleek.

Earl Stone (1926 -)
Born: Alachua, Florida.

Earl Stone graduated from Auburn University in 1949 after service in the U.S. Navy during World War II. He worked in the electrical appliance business and as a heating and air conditioning contractor until the mid-1950s, when he began installing irrigation systems on golf courses. This led to jobs rebuilding greens and in 1958 to a commission to design and build an entire course. An admirer of golf architect Dick Wilson's work, Stone designed courses in the Southeast over the next twenty-five years.

Courses by: Earl Stone
Alabama: Camden State Park GC (1970); Deer Run GC, Moulton (9, 1980); Frank House Muni, Bessemer (1972); Gulf Shores GC (1965); Gulf State Park GC, Gulf Shores (1972); Holly Hills CC, Bay Minette (9, 1966); Joe Wheeler State Park GC, Rogersville (1974); Lake Guntersville State Park GC, Guntersville (1972); Little Mountain State Park GC, Gunthersville (1972); McFarland Park GC, Florence (1973); Moulton Muni; Oak Mountain State Park GC, Pelham (1972); St. Andrews CC, Mobile (1971).

Arkansas: Rivercliff GC, Bull Shoals (9, 1977).

Florida: Indian Bayou G&CC, Destin (1978).

Kentucky: Western Hills Muni, Hopkinsville (1985).

Mississippi: Briarwood CC, Meridian (1967); Broadwater Beach Hotel GC (Fun Course), Gulfport (Par 3, 9, 1968); Broadwater Beach Hotel GC (Sun Course), Gulfport (1968); Gulfport Naval Air Station GC (9, 1978); Hickory Hills CC, Gautier (1965); Longfellow House GC, Pascagoula (Par 3, 9, 1981); Pine Burr CC, Wiggens (9, 1977); Riverside Muni, Jackson (9, 1974); Waynesboro CC (9, 1960).

Bahrain: Bahrain Equestrain & Racing C, Manama (1980).

Courses Remodeled & Added to by: Earl Stone
Alabama: CC of Mobile (A.9, 1966); Lake Forest CC, Daphne (R.9, 1978); Lake Forest CC, Daphne (A.9, 1978); Skyline CC, Mobile (A.9, 1974).

Florida: Crestview CC (A.9, 1985).

Mississippi: Broadwater Beach Hotel GC (Sea Course), Gulfport (A.9, 1962); Broadwater Beach Hotel GC (Sea Course), Gulfport (R.9, 1962); Diamond Head Y&CC, Bay St. Louis (A.9, 1977); Rainbow Bay GC, Biloxi (R.12, 1976); Rainbow Bay GC, Biloxi (A.6, 1976).

David Strath (1840 - 1879)
Born: St. Andrews, Scotland. Died: En route to Australia at age 39.

Davie Strath served as greenkeeper at North Berwick from 1876 to 1878. He formalized the course and extended it to eighteen holes, and his revisions to the Perfection (hole number 14) and the Redan (hole number 15) made those holes famous worldwide. The Redan's concept was subsequently adapted repeatedly on courses throughout the world by many golf architects.

A contemporary competitor of Young Tom Morris, Strath left North Berwick to seek his fortune in Australia. He developed consumption and died aboard a steamship enroute.

Herbert Bertram Strong (1879 - 1944)
Born: Ramsgate, Kent, England. Died: Fort Pierce, Florida at age 65.

Herbert Strong began his golf career as professional and club maker at St. Georges GC, Sandwich, Kent, England. In 1905 he emigrated to New York, becoming professional at Apawamis Club in Rye. Six years later he moved to Inwood GC in Far Rockaway and, while there, remodeled the course. This led to other design jobs, and within a few years, Strong was devoting virtually all his time to golf course architecture.

Throughout his career, Strong did his own surveying and usually remained at the sites to supervise construction. He was assisted on some of his later jobs by younger brother Leonard, who later became a prominent course superintendent. (Curiously, while Strong never made much of the fact, Leonard claimed that Herbert had invented the first golf pull cart in the 1920s but someone else had obtained a patent on such a device before Herbert was able to apply.)

Like many architects of that era, Herbert Strong was a victim of the Depression. He lost a fortune when the golf course market collapsed, although he remained in the golf business until the end. In his day he had been a fine player and considered among the longest drivers, having nearly a dozen holes-in-one to his credit, including one of 320 yards. He was a charter member of the PGA and served as its first treasurer from 1917 to 1919.

Courses by: Herbert Strong
Florida: Clearwater CC (1920); Indian Hills G&CC, Fort Pierce; Lakewood CC, St. Petersburg; Ponte Vedra C (Ocean Course), Ponte Vedra Beach (1932); Rio Mar CC, Vero Beach (9, 1919); Royal Park G&CC, Vero Beach (NLE); Vero Beach CC (1929).

Maryland: Rodgers Forge CC, Baltimore (1923), with George Low Sr; Sherwood Forest GC, Annapolis (1920); Woodholme CC, Pikesville (1927).

New Jersey: Aviation Y&CC, Bendix (NLE, 1937); Braidburn CC (Lake Course), Florham Park; Linwood CC.

New York: Engineers GC, Roslyn (1918); Huntington G & Marine C, Huntington (1915); Island Hills CC, Sayville; Island's End G&CC; Metropolis CC, White Plains .

Ohio: Canterbury CC, Shaker Heights (1922); Lake Forest CC, Hudson (1931).

Pennsylvania: Saucon Valley CC (Saucon Course), Bethlehem (1922).

Vermont: Lake Shore CC, Burlington (9, 1928).

Virginia: Army-Navy CC (Fairfax Course), Fairfax .

West Virginia: Guyen G&CC, Huntington (1918).

Ontario: Lakeview G&CC, Toronto .

Quebec: Laval sur le Lac GC; Manoir Richelieu GC, Murray Bay (1927); Royal Quebec CC (Kent Course) (NLE, 1923); St. Andrew CC, Saint-Andre .

Cuba: Veradera Beach CC, Havana .

Courses Remodeled & Added to by: Herbert Strong
New Jersey: Knickerbocker CC, Tenafly (R.); Mountain Ridge CC, West Caldwell (R.).

New York: Beacon CC (R.9, 1929); Beacon CC (A.9, 1929); Deepdale GC, Great Neck (NLE, R.); Inwood CC, Far Rockaway (R., 1911); Nassau CC, Glen Cove (A.3, 1924), with George Low Sr; Nassau CC, Glen Cove (R., 1924), with George Low Sr.

Pennsylvania: CC of Harrisburg (R.).

John Hamilton Stutt (1924 -) BAGCA, Founding Member; Chairman, 1975, President, 1980.
Born: Scotland.

J. Hamilton Stutt attended Glasgow Academy and received a B.S. degree in Mathematics and Botany from St. Andrews University, where he was a member of the golf and tennis teams. As a boy, he accompanied his father, John R. Stutt, and his father's business associate, James Braid, to many construction sites. Following service with the Royal Air Force during World War II, he entered his father's golf course and sports ground construction firm. At the same time, he began studying civil engineering and surveying at Strathclyde University. Over the next fifteen years Stutt constructed many golf courses, several of them planned by golf architects P.M. Ross and J.S.M. Morrison. Ross and Morrison instructed and encouraged Stutt in course design, and by 1949 he began doing design work on his own. In the course of the next decade, Stutt gradually gave up the family construction business to devote full time to golf course architecture.

Hamilton Stutt was the author of *Restoration of Derelict Land for Golf*, a booklet published by the Golf Development Council. In addition to his native tongue, Stutt spoke French, German, Spanish and Norwegian. Such fluency helped him land projects in Europe, Scandinavia and the Middle East.

Courses by: J. Hamilton Stutt
England: Blyth GC, Northumberland (1976); Bramshott Hill GC, Hampshire (1974); Carlyon Bay GC, Cornwall; Deane Muni, Somerset (Precision); Ferndown GC (New Course), Dorset (1970); Knighton Heath GC, Dorset (1976); Meon Valley CC, Hampshire (1976); Middlesbrough Muni, Yorkshire (1977); Ramsey GC, Cambridgeshire (1964); Rushyford GC, Aycliffe, Durham (1983); St. Mellion G&CC, Cornwall (1976); Vivary GC (Precision); Westwood GC, Staffordshire .

France: Corsica GC (Par 3); Normandie GC (9); Piencort GC, Normandy .

Ireland: Wexford GC, County Wexford (9, 1961).

Lebanon: Delhamyeh CC, Beirut .

Scotland: Ardeer GC, Ayrshire (1980); Cumbernauld GC, Dumbartonshire (1977); Fort William GC, Invernesshire (1974); Glennoch G&CC, Firth of Clyde (1974); Glenrothes GC, Fife (1958), with Fraser Middleton; Murrayshall G&CC, Perthshire (1981).

247

Spain: Costa Brava GC, Gerona (1962); Coto de Donana, Seville (1985).
Courses Remodeled & Added to by: J. Hamilton Stutt
England: Ashley Wood GC, Dorset (R.9, 1983); Ashridge GC, Hertfordshire (R.); Blandford GC (R.); Brockenhurst Manor GC (R.); Came Down GC (R.); Cowes GC (A.9); Launceston GC, Cornwall (A.9); Lee-on-the-Solent GC (R.); Marlborough GC, Wiltshire (A.9); Middlesborough GC (R.); Morpeth GC, Northumberland (R.); Mullion GC, Cornwall (R.); Parkstone GC, Dorset (R.); Royal Eastbourne GC, Sussex (R.); Ryde GC, Isle of Wight (R.); South Herts GC, London (R.); Southampton GC, Hampshire (R.); St. George's Hill GC, Surrey (R.); Ventnor GC (R.); Whitby GC, Yorkshire (R.).
France: International C du Lys, Chantilly (R., 1980).
Ireland: Dundalk GC (R.); Rosslare GC (R.); Wexford GC, County Wexford (A.9, 1984).
Isle of Man: Shanklin & Sandown GC (R.).
Scotland: Colville Park GC (R.); Inverurie GC, Aberdeenshire (R.); Irvine GC, Ayrshire (R.); Kirkcaldy GC, Fife (R.); Monifieth GC, Angus (R.); Prestwick GC, Ayrshire (R., 1979); Prestwick St. Cuthbert GC, Ayrshire (R.); Strathaven GC, Lanarkshire (R.).
Wales: Pyle and Kenfig GC (R.).
West Germany: Frankfurter GC (R., 1952), with J.S.F. Morrison.

John R. Stutt (1897 -)
Born: Paisley, Scotland.
In 1923 John Stutt founded the landscape and sports ground construction firm of John R. Stutt Ltd. Soon branching into golf, Stutt built some eighty-two courses by 1939, most to the plans of James Braid, with whom Stutt became associated in 1923.
The Braid-Stutt team lasted until Braid's death in 1950. In the beginning Braid did all the course planning, but he encouraged Stutt to take on some of the design work as well as construction. Eventually, Stutt became architect and builder of numerous courses of his own. A majority of his career, however, was spent building courses done by Braid and other architects, including John Morrison and Theodore Moone.
Courses by: John R. Stutt
England: Arcot Hall GC, Northumberland , with James Braid; Clitheroe GC, Lancashire , with James Braid; Drayton Park GC, Birmingham , with James Braid; Eaglescliffe GC, County Durham , with James Braid; Exeter G&CC, Countess Wear, Devon , with James Braid; Finchley GC, London , with James Braid; Fulford Heath GC (1934), with James Braid; Hainault Forest GC (Course No. 2), Essex; Kedleston Park GC, Derbyshire (1947), with J.S.F. Morrison; Kingswood GC, Surrey , with James Braid; Mere G&CC, Surrey (1934), with James Braid and George Duncan; Middlesborough GC, with James Braid; Orsett GC, Essex , with James Braid; Oswestry GC, Shropshire , with James Braid; Perranporth GC (1927), with James Braid; Petersborough Milton GC, Northamptonshire , with James Braid; Royal Blackheath GC (1923), with James Braid; Scarborough North Cliff GC, Yorkshire (1927), with James Braid; Tiverton GC, Devon , with James Braid; Torquay GC, Devonshire , with James Braid; Truro GC, Cornwall , with James Braid.
Ireland: Mullingar GC, County Westmeath (1932), with James Braid.
Isle of Man: Ramsey GC, Cambridgeshire (1935), with James Braid.
Northern Ireland: Carnalea GC (1927), with James Braid.
Scotland: Belleisle GC, Ayrshire (1927), with James Braid; Blairgowrie GC (Wee Course), Perthshire , with James Braid; Boat-of-Garten GC, Invernesshire , with James Braid; Buchanan Castle GC, Stirlingshire (1936), with James Braid; Cawder GC (Cawder Course) (1933), with James Braid; Cawder GC (Keir Course) (1933), with James Braid; Countess Wear GC; Crow Wood GC, Glasgow (1925), with James Braid; Dalmahoy GC (East Course), Midlothian (1926), with James Braid; Dalmahoy GC (West Course), Midlothian (1926), with James Braid; Downfield GC, Dundee (1932), with James Braid; Hamilton GC, Lanarkshire , with James Braid; Hayston GC, Glasgow (1926), with James Braid; Hilton Park GC (Allender Course), Dunbarton , with James Braid; Ingliston GC, with James Braid; Musselburgh GC (1937), with James Braid; Ratho Park GC, Edinburgh (1928), with James Braid; Royal Musselburgh GC, East Lothian (1925), with James Braid; Seafield GC (1930), with James Braid; Stornoway GC, Isle of Lewis (1947).
Wales: Welshpool GC, Powys (1929), with James Braid.
Courses Remodeled & Added to by: John R.Stutt
England: Leamington and County GC (R.), with James Braid; Meyrick Park GC, Hampshire (R.); Parkstone GC, Dorset (R., 1927), with James Braid; Ruislip GC, Middlesex (A.9, 1938); Sherwood Forest GC, Nottinghamshire (R., 1935), with James Braid; Wallasey GC, Cheshire (R., 1929), with James Braid.
Ireland: Howth GC (A.9, 1929), with James Braid; Howth GC (R.9, 1929), with James Braid; Waterford GC, County Waterford (A.9, 1934), with James Braid; Waterford GC, County Waterford (R.9, 1934), with James Braid.
Northern Ireland: Bangor GC, County Donegal (R., 1932), with James Braid.
Scotland: Blairgowrie GC (Rosemount Course) (R.10, 1934), with James Braid; Blairgowrie GC (Rosemount Course) (A.8, 1934), with James Braid; Carnoustie GC, Angus (R., 1926), with James Braid; Cathcart Castle GC, Glasgow (R.); Cochrane Castle GC, Renfrewshire (A.10, 1949), with James Braid; Cochrane Castle GC, Renfrewshire (R., 1949), with James Braid; Dunfermline GC, Fife (R.); Eastwood GC, Renfrewshire (R.); Edzell GC (R., 1934), with James Braid; Lanark GC, Lanarkshire (R.); Prestwick GC, Ayrshire (R., 1930), with James Braid; Stranraer GC, Wigtownshire (R.).

John Sutherland
John Sutherland served as secretary of Royal Dornoch GC in Scotland for fifty years, from the 1880s to the late 1920s. A lifelong student of course architecture and greenkeeping, he exerted an enormous influence on Donald Ross during the years Ross worked as pro/greenkeeper at Dornoch. The two made a point of walking the course every evening to see where improvements could be made. They constantly experimented with grasses and often discussed what constituted a good golf hole.
Sutherland also did some designing on his own, including a private course for his friend Andrew Carnegie, the American steel magnate, at Carnegie's Scottish estate, Skibo Castle.
Courses by: John Sutherland
Scotland: Skibo Castle GC (1898); Tarbat GC (9).
Courses Remodeled & Added to by: John Sutherland
Scotland: Royal Dornoch GC, Sutherland (R.9); Royal Dornoch GC, Sutherland (A.9); Tain GC, Rossshire (R.).

John Henry Taylor (1871 - 1963)
Born: Devonshire, England. Died: Devonshire, England at age 92.
J.H. Taylor, one of British golf's "Great Triumvirate," originally trained as a gardener at the boyhood home of Horace Hutchinson. He served as assistant greenkeeper at Westward Ho! and later as pro/greenkeeper at Burnham, Winchester, Wimbledon, and for many years at Royal MidSurrey. He won the British Open five times, as well as many other major championships.
Taylor used his enormous influence to promote public golf courses in England. He had laid out several courses before World War I and continued to plan new ones as part of a design-and-build partnership with F.G. Hawtree. Founded in 1924, the firm of Hawtree and Taylor was active until World War II.
Taylor had little formal education, having left school by age eleven, but he was an avid reader and insisted on writing his memoirs, *Golf, My Life's Work*, without the assistance of a ghost writer.
Courses by: J.H. Taylor
Egypt: Heliopolis Sporting C, Cairo (9, 1905).
England: Addington Court GC (Lower Course), Surrey (1931), with F.G. Hawtree; Addington Court GC (Old Course), Surrey (1931), with F.G. Hawtree; Addington Palace GC, Surrey (1923), with F.G. Hawtree; Batchwood Hall GC, St. Albans (1936), with F.G. Hawtree; Bigbury GC (1923), with F.G. Hawtree; Came Down GC; Chadwell Springs GC, Hertfordshire (9); Chigwell GC, Essex (1925), with F.G. Hawtree; Clevedon GC, Avon (1909); Cock Moor Woods GC, Birmingham (1926), with F.G. Hawtree; Easingwold GC, North Yorkshire (1930), with F.G. Hawtree; Eastbourne Downs GC, Sussex (1908); Elfordleigh GC, Devon (1932), with F.G. Hawtree; Gorleston GC, Suffolk (1926), with F.G. Hawtree; Hainault Forest GC (Course No. 1), Essex (1920); Harborne Church Farm GC, Birmingham (1926), with F.G. Hawtree; Harpenden GC, Hertfordshire (1931), with F.G. Hawtree; Heaton Park GC, Lancashire (1911); High Post GC, Wiltshire (1922), with F.G. Hawtree; Highwoods GC, Bexhill-on-Sea (1925), with F.G. Hawtree; Hill Barn GC, Sussex (1935), with F.G. Hawtree; Hollingbury Park GC, Sussex (1922), with F.G. Hawtree; Ifield G&CC, Sussex (1927), with F.G. Hawtree; Ipswich GC, Purdis Heath (1921), with F.G. Hawtree; Knowle GC, Gloucestershire , with F.G. Hawtree; Lickey Hills GC, Birmingham , with F.G. Hawtree; Marston Green Muni, Birmingham (NLE), with F.G. Hawtree; Norfolk GC; Norwich Muni, with F.G. Hawtree; Pinner Hill GC, Middlesex (1929), with F.G. Hawtree; Pype Hayes Muni, Warwickshire (1932), with F.G. Hawtree; Queens Park GC, Bournemouth (1905); Richmond Park GC (Dukes Course), London (1923), with F.G. Hawtree; Richmond Park GC (Princes Course), London (1923), with F.G. Hawtree; Rickmansworth GC, Hertfordshire (1937), with F.G. Hawtree; Royal Ascot GC, Berkshire (1905); Royal Mid-Surrey GC (Ladies Course); Ruislip GC, Middlesex (1938), with F.G. Hawtree; Salisbury & South Wilts GC, Wiltshire (1894); Seaford GC, Sussex (1906); Selsdon Park Hotel GC, Surrey (1929), with F.G. Hawtree; Southampton GC, Hampshire (27, 1935), with F.G. Hawtree; Southcliffe and Canwick GC, Lincolnshire , with F.G. Hawtree; Stratford-On-Avon GC, Warwickshire (1928); Swinton Park GC, Lancashire (1926), with F.G. Hawtree; Tinsley Park GC, Yorkshire , with F.G. Hawtree; Warren GC, Cheshire (9, 1911), with F.G. Hawtree; Wells-by-the-Sea GC (Par 3, 9), with F.G. Hawtree; Welwyn Garden City GC, Hertfordshire (1922), with F.G. Hawtree; White Webbs Muni, Enfield, Middlesex (1932), with F.G. Hawtree; Woodlands Manor GC, Sevenoaks (1928), with F.G. Hawtree; Woolacombe Bay Hotel GC (Par 3, 9), with F.G. Hawtree; Wyke Green GC, Middlesex (1928), with F.G. Hawtree.
Ireland: Arklow GC, County Wicklow (1926), with F.G. Hawtree.
Scotland: Hilton Park GC (Hilton Course) (1922), with F.G. Hawtree.
Sweden: Bastad GC (1928), with F.G. Hawtree.
Wales: Holywell GC, Clywed (9), with F.G. Hawtree; Rhuddlan GC, Clwyd (1930), with F.G. Hawtree.
Courses Remodeled & Added to by: J.H. Taylor
England: Aldeburgh GC, Suffolk (R., 1906); Coventry GC (R.); Filton GC (A.9), with F.G. Hawtree; Filton GC (R.9), with F.G. Hawtree; Hainault Forest GC (Course No. 1), Essex (A.9), with F.G. Hawtree; Hull GC, Yorkshire (R.), with F.G. Hawtree; Littlehampton GC, Sussex (A.9), with F.G. Hawtree; Littlehampton GC, Sussex (R.9), with F.G. Hawtree; Notts GC, Nottinghamshire (R.); Royal Birkdale GC, Southport (R., 1932), with F.G. Hawtree; Royal Mid-Surrey GC, Surrey (R., 1918); Sidmouth GC, Devon (R.); Sidmouth GC, Devon (A.9, 1908); Sonning GC, Berkshire (R.9), with F.G. Hawtree; Sonning GC, Berkshire (A.9), with F.G. Hawtree; West Middlesex GC, Middlesex (A.9), with F.G. Hawtree; West Wiltshire GC (R.); Willingdon GC, Sussex (R.); York GC, Yorkshire (R.).
Scotland: Machrihanish GC, Argyllshire (R., 1914); Morton Hall GC (R., 1906); Royal Dornoch GC, Sutherland (R., 1907); Williamwood GC, Glasgow (R.), with F.G. Hawtree.
Wales: Ashburnham GC (R., 1914), with F.G. Hawtree; Royal Porthcawl GC, Mid Glamorgan (A.4, 1925), with F.G. Hawtree; Royal Porthcawl GC, Mid Glamorgan (R., 1925), with F.G. Hawtree.

Alec Ternyei, born Elek Viktor Ternyey (1909 - 1983)
Born: Briarcliff, New York. Died: Port St. Lucie, Florida at age 74.
The son of Hungarian immigrants, Elek Ternyey became a caddie at age nine and within a year was working for the club professional, cleaning up after club-making sessions. By observing the club maker and by salvaging old parts, Ternyey soon became adept at club making and repaired many a club for fellow caddies. Leaving high school at the age of sixteen, Ternyey turned professional and worked as an apprentice to Englewood (N.J.) CC professional Cyril Walker. He became a member of the PGA of America at eighteen and in the manner of star golfer Gene Sarazen, modified his name to Alec Ternyei. The "Alec" he once explained, had a Scottish ring to it, while the "Ternyei" was a concession to those who constantly misspelled

his last name.

After stints at Knickerbocker CC and Maidstone CC, Ternyei got his first head professional job in 1931 at Rivervale CC in New Jersey. Over the next twenty-five years he worked as professional at several New Jersey clubs, played in local and regional PGA events and earned a fine reputation as an expert club maker. He also served in the Air Force during World War II.

In the late 1950s Ternyei designed and built his first golf course. He resigned his professional duties in the Sixties to devote his full energies to golf architecture and prided himself on the fact that he personally constructed the dozen courses he designed in the New Jersey area. In 1970 Ternyei retired to a teaching professional position in Florida.

Courses by: Alec Ternyei

Florida: Crystal Lago CC, Pompano Beach (1972).

New Jersey: Beacon Hill CC, Atlantic Heights (1962); Beaver Brook GC, Clinton (1965); Glenhurst CC, Watchung (1966); Green Pond GC (9, 1964); High Mountain CC, Franklin Lakes (1968); Pines GC, Emerson (1963); Princeton Hills Golf Academy, Princeton (1970).

Courses Remodeled & Added to by: Alec Ternyei

New Jersey: Englewood CC (R., 1961).

Pennsylvania: Wynding Brook CC, Milton (A.9, 1957).

William G. Teufel (1926 -) ASGCA
Born: Fairbanks, Alaska.

William Teufel attended Washington State University and obtained a Bachelor of Science degree in Landscape Architecture from the University of Oregon. In 1956 Teufel established a landscape architecture firm in Seattle. In the early Sixties his company, William G. Teufel and Associates, branched into golf course architecture, primarily in the planning of golf course residential development layouts.

Courses by: William Teufel

Washington: Enumclaw GC (9, 1978); Fairwood G&CC, Renton (1966); Fort Lewis GC, Olympia (9, 1976); Hat Island G&CC (1969); Quincy G&CC (1986); Tam O'Shanter CC, Bellevue (1964); Twin Lakes G&CC, Federal Way (1965); Useless Bay G&CC, Whidbey Island (1968); Wing Point G&CC, Bainbridge Island (9, 1963).

Courses Remodeled & Added to by: William Teufel

Montana: Green Meadow CC, Helena (A.9, 1974).

Washington: Foster G Links, Tukwila (R., 1986); Inglewood CC, Kenmore (R., 1985); Kitsap G&CC, Bremerton (R., 1981); Useless Bay G&CC, Whidbey Island (R., 1982); Vashon Island G&CC (R., 1983).

David C. Thomas (1934 -)
Born: Newcastle-upon-Tyne, England.

David Thomas competed on the British, European and American professional golf circuits for over two decades with mixed success. He won the Belgian, Dutch and French Opens, but was never able to win the British Open, losing it in a playoff in 1958 and by a stroke in 1966. A four-time member of Ryder Cup teams, Thomas represented his adopted homeland of Wales in a dozen World Cup competitions.

In the late Sixties, Thomas became interested in golf course design. Teaming with fellow professional golfer Peter Alliss, he laid out and built several courses, including The Belfry, home of the British PGA.

In the late Seventies Thomas and Alliss abandoned course architecture to concentrate on the more lucrative business of course construction.

Courses by: David Thomas

England: Belfry GC (Brabazon Course) (1979), with Peter Alliss; Belfry GC (Derby Course) (1979), with Peter Alliss; Chapel-en-le-Firth GC, Derbyshire; Dewsbury District GC, with Peter Alliss; Hessle GC, with Peter Alliss; Hill Valley G&CC (27, 1975), with Peter Alliss; King's Lynn GC (1975), with Peter Alliss; Thorpe Wood GC (1975), with Peter Alliss.

Northern Ireland: Clandeboye GC (New Course), County Down (1973), with Peter Alliss and T.J.A.McAuley.

Scotland: Blairgowrie GC (Lansdowne Course), Perthshire (9, 1974), with Peter Alliss.

Courses Remodeled & Added to by: David Thomas

France: Golf de La Baule (R., 1977), with Peter Alliss; *Ireland:* Dundalk GC (A.9, 1975), with Peter Alliss; Dundalk GC (R., 1975), with Peter Alliss.

Northern Ireland: Ballyclare GC (R.9, 1973), with Peter Alliss and T.J.A. McAuley.

Scotland: Blairgowrie GC (Rosemount Course) (R., 1974), with Peter Alliss; Haggs Castle GC (R.), with Peter Alliss; Turnberry GC (Ailsa Course), Ayrshire (R., 1976), with Peter Alliss.

George Clifford Thomas Jr. (1873 - 1932)
Born: Philadelphia, Pennsylvania. Died: Beverly Hills, California at age 58.

George C. Thomas Jr., scion of a prominent Philadelphia family, was educated at Episcopal Academy and at the University of Pennsylvania. He worked with his father in the banking firm of Drexel & Co. until 1907, but his early avocation was gardening. He was a nationally recognized authority on the care and breeding of roses and wrote several books about them.

Thomas was a marginal golfer but was interested in the landscaping aspects of golf course design. His first course, a nine-hole layout at Marion, Massachusetts was staked out in the early 1900s. Thomas went on to design other courses in the East and to study the various techniques of prominent architects. He worked as a club committeeman with Donald Ross at Flourtown CC and Sunnybrook CC in Pennsylvania and with A.W. Tillinghast on a second course for Philadelphia Cricket Club. He also observed the works-in-progress of his friends Hugh Wilson at Merion and George Crump at Pine Valley. In 1908 Thomas designed Mount Airy CC (later Whitemarsh Valley CC), built on his family estate at Chestnut Hill, Pennsylvania. The family home served for years as the clubhouse.

During World War I, Thomas served in Europe with the U.S. Army Corps as captain of a unit rumored to have been totally outfitted at his expense. In 1919 he moved to California, ostensibly to carry on his rose breeding. He devoted much of his time, however, to course architecture and over the next ten years designed and

built some twenty-five courses, many with the assistance of William P. Bell. Throughout his career, Thomas never accepted a fee for his services as course designer.

Thomas's classic work, *Golf Architecture in America: Its Strategy and Construction*, was published in 1927, but soon after its appearance the author began to lose interest in the subject. Thomas spent his last years working on a book about Pacific game fish.

Courses by: George C. Thomas Jr

California: Baldwin Hills GC, Los Angeles (NLE, 1926), with William P. Bell; Bel-Air CC, Los Angeles (1927), with William P. Bell and Jack Neville; El Caballero CC, Tarzana (NLE, 1926), with William P. Bell; Fox Hills GC (NLE, 1926), with William P. Bell; Griffith Park GC (Harding Course) (1926); Los Angeles CC (North Course) (1921); Ojai Valley Inn & CC, Ojai (1925), with William P. Bell; Palos Verdes CC (1924), with William P. Bell; Red Hill CC, Cucamonga (9, 1921); Riviera CC (1927), with William P. Bell; Saticoy Public Links, Saticoy (9, 1921).

Massachusetts: Marion GC (9).

New Jersey: Spring Lake G&CC (1910).

Pennsylvania: Whitemarsh Valley CC, Chestnut Hill (1908).

Courses Remodeled & Added to by: George C. Thomas Jr

California: Griffith Park GC (Wilson Course), Los Angeles (R., 1923); La Cumbre G&CC, Santa Barbara (A.9, 1920), with William P. Bell; La Cumbre G&CC, Santa Barbara (R.9, 1920), with William P. Bell; Los Angeles CC (South Course) (R., 1921).

John Alexander "Jack" Thompson (1920 -)
Born: Winnipeg, Manitoba, Canada.

Jack Thompson (no relation to legendary Canadian golf architect Stanley Thompson) graduated from the American School of Landscape Design in Chicago in 1938. After World War II he formed a garden supply and landscape contracting firm in Canada.

While a contractor, Thompson formed an association with Alexander Mann, a golf course designer and turfgrass consultant from Aberdeen, Scotland. Thompson worked closely with Mann on the renovation and redesign of numerous courses from 1946 until Mann's death in 1952, and credited the Scot with providing his formal education in golf course architecture. After 1952 Thompson returned full time to his landscape contracting business until 1966, when he branched into golf course and landscape architecture.

Courses by: John A. Thompson

Alberta: Black Bull G&CC, Mam-E-O Beach (9).

Manitoba: Carmen G&CC; Hecla GC (1975); Minnedosa G&CC (9).

Saskatchewan: Craig GC, Regina (9); Tor Hill GC, Regina .

Courses Remodeled & Added to by: John A.Thompson

Manitoba: Southwood G&CC, Winnipeg (R.); Steinback Fly Inn GC (A.9).

Stanley Thompson (1894 - 1952) ASGCA, Charter Member; President, 1949.
Born: Scotland. Died: Toronto, Ontario, Canada at age 58.

Stanley Thompson emigrated with his family to Toronto, before the first World War. He was one of five brothers (Nicol, William, Matthew, Stanley and Frank), all of whom became internationally-known professional or amateur golfers. Stanley attended Ontario Agricultural College in Guelph but left in 1915 to serve with the Canadian Expeditionary Force in France.

In 1921 Thompson entered practice as a course architect and landed a few modest projects in Toronto. His first eighteen-hole design was Southwood GC in Winnipeg. After courses in Winnipeg and Toronto, Thompson produced in quick succession two of his greatest triumphs, Banff Springs and Jasper Park, both in the Canadian Rockies. Banff was built for the Canadian Pacific Railway and officially opened by the Price of Wales. Jasper was done for the Canadian National Railway and opened by Field Marshall Haig. Both dramatic mountain layouts met with worldwide acclaim. They exhibited a degree of strategic design unprecedented in North America, and Thompson's fame spread as a result. Even Winston Churchill, hardly a golf devotee, enjoyed his rounds at Banff on his visits to Canada between the Wars.

Thompson, nicknamed "the Toronto Terror," was one of the more colorful figures in golf design history. Many close to him felt him to be a genius and recognized depth beneath his flamboyance. He made and spent fortunes. But he was also conscientious in the training of a number of assistants who later made names for themselves in course architecture, including Robert Trent Jones (who became his partner in the firm of Thompson-Jones & Co. Ltd.), Howard Watson, C.E. Robinson, Norman Woods, Kenneth Welton, Robert Moote and Geoffrey S. Cornish.

Shortly after his death in 1952, the *Ottawa Citizen* eulogized him with these words: "Stanley Thompson has left a mark on the Canadian landscape from coast to coast. No man could ask for a more handsome set of memorials." In 1980 he was inducted posthumously into the Canadian Hall of Fame.

Courses by: Stanley Thompson

Florida: Floridale GC, Milford (NLE); Nealhurst GC, Jacksonville (NLE).

Minnesota: North Oaks CC, St. Paul (1951).

New York: Carlton Island GC (NLE), with Robert Trent Jones; Midvale G&CC, Penfield (1931), with Robert Trent Jones; Onondaga G&CC, Fayetteville .

Ohio: Beechmont CC, Cleveland; Chagrin Valley CC, Chagrin Falls (1925); Sleepy Hollow GC, Cleveland (1923); Squaw Creek CC, Vienna (18, 1924); Trumbull CC, Warren .

Washington: Tacoma C&GC.

Alberta: Banff Springs GC, Banff (1927); Jasper Park GC (1925); Waterton National Park GC (1935).

British Columbia: Capilano G&CC, West Vancouver (1937).

Manitoba: Clear Lake GC, Riding Mtn. Nat. Pk. (1934); Glendale G&CC, Winnipeg; Niakwa G&CC, Winnipeg; Pine Ridge G&CC, Winnipeg; Southwood G&CC, Winnipeg .

New Brunswick: Fundy National Park GC, Alma; Moncton G&CC.

Nova Scotia: Cape Breton Highlands National Park GC, Keltic Lodge (1935); Digby Pines GC, Digby (1932); Halifax G&CC (Old Ashburn) (1922); Lingan GC, Sydney (1922).

Ontario: Allandale GC (9); Aurora GC (9); Bayview GC; Beach Grove G&CC,

Walkerville (1922); Big Bay G&CC, Lake Simcoe (9); Bigwin Island GC, Lake of Bays; Briars G&CC, Jackson Point (9, 1922); Burlington G&CC, Hamilton; Cataraqui G&CC, Kingston; Cedarbrook G&CC, Toronto (1922); Chedoke GC (New Course), Hamilton (1950); Civic GC, Kitchener (9); Credit Valley G&CC, Toronto (9); Dundas Valley G&CC; Erie Downs G&CC; Essex GC, St. Thomas; Fort William G&CC (9, 1925); Geneva G&CC; Glen Mawr GC, Toronto (1931); Highland GC, London (1921); Humber Valley G&CC, Toronto (1921); Islington GC, Toronto (1924); Kawartha GC, Peterboro; Kenogamisis GC, Geraldton (9); Kenora G&CC; Ladies GC of Toronto (1924); Mardon Lodge GC, Barrie (9); Minaki Lodge GC, Minaki (9, 1928); Muskoka Beach GC, Gravenhurst (9, 1922); Muskoka Lakes G&CC, Port Carling; North Bay GC (9, 1922); Northwood G&CC, Toronto; Oakdale G&CC, Downsview; Orchard Beach G&CC, Lake Simcoe (9, 1926); Owen Sound GC (9); Peninsula GC, Marathon (9); Peninsula Park GC, Portage (9); Rio Vista GC, Bridgeburg (9); Shoreacres GC; Sir Harry Oakes Private Course, Niagara Falls (9); St. Andrews GC, Toronto (NLE, 27); St. Catharines G&CC; St. George's G&CC, Islington (1929); St. Thomas G&CC (9); Sunningdale CC (Old Course), London (1937); Thunder Bay G&CC; Uplands G&CC (18, 1922); Whirlpool GC, Niagara Falls (1947).

Prince Edward Island: Green Gables GC, Charlottetown (1939).

Quebec: Arvida GC (9); International C, Richford; Ki-8-EB GC, Three Rivers; Lachute GC; Le Chateau Montebello GC, Montebello (1931); Lucerne-in-Quebec GC, Montebello; Marlborough GC, Montreal (NLE, 27); Noranda Mines GC (9, 1934); Saguenay CC, Arvida (9, 1927).

Saskatchewan: Waskesiu Lake GC.

Brazil: Itanhanga GC, Tijuca (1922); Teresopolis GC (1932).

Colombia: Medellin GC, with Clinton E. Robinson; San Andres GC, Bogota (1946).

Jamaica: Constant Springs GC (1930).

Courses Remodeled & Added to by: Stanley Thompson

Florida: Hyde Park GC, Jacksonville (R.).

Minnesota: Somerset CC, St. Paul (R.).

New York: Bonnie Briar CC, Larchmont (R., 1936), with Robert Trent Jones; Fort Erie GC (A.9); Fort Erie GC (R.9); Lockport CC (R.); Stafford CC (R., 1931), with Robert Trent Jones.

Nova Scotia: Sydney GC (R.); Truro GC (R.).

Ontario: Brampton G&CC (R.); Brantford G&CC (R.); Brockville CC (R.9); Chedoke GC (Old Course), Hamilton (R., 1950); Lake Shore G&CC, Toronto (R.); Lambton G&CC, Toronto (R., 1930); Mississauga G&CC, Port Credit (R., 1928); Norway Point GC (R.9); Oshawa GC (R.); Peterborough G&CC (R.); Sault St. Marie CC (R.); Scarboro G&CC, Toronto (R., 1927); Thornhill GC (R., 1922); York Downs CC, Toronto (NLE, R.).

Quebec: Beaconsfield G&CC, Montreal (R., 1940).

Saskatchewan: Hillcrest GC (R.).

Brazil: Gavea G&CC (R., 1932); Sao Paulo GC (R., 1935).

Peter William Thomson, C.B.E. (1929 -   )
Born: Melbourne, Australia.

Five time British Open champion and winner of seventy-five other professional golf tournaments, Peter Thomson was as close to being a Renaissance Man of Golf as any person in the late Twentieth Century. He was a lively and sometimes acerbic writer and columnist for the Melbourne Herald and Melbourne Age. He was a respected critic of golf courses, and co-authored *The World Atlas of Golf*. He served as a member of the Australian Parliament, as a television commentator on golf broadcasts, as president of the Australian PGA, as special advisor for the Asia golf circuit (which he was instrumental in founding) and as a member of the India Golf Union. Thomson was also deeply involved in golf course architecture. In his younger days he served as a consultant to British designer John D. Harris, and eventually became his partner. After Harris' death, he teamed with another Harris associate, Michael Wolveridge, in the design and remodeling of courses throughout the Far East and Australia.

Courses by: Peter Thomson

California: Bixby GC, Long Beach (Precision, 9, 1980), with Ronald Fream and Michael Wolveridge.

Washington: Canyon Lakes G&CC, Kennewick (1981), with Michael Wolveridge, Ronald Fream and John Steidel; Kayak Point GC, Stanwood (1974), with Michael Wolveridge, Ronald Fream and Terry Storm; Tapps Island GC, Sumner (9, 1981), with Ronald Fream and Michael Wolveridge.

Australia: Alice Springs GC (1982), with Michael Wolveridge; Collier Park GC, Perth (1984), with Michael Wolveridge; Darwin GC (1983), with Michael Wolveridge; Desert Springs CC, Alice Springs (1984), with Michael Wolveridge; Fairway Park GC, Mandurah (1984), with Michael Wolveridge; Gold Coast CC, Surfers' Paradise (1984), with Michael Wolveridge; Hall's Head Resort GC, Mandurah (1984), with Michael Wolveridge; Iwasaki Resort GC, Yeppoon (1984), with Michael Wolveridge; Lake Ross GC, Marulan (1984), with Michael Wolveridge; Midlands GC, Victoria (1975), with Michael Wolveridge; North Lakes CC, Victoria , with Michael Wolveridge; Tasmanian Casino CC, Launceston (1982), with Michael Wolveridge; Thurgoona G&CC, Albury (27, 1983), with Michael Wolveridge; Tura Beach CC, Merimbula (1982), with Michael Wolveridge.

England: Telford Hotel G&CC, Great Hay (1979), with John Harris and Michael Wolveridge.

Fiji: Fijian Hotel GC (Precision, 9, 1973), with Michael Wolveridge and Ronald Fream.

Hong Kong: Royal Hong Kong GC (Eden Course), Fanling (1968), with John Harris and Michael Wolveridge.

India: Bangladore GC (1982), with Michael Wolveridge; Gulmarg GC, Cashmere (1973), with Michael Wolveridge; Karnataka GC, Bangalore (1984), with Michael Wolveridge.

Indonesia: Bali Handara CC, Pancasari (1975), with John Harris, Michael Wolveridge and Ronald Fream; Jagorawi G&CC, Chibinong (1978), with Michael Wolveridge and Ronald Fream; National GC, Jakarta Pusat , with Michael Wolveridge and Ronald Fream.

Japan: Chigusa CC (27, 1973), with Michael Wolveridge; Fujioka CC, Magoya (1971), with Michael Wolveridge and Tameshi Yamada; Hammamatsu CC, with

Michael Wolveridge; Ibusuki CC (New Course), Kagoshima (1978), with Michael Wolveridge; Korakuen CC, Sapporo (27, 1974), with Michael Wolveridge; Meihan Kokusai CC, Sapporo (1975); Naie GC, Sapporo (1976), with Michael Wolveridge; Nambu Fuji GC, Kwate (1974), with John Harris and Michael Wolveridge; Takaha Royal CC, Fukuoka (1976), with Michael Wolveridge; Three Lakes CC, Kuwana (1976), with Michael Wolveridge; Tokuyama CC (1975), with Michael Wolveridge; Yoro CC, Nagoya (1977), with Michael Wolveridge; Zen CC, Himeji (1977), with Michael Wolveridge.

Mauritius: Case Noyale GC, Port Louis (1972), with Michael Wolveridge.

New Zealand: Harewood GC, Christchurch (1967), with John Harris and Michael Wolveridge; Karori GC, Wellington (1968), with John Harris and Michael Wolveridge; Maramarua GC, Pokeno (1969), with John Harris and Michael Wolveridge; Taieri GC, Mosgiel (1967), with John Harris and Michael Wolveridge; Wairakei International GC, Taupo (1975), with John Harris and Michael Wolveridge.

Portugal: Estoril Sol GC, Estoril (Precision, 9, 1976), with John Harris, Michael Wolveridge and Ronald Fream.

Scotland: Inverness GC, Invernesshire (1968), with John Harris and Michael Wolveridge.

Singapore: Sentosa Island GC (Serapong Course) (1983), with Michael Wolveridge and Ronald Fream.

St. Kitts: Royal St. Kitts GC (1977), with John Harris, Michael Wolveridge and Ronald Fream.

Tonga: Tonga GC, with Michael Wolveridge.

Trinidad and Tobago: Balandra Beach GC (1982), with Michael Wolveridge and Ronald Fream; St. Andrews GC, Maraval (1975), with John Harris, Michael Wolveridge and Ronald Fream.

Tunisia: El Kantaoui GC, Soussenord (1977), with John Harris, Michael Wolveridge and Ronald Fream.

Courses Remodeled & Added to by: Peter Thomson

California: Almaden G&CC, San Jose (R., 1979), with Michael Wolveridge and Ronald Fream; Hacienda CC, La Habra (R., 1978), with Michael Wolveridge and Ronald Fream; Marine Memorial GC, Santa Ana (R., 1980), with Michael Wolveridge and Ronald Fream; Miramar Memorial GC, San Diego (R., 1981), with Michael Wolveridge and Ronald Fream; San Juan Hills CC, San Juan Capistrano (R., 1981), with Michael Wolveridge and Ronald Fream.

Nevada: Edgewood Tahoe CC, Stateline (R., 1980), with Michael Wolveridge and Ronald Fream.

Oregon: Sunriver CC (South Course) (R., 1978), with Michael Wolveridge and Ronald Fream.

Washington: Broadmoor GC, Seattle (R.2, 1982), with Michael Wolveridge and Ronald Fream; Cedarcrest GC, Marysville (R., 1982), with Michael Wolveridge and Ronald Fream; Manito G&CC, Spokane (R., 1979), with Michael Wolveridge and Ronald Fream; Seattle GC (R.2, 1981), with Michael Wolveridge and Ronald Fream; West Seattle GC, Seattle (R., 1979), with Michael Wolveridge and Ronald Fream.

Alberta: Glendale CC, Edmonton (R.3, 1981), with Michael Wolveridge and Ronald Fream.

Australia: Cottesloe GC (R.), with Michael Wolveridge; Kingston Heath GC, Cheltenham (R.), with Michael Wolveridge; Kooyonga GC (R.), with Michael Wolveridge; Lake Karrinyup CC, Perth (R., 1977), with Michael Wolveridge; Lake Karrinyup GC, Perth (A.9, 1977), with Michael Wolveridge; Metropolitan GC (R.), with Michael Wolveridge; Middlemore GC (R.), with Michael Wolveridge; Peninsula G&CC (R.), with Michael Wolveridge; Royal Adelaide GC, Seaton (R.), with Michael Wolveridge; Royal Canberra GC, Yarralumia (R.), with Michael Wolveridge; Royal Perth GC (R.), with Michael Wolveridge; Royal Sydney GC, Sydney (R.), with Michael Wolveridge; Sandringham GC, Melbourne (A.9), with Michael Wolveridge; Sorrento GC (R.), with Michael Wolveridge; Southern GC, Melbourne (R., 1978), with Michael Wolveridge; Southern GC, Melbourne (A.9, 1978), with Michael Wolveridge; Victoria GC, Cheltenham (R., 1983), with Michael Wolveridge; Yarrawonga GC, Victoria (A.9, 1980), with Michael Wolveridge.

Hong Kong: Royal Hong Kong GC (New Course) (R., 1970), with Michael Wolveridge; Royal Hong Kong GC (Old Course) (R., 1976), with Michael Wolveridge.

India: Bombay Presidency GC (R., 1980), with Michael Wolveridge; Delhi GC (R., 1974), with Michael Wolveridge; Delhi GC (A.9, 1974), with Michael Wolveridge; Royal Calcutta GC, Calcutta (R., 1969), with Michael Wolveridge.

Indonesia: Kebayoran GC, Jajarta (R., 1980), with Michael Wolveridge and Ronald Fream; Yani GC (R.), with Michael Wolveridge.

Malaysia: Gentling Highlands GC (R., 1984), with Michael Wolveridge and Ronald Fream.

New Zealand: Akarana GC (R., 1972), with Michael Wolveridge; Ashburton GC (R., 1977), with Michael Wolveridge; Auckland GC (R.), with Michael Wolveridge; Hastings GC (R., 1972), with Michael Wolveridge; Miramar GC, Wellington (R., 1977), with Michael Wolveridge; Nelson GC (R., 1967), with John Harris and Michael Wolveridge; North Shore GC (R., 1969), with John Harris and Michael Wolveridge; Rarotonga GC, Cook Islands (A.9, 1984), with Michael Wolveridge; Russley GC (R., 1967), with John Harris and Michael Wolveridge; Timaru GC (R., 1968), with John Harris and Michael Wolveridge.

Albert Warren Tillinghast (1874 - 1942)
Born: North Philadelphia, Pennsylvania. Died: Toledo, Ohio at age 67.

A.W. Tillinghast, known in his day as "Tillie the Terror," was an outstanding golf architect in his day and also one of the most colorful characters in the history of golf.

The only child of a wealthy Philadelphia couple, Tillinghast was a spoiled, pampered youth. He ran with a local gang of boys—called the Kelly Street Gang—who seemed bent on engaging in the most scandalous behavior that could be attempted in the late 1890s.

At the age of 20, Tillinghast abruptly left the band of ruffians, joined a more refined social circle and married a lovely young woman named Lillian. He then worked hard to develop an aristocratic image. He took on the trappings of a connoisseur and raconteur, collected beautiful pieces of furniture, china and art, and wrote self-published novels full of maudlin prose. He lived the life of a sportsman, dabbling in cricket, billiards, polo and bridge.

Tillinghast also became enthralled with golf during a visit to St. Andrews, Scotland. He took lessons from Old Tom Morris and returned each summer for several years to visit the grand old man of the game. In the States, Tillinghast competed in the U.S. Amateur on several occasions between 1905 and 1915, acquitting himself well in matches lost to such golfing luminaries as Walter Travis, Chandler Egan and Chick Evans.

In 1906, at the behest of Charles Worthington (who had made a fortune with his pump company), Tillinghast somewhat audaciously laid out a golf course on the Worthington family's farm at Shawnee-on-Delaware, Pennsylvania. He was 32 years old.

It was about the first honest work Tillie had ever done in his life, and he found that he not only enjoyed it, but also that he was good at it. He formed a design-and-construction firm that immediately became a success, and Tillinghast was a millionaire from his own efforts by the mid-1920s.

He honed his aristocratic image even further during his years as a golf designer. From his home in Harrington Park, N.J., Tillie routinely rode a chauffeured limousine to his office in midtown Manhattan. Not one to slave over working drawings and detailed plans, Tillie preferred to tromp through the thick brush of a course site—always dressed in the garb of a Wall Street banker—and lay out the course with his perceptive eye and uncanny intuition. During course construction, he would routinely appear in his three-piece suit, plant a shooting stick in the shade, settle his bulk on it, sip from a flask and shout directions all day long to the laborers.

His glorious career, which included outstanding designs such as Winged Foot and Baltusrol, lasted until the Great Depression, when a series of ill-advised investments (into such things as a Broadway show) left Tillinghast nearly a pauper. He then worked for the PGA of America, touring members' courses and recommending changes. Most clubs were struggling to simply avoid foreclosure and had little need for a keen expert's opinion on the weaknesses of their courses. Still, Tillie dutifully performed his assignments, emphasizing the savings that could result if they followed his suggestions.

Tillinghast gave that up after a couple of seasons and, figuring that Hollywood was the last bastion of wealth in America, moved to Beverly Hills, Calif. and opened an antique shop. His own family's furniture and art collections supplied most of the stock. When this venture failed, so did his health. He moved in with a daughter in Toledo, Ohio, where he died shortly after, nearly forgotten by the golfing world.

Tillinghast was an accomplished artist and prolific golf writer as well as an architect. He also coined the word "birdie" to describe a hole shot in one less stroke than par.

Courses by: A.W. Tillinghast

California: San Francisco GC (1915).

Florida: Atlantic Beach CC (NLE, 1918); Davis Shores CC, St. Augustine (NLE, 1926).

Kansas: Indian Hills CC, Prairie Village (1926); Kansas City CC, Shawnee Mission (1926).

Maryland: Baltimore CC (Five Farms Course) (1926).

Massachusetts: Berkshire Hills CC, Pittsfield (1926).

Minnesota: Golden Valley GC, Minneapolis (1924).

New Jersey: Alpine CC (1931); Baltusrol GC (Lower Course), Springfield (1922); Baltusrol GC (Upper Course), Springfield (1922); Forest Hill Field C, Bloomfield; Mountain Ridge CC, West Caldwell (1928); Myosotis CC, Eatontown (NLE); Norwood CC, Long Branch (NLE); Ridgewood CC (27, 1929); Shackamaxon G&CC, Westfield (1917); Somerset Hills CC, Bernardsville (1917); Wilton Grove CC (1916).

New York: Bethpage State Park GC (Black Course), Farmingdale (1936); Bethpage State Park GC (Blue Course), Farmingdale (1935); Bethpage State Park GC (Red Course), Farmingdale (1935); Binghampton CC, Endwell (1918); Bluff Point CC, Lake Champlain; CC of Ithaca (NLE); Elmwood CC, White Plains (1928); Fenway GC, White Plains (1924); Fresh Meadow CC, Flushing (NLE); Harmon CC, Lebanon (9, 1918); Jackson Heights GC, Jamaica (Par 3, 9, 1925); North Hempstead GC; North Shore CC, Long Island; Oswego CC (9); Port Jervis CC (9, 1922); Rainey Estate GC, Huntington (3); Southward Ho! CC, Bayshore (1924); Winged Foot GC (East Course), Mamaroneck (1923); Winged Foot GC (West Course), Mamaroneck (1923).

North Carolina: Myers Park CC, Charlotte (9, 1921).

Ohio: Lakewood CC, Westlake (1920).

Oklahoma: Oaks CC, Tulsa (1924); Tulsa CC (1920).

Pennsylvania: Cedarbrook CC, Philadelphia (NLE); Irem Temple CC, Wilkes Barre; New Castle CC (1923); Shawnee CC, Shawnee-on-Delaware (1908); Sunnehanna CC, Johnstown (1923); Wyoming Valley CC, Wilkes Barre (1923).

Rhode Island: Clarke Estate GC (9, 1928).

South Carolina: Rock Hill CC (9).

Tennessee: Johnson City CC; Kingsport CC.

Texas: Brackenridge Park GC, San Antonio (1915); Brook Hollow GC, Dallas (1921); Cedar Crest GC, Dallas; Fort Sam Houston GC, San Antonio; Oak Hill CC {formerly Alamo CC}, San Antonio (1921).

Vermont: Marble Island G&YC, Essex Junction (9).

Virginia: Hermitage CC, Richmond (1916).

Quebec: Anglo-American Club, Lec. L'Achign; Elm Ridge CC, Montreal (NLE).

Courses Remodeled & Added to by: A.W. Tillinghast

Connecticut: Brooklawn CC, Bridgeport (R., 1928).

Illinois: Westmoreland CC, Wilmette (R., 1925).

Minnesota: Rochester G&CC (A.9, 1925); Rochester G&CC (R.9, 1925).

Missouri: Swope Park GC, Kansas City (R., 1934).

New Jersey: Essex County CC (East Course) (R.); Essex County CC (West Course), West Orange (R.); Seaview GC (Bay Course), Absecon (R.); Spring Lake G&CC (R.); Suburban GC, Union (R.); Upper Montclair CC, Clifton (NLE, R.).

New York: Bethpage State Park GC (Green Course), Farmingdale (R., 1935); Bluff Point CC, Lake Champlain (R., 1916); Bonnie Briar CC, Larchmont (R.); Elmira CC (A.9, 1933); Hempstead CC (A.9, 1916); Island Hills CC, Sayville (R., 1927); Meadow Brook C, Westbury (NLE, R.); Mount Kisco CC (R.); Quaker Ridge CC, Scarsdale (A.9, 1926); Quaker Ridge CC, Scarsdale (R.9, 1926); Rockaway Hunting C, Cedarhurst (A.7, 1933); Rockaway Hunting C, Cedarhurst (R., 1933); Rockwood Hall CC, Tarrytown (R., 1929); Rockwood Hall CC, Tarrytown (A.5, 1929); Sands Point CC, Port Washington (R.9); Sands Point CC, Port Washington (A.9); Scarsdale GC, Hartsdale (R., 1929); Scarsdale GC, Hartsdale (A.6, 1929); Sleepy Hollow GC, Scarboro-on-Hudson (A.5, 1933); Sleepy Hollow GC, Scarboro-on-Hudson (R., 1933); St. Albans CC (R.); Sunningdale CC, Scarsdale (R.); Wolferts Roost CC, Albany (R.); Wykagyl CC, New Rochelle (R., 1931).

Ohio: Inverness C, Toledo (R., 1930).

Pennsylvania: Aronimink GC, Newton Square (NLE, R.); Bedford Springs C0 (R.); Conyngham Valley CC (R.); Fox Hill CC, Exeter (R.); Galen Hall GC, Wernersville (R., 1917); Nemacolin CC, Beallsville (R.); Old York Road CC, Jenkintown (NLE, R.); Philadelphia Cricket C (R.); Pittsburgh Field C (R.); St. Davids GC, Philadelphia (R.); Valley CC, Conyngham (R.); Wanango CC, Reno (R.); Williamsport CC (R.).

Rhode Island: Newport CC (R.9); Newport CC (A.9).

Texas: San Antonio CC (R.).

Virginia: Roanoke CC (R.).

Wisconsin: Blackhawk CC, Madison (R., 1937).

Ontario: Scarboro G&CC, Toronto (R., 1926).

Wallace Bancroft Timmons (1915 - 1983)

Born: Maryland. Died: Birmingham, Alabama at age 68.

Bancroft Timmons gained his first golf course experience as a boy when he maintained the Ocean City (Md.) GC after school and on weekends for $15.00 a week. A fine athlete, Timmons pursued a baseball career and played several seasons in a semi-pro league around the Eastern shore. In the late '30s Timmons joined the Automobile Association of America, working as office manager in Virginia and later West Virginia. When he was transferred to the Alabama Motorists Association in Birmingham in 1948, Timmons was surprised by the lack of courses in the area. He helped organize Green Valley CC and laid out its original nine. Timmons practiced golf design as a hobby in the Birmingham area for over 30 years, often donating his service and, on at least one occasion, parcels of land. Timmons never professed to be a course architect, preferring to call his role that of "golf promoter".

Courses by: Bancroft Timmons

Alabama: Buxahatchee CC, Calera; Cahawba Falls CC, Centerville (9); Chace Lake CC, Montgomery (1966); Green Valley CC, Birmingham (9, 1960); Pine Crest CC, Gardendale (9); Shades Valley CC; Terry Walker G&CC, Leeds (1961).

Howard C. Toomey (- 1933)

An engineer specializing in railroad construction. Howard Toomey formed the partnership of Toomey and Flynn with William S. Flynn shortly after World War I and was responsible for much of the firm's construction.

Courses by: Howard Toomey

Florida: Boca Raton Hotel & C (1928), with William S. Flynn; Boca Raton Hotel & C (North Course) (NLE, 1928), with William S. Flynn; Cleveland Heights G&CC, Lakeland (1925), with William S. Flynn; Indian Creek CC, Miami Beach (1930), with William S. Flynn; Normandy Shores GC, Miami Beach (1916), with William S. Flynn.

Illinois: Mill Road Farm GC, Lake Forest (NLE, 1927), with William S. Flynn.

New Jersey: Seaview GC (Pines Course), Absecon (9, 1931), with William S. Flynn; Springdale CC, Princeton (1928), with William S. Flynn; Woodcrest CC, Cherry Hill , with William S. Flynn.

New York: Shinnecock Hills GC, Southampton (1931), with William S. Flynn.

Ohio: The Country Club, Cleveland (1931), with William S. Flynn.

Pennsylvania: Green Valley CC, Lafayette Hills (1924), with William S. Flynn; Huntingdon Valley CC, Abington (1927), with William S. Flynn; Lehigh CC, Emmaus (1926), with William S. Flynn; Philadelphia CC, Gladwyne (1927), with William S. Flynn; Philmont CC (North Course), Philadelphia (1924), with William S. Flynn; Rolling Green CC, Springfield (1926), with William S. Flynn.

Virginia: CC of Virginia (James River Course), Richmond (1928), with William S. Flynn.

Courses Remodeled & Added to by: Howard Toomey

Massachusetts: The Country Club, Brookline (A.9, 1927), with William S. Flynn.

Pennsylvania: Merion GC (East Course), Ardmore (R., 1925), with William S. Flynn.

Walter James Travis (1862 - 1927)

Born: Maldon, Australia. Died: Denver, Colorado at age 65.

Educated at public schools and at Trinity College in Australia, Walter Travis emigrated to the United States at age twenty-three. Although he did not take up golf until he was thirty-five, he was soon the winner of the U.S. Amateur (1900, 1901 and 1903), and the British Amateur (1904) and was runner-up in the 1902 U.S. Open. In addition, he was founder and editor of American Golfer magazine and author of *The Art of Putting* and *Practical Golf*. He was known in golf circles as the "Grand Old Man".

Travis, unlike his contemporary C. B. Macdonald, often criticized British golf and in turn was not often treated kindly by the British press. He was originally appointed to Macdonald's select committee for The National Golf Links but was later dropped from it.

Walter Travis created many distinguished courses in the Eastern U.S. after learning the design trade as a consultant to John Duncan Dunn. He was particularly fond of the state of Vermont and was buried at Manchester near Ekwanok CC, one of his favorites.

Courses by: Walter J. Travis

Connecticut: Round Hill C, Greenwich (1922).

Georgia: Jekyll Island GC (Oceanside Course) (9, 1926); Sea Island GC (Plantation 9), St. Simons Island (9, 1927).

Maine: Cape Arundel GC, Kennebunkport (1900), with John Duncan Dunn.

Michigan: Lochmoor C, Grosse Pointe Woods (1919).

New Jersey: Canoe Brook CC (South Course), Summit (1917); Hollywood GC, Deal (1913); North Jersey CC, Wayne (1915); White Beeches G&CC, Haworth .

New York: CC of Troy; Garden City CC (1916); Old Country Club, Flushing (NLE); Orchard Park CC, Buffalo (1928); Stafford CC (1928); Westchester CC (South Course), Rye (1922); Westchester CC (West Course), Rye (1922); Yahnunda-

sis GC, Utica .
Ohio: Youngstown CC.
Pennsylvania: CC of Scranton (1927).
Vermont: Ekwanok CC, Manchester (1900), with John Duncan Dunn; Equinox G Links, Manchester (1925).
Ontario: Cherry Hill GC, Ontario (1917); Welland CC, Ontario .
Washington, D.C.: West Potomac Park GC (9, 1920), with Dr. Walter S. Harban.
Courses Remodeled & Added to by: Walter J. Travis
Connecticut: CC of New Canaan (R.9).
Kentucky: Louisville CC (R.9); Louisville CC (A.9).
Maryland: Columbia CC (R.).
Massachusetts: Essex CC, Manchester (R.), with John Duncan Dunn.
New York: Garden City GC (R., 1926); Grover Cleveland Muni, Buffalo (R., 1926).

William Henry Tucker Sr. (1871 - 1954)
Born: Redhill, Surrey, England. Died: Albuquerque, New Mexico at age 83.
William H. Tucker learned the art of sod rolling from his father, an employee of the Wimbledon Commons. He served as professional at two English clubs as a teenager, and then worked on course construction crews for Tom and Young Willie Dunn in England, France and Switzerland.
In 1895 Tucker emigrated to the United States, joining his brother Samuel, who was professional at St. Andrews GC in New York. They formed the equipment firm of Tucker Brothers, and their handmade "Defiance" brand clubs were sold for years. When St. Andrews moved to a new site, Tucker was hired to construct it to the design of Harry Tallmadge and to serve as greenkeeper. Within a year of the course's opening, he had rearranged some holes and built several new ones.
Tucker laid out several other courses in the New York area while at St. Andrews and later at Ardsley CC. He also worked in the early 1900s as pro-greenkeeper at Chevy Chase Club near Washington, D.C., where he collaborated with Dr. Walter S. Harban, the wealthy and eccentric dentist to Presidents who dabbled in course design and maintenance. In the 1920s Tucker and his son, William H. Tucker Jr., established a full-time golf architecture firm with offices in New York, Los Angeles and Portland. After World War II, he retired to Albuquerque, N.M. where he designed, built and maintained the University of New Mexico course. It is estimated that Tucker designed or remodeled over 120 courses in his career.
Tucker was also a nationally known turfgrass expert and in his New York days had been called upon to install and nurture the original turf at such sports facilities as Yankee Stadium and the West Side Tennis Club (better known as Forest Hills).
Courses by: William H. Tucker
Colorado: Green Gables CC, Denver (9, 1928); Overland Park Muni, Denver (9).
Maryland: Argyle CC, Chevy Chase , with Dr. Walter S. Harban; Bannockburn G&CC, Glen Echo (NLE), with Dr. Walter S. Harban.
Nebraska: CC of Lincoln (1923), with Gregor MacMillan; Hillcrest CC, Lincoln (1925), with Gregor MacMillan; Pioneer Park GC, Lincoln (1932), with Gregor MacMillan.
New Jersey: Phelps Manor GC, Teaneck (1924); Preakness Hills CC, Paterson (1927).
New Mexico: Portales CC (9); Riverside CC, Carlsbad (1946), with William H. Tucker Jr; Univ of New Mexico GC (North Crs.), Albuquerque (1951).
New York: Antlers CC (18, 1928); Clearview GC, Bayside (1925); Douglaston Park GC, Douglaston (1926); Maidstone C, East Hampton (9, 1896); St. Andrews GC, Hastings-on-Hudson (1898).
Pennsylvania: Bala CC, Philadelphia (9).
Vermont: Woodstock CC (NLE, 1906).
Washington: Jackson Park Muni, Seattle , with Frank James; Linden G&CC, Puyallup (9), with Frank James and Gregor MacMillan; Olympia G&CC (9), with Frank James; Roche Harbor GC, San Juan , with Frank James and Gregor MacMillan; Sands Point CC, Seattle (1928), with Frank James.
Courses Remodeled & Added to by: William H. Tucker
New Mexico: Univ of New Mexico GC (North Crs.), Albuquerque (NLE, Par 3, A.9).
New York: Ardsley CC, Ardsley-on-Hudson (A.9).
Pennsylvania: Philadelphia CC (NLE, R.).

William Henry Tucker Jr. (1895 - 1962)
Born: New York. Died: Los Angeles, California at age 67.
William H. Tucker Jr. was the son of pioneer golf course architect and builder William H. Tucker. He joined his father's business after service in World War I and, except for a stint in World War II, worked most of his life on the design, construction and maintenance of courses for his father.
Tucker Jr. did not work under his own name until after his father's death in 1954, although some of the courses that bore the name of the father were actually his designs. He practiced on his own for slightly less than a decade, designing courses mainly in the Southwest from his base in Los Angeles.
Courses by: William H. Tucker Jr
Arizona: Glendale Muni (NLE).
California: Anderson Tucker Oaks GC, Anderson (9, 1964); Elkins Ranch GC, Fillmore (1962); Fletcher Hills CC, Santee (1960); Ontario National GC (Course No. 1); Ontario National GC (Course No. 2) (Par 3).
New Mexico: Riverside CC, Carlsbad (1946), with William H. Tucker.

The Tufts Family
James Walker Tufts (1835 - 1902)
Born: Charlestown, Massachusetts. Died: Pinehurst, North Carolina at age 67.
James Tufts, a cousin of Charles Tufts (who donated the land for the campus of Tufts University in Medford, Mass.) became an apprentice druggist at the age of sixteen. By age twenty-one the enterprising Tufts owned three stores and was on his way to becoming a tycoon in the soda fountain business. One of the first to foresee the coming popularity of soda fountains, Tufts installed them in his stores and developed and marketed extracts and dispensers. He also created a line of silver-plated accessories based on his own more efficient method of silver plating which sold

nationwide. In 1891 Tufts consolidated his booming business with several others to become the American Soda Fountain Company.
But Tufts remained as head of his organization for only four years. Turning the operation over to his son, he moved south for his health, settling in central North Carolina. There he bought 5,000 acres of barren sand hills for $7,500. Many claimed this proved Tarheel woodsmen to be better businessmen than Yankee merchants, but Tufts was so enamored with the place that he dreamed of developing it into a resort. He hired eminent landscape architect Frederick Law Olmstead to lay out a formal village, built several hotels and negotiated for a railroad spur. The resort was named Pinehurst.
Pinehurst proved a popular winter retreat, and in 1898 Tufts and a friend, Dr. D. LeRoy Culver, laid out a primitive nine-hole course for guests. A year later they added nine more. This was the beginning of what would become the largest single golf resort in the world.
In 1900 Tufts met a young Scottish professional golfer in Massachusetts and hired him to become winter pro at Pinehurst and to develop its courses. The young golfer, Donald J. Ross, began an association with Pinehurst in the winter of 1901 that would last the rest of his life.
James W. Tufts died in 1902 while his proudest accomplishment, Pinehurst, was still evolving.

Leonard Tufts (1870 - 1945)
Born: Medford, Massachusetts. Died: Pinehurst, North Carolina at age 75.
Leonard Tufts, who attended the Massachusetts Institute of Technology, worked for his father in the soda fountain business after leaving college. Though not yet 26 at the time of his father's retirement, Leonard was placed on the executive staff of the giant American Soda Fountain Company. But he was more interested in the new Pinehurst resort his father was building in North Carolina.
Tufts assisted his father and Dr. Culver in building Pinehurst's first course in 1898. Although this was his only active golf design experience, he was instrumental in the early 1900s in convincing Donald Ross to rebuild the course and eventually add several others to the resort, in accordance with James Tufts' dream.
Leonard Tufts became Director of Pinehurst after his father's death. In 1906 he terminated all executive involvement with American Soda Fountain, devoting full time to the resort. He became nationally known for his cattle-breeding experiments, begun originally in an effort to supply fresh milk and butter to the Pinehurst guests.
Tufts resigned his control of Pinehurst in 1930 due to ill health, but he continued to reside there and assisted his eldest son Richard in running the resort. He died of pneumonia in 1930, leaving three sons and a daughter.

Richard Sise Tufts (1896 - 1980)
Born: Medford, Massachusetts. Died: Pinehurst, North Carolina at age 84.
Richard Tufts, son of Leonard Tufts and Gertrude Sise Tufts, learned his golf at Pinehurst from Donald Ross. Starting at the age of 8, he ultimately became the most proficient golfer of the Tufts clan. Upon graduation from Harvard in 1917, he served with the U.S. Navy in World War I and then returned to Pinehurst to work with his father. He took over in 1930 after his father's retirement and continued as director of Pinehurst Inc. into the 1960s.
A lifelong friend of Donald Ross and devotee of his work, Tufts dabbled in course design after the great architect's death. He laid out a new Pinehurst No. 4 course in the early 1950s because the original No. 4 (a Ross design) had been abandoned during World War II in an austerity measure. He revised several holes of Pinehurst No. 2 for the 1962 US Amateur and he also assisted golf architect Ellis Maples with the routing of Pinehurst No. 5 in the 1960s.
Richard Tufts was involved in every facet of golf administration and was often consulted in setting up courses for championship play. At one time or another he served on every committee of the USGA and was its President in 1956-'57. He was awarded the Richardson Award in 1950 by the GWAA for outstanding contributions to the game, and the Bob Jones Award in 1966 by the USGA for distinguished sportsmanship in golf. He also wrote many articles on golf, some pertaining to golf architecture, and was author of *The Principles Behind the Rules of Golf* (1960) and *The Scottish Invasion: A Brief Review of American Golf in Relation to Pinehurst* (1962).
In 1971 Tufts' two brothers, who owned a majority of the stock in Pinehurst Inc., voted to sell the grand old resort. Undaunted, Richard Tufts helped his son Peter start a new golf resort a short distance away. In the late 1970s he was pleased to see the Pinehurst management restore the courses, particularly the masterful No. 2.

Peter Vail Tufts
Born: Pinehurst, North Carolina.
Peter Tufts, son of Richard S. Tufts and Alice Vail Tufts and godson of Donald Ross, worked his way up to the management of Pinehurst. Beginning as manager of laundry and garage facilities, he worked on course maintenance crews, served as club manager and was finally appointed golf operations manager at Pinehurst in the 1960s. When the resort was sold in 1971, he resigned his position, and he and his father searched for a new location in which to carry on their family traditions. They established Seven Lakes GC in nearby West End, N.C., a residential housing complex.
Peter Tufts designed and supervised construction of the Seven Lakes course, his first experience in golf architecture. When the course opened in 1976, he was quick to downplay any comparison with Donald Ross works. Nevertheless Tufts, who grew up playing Ross's courses in the company of the great designer, professed his admiration for Ross designs and announced his hope of someday reestablishing the Ross philosophy of course design.
In 1977 Tufts opened his own course design firm and soon landed a few promising contracts, including partial renovation of the famous Pinehurst No. 2. There he set about restoring some of the original Ross mounds, removing the Bermuda roughs and redefining the fairway contours. For a man who had hoped to someday practice the art as Donald Ross had, it was the fulfillment of a dream.

Alfred H. Tull (1897 - 1982) ASGCA
Born: England. Died: Fort Myers, Florida at age 85.

Alfred Tull moved with his family to Canada in 1907 and to the United States in 1914. He began his career as a construction superintendent for Walter Travis in 1921, then worked for A.W. Tillinghast in 1922. In 1923 he took a similar position with Devereux Emmet.

Tull's association with Emmet and his son lasted for twelve years, culminating in the design partnership of Emmet, Emmet and Tull. He entered private practice as a course architect in 1935 following Emmet's death.

Clients and others he worked with were struck by Tull's remarkable ability to lay out individual holes and establish a circuit by walking the land and staking the holes without resort to a topographical plan. Later he would place his circuit on a topo to convey his ideas to others.

Courses by: Alfred H. Tull
Arkansas: Rosswood CC, Pine Bluff (1961).
Connecticut: CC of Darien (1958); Fulton Estate GC, Salisbury (1933), with Devereux Emmet; Hob Nob Hill GC, Salisbury (NLE, 1934), with Devereux Emmet; Keney Park GC, Hartford (1927), with Devereux Emmet; Oak Hill GC, Norwalk (1967); Pilgrim's Harbor CC, Wallingford (9, 1970); Pine Tree CC, Brooksville (9, 1953); Rolling Hills CC, Wilton (1965).
Delaware: Brandywine CC, Wilmington (1951); DuPont CC (DuPont Course), Wilmington (1950); DuPont CC (Nemours Course), Wilmington (1938); Hercules CC, Wilmington (9, 1937); Seaford CC (9, 1941).
Maryland: Norbeck CC, Rockville (1952); Woodmont CC, Bethesda (NLE, 9, 1948); Woodmont CC, Rockville (1951).
Massachusetts: Cape Cod CC, North Falmouth (9, 1929), with Devereux Emmet; Jug End Inn GC, Egremont (9, 1961); Ledgemont CC, Seekonk (1948).
New Jersey: Ashbrook GC, Scotch Plains (1951); Canoe Brook CC (North Course), Millburn (1949); Cooper River CC, Camden (NLE, 1929), with Devereux Emmet; Greenacres CC, Lawrence (1932), with Devereux Emmet; Mendham G&TC (1967); Rockleigh GC (Rockleigh Course), Hackensack (1958).
New York: Bethpage State Park GC (Yellow Course), Farmingdale (1958); Broadmoor CC, New Rochelle (NLE, 1929), with Devereux Emmet; Concord Hotel GC (Challenger Course), Kiamesha Lake (9, 1951); Concord Hotel GC (International Course), Kiamesha Lake (1951); Graham F Vanderbilt Estate GC, Manhasset (4); Hampshire CC, Mamaroneck (1927), with Devereux Emmet; Harbor Hills CC, Port Jefferson (1955); Harrison Williams Private Course, Bayville (3, 1932), with Devereux Emmet; Huntington Crescent CC, Huntington (1931), with Devereux Emmet; Huntington Crescent CC (West Course), Huntington (NLE, 1931), with Devereux Emmet; Indian Hills GC, Pine Bush (Par 3, 9, 1965); Lake Anne CC, Monroe (9, 1963); Mayflower GC, New York (NLE, 1930), with Devereux Emmet; Morningside Hotel GC, Hurleyville (1961); Muttontown G&CC, East Norwich (1959); Nassau CC, Glen Cove (1927), with Devereux Emmet; Nevele GC, Ellenville (1963); Pine Ridge CC, Newcastle (1954); Poxebogue GC, Bridgehampton (9, 1962); Rockwood Hall CC, Tarrytown (1929), with Devereux Emmet; Schuyler Meadows C, Loudonville (1928), with Devereux Emmet; Seawane C, Hewlitt Harbor (1927), with Devereux Emmet; Sunken Meadow Park GC, Northport (1968); Tennanah Lake House GC, Roscoe (1960); Vanderbilt Estate GC, Manhasset (NLE, 9, 1929), with Devereux Emmet; Vernon Hills CC, Mt. Vernon (1928), with Devereux Emmet.
North Carolina: Hog Back Mountain C, Tryon (NLE, 9, 1931), with Devereux Emmet; Old Fort CC (9).
Pennsylvania: Lawrence Park GC, Erie (1941); Radley Run CC, West Chester (1964); Valley Forge V.A.Hospital GC (1943).
South Carolina: Georgetown CC (9, 1956).
Virginia: Brook Manor CC, Brooke (1955); Westwood CC, Vienna (1953).
Newfoundland: Blomidon Club, Corner Brook (1967).
Bahamas: Cable Beach Hotel & GC, Nassau (1928), with Devereux Emmet.
Bermuda: Southampton Princess GC (Par 3, 1964).
Dominican Republic: Campo de G Bella Vista, Cuidad Trujillo (1958).
Puerto Rico: Ponce GC (9, 1953).
Virgin Islands: Estate Carlton GC, St. Croix (9, 1960).

Courses Remodeled & Added to by: Alfred H. Tull
Alabama: CC of Mobile (R., 1967).
Connecticut: CC of New Canaan (A.9, 1947); Meriden Park Muni (R., 1968); Silver Spring CC, Ridgefield (R.); Silvermine CC, Norwalk (R.).
Delaware: Henry F. DuPont Private Course, Wilmington (R., 1929), with Devereux Emmet; Hercules CC, Wilmington (A.9, 1941); Hercules CC, Wilmington (A.9, 1966).
Maryland: Congressional CC (Blue Course), Bethesda (R., 1951); Green Hill Y&CC, Salisbury (R., 1951); Woodmont CC, Rockville (A.9, 1955).
Massachusetts: Belmont CC (R., 1969); Cape Cod CC, North Falmouth (A.9); Green Hill Muni, Worcester (R., 1962).
New Jersey: Fairmont CC, Chatham (R., 1968); Galloping Hills GC, Union (R., 1953); Passaic County CC, Wayne (A.9, 1955); White Beeches G&CC, Haworth (R., 1950).
New York: Apawamis C, Rye (R., 1962); Bonnie Briar CC, Larchmont (R., 1928), with Devereux Emmet; Bonnie Briar CC, Larchmont (R., 1954); Elmwood CC, White Plains (R., 1954); Fairview CC, Elmsford (R., 1964); Glen Head CC (R., 1968); Green Meadow CC, Rye (R., 1947); Huntington CC (R., 1928), with Devereux Emmet; Maidstone C, East Hampton (R., 1965); Middle Bay CC, Oceanside (R., 1955); Old Country Club, Flushing (NLE, R., 1928), with Devereux Emmet; Pelham CC (R., 1954); Red Hook GC (R., 1967); Rockland CC, Sparkill (R., 1965); Waccabuc CC (R., 1967); Westchester CC (West Course), Rye (R., 1969); Wheatley Hills CC, Williston (R., 1929); Wheatley Hills GC, East Williston (R., 1929), with Devereux Emmet.
Oklahoma: Walnut Hills CC, Oklahoma City (R., 1968).
Bermuda: St. George Hotel GC, Warwick (R., 1928), with Devereux Emmet.
Puerto Rico: Berwind CC, Rio Grande (NLE, A.9, 1959).

Herbert James Tweedie (- 1921)
Born: Hoylake, Cheshire, England. Died: Chicago, Illinois.

H.J. Tweedie came to the United States with his brother L.P. in 1887. Both avid golfers from Royal Liverpool Club, they settled in Chicago and managed the A.G.

Spalding & Bros. sporting goods store.

The Tweedies became friends of C.B. Macdonald and were members of his original Chicago Golf Club. When Chicago GC was moved to Wheaton, Ill., Tweedie and others organized Belmont GC at the old site and built a new course there. Over the next ten years, Tweedie built a number of Chicago-area clubs. He also continued to manage the Spalding concern until his death, when his son Douglas assumed the position.

Courses by: H.J. Tweedie
Illinois: Belmont GC; Bryn Mawr GC, Chicago; Exmoor CC, Highland Park; Flossmoor CC {formerly Homewood CC} (1898); Glen View GC, Golf (1904); La Grange CC (NLE, 9, 1899); Midlothian CC (1898); Park Ridge CC (1906); Ridge CC, Chicago (1902); Rockford CC (1899); Washington Park CC, Chicago (NLE); Westward Ho CC, Oak Park (NLE).
Wisconsin: Maple Bluff CC, Madison (NLE, 1900).

Courses Remodeled & Added to by: H.J. Tweedie
Illinois: Onwentsia C, Lake Forest (A.9, 1898), with James Foulis, Robert Foulis and H.J. Whigham.

Kenneth Tyson (- 1983)
Died: Tacoma, Washington.

A golf professional in the Pacific Northwest for 34 years, Ken Tyson owned and operated a succession of golf courses which he designed or remodeled.

Courses by: Kenneth Tyson
Washington: Gold Mountain GC, Bremerton; Lake Spanaway GC, Tacoma (1967); Madrona Links, Gig Harbor (9, 1978).

Courses Remodeled & Added to by: Kenneth Tyson
Washington: Elks Allenmore GC, Tacoma (R.); Everett Muni (R.).

Lawrence E. Van Etten (1865 - 1951)
Born: Kingston, New York. Died: New Rochelle, New York at age 85.

Lawrence Van Etten attended Princeton University, where he received an Engineering Degree in 1886 and later a law degree as well. For most of his life he worked as a civil engineer, planning and developing residential subdivision in metropolitan New York.

Van Etten was also a prominent player in the early days of American golf and won many local titles. His golfing abilities and engineering training provided excellent course design background, and he planned many in the New York area. Though most were eventually abandoned, Wykagyl CC in New Rochelle, where Van Etten maintained a lifelong membership, retained his design in modified form since its inception.

Courses by: Lawrence Van Etten
New Jersey: Deal GC, Deal Beach (1898).
New York: Knollwood CC, Elmsford (NLE, 1898); Pelham Bay Park GC (Pelham Course), Bronx; Pelham CC (NLE, 9, 1908); Wykagyl CC, New Rochelle (1905).

John R. Van Kleek (- 1957)
Died: Tryon, North Carolina.

After graduating with a degree in Landscape Architecture from Cornell University, John Van Kleek formed a partnership with Wayne Stiles of Boston, Massachusetts. Van Kleek managed the firm's St. Petersburg, Fla. office. The firm was one of the nation's busiest by the mid-1920s. The Stiles and Van Kleek partnership was dissolved in the late Twenties, but each continued a modest practice on his own until after World War II.

Courses by: John Van Kleek
Alabama: Highland Park GC, Birmingham , with Wayne Stiles.
Connecticut: Paul Block Private Course, Greenwich (9), with Wayne Stiles.
Florida: Highland Park C, Lake Wales (1925), with Wayne Stiles; Holly Hill G&CC, Davenport (NLE), with Wayne Stiles; Kenilworth Lodge GC, Sebring (NLE), with Wayne Stiles; Lake Jovita GC, with Wayne Stiles; Palmetto G&CC, with Wayne Stiles; Pasadena GC, St. Petersburg (1923), with Wayne Stiles and Walter Hagen; Tarpon Springs CC (1927), with Wayne Stiles.
Georgia: Glen Arven GC, Thomasville (1929), with Wayne Stiles; Radium CC, Albany (1927), with Wayne Stiles.
Maine: Boothbay Harbor CC (9), with Wayne Stiles; Brunswick GC (9), with Wayne Stiles; Wawenock GC, Damariscotta (9), with Wayne Stiles; Wilson Lake CC (9), with Wayne Stiles.
Massachusetts: Berkshire Hunt & CC, Lenox (1930), with Wayne Stiles; Cranwell School GC, Lenox , with Wayne Stiles; D.W. Field Muni, Brockton (1927), with Wayne Stiles; Franconia Muni, Springfield (1930), with Wayne Stiles; Haverhill CC, with Wayne Stiles; Marlborough CC, Marlboro (9), with Wayne Stiles; Memorial Muni, Springfield (NLE), with Wayne Stiles; Newton Commonwealth GC, Newton , with Wayne Stiles; Pine Brook CC, Weston , with Wayne Stiles; Putterham Meadows Muni, Brookline , with Wayne Stiles; Taconic GC, Williamstown (1927), with Wayne Stiles; Thorny Lea GC, Brockton (1925), with Wayne Stiles; Unicorn CC, Stoneham , with Wayne Stiles; Weld GC, with Wayne Stiles.
New Hampshire: CC of New Hampshire {formerly Kearsarge Valley CC}, North Conway (R., 1930), with Wayne Stiles; Hooper GC, Walpole (9), with Wayne Stiles; Mojalaki CC, Franklin (9), with Wayne Stiles; Nashua CC (9, 1916), with Wayne Stiles.
New Jersey: Brigantine CC (1927), with Wayne Stiles; Wildwood G&CC, Cape May Court House (1923), with Wayne Stiles.
New Mexico: Albuquerque CC (1929).
New York: Forest Park GC, Queens (1934); IBM CC, Endicott (1938); Kissena GC, Flushing (1934); Pelham Bay Park GC (Split Rock Course), Bronx (1934); Whiteface Inn & GC, Lake Placid (1935).
North Carolina: Hamilton Lakes CC, Chimney Rock , with Wayne Stiles; Lake Lure Muni (9, 1935).
Colombia: CC of Bogota (East Course) (1950); CC of Bogota (West Course) (1947).
Venezuela: Carabelleda G&YC, Macuto (9, 1949).

Courses Remodeled & Added to by: John Van Kleek
Maine: Augusta CC, Augusta (A.9, 1926), with Wayne Stiles; North Haven GC (R.), with Wayne Stiles; Prouts Neck GC (A.9), with Wayne Stiles; Prouts Neck GC (R.9), with Wayne Stiles.
Massachusetts: Monoosnock CC, Leominster (R.9), with Wayne Stiles; Oak Hill CC, Fitchburg (A.9), with Wayne Stiles.
New Hampshire: Crawford Notch CC (R.), with Wayne Stiles.
New York: Dyker Beach GC, Brooklyn (R.), 1935); La Tourette Muni, Staten Island (A.9, 1935); La Tourette Muni, Staten Island (R.9, 1935); Pelham Bay Park GC (Pelham Course), Bronx (R., 1934).
Vermont: Rutland CC (A.9), with Wayne Stiles; Rutland CC (R.9), with Wayne Stiles; Woodstock CC (R.9, 1924), with Wayne Stiles; Woodstock CC (9, 1924), with Wayne Stiles.

Harry Vardon (1870 - 1937)
Born: Grouville, Isle of Jersey. Died: London, England at age 67.
Harry Vardon became one of Britain's "Great Triumvirate" of professional golfers. He won a record six British Opens and one U.S. Open. Despite demand for his services as a course architect, his planning was limited by poor health.
Courses by: Harry Vardon
England: Brocton Hall GC, Staffordshire (1923); Letchworth GC, Hertfordshire (1905); Little Aston GC, Staffordshire (1908); Mendip GC, Avon (9, 1908); Moore Place GC, Oxney (1909); Saffron Walden GC, Cambridgeshire (1919); Sandy Lodge GC (1910), with H.S. Colt; Tadmarton Heath GC, Banbury (9, 1922); Woodhall Spa GC, Lincolnshire (1905).
France: Montreux GC (9).
Scotland: Kingussie GC, Invernesshire.
Wales: Aberystwyth GC, Dyfed (1911); Knighton GC, Powys (1908); Llandrindod Wells GC, Powys (1905).
Courses Remodeled & Added to by: Harry Vardon
England: Ganton GC (R., 1899); South Herts GC, London (R.); West Herts GC, Hertfordshire (R., 1910).
Ireland: Bundoran GC, County Donegal (R.).
Northern Ireland: Royal County Down GC, Newcastle (R., 1908); Royal County Down GC, Newcastle (R., 1919).

Tom Vardon (1874 - 1938)
Born: Grouville, Isle of Jersey. Died: Minneapolis, Minnesota at age 64.
Tom Vardon, younger brother of the legendary Harry Vardon, decided at an early age to become a golf professional. After landing an assistant's job in England, he found one for Harry.
They both played competitively, but Tom never had much success. After the turn of the century, he sailed for America where he landed the head professional position at Onwentsia C near Chicago. In 1914 he moved to a similar position at White Bear Yacht C near Minneapolis, where he remained the rest of his life.
While in Minnesota, Vardon designed some fine courses throughout that and surrounding states, including Minot CC in North Dakota.

George Von Elm (1901 - 1961)
Born: Salt Lake City, Utah. Died: Pocatello, Idaho at age 60.
George Von Elm was well known as an amateur golfer between the First and Second World Wars and had an impressive record in both the British and U.S. Opens. After his retirement from active competition, Von Elm designed several courses in the western United States.
Courses by: George Von Elm
California: Shadow Mountain GC, Palm Desert (1960).
Idaho: Blackfoot Muni (9, 1957).
Courses Remodeled & Added to by: George Von Elm
California: Hacienda CC, La Habra (R., 1959).
Idaho: Sun Valley GC (R., 1962).

Brent H. Wadsworth
A graduate landscape architect, Brent Wadsworth joined golf architect Edward Lawrence Packard in a golf and landscape architect partnership in 1954. Packard and Wadsworth was dissolved in 1957 when Wadsworth left to form his own firm specializing in golf course construction. He occasionally participated in course designs after that, including laying out Fox Bend GC, Oswego, Ill., a daily-fee course near his corporate headquarters built to showcase the company's talents.
Courses by: Brent Wadsworth
Illinois: Belk Park GC, Wood River (9, 1957), with Edward Lawrence Packard; Coal Creek CC, Atkinson (9, 1958), with Edward Lawrence Packard; Fox Bend CC, Oswego (1970); Granite City GC (9, 1958), with Edward Lawrence Packard; Jerseyville CC (9, 1958), with Edward Lawrence Packard; Vermillion Hills CC, Danville (9, 1959), with Edward Lawrence Packard.
Michigan: Spring Meadows CC, Linden (1965), with Edward Lawrence Packard.
Missouri: Whiteman AFB GC, Sedalia (9, 1958), with Edward Lawrence Packard.
New York: Wayne GC, Lyons (9, 1957), with Edward Lawrence Packard.
Ohio: Silver Lake CC, Akron (1959), with Edward Lawrence Packard.
Wisconsin: Black River Falls GC (9, 1956), with Edward Lawrence Packard.
Courses Remodeled & Added to by: Brent Wadsworth
Illinois: Calumet CC, Homewood (R.12, 1957), with Edward Lawrence Packard; Danville CC (A.9, 1958), with Edward Lawrence Packard; Greenville CC (R., 1958), with Edward Lawrence Packard; Sunset Hills CC, Edwardsville (A.9, 1957), with Edward Lawrence Packard.
Indiana: Gary CC, Merrillville (R., 1958), with Edward Lawrence Packard.
Iowa: Fort Dodge CC (R.9, 1958), with Edward Lawrence Packard.
Minnesota: Westfield CC, Winona (R., 1960), with Edward Lawrence Packard.
Missouri: Cape Girardeau CC (R.2, 1957), with Edward Lawrence Packard; Cape Girardeau CC (A.2, 1957), with Edward Lawrence Packard.
Ohio: Wright-Patterson AFB GC, Dayton (R.9, 1958), with Edward Lawrence

Packard; Wright-Patterson AFB GC, Dayton (A.9, 1958), with Edward Lawrence Packard.
Wisconsin: Watertown CC (A.9, 1961), with Edward Lawrence Packard.

Charles Dudley Wagstaff (1894 - 1977)
Born: Tipton, Indiana. Died: Boca Raton, Florida at age 82.
C.D. Wagstaff attended the University of Illinois, where he was captain of the varsity gymnastics team, and graduated in 1918 with a B.S. Degree in Landscape Architecture.
After serving in the U.S. Navy for two years, the diminutive Wagstaff (5'3", 110 pounds) moved to Glenview, Ill. where he formed a landscape and golf course architecture business in 1923. Over the next 46 years he worked on many prominent landscaping projects, including the Chicago World's Fair of 1933, the Great Lakes Exposition in Cleveland in 1936, and the La Gorce Island housing project in Florida.
But Wagstaff devoted much of his attention to golf course design and construction, creating such well-known Illinois layouts as Tam O'Shanter CC, Kildeer CC [later Twin Orchards CC] and, after World War II, thirty-six holes for the University of Illinois.
In his later years Wagstaff was assisted by Donald R. Anderson and by his son Charles Jr. C.D. Wagstaff disbanded his firm in 1969 and retired to Florida, where he died in 1977.
Courses by: C.D. Wagstaff
Illinois: Bonnie Dundee GC, Dundee; Brookridge CC, Park Ridge; Brookwood CC, Addison; Elsbert Farm GC, Chicago (3, 1964); Great Lakes NTC GC, North Chicago (9); Grigsby CC, Chicago; Indian Boundary CC, Chicago; Mauh-Na-Tee-See CC, Rockford; Olympic G&CC, Arlington Heights (1927); Park Hills GC (East Course), Freeport (1953); Park Hills GC (West Course), Freeport (1964); Park Lake GC, DesPlaines; Sandy Hollow Muni, Rockford; Tam O'Shanter CC, Niles (NLE, 1925); Twin Orchards CC (Red Course), Long Grove (1928); Twin Orchards CC (White Course), Long Grove (1928); Twin Ponds GC, Crystal Lake (Par 3, 9, 1964); University of Illinois GC (Blue Course), Champaign (1964); University of Illinois GC (Orange Crs.), Champaign (1950); Wheeling GC; Winnetka Park GC.
Iowa: Emeis Park GC, Davenport (1961); Sheaffer Memorial Park GC, Fort Madison (1962); Starhaven GC, Keokuk (3, 1969).
Michigan: Leland CC (1965); Sugarloaf Mountain GC, Cedar (1966).
Missouri: Greenbriar Hills CC, Kirkwood (9, 1937).
North Carolina: Sippihaw CC, Fuquay-Varina (9, 1961).
Courses Remodeled & Added to by: C.D. Wagstaff
Illinois: Barrington Hills CC, Barrington (R.); Hickory Hills CC, Palos Park (Precision, A., 1963); Mission Hills CC, Northbrook (Par 3, A.); Oregon CC, Rockford (R., 1949); Rockford CC (R.); Sunset Ridge CC, Northbrook (R., 1926); Winnetka Park GC (Par 3, A.18, 1961).
Missouri: Greenbriar Hills CC, Kirkwood (A.9, 1958).

Robert C. Walker (1948 -) ASGCA
Born: Sherman, Texas.
Robert Walker received a B.S. degree in Engineering and Architecture from East Texas State University in 1971, and later undertook post-graduate studies in Soil Science and Parks and Recreation at Texas A & M University. He was employed in 1972 with the Club Corporation of America, where he worked with golf architects Ralph Plummer and Joe Finger. In 1974 he joined the firm of Edwin B. Seay Inc., which soon associated with Arnold Palmer. In 1979 the Palmer Course Design Co. was formed, with Seay and Walker serving as its principal designers. In 1986 Walker left Palmer Course Design and formed his own architectural firm based in Florida.
Courses by: Bob Walker
Florida: Grenelefe G&RC (East Course), Haines City (1977), with Arnold Palmer and Ed Seay; Matanzas Woods GC, Palm Coast (1986), with Arnold Palmer and Ed Seay; Pine Lakes GC, Palm Coast (1980), with Arnold Palmer and Ed Seay; Saddlebrook G&TC (Palmer Course) (1986), with Arnold Palmer and Ed Seay; Spessard Holland GC, Melbourne (Precision, 1977), with Arnold Palmer and Ed Seay.
Maryland: Prince Georges G&CC, Mitchellville (1981), with Arnold Palmer and Ed Seay.
Michigan: Shanty Creek GC (Legend Course) (1985), with Arnold Palmer and Ed Seay.
British Columbia: Whistler Village GC (1980), with Arnold Palmer and Ed Seay.
China: Chung-Shan GC (1985), with Arnold Palmer and Ed Seay.
Japan: Minakami Kogen GC (Lower Course) (1986), with Arnold Palmer and Ed Seay; Minakami Kogen GC (Upper Course) (1986), with Arnold Palmer and Ed Seay; Niseko GC, Sapporo (1986), with Arnold Palmer and Ed Seay; Niseko Kogen GC, Sapporo (1986), with Arnold Palmer and Ed Seay; Tsugaru Kogen GC, Amori (1986), with Arnold Palmer and Ed Seay.
Mexico: Nuevo Vallarta GC (27, 1980), with Arnold Palmer and Ed Seay.
Courses Remodeled & Added to by: Bob Walker
Arizona: Scottsdale CC (R., 1986), with Arnold Palmer and Ed Seay.
Florida: Hidden Hills CC, Jacksonville (R., 1986), with Arnold Palmer and Ed Seay; Sawgrass GC (Oceanside Course), Ponte Vedra Beach (A.9, 1985), with Arnold Palmer, Ed Seay and Harrison Minchew.

David L. Wallace
David Wallace's first golf design experience was his collaboration with Mark Mahannah on the addition of a second course at Sandpiper Resort in Florida, where he was employed as superintendent of grounds. In the 1970s, based in Tampa, Wallace created a score of courses along Florida's west coast.
Courses by: David Wallace
Florida: Burnt Store GC, Punta Gorda (9, 1970); Cove Cay G&TC, Clearwater (1972); Deltona G&CC (1964); Grenelefe G&RC (West Course), Haines City (1973); High Point CC, Naples (Par 3, 1972); Lake Region Y&CC, Winter Haven (1964); Lely Community GC; Lely G&CC, Naples (1975); Lucerne GC, Winter Haven (Par 3, 1967); Marco Island CC (1966); Mission Valley G&CC, Laurel (1969); Port Charlotte CC (9, 1962); Royal Poinciana GC (Cypress Course), Naples (1970); Royal Poinciana GC (Pines Course), Naples (1969); Sandpiper Bay CC (Saints

254

Course), Port St. Lucie (1963); Southridge GC, Delano (1968); Spring Hill G&CC (1969); Willow Brook GC, Winter Haven (1968).

Courses Remodeled & Added to by: David Wallace

Florida: Gasparilla Inn & CC, Boca Grande (R.); Riviera CC, Ormand Beach (A.9, 1968); Rocky Point GC, Tampa (A.9).

Lawrence Buddo Waters (1875 - 1960)

Born: St. Andrews, Scotland. Died: Salisbury, Rhodesia at age 85.

A native of St. Andrews, Laurie Waters apprenticed under Old Tom Morris. In 1901 he emigrated to South Africa, where he won the first South African Open, introduced grass greens, laid out several courses and became known as the "Father of South African Golf."

Courses by: Laurie Waters

South Africa: Durban CC (1920), with George Waterman; Royal Johannesburg GC (West Course) (1920).

Zimbabwe: Royal Salisbury GC (1922); Ruma CC (1948), with George Waterman.

Howard Watson (1907 -) ASGCA, President, 1958.

Born: Dresden, Ontario, Canada.

Howard Watson attended the University of Toronto, majoring in Bacteriology at the School of Agriculture in Guelph. He met golf architect Stanley Thompson through a classmate, Edwin I. Wood, who later became a prominent Canadian landscape architect. Thompson started Watson and another classmate, C.E. "Robbie" Robinson, on their respective careers on the same day in June 1929 at Royal York GC, then under construction in Toronto. Both went on to become well-known designers.

In 1930 Watson was sent to work with Robert Trent Jones in Rochester, N.Y. in the newly formed Thompson, Jones & Co. As the Depression progressed, he became involved in a variety of occupations in addition to his work at Thompson, Jones. He worked as greenkeeper at Port Arthur (Ontario) GC, as a turf consultant in Toronto, and as a diamond driller, mucker boss and blasting foreman at Noranda Mines in Quebec. During the war years he served overseas with the Royal Canadian Engineers.

Watson remodeled the Noranda Mines course and did his first solo design at Seaforth, Ontario in the Thirties. In 1945 Watson rejoined Stanley Thompson, remaining until 1949 when he established Canadian Golf Landscaping Ltd. in Quebec. He was joined in this business by his son John in 1969.

Courses by: Howard Watson

Florida: Pembroke Lakes G&CC, Hollywood (27, 1974), with John Watson.

New York: O'Brien Estate GC, Plattsburg (1962).

Vermont: A.D. Dana Estate GC, Stowe (9, 1966).

Manitoba: Pinawa GC (9, 1964).

New Brunswick: Pokemouche GC, Caraquet (9, 1974), with John Watson.

Ontario: Aguasabon GC, Terrace Bay (1955); Bay of Quinte GC, Bellville (1964); Board of Trade CC (East Course), Woodbridge (1963); Board of Trade CC (West Course), Woodbridge (1963); Brian Thicke Estate GC, Orangeville (1974); Brockville GC (Course No. 1) (1966); Brockville GC (Course No. 2) (1966); Cherry Downs GC, Claremont (27, 1962); Chrysler Memorial Park GC, Morrisburg (9, 1958); Crang Estate GC, Toronto (9, 1953); Deep River GC (9, 1952), with Robert Moote; Don Valley Muni, Toronto (1956); Downsview G&CC, Toronto (27, 1955), with Robert Moote; F.A.McConnel Private Course, Caledon (3, 1954); Flemingdon Park GC, Toronto (9, 1959); Kanata GC, Ottawa (9, 1966); Manderly GC, North Gower (1962); Manitouwadge GC (1971); Pine Valley GC, Woodbridge (NLE, 1960); Pineview GC (No. 1 Course), Ottawa (1968); Pineview GC (No. 2 Course), Ottawa (1968); R.H. Storrer Estate GC, Woodbridge (1966); Rideau View CC, Manotick (1957); Scarlett Woods GC, Toronto (1972); Seaforth GC (9, 1933); Spruce Needles GC, Timmins (1959); Sumner Heights GC, Cornwall (9, 1968); Tam O'Shanter Muni, Toronto (1974), with John Watson; Upper Canada CC, Oakville (1964); Woodbine Downs GC, Toronto (1960).

Quebec: Asbestos G&CC (1966); Bonaventure GC, Fauvel (9, 1973), with John Watson; Bonniebrook GC, St. Colomban (1966); Carling Lake GC, Pine Hill (1961); Cedarbrook GC, Ste. Sophie (1959); Champlain GC, Ville, Brossard (1963); Chicoutimi GC (1955); Club d'G Triangle Dor, St. Remi (1968); Club de G de Joliette (1951); Club de G du Bic, Rimouski (1962); Club de G le Portage, L'Assomtion (1963); Club de G Adstock (9), with John Watson; Club de G Berthier, Berthierville (1959); Club de G Bromont, Shefford (1963); Club de G Cap Rouge (1959); Club de G Chambly (1960); Club de G Chicoutina (Course No. 1); Club de G Chicoutina (Course No. 2); Club de G Granby-St. Paul (New Crs.), with John Watson; Club de G Lac Beuport (1961); Club de G Laprairie, Montreal (27, 1963); Club de G Les Dunes (Course No. 2) 2), Sorel (1952); Club de G Longchamps, Sherbrooke (1969), with John Watson; Club de G St. Michel (St. Michel) (1960); Club de G St. Michel (Vaudrevil) (1960); Club de G St. Patrick, with John Watson; Club de G Valle du Parc, Grandmere (1972); Club de G Vielles Forges, Trois-Rivieres (1974), with John Watson; Concordia GC, Ste. Therese (1962); Cowansville GC (1963); Dorval GC (1974); Douglas H. Keen Estate GC, Austin (9, 1974); Grey Rocks GC, St. Jovite; Harve des Isles GC, Montreal (1966); Hillsdale G&CC (Dale Course), St. Therese (1958); Hillsdale G&CC (Hill Course), St. Therese (1953); Hudson G & Curling C, Hudson Heights (1969); Ile Bourdon GC, Montreal (1969); Lac Thomas GC, St. Didace (9, 1962); Le Chantecler GC; Le Seigneurie de Vaudrevil GC, Louisville (1969); Lennoxville GC (1964); Leonard Wheatley Private Course, Hillhead (3, 1962); Mont Adstock GC, Thetford Mines (9, 1972), with John Watson; Mont St. Anne GC (Course No. 0, St. Anne de Beaupre (1972), with John Watson; Mont St. Anne GC (Course No.2), St. Anne de Beaupre (9, 1974), with John Watson; Mont St. Marie GC, St. Marie de Bauce (9, 1967); Mountain Ranches GC, Rigaud (1963); Nun's Island GC, Montreal (1967); Pinegrove G&CC, Montreal (27, 1958); Royal Quebec CC (Quebec Course), Boischatel (9, 1958); Salzborg GC, Morin Heights (1954); Shawinigan G&CC (1962); St. Georges GC, St. Georges de Beauc (1959); St. Laurent GC, I'le D'Orleans (1971), with John Watson; St. Luc GC (1974); Ste. Marguerite GC, Sept Isles (9, 1954); Val Morin GC (9, 1973), with John Watson; Wentworth GC, Ile Perrot (1969).

Colombia: Club Campestre de Cucuta (1958); CC de Manizales, Calais (1953), with Robert Moote; CC El Rodeo, Mendellin (1953), with Robert Moote; CC Militar, Melgar (1954).

Jamaica: Caymanas G&CC, Spanish Town (1955).

Courses Remodeled & Added to by: Howard Watson

Maine: Aroostook Valley GC, Fort Fairfield (A.9, 1958); Aroostook Valley GC, Fort Fairfield (R.9, 1958).

New York: Wheatley Hills CC, Williston (A.9, 1962).

Vermont: Barre CC (A.9, 1969).

Ontario: Carlton Yacht & GC, Manotick (R.1, 1980); Don Valley Muni, Toronto (A.9, 1973), with John Watson; Don Valley Muni, Toronto (R., 1973), with John Watson; Forest Hills GC, Toronto (R.27, 1956); Idylwylde GC, Sudbury (R.9, 1961); Idylwylde GC, Sudbury (A.9, 1961); Larrimac GC, Ottawa (R.9, 1973); Mississauga G&CC, Port Credit (R.3, 1973); Mississauga G&CC, Port Credit (A.9, 1973); North Bay G&CC (A.9, 1963); North Bay G&CC (R.9, 1963); Rosedale CC, Toronto (R., 1951); Scarlett Woods GC, Toronto (A.9, 1971), with John Watson; Thornhill GC (R., 1954); Toronto GC (R.9, 1962); Toronto GC (A.5, 1968).

Quebec: Beaconsfield G&CC, Montreal (R.6, 1970); Candiac GC (R., 1974), with John Watson; CdG Charny (A.9, 1971), with John Watson; CdG Charny (R.9, 1971); Club de G Alpin, Ste. Brigitte de Lav (R., 1972); Club de G Baie Comeau, Hauterire (A.9, 1973), with John Watson; Club de G Chaudiere, Hull (R.5, 1973), with John Watson; Club de G Granby-St. Paul (Old), Granby (R., 1974), with John Watson; Club de G Grand Pabos, Chandler (R.9, 1972); Club de G Grand Pabos, Chandler (A.9, 1972); Club de G Les Dunes (Course No. 1), Sorel (R., 1952); Club de G Port, Port Alfred (R.9, 1963); Club de G St. Marie, St. Marie de Bauce (R.2, 1970), with John Watson; Club de G Victoriaville (A.9); Club de G Victoriaville (R.9, 1960); Fort Preval GC, Preval (R.9, 1974); Fort Preval GC, Preval (A.5, 1974), with John Watson; Grandmere GC (R.3, 1967); Green Valley GC (R., 1965); Islesmere G&CC (A.9, 1965); Kanawaki GC (R.9, 1963); Kanawaki GC (R.3, 1976), with John Watson; Ki-8-EB GC, Three Rivers (R.2, 1974); Knowlton GC, Brome (A.9, 1970); Knowlton GC, Brome (R.9, 1970); La Tuque G & Curling C (A.9, 1969); La Tuque G & Curling C (R.9, 1969); Lachute GC (A.18, 1956); Lachute GC (R.9, 1956); Laval sur le Lac GC (R.9, 1966); Levis GC (R., 1956); Lorette GC, Quebec (R.9, 1962); Marlborough GC, Montreal (R., 1964); Mont St. Marie GC, St. Marie de Bauce (R.2, 1970), with John Watson; Mont Tremblant GC (R.9, 1974); New Glasgow GC (R., 1974); Noranda Mines GC (R.9, 1935); Riviere Du Loup GC (A.9, 1974), with John Watson; Riviere Du Loup GC (R.9, 1974), with John Watson; Royal Ottawa GC, Hull (R.27, 1966); Royal Ottawa GC, Hull (A.9, 1966); Royal Quebec CC (Quebec Course), Boischatel (R.9, 1966), with John Watson; Royal Quebec CC (Royal Course), Boischatel (A.2, 1974), with John Watson; Thetford Mines G & Curling C (R.9, 1971), with John Watson; Thetford Mines G & Curling C (A.9, 1971), with John Watson; Val Morin GC (R., 1971); Whitlock G&CC, Hudson Heights (A.9, 1961); Whitlock G&CC, Hudson Heights (R., 1970).

Jamaica: Upton G&CC, Ocho Rios (R.9, 1961).

John Watson (1933 -) ASGCA, President, 1985.

Born: Toronto, Ontario, Canada.

John Watson served for 16 years as a pilot in the Royal Canadian Air Force, resigning his commission in 1967 to accept a flight test position with North American Rockwell. In 1969 he joined the practice of his father, golf architect Howard Watson, training under and working with him on some twenty projects. He entered private practice under the firm name of John Watson Golf Design Ltd. in 1975.

Courses by: John Watson

Florida: Pembroke Lakes G&CC, Hollywood (27, 1974), with Howard Watson.

New Brunswick: Pokemouche GC, Caraquet (9, 1974), with Howard Watson.

Ontario: Amberwood Village GC, Stittsville (9, 1977); Tam O'Shanter Muni, Toronto (1974), with Howard Watson.

Quebec: Bonaventure GC, Fauvel (9, 1973), with Howard Watson; CdG Montcalm, St-Liquori (1976); Club de G Adstock (9), with Howard Watson; Club de G Deaux, St. Eustache (1987); Club de G Des Saules, Rimouski (9, 1985); Club de G Gaspesien, St. Anne des Morts (9, 1986); Club de G Granby-St. Paul (New Crs.), with Howard Watson; Club de G Longchamps, Sherbrooke (1969), with Howard Watson; Club de G Montcalm, St. Liguori (9, 1986); Club de G Montevilla, Montebello (9, 1983); Club de G St. Luc (9, 1976); Club de G St. Patrick, with Howard Watson; Club de G Terrebonne (9, 1977); Club de G Vielles Forges, Trois-Rivieres (1974), with Howard Watson; Deux Montagnes GC (36, 1984); Estrimont GC, Mont Orford (1986); Mont Adstock GC, Thetford Mines (9, 1972), with Howard Watson; Mont St. Anne GC (Course No. 0, St. Anne de Beaupre (1972), with Howard Watson; Mont St. Anne GC (Course No.2), St. Anne de Beaupre (9, 1974), with Howard Watson; St. Laurent GC, I'le D'Orleans (1971), with Howard Watson; Val Morin GC (9, 1973), with Howard Watson; Val Niegette GC, Rimouski (1984).

Courses Remodeled & Added to by: John Watson

New Brunswick: Pokemouche GC, Caraquet (R.9, 1977); Pokemouche GC, Caraquet (A.9, 1983).

Ontario: Carlton Yacht & GC, Manotick (R.1, 1980); Don Valley Muni, Toronto (R., 1973), with Howard Watson; Don Valley Muni, Toronto (A.9, 1973), with Howard Watson; Fort William G&CC (R.13, 1985); Hylands GC (R.1, 1981); Larrimac GC, Ottawa (A.3, 1974); Scarlett Woods GC, Toronto (A.9, 1971), with Howard Watson; St. Andrews GC, Toronto (R.3, 1981); Strathcona GC, Huntsville (R.13, 1985).

Quebec: Bonaventure GC, Fauvel (A.9, 1975); Candiac GC (R., 1974), with Howard Watson; Candiac GC (R.2, 1976); CdG Charny (A.9, 1971), with Howard Watson; Club de G de Joliette (R.10, 1982); Club de G du Bic, Rimouski (R.5, 1986); Club de G Alpin, Ste. Brigitte de Lav (R.3, 1973); Club de G Baie Comeau, Hauterire (A.9, 1973), with Howard Watson; Club de G Baie Comeau, Hauterire (A.9, 1976); Club de G Baie Comeau, Hauterire (R.2, 1976); Club de G Chaudiere, Hull (R.5, 1973), with Howard Watson; Club de G Granby-St. Paul (Old), Granby (R., 1974), with Howard Watson; Club de G Sorel Tracy, Tracy (R.6, 1976); Club de G Sorel Tracy, Tracy (A.9, 1976); Club de G Sorel Tracy, Tracy (R.4, 1977); Club de G St. Luc (A.9, 1985); Club de G St. Marie, St. Marie de Bauce (R.2, 1970), with Howard Watson; Club de G St. Patrick (R.9, 1974); Club de G St. Patrick (A.9, 1974); Club de G Terrebonne (A.18, 1985); Fort Preval GC, Preval (A.5, 1974), with Howard Watson; Green Valley GC (R.7, 1980); Hillsdale G&CC (Dale Course), St. Therese (R.1, 1976); Hillsdale G&CC (Hill Course), St. Therese (R.1, 1974); Kanawaki GC (R.3, 1976), with Howard Watson; Ki-8-EB GC, Three Rivers (R.2, 1975); Larrimac GC, Chelsea (R.3, 1975); Laval sur le Lac GC (R.3, 1984); Massawippi

GC, North Hatley (R.7, 1986); Milby GC, Lennoxville (R.3, 1985); Mont Adstock GC, Thetford Mines (R.9, 1975); Mont St. Anne GC (Course No.2), St. Anne de Beaupre (A.9, 1980); Mont St. Marie GC, St. Marie de Bauce (R.2, 1970), with Howard Watson; Mont St. Marie GC, St. Marie de Bauce (A.9, 1980); Pinegrove G&CC, Montreal (R.3, 1981); Riviere Du Loup GC (R.9, 1974), with Howard Watson; Riviere Du Loup GC (A.9, 1974), with Howard Watson; Rosemere G&CC (R.3, 1979); Royal Ottawa GC, Hull (R.4, 1986); Royal Ottawa GC, Hull (A.2, 1986); Royal Quebec CC (Quebec Course), Boischatel (R.9, 1966), with Howard Watson; Royal Quebec CC (Royal Course), Boischatel (A.2, 1974), with Howard Watson; St. Luc GC (A.9); Thetford Mines G & Curling C (R.9, 1971), with Howard Watson; Thetford Mines G & Curling C (A.9, 1971), with Howard Watson.

Richard Watson (1932 -)
Born: Fairbury, Nebraska.

Dick Watson attended Fairbury Junior College and Doane College, and received a B.S. degree in Zoology from Nebraska University. He then served for four years with the U.S. Navy, learning to play golf while stationed in Pensacola, Florida. Upon his return to Nebraska, he was employed as district sales manager with a major pharmaceutical company and continued to play golf. Watson competed successfully in many local and regional tournaments and won the 1962 Lincoln Publinks title.

In 1963 Watson resigned to build and operate a par-3 course in Lincoln. He retained Denver golf architect Henry Hughes to assist him with the project. Hughes stayed in Nebraska to build several small town courses, and Watson collaborated on both design and construction phases. The two formed a partnership in the mid-1960s, planning several courses in the Midwest.

In 1970 Hughes retired to Colorado, and Watson continued to practice on his own in Nebraska. He had designed or remodeled some forty courses by the end of the 1970s, when he gradually began to concentrate on constructing layouts for other architects.

Courses by: Richard Watson
California: Suncrest CC, Palm Desert (Precision, 9, 1980).
Iowa: Beacon Hills GC, Creston (Precision, 9); Lake Panorama National GC, Panora (1972); Lake Panorama Par 3 GC, Panora (Par 3, 9, 1973).
Kansas: Belleville CC (9, 1968), with Henry B. Hughes; Indian Hills Muni, Chapman (9, 1977); Rolling Meadows GC, Junction City (1981), with Keith Evans; Scott County GC, Scott City (9, 1968), with Henry B. Hughes.
Kentucky: Doe Valley G&CC, Brandenberg (1973).
Missouri: Nehai Tonkayea GC, Marceline (Par 3, 9, 1977).
Montana: Larchmont Muni, Missoula (1982), with Keith Hellstrom.
Nebraska: Ashland CC (9, 1968), with Henry B. Hughes; Atkinson-Stuart GC (9, 1969), with Henry B. Hughes; Bloomfield-Wausa GC (9, 1969), with Henry B. Hughes; Colonial GC, Lincoln (NLE, Par 3, 9, 1964), with Henry B. Hughes; Friend CC (9, 1967), with Henry B. Hughes; Mid-County GC, Arapahoe (9, 1968), with Henry B. Hughes; Pine Lake GC, Lincoln (Par 3, 9, 1973); Tara Hills GC, Papillion (Precision, 9, 1978), with Keith Evans; Wayne CC (1969), with Henry B. Hughes.
South Dakota: Lakeview Muni, Brandon (9, 1979); Mitchell CC (9).
Texas: Colony Creek CC, Victoria (1985); Treasure Hills CC (1986).
Virginia: Massanuetten Mountain Greens GC, Harrisburg (9, 1975); Summit GC at Lake Holiday, Winchester (1972).
West Virginia: Claymont Chase CC (9).
Wyoming: Midway GC, Greybull (9, 1970), with Henry B. Hughes; Riverton GC (9).

Courses Remodeled & Added to by: Richard Watson
Kansas: Great Bend Petroleum C, Great Bend (A.9, 1981).
Nebraska: Ashland CC (A.9, 1982).

William Watson
Willie Watson emigrated to the United States from Scotland in 1898 to help Robert Foulis lay out and build the original nine holes at Minikahda CC in Minneapolis. He remained at Minikahda as pro-greenkeeper during the summer months, and served as golf instructor at Hotel Green GC in Pasadena, Calif. during the winter. He also began laying out golf courses on his own.

Prior to World War I, most of Watson's design work was done in Minnesota, Michigan and Illinois. Following the War he was based in Los Angeles until 1931. He then became professional at Charlevoix (Mich.) CC when golf course construction was severely curtailed by the Depression.

Courses by: William Watson
California: Coronado GC (NLE, 3, 1922); Diablo G&CC (1914); East Bay CC, Oakland; Fort Washington G&CC, Pinedale (1923); Harding Park GC, San Francisco (1925); Hillcrest CC, Los Angeles (1920); Hotel Green GC, Pasadena (NLE, 9, 1901); Lake Arrowhead CC (NLE); Mira Vista G&CC {formerly Berkeley CC}, Berkeley (1921), with Robert Hunter; Mount Diablo CC; Olympic C (Ocean Course), San Francisco (1924), with Sam Whiting; Orinda CC (1924); Sonoma National GC (1928), with Sam Whiting; Sunset Canyon GC, Burbank (NLE, Par 3, 9, 1921).
Illinois: Momence CC (9, 1928); Olympia Fields CC (Course No.3) (NLE, 1919).
Michigan: Belvedere GC, Charlevoix (1917); Charlevoix Muni (9).
Minnesota: Interlachen CC, Edina (1910); Minikahda C, Minneapolis (9, 1906), with Robert Foulis.

Courses Remodeled & Added to by: William Watson
California: Annandale CC, Pasadena (R., 1928); Brentwood CC (R.); Burlingame CC, Hillsborough (R.).

William R. Watts (1932 -)
Born: Miami, Florida.

Billy Watts attended the University of Miami, where he was a member of the golf team. A lifelong amateur golfer, he won more than thirty local and regional titles in southern Florida.

In the late 1950s Watts designed and built Sunrise CC, which he owned and managed. Over the next twenty years he designed a dozen other courses along the Gold Coast area of Florida.

Courses by: Bill Watts
Florida: Arrowhead CC, Ft. Lauderdale (1968); Broken Woods G&RC, Coral Springs (Precision); Deer Creek G&CC, Deerfield Beach (1971); Foxcroft CC, Miramar (1968); Hollywood Lakes CC (East Course) (1965); Hollywood Lakes CC (West Course) (1967); Lago Mar CC, Ft. Lauderdale (1970); Miami Lakes Inn & CC (Championship) (1963); Sun 'n Lake CC, Lake Placid (Precision, 1969); Sunrise CC, Ft. Lauderdale (1960).
Georgia: Innsbruck GC, Cleveland (1987); Sky Valley CC, Dillard.

Ernest W. Way (- 1943)
Born: Westward Ho! Devonshire, England. Died: Miami, Florida.

Ernest Way was the son of an English cabinetmaker and brother of golfers Ed, Jack and Bert Way. He and Jack emigrated to the United States around 1905 to join their elder brother Bert, already a successful golfer in America at the time. After brief jobs at golf clubs in Pittsburgh and Richmond, Va. Ernest moved to Detroit GC, whose course Bert had just built. He remained as head professional at Detroit until 1919 and during his tenure supervised construction of the club's two Donald Ross courses. Jack meantime became the professional of Canterbury CC near Cleveland, where he remodeled the course and added three holes in the early 1920s.

A charter member of the Michigan PGA and a member of both the PGA of America and the GCSAA, Ernest resigned from Detroit GC to design and build courses in Michigan in the 1920s. He returned to his position as course superintendent at Detroit in the 1930s, but ill health forced him to retire in 1937. He then moved to Florida, where he resided until his death.

Courses by: Ernest Way
Florida: Hotel Indiatlantic GC, Melbourne (NLE).
Michigan: Belle Isle Muni, Detroit (NLE, 9, 1922); Birch Hill GC, Detroit (NLE); Edgewood CC, Union Lakes; Pontiac CC.

William H. "Bert" Way (1873 - 1963)
Born: Westward Ho! Devonshire, England. Died: Miami, Florida at age 90.

Bert Way and his brothers grew up alongside the Royal North Devon GC. All were proficient golfers who moved to America to further their careers. The first of his family to emigrate to the United States, Bert took a roundabout route. He had worked as an apprentice to Tom and Young Willie Dunn in England and Biarritz, France. When Dunn traveled to America to build Shinnecock Hills, Bert Way soon followed.

In 1896 Bert found one of the few available club professional jobs in the U.S. at Meadow Brook Club in New York, where he worked for $100.00 a month. His duties left him plenty of time to work on his game, and he soon became a successful tournament golfer. In 1899 he was joint runner-up in the U.S. Open, though a distant eleven shots behind the winner Willie Smith.

By that time, Bert had relocated in Detroit, Mich. where he laid out several courses. He was also active in the Cleveland, Ohio area. In 1909 he designed Mayfield (Ohio) CC and remained as its professional until 1952. While in that capacity he introduced John D. Rockefeller to golf. Bert continued to design and remodel courses while at Mayfield, and his best-known creation was the original Firestone CC in Akron, which was considerably toughened by Robert Trent Jones in the 1950s.

A member of the PGA of America, Bert was especially active in Senior golf activities. He served as PGA Senior President in 1946, won several Senior events and was at one time the oldest living PGA professional. He died in Miami in August of 1963, just two weeks short of his 91st birthday.

Courses by: William "Bert" Way
Kentucky: Sundowner GC, Ashland (9, 1953).
Michigan: CC of Detroit, Lake St. Clair (NLE, 1898); Detroit GC (NLE, 1905).
Ohio: Aurora CC (1926); Dover Bay CC (9, 1904); Euclid Heights CC (NLE, 1900); Firestone CC (South Course), Akron (1929); Firestone Public GC, Arkon (NLE, 1929); Mayfield CC, South Euclid (1911), with Herbert Barker.

Henry James Whigham (1869 - 1954)
Born: Prestwick, Scotland. Died: Southampton, New York at age 85.

H.J. Whigham, descended from one of Prestwick's oldest golfing families, was the son of a golfing friend that C.B. Macdonald first met as an undergraduate at St. Andrews University. An Oxford graduate, Whigham traveled to the United States in 1895 to lecture on English literature and political economy at the university level. Shortly after his arrival, he became drama critic for the Chicago Tribune, a post from which he took time off in 1896 and 1897 to win the U.S. Amateur Championship.

From 1896 to 1907 Whigham served as war correspondent for several British and American newspapers, covering the Battle of San Juan (where he was captured), the Boer War, the Boxer Rebellion of 1899, the Macedonian Rebellion and the Russo-Japanese War. He returned to the United States in 1908, became editor of Metropolitan and Town and Country magazines. He was author of How to Play Golf and of books on a variety of other subjects, from The Persian Problem (1903) to one on the New Deal in 1936.

In his first years in the United States, Whigham had staked out the original Onwentsia Club in Chicago in collaboration with H.J. Tweedie and James and Robert Foulis. After his marriage in 1909 to C.B. Macdonald's daughter Frances, he assisted his father-in-law in planning The National Golf Links of America. Whigham took a friendly interest in Macdonald's design work and studied the work of other early golf architects on the East Coast. He did little other design work himself.

Jack White (1873 - 1949)
Born: Dirleton, Scotland. Died: London, England at age 76.

Jack White, professional golfer at Sunningdale in England for many years, won the British Open in 1904. He assisted Willie Park Jr. with the design and construction of several courses and consulted on modifications to numerous established layouts in the London area. He also laid out a few original designs himself.

Robert White (1874 - 1959) ASGCA, Charter Member.
Born: St. Andrews, Scotland. Died: Myrtle Beach, South Carolina at age 85.

In 1894 Robert White emigrated from St. Andrews to the United States to study agronomy. For a short period around 1895 he served as pro-greenkeeper at Myopia Hunt Club in Massachusetts and in 1902 moved to Ravisloe CC in Illinois. Later he was professional at Wykagyl CC in New Rochelle, New York. During his career, White laid out a number of courses at which he remained as pro-superintendent. He also planned and revised many others.

White became the first President of the PGA of America in 1916, was a founding member of the ASGCA, a pioneer in scientific turfgrass management and a leading golf businessman.

Courses by: Robert White

Connecticut: Fairchild Wheeler GC (Course No. 1), Bridgeport; Fairchild Wheeler GC (Course No. 2), Bridgeport; Shorehaven GC, Norwalk; Silver Spring CC, Ridgefield.

Kentucky: Louisville CC (9).

Massachusetts: North Salem Links, Salem (NLE, 9, 1895).

New Jersey: Green Brook CC, Caldwell (1923); Harkers Hollow GC, Phillipsburg; Lake Hopatcong GC (1918); Manasquan River G&CC, Brielle.

New York: Richmond County CC, Staten Island (1916).

Pennsylvania: Berkleigh CC, Kutztown (1926); Glen Brook CC, Stroudsburg (1924); Longue Vue C, Verona (1920); Skytop C (1927); Water Gap CC, Delaware Watergap (1923); Wiscasset GC (9, 1924).

South Carolina: Kingstree CC (1925); Pine Lakes International GC, Myrtle Beach (1927).

Washington, D.C.: East Potomac Park GC (9).

Courses Remodeled & Added to by: Robert White

Illinois: Ravisloe CC, Homewood (R.).

New Jersey: Colonia CC (A., 1937); Echo Lake CC, Westfield (R.6, 1919).

New York: Rockland CC, Sparkhill (R.9, 1929); Wykagyl CC, New Rochelle (R., 1923).

Ohio: Cincinnati CC (A.9); Cincinnati CC (R.9).

Pennsylvania: Buck Hill Inn & CC, Buck Hill Falls (A.9).

Sam Whiting (1880 - 1956)
Died: San Francisco, California at age 76.

Sam Whiting was professional at Lakeside G&CC from 1920 to 1924, when the course was sold to the Olympic Club of San Francisco. Whiting was then hired as superintendent of the Lakeside Course of Olympic and in that capacity supervised construction in 1924 of a second eighteen, the Ocean Course designed by Willie Watson. He also supervised construction of Watson's design of Harding Park Muni.

Whiting is often credited with remodeling Olympic's Lakeside Course in 1924, but in fact Watson planned the changes. Whiting was indeed responsible for the massive tree-planting program that eventually made Lakeside one of the tightest courses in the country. He is also credited with building Sonoma National GC in California, but records are unclear as to whether he built it to his own design or to that of Watson's. In either case, Whiting's work was a good example of the overlapping roles of architect, superintendent and professional so prevalent in the history of course design.

Sam Whiting continued as superintendent at Olympic until his poor health forced his retirement in 1954. It was a disappointment to him that he was unable to handle the course for the U.S. Open scheduled there in the following year.

Ronald Edward Whitten (1950 -)
Born: Omaha, Nebraska.

Ron Whitten received a B.S. degree in 1972 from the University of Nebraska and a J.D. degree in 1977 from the Washburn University School of Law. A practicing trial attorney, he served as both an Assistant District Attorney and Assistant City Attorney in Topeka, Kansas.

Whitten's interest in golf course design began in 1967 when he visited Chicago GC and Beverly CC courses in Illinois. He began compiling information about courses and course architects in 1969, eventually establishing one of the world's most complete data banks on the subject. In 1974 Whitten was a contributor to Frank Hannigan's article on golf architect A.W. Tillinghast that appeared in the USGA Journal. Six years later he began writing extensively about golf course design and designers, co-authoring with Geoffrey S. Cornish a history on course architecture, *The Golf Course.* His articles on golf design appeared in every major American golf magazine. A devoted student of the subject, Whitten interviewed and spent time with nearly every practicing golf architect of his day. In 1985 he became Contributing Editor on Golf Architecture for Golf Digest magazine.

Benjamin J. Wihry (1913 -) ASGCA
Born: Haverhill, Massachusetts.

Ben Wihry received B.S. and Landscape Architecture degrees from the University of Massachusetts in 1935 and 1941. He was employed as a recreational planner for the U.S. Forest Service from 1935 to 1940, and from 1941 to 1946 served with the U.S. Army Corps of Engineers.

In 1946 Wihry entered private practice in planning, engineering and landscape architecture. His firm, Miller, Wihry, Lee Inc. of Louisville, Ky., branched into golf course architecture around 1964, after Wihry had worked with and studied under his friend and former classmate, Edward Lawrence Packard.

Courses by: Benjamin Wihry

Indiana: Elks Lodge GC, Jeffersonville (9, 1969).

Kentucky: Barren River State Park GC, Glasgow (Par 3, 1979); Bobby Nichols GC, Louisville (9, 1964); Chenoweth GC, Jeffersontown (9, 1967); Danville CC (1974); Eagle's Nest CC, Somerset (1979); Eastern Kentucky Univ GC, Richmond (1972); Elizabethtown GC (Par 3, 9, 1968), with Morgan Boggs; Hunting Creek CC, Prospect (1965); Long Run GC, Anchorage (9, 1965); Rough River State Park GC, Falls of Rough (Par 3, 9, 1973); Sun Valley GC, Louisville (9, 1972).

Tennessee: Nashboro Village CC, Nashville (1974); Paris Landing State Park GC (1970); Rock Island State Park GC; Swan Lake CC, Clarksville (1977); Winfield Dunn GC (1973).

Courses Remodeled & Added to by: Benjamin Wihry

Kentucky: Iroquois GC, Louisville (A.9, 1964); Iroquois GC, Louisville (R.3, 1964); Lexington CC (A.5, 1975); Lexington CC (R.4, 1975); Louisville CC (R.1, 1974); Louisville CC (A.1, 1974); Seneca Muni, Louisville (R.8, 1972); Shelbyville CC (A.2, 1974).

Willard G. Wilkinson (1889 - 1979) ASGCA
Born: Wimbledon, England. Died: Phoenix, Arizona at age 90.

After service with the Royal Flying Corps during World War I, Willard Wilkinson moved to the United States where he attended Rutgers University and then went to work as assistant to golf architect A.W. Tillinghast. Eventually he became Vice-President of A.W. Tillinghast Golf Construction Company Inc., and during these years supervised construction at Winged Foot, Baltusrol and other renowned layouts.

In 1924 Wilkinson entered private practice, aided by his former employer, who arranged for him to complete three Tillinghast courses and receive the fees still due on them. He went on to design eighty-seven courses and remodel sixteen in the continental United States, Hawaii (where he resided for many years), the Philippines, Guam, Japan and Tahiti. He was assisted by his son, Col. Robert N. Wilkinson (USAF, ret.) during several of the years when his practice was based in Honolulu. Wilkinson moved to Arizona shortly after his retirement in 1969.

Courses by: Willard Wilkinson

Hawaii: Fort Shafter GC, Honolulu (9, 1950); Hilo Muni (1951); Kauai Surf G&CC, Kauai (NLE, 9, 1967); Pacific Palisades GC, Pearl City (Par 3, 1962); Pali GC, Honolulu (1957).

New Jersey: Galloping Hills GC, Union; Jumping Brook GC, Neptune (1925); Locust Grove GC, Rahway (1925); Prescott Hills GC, Plainfield (1926).

New York: Cortland CC (1947); Malone GC (9, 1939).

Japan: Hayana International GC (1967).

Philippines: Binicitan GC, Manila; Subic Bay GC (1966).

Tahiti: Atimoona G&CC (1965).

Courses Remodeled & Added to by: Willard Wilkinson

Hawaii: Mid-Pacific CC, Honolulu (A.9, 1949); Mid-Pacific CC, Honolulu (R.9, 1949).

New Jersey: Echo Lake CC, Westfield (R.3, 1928).

New York: Bellevue CC, Syracuse (R., 1947); Bellevue CC, Syracuse (A.3, 1947).

John Harold Williams Sr. (1920 -)
Born: Alabama.

Harold Williams attended the University of Alabama and served in the military for four and a half years during World War II. He became a professional golfer in 1945, joining the PGA of America and becoming a charter member of the Alabama PGA.

Williams owned and operated Meadowbrook Golf Club in Tuscaloosa, Ala. until 1962. He played frequently on the PGA Tour during that time and won the Alabama Open once, the Mississippi Open twice and the Alabama PGA Championship on several occasions.

Williams began designing golf courses in Alabama on a part-time basis in the late 1950s.

Courses by: Harold Williams

Alabama: Canoe Creek CC, Gadsen; Grayson Valley CC, Birmingham; Indian Hills CC, Tuscaloosa (1960), with Thomas H. Nicol; Indian Oaks CC, Anniston (1968); Pine Harbor Champions G&CC, Pell City; Terrapin Hills GC, Ft. Payne; The Country Club, Reform (9); University of Alabama GC, Tuscaloosa (9, 1959), with Thomas H. Nicol.

Courses Remodeled & Added to by: Harold Williams

Alabama: Anniston CC (R.).

Joseph B. Williams

Joseph Williams served as superintendent at the Santa Clara (California) CC in the 1960s and then designed Shorecliffs CC in San Clemente and became its superintendent. He later planned several more courses in the Southwest.

Courses by: Joseph B. Williams

California: Bishop GC (9, 1963); Golden Hills GC, Tehachapi (1966); Navy GC (Destroyer Course), Cypress; Richard Nixon Estate GC, San Clemente (1, 1970); Shorecliffs GC, San Clemente (1964); Tahoe Donner GC, Truckee (1975).

Utah: Roosevelt Muni (1973); Tri-City GC, American Fork; Valley View GC, Layton (1979).

Tom Williamson (1880 - 1950)
Born: England. Died: England at age 70.

Tom Williamson's career as a pro-greenkeeper and club maker at Notts Golf Club spanned more than half a century, from 1896 until his death in 1950. He laid out numerous courses on the side and in 1919 claimed to have worked on all but one of the courses within a fifty-mile radius of Nottingham. Over the years he designed or remodeled some sixty courses and was assisted by his brother Hugh with the construction of several. Tom Williamson was an early advocate of plasticine models of new greens.

Courses by: Tom Williamson

England: Ashover GC, Derbyshire; Beeston Fields GC, Nottinghamshire (1923); Garforth GC, Yorkshire (1913); Hillsborough GC, Yorkshire (1920); Ladbrook Park GC, Warwickshire (1908); Longcliffe GC, Leicestershire (1905); Louth GC, Lincolnshire (1919); Mapperley GC, Nottinghamshire (1913); Matlock GC, Derbyshire (1907); Melton Mowbray GC, Leicestershire (1925); Nuneaton GC, Warwickshire (1906); Radcliffe on Trent GC, Nottinghamshire (1909); Retford GC, Nottinghamshire (1921); Rothley Park GC, Leicestershire (1911); Rushcliffe GC, Nottinghamshire (1910); Scraptoft GC, Leicestershire (1928); Serlby Park GC, Yorkshire (9, 1905); Sleaford GC, Lincolnshire (1905); Southwell GC, Nottinghamshire (NLE); Stanton-on-the-Wolds, Nottinghamshire (1928); Tipworth GC; Trentham Park GC, Staffordshire (1936); Wollaton Park GC, Nottinghamshire (1927); Worksop GC, Nottinghamshire (1914).

Courses Remodeled & Added to by: Tom Williamson

England: Belton Park GC, Lincolnshire (R.); Birstall GC, Leicestershire (R.); Bulwell Forest GC (R.); Burton-on-Trent GC, Derbyshire (R.); Buxton and High Peak GC, Derbyshire (R.); Cavendish GC, Derbyshire (R., 1925); Chatsworth GC, Derbyshire (R.); Chesterfield GC, Derbyshire (R.); Chilwell Manor GC, Nottinghamshire (R.); Edgbaston GC, Warwickshire (R.); Erewash Valley GC, Derbyshire (R.); Grimsby GC, Lincolnshire (R.); Leek GC, Staffordshire (R.); Lees Hall GC, Yorkshire (R.); Mullion GC, Cornwall (R.); Notts GC, Nottinghamshire (R.); Radcliffe on Trent GC, Nottinghamshire (R.); Renishaw GC, Yorkshire (R.); Rushden & District GC, North Hants (R., 1919); Sandilands GC, Sutton-on-Sea (R.); Sherwood Forest GC, Nottinghamshire (R.); Sickleholme GC, Yorkshire (R.); Wellingborough GC, Northhamptonshire (R.); West Runton GC, Norfolk (NLE, R.).

Switzerland: Zumikon G&CC, Zurich-Zumikon (R.).

Louis Sibbett "Dick" Wilson (1904 - 1965)

Born: Philadelphia, Pennsylvania. Died: Boynton Beach, Florida at age 61.

Dick Wilson was a fine athlete as a youth and attended the University of Vermont on a football scholarship. As a youngster, he had served as water boy for a construction crew at Merion West. After leaving college, Dick returned to Merion and worked on Toomey and Flynn's crew during the revision of Merion's East Course in 1926.

Wilson remained with Toomey and Flynn, becoming a construction superintendent and later a design associate. He was credited with making major contributions to Flynn's design of Shinnecock Hills GC on Long Island which opened in 1931, but in truth he supervised its construction to Flynn's plans. In the early '30s Wilson moved to Florida to construct Indian Creek Club in Miami Beach. But Toomey's death and the decline of business due to the Depression forced Wilson to take a job as pro/greenkeeper at Delray Beach CC. He remained there until World War II, teaching the game to visiting tourists. Among the frequent visitors to Wilson's course were Mr. and Mrs. Paul Dye of Ohio, parents of Pete and Roy Dye.

He spent the war years constructing and camouflaging airfields. In 1945 Wilson formed his own golf design company in association with a Miami earthmoving firm, the Troup Brothers. His early post-war works, especially West Palm Beach CC and NCR CC in Dayton, Ohio, established Dick Wilson as one of the most sought-after architects of the 1950s and '60s. Wilson did relatively few courses in the later years of his life in an attempt to give personal attention to each work bearing his name. He maintained a staff of loyal and talented assistants who handled much of the actual design and construction work on some projects, including Joseph L. Lee, Frank Batto, Robert von Hagge, Ward Northrup and Robert Simmons.

Courses by: Dick Wilson

Arizona: Moon Valley CC, Phoenix (1958), with Bob Simmons.

Arkansas: Blytheville CC (9, 1957), with Bob Simmons.

California: La Costa CC (Gold Course), Carlsbad (1964), with Joe Lee; Sunnylands GC, Rancho Mirage (9, 1962), with Joe Lee.

Delaware: Bidermann GC, Wilmington , with Joe Lee; Wilmington CC (North Course), Greenville (1962).

Florida: Bay Hill C, Orlando (1961), with Joe Lee, Robert von Hagge and Bob Simmons; Blackburn Estate GC, Fort Myers (3); Cape Coral CC (1963), with Robert von Hagge; Cypress Lake CC, Ft. Myers (1960), with Robert von Hagge; Doral CC (Blue Course), Miami (1962), with Robert von Hagge; Doral CC (Red Course), Miami (1962), with Robert von Hagge; Golden Gate CC, Naples (1965), with Robert von Hagge; Harder Hall Hotel GC, Sebring (1958), with Joe Lee; Hole-in-the-Wall GC, Naples (1958), with Joe Lee; JDM CC (East Course), Palm Beach Gardens (1964), with Joe Lee; JDM CC (North Course), Palm Springs Gardens (9, 1964), with Joe Lee; JDM CC (South Course), Palm Springs Gardens (9, 1964), with Joe Lee; Lone Palm GC, Lakeland (1965), with Joe Lee; Melreese GC, Miami (1962), with Joe Lee; Palm Beach Par 3 GC (9, 1961), with Joe Lee; Palm-Aire West CC (Champions Course) {formerly DeSoto Lakes G&CC}, Sarasota (1958); Palmetto GC, South Miami (1960), with Bob Simmons; Pine Tree CC, Delray Beach (1962), with Joe Lee and Robert von Hagge; Royal Oak G&CC, Titusville (1964), with Robert von Hagge; Tamarac CC, Ft. Lauderdale (1961), with Robert von Hagge; Tequesta CC, Jupiter (1958), with Joe Lee; West Palm Beach CC (1947); Westview GC, Miami (9, 1949).

Georgia: Callaway Gardens GC (Lakeview Course), Pine Mountain (9, 1952); Callaway Gardens GC (Mountainview Crs), Pine Mountain (1963), with Joe Lee; Canongate GC, Palmetto (1965), with Joe Lee; Jekyll Island GC (Oleander Course) (1961), with Joe Lee; Mystery Valley CC, Lithonia (1965), with Joe Lee; Sea Island GC (Retreat 9) (9, 1959), with Joe Lee.

Illinois: Cog Hill GC (Course No. 3), Lemont (1964), with Joe Lee; Cog Hill GC (Course No. 4), Lemont (1964), with Joe Lee.

Louisiana: Oakbourne CC, Lafayette (1958), with Bob Simmons.

Mississippi: CC of Jackson (27, 1963), with Robert von Hagge.

Nevada: Desert Rose GC, Las Vegas (1964), with Joe Lee.

New Jersey: Bedens Brook C, Skillman (1964), with Joe Lee.

New York: Cavalry C, Manlius (1966), with Joe Lee; Deepdale CC, Manhasset (1956); Garrison GC {formerly North Redoubt C} (1963); Meadow Brook C, Jericho (1955).

Ohio: Coldstream CC, Cincinnati (1960), with Joe Lee, Robert von Hagge and Bob Simmons; NCR CC (North Course), Dayton (1954); NCR CC (South Course), Dayton (1954).

Pennsylvania: Laurel Valley CC, Ligonier (1960), with Bob Simmons; Radnor Valley CC, Villanova (1953), with X.G. Hassenplug; Westmoreland CC, Export (1948), with X.G. Hassenplug.

Tennessee: Town'N Country GC, Chattanooga (Par 3, 1963), with Bob Simmons.

Virginia: Elizabeth Manor GC, Portsmouth (1951); Glen Oak CC, Danville (9, 1951); Hidden Valley CC, Salem (1952); Kinderton CC, Clarksville (1947).

West Virginia: Fincastle CC, Bluefield (1963), with Bob Simmons; Greenbriar GC (Lakeside Course), Wht. Sulphur Springs (1962), with Bob Simmons.

Quebec: Royal Montreal GC (Black Course), Ile Bizard (9, 1959), with Bob Simmons; Royal Montreal GC (Blue Course), Ile Bizard (1959), with Bob Simmons; Royal Montreal GC (Red Course), Ile Bizard (1959), with Bob Simmons.

Bahamas: Bahamas Princess Hotel & CC (Emerald), Freeport (1965), with Joe Lee and Bob Simmons; Lucaya Park G&CC, Freeport (1964), with Joe Lee and Bob

Simmons; Lyford Cay C, New Providence (1960), with Joe Lee and Bob Simmons; Paradise Island G&CC, Nassau (1962), with Joe Lee and Bob Simmons; Treasure Cay GC, Abaco (1966), with Joe Lee.

Cuba: Villa Real GC, Havana (1957), with Joe Lee.

Venezuela: Lagunita CC, Caracas (1958), with Bob Simmons.

Courses Remodeled & Added to by: Dick Wilson

California: Bel-Air CC, Los Angeles (R., 1961).

Florida: Dunedin CC (R., 1960); Gulfstream GC, Delray Beach (R., 1958), with Joe Lee; Indian Creek CC, Miami Beach (R.), with Joe Lee; Lake Worth Muni (R.); Lakewood CC, St. Petersburg (R., 1957); Riviera CC, Coral Gables (R., 1962); Seminole GC, North Palm Beach (R., 1947).

Georgia: Callaway Gardens GC (Lakeview Course), Pine Mountain (A.9, 1963), with Joe Lee.

Illinois: Cog Hill CC (Course No. 1), Lemont (R., 1963), with Joe Lee; Cog Hill GC (Course No. 2), Lemont (R., 1963), with Joe Lee.

New Jersey: Hollywood GC, Deal (R., 1956).

New York: Deepdale CC, Manhasset (R., 1962); Scarsdale GC, Hartsdale (R., 1956); Winged Foot GC (West Course), Mamaroneck (R.3, 1958).

Ohio: Columbus CC (R., 1962); Inverness C, Toledo (R., 1956); Moraine CC, Dayton (R., 1955); Scioto CC, Columbus (R., 1963), with Joe Lee and Robert von Hagge.

Pennsylvania: Aronimink GC, Newton Square (R., 1961); Merion GC (East Course), Ardmore (R., 1965); Penn Hills C, Bradford (A.9; Penn Hills C, Bradford (R.9).

Texas: Colonial CC, Fort Worth (R., 1956).

Australia: Metropolitan GC (R.11, 1961); Metropolitan GC (A.8, 1961); Royal Melbourne GC (East Course), Black Rock (R., 1959); Royal Melbourne GC (West Course), Black Rock (R., 1959).

Mexico: Club Campestre, Mexico City (R.), with Bob Simmons.

Hugh Irvine Wilson (1879 - 1925)

Born: Philadelphia, Pennsylvania. Died: Bryn Mawr, Pennsylvania at age 45.

Hugh Wilson graduated in 1902 from Princeton University where he had been captain of the golf team. Following college, he joined a Philadelphia insurance brokerage firm and eventually became its president.

A lifelong amateur golfer, Wilson was a member of Aronimink GC and Merion Cricket Club. In 1910 he was chosen to make a survey of great British courses in preparation for a new Merion course. Wilson spent seven months in England and Scotland, returning with armloads of sketches and notes, and proceeded, with the assistance of Richard S. Francis, to lay out a new course for Merion in Ardmore, Pennsylvania. With the exception of later changes to four holes and some re-bunkering, Merion East remained as Wilson designed it in 1912.

Hugh Wilson also planned the West course at Merion (1914) and Cobbs Creek Municipal GC in Philadelphia (1917). With the assistance of his brother Alan, he finished the remaining four holes at Pine Valley after George Crump's death in 1919. He also consulted with his friend William S. Flynn on the design of The Kittansett Club in Marion, Mass., a design not executed in its entirety.

Courses by: Hugh Wilson

Pennsylvania: Cobbs Creek Muni, Philadelphia (1917); Merion GC (East Course), Ardmore (1912); Merion GC (West Course), Ardmore (1914).

Courses Remodeled & Added to by: Hugh Wilson

New Jersey: Pine Valley GC, Clementon (A.4, 1921), with Alan Wilson.

Thomas Winton (1871 - 1944)

Born: Montrose, Scotland. Died: Tuckahoe, New York at age 73.

Tom Winton, descended from a Scottish golfing family, was the son of James Winton, longtime pro and club maker at Montrose. Tom's brothers all became professionals and club makers. Tom studied under his father as well but moved to London at the turn of the century. There he became involved in golf course construction, working for several architects on construction of such courses as Coombe Hill and South Herts.

At the outbreak of World War I, Winton joined Willie Park Jr.'s crew and moved to the United States. But business was slow there also, so Winton took a position as superintendent for the Westchester (N.Y.) County Park Commission, where he remained for many years. He was in charge of maintaining the county's golf courses and other parks, and with constructing new facilities as well. In this capacity he designed several public courses in the New York suburbs.

Winton soon found additional design jobs and in the 1920s was active along the Eastern seaboard, laying out courses and supervising their construction. When design business fell off in the Depression, he continued in his park commission position and also served as a maintenance consultant for several New York clubs.

Courses by: Tom Winton

Connecticut: Mill River CC, Stratford (1923).

Massachusetts: Woods Hole GC, Falmouth.

New Jersey: Cranmoor CC, Toms River (1925); Hopewell Valley GC, Hopewell Junction (1927).

New York: Amityville CC; Colgate Univ GC, Hamilton (NLE); Corning CC; Kingsridge CC, Portchester (1929); Maplemoor CC, White Plains (1927), with Archie Capper; Mohansic Park GC, Yorktown Heights (1925); Mount Kisco CC; Saxon Woods GC, Mamaroneck (1930); Sprain Brook GC, Yonkers (27, 1928); Westport GC (1928).

Virginia: Lynn Haven CC, Norfolk.

Courses Remodeled & Added to by: Tom Winton

Kentucky: Big Spring CC, Louisville (R.).

Maryland: Congressional CC (Blue Course), Bethesda (R., 1927).

New York: Apawamis C, Rye (R.); Hollow Brook G&CC, Peekskill (R.); Maplemoor CC, White Plains (R.); Siwanoy CC, Bronxville (R.); Sleepy Hollow GC, Scarboro-on-Hudson (R.); Sunset Hill GC, Ossining (R., 1929); Westchester CC (South Course), Rye (R.).

Theodore J. Wirth (1927 -   )
Born: New Orleans, Louisiana.

Ted Wirth attended St. Thomas College, Kansas University and Iowa State University, where he received a B.S. degree in Landscape Architecture in 1950. After working as a park planner with the National Park Service for ten years, he entered private practice as a landscape architect in Montana in the early 1960s. Wirth served as President of the National Council of Park and Recreation Consultants and as Vice-President of the ASLA. Branching into golf course design in the late 1960s, he had planned several courses in the Montana area by the end of the 1970s.
Courses by: Theodore Wirth
Montana: Ennis GC (9); Laurel G&RC (1968); Point North GC, Billings (1978), with Dave Bennett; Riverside GC, Bozeman; Valley View GC, Bozeman.
Wyoming: Powell Muni (9, 1971).

Gordon C. Witteveen
A graduate of Ontario (Canada) Agricultural College in Guelph, Gordon Witteveen was course superintendent at Northwood CC in Toronto and Board of Trade CC in Woodbridge, Ontario.

He also served as national President of the CGCSA. While at Board of Trade, he altered some holes and designed an additional nine hole precision course for the club. Working alone and sometimes with well-known Toronto landscape architect Alexander Budrevics, Witteveen designed and remodeled several other Ontario courses in the 1970s and '80s.
Courses by: Gordon Witteveen
Ontario: Board of Trade CC (South Course), Woodbridge (Precision, 9, 1981); Loch March GC, Kanata (1987); Nottawasage Inn GC, Alliston (1986); Sawmill GC, Fenwick (1977); Warkworth GC (9, 1969).
Courses Remodeled & Added to by: Gordon Witteveen
Ontario: Bay of Quinte GC, Bellville (R.3); Board of Trade CC (East Course), Woodbridge (R.4); Warkworth GC (A.9, 1977).

Eugene F. "Skip" Wogan (1890 - 1957)
Born: Roxbury, Massachusetts. Died: Manchester, Massachusetts at age 67.

Skip Wogan attended public schools in Watertown, Massachusetts and after graduation went to work as assistant professional under Donald Ross at Essex CC in Manchester.

Upon Ross' resignation from Essex in 1913, Wogan succeeded him and remained as its head professional and grounds manager until his death. He also carried on a design practice on the side, planning a number of courses in Massachusetts and other eastern states. Wogan's son Philip became a course architect and two other sons, Louis and Richard, became contractors specializing in golf construction.
Courses by: Eugene "Skip" Wogan
Maine: Mingo Springs GC, Rangeley; Webhannett GC, Kennebunkport; Willowdale GC, Scarborough.
Massachusetts: Arlmont CC, Arlington (9); Bellevue CC, Melrose (9); Blue Hill CC, Canton; Bristol County CC (9); Cape Ann GC, Essex (9); Herring Run CC, Taunton (9); Labour-in-Vain GC, Ipswich (NLE, 9); Merrimack GC, Methuen; Sankaty Head GC, Nantucket (1925); Walpole CC (NLE, 9).
New Jersey: Picatinny GC, Dover.
Courses Remodeled & Added to by: Eugene "Skip" Wogan
Massachusetts: Bear Hill GC, Wakefield (R.); Beverly G&TC (R.); Essex CC, Manchester (R.); Needham GC (A.9); Tedesco CC, Marblehead (R.).

Philip A. Wogan (1918 -   ) ASGCA
Born: Beverly, Massachusetts.
Philip Wogan attended North Carolina State, Penn State, Lehigh University and Boston University, where he received a Bachelor's degree in Biology and a Master's degree in Education. From 1947 to 1956 he taught biology on the high school level and during the same years assisted his father, Skip Wogan, in golf course design on a part-time basis.

In 1956 Wogan retired from teaching to devote full time to golf architecture. After his father's death in 1958, he continued the practice on his own. Employing his joint background in biology and course design, he became a leading authority on the relationship of golf courses to the environment and prepared the ASGCA's widely distributed paper on the subject.
Courses by: Phil Wogan
Maine: Bar Harbor GC, Trenton (1968); Bucksport G&CC (9, 1969); Martindale CC, Auburn (9, 1963); Tidewater GC, Trenton (1968); Val Halla CC, Cumberland (9, 1965).
Massachusetts: CC of Billerica (9, 1971); Halifax CC (1969); New Meadows GC, Topsfield (9, 1963); Oxford G&RC; Pembroke CC (1973); Rockland CC (Par 3, 1955); Rowley CC (9, 1970).
New Hampshire: Charmingfare Links, Candia (1964); East Kingston GC (9); Hoodkroft CC, Derry (9, 1971).
Rhode Island: Lindbrook CC, Hope Valley (Par 3, 1968); Pond View GC, Westerly (9); Spring Haven GC (Par 3, 9).
Courses Remodeled & Added to by: Phil Wogan
Maine: Val Halla CC, Cumberland (A.9, 1986).
Massachusetts: Blue Hill CC, Canton (A.9, 1955); Essex CC, Manchester (R.); Franklin CC (A.9); Franklin CC (A.10, 1974); Juniper Hills GC, Northboro (R.4, 1972); Myopia Hunt C, Hamilton (R.1, 1981); Putterham Meadows Muni, Brookline (R.2, 1962); Rockport GC (R.2).
New Hampshire: Cochecho CC, Dover (A.9, 1965); Manchester CC (R.4, 1985); North Conway CC (A.9, 1974); Rochester CC (A.9, 1964).
New York: Onondaga G&CC, Fayetteville (R.2, 1982), with Samuel Mitchell.
Rhode Island: Lindbrook CC, Hope Valley (R., 1986).

Michael Stephen Wolveridge (1937 -   )
Born: Essex, England.
After playing for a time on the PGA Tour in the United States, Michael Wolveridge worked with golf architect John Harris and professional golfer Peter

Thomson in the 1960s in New Zealand and other countries. In 1976 he formed a partnership with Peter Thomson and American Ronald Fream. The firm of Thomson, Wolveridge, Fream and Associates worked on an international scale in course design and construction. Fream left after a few years, so Wolveridge and Thomson worked as a team, and were as active as any "Down Under" firm in the 1980s.
Courses by: Michael Wolveridge
California: Bixby GC, Long Beach (Precision, 9, 1980), with Ronald Fream and Peter Thomson.
Washington: Canyon Lakes G&CC, Kennewick (1981), with Peter Thomson, Ronald Fream and John Steidel; Kayak Point GC, Stanwood (1974), with Peter Thomson, Ronald Fream and Terry Storm; Tapps Island GC, Sumner (9, 1981), with Ronald Fream and Peter Thomson.
Australia: Alice Springs GC (1982), with Peter Thomson; Collier Park GC, Perth (1984), with Peter Thomson; Darwin GC (1983), with Peter Thomson; Desert Springs CC , Alice Springs (1984), with Peter Thomson; Fairway Park GC, Mandurah (1984), with Peter Thomson; Gold Coast CC, Surfers' Paradise (1984), with Peter Thomson; Hall's Head Resort GC, Mandurah (1984), with Peter Thomson; Iwasaki Resort GC, Yeppoon (1984), with Peter Thomson; Lake Ross GC, Marulan (1984), with Peter Thomson; Midlands GC, Victoria (1975), with Peter Thomson; North Lakes CC, Victoria , with Peter Thomson; Tasmanian Casino CC, Launceston (1982), with Peter Thomson; Thurgoona GC, Albury (27, 1983), with Peter Thomson; Tura Beach CC, Merimbula (1982), with Peter Thomson.
England: Southwood GC, Hampshire (9, 1977), with John Harris; Telford Hotel G&CC, Great Hay (1979), with John Harris and Peter Thomson; Washington GC, Dunham (1979), with John Harris.
Fiji: Fijian Hotel GC (Precision, 9, 1973), with Peter Thomson and Ronald Fream.
Hong Kong: Royal Hong Kong GC (Eden Course), Fanling (1968), with John Harris and Peter Thomson.
India: Bangladore GC (1982), with Peter Thomson; Gulmarg GC, Cashmere (1973), with Peter Thomson; Karnataka GC, Bangalore (1984), with Peter Thomson.
Indonesia: Bali Handara CC, Pancasari (1975), with John Harris, Peter Thomson and Ronald Fream; Jagorawi G&CC, Chibinong (1978), with Peter Thomson and Ronald Fream; National GC, Jakarta Pusat , with Peter Thomson and Ronald Fream.
Japan: Chigusa CC (27, 1973), with Peter Thomson; Fujioka CC, Magoya (1971), with Peter Thomson and Tameshi Yamada; Hammamatsu CC, with Peter Thomson; Ibusuki CC (New Course), Kagoshima (1978), with Peter Thomson; Korakuen CC, Sapparo (27, 1974), with Peter Thomson; Naie GC, Sapporo (1976), with Peter Thomson; Nambu Fuji GC, Kwate (1974), with John Harris and Peter Thomson; Takaha Royal CC, Fukuoka (1976), with Peter Thomson; Three Lakes CC, Kuwana (1976), with Peter Thomson; Tokuyama CC (1975), with Peter Thomson; Yoro CC, Nagoya (1977), with Peter Thomson; Zen CC, Himeji (1977), with Peter Thomson.
Mauritius: Case Noyale GC, Port Louis (1972), with Peter Thomson.
New Zealand: Harewood GC, Christchurch (1967), with John Harris and Peter Thomson; Karori GC, Wellington (1968), with John Harris and Peter Thomson; Maramarua GC, Pokeno (1969), with John Harris and Peter Thomson; Taieri GC, Mosgiel (1967), with John Harris and Peter Thomson; Wairakei International GC, Taupo (1975), with John Harris and Peter Thomson.
Portugal: Estoril Sol GC, Estoril (Precision, 9, 1976), with John Harris, Peter Thomson and Ronald Fream.
Scotland: Dougalston GC, Glasgow (1977), with John Harris; Inverness GC, Invernesshire (1968), with John Harris and Peter Thomson.
Singapore: Sentosa Island GC (Serapong Course) (1983), with Peter Thomson and Ronald Fream.
St. Kitts: Royal St. Kitts GC (1977), with John Harris, Peter Thomson and Ronald Fream.
Tonga: Tonga GC, with Peter Thomson.
Trinidad and Tobago: Balandra Beach GC (1982), with Peter Thomson and Ronald Fream; St. Andrews GC, Maraval (1975), with John Harris, Peter Thomson and Ronald Fream.
Tunisia: El Kantaoui GC, Soussenord (1977), with John Harris, Peter Thomson and Ronald Fream.
Courses Remodeled & Added to by: Michael Wolveridge
California: Almaden G&CC, San Jose (R., 1979), with Peter Thomson and Ronald Fream; Hacienda CC, La Habra (R., 1978), with Peter Thomson and Ronald Fream; Marine Memorial GC, Santa Ana (R., 1980), with Peter Thomson and Ronald Fream; Miramar Memorial GC, San Diego (R., 1981), with Peter Thomson and Ronald Fream; San Juan Hills CC, San Juan Capistrano (R., 1981), with Peter Thomson and Ronald Fream.
Nevada: Edgewood Tahoe CC, Stateline (R., 1980), with Peter Thomson and Ronald Fream.
Oregon: Sunriver CC (South Course) (R., 1978), with Peter Thomson and Ronald Fream.
Washington: Broadmoor GC, Seattle (R.2, 1982), with Peter Thomson and Ronald Fream; Cedarcrest GC, Marysville (R., 1982), with Peter Thomson and Ronald Fream; Manito G&CC, Spokane (R., 1979), with Peter Thomson and Ronald Fream; Seattle GC (R.2, 1981), with Peter Thomson and Ronald Fream; West Seattle GC, Seattle (R., 1979), with Peter Thomson and Ronald Fream.
Alberta: Glendale CC, Edmonton (R.3, 1981), with Peter Thomson and Ronald Fream.
Australia: Cottesloe GC (R.), with Peter Thomson; Kingston Heath GC, Cheltenham (R.), with Peter Thomson; Kooyonga GC (R.), with Peter Thomson; Lake Karrinyup CC, Perth (A.9, 1977), with Peter Thomson; Lake Karrinyup CC, Perth (R., 1977), with Peter Thomson; Metropolitan GC (R.), with Peter Thomson; Middlemore GC (R.), with Peter Thomson; Peninsula G&CC (R.), with Peter Thomson; Royal Adelaide GC, Seaton (R.), with Peter Thomson; Royal Canberra GC, Yarralumia (R.), with Peter Thomson; Royal Perth GC (R.), with Peter Thomson; Royal Sydney GC, Sydney (R.), with Peter Thomson; Sandringham GC, Melbourne (A.9), with Peter Thomson; Sorrento GC (R.), with Peter Thomson; Southern GC, Melbourne (A.9, 1978), with Peter Thomson; Southern GC, Melbourne (R., 1978), with Peter Thomson; Victoria GC, Cheltenham (R., 1983), with Peter Thomson; Yarrawonga GC, Victoria (A.9, 1980), with Peter Thomson.
Hong Kong: Royal Hong Kong GC (New Course) (R., 1970), with Peter Thomson;

Royal Hong Kong GC (Old Course) (R., 1976), with Peter Thomson.
India: Bombay Presidency GC (R., 1980), with Peter Thomson; Delhi GC (A.9, 1974), with Peter Thomson; Delhi GC (R., 1974), with Peter Thomson; Royal Calcutta GC, Calcutta (R., 1969), with Peter Thomson.
Indonesia: Kebayoran GC, Jajarta (R., 1980), with Peter Thomson and Ronald Fream; Yani GC (R.), with Peter Thomson.
Malaysia: Gentling Highlands GC (R., 1984), with Peter Thomson and Ronald Fream.
New Zealand: Akarana GC (R., 1972), with Peter Thomson; Ashburton GC (R., 1977), with Peter Thomson; Auckland GC (R.), with Peter Thomson; Hastings GC (R., 1972), with Peter Thomson; Miramar GC, Wellington (R., 1977), with Peter Thomson; Nelson GC (R., 1967), with John Harris and Peter Thomson; North Shore GC (R., 1969), with John Harris and Peter Thomson; Rarotonga GC, Cook Islands (A.9, 1984), with Peter Thomson; Russley GC (R., 1967), with John Harris and Peter Thomson; Timaru GC (R., 1968), with John Harris and Peter Thomson.
Spain: Real Sociedad Hipica Espanola (R.), with John Harris.

Norman H. Woods ASGCA
Norman Woods attended the Ontario Agricultural College at Guelph in the early 1930s and later became associated with golf architect Stanley Thompson. He worked on over fifty projects for the legendary designer. After Thompson's death in the early 1950s, Woods began his own practice in British Columbia.
Courses by: Norman H. Woods
Montana: Hilands GC, Billings (9, 1950), with Gregor MacMillan; Marias Valley G&CC, Shelby (1971); Signal Point CC, Fort Benton (9).
Pennsylvania: Lords Valley CC, Hawley (1963).
Washington: Capital City GC, Olympia; Nile CC, Edmonds.
Alberta: Broadmoor CC; Henderson Lake GC, Lethbridge; Indian Hills GC, Calgary; Stoney Plain GC; Willow Park CC, Calgary.
British Columbia: Harrison GC, Harrison Hotel (9, 1961); Hirsch Creek CC, Kitimat; Kokanee Springs CC, Crawford Bay (1968); Mission GC; Pine Hills G&CC, Penticton (Par 3, 9); Tsawwassen G&CC (1966), with Jack Reimer.
Manitoba: Falcon Beach Lake CC; Grand Beach GC; Rossmere G&CC, Winnipeg; St. Charles CC (West Nine), Winnipeg (9, 1954).
Courses Remodeled & Added to by: Norman H. Woods
Washington: Lake Wilderness CC, Maple Valley (A.9).
British Columbia: Penticton G&CC (A.9); Rebelstoke GC (A.9, 1976); Shaughnessy G&CC, Vancouver (R., 1969); Shuswap Lake Estates G&CC, Blind Bay (R., 1977).
Manitoba: Birds Hill GC (R.).
Ontario: Kimberley GC (A.9, 1980).

Charles Campbell Worthington (1854 - 1944)
C.C. Worthington was famed as a pump manufacturer and later as a developer of mowing and other types of golf course maintenance equipment. Around 1900 he laid out several rudimentary courses on estates in the eastern United States. These included a six-hole course on his own estate at Irvington-on-Hudson, N.Y., Manwallimink GC at Shawnee-on-Delaware, Penn. (built in 1898 on one of his properties, believed to have been the largest private estate east of the Mississippi), and the nine-hole Calendo GC in Pennsylvania.
Worthington started A.W. Tillinghast on his road to fame as a course architect when he hired him to design a course at Shawnee-on-Delaware in 1907. This was Tillinghast's first project. Worthington was also the grandfather of several men whose careers in the development and production of maintenance equipment were significant in the business world of golf. They included Edmund (Ross), Chester and Charles Sawtelle, and Edward Worthington Jr.

George Wright (1847 - 1937)
Born: Yonkers, New York. Died: Boston, Massachusetts at age 90.
The founder of Wright and Ditson Sporting Goods of Boston, Mass., George Wright laid out several informal courses in the 1890s in parks and vacant lots in the Boston area. Among these were a course at Franklin Park, the original Allston GC and an early version of Wollaston GC. They were laid out in an attempt to popularize the then recently introduced game of golf and thus increase the sales of playing equipment imported from Great Britain. His promotional efforts led many to consider George Wright as the "Father of Golf in New England."

Arthur M. Young (1917 -   )
Born: Kalamazoo, Michigan.
Arthur Young attended Northwestern University and was employed as a CPA with Swift & Co. in Chicago. He served in the U.S. Army during World War II and the Korean Conflict, and then resigned his accounting position to build his first golf course in Shelbyville, Mich. in the early 1950s. After operating that course for several years as a member of the PGA of America, Young designed and built other small town courses in Michigan.
Young moved to Florida in the late 1960s and designed and built several precision courses which he owned and operated. In the 1970s he retired to operate Crane Creek GC, which he helped Charles Ankrom design.
Courses by: Arthur Young
Florida: Holiday CC, Lake Park (Precision, 1969); Holiday CC, Stuart (Precision, 1971); Indian Pines GC, Fort Pierce (Precision, 1971); Martin Downs CC (Crane Creek Course) (1976), with Chuck Ankrom.
Michigan: Shelbyville GC (9, 1955); Whiffletree Hill GC, Concord (1970).
Courses Remodeled & Added to by: Arthur Young
Michigan: Duck Lake GC, Albion (A.9); Shelbyville GC (A.9, 1960).

Albert Zikorus (1921 -   ) ASGCA
Born: Needham, Massachusetts.
After caddying at Needham GC and Wellesley CC, Al Zikorus attended the winter school for turfgrass managers at the University of Massachusetts and then served

overseas with the U.S. Army Air Force. After the war he became superintendent at Ould Newbury CC, Wellesley CC, and finally Woodbridge CC in Connecticut.
Zikorus was associated in course design with golf architect William F. Mitchell for a short time. He then worked with Orrin Smith until Smith's retirement in the mid-1950s. Zikorus took over Smith's practice and ultimately planned many courses on his own. Several of these were built by his brothers Walter and Edward, who operated a course construction company.
Courses by: Al Zikorus
Connecticut: Deercrest CC, Greenwich (1957), with Orrin Smith; Elmcrest CC, East Longmeadow (1964); Glastonbury Hills CC (1965); Great Hills CC, Seymour (9, 1960); Harry Greens GC, Prospect (Par 3, 9, 1965); Heritage Village CC, Southbury (1966); Highland Greens GC (Par 3, 9); Hillandale CC, Trumbull (1960); Prospect CC (1961); Riverview CC, Milford (1961); Stony Brook CC, Litchfield (9, 1964); Tashua Knolls G&RC, Trumbull (1971); Timberlin GC, Berlin (1970); Tunxis Plantation CC, Farmington (27, 1961); Wallingford CC (6, 1961); Washington CC (9, 1964); Woodhaven CC, Bethany (1968).
Massachusetts: Billerica GC (Par 3, 9, 1952), with William F. Mitchell; Hampden CC (1964); Ludlow Muni, Chicopee (9), with Orrin Smith; Twin Hills CC; Walpole CC (1973); Wyckoff Park GC, Holyoke (1966).
New Hampshire: Portsmouth AFB GC (1960).
New Jersey: Lakeshore CC, Oradell (1965).
New York: Bel Aire CC, Armonk (1963); Cedar Brook CC, Brookville (1960); Lakeover CC, Bedford Village (1967); Plattsburgh AFB GC (1960).
South Carolina: Green River CC, Chesterfield (9, 1966).
Courses Remodeled & Added to by: Al Zikorus
Connecticut: Alling Memorial GC, New Haven (R., 1972); Banner Lodge GC, Moodus (A.9, 1965); Crestbrook CC, Watertown (A.9, 1980); East Hartford GC (A.9, 1956), with Orrin Smith; Greenwoods CC, Torrington (R.1, 1961); High Ridge CC, Stamford (R.2, 1951), with William F. Mitchell; Hyfield CC, Middleburg (R.9, 1954), with Orrin Smith; Hyfield CC, Middleburg (A.9, 1954); Hyfield CC, Middleburg (R., 1964); Minnechaug GC, Glastonbury (R.9, 1951), with William F. Mitchell; New Haven CC (R.1, 1957); Pine Orchards CC, Brantford (A.4, 1961); Racebrook CC, Orange (R.2, 1957); Rockledge CC, West Hartford (R.9, 1954), with Orrin Smith; Rockrimmon CC, Stamford (A.9, 1953), with Orrin Smith; Stanley GC, New Britain (A.9, 1958), with Orrin Smith; Wepaug CC, Orange (R.13, 1961); Woodway CC, Darien (R.1, 1961).
Massachusetts: Cohasset CC, Quincy (R.9, 1971); Colonial GC, Lynnfield (R.5, 1954), with William F. Mitchell; Framingham CC (A.5, 1954), with Orrin Smith; Quincy CC (R.), with Orrin Smith; Red Hill CC, Reading (A.9, 1951), with William F. Mitchell; Red Hill CC, Reading (R.9, 1951), with William F. Mitchell; Winthrop GC (R., 1950), with William F. Mitchell.
New York: Lake Success GC (R.9, 1958), with Orrin Smith; Lake Success GC (A.9, 1958), with Orrin Smith; Orange County CC, Middletown (R.3, 1961); Somers CC (R.9, 1961); Somers CC (A.9, 1961).
Virginia: Langley AFB GC (A.9, 1969).

Benjamin W. Zink
A charter member of the GCSAA, Ben Zink served as superintendent at Acadia CC and later at Kirtland CC, both in Ohio. His design firm, Ben W. Zink and Son, planned a number of courses in Ohio and Florida.
Courses by: Ben W. Zink
Florida: Palm River CC, Naples (1960).
Ohio: Aqua Marine Swim C (Par 3); Erie Shores GC, North Madison (1958); Hemlock Springs GC, Harpersfield; Pebble Brook CC, Cleveland; Shawnee Hills GC, Cleveland (9, 1957); Shelby CC; Tomahawk CC, Welshfield (1963).
Courses Remodeled & Added to by: Ben W. Zink
Ohio: Lander Haven CC (A.9, 1955);

PART THREE

A MASTER LIST OF GOLF COURSES CROSS-REFERENCED TO DESIGNERS.

This Master List was computer generated, and therefore follows a literal alphabetical format. A name beginning with an initial (e.g.: R.H. Storrer Estate GC) precedes all other names beginning with the same first letter. A name consisting of all capital letters (e.g.: TPC at Avenal) follows all other names beginning with the same first letter. A name consisting of more than one word will precede a similar name consisting of just a single word (e.g.: Spring Brook precedes Springbrook CC). Course names beginning with a numeral follow all courses beginning with a letter.

When two or more architects were involved in a partnership or joint effort, it is often impossible to now ascertain which architect took the most active role in a particular design. However, an effort has been made to list the Architect of Record first in all listings of such collaborations.

Abbreviations used are the same as appear in Section II, and are explained in the preface preceding those Profiles.

An effort has been made to list work on an individual course by different architects chronologically.

If an architect's name appears in italics on the master list, that person is not profiled in Part Two.

With some 21,000 links and courses in existence around the world, there are many layouts yet to be identified and included in the master list. This compilation is an ongoing project. The authors welcome additions, deletions and corrections so that an even more accurate and complete listing can be prepared.

A.C. Read GC (Mainside Course) (R)
Florida
Bill Amick

A.C. Read GC (Seaside Course)
Pensacola, Florida
Bill Amick

A.D. Dana Estate GC
Stowe, Vermont
Howard Watson

A.H. Blank GC
Des Moines, Iowa
Edward Lawrence Packard

A.H. Blank GC (A. 9)
Iowa
Edward Lawrence Packard,
Roger Packard

A.L. Gustin Jr. Memo. GC
Columbia, Missouri
Floyd Farley

A-Ga-Ming GC
Elk Rapids, Michigan
Roy Wetmore

A-Ga-Ming GC (A. 9)
Michigan
Chick Harbert

Aalborg GC (A. 9)
Denmark
John Harris

Abbey Hill GC
Buckinghamshire, England
J.J.F. Pennink, C.D. Lawrie

Abbey Leix GC (R)
Ireland
Eddie Hackett

Abbey Springs GC
Fontana, Wisconsin
Ken Killian, Dick Nugent

Abbeydale GC
Yorkshire, England
Herbert Fowler

Abenaqui C (R)
New Hampshire
Geoffrey S. Cornish, William G. Robinson

Abenaqui CC (R. 3)
New Hampshire
Manny Francis

Abercrombie CC (A. 9)
Nova Scotia
Clinton E. Robinson

Abercrombie CC (R)
England
H.S. Colt

Aberdeen G&CC
Boynton Beach, Florida
Desmond Muirhead

Aberdeen Proving Grounds GC
Maryland
Edmund B. Ault

Aberdour GC (A. 3)
Scotland
Fraser Middleton

Aberdovey GC (R)
Wales
H.S. Colt

Aberdovey GC (R)
Wales
James Braid

Aberdovey GC (R)
Wales
Herbert Fowler

Abergele and Pensare GC
Clwyd, Wales
F.G. Hawtree, Fred W. Hawtree

Aberystwyth GC
Dyfed, Wales
Harry Vardon

Abidjan GC
Ivory Coast
Pier Mancinelli

Abiko CC
Japan
Rokuro Akaboshi, Shiro Akaboshi

Abilene CC (R)
Kansas
Dewitt "Maury" Bell

Abilene CC (R. 1)
Texas
Marvin Ferguson

Abingdon CC
Illinois
Tom Bendelow

Abington CC
Pennsylvania
Robert Strange

Abitibi GC
Iroquois Falls, Ontario
Willie Park Jr

Abridge GC
England
Henry Cotton

Acacia CC
Harlem, Illinois
William B. Langford, Theodore J. Moreau

Acacia CC (R) NLE
Illinois
Robert Bruce Harris

Acacia CC
South Euclid, Ohio
Donald Ross, Sandy Alves

Acadian Hills CC
Lafayette, Louisiana
Luca Barbato

Acadian Hills CC (R)
Louisiana
Jay Riviere

Acapulco CC
Mexico
John Bredemus

Acapulco CC (R. 9)
Mexico
Percy Clifford

Acapulco CC (A. 9)
Mexico
Percy Clifford

Acapulco Princess CC
Mexico
Ted Robinson

Acres of Fun GC
Greenfield, Indiana
Gary Kern

Acton GC
England
Willie Park Jr

Adam Springs G&CC
Cobb, California
Jack Fleming

Adams Park Muni
Bartlesville, Oklahoma
Floyd Farley

Addington Court GC (Lower Course)
Surrey, England
F.G. Hawtree, J.H. Taylor

Addington Court GC (New Course)
Surrey, England
Fred W. Hawtree

Addington Court GC (Old Course)
Surrey, England
F.G. Hawtree, J.H. Taylor

Addington GC (New Course)
Surrey, England
J.F. Abercromby

Addington GC (Old Course)
Surrey, England
J.F. Abercromby

Addington Palace GC
Surrey, England
F.G. Hawtree, J.H. Taylor

Addison Pinnacle CC
New York
Geoffrey S. Cornish, William G. Robinson

Adios CC
Deerfield Beach, Florida
Arnold Palmer, Ed Seay

Adirondacks C NLE
Lake Placid, New York
Alister Mackenzie

Adolfo Siro GC
Argentina
Mungo Park II

Adventure Inn GC NLE
Hilton Head Island, South Carolina
George W. Cobb

Agate Beach GC
Newport, Oregon
Frank Stenzel

Agate Beach GC (R. 9)
Oregon
Fred Federspiel

Agawam Hunt C
Providence, Rhode Island
Willie Park Jr

Agawam Hunt C (R)
Rhode Island
Donald Ross

Agawam Hunt C (R)
Rhode Island
Geoffrey S. Cornish

Agesta GC (A. 4)
Sweden
Jan Sederholm

Agesta GC (A. 9)
Sweden
Jan Sederholm

Agesta GC (A.13)
Sweden
Jan Sederholm

Aguasabon GC
Terrace Bay, Ontario
Howard Watson

Ahwatukee Lakes CC
Phoenix, Arizona
Gary Panks

Airco GC
Tampa, Florida
Chic Adams

Airdrie GC
Lanarkshire, Scotland
James Braid

Airport GC NLE
Oklahoma City, Oklahoma
Arthur Jackson

Airport Inn GC (A. 9)
Florida
William Bulmer

Airways GC
Fresno, California
Bert Stamps

Akarana GC (R)
New Zealand
Peter Thomson, Michael Wolveridge

Al Amin Temple CC
Little Rock, Arkansas
William B. Langford, Theodore J. Moreau

Ala Wai GC
Waikiki, Hawaii
Donald MacKay

Ala Wai GC (A. 9)
Hawaii
Donald MacKay

Ala Wai GC (R)
Hawaii
Bob Baldock

Ala Wai GC (R)
Hawaii
Robin Nelson

Alabang G&CC
Philippines
Robert Trent Jones Jr

Alamance CC
Burlington, North Carolina
Donald Ross

Alamance CC (R)
North Carolina
Willard Byrd, Clyde Johnston

Alameda Muni (Earl Fry Course)
California
William P. Bell

Alameda Muni (Jack Clark Course)
California
William F. Bell

Alameda Muni (Jack Clark Course) (R)
California
Desmond Muirhead

Alameda Muni (Jack Clark Course) (R)
California
Robert Muir Graves

Alamo CC now known as Oak Hill CC

Aland GC
Finland
Jan Sederholm

Alanwood GC
Sarver, Pennsylvania
X.G. Hassenplug

Alaqua CC
Florida
Karl Litten, Gary Player

Alassio GC
Italy
John Harris

Albany CC (A. 9)
Minnesota
Willie Kidd

Albany CC
New York
Robert Trent Jones

Albany CC (R) NLE
New York
Willie Ogg

Albany CC
Vermont
Walter Barcomb

Albarella GC
Rovigo, Italy
John Harris, *M. Croze*

Albemarle CC
West Newton, Massachusetts
Wayne Stiles

Albermarle Farms GC
Virginia
Arnold Palmer, Ed Seay

Albuquerque CC
New Mexico
John Van Kleek

Albuquerque CC (R)
New Mexico
Warren Cantrell

Albuquerque CC (R)
New Mexico
Leon Howard

Alcester GC
South Dakota
Ralph Gobel

Alcoma CC
Pennsylvania
Emil Loeffler, *John McGlynn*

Alcoma CC (R)
Pennsylvania
Ferdinand Garbin

Aldeburgh GC
Suffolk, England
Willie Fernie

Aldeburgh GC (R)
England
Willie Park Jr
Aldeburgh GC (R)
England
J.H. Taylor
Alden Pines GC
Pineland, Florida
Gordon G. Lewis
Alderbrook G&CC
Union, Washington
Roy L. Goss, *Glen Proctor*
Alderney GC
Channel Islands
J.J.F. Pennink
Alderwood CC NLE
Portland, Oregon
A. Vernon Macan
Alderwood CC (R)
Oregon
A. Vernon Macan
Alexandria G&CC
Mississippi
Tom Bendelow
Algona CC
Iowa
Willie Dunn Jr
Algonquin CC
Glendale, Missouri
Robert Foulis
Algonquin CC (R)
Missouri
Geoffrey S. Cornish, Brian Silva
Algonquin Hotel GC
St. Andrews, New Brunswick
Donald Ross
Alhambra G&CC
Orlando, Florida
Bill Amick
Alhambra Muni
California
William F. Bell
Alhambra Muni (A. 9)
California
Algie Pulley
Alhambra Muni (R. 9)
California
Algie Pulley
Alice CC
Texas
Ralph Plummer
Alice Springs GC
Australia
Peter Thomson, Michael
Wolveridge
Alisal GC
California
William F. Bell
Aliwal North GC
South Africa
John Watt
All-American GC
Sharpes, Florida
Robert Trent Jones
All-View GC
Maryland
Edmund B. Ault
All-View GC (R)
Maryland
Desmond Muirhead
Alladin Hotel GC NLE
Las Vegas, Nevada
Bob Baldock
Allandale GC
Ontario
Stanley Thompson
Allegheny CC
Sewickley, Pennsylvania
Tom Bendelow
Allegheny CC (A. 3)
Pennsylvania
Herbert Fowler
Allegheny CC (R)
Pennsylvania
Herbert Fowler
Allegheny CC (R. 3)
Pennsylvania
Donald Ross
Allegheny CC (R)
Pennsylvania
Ed Seay
Allen CC
Louisiana
Vernon Meyer

Allendale CC
New Bedford, Massachusetts
Geoffrey S. Cornish
Alliance CC (R)
Ohio
Ferdinand Garbin
Alling Memorial GC
New Haven, Connecticut
Robert D. Pryde
Alling Memorial GC (R)
Connecticut
Al Zikorus
Allston CC NLE
Massachusetts
George Wright
Almaden G&CC
San Jose, California
Jack Fleming
Almaden G&CC (R. 1)
California
Robert Muir Graves
Almaden G&CC (R)
California
Peter Thomson, Michael
Wolveridge, Ronald Fream
Almanor West GC
California
Doug Pohlson
Almerimar GC
Almeria, Spain
Ron Kirby, Gary Player, Denis
Griffiths
Alnmouth GC
Northumberland, England
Mungo Park
Alnmouth GC (R)
England
P.M. Ross
Aloha Golf
Spain
Javier Arana
Alondra Park GC (Course No. 1)
Lawndale, California
William P. Bell, William H.
Johnson
**Alondra Park GC (Course No. 1)
(R)**
California
Ted Robinson
Alondra Park GC (Course No. 2)
Lawndale, California
Cecil B. Hollingsworth
Alpine Bay Y&CC
Alpine, Alabama
Robert Trent Jones, Rees Jones
Alpine CC
Comstock Park, Michigan
Mark DeVries
Alpine CC
New Jersey
A.W. Tillinghast
Alpine CC (R)
New Jersey
William Gordon
Alpine CC
Granston, Rhode Island
Geoffrey S. Cornish
Alpine CC
American Fork, Utah
William H. Neff
Alpine Resort GC
Wisconsin
Francis H. "Fritz" Schaller
Alpine Valley GC
Georgia
Ron Kirby
Alpino Di Stresa GC
Italy
James Gannon
Alta Mesa CC
Mesa, Arizona
Dick Phelps
Alta Sierra CC
Grass Valley, California
Bob Baldock, Robert L. Baldock
Alta Vista CC
Placentia, California
Harry Rainville
Alta Vista CC (A. 9)
California
Harry Rainville, David Rainville
Altadena GC
California
William P. Bell

Alto Lakes G&CC
New Mexico
Milt Coggins
Alto Lakes G&CC (A. 9)
New Mexico
Arthur Davis, Ron Kirby, Gary
Player
Alton Beach GC NLE
Miami, Florida
Willie Park Jr
Alton GC
Hampshire, England
Willie Park Jr
Alton Jones Estate GC
Albemarle, Virginia
James Root
Altus CC
New Mexico
Ralph Plummer
Altus GC (A. 9)
Oklahoma
Floyd Farley
Alva G&CC
Oklahoma
Floyd Farley
Alvamar CC
Lawrence, Kansas
Melvin Anderson
Alvamar CC (A. 9)
Kansas
Melvin Anderson
Alvamar GC
Lawrence, Kansas
Bob Dunning
Alwoodley GC
Leeds, England
Alister Mackenzie, H.S. Colt
Alyth GC
Tayside, Scotland
Old Tom Morris
Alyth GC (R)
Scotland
James Braid
Amana Colonies GC
Amana, Iowa
William James Spear
Amarillo CC
Texas
William A. McConnell
Amarillo CC (R)
Texas
Warren Cantrell
Amarillo CC (R)
Texas
Don Sechrest
Amarillo Muni
Texas
Joseph S. Finger
Ambassador Hotel GC NLE
Los Angeles, California
Herbert Fowler
Amberwood Village GC
Stittsville, Ontario
John Watson
Ambo Chesterfield GC
Missouri
Walter F. Ambo
Ambridge CC
Pennsylvania
Emil Loeffler, *John McGlynn*
Amelia Island Plantation GC
Fernadina Beach, Florida
Pete Dye
American Golfers C
Fort Lauderdale, Florida
Robert Trent Jones
American Legion GC (R)
Georgia
Hugh Moore
American Legion GC
Iowa
Chic Adams
**Americana Canyon Hotel GC
formerly known as Canyon GC**
California
William F. Bell
Americana Canyon Hotel GC (R)
California
William F. Mitchell
Americana Great Gorge GC
McAfee, New Jersey
George Fazio, Tom Fazio

**Americana Lake Geneva GC
(Briarpatch)**
Wisconsin
Pete Dye, Jack Nicklaus
**Americana Lake Geneva GC
(Brute)**
Lake Geneva, Wisconsin
Robert Bruce Harris
Amery GC (R. 9)
Wisconsin
Don Herfort
Ames G&CC
Iowa
Don Sechrest
Amherst Audubon GC
Williamsville, New York
William Harries
Amherst CC
New Hampshire
William F. Mitchell
Amherst GC
Massachusetts
Walter Hatch
Amityville CC
New York
Tom Winton
Ammonoosuc Inn & GC
New Hampshire
Ralph Barton
Ampfield Par 3 GC
England
Henry Cotton
Amsterdam Muni
New York
Robert Trent Jones
Anaconda CC
Montana
Gregor MacMillan
Anaheim Hills GC
California
Richard Bigler
Anasazi GC
Phoenix, Arizona
Roy Dye, Gary Grandstaff
Anasazi GC (R)
Arizona
Arthur Jack Snyder
Anasazi GC (R.18)
Arizona
Greg Nash
Anchorage Muni
Alaska
William Newcomb
Ancil Hoffman GC
Sacramento, California
William F. Bell
Anderson AFB GC
Guam
Joe Lee
Anderson CC (A. 9)
Indiana
William H. Diddel
Anderson CC (R. 9)
Indiana
William H. Diddel
Anderson CC
South Carolina
Tom Bendelow
Anderson GC
Killeen, Texas
Perry Maxwell, Press Maxwell
Anderson Tucker Oaks GC
Anderson, California
William H. Tucker Jr
Andorra Springs GC
Lafayette Hill, Pennsylvania
Horace W. Smith
Andover GC
Massachusetts
W.H. Follett
Andrews AFB GC (East Course)
Maryland
Frank Murray, Russell Roberts
Andrews AFB GC (West Course)
Maryland
Frank Murray
Andrews County GC
Texas
Warren Cantrell
Andros Island CC NLE
Bahamas
George W. Cobb

Androscoggin Valley CC
New Hampshire
Alex Chisholm
Angel Fire GC
Eagle Nest, New Mexico
Ron Garl
Angelholm GC
Sweden
Jan Sederholm
Anglesey GC
Wales
Fred W. Hawtree, Martin
Hawtree
Anglo-American Club
Lec. L'Achign, Quebec
A.W. Tillinghast
Ankara GC
Turkey
George Wadsworth
Ankeny G&CC
Iowa
Leo Johnson
Annandale CC (R)
California
William Watson
Annandale CC (A. 2)
California
William P. Bell
Annandale CC (R. 2)
California
William P. Bell
Annandale CC (R)
California
Robert Trent Jones, Robert Trent
Jones Jr
Annandale GC (R)
California
Walter Fovargue
Annandale GC (R)
California
Norman Macbeth
Annandale GC (R. 4)
California
Jack Croke
Annandale GC
Jackson, Mississippi
Jack Nicklaus, Jay Morrish, Bob
Cupp, Scott Miller
Annanhill GC
Ayrshire, Scotland
Fraser Middleton
Annapolis Roads GC
Maryland
Charles Banks
Anniston CC (R)
Alabama
Harold Williams
Anniston CC (R)
Alabama
Ed Seay
Ansley GC
Atlanta, Georgia
Ward Northrup
Antelope Hills GC
Prescott, Arizona
Lawrence Hughes
Antelope Valley CC
Palmdale, California
William F. Bell
Antigo & Bass Lake CC
Antigo, Wisconsin
Edward Lawrence Packard
Antioch Muni
California
Bob Baldock
Antioch Muni (A. 9)
California
Bob Baldock
**Antlers CC now known as
Arrowhead GC**
Antlers CC
New York
William H. Tucker
Antonio GC
Toronto, Ontario
Clinton E. Robinson
Antrim Dells GC
Atwood, Michigan
Bruce Matthews, Jerry Matthews
Antwerp GC
Belgium
Seymour Dunn

Apache CC now known as Golden Hills Resort GC

Apache Wells CC
Mesa, Arizona
Arthur Jack Snyder

Apache Wells CC (A. 9)
Arizona
Milt Coggins

Apawamis C
Rye, New York
William F. Davis

Apawamis C
Rye, New York
Willie Dunn Jr, *Maturin Ballou*

Apawamis C (R)
New York
Tom Winton

Apawamis C (R)
New York
Peter W. Lees

Apawamis C (A. 9)
New York
Tom Bendelow

Apawamis C (R)
New York
Alfred H. Tull

Apawamis C (R)
New York
George Fazio, Tom Fazio

Apollo Beach G & Sea C
Florida
Robert Trent Jones, Frank Duane

Apollo Beach G & Sea C (A. 9)
Florida
Robert Trent Jones, Roger Rulewich

Appanoose G&CC (R)
Iowa
Charles Calhoun

Apple Creek G&CC
Bismarck, North Dakota
Robert Bruce Harris

Apple Orchard CC (R. 4)
Illinois
David Gill

Apple Ridge CC
New Jersey
Clinton Carlough

Apple Ridge CC
Mahwah, New Jersey
Hal Purdy

Apple Valley CC
California
William P. Bell, William F. Bell

Apple Valley CC (A. 9)
California
William F. Bell

Apple Valley CC
Bartlett, Illinois
Edward Lawrence Packard

Apple Valley GC
Lake Lure, North Carolina
Ellis Maples, Dan Maples

Apple Valley GC
Howard, Ohio
William Newcomb

Applewood GC
Golden, Colorado
Press Maxwell

Applewood Muni
Omaha, Nebraska
Leon Howard

Appomattox CC
Virginia
Fred Findlay, *Ben Loving*

April Sound CC
Conroe, Texas
Carlton E. Gipson

Aptos Seascape GC now known as Rio Del Mar GC

Aqua Caliente GC now known as Tijuana CC

Aqua Marine Swim C
Ohio
Ben W. Zink

Arbor Hills CC
Michigan
Arthur Ham

Arcadia GC
Florida
Ted Eller

Arcadian Shores G&RC
Myrtle Beach, South Carolina
Rees Jones

Arcola CC
Paramus, New Jersey
Harry Auchterlonie

Arcola CC (R)
New Jersey
Robert Trent Jones, Frank Duane

Arcot Hall GC
Northumberland, England
James Braid, John R. Stutt

Ardee GC (R)
Ireland
Eddie Hackett

Ardee GC (A. 9)
Ireland
Eddie Hackett

Ardeer GC
Ayrshire, Scotland
J. Hamilton Stutt

Ardsley CC
Ardsley-on-Hudson, New York
Willie Dunn Jr

Ardsley CC (A. 9)
New York
William H. Tucker

Ardsley CC (R)
New York
Stephen Kay

Arenzano G&TC
Italy
Donald Harradine

Argyle CC
Chevy Chase, Maryland
William H. Tucker, Dr. Walter S. Harban

Argyle CC (R)
Maryland
Edmund B. Ault, Al Jamison

Arikikapakapa GC
New Zealand
Charles H. Redhead

Arima Royal GC
Hyogo, Japan
O. Ueda

Arispie Lake CC
Princeton, Illinois
John Darrah

Arizona Biltmore GC (Adobe Course)
Phoenix, Arizona
William P. Bell

Arizona Biltmore GC (Links Course)
Phoenix, Arizona
William Johnston

Arizona City CC
Arizona
Arthur Jack Snyder

Arizona CC
Phoenix, Arizona
Ernest Suggs, Willie Wansa

Arizona CC (R)
Arizona
Gary Panks

Arizona CC (R. 4)
Arizona
Joseph S. Finger

Arizona CC (R)
Arizona
Johnny Bulla

Arizona CC (R)
Arizona
Tom Clark, Bill Love

Arkansas City CC
Kansas
Perry Maxwell

Arkansas City CC (A. 9)
Kansas
Dick Metz

Arklow GC
County Wicklow, Ireland
F.G. Hawtree, J.H. Taylor

Arklow GC (A. 9)
Ireland
Eddie Hackett

Arlington GC NLE
Arlington Heights, Illinois
David Gill

Arlington Lakes GC
Arlington Heights, Illinois
David Gill, Garrett Gill

Arlington Park GC
Arlington Heights, Illinois
David Gill

Arlmont CC
Arlington, Massachusetts
Eugene "Skip" Wogan

Armour Fields GC NLE
Kansas City, Missouri
Smiley Bell

Army GC
England
Col R.E. Bagot

Army GC (R)
England
C.K. Cotton, J.J.F. Pennink

Army-Navy CC (Arlington Course)
Arlington, Virginia
Major Richard D. Newman

Army-Navy CC (Arlington Course) (R. 5)
Virginia
Buddy Loving, Algie Pulley

Army-Navy CC (Arlington Course) (R. 3)
Virginia
Edmund B. Ault

Army-Navy CC (Arlington Course) (R. 5)
Virginia
Edmund B. Ault, Tom Clark,Bill Love

Army-Navy CC (Fairfax Course)
Fairfax, Virginia
Herbert Strong

Army-Navy CC (Fairfax Course) (R)
Virginia
George W. Cobb

Army-Navy CC (Fairfax Course) (R)
Virginia
Edmund B. Ault

Army-Navy CC (Fairfax Course) (R. 2)
Virginia
Buddy Loving, Algie Pulley

Army-Navy CC (Fairfax Course) (R. 2)
Virginia
Edmund B. Ault, Brian Ault,Bill Love

Aroma Park GC
Kankakee, Illinois
William B. Langford

Aronimink GC NLE
Philadelphia, Pennsylvania
Alex Findlay

Aronimink GC
Newton Square, Pennsylvania
Donald Ross

Aronimink GC (R) NLE
Pennsylvania
A.W. Tillinghast

Aronimink GC (R)
Pennsylvania
Dick Wilson

Aronimink GC (R)
Pennsylvania
George Fazio, Tom Fazio

Aroostook Valley GC (A. 9)
Maine
Howard Watson

Aroostook Valley GC (R. 9)
Maine
Howard Watson

Arrowbrook CC
Chesterfield, Indiana
John Darrah

Arrowbrook CC
Bordentown, New Jersey
Hal Purdy

Arrowhead CC
Ft. Lauderdale, Florida
Bill Watts

Arrowhead CC
Chillicothe, Illinois
William James Spear

Arrowhead CC (North Course)
Glendale, Arizona
Arnold Palmer, Ed Seay,Harrison Minchew

Arrowhead CC (South Course)
Glendale, Arizona
Arnold Palmer, Ed Seay,Harrison Minchew

Arrowhead GC
Littleton, Colorado
Robert Trent Jones Jr, Gary Roger Baird

Arrowhead GC
Jasper, Georgia
Arthur Davis

Arrowhead GC formerly known as Antlers CC
Wheaton, Illinois
Stanley Pelchar

Arrowhead GC (A. 9)
Illinois
David Gill

Arrowhead GC
Alexandria, Minnesota
Donald G. Brauer, Emile Perret

Arrowhead GC
Molalla, Oregon
Kip Kappler

Arrowhead Park GC
Minster, Indiana
Bob Simmons

Arrowhead State Park GC
Eufaula, Oklahoma
Floyd Farley

Arrowhead State Park GC (A. 9)
Oklahoma
Dave Bennett

Arroyo del Oso GC
Albuquerque, New Mexico
Arthur Jack Snyder

Arroyo Seco GC
Banning, California
William H. Johnson

Artesia CC
New Mexico
Ralph Plummer

Arthur Pack GC
Tucson, Arizona
Dave Bennett

Arthur Raymond GC
Columbus, Ohio
Robert Trent Jones

Artondale G&CC (R)
Washington
Robert Muir Graves

Aruba GC (R. 9)
Aruba
C.H. Anderson

Arvida GC
Quebec
Stanley Thompson

Asbestos G&CC
Quebec
Howard Watson

Asbury Park GC (R)
New Jersey
Hal Purdy

Ascarte Park Muni
El Paso, Texas
George Hoffman

Ashbourne GC (R)
England
J.J.F. Pennink

Ashbrook GC
Scotch Plains, New Jersey
Alfred H. Tull

Ashburnham GC
Wales
Charles Gibson

Ashburnham GC (A. 9)
Wales
William Tate

Ashburnham GC (R)
Wales
F.G. Hawtree, J.H. Taylor

Ashburnham GC (R)
Wales
C.K. Cotton

Ashburnham GC (A. 1)
Wales
C.K. Cotton

Ashburton GC (R)
New Zealand
Peter Thomson, Michael Wolveridge

Asheville CC formerly known as Beaver Lake GC
North Carolina
Donald Ross

Asheville Muni
North Carolina
Donald Ross

Ashford Castle GC
County Galway, Ireland
Eddie Hackett

Ashiya CC
Hyogo, Japan
Y. Yasuda, Y. Sato

Ashland CC
Nebraska
Henry B. Hughes, Richard Watson

Ashland CC (A. 9)
Nebraska
Richard Watson

Ashley Wood GC
Dorset, England
Tom Dunn

Ashley Wood GC (R. 9)
England
J. Hamilton Stutt

Ashludie GC
Angus, Scotland
Willie Park Jr

Ashover GC
Derbyshire, England
Tom Williamson

Ashridge GC
Hertfordshire, England
Sir Guy Campbell, C.K. Hutchison,S.V. Hotchkin

Ashridge GC (R)
England
J. Hamilton Stutt

Ashridge GC (R)
England
Tom Simpson

Ashton-in-Makerfield GC (A. 9)
England
Fred W. Hawtree

Asiago GC
Italy
A. Girardi

Askernish GC
Western Isles, Scotland
Old Tom Morris

Askersunds GC
Ammeberg, Sweden
Ronald Fream

Aspen Grove GC
Winfield, British Columbia
V. Norbraten

Aspen Muni
Colorado
Frank Hummel

Aspen Valley GC
Flagstaff, Arizona
Jeff Hardin, Greg Nash

Aspen Valley GC (A. 9)
Arizona
Jeff Hardin, Greg Nash

Aspetuck Valley CC
Weston, Connecticut
Hal Purdy

Aspley Guise & Woburn Sands GC
Buckinghamshire, England
Sandy Herd, *Charles Willmott*

Assoc. Sportive du G de Meribel
France
Michael G. Fenn

Astorhurst CC
Bedford, Ohio
Harold Paddock

Astoria G&CC
Warrenton, Oregon
George Junor

Asuncion GC
Paraguay
Alberto Serra

Atalaya Park Hotel G&CC
Spain
Bernhard von Limburger

Atascadero CC NLE
California
John Duncan Dunn

Atascocita CC
Humble, Texas
Ralph Plummer

Athens CC
Alabama
William Burton

Athens CC
Georgia
Donald Ross

Athens CC (R)
Georgia
Hugh Moore
Athens CC (A. 9)
Georgia
George W. Cobb, John LaFoy
Athens CC
Ohio
Donald Ross
Athlone GC (R)
Ireland
C.K. Cotton
Atimoona G&CC
Tahiti
Willard Wilkinson
Atkinson-Stuart GC
Nebraska
Henry B. Hughes, Richard
Watson
Atlanta Athletic C (Course No.
1) now known as East Lake CC
Atlanta Athletic C (Course No.
2) now known as East Lake CC
(Course No. 2)
Atlanta Athletic C (Highlands
Course)
Duluth, Georgia
Robert Trent Jones
Atlanta Athletic C (Highlands
Course) (A. 9)
Georgia
Joseph S. Finger
Atlanta Athletic C (Highlands
Course) (R)
Georgia
George Fazio, Tom Fazio
Atlanta Athletic C (Highlands
Course) (R)
Georgia
Tom Fazio
Atlanta Athletic C (Riverside
Course)
Duluth, Georgia
Robert Trent Jones
Atlanta CC
Marietta, Georgia
Willard Byrd, Joseph S. Finger
Atlanta CC (R)
Georgia
Bob Cupp, Jay Morrish
Atlantic Beach CC NLE
Florida
A.W. Tillinghast
Atlantic City CC NLE
New Jersey
John Reid
Atlantic City CC
Northfield, New Jersey
William S. Flynn
Atlantic City CC (A.13) NLE
New Jersey
Willie Park Jr
Atlantic City CC (R) NLE
New Jersey
Willie Park Jr
Atlantic City Electric Co. GC
Somers Point, New Jersey
Hal Purdy
Atlantic Pines CC NLE
New Jersey
James MacMillan
Atlantis GC
Florida
William F. Mitchell
Atlantis GC (A. 9)
Florida
Bob Simmons
Atlantis GC
Tuckerton, New Jersey
George Fazio
Atlantis Inn & CC
Florida
Bob Simmons
Atlas Valley GC formerly known
as Flint GC
Michigan
Tom Bendelow
Atoka Muni
Oklahoma
Floyd Farley
Atsugi International CC (East
Course)
Kanagawa, Japan
Jun Mizutani

Atsugi International CC (East
Course) (R)
Japan
Jay Morrish, Bob Cupp
Atsugi International CC (West
Course)
Kanagawa, Japan
Jun Mizutani
Atsugi International CC (West
Course) (R)
Japan
Jay Morrish, Bob Cupp
Atwood GC
Rockford, Illinois
Charles Maddox
Auburn Center GC
Oregon
Wayne Larson, Sue Larson
Auburn CC
New York
Tom Bendelow
Auckland GC
Middlewood, New Zealand
F.G. Hood
Auckland GC (R)
New Zealand
Peter Thomson, Michael
Wolveridge
Audubon CC NLE
Louisville, Kentucky
Tom Bendelow
Audubon CC
Louisville, Kentucky
William B. Langford, Theodore J.
Moreau
Audubon State Park GC
Henderson, Kentucky
Edward Lawrence Packard
Auglaize C
Defiance, Ohio
William James Spear
Augsburg GC
West Germany
Bernhard von Limburger
Augsburg GC (R)
West Germany
Donald Harradine, Peter Harradine
Augusta CC
Georgia
David Ogilvie
Augusta CC (R)
Georgia
Donald Ross
Augusta CC (R)
Georgia
Hugh Moore
Augusta CC (R)
Georgia
Seth Raynor
Augusta CC (R)
Georgia
Bob Cupp
Augusta CC
Kansas
Charles Bland
Augusta CC
Augusta, Maine
Donald Ross
Augusta CC (A. 9)
Maine
Wayne Stiles, John Van Kleek
Augusta CC (R)
Maine
Orrin Smith, William F. Mitchell
Augusta CC
Staunton, Virginia
Fred Findlay
Augusta Golferama
Georgia
Luther O. "Luke" Morris
Augusta National GC
Augusta, Georgia
Alister Mackenzie, Robert Tyre
"Bobby" Jones Jr
Augusta National GC
Augusta, Georgia
George W. Cobb, Robert Tyre
"Bobby" Jones Jr
Augusta National GC (R)
Georgia
Perry Maxwell
Augusta National GC (R. 3)
Georgia
Robert Trent Jones

Augusta National GC (R)
Georgia
George W. Cobb
Augusta National GC (R)
Georgia
George Fazio
Augusta National GC (R. 1)
Georgia
Joseph S. Finger, Byron Nelson
Augusta National GC (R)
Georgia
Jay Morrish, Bob Cupp,Scott
Miller
Augusta National GC (R)
Georgia
Jack Nicklaus, Bob Cupp
Augusta National GC (A. 2)
Georgia
Tom Fazio
Aurora CC
Illinois
Tom Bendelow
Aurora CC
Louisiana
Tom Bendelow
Aurora CC
Ohio
William "Bert" Way
Aurora GC
Ontario
Stanley Thompson
Aurora Highlands GC
Aurora, Ontario
Renee Muylaert, Charles Muylaert
Aurora Hills GC
Aurora, Colorado
Henry B. Hughes
Ausable C
New York
Seymour Dunn
Austin CC
Minnesota
William H. Livie
Austin CC
Texas
Pete Dye, Alice Dye
Australian GC
Kensington, Australia
Alister Mackenzie
Australian GC (R)
Australia
Sloan Morpeth
Australian GC (R)
Australia
Jack Nicklaus, Jay Morrish,Bob
Cupp
Automobile C NLE
Grandview, Missouri
James Dalgleish
Automobile C of Peoria NLE
Illinois
Tom Bendelow
Ava G&CC
Missouri
Floyd Farley
Avalon Lakes GC
Warren, Ohio
Pete Dye, William Newcomb
Aviation Y&CC
Maryland
Edmund B. Ault
Aviation Y&CC (R)
Maryland
George W. Cobb
Aviation Y&CC NLE
Bendix, New Jersey
Herbert Strong
Avila G&CC
Tampa, Florida
Ron Garl
Avon CC
Connecticut
Robert J. Ross
Avon CC (A. 9)
Connecticut
Geoffrey S. Cornish, William G.
Robinson
Avon CC (R.18)
Connecticut
Geoffrey S. Cornish, William G.
Robinson
Avon Fields GC
Cincinnati, Ohio
William B. Langford, Theodore J.
Moreau

Avon Fields GC (R)
Ohio
William H. Diddel
Avon Oaks CC
Ohio
Harold Paddock
Avon Oaks CC (R. 6)
Ohio
Geoffrey S. Cornish, William G.
Robinson
Avondale-on-Hayden GC
Hayden Lake, Idaho
Mel "Curley" Hueston
Azalea City GC
Mobile, Alabama
Robert Bruce Harris
Azalea Sands GC
North Myrtle Beach, South
Carolina
Gene Hamm
Azuza Green GC
California
Bob Baldock
B.L. England GC
Beesley Point, New Jersey
Hal Purdy
Babe Zaharias GC
Tampa, Florida
Ron Garl
Baberton GC
Edinburgh, Scotland
Willie Park
Babson Park G&YC NLE
Florida
Seth Raynor
Back Acres CC (R. 9)
Mississippi
John Darrah
Back Acres CC (A. 9)
Mississippi
John Darrah
Back O'Beyond GC
Brewster, New York
Edward Ryder, Val Carlson
Bacon Park GC
Savannah, Georgia
Donald Ross
Bacon Park GC (R. 9)
Georgia
J. Porter Gibson
Bacon Park GC (A. 3)
Georgia
J. Porter Gibson
Bacon Park GC (R)
Georgia
Joseph S. Finger
Bacon Park GC (R)
Georgia
Ron Kirby, Denis Griffiths
Bacon Park GC (A. 9)
Georgia
Ron Kirby, Denis Griffiths
Bad Driburger GC
West Germany
Karl Hoffmann, Bernhard von
Limburger
Bad Kissengen GC
West Germany
C.S. Butchart
Bad Ragaz GC
Switzerland
Fred W. Hawtree
Bad Raqaz GC (R) NLE
Switzerland
Donald Harradine
Bad Waldsee GC
West Germany
Bernhard von Limburger
Bad Worishoffen GC
West Germany
Donald Harradine
Badgastein GC
Austria
Bernhard von Limburger
Baederwood GC
Pennsylvania
John Reid
Baederwood GC (R)
Pennsylvania
C.H. Alison, H.S. Colt
Bahama Reef CC
Bahamas
Byrecton Scott

Bahamas Princess Hotel & CC
(Emerald)
Freeport, Bahamas
Dick Wilson, Joe Lee,Bob
Simmons
Bahamas Princess Hotel & CC
(Ruby)
Freeport, Bahamas
Joe Lee
Bahia de Banderas
Mexico
Percy Clifford
Bahnfyre GC
St. Louis, Missouri
Marvin Ferguson
Bahrain Equestrain & Racing C
Manama, Bahrain
Earl Stone
Bainbridge CC
Georgia
Les Hall
Baiting Hollow CC
Riverhead, New York
Robert Trent Jones
Bajamar GC
Mexico
Percy Clifford
Baker GC
Oregon
George Junor
Baker Park GC
Minnesota
Don Herfort
Bakersfield CC
California
William F. Bell, William P. Bell
Bala CC
Philadelphia, Pennsylvania
William H. Tucker
Bala CC (R. 9)
Pennsylvania
William S. Flynn
Bala CC (A. 9)
Pennsylvania
William S. Flynn
Balandra Beach GC
Trinidad and Tobago
Peter Thomson, Michael
Wolveridge,Ronald Fream
Balbirnie Park GC
Scotland
Fraser Middleton
Balboa GC
Hot Springs Village, Arkansas
Tom Clark, Edmund B. Ault
Balboa Park GC
San Diego, California
William P. Bell
Balbriggan GC (R)
Ireland
Eddie Hackett
Balbriggan GC (A. 9)
Ireland
Bobby Browne
Bald Head Island CC
North Carolina
George W. Cobb
Bald Mountain GC
Detroit, Michigan
Wilfrid Reid, William Connellan
Bald Peak Colony C
New Hampshire
Donald Ross
Baldoc CC
Erwin, Pennsylvania
Orrin Smith
Baldwin Hills GC NLE
Los Angeles, California
George C. Thomas Jr, William P.
Bell
Bali Handara CC
Pancasari, Indonesia
John Harris, Peter
Thomson,Michael Wolveridge,
Ronald Fream
Bali International GC
Indonesia
George Hadi
Ballaghadereen GC
Ireland
Paddy Skerritt
Ballina GC (R)
Ireland
Eddie Hackett

Ballinasloe GC (R)
Ireland
Eddie Hackett
Ballinrobe GC (R)
Ireland
Eddie Hackett
Ballochmyle GC (A. 9)
Scotland
Fraser Middleton
Ballston Spa & CC (R. 9)
New York
Pete Craig
Ballston Spa & CC (A. 9)
New York
Pete Craig
Ballwin Muni GC
Missouri
Homer Herpel
Ballybofey & Stranorlar GC (A. 9)
Ireland
Eddie Hackett
Ballybunion GC
Ireland
P. Murphy
Ballybunion GC (New Course)
County Kerry, Ireland
Robert Trent Jones, Roger Rulewich,Cabell Robinson
Ballybunion GC (Old Course) (R. 9)
Ireland
James Braid
Ballybunion GC (Old Course) (A. 9)
Ireland
James Braid
Ballybunion GC (Old Course) (R)
Ireland
Tom Simpson, *Molly Gourlay*
Ballybunion GC (Old Course) (R)
Ireland
Eddie Hackett
Ballyclare GC (R. 9)
Northern Ireland
Peter Alliss, David Thomas,T.J.A. McAuley
Ballyliffin GC (R)
Ireland
Eddie Hackett
Balmoral GC
Belfast, Northern Ireland
P.M. Ross
Balmore GC
Glasgow, Scotland
James Braid
Balnagask GC
Aberdeen, Scotland
Fred W. Hawtree, Martin Hawtree
Balsams Hotel GC (Panorama Course)
Dixville Notch, New Hampshire
Donald Ross
Baltimore CC (Five Farms Course)
Maryland
A.W. Tillinghast
Baltimore CC (Roland Park Course) NLE
Maryland
Willie Dunn Jr
Baltimore CC (West Course)
Maryland
Edmund B. Ault
Baltinglass GC (R)
Ireland
Eddie Hackett
Baltusrol GC NLE
Springfield, New Jersey
Louis Keller
Baltusrol GC (Lower Course)
Springfield, New Jersey
A.W. Tillinghast
Baltusrol GC (Lower Course) (R)
New Jersey
Robert Trent Jones
Baltusrol GC (Upper Course)
Springfield, New Jersey
A.W. Tillinghast

Bamm Hollow CC
Middletown, New Jersey
Hal Purdy, Malcolm Purdy
Bancroft GC
Zimbabwe
Robert G. Grimsdell
Bandon Face Rock GC
Oregon
Lee Smith
Bandon GC (R)
Ireland
Eddie Hackett
Bandon GC (R)
Ireland
J.J.F. Pennink
Banff Springs GC
Banff, Alberta
Stanley Thompson
Bangladore GC
India
Peter Thomson, Michael Wolveridge
Bangor GC (R)
Northern Ireland
P.M. Ross
Bangor GC (R)
Northern Ireland
James Braid, John R. Stutt
Bangor GC (R. 1)
Northern Ireland
T.J.A. McAuley
Bangor Muni
Maine
Geoffrey S. Cornish
Bangpoo GC
Thailand
Arnold Palmer, Ed Seay
Banksville CC (A)
New York
Edward Ryder
Banner Lodge GC (A. 9)
Connecticut
Al Zikorus
Banning Muni
California
William F. Bell
Bannockburn G&CC NLE
Glen Echo, Maryland
William H. Tucker, Dr. Walter S. Harban
Banstead Downs GC
England
Wilfrid Reid
Bantry GC
County Cork, Ireland
Eddie Hackett
Banyan GC
West Palm Beach, Florida
Joe Lee, Rocky Roquemore
Banyan GC
Hawaii
Col. Alex Kahapea
Bar Harbor GC
Trenton, Maine
Phil Wogan
Bar-K GC
Lago Vista, Texas
Leon Howard
Baraboo CC
Wisconsin
Edward Lawrence Packard
Barbados G&CC
Christchurch, Barbados
John Harris
Barbara Worth GC (R)
California
Lawrence Hughes
Barcoven GC (R)
Ontario
Clinton E. Robinson
Bardmoor CC (East Course)
Largo, Florida
William H. Diddel
Bardmoor CC (East Course) (R)
Florida
Tom Fazio
Bardmoor CC (East Course) (R)
Florida
Edmund B. Ault
Bardmoor CC (North Course)
Largo, Florida
William H. Diddel

Bardmoor CC (South Course)
Largo, Florida
William H. Diddel
Barefoot Bay G&CC
Sebastian, Florida
Joe Lee
Barlassina CC
Milano, Italy
Donald Harradine
Barlassina CC (R)
Italy
John Harris
Barnehurst GC
Kent, England
James Braid
Barnham Broom GC
Norwich, England
J.J.F. Pennink
Barnton GC
England
Willie Park Jr
Baron Edward de Rothchild Estate GC
France
Tom Simpson
Baron Henri de Rothchild Estate GC
France
Tom Simpson
Barquisimeto CC
Venezuela
Joe Lee
Barranquilla CC NLE
Colombia
Frank Applebye
Barranquilla CC
Colombia
Ward Northrup
Barre CC
Vermont
Wayne Stiles
Barre CC (A. 9)
Vermont
Howard Watson
Barren River State Park GC
Glasgow, Kentucky
Benjamin Wihry
Barrie GC
Ontario
Robert Moote, *David Moote*
Barrington Hills CC
Barrington, Illinois
George O'Neill, *Jack Croke,*Joseph A. Roseman
Barrington Hills CC (R)
Illinois
C.D. Wagstaff
Barrington Hills CC (R. 1)
Illinois
William B. Langford
Barrington Hills CC (R)
Illinois
Edward Lawrence Packard
Barrington Hills CC (R)
Illinois
Roger Packard
Bartlett CC (R)
New York
Robert Trent Jones, Frank Duane
Bartlett Hills G&CC
Bartlett, Illinois
Charles Maddox, *Frank P. MacDonald*
Bartlett Hills G&CC (R. 1)
Illinois
Ken Killian
Barton Creek C
Austin, Texas
Tom Fazio
Barton CC
Vermont
Andrew Freeland
Barton Hills CC
Ann Arbor, Michigan
Donald Ross
Barton Hills CC (R)
Michigan
William Newcomb
Barton Hills CC (R)
Michigan
William H. Diddel
Barton Hills CC (R)
Michigan
Arthur Hills, Steve Forrest

Barton-on-Sea GC
England
H.S. Colt
Barwick GC
Delray Beach, Florida
John Strom, John Carpenter
Basel G&CC
Switzerland
Karl Hoffmann, Bernhard von Limburger
Bash Recreation GC NLE
Dublin, Ohio
Jack Kidwell
Basildon GC
Essex, England
J.J.F. Pennink
Basin Harbor C
Vermont
Alex "Nipper" Campbell
Basin Harbor C (R)
Vermont
Geoffrey S. Cornish
Basin Harbor C (R)
Vermont
William F. Mitchell
Basingstoke GC
England
James Braid
Bass River GC (R)
Massachusetts
Donald Ross
Bass Rocks GC
Gloucester, Massachusetts
Herbert Leeds
Bastad GC
Sweden
F.G. Hawtree, J.H. Taylor
Batchwood Hall GC
St. Albans, England
F.G. Hawtree, J.H. Taylor
Bath GC
England
Tom Dunn
Bathgate GC
East Lothian, Scotland
Willie Park
Baton Rouge CC
Louisiana
Bert Stamps
Baton Rouge CC (R)
Louisiana
Joe Lee
Baton Rouge CC (R)
Louisiana
Joseph S. Finger
Baton Rouge Muni NLE
Louisiana
Tom Bendelow
Battle Creek CC
Michigan
Willie Park Jr
Battle Creek CC (R)
Michigan
William Newcomb
Battlecreek GC
Salem, Oregon
Lynn Baxter
Battleground CC
Freehold, New Jersey
Hal Purdy
Battleground CC (Routing)
Freehold, New Jersey
James Gilmore Harrison
Battlement Mesa CC
Parachute, Colorado
Joseph S. Finger, Ken Dye
Bay of Quinte GC
Bellville, Ontario
Howard Watson
Bay of Quinte GC (A. 9)
Ontario
Clinton E. Robinson, Robert Moote
Bay of Quinte GC (R. 3)
Ontario
Gordon Witteveen
Bay City CC (R. 9) NLE
Maine
Robert Bruce Harris
Bay City CC (A. 9) NLE
Maine
Robert Bruce Harris

Bay City CC
Michigan
Edward Lawrence Packard
Bay Hill C
Orlando, Florida
Dick Wilson, Joe Lee,Robert von Hagge, Bob Simmons
Bay Hill C (A. 9)
Florida
Bob Simmons
Bay Hill C (R)
Florida
Arnold Palmer
Bay Hills GC
Maryland
Edmund B. Ault
Bay Hills GC
Nebraska
Larry Hagewood
Bay Park GC
East Rockaway, New York
David Gordon
Bay Point Y&CC (Club Meadows Course)
Panama City, Florida
Willard Byrd
Bay Point Y&CC (Lagoon Legend Course)
Panama City, Florida
Robert von Hagge, Bruce Devlin
Bay Pointe GC
Michigan
Ernest Fuller
Bay Ridge GC
Wisconsin
William E. Davis
Bay Tree Golf Plantation (Gold Course)
South Carolina
Russell Breeden, George Fazio,Tom Fazio
Bay Tree Golf Plantation (Green Course)
South Carolina
Russell Breeden, George Fazio,Tom Fazio
Bay Tree Golf Plantation (Silver Course)
South Carolina
Russell Breeden, George Fazio,Tom Fazio
Bay Valley GC
Bay City, Michigan
Desmond Muirhead, Jack Nicklaus
Bay View GC
Honolulu, Hawaii
Jimmy Ukauka
Bay West Lodge & CC
Florida
Chic Adams
Bayerwald G und Land C
Waldkirchen, West Germany
Donald Harradine
Baymeadows GC
San Francisco, California
Jack Fleming
Baymeadows GC
Jacksonville, Florida
Desmond Muirhead
Bayou Barriere GC
New Orleans, Louisiana
Jimmy Self
Bayou Bend CC (R)
Louisiana
Jay Riviere
Bayou De Siard CC
Monroe, Louisiana
Perry Maxwell, Press Maxwell
Bayou De Siard CC (R)
Louisiana
John Cochran
Bayou G&CC
Oregon
William Sander
Bayou GC
Texas City, Texas
Joseph S. Finger
Bayreuth GC
West Germany
Bernhard von Limburger
Bayshore GC NLE
Miami Beach, Florida
H.C.C. Tippetts

Bayshore GC (R) NLE
Florida
Red Lawrence
Bayshore Muni
Miami Beach, Florida
Robert von Hagge, Bruce Devlin
Bayside CC
San Diego, California
William P. Bell
Bayside CC NLE
Rhode Island
Seth Raynor
Bayside Links NLE
New York
Tom Wells
Bayside Links (R)
New York
Alister Mackenzie
Bayside Muni
Eureka, California
H. Chandler Egan
Bayview G&CC
Thornhill, Ontario
Clinton E. Robinson
Bayview G&CC (R)
Ontario
Robert Moote
Bayview GC
Ontario
Stanley Thompson
Baywood CC NLE
Houston, Texas
Joseph S. Finger
Baywood CC (R)
Texas
Jay Riviere
Baywood G&CC
Arcata, California
Bob Baldock
Baywood G&CC (R)
California
Robert Muir Graves
Beach Grove G&CC
Walkerville, Ontario
Stanley Thompson
Beach Grove G&CC (R)
Ontario
Clinton E. Robinson
Beachwood GC
North Myrtle Beach, South
  Carolina
Gene Hamm
Beacon CC (A. 9)
New York
Herbert Strong
Beacon CC (R. 9)
New York
Herbert Strong
Beacon Hill CC
Atlantic Heights, New Jersey
Alec Ternyei
Beacon Hills GC
Creston, Iowa
Richard Watson
Beacon Light GC
Columbus, Ohio
Wright McCallip
Beacon Park GC
West Lancashire, England
D.M.A. Steel
Beacon Woods CC
New Port Richey, Florida
Bill Amick
Beaconsfield G&CC
Montreal, Quebec
Willie Park Jr
Beaconsfield G&CC (R)
Quebec
Clinton E. Robinson
Beaconsfield G&CC (R)
Quebec
Stanley Thompson
Beaconsfield G&CC (R. 6)
Quebec
Howard Watson
Beaconsfield GC
England
H.S. Colt
Beale AFB CC
California
Bob Baldock
Beamish Park GC
England
Sir Guy Campbell, Henry Cotton

Bear Creek CC
Redmond, Washington
Jack Frei
Bear Creek G&RC (East Course)
Dallas-Ft. Worth, Texas
Ted Robinson
Bear Creek G&RC (West Course)
Dallas-Ft. Worth, Texas
Ted Robinson
**Bear Creek Golf World
  (Executive Crs.)**
Houston, Texas
Bruce Littell
**Bear Creek Golf World (Masters
  Course)**
Houston, Texas
Jay Riviere
**Bear Creek Golf World
  (Presidents Crs.)**
Houston, Texas
Bruce Littell
Bear Creek GC
Wildomar, California
Jack Nicklaus, Jay Morrish, Bob
  Cupp, Scott Miller
Bear Creek GC
Golden, Colorado
Arnold Palmer, Ed Seay
Bear Creek GC
Oregon
Shirley Stone
Bear Creek GC
Hilton Head Island, South
  Carolina
Rees Jones
Bear Creek GC
Spartanburg, South Carolina
Russell Breeden, *Dan Breeden*
Bear Hill GC
Wakefield, Massachusetts
Alex Findlay
Bear Hill GC (R)
Massachusetts
Eugene "Skip" Wogan
Bear Hill GC (R)
Massachusetts
William F. Mitchell
Bear Lake West GC
Fish Haven, Idaho
Keith Downs
Bear Lakes CC
West Palm Beach, Florida
Jack Nicklaus, Bob Cupp
Bear Valley GC
California
Bob Baldock
Bear's Paw CC
Naples, Florida
Jack Nicklaus, Jay Morrish, Bob
  Cupp, Scott Miller
Beatrice CC
Nebraska
Tom Bendelow
**Beau Chene G&RC (Magnolia
  Course)**
Mandeville, Louisiana
Joe Lee, Rocky Roquemore
**Beau Chene G&RC (Magnolia
  Course) (A. 9)**
Louisiana
Joe Lee
**Beau Chene G&RC (Oak
  Course)**
Mandeville, Louisiana
Joe Lee, Rocky Roquemore
Beau Desert GC
Staffordshire, England
Herbert Fowler
Beauclerc CC
Jacksonville, Florida
Robert Trent Jones
Beauclerc CC (A. 9)
Florida
George W. Cobb
Beaumont CC
Hollidayburg, Pennsylvania
James Gilmore Harrison
Beaumont CC
Texas
Alex Findlay
Beaver Brook G&CC
Knoxville, Tennessee
Lon Mills

Beaver Brook GC
Clinton, New Jersey
Alec Ternyei
Beaver Creek CC
Lake Montezuma, Arizona
Arthur Jack Snyder
Beaver Creek CC
Hagerstown, Maryland
Reuben Hines
Beaver Creek GC
Avon, Colorado
Robert Trent Jones Jr, Don Knott
Beaver Creek Meadows CC
Ohio
*Bruce Weber, Mark Weber, Steve
  Weber*
Beaver Hill CC
Martinsville, Virginia
Ferdinand Garbin
Beaver Hills CC
Cedar Falls, Iowa
Edward Lawrence Packard
Beaver Island GC
Grand Island, New York
William Harries, *A. Russell Tryon*
**Beaver Lake GC now known as
  Asheville CC**
Beaver Lakes CC
Aliquippa, Pennsylvania
Ferdinand Garbin
Beaver Meadow CC
New York
Russell D. Bailey
Beaver Meadows Muni (A. 9)
New Hampshire
Geoffrey S. Cornish, William G.
  Robinson
Beaver Valley CC
Beaver Falls, Pennsylvania
Emil Loeffler, *John McGlynn*
Beaver Valley CC (R. 9)
Pennsylvania
James Gilmore Harrison,
  Ferdinand Garbin
Beaver Valley CC (A. 9)
Pennsylvania
James Gilmore Harrison,
  Ferdinand Garbin
Beavers Bend State Park GC
Broken Bow, Oklahoma
Floyd Farley
Beaverstown GC
Ireland
Eddie Hackett
Bebington GC (A. 9)
England
Fred W. Hawtree
Beckenham Place Park GC
England
Tom Dunn
Beckett Ridge G&CC
Cincinnati, Ohio
Jack Kidwell, Michael Hurdzan
Bedale GC (R)
England
J.J.F. Pennink
Bedens Brook C
Skillman, New Jersey
Dick Wilson, Joe Lee
Bedford AFB GC
Massachusetts
Manny Francis
Bedford AFB GC (R)
Massachusetts
Brian Silva, Geoffrey S. Cornish
Bedford G&TC (R. 9)
New York
Geoffrey S. Cornish
Bedford G&TC (R. 9)
New York
Devereux Emmet
Bedford G&TC (A. 9)
New York
Devereux Emmet
Bedford Springs C0
Pennsylvania
Arthur M. Goss
Bedford Springs C0 (R)
Pennsylvania
A.W. Tillinghast
Bedford Springs C0 (R)
Pennsylvania
Donald Ross

Bedford Springs C0 (R)
Pennsylvania
James Gilmore Harrison
Bedford Valley CC
Battle Creek, Michigan
William F. Mitchell
Bedlingtonshire GC
Northumberland, England
J.J.F. Pennink
Bedouin Hills GC
Saudi Arabia
John Arnold
Bedwell Park GC
England
Fred W. Hawtree, Martin
  Hawtree
Beech Mountain GC
Banner Elk, North Carolina
Willard Byrd
Beech Park Rathcoole GC
County Dublin, Ireland
Eddie Hackett
Beechmont CC
Cleveland, Ohio
Stanley Thompson
Beechwood CC
Ahoskie, North Carolina
Russell Breeden
Beechwood GC
LaPorte, Indiana
William H. Diddel
Beechwood GC (R. 9)
Ontario
Robert Moote
Beechwood GC (A. 9)
Ontario
Robert Moote
Beeson Park CC
Winchester, Indiana
William H. Diddel
Beeston Fields GC
Nottinghamshire, England
Tom Williamson
Beeville CC
Texas
George Albrecht
Beijing GC (North Course)
China
Brad Benz, Mike Poellot, Mark
  Rathert
Beijing GC (South Course)
China
Brad Benz, Mike Poellot, Mark
  Rathert
Bel Aire CC
Armonk, New York
Al Zikorus
Bel Aire G&CC
Bowie, Maryland
Frank Murray, Russell Roberts
Bel Campo GC
Connecticut
Joseph Brunoli
Bel-Air CC
Los Angeles, California
George C. Thomas Jr, William P.
  Bell, Jack Neville
Bel-Air CC (R. 3)
California
William H. Johnson
Bel-Air CC (R)
California
Dick Wilson
Bel-Air CC (R. 1)
California
George Fazio
Bel-Air CC (R)
California
William F. Bell
Bel-Air CC (R. 1)
California
Robert Trent Jones Jr, Gary
  Roger Baird
Bel-Mar GC
Illinois
Tom Bendelow
Bel-Meadow G&CC
Mount Clare, West Virginia
Robert Trent Jones
Belfry GC (Brabazon Course)
England
Peter Alliss, David Thomas

Belfry GC (Derby Course)
England
Peter Alliss, David Thomas
Belgrade Hotel GC
Belgrade Lakes, Maine
Alex Findlay
Belham River Valley GC
Montserrat
Edmund B. Ault
Belk Park GC
Wood River, Illinois
Edward Lawrence Packard, Brent
  Wadsworth
Belk Park GC (A. 9)
Illinois
Edward Lawrence Packard
Bella Vista CC
Arkansas
Joseph S. Finger
Bella Vista CC (R)
Arkansas
Edmund B. Ault
Bellach GC
Austria
Bernhard von Limburger
Bellaire GC
Phoenix, Arizona
Red Lawrence, Jeff Hardin, Greg
  Nash
Belle Glade Muni
Florida
Karl Litten, Gary Player
Belle Haven CC
Alexandria, Virginia
Leonard Macomber
Belle Haven CC (R)
Virginia
George W. Cobb
Belle Haven CC (R)
Virginia
Edmund B. Ault
Belle Isle Muni NLE
Detroit, Michigan
Ernest Way
Belle Meade CC
Thomson, Georgia
Boone A. Knox, Nick Price
Belle Meade CC
Nashville, Tennessee
Donald Ross
Belle Meade CC (R)
Tennessee
Robert Trent Jones
Belle Meade CC (R)
Tennessee
Gary Roger Baird
Belle Terre CC
LaPlace, Louisiana
David Pfaff
Belleclaire G Links
Bayside, New York
Tom Wells
Bellefonte CC (R)
Kentucky
James Gilmore Harrison,
  Ferdinand Garbin
Belleisle GC
Ayrshire, Scotland
James Braid, John R. Stutt
Bellerive CC NLE
Normandy, Missouri
Robert Foulis
Bellerive CC
Creve Coeur, Missouri
Robert Trent Jones, Frank Duane
Bellerive CC (R. 1)
Missouri
Ron Kirby, Denis Griffiths
Belles Springs GC
Pennsylvania
Edmund B. Ault
**Belleview-Biltmore Hotel & C
  (East)**
Clearwater, Florida
Donald Ross
**Belleview-Biltmore Hotel & C
  (East) (R)**
Florida
Hal Purdy, Malcolm Purdy
**Belleview-Biltmore Hotel & C
  (West)**
Florida
John Duncan Dunn

267

Belleview-Biltmore Hotel & C
(West) (A. 9)
Florida
Donald Ross
Belleview-Biltmore Hotel & C
(West) (R. 9)
Florida
Donald Ross
Belleview-Biltmore Hotel & C
(West) (R)
Florida
Hal Purdy, Malcolm Purdy
Belleville CC
Kansas
Henry B. Hughes, Richard
Watson
Belleville G&CC (A. 9)
Ontario
Clinton E. Robinson
Belleville GC NLE
Kansas
Mike Ahearn
Bellevue CC
Melrose, Massachusetts
Eugene "Skip" Wogan
Bellevue CC
Syracuse, New York
Donald Ross
Bellevue CC (R)
New York
Willard Wilkinson
Bellevue CC (A. 3)
New York
Willard Wilkinson
Bellevue CC (A. 4)
New York
Frank Duane
Bellevue CC (R.14)
New York
Frank Duane
Bellevue CC
Sewickley, Pennsylvania
John Moorhead
Bellevue Muni
Washington
David W. Kent
Bellport GC (R)
New York
Robert Trent Jones
Bellwood CC
Texas
Tyrus Stroud
Belmont CC
Fresno, California
Bert Stamps
Belmont CC (R)
California
Bob Baldock
Belmont CC
Massachusetts
Donald Ross
Belmont CC (R)
Massachusetts
Orrin Smith
Belmont CC (R)
Massachusetts
Alfred H. Tull
Belmont CC
Perrysburg, Ohio
Robert Bruce Harris
Belmont CC (R)
Ohio
Arthur Hills
Belmont GC
Illinois
H.J. Tweedie
Belmont Hotel & C
Warwick, Bermuda
Devereux Emmet
Belmont Hotel & C (A. 9)
Bermuda
Devereux Emmet
Beloit CC
Wisconsin
Stanley Pelchar
Belton Muni
Missouri
Bob Baldock
Belton Park GC (R)
England
Tom Williamson
Belvedere CC
Hot Springs, Arkansas
Herman Hackbarth

Belvedere CC NLE
West Palm Beach, Florida
Sheffield A. Arnold
Belvedere G & Winter C (R)
Prince Edward Island
Clinton E. Robinson
Belvedere GC
Charlevoix, Michigan
William Watson
Belvedere Plantation CC
Hampstead, North Carolina
Russell T. Burney
Belvedere Plantation CC (A. 9)
North Carolina
Gene Hamm
Belvoir Park GC
Belfast, Northern Ireland
C.S. Butchart
Belvoir Park GC (R)
Northern Ireland
H.S. Colt, C.H. Alison
Ben Geren GC
Ft. Smith, Arkansas
Marvin Ferguson
Benbrook Muni
Ft. Worth, Texas
Ralph Plummer
Bend G&CC
Oregon
H. Chandler Egan
Bend G&CC (A. 9)
Oregon
Bob Baldock, Robert L. Baldock
Bend Muni
Oregon
Gene "Bunny" Mason
Bendinat GC
Spain
Fred W. Hawtree, Martin
Hawtree
Bendix Estate GC
Illinois
Jack Kohr
Benghazi GC
Libya
J.J.F. Pennink
Bennett Valley GC
Santa Rosa, California
Ben Harmon
Benona Shores GC
Shelby, Michigan
Warner Bowen
Benson GC
Minnesota
Joel Goldstrand
Benson Park GC
Omaha, Nebraska
Edward Lawrence Packard
Bent Creek CC
Louisville, Kentucky
Bob Simmons
Bent Creek Mountain Inn CC
formerly known as Cobbly
Nob G Links
Gatlinburg, Tennessee
Arthur Davis, Ron Kirby,Gary
Player
Bent Oak GC
Oak Grove, Missouri
Bob Simmons
Bent Pine GC
Vero Beach, Florida
Joe Lee
Bent Tree CC
Jasper, Georgia
Joe Lee
Bent Tree G&RC
Sarasota, Florida
William B. Lewis
Bent Tree GC
Dallas, Texas
Desmond Muirhead
Benton CC
Illinois
Robert Bruce Harris
Benton CC
Indiana
William H. Diddel
Benton G&CC
Kentucky
Alex McKay
Bentwinds G&CC
Fuquay-Varina, North Carolina
Tom Hunter

Bentwood CC
San Angelo, Texas
Billy Martindale
Benvenue CC
Rocky Mount, North Carolina
Donald Ross
Bergamo L'Albenza GC
Italy
Henry Cotton
Bergen Park GC (R)
Illinois
Edward Lawrence Packard
Bergen Point Muni
Babylon, New York
William F. Mitchell
Bergisch Land und GC (R)
West Germany
Bernhard von Limburger
Berkeley CC now known as Mira
Vista G&CC
Berkeley CC
Moncks Corner, South Carolina
George W. Cobb
Berkeley Hills CC
Norcross, Georgia
Arthur Davis, Ron Kirby,Gary
Player
Berkeley Township GC
New Jersey
Nicholas Psiahas
Berkhampsted GC
Hertfordshire, England
C.J. Gilbert
Berkhampsted GC (R)
England
Willie Park, Willie Park Jr
Berkhampsted GC (R.12)
England
James Braid
Berkhampsted GC (A. 6)
England
James Braid
Berkleigh CC
Kutztown, Pennsylvania
Robert White
Berksdale GC
Bella Vista, Arkansas
Edmund B. Ault
Berkshire CC
Reading, Pennsylvania
Willie Park Jr
Berkshire GC (Blue Course)
Surrey, England
Herbert Fowler, Tom Simpson
Berkshire GC (Red Course)
England
Herbert Fowler, Tom Simpson
Berkshire Hills CC
Pittsfield, Massachusetts
A.W. Tillinghast
Berkshire Hills CC (R. 4)
Massachusetts
Geoffrey S. Cornish, William G.
Robinson
Berkshire Hunt & CC
Lenox, Massachusetts
Wayne Stiles, John Van Kleek
Berlin G&CC
East Germany
C.S. Butchart
Bermuda Dunes CC
California
William F. Bell
Bermuda Dunes CC (A. 9)
California
Robert L. Baldock
Bermuda Run G&CC
Clemmons, North Carolina
Ellis Maples, Ed Seay
Bermuda Run G&CC (A. 9)
North Carolina
Dan Maples
Bernardo Heights CC
Rancho Bernardo, California
Ted Robinson
Berrien Hills CC (R)
Michigan
Ken Killian, Dick Nugent
Berry Hills CC
Charleston, West Virginia
William Gordon
Berwick-upon-Tweed GC
Northumberland, England
Willie Park

Berwick-upon-Tweed GC (A. 9)
England
Fred W. Hawtree
Berwick-upon-Tweed GC (R)
England
James Braid
Berwind CC
Rio Grande, Puerto Rico
Frank Murray
Berwind CC (A. 9) NLE
Puerto Rico
Alfred H. Tull
Betchworth Park GC (R)
England
Tom Simpson
Bethel Island GC
California
Bob Baldock, Robert L. Baldock
Bethesda CC
Maryland
Fred Findlay
Bethesda CC (A. 9)
Maryland
Edmund B. Ault
Bethesda CC (R. 9)
Maryland
Edmund B. Ault
Bethesda Naval Hospital GC (R.
9)
Maryland
Edmund B. Ault
Bethlehem CC (R)
New Hampshire
Wayne Stiles
Bethlehem Muni
Pennsylvania
William Gordon, David Gordon
Bethlehem Steel C
Hellertown, New York
William Gordon, David Gordon
Bethlehem Steel Club (A. 9)
Pennsylvania
William Gordon, David Gordon
Bethlehem Steel Club (R)
Pennsylvania
William Gordon, David Gordon
Bethpage State Park GC (Black
Course)
Farmingdale, New York
A.W. Tillinghast
Bethpage State Park GC (Blue
Course)
Farmingdale, New York
A.W. Tillinghast
Bethpage State Park GC (Blue
Course) (R)
New York
Frank Duane
Bethpage State Park GC (Green
Course) (R)
New York
Frank Duane
Bethpage State Park GC (Green
Course) (R)
New York
A.W. Tillinghast
Bethpage State Park GC (Red
Course)
Farmingdale, New York
A.W. Tillinghast
Bethpage State Park GC (Red
Course) (R)
New York
Frank Duane
Bethpage State Park GC (Yellow
Course)
Farmingdale, New York
Alfred H. Tull
Bethpage State Park GC (Yellow
Course) (R)
New York
Frank Duane
Beverly CC
Chicago, Illinois
Donald Ross
Beverly CC (R. 4)
Illinois
William B. Langford
Beverly G&TC (R)
Massachusetts
Eugene "Skip" Wogan
Beverly GC
Copetown, Ontario
Clinton E. Robinson, Robert
Moote

Beverly Shores CC
Indiana
Charles Maddox, *Frank P.
MacDonald*
Bevico CC
Memphis, Tennessee
John W. Frazier
Bey-Lea GC
Toms River, New Jersey
Hal Purdy
Biddeford and Saco CC
Maine
Donald Ross
Biddeford and Saco CC (A. 9)
Maine
Brian Silva, Geoffrey S. Cornish
Bide-A-Wee CC
Portsmouth, Virginia
Fred Findlay, *Ben Loving*
Bidermann GC
Wilmington, Delaware
Dick Wilson, Joe Lee
Bielefelder GC
Bielefeld, West Germany
Donald Harradine
Big Bay G&CC
Lake Simcoe, Ontario
Stanley Thompson
Big Canoe GC
Lake Sconti, Georgia
Joe Lee, Rocky Roquemore
Big Canyon CC
Newport Beach, California
Robert Muir Graves
Big Cypress at Royal Palm CC
Florida
Chuck Ankrom
Big Cypress GC now known as
Winter Springs GC
Big Elm CC
Kentucky
Robert Lee
Big Foot CC
Fontana, Wisconsin
Tom Bendelow
Big Foot CC (R)
Wisconsin
Roger Packard
Big Foot CC (R)
Wisconsin
Dick Nugent
Big Oaks CC
Illinois
Edward B. Dearie Jr
Big Pine GC
Attica, Indiana
Robert Beard
Big Rapids CC
Michigan
Jack Daray
Big Sky GC
Montana
Frank Duane, Arnold Palmer
Big Spring CC
Louisville, Kentucky
George Davies
Big Spring CC (R)
Kentucky
Tom Winton
Big Spring CC (R)
Kentucky
William H. Diddel
Big Spring CC (R)
Kentucky
Edward Lawrence Packard
Big Spring CC (R)
Kentucky
Arthur Hills, Steve Forrest
Big Spring Muni
Texas
William Cantrell
Big Springs CC
Texas
Warren Cantrell
Big Tee GC
Buena Park, California
William H. Johnson
Bigbury GC
England
F.G. Hawtree, J.H. Taylor
Biggar GC
Lanarkshire, Scotland
Willie Park

Bigwin Island GC
Lake of Bays, Ontario
Stanley Thompson
Bigwood GC
Sun Valley, Idaho
Robert Muir Graves
Bigwood GC (R)
Idaho
Robert Muir Graves
Bill Roberts Muni
Helena, Montana
Robert Muir Graves
Billerica CC
Massachusetts
William F. Mitchell, Al Zikorus
Billingham GC
Durham, England
J.J.F. Pennink
Billings G&CC
Montana
Tom Bendelow
Biloxi CC NLE
Mississippi
Tom Bendelow
Biltmore CC
Barrington, Illinois
Leonard Macomber
Biltmore CC (R)
Illinois
William B. Langford
Biltmore CC (R)
Illinois
Edward Lawrence Packard
Biltmore Forest GC
Asheville, North Carolina
Donald Ross
Binbrook GC
Hamilton, Ontario
Renee Muylaert
Binder Park Muni
Michigan
Arch Flannery
Bing Mahoney GC
Sacramento, California
Michael J. McDonagh
Binghampton CC
Endwell, New York
A.W. Tillinghast
Binghampton CC (R)
New York
William Gordon, David Gordon
Binicitan GC
Manila, Philippines
Willard Wilkinson
Birch Bay GC
Washington
William G. Robinson
Birch Hill GC NLE
Detroit, Michigan
Ernest Way
Birch Hills GC
Brea, California
Harry Rainville, David Rainville
Birchwood CC
Westport, Connecticut
Orrin Smith
Birchwood CC (R)
Connecticut
William F. Mitchell
Birchwood Farm G&CC
Harbor Springs, Michigan
Bruce Matthews, Jerry Matthews
Birchwood GC (A. 9)
Ohio
Ferdinand Garbin
Birchwood GC (R. 9)
Ohio
Ferdinand Garbin
Birchwood GC
Cheshire, England
T.J.A. McAuley
Bird Bay G&CC
Venice, Florida
Ron Garl
Birds Hill GC
Manitoba
Tom Bendelow
Birds Hill GC (R)
Manitoba
Norman H. Woods
Birdwood GC
Charlottesville, Virginia
Lindsay Ervin

Birmingham CC
Michigan
Tom Bendelow
Birmingham CC (A. 9)
Michigan
Tom Bendelow
Birmingham CC (R)
Michigan
Wilfrid Reid, William Connellan
Birmingham CC (R)
Michigan
William H. Diddel
Birmingham CC (R. 3)
Michigan
Bruce Matthews, Jerry Matthews
Birmingham CC (R)
Michigan
Arthur Hills, Steve Forrest
Birmingham VA Hospital GC
California
William P. Bell
Birnam Wood GC
Santa Barbara, California
Robert Trent Jones, Robert Trent
Jones Jr
Birnam Wood GC (R)
California
Robert Trent Jones Jr, Gary
Roger Baird
Birnamwood GC
Burnsville, Minnesota
Don Herfort
Birr GC (R)
Ireland
Eddie Hackett
Birstall GC (R)
England
Tom Williamson
Bishop GC
California
Joseph B. Williams
Bitterroot River CC
Montana
William F. Bell
Bixby GC
Long Beach, California
Ronald Fream, Peter
Thomson,Michael Wolveridge
Black Bull G&CC
Mam-E-O Beach, Alberta
John A. Thompson
**Black Butte Ranch GC (Big
Meadows)**
Sisters, Oregon
Robert Muir Graves
**Black Butte Ranch GC (Glaze
Meadows Crs)**
Sisters, Oregon
Gene "Bunny" Mason
Black Canyon GC NLE
Phoenix, Arizona
Arthur Jack Snyder
Black Hall C
Old Lyme, Connecticut
Robert Trent Jones, Roger
Rulewich
Black Knight CC (R)
West Virginia
Ferdinand Garbin
Black Lake CC
California
Joe Novak
Black Mountain CC (R. 9)
North Carolina
Ross Taylor
Black Mountain CC (A. 9)
North Carolina
Ross Taylor
Black Mountain G&CC
Henderson, Nevada
Bob Baldock
Black Mountain G&CC (A.18)
Nevada
Robert L. Baldock
Black River CC
Michigan
Fred L. Riggin
Black River CC (A. 9)
Michigan
Wilfrid Reid, William Connellan
Black River CC (R. 9)
Michigan
William H. Diddel

Black River CC (A. 9)
Michigan
William H. Diddel
Black River Falls GC
Wisconsin
Edward Lawrence Packard, Brent
Wadsworth
Blackberry Farm GC
Cupertino, California
Robert Muir Graves
Blackburn Estate GC
Fort Myers, Florida
Dick Wilson
Blackfoot Muni
Idaho
George Von Elm
Blackhawk CC
Danville, California
Robert von Hagge, Bruce Devlin
Blackhawk CC (R)
Wisconsin
A.W. Tillinghast
Blackhawk CC (R)
Wisconsin
Ken Killian, Dick Nugent
Blackhawk GC
Galena, Ohio
Jack Kidwell
Blackhill Wood GC
Staffordshire, England
J.J.F. Pennink, D.M.A. Steel
Blackhorse GC
Downers Grove, Illinois
Charles Maddox
Blackledge CC
Hebron, Connecticut
Geoffrey S. Cornish, William G.
Robinson
**Blacklick Woods Metro Park GC
(No. 1)**
Reynoldsburg, Ohio
Jack Kidwell
**Blacklick Woods Metro Park GC
(No. 1) (A.13)**
Ohio
Jack Kidwell
**Blacklick Woods Metro Park GC
(No.2)**
Reynoldsburg, Ohio
Jack Kidwell
Blacklion GC
County Levon, Ireland
Eddie Hackett
Blacklion GC (R)
Ireland
Eddie Hackett
Blackmoor GC
England
H.S. Colt
Blackpool Park GC
Lancashire, England
Alister Mackenzie
Blacksburg CC (Valley Course)
Virginia
Ferdinand Garbin
Blackwell Grange GC (R)
England
J.J.F. Pennink
Blackwell GC
Worcestershire, England
Herbert Fowler
Blackwood CC
Gloucester Township, New Jersey
Alex Findlay
Blackwood CC
Douglasville, Pennsylvania
William Gordon, David Gordon
Blair Academy GC
New Jersey
Duer Irving Sewall
Blair Hampton GC
Minden, Ontario
Robert Moote, *David Moote*
**Blairgowrie GC (Lansdowne
Course)**
Perthshire, Scotland
Peter Alliss, David Thomas
**Blairgowrie GC (Rosemount
Course)**
Scotland
Tom Dunn
**Blairgowrie GC (Rosemount
Course) (R. 9)**
Scotland
Alister Mackenzie

**Blairgowrie GC (Rosemount
Course) (A. 9)**
Scotland
Alister Mackenzie
**Blairgowrie GC (Rosemount
Course) (R.10)**
Scotland
James Braid, John R. Stutt
**Blairgowrie GC (Rosemount
Course) (A. 8)**
Scotland
James Braid, John R. Stutt
**Blairgowrie GC (Rosemount
Course) (R)**
Scotland
Peter Alliss, David Thomas
Blairgowrie GC (Wee Course)
Perthshire, Scotland
James Braid, John R. Stutt
Blairmore and Strone GC
Argyll, Scotland
James Braid
Blairsville CC
Pennsylvania
James Gilmore Harrison,
Ferdinand Garbin
Blakely CC
Georgia
Hugh Moore
Blandford GC (R)
England
J. Hamilton Stutt
Bled GC
Yugoslavia
Donald Harradine
Blind Brook C (Routing)
Portchester, New York
Seth Raynor
Blind Brook CC
Portchester, New York
George Low Sr
Bloemfontein GC
South Africa
John Watt
Blomidon Club
Corner Brook, Newfoundland
Alfred H. Tull
Bloomfield Hills CC
Michigan
Tom Bendelow
Bloomfield Hills CC (R)
Michigan
Donald Ross
Bloomfield Hills CC (R)
Michigan
Robert Trent Jones
Bloomfield Hills CC (R)
Michigan
Robert Trent Jones, Roger
Rulewich
Bloomfield Hills CC (R)
Michigan
Arthur Hills, Steve Forrest
Bloomfield-Wausa GC
Nebraska
Henry B. Hughes, Richard
Watson
Bloomingdale Golfers C
Valrico, Florida
Ron Garl
Bloomington CC
Illinois
Tom Bendelow
Bloomington CC (A. 9)
Illinois
William B. Langford
Bloomington CC (R)
Illinois
Edward Lawrence Packard
Bloomington CC
Minnesota
Paul Coates
Bloomington CC
St. George, Utah
William H. Neff
Bloomington Hills CC
Utah
David Bingaman
Bloomington Hills CC (R)
Utah
William Howard Neff
Bloomsburg CC (R)
Pennsylvania
James Gilmore Harrison

Blossom Trails GC
Benton Harbor, Michigan
Bruce Matthews
Bloxwich GC
England
J. Sixsmith
Blue Ash GC
Ohio
Jack Kidwell, Michael Hurdzan
Blue Hill CC
Canton, Massachusetts
Eugene "Skip" Wogan
Blue Hill CC (A. 9)
Massachusetts
Phil Wogan
Blue Hill CC (R. 6)
Massachusetts
Manny Francis
Blue Hill CC (R)
Massachusetts
Brian Silva, Geoffrey S. Cornish
Blue Hill GC (R)
New Jersey
Frank Duane
Blue Hill GC (R)
New York
Edmund B. Ault
Blue Hill GC (R)
New York
Stephen Kay
Blue Hill GC NLE
Nassau, Bahamas
C.C. Shaw
Blue Hills CC
Kansas City, Missouri
Bob Dunning
Blue Hills CC (R) NLE
Missouri
Orrin Smith, James Gilmore
Harrison
Blue Knob Resort GC
Claysburg, Pennsylvania
Ferdinand Garbin
Blue Lake Estates GC
Marble Falls, Texas
Joseph S. Finger
Blue Lake GC
Tennessee
Edmund B. Ault
Blue Lake Springs GC
Arnold, California
Bob Baldock
Blue Mound G&CC NLE
Milwaukee, Wisconsin
Tom Bendelow
Blue Mound G&CC
Wauwautosa, Wisconsin
Seth Raynor
Blue Mound G&CC (R. 3)
Wisconsin
David Gill
Blue Mound G&CC (R)
Wisconsin
Ken Killian, Dick Nugent
Blue Mountain G&CC
Collingwood, Ontario
Clinton E. Robinson
Blue Mountain GC
Linglestown, Pennsylvania
David Gordon
Blue Mountain GC (A. 9)
Ontario
William G. Robinson, John F.
Robinson
Blue Ridge CC (R)
Pennsylvania
James Gilmore Harrison,
Ferdinand Garbin
Blue Ridge CC (R)
Pennsylvania
William F. Mitchell
Blue Rock GC
South Yarmouth, Massachusetts
Geoffrey S. Cornish
Blue Rock Springs GC
Vallejo, California
Jack Fleming
Blue Skies CC
Yucca Valley, California
William F. Bell
Blue Springs G&CC
Missouri
John S. Davis

269

Blueberry Hill GC
Warren, Pennsylvania
James Gilmore Harrison,
  Ferdinand Garbin
Blueberry Hill GC (A. 9)
Pennsylvania
Ferdinand Garbin
Bluebonnet CC
Navasota, Texas
Jay Riviere
Bluefield CC (R)
West Virginia
I.C. "Rocky" Schorr
Bluegrass CC
Hendersonville, Tennessee
Robert Bruce Harris
Bluegrass CC (A. 2)
Tennessee
Robert Bruce Harris
Bluegrass CC (R)
Tennessee
Robert Bruce Harris
Bluewater Bay GC
Niceville, Florida
Tom Fazio
Bluewater Bay GC (A. 9)
Florida
Tom Fazio
Bluff Point CC
Lake Champlain, New York
A.W. Tillinghast
Bluff Point CC (R)
New York
A.W. Tillinghast
Bluff Point CC (R)
New York
George Low Sr
Bluffs CC
Louisiana
Arnold Palmer, Ed Seay, Harrison
  Minchew
Blumisberg G&CC
Bern, Switzerland
Bernhard von Limburger
Blyth GC
Northumberland, England
J. Hamilton Stutt
Blythe Muni
California
William F. Bell
Blythefield CC
Belmont, Michigan
William B. Langford, Theodore J.
  Moreau
Blythefield CC (R. 5)
Michigan
Bruce Matthews, Jerry Matthews
Blythefield CC (R)
Michigan
Jay Riviere
Blythefield CC (R. 1)
Michigan
Jerry Matthews
Blytheville CC
Arkansas
Dick Wilson, Bob Simmons
Blytheville CC (R. 9)
Arkansas
Joseph S. Finger
Blytheville CC (A. 9)
Arkansas
Joseph S. Finger
Boar's Head Inn GC
Charlottesville, Virginia
Buddy Loving
Board of Trade CC (East Course)
Woodbridge, Ontario
Howard Watson
**Board of Trade CC (East Course)
(R. 4)**
Ontario
Gordon Witteveen
**Board of Trade CC (South
  Course)**
Woodbridge, Ontario
Gordon Witteveen
**Board of Trade CC (West
  Course)**
Woodbridge, Ontario
Howard Watson
**Board of Trade CC (West
  Course) (A. 9)**
Ontario
Arthur Hills

**Board of Trade CC (West
  Course) (R. 9)**
Ontario
Arthur Hills
Boat-of-Garten GC
Invernesshire, Scotland
James Braid, John R. Stutt
Bob O'Link CC
Highland Park, Illinois
Donald Ross
Bob O'Link CC (R)
Illinois
C.H. Alison, H.S. Colt
Bob O'Link CC (R)
Illinois
Edward Lawrence Packard
Bob O'Link CC (R)
Illinois
Ken Killian, Dick Nugent
Bob O'Link CC
Novi, Michigan
Wilfrid Reid, William Connellan
**Bobby Jones Muni (American
  Course)**
Sarasota, Florida
Donald Ross
**Bobby Jones Muni (American
  Course) (R)**
Florida
R. Albert Anderson
**Bobby Jones Muni (British
  Course)**
Sarasota, Florida
Donald Ross
**Bobby Jones Muni (Executive
  Course)**
Sarasota, Florida
Lane Marshall
Bobby Nichols GC
Louisville, Kentucky
Benjamin Wihry
Boca Del Mar G&TC
Boca Raton, Florida
Robert von Hagge, Bruce Devlin
Boca Delray G&CC
Delray Beach, Florida
Karl Litten
Boca G&TC
Boca Raton, Florida
Joe Lee
Boca Greens GC
Boca Raton, Florida
Joe Lee
Boca Grove Plantation GC
Boca Raton, Florida
Karl Litten
Boca Lago G&CC (East Course)
Boca Raton, Florida
Robert von Hagge, Bruce Devlin
Boca Lago G&CC (West Course)
Boca Raton, Florida
Robert von Hagge, Bruce Devlin
Boca Pointe CC
Boca Raton, Florida
Bob Cupp, Jay Morrish
Boca Raton Hotel & C
Florida
William S. Flynn, Howard
  Toomey
Boca Raton Hotel & C (R)
Florida
Red Lawrence
Boca Raton Hotel & C (R)
Florida
Robert Trent Jones
**Boca Raton Hotel & C
  (Lakeview Crs)**
Florida
Dick Bird
**Boca Raton Hotel & C (North
  Course) NLE**
Florida
William S. Flynn, Howard
  Toomey
Boca Raton Muni
Florida
Chuck Ankrom
Boca Rio GC
Boca Raton, Florida
Robert von Hagge
Boca Teeca CC
Boca Raton, Florida
Mark Mahannah

Boca West C (Course No. 1)
Boca Raton, Florida
Desmond Muirhead
Boca West C (Course No. 1) (R)
Florida
Desmond Muirhead
Boca West C (Course No. 2)
Boca Raton, Florida
Desmond Muirhead
Boca West C (Course No. 4)
Boca Raton, Florida
Joe Lee
Boca West CC (Course No. 3)
Boca Raton, Florida
Robert von Hagge, Bruce Devlin
Boca Woods CC (North Course)
Boca Raton, Florida
Karl Litten
Boca Woods CC (South Course)
Boca Raton, Florida
Joe Lee
Bocaire CC
Boca Raton, Florida
Joe Lee, Rocky Roquemore
Bodega Harbour GC
California
Robert Trent Jones Jr, Gary
  Roger Baird
Bodenstown GC
County Kildare, Ireland
Eddie Hackett
Bogey CC
St. Louis, Missouri
Robert Foulis
Bognor Regis GC
Sussex, England
James Braid
Bogue Banks CC
Atlantic Beach, North Carolina
Maurice Brackett
Boiling Springs GC
Woodward, Oklahoma
Don Sechrest
Bois de Sioux GC
Wahpeton, North Dakota
Robert Bruce Harris
Bois le Roe GC
France
Robert Berthet
Boldmere GC
England
Carl Bretherston
Bolen GC
Ohio
Robert Morrison
Bolling AFB GC
Virginia
Edmund B. Ault, Al Jamison
Bologna GC
Italy
Henry Cotton
Bolton Field GC
Columbus, Ohio
Jack Kidwell
Bombay Presidency C
India
C.R. Clayton
Bombay Presidency GC (R)
India
Peter Thomson, Michael
  Wolveridge
Bomun Lake GC
Kyongju, South Korea
Edward Lawrence Packard,
  Roger Packard
Bon Air CC
Glen Rock, Pennsylvania
William Gordon, David Gordon
Bon Air GC
Kentucky
Taylor Boyd
**Bon Air Vanderbilt Hotel GC
  (Lake Crs)**
Augusta, Georgia
Seth Raynor
**Bon Air-Vanderbilt Hotel GC
  (Hill Crs) (R)**
Georgia
Donald Ross
Bon Vivant CC
Bourbonnais, Illinois
Ray Didier

Bonaventure CC (East Course)
Fort Lauderdale, Florida
Joe Lee
Bonaventure CC (West Course)
Fort Lauderdale, Florida
Charles Mahannah
Bonaventure GC
Fauvel, Quebec
Howard Watson, John Watson
Bonaventure GC (A. 9)
Quebec
John Watson
Bonita Bay C
Bonita Springs, Florida
Arthur Hills, Steve Forrest, Mike
  Dasher
Bonita GC
California
William F. Bell
Bonita Springs G&CC
Florida
William Maddox
Bonn-Godesberg GC
West Germany
John Harris
Bonneville Muni
Salt Lake City, Utah
William F. Bell, William P. Bell
Bonneville Muni (A. 9)
Utah
William F. Bell, William H. Neff
Bonnie Brae GC
South Carolina
Russell Breeden
Bonnie Briar CC
Larchmont, New York
Archie Capper
Bonnie Briar CC (R)
New York
A.W. Tillinghast
Bonnie Briar CC (R)
New York
Devereux Emmet, Alfred H. Tull
Bonnie Briar CC (R)
New York
Robert Trent Jones, Stanley
  Thompson
Bonnie Briar CC (R)
New York
Alfred H. Tull
Bonnie Brook CC
Waukegan, Illinois
James Foulis
Bonnie Crest CC
Montgomery, Alabama
Weldon W. Doe
Bonnie Dundee GC
Dundee, Illinois
C.D. Wagstaff
Bonnie View CC (R)
Maryland
Edmund B. Ault
Bonnie View GC
Eaton, Michigan
Henry Chisholm
Bonnie View GC (R. 4)
Michigan
Bruce Matthews, Jerry Matthews
Bonnie View GC (A. 2)
Michigan
Bruce Matthews, Jerry Matthews
Bonniebrook GC
St. Colomban, Quebec
Howard Watson
Bookcliff CC
Grand Junction, Colorado
Henry B. Hughes
Bookcliff CC (A. 5)
Colorado
Press Maxwell
Boone Aire GC
Florence, Kentucky
Robert von Hagge
Boone CC
North Carolina
Ellis Maples
Boonsboro CC
Lynchburg, Virginia
Fred Findlay
Boonsboro CC (R)
Virginia
Rees Jones

Boonville GC
Indiana
Tom Bendelow
Boothbay Harbor CC
Maine
Wayne Stiles, John Van Kleek
Boothferry GC
Yorkshire, England
D.M.A. Steel
Bootle GC
Lancashire, England
Tom Simpson
Boots Randolph GC
Cadiz, Kentucky
Edward Lawrence Packard
Borden G&CC
Amiens, France
P.M. Ross
Borden G&CC (R. 9)
France
J.J.F. Pennink
Borden G&CC (R)
France
J.J.F. Pennink
Borris GC
County Carlow, Ireland
Col. J.H. Curry
Borris GC (R)
Ireland
Eddie Hackett
Borth and Ynyslas GC (R)
Wales
H.S. Colt
Boscobel G&CC
South Carolina
Fred Bolton
Boskogens GC (R)
Sweden
Jan Sederholm
Bosques De San Isidro GC
Guadalajara, Mexico
Lawrence Hughes
**Bosques Del Lago CC (East
  Course)**
Mexico City, Mexico
Joseph S. Finger
**Bosques Del Lago CC (West
  Course)**
Mexico City, Mexico
Joseph S. Finger
Botany Woods GC
Greenville, South Carolina
George W. Cobb
Boughton Ridge GC
Bollingbrook, Illinois
Roger Packard
Boulder City GC
Nevada
Harry Rainville, David Rainville
Boulder City GC (A. 9)
Nevada
Greg Nash
Boulder Creek GC
California
Jack Fleming
Boulder CC NLE
Colorado
Tom Bendelow
Boulder CC
Colorado
Press Maxwell
Boulders GC
Carefree, Arizona
Red Lawrence
Boulders GC (A. 9)
Arizona
Arthur Jack Snyder
Boulders GC (R. 2)
Arizona
Arthur Jack Snyder
Boulders GC (R)
Arizona
Jay Morrish
Boulders GC (A. 9)
Arizona
Jay Morrish
Boundary Oaks GC
California
Robert Muir Graves
Bountiful Muni
Utah
William H. Neff, William Howard
  Neff

Bow Creek GC
Virginia
Fred Sappenfield
Bowden Muni
Macon, Georgia
Hugh Moore
Bowden Muni (A. 9)
Georgia
Ward Northrup
Bowling Green CC
Kentucky
William B. Langford, Theodore J. Moreau
Bowling Green GC
Milton, New Jersey
Geoffrey S. Cornish, William G. Robinson
Bowling Green University GC (R)
Ohio
Arthur Hills
Bowling Green University GC (R. 9)
Ohio
X.G. Hassenplug
Bowman's Mt Hood GC
Oregon
George Walle, Ralph Shattuck
Bowman's Mt Hood GC (A. 9)
Oregon
Gene Bowman
Bowman's Mt Hood GC (Rippling River 9)
Oregon
Gene Bowman
Bowmanville CC
Ontario
Clinton E. Robinson
Bowness GC
Calgary, Alberta
Willie Park Jr
Bowring Park GC
Liverpool, England
Fred W. Hawtree
Boyce Hill GC (R. 9)
England
F.G. Hawtree
Boyle GC
County Roscommon, Ireland
Eddie Hackett
Boyne Highlands GC (Heather Course)
Harbor Springs, Michigan
Robert Trent Jones
Boyne Highlands GC (Heather Course) (A. 9)
Michigan
William Newcomb
Boyne Highlands GC (Moor Course)
Harbor Springs, Michigan
Robert Trent Jones
Boyne Highlands GC (Moor Course) (A. 9)
Michigan
William Newcomb
Boyne Highlands GC (Ross Memorial Crs)
Harbor Springs, Michigan
William Newcomb
Boyne Mountain GC (Alpine Course)
Boyne Falls, Michigan
William Newcomb
Boyne Mountain GC (Executive Course)
Boyne Falls, Michigan
William Newcomb
Boyne Mountain GC (Monument Course)
Boyne Falls, Michigan
William Newcomb, Stephen Kay
Boynton Beach Muni
Florida
Robert von Hagge, Bruce Devlin
Brackenridge Park GC
San Antonio, Texas
A.W. Tillinghast
Brackenwood Muni
Cheshire, England
Fred W. Hawtree
Bradford GC
Pennsylvania
James Gilmore Harrison, Ferdinand Garbin

Bradford GC
Yorkshire, England
Herbert Fowler
Bradford GC (A.13)
England
Old Tom Morris
Brae Burn CC
West Newton, Massachusetts
Donald Ross
Brae Burn CC (R)
Massachusetts
Donald Ross
Brae Burn CC (R. 2)
Massachusetts
Geoffrey S. Cornish, William G. Robinson
Brae Burn CC
Purchase, New York
Frank Duane
Brae Burn CC
Bellaire, Texas
John Bredemus
Brae Burn CC (R)
Texas
Ralph Plummer
Brae Burn CC (R. 4)
Texas
Joseph S. Finger
Brae Burn CC (R. 4)
Texas
Marvin Ferguson
Brae Burn CC
Bellevue, Washington
Al Smith
Brae Burn GC
Plymouth, Michigan
Wilfrid Reid, William Connellan
Brae Burn Links NLE
Copley, Ohio
L.M. Latta
Braemar CC (East Course)
Tarzana, California
Ted Robinson
Braemar CC (West Course)
Tarzana, California
Ted Robinson
Braemar GC
Edina, Minnesota
Dick Phelps
Braid Hills GC
Edinburgh, Scotland
Robert Ferguson, Peter McEwan
Braidburn CC (Lake Course)
Florham Park, New Jersey
Herbert Strong
Braidburn CC (Lake Course) (R. 9)
New Jersey
Duer Irving Sewall
Braidburn CC (Lake Course) (A. 9)
New Jersey
Hal Purdy, Malcolm Purdy
Braidwood GC
Illinois
Homer Fieldhouse
Brainerd Muni
Chattanooga, Tennessee
Donald Ross, Walter Hatch
Brainroe GC
County Wicklow, Ireland
Fred W. Hawtree, Martin Hawtree
Braintree GC
Essex, England
Fred W. Hawtree
Braintree Muni (A.11)
Massachusetts
Samuel Mitchell
Braintree Muni (R)
Massachusetts
Samuel Mitchell
Bramley GC
England
Charles H. Mayo
Bramley GC (R)
England
James Braid
Brampton GC (R. 9)
Ontario
Stanley Thompson
Bramshaw GC (Manor Course)
England
Tom Dunn

Bramshaw GC (Manor Course) (R)
England
W. Wiltshire
Bramshott Hill GC
Hampshire, England
J. Hamilton Stutt
Brancepeth Castle GC
Durham, England
H.S. Colt, C.H. Alison, Alister Mackenzie
Branchwood GC
Bella Vista, Arkansas
Tom Clark, Edmund B. Ault
Brandermill CC
Midlothian, Virginia
Ron Kirby, Gary Player, Denis Griffiths
Brandon GC (R)
Ireland
Eddie Hackett
Brandon Wood GC
Coventry, England
J.J.F. Pennink
Brandywine Bay GC
Morehead City, North Carolina
Robert von Hagge, Bruce Devlin
Brandywine CC
Wilmington, Delaware
Alfred H. Tull
Brandywine CC (R. 7)
Delaware
Brian Ault, Bill Love
Brandywine CC
Maumee, Ohio
Earl F. Yesberger
Branson Bay GC
Mason, Michigan
Phil Shirley
Brantford G&CC
Ontario
George Cumming, *Nicol Thompson*
Brantford G&CC (R)
Ontario
Clinton E. Robinson, Robert Moote
Brantford G&CC (R)
Ontario
Clinton E. Robinson
Brantford G&CC (R)
Ontario
Stanley Thompson
Brasilia GC
Brazil
Robert Trent Jones
Brattleboro CC
Vermont
Wayne Stiles
Brattleboro CC (R)
Vermont
William F. Mitchell
Bray GC (R. 9)
Ireland
Cecil Barcroft
Brazoria Bend GC
Houston, Texas
Frank Cope
Brea GC
California
Harry Rainville
Breakers Beach CC NLE
Northbrook, Illinois
Leonard Macomber
Breakers GC (Ocean Course)
Palm Beach, Florida
Alex Findlay
Breakers GC (Ocean Course) (R. 9)
Florida
William B. Langford, Theodore J. Moreau
Breakers GC (Ocean Course) (A. 9)
Florida
William B. Langford
Breakers GC (Ocean Course) (R)
Florida
Joe Lee
Breakers GC (West Course)
West Palm Beach, Florida
Willard Byrd
Brean GC
England
A.H. Clarke

Breathnach CC
Akron, Ohio
Harold Paddock
Brechin GC
Angus, Scotland
James Braid
Brechtel Memorial Park GC (A. 9)
Louisiana
Richard W. LaConte, Ted McAnlis
Brechtel Memorial Park GC (R. 9)
Louisiana
Richard W. LaConte, Ted McAnlis
Breckenridge GC
Colorado
Jack Nicklaus, Bob Cupp
Breckenridge GC
Minnesota
Robert Bruce Harris
Breckenridge GC
Texas
Tom Bendelow
Breezy Bend CC (R)
Manitoba
Geoffrey S. Cornish, William G. Robinson
Breitenloo GC
Zurich, Switzerland
Donald Harradine
Breitenloo GC (R)
Switzerland
J.J.F. Pennink
Brentwood CC (R)
California
Max Behr
Brentwood CC (R)
California
William Watson
Brentwood CC (R. 3)
California
Ronald Fream
Brentwood GC
Jacksonville, Florida
Donald Ross
Breslau GC
West Germany
Karl Hoffmann
Breton Bay CC
Leonardtown, Maryland
J. Porter Gibson
Bretton Woods GC
Germantown, Maryland
Edmund B. Ault
Bretton Woods GC
Mt. Washington Hotel, New Hampshire
Donald Ross
Bretwood GC
Keene, New Hampshire
Geoffrey S. Cornish, William G. Robinson
Brewster Green GC NLE
Massachusetts
Orrin Smith
Brewster Green GC (A. 2) NLE
Massachusetts
Geoffrey S. Cornish, William G. Robinson
Brian Thicke Estate GC
Orangeville, Ontario
Howard Watson
Briar Bay GC
Miami, Florida
Robert von Hagge, Bruce Devlin
Briar Creek CC
Sylvania, Georgia
Bill Amick
Briar Hall CC
Briarcliff Manor, New York
Devereux Emmet
Briar Ridge CC
Dyer, Indiana
Roger Packard
Briarcliff G&CC
Rainier, Washington
Fred Federspiel
Briarcliff Lodge GC
New York
Devereux Emmet

Briarcrest CC
Bryan, Texas
Marvin Ferguson
Briardale Greens Muni
Euclid, Ohio
Richard W. LaConte, Ted McAnlis
Briars G&CC
Jackson Point, Ontario
Stanley Thompson
Briarwood CC formerly known as Briergate CC
Deerfield, Illinois
C.H. Alison, H.S. Colt
Briarwood CC (R)
Illinois
Robert Bruce Harris
Briarwood CC
Meridian, Mississippi
Earl Stone
Briarwood CC
Montana
Brad Benz, Mike Poellot
Briarwood CC
Sun City West, Arizona
Jeff Hardin, Greg Nash, *John W. Meeker, Tom Ryan*
Briarwood GC
Broadview Heights, Ohio
Ted McAnlis
Briarwood GC (A. 9)
Ohio
Ted McAnlis
Brickendon Grange G&CC
England
C.K. Cotton, J.J.F. Pennink
Bridgeport CC
West Virginia
James Gilmore Harrison, Ferdinand Garbin
Bridgeport Fairways
Connestoga, Ontario
Clinton E. Robinson
Bridgeton GC (R)
Maine
Orrin Smith, William F. Mitchell
Bridgman GC
Michigan
George B. Ferry
Bridgton Highlands GC
Maine
Ralph Barton
Bridport and West Dorset GC
England
James Braid
Briergate CC now known as Briarwood CC
Brigantine CC
New Jersey
Wayne Stiles, John Van Kleek
Brigham City G&CC
Utah
Mick Riley
Brigham City G&CC (A. 9)
Utah
William Howard Neff
Bright Leaf GC
Harrodsburg, Kentucky
Buck Blankenship
Brightmoor CC
Michigan
Donald Ross
Brighton and Hove GC
Sussex, England
Tom Dunn
Brighton and Hove GC (R)
England
Willie Park Jr
Brighton and Hove GC (A. 9)
England
James Braid
Brighton Park GC
Tonawanda, New York
William Harries, *A. Russell Tryon*
Brightondale Muni
Wisconsin
Edmund B. Ault
Brightwood G&CC
Dartmouth, Nova Scotia
Willie Park Jr
Brightwood G&CC (R)
Nova Scotia
Donald Ross

Brightwood G&CC (R)
Nova Scotia
Robert Moote
Brightwood Hills GC
New Brighton, Minnesota
Leo Johnson
Brioni GC
Italy
Archie Kitts, M. Lauber
Brioni GC (R)
Italy
M. Lauber
Brioni GC (A. 2)
Italy
M. Lauber
Bristol County CC
Massachusetts
Eugene "Skip" Wogan
Bristol Harbor Village GC
Canandaigua, New York
Robert Trent Jones, Rees Jones
Bristolwood GC
Bristol, Pennsylvania
George Fazio
Britannia GC
Cayman Islands
Jack Nicklaus, Bob Cupp
Broad Bay Point G&CC
Virginia Beach, Virginia
Tom Clark, Edmund B. Ault
Broadmoor CC
Shareville, Indiana
R. Albert Anderson
Broadmoor CC
Indianapolis, Indiana
Donald Ross
Broadmoor CC NLE
New Rochelle, New York
Devereux Emmet, Alfred H. Tull
Broadmoor CC
Alberta
Norman H. Woods
Broadmoor GC (A)
Michigan
Mark DeVries
Broadmoor GC
Portland, Oregon
George Junor
Broadmoor GC (R)
Oregon
William Sander
Broadmoor GC
Seattle, Washington
A. Vernon Macan
Broadmoor GC (R. 2)
Washington
Peter Thomson, Michael
  Wolveridge,Ronald Fream
Broadmoor GC (East Course)
Colorado Springs, Colorado
Donald Ross, Walter Hatch
Broadmoor GC (East Course) (A. 9)
Colorado
Robert Trent Jones
Broadmoor GC (South Course)
Colorado Springs, Colorado
Arnold Palmer, Ed Seay
Broadmoor GC (West Course)
Colorado Springs, Colorado
Donald Ross, Walter Hatch
Broadmoor GC (West Course) (A. 9)
Colorado
Robert Trent Jones
Broadmoore CC
Moore, Oklahoma
Floyd Farley
Broadmore CC
Idaho
T.R. Scott
Broadstone GC
Dorset, England
Tom Dunn
Broadstone GC (A. 8)
England
H.S. Colt
Broadstone GC (R)
England
Herbert Fowler
Broadstone GC (R)
England
Willie Park, Willie Park Jr

Broadstone GC (R)
England
H.S. Colt
Broadview GC
Pataskala, Ohio
Jack Kidwell
Broadwater Beach Hotel GC (Fun Course)
Gulfport, Mississippi
Earl Stone
Broadwater Beach Hotel GC (Sea Course)
Gulfport, Mississippi
Charles G. Nieman
Broadwater Beach Hotel GC (Sea Course) (R. 9)
Mississippi
Earl Stone
Broadwater Beach Hotel GC (Sea Course) (A. 9)
Mississippi
Earl Stone
Broadwater Beach Hotel GC (Sun Course)
Gulfport, Mississippi
Earl Stone
Brock Park GC
Texas
A.C. Ray
Brockenhurst Manor GC
England
H.S. Colt
Brockenhurst Manor GC (R)
England
J. Hamilton Stutt
Brockton CC
Brockton, Massachusetts
Alex Findlay
Brockville CC (R. 9)
Ontario
Stanley Thompson
Brockville CC (A. 9)
Ontario
Clinton E. Robinson
Brockville GC (Course No. 1)
Ontario
Howard Watson
Brockville GC (Course No. 2)
Ontario
Howard Watson
Brockway GC
Kings Beach, California
John Duncan Dunn
Brocton Hall GC
Staffordshire, England
Harry Vardon
Brocton Hall GC (R)
England
Reginald Beale
Broken Sound CC
Boca Raton, Florida
Joe Lee
Broken Sound GC
Boca Raton, Florida
Joe Lee
Broken Woods G&RC
Coral Springs, Florida
Bill Watts
Broken Woods G&RC (R)
Florida
Edmund B. Ault
Bromborough GC (R)
England
Fred W. Hawtree, A.H.F. Jiggens
Bromley GC
England
Tom Dunn
Brook Hill GC
Brookville, Indiana
Gary Kern
Brook Hollow GC
Dallas, Texas
A.W. Tillinghast
Brook Hollow GC (R)
Texas
Ralph Plummer
Brook Manor CC
Brooke, Virginia
Alfred H. Tull
Brook Valley G&CC
Greenville, North Carolina
Ellis Maples, Ed Seay

Brookdale CC
Tacoma, Washington
Al Smith
Brooke Hills Park GC
Wellsburg, West Virginia
X.G. Hassenplug
Brookfield CC
Clarence, New York
William Harries
Brookfield Hills GC
Wisconsin
Robert von Hagge, Bruce Devlin
Brookfield West G&CC
Atlanta, Georgia
George W. Cobb
Brookhaven CC NLE
Georgia
Herbert Barker
Brookhaven CC (Championship Course)
Dallas, Texas
Press Maxwell
Brookhaven CC (Masters Course)
Dallas, Texas
Press Maxwell
Brookhaven CC (Presidents Course)
Dallas, Texas
Press Maxwell
Brookhaven GC
New York
George Pulver
Brookhill GC
Rantoul, Illinois
Edward Lawrence Packard
Brookhill GC (A. 9)
Illinois
Roger Packard
Brooklawn CC (R)
Connecticut
A.W. Tillinghast
Brooklea CC
Rochester, New York
Donald Ross
Brooklea CC (R)
New York
William Harries
Brooklea CC (R)
New York
Bob Cupp
Brooklea GC (R)
Ontario
Robert Moote
Brookmeadow GC
Canton, Massachusetts
Samuel Mitchell
Brookridge CC
Park Ridge, Illinois
C.D. Wagstaff
Brookridge CC (R)
Illinois
Charles Maddox, *Frank P. MacDonald*
Brookridge G&CC
Overland Park, Kansas
Chic Adams
Brooks CC
Okoboji, Iowa
Warren Dickinson
Brookshire CC
Wiliamston, Michigan
Bruce Matthews
Brookshire GC
Carmel, Indiana
William H. Diddel
Brookside CC
Canton, Ohio
Donald Ross
Brookside CC (R. 2)
Ohio
Jack Kidwell, Michael Hurdzan
Brookside CC (A. 9)
Pennsylvania
William Gordon, David Gordon
Brookside CC (R. 9)
Pennsylvania
William Gordon, David Gordon
Brookside CC (R. 9)
Pennsylvania
James Gilmore Harrison, Ferdinand Garbin
Brookside CC (A. 9)
Pennsylvania
James Gilmore Harrison, Ferdinand Garbin

Brookside GC
Kingsley, Iowa
Leo Johnson
Brookside GC
Michigan
David Snider
Brookside GC
Reno, Nevada
Bob Baldock
Brookside GC
Oklahoma City, Oklahoma
Floyd Farley
Brookside GC
Agincourt, Ontario
Renee Muylaert
Brookside Muni (Course No.1)
Pasadena, California
William P. Bell
Brookside Muni (Course No.2)
Pasadena, California
William P. Bell
Brookside Muni (Course No.2) (R)
California
Desmond Muirhead
Brookside Park GC
Ashland, Ohio
X.G. Hassenplug
Brookside Park GC (A. 9)
Ohio
Jack Kidwell, Michael Hurdzan
Brooksville G&CC
Florida
William F. Mitchell
Brookview CC
Surprise, Arizona
Gary Grandstaff
Brookview CC (R)
Arizona
Arthur Jack Snyder
Brookview CC
Minneapolis, Minnesota
Charles Maddox
Brookview CC (R. 9)
Minnesota
Fred Sicora
Brookview CC (R)
Minnesota
Dick Phelps
Brookview CC (R)
Minnesota
Donald G. Brauer, Paul S. Fjare
Brookview CC (A. 9)
Minnesota
Donald G. Brauer, Emile Perret
Brookwood CC
Addison, Illinois
C.D. Wagstaff
Brookwood CC (R)
Illinois
Edward Lawrence Packard, Roger Packard
Brookwood CC
Rochester, Michigan
William Newcomb
Brookwood GC
Buchanan, Michigan
William James Spear
Broome Manor GC
Wiltshire, England
Fred W. Hawtree, Martin Hawtree
Broome Park GC
Kent, England
J.J.F. Pennink, D.M.A. Steel
Broomie Knowe GC
Midlothian, Scotland
Ben Sayers
Broomie Knowe GC (R)
Scotland
James Braid
Brora GC
Sutherland, Scotland
James Braid
Brown County GC
Green Bay, Wisconsin
Edward Lawrence Packard
Brown Deer Park GC
Milwaukee, Wisconsin
George Hansen
Brown's Lake GC (R. 2)
Wisconsin
David Gill

Browns Mill GC
Atlanta, Georgia
George W. Cobb
Browns Run CC
Middleton, Ohio
William Gordon, David Gordon
Brownsville CC
Texas
Don Sechrest
Brownwood CC
Texas
Leon Howard
Bruce Memorial GC
Greenwich, Connecticut
Robert Trent Jones
Brudenell G&CC
Montague, Prince Edward Island
Clinton E. Robinson
Brunswick CC
Georgia
Donald Ross
Brunswick GC
Maine
Wayne Stiles, John Van Kleek
Brunswick GC (A. 9)
Maine
Geoffrey S. Cornish, William G. Robinson
Bruntsfield Links
Davidson's Main, Scotland
Willie Park Jr
Bruntsfield Links (R)
Scotland
James Braid
Bruntsfield Links (R) NLE
Scotland
Willie Park, Mungo Park
Bruntsfield Links (R)
Scotland
Fred W. Hawtree
Bruntsfield Links (A. 7)
Scotland
Fred W. Hawtree
Bryan CC
Ohio
Harold Paddock
Bryan Muni (R.13)
Texas
I.F. "Fred" Marberry
Bryan Muni (R. 6)
Texas
Marvin Ferguson
Bryan Park GC (Course No. 2)
Greensboro, North Carolina
Rees Jones
Bryan Park GC (Course No.1)
Greensboro, North Carolina
George W. Cobb, John LaFoy
Bryanston CC
South Africa
C.H. Alison
Bryce Mountain GC
Virginia
Edmund B. Ault
Bryn Llawen GC
Ivyville, Pennsylvania
Garrett J. Renn
Bryn Mawr GC
Chicago, Illinois
H.J. Tweedie
Bryn Mawr GC
Lincolnwood, Illinois
William B. Langford, Theodore J. Moreau
Bryn Mawr GC (R)
Illinois
William B. Langford
Bryn Mawr GC (R)
Illinois
Edward Lawrence Packard
Bryn Mawr GC (R)
Illinois
Bob Cupp, Jay Morrish
Bryn Mawr GC (A)
Illinois
Roger Packard
Bryn Meadows G&CC
Wales
Edgar Jefferies
Brynhill GC
Glamorganshire, Wales
Willie Park Jr

Brynhill GC (R)
Wales
C.K. Cotton
Brynhill GC (R)
Wales
Willie Park Jr
Brynwood CC
Milwaukee, Wisconsin
William H. Diddel
Brynwood CC (R. 6)
Wisconsin
David Gill
Brynwood CC (R)
Wisconsin
Ken Killian, Dick Nugent
Brynwood CC (A. 2)
Wisconsin
Bruce Matthews, Jerry Matthews
Brynwood CC (R. 1)
Wisconsin
Bruce Matthews, Jerry Matthews
Buccaneer Hotel GC
Virgin Islands
Robert Joyce
Buchanan Castle GC
Stirlingshire, Scotland
James Braid, John R. Stutt
Buchanan Fields GC
Concord, California
Jack Fleming
Buck Hill Inn & CC
Buck Hill Falls, Pennsylvania
Donald Ross
Buck Hill Inn & CC (A. 9)
Pennsylvania
Robert White
Buck Hill Inn & CC (R)
Pennsylvania
William Gordon, David Gordon
Buckeye Hills CC
Washington Court Hou, Ohio
X.G. Hassenplug
Buckingham CC
Dallas, Texas
Ralph Plummer
Buckingham GC
California
James Young
Bucknell University GC (A. 9)
Pennsylvania
Edmund B. Ault
Bucks County GC
Jamison, Pennsylvania
William Gordon, David Gordon
Bucksport G&CC
Maine
Phil Wogan
Bude and North Cornwall GC
England
Tom Dunn
Budock Vean Hotel GC
England
James Braid
Buena Vista CC
Vincennes, Indiana
William B. Langford
Buena Vista CC
Buena, New Jersey
William Gordon, David Gordon
Buena Vista GC
California
Lance Hopper
Buenaventura Lakes CC
Kissimmee, Florida
Ward Northrup
Buffalo Creek GC
Manatee, Florida
Ron Garl
Buffalo Dunes Muni
Garden City, Kansas
Frank Hummel
Buffalo Grove GC
Illinois
Ken Killian, Dick Nugent
Buffalo Hill GC (A. 9)
Montana
Robert Muir Graves
Buffalo Hill GC (R)
Montana
Robert Muir Graves
Buffalo Muni
Wyoming
Frank Hummel

Buford Ellington GC
Horton State Park, Tennessee
Charles M. Graves
Bukit Jambul CC
Malaysia
Robert Trent Jones Jr
Bull Bay GC
Gwynedd, Wales
Herbert Fowler
Bull Creek GC
Columbus, Georgia
Joe Lee
Bulls Eye CC
Wisconsin Rapids, Wisconsin
Leonard Macomber
Bulls Eye CC (A. 9)
Wisconsin
Edward Lawrence Packard
Bulwell Forest GC
England
Tom Dunn
Bulwell Forest GC (R)
England
Tom Williamson
Bundoran GC
County Donegal, Ireland
C.S. Butchart
Bundoran GC (R)
Ireland
Harry Vardon
Bunker Hill CC
Brush, Colorado
Frank Hummel
Bunker Hill CC
Maryland
Charles B. Schalestock
Bunker Hill GC
Medina, Ohio
Walter Kennedy
Bunker Hills Muni
Coon Rapids, Minnesota
David Gill
Bunn Park GC (R)
Illinois
Edward Lawrence Packard
Burhill GC
Surrey, England
Tom Dunn
Burhill GC (R. 9)
England
Willie Park Jr
Burhill GC (A. 9)
England
H.S. Colt
Burke Lake Park GC
Annandale, Virginia
Leon Howard
Burleigh CC
Australia
James D. Scott
Burlingame CC
Hillsborough, California
Tom Nicoll
Burlingame CC (R)
California
William Watson
Burlington County CC
Mount Holly, New Jersey
John Finley
Burlington CC
Vermont
Donald Ross
Burlington CC
Wisconsin
James Foulis
Burlington G&CC
Hamilton, Ontario
Stanley Thompson
Burlington GC
Iowa
Ben Knight
Burlington GC (R. 9)
Iowa
Edward Lawrence Packard
Burlington GC (A. 9)
Iowa
Edward Lawrence Packard
Burlington GC
Kentucky
Buck Blankenship
Burlington GC
Greensboro, North Carolina
Gene Hamm

Burlington GC (R)
Ontario
Robert Moote
Burnaby Mountain GC (R)
British Columbia
Clinton E. Robinson
Burnet Park Muni
New York
Larry Murphy
Burnham and Berrow GC (A. 9)
England
Fred W. Hawtree
Burnham Woods CC
Illinois
Stanley Pelchar
Burning Ridge GC (East Course)
Myrtle Beach, South Carolina
Gene Hamm
Burning Ridge GC (West Course)
Myrtle Beach, South Carolina
Gene Hamm
Burning Tree C
Bethesda, Maryland
C.H. Alison, H.S. Colt
Burning Tree C (R)
Maryland
William S. Flynn
Burning Tree C (R)
Maryland
Edmund B. Ault
Burning Tree C (R)
Maryland
Robert Trent Jones
Burning Tree CC
Greenwich, Connecticut
Hal Purdy
Burning Tree G&CC
Mount Clemens, Michigan
Lou Powers
Burning Tree GC
White Oak, Ohio
Edward Lawrence Packard
Burningtree CC
Decatur, Alabama
George W. Cobb
Burns Park Muni
North Little Rock, Arkansas
Joseph S. Finger
Burns Park Muni (A. 9)
Arkansas
Joseph S. Finger
Burnt Store GC
Punta Gorda, Florida
David Wallace
Burnt Store Marina GC
Punta Gorda, Florida
Ron Garl
Burntisland Golf House C (R)
Scotland
Willie Park Jr
Burswood Island GC
Perth, Australia
Robin Nelson
Burton-on-Trent GC (R)
England
Tom Williamson
Bury St. Edmonds GC
England
Ted Ray
Bury St. Edmonds GC (R)
England
J.J.F. Pennink
Buscot Park GC
England
Tom Dunn
Bush Hill Park GC (R)
England
James Braid
Bushey G & Squash C
Hertfordshire, England
J.J.F. Pennink, D.M.A. Steel
Bushfield CC
Virginia
Edmund B. Ault, Al Jamison
Bushfoot GC
Northern Ireland
John Harris
Butler County GC
Ohio
Tom Bendelow
Butler CC
Pennsylvania
Tom Bendelow

Butler CC (R)
Pennsylvania
Emil Loeffler, *John McGlynn*
Butler CC (R. 9)
Pennsylvania
Leonard Macomber
Butler CC (A. 9)
Pennsylvania
Leonard Macomber
Butler CC (R)
Pennsylvania
Edmund B. Ault
Butler CC (R)
Pennsylvania
Ferdinand Garbin
Butler National GC
Oak Brook, Illinois
George Fazio, Tom Fazio
Butte Creek G&CC
California
Bob Baldock, Robert L. Baldock
Butte CC
Montana
Alex Findlay
Butte Des Morts GC
Wisconsin
Frank Taylor
Butterfield CC
Hinsdale, Illinois
William B. Langford, Theodore J. Moreau
Butterfield CC (R)
Illinois
Edward Lawrence Packard
Butterfield CC (R)
Illinois
Ken Killian, Dick Nugent
Buttermilk Falls GC
Georgetown, Ohio
Jack Kidwell, Michael Hurdzan
Butternut Ridge CC
North Olmstead, Ohio
Harold Paddock
Buttonville GC
Ontario
Renee Muylaert, *Charles Muylaert*
Buxahatchee CC
Calera, Alabama
Bancroft Timmons
Buxton and High Peak GC (R)
England
Alister Mackenzie
Buxton and High Peak GC (R)
England
Tom Williamson
Byrncliff CC
Varysborg, New York
William Harries
Byrnewood GC
New Jersey
J.E. Wells
Byron Meadows CC
Batavia, New York
William Harries
C.F.B. Borden GC (R)
Ontario
Clinton E. Robinson
Ca' Della Nave GC
Italy
Arnold Palmer, Ed Seay
Cabarrus CC
Concord, North Carolina
George W. Cobb
Cabinet View CC
Libby, Montana
Gregor MacMillan
Cable Beach Hotel & GC
Nassau, Bahamas
Devereux Emmet, Alfred H. Tull
Cabool-Mountain Grove CC
Cabool, Missouri
Floyd Farley
Cacapon Springs GC
Berkeley Springs, West Virginia
Robert Trent Jones
Cactus Heights GC
South Dakota
Clifford A. Anderson
Cadillac CC
Michigan
Paul Blick
Cadillac CC (R. 1)
Michigan
Bruce Matthews, Jerry Matthews

Caernarvonshire GC (R)
Wales
J.J.F. Pennink
Caesarea G&CC
Isreal
Fred Smith
Cahawba Falls CC
Centerville, Alabama
Bancroft Timmons
Cahir Park GC
County Tipperary, Ireland
Eddie Hackett
Cairndnu GC (R)
Northern Ireland
Eddie Hackett
Cairo CC
Georgia
R. Albert Anderson
Calabasas Park CC
California
Robert Trent Jones, Robert Trent Jones Jr
Calais GC (R)
France
J.J.F. Pennink
Calatagan GC
Philippines
Robert Trent Jones Jr, Don Knott
Calcot Park GC
England
H.S. Colt
Caldwell GC
Glasgow, Scotland
George Fernie
Caledonia Springs GC
Ontario
Tom Bendelow
Calendo GC
Pennsylvania
C.C. Worthington
Calero Hills CC
San Jose, California
Jack Fleming
Calgary G&CC
Alberta
Willie Park Jr
Calgary G&CC (R)
Alberta
William G. Robinson
Calgary Muni
Alberta
Tom Bendelow
Calgary St. Andrews GC
Alberta
Willie Park Jr
Calhoun C
St. Matthews, South Carolina
Ellis Maples
California CC
Whittier, California
William F. Bell
California CC (R. 9)
California
Max Behr
California CC (A. 9)
California
Max Behr
California CC
Missouri
Chet Mendenhall
California GC
Cincinnati, Ohio
William H. Diddel
California GC (A. 5)
Ohio
Jack Kidwell, Michael Hurdzan
California GC of San Francisco
California
A. Vernon Macan
California GC of San Francisco (R)
California
Alister Mackenzie
California GC of San Francisco (R)
California
Robert Trent Jones, Robert Trent Jones Jr
Calimesa G&CC
California
William F. Bell
Callan GC
County Kilkenay, Ireland
P. Mahon

Callan GC (R)
Ireland
Eddie Hackett
Callander GC
Stirlingshire, Scotland
Old Tom Morris
Callaway Gardens GC (Gardensview Crs)
Pine Mountain, Georgia
Joe Lee
Callaway Gardens GC (Lakeview Course)
Pine Mountain, Georgia
Dick Wilson
Callaway Gardens GC (Lakeview Course) (A. 9)
Georgia
Dick Wilson, Joe Lee
Callaway Gardens GC (Mountainview Crs)
Pine Mountain, Georgia
Dick Wilson, Joe Lee
Callaway Gardens GC (Skyview Course)
Pine Mountain, Georgia
Joe Lee
Callemont CC
Pennsylvania
Robert L. Elder
Caloosa CC
Sun City Center, Florida
Mark Mahannah, Charles Mahannah
Calumet CC
Homewood, Illinois
Donald Ross
Calumet CC (R) NLE
Illinois
James Foulis
Calumet CC (R.12)
Illinois
Edward Lawrence Packard, Brent Wadsworth
Calusa CC
Miami, Florida
Mark Mahannah
Calvada Valley G&CC
Pahrump, Nevada
William F. Bell
Camargo C
Cincinnati, Ohio
Seth Raynor
Camargo C (R)
Ohio
Robert von Hagge
Camargo C (R. 1)
Ohio
Jack Kidwell
Camarillo Springs CC
California
Ted Robinson
Camberley Heath GC
Surrey, England
H.S. Colt
Camberley Heath GC (R)
England
Tom Simpson
Cambrian GC
San Jose, California
George E. Santana
Cambridge GC
Ontario
Clinton E. Robinson
Cambridgeshire Hotel GC
England
Fraser Middleton
Camden CC
South Carolina
Donald Ross
Camden State Park GC
Alabama
Earl Stone
Came Down GC
England
J.H. Taylor
Came Down GC (R)
England
J. Hamilton Stutt
Camelback GC (Indian Bend Course)
Scottsdale, Arizona
Arthur Jack Snyder

Camelback GC (Padre Course)
Scottsdale, Arizona
Red Lawrence
Camelback GC (Padre Course) (R. 2)
Arizona
Arthur Jack Snyder
Camelot CC
Mesa, Arizona
Milt Coggins
Camelot CC (A. 9)
Arizona
Milt Coggins
Camelot CC
Lomira, Wisconsin
Homer Fieldhouse
Camelot GC
Tennessee
Robert Thomason
Cameron Park CC
Shingle Springs, California
Bert Stamps
Camino Del Mar CC
Boca Raton, Florida
Joe Lee
Camino Heights GC
California
Bert Stamps
Camp Chic-a-mee GC
Levering, Michigan
Elmer Dankert
Camp Crowder GC
Missouri
Smiley Bell
Camp David GC
Maryland
Robert Trent Jones
Campbell River G&CC
British Columbia
Jock McKinn, Ben Fellows
Campbelltown GC
Sydney, Australia
Robert von Hagge, Bruce Devlin
Camperdown GC
Australia
Colin Campbell
Camperdown GC (A. 9)
Australia
Colin Campbell
Camperdown GC
Scotland
Fraser Middleton
Campestre de Lagunero
Mexico
Percy Clifford
Campo de G Bella Vista
Cuidad Trujillo, Dominican Republic
Alfred H. Tull
Campo de G El Saler
Spain
Javier Arana
Campo de G Somosaguas
Madrid, Spain
John Harris
Campo Carlo Magno GC (R)
Italy
Henry Cotton
Campobello Provincial Park GC
New Brunswick
Geoffrey S. Cornish, William G. Robinson
Canaan Valley State Park GC
West Virginia
Geoffrey S. Cornish, William G. Robinson
Canada Hills CC (Course No. 1)
Tucson, Arizona
Jeff Hardin, Greg Nash
Canada Hills CC (Course No. 2)
Tuscon, Arizona
Jeff Hardin
Candiac GC (R)
Quebec
Howard Watson, John Watson
Candiac GC (R. 2)
Quebec
John Watson
Candlestone GC
Belding, Michigan
Bruce Matthews, Jerry Matthews
Candlewood CC
Whittier, California
Harry Rainville

Candlewood CC (R. 6)
California
Ted Robinson
Cando GC
North Dakota
Leo Johnson
Candywood GC
Vienna, Ohio
Homer Fieldhouse
Cane Patch Par 3 GC
Myrtle Beach, South Carolina
Edmund B. Ault
Canlubang GC
Philippines
Robert Trent Jones Jr
Cannes CC
France
Wilfrid Reid
Cannes CC (R)
France
Robert Berthet
Canoa Hills GC
Green Valley, Arizona
Dave Bennett
Canoe Brook CC (North Course) NLE
Millburn, New Jersey
C.H. Alison, H.S. Colt
Canoe Brook CC (North Course)
Millburn, New Jersey
Alfred H. Tull
Canoe Brook CC (North Course) (R) NLE
New Jersey
Carroll P. Bassett
Canoe Brook CC (North Course) (R)
New Jersey
William Gordon, David Gordon
Canoe Brook CC (North Course) (R)
New Jersey
Robert Trent Jones, Rees Jones
Canoe Brook CC (South Course)
Summit, New Jersey
Walter J. Travis
Canoe Brook CC (South Course) (R)
New Jersey
William Gordon, David Gordon
Canoe Brook CC (South Course) (R)
New Jersey
Rees Jones
Canoe Creek CC
Gadsen, Alabama
Harold Williams
Canon del Oro CC
Sedona, Arizona
Arthur Jack Snyder
Canongate GC
Orlando, Florida
Joe Lee
Canongate GC
Palmetto, Georgia
Dick Wilson, Joe Lee
Canongate-on Lanier GC
Cumming, Georgia
Joe Lee, Rocky Roquemore
Canons Brook GC
England
Henry Cotton
Canterbury CC
Shaker Heights, Ohio
Herbert Strong
Canterbury CC (R)
Ohio
Geoffrey S. Cornish, William G. Robinson
Canterbury Green GC
Fort Wayne, Indiana
Robert Beard
Canterbury Place GC
Crystal Lake, Illinois
Bob Lohmann
Cantigny GC
Wheaton, Illinois
Roger Packard
Canton Park District GC (A. 9)
Ohio
Edward Lawrence Packard
Canton Public GC
Connecticut
Robert J. Ross

Canyon Creek CC now known as Club at Sonterra (South Course)
Canyon CC
Palm Springs, California
William F. Bell
Canyon CC (R)
California
William F. Mitchell
Canyon GC now known as Americana Canyon Hotel GC
Canyon Lake GC
California
Ted Robinson
Canyon Lakes CC
Danville, California
Ted Robinson
Canyon Lakes G&CC
Kennewick, Washington
Peter Thomson, Michael Wolveridge, Ronald Fream, John Steidel
Canyon Meadows G&CC (R)
Alberta
William G. Robinson
Canyon Mesa GC
Sedona, Arizona
Arthur Jack Snyder
Canyon Ridge CC
New Jersey
Gerald C. Roby
Canyon Springs GC
Twin Falls, Idaho
Max Mueller
Cape Ann GC
Essex, Massachusetts
Eugene "Skip" Wogan
Cape Arundel GC
Kennebunkport, Maine
John Duncan Dunn, Walter J. Travis
Cape Breton Highlands National Park GC
Keltic Lodge, Nova Scotia
Stanley Thompson
Cape Cod CC
North Falmouth, Massachusetts
Devereux Emmet, Alfred H. Tull
Cape Cod CC (A. 9)
Massachusetts
Alfred H. Tull
Cape Coral CC
Florida
Dick Wilson, Robert von Hagge
Cape Coral Executive GC
Florida
Sid Clarke
Cape Coral Muni
Florida
Arthur Hills, Steve Forrest, Mike Dasher
Cape Eleuthera GC
Bahamas
Robert von Hagge, Bruce Devlin
Cape Fear CC
Wilmington, North Carolina
Donald Ross
Cape Fear CC (R)
North Carolina
John LaFoy
Cape G&CC
Wilmington, North Carolina
Gene Hamm
Cape Girardeau CC
Missouri
Al Linkogel
Cape Girardeau CC (R. 2)
Missouri
Edward Lawrence Packard, Brent Wadsworth
Cape Girardeau CC (A. 2)
Missouri
Edward Lawrence Packard, Brent Wadsworth
Cape Girardeau CC (A. 9)
Missouri
David Gill
Cape Girardeau CC (R. 9)
Missouri
David Gill
Cape Royale CC
Texas
Bruce Littell

Capehart GC
Bellevue, Nebraska
Robert Trent Jones
Capilano G&CC
West Vancouver, British Columbia
Stanley Thompson
Capital City C
Georgia
Herbert Barker
Capital City C (R)
Georgia
George W. Cobb
Capital City C (R)
Georgia
Arthur Hills, Mike Dasher
Capital City CC
Tallahassee, Florida
John Budd
Capital City CC (R)
Florida
R. Albert Anderson
Capital City GC
Olympia, Washington
Norman H. Woods
Capitol Hills CC
Philippines
Francisco D. Santana
Capri Isles GC
Venice, Florida
Lane Marshall
Caprock G&CC
Lubbock, Texas
Warren Cantrell
Captains GC
Brewster, Massachusetts
Brian Silva, Geoffrey S. Cornish
Carabelleda G&YC
Macuto, Venezuela
John Van Kleek
Carambola Beach GC formerly known as Fountain Valley GC
Frederiksted, Virgin Islands
Robert Trent Jones
Carbondale CC
Illinois
William H. Diddel
Card Sound GC
North Key Largo, Florida
Robert von Hagge, Bruce Devlin
Cardiff GC
Alberta
William G. Robinson
Cardinal Creek GC (R)
Illinois
Gary Kern
Cardinal GC
Greensboro, North Carolina
Pete Dye
Cardross GC
Dumbartonshire, Scotland
Willie Fernie
Cariari International CC
San Jose, Costa Rica
George Fazio, Tom Fazio
Carimate Parco GC
Italy
Pier Mancinelli
Carimate Parco GC (R)
Italy
Pier Mancinelli
Carl E. Smock GC
Indianapolis, Indiana
Bob Simmons
Carleton Glen GC
Michigan
Joseph E. Milosch
Carling Lake GC
Pine Hill, Quebec
Howard Watson
Carlinville GC
Illinois
Edward Lawrence Packard
Carlisle GC
Cumberland, England
Theodore Moone
Carlisle GC (R)
England
J.J.F. Pennink
Carlisle GC (R)
England
P.M. Ross
Carlisle Race Track GC
Cumbria, England
D.M.A. Steel

Carlow GC (R)
Ireland
Eddie Hackett
Carlow GC (R)
Ireland
Tom Simpson, *Molly Gourlay*
Carlton Island GC NLE
New York
Stanley Thompson, Robert Trent
Jones
Carlton Oaks CC
California
William W. Mast
Carlton Yacht & GC (R. 1)
Ontario
Howard Watson
Carlton Yacht & GC (R. 1)
Ontario
John Watson
Carlyon Bay GC
Cornwall, England
J. Hamilton Stutt
Carmack Lake GC
Converse, Texas
Donald Carmack
Carmel CC (North Course)
Charlotte, North Carolina
George W. Cobb
Carmel CC (North Course) (R)
North Carolina
Rees Jones
Carmel CC (South Course)
Charlotte, North Carolina
Ellis Maples
Carmel CC (South Course) (A. 9)
North Carolina
Ellis Maples, Ed Seay
Carmel CC (South Course) (R)
North Carolina
Rees Jones
Carmel Mountain Ranch GC
Rancho Bernardo, California
Ronald Fream
Carmel Valley G&CC
Carmel, California
Robert Muir Graves
Carmel Valley Ranch GC
Carmel, California
Pete Dye, David Pfaff
Carmen G&CC
Manitoba
John A. Thompson
Carnalea GC
Northern Ireland
James Braid, John R. Stutt
Carnoustie G&CC
Burns Lake, British Columbia
Mel Forbes, Peggy Forbes
Carnoustie GC
Angus, Scotland
Allan Robertson
Carnoustie GC (R)
Scotland
Willie Park Jr
Carnoustie GC (R)
Scotland
Old Tom Morris
Carnoustie GC (A. 6)
Scotland
Old Tom Morris
Carnoustie GC (R)
Scotland
James Braid, John R. Stutt
Carnoustie GC (Burnside
Course)
Angus, Scotland
James Braid
Caro GC
Michigan
F.L. Clark
Carolina G&CC
Charlotte, North Carolina
Donald Ross
Carolina Pines G&CC (R)
North Carolina
Gene Hamm
Carolina Sands GC
White Lake, North Carolina
Willard Byrd
Carolina Shores GC
Calabash, North Carolina
Tom Jackson

Carolina Trace G&CC
Sanford, North Carolina
Robert Trent Jones, Roger
Rulewich
Carolina Trace GC
Harrison, Ohio
Robert von Hagge
Caroline CC
Maryland
Edmund B. Ault
Carper Valley GC
Virginia
Fred Findlay
Carradam CC
Irwin, Pennsylvania
James Gilmore Harrison,
Ferdinand Garbin
Carriage Hills G&CC
Pensacola, Florida
Brent Lane
Carrick-on-Shannon GC (R)
Ireland
Eddie Hackett
Carrick-on-Suir GC (R)
Ireland
Eddie Hackett
Carrol Lake GC
McKenzie, Tennessee
R. Albert Anderson
Carroll County GC
Berryville, Arkansas
Herman Hackbarth
Carroll CC NLE
Iowa
Jack Hawkins
Carroll Park Muni
Baltimore, Maryland
Gus Hook
Carrollton CC (R. 9)
Pennsylvania
Marvin Ferguson
Carrollwood Village G&TC
Florida
Edmund B. Ault
Carson City Muni
Nevada
Bob Baldock
Carstairs G&CC
Alberta
William G. Robinson
Carswell AFB GC
Texas
Charles B. Akey
Carter Caves State Park GC
Olive Hill, Kentucky
Hal Purdy
Carter CC
Lebanon, New Hampshire
Donald Ross
Cartersville CC (R. 9)
Georgia
Arthur Davis, Ron Kirby, Gary
Player
Cartersville CC (A. 9)
Georgia
Arthur Davis, Ron Kirby, Gary
Player
Carthage Muni
Missouri
Tom Bendelow
Carthage Muni (A. 9)
Missouri
Don Sechrest
Carthage Muni (R. 9)
Missouri
Don Sechrest
Cary CC
Indiana
R. Albert Anderson
Casa de Campo (Links Course)
La Ramona, Dominican Republic
Pete Dye, Alice Dye, *Lee Schmidt*
Casa de Campo (Teeth of the
Dog Course)
La Romana, Dominican Republic
Pete Dye
Casa de Mar G&CC
Nevada
Bob Baldock
Casa Blanca GC
Laredo, Texas
Leon Howard

Casaview CC NLE
Dallas, Texas
Leon Howard
Cascade Fairways GC
Orem, Utah
William H. Neff
Cascade GC
Idaho
Bob Baldock
Cascade Hills CC
Grand Rapids, Michigan
Jack Daray
Cascade Hills CC (R)
Michigan
David Gill
Cascade Hills CC (R)
Michigan
Edward Lawrence Packard
Cascade Hills CC (R)
Michigan
Bruce Matthews, Jerry Matthews
Cascade Hills CC (R. 9)
Michigan
Jerry Matthews
Cascades GC
Virginia Hot Springs, Virginia
William S. Flynn
Cascades GC (R)
Virginia
Robert Trent Jones
Case Leasing GC
Celina, Michigan
Robert Beard
Case Noyale GC
Port Louis, Mauritius
Peter Thomson, Michael
Wolveridge
Casey GC
Pacific, Missouri
Gary Kern
Casino C
San Salvador, El Salvador
Fred W. Hawtree
Caslano GC (R)
Switzerland
Edmund B. Ault
Casper CC
Wyoming
James Mason
Casper CC NLE
Wyoming
Tom Bendelow
Casper CC (A. 9)
Wyoming
Bob Baldock
Casper CC (R. 9)
Wyoming
Bob Baldock
Casper CC (R)
Wyoming
Robert Muir Graves
Casper Muni (R)
Wyoming
Robert Muir Graves
Casselberry G&CC
Florida
Paul McClure
Casselberry G&CC (R. 9)
Florida
Lloyd Clifton
Casselberry G&CC (A. 9)
Florida
Lloyd Clifton
Casta del Sol GC
Mission Viejo, California
Ted Robinson
Castine GC
Maine
Willie Park Jr
Castle AFB GC
California
Bob Baldock
Castle Eden and Peterlee GC (R)
England
Henry Cotton
Castle GC
Dublin, Ireland
Cecil Barcroft, *Tom Hood*, W.C.
Pickeman
Castle GC (R)
Ireland
Eddie Hackett

Castle GC (R)
Ireland
H.S. Colt
Castle Harbour GC
Tuckerstown, Bermuda
Charles Banks
Castle Hawk GC
Lancashire, England
E. Jones
Castle Inn GC NLE
Bermuda
Devereux Emmet
Castle Pines GC
Castle Rock, Colorado
Jack Nicklaus, Jay Morrish, Bob
Cupp, Scott Miller
Castle Rock GC
Pembroke, Virginia
Ferdinand Garbin
Castle View T&CC
Atlanta, Georgia
Chic Adams
Castlebar GC (R. 9)
Ireland
Eddie Hackett
Castlebar GC (A. 9)
Ireland
Eddie Hackett
Castlebar GC (R. 4)
Ireland
Paddy Skerritt
Castlebrook G&CC
Lowell, Indiana
William James Spear
Castlecoole GC (A. 1)
Northern Ireland
T.J.A. McAuley
Castlefalfi GC
Italy
Pier Mancinelli
Castlerea GC (R)
Ireland
Eddie Hackett
Castlerock GC
County Londonderry, Northern
Ireland
Ben Sayers
Castlerock GC (R)
Northern Ireland
Eddie Hackett
Castlerock GC (A. 9)
Northern Ireland
J.J.F. Pennink
Castletown GC
Isle of Man
Old Tom Morris
Castletown GC (R)
Isle of Man
Alister Mackenzie
Castletown GC (R)
Isle of Man
P.M. Ross
Castletroy GC
County Limerick, Ireland
Ronnie Deakin
Castletroy GC (R)
Ireland
Eddie Hackett
Castlewood CC (A. 9)
Mississippi
Dave Bennett
Castlewood CC (Hill Course)
Pleasanton, California
William P. Bell
Castlewood CC (Valley Course)
Pleasanton, California
William P. Bell
Castro CC
Texas
Leon Howard
Cat Island CC
Fripp Island, South Carolina
George W. Cobb, *Byron Comstock*
Catalina GC
Avalon, California
John Duncan Dunn
Cataraqui G&CC
Kingston, Ontario
Stanley Thompson
Catatonk GC
Candor, New York
Hal Purdy

Catawba Cliffs CC
Port Clinton, Ohio
William J. Rockefeller
Catawba CC
Newton, North Carolina
Donald Ross
Catawba Island C
Port Clinton, Ohio
Gary Grandstaff
Cathcart Castle GC (R)
Scotland
John R. Stutt
Cathedral Canyon CC
Cathedral City, California
David Rainville
Cathedral Canyon CC (A. 9)
California
David Rainville
Catskills Village GC NLE
New York
John Duncan Dunn
Cavalier G&YC
Virginia
Charles Banks
Cavaliers CC
New Castle, Delaware
Frank Murray, Russell Roberts
Cavalry C
Manlius, New York
Dick Wilson, Joe Lee
Cave Creek Muni
Phoenix, Arizona
Arthur Jack Snyder
Cavendish GC
Derbyshire, England
Alister Mackenzie
Cavendish GC (R)
England
Tom Williamson
Cawder GC (Cawder Course)
Scotland
James Braid, John R. Stutt
Cawder GC (Keir Course)
Scotland
James Braid, John R. Stutt
Caymanas G&CC
Spanish Town, Jamaica
Howard Watson
Cazenovia CC
New York
Seymour Dunn
Cazenovia CC (A. 9)
New York
Hal Purdy
CdG Charny (A. 9)
Quebec
Howard Watson, John Watson
CdG Charny (R. 9)
Quebec
Howard Watson
CdG Montcalm
St-Liquori, Quebec
John Watson
Ceann Sibeal GC
County Kerry, Ireland
Eddie Hackett
Cedar Bend GC
Oregon
John Zoller
Cedar Brae G&CC
East Toronto, Ontario
Clinton E. Robinson
Cedar Brook CC
Brookville, New York
Al Zikorus
Cedar Brook CC
Elkin, North Carolina
Ellis Maples, Ed Seay
Cedar Brook GC
London, Ontario
Robert Moote
Cedar Creek GC
Leo, Indiana
Robert Beard
Cedar Creek GC
Battle Creek, Michigan
Robert Beard
Cedar Crest GC
Antioch, Illinois
George O'Neill
Cedar Crest GC
Dallas, Texas
A.W. Tillinghast

Cedar Crest GC (R)
Texas
John Bredemus
Cedar Glen GC (R)
Massachusetts
Orrin Smith, William F. Mitchell
Cedar Glenn G&CC (A. 9)
Ontario
John F. Robinson
Cedar Hills GC
Omaha, Nebraska
Harold Glissmann
Cedar Knob CC
Somers, Connecticut
Geoffrey S. Cornish
Cedar Knoll CC
Ashland, Kentucky
James Gilmore Harrison
Cedar Lake GC
Indiana
R. Albert Anderson
Cedar Links GC
Medford, Oregon
Dale Coverstone
Cedar Point C
Norfolk, Virginia
Arthur Jack Snyder
Cedar Point C (R)
Virginia
Tom Clark
Cedar Rapids CC NLE
Iowa
Tom Bendelow
Cedar Rapids CC
Iowa
Donald Ross
Cedar Ridge CC
Broken Arrow, Oklahoma
Joseph S. Finger
Cedar Ridges GC
Rangley, Colorado
Frank Hummel
Cedar Rock CC
Lenoir, North Carolina
Ellis Maples
Cedar Rocks CC
Wheeling, Pennsylvania
Emil Loeffler, *John McGlynn*
Cedar Springs GC
Waupacas, Wisconsin
Homer Fieldhouse
Cedar Valley GC
Guthrie, Oklahoma
Floyd Farley
Cedar Valley GC (A. 9)
Oklahoma
Floyd Farley
Cedar Valley GC (A. 9)
Oklahoma
Floyd Farley
Cedar Valley GC
Antigua and Barbuda
Ralph Aldridge
Cedarbrook CC NLE
Philadelphia, Pennsylvania
A.W. Tillinghast
Cedarbrook CC
Blue Bell, Pennsylvania
William F. Mitchell
Cedarbrook CC (R) NLE
Pennsylvania
Donald Ross
Cedarbrook G&CC
Toronto, Ontario
Stanley Thompson
Cedarbrook GC
Smithton, Pennsylvania
James Gilmore Harrison,
  Ferdinand Garbin
Cedarbrook GC
Ste. Sophie, Quebec
Howard Watson
Cedarcrest GC (R)
Washington
Peter Thomson, Michael
  Wolveridge,Ronald Fream
Cedarcrest GC (R. 2)
Washington
John Steidel
Cedardell GC
Plano, Illinois
Leonard Macomber

Cedarholm Muni
Minnesota
Paul Coates
Cedarhurst CC
Ohio
William H. Livie
Cedarwood CC
Matthews, North Carolina
Ellis Maples
Centennial Acres GC
Sunfield, Michigan
Warner Bowen
Centennial CC
Chattanooga, Tennessee
Arthur Davis
Centennial Downs GC
Littleton, Colorado
Dick Phelps
Centennial GC NLE
Littleton, Colorado
Jack Fleming
Center Square GC
Pennsylvania
Edmund B. Ault
Centerbrook GC
Brooklyn, Minnesota
Donald G. Brauer, Paul S. Fjare
Centerville G&CC
Iowa
Tom Bendelow
Centerwood CC
Gig Harbor, Washington
Robert Muir Graves, Damian
  Pascuzzo
Central City CC
Kentucky
Harold England
Central Valley GC
New York
Hal Purdy
Centralia CC
Missouri
Chet Mendenhall
Centre Hills CC
State College, Pennsylvania
Alex Findlay
Centre Hills CC (R)
Pennsylvania
James Gilmore Harrison
Centre Hills CC (A. 9)
Pennsylvania
Robert Trent Jones
Centro Deportivo GC
Acapulco, Mexico
Percy Clifford
Century GC
West Palm Beach, Florida
Joe Lee
Century GC
White Plains, New York
C.H. Alison, H.S. Colt
Century GC (R)
New York
Robert Trent Jones, Frank Duane
Century Hills CC
Rocky Hill, Connecticut
Geoffrey S. Cornish, William G.
  Robinson
Century Village GC
Deerfield Beach, Florida
Joe Lee
Century XXI Club
Germantown, Maryland
Algie Pulley
Cerritos Iron-Wood Nine GC
Cerritos, California
Ted Robinson
**Cerromar Beach GC (North
  Course)**
Dorado Beach, Puerto Rico
Robert Trent Jones, Roger
  Rulewich
**Cerromar Beach GC (South
  Course)**
Dorado Beach, Puerto Rico
Robert Trent Jones, Roger
  Rulewich
Cervino GC
Cervinia, Italy
Donald Harradine
Cervino GC (A. 9)
Italy
Fred W. Hawtree

Chabre GC
Somerset, Wisconsin
John R. Nelson
Chace Lake CC
Montgomery, Alabama
Bancroft Timmons
Chadron CC
Nebraska
Frank Hummel
Chadwell Springs GC
Hertfordshire, England
J.H. Taylor
Chagrin Valley CC
Chagrin Falls, Ohio
Stanley Thompson
Chain O'Lakes GC (R)
Indiana
Ken Killian, Dick Nugent
Chalk Mountain Muni
Atascadero, California
Robert Muir Graves
Chamberlain CC
South Dakota
Robert Bruce Harris
Chambersburg CC (R)
Pennsylvania
David Gordon, William Gordon
Chambersburg CC (A. 9)
Pennsylvania
Brian Ault, Edmund B. Ault
Chamonix GC (R)
France
Robert Trent Jones, Cabell
  Robinson
Champaign CC
Illinois
Tom Bendelow
Champaign CC (R)
Illinois
Edward Lawrence Packard
Champion Lakes GC
Bolivar, Pennsylvania
Paul E. Erath
**Champions GC (Cypress Creek
  Course)**
Houston, Texas
Ralph Plummer
**Champions GC (Jackrabbit
  Course)**
Houston, Texas
George Fazio
Champlain GC
Ville, Brossard, Quebec
Howard Watson
Chantilly Manor CC
Rising Sun, Maryland
Russell Roberts
Chantilly National G&CC
Virginia
Edmund B. Ault, Al Jamison
Chanute AFB GC
Rantoul, Illinois
Edward Lawrence Packard
Chanute AFB GC (A. 9)
Illinois
Edward Lawrence Packard
Chaparral CC
Palm Desert, California
Ted Robinson
Chaparral CC
Sequin, Texas
Leon Howard
Chapel Hill CC
North Carolina
Fred Findlay
Chapel Hill CC (R)
North Carolina
George W. Cobb
Chapel Hill CC (R)
North Carolina
Gene Hamm
Chapel Hills GC
Ashtabula, Ohio
Richard W. LaConte
Chapel Woods GC
Lee's Summit, Missouri
Ray Bondurant
Chapel-en-le-Firth GC
Derbyshire, England
David Thomas
Chappaqua CC NLE
New York
Tom Bendelow

Chappel G&RC (R. 9)
Ontario
Donald G. Brauer, Emile Perret
Chappel G&RC (A. 9)
Ontario
Donald G. Brauer, Emile Perret
Chappell CC
Nebraska
Frank Hummel
Chappequa CC
Mt. Kisco, New York
Donald Ross
Chapultepec CC
Mexico
Willie Smith, *Alex Smith*
Chapultepec CC (R)
Mexico
Percy Clifford
Charbonneau GC
Wilsonville, Oregon
Ted Robinson
Chardonnay CC
Napa, California
Algie Pulley
Charles City CC NLE
Iowa
William H. Livie
Charles City CC
Iowa
Dick Phelps
Charles River CC
Newton Centre, Massachusetts
Donald Ross
Charles River CC (R)
Massachusetts
William F. Mitchell
Charles Schwab Estate GC
Loretto, Pennsylvania
Donald Ross
Charles T. Myers GC
North Carolina
Bill Love
Charleston AFB GC
South Carolina
George W. Cobb
Charleston Muni
South Carolina
John E. Adams
Charleville GC (R)
Ireland
Eddie Hackett
Charlevoix Muni
Michigan
William Watson
Charlie Chaplin Estate GC
Beverly Hills, California
Alister Mackenzie
Charlotte CC
Michigan
Tom Bendelow
Charlotte CC (R)
North Carolina
Donald Ross
Charlotte CC (R)
North Carolina
Hugh Moore
Charlotte CC (R)
North Carolina
Robert Trent Jones
Charlotte CC (R)
North Carolina
Robert Trent Jones
Charmingfare Links
Candia, New Hampshire
Phil Wogan
Charnita CC
Pennsylvania
Edmund B. Ault
Charnwood Forest GC
Leicester, England
James Braid
Chartiers CC
Pittsburgh, Pennsylvania
Willie Park Jr
Chartiers CC (R)
Pennsylvania
Emil Loeffler, *John McGlynn*
Chartiers CC (R)
Pennsylvania
X.G. Hassenplug
Chartwell G&CC
Maryland
Edmund B. Ault, Al Jamison

Chase Hammond Muni
Muskegon, Michigan
Mark DeVries
**Chase Oaks GC (Blackjack
  Course)**
Plano, Texas
Robert von Hagge, Bruce Devlin
**Chase Oaks GC (Sawtooth
  Course)**
Plano, Texas
Robert von Hagge, Bruce Devlin
Chaska GC
Greenville, Wisconsin
Edward Lawrence Packard,
  Roger Packard
Chatham CC
Virginia
Gene Hamm
Chatham G&CC
Ontario
Clinton E. Robinson
Chatmoss CC
Martinsville, Virginia
Ellis Maples
Chatsworth GC (R)
England
Tom Williamson
Chattahoochee GC
Abbeville, Alabama
Bill Amick
Chattahoochee GC
Gainesville, Georgia
Robert Trent Jones, Frank Duane
Chattanooga G&CC
Tennessee
Donald Ross
Chattanooga G&CC (R)
Tennessee
Alex McKay
Chattanooga G&CC (R. 4)
Tennessee
Arthur Davis
Chattanooga G&CC (R)
Tennessee
Gary Roger Baird
Chatuge Shores CC
Hayesville, North Carolina
John V. Townsend
Chautauqua GC
New York
Seymour Dunn
Chautauqua GC (A. 9)
New York
Donald Ross
Chautauqua GC (R. 9)
New York
Donald Ross
Chautauqua GC (R)
New York
X.G. Hassenplug
Chautauqua GC (Course No. 2)
New York
X.G. Hassenplug
Cheat Lake GC
Morgantown, West Virginia
James Gilmore Harrison
Chedoke GC (New Course)
Hamilton, Ontario
Stanley Thompson
Chedoke GC (Old Course) (R)
Ontario
Stanley Thompson
Cheeca Lodge GC
Florida
Bob Cupp, Jay Morrish
Chelmsford GC
Essex, England
John Harris
Chemay Estate GC
France
Seymour Dunn
Chemnitzer GC
Slauv-Floeha, East Germany
Karl Hoffmann, Bernhard von
  Limburger
Chemung Hills CC (R)
Michigan
Arthur Hills, Steve Forrest
Chemung Hills GC (A. 9)
Michigan
William Newcomb, Stephen Kay
Chenango Valley GC
Binghampton, New York
Hal Purdy

Chenequa GC
Hartland, Wisconsin
Tom Bendelow
Chenequa GC (A. 9)
Wisconsin
Edward Lawrence Packard
Chennault GC
Monroe, Louisiana
Winnie Cole
Chenoweth GC
Jeffersontown, Kentucky
Benjamin Wihry
Cherokee CC (R)
Tennessee
Alex McKay
Cherokee CC (R)
Tennessee
Dan Maples
Cherokee CC
Jacksonville, Texas
Carl Gregory
Cherokee CC
Madison, Wisconsin
David Gill
Cherokee Grove GC
Grove, Oklahoma
Vince Bizik
Cherokee GC
Centre, Alabama
Neil R. Bruce
Cherokee GC
Louisville, Kentucky
Tom Bendelow
Cherokee GC (R)
Kentucky
Alex McKay
Cherokee GC (R)
Kentucky
Edward Lawrence Packard
Cherokee Hills CC
Bellefontaine, Ohio
Wilton Ede
Cherokee National G&CC
Gaffney, South Carolina
J. Porter Gibson
Cherokee Town & CC (Hillside Course)
Dunwoody, Georgia
David Gill
Cherokee Town & CC (Hillside Course) (R)
Georgia
Willard Byrd
Cherokee Town & CC (Riverside Course)
Dunwoody, Georgia
Willard Byrd
Cherokee Town & CC (Riverside Course) (A. 9)
Georgia
Joe Lee, Rocky Roquemore
Cherokee Village CC (North Course)
Arkansas
Edmund B. Ault
Cherokee Village CC (South Course)
Arkansas
Edmund B. Ault
Cherry Chase CC
Sunnyvale, California
Bob Amyx
Cherry Downs GC
Claremont, Ontario
Howard Watson
Cherry Hill GC
Massachusetts
David Maxon
Cherry Hill GC
Ontario, Ontario
Walter J. Travis
Cherry Hill GC (R)
Ontario
Clinton E. Robinson
Cherry Hills CC
Englewood, Colorado
William S. Flynn
Cherry Hills CC (R)
Colorado
Press Maxwell
Cherry Hills CC (A. 9)
Colorado
Press Maxwell

Cherry Hills CC (R)
Colorado
Arnold Palmer, Ed Seay
Cherry Hills CC
Flossmoor, Illinois
Harry Collis, Jack Daray
Cherry Hills CC (A. 9)
Illinois
David Gill
Cherry Hills CC (R)
Illinois
Gary Kern
Cherry Hills CC (Course No. 2) NLE
Flossmoor, Illinois
Joe Meister
Cherry Hills GC
Sun City, California
Milt Coggins
Cherry Lane GC
Meridian, Idaho
Bob Baldock, Robert L. Baldock
Cherry Lodge GC
Kent, England
John Day
Cherry Point GC
North Carolina
George W. Cobb
Cherry Ridge GC
Elyria, Ohio
Harold Paddock
Cherry Valley CC (R)
New Jersey
Willie Park Jr
Cherry Valley CC (R.12)
New Jersey
Frank Duane
Cherry Valley CC
Garden City, New York
Devereux Emmet
Cherry Valley CC (R)
New York
Robert Trent Jones, Frank Duane
Chesapeake CC
Lusby, Maryland
James Thompson
Chester CC
Illinois
Bill Amick
Chester GC
Greenville, South Carolina
Russell Breeden
Chester GC
England
Fred W. Hawtree, A.H.F. Jiggens
Chester River Y&CC
Chestertown, Maryland
Alex Findlay
Chester River Y&CC (R)
Maryland
Edmund B. Ault
Chester Valley CC
Pennsylvania
Perry Maxwell
Chester Valley CC (R)
Pennsylvania
George Fazio
Chester W. Ditto Muni
Arlington, Texas
Ken Killian, Dick Nugent, Jeff Brauer
Chesterfield GC (R)
England
Tom Williamson
Chestnut Hill CC
Newton, Massachusetts
Samuel Mitchell
Chestnut Hill CC
Ravenna, Ohio
Harold Paddock
Chestnut Park GC
Herts, England
Fred W. Hawtree
Chestnut Ridge CC
Lutherville, Maryland
Alex McKay
Chestnut Ridge CC (R. 9)
Maryland
Russell Roberts
Chestnut Ridge CC (A. 9)
Maryland
Russell Roberts

Chestnut Ridge CC
Indiana, Pennsylvania
James Gilmore Harrison, Ferdinand Garbin
Chestuee G&CC
Etawah, Tennessee
Bill Amick
Cheval Polo & CC
Tampa, Florida
Karl Litten
Cheviot Hills GC
Raleigh, North Carolina
Gene Hamm
Chevy Chase CC
Glendale, California
William F. Bell, William P. Bell
Chevy Chase CC (R. 9)
California
Harry Rainville, David Rainville
Chevy Chase CC
Wheeling, Illinois
Tom Bendelow
Chevy Chase CC (R)
Illinois
Ken Killian, Dick Nugent
Chevy Chase CC NLE
Kansas City, Kansas
James Dalgleish
Chevy Chase CC
Maryland
Donald Ross
Chevy Chase CC (R)
Maryland
C.H. Alison, H.S. Colt
Chevy Chase CC (R)
Maryland
Robert Trent Jones
Cheyenne CC NLE
Wyoming
Tom Bendelow
Cheyenne CC
Wyoming
Herbert Lockwood
Chiba CC
Japan
Kinya Fujita
Chicago G & Saddle C NLE
Chicago, Illinois
Charles Maddox, *Frank P. MacDonald*
Chicago GC
Wheaton, Illinois
Charles Blair Macdonald
Chicago GC (R)
Illinois
Seth Raynor
Chicago GC now known as Downers Grove GC
Chicago Lakes GC
Lindstrom, Minnesota
Donald G. Brauer, Paul S. Fjare
Chickaming GC
Michigan
Harry Collis
Chickasaw CC
Memphis, Tennessee
William B. Langford
Chickasaw Point GC
Fair Play, South Carolina
Russell Breeden
Chickasha CC
Oklahoma
Woody Kerr
Chicopee Muni
Massachusetts
Geoffrey S. Cornish
Chicora CC (R)
North Carolina
Gene Hamm
Chicoutimi GC
Quebec
Howard Watson
Chiemsee GC
Prien, West Germany
Donald Harradine
Chiemsee GC (A. 9)
West Germany
J.F. Dudok Van Heel
Chigusa CC
Japan
Peter Thomson, Michael Wolveridge

Chigwell GC
Essex, England
F.G. Hawtree, J.H. Taylor
Chihuahua CC
Mexico
Percy Clifford
Chilliwack G&CC
British Columbia
Ernest Brown
Chilwell Manor GC (R)
England
Tom Williamson
Chimney Rock GC
Napa, California
Bob Baldock, Robert L. Baldock
China Lake GC
California
William F. Bell
Chingford GC
England
Willie Dunn Jr
Chinguacousy CC
Brampton, Ontario
Renee Muylaert
Chippanee GC
Bristol, Connecticut
Herbert Lagerblade
Chippenham GC (R)
England
J.J.F. Pennink
Chippewa CC
Barberton, Ohio
James Gilmore Harrison, Ferdinand Garbin
Chippewa CC (A. 9)
Ohio
Ferdinand Garbin
Chippewa CC (A. 9)
Pennsylvania
Ferdinand Garbin
Chippewa CC (R. 9)
Pennsylvania
James Gilmore Harrison, Ferdinand Garbin
Chippewa CC (A. 9)
Pennsylvania
James Gilmore Harrison, Ferdinand Garbin
Chipping Sodbury GC
Avon, England
Fred W. Hawtree
Chiselhurst GC
Kent, England
Tom Dunn
Chiselhurst GC (R)
England
Willie Park Jr
Chockoyette CC
Roanoke Rapids, North Carolina
Ellis Maples, Ed Seay
Chorley GC
England
Fred W. Hawtree, A.H.F. Jiggens
Christchurch CC NLE
New Zealand
Denis O'Rorke, L.B. Wood
Christchurch CC
Shirley, New Zealand
Des Soutar
Christiana CC
Elkhart, Indiana
William B. Langford, Theodore J. Moreau
Christiana CC (A. 9)
Indiana
William B. Langford
Christina Lake GC
British Columbia
Reg Stone, Roy Stone
Christmas Lake G&CC
Santa Claus, Indiana
Edmund B. Ault
Christmas Valley GC
Oregon
Joe Ward
Christown G&CC
Phoenix, Arizona
Milt Coggins
Chromonix CC
Hugo, Minnesota
Don Herfort
Chrysler Memorial Park GC
Morrisburg, Ontario
Howard Watson

Chuckie Creek CC
Bowling Green, Ohio
Harold Paddock
Chula Vista Muni
Bonita, California
Harry Rainville
Chulmleigh GC
North Devon, England
J.W.D. Goodban, W.G. Mortimer
Chung-Shan GC
China
Arnold Palmer, Ed Seay, Bob Walker
Church Stretton GC
Shropshire, England
James Braid
Churchill Valley CC (R)
Pennsylvania
James Gilmore Harrison, Ferdinand Garbin
Churston GC (R)
England
H.S. Colt
Churubusco CC
Mexico City, Mexico
John Bredemus
Churubusco CC (R)
Mexico
Robert Trent Jones Jr
Churubusco CC (R)
Mexico
Manny Francis
Cielo Vista GC
El Paso, Texas
Marvin Ferguson
Cimarron CC
McAllen, Texas
Dave Bennett
Cimarron CC
East Oakdale, Minnesota
Don Herfort
Cimarron Hills GC
Colorado Springs, Colorado
Press Maxwell
Cincinnati CC (R)
Ohio
William Newcomb
Cincinnati CC (R. 9)
Ohio
Robert White
Cincinnati CC (A. 9)
Ohio
Robert White
Cincinnati CC (A. 4)
Ohio
William Newcomb
Circle Bar GC
Westfir, Oregon
Clarence Sutton
Circle J GC
Newhall, California
William P. Bell
Circle R Ranch GC
Escondido, California
Jack Daray
Circle R Ranch GC (R)
California
Jack Daray Jr
Circleston CC
Georgia
Sid Clarke
Circolo G Lido di Venezia (A. 9)
Italy
C.K. Cotton, John Harris
Circolo G Lido di Venezia (R. 9)
Italy
John Harris
Cirencester GC
Gloucestershire, England
John Harris
Citrus Hills G&CC (Meadows Course)
Hernando, Florida
Phil Friel
Citrus Hills G&CC (Oaks Course)
Hernando, Florida
Mike Andrijiszyn
Citrus Springs CC
Florida
Charles Almony
City of Derry GC
Londonderry, Northern Ireland
Willie Park Jr

277

City of Derry GC (A. 9)
Northern Ireland
Eddie Hackett
City of Newcastle GC
Northumberland, England
Old Tom Morris
City of Newcastle GC (R)
England
Alister Mackenzie
City Park GC
Pueblo, Colorado
Tom Bendelow
City Park GC (R)
Colorado
John Cochran
City Park GC (Course No. 1)
New Orleans, Louisiana
Richard Koch
City Park GC (Course No. 1) (R)
Louisiana
Ralph Plummer
City Park GC (Course No. 1) (R. 3)
Louisiana
Bill Amick
City Park GC (Course No. 2)
New Orleans, Louisiana
Richard Koch
Civic GC
Kitchener, Ontario
Stanley Thompson
Civitan Park Muni
Farmington, New Mexico
Arthur Jack Snyder
Clacton-on-Sea GC
Essex, England
Jack White
Clairville GC
Toronto, Ontario
William G. Robinson
Clandeboye GC (New Course)
County Down, Northern Ireland
Peter Alliss, David Thomas, T.J.A. McAuley
Clandeboye GC (Old Course)
County Down, Northern Ireland
Bernhard von Limburger, T.J.A. McAuley,*William Rennick Robinson*
Clandeboye GC (Old Course) (R)
Northern Ireland
Bernhard von Limburger, T.J.A. McAuley
Claremont CC
Oakland, California
Jim Smith
Claremont CC (R)
California
Alister Mackenzie
Claremont CC (R)
New Hampshire
Orrin Smith, William F. Mitchell
Claremorris GC (R)
Ireland
Eddie Hackett
Clarendon G&CC
Manning, South Carolina
Ed Riccoboni
Clark Estate GC
Windlesham, England
Tom Simpson
Clarke Estate GC
Rhode Island
A.W. Tillinghast
Clarkesdale CC
Mississippi
William B. Langford, Theodore J. Moreau
Clarksburg CC (A. 9)
West Virginia
Edmund B. Ault
Clarksburg CC (R. 9)
West Virginia
Edmund B. Ault
Clarkston G&CC
Washington
Keith Hellstrom
Clarksville CC
Tennessee
George W. Cobb
Clay Center CC
Kansas
Floyd Farley

Clay County CC
Henrietta, Texas
Bruce Littell
Claycrest CC
Liberty, Missouri
Chet Mendenhall
Claymont Chase CC
West Virginia
Richard Watson
Clear Brook GC
Cranbury, New Jersey
Hal Purdy, Malcolm Purdy
Clear Creek GC
Killeen, Texas
Leon Howard
Clear Lake CC (Routing)
Houston, Texas
Milt Coggins
Clear Lake GC
Salem, Oregon
Felix Riedel
Clear Lake GC
Houston, Texas
Jay Riviere
Clear Lake GC
Riding Mtn. Nat. Pk., Manitoba
Stanley Thompson
Clear Lake Riviera GC
Lower Lake, California
Edward Defilice
Clearbrook CC
Saugatuck, Michigan
Charles Darl Scott
Clearcrest CC NLE
Evansville, Indiana
Robert Bruce Harris
Clearcrest CC (A. 9)
Indiana
Roger Packard
Clearfield-Curwensville CC
Pennsylvania
Alex Findlay
Clearview CC
Lincoln Park, New Jersey
Hal Purdy
Clearview GC
Bayside, New York
William H. Tucker
Clearwater Bay CC
Hong Kong
Brad Benz, Mike Poellot
Clearwater CC
Florida
Herbert Strong
Clearwater CC (R)
Florida
George Low Sr
Clearwater CC (R)
Florida
Perry Maxwell
Clearwater CC (R)
Florida
Joe Lee
Clearwater CC (R)
Florida
Joe Lee
Clearwater G Park
Florida
Ron Garl
Clearwater Greens GC
Kansas
Dave Trufelli
Cleary Lake GC (R)
Minnesota
Don Herfort
Cleburne Muni
Texas
Leon Howard
Cleghorn Plantation G&CC
Rutherfordton, North Carolina
George W. Cobb
Clemson University GC
South Carolina
George W. Cobb, John LaFoy
Clerbrook CC
Florida
Dean Refram
Clevedon GC
Avon, England
J.H. Taylor
Cleveland CC (R)
North Carolina
John LaFoy

Cleveland CC (R)
Tennessee
Bert Stamps
Cleveland CC (R)
Tennessee
Gene Hamm
Cleveland G Links (R)
England
Old Tom Morris
Cleveland G Links (A. 9)
England
Old Tom Morris
Cleveland Heights G&CC
Lakeland, Florida
William S. Flynn, Howard Toomey
Cleveland Heights G&CC (R. 3)
Florida
Ron Garl
Cleveland Heights G&CC (A. 9)
Florida
Ron Garl
Clewiston CC
Florida
R. Albert Anderson
Cliff CC
Ogunquit, Maine
Donald Ross
Cliffside CC
Simsbury, Connecticut
Geoffrey S. Cornish
Clifton Highlands GC
Prescott, Wisconsin
Homer Fieldhouse
Clifton Park Muni (R)
Maryland
Gus Hook
Clifton Springs CC
New York
Pete Craig
Clingendael GC
Netherlands
John Duncan Dunn
Clinton CC
Connecticut
Geoffrey S. Cornish, William G. Robinson
Clinton CC
Iowa
Tom Bendelow
Clinton CC
Lockhaven, Pennsylvania
Edmund B. Ault, Brian Ault
Clinton CC NLE
Lockhaven, Pennsylvania
Alex Findlay
Clinton Muni
Iowa
William James Spear
Clinton Springs CC
Wheeling, West Virginia
William Gordon, David Gordon
Clinton Valley CC
Detroit, Michigan
David T. Millar
Clitheroe GC
Lancashire, England
James Braid, John R. Stutt
Clongowes Wood College GC
County Kildare, Ireland
Eddie Hackett
Clonmel GC (A. 9)
Ireland
Eddie Hackett
Clontarf GC (R)
Ireland
Eddie Hackett
Clovelly CC
South Africa
Campbell Ross
Cloverleaf GC
Pennsylvania
Wynn Tredway
Clovernook CC
Cincinnati, Ohio
William B. Langford, Theodore J. Moreau
Clovernook CC (R)
Ohio
William H. Diddel
Clovernook CC (R)
Ohio
Arthur Hills, Steve Forrest

Club at Falcon Point
Katy, Texas
Robert von Hagge, Bruce Devlin
Club at Morningside
Rancho Mirage, California
Jack Nicklaus, Jay Morrish,Bob Cupp, Scott Miller
Club at Pelican Bay
Naples, Florida
Arthur Hills, Steve Forrest
Club at Sonterra (North Course)
San Antonio, Texas
Robert von Hagge, Bruce Devlin
Club at Sonterra (South Course) formerly known as Canyon Creek CC
Texas
Press Maxwell
Club at Sonterra (South Course) (R)
Texas
Ralph Plummer
Club d'Amiens
France
P.M. Ross
Club d'G Triangle Dor
St. Remi, Quebec
Howard Watson
Club de la Barouge
Mazamet, France
Tom Simpson, P.M. Ross
Club de la Barouge (A. 9)
France
Fred W. Hawtree, Martin Hawtree
Club de la Cordeliere
Chaource, France
Tom Simpson
Club de Campo de Malaga
Torremolinos, Spain
Tom Simpson, P.M. Ross
Club de G de Caracas
Venezuela
Dave Bennett
Club de G de Joliette
Quebec
Howard Watson
Club de G de Joliette (R.10)
Quebec
John Watson
Club de G de Mexico
Mexico
Lawrence Hughes, Percy Clifford
Club de G du Bic
Rimouski, Quebec
Howard Watson
Club de G du Bic (R. 5)
Quebec
John Watson
Club de G le Portage
L'Assomtion, Quebec
Howard Watson
Club de G Acozac
Mexico
Lawrence Hughes
Club de G Adstock
Quebec
Howard Watson, John Watson
Club de G Alpin (R)
Quebec
Howard Watson
Club de G Alpin (R. 3)
Quebec
John Watson
Club de G Avandara
Mexico
Percy Clifford
Club de G Baie Comeau
Hauterire, Quebec
Clinton E. Robinson, Robert Moote
Club de G Baie Comeau (A. 9)
Quebec
Howard Watson, John Watson
Club de G Baie Comeau (A. 9)
Quebec
John Watson
Club de G Baie Comeau (R. 2)
Quebec
John Watson
Club de G Baru
Colombia
Percy Clifford

Club de G Bellavista
Mexico City, Mexico
Percy Clifford
Club de G Bellavista (R)
Mexico
Manny Francis
Club de G Berthier
Berthierville, Quebec
Howard Watson
Club de G Bromont
Shefford, Quebec
Howard Watson
Club de G Bugambillian
Guadalajara, Mexico
Percy Clifford
Club de G Cap Rouge
Quebec
Howard Watson
Club de G Cerdana
Spain
Javier Arana
Club de G Cerro Alto
Mexico
Percy Clifford
Club de G Chambly
Quebec
Howard Watson
Club de G Chaudiere (R. 5)
Quebec
Howard Watson, John Watson
Club de G Chicoutina (Course No. 1)
Quebec
Howard Watson
Club de G Chicoutina (Course No. 2)
Quebec
Howard Watson
Club de G Costalita
Malaga, Spain
Pepe Gancedo
Club de G Deaux
St. Eustache, Quebec
John Watson
Club de G Des Saules
Rimouski, Quebec
John Watson
Club de G Dos Mares
Ensenada, Mexico
Percy Clifford
Club de G Erandeni
Mexico
Percy Clifford
Club de G Gaspesien
St. Anne des Morts, Quebec
John Watson
Club de G Granby-St. Paul (New Crs.)
Quebec
Howard Watson, John Watson
Club de G Granby-St. Paul (Old) (R)
Quebec
Howard Watson, John Watson
Club de G Grand Pabos (A. 9)
Quebec
Howard Watson
Club de G Grand Pabos (R. 9)
Quebec
Howard Watson
Club de G Hacienda
Mexico City, Mexico
Percy Clifford
Club de G Hacienda (R)
Mexico
Harry C. Offutt
Club de G Hermosillo NLE
Mexico
John Bredemus
Club de G Ile Perrot (R)
Quebec
Robert Moote
Club de G La Canada
Mexico City, Mexico
Percy Clifford
Club de G La Villa Rica
Vera Cruz, Mexico
Percy Clifford
Club de G Lac Beuport
Quebec
Howard Watson
Club de G Laguna
Mexico
Percy Clifford

Club de G Laprairie
Montreal, Quebec
Howard Watson
Club de G Les Dunes (Course
No. 1) (R)
Quebec
Howard Watson
Club de G Les Dunes (Course
No. 2) 2)
Sorel, Quebec
Howard Watson
Club de G Llavaneras
Spain
James Gannon
Club de G Llavaneras (R)
Spain
Fred W. Hawtree
Club de G Longchamps
Sherbrooke, Quebec
Howard Watson, John Watson
Club de G Los Monteros
Spain
Javier Arana
Club de G Mijas (Los Lagos
Course)
Fuengirola, Malaga, Spain
Robert Trent Jones, Cabell
Robinson
Club de G Mijas (Los Olivos
Course)
Fuengirola, Malaga, Spain
Robert Trent Jones, Cabell
Robinson
Club de G Montcalm
St. Liguori, Quebec
John Watson
Club de G Monte Castillo
Mexico
Percy Clifford
Club de G Montevilla
Montebello, Quebec
John Watson
Club de G Morelia
Mexico
Percy Clifford
Club de G Obregon
Sonora, Mexico
Percy Clifford
Club de G Panama
Panama
Jay Riviere
Club de G Piramides
Mexico
Percy Clifford
Club de G Poniente Magaluf
Mallorca, Spain
John Harris
Club de G Port (R. 9)
Quebec
Howard Watson
Club de G Ranchitos
Morales, Mexico
Percy Clifford
Club de G Rio Seco
Valles, Mexico
Percy Clifford
Club de G San Andres de
Llavaneras
Barcelona, Spain
James Gannon
Club de G San Andres de
Llavaneras (R)
Spain
Fred W. Hawtree
Club de G San Carlos
Toluca, Mexico
Percy Clifford
Club de G San Gasper
Mexico
Percy Clifford
Club de G San Luis
Mexico
Percy Clifford
Club de G Santa Anita
Mexico
Lawrence Hughes
Club de G Santo Domingo
Chile
A. Macdonald
Club de G Sorel Tracy (A. 9)
Quebec
John Watson

Club de G Sorel Tracy (R. 6)
Quebec
John Watson
Club de G Sorel Tracy (R. 4)
Quebec
John Watson
Club de G St. Luc
Quebec
John Watson
Club de G St. Luc (A. 9)
Quebec
John Watson
Club de G St. Marie (R. 2)
Quebec
Howard Watson, John Watson
Club de G St. Michel (St.
Michel)
Quebec
Howard Watson
Club de G St. Michel (Vaudrevil)
Quebec
Howard Watson
Club de G St. Patrick
Quebec
Howard Watson, John Watson
Club de G St. Patrick (A. 9)
Quebec
John Watson
Club de G St. Patrick (R. 9)
Quebec
John Watson
Club de G Tabashines
Morales, Mexico
Percy Clifford
Club de G Tequisquiapan
Queretaro, Mexico
Joseph S. Finger
Club de G Terramar
Sitges, Spain
Tom Simpson
Club de G Terramar (A. 9)
Spain
Fred W. Hawtree
Club de G Terrebonne
Quebec
John Watson
Club de G Terrebonne (A.18)
Quebec
John Watson
Club de G Ulzama
Spain
Javier Arana
Club de G Ulzama
Spain
Javier Arana
Club de G Valle du Parc
Grandmere, Quebec
Howard Watson
Club de G Vallescondido
Mexico City, Mexico
Percy Clifford
Club de G Victoriaville (A. 9)
Quebec
Howard Watson
Club de G Victoriaville (R. 9)
Quebec
Howard Watson
Club de G Vidago
Portugal
P.M. Ross
Club de G Vielles Forges
Trois-Rivieres, Quebec
John Watson, Howard Watson
Club de Lyon
France
Fred W. Hawtree
Club de Lyon (A. 9)
France
Michael G. Fenn
Club de Palmola
Toulouse, France
Michael G. Fenn
Club de Rouen
France
Willie Park Jr
Club de Strasbourg
France
Donald Harradine
Club de Toulouse
France
Michael G. Fenn
Club de Valescure
France
John Harris

Club du Mans Mulsanne
Le Mans, France
J.J.F. Pennink
Club of Prestwick
Danville, Indiana
Bob Simmons
Club Atlas Campo de Golf
Guadalajara, Mexico
Joseph S. Finger
Club Campestre (R)
Mexico
Dick Wilson, Bob Simmons
Club Campestre de
Bucaramanga
Chile
Mark Mahannah, *Jaime Saenz*
Club Campestre de Cucuta
Colombia
Howard Watson
Club Campestre de Hermosillo
San Buenaventura, Mexico
Lawrence Hughes
Club Campestre de Leon
Mexico
Mario D. Schjetnan
Club Campestre de Leon (A. 9)
Mexico
Joseph S. Finger
Club Campestre de Queretaro
Mexico
Percy Clifford
Club Campestre de Saltillo
Mexico
George Hoffman
Club Campestre Agunero
Mexico
Percy Clifford
Club Campestre Cartagena
Colombia
Ward Northrup
Club Campestre Torreon
Mexico
Percy Clifford
Club Del Lago
Conroe, Texas
Jay Riviere, *Dave Marr*
Club Lagos De Caujarel
Barranquilla, Colombia
Joe Lee
Club Lomas de Cocoyoc
Morales, Mexico
Mario D. Schjetnan
Club Portales Del Centenario
Argentina
Angel Reartes
Club Santiago Manzanillo
Mexico
Lawrence Hughes
Clyne GC
Wales
H.S. Colt
Coachman's Inn GC
Wisconsin
R.C. Greaves
Coal Creek CC
Atkinson, Illinois
Edward Lawrence Packard, Brent
Wadsworth
Coal Ridge CC
West Virginia
Pete Dye
Coatesville CC
Pennsylvania
Alex Findlay
Cobb's Glen CC
Anderson, South Carolina
George W. Cobb, John LaFoy
Cobbly Nob G Links now known
as Bent Creek Mountain Inn
CC
Cobbs Creek Muni
Philadelphia, Pennsylvania
Hugh Wilson
Cochecho CC
Dover, New Hampshire
Wayne Stiles
Cochecho CC (A. 9)
New Hampshire
Phil Wogan
Cochiti Lake GC
New Mexico
Robert Trent Jones Jr

Cochrane Castle GC
Renfrewshire, Scotland
Charles Hunter
Cochrane Castle GC (R)
Scotland
Willie Fernie
Cochrane Castle GC (A.10)
Scotland
James Braid, John R. Stutt
Cochrane Castle GC (R)
Scotland
James Braid, John R. Stutt
Cock Moor Woods GC
Birmingham, England
F.G. Hawtree, J.H. Taylor
Cockermouth GC (R. 2)
England
James Braid
Cocoa Beach Muni
Florida
Mark Mahannah
Coeur D'Alene GC
Idaho
Mel "Curley" Hueston
Coffeyville CC
Kansas
Smiley Bell
Coffeyville CC (R)
Kansas
Bob Dunning
Coffin Muni
Indianapolis, Indiana
William H. Diddel
Coffin Muni (R)
Indiana
William H. Diddel
Cog Hill CC (Course No. 1)
Lemont, Illinois
Bert F. Coghill
Cog Hill CC (Course No. 1) (R)
Illinois
Dick Wilson, Joe Lee
Cog Hill GC (Course No. 2)
Lemont, Illinois
Bert F. Coghill
Cog Hill GC (Course No. 2) (R)
Illinois
Dick Wilson, Joe Lee
Cog Hill GC (Course No. 3)
Lemont, Illinois
Dick Wilson, Joe Lee
Cog Hill GC (Course No. 4)
Lemont, Illinois
Dick Wilson, Joe Lee
Cog Hill GC (Course No. 4) (R)
Illinois
Joe Lee
Cohanzick CC
Bridgeton, New Jersey
Alex Findlay
Cohasset GC
Quincy, Massachusetts
Donald Ross
Cohasset GC (R. 9)
Massachusetts
Al Zikorus
Coherie CC
Clinton, North Carolina
Ellis Maples
Colchester GC
Essex, England
James Braid
Cold Ashby GC
Northamptonshire, England
Fred W. Hawtree
Cold Norton GC
England
Fred W. Hawtree
Cold Spring G&CC
Cold Spring Harbor, New York
Donald Ross
Cold Spring G&CC (R)
New York
Robert Trent Jones, Rees Jones
Cold Spring GC
New Hampshire
Geoffrey S. Cornish, William G.
Robinson
Cold Spring Harbor CC
New York
Seth Raynor
Cold Springs G&CC (A. 9)
California
Bert Stamps

Coldstream CC
Cincinnati, Ohio
Dick Wilson, Joe Lee, Robert von
Hagge, Bob Simmons
Coldstream GC
East Hempstead, New York
Devereux Emmet
Coldwater CC
Michigan
Robert Beard
Coldwater CC
Michigan
George Parker
Cole Park GC (R)
Kentucky
Edward Lawrence Packard
Colfax GC (R)
Iowa
Charles Calhoun
Colgate Univ GC NLE
Hamilton, New York
Tom Winton
College of the Sequoias GC
Fresno, California
Bob Baldock
College GC
Delhi, New York
Pete Craig
College Hill GC (R)
New York
William F. Mitchell
Collier Park GC
Perth, Australia
Peter Thomson, Michael
Wolveridge
Collindale GC
Fort Collins, Colorado
Frank Hummel
Colonia CC
New Jersey
Tom Bendelow
Colonia CC (A)
New Jersey
Robert White
Colonia CC (R)
New Jersey
Hal Purdy
Colonia CC (R)
New Jersey
Frank Duane
Colonial CC
Thomasville, North Carolina
Gene Hamm
Colonial CC
Harrisburg, Pennsylvania
William Gordon, David Gordon
Colonial CC NLE
Memphis, Tennessee
William B. Langford
Colonial CC
Fort Worth, Texas
John Bredemus
Colonial CC (A. 3)
Texas
Perry Maxwell
Colonial CC (R)
Texas
Dick Wilson
Colonial CC (R)
Texas
Robert Trent Jones
Colonial CC (R)
Texas
Jay Morrish, Bob Cupp
Colonial CC (North Course)
Cordova, Tennessee
Joseph S. Finger
Colonial CC (South Course)
Cordova, Tennessee
Joseph S. Finger
Colonial CC (South Course) (R)
Tennessee
Bob Cupp
Colonial G&CC
Hanrahan, Louisiana
Ernest Penfold
Colonial Gardens GC
Ohio
James Root
Colonial GC (R. 5)
Massachusetts
William F. Mitchell, Al Zikorus

Colonial GC (A. 9)
Massachusetts
William F. Mitchell
Colonial GC NLE
Lincoln, Nebraska
Henry B. Hughes, Richard
   Watson
Colonial GC
Uniontown, Pennsylvania
William Gordon, David Gordon
Colonial Oaks GC
Fort Wayne, Indiana
Richard Chilcote, Pat Riley
Colonial Palms GC
Miami, Florida
John E. O'Connor
Colonial Park CC
Clovis, New Mexico
Warren Cantrell
Colonial Park CC (A. 9)
New Mexico
Ray Hardy
Colonial Valley GC
Grants Pass, Oregon
John Nelson
Colonie CC
Albany, New York
Geoffrey S. Cornish
Colonie Muni
New York
William F. Mitchell
Colonie Muni (A. 9)
New York
Robert Trent Jones, Roger
   Rulewich
Colony Creek CC
Victoria, Texas
Richard Watson
Colony CC
Algonac, New York
C.H. Alison, H.S. Colt
Colony West GC
Tamarac, Florida
Robert von Hagge, Bruce Devlin
Colony West GC (Course No. 2)
Tamarac, Florida
Robert von Hagge, Bruce Devlin
Colorado Springs CC
Colorado
John Montieth
Colorado Springs CC (A. 9)
Colorado
Dick Phelps
Columbia CC
Maryland
Herbert Barker
Columbia CC (R)
Maryland
Walter J. Travis
Columbia CC (R)
Maryland
George Fazio, Tom Fazio
Columbia CC (R)
Maryland
William S. Flynn
Columbia CC
Missouri
Tom Bendelow
Columbia CC (R)
Missouri
Smiley Bell
Columbia CC (R)
Missouri
Edward Lawrence Packard
Columbia CC (A. 9)
Missouri
Roger Packard
Columbia CC
South Carolina
Ellis Maples
Columbia G&CC
Hudson, New York
Hal Purdy
Columbia GC
Illinois
Al Linkogel
Columbia Hills CC
Columbia Station, Ohio
Harold Paddock
Columbia Lakes CC
West Columbia, Texas
Jack B. Miller

Columbia Lakes CC (R)
Texas
Tom Fazio
Columbia Muni
Missouri
Smiley Bell
Columbia Park Muni (R)
Minnesota
Edward Lawrence Packard
Columbia-Edgewater CC
Portland, Oregon
A. Vernon Macan
Columbia-Edgewater CC (R)
Oregon
Robert Muir Graves
Columbia-Edgewater CC (R)
Oregon
William F. Bell
Columbian C
Carrollton, Texas
Ralph Plummer
Columbian C (A. 9)
Texas
Leon Howard
Columbian C (R. 6)
Texas
Joseph S. Finger
Columbine CC
Littleton, Colorado
Henry B. Hughes
Columbine CC (R)
Colorado
Press Maxwell
Columbine CC (R)
Colorado
Henry B. Hughes
Columbus CC
Indiana
William H. Diddel
Columbus CC
Mississippi
John W. Frazier
Columbus CC (R. 9)
Mississippi
Brian Ault
Columbus CC
Ohio
Donald Ross
Columbus CC (A. 9)
Ohio
Donald Ross
Columbus CC (R)
Ohio
Orrin Smith
Columbus CC (R. 2)
Ohio
Robert Bruce Harris
Columbus CC (R)
Ohio
Dick Wilson
Columbus Park GC
Chicago, Illinois
Tom Bendelow
Colville Park GC
Scotland
James Braid
Colville Park GC (R)
Scotland
J. Hamilton Stutt
Colwood National GC
Portland, Oregon
A. Vernon Macan
Combat Center GC
Twenty Nine Palms, California
David W. Kent
Commack Hills G&CC
New York
Alex McKay
Commonwealth GC
Victoria, Australia
S. Berriman
Community GC (A. 9)
Ohio
Earl Shock
Como Muni (Course No. 2)
St. Paul, Minnesota
Don Herfort
Compton GC
Los Angeles, California
William H. Johnson
Comstock CC
Davis, California
Bob Baldock

Comte de Rougemont Estate GC
France
Tom Simpson
Concho Valley GC
St. John's, Arizona
Arthur Jack Snyder
Conchos Lake GC
Conchos, New Mexico
Leon Howard
Concord CC
Massachusetts
Donald Ross
Concord CC (A. 9)
Massachusetts
William F. Mitchell
Concord CC
New Hampshire
Ralph Barton
Concord Green GC
Libertyville, Illinois
Ken Killian, Dick Nugent
Concord GC
Tennessee
Arthur Davis
**Concord Hotel GC (Challenger
   Course)**
Kiamesha Lake, New York
Alfred H. Tull
**Concord Hotel GC
   (Championship Course)**
Kiamesha Lake, New York
Joseph S. Finger
**Concord Hotel GC (International
   Course)**
Kiamesha Lake, New York
Alfred H. Tull
Concordia GC
New Jersey
Brian Ault, Bill Love
Concordia GC
Ste. Therese, Quebec
Howard Watson
Concordville CC (A. 4)
Pennsylvania
Geoffrey S. Cornish, William G.
   Robinson
Condon GC
Oregon
Don Lehman
Conestoga CC
Lancaster, Pennsylvania
William Gordon
Conestoga CC (R)
Pennsylvania
Ferdinand Garbin
Conestoga G&TC
Ontario
Clinton E. Robinson
Conewango Valley CC (R)
Pennsylvania
Edmund B. Ault
Confederate Hills CC
Highland Springs, Virginia
Buddy Loving, Algie Pulley
Congleton GC
England
Fred W. Hawtree, A.H.F. Jiggens
Congress Lake C
Hartville, Ohio
Willie Park Jr
Congress Lake C (R)
Ohio
William Newcomb
Congress Lake C (R)
Ohio
Donald Ross
Congressional CC (Blue Course)
Bethesda, Maryland
Devereux Emmet
**Congressional CC (Blue Course)
   (R)**
Maryland
Tom Winton
**Congressional CC (Blue Course)
   (R)**
Maryland
Donald Ross
**Congressional CC (Blue Course)
   (R)**
Maryland
Alfred H. Tull
**Congressional CC (Blue Course)
   (A. 9)**
Maryland
Robert Trent Jones

**Congressional CC (Blue Course)
   (R. 9)**
Maryland
Robert Trent Jones
**Congressional CC (Blue Course)
   (R)**
Maryland
Robert Trent Jones, Roger
   Rulewich
**Congressional CC (Blue Course)
   (R. 2)**
Maryland
Edmund B. Ault, Tom Clark, Bill
   Love
Congressional CC (Gold Course)
Bethesda, Maryland
Devereux Emmet
**Congressional CC (Gold Course)
   (A. 9)**
Maryland
George Fazio, Tom Fazio
Conneaut Shores CC
Ohio
J. Thomas Francis
**Connecticut GC formerly known
   as Golf Club at Aspetuck**
Easton, Connecticut
Geoffrey S. Cornish, William G.
   Robinson
Connell Lake G&CC
Inverness, Florida
William L. Campbell
Connemara GC
County Galway, Ireland
Eddie Hackett
Connestee Falls CC
Brevard, North Carolina
George W. Cobb
Constant Springs CC
Jamaica
Stanley Thompson
Contea di Gradella GC
Milan, Italy
Pier Mancinelli
Continental CC
Wildwood, Florida
Ron Garl
Continental Foothills GC
Cave Creek, Arizona
Bob Cupp
Continental GC
Scottsdale, Arizona
Jeff Hardin, Greg Nash
Contra Costa CC (R)
California
Robert Muir Graves
Conyngham Valley CC (R)
Pennsylvania
A.W. Tillinghast
Cooden Beach GC
Sussex, England
Willie Park Jr
Cookeville G&CC
Tennessee
Hooper Elblen, Tom Thaxton
Cool Creek CC
Pennsylvania
Chester Ruby
Coollattin GC (R)
Ireland
Eddie Hackett
Coombe Hill GC
England
J.F. Abercromby, Willie Park Jr
Coonskin Park GC
Charleston, West Virginia
X.G. Hassenplug
Cooper Colony CC
Hollywood, Florida
Pat Pattison
Cooper Hill GC
New Jersey
W.F. Pease
Cooper River CC NLE
Camden, New Jersey
Devereux Emmet, Alfred H. Tull
Coos CC
Coos Bay, Oregon
H. Chandler Egan
Coosa CC (R)
Georgia
George W. Cobb

Coosa CC (R)
Georgia
Arthur Davis
Copeland Hills CC
Columbiana, Ohio
R. Albert Anderson
Copenhagen GC
Denmark
John Harris
Copper Creek GC
Copper Mountain, Colorado
Perry Dye
Copper GC
Utah
Mick Riley
Copper Mountain GC NLE
Colorado
Dick Phelps, Brad Benz
**Copper Mountain GC (A. 9)
   NLE**
Colorado
Dick Phelps
Copt Heath GC
Warwickshire, England
H.S. Colt
Copthorne GC
Sussex, England
James Braid
Coquille Valley Elks CC
Oregon
Clarence Sutton
Coral Creek G&CC
Fisherville, Ontario
Clinton E. Robinson
**Coral Gables Biltmore GC
   formerly known as Miami
   Biltmore GC (North Course)**
Coral Gables, Florida
Donald Ross
Coral Gables Biltmore GC (R)
Florida
William B. Langford
Coral Gables Biltmore GC (R)
Florida
Mark Mahannah
Coral Harbour GC NLE
Nassau, Bahamas
George Fazio
Coral Ridge CC
Fort Lauderdale, Florida
Robert Trent Jones
Corballis GC
County Dublin, Ireland
Fred W. Hawtree, A.H.F. Jiggens
Corballis GC (R)
Ireland
Eddie Hackett
Corfu G&CC
Corfu, Greece
Donald Harradine
Corhampton GC (R. 9)
England
J.J.F. Pennink, C.D. Lawrie
Corhampton GC (A. 9)
England
J.J.F. Pennink
Cork GC
County Cork, Ireland
David Brown
Cork GC (R. 9)
Ireland
Tom Dunn
Cork GC (R. 9)
Ireland
Alister Mackenzie
Cork GC (A. 9)
Ireland
Alister Mackenzie
Cork GC (R)
Ireland
C.K. Cotton, J.J.F. Pennink, C.D.
   Lawrie
Cornell University GC
Ithaca, New York
Robert Trent Jones
Corning CC
New York
Tom Winton
Cornwells CC
Cornwells Heights, Pennsylvania
William Gordon, David Gordon
Corona National GC
Corona, California
Lawrence Hughes

Coronado Beach GC
Panama City, Panama
George Fazio, Tom Fazio
Coronado G&CC
El Paso, Texas
Lawrence Hughes
Coronado G&CC (R)
Texas
Marvin Ferguson
Coronado GC
Scottsdale, Arizona
Arthur Jack Snyder
Coronado GC (A. 9)
Arizona
Milt Coggins
Coronado GC
Hot Springs Village, Arkansas
Edmund B. Ault, Tom Clark
Coronado GC NLE
California
William Watson
Coronado GC
California
Jack Daray
Coronado GC (R)
California
William F. Bell
Corpus Christi CC NLE
Texas
Tom Bendelow
Corpus Christi CC
Texas
Robert Trent Jones, Frank Duane
Corpus Christi G Center
Texas
Leon Howard
Corral De Tierra CC
Salinas, California
Bob Baldock
Corral De Tierra CC (R)
California
Gary Roger Baird
Corry Muni
Pennsylvania
Edmund B. Ault
Corsica GC
France
J. Hamilton Stutt
Cortez GC
Hot Springs Village, Arkansas
Edmund B. Ault
Cortez Muni
Colorado
Press Maxwell
Cortez Muni (A. 9)
Colorado
Press Maxwell
Cortland CC
New York
Willard Wilkinson
Corvallis CC (A. 9)
Oregon
Fred Federspiel
Coshocton T&CC
Ohio
Tom Bendelow
Costa Brava GC
Gerona, Spain
J. Hamilton Stutt
Costa Del Sol G&RC
Florida
Bob Cupp
Costa Mesa G&CC (Los Lagos Course)
California
William F. Bell
Costa Mesa G&CC (Mesa Linda Course)
California
William F. Bell
Costa Teguise GC
Lanzarote, Canary Islands
John Harris
Costebelle Golf Links
Hyeres, France
Willie Park Jr
Coto de Caza GC
California
Robert Trent Jones Jr, Don Knott
Coto de Donana
Seville, Spain
J. Hamilton Stutt

Cotswold Hills GC
England
M.D. Little
Cottesloe GC (R)
Australia
Peter Thomson, Michael
  Wolveridge
Cottesmore GC (New Course)
England
M. Rogerson
Cotton Bay C
Eleuthera, Bahamas
Robert Trent Jones
Cotton Dike C
Dataw Island, South Carolina
Tom Fazio
Cotton Valley CC
Texas
Lee Singletary
Cottonwood C (A. 9)
Utah
William H. Neff
Cottonwood C (R. 9)
Utah
William H. Neff
Cottonwood Creek Muni
Waco, Texas
Joseph S. Finger, Ken Dye
Cottonwood CC
Sunlakes, Arizona
Jeff Hardin, Greg Nash
Cottonwood CC
Glendive, Montana
Leo Johnson
Cottonwood CC (Ivanhoe Course)
California
O.W. Moorman, A.C. Sears
Cottonwood CC (Monte Vista Course)
California
O.W. Moorman, A.C. Sears
Coubert GC
France
Tom Dunn
Council Bluffs CC (R) NLE
Iowa
Henry C. Glissmann, Harold
  Glissmann
Council Grove CC (R. 9)
Kansas
Leo Johnson
Countess Wear GC
Scotland
John R. Stutt
Country Club Lake
Dumfries, Virginia
Buddy Loving, Algie Pulley
Country Club Villages of America
Ohio
Edmund B. Ault
Country Lakes Village CC
Naperville, Illinois
Rolf C. Campbell
Country Meadows GC
Peoria, Arizona
Jeff Hardin, Greg Nash
Country Squire Inn GC
Eugene, Oregon
Gary Washburn
Country View GC
St. Paul, Minnesota
Don Herfort
Countryside CC
Clearwater, Florida
Edward Lawrence Packard,
  Roger Packard
Countryside CC
Roanoke, Virginia
Ellis Maples, Ed Seay
Countryside GC (R)
Illinois
Ken Killian, Dick Nugent
Countryside GC (R)
Illinois
Bob Lohmann
Countryside West GC
DeKalb, Illinois
Edward Lawrence Packard
County Caven GC (A. 9)
Ireland
Eddie Hackett

County Longford GC (A. 9)
Ireland
Eddie Hackett
County Louth GC (R)
Ireland
Cecil Barcroft, *N. Halligan*
County Louth GC (R)
Ireland
Tom Simpson, *Molly Gourlay*
County Sligo GC
Ireland
H.S. Colt, C.H. Alison, Alister
  Mackenzie
County Sligo GC (R)
Ireland
Eddie Hackett
Courthouse CC
Fairfax, Virginia
Reuben Hines
Courtland Hills GC
Rockford, Michigan
Mark DeVries
Courtown GC
County Wexford, Ireland
C.K. Cotton, John Harris
Courtown GC (R)
Ireland
Eddie Hackett
Cove Cay G&TC
Clearwater, Florida
David Wallace
Cove Creek CC
Stevensville, Maryland
Lindsay Ervin
Coventry GC
England
Peter Paxton
Coventry GC (R)
England
J.H. Taylor
Covered Bridge GC (R)
New Jersey
Hal Purdy, Malcolm Purdy
Coves At Bird Island GC
Afton, Oklahoma
Jay Morrish
Cowal GC
Argyll, Scotland
James Braid
Cowansville GC
Quebec
Howard Watson
Cowdray Park GC
England
J.F. Abercromby, Herbert Fowler
Cowdray Park GC (R. 2)
England
Herbert Fowler
Cowes GC (A. 9)
England
J. Hamilton Stutt
Cowichan G&CC
British Columbia
A. Vernon Macan
Cowichan G&CC (A. 9)
British Columbia
Ken Worthington
Crab Meadow GC
Northport, New York
William F. Mitchell
Crab Meadow GC (R. 3)
New York
Stephen Kay
Crackerneck CC
Blue Springs, Missouri
Charles Maddox, William
  Maddox
Cradoc GC
Powys, Wales
J.J.F. Pennink
Crag Burn C
Elma, New York
Robert Trent Jones, Rees Jones
Cragie Brae GC
Leroy, New York
James Gilmore Harrison,
  Ferdinand Garbin
Craig Gowan GC
Woodstock, Ontario
Clinton E. Robinson, Robert
  Moote
Craig GC
Regina, Saskatchewan
John A. Thompson

Craig Ranch GC
Las Vegas, Nevada
John F. Stinson, John C. Stinson
Craig Wood CC
New York
Seymour Dunn
Craigie Hill GC
Perth, Scotland
J. Anderson
Craigowan G&CC
Woodstock, Ontario
Clinton E. Robinson
Crail GC
Fife, Scotland
Old Tom Morris
Cramer Mountain CC
Cramerton, North Carolina
Dan Maples
Cranberry Valley GC
Harwich, Massachusetts
Geoffrey S. Cornish, William G.
  Robinson
Cranbrook GC
British Columbia
Reid Geddes, Arch Finlay, Frank
  Fergie
Cranbrook GC
Kent, England
John Harris
Crandon GC
Wisconsin
Charles Maddox, *Frank P.
  MacDonald*
Crane Creek CC
Boise, Idaho
Bob Baldock
Crane Creek CC (R. 2)
Idaho
Robert Muir Graves
Crang Estate GC
Toronto, Ontario
Howard Watson
Cranmoor CC
Toms River, New Jersey
Tom Winton
Crans Sur Sierre GC
Switzerland
Sir Arnold Lunn
Crans Sur Sierre GC (R. 9)
Switzerland
Elysee Bonvin
Crans Sur Sierre GC (A. 9)
Switzerland
Elysee Bonvin
Cranston CC
Rhode Island
Geoffrey S. Cornish, William G.
  Robinson
Cranwell School GC
Lenox, Massachusetts
Wayne Stiles, John Van Kleek
Crater C
Virginia
Fred Findlay
Crawford County GC
Robinson, Illinois
Tom Bendelow
Crawford County GC (A. 9)
Illinois
William James Spear
Crawford CC (R)
New York
Seth Raynor
Crawford Notch CC (R)
New Hampshire
Wayne Stiles, John Van Kleek
Crawfordsville Muni
Indiana
William H. Diddel
Cray Valley GC
Kent, England
John Day
Cream Ridge GC
New Jersey
Frank Miscoski
Credit Island GC
Davenport, Iowa
William B. Langford, Theodore J.
  Moreau
Credit Valley G&CC
Toronto, Ontario
Stanley Thompson

Credit Valley G&CC (R)
Ontario
Clinton E. Robinson
Credit Valley G&CC (R. 3)
Ontario
Robert Moote, *David Moote*
Creek C
Locust Valley, New York
Charles Blair Macdonald, Seth
  Raynor
Creek C (R)
New York
William S. Flynn
Creigiau GC (A. 9)
Wales
Fraser Middleton
Crescent CC
Missouri
Roger Packard
Crescent Hill GC (R)
Kentucky
Alex McKay
Cress Creek CC
Naperville, Illinois
David Gill
Crest Hills CC
Cincinnati, Ohio
Bob Simmons
Crestbrook CC
Watertown, Connecticut
Geoffrey S. Cornish
Crestbrook CC (A. 9)
Connecticut
Al Zikorus
Crestmont CC
West Orange, New Jersey
Donald Ross
Crestmont CC (R. 3)
New Jersey
Frank Duane
Crestmont CC (R)
New Jersey
Robert Trent Jones, Roger
  Rulewich
Crestview CC
Florida
Bill Amick
Crestview CC (A. 9)
Florida
Earl Stone
Crestview CC
Agawam, Massachusetts
Geoffrey S. Cornish
Crestview CC (North Course)
Wichita, Kansas
Robert Trent Jones, Robert Trent
  Jones Jr
Crestview CC (South Course)
Wichita, Kansas
Robert Trent Jones, Robert Trent
  Jones Jr
Crestview CC (South Course) (A. 9)
Kansas
Robert Trent Jones Jr
Crestview GC
Muncie, Indiana
Robert Beard
Crestview Hills GC
Waldport, Oregon
Willard Hill
Crestwicke CC
Bloomington, Illinois
Edward Lawrence Packard,
  Roger Packard
Crestwood CC (R. 3)
Kansas
Floyd Farley
Crestwood CC (A. 9)
Kansas
Floyd Farley
Crestwood CC
Rehoboth, Massachusetts
Geoffrey S. Cornish
Crestwood Hills GC
Anita, Iowa
Kenneth Turner
Crieff GC
Perthshire, Scotland
Willie Park
Crieff GC (R)
Scotland
James Braid

Cripple Creek CC NLE
Connecticut
Dewitt "Maury" Bell
Cripple Creek G&CC
Bethany Beach, Delaware
Algie Pulley
Crispin Center GC
Wheeling, West Virginia
Devereux Emmet
Croara CC
Croara dei Gazzola, Italy
R. Buratti
Croasdaile CC
Durham, North Carolina
George W. Cobb
Crockery Hills GC (R. 5)
Michigan
Bruce Matthews, Jerry Matthews
Crockery Hills GC (A. 9)
Michigan
Bruce Matthews, Jerry Matthews
Crockett Springs National G&CC
now known as Nashville
G&AC
Crofton GC
Maryland
Edmund B. Ault
Croham Hurst GC
Surrey, England
James Braid, F.G. Hawtree
Crooked Creek CC
Indiana
Roger Packard
Crooked Creek G&CC
Miami, Florida
Frank Murray
Crooked Creek G&CC (R)
Florida
Bob Cupp
Crooked Creek GC
Saginaw, Michigan
Donald Bray
Crooked Creek GC
Hendersonville, North Carolina
Alex Guin
Crooked River Ranch GC
Redmond, Oregon
Gene "Bunny" Mason
Crooked Stick GC
Carmel, Indiana
Pete Dye
Crooked Stick GC (R)
Indiana
Pete Dye
Crooked Stick GC (R)
Indiana
Pete Dye
Crookhill Park GC
Yorkshire, England
J.J.F. Pennink
Cross Creek GC
Fort Myers, Florida
Arthur Hills, Steve Forrest, Mike
Dasher
Cross Creek CC
Atlanta, Georgia
Arthur Davis, *James T. Shirley*
Cross Creek CC
Mount Airy, North Carolina
Joe Lee, Rocky Roquemore
Cross Creek GC (R. 9)
Pennsylvania
Ferdinand Garbin
Cross Creek GC (A. 9)
Pennsylvania
Ferdinand Garbin
Cross Roads CC
Lawrenceville, Illinois
Tom Bendelow
Cross Roads GC
Seattle, Washington
Al Smith
Crossings G&CC formerly
known as Half Sinke GC
Richmond, Virginia
Joe Lee
Crow Canyon CC
Danville, California
Ted Robinson
Crow River CC
Hutchinson, Minnesota
Robert Prochnow

Crow Valley CC
Bettendorf, Iowa
John Cochran
Crow Wood GC
Glasgow, Scotland
James Braid, John R. Stutt
Crown Colony CC
Lufkin, Texas
Robert von Hagge, Bruce Devlin
Crown Mines GC (R)
South Africa
Gary Player, *Sidney Brews, Dr. Van
Vincent*
Crown Point CC
Springfield, Vermont
William F. Mitchell
Crown Point CC (A. 9)
Vermont
William F. Mitchell
Cruden Bay G&CC
Aberdeen, Scotland
Herbert Fowler, Tom Simpson
Crumpin Fox C
Bernardston, Massachusetts
Robert Trent Jones, Roger
Rulewich
Crystal Downs CC
Frankfort, Michigan
Eugene Goebel
Crystal Downs CC (R. 9)
Michigan
Alister Mackenzie, Perry Maxwell
Crystal Downs CC (A. 9)
Michigan
Alister Mackenzie, Perry Maxwell
Crystal Downs CC (R)
Michigan
Geoffrey S. Cornish, Brian Silva
Crystal Lago CC
Pompano Beach, Florida
Alec Ternyei
Crystal Lago CC (R)
Florida
Rees Jones, Keith Evans
Crystal Lake CC
Pompano Beach, Florida
Pat Pattison
Crystal Lake CC
Illinois
George O'Neill, Joseph A.
Roseman, *Jack Croke*
Crystal Lake CC (R)
Illinois
Ken Killian, Dick Nugent
Crystal Lake CC (R)
Illinois
Bob Lohmann
Crystal Lake CC
St. Louis, Missouri
William H. Diddel
Crystal Lake GC
Beulah, Michigan
Bruce Matthews, Jerry Matthews
Crystal Lakes CC (A. 9)
Montana
William G. Robinson
Crystal Lakes GC
Okeechobee, Florida
Chuck Ankrom
Crystal Mountain GC
Thomasville, Michigan
William Newcomb
Crystal River CC (R)
Florida
Mark Mahannah
Crystal Springs GC (R)
California
William P. Bell
Crystal Springs GC
Haverhill, Massachusetts
Geoffrey S. Cornish
Crystal Springs GC
Pineville, North Carolina
John J. Criscione, Gene Thomas
Crystalaire CC
California
William F. Bell
Cuddington GC
England
H.S. Colt, J.S.F. Morrison, C.H.
Alison
Cuernavaca CC
Mexico
I.D. Gonzales

Cullen GC (R)
Scotland
Old Tom Morris
Culver Military Academy GC
Indiana
William B. Langford
Cumberland CC (R.11)
Maryland
X.G. Hassenplug
Cumberland CC
Carlisle, Pennsylvania
James Gilmore Harrison,
Ferdinand Garbin
Cumberland Lake CC
Birmingham, Alabama
Bill Amick
Cumbernauld GC
Dumbartonshire, Scotland
J. Hamilton Stutt
Cummaquid GC (A. 9)
Massachusetts
Henry Mitchell
Current River CC
Doniphan, Missouri
Floyd Farley
Currie Park GC
Wauwautosa, Wisconsin
George Hansen
Curtis Creek CC
Indiana
Leonard Macomber
Custer GC
South Dakota
John W. Gillum
Custer Hill GC
Fort Riley, Kansas
Robert Trent Jones
Cutten Fields CC
Guelph, Ontario
Chick Evans
Cutter Sound CC
Stuart, Florida
Mark McCumber
Cuyuna CC (A. 9)
Minnesota
Don Herfort
Cuyuna CC (R. 9)
Minnesota
Don Herfort
Cypress Bay GC
North Myrtle Beach, South
Carolina
Russell Breeden
Cypress Creek CC
Boynton Beach, Florida
Robert von Hagge
Cypress Creek CC
Orlando, Florida
Lloyd Clifton
Cypress Greens CC
Sun City Center, Florida
Ron Garl
Cypress Hills GC
Colma, California
Jack Fleming
Cypress Lake CC
Ft. Myers, Florida
Dick Wilson, Robert von Hagge
Cypress Lake CC (R)
Florida
Arthur Hills, Steve Forrest
Cypress Lakes GC
Travis AFB, California
Joseph S. Finger
Cypress Lakes GC
Hope Hills, North Carolina
L.B. Floyd
Cypress Point C
Pebble Beach, California
Alister Mackenzie, Robert Hunter
Cypress Point C (R. 1)
California
Robert Trent Jones
Cypress Point GC
Virginia Beach, Virginia
Tom Clark, Edmund B. Ault
Cypress Run CC
Tarpon Springs, Florida
Edward Lawrence Packard
Cypresswood G&RC
Winter Haven, Florida
Ron Garl

CC at Heathrow
Lake Mary, Florida
Ron Garl
CC at Muirfield Village
Dublin, Ohio
Jack Nicklaus, Jay Morrish, Bob
Cupp
CC de Manizales
Calais, Colombia
Howard Watson, Robert Moote
CC of the Rockies
Avon, Colorado
Jack Nicklaus, Jay Morrish, Bob
Cupp
CC of the South
Alpharetta, Georgia
Jack Nicklaus, *Tom Pearson*
CC of Alabama
Eufaula, Alabama
Ron Kirby, Denis Griffiths
CC of Ashland
Ohio
Willie Park Jr
**CC of Austin now known as
Riverside GC**
CC of Beloit NLE
Wisconsin
Tom Bendelow
CC of Billerica
Massachusetts
Phil Wogan
CC of Birmingham (East Course)
Alabama
Donald Ross
**CC of Birmingham (East Course)
(R)**
Alabama
George W. Cobb
**CC of Birmingham (West
Course)**
Alabama
Donald Ross
**CC of Birmingham (West
Course) (R)**
Alabama
Robert Trent Jones
**CC of Birmingham (West
Course) (R)**
Alabama
Pete Dye, P.B. Dye
CC of Bogota
Colombia
Charles Banks
CC of Bogota (East Course)
Colombia
John Van Kleek
CC of Bogota (West Course)
Colombia
John Van Kleek
CC of Brevard
Florida
R. Albert Anderson
CC of Bristol NLE
Tennessee
Alex Findlay
CC of Bristol
Tennessee
Alex McKay
CC of Buffalo
Williamsville, New York
Donald Ross
CC of Buffalo (R)
New York
Robert Trent Jones
CC of Buffalo (R)
New York
Geoffrey S. Cornish, William G.
Robinson
CC of Callawassie
Callawassie Island, South
Carolina
Tom Fazio
CC of Castle Pines
Castle Rock, Colorado
Jack Nicklaus, Scott Miller
CC of Chapala
Mexico
Harry C. Offutt
CC of Charleston
South Carolina
Seth Raynor
CC of Charleston NLE
South Carolina
Tom Bendelow

CC of Charleston
West Virginia
George W. Cobb
CC of Colorado
Colorado Springs, Colorado
Pete Dye, Roy Dye
CC of Columbus
Georgia
Donald Ross, J.B. McGovern
CC of Connersville
Indiana
Tom Bendelow
CC of Connersville (A. 9)
Indiana
Bob Simmons
CC of Coral Springs
Florida
Edmund B. Ault
CC of Culpepper
Virginia
Fred Findlay, *Ben Loving*
CC of Cuzcatlan
El Salvador
Fred W. Hawtree
CC of Darien
Connecticut
Alfred H. Tull
CC of Darien (R)
Connecticut
Hal Purdy, Malcolm Purdy
CC of Darien (R. 3)
Connecticut
Geoffrey S. Cornish
CC of Decatur
Illinois
Tom Bendelow
CC of Decatur (R)
Illinois
Edward Lawrence Packard
CC of Decatur (R)
Illinois
Edward Lawrence Packard
CC of Decatur (R)
Illinois
Edward Lawrence Packard,
Roger Packard
CC of Detroit NLE
Lake St. Clair, Michigan
William "Bert" Way
CC of Detroit
Grosse Pointe Farms, Michigan
H.S. Colt
CC of Detroit (R)
Michigan
C.H. Alison, H.S. Colt
CC of Detroit (R)
Michigan
Robert Trent Jones
CC of Detroit (R)
Michigan
Bruce Matthews, Jerry Matthews
CC of Detroit (A. 9)
Michigan
Robert Trent Jones
CC of Detroit (R)
Michigan
Arthur Hills, Steve Forrest
CC of Detroit (R)
Michigan
Geoffrey S. Cornish, Brian Silva
CC of Fairfax
Virginia
William Gordon
CC of Fairfax (A. 9)
Virginia
Robert Trent Jones
CC of Fairfax (R)
Virginia
Buddy Loving, Algie Pulley
CC of Fairfield
Connecticut
Seth Raynor
CC of Fairfield (R. 2)
Connecticut
Geoffrey S. Cornish
CC of Farmington
Connecticut
Willie Park Jr
CC of Farmington (R)
Connecticut
Orrin Smith
CC of Farmington (R. 1)
Connecticut
Geoffrey S. Cornish

CC of Florida
Delray Beach, Florida
Robert Bruce Harris
CC of Fort Collins
Colorado
Henry B. Hughes
CC of Fort Collins (R)
Colorado
John Cochran
CC of Fort Collins (A. 9)
Colorado
Henry B. Hughes
CC of Green Valley
Arizona
Red Lawrence
CC of Harrisburg
Pennsylvania
William S. Flynn
CC of Harrisburg (R)
Pennsylvania
Herbert Strong
CC of Havana
Cuba
Donald Ross
CC of Hilton Head
Hilton Head Island, South
    Carolina
Rees Jones
CC of Hudson
Ohio
Harold Paddock
CC of Hudson (R)
Ohio
Geoffrey S. Cornish
CC of Indianapolis
Indiana
William H. Diddel
CC of Indianapolis (R)
Indiana
Pete Dye
CC of Ithaca NLE
New York
A.W. Tillinghast
CC of Ithaca
New York
Geoffrey S. Cornish
CC of Ithaca (R) NLE
New York
Robert Trent Jones
CC of Jackson
Michigan
Arthur Ham
CC of Jackson NLE
Mississippi
Tom Bendelow
CC of Jackson
Mississippi
Dick Wilson, Robert von Hagge
CC of Jackson (R. 9)
Mississippi
Tom Clark
CC of Johnston County
Smithfield, North Carolina
Ellis Maples, Ed Seay
CC of Lansing
Michigan
William B. Langford, Theodore J.
    Moreau
CC of Lansing (R)
Michigan
Edward Lawrence Packard
CC of Lansing (R)
Michigan
Edward Lawrence Packard,
    Roger Packard
CC of Lansing (R. 1)
Michigan
Jerry Matthews
CC of Laurel
Mississippi
Seymour Dunn
CC of Lincoln
Nebraska
William H. Tucker, Gregor
    MacMillan
CC of Lincoln (R. 3)
Nebraska
Pete Dye
CC of Little Rock
Arkansas
Herman Hackbarth
CC of Little Rock (R)
Arkansas
William H. Diddel

CC of Little Rock (R. 3)
Arkansas
Joseph S. Finger
CC of Little Rock (R)
Arkansas
Edmund B. Ault
CC of Little Rock (R)
Arkansas
Tom Clark
CC of Louisiana
Baton Rouge, Louisiana
Jack Nicklaus, *Tom Pearson*
CC of Miami (East Course)
Hialeah, Florida
Robert Trent Jones, Frank Duane
**CC of Miami (North Course)
    NLE**
Hialeah, Florida
Robert Trent Jones, Frank Duane
CC of Miami (South Course)
Hialeah, Florida
Bill Dietsch
CC of Miami (West Course)
Hialeah, Florida
Robert Trent Jones, Frank Duane
CC of Missouri
Columbia, Missouri
Marvin Ferguson
CC of Mobile
Alabama
Donald Ross
CC of Mobile (R)
Alabama
Willard Byrd, Clyde Johnston
CC of Mobile (A. 9)
Alabama
Earl Stone
CC of Mobile (R)
Alabama
Alfred H. Tull
CC of Montreal
St. Laurent, Quebec
Albert Murray
CC of Montreal (R)
Quebec
Roy Dye
CC of Morristown
Tennessee
William B. Langford
CC of Naples
Florida
William H. Diddel
CC of New Bedford
Massachusetts
Willie Park Jr
CC of New Bedford (R)
Massachusetts
Donald Ross
CC of New Canaan
Connecticut
Willie Park Jr
CC of New Canaan (R. 9)
Connecticut
Walter J. Travis
CC of New Canaan (A. 9)
Connecticut
Alfred H. Tull
CC of New Canaan (R)
Connecticut
Robert Trent Jones, Frank Duane
**CC of New Hampshire formerly
    known as Kearsarge Valley CC**
North Conway, New Hampshire
Wayne Stiles, John Van Kleek
CC of New Hampshire (R. 9)
New Hampshire
William F. Mitchell
CC of New Hampshire (A. 9)
New Hampshire
William F. Mitchell
**CC of New Seabury (Blue
    Course)**
South Mashpee, Massachusetts
William F. Mitchell
**CC of New Seabury (Blue
    Course) (R)**
Massachusetts
Rees Jones
**CC of New Seabury (Green
    Course)**
South Mashpee, Massachusetts
William F. Mitchell

**CC of New Seabury (Green
    Course) (R)**
Massachusetts
Rees Jones
**CC of North Carolina (Cardinal
    Course)**
Pinehurst, North Carolina
Willard Byrd
**CC of North Carolina (Cardinal
    Course) (A. 9)**
North Carolina
Robert Trent Jones
**CC of North Carolina (Dogwood
    Course)**
Pinehurst, North Carolina
Ellis Maples, Willard Byrd
**CC of North Carolina (Dogwood
    Course) (R)**
North Carolina
Robert Trent Jones
**CC of North Carolina (Dogwood
    Course) (R)**
North Carolina
Rees Jones
**CC of Northampton County (A.
    6)**
Pennsylvania
David Gordon
**CC of Northampton County
    (R.12)**
Pennsylvania
David Gordon
CC of Norwood
Massachusetts
Samuel Mitchell
CC of Orangeburg
South Carolina
Ellis Maples
CC of Orlando
Florida
Donald Ross
CC of Orlando (R)
Florida
Robert Trent Jones, Frank Duane
CC of Paducah NLE
Kentucky
Tom Bendelow
CC of Paducah
Kentucky
Robert Trent Jones
CC of Paducah (A. 9)
Kentucky
Robert Trent Jones, Roger
    Rulewich
CC of Peoria
Illinois
F.M. Birks
CC of Petersburg NLE
Virginia
Donald Ross
CC of Petersburg
Virginia
Edmund B. Ault
CC of Pittsfield
Massachusetts
Donald Ross
CC of Pittsfield (R)
Massachusetts
Wayne Stiles
CC of Rochester NLE
New York
Alex Findlay
CC of Rochester
New York
Donald Ross
CC of Rochester (R)
New York
Robert Trent Jones
CC of Rochester (A. 3)
New York
Robert Trent Jones
CC of Rochester (R)
New York
Arthur Hills, Steve Forrest
CC of Salisbury (R)
North Carolina
Donald Ross, Walter I. Johnson
CC of Sapphire
North Carolina
George W. Cobb
CC of Sapphire (R. 1)
North Carolina
John LaFoy

**CC of Sarasota now known as
    TPC at Prestancia (Course No.
    1)**
CC of Savannah NLE
Georgia
Tom Bendelow
CC of Scranton
Pennsylvania
Walter J. Travis
CC of Scranton (A. 9)
Pennsylvania
Art Wall
CC of Scranton (R)
Pennsylvania
Geoffrey S. Cornish, Brian Silva
CC of South Carolina
Florence, South Carolina
Ellis Maples, Ed Seay
CC of Spartanburg (A. 9)
South Carolina
George W. Cobb
CC of Spartanburg (R. 9)
South Carolina
George W. Cobb
CC of Spartanburg (R)
South Carolina
John LaFoy
CC of Terre Haute
Indiana
Tom Bendelow
CC of Terre Haute (R. 9)
Indiana
William H. Diddel
CC of Terre Haute (A. 9)
Indiana
William H. Diddel
CC of Troy
New York
Walter J. Travis
**CC of Virginia (James River
    Course)**
Richmond, Virginia
William S. Flynn, Howard
    Toomey
**CC of Virginia (James River
    Course) (R)**
Virginia
Fred Findlay
**CC of Virginia (James River
    Course) (R)**
Virginia
George O'Neill
**CC of Virginia (James River
    Course) (R. 3)**
Virginia
Buddy Loving
**CC of Virginia (Tuckahoe
    Course)**
Richmond, Virginia
Edmund B. Ault
**CC of Virginia (Tuckahoe
    Course) (A. 9)**
Virginia
Joe Lee, Rocky Roquemore
**CC of Virginia (Westhampton
    Course)**
Virginia
Herbert Barker
**CC of Virginia (Westhampton
    Course) (R)**
Virginia
Fred Findlay
CC of Waterbury
Connecticut
Donald Ross
**CC of Whispering Pines (East
    Course)**
North Carolina
Ellis Maples
**CC of Whispering Pines (South
    Course)**
North Carolina
Ellis Maples, Dan Maples
**CC of Whispering Pines (West
    Course)**
North Carolina
Ellis Maples, Ed Seay
CC of York
Pennsylvania
Donald Ross
CC of York (R)
Pennsylvania
William S. Flynn

CC El Rodeo
Mendellin, Colombia
Howard Watson, Robert Moote
CC Militar
Melgar, Colombia
Howard Watson
D.W. Field Muni
Brockton, Massachusetts
Wayne Stiles, John Van Kleek
D.W. Field Muni (A. 2)
Massachusetts
Samuel Mitchell
D'Allegre Estate GC
France
Seymour Dunn
Da-De-Co GC
Ottawa, Illinois
Edward Lawrence Packard
Dacca GC
Bangladesh
J.J.F. Pennink
Dad Miller Muni
Anaheim, California
Dick Miller, Wynn Priday
Dahlgreen GC
Chaska, Minnesota
Donald G. Brauer, Emile Perret
Daisifu Central CC
Fukoka, Japan
Robert von Hagge, Bruce Devlin
Dale GC
Shetland, Scotland
Fraser Middleton
Dalewood G&Curling C
Port Hope, Ontario
Clinton. E. Robinson
Dallas Athletic C (Blue Course)
Mesquite, Texas
Ralph Plummer
**Dallas Athletic C (Blue Course)
    (R)**
Texas
Jack Nicklaus, Scott Miller
Dallas Athletic C (Gold Course)
Mesquite, Texas
Ralph Plummer
Dallas CC
Texas
Tom Bendelow
Dallas CC (R)
Texas
Ralph Plummer
Dallas CC (R)
Texas
Jay Morrish
Dalmahoy GC (East Course)
Midlothian, Scotland
James Braid, John R. Stutt
Dalmahoy GC (West Course)
Midlothian, Scotland
James Braid, John R. Stutt
Dalmilling GC
Ayrshire, Scotland
Fraser Middleton
Dalton CC (R)
Georgia
Ron Kirby, Denis Griffiths
Dania CC
Florida
Red Lawrence
Danville CC
Illinois
William H. Diddel
Danville CC (A. 9)
Illinois
Edward Lawrence Packard, Brent
    Wadsworth
Danville CC
Indiana
William H. Diddel
Danville CC
Kentucky
Benjamin Wihry
Danville CC (R)
North Carolina
Gene Hamm
Danville CC
Pennsylvania
William Gordon, David Gordon
Danville CC (R)
Virginia
Gene Hamm

Danville Elks C
Illinois
William James Spear
Danville VA Hospital GC
Illinois
Charles Maddox
Darenth Valley GC
England
R. Tempest
Darlington County GC
New Jersey
Nicholas Psiahas
Darlington CC (A. 9)
South Carolina
Roland "Robby" Robertson
Darlington GC
Durham, England
Alister Mackenzie
Darlington GC (R)
England
J.J.F. Pennink
Dartford GC (R)
England
J.J.F. Pennink
Darwin GC
Australia
Peter Thomson, Michael Wolveridge
Dauphin G&CC (A. 9)
Manitoba
William G. Robinson
Dave White Muni
Casa Grande, Arizona
Gary Panks
Davenport CC
Iowa
C.H. Alison, H.S. Colt
Davenport CC (R. 2)
Iowa
Ted Lockie
Davenport GC
Cheshire, England
Fraser Middleton
Davis Park GC
Kaysville, Utah
William H. Neff
Davis Park GC (R)
Utah
William Howard Neff
Davis Shores CC NLE
St. Augustine, Florida
A.W. Tillinghast
Davison CC
Michigan
Frederick A. Ellis
Davos GC (R. 9)
Switzerland
Donald Harradine
Davos GC (A. 9)
Switzerland
Donald Harradine
Dawn Hill CC
Arkansas
Virgil Brookshire
Dawson CC
Georgia
Hugh Moore
Dayton CC
Ohio
Geoffrey S. Cornish, William G. Robinson
Dayton GC
Aurora, Missouri
Horton Smith
Dayton GC
Ohio
Willie V. Hoare
Daytona Beach G&CC (North Course)
Florida
Amos Deatherage
Daytona Beach G&CC (South Course)
Florida
Donald Ross
De Dommel GC
Hertogenbosch, Netherlands
J.F. Dudok Van Heel
Deaconsbank GC
Glasgow, Scotland
James Braid
Deal GC
Deal Beach, New Jersey
Lawrence Van Etten

Deane Muni
Somerset, England
J. Hamilton Stutt
Deangate Ridge GC
Kent, England
Fred W. Hawtree
Dearborn CC
Michigan
Donald Ross
Dearborn CC (R)
Michigan
Clinton E. Robinson
Dearborn CC (R. 1)
Michigan
Jerry Matthews
Dearborn Hills CC
Dearborn, Michigan
Walter Hagen, Mike Brady
Dearhurst GC
Hidden Valley, Ontario
Clinton E. Robinson
Debordieu Colony CC NLE
Pawley's Island, South Carolina
Wallace F. Pate
Debordieu Colony CC
Pawley's Island, South Carolina
Pete Dye, P.B. Dye
Decatur CC (A. 9)
Alabama
David Gill
Decatur CC (R. 9)
Alabama
David Gill
Decatur GC
Indiana
Robert Bruce Harris
Dedham Hunt & Polo C
Massachusetts
Alex Findlay
Dedham Hunt & Polo C (R. 2)
Massachusetts
Geoffrey S. Cornish, William G. Robinson
Dedham Hunt & Polo C (R)
Massachusetts
Willie Ogg
Deep Cliff GC
Cupertino, California
Clark Glasson
Deep Creek GC
Port Charlotte, Florida
Mark McCumber
Deep River GC
Ontario
Howard Watson, Robert Moote
Deep Springs CC
Madison, North Carolina
Ellis Maples, Ed Seay
Deep Springs CC (A. 9)
North Carolina
Ellis Maples, Dan Maples
Deepdale CC
Manhasset, New York
Dick Wilson
Deepdale CC (R)
New York
Dick Wilson
Deepdale GC NLE
Great Neck, New York
Charles Blair Macdonald, Seth Raynor
Deepdale GC (R) NLE
New York
Herbert Strong
Deer Creek G&CC
Deerfield Beach, Florida
Bill Watts
Deer Creek GC
Park Forest, Illinois
Edward Lawrence Packard, Roger Packard
Deer Creek State Park GC
Mt. Sterling, Ohio
Jack Kidwell, Michael Hurdzan
Deer Park GC
Valentine, Nebraska
Leon Pounders
Deer Park GC
Utica, New Jersey
Hal Purdy
Deer Run CC (R)
Florida
Lloyd Clifton

Deer Run GC
Moulton, Alabama
Earl Stone
Deer Run GC
Lehigh, Florida
Gordon G. Lewis
Deer Run Muni
Newport News, Virginia
Edmund B. Ault
Deer Run Muni (R.27)
Virginia
Ron Kirby, Denis Griffiths
Deer Run Muni (A. 9)
Virginia
Ron Kirby, Denis Griffiths
Deer Track CC (North Course)
Myrtle Beach, South Carolina
J. Porter Gibson
Deer Track CC (South Course)
Myrtle Beach, South Carolina
J. Porter Gibson
Deer Trail CC
Woodville, Texas
Leon Howard
Deercrest CC
Greenwich, Connecticut
Orrin Smith, Al Zikorus
Deerfield CC
Deerfield Beach, Florida
William F. Mitchell
Deerfield CC
Madison, Mississippi
Joseph S. Finger, Ken Dye
Deerfield CC
New York
Pete Craig
Deerfield CC (R. 9)
West Virginia
Jack Kidwell, Michael Hurdzan
Deerfield CC (A. 9)
West Virginia
Jack Kidwell, Michael Hurdzan
Deerfield Park GC
Riverswood, Illinois
Edward Lawrence Packard
Deerpath Park GC
Lake Forest, Illinois
Alex Pirie
Deerpath Park GC (R)
Illinois
Edward Lawrence Packard
Deerpath Park GC (R)
Illinois
Ken Killian, Dick Nugent
Deerpath Park GC (R)
Illinois
Ken Killian, Dick Nugent
Deerpath Park GC (R)
Illinois
Dick Nugent
Deerwood CC
Jacksonville, Florida
George W. Cobb
Deerwood CC (R)
Florida
Willard Byrd
Deerwood GC
Kingwood, Texas
Joseph S. Finger, Ken Dye
Deeside GC (A. 9)
Scotland
D.M.A. Steel
Defence GC
Bloemfontein, South Africa
Robert G. Grimsdell
Del Bosque CC
Mexico
Percy Clifford
Del Lago GC
Mexico
Percy Clifford
Del Mar CC
Ellwood City, Pennsylvania
Emil Loeffler, John McGlynn
Del Paso CC
California
John L. Black
Del Paso CC (R)
California
Herbert Fowler
Del Paso CC (R)
California
William F. Bell

Del Paso CC (R)
California
Gary Roger Baird
Del Paso CC (R)
California
Robert Muir Graves, Damian Pascuzzo
Del Rio G&CC
Brawley, California
William P. Bell
Del Safari CC
Palm Desert, California
Jimmy Hines
Del Tura CC
North Fort Myers, Florida
Ron Garl
Del-Aire CC
Delray Beach, Florida
Joe Lee
Delamere Forest GC
Cheshire, England
Herbert Fowler
Delamere Forest GC (R)
England
Fred W. Hawtree
Delano GC
California
Bert Stamps
Delapre GC
England
John Jacobs
Delaware CC
Ohio
Donald Ross
Delaware GC (R)
Indiana
Gary Kern
Delcastle Farms GC
Delaware
Edmund B. Ault
Delhamyeh CC
Beirut, Lebanon
J. Hamilton Stutt
Delhi GC (A. 9)
India
Peter Thomson, Michael Wolveridge
Delhi GC (R)
India
Peter Thomson, Michael Wolveridge
Delkenheim GC
West Germany
Bernhard von Limburger
Dellwood CC (R)
New York
William F. Mitchell
Dellwood CC (R)
New York
Robert Trent Jones
Dellwood National GC
White Bear Lake, Minnesota
Don Herfort
Delmar CC NLE
California
Charles Maud
Delphos CC
Ohio
Leonard Schmutte
Delray Beach G&CC
Florida
Donald Ross
Delray Beach G&CC (R)
Florida
Robert Bruce Harris
Delray Beach G&CC (A. 9)
Florida
Red Lawrence
Delray Dunes G&CC
Delray Beach, Florida
Pete Dye, Jack Cabler
Delray Dunes G&CC (R)
Florida
Pete Dye
Deltona G&CC
Florida
David Wallace
Demor Hills CC
Morenci, Michigan
Harold Paddock
Dempster GC NLE
Chicago, Illinois
Tom Bendelow

Denbigh GC
Wales
J. Stockton
Denham GC
England
H.S. Colt
Denham GC (R)
England
James Braid
Denison CC
Iowa
William Ada
Dennis Highlands GC
Dennis, Massachusetts
Michael Hurdzan, Jack Kidwell
Dennis Pines Muni
Dennis, Massachusetts
Henry Mitchell
Denton CC
Texas
Ralph Plummer
Denton GC
England
B. Allen
Denver CC
Colorado
James Foulis
Denver CC (R)
Colorado
William S. Flynn
Denver CC (R)
Colorado
William H. Diddel
Denver CC (R)
Colorado
Press Maxwell
Denver CC (R. 3)
Colorado
John Cochran
Denver CC (R)
Colorado
Ed Seay
Dereham GC
England
E.C. Gray
Derrick C
Edmonton, Alberta
William Brinkworth
Derrydale GC
Brampton, Ontario
Renee Muylaert
Des Moines G&CC (Blue Course)
West Des Moines, Iowa
Pete Dye
Des Moines G&CC (Red Course)
West Des Moines, Iowa
Pete Dye
Desaru Resort GC
Malaysia
Robert Trent Jones Jr
Desert Air CC
Rancho Mirage, California
Jimmy Hines
Desert Aire CC
Palmdale, California
Ted Robinson
Desert Falls CC
Palm Desert, California
Ronald Fream
Desert Forest GC
Carefree, Arizona
Red Lawrence
Desert Forest GC (R. 2)
Arizona
Arthur Jack Snyder
Desert Highlands GC
Scottsdale, Arizona
Jack Nicklaus, Jay Morrish, Bob Cupp, Scott Miller
Desert Hills CC
Tucson, Arizona
Dave Bennett
Desert Horizons CC
Indian Wells, California
Ted Robinson
Desert Inn & CC
Las Vegas, Nevada
Lawrence Hughes
Desert Inn & CC (R)
Nevada
Donald Collett

Desert Island CC
Rancho Mirage, California
Desmond Muirhead
Desert Island CC (R)
California
Stan Leonard, *Philip Tattersfield*
Desert Mountain GC (Cochise
   Course)
Carefree, Arizona
Jack Nicklaus, Scott Miller
Desert Mountain GC (Geronimo
   Course)
Carefree, Arizona
Jack Nicklaus, Scott Miller
Desert Mountain GC (Renegade
   Course)
Carefree, Arizona
Jack Nicklaus, Scott Miller
Desert Princess CC
Cathedral City, California
David Rainville
Desert Rose GC
Las Vegas, Nevada
Dick Wilson, Joe Lee
Desert Rose GC (R)
Nevada
Jeff Brauer, *Jim Colbert*
Desert Sands G&CC
Mesa, Arizona
Arthur Jack Snyder
Desert Springs CC
Alice Springs, Australia
Peter Thomson, Michael
   Wolveridge
Desert Springs GC
Palm Desert, California
Ted Robinson
Detroit CC
Detroit Lakes, Minnesota
Tom Bendelow
Detroit CC (A. 9)
Minnesota
Don Herfort
Detroit GC NLE
Michigan
William "Bert" Way
Detroit GC (North Course)
Michigan
Donald Ross
Detroit GC (North Course) (R)
Michigan
Robert Trent Jones
Detroit GC (North Course) (R)
Michigan
Arthur Hills
Detroit GC (South Course)
Michigan
Donald Ross
Detroit GC (South Course) (R)
Michigan
Robert Trent Jones
Detwiler GC
Toledo, Ohio
Arthur Hills
Deux Montagnes GC
Quebec
John Watson
Devil's Head Lodge GC
Merrimac, Wisconsin
Arthur Johnson
Devil's Knob GC
Wintergreen, Virginia
Ellis Maples, Dan Maples
Devon CC
Pennsylvania
Lemeul C. Altemus
Devonshire GC
Chatsworth, California
William H. Johnson
Dewsbury District GC
England
Peter Alliss, David Thomas
DeAnza Desert CC
Borrego Springs, California
Lawrence Hughes
DeAnza Palm Springs Mobile CC
Cathedral City, California
Ted Robinson
DeBell GC
Burbank, California
William F. Bell, William H.
   Johnson

DeBell GC (R)
California
William F. Bell
DeBell GC (R)
California
Richard Bigler
DeCordova Bend CC
Granbury, Texas
Leon Howard
DeLavega CC
Santa Cruz, California
Bert Stamps
DeLavega CC (R. 2)
California
Ronald Fream
DeSoto GC
Hot Springs Village, Arkansas
Edmund B. Ault
DeSoto Lakes G&CC now known
   as Palm-Aire West CC
   (Champions Course)
Diablo Creek GC
Concord, California
Bob Baldock
Diablo Creek GC (R. 5)
California
Robert Muir Graves
Diablo G&CC
California
William Watson
Diablo G&CC (R. 2)
California
Robert Muir Graves
Diablo Hills GC
Walnut Creek, California
Robert Muir Graves
Diamond Bar GC
California
William F. Bell
Diamond Head Y&CC
Bay St. Louis, Mississippi
Bill Atkins
Diamond Head Y&CC (A. 9)
Mississippi
Earl Stone
Diamond Hill GC
Valrico, Florida
Ken Snow, Robert Greenwell
Diamond Hills G&CC
Florida
Chic Adams
Diamond Oaks CC
Roseville, California
Ted Robinson
Diamond Oaks G&CC
Fort Worth, Texas
Charles B. Akey
Diamond Ridge GC
Maryland
Edmund B. Ault
Diamondhead GC
Hot Springs, Arkansas
Norman Henderson
Diboll Muni
Texas
Leon Howard
Dickinson Muni
North Dakota
Abe Espinosa
Digby Pines GC
Digby, Nova Scotia
Stanley Thompson
Dighton GC
Massachusetts
Samuel Mitchell
Dinard GC (R)
France
Willie Park Jr
Dinsmore CC NLE
Staatsburg, New York
Robert P. Huntington
Dinsmore GC
Staatsburg, New York
Hal Purdy
Diplomat CC
Hollywood, Florida
Red Lawrence
Diplomatic C
Bucharest, Romania
Donald Harradine
Discovery Bay CC
Sacramento, California
Ted Robinson

Disney World GC (Magnolia
   Course)
Lake Buena Vista, Florida
Joe Lee, Rocky Roquemore
Disney World GC (Palm Course)
Lake Buena Vista, Florida
Joe Lee, Rocky Roquemore
Disney World GC (Wee Links)
Lake Buena Vista, Florida
Ron Garl
Disneyland Hotel GC NLE
Anaheim, California
Desmond Muirhead
Diversey GC NLE
Chicago, Illinois
Tom Bendelow
Dix Hills GC (R)
New York
Stephen Kay
Dixie GC
Laurel, Mississippi
Charles N. Clark
Dixon CC
Illinois
Tom Bendelow
Dixon Landing CC NLE
Milpatas, California
Algie Pulley
Dixville Notch GC
New Hampshire
George Thom
Djakarta GC
Batavia, Indonesia
Tom Simpson
Djurslands GC
Denmark
Frederik Dreyer
Dobbins AFB GC
Georgia
Chic Adams
Dobson Ranch GC
Mesa, Arizona
Red Lawrence, Jeff Hardin,Greg
   Nash
Dodge City CC
Kansas
Harry Robb
Dodge City CC (A. 9)
Kansas
Don Sechrest
Dodge Point GC
Dodgeville, Wisconsin
Homer Fieldhouse
Dodger Pines CC
Vero Beach, Florida
Dick Bird, Walter O'Malley,Ira Hoyt
Doe Valley G&CC
Brandenberg, Kentucky
Richard Watson
Doering Estate GC
Chicago, Illinois
William B. Langford, Theodore J.
   Moreau
Dogwood Hills GC
Osage Beach, Missouri
Herman Hackbarth
Dogwood Lakes CC
Florida
James Root
Dolphin Head GC
Hilton Head Island, South
   Carolina
Arthur Davis, Ron Kirby,Gary
   Player
Dom Pedro Vilamoura GC
Portugal
J.J.F. Pennink
Dominion CC
San Antonio, Texas
William Johnston
Don Hawkins Muni
Birmingham, Alabama
Jack Daray
Don Valley Muni
Toronto, Ontario
Howard Watson
Don Valley Muni (R)
Ontario
Howard Watson, John Watson
Don Valley Muni (A. 9)
Ontario
Howard Watson, John Watson

Donabate GC (R)
Ireland
Eddie Hackett
Donalsonville CC
Georgia
Bill Amick
Donaveschingen GC
West Germany
Karl Hoffmann
Doncaster GC (R)
England
J.J.F. Pennink
Doncaster GC (R. 7)
England
Fred W. Hawtree, Martin
   Hawtree
Donegal Town GC
County Donegal, Ireland
Eddie Hackett
Donneybrook GC NLE
San Bernardino, California
William H. Johnson
Dooks GC (R)
Ireland
Eddie Hackett
Doon Valley GC
Kitchener, Ontario
Clinton E. Robinson, Robert
   Moote
Doornsche GC NLE
Utrecht, Netherlands
John Duncan Dunn
Dorado del Mar GC
Dorado, Puerto Rico
James Gilmore Harrison,
   Ferdinand Garbin
Dorado del Mar GC (R)
Puerto Rico
Edmund B. Ault
Dorado Beach GC (East Course)
Dorado, Puerto Rico
Robert Trent Jones, Frank Duane
Dorado Beach GC (East Course)
   (A. 9)
Puerto Rico
Robert Trent Jones, Frank Duane
Dorado Beach GC (West Course)
Dorado, Puerto Rico
Robert Trent Jones, Frank Duane
Dorado Beach GC (West Course)
   (A. 9)
Puerto Rico
Robert Trent Jones, Frank Duane
Dorado CC
Tucson, Arizona
Ted Robinson
Doral CC (Blue Course)
Miami, Florida
Dick Wilson, Robert von Hagge
Doral CC (Blue Course) (R)
Florida
Robert von Hagge, Bruce Devlin
Doral CC (Gold Course)
Miami, Florida
Robert von Hagge, Bruce Devlin
Doral CC (Gold Course) (R)
Florida
Robert von Hagge, Bruce Devlin
Doral CC (Green Course)
Miami, Florida
Robert von Hagge
Doral CC (Red Course)
Miami, Florida
Dick Wilson, Robert von Hagge
Doral CC (Red Course) (R)
Florida
Robert von Hagge, Bruce Devlin
Doral CC (White Course)
Miami, Florida
Robert von Hagge
Doral Park CC (Silver Course)
Miami, Florida
Robert von Hagge, Bruce Devlin
Dorcester GC
Fairfield Glade, Tennessee
Bob Greenwood
Dorking GC
Surrey, England
James Braid
Dorlon Park GC
Columbiana, Ohio
Richard W. LaConte

Dornick Hills G&CC
Ardmore, Oklahoma
Perry Maxwell
Dornick Hills G&CC (R. 9)
Oklahoma
Perry Maxwell
Dornick Hills G&CC (A. 9)
Oklahoma
Perry Maxwell
Dornick Hills G&CC (R)
Oklahoma
Dick Nugent
Dortmunder GC
Dortmund, West Germany
Bernhard von Limburger
Dorval GC
Quebec
Howard Watson
Dorval Muni (Dorval Course)
Quebec
Graham Cooke
Dorval Muni (Oakville Course)
Quebec
Graham Cooke
Dos Rios CC
Gunnison, Colorado
John Cochran
Dos Rios CC (A. 9)
Colorado
Dick Phelps, Brad Benz,Mike
   Poellot
Dothan CC
Alabama
Hugh Moore
Double Eagle GC
Eagle Bend, Minnesota
Joel Goldstrand
Doublegate Plantation CC
Albany, Georgia
George W. Cobb
Dougalston GC
Glasgow, Scotland
John Harris, Michael Wolveridge
Douglas CC
Arizona
A.H. Jolly
Douglas GC
County Cork, Ireland
Alister Mackenzie
Douglas GC (R)
Ireland
Eddie Hackett
Douglas H. Keen Estate GC
Austin, Quebec
Howard Watson
Douglas Highlands GC
Colorado
Dick Phelps
Douglas Muni
Isle of Man
Alister Mackenzie
Douglasdale Estates GC
Alberta
William G. Robinson
Douglaston Park GC
Douglaston, New York
William H. Tucker
Douglaston Park GC (R. 5)
New York
Frank Duane
Dover AFB GC
Delaware
Edmund B. Ault, Al Jamison
Dover Bay CC
Ohio
William "Bert" Way
Dover CC (R. 9)
Delaware
Edmund B. Ault
Dover CC
New Hampshire
Wayne Stiles
Dover CC (R)
New Hampshire
Orrin Smith, William F. Mitchell
Downers Grove GC formerly
   known as Chicago GC
Belmont, Illinois
Charles Blair Macdonald
Downers Grove GC (R. 3)
Illinois
David Gill

Downey VA Hospital GC
Chicago, Illinois
Charles Maddox
Downfield GC
Dundee, Scotland
James Braid, John R. Stutt
Downfield GC (R)
Scotland
C.K. Cotton
Downing Muni
Erie, Pennsylvania
James Gilmore Harrison,
  Ferdinand Garbin
Downingtown Inn GC
Pennsylvania
George Fazio
Downshire GC
Berkshire, England
Fred W. Hawtree
Downsview G&CC
Toronto, Ontario
Howard Watson, Robert Moote
Dows CC
Iowa
Arthur E. Cott
Doylestown CC
Pennsylvania
William S. Flynn
Dragon Lake GC
British Columbia
Jack Reimer
Dragon Valley GC
Yongpyeong, South Korea
Ronald Fream
Drayton Park GC
Birmingham, England
James Braid, John R. Stutt
Dretzka Muni
Madison, Wisconsin
Evert Kincaid
Driffield GC
England
C.H. Websdale
Driftwood G&CC
Bayou La Batre, Alabama
Telfair Ghioto
Dromoland Castle GC
Ireland
B.E. Wiggington
Drottningholms GC
Sweden
Nils Skold, Rafael Sundblom
Druid Hills CC
Atlanta, Georgia
Herbert Barker
Druid Hills CC (R)
Georgia
Ron Kirby
Druid Hills CC (R)
Georgia
Arthur Hills, Mike Dasher
Druid Hills GC
Fairfield Glade, Tennessee
Leon Howard
Drumlins GC
Syracuse, New York
Leonard Macomber
Dry Creek GC
Galt, California
Jack Fleming
Dryden G&CC
Ontario
Clinton E. Robinson, Robert
  Moote
Dryden Park Muni
California
William F. Bell
Duamyre CC NLE
Enfield, Massachusetts
Orrin Smith
Dubb's Dread GC
Butler, Pennsylvania
John Aubrey
Dublin and County GC
Ireland
Eddie Hackett
Dublin CC (A. 9)
Georgia
George W. Cobb
Dublin CC (R. 9)
Georgia
George W. Cobb

Dublin Sports C
County Dublin, Ireland
Eddie Hackett
Dubs Dread GC
Piper, Kansas
Bob Dunning
Dubsdread CC
Orlando, Florida
Tom Bendelow
Dubsdread CC (R)
Florida
Lloyd Clifton
Dubuque G&CC
Iowa
Tom Bendelow
Dubuque G&CC (R. 9)
Iowa
Roger Packard
Duc de Gramont Estate GC
France
Tom Simpson
Duck Creek CC
Ravenna, Ohio
Richard W. LaConte
Duck Creek Park GC
Davenport, Iowa
William B. Langford
Duck Creek Park GC (R)
Iowa
Robert Bruce Harris
Duck Lake GC
Albion, Michigan
Tom Bendelow
Duck Lake GC (A. 9)
Michigan
Arthur Young
Duck Woods GC
Kitty Hawk, North Carolina
Ellis Maples, Ed Seay
Duck Woods GC (R. 7)
North Carolina
Brian Ault, Tom Clark
Duddington GC
Edinburgh, Scotland
Willie Park, Willie Park Jr
Duff House Royal GC
Banff, Scotland
Alister Mackenzie
Duff House Royal GC (R)
Scotland
Alister Mackenzie, *Charles A.
  Mackenzie*
Dugway GC
Utah
William F. Bell
**Duke of Marlborough GC now
  known as Marlboro CC**
Duke Estate GC NLE
Somerville, New Jersey
Robert Trent Jones
Duke University GC
Durham, North Carolina
Robert Trent Jones, Frank Duane
Dullatur GC
Glasgow, Scotland
James Braid
Dumfries & County GC (R)
Scotland
P.M. Ross
Dumfries and Galloway GC (R)
Scotland
Theodore Moone
Dun Laoghaire GC
Dublin, Ireland
H.S. Colt
Dun Laoghaire GC (R)
Ireland
Eddie Hackett
Dun Roamin GC
Gilbertsville, Massachusetts
Manny Francis
Dun Rovin CC
Northville, Michigan
Bruce Matthews
Dunbar GC
East Lothian, Scotland
Old Tom Morris
Dunblane GC
Perthshire, Scotland
Old Tom Morris
Dundalk GC
Ireland
James Braid

Dundalk GC (R)
Ireland
J. Hamilton Stutt
Dundalk GC (R)
Ireland
Peter Alliss, David Thomas
Dundalk GC (A. 9)
Ireland
Peter Alliss, David Thomas
Dundas Valley G&CC
Ontario
Stanley Thompson
Dundas Valley G&CC (R)
Ontario
Clinton E. Robinson
Dundee CC
Illinois
Harry Collis, *Jack Croke*
Dundee GC NLE
Omaha, Nebraska
*Henry C. Glissmann, Harold
  Glissmann*
Dundee Park GC NLE
Omaha, Nebraska
Harry Lawrie
Dundee Resort GC
Cape Breton, Nova Scotia
Robert Moote
Dundee Resort GC (A. 9)
Nova Scotia
Robert Moote
Dunedin CC
Florida
Donald Ross
Dunedin CC (R)
Florida
Dick Wilson
Dunedin CC (R)
Florida
Arthur Hills
Dunes CC
Sanibel Island, Florida
Mark McCumber
Dunes G&BC
Myrtle Beach, South Carolina
Robert Trent Jones
Dunes G&BC (R)
South Carolina
Robert Trent Jones, Roger
  Rulewich
Dunes Hotel CC
Las Vegas, Nevada
William F. Bell
Dunfermline GC (R)
Scotland
John R. Stutt
Dunfey's GC
Hyannis, Massachusetts
Geoffrey S. Cornish, William G.
  Robinson
Dungarvan GC
County Waterford, Ireland
Eddie Hackett
Dungarvan GC (R)
Ireland
Eddie Hackett
Dunham Muni
Cincinnati, Ohio
Arthur Hills
Dunmurry GC
Northern Ireland
T.J.A. McAuley
Dunmurry GC (R)
Northern Ireland
J.J.F. Pennink
Dunnikier Park GC
Fife, Scotland
Fraser Middleton
Dunstable Downs GC
Bedfordshire, England
James Braid
Dunwoody CC
Georgia
Willard Byrd
Duquesne GC (R)
Pennsylvania
Ferdinand Garbin
Durand-Eastman Park GC
Rochester, New York
Robert Trent Jones
Durango Muni
Colorado
Frank Hummel

Durant CC
Oklahoma
Leon Howard
Durban CC
South Africa
Laurie Waters, *George Waterman*
Durban CC (R)
South Africa
S.V. Hotchkin
Durban CC (R)
South Africa
Robert G. Grimsdell
Duren GC
Bad Duren, West Germany
Bernhard von Limburger
Duren GC (A. 9)
West Germany
J.J.F. Pennink
**Dusseldorf Land und GC (East
  Course)**
West Germany
Bernhard von Limburger
**Dusseldorf Land und GC (West
  Course)**
West Germany
Bernhard von Limburger
Dusseldorfer GC
West Germany
Fred W. Hawtree
Duxbury Park GC
Lancashire, England
Fred W. Hawtree, Martin
  Hawtree, A.H.F. Jiggens
Duxbury YC
Massachusetts
Wayne Stiles
Duxbury YC (R)
Massachusetts
William F. Mitchell
Duxbury YC (A. 9)
Massachusetts
Geoffrey S. Cornish, William G.
  Robinson
DuBois CC (R. 9)
Pennsylvania
X.G. Hassenplug
DuPont CC NLE
Wilmington, Delaware
Wilfrid Reid
DuPont CC (DuPont Course)
Wilmington, Delaware
Alfred H. Tull
DuPont CC (DuPont Course) (R)
Delaware
William Gordon, David Gordon
DuPont CC (DuPont Course) (R)
Delaware
Geoffrey S. Cornish, William G.
  Robinson
DuPont CC (Louviers Course)
Wilmington, Delaware
William Gordon, David Gordon
**DuPont CC (Louviers Course)
  (R)**
Delaware
Geoffrey S. Cornish, William G.
  Robinson
DuPont CC (Montchanin Course)
Newark, Delaware
William Gordon, David Gordon
**DuPont CC (Montchanin Course)
  (R)**
Delaware
Geoffrey S. Cornish, William G.
  Robinson
DuPont CC (Nemours Course)
Wilmington, Delaware
Alfred H. Tull
**DuPont CC (Nemours Course)
  (R)**
Delaware
William Gordon, David Gordon
**DuPont CC (Nemours Course)
  (R)**
Delaware
Geoffrey S. Cornish, William G.
  Robinson
DuPont GC (R. 9)
Virginia
Gene Hamm
DuPont GC (A. 9)
Virginia
Gene Hamm

DuWayne Motel GC
Chicago, Illinois
Charles Maddox
Dwan GC
Bloomington, Minnesota
David Gill
Dwight D. Eisenhower GC
Annapolis, Maryland
Edmund B. Ault
Dyess AFB GC
Abilene, Texas
Leon Howard
Dyke GC (R)
England
F.G. Hawtree, Fred W. Hawtree
Dykeman Park Muni
Logansport, Indiana
William B. Langford, Theodore J.
  Moreau
Dyker Beach GC
Brooklyn, New York
Tom Bendelow
Dyker Beach GC (R)
New York
John Van Kleek
Dyker Meadow GC NLE
Brooklyn, New York
Tom Bendelow
Dysart G&CC
Iowa
Dick Phelps
**E. Gaynor Brennan GC formerly
  known as Hubbard Heights
  CC**
Stamford, Connecticut
Maurice McCarthy
Eagle Bend GC
Montana
Bill Hull
Eagle Bluff CC
Hurley, Wisconsin
Homer Fieldhouse
Eagle Creek G&TC
Naples, Florida
Edward Lawrence Packard
Eagle Creek Muni
Indianapolis, Indiana
Pete Dye, David Pfaff
Eagle Crest GC
Cline Falls, Oregon
Gene "Bunny" Mason
Eagle CC
Broomfield, Colorado
Leon Howard
Eagle CC (A. 9)
Colorado
Dick Phelps
Eagle CC (R. 9)
Colorado
Dick Phelps
Eagle Glen GC
Elmendorf AFB, Alaska
Robert Trent Jones, Robert Trent
  Jones Jr
Eagle Hills GC
Idaho
C. Edward Trout
Eagle Hills GC (A. 9)
Idaho
Bob Baldock, Robert L. Baldock
Eagle Landing GC
Hanahan, South Carolina
Bill Amick
Eagle Lodge GC
Lafayette Hill, Pennsylvania
Rees Jones
Eagle Nest GC
North Myrtle Beach, South
  Carolina
Gene Hamm
Eagle Point Park GC
Clinton, Illinois
Robert Bruce Harris
Eagle Ridge CC
Ft. Myers, Florida
Gordon G. Lewis
Eagle Ridge GC (North Course)
Galena, Illinois
Roger Packard
Eagle Ridge GC (South Course)
Galena, Illinois
Roger Packard

Eagle River CC (R. 3)
Wisconsin
Don Herfort
Eagle River CC (A. 9)
Wisconsin
Don Herfort
Eagle Vail CC
Avon, Colorado
Robert von Hagge, Bruce Devlin
Eagle Valley Muni
Carson City, Nevada
Arthur Jack Snyder
Eagle's Nest CC
Somerset, Kentucky
Benjamin Wihry
Eagle's Nest CC
Blue Mountain Lake, New York
Tom Bendelow
Eaglehead G&CC
New Market, Maryland
William F. Mitchell
Eagles Nest GC
Silverthorne, Colorado
Dick Phelps
Eaglescliffe GC
County Durham, England
James Braid, John R. Stutt
Eaglescliffe GC (R)
England
Henry Cotton
Eaglesmere CC (R)
Pennsylvania
William S. Flynn
Eaglewood CC
Hobe Sound, Florida
Ward Northrup
Earl F. Elliot Park GC
Rockford, Illinois
Edward Lawrence Packard
Earl Grey GC (R)
Alberta
Clinton E. Robinson
Earlington G&CC (R)
Washington
David Craig
Earlville Island GC
Earlville, Illinois
Joe Meister
Earlywine Park GC
Oklahoma City, Oklahoma
Floyd Farley
Easingwold GC
North Yorkshire, England
F.G. Hawtree, J.H. Taylor
East Aurora CC (A. 9)
New York
William Harries, *A. Russell Tryon*
East Aurora CC (R. 9)
New York
William Harries, *A. Russell Tryon*
East Bay CC
Oakland, California
William Watson
East Bay CC
Largo, Florida
William F. Mitchell
East Bay GC
Provo, Utah
William Howard Neff
East Berkshire GC
England
Peter Paxton
East Cork GC
County Cork, Ireland
John Harris
East Cork GC (R)
Ireland
Eddie Hackett
East Hartford GC
Connecticut
Orrin Smith
East Hartford GC (A. 9)
Connecticut
Orrin Smith, Al Zikorus
East Herts GC
Hertfordshire, England
D. Hunt, D. Lewis
East Kilbride GC
Lanarkshire, Scotland
Fred W. Hawtree
East Kingston GC
New Hampshire
Phil Wogan

East Lake CC formerly known as
Atlanta Athletic C (Course No.
1)
Atlanta, Georgia
Tom Bendelow
East Lake CC (R)
Georgia
Donald Ross
East Lake CC (R)
Georgia
George W. Cobb
East Lake CC (Course No. 2)
formerly known as Atlanta
Athletic C (Course No. 2) NLE
Atlanta, Georgia
Donald Ross
East Lake CC (Course No. 2) (R)
Georgia
Chic Adams
East Lake Woodlands G&CC
(North Course)
Oldsmar, Florida
Robert von Hagge, Bruce Devlin
East Lake Woodlands G&CC
(South Course)
Oldsmar, Florida
Tom Jackson
East Lakes GC
Palm Beach Gardens, Florida
George Fazio, Tom Fazio
East Liverpool CC
Ohio
Willie Park Jr
East Liverpool CC (A. 9)
Ohio
Sandy Alves
East London CC (R)
South Africa
S.V. Hotchkin
East Mountain Muni
Waterbury, Connecticut
William Gordon, David Gordon
East Orange Muni
New Jersey
Tom Bendelow
East Park GC
London, Ontario
Clinton E. Robinson
East Potomac Park GC
Washington, D.C.
Robert White
East Potomac Park GC (R)
Washington, D.C.
William S. Flynn
East Ridge CC
Shreveport, Louisiana
Press Maxwell
East Ridge CC NLE
Lincoln, Nebraska
Orrin Smith
East Shore CC
Culver, Indiana
William B. Langford, Theodore J.
Moreau
Eastbourne Downs GC
Sussex, England
J.H. Taylor
Eastern Hills CC
Garland, Texas
Ralph Plummer
Eastern Hills CC (R. 5)
Texas
Marvin Ferguson
Eastern Kentucky Univ GC
Richmond, Kentucky
Benjamin Wihry
Eastern Shore Y&CC
Onancock, Virginia
Russell Roberts
Eastern Shore Y&CC (R)
Virginia
Edmund B. Ault
Eastham Lodge GC
Cheshire, England
Fred W. Hawtree, Martin
Hawtree,A.H.F. Jiggens
Easthampstead Park GC
Wokingham, England
Fred W. Hawtree
Eastman Lake CC
Grantham, New Hampshire
Geoffrey S. Cornish, William G.
Robinson

Eastmoreland GC
Portland, Oregon
H. Chandler Egan
Eastmoreland GC (R)
Oregon
John Junor
Easton CC
Massachusetts
Samuel Mitchell
Easton CC (A. 9)
Massachusetts
Samuel Mitchell
Eastover CC
New Orleans, Louisiana
Joe Lee, Rocky Roquemore
Eastpointe CC
Palm Beach Gardens, Florida
George Fazio, Tom Fazio
Eastward Ho! CC
Chatham, Massachusetts
Herbert Fowler
Eastwood Fairways GC
Louisiana
Tommy Moore
Eastwood GC
Renfrewshire, Scotland
Theodore Moone
Eastwood GC (R)
Scotland
John R. Stutt
Eastwood Muni
Ft. Myers, Florida
Robert von Hagge, Bruce Devlin
Eaton Canyon GC
California
William F. Bell
Eaton GC
Cheshire, England
Fred W. Hawtree
Echo Farms G&CC
Wilmington, North Carolina
Gene Hamm
Echo Farms G&CC (R)
North Carolina
Clement B. "Johnny" Johnston,
Clyde Johnston
Echo Hills GC
Hemet, California
Ed Dover
Echo Hills GC (R)
Kansas
Bert Henderson
Echo Lake CC
Detroit, Michigan
William H. Diddel
Echo Lake CC
Westfield, New Jersey
Donald Ross, George Low Sr
Echo Lake CC (R. 6)
New Jersey
Robert White
Echo Lake CC (R. 3)
New Jersey
Willard Wilkinson
Echo Lake CC (A. 3)
New Jersey
Geoffrey S. Cornish, William G.
Robinson
Echo Lake CC (R. 3)
New Jersey
Geoffrey S. Cornish, William G.
Robinson
Echo Mesa GC
Sun City West, Arizona
Greg Nash
Echo Valley G&CC
Des Moines, Iowa
Edward Lawrence Packard
Eden Isles CC
Slidell, Louisiana
Edmund B. Ault, Brian Ault
Eden Isles CC (R. 1)
Louisiana
Tom Clark
Edenvale GC (R)
Minnesota
Don Herfort
Edgbaston GC
Warwickshire, England
H.S. Colt
Edgbaston GC (R)
England
Tom Williamson

Edgebrook GC NLE
Illinois
James Foulis
Edgebrook GC
Sandwich, Illinois
Ken Killian, Dick Nugent
Edgebrook GC
South Dakota
Donald K. Rippel
Edgecreek GC
Van Wert, Ohio
William James Spear
Edgemont GC
Philadelphia, Pennsylvania
Tony Pedone
Edgewater GC
Richland, California
T.R. Fritz
Edgewater GC NLE
Chicago, Illinois
Harry Turpie
Edgewater GC now known as
Rainbow Bay GC
Edgewater Muni
Pasco, Washington
A. Vernon Macan
Edgewood in the Pines GC
Hazilton, Pennsylvania
David Gordon
Edgewood CC
Virden, Illinois
Charles Maddox
Edgewood CC
Anderson, Indiana
Marion Collins
Edgewood CC
Southwick, Massachusetts
Geoffrey S. Cornish
Edgewood CC
Union Lakes, Michigan
Ernest Way
Edgewood CC
Pittsburgh, Pennsylvania
Donald Ross
Edgewood CC (R)
Pennsylvania
Emil Loeffler
Edgewood CC (R)
Pennsylvania
James Gilmore Harrison,
Ferdinand Garbin
Edgewood GC
Charleston, West Virginia
Alex McKay
Edgewood GC now known as
TPC of Connecticut
Edgewood GC
Polo, Illinois
Tom Bendelow
Edgewood Muni (R)
North Dakota
Robert Bruce Harris
Edgewood Tahoe CC
Stateline, Nevada
George Fazio, Tom Fazio
Edgewood Tahoe CC (R)
Nevada
Peter Thomson, Michael
Wolveridge,Ronald Fream
Edgewood Valley CC
LaGrange, Illinois
William H. Diddel
Edinburg CC
Texas
John Bredemus
Edison CC
Rexford, New York
Devereux Emmet
Edmondstown GC (R)
Ireland
Eddie Hackett
Edmonton G&CC
Alberta
William Brinkworth
Edmonton G&CC (R)
Alberta
William G. Robinson
Edmore GC
Michigan
Carol O. Hegenauer
Edmund Orgill GC
Millington, Tennessee
Press Maxwell

Edmunston GC (R)
New Brunswick
Albert Murray
Edmunston GC (A.11)
New Brunswick
Albert Murray
Edwalton GC
Nottinghamshire, England
J.J.F. Pennink
Edwin R. Carr Estate GC
Virginia
Edmund B. Ault, Al Jamison
Edzell GC
Scotland
Archie Simpson
Edzell GC (R)
Scotland
James Braid, John R. Stutt
Effingham CC (A. 9)
Illinois
William James Spear
Effingham GC
England
H.S. Colt, C.H. Alison
Eglin AFB GC
Niceville, Florida
William B. Langford, Theodore J.
Moreau
Eglin AFB GC (A. 9)
Florida
Bill Amick
Eindhoven GC
Netherlands
H.S. Colt, C.H. Alison,J.S.F.
Morrison
Eisenhower College GC
Seneca, New York
George W. Cobb
Eisenhower GC (Blue Course)
US Air Force Academy, Colorado
Robert Trent Jones, Robert Trent
Jones,Frank Duane
Eisenhower GC (Silver Course)
US Air Force Academy, Colorado
Frank Hummel
Eisenhower Park GC (Blue
Course)
East Meadow, New York
Robert Trent Jones
Eisenhower Park GC (Red
Course)
East Meadow, New York
Devereux Emmet
Eisenhower Park GC (White
Course)
East Meadow, New York
Robert Trent Jones
Ekwanok CC
Manchester, Vermont
John Duncan Dunn, Walter J.
Travis
Ekwanok CC (R. 8)
Vermont
Geoffrey S. Cornish
El Bosque CC
Mexico
Percy Clifford
El Bosque GC
Valencia, Spain
Robert Trent Jones, Cabell
Robinson
El Caballero CC NLE
Tarzana, California
George C. Thomas Jr, William P.
Bell
El Caballero CC
Tarzana, California
William H. Johnson
El Caballero CC (R)
California
Robert Trent Jones
El Camino CC
Oceanside, California
William H. Johnson
El Campestre Chiluca
Mexico City, Mexico
Lawrence Hughes
El Campo CC
Texas
Jay Riviere
El Cariso GC
Sylmar, California
Robert Muir Graves

El Cerrito G&CC (R)
California
Robert Muir Graves
El Cid G&CC
Mazatlan, Mexico
Manore Orthoco
El Cid G&CC (A. 9)
Mexico
Lawrence Hughes
El Conquistador CC
Bradenton, Florida
Mark Mahannah
El Conquistador GC NLE
Valparaiso, Florida
George O'Neill
El Conquistador Hotel & C NLE
Fujardo, Puerto Rico
Robert von Hagge
El Conquistador Hotel GC
Tucson, Arizona
Jeff Hardin, Greg Nash
El Dorado CC
Greenwood, Indiana
Pete Dye, Alice Dye
El Dorado CC (A. 9)
Indiana
Gary Kern
El Dorado CC (R. 9)
Indiana
Gary Kern
El Dorado CC
Kansas
Smiley Bell
El Dorado CC
McKinney, Texas
Gary Roger Baird
El Dorado GC
Humble, Texas
George Fazio
El Dorado Hills GC
California
Robert Trent Jones, Frank Duane
El Dorado Park GC (R.12)
California
Ted Robinson
El Kantaoui GC
Soussenord, Tunisia
John Harris, Peter
    Thomson,Michael Wolveridge,
    Ronald Fream
El Macero CC
California
Bob Baldock
El Macero CC (R)
California
Robert Muir Graves, Damian
    Pascuzzo
El Merrie Del CC NLE
Florida
John Duncan Dunn
El Mirador Hotel GC NLE
Palm Springs, California
Gregor MacMillan
El Monte GC
Ogden, Utah
Mick Riley
El Morro GC
Puerto La Cruz, Venezuela
Edward Lawrence Packard,
    Roger Packard
El Niguel CC
South Laguna, California
David W. Kent
El Paraiso GC
Spain
Arthur Davis, Ron Kirby,Gary
    Player
El Paso CC
Texas
Tom Bendelow
El Paso CC (R)
Texas
Ronald Fream
El Prado CC (Butterfield Stage
    Course)
Chino, California
Harry Rainville, David Rainville
El Prado CC (Chino Creek
    Course)
Chino, California
Harry Rainville, David Rainville
El Rancho Verde CC
Rialto, California
Harry Rainville

El Rancho Verde CC
San Jose, California
George E. Santana
El Reno CC
Oklahoma
Floyd Farley
El Rincon C
Bogota, Colombia
Robert Trent Jones, Frank Duane
El Rincon C (A)
Colombia
Robert Trent Jones, Frank Duane
El Rio GC
Tuscon, Arizona
William P. Bell
El Rivino CC
Riverside, California
Joseph Calwell
El Toro USMC GC
California
William Foley
Elanora CC
Australia
Des Soutar
Elba Dell'Acquabone GC
Italy
G. Albertini
Elba GC
Italy
Pier Mancinelli
Elbel Park GC
South Bend, Indiana
William James Spear
Elcona CC
Elkhart, Indiana
William H. Diddel
Elcona CC (R)
Indiana
Bruce Matthews, Jerry Matthews
Elden Hills GC
Flagstaff, Arizona
Bob Baldock
Elden Hills GC (R)
Arizona
William Johnston
Eldorado CC
Palm Desert, California
Lawrence Hughes
Eldorado GC
Mason, Michigan
Bruce Matthews, Jerry Matthews
Eldorado GC (A. 9)
Michigan
Bruce Matthews, Jerry Matthews
Elephant Butte G&CC
Truth or Consequence, New
    Mexico
Dick Phelps, Brad Benz
Elephant Hills GC
Victoria Falls, Zimbabwe
Gary Player, *Sidney Brews,Dr. Van
    Vincent*
Elfordleigh GC
Devon, England
F.G. Hawtree, J.H. Taylor
Elgin CC
Illinois
Edward Lawrence Packard
Elgin CC (A. 9)
Illinois
Tom Bendelow
Elgin CC (R. 9) NLE
Illinois
Tom Bendelow
Elgin CC (R)
Illinois
Ken Killian, Dick Nugent
Elgin House GC
Port Carling, Ontario
Clinton E. Robinson
Elgin Wing Park GC
Illinois
Tom Bendelow
Elie Golf House C
Fife, Scotland
Old Tom Morris
Elie Golf House C (R)
Scotland
James Braid
Elizabeth City GC
North Carolina
J. Porter Gibson

Elizabeth Manor GC
Portsmouth, Virginia
Dick Wilson
Elizabethtown GC
Kentucky
Benjamin Wihry, *Morgan Boggs*
Elk City G&CC
Oklahoma
Bob Dunning
Elk City G&CC (R)
Oklahoma
Don Sechrest
Elk County CC (R. 9)
Pennsylvania
X.G. Hassenplug
Elk Island National Park GC
Alberta
William Brinkworth
Elk River CC
Minnesota
Willie Kidd
Elk River GC
Banner Elk, North Carolina
Jack Nicklaus, Bob Cupp
Elkhart GC (R. 9)
Kansas
Leo Johnson
Elkhorn GC
Orcutt, California
Ed Burns
Elkhorn GC
Lodi, California
Bert Stamps
Elkhorn GC
Sun Valley, Idaho
Robert Trent Jones, Robert Trent
    Jones Jr
Elkhorn Valley GC
Orcutt, Oregon
Don Cutler
Elkins Lake GC
Huntsville, Texas
Ralph Plummer
Elkins Ranch GC
Fillmore, California
William H. Tucker Jr
Elkridge CC
Baltimore, Maryland
Tom Bendelow
Elkridge CC (R)
Maryland
Robert Trent Jones
Elkridge CC (R)
Maryland
Edmund B. Ault
Elks Allenmore GC (R)
Washington
Kenneth Tyson
Elks CC
Seymour, Indiana
Harold England
Elks CC
West Lafayette, Indiana
William H. Diddel
Elks CC
Marion, Indiana
William H. Diddel
Elks CC
Elkhart, Indiana
Hal Purdy
Elks CC (R. 9)
Indiana
Gene Conway
Elks CC (A. 3)
Indiana
Gene Conway
Elks CC
Benton Harbor, Michigan
Charles Maddox
Elks CC
Columbus, Nebraska
Dick Phelps
Elks CC
Hamilton, Ohio
John Duncan Dunn
Elks CC
Columbus, Ohio
Donald Ross
Elks CC
Duncan, Oklahoma
Perry Maxwell
Elks CC (A. 9)
Oklahoma
Floyd Farley

Elks GC (R)
Alberta
Claude Muret
Elks Lodge GC
Jeffersonville, Indiana
Benjamin Wihry
Ellendale CC
Houma, Louisiana
Joseph S. Finger
Ellesmere GC (R)
England
J.J.F. Pennink
Ellington Ridge CC
Connecticut
Geoffrey S. Cornish
Ellinwood CC
Athol, Massachusetts
Donald Ross, Walter Hatch
Ellinwood CC
Athol, Massachusetts
Donald Ross
Ellinwood CC (A. 9)
Massachusetts
Geoffrey S. Cornish, William G.
    Robinson
Ellis CC
Kansas
Dewey Longworth
Ellis Park Muni NLE
Cedar Rapids, Iowa
Tom Bendelow
Ellis Park Muni
Cedar Rapids, Iowa
William B. Langford
Ellwood Greens CC
DeKalb, Illinois
Charles Maddox
Elm Park G & Sports C (R)
Ireland
Eddie Hackett
Elm Park G & Sports C (R)
Ireland
John Harris
Elm Ridge CC NLE
Montreal, Quebec
A.W. Tillinghast
Elm Ridge CC (Course No. 1)
    (R)
Manitoba
Geoffrey S. Cornish, William G.
    Robinson
Elm Ridge CC (Course No. 1)
Ile Bizard, Quebec
William Gordon, David Gordon
Elm Ridge CC (Course No. 1)
    (R)
Quebec
Clinton E. Robinson
Elm Ridge CC (Course No. 2)
Ile Bizard, Quebec
William Gordon, David Gordon
Elma Meadows GC
Elma, New York
William Harries, *A. Russell Tryon*
Elmbrook GC (R. 3)
Michigan
Jerry Matthews
Elmcrest CC
East Longmeadow, Connecticut
Al Zikorus
Elmgate CC now known as
    Glenview Park GC
Elmhurst G Links
Winnepeg, Manitoba
Donald Ross
Elmhurst G Links (R. 2)
Manitoba
Geoffrey S. Cornish, William G.
    Robinson
Elmhurst G Links (R. 3)
Manitoba
Clinton E. Robinson
Elmhurst G Links (A. 9)
Manitoba
Donald Ross
Elmira CC
New York
Willie Dunn Jr
Elmira CC (A. 9)
New York
A.W. Tillinghast
Elmira CC (A. 7)
New York
Ferdinand Garbin

Elmsford CC
White Plains, New York
Tom Wells
Elmwood CC
White Plains, New York
A.W. Tillinghast
Elmwood CC (R)
New York
Alfred H. Tull
Elmwood CC (R. 1)
New York
Frank Duane
Elmwood G&CC
Marshalltown, Iowa
Tom Bendelow
Elmwood G&CC
Saskatchewan
William Brinkworth
Elmwood Park GC
Sioux Falls, South Dakota
Edward Lawrence Packard
Elmwood Park GC (A. 9)
South Dakota
Charles Maddox
Elmwood Park GC (R)
South Dakota
Don Herfort
Elmwood Park Muni
Nebraska
Tom Bendelow
Elsbert Farm GC
Chicago, Illinois
C.D. Wagstaff
Eltham Warren GC
England
Tom Dunn
Ely City GC
England
Henry Cotton
Ely Park GC
Binghamton, New York
Ernest E. Smith
Ely Park GC (A)
New York
Ernest E. Smith
Elyria CC
Ohio
William S. Flynn
Elyria CC (R. 2)
Ohio
Jack Kidwell, Michael Hurdzan
Embassy C
Armonk, New York
Orrin Smith
Emeis Park GC
Davenport, Iowa
C.D. Wagstaff
Emerald Green GC
Rock Hill, New York
William F. Mitchell
Emerald Hills CC
Hollywood, Florida
Robert von Hagge, Bruce Devlin
Emerald Hills Elks GC
Redwood City, California
Clark Glasson
Emerald Hills GC
Redwood City, California
Ellis W. Van Gorder
Emerald Hills GC
Arnolds Park, Iowa
Leo Johnson
Emerald Valley GC
Creswell, Oregon
Bob Baldock, Robert L. Baldock
Emerates GC
Dubai, United Arab Emirates
Karl Litten
Emmettsburg G&CC
Iowa
Henry C. Glissmann, Harold
    Glissmann
Emorywood CC (R. 9)
North Carolina
Ellis Maples
Emorywood CC (R)
North Carolina
Willard Byrd, Clyde Johnston
Empire G&CC
Vernal, Utah
Mick Riley
Emporia CC
Kansas
Harry Robb

Emporia CC
Virginia
Jim Reynolds
Emporia Muni
Kansas
Frank Hummel
Emporium CC (R. 9)
Pennsylvania
Ferdinand Garbin
Emporium CC (A. 9)
Pennsylvania
Ferdinand Garbin
Empress Josephine GC
Martinique
Robert Trent Jones, Roger
  Rulewich
En-Joie CC
Endicott, New York
Ernest E. Smith
En-Joie CC (R)
New York
William F. Mitchell
En-Joie CC (R. 2)
New York
Pete Dye, *David Postlethwaite*
Encanto Muni
Phoenix, Arizona
William P. Bell
Encanto Muni (R)
Arizona
Gary Panks
Encanto Muni (A. 9)
Arizona
William P. Bell, William F. Bell
Encinal GC
Alameda, California
William Lock
Enderlin GC (R. 9)
North Dakota
Don Herfort
Endwell Greens GC
Johnson City, New York
Geoffrey S. Cornish, William G.
  Robinson
Enfield GC
England
Tom Dunn
Enfield GC (R)
England
James Braid
Engineers GC
Roslyn, New York
Herbert Strong
Engineers GC (R)
New York
Devereux Emmet
Engineers GC (R)
New York
William Gordon, David Gordon
Engineers GC (R. 3)
New York
Frank Duane
Engineers GC (R.18)
New York
Frank Duane
Englewood CC (R)
New Jersey
Donald Ross
Englewood CC (R)
New Jersey
Alec Ternyei
Englewood G&CC
Florida
R. Albert Anderson
Englewood G&CC (R)
Florida
Steve Smyers
Englewood Muni
Colorado
Dick Phelps, Brad Benz,Mike
  Poellot
English Hills GC
Walker, Michigan
Mark DeVries
English Hills GC (A. 9)
Michigan
Jerry Matthews
English Turn CC
Gretna, Louisiana
Jack Nicklaus, *Tom Pearson*
Enmore Park GC
Somerset, England
Fred W. Hawtree, A.H.F. Jiggens

Enmore Park GC (A. 9)
England
Fred W. Hawtree, A.H.F. Jiggens
Ennis GC
Montana
Theodore Wirth
Ennis GC (R)
Ireland
Eddie Hackett
Enniscorthy GC (R)
Ireland
Eddie Hackett
Enniscrone GC
County Sligo, Ireland
Eddie Hackett
Enniskillen GC
County Fermanagh, Northern
  Ireland
T.J.A. McAuley
Enniskillen GC (R)
Northern Ireland
Eddie Hackett
Enoch Hills GC
Alberta
William G. Robinson
Enumclaw GC
Washington
William Teufel
Enzesfeld G&CC
Austria
John Harris
Equinox G Links NLE
Manchester, Vermont
George A. Orvis
Equinox G Links
Manchester, Vermont
Walter J. Travis
Equinox G Links (R)
Vermont
William F. Mitchell
Erding-Grunbach GC
West Germany
Donald Harradine
Erewash Valley GC
Derbyshire, England
Tom Dunn
Erewash Valley GC (R)
England
Tom Williamson
Erie Downs G&CC
Ontario
Stanley Thompson
Erie MacCaune CC
Erie, Pennsylvania
James Gilmore Harrison
Erie Shores GC
North Madison, Ohio
Ben W. Zink
Errol Estates Inn & CC
Apopka, Florida
Joe Lee
Erskine Muni
South Bend, Indiana
William H. Diddel
Erskine Park GC
Michigan
George O'Neill, *Chick Evans*
Esbo GC
Finland
Jan Sederholm
Escanaba CC
Michigan
Tom Bendelow
Escondido CC
California
Harry Rainville, David Rainville
Escorpion GC
Valencia, Spain
Ron Kirby, Gary Player,Denis
  Griffiths
Eseeola Lodge GC NLE
North Carolina
Alex Findlay
Esquire CC
Huntington, West Virginia
X.G. Hassenplug
Essener GC Haus Oefte
Essen, West Germany
Karl Hoffmann, Bernhard von
  Limburger
Essex County Club
Hempstead, New York
Donald Ross

Essex County CC (East Course)
New Jersey
Tom Bendelow
**Essex County CC (East Course)
(R)**
New Jersey
A.W. Tillinghast
**Essex County CC (East Course)
(A. 9) NLE**
New Jersey
Alex Findlay
**Essex County CC (East Course)
(A)**
New Jersey
David S. Hunter
**Essex County CC (East Course)
(R)**
New Jersey
David S. Hunter
**Essex County CC (East Course)
(R)**
New Jersey
Donald Ross
**Essex County CC (East Course)
(R)**
New Jersey
Robert Trent Jones
Essex County CC (West Course)
West Orange, New Jersey
Charles Banks
**Essex County CC (West Course)
(R)**
New Jersey
A.W. Tillinghast
**Essex County CC (West Course)
(R. 9)**
New Jersey
Frank Duane
Essex CC NLE
Manchester, Massachusetts
Herbert Leeds
Essex CC
Manchester, Massachusetts
Donald Ross
Essex CC (R)
Massachusetts
Eugene "Skip" Wogan
Essex CC (R)
Massachusetts
Phil Wogan
Essex CC (R)
Massachusetts
John Duncan Dunn, Walter J.
  Travis
Essex Fells CC
New Jersey
Donald Ross
Essex Fells CC (R)
New Jersey
Hal Purdy, Malcolm Purdy
Essex G&CC
LaSalle, Ontario
Donald Ross
Essex G&CC (R)
Ontario
Arthur Hills
Essex G&CC (A. 2)
Ontario
Bruce Matthews, Jerry Matthews
Essex GC
St. Thomas, Ontario
Stanley Thompson
Estate Carlton GC
St. Croix, Virgin Islands
Alfred H. Tull
Estes Park GC
Colorado
Henry B. Hughes
Estoril GC
Portugal
Jean Gassiat
Estoril GC (R. 9)
Portugal
P.M. Ross
Estoril GC (A. 9)
Portugal
P.M. Ross
Estoril Sol GC
Estoril, Portugal
John Harris, Peter
  Thomson,Michael Wolveridge,
  Ronald Fream

Estrimont GC
Mont Orford, Quebec
John Watson
Ethelwood CC
Richmond, Virginia
William Gordon, David Gordon
Eton College GC
Windsor, England
J.J.F. Pennink
Etowah Valley CC
North Carolina
Edmund B. Ault
Euclid Heights CC NLE
Ohio
William "Bert" Way
**Euclid Hill CC now known as
  Silver Lake GC (North Course)**
Springfield, Oregon
H. Chandler Egan
Eugene CC NLE
Oregon
Robert Trent Jones, Robert Trent
  Jones Jr
Eugene CC (R)
Oregon
Gary Roger Baird
Eugene Grace Estate GC
Bethlehem, Pennsylvania
Perry Maxwell
Eureka GC (R. 9)
Kansas
Leo Johnson
Eureka Muni
California
Bob Baldock, Robert L. Baldock
Eureka Muni (A. 6)
California
Bob Baldock, Robert L. Baldock
Eustis CC NLE
Florida
C.S. Butchart
Evan Heights GC (R. 9)
Georgia
Arthur Davis
Evanston GC
Skokie, Illinois
Donald Ross
Evanston GC (R)
Illinois
Ken Killian, Dick Nugent
Evanston GC (R)
Illinois
Bob Cupp
Evanston GC NLE
Kansas City, Missouri
Tom Bendelow
Evanston GC (R)
Missouri
James Dalgleish
Evansville CC
Indiana
William H. Diddel
Everett G&CC
Washington
Ted Robinson
Everett G&CC (R. 1)
Washington
John Steidel
Everett Muni
Washington
Al Smith
Everett Muni (R)
Washington
Kenneth Tyson
Everglades C
Palm Beach, Florida
Seth Raynor
Everglades C (A. 9)
Florida
Seth Raynor
Everglades C (R)
Florida
William B. Langford, Theodore J.
  Moreau
Everglades C (R)
Florida
Mark Mahannah
Everglades C (R)
Florida
George Fazio, Tom Fazio
Everglades C (R)
Florida
Ron Kirby, Denis Griffiths

Evergreen CC
Hudson, Michigan
Robert Beard
Evergreen CC
Haymarket, Virginia
Buddy Loving, Algie Pulley
Evergreen GC
Mt. Angel, Oregon
Bill Schaefer
Evergreen GC
Elkhorn, Wisconsin
Ken Killian, Dick Nugent
Excelsior Springs CC
Missouri
Tom Bendelow
Excelsior Springs CC (A. 9) NLE
Missouri
Perry Maxwell
Excelsior Springs CC (R)
Missouri
Smiley Bell
Excelsior Springs CC (A. 9)
Missouri
Bob Dunning
Excelsior Springs CC (R)
Missouri
Chet Mendenhall
Exeter CC (R)
New Hampshire
Manny Francis
Exeter CC
Rhode Island
Geoffrey S. Cornish
Exeter G&CC
Countess Wear, Devon, England
James Braid, John R. Stutt
Exeter Muni
California
Bob Baldock
Exmoor CC
Highland Park, Illinois
H.J. Tweedie
Exmoor CC (R)
Illinois
Donald Ross
Exmoor CC (R)
Illinois
Ken Killian, Dick Nugent
F.A. McConnel Private Course
Caledon, Ontario
Howard Watson
Fair Oaks Ranch G&CC
Boerne, Texas
Ron Kirby, Gary Player,Denis
  Griffiths
Fair Oaks Ranch G&CC (A. 9)
Texas
Ron Kirby, Denis Griffiths
Fairbanks Ranch CC
Rancho Santa Fe, California
Ted Robinson
Fairborn CC
Ohio
William H. Diddel
Fairbury CC (R. 1)
Nebraska
Jeff Brauer
**Fairchild Wheeler GC (Course
  No. 1)**
Bridgeport, Connecticut
Robert White
**Fairchild Wheeler GC (Course
  No. 2)**
Bridgeport, Connecticut
Robert White
Fairfield CC
Winnsboro, South Carolina
Robert Renaud
Fairfield Harbour GC
New Bern, North Carolina
Dominic Palombo
Fairfield Mountains GC
Lake Lure, North Carolina
William B. Lewis
**Fairfield Ocean Ridge GC
  formerly known as Oristo
  G&RC**
Edisto Island, South Carolina
Tom Jackson
Fairfield Plantation CC
Carrollton, Georgia
Willard Byrd

Fairgreen CC
New Smyrna Beach, Florida
Bill Amick
Fairington G&TC now known as Metropolitan G&TC
Fairlawn CC
East Poland, Maine
Chic Adams
Fairlawn CC
Akron, Ohio
William B. Langford, Theodore J. Moreau
Fairlawn CC (R)
Ohio
Edward Lawrence Packard
Fairlawn CC (R)
Ohio
Arthur Hills
Fairless Hills GC
Morrisville, Pennsylvania
Marion V. Packard
Fairmede CC NLE
Florida
John Duncan Dunn
Fairmont CC (R)
New Jersey
Alfred H. Tull
Fairmount CC
Chatham, New Jersey
Hal Purdy
Fairmount Hot Springs CC
British Columbia
C.L. Wilder
Fairview CC
Greenwich, Connecticut
Robert Trent Jones, Rees Jones
Fairview CC NLE
Elmsford, New York
Donald Ross
Fairview CC (R)
New York
Alfred H. Tull
Fairview G&CC
Quentin, Pennsylvania
Frank Murray, Russell Roberts
Fairview GC
Wayne, Indiana
Donald Ross
Fairview GC (A. 9)
Indiana
Everett A. Monroe
Fairview GC
New Jersey
William F. Mitchell
Fairview Muni (R. 2)
Missouri
Melvin Anderson
Fairway Glen GC
Santa Clara, California
Bob Baldock
Fairway GC
Orlando, Florida
Bill Amick
Fairway Oaks G&CC
Abilene, Texas
Ron Garl
Fairway Park GC
Mandurah, Australia
Peter Thomson, Michael Wolveridge
Fairway Pines GC
Painesville, Ohio
X.G. Hassenplug
Fairway-to-the-Stars GC NLE
Las Vegas, Nevada
Louis Prima
Fairways GC
Warrington, Pennsylvania
William Gordon, David Gordon
Fairwood G&CC
Renton, Washington
William Teufel
Fairwood Park GC
Swansea, Wales
Fred W. Hawtree
Fairyland CC now known as Lookout Mountain GC
Fakenham GC
Norfolk, England
J.J.F. Pennink, C.D. Lawrie
Falcon Beach Lake CC
Manitoba
Norman H. Woods

Falconhead GC
Burneyville, Oklahoma
Bob Dunning, *Waco Turner*
Falkenstein GC
West Germany
H.S. Colt, C.H. Alison, J.S.F. Morrison
Falkenstein GC (R)
West Germany
Bernhard von Limburger
Fall Creek Falls State Park GC
Pikesville, Tennessee
Joe Lee, Rocky Roquemore
Fall River CC
Massachusetts
Willie Park Jr
Fall River CC (A. 9)
Massachusetts
Geoffrey S. Cornish, William G. Robinson
Fall River Valley G&CC
Fall River Mills, California
Clark Glasson
Fallbrook CC
California
Harry Rainville
Falling Creek GC
Kinston, North Carolina
Gene Hamm
Falls G&CC
New Ulm, Texas
Jay Riviere, *Dave Marr*
Falls Road Muni
Maryland
Edmund B. Ault, Al Jamison
Fallsview Hotel GC
Ellenville, New York
Robert Trent Jones, Frank Duane
Falsterbo GC
Sweden
Gunnar Bauer
Far Corner Farm GC
West Boxford, Massachusetts
Geoffrey S. Cornish, William G. Robinson
Fargo CC (A. 9)
North Dakota
Robert Bruce Harris
Faribault CC
Minnesota
Willie Kidd
Faries Park GC
Decatur, Illinois
Edward Lawrence Packard
Farm Neck GC
Martha's Vineyard, Massachusetts
Geoffrey S. Cornish, William G. Robinson
Farm Neck GC (A. 9)
Massachusetts
Patrick Mulligan
Farmington CC (R)
Michigan
William Newcomb
Farmington CC (R)
Michigan
Bruce Matthews, Jerry Matthews
Farmington CC
New Mexico
Warren Cantrell
Farmington CC
Germantown, Tennessee
Press Maxwell
Farmington CC
Charlottesville, Virginia
Fred Findlay
Farmington CC (A. 9)
Virginia
Ben Loving, Buddy Loving
Farmington CC (R)
Virginia
Buddy Loving
Farmington Woods CC
Farmington, Connecticut
Desmond Muirhead
Farms CC
Wallingford, Connecticut
Geoffrey S. Cornish
Farms Motel GC
Vermont
Geoffrey S. Cornish, William G. Robinson

Farnham Park GC
Folly Hill, England
Henry Cotton
Farnham Park GC
Stoke Poges, England
J.J.F. Pennink, D.M.A. Steel
Farnham Park GC (A. 9)
England
Fred W. Hawtree, Martin Hawtree
Farwell CC
Texas
Warren Cantrell
Fawn C
New York
Seymour Dunn
Fawn Creek GC
Alamosa, Iowa
Gordon Cunningham
Fawn Crest GC
Michigan
Ron Weber
Feather River Inn GC
Blairsden, California
Harold Sampson
Feather River Park GC
California
Bert Stamps
Feather Sound CC
St. Petersburg, Florida
Joe Lee
Feldafing GC
West Germany
Karl Hoffmann, Bernhard von Limburger
Felixstowe Ferry GC NLE
Suffolk, England
Tom Dunn
Felixstowe Ferry GC
Suffolk, England
Alister Mackenzie
Felixstowe Ferry GC (R) NLE
England
Willie Fernie
Felixstowe Ferry GC (A. 4)
England
Tom Simpson
Felixstowe Ferry GC (R)
England
Tom Simpson
Felixstowe Ferry GC (R)
England
Sir Guy Campbell, Henry Cotton
Fellows Creek GC
Wayne, Michigan
Bruce Matthews, Jerry Matthews
Fellows Creek GC (A. 9)
Michigan
Jerry Matthews
Fendrich GC
Evansville, Indiana
William H. Diddel
Fendrich GC (R)
Indiana
Edmund B. Ault
Fenway GC
White Plains, New York
A.W. Tillinghast
Fermoy GC
County Cork, Ireland
John Harris
Fermoy GC (R)
Ireland
Eddie Hackett
Fernandina Beach GC
Florida
Ed Matteson
Fernandina Beach GC (A. 9)
Florida
Joe Lee
Ferncliffe CC
New Hampshire
Alex Findlay
Ferndown GC (New Course)
Dorset, England
J. Hamilton Stutt
Ferndown GC (Old Course)
England
Harold Hilton
Fernwood CC
McComb, Mississippi
George C. Curtis

Fernwood Resort GC
Pennsylvania
Nicholas Psiahas
Fianna Hills GC
Fort Smith, Arkansas
James L. Holmes
Fiddler's Elbow CC
Bedminster, New Jersey
Hal Purdy
Fiddlers Green GC
Eugene, Oregon
John Zoller
Fiddlesticks CC (Long Mean Course)
Fort Myers, Florida
Ron Garl
Fiddlesticks CC (Wee Friendly Course)
Fort Myers, Florida
Ron Garl
Field C of Omaha
Nebraska
Harry Lawrie
Fig Garden GC
Fresno, California
Nick Lombardo
Fijian Hotel GC
Fiji
Peter Thomson, Michael Wolveridge, Ronald Fream
Filton GC (R. 9)
England
F.G. Hawtree, J.H. Taylor
Filton GC (A. 9)
England
F.G. Hawtree, J.H. Taylor
Fincastle CC
Bluefield, West Virginia
Dick Wilson, Bob Simmons
Fincastle CC (R)
West Virginia
John LaFoy
Finchley GC
London, England
James Braid, John R. Stutt
Finger Lakes GC
Ithaca, New York
David Gordon
Finham Park GC (R. 3)
England
Fred W. Hawtree
Finkbine GC
Iowa City, Iowa
Robert Bruce Harris
Finley GC
Univ of N Carolina, North Carolina
George W. Cobb
Fioranello GC
Italy
D. Mezzacane
Fircrest GC
Tacoma, Washington
A. Vernon Macan
Firefly CC
Seekonk, Massachusetts
Donald Hoenig
Firenze GC
Italy
Charles Blanchford
Firestone CC (North Course)
Akron, Ohio
Robert Trent Jones, Roger Rulewich
Firestone CC (South Course)
Akron, Ohio
William "Bert" Way
Firestone CC (South Course) (R)
Ohio
Robert Trent Jones
Firestone CC (South Course) (R)
Ohio
Jack Nicklaus, *Tom Pearson*
Firestone Public GC NLE
Arkon, Ohio
William "Bert" Way
Firethorn GC
Lincoln, Nebraska
Pete Dye
Firewheel Muni (Course No. 1)
Garland, Texas
Dick Phelps, Brad Benz, Mike Poellot

Firewheel Muni (Course No. 2)
Garland, Texas
Dick Phelps
Fishers Island GC
New York
Seth Raynor
Fitzsimons GC
Denver, Colorado
Joseph Wheeler
Five-by 80 GC
Menlo, Iowa
Harold Glissmann
Flagstaff Hill GC
Australia
D.N. Hillan
Flagtree CC
Fairmont, North Carolina
J. Porter Gibson
Flaine GC
France
Robert Berthet
Flanders Valley GC
New Jersey
Hal Purdy
Flanders Valley GC (A. 9)
New Jersey
Rees Jones, Keith Evans
Flat Creek GC
Peachtree City, Georgia
Joe Lee
Flat Creek GC (A. 9)
Georgia
Joe Lee, Rocky Roquemore
Flatirons CC
Boulder, Colorado
Robert Bruce Harris
Flaxmere GC
Hastings, New Zealand
John Harris
Fleetwood GC
England
J.A. Steer
Fleming Park GC
Hampshire, England
J.J.F. Pennink
Flemingdon Park GC
Toronto, Ontario
Howard Watson
Fletcher Hills CC
Santee, California
William H. Tucker Jr
Flinders CC
Victoria, Australia
Alister Mackenzie
Flint Elks CC
Flint, Michigan
Bruce Matthews, Jerry Matthews
Flint GC
Michigan
Willie Park Jr
Flint GC now known as Atlas Valley GC
Flint GC
Wales
James Braid
Flora GC
Illinois
Robert Bruce Harris
Florence CC (R)
South Carolina
John LaFoy
Florham Park CC
New Jersey
Hal Purdy
Florida CC NLE
Jacksonville, Florida
Donald Ross
Floridale GC NLE
Milford, Florida
Stanley Thompson
Flossmoor CC formerly known as Homewood CC
Illinois
H.J. Tweedie
Flossmoor CC (R)
Illinois
Harry Collis
Flourtown CC NLE
Philadelphia, Pennsylvania
Donald Ross
Flourtown CC (R) NLE
Pennsylvania
Perry Maxwell

Floyd CC
Virginia
Gene Hamm
Floydada CC
Texas
Curt Wilson
Flushing GC NLE
New York
Tom Bendelow
Flushing Valley CC
Flushing, Michigan
Wilfrid Reid
Folmont Resort GC
Somerset, Pennsylvania
Ferdinand Garbin
Fonderlac CC (A. 9)
Ohio
William Newcomb
Fontainbleau GC (R)
France
Fred W. Hawtree
Fontainbleau GC (A. 4)
France
Fred W. Hawtree
Fontainebleau Park CC (East Course)
Miami, Florida
Mark Mahannah
Fontainebleau Park CC (West Course)
Miami, Florida
Mark Mahannah, Charles Mahannah
Foothills GC
Lakewood, Colorado
Dick Phelps
Forbes GC
Topeka, Kansas
Bob Baldock
Forbes GC (R)
Kansas
L.J. "Dutch" McClellan
Ford's Colony CC
Williamsburg, Virginia
Ellis Maples, Dan Maples
Fore Lakes GC
Salt Lake City, Utah
William H. Neff, William Howard Neff
Forest of Arden GC
Warwickshire, England
J.B. Tomlinson
Forest Akers GC (West Course)
East Lansing, Michigan
Bruce Matthews
Forest Cove CC
Humble, Texas
John A. Plumbley
Forest CC (Bobcat Course)
Fort Myers, Florida
Gordon G. Lewis
Forest CC (Deer Course)
Fort Myers, Florida
Gordon G. Lewis
Forest CC (Deer Course) (A. 9)
Florida
Gordon G. Lewis
Forest Dale GC
Salt Lake City, Utah
Mick Riley
Forest Dale GC (R)
Utah
William Howard Neff
Forest Heights CC
Statesboro, Georgia
George W. Cobb
Forest Heights GC
Jamestown, New York
Alfred A. Schardt
Forest Highlands GC
Flagstaff, Arizona
Jay Morrish, *Tom Weiskopf*
Forest Hill Field C
Bloomfield, New Jersey
A.W. Tillinghast
Forest Hill Field C (R)
New Jersey
Charles Banks
Forest Hill Field C (R)
New Jersey
Rees Jones
Forest Hill GC
West Palm Beach, Florida
Hans Schmeisser

Forest Hill GC
Augusta, Georgia
Donald Ross
Forest Hill GC (R)
Georgia
Arnold Palmer, Ed Seay, Harrison Minchew
Forest Hill GC
Bloomfield, New Jersey
Tom Bendelow
Forest Hills CC
Rockford, Illinois
Charles Maddox
Forest Hills CC
Richmond, Indiana
William H. Diddel
Forest Hills CC
Columbia, Missouri
John Gavin
Forest Hills GC
Michigan
Harry E. Flora
Forest Hills GC (R. 1)
Michigan
Jerry Matthews
Forest Hills GC (R. 8)
Michigan
Mark DeVries
Forest Hills GC (A.10)
Michigan
Mark DeVries
Forest Hills GC NLE
Cornelius, Oregon
William Martin
Forest Hills GC
Oregon
William F. Bell, William P. Bell
Forest Hills GC (R.27)
Ontario
Howard Watson
Forest Hils CC
Florida
J. Franklyn Meehan
Forest Hotel G&CC
Ontario
Norm Anders
Forest Hotel G&CC (A. 9)
Ontario
Norm Anders
Forest Lake CC
Bloomfield Hills, Michigan
William H. Diddel
Forest Lake CC (A. 4)
Michigan
William H. Diddel
Forest Lake CC (R)
Michigan
William H. Diddel
Forest Lake CC (R)
Michigan
Arthur Hills, Steve Forrest
Forest Lake CC now known as River Bend G&CC
Forest Lakes C
Columbia, South Carolina
Maurice McCarthy
Forest Lakes CC
Sarasota, Florida
R. Albert Anderson
Forest Little GC
County Dublin, Ireland
Fred W. Hawtree, A.H.F. Jiggens
Forest Little GC (R)
Ireland
Eddie Hackett
Forest Meadows GC
California
Robert Trent Jones Jr
Forest Oaks CC
Greensboro, North Carolina
Ellis Maples
Forest Park CC (A. 9)
Virginia
Gene Hamm
Forest Park CC (R. 9)
Virginia
Gene Hamm
Forest Park GC
Brazil, Indiana
William H. Diddel
Forest Park GC
Valparaiso, Indiana
William James Spear

Forest Park GC
Bronx, New York
Tom Bendelow
Forest Park GC
Queens, New York
John Van Kleek
Forest Park GC (R)
New York
Lindsay Ervin
Forest Park Muni
Noblesville, Indiana
William Newcomb
Forest Park Muni (R)
Maryland
Gus Hook
Forest Park Muni
St. Louis, Missouri
Robert Foulis
Forest Preserve National GC
Oak Forest, Illinois
Ken Killian, Dick Nugent, Bob Lohmann
Forfar GC
Angus, Scotland
James Braid
Formby GC
England
Willie Park Jr
Formby GC (R)
England
H.S. Colt
Formosa G&CC
Taiwan
Arnold Palmer, Ed Seay
Forres GC
Morayshire, Scotland
Andrew Kirkaldy
Forres GC (R)
Scotland
James Braid
Forres GC (R)
Scotland
Willie Park
Forsgate CC (East Course)
New Jersey
Charles Banks
Forsgate CC (West Course)
Jamesburg, New Jersey
Hal Purdy
Forsyth CC
Winston-Salem, North Carolina
Donald Ross
Forsyth CC (R)
North Carolina
Willard Byrd
Fort Augustus GC
Invernesshire, Scotland
James Braid
Fort Belvoir GC
Virginia
Robert Trent Jones
Fort Belvoir GC (R. 9)
Virginia
Edmund B. Ault
Fort Belvoir GC (A. 9)
Virginia
Edmund B. Ault
Fort Benning GC (Lakeside Course)
Georgia
Lester Lawrence
Fort Benning GC (Pineside Course)
Georgia
Lester Lawrence
Fort Benning GC (Pineside Course) (A. 9)
Georgia
Robert Trent Jones
Fort Cobb Lake State Park GC
Lake Cobb, Oklahoma
Floyd Farley
Fort Cobb Lake State Park GC (A. 9)
Oklahoma
Don Sechrest
Fort Devens GC
Massachusetts
Melvin B. Lucas Jr.
Fort Dodge CC
Iowa
Tom Bendelow

Fort Dodge CC (R. 9)
Iowa
Edward Lawrence Packard, Brent Wadsworth
Fort Douglas VA Hospital GC
Utah
Mick Riley
Fort DuPont Muni
Washington, D.C.
William Gordon
Fort Erie GC
New York
Tom Bendelow
Fort Erie GC (A. 9)
New York
Stanley Thompson
Fort Erie GC (R. 9)
New York
Stanley Thompson
Fort Eustis GC
Maryland
George W. Cobb
Fort Frances GC
Ontario
Clinton E. Robinson
Fort Harrison GC
Indiana
William H. Diddel
Fort Hays CC
Hays, Kansas
Dewey Longworth
Fort Hays CC (R. 9)
Kansas
Chet Mendenhall
Fort Huachuca GC
Arizona
Milt Coggins
Fort Huachuca GC (A. 9)
Arizona
Milt Coggins, Gary Panks
Fort Irwin GC (R)
California
Desmond Muirhead
Fort Jackson GC
Columbia, South Carolina
George W. Cobb
Fort Jackson GC (R. 4)
South Carolina
John LaFoy
Fort Lauderdale CC (North Course)
Florida
Joseph A. Roseman
Fort Lauderdale CC (North Course) (R)
Florida
Red Lawrence
Fort Lauderdale CC (South Course)
Florida
Red Lawrence
Fort Leavenworth GC (A. 9)
Kansas
Art F. Hall
Fort Leonard Wood GC
Missouri
Floyd Farley
Fort Lewis GC
Olympia, Washington
William Teufel
Fort McClellan GC
Alabama
George W. Cobb
Fort McPherson GC (R)
Georgia
George W. Cobb
Fort Meade GC (Meade Course)
Maryland
Major Robert B. McClure
Fort Meade GC (Parks Course)
Maryland
George W. Cobb
Fort Mitchell CC
Covington, Kentucky
Tom Bendelow
Fort Mitchell CC (R)
Kentucky
Arthur Hills
Fort Mitchell CC (R)
Kentucky
Arthur Hills, Steve Forrest
Fort Monmouth GC
New Jersey
Seymour Dunn

Fort Morgan Muni (R. 9)
Colorado
Henry B. Hughes
Fort Morgan Muni (A. 9)
Colorado
Henry B. Hughes
Fort Myers G&CC
Florida
Donald Ross
Fort Ord GC (Bayonet Course)
California
Major Robert B. McClure, Lawson Little
Fort Preval GC
Preval, Quebec
William F. Mitchell
Fort Preval GC (R. 9)
Quebec
Howard Watson
Fort Preval GC (A. 5)
Quebec
Howard Watson, John Watson
Fort Riley Officer's GC
Kansas
Major Richard D. Newman
Fort Royal GC
County Donegal, Northern Ireland
T.J.A. McAuley
Fort Sam Houston GC
San Antonio, Texas
A.W. Tillinghast
Fort Shafter GC
Honolulu, Hawaii
Willard Wilkinson
Fort Sheridan GC
Illinois
Edward B. Dearie Jr
Fort Sill GC
Oklahoma
Lefty Mace
Fort Sill GC (R)
Oklahoma
Don Sechrest
Fort Smith CC
Arkansas
Alex Findlay
Fort Walton Beach Muni
Florida
Bill Amick
Fort Washington G&CC
Pinedale, California
William Watson
Fort Washington G&CC (R)
California
Bob Baldock
Fort Wayne CC (R)
Indiana
William H. Diddel
Fort Wayne CC (R. 3)
Indiana
Bruce Matthews, Jerry Matthews
Fort Wayne CC (R)
Indiana
Rees Jones
Fort William G&CC
Ontario
Stanley Thompson
Fort William G&CC (R.13)
Ontario
John Watson
Fort William GC
Invernesshire, Scotland
J. Hamilton Stutt
Fort Worth GC NLE
Texas
Tom Bendelow
Fort Yukon AFB GC
Alaska
Richard Carpenter, Charles F. Scholer
Fortrose and Rosemarkie
Invernesshire, Scotland
James Braid
Fortune Hills GC
Freeport, Bahamas
Joe Lee
Fortwilliam GC
Belfast, Northern Ireland
C.S. Butchart
Forty Niners CC
Tuscon, Arizona
William F. Bell

Foster G Links (R)
Washington
William Teufel
Fostoria CC (A.10)
Ohio
Jack Kidwell
Fostoria CC (R)
Ohio
Jack Kidwell
Fountain of the Sun GC
Mesa, Arizona
Red Lawrence
Fountain Grove GC
Santa Rosa, California
Ted Robinson
Fountain Head CC
Hagerstown, Maryland
Donald Ross, Walter Hatch
Fountain Head CC (R)
Maryland
Edmund B. Ault
**Fountain Valley GC now known
   as Carambola Beach GC**
Fountaingate CC
Ooltewah, Tennessee
Gary Roger Baird
Fountainhead State Park GC
Oklahoma
Floyd Farley
Fountains G&RC (North Course)
Lake Worth, Florida
Robert von Hagge, Bruce Devlin
Fountains G&RC (South Course)
Lake Worth, Florida
Robert von Hagge, Bruce Devlin
Fountains G&RC (West Course)
Lake Worth, Florida
Robert von Hagge, Bruce Devlin
Fountains GC
Escondido, California
David Rainville
Four Hills CC
Albuquerque, New Mexico
Bob Baldock
Four Lakes GC
County Dublin, Ireland
Phil Lawlor
Four Oaks GC (A. 9)
Kansas
Floyd Farley
Four Seasons CC
Wrens, Georgia
R. Albert Anderson
Four Seasons CC
Smithville, Tennessee
R. Albert Anderson
Four Seasons G&CC
Lake Ozark, Missouri
Robert Trent Jones, Roger
   Rulewich
Four Seasons GC
Jennerstown, Pennsylvania
Ferdinand Garbin
Four Seasons GC (A.18)
Pennsylvania
Ferdinand Garbin
Four Seasons GC
Pembine, Wisconsin
Stanley Pelchar
Four Ways GC
Johannesburg, South Africa
Gary Player, *Sidney Brews,Dr. Van
   Vincent*
Fox Acres CC
Red Feather Lake, Colorado
John Cochran
Fox Bend CC
Oswego, Illinois
Brent Wadsworth
Fox Chapel GC
Pittsburgh, Pennsylvania
Seth Raynor
Fox Chapel GC (R)
Pennsylvania
James Gilmore Harrison
Fox Chapel GC (R)
Pennsylvania
Paul E. Erath
Fox Cliff CC
Martinsville, Indiana
William H. Diddel
Fox Creek CC
Ballwin, Missouri
Homer Herpel

Fox Den CC
Knoxville, Tennessee
Willard Byrd
Fox Hill CC (R)
Pennsylvania
A.W. Tillinghast
Fox Hills CC
Mishicot, Wisconsin
Bob Lohmann
Fox Hills GC NLE
California
George C. Thomas Jr, William P.
   Bell
Fox Hills GC
New York
Tom Bendelow
Fox Hills GC (R)
New York
Donald Ross
Fox Hollow GC
Somerville, New Jersey
Hal Purdy
Fox Lake CC
Illinois
Harry Hall King
Fox Lake CC (R)
Illinois
Ken Killian, Dick Nugent
Fox Lake CC (A. 9)
Wisconsin
Homer Fieldhouse
Fox Meadows CC
Memphis, Tennessee
Chic Adams
Fox River CC
Green Bay, Wisconsin
Tom Bendelow
Fox Run GC
Elk Grove, Illinois
William Newcomb, Stephen Kay
Fox Run GC
Ludlow, Vermont
Frank Duane
Fox Valley CC
Batavia, Illinois
Joe Meister
Foxborough CC
Massachusetts
Geoffrey S. Cornish
Foxborough CC (A. 9)
Massachusetts
Geoffrey S. Cornish, William G.
   Robinson
Foxbury CC
Pennsylvania
James Gilmore Harrison
Foxcreek GC
Atlanta, Georgia
John LaFoy
Foxcroft CC
Miramar, Florida
Bill Watts
Foxfire CC
Sarasota, Florida
Lane Marshall
Foxfire CC
Naples, Florida
Arthur Hills, Steve Forrest,Mike
   Dasher
Foxfire CC (Course No. 1)
Pinehurst, North Carolina
Gene Hamm
Foxfire CC (Course No. 2)
Pinehurst, North Carolina
Gene Hamm
Foxfire CC (Course No. 2) (A. 9)
North Carolina
Gene Hamm
Foxfire GC (A. 6)
Ohio
Jack Kidwell
Foxfire GC (A. 9)
Ohio
Jack Kidwell, Michael Hurdzan
Foxhill CC
Longmont, Colorado
Frank Hummel
Foxhills GC (Chertsey Course)
Surrey, England
Fred W. Hawtree
Foxhills GC (Longcross Course)
Surrey, England
Fred W. Hawtree

Foxrock GC (R)
Ireland
Eddie Hackett
Framingham CC
Massachusetts
Orrin Smith
Framingham CC (A. 2)
Massachusetts
Geoffrey S. Cornish, William G.
   Robinson
Framingham CC (R)
Massachusetts
Manny Francis
Framingham CC (A. 5)
Massachusetts
Orrin Smith, Al Zikorus
Framingham CC (A. 9)
Massachusetts
William F. Mitchell
Frances Miller Memorial GC
Murray State Univ., Kentucky
Jack Kidwell, Michael Hurdzan
Francis Ii Brown GC
Mauna Lani Resort, Hawaii
*Homer Flint, Raymond F.
   Cain,*Robin Nelson
Francis Lake GC
Valdosta, Georgia
Willard Byrd
Francisco Grande CC
Casa Grande, Arizona
Ralph Plummer
Franconia Muni
Springfield, Massachusetts
Wayne Stiles, John Van Kleek
Franconia Muni (R. 7)
Massachusetts
Geoffrey S. Cornish, William G.
   Robinson
Francourt Farms GC
Elmira, New York
Pete Craig
Frank G Clement GC
Dickson, Tennessee
George W. Cobb
Frank House Muni
Bessemer, Alabama
Earl Stone
Frankenmuth GC (R. 2)
Michigan
Jerry Matthews
Frankenmuth GC (A. 1)
Michigan
Jerry Matthews
Frankfort CC
Kentucky
William H. Diddel
Frankfort GC
Indiana
Charles Maddox
Frankfurter GC
West Germany
H.S. Colt, C.H. Alison,J.S.F.
   Morrison
Frankfurter GC (R)
West Germany
Bernhard von Limburger
Frankfurter GC (R)
West Germany
J.S.F. Morrison, J. Hamilton Stutt
Franklin Canyon GC
Rodeo, California
Robert Muir Graves
Franklin County CC
West Frankfort, Illinois
William B. Langford, Theodore J.
   Moreau
Franklin CC (R)
Massachusetts
Wayne Stiles
Franklin CC (A. 9)
Massachusetts
Phil Wogan
Franklin CC (A. 2)
Massachusetts
William F. Mitchell
Franklin CC (R)
Massachusetts
William F. Mitchell
Franklin CC (R)
Massachusetts
William F. Mitchell

Franklin CC (A.10)
Massachusetts
Phil Wogan
Franklin Hills CC
Franklin Woods, Michigan
Donald Ross
Franklin Park GC NLE
Boston, Massachusetts
George Wright
Franklin Park GC (R)
Massachusetts
Willie Campbell
Frear Park GC
Troy, New York
Robert Trent Jones
Fred Enke Muni
Tucson, Arizona
Brad Benz, Mike Poellot,Mark
   Rathert
Frederick GC (R)
Oklahoma
Arthur Jackson
Fredericksburg CC (A. 9)
Virginia
James Gilmore Harrison
Fredericksburg CC (A. 9)
Virginia
James Gilmore Harrison
Fredericksburg CC (R. 1)
Virginia
Bill Love
Fredericton GC (R. 1)
New Brunswick
Clinton E. Robinson
Fredericton GC (R. 2)
New Brunswick
Geoffrey S. Cornish, William G.
   Robinson
Freeport CC
Illinois
Harry Collis
Freeport CC (R. 2)
Illinois
Robert Bruce Harris
Freestone CC
Teague, Texas
Leon Howard
Freiburger GC
Freiburg, West Germany
Bernhard von Limburger
Fremont County GC
St. Anthony, Idaho
Marvin J. Aslett
Fremont CC (R)
Ohio
Edward Lawrence Packard
Fremont CC (R)
Ohio
Arthur Hills, Mike Dasher
Fremont GC
Nebraska
Tom Bendelow
Fremont GC (R)
Nebraska
Harold Glissmann
Fremont GC (A.11)
Nebraska
David Gill
Fremont GC (R. 7)
Nebraska
David Gill
Fremont Hills CC
Nixa, Missouri
Press Maxwell
French Lick CC (Hill Course)
Indiana
Donald Ross
**French Lick CC (Hill Course)
   (R)**
Indiana
Hal Purdy
French Lick GC (Valley Course)
Indiana
Tom Bendelow
**French Lick GC (Valley Course)
   (R)**
Indiana
Sandy Alves
**French Lick GC (Valley Course)
   (R)**
Indiana
Hal Purdy

Frenchman's Bend CC
Louisiana
Arnold Palmer, Ed Seay
**Frenchman's Creek GC (North
   Course)**
North Palm Beach, Florida
Gardner Dickinson
**Frenchman's Creek GC (North
   Course) (R)**
Florida
Bob Cupp, Jay Morrish
**Frenchman's Creek GC (South
   Course)**
North Palm Beach, Florida
Gardner Dickinson
**Frenchman's Creek GC (South
   Course) (R)**
Florida
Bob Cupp, Jay Morrish
Fresh Meadow CC NLE
Flushing, New York
A.W. Tillinghast
**Fresh Meadow CC formerly
   known as Lakeville CC**
Great Neck, New York
C.H. Alison, H.S. Colt
Fresh Meadow CC (R)
New York
Orrin Smith, William F. Mitchell
Fresh Meadow G&CC (R)
Illinois
William B. Langford
Fresh Pond Muni
Cambridge, Massachusetts
Walter I. Johnson
Fresh Pond Muni (A. 9)
Massachusetts
Geoffrey S. Cornish, William G.
   Robinson
Freshwater Bay GC (R)
England
F.G. Hawtree
Fresno West G&CC
California
Bob Baldock, Robert L. Baldock
Friend CC
Nebraska
Henry B. Hughes, Richard
   Watson
Friendly Hills CC
Whittier, California
Jimmy Hines
**Frilford Heath GC (Green
   Course) (R. 9)**
England
C.K. Cotton, J.J.F. Pennink
**Frilford Heath GC (Green
   Course) (A. 9)**
England
C.K. Cotton, J.J.F. Pennink
**Frilford Heath GC (Red Course)
   (R. 9)**
England
C.K. Cotton, J.J.F. Pennink
**Frilford Heath GC (Red Course)
   (A. 9)**
England
C.K. Cotton, J.J.F. Pennink
Frinton GC
Frinton-on-Sea, England
Tom Dunn
Frinton GC (R)
England
Willie Park, Willie Park Jr
Fripp Island CC
South Carolina
George W. Cobb
Fripp Island CC (R)
South Carolina
George W. Cobb, John LaFoy
Frisch Auf Valley CC
LaGrange, Texas
Jay Riviere
Frontier GC
Canby, Oregon
Joe Sisul
Frosty Valley CC
Danville, Pennsylvania
William Gordon, David Gordon
Frosty Valley CC (R)
Pennsylvania
Ferdinand Garbin

Fruitport CC
Muskegon, Michigan
David Snider
Fuji CC
Japan
C.H. Alison
Fuji Lakeside GC
Japan
Makoto Harada
Fujioka CC
Magoya, Japan
Peter Thomson, Michael
  Wolveridge,*Tameshi Yamada*
Fulford GC
Yorkshire, England
Alister Mackenzie
Fulford Heath GC
England
James Braid, John R. Stutt
Fullerton G&CC
California
William F. Bell
Fullerton Muni (A. 9)
California
Ted Robinson
Fulton Estate GC
Salisbury, Connecticut
Devereux Emmet, Alfred H. Tull
Fulwell GC
Middlesex, England
J.S.F. Morrison
Fundy National Park GC
Alma, New Brunswick
Stanley Thompson
Furano CC
Japan
Arnold Palmer, Ed Seay
Fureso GC
Sweden
Jan Sederholm
Furnace Brook CC (R)
Massachusetts
William F. Mitchell
Furnace Creek GC
California
William P. Bell
Furnace Creek GC (A. 9)
California
William F. Bell
Furnas GC
Azores Islands
P.M. Ross
Furth GC
West Germany
Bernhard von Limburger
Futurama GC
Sarasota, Florida
R. Albert Anderson
Gables GC NLE
Florida
John Duncan Dunn
Gabriola G&CC (A)
British Columbia
Dan Kitsul
Gadsden CC
Quincy, Florida
Joe Lee
Gagetown GC
Oromocto, New Brunswick
Clinton E. Robinson
Gaines County GC
Seminole, Texas
C. William Keith
Gainesville G&CC
Florida
George W. Cobb
Gainesville Muni NLE
Georgia
Donald Ross
Gainesville Muni
Texas
Ralph Plummer
Gainey Ranch GC
Scottsdale, Arizona
Brad Benz, Mike Poellot,Mark
  Rathert
Galaglades G & CC
Cambridge, Ontario
Clinton E. Robinson
Galen Hall GC
Wernersville, Pennsylvania
Alex Findlay

Galen Hall GC (R)
Pennsylvania
A.W. Tillinghast
Galen Hall GC (R)
Pennsylvania
William Gordon, David Gordon
Galion CC (A. 9)
Ohio
Jack Kidwell
Gallaghers Canyon GC
Kelowna, British Columbia
William G. Robinson
Galloping Hills GC
Union, New Jersey
Willard Wilkinson
Galloping Hills GC (R)
New Jersey
Robert Trent Jones
Galloping Hills GC (R)
New Jersey
Alfred H. Tull
Galloping Hills GC (R)
New Jersey
Robert Trent Jones
Galls GC (R)
Minnesota
Don Herfort
Gallup Muni
New Mexico
Leon Howard
Galt G & Curling C
Ontario
Robert Moote, *David Moote*
Galveston CC
Texas
John Bredemus
Galveston CC (R. 6)
Texas
Joseph S. Finger
Galveston Muni NLE
Texas
John Bredemus
Galveston Muni
Texas
Donald Ross
Galway GC
County Galway, Ireland
Alister Mackenzie
Gambel G Links NLE
Carefree, Arizona
Roy Dye, Gary Grandstaff
Ganstead Park GC
Yorkshire, England
Ted Eltherington
Ganton GC
England
Tom Dunn
Ganton GC (R)
England
C.K. Hutchison
Ganton GC (R)
England
Herbert Fowler
Ganton GC (R)
England
Harry Vardon
Ganton GC (R)
England
Ted Ray
Ganton GC (R)
England
James Braid
Ganton GC (R)
England
Harold Hilton
Ganton GC (R)
England
H.S. Colt
Ganton GC (R)
England
C.K. Cotton
Garden of Eden GC
Momence, Illinois
Stanley Pelchar
Garden City CC (R)
Kansas
Smiley Bell
Garden City CC
New York
Walter J. Travis
Garden City CC (R. 6)
New York
Frank Duane

Garden City GC
New York
Devereux Emmet
Garden City GC (R)
New York
Walter J. Travis
Garden City GC (R)
New York
Robert Trent Jones
Garden City GC (R)
New York
Robert Trent Jones, Frank Duane
Gardiner's Bay CC (R. 9)
New York
Seth Raynor
Gardiner's Bay CC (A. 9)
New York
Seth Raynor
Gardiner's Bay CC (R)
New York
William F. Mitchell
Gardner Muni (R. 2)
Massachusetts
Samuel Mitchell
Garfield Muni
Chicago, Illinois
Tom Bendelow
Garforth GC
Yorkshire, England
Tom Williamson
Garforth GC (R. 1)
England
Charles A. Mackenzie
Garlenda GC
Italy
John Harris
Garmish-Partnekirchen GC
West Germany
Karl Hoffmann, Bernhard von
  Limburger
Garmish-Partnekirchen GC (R)
West Germany
Donald Harradine
Garner Lake GC
Edwardsburg, Michigan
Bruce L. Dustin
Garrats Hall GC
England
Wilfrid Reid
Garrett CC
Indiana
Tom Bendelow
**Garrison GC formerly known as
  North Redoubt C**
New York
Dick Wilson
Garrison's Lake GC
Delaware
Edmund B. Ault
Gary CC
Merrillville, Indiana
William B. Langford, Theodore J.
  Moreau
Gary CC (R)
Indiana
Edward Lawrence Packard, Brent
  Wadsworth
Gary Player CC
Sun City, Bophutatswana
Ron Kirby, Gary Player,Denis
  Griffiths
Gaschwitz GC
Leipzig, East Germany
Karl Hoffmann, Bernhard von
  Limburger
Gasparilla Inn & CC (R)
Florida
David Wallace
Gassin GC
St. Tropez, France
Pier Mancinelli
Gaston CC
Gastonia, North Carolina
Ellis Maples
Gastonia National GC
Gaston, North Carolina
J. Porter Gibson
Gates Four G&CC
Fayetteville, North Carolina
Willard Byrd
Gates Park GC
Waterloo, Iowa
Robert Bruce Harris

Gateway GC
Land O'Lakes, Wisconsin
Robert Bruce Harris
Gatlinburg G&CC
Tennessee
William B. Langford
Gatlinburg G&CC (R)
Tennessee
Ellis Maples, Dan Maples
Gator Creek GC
Sarasota, Florida
Joe Lee
Gator Hole GC
North Myrtle Beach, South
  Carolina
Rees Jones
Gator Trace GC
Ft. Pierce, Florida
Arthur Hills, Steve Forrest,Mike
  Dasher
Gatton Manor Hotel & GC
Surrey, England
John Harris
Gavea G&CC
Brazil
Arthur Davidson
Gavea G&CC (R)
Brazil
Stanley Thompson
Gay Hill CC
Galax, Virginia
Gene Hamm
Gaylord CC
Michigan
Wilfrid Reid
Gaylord CC (R)
Michigan
Robert W. Bills, Donald L. Childs
Gelpenberg GC
Zweeloo, Netherlands
J.J.F. Pennink
Gem Lake GC
Minnesota
Paul Coates
Gene List Muni
Bellflower, California
Harry Rainville
Geneganslet GC
Greene, New York
Ernest E. Smith
General Blanchard GC
Davis Monthan AFB, Arizona
Bob Baldock
General Butler State Park GC
Carrollton, Kentucky
Hal Purdy
General Electric AA GC
Massachusetts
Rowland Armacost
General Washington CC
Audubon, Pennsylvania
William F. Mitchell
Generals GC
Crownsville, Maryland
Edmund B. Ault
Geneva G&CC NLE
Muscatine, Iowa
Tom Bendelow
Geneva G&CC
Muscatine, Iowa
David Gill, Garrett Gill
Geneva G&CC
Ontario
Stanley Thompson
Geneva G&CC
Switzerland
Robert Trent Jones, Cabell
  Robinson
Geneva G&CC (R) NLE
Switzerland
Donald Harradine
Geneva Lake Y&GC (R)
Wisconsin
Tom Bendelow
Geneva-on-the-Lake GC
Ohio
James Gilmore Harrison
Geneva-on-the-Lake GC (A. 9)
Ohio
James Gilmore Harrison
Gentling Highlands GC (R)
Malaysia
Peter Thomson, Michael
  Wolveridge,Ronald Fream

George GC
Cape Province, South Africa
Hendrik J. Raubenheimer
George Wright Muni
Boston, Massachusetts
Donald Ross
Georgetown CC
South Carolina
Alfred H. Tull
Georgetown GC
Ann Arbor, Michigan
Charles Maddox, *Charles Maddox
  Jr*
Georgetown GC
Ontario
Clinton E. Robinson, Robert
  Moote
Geysteren G&CC
Eindhoven, Netherlands
J.J.F. Pennink
Giant Oak CC
Temperance, Michigan
Arthur Hills
Gibson Island GC
Maryland
Charles Blair Macdonald, Seth
  Raynor
Gibson Woods Muni
Monmouth, Illinois
Homer Fieldhouse
Gillespie GC NLE
Sarasota, Florida
John Hamilton Gillespie
Gillette CC
Wyoming
Frank Hummel
Glacier View GC
West Glacier, Montana
Bob Baldock, Robert L. Baldock
Glacier View GC (R)
Montana
Ronald Fream, *Terry Storm*
Glade Springs CC
Beckley, West Virginia
George W. Cobb
Glades CC (Course No. 1)
Naples, Florida
B. Dudley Gray
Glades CC (Course No. 2)
Naples, Florida
B. Dudley Gray
Gladestone CC
Michigan
A.H. Jolly
Glamorganshire GC
Wales
Willie Park Jr
Glamorganshire GC (R)
Wales
Tom Simpson
Glasgow AFB GC
Montana
Bob Baldock
Glasgow GC
Scotland
Old Tom Morris
Glasgow Killermont GC (R)
Scotland
Willie Park Jr
Glastonbury Hills CC
Connecticut
Al Zikorus
Glastonbury Hills CC (R)
Connecticut
William F. Mitchell
Glastonbury Hills CC (R. 4)
Connecticut
Geoffrey S. Cornish, William G.
  Robinson
Glen Abbey GC
Florida
Dominic Palombo
Glen Abbey GC
Oakville, Ontario
Jack Nicklaus, Jay Morrish,Bob
  Cupp
Glen Acres CC
Bothel, Washington
George S. "Pop" Merrit
Glen Arven CC
Thomasville, Georgia
Wayne Stiles, John Van Kleek

293

Glen Arven CC (R. 4)
Georgia
Hugh Moore
Glen Avon GC
California
William H. Johnson
Glen Brook CC
Stroudsburg, Pennsylvania
Robert White
Glen Cannon GC
Brevard, North Carolina
William B. Lewis
Glen Cedars GC
Markham, Ontario
Renee Muylaert
Glen Cove Muni
New York
William F. Mitchell
Glen Eagles GC
Bolton, Ontario
Renee Muylaert
Glen Echo CC
Normandy, Missouri
James Foulis, Robert Foulis
Glen Echo CC (R)
Missouri
Robert Foulis
Glen Falls CC
New York
Donald Ross
Glen Garden CC (A. 9)
Texas
John Bredemus
Glen Garden CC (R. 9)
Texas
John Bredemus
Glen GC (R)
Scotland
P.M. Ross
Glen Head CC formerly known as Women's National G&CC
New York
Devereux Emmet
Glen Head CC (R)
New York
William S. Flynn
Glen Head CC (R)
New York
William F. Mitchell
Glen Head CC (R)
New York
Alfred H. Tull
Glen Head CC (R)
New York
Stephen Kay
Glen Lakes CC (R)
Texas
Ralph Plummer
Glen Lakes GC
Glendale, Arizona
Milt Coggins
Glen Lawrence G&CC
Kinston, Ontario
W.C. Harvey, D.H. Green
Glen Lawrence G&CC (R)
Ontario
Clinton E. Robinson
Glen Mawr GC
Toronto, Ontario
Stanley Thompson
Glen Oak C
Old Westbury, New York
Joseph S. Finger
Glen Oak GC
Glen Ellyn, Illinois
Tom Bendelow
Glen Oak CC (R)
Illinois
William B. Langford, Theodore J. Moreau
Glen Oak CC (R. 4)
Illinois
David Gill
Glen Oak CC (R)
Illinois
Ken Killian
Glen Oak CC
Waverly, Pennsylvania
James Gilmore Harrison, Ferdinand Garbin
Glen Oak CC
Danville, Virginia
Dick Wilson

Glen Oaks GC
Clearwater, Florida
Hans Schmeisser
Glen Ridge CC
New Jersey
Willie Park Jr
Glen Ridge CC NLE
New Jersey
Tom Bendelow
Glen Ridge CC (R)
New Jersey
Robert Trent Jones
Glen Ridge CC (R)
New Jersey
Robert Trent Jones, Roger Rulewich
Glen View GC
Golf, Illinois
H.J. Tweedie
Glen View GC (R)
Illinois
William S. Flynn
Glen View GC (R)
Illinois
George O'Neill, Joseph A. Roseman
Glenbard GC NLE
Glen Ellyn, Illinois
Robert Bruce Harris
Glenbervie GC
Stirlingshire, Scotland
James Braid
Glenbrook CC (R)
Nevada
Robert Muir Graves
Glenbrook CC
East Brunswick, New Jersey
Hal Purdy
Glencoe G & CC (Forest Course)
Calgary, Alberta
Robert Trent Jones Jr, Don Knott, Gary Linn
Glencoe G & CC (Meadow Course)
Calgary, Alberta
Robert Trent Jones Jr, Don Knott, Gary Linn
Glencoe GC (R)
Illinois
Ken Killian, Dick Nugent
Glencoe GC (R)
Illinois
Ken Killian, Dick Nugent, Bob Lohmann
Glencorse GC
Midlothian, Scotland
Willie Park
Glencruitten GC
Argyll, Scotland
James Braid
Glendale CC NLE
Bloomingdale, Illinois
Tom Bendelow
Glendale CC
Bellevue, Washington
Al Smith
Glendale CC (R. 3)
Alberta
Peter Thomson, Michael Wolveridge, Ronald Fream
Glendale G&CC
Bothel, Washington
Al Smith
Glendale G&CC
Winnipeg, Manitoba
Stanley Thompson
Glendale G&CC (R)
Ontario
Clinton E. Robinson
Glendale Lakes GC
Glendale Heights, Illinois
Dick Nugent
Glendale Muni NLE
Arizona
William H. Tucker Jr
Glendale Park Muni
Salt Lake City, Utah
William F. Bell
Glendora CC
California
E. Warren Beach
Glendora CC (R. 9)
California
William H. Johnson

Glendora CC (R)
California
Robert Trent Jones, Robert Trent Jones Jr, Gary Roger Baird
Glendoveer GC (East Course)
Portland, Oregon
Frank Stenzel
Glendoveer GC (East Course) (R)
Oregon
John Junor
Glendoveer GC (East Course) (R)
Oregon
John Junor
Glendoveer GC (West Course)
Portland, Oregon
Frank Stenzel
Gleneagle CC
Colorado Springs, Colorado
Frank Hummel
Gleneagles CC (East Course)
Delray Beach, Florida
Karl Litten
Gleneagles CC (King's Course)
Plano, Texas
Robert von Hagge, Bruce Devlin
Gleneagles CC (Queen's Course)
Texas
Robert von Hagge, Bruce Devlin
Gleneagles CC (West Course)
Delray Beach, Florida
Karl Litten
Gleneagles GC (Red Course)
Lemont, Illinois
Charles Maddox, *Frank P. MacDonald*
Gleneagles GC (White Course)
Lemont, Illinois
Charles Maddox, *Frank P. MacDonald*
Gleneagles Hotel GC (Glendevon Course)
Perthshire, Scotland
T.J.A. McAuley
Gleneagles Hotel GC (Kings Course)
Perthshire, Scotland
James Braid, C.K. Hutchison
Gleneagles Hotel GC (Princes Course)
Scotland
James Alexander, I. Marchbanks, T. Telford
Gleneagles Hotel GC (Queen's Course)
Perthshire, Scotland
James Braid, C.K. Hutchison
Gleneagles Hotel GC (Queen's Course) (R)
Scotland
James Alexander
Gleneagles International GC (R)
California
Robert Muir Graves
Glenelg GC
Australia
V. Morcomb
Glenhardie CC
Wayne, Pennsylvania
David Gordon
Glenhaven CC
Oelwein, Iowa
Dick Phelps, *Emile Perret, Donald G. Brauer*
Glenhaven G&CC
Milpitas, California
Jack Fleming
Glenhurst CC
Watchung, New Jersey
Alec Ternyei
Glenmoor CC
Englewood, Colorado
Pete Dye
Glenmore G&CC
Jordan, Utah
William H. Neff
Glenn G&CC
Willows, California
Ben Harmon
Glennoch G&CC
Firth of Clyde, Scotland
J. Hamilton Stutt
GlennDale CC (R)
Maryland
Ray Shields, Roy Shields

Glenoaks CC
Japan
Brad Benz, Mike Poellot
Glenora GC
Australia
Des Soutar
Glenrochie CC
Abington, Virginia
Alex McKay
Glenrothes GC
Fife, Scotland
J. Hamilton Stutt, Fraser Middleton
Glenview Muni
Cincinnati, Ohio
Arthur Hills
Glenview NAS GC (Course No. 2)
Illinois
Joseph A. Roseman
Glenview NAS GC (Course No.1)
Illinois
Joseph A. Roseman
Glenview Park GC formerly known as Elmgate CC
Glenview, Illinois
Joseph A. Roseman
Glenview Park GC (R)
Illinois
Edward Lawrence Packard
Glenview Park GC (R)
Illinois
Ken Killian
Glenwood CC
New Jersey
Hal Purdy
Glenwood CC
Farmingdale, New York
Devereux Emmet
Glenwood CC
Richmond, Virginia
Fred Findlay
Glenwood GC
Virginia Beach, Virginia
Rees Jones
Glenwood Hall CC
Perry Park, Kentucky
Bob Simmons
Glenwood Muni
Ashland, Ohio
X.G. Hassenplug
Glenwood Muni
Columbia, South Carolina
R.B. Jennings
Glenwood Park Muni
Erie, Pennsylvania
Charles Hymers
Glenwood Springs GC
Colorado
Henry B. Hughes
Glenwoodie GC
Chicago Heights, Illinois
Harry Collis, Jack Daray
Glenwoodie GC (R)
Illinois
Joe Lee
Glimmerglass State Park GC
East Springfield, New York
Frank Duane
Glyfada GC
Athens, Greece
Donald Harradine
Glyfada GC (R)
Greece
Robert Trent Jones, Cabell Robinson
Glynhir GC
Llandeilo, Wales
Fred W. Hawtree
Goderich GC (R)
Ontario
Robert Moote
Godwin Glen GC
South Lyon, Michigan
Bruce Matthews, Jerry Matthews
Goettingen GC
West Germany
Donald Harradine
Goffstown CC
New Hampshire
William F. Mitchell
Gog Magog GC
Cambridgeshire, England
Willie Park Jr

Gog Magog GC (A. 9)
England
Fred W. Hawtree
Gold Canyon Ranch GC
Apache Junction, Arizona
Jeff Hardin, Greg Nash
Gold Coast CC
Surfers' Paradise, Australia
Peter Thomson, Michael Wolveridge
Gold Hills CC
Redding, California
Bob Baldock, Robert L. Baldock
Gold Mountain GC
Bremerton, Washington
Kenneth Tyson
Golden Acres CC
Schaumberg, Illinois
William B. Langford, Theodore J. Moreau
Golden Eagle GC
Tallahassee, Florida
Tom Fazio
Golden Gate CC
Naples, Florida
Dick Wilson, Robert von Hagge
Golden Gate Fields GC
Albany, California
Jack Fleming
Golden Gate GC
San Francisco, California
Jack Fleming
Golden Hills G&TC
Ocala, Florida
Charles Pace, Lee Popple
Golden Hills GC
Tehachapi, California
Joseph B. Williams
Golden Hills Resort GC formerly known as Apache CC
Mesa, Arizona
Arthur Jack Snyder
Golden Hills Resort GC (R)
Arizona
Arthur Jack Snyder
Golden Horseshoe GC
Williamsburg, Virginia
Robert Trent Jones
Golden Horseshoe GC (Spotswood 9)
Williamsburg, Virginia
Robert Trent Jones
Golden Ocala G&CC
Ocala, Florida
Ron Garl
Golden Sands GC
Cecil, Wisconsin
Homer Fieldhouse
Golden Tee GC
Sarasota, Florida
R. Albert Anderson
Golden Tee GC
Sharonville, Ohio
R. Albert Anderson
Golden Triangle GC
Beltville, Maryland
Robert Trent Jones, Roger Rulewich
Golden Triangle GC (A. 9)
Maryland
Robert Trent Jones, Roger Rulewich
Golden Valley GC
Minneapolis, Minnesota
A.W. Tillinghast
Golden Valley GC
Japan
Robert Trent Jones Jr, Gary Linn
Goldman Hotel GC
East Orange, New Jersey
Frank Duane
Golf d'Ormesson
France
John Harris
Golf de Bercuit
Grez Doiceau, Belgium
Robert Trent Jones
Golf de Besancon
France
Michael G. Fenn
Golf de Biarritz
France
Willie Dunn Jr, Tom Dunn

Golf de Biarritz (R)
France
H.S. Colt
Golf de Bondues
Roubaix, France
Fred W. Hawtree
Golf de Bondues (A. 9)
France
Robert Trent Jones
Golf de Bondues (R.18)
France
Robert Trent Jones
Golf de Bourgogne
Dijon, France
Michael G. Fenn
Golf de Cabo Negro
Morocco
Fred W. Hawtree
Golf de Chaumont en Vexin
Paris, France
Donald Harradine
Golf de Chiberta
Biarritz, France
Tom Simpson
Golf de Claris
France
Michael G. Fenn
Golf de Clermont-Ferrand
France
Michael G. Fenn
Golf de Cornouaille
Quimper, France
Fred W. Hawtree
Golf de Dieppe
France
Willie Park Jr
Golf de Dieppe (R)
France
Tom Simpson
Golf de Dinard
France
John Duncan Dunn, Tom Dunn
Golf de Domont
Paris, France
Fred W. Hawtree
Golf de Fountainbleau
France
Tom Simpson
Golf de Hardelot
France
John Duncan Dunn
Golf de Hardelot (R)
France
Tom Simpson, P.M. Ross
Golf de Hossegor
France
Tom Simpson
Golf de La Baule (R)
France
Peter Alliss, David Thomas
Golf de Lann-Rohou
Brest, France
Michael G. Fenn
Golf de Lyon
France
Fred W. Hawtree
Golf de Memillon
France
Tom Simpson
Golf de Metz Cherisey
Metz, France
Fred W. Hawtree
Golf de Morfontaine
Senlis, France
Tom Simpson
Golf de Nancy-Aingeray (R)
France
Michael G. Fenn
Golf de Nantes
France
J.J.F. Pennink
Golf de Rochefort en Yvelines
Paris, France
Fred W. Hawtree
Golf de Seraincourt
Meulan, France
Fred W. Hawtree
Golf de St. Francois
Guadeloupe
Robert Trent Jones, Roger
  Rulewich
Golf de St. Laurent
France
Michael G. Fenn

Golf de St. Samson
Pleumeur-Bodou, France
Fred W. Hawtree
Golf de Toulouse (A. 9)
France
Fred W. Hawtree
Golf de Touraine
Tours, France
Michael G. Fenn
Golf de Valbonne
France
Donald Harradine
Golf de Valcros
France
Fred W. Hawtree
Golf de Valliere
France
Tom Simpson
Golf de Vaudreuil
France
Fred W. Hawtree
Golf de Vaux de Cernay
France
Tom Simpson
Golf de Villard-de-Lans
France
Tom Simpson
Golf de Voisins
France
Tom Simpson
**Golf des Chateaux de
  Villarceaux**
France
John Harris
Golf du Clair Vallon
Clairis, France
Michael G. Fenn
Golf du Parc Carleton
Quebec
William F. Mitchell
Golf du Prieure (East Course)
Sailly, France
Fred W. Hawtree
Golf du Prieure (West Course)
Sailly, France
Fred W. Hawtree
Golf und Land C Cologne
West Germany
Karl Hoffmann, Bernhard von
  Limburger
Golf und Landclub Oswestfalen
Lippe, West Germany
Bernhard von Limburger
Golf City Par 3 GC
Corvallis, Oregon
Ed Burns
**Golf Club at Aspetuck now
  known as Connecticut GC**
Golf Club at Fossil Creek
Fort Worth, Texas
Arnold Palmer, Ed Seay
Golf Club d'Aix-les-bains
France
Wilfrid Reid
Golf Club d'Arcahon
France
Charles Blanchford
Golf Club d'Ozoir-la-Ferriere
France
Tom Simpson
Golf Club de Brotel
Hieres-sur-Amby, France
Michael G. Fenn
Golf Club de Campagne
Nimes, France
Donald Harradine
Golf Club de Pals
Gerona, Spain
Fred W. Hawtree
Golf Club de Pals (A. 9)
Spain
Fred W. Hawtree
Golf Club de Quiberon
France
Michael G. Fenn
Golf Club de Reims
France
Michael G. Fenn
Golf Club de Reims
France
Michael G. Fenn
Golf Club de Schoot
Sint Oedenrode, Netherlands
J.F. Dudok Van Heel

**Golf Club de St. Cloud (Green
  Course)**
France
H.S. Colt
**Golf Club de St. Cloud (Yellow
  Course)**
France
J.S.F. Morrison, H.S. Colt
Golf Club de Touquet NLE
Le Touquet, France
Allen Stoneham
**Golf Club de Touquet (Forest
  Course)**
France
H.S. Colt
**Golf Club de Touquet (Forest
  Course) (R)**
France
P.M. Ross
**Golf Club de Touquet (Sea
  Course)**
France
H.S. Colt, J.S.F. Morrison,C.H.
  Alison
Golf Club de Uruguay
Montevideo, Uruguay
Alister Mackenzie
Golf Club de Villette-D'Anthon
France
Michael G. Fenn
Golf Club of Delray
Florida
Bill Dietsch
Golf Club of Illinois
Algonquin, Illinois
Dick Nugent
Golf Club of Indiana
Lebanon, Indiana
Charles Maddox
Golf Club of Kentucky
Crestwood, Kentucky
Larry Fitch
Golf Club of Lebanon
Beirut, Lebanon
J.J.F. Pennink
Golf Club of Oklahoma
Broken Arrow, Oklahoma
Tom Fazio
Golf Club Broekpolder
Vlaardingen, Netherlands
J.J.F. Pennink
Golf Club Nordsec-Kurhof
Wik-Auf-Fuhr, West Germany
J.J.F. Pennink
Golf D'Atimaona CC
Papeete, Tahiti
Bob Baldock, Robert L. Baldock
**Golf Guadalamina (North
  Course)**
Spain
Javier Arana
**Golf Guadalamina (South
  Course)**
Spain
Javier Arana
Golf Hammock CC
Sebring, Florida
Ron Garl
Golf Hill G&CC
Fatogue, New York
Frank Duane
Golf Ile de Berder
France
Wilfrid Reid
Golf Les Bordes
France
Robert von Hagge, Bruce Devlin
Golf Park G Links NLE
Florida
H.C.C. Tippetts
Golf Puy de Dome
France
Michael G. Fenn
Golf Rio Real
Spain
Javier Arana
Golf Village GC
Neenah, Wisconsin
Homer Fieldhouse
Golf 72 (Higashi Course)
Japan
Robert Trent Jones, Robert Trent
  Jones Jr

Golf 72 (Karuizawa Course)
Japan
Robert Trent Jones Jr
Golf 72 (Kita Course)
Japan
Robert Trent Jones, Robert Trent
  Jones Jr
Golf 72 (Minami Course)
Japan
Robert Trent Jones, Robert Trent
  Jones Jr
Golf 72 (Nishi Course)
Japan
Robert Trent Jones, Robert Trent
  Jones Jr
Golfcrest CC NLE
Houston, Texas
Ralph Plummer
Golfcrest CC
Houston, Texas
Joseph S. Finger
Golfland GC
Georgia
Chic Adams
Golfland GC (R)
Ontario
Clinton E. Robinson
Golfmohr GC
East Moline, Illinois
Ted Lockie
Goodwin Park Muni (R)
Connecticut
Everett Pyle
Goodyear G&CC (Blue Course)
Litchfield Park, Arizona
Robert Trent Jones
Goodyear G&CC (Gold Course)
Litchfield Park, Arizona
Robert Trent Jones
Goodyear G&CC (West Course)
Litchfield Park, Arizona
Red Lawrence, Jeff Hardin,Greg
  Nash
Goose Creek CC
Leesburg, Virginia
William Gordon
Goose Island Lake GC
Texas
Bruce Littell
Goosepond Colony GC
Scottsboro, Alabama
George W. Cobb
Gordon Lakes GC
Fort Gordon, Georgia
Robert Trent Jones, Rees Jones
Gordon Trent GC
Martinsville, Virginia
Al Jamison, *Claude Bingham*
Gorleston GC
Suffolk, England
F.G. Hawtree, J.H. Taylor
Gormley Green GC
Ontario
Renee Muylaert
Gormley Green GC (R. 9)
Ontario
Renee Muylaert, *Charles Muylaert*
Gort GC (R)
Ireland
Eddie Hackett
Goshen Plantation CC
Augusta, Georgia
Ellis Maples, Ed Seay
Gotts Park GC
England
T.R. Trigg
Gourock GC
Scotland
Henry Cotton
Governors Island GC
New York
Fred J. Roth
Gowan Brae GC
Bathurst, New Brunswick
Clinton E. Robinson, Robert
  Moote
Gowanda CC
New York
A. Russell Tryon
Gowrie G&CC
Iowa
Charles Calhoun

Gracewil CC (East Course)
Grand Rapids, Michigan
Maurie Wells
Gracewil GC (West Course)
Grand Rapids, Michigan
Morris Wilson
Gracewil Pines GC
Michigan
Morris Wilson
Graham F Vanderbilt Estate GC
Manhasset, New York
Alfred H. Tull
Grain Valley GC
Missouri
John S. Davis, Robert Stone
Gramont Estate GC
France
Tom Simpson
Granada Farms CC
Granite, North Carolina
Tom Jackson
Granada GC
Coral Gables, Florida
William B. Langford, Theodore J.
  Moreau
Granbury GC
Texas
Leon Howard
Grand Bahama Hotel & CC
Freeport, Bahamas
Mark Mahannah
Grand Beach CC
Michigan
Tom Bendelow
Grand Beach CC (A.27)
Michigan
William H. Livie
Grand Beach GC
Manitoba
Norman H. Woods
Grand Blanc GC
Michigan
Bruce Matthews, Jerry Matthews
Grand Cypress Golf Academy
Orlando, Florida
Jack Nicklaus, Bob Cupp
Grand Cypress GC
Orlando, Florida
Jack Nicklaus, Bob Cupp
Grand Cypress GC (A. 9)
Florida
Jack Nicklaus, Bob Cupp
Grand Falls GC (R)
New Brunswick
Robert Moote
Grand Forks CC
North Dakota
Robert Bruce Harris
Grand Haven GC
Michigan
Bruce Matthews, Jerry Matthews
Grand Hotel GC (R. 4)
Michigan
Jerry Matthews
Grand Island Muni
Nebraska
Frank Hummel
Grand Lake GC (R. 9)
Colorado
Dick Phelps, Brad Benz
Grand Lake GC (A. 9)
Colorado
Dick Phelps, Brad Benz
Grand Ledge GC
Michigan
Stephen Lipkowitz
Grand Marais GC
East St. Louis, Illinois
Joseph A. Roseman
Grand Prairie GC
Kalamazoo, Indiana
William James Spear
Grand Prairie Muni
Texas
Ralph Plummer
Grand Rapids CC
Michigan
Willie Park Jr
**Grand Traverse GC (Newcombe
  Course)**
Acme, Michigan
William Newcomb, Stephen Kay

Grand Traverse GC (Newcombe Course) (R)
Michigan
Bob Cupp
Grand Traverse GC (The Bear Course)
Acme, Michigan
Jack Nicklaus, Bob Cupp
Grandfather G&CC
Linville, North Carolina
Ellis Maples, Ed Seay
Grandmere GC (R. 3)
Quebec
Howard Watson
Grandview CC (R)
Ohio
Richard W. LaConte, Ted McAnlis
Grandview GC
Sun City West, Arizona
Greg Nash
Grandview GC (R)
Pennsylvania
James Gilmore Harrison
Grandview GC
Hortonville, Wisconsin
Ted Lockie
Grandview Muni
Springfield, Missouri
Perry Maxwell, Press Maxwell
Grange GC (R)
England
T.J.A. McAuley
Grange GC
Dublin, Ireland
Tom Hood
Grange GC (R)
Ireland
W. Wiltshire
Grange-over-Sands GC
Cumbria, England
Alister Mackenzie
Grangemouth Muni
Shirlingshire, Scotland
Fred W. Hawtree
Granit Hotel GC
Kerhonkson, New York
Lou Block
Granite City GC
Illinois
Edward Lawrence Packard, Brent Wadsworth
Granliden Hotel GC
Lake Sunapee, New Hampshire
Alex Findlay
Grant Park GC
Milwaukee, Wisconsin
George Hansen
Grant's Pass CC (R)
Oregon
Bob Baldock, Robert L. Baldock
Grant's Pass CC (A.14)
Oregon
Bob Baldock, Robert L. Baldock
Grantown GC
Morayshire, Scotland
Willie Park
Grantwood CC
Solon, Ohio
Harold Paddock
Granville Inn GC
Granville, Ohio
Donald Ross
Grapevine Muni
Texas
Joseph S. Finger, Ken Dye, Byron Nelson
Grasmere GC
Falmouth, Massachusetts
Geoffrey S. Cornish, William G. Robinson
Grassy Brook GC
Alder Creek, New York
Geoffrey S. Cornish, William G. Robinson
Gray Gables CC
Laramie, Wyoming
Herbert Lockwood
Graysburg Hills GC
Chuckey, Tennessee
Rees Jones
Grayson Valley CC
Birmingham, Alabama
Harold Williams

Grayson Valley CC (R)
Alabama
John LaFoy
Great Bend Petroleum C (A. 9)
Kansas
Richard Watson
Great Cove GC
Pennsylvania
Edmund B. Ault
Great Harbour Cay CC
Berry Island, Bahamas
Joe Lee
Great Hills CC
Seymour, Connecticut
Al Zikorus
Great Hills GC
Austin, Texas
Don January, Billy Martindale
Great Island GC
Massachusetts
Alex Findlay
Great Lakes NTC GC
North Chicago, Illinois
C.D. Wagstaff
Great Lakes NTC GC (A. 9)
Illinois
Ken Killian, Dick Nugent
Great Oaks CC
Rochester, Michigan
William Newcomb
Great Smokies Hilton GC
Asheville, North Carolina
William B. Lewis
Great Southwest GC
Arlington, Texas
Ralph Plummer, Byron Nelson
Great Southwest GC (R)
Texas
Ken Killian, Dick Nugent, Jeff Brauer
Greeley CC
Colorado
Tom Bendelow
Greeley CC (A. 9)
Colorado
Press Maxwell
Greeley CC (R. 9)
Colorado
Press Maxwell
Green Acres CC
Northbrook, Illinois
George O'Neill
Green Acres CC (R)
Illinois
Joseph A. Roseman
Green Acres CC (R. 1)
Illinois
Ken Killian, Dick Nugent
Green Acres CC
Kokomo, Indiana
Bob Simmons
Green Acres GC
Dexter, Georgia
Arthur Davis
Green Brook CC
Caldwell, New Jersey
Robert White
Green Brook CC (R)
New Jersey
Maurice McCarthy
Green Brook CC (R)
New Jersey
Robert Trent Jones
Green Brook CC (R)
New Jersey
Hal Purdy, Malcolm Purdy
Green Gables CC
Denver, Colorado
William H. Tucker
Green Gables CC (A. 9)
Colorado
James L. Haines
Green Gables GC
Charlottetown, Prince Edward Island
Stanley Thompson
Green Gables GC (R)
Prince Edward Island
Clinton E. Robinson
Green Gables GC (A. 9)
Prince Edward Island
Clinton E. Robinson

Green Harbor CC
Marshfield, Massachusetts
Manny Francis
Green Haven GC (R. 3)
Minnesota
David Gill
Green Hill Muni
Wilmington, Delaware
Wilfrid Reid
Green Hill Muni (R)
Delaware
Edmund B. Ault
Green Hill Muni NLE
Worcester, Massachusetts
Willie Ogg
Green Hill Muni
Worcester, Massachusetts
William F. Mitchell
Green Hill Muni (R)
Massachusetts
Alfred H. Tull
Green Hill Y&CC (R)
Maryland
Alfred H. Tull
Green Hills CC
Millbrae, California
Alister Mackenzie, Robert Hunter, H. Chandler Egan
Green Hills CC (R)
California
Robert Muir Graves
Green Hills CC (R)
California
Gary Roger Baird
Green Hills CC (A. 9)
Illinois
Gary Kern
Green Hills CC
Willard, Missouri
Floyd Farley
Green Hills CC
Rochester, New York
Pete Craig, *Joseph Demino*
Green Hills CC
West Virginia
Edmund B. Ault
Green Hills G&CC
Selma, Indiana
William H. Diddel
Green Hills G&CC (R)
Indiana
William H. Diddel
Green Hills GC
Linwood, Michigan
William Newcomb
Green Island CC
Columbus, Georgia
George W. Cobb
Green Island CC (R)
Georgia
Joe Lee, Rocky Roquemore
Green Knoll GC
Somerset, New Jersey
William Gordon, David Gordon
Green Lakes State Park GC
Fayetteville, New York
Robert Trent Jones
Green Lakes State Park GC (R)
New York
William F. Mitchell
Green Meadow CC
Helena, Montana
Gregor MacMillan
Green Meadow CC (R)
Montana
Gregor MacMillan
Green Meadow CC (A. 9)
Montana
William Teufel
Green Meadow CC (R)
New York
Alfred H. Tull
Green Meadow CC now known as Willow Ridge CC
Green Meadow CC
Marysville, Tennessee
William B. Langford
Green Meadow CC (R)
Tennessee
Willard Byrd
Green Meadows CC
Augusta, Georgia
Bill Amick

Green Meadows CC
Katy, Texas
Jay Riviere
Green Park-Norwood GC NLE
Blowing Rock, North Carolina
Seth Raynor
Green Pond CC
Bethlehem, Pennsylvania
Alex Findlay
Green Pond GC
New Jersey
Alec Ternyei
Green Ridge CC
Grand Rapids, Michigan
Tom Bendelow
Green Ridge CC (R)
Michigan
William Newcomb
Green Ridge CC (R)
Michigan
Bruce Matthews
Green Ridge CC (R)
Michigan
Bruce Matthews
Green River CC
Chesterland, South Carolina
Al Zikorus
Green River CC
Waynesboro, Tennessee
Robert Renaud
Green River CC (Orange Course)
Corona, California
Lawrence Hughes
Green River CC (Riverside Course)
Corona, California
Cary Bickler
Green Spring Valley Hunt C (R. 9)
Maryland
Robert Trent Jones
Green Spring Valley Hunt C (A. 9)
Maryland
Robert Trent Jones
Green Tree GC
California
William F. Bell
Green Valley CC
Birmingham, Alabama
Bancroft Timmons
Green Valley CC (R. 9)
Alabama
George W. Cobb
Green Valley CC (A. 9)
Alabama
George W. Cobb
Green Valley CC
Suisun, California
Elmer G. Border
Green Valley CC (R)
California
Robert Muir Graves
Green Valley CC
Clermont, Florida
R. Albert Anderson
Green Valley CC NLE
Roxborough, Pennsylvania
Willie Park Jr
Green Valley CC
Lafayette Hills, Pennsylvania
William S. Flynn, Howard Toomey
Green Valley CC (R)
Pennsylvania
J.B. McGovern
Green Valley CC
Greenville, South Carolina
George W. Cobb
Green Valley CC
Kingsport, Tennessee
Lon Mills
Green Valley CC
St. George, Utah
Mark Dixon Ballif
Green Valley G&CC (R)
North Carolina
Gene Hamm
Green Valley GC
Greensboro, North Carolina
George W. Cobb
Green Valley GC
Kings Mountain, North Carolina
Ellis Maples, Dan Maples

Green Valley GC
Quebec
George Cumming
Green Valley GC (R)
Quebec
Howard Watson
Green Valley GC (R. 7)
Quebec
John Watson
Green Valley Muni
Sioux City, Iowa
David Gill
Greenacres CC
Lawrence, New Jersey
Devereux Emmet, Alfred H. Tull
Greenacres CC (R)
New Jersey
William Gordon, David Gordon
Greenacres CC (R. 2)
New Jersey
Brian Ault, Tom Clark, Bill Love
Greenacres GC
British Columbia
Heinz Knoedler
Greenbriar GC (Lakeside Course)
Wht. Sulphur Springs, West Virginia
Dick Wilson, Bob Simmons
Greenbriar Hills CC
Kirkwood, Missouri
C.D. Wagstaff
Greenbriar Hills CC (R)
Missouri
Don Sechrest
Greenbriar Hills CC (A. 9)
Missouri
C.D. Wagstaff
Greenbrier G&CC
Lexington, Kentucky
William Newcomb
Greenbrier GC
New Bern, North Carolina
Rees Jones
Greenbrier GC
Chesapeake, Virginia
Rees Jones
Greenbrier GC (Greenbrier Course)
White Sulphur Spgs, West Virginia
George O'Neill
Greenbrier GC (Greenbrier Course) (R)
West Virginia
Jack Nicklaus, Jay Morrish, Bob Cupp
Greenbrier GC (Lakeside Course) NLE
White Sulphur Spgs, West Virginia
Alex Findlay
Greenbrier GC (Old White Course)
White Sulphur Spgs, West Virginia
Charles Blair Macdonald, Seth Raynor
Greenbrier Valley GC
West Virginia
R. Vaughn
Greendale Muni
Alexandria, Virginia
Leon Howard, *Charles Howard*
Greene County GC
Waynesburg, Pennsylvania
Emil Loeffler, *John McGlynn*
Greene CC
Yellow Springs, Ohio
William H. Diddel
Greene Hills C
Stanardsville, Virginia
Buddy Loving
Greenfield CC (R. 9)
Indiana
Gary Kern
Greenfield CC (A. 9)
Indiana
Gary Kern
Greenfield CC
Massachusetts
Ralph Barton

Greenfield CC
Massachusetts
Alex Findlay
Greenfield CC (R)
Massachusetts
Ralph Barton
Greenfield Park GC
West Allis, Wisconsin
George Hansen
Greenhills CC
Lambeth, Ontario
Renee Muylaert, *Charles Muylaert*
Greenisland GC (A. 9)
Northern Ireland
Fraser Middleton
Greenisland GC (R)
Northern Ireland
Fraser Middleton
Greenlea GC
Boring, Oregon
Walt Markham
Greenleaf G&RC
Invergrove, Minnesota
Donald G. Brauer, Emile Perret
Greenock CC
Lee, Massachusetts
Donald Ross, Walter Hatch
Greenock CC
Renfrewshire, Scotland
James Braid
Greenore GC (R)
Ireland
Eddie Hackett
Greens G&RC
Oklahoma City, Oklahoma
Don Sechrest
Greensboro CC (Carlson Farms Course)
North Carolina
Ellis Maples
Greensboro CC (Carlson Farms Course) (R. 1)
North Carolina
John LaFoy
Greensboro CC (Irving Park Course)
North Carolina
Donald Ross
Greensboro CC (Irving Park Course) (R)
North Carolina
George W. Cobb
Greensburg CC
Pennsylvania
Tom Bendelow
Greenshire GC
Waukegan, Illinois
Ken Killian, Dick Nugent
Greentree CC
Carmel, Indiana
William H. Diddel
Greenview Cove GC
West Palm Beach, Florida
Ted McAnlis
Greenview GC
Centralia, Illinois
Tom Bendelow
Greenview GC
Central Square, New York
Hal Purdy
Greenville CC (R)
Illinois
Edward Lawrence Packard, Brent Wadsworth
Greenville CC
Kentucky
Alex McKay
Greenville CC
Pennsylvania
James Gilmore Harrison
Greenville CC (R. 9)
Pennsylvania
Ferdinand Garbin
Greenville CC (A. 9)
Pennsylvania
Ferdinand Garbin
Greenville CC (Chanticleer Course)
South Carolina
Robert Trent Jones
Greenville CC (Riverside Course)
South Carolina
William B. Langford

Greenville CC (Riverside Course) (R)
South Carolina
George W. Cobb
Greenville CC (Riverside Course) (R)
South Carolina
Russell Breeden
Greenville Muni
Mississippi
Leon Howard
Greenway Park GC
Broomfield, Colorado
Dick Phelps
Greenwich CC
Connecticut
Seth Raynor
Greenwich CC (R)
Connecticut
Donald Ross
Greenwich CC (R)
Connecticut
Robert Trent Jones
Greenwood CC
South Carolina
George W. Cobb
Greenwood CC (A. 9)
South Carolina
George W. Cobb
Greenwoods CC (R. 1)
Connecticut
Al Zikorus
Grenada G&CC
St. George, Grenada
Ewart Hughes
Grenelefe G&RC (East Course)
Haines City, Florida
Arnold Palmer, Ed Seay, Bob Walker
Grenelefe G&RC (South Course)
Haines City, Florida
Ron Garl
Grenelefe G&RC (West Course)
Haines City, Florida
David Wallace
Grenelefe G&RC (West Course)(Routing)
Haines City, Florida
Robert Trent Jones
Gresham G&CC
Oregon
Eddie Hogan, Sam Walsborn
Grey Rocks GC
St. Jovite, Quebec
Howard Watson
Greylock Glen CC
Adams, Massachusetts
Geoffrey S. Cornish, William G. Robinson
Greynold Park GC
Miami Beach, Florida
Mark Mahannah
Greystones GC (R)
Ireland
Eddie Hackett
Griffin CC (A. 9)
Georgia
Willard Byrd, Clyde Johnston
Griffin Gate GC
Lexington, Kentucky
Rees Jones
Griffith Park GC (Coolidge Course)
Los Angeles, California
William H. Johnson
Griffith Park GC (Harding Course)
California
George C. Thomas Jr
Griffith Park GC (Harding Course) (R. 9)
California
William H. Johnson
Griffith Park GC (Los Feliz Course)
Los Angeles, California
William H. Johnson
Griffith Park GC (Roosevelt Course)
Los Angeles, California
William H. Johnson
Griffith Park GC (Wilson Course)
Los Angeles, California
Tom Bendelow

Griffith Park GC (Wilson Course) (R)
California
George C. Thomas Jr
Griffith Park GC (Wilson Course) (R)
California
William H. Johnson
Griffiths Park GC
Akron, Ohio
Harold Paddock
Grigsby CC
Chicago, Illinois
C.D. Wagstaff
Grimball GC
Savannah, Georgia
Ron Kirby, Denis Griffiths
Grimsby GC
Lincolnshire, England
S.V. Hotchkin
Grimsby GC (R)
England
Tom Williamson
Grimsby GC (R)
England
Fred W. Hawtree
Grindstone Inn GC
Winter Harbor, Maine
Alex Findlay
Grosse Ile G&CC
Michigan
Donald Ross
Grosse Ile G&CC (R)
Michigan
Wilfrid Reid, William Connellan
Grosse Ile G&CC (R)
Michigan
Arthur Hills, Steve Forrest
Grossinger's GC
New York
Andrew Carl Salerno
Grossinger's GC (R)
New York
William F. Mitchell
Grossinger's GC (R)
New York
Joseph S. Finger
Grossinger's GC (A. 9)
New York
Joseph S. Finger
Grove City CC
Pennsylvania
Tom Bendelow
Grove Park GC
Jackson, Mississippi
Sonny Guy
Grove Park Inn CC
Asheville, North Carolina
Willie Park Jr
Groveport GC (A. 9)
Ohio
Jack Kidwell
Groveport GC (R)
Ohio
Jack Kidwell, Michael Hurdzan
Grover Cleveland Muni (R)
New York
Walter J. Travis
Grover Keaton Muni
Dallas, Texas
Dave Bennett
Grunow Estate GC
Lake Geneva, Wisconsin
Alfred F. Hackbarth
Guadalajara CC
Mexico
John Bredemus
Guadalajara CC (A. 9)
Mexico
John Bredemus
Guadalajara CC (R)
Mexico
Lawrence Hughes
Guataparo GC
Valencia, Venezuela
Joe Lee, Rocky Roquemore
Guggenheim Estate GC
New York
William Mackie
Guilford GC
British Columbia
Jack Reimer

Guilin-Lijiang G&CC
China
Ronald Fream
Gulf Harbors GC
New Port Richey, Florida
Don Rawley
Gulf Hills GC
Mississippi
Jack Daray
Gulf Hills GC (R)
Mississippi
Tom Clark
Gulf Shores GC
Alabama
Earl Stone
Gulf State Park GC
Gulf Shores, Alabama
Earl Stone
Gulfport Naval Air Station GC
Mississippi
Earl Stone
Gulfstream GC
Delray Beach, Florida
Donald Ross
Gulfstream GC (R)
Florida
Dick Wilson, Joe Lee
Gulfstream GC (R. 3)
Florida
Mark Mahannah
Gull Lake CC
Richland, Michigan
William F. Mitchell
Gull Lakeview GC (East Course)
Augusta, Michigan
Charles Darl Scott
Gull Lakeview GC (West Course)
Michigan
Charles Darl Scott
Gullane GC (Course No. 1)
East Lothian, Scotland
Willie Park
Gullane GC (Course No. 1) (R)
Scotland
Willie Park Jr
Gullane GC (Course No. 2)
East Lothian, Scotland
Willie Park Jr
Gullane GC (Course No. 3)
East Lothian, Scotland
Willie Park Jr
Gulmarg GC
Cashmere, India
Peter Thomson, Michael Wolveridge
Gulph Mills GC
King of Prussia, Pennsylvania
Donald Ross
Gulph Mills GC (R)
Pennsylvania
William S. Flynn
Gulph Mills GC (R)
Pennsylvania
Perry Maxwell
Gulph Mills GC (R)
Pennsylvania
Wayne Stiles
Gulph Mills GC (R)
Pennsylvania
J.B. McGovern
Gulph Mills GC (R. 7)
Pennsylvania
William Gordon, David Gordon
Gulph Mills GC (R. 4)
Pennsylvania
Robert Trent Jones
Gunpowder CC
Maryland
Robert Milligan
Gus Wortham Park GC
Houston, Texas
Willie Maquire
Gut Steinberg GC
West Germany
Bernhard von Limburger
Guthrie CC
Oklahoma
Alex Findlay
Guyen G&CC
Huntington, West Virginia
Herbert Strong
Guyen G&CC (R. 3)
West Virginia
X.G. Hassenplug

Gweedore GC (R)
Ireland
Eddie Hackett
GMG Hachioji GC
Japan
Y. Kawanami, M. Komatsubara
H. Smith Richardson GC
Connecticut
Hal Purdy, Malcolm Purdy
H. Smith Richardson Muni
Fairfield, Connecticut
Hal Purdy, Malcolm Purdy
H.P. Whitney Estate GC
Manhasset, New York
Charles Blair Macdonald, Seth Raynor
Haagsche G&CC
Netherlands
H.S. Colt, C.H. Alison, J.S.F. Morrison
Haagsche G&CC (R)
Netherlands
Sir Guy Campbell
Haagsche GC NLE
Netherlands
Tom Dunn
Haagsche GC (A. 9) NLE
Netherlands
J.F. Abercromby
Hacienda CC
La Habra, California
Max Behr
Hacienda CC (R)
California
William P. Bell
Hacienda CC (R)
California
George Von Elm
Hacienda CC (R. 2)
California
Ted Robinson
Hacienda CC (R)
California
Robert Trent Jones, Robert Trent Jones Jr
Hacienda CC (R)
California
Peter Thomson, Michael Wolveridge, Ronald Fream
Hacienda Hotel Par 3 GC
Bakersfield, California
Bob Baldock
Hacienda Hotel Par 3 GC NLE
Las Vegas, Nevada
Bob Baldock
Hacienda San Gaspar GC
Cuernavaca, Mexico
Joseph S. Finger
Hackberry Creek CC
Irving, Texas
Joseph S. Finger, Ken Dye
Hackensack CC NLE
New Jersey
Tom Bendelow
Hackensack CC
New Jersey
Charles Banks
Hadley Wood GC
Hertfordshire, England
Alister Mackenzie
Hagerstown CC
Maryland
Donald Ross
Hagerstown Muni
Maryland
Frank Murray, Russell Roberts
Haggin Oaks GC (North Course)
Sacramento, California
Michael J. McDonagh
Haggin Oaks Muni (South Course)
Sacramento, California
Alister Mackenzie
Haggs Castle GC (R)
Scotland
Peter Alliss, David Thomas
Haig Point GC
Daufuskie Island, South Carolina
Rees Jones
Hainault Forest GC (Course No. 1)
Essex, England
J.H. Taylor

Hainault Forest GC (Course No. 1) (A. 9)
England
F.G. Hawtree, J.H. Taylor
Hainault Forest GC (Course No. 2)
Essex, England
John R. Stutt
Hakone CC
Kanagawa, Japan
Shiro Akaboshi
Haleakala Ranch GC NLE
Maui, Hawaii
Charles Dole
Half Moon Bay CC
California
Frank Duane, Arnold Palmer
Half Moon-Rose Hall GC
Montego Bay, Jamaica
Robert Trent Jones, Frank Duane
Half Sinke GC now known as Crossings G&CC
Halie Plantation GC
Gainesville, Florida
Joe Lee
Halifax Bradley Hall GC
Yorkshire, England
J.J.F. Pennink, D.M.A. Steel
Halifax CC
Massachusetts
Phil Wogan
Halifax G&CC (New Ashburn)
Nova Scotia
Geoffrey S. Cornish, William G. Robinson
Halifax G&CC (Old Ashburn)
Nova Scotia
Stanley Thompson
Hall's Head Resort GC
Mandurah, Australia
Peter Thomson, Michael Wolveridge
Halloud Muni (A. 9)
Virginia
Russell Breeden
Hallowes GC
Yorkshire, England
George Duncan
Halmstad GC
Sweden
Rafael Sundblom
Halmstad GC (R)
Sweden
J.J.F. Pennink
Halmstad GC (A. 9)
Sweden
J.J.F. Pennink
Ham Manor GC
Sussex, England
H.S. Colt, C.H. Alison, J.S.F. Morrison
Hamburg-Ahrensburg GC
Hamburg, West Germany
Bernhard von Limburger
Hamburg-Ahrensburg GC (R)
West Germany
Robert Trent Jones, Cabell Robinson
Hamburg-Falkenstein GC (R)
West Germany
Bernhard von Limburger
Hamburg-Waldorfer GC
Hoisbuettel, West Germany
Bernhard von Limburger
Hamburg-Waldorfer GC (R)
West Germany
Bernhard von Limburger
Hamburger GC
Luneburger Heide, West Germany
Herbert E. Gaertner
Hamburger Land und GC
West Germany
H.S. Colt, C.H. Alison, J.S.F. Morrison
Hamilton County GC
Ohio
Tom Bendelow
Hamilton CC
Montana
Gregor MacMillan
Hamilton CC (A. 9)
Montana
Edward A. Hunnicutt

Hamilton CC
Ohio
Donald Ross
Hamilton G&CC
Ancaster, Ontario
H.S. Colt
Hamilton G&CC (R)
Ontario
William H. Diddel
Hamilton G&CC (A. 9)
Ontario
Clinton E. Robinson
Hamilton G&CC (R)
Ontario
Rees Jones
Hamilton G&CC (Ladies 9)
Ancaster, Ontario
H.S. Colt
Hamilton GC
St. Andrews, New Zealand
F.G. Hood, Harry T. Gillies, Arthur D.S. Duncan
Hamilton GC
Lanarkshire, Scotland
James Braid, John R. Stutt
Hamilton Lakes CC
Chimney Rock, North Carolina
Wayne Stiles, John Van Kleek
Hamilton Muni
Evansville, Indiana
William H. Diddel
Hamilton Muni
Ohio
William H. Diddel
Hamlet of Delray Beach GC
Florida
Joe Lee, Rocky Roquemore
Hammamatsu CC
Japan
Peter Thomson, Michael Wolveridge
Hammersley Hill GC
Pawling, New York
William F. Mitchell
Hammock CC
Larchmont, New York
Nicholas Demane
Hammond CC
Indiana
Tom Bendelow
Hampden CC
Massachusetts
Al Zikorus
Hampshire CC
Dowagiac, Michigan
Edward Lawrence Packard
Hampshire CC
Mamaroneck, New York
Devereux Emmet, Alfred H. Tull
Hampshire CC (R)
New York
Edmund B. Ault
Hampshire CC (R. 4)
New York
Frank Duane
Hampstead GC
England
Tom Dunn
Hampstead GC at Lido
Long Beach, New York
Robert Trent Jones, Frank Duane
Hampton GC
New York
Frank Duane
Hampton GC formerly known as Hampton Rhodes GC
Virginia
Donald Ross
Hampton GC (R)
Virginia
Edmund B. Ault
Hampton Muni GC
Rochester, Michigan
William Newcomb
Hampton Rhodes GC now known as Hampton GC
Hana Ranch G Park (R. 3)
Hawaii
Robin Nelson
Hanayashiki GC (Hirono Course)
Hyogo, Japan
R. Shimaumura

Hanayashiki GC (Yokawa Course)
Hyogo, Japan
O. Ueda
Hancock Muni NLE
New York
Robert Trent Jones
Handsworth GC (R)
England
H.S. Colt
Hangman Valley Muni
Spokane, Washington
Bob Baldock, Robert L. Baldock
Hankley Common GC (A. 9)
England
James Braid
Hankley Common GC (R. 9)
England
James Braid
Hannastown CC
Greensburg, Pennsylvania
Emil Loeffler, *John McGlynn*
Hannibal CC NLE
Missouri
Tom Bendelow
Hanno GC
Saitama, Japan
Ichisuke Izumi
Hanover CC
Dartmouth College, New Hampshire
Ralph Barton
Hanover CC (R)
New Hampshire
Orrin Smith, William F. Mitchell
Hanover CC (R)
New Hampshire
Geoffrey S. Cornish, William G. Robinson
Hanover CC (R)
Pennsylvania
William Gordon
Hanover CC (R)
Pennsylvania
Ferdinand Garbin
Hanover CC
Ashland, Virginia
Jim Reynolds
Hanover GC
Garbson, West Germany
Herbert E. Gaertner
Hanover GC (R)
West Germany
Karl Hoffmann, Bernhard von Limburger
Happy Acres CC
Webster, New York
James Gilmore Harrison, Ferdinand Garbin
Happy Hollow C
Omaha, Nebraska
William B. Langford, Theodore J. Moreau
Happy Hollow C (R)
Nebraska
James L. Holmes
Happy Hollow C (R)
Nebraska
William H. Diddel
Happy Hollow C (R)
Nebraska
David Gill
Happy Hunting C
Lenexa, Kansas
Bob Dunning
Happy Valley CC
Wilson, North Carolina
Willard Byrd
Harbor City Muni
Eau Gaullie, Florida
R. Albert Anderson
Harbor City Muni (R)
Florida
Bill Amick
Harbor Hills CC
Port Jefferson, New York
Alfred H. Tull
Harbor Park GC
Wilmington, California
William H. Johnson
Harbor Point GC (A. 3)
Michigan
David Gill

Harbor Point GC (R.15)
Michigan
David Gill
Harborne Church Farm GC
Birmingham, England
F.G. Hawtree, J.H. Taylor
Harborne GC (R)
England
H.S. Colt
Harbour Pointe GC
New Bern, North Carolina
Rees Jones, Keith Evans
Harbour Ridge CC (Golden Marsh Course)
Stuart, Florida
Joe Lee
Harbour Town G Links
Hilton Head Island, South Carolina
Pete Dye, Alice Dye, Jack Nicklaus
Harbour Town G Links (R)
South Carolina
Pete Dye
Harbour Trees GC
Noblesville, Indiana
Pete Dye, David Pfaff
Harder Hall Hotel GC
Sebring, Florida
Dick Wilson, Joe Lee
Harder Hall Hotel GC (R)
Florida
Gordon G. Lewis
Harding Park GC
San Francisco, California
William Watson
Harding Park GC (R)
California
Jack Fleming
Harding Park GC (Fleming Nine)
San Francisco, California
Jack Fleming
Hardscrabble CC
Fort Smith, Arkansas
Herman Hackbarth
Hardscrabble CC (R)
Arkansas
James L. Holmes
Hardscrabble CC (R)
Arkansas
Marvin Ferguson
Harewood GC
Christchurch, New Zealand
John Harris, Peter Thomson, Michael Wolveridge
Harker Heights Muni
Texas
Leon Howard
Harkers Hollow GC
Phillipsburg, New Jersey
Robert White
Harlem GC NLE
Forest Park, Illinois
Tom Bendelow
Harlem Hills CC
Rockford, Illinois
Harry Collis
Harlingen CC
Texas
Leon Howard
Harlingen CC (R)
Texas
Dick Nugent
Harlingen Muni NLE
Texas
John Bredemus
Harlington Muni
Texas
Dennis W. Arp
Harmon CC
Lebanon, New York
A.W. Tillinghast
Harmony Farm CC NLE
Jane Lew, West Virginia
Arthur Jack Snyder
Harmony Landing CC
Goshen, Kentucky
Hal Purdy
Harney's GC
Falmouth, Massachusetts
Paul Harney
Harold Lloyd Estate GC NLE
Beverly Hills, California
Alister Mackenzie

Harpenden GC
Hertfordshire, England
F.G. Hawtree, J.H. Taylor
Harrington G&CC
Washington
Robert Dean Putnam
Harrison GC
Harrison Hotel, British Columbia
Norman H. Woods
Harrison Heights GC NLE
Omaha, Nebraska
Henry C. Glissmann, Harold Glissmann
Harrison Hills CC
Attica, Indiana
William B. Langford, Theodore J. Moreau
Harrison Lake GC
Columbus, Indiana
Bob Simmons
Harrison Williams Private Course
Bayville, New York
Devereux Emmet, Alfred H. Tull
Harrogate GC
Yorkshire, England
Sandy Herd, George Duncan
Harrogate GC (R)
England
George Duncan
Harrogate GC (R)
England
Alister Mackenzie
Harrow School GC
Middlesex, England
J.J.F. Pennink, D.M.A. Steel
Harry Brownson CC
Shelton, Connecticut
Edward Ryder, *Val Carlson*
Harry Greens GC
Prospect, Connecticut
Al Zikorus
Harsens Island GC
Michigan
Wilfrid Reid, William Connellan
Hartepool GC
Durham, England
Willie Park Jr
Hartford CC (R. 9)
Wisconsin
Ken Killian, Dick Nugent
Hartford CC (A. 9)
Wisconsin
Ken Killian, Dick Nugent
Hartford Estate GC
Charleston, South Carolina
Wayne Stiles
Hartford GC
West Hartford, Connecticut
Donald Ross
Hartford GC (R)
Connecticut
Orrin Smith, William F. Mitchell
Hartford GC (R)
Connecticut
William Gordon, David Gordon
Hartford GC (R)
Connecticut
Robert Trent Jones
Hartford GC (R. 2)
Connecticut
Geoffrey S. Cornish, William G. Robinson
Hartsbourne CC
Hertfordshire, England
F.G. Hawtree, Fred W. Hawtree
Hartwellville CC NLE
Vermont
William S. Flynn
Harve des Isles GC
Montreal, Quebec
Howard Watson
Harve Elks CC (R)
Montana
William H. Diddel
Harz GC
Bad Harzburg, West Germany
Bernhard von Limburger
Hastings and St. Leonards GC
England
Tom Dunn
Hastings CC
Michigan
Jack Daray

Hastings CC
Minnesota
Paul Coates
Hastings CC (R)
Minnesota
Don Herfort
Hastings GC
Sussex, England
J.J.F. Pennink
Hastings GC NLE
Sussex, England
Tom Dunn
Hastings GC (R)
New Zealand
Peter Thomson, Michael
  Wolveridge
Hat Island G&CC
Washington
William Teufel
Hatch Point CC
Victoria, British Columbia
William G. Robinson
Hatchford Brook Muni
Birmingham, England
Fred W. Hawtree
Hatherly CC (A. 3)
Massachusetts
Samuel Mitchell
Hatherly CC (R. 2)
Massachusetts
Samuel Mitchell
Hattiesburg CC
Mississippi
Press Maxwell
Haulover Beach GC
Miami, Florida
Mark Mahannah
Havana Biltmore GC
Cuba
Donald Ross
Havana Biltmore GC (R)
Cuba
Mark Mahannah
Havana CC
Florida
Bill Amick
Haven CC
Green Valley, Arizona
Arthur Jack Snyder
Havenhurst GC
New Haven, Indiana
Robert Beard
Haverhill CC
Massachusetts
Wayne Stiles, John Van Kleek
Hawaii CC
Honolulu, Hawaii
Red Uldrick
**Hawaii Kai CC (Championship
  Course)**
Honolulu, Hawaii
William F. Bell
**Hawaii Kai CC (Executive
  Course)**
Honolulu, Hawaii
Robert Trent Jones
**Hawaii Kai CC (Executive
  Course) (R)**
Hawaii
William F. Bell
Hawk Creek GC
Neskowin, Oregon
Harold Schlicting
Hawk Valley GC
Bowmansville, Pennsylvania
William Gordon, David Gordon
Hawk's Nest G&CC
Vero Beach, Florida
George Fazio, *Jim Fazio*
Hawkhurst G & CC
Kent, England
J.J.F. Pennink
Hawthorn Ridge GC
Aledo, Illinois
William James Spear
Hawthorne CC
Maryland
Edmund B. Ault, Al Jamison
Hawthorne Hills CC
Indianapolis, Indiana
William H. Diddel
Hawthorne Hills CC
Lima, Ohio
Harold Paddock

Hawthorne Valley CC
Cleveland, Ohio
Donald Ross, Walter Hatch
Hawthorne Valley G&CC
Mississauga, Ontario
Clinton E. Robinson, Robert
  Moote
Hayana International GC
Japan
Willard Wilkinson
Hayling GC (R)
England
Tom Simpson
Haystack CC NLE
Wilmington, Vermont
Desmond Muirhead
Hayston GC
Glasgow, Scotland
James Braid, John R. Stutt
Hayward GC
California
Dick Fry
Hazelden CC
Indiana
Tom Bendelow
Hazelhead Muni (Course No. 1)
Aberdeen, Scotland
Alister Mackenzie
Hazelhead Muni (Course No. 2)
Aberdeen, Scotland
Brian Huggett, Neil Coles
Hazeltine National GC
Chaska, Minnesota
Robert Trent Jones
Hazeltine National GC (R)
Minnesota
Robert Trent Jones, Roger
  Rulewich
Headingley GC
Leeds, England
Willie Park
Headingley GC (R)
England
Alister Mackenzie
Heart River GC (A. 9)
North Dakota
Dick Phelps, Brad Benz, Mike
  Poellot
Heart River GC (R. 9)
North Dakota
Dick Phelps, Brad Benz, Mike
  Poellot
Hearthstone CC
Houston, Texas
Jay Riviere
Heartwell GC
Long Beach, California
William F. Bell
Heath GC (R)
Ireland
Eddie Hackett
Heather Farms GC
Walnut Creek, California
Bob Baldock
Heather Gardens CC
Aurora, Colorado
Dick Phelps
Heather Glen GC
Little River, South Carolina
Willard Byrd, Clyde Johnston
Heather Highlands GC
Holly, Michigan
Robert Bruce Harris
Heather Hills CC
Indianapolis, Indiana
Pete Dye, Alice Dye
Heather Hills GC
Florida
R. Albert Anderson
Heather Ridge CC
Aurora, Colorado
Dick Phelps
Heatherwood GC
Birmingham, Alabama
Arthur Davis
Heaton Park GC
Lancashire, England
J.H. Taylor
Hecla GC
Manitoba
John A. Thompson
Hedeland GC
Denmark
Jan Sederholm

Heidelberg CC
Pennsylvania
John H. Guenther Jr
Heidelberg G & Sports C
West Germany
Bernhard von Limburger
Heidelberg G & Sports C (R)
West Germany
Donald Harradine
Height Park CC
Davis, Oregon
Ernest Schneiter
Helensburgh GC
Scotland
Old Tom Morris
Helfrich Muni
Indiana
Tom Bendelow
Heliopolis Sporting C
Cairo, Egypt
J.H. Taylor
Hell's Point GC
Virginia Beach, Virginia
Rees Jones, Keith Evans
Helsingor GC
Denmark
Anders Amilon
Helsingor GC (R)
Denmark
Jorn Larsen
Helsinki GC
Sweden
Ture Bruce
Hemet West GC
Hemet, California
Harry Rainville
Hemlock Springs GC
Harpersfield, Ohio
Ben W. Zink
Hempstead CC
New York
Peter W. Lees
Hempstead CC (A. 9)
New York
A.W. Tillinghast
Hempstead CC
Texas
Leon Howard
Henbury GC (R)
England
F.G. Hawtree
Hendaye GC
France
John Duncan Dunn
Henderson CC (R. 9)
North Carolina
Gene Hamm
Henderson CC (A. 9)
North Carolina
Gene Hamm
Henderson G&CC
Kentucky
William B. Langford, Theodore J.
  Moreau
Henderson Lake GC
Lethbridge, Alberta
Norman H. Woods
Hendersonville CC
North Carolina
Donald Ross
Hendon GC
Middlesex, England
Willie Park, Willie Park Jr
Hendon GC (R)
England
H.S. Colt
Hendry Isles GC
Moore Haven, Florida
B. Dudley Gray
Henley GC
England
James Braid
**Henry F. DuPont Private Course
  (R)**
Delaware
Devereux Emmet, Alfred H. Tull
Henson Creek GC
Maryland
Edmund B. Ault
Hercules CC
Wilmington, Delaware
Alfred H. Tull

Hercules CC (A. 9)
Delaware
Alfred H. Tull
Hercules CC (A. 9)
Delaware
Alfred H. Tull
Hercules Powder C (R)
Delaware
William S. Flynn
Heretaunga GC
Wellington, New Zealand
Alister Mackenzie
Heritage GC
Pawley's Island, South Carolina
Dan Maples
Heritage Harbour GC
Maryland
Tom Clark, Brian Ault, Edmund
  B. Ault
Heritage Hills of Westchester
Somers, New York
Geoffrey S. Cornish, William G.
  Robinson
**Heritage Hills of Westchester (A.
  9)**
New York
Geoffrey S. Cornish
Heritage Hills GC
Lakeville, Massachusetts
Geoffrey S. Cornish, William G.
  Robinson
Heritage Hills GC
McCook, Nebraska
Dick Phelps, Brad Benz
Heritage Hills GC
Claremore, Oklahoma
Don Sechrest
Heritage Ridge GC
Stuart, Florida
Ted McAnlis
Heritage Ridge GC (R. 9)
Florida
Chuck Ankrom
Heritage Ridge GC (A. 9)
Florida
Chuck Ankrom
Heritage Village CC
Southbury, Connecticut
Al Zikorus
Heritage Village CC (A. 9)
Connecticut
Theodore Manning
Hermann Park GC
Houston, Texas
John Bredemus
Hermann Park GC (R. 9)
Texas
Ralph Plummer
Hermitage CC
Richmond, Virginia
A.W. Tillinghast
Hermitage CC (R)
Virginia
Donald Ross
Hermitage CC (R)
Virginia
David Gordon
Hermitage CC (A. 9)
Virginia
Edmund B. Ault
Hermitage CC (R)
Virginia
Edmund B. Ault
Hermitage GC
Old Hickory, Tennessee
Gary Roger Baird
Hermitage GC (R)
Ireland
Eddie Hackett
Hermitage Woods GC
Nashville, Tennessee
James King
Herndon Centennial Muni
Virginia
Edmund B. Ault
Herrenalb-Bernbach GC
West Germany
Bernhard von Limburger
Herring Run CC
Taunton, Massachusetts
Eugene "Skip" Wogan
Hershey CC (East Course)
Pennsylvania
George Fazio

Hershey CC (West Course)
Pennsylvania
Maurice McCarthy
Hershey Pocono GC
White Haven, Pennsylvania
Geoffrey S. Cornish, William G.
  Robinson
Hershey's Mill GC
Malvern, Pennsylvania
David Gordon
Hesperia G&CC
California
William F. Bell
Hessle GC
England
Peter Alliss, David Thomas
Hesston Muni
Kansas
Frank Hummel
Hexham GC (R)
England
C.K. Cotton, J.J.F. Pennink
Heysham GC
Lancashire, England
Sandy Herd, F.G. Hawtree
Heythrop College GC
England
Tom Simpson
Hi Cedars GC
Orting, Washington
Roy L. Goss, *Glen Proctor*
Hi-Line GC
Goshen College, Indiana
John Ingold
Hiawatha CC (R)
New York
William F. Mitchell
Hiawatha GC
Mt. Vernon, Ohio
Jack Kidwell
Hickleton GC
Yorkshire, England
Brian Huggett, Neil Coles, *Roger
  Dyer*
Hickman AFB GC
Oahu, Hawaii
Bob Baldock, Robert L. Baldock
Hickman AFB GC (R)
Hawaii
Robin Nelson
Hickman GC
Wayne, New Jersey
Hal Purdy
Hickory Flat GC
West Lafayette, Ohio
Jack Kidwell
Hickory Grove CC
Fennimore, Wisconsin
William James Spear
Hickory Hill GC
Lawrence, Massachusetts
Manny Francis
Hickory Hills CC
Palos Park, Illinois
James Foulis
Hickory Hills CC (A. 9)
Illinois
William B. Langford
Hickory Hills CC (A)
Illinois
C.D. Wagstaff
Hickory Hills CC
Liberty, Kentucky
Buck Blankenship
Hickory Hills CC
Grand Rapids, Michigan
Mark DeVries
Hickory Hills CC
Gautier, Mississippi
Earl Stone
Hickory Hills CC (R)
Missouri
Bob Dunning
Hickory Hills CC (R)
Missouri
Edmund B. Ault
Hickory Hills CC
Georgesville, Ohio
Jack Kidwell, Michael Hurdzan
Hickory Hills GC (R. 9)
Michigan
William Newcomb

Hickory Hills GC (A. 9)
Michigan
William Newcomb

Hickory Knob State Park GC
McCormack, South Carolina
Tom Jackson

Hickory Point GC
Decatur, Illinois
Edward Lawrence Packard

Hickory Ridge CC
Amherst, Massachusetts
Geoffrey S. Cornish, William G. Robinson

Hidden Creek CC
Virginia
Edmund B. Ault

Hidden Greens GC
Hastings, Minnesota
Joel Goldstrand

Hidden Hills CC
Jacksonville, Florida
David Gordon

Hidden Hills CC (R)
Florida
Arnold Palmer, Ed Seay, Bob Walker

Hidden Hills CC
Stone Mountain, Georgia
Joe Lee, Rocky Roquemore

Hidden Hills GC
Austin, Texas
Arnold Palmer, Ed Seay

Hidden Lake GC
Osage Beach, Missouri
Robert von Hagge

Hidden Lakes CC
Derby, Kansas
Floyd Farley

Hidden Valley C
Gaylord, Michigan
William H. Diddel

Hidden Valley CC
Reno, Nevada
William F. Bell

Hidden Valley CC
Willow Springs, North Carolina
Henry Dupree

Hidden Valley CC
Reading, Pennsylvania
James Gilmore Harrison

Hidden Valley CC
Pittsburgh, Pennsylvania
Edmund B. Ault

Hidden Valley CC (R. 9)
Pennsylvania
James Gilmore Harrison, Ferdinand Garbin

Hidden Valley CC (A. 9)
Pennsylvania
James Gilmore Harrison, Ferdinand Garbin

Hidden Valley CC (R)
Pennsylvania
Joe Lee

Hidden Valley CC NLE
Salt Lake City, Utah
William P. Bell

Hidden Valley CC
Draper, Utah
William F. Bell

Hidden Valley CC (A. 9)
Utah
William H. Neff, William Howard Neff

Hidden Valley CC
Salem, Virginia
Dick Wilson

Hidden Valley GC
Boca Raton, Florida
Pat Pattison

Hidden Valley GC
Miami, Florida
Bob Cupp

Hidden Valley GC
Lawrenceburg, Indiana
Jack Kidwell, Michael Hurdzan

Hidden Valley GC
Eureka, Missouri
Tim Boyd

Hidden Valley GC (A. 9)
Missouri
Tim Boyd

Hidden Valley GC
New Philadelphia, Ohio
James Gilmore Harrison, Ferdinand Garbin

Hidden Valley GC
Cottage Grove, Oregon
Ray Vincent

Hidden Valley GC
Pottstown, Pennsylvania
James Gilmore Harrison, Ferdinand Garbin

Hidden Valley GC
Edmonton, Alberta
Ron Garl

Hidden Valley GC
Ontario
Clinton E. Robinson

Hidden Valley Lake GC
California
William F. Bell

Hideaway CC
Fort Myers, Florida
Ron Garl

Hideout GC
Lake Ariel, Pennsylvania
Bob Baldock

Higashi Ibaragi CC
Ibaragi, Japan
Arthur Hills

Higashi Matsuyama GC
Saitama, Japan
Kinya Fujita

Higby Hills CC
Utica, New York
Geoffrey S. Cornish, William G. Robinson

High Elms GC
Kent, England
Fred W. Hawtree, Martin Hawtree

High Hampton Inn GC (R)
North Carolina
George W. Cobb

High Meadows GC
Roaring Gap, North Carolina
George W. Cobb

High Meadows GC (R)
North Carolina
John LaFoy

High Mountain CC
Franklin Lakes, New Jersey
Alec Ternyei

High Point CC
Naples, Florida
David Wallace

High Post GC
Wiltshire, England
F.G. Hawtree, J.H. Taylor

High Ridge CC (R. 2)
Connecticut
William F. Mitchell, Al Zikorus

High Ridge CC
Boynton Beach, Florida
Joe Lee

High Ridge GC (R)
Connecticut
William F. Mitchell

High Vista CC
Arden, North Carolina
Tom Jackson

Highgate GC (R)
England
C.S. Butchart

Highland Burne GC NLE
Michigan
Warner Bowen

Highland CC
LaGrange, Georgia
Donald Ross

Highland CC (A. 9)
Georgia
Joseph S. Finger

Highland CC NLE
Fort Thomas, Kentucky
Tom Bendelow

Highland CC
Fort Thomas, Kentucky
William H. Diddel

Highland CC (R)
Kentucky
Willard Byrd

Highland CC (R)
Kentucky
Edmund B. Ault

Highland CC (A. 9)
Kentucky
Arthur Hills, Steve Forrest, Mike Dasher

Highland CC
Omaha, Nebraska
William B. Langford, Theodore J. Moreau

Highland CC (R)
Nebraska
David Gill

Highland CC
Fayetteville, North Carolina
Donald Ross

Highland CC
Pittsburgh, Pennsylvania
Emil Loeffler, *John McGlynn*

Highland CC (R)
Pennsylvania
James Gilmore Harrison

Highland CC (R)
Pennsylvania
Ferdinand Garbin

Highland CC (R)
Pennsylvania
Ferdinand Garbin

Highland CC (A. 3)
Pennsylvania
Ferdinand Garbin

Highland G&CC NLE
Indianapolis, Indiana
Tom Bendelow

Highland G&CC
Indianapolis, Indiana
Willie Park Jr, William H. Diddel

Highland Greens GC
Connecticut
Al Zikorus

Highland GC
Grand Rapids, Michigan
Donald Ross

Highland GC
Tacoma, Washington
Ted Robinson

Highland GC
London, Ontario
Stanley Thompson

Highland Hills GC
Dewitt, Michigan
Bruce Matthews, Jerry Matthews

Highland Hills Muni (A. 9)
Colorado
Frank Hummel

Highland Lake Estates GC
Jackson, Mississippi
Ward Northrup

Highland Lake GC
Richmond, Indiana
Bob Simmons

Highland Lakes GC
Palm Harbor, Florida
Lloyd Clifton

Highland Lakes GC
Kingsland, Texas
Leon Howard

Highland Links
Norfolk, Virginia
Luther O. "Luke" Morris

Highland Meadows CC
Sylvania, Ohio
Sandy Alves

Highland Meadows CC (R)
Ohio
Arthur Hills

Highland Muni
Pocatello, Idaho
Perley A. Hill

Highland Park C
Lake Wales, Florida
Wayne Stiles, John Van Kleek

Highland Park CC (A. 9)
New York
Geoffrey S. Cornish, William G. Robinson

Highland Park GC
Birmingham, Alabama
Wayne Stiles, John Van Kleek

Highland Park GC (R. 3)
Illinois
William B. Langford, Theodore J. Moreau

Highland Park GC (R. 5)
Illinois
Ken Killian, Dick Nugent

Highland Park GC
Mason City, Iowa
David Gill

Highland Park GC
Grand Rapids, Michigan
Tom Bendelow

Highland Park GC (A. 9)
Minnesota
Donald G. Brauer, Emile Perret

Highland Park GC (Blue Course)
Ohio
Sandy Alves

Highland Park GC (Red Course)
Ohio
Sandy Alves

Highland Springs CC
Rock Island, Illinois
William James Spear

Highland Springs CC
Ohio
Harold Paddock

Highland Springs GC
Wellsburg, Pennsylvania
James Gilmore Harrison, Ferdinand Garbin

Highland Woods GC
Hoffman Estates, Illinois
William James Spear

Highlands CC
North Carolina
Donald Ross

Highlands Falls CC
Highlands, North Carolina
Bill Amick

Highlands Falls CC (R. 5)
North Carolina
Joe Lee, Rocky Roquemore

Highlands Falls CC (A.13)
North Carolina
Joe Lee, Rocky Roquemore

Highlands GC
Edmonton, Alberta
William Brinkworth

Highwoods GC
Bexhill-on-Sea, England
F.G. Hawtree, J.H. Taylor

Hilaman Park GC
Tallahassee, Florida
Edward Lawrence Packard, Roger Packard

Hilands GC
Billings, Montana
Norman H. Woods, Gregor MacMillan

Hill Barn GC
Sussex, England
F.G. Hawtree, J.H. Taylor

Hill Crest CC (A. 9)
Pennsylvania
James Gilmore Harrison

Hill Muni
Chickasha, Oklahoma
Donald Sparks

Hill Valley G&CC
England
Peter Alliss, David Thomas

Hillandale CC
Trumbull, Connecticut
Al Zikorus

Hillandale CC
Durham, North Carolina
Donald Ross

Hillandale CC (R)
North Carolina
George W. Cobb

Hillandale GC
Huntington, New York
Hal Purdy

Hillcrest Acres GC
Barrington, Illinois
David Gill

Hillcrest CC
Los Angeles, California
William Watson

Hillcrest CC (A. 9)
California
William F. Bell, William P. Bell

Hillcrest CC (R. 6)
California
Robert Muir Graves

Hillcrest CC (R. 9)
Colorado
Henry B. Hughes

Hillcrest CC (R. 9)
Colorado
Henry B. Hughes

Hillcrest CC
Boise, Idaho
A. Vernon Macan

Hillcrest CC (A. 9)
Idaho
A. Vernon Macan

Hillcrest CC (R. 6)
Idaho
Robert Muir Graves

Hillcrest CC
Long Grove, Illinois
Robert Bruce Harris

Hillcrest CC (R)
Illinois
Ken Killian, Dick Nugent

Hillcrest CC
Indianapolis, Indiana
William H. Diddel

Hillcrest CC
Kansas City, Missouri
Donald Ross

Hillcrest CC (R. 4)
Missouri
Marvin Ferguson

Hillcrest CC (R. 1)
Missouri
Bill Amick

Hillcrest CC
Lincoln, Nebraska
William H. Tucker, Gregor MacMillan

Hillcrest CC NLE
Cincinnati, Ohio
William B. Langford, Theodore J. Moreau

Hillcrest CC
Bartlesville, Oklahoma
Perry Maxwell

Hillcrest CC (R. 9)
Oklahoma
Floyd Farley

Hillcrest CC (R)
Oklahoma
Don Sechrest

Hillcrest CC
Pennsylvania
Emil Loeffler, *John McGlynn*

Hillcrest CC (A. 9)
Pennsylvania
James Gilmore Harrison

Hillcrest CC
Lubbock, Texas
Ralph Plummer

Hillcrest East GC
Florida
Mark Mahannah

Hillcrest G&CC
Hollywood, Florida
Robert von Hagge

Hillcrest G&CC
Batesville, Indiana
D. Robertson Smith

Hillcrest G&CC (R. 9)
Indiana
William H. Diddel

Hillcrest G&CC (R. 9)
Indiana
Michael Hurdzan, Jack Kidwell

Hillcrest G&CC (A. 9)
South Dakota
Homer Fieldhouse

Hillcrest GC
Sun City West, Arizona
Jeff Hardin, Greg Nash, *John W. Meeker, Tom Ryan*

Hillcrest GC
Washington, Illinois
Al Linkogel

Hillcrest GC (R)
Saskatchewan
Stanley Thompson

Hillcrest Muni
Coffeyville, Kansas
Smiley Bell

Hillcrest Muni
Owensboro, Kentucky
Alex McKay

Hilldale GC
Hoffman Estates, Illinois
Robert Trent Jones, Roger Rulewich

Hillendale CC
Phoenix, Maryland
William Gordon, David Gordon
Hillendale CC (R)
Maryland
Edmund B. Ault
Hillendale CC (R)
Maryland
George Fazio
Hillerod GC (A. 9)
Denmark
Jan Sederholm
Hillerod GC (R. 9)
Denmark
Jan Sederholm
Hillman's GC
New Jersey
Geoffrey S. Cornish
Hillmoor CC
Lake Geneva, Wisconsin
James Foulis
Hills of Lakeway Golf Academy
Lakeway, Texas
Jack Nicklaus, Jay Morrish, Bob
Cupp, Scott Miller
Hills of Lakeway GC
Lakeway, Texas
Jack Nicklaus, Jay Morrish, Bob
Cupp, Scott Miller
Hillsboro CC
Boca Raton, Florida
*W.C. Nicolaysen, Mark M.
Nicolaysen*
Hillsboro CC (R. 9)
Illinois
Edward Lawrence Packard
Hillsboro CC (A. 9)
Illinois
Edward Lawrence Packard
Hillsborough GC
Yorkshire, England
Tom Williamson
Hillsdale G&CC
Michigan
Tom Bendelow
Hillsdale G&CC (R. 9)
Michigan
Harold Paddock
Hillsdale G&CC (A. 9)
Michigan
Harold Paddock
Hillsdale G&CC (R)
Michigan
Arthur Ham
Hillsdale G&CC (Dale Course)
St. Therese, Quebec
Howard Watson
**Hillsdale G&CC (Dale Course)
(R. 1)**
Quebec
John Watson
Hillsdale G&CC (Hill Course)
St. Therese, Quebec
Howard Watson
**Hillsdale G&CC (Hill Course)
(R. 1)**
Quebec
John Watson
Hillsdale GC
Bellwood, Illinois
Tom Bendelow
Hillsgrove GC
Rhode Island
Geoffrey S. Cornish
Hillside G&TC NLE
Plainfield, New Jersey
Tom Bendelow
Hillside GC (A. 9)
England
Fred W. Hawtree
Hillside GC (R. 9)
England
Fred W. Hawtree
Hillside Muni NLE
Illinois
Tom Bendelow
Hillsview GC (A. 9)
California
Richard Bigler
Hillsview GC
Pierre, South Dakota
Charles Maddox

Hilltop & Manwood Farm GC
Birmingham, England
Fred W. Hawtree, Martin
Hawtree
Hilltop GC (R)
Ohio
Ferdinand Garbin
Hilltop Lakes GC
Normangee, Texas
Ralph Plummer
Hilltop Lakes GC (A. 9)
Texas
Leon Howard
Hillview CC
Indiana
Bob Simmons
Hillview CC
North Reading, Massachusetts
William F. Mitchell
Hillwood CC
Nashville, Tennessee
Bubber Johnson
Hillwood CC (A. 9)
Tennessee
Bubber Johnson
Hilly Dale CC
Carmel, New York
Orrin Smith
Hilo Muni
Hawaii
Willard Wilkinson
**Hilton Park GC (Allender
Course)**
Dunbarton, Scotland
James Braid, John R. Stutt
Hilton Park GC (Hilton Course)
Scotland
F.G. Hawtree, J.H. Taylor
Hilversum GC
Netherlands
John Duncan Dunn
Himmerland GC
Sweden
Jan Sederholm
Hinckley Hills GC
Hinckley, Ohio
Harold Paddock
Hindman Park GC
Little Rock, Arkansas
Leon Howard
Hinsdale GC
Illinois
Donald Ross
Hinsdale GC (R)
Illinois
Edward Lawrence Packard,
Roger Packard
Hinsdale Par 3 GC
Illinois
Edward Lawrence Packard
Hirona CC
Japan
C.H. Alison
Hirsch Creek CC
Kitimat, British Columbia
Norman H. Woods
Hiwan GC
Evergreen, Colorado
Press Maxwell
Hob Nob Hill GC NLE
Salisbury, Connecticut
Devereux Emmet, Alfred H. Tull
Hobart CC
Oklahoma
Bob Dunning
Hobbit's Glen GC
Columbia, Maryland
Edmund B. Ault
Hobble Creek GC
Springville, Utah
William F. Bell
Hobbs CC (A. 9)
New Mexico
Warren Cantrell
Hobbs CC (R. 9)
New Mexico
Warren Cantrell
Hobe Sound CC
Florida
Ernest E. Smith
Hodge Park Muni
Kansas City, Missouri
Larry Runyon, Michael H. Malyn

Hodogayo CC
Yokohama, Japan
Walter Fovargue
Hodogayo CC (R)
Japan
Rokuro Akaboshi, Shiro Akaboshi
Hog Back Mountain C NLE
Tryon, North Carolina
Devereux Emmet, Alfred H. Tull
Hog Neck GC
Easton, Maryland
Lindsay Ervin
Hogan Park GC (A. 9)
Texas
Ron Kirby, Denis Griffiths
Hohenstauffen GC
Goppingen, West Germany
Donald Harradine
Hokkaido CC (Ohnuma Course)
Japan
Robert Trent Jones Jr
Holden GC (R)
Massachusetts
William F. Mitchell
Holdrege CC (A. 9)
Nebraska
Jeff Brauer
Hole-in-the-Wall GC
Naples, Florida
Dick Wilson, Joe Lee
Hole-in-the-Wall GC (R)
Florida
Arthur Hills, Steve Forrest
Holiday Beach GC
Breckenridge, Kentucky
Morgan Boggs
Holiday CC
Lake Park, Florida
Arthur Young
Holiday CC
Stuart, Florida
Arthur Young
Holiday Greens GC
Michigan
William Newcomb, Stephen Kay
Holiday Hills CC
Branson, Missouri
Bob Dunning
Holiday Inn GC
Crete, Illinois
Arthur Davis, Ron Kirby
Holiday Inn GC (R)
Michigan
William Newcomb, Stephen Kay
Holiday Inn GC
Sarnia, Ontario
Clinton E. Robinson
Holiday Island GC
Arkansas
John Allen
Holiday Park GC
Saskatoon, Saskatchewan
Clinton E. Robinson
Holiday Springs CC
Margate, Florida
Robert von Hagge, Bruce Devlin
Holland Lake GC
Sheridan, Michigan
Warner Bowen
Holland Lake GC (A. 9)
Michigan
Jerry Matthews
Holland Lake GC (R. 1)
Michigan
Jerry Matthews
Hollingbury Park GC
Sussex, England
F.G. Hawtree, J.H. Taylor
Hollis Memorial GC (R)
Massachusetts
Samuel Mitchell
Hollis Memorial GC (A.11)
Massachusetts
Samuel Mitchell
Hollow Acres GC
Delphi, Indiana
R. Albert Anderson
Hollow Brook G&CC
Peekskill, New York
Mungo Park II
Hollow Brook G&CC (R)
New York
Tom Winton

Hollows GC
Virginia
Brian Ault, Tom Clark
Holly Forest GC
Sapphire, North Carolina
Ron Garl
Holly Hill CC
Frederick, Maryland
Robert L. Elder
Holly Hill CC
Frederick, Maryland
Russell Roberts
Holly Hill CC
South Carolina
Ed Riccoboni
Holly Hill G&CC NLE
Davenport, Florida
Wayne Stiles, John Van Kleek
Holly Hills CC
Bay Minette, Alabama
Earl Stone
Holly Hills CC
Cordova, Tennessee
Marvin Ferguson
Holly Lake Ranch GC
Hawkins, Texas
Leon Howard
Holly Ridge GC
South Sandwich, Massachusetts
Geoffrey S. Cornish, William G.
Robinson
Holly Tree CC
Greenville, South Carolina
George W. Cobb, John LaFoy
Hollybrook G&CC
Hollywood, Florida
William F. Mitchell
Hollytree CC
Tyler, Texas
Robert von Hagge, Bruce Devlin
Hollywood Beach Hotel CC
Florida
H.C.C. Tippetts
Hollywood Beach Hotel CC (R)
Florida
Mark Mahannah
Hollywood GC
Fort Walton Beach, Florida
Bill Amick
Hollywood GC NLE
Deal, New Jersey
Tom Bendelow
Hollywood GC
Deal, New Jersey
Walter J. Travis
Hollywood GC (R)
New Jersey
Dick Wilson
**Hollywood Lakes CC (East
Course)**
Florida
Bill Watts
**Hollywood Lakes CC (West
Course)**
Florida
Bill Watts
Holmes Park Muni
Lincoln, Nebraska
Floyd Farley
Holston Hills CC
Knoxville, Tennessee
Donald Ross
Holston Hills CC (R. 3)
Tennessee
Alex McKay
Holston Hills CC
Marion, Virginia
Edmund B. Ault
Holyhead GC
Wales
James Braid
Holywell GC
Clywed, Wales
F.G. Hawtree, J.H. Taylor
Home Park GC
Surrey, England
James Braid
Homelinks GC
Olmstead Falls, Ohio
Harold Paddock
Homestead AFB GC
Florida
Mark Mahannah

Homestead AFB GC (A. 9)
Florida
Bob Cupp
Homestead AFB GC (R. 9)
Florida
Bob Cupp
Homestead CC NLE
Prairie Village, Kansas
James Dalgleish
Homestead GC
Spring Lake, New Jersey
Donald Ross
Homestead GC
Tipp City, Ohio
Bill Amick
**Homestead Mine GC now known
as Tomahawk Lake GC**
**Homewood CC now known as
Flossmoor CC**
Hominy Hill GC
Colts Neck, New Jersey
Robert Trent Jones
Homosassa CC NLE
Florida
Harry Collis
Honey Hill CC
Newport, New York
Geoffrey S. Cornish, William G.
Robinson
Honey Run G&CC
Pennsylvania
Edmund B. Ault
Honeywell CC
Orchard Gardens, Minnesota
Dick Phelps
Honeywell GC
Wabash, Indiana
William H. Diddel
Honeywell GC (A. 9)
Indiana
Steve Forrest
Honolulu International CC
Hawaii
Frank Duane, Arnold Palmer
Honors C
Brighton, Michigan
Arthur Hills, Steve Forrest, Mike
Dasher
Honors Course
Ooltewah, Tennessee
Pete Dye, P.B. Dye
Hood River GC
Oregon
H. Chandler Egan, *Hugh Junor*
Hoodkroft CC
Derry, New Hampshire
Phil Wogan
Hook & Slice GC
Oklahoma City, Oklahoma
Floyd Farley
Hooks G&CC
Hook, Sweden
Sig Edberg
Hooks G&CC (A. 9)
Sweden
Sig Edberg
Hooks G&CC (A. 8)
Sweden
Sig Edberg
Hooper GC
Walpole, New Hampshire
Wayne Stiles, John Van Kleek
Hoosier Links
New Palestine, Indiana
Charles Maddox
Hop Meadow CC
Simsbury, Connecticut
Geoffrey S. Cornish
Hope Valley CC
Durham, North Carolina
Donald Ross
Hope Valley CC (R)
North Carolina
Perry Maxwell
Hope Valley CC (R)
North Carolina
Dan Maples
Hopedale CC (R)
Massachusetts
Geoffrey S. Cornish
Hopewell CC
Virginia
Fred Findlay

Hopewell Valley GC
Hopewell Junction, New Jersey
Tom Winton
Hopewood GC
England
H.S. Colt
Hopkinsville G&CC
Kentucky
John Darrah
Horizon City CC
El Paso, Texas
Jack Harden
Horizon CC
Belen, New Mexico
Red Lawrence
Hornby Towers GC
Ontario
Robert Moote, *David Moote*
Horse Thief G&CC
Tehachapi, California
Bob Baldock, Robert L. Baldock
Horseshoe Bay CC (Apple Rock Course)
Marble Falls, Texas
Robert Trent Jones, Roger Rulewich
Horseshoe Bay CC (Ram Rock Course)
Marble Falls, Texas
Robert Trent Jones, Roger Rulewich
Horseshoe Bay CC (Slick Rock Course)
Marble Falls, Texas
Robert Trent Jones, Robert Trent Jones Jr,Gary Roger Baird
Horseshoe Bend CC
Roswell, Georgia
Joe Lee, Rocky Roquemore
Horseshoe GC
Cummings Cove, North Carolina
Bob Cupp
Horseshoe Valley GC
Barrie, Ontario
Renee Muylaert, *Charles Muylaert*
Horton Smith Muni
Springfield, Missouri
Tom Talbot
Hospitality Muni
Winslow, Arizona
Arthur Jack Snyder
Host Farms GC (Executive Course)
Lancaster, Pennsylvania
Geoffrey S. Cornish, William G. Robinson
Hot Springs G&CC (Arlington course)
Arkansas
William H. Diddel
Hot Springs G&CC (Arlington course) (R)
Arkansas
Smiley Bell
Hot Springs G&CC (Course No. 2)
Arkansas
Bert Meade
Hot Springs G&CC (Majestic Course)
Arkansas
Willie Park Jr
Hot Springs G&CC (Majestic Course) (R)
Arkansas
William H. Diddel
Hot Springs G&CC (Majestic Course) (R)
Arkansas
Smiley Bell
Hotchkiss School GC
Lakeville, Connecticut
Seth Raynor
Hotchkiss School GC (R)
Connecticut
Charles Banks
Hotel Champlain GC
Lake Bluff, New York
George Low Sr
Hotel Frascati GC NLE
Bermuda
Devereux Emmet

Hotel Green GC NLE
Pasadena, California
William Watson
Hotel Hershey GC
Hershey, Pennsylvania
Maurice McCarthy
Hotel Indiatlantic GC NLE
Melbourne, Florida
Ernest Way
Houghton GC (R)
South Africa
Sidney Brews
Hound Ear CC
Blowing Rock, North Carolina
George W. Cobb
Hound Ear CC (R)
North Carolina
Tom Jackson
Houndslake CC
Aiken, South Carolina
Joe Lee, Rocky Roquemore
Hounslow Heath GC
Middlesex, England
Fraser Middleton
Houston CC
Texas
Robert Trent Jones
Houston CC now known as Houston GC
Houston Golf Academy
Texas
Bruce Littell
Houston GC formerly known as Houston CC
Texas
Donald Ross
Houston GC (R)
Texas
Ralph Plummer
Houston Lake CC
Perry, Georgia
O.C. Jones
Houston Levee CC
Germantown, Tennessee
George C. Curtis
Houston Levee CC (A. 9)
Tennessee
Kevin Tucker
Hoveringham GC
Yorkshire, England
E. Baker, M. Baker
Howell Park GC
Farmingdale, New Jersey
Frank Duane
Howell Park GC (R)
New Jersey
Geoffrey S. Cornish, Brian Silva
Howstrake GC (R)
Isle of Man
T.J.A. McAuley
Howth Castle GC
County Dublin, Ireland
Fred W. Hawtree
Howth GC
Ireland
Cecil Barcroft
Howth GC (A. 9)
Ireland
James Braid, John R. Stutt
Howth GC (R. 9)
Ireland
James Braid, John R. Stutt
Hoylake Muni GC
England
James Braid
Hoyt Park GC
Portland, Oregon
Ed Erickson, David Duval
Hubbard Heights CC now known as E. Gaynor Brennan GC
Huddersfield GC
Yorkshire, England
Tom Dunn
Huddersfield GC (R)
England
Herbert Fowler
Huddersfield GC (R)
England
Tom Simpson
Hudson CC
Minnesota
Leo J. Feser

Hudson CC (A. 9)
Wisconsin
Don Herfort
Hudson CC (R. 9)
Wisconsin
Don Herfort
Hudson G & Curling C
Hudson Heights, Quebec
Howard Watson
Hudson River GC NLE
Yonkers, New York
Donald Ross
Hueston Woods State Park
Oxford, Ohio
Jack Kidwell
Hughes C
Houston, Texas
A. B. "Monk" Keith
Huguenot Manor GC
New Paltz, New York
Hal Purdy
Hull GC (R)
England
F.G. Hawtree, J.H. Taylor
Hulman Links of Terre Haute
Indiana
David Gill, Garrett Gill
Hulta GC
Sweden
Jan Sederholm
Humber Valley G&CC
Toronto, Ontario
Stanley Thompson
Humberstone Heights GC
Leicestershire, England
Fred W. Hawtree, Martin Hawtree
Humewood CC
Port Elizabeth, South Africa
S.V. Hotchkin
Hunsley Hills CC
Canyon, Texas
Henry B. Hughes
Hunstanton GC
Norfolk, England
George Fernie
Hunstanton GC (R. 9)
England
James Braid
Hunstanton GC (A. 9)
England
James Braid
Hunstanton GC (R. 3)
England
James Sherlock
Hunt Valley Inn & CC
Maryland
Edmund B. Ault
Hunt Valley Inn & CC (R. 9)
Maryland
Algie Pulley
Hunter's Creek CC
Kissimmee, Florida
Lloyd Clifton
Huntercombe GC
Oxfordshire, England
Willie Park Jr
Hunters Run GC (East Course)
Boynton Beach, Florida
Robert von Hagge, Bruce Devlin
Hunters Run GC (North Course)
Boynton Beach, Florida
Robert von Hagge, Bruce Devlin
Hunters Run GC (South Course)
Boynton Beach, Florida
Robert von Hagge, Bruce Devlin
Hunting Creek CC
Prospect, Kentucky
Benjamin Wihry
Hunting Hills CC
Roanoke, Virginia
Fred Findlay, *Ben Loving*,Buddy Loving
Hunting Hills CC (R)
Virginia
Buddy Loving
Huntingdale GC
Victoria, Australia
C.H. Alison, *S. Berriman*
Huntingdon Valley CC
Abington, Pennsylvania
William S. Flynn, Howard Toomey

Huntingdon Valley CC (R) NLE
Pennsylvania
Emil Loeffler
Huntington Crescent CC
Huntington, New York
Devereux Emmet, Alfred H. Tull
Huntington Crescent CC (R)
New York
Orrin Smith, William F. Mitchell
Huntington Crescent CC (R. 2)
New York
Stephen Kay
Huntington Crescent CC (West Course) NLE
Huntington, New York
Devereux Emmet, Alfred H. Tull
Huntington Crescent CC (West Course) (R)
New York
Orrin Smith, William F. Mitchell
Huntington CC
Indiana
Tom Bendelow
Huntington CC
New York
Devereux Emmet
Huntington CC (R)
New York
Devereux Emmet, Alfred H. Tull
Huntington CC (R)
New York
Robert Trent Jones, Frank Duane
Huntington CC (R)
New York
William F. Mitchell
Huntington CC
West Virginia
Tom Bendelow
Huntington Elks CC
Martha, West Virginia
X.G. Hassenplug
Huntington G & Marine C
Huntington, New York
Herbert Strong
Huntington GC NLE
New York
Tom Bendelow
Huntington GC (R)
Ontario
Clinton E. Robinson, Robert Moote
Huntington Hills GC
Spartanburg, South Carolina
Russell Breeden
Huntington Park GC
Louisiana
Tommy Moore
Huntington Seacliff CC now known as Seacliff CC
Huntsville Muni
Alabama
Bob Baldock
Huntsville Muni (R)
Alabama
Ron Kirby, Denis Griffiths
Hurlburt Field GC
Florida
Dave Bennett
Hurlingham G&CC
Argentina
George Gadd, Arthur Havers
Huron CC (A. 9)
South Dakota
Dick Phelps, Brad Benz
Huron CC (R. 9)
South Dakota
Dick Phelps, Brad Benz
Huron Hills GC
Ann Arbor, Michigan
Tom Bendelow
Huron Pines G&CC
Blind River, Ontario
Clinton E. Robinson
Hurricane Creek CC
Anna, Texas
Leon Howard
Hurstborne CC
Louisville, Kentucky
Chic Adams
Hutchinson CC NLE
Kansas
Tom Bendelow

Hutt GC (R)
New Zealand
John Harris
Huyton & Prescot GC (R)
England
Fred W. Hawtree, A.H.F. Jiggens
Hy Pointe CC
Grand Rapids, Michigan
Jack Daray
Hyannisport C (R)
Massachusetts
Donald Ross
Hyatt Pattaya GC
Thailand
Ichisuke Izumi
Hyde Estate GC
France
Tom Simpson
Hyde Manor GC
Vermont
Horace Rollins, George Sargent
Hyde Park CC NLE
Cincinnati, Ohio
Tom Bendelow
Hyde Park CC (R)
Ohio
Arthur Hills, Steve Forrest
Hyde Park GC
Jacksonville, Florida
Donald Ross
Hyde Park GC (R)
Florida
Stanley Thompson
Hyde Park GC
Cincinnati, Ohio
Donald Ross
Hyde Park Muni (North Course)
Niagara Falls, New York
William Harries
Hyde Park Muni (North Course) (R)
New York
William Gordon, David Gordon
Hyde Park Muni (South Course)
Niagara Falls, New York
William Harries
Hyde Park Muni (South Course) (A. 9)
New York
William Gordon, David Gordon
Hyde Park Muni (South Course) (R. 9)
New York
William Gordon, David Gordon
Hydeaway GC
Tecumseh, Ontario
Nick Panasi
Hydeaway GC (A. 9)
Ontario
Nick Panasi
Hyfield CC (A. 9)
Connecticut
Orrin Smith
Hyfield CC (R. 9)
Connecticut
Orrin Smith, Al Zikorus
Hyfield CC (A. 9)
Connecticut
Al Zikorus
Hyfield CC (R)
Connecticut
Al Zikorus
Hyland Greens CC
Minnesota
Paul Coates
Hyland Hills CC
Bloomfield, Colorado
Henry B. Hughes
Hyland Hills CC (A. 9)
Colorado
Frank Hummel
Hyland Hills GC
Southern Pines, North Carolina
Tom Jackson
Hylands GC (R. 1)
Ontario
John Watson
Hyperion Field C
Grimes, Iowa
Tom Bendelow
Hyperion Field C (R)
Iowa
Warren Dickinson

Hyperion Field C (R)
Iowa
Roger Packard
Hythe Imperial GC
Kent, England
P.M. Ross
HV-JAC GC
Delaware, Ohio
Jack Kidwell
I Roveri GC
Turin, Italy
Robert Trent Jones, Cabell
Robinson
Ibusuki CC (New Course)
Kagoshima, Japan
Peter Thomson, Michael
Wolveridge
Ida Grove G&CC
Iowa
Harold Glissmann
Idaho Falls CC
Idaho
William F. Bell
Idle Hour CC (R)
Georgia
Willard Byrd
Idle Hour CC
Lexington, Kentucky
Donald Ross, J.B. McGovern
Idle Hour CC (R)
Kentucky
Bob Simmons
Idlewild CC
Flossmoor, Illinois
Al Naylor
Idlewild CC (R)
Illinois
William B. Langford
Idyllwild CC
California
John Duncan Dunn
Idylwylde GC (A. 9)
Ontario
Howard Watson
Idylwylde GC (R. 9)
Ontario
Howard Watson
Idylwylde GC (R. 1)
Ontario
Robert Moote
Ifield G&CC
Sussex, England
F.G. Hawtree, J.H. Taylor
Iga Ueno CC
Japan
Arnold Palmer, Ed Seay
Ile Bourdon GC
Montreal, Quebec
Howard Watson
Ilkley GC
Yorkshire, England
Alister Mackenzie
Illahee Hills CC
Oregon
William F. Bell
Illenwick Fields GC
Bensenville, Illinois
Jack Daray
Illini CC
Springfield, Illinois
Tom Bendelow
Illini CC (A. 9)
Illinois
Robert Bruce Harris
Illini CC (R. 9)
Illinois
Robert Bruce Harris
Illini CC (R)
Illinois
Edward Lawrence Packard
Illinois State Univ. GC
Normal, Illinois
Robert Bruce Harris
Illinois Valley GC
Cave Junction, Oregon
Bob Baldock, Robert L. Baldock
Immingham GC
Lincolnshire, England
J.J.F. Pennink
Immingham GC (A. 9)
England
Fred W. Hawtree, Martin
Hawtree

Imperial CC
Teheran, Iran
Jack Armitage
Imperial GC
Brea, California
Harry Rainville, David Rainville
Imperial GC (East Course)
Naples, Florida
Arthur Hills
Imperial GC (West Course)
Naples, Florida
Ward Northrup
Imperial Lakes GC
Palmetto, Florida
Ted McAnlis
Imperial Sports C
Teheran, Iran
Fred W. Hawtree
Imperialakes CC
Mulberry, Florida
Ron Garl
Incline Green GC
Incline Village, Nevada
Robert Trent Jones, Robert Trent
Jones Jr,Gary Roger Baird
Incline Village GC
Nevada
Robert Trent Jones
Independence CC
Kansas
Tom Manley
Independence CC (R)
Kansas
Smiley Bell
Independence Green GC
Farmington, Michigan
Bruce Matthews, Jerry Matthews
Indian Bayou G&CC
Destin, Florida
Earl Stone
Indian Boundary CC
Chicago, Illinois
C.D. Wagstaff
Indian Canyon GC
Spokane, Washington
H. Chandler Egan
Indian Creek CC
Miami Beach, Florida
William S. Flynn, Howard
Toomey
Indian Creek CC (R)
Florida
Dick Wilson, Joe Lee
Indian Creek CC
Abilene, Texas
Ralph Plummer
Indian Creek GC
Jupiter, Florida
Lamar K. Smith
Indian Creek GC (Course No. 1)
Carrollton, Texas
Dick Phelps, Brad Benz,Mike
Poellot
Indian Creek GC (Course No. 2)
Carrollton, Texas
Dick Phelps
Indian Head GC (R. 9)
Maryland
Edmund B. Ault
Indian Hill C (R)
Illinois
Donald Ross
Indian Hill GC (R)
California
William P. Bell
Indian Hills CC
Tuscaloosa, Alabama
Harold Williams, *Thomas H. Nicol*
Indian Hills CC (R)
California
Bob Baldock, Robert L. Baldock
Indian Hills CC
Newington, Connecticut
Robert J. Ross
Indian Hills CC
Marietta, Georgia
Joe Lee, Rocky Roquemore
Indian Hills CC
Prairie Village, Kansas
A.W. Tillinghast
Indian Hills CC (R)
Kansas
Floyd Farley

Indian Hills CC (R)
Kansas
Bob Dunning
Indian Hills CC
Bowling Green, Kentucky
William B. Langford
Indian Hills CC
North St. Paul, Minnesota
Don Herfort
Indian Hills G&CC
Fort Pierce, Florida
Herbert Strong
Indian Hills Lakes GC
Fairfield Bay, Arkansas
Leon Howard, *Charles Howard*
Indian Hills GC (R)
Arkansas
Edmund B. Ault
Indian Hills GC
Mt. Vernon, Illinois
Thomas A. Puckett
Indian Hills GC (R)
Michigan
Bruce Matthews, Jerry Matthews
Indian Hills GC NLE
Omaha, Nebraska
Henry C. Glissmann, Harold
Glissmann
Indian Hills GC
Pine Bush, New York
Alfred H. Tull
Indian Hills GC
Brookings, South Dakota
Donald G. Brauer, Emile Perret
Indian Hills GC
Calgary, Alberta
Norman H. Woods
Indian Hills GC
Ontario
Russ Axford
Indian Hills Muni
Chapman, Kansas
Richard Watson
Indian Island Park GC
Riverhead, New York
William F. Mitchell
Indian Lake GC
Manistique, Michigan
John Barr
Indian Lake GC (R. 3)
Michigan
Bruce Matthews, Jerry Matthews
Indian Lake GC (A. 9)
Pennsylvania
X.G. Hassenplug, Arnold Palmer
Indian Lakes CC (A. 9)
Florida
George W. Cobb
Indian Lakes CC (R. 9)
Florida
George W. Cobb
**Indian Lakes CC (Iroquois Trail
Course)**
Bloomingdale, Illinois
Robert Bruce Harris
**Indian Lakes CC (Sioux Trail
Course)**
Bloomingdale, Illinois
Robert Bruce Harris
Indian Lakes GC
Florida
William L. Campbell
Indian Lakes GC
Batesville, Indiana
Robert Renaud
Indian Meadow CC
Westboro, Massachusetts
Geoffrey S. Cornish
Indian Oaks CC
Anniston, Alabama
Harold Williams
Indian Oaks CC
Phoenix City, Alabama
Willard Byrd
Indian Pines G&TC
Mi-Wuk Village, California
Clark Glasson
Indian Pines GC
Fort Pierce, Florida
Arthur Young
Indian Pines GC
Rockledge, Florida
Robert Renaud

Indian Ridge CC
Andover, Massachusetts
Geoffrey S. Cornish
Indian Ridge GC
Hobart, Indiana
Stanley Pelchar
Indian River GC
Michigan
Wilfrid Reid, William Connellan
Indian River Plantation GC
Florida
Chuck Ankrom
Indian Run GC
Scotts, Michigan
Charles Darl Scott
Indian Run GC (A. 9)
Michigan
Bruce Matthews, Jerry Matthews
Indian Spring C (Chief Course)
Silver Spring, Maryland
William Gordon, David Gordon
Indian Spring C (Valley Course)
Silver Spring, Maryland
William Gordon, David Gordon
Indian Spring CC (East Course)
Boynton Beach, Florida
Robert von Hagge, Bruce Devlin
Indian Spring CC (West Course)
Boynton Beach, Florida
Robert von Hagge, Bruce Devlin
Indian Spring GC (A. 9)
Illinois
Edward Lawrence Packard
Indian Springs CC
Palm Springs, California
John Gurley, Hoagy Carmichael
Indian Springs CC
Barbourville, Kentucky
Alex McKay
**Indian Springs CC (River
Course)**
Broken Arrow, Oklahoma
George Fazio
**Indian Springs CC (Windmill
Course)**
Broken Arrow, Oklahoma
Don Sechrest
Indian Trail CC
Palm Beach, Florida
Mark Mahannah
Indian Tree GC
Arvada, Colorado
Dick Phelps
Indian Valley CC
Burlington, North Carolina
Ellis Maples, Ed Seay
Indian Valley CC
Telford, Pennsylvania
William Gordon, David Gordon
Indian Valley GC
Novato, California
Robert Nyberg
Indian Valley CC
Cincinnati, Ohio
William H. Diddel
Indian Village CC
Lafayette, Indiana
Edward Lawrence Packard
Indian Wells CC
California
Harry Rainville
Indian Wells CC (R)
California
Ted Robinson
**Indian Wells G Resort (East
Course)**
California
Ted Robinson
**Indian Wells G Resort (West
Course)**
California
Ted Robinson
Indian Wells GC
Myrtle Beach, South Carolina
Gene Hamm
Indian Wells GC
Burlington, Ontario
Renee Muylaert
Indian Wood G&CC
Matteson, Illinois
Harry Collis
Indiana CC NLE
Pennsylvania
Willie Park Jr

Indiana CC
Pennsylvania
James Gilmore Harrison,
Ferdinand Garbin
Indiana CC (R)
Pennsylvania
Edmund B. Ault
Indiana Univ. GC
Bloomington, Indiana
Jim Soutar
Indianfield G&CC
Caro, Michigan
William Newcomb, *Jim Lipe*
Indianwood G&CC
Indiantown, Florida
Ted McAnlis
**Indianwood G&CC (New
Course)**
Lake Orion, Michigan
Bob Cupp, *Jerry Pate*
Indianwood G&CC (Old Course)
Lake Orion, Michigan
Wilfrid Reid, William Connellan
**Indianwood G&CC (Old Course)
(R)**
Michigan
Arthur Hills, Steve Forrest
Indies Inn GC
Duck Key, Florida
C.H. Anderson
Indigo Lakes CC
Daytona Beach, Florida
Lloyd Clifton
Indigo Run GC
Hilton Head Island, South
Carolina
Willard Byrd, Clyde Johnston
Indio Muni
California
Lawrence Hughes
Indole G&CC
New York
Seymour Dunn
**Industry Hills GC (Eisenhower
Course)**
California
William F. Bell
**Industry Hills GC (Zaharias
Course)**
California
William F. Bell
Ine's Lodge GC
Laurinburg, North Carolina
Tom Jackson
Ingersoll Muni
Illinois
Tom Bendelow
Ingestre GC
Staffordshire, England
Fred W. Hawtree, Martin
Hawtree
Ingleside Augusta CC
Saunton, Virginia
Fred Findlay
Ingleside GC NLE
San Francisco, California
Robert Johnstone
Inglewood CC
Kenmore, Washington
A. Vernon Macan, Robert
Johnstone
Inglewood CC (R)
Washington
William Teufel
Inglewood GC
California
Ted Robinson
Inglewood Muni (A. 9)
Alberta
William G. Robinson
Ingliston GC
Scotland
James Braid, John R. Stutt
Ingol G & Squash C
Lancashire, England
J.J.F. Pennink, D.M.A. Steel
Inn of the Mountain Gods GC
Mescalero, New Mexico
Ted Robinson
Innellan GC
Argyllshire, Scotland
Willie Park, Willie Park Jr

303

Innerleithen GC
Peebleshire, Scotland
Willie Park
Innis Arden GC (R)
Connecticut
Robert Trent Jones
Innis Arden GC (R)
Connecticut
Frank Duane
Innis Arden GC (R. 3)
Connecticut
Geoffrey S. Cornish, Brian Silva
Innisbrook GC (Copperhead Course)
Tarpon Springs, Florida
Edward Lawrence Packard,
  Roger Packard
Innisbrook GC (Island Course)
Tarpon Springs, Florida
Edward Lawrence Packard
Innisbrook GC (Sandpiper Course)
Tarpon Springs, Florida
Edward Lawrence Packard,
  Roger Packard
Innisfail G&CC (A. 9)
Alberta
William G. Robinson
Innsbruck GC
Cleveland, Georgia
Bill Watts
Innsbruck-Igls GC
Austria
G. Hauser
Intercollegiate GC NLE
New York
Devereux Emmet
Intercontinental GC
West Germany
Bernhard von Limburger
Interlachen CC
Winter Park, Florida
Joe Lee
Interlachen CC
Edina, Minnesota
William Watson
Interlachen CC (R)
Minnesota
Donald Ross
Interlachen CC (R)
Minnesota
Robert Trent Jones
Interlachen CC (R)
Minnesota
Donald G. Brauer, Emile Perret
Interlachen CC (R)
Minnesota
Brian Silva, Geoffrey S. Cornish
Interlaken GC (A. 9)
Minnesota
Don Herfort
Interlaken GC (R. 9)
Minnesota
Don Herfort
Interlaken-Unterseen GC
Switzerland
Donald Harradine
International C
Richford, Quebec
Stanley Thompson
International C du Lys
Chantilly, France
Tom Simpson
International C du Lys (R)
France
J. Hamilton Stutt
International G&CC
Orlando, Florida
Joe Lee
International GC
Bolton, Massachusetts
Geoffrey S. Cornish
International GC (R)
Massachusetts
Robert Trent Jones
International Town & CC (R)
Virginia
Edmund B. Ault
Interstate Park GC NLE
New York
John Duncan Dunn
Intervale GC
Manchester, New Hampshire
Alex Findlay

Inverallochy GC
Aberdeen, Scotland
James Gibbs
Invercargill GC
New Zealand
A.M. Howden
Invergordon GC (A. 9)
Scotland
Fraser Middleton
Inverness C
Toledo, Ohio
Bernard Nicholls
Inverness C (R. 9)
Ohio
Donald Ross
Inverness C (A. 9)
Ohio
Donald Ross
Inverness C (R)
Ohio
A.W. Tillinghast
Inverness C (R)
Ohio
Dick Wilson
Inverness C (A. 9)
Ohio
Robert Bruce Harris
Inverness C (R. 9)
Ohio
Robert Bruce Harris
Inverness C (R)
Ohio
Arthur Hills
Inverness C (A. 4)
Ohio
George Fazio, Tom Fazio
Inverness C (R)
Ohio
George Fazio, Tom Fazio
Inverness C (R)
Ohio
Arthur Hills, Steve Forrest
Inverness CC
Birmingham, Alabama
George W. Cobb
Inverness GC
Englewood, Colorado
Press Maxwell
Inverness GC (R)
Illinois
Edward Lawrence Packard
Inverness GC
Invernesshire, Scotland
John Harris, Peter
  Thomson, Michael Wolveridge
Inverrary CC (East Course)
Lauderhill, Florida
Robert Trent Jones, Rees Jones
Inverrary CC (South Course)
Lauderhill, Florida
Robert Trent Jones, Rees Jones
Inverrary CC (West Course)
Lauderhill, Florida
Robert Trent Jones, Rees Jones
Inverurie GC (R)
Scotland
J. Hamilton Stutt
Inwood CC (R)
New York
Herbert Strong
Inwood CC (R)
New York
Hal Purdy
Inwood CC (R)
New York
Frank Duane
Inwood Forest CC
Houston, Texas
Donald Collett
Inwood Forest CC (A. 9)
Texas
Jay Riviere
Inwood GC (R)
Illinois
Edward Lawrence Packard
Iola Community GC
Wisconsin
Edward Lawrence Packard
Iola CC NLE
Kansas
Harry Robb
Iowa City CC NLE
Iowa
Tom Bendelow

Ipswich GC
Purdis Heath, England
F.G. Hawtree, J.H. Taylor
Ipswich GC NLE
England
James Braid
Ipswich GC (A. 9)
England
Fred W. Hawtree, A.H.F. Jiggens
Irem Temple CC
Wilkes Barre, Pennsylvania
A.W. Tillinghast
Iron Masters CC
Pennsylvania
Edmund B. Ault
Iron Mountain GC
Mission, Ontario
William L. Overdorf
Iron River CC
Michigan
William B. Langford, Theodore J.
  Moreau
Irondequoit CC
Rochester, New York
Donald Ross
Irondequoit CC (A. 9)
New York
J.B. McGovern
Ironhorse GC
West Palm Beach, Florida
Arthur Hills, Steve Forrest,Mike
  Dasher
Ironshore CC
Montego Bay, Jamaica
Robert Moote, *David Moote*
Ironton CC
Ohio
Harold Paddock
Ironwood CC
Longwood, Florida
Karl Litten, Gary Player
Ironwood CC (North Course)
Palm Desert, California
Ted Robinson
Ironwood CC (Short Course)
Palm Desert, California
Arnold Palmer, Ed Seay
Ironwood CC (South Course)
Palm Desert, California
Desmond Muirhead
Ironwood CC (South Course) (R)
California
Ted Robinson
Ironwood GC
Arizona
Arthur Jack Snyder
Ironwood GC
Byron Center, Michigan
George Woolferd
Ironwood GC
Cookeville, Tennessee
L. Wesley Flatt
Iroquois GC
Louisville, Kentucky
Robert Bruce Harris
Iroquois GC (A. 9)
Kentucky
Edward Lawrence Packard
Iroquois GC (A. 9)
Kentucky
Benjamin Wihry
Iroquois GC (R. 3)
Kentucky
Benjamin Wihry
Irvine Coast CC
California
William F. Bell, William P. Bell
Irvine Coast CC (R)
California
Harry Rainville, David Rainville
Irvine Coast CC (R)
California
William F. Bell
Irvine GC (R)
Scotland
J. Hamilton Stutt
Irvine Ravenspark GC
Ayrshire, Scotland
J. Walker
Irving CC NLE
Texas
Press Maxwell

Irwin CC (R)
Pennsylvania
James Gilmore Harrison
Irwindale Muni
California
Bob Baldock, Robert L. Baldock
Is Molas GC
Sardinia
Pier Mancinelli
Isla de la Piedra GC
Mazatlan, Mexico
Robert Trent Jones Jr, Gary
  Roger Baird
Isla de la Piedra GC (A. 9)
Mexico
Robert Trent Jones Jr
Isla del Sol GC
St. Petersburg, Florida
Mark Mahannah, Charles
  Mahannah
Island of Rhodes GC
Rhodes, Greece
Donald Harradine
Island C
St. Simons Island, Georgia
Joe Lee, Rocky Roquemore
Island Dunes GC
Jensen Beach, Florida
Joe Lee
Island G Links NLE
Garden City, New York
Devereux Emmet
Island Green GC
Myrtle Beach, South Carolina
William Mooney
Island GC
Fort Walton Beach, Florida
Bill Amick
Island GC (R)
Ireland
Eddie Hackett
Island Hills CC
Sayville, New York
Herbert Strong
Island Hills CC (R)
New York
A.W. Tillinghast
Island Hills CC (R)
New York
William F. Mitchell
Island Valley GC
Rochester, New York
Pete Craig
Island View GC
Winona, Minnesota
Willie Kidd
Island's End G&CC
New York
Herbert Strong
Isle of Purbeck GC (Purbeck Course)
Dorset, England
H.S. Colt
Isle Dauphine CC
Alabama
Charles Maddox
Isles of Scilly GC
England
Horace Hutchinson
Islesmere G&CC
Quebec
Willie Park Jr
Islesmere G&CC (A. 9)
Quebec
Howard Watson
Isleworth G&CC
Windermere, Florida
Arnold Palmer, Ed Seay
Islington GC
Toronto, Ontario
Stanley Thompson
Itanhanga GC
Tijuca, Brazil
Stanley Thompson
Itanhanga GC (R)
Brazil
Robert Trent Jones
Itasca CC (R)
Illinois
Robert Bruce Harris
Ito International GC
Shizuoko, Japan
Kinya Fujita

Ives Groves GC
Racine, Wisconsin
David Gill
Ives Hill CC
Watertown, New York
Maurice McCarthy
Ives Hill CC (R)
New York
Peter W. Lees
Ives Hill CC (A. 9)
New York
Geoffrey S. Cornish, William G.
  Robinson
Ivinghoe GC
England
R. Garrad
Ivy Creek Farm GC
Virginia
Bill Love
Ivy Hill CC
Forrest, Virginia
J. Porter Gibson
Iwasaki Resort GC
Yeppoon, Australia
Peter Thomson, Michael
  Wolveridge
Iyanough Hills GC
Hyannis, Massachusetts
Geoffrey S. Cornish, William G.
  Robinson
Izcaragua CC
Caracas, Venezuela
Joe Lee, Rocky Roquemore
IBM CC
Endicott, New York
John Van Kleek
IBM CC
Poughkeepsie, New York
Robert Trent Jones
IBM CC (A. 9)
New York
Robert Trent Jones
IBM CC (R. 9)
New York
Robert Trent Jones
IBM CC (R)
New York
William F. Mitchell
IBM CC (R)
New York
Robert Trent Jones
IBM CC (R. 9)
New York
Hal Purdy
IBM CC (R. 1)
New York
Frank Duane
IBM CC (R)
New York
Robert Trent Jones, Roger
  Rulewich
IBM GC
San Jose, California
Jack Fleming
J.C. Long Estate GC
Mt. Pleasant, South Carolina
George W. Cobb
J.J. Lynn Estate GC NLE
Kansas City, Missouri
Orrin Smith
Jablonna GC
Warsaw, Poland
J.J.F. Pennink
Jacaranda CC (East Course)
Plantation, Florida
Mark Mahannah
Jacaranda CC (West Course)
Plantation, Florida
Mark Mahannah, Charles
  Mahannah
Jacaranda West CC
Venice, Florida
Mark Mahannah, Charles
  Mahannah
Jack Nicklaus Sports Center (Bruin)
Mason, Ohio
Desmond Muirhead, Jack
  Nicklaus
Jack Nicklaus Sports Center (Grizzly)
Mason, Ohio
Desmond Muirhead, Jack
  Nicklaus

Jackpot GC
Nevada
Robert Muir Graves
Jackson CC (A. 9)
Illinois
David Gill
Jackson Heights GC
Jamaica, New York
A.W. Tillinghast
Jackson Hole G&TC
Wyoming
Bob Baldock
Jackson Hole G&TC (R)
Wyoming
Robert Trent Jones, Robert Trent
Jones Jr
Jackson Park Muni
Seattle, Washington
William H. Tucker, Frank James
Jacksonville CC
Illinois
Tom Bendelow
Jacksonville CC (A. 9)
Illinois
Edward Lawrence Packard
Jacksonville CC
North Carolina
George W. Cobb
Jagorawi G&CC
Chibinong, Indonesia
Peter Thomson, Michael
Wolveridge,Ronald Fream
James Baird State Park GC
Pleasant Valley, New York
Robert Trent Jones
James Connally GC
Waco, Texas
Ralph Plummer
James D. Rothchild Estate GC
England
Tom Simpson
James H. Ager Jr GC
Lincoln, Nebraska
Floyd Farley
James L. Key Muni
Atlanta, Georgia
Willie Ogg
James River CC
Newport News, Virginia
James McMenamin
Jamestown CC
St. James, Missouri
Floyd Farley
Jamestown CC
North Dakota
Robert Bruce Harris
Jamestown Park GC
Jamestown, North Carolina
John V. Townsend
Janley Hills GC
New York
Pete Craig
Jasper Muni
Indiana
William Newcomb
Jasper Muni (A. 9)
Indiana
Gary Kern
Jasper Park GC NLE
Jasper, Alberta
Sir Arthur Conan Doyle
Jasper Park GC
Alberta
Stanley Thompson
Jasper Park GC (R)
Alberta
William Brinkworth
Jawbone Creek GC
Harlowton, Montana
Frank Hummel
Jedburgh GC
Roxburghshire, Scotland
Willie Park
Jefferson City CC
Missouri
Robert Foulis
Jefferson City CC (A. 9)
Missouri
Edward Lawrence Packard
Jefferson City CC (R)
Missouri
Edward Lawrence Packard

Jefferson CC
Monticello, Florida
Bill Amick
Jefferson High School GC
Jefferson, Kentucky
Hal Purdy
Jefferson Park GC
Fairfax, Maryland
Algie Pulley
Jefferson Park Muni
Washington
Tom Bendelow
Jefferson-Lakeside CC
Richmond, Virginia
Donald Ross
Jekyll Island GC NLE
Georgia
Willie Dunn Jr
**Jekyll Island GC (Indian
Mounds Course)**
Georgia
Joe Lee
**Jekyll Island GC (Oceanside
Course)**
Georgia
Walter J. Travis
**Jekyll Island GC (Oceanside
Course) (R. 3)**
Georgia
Hugh Moore
**Jekyll Island GC (Oleander
Course)**
Georgia
Dick Wilson, Joe Lee
**Jekyll Island GC (Pine Lakes
Course)**
Georgia
Joe Lee
**Jekyll-Hyde GC now known as
Reservation GC**
Jenny Wiley State Park GC
Pikeville, Kentucky
Hal Purdy
Jeremy Ranch GC
Park City, Utah
Arnold Palmer, Ed Seay
Jerseyville CC
Illinois
Edward Lawrence Packard, Brent
Wadsworth
Jester Park GC
Granger, Iowa
Dick Phelps
Jesup G&CC
Iowa
Charles Calhoun
Jidda GC
Saudi Arabia
George Wadsworth
Jockey C (Blue Course)
San Isidro, Argentina
Alister Mackenzie
Jockey C (Blue Course) (R)
Argentina
Ronald Fream
Jockey C (Red Course)
San Isidro, Argentina
Alister Mackenzie
Jockey C (Red Course) (R)
Argentina
Ronald Fream
Joe Wheeler State Park GC
Rogersville, Alabama
Earl Stone
John Blumberg Muni
Winnipeg, Manitoba
Clinton E. Robinson
John Conrad GC
Midwest City, Oklahoma
Floyd Farley
John F. Kennedy Muni
Denver, Colorado
Henry B. Hughes
John Knox Village GC
Missouri
Larry Runyon, Michael H. Malyn
**John O'Gaunt GC (Carthagena
Course)**
Bedfordshire, England
Willie Dunn Jr
**John O'Gaunt GC (Carthagena
Course) (R)**
England
Fred W. Hawtree

John's Island C (North Course)
Vero Beach, Florida
Pete Dye
John's Island C (South Course)
Vero Beach, Florida
Pete Dye, Jack Nicklaus
**John's Island C (South Course)
(R)**
Florida
Joe Lee
John's Island C (West Course)
Vero Beach, Florida
Tom Fazio
Johnson City CC
Tennessee
A.W. Tillinghast
Johnstown Elks CC
Pennsylvania
James Gilmore Harrison
Joliet CC
Illinois
Tom Bendelow
Jolly Acres GC
South Dakota
Clifford A. Anderson
Jonathan Par 30 GC
Chaska, Minnesota
Robert Trent Jones
Jonathan's Landing GC
Jupiter, Florida
George Fazio, Tom Fazio
Jones Creek GC
Augusta, Georgia
Rees Jones, Keith Evans
Jonesboro CC
Arkansas
William M. Martin
Jonesco GC
Gray, Georgia
Ernie Schrock
Joondalup GC
Australia
Robert Trent Jones Jr, Don Knott
Joplin CC NLE
Missouri
Tom Bendelow
Joplin CC (R) NLE
Missouri
Orrin Smith
Jordan Point CC
Hopewell, Virginia
Russell Breeden
Juarez CC
Mexico
George Hoffman
Jug End Inn GC
Egremont, Massachusetts
Alfred H. Tull
Jumping Brook GC
Neptune, New Jersey
Willard Wilkinson
Jumping Brook GC (R)
New Jersey
Nicholas Psiahas
Juniata GC
Philadelphia, Pennsylvania
Edmund B. Ault
Juniper CC
Redmond, Oregon
Fred Sparks
Juniper Hills GC
Frankfort, Kentucky
Buck Blankenship
Juniper Hills GC
Massachusetts
Homer Darling
Juniper Hills GC (A. 9)
Massachusetts
Geoffrey S. Cornish
Juniper Hills GC (R. 4)
Massachusetts
Phil Wogan
Junko CC
Venezuela
Charles Banks
Jupiter Dunes GC
Jupiter, Florida
Bob Erickson
Jupiter Dunes GC (R)
Florida
Ward Northrup
Jupiter Hills C (Hills Course)
Jupiter, Florida
George Fazio

**Jupiter Hills C (Hills Course)
(R)**
Florida
George Fazio, Tom Fazio
**Jupiter Hills C (Hills Course)
(A. 3)**
Florida
George Fazio, Tom Fazio
Jupiter Hills C (Village Course)
Jupiter, Florida
George Fazio, Tom Fazio
Jupiter Island C
Jupiter, Florida
William H. Diddel
Jupiter Island C (R)
Florida
George Fazio, Tom Fazio
Jupiter West GC
Jupiter, Florida
Ward Northrup
Jurong CC (R)
Singapore
Ronald Fream
Jurupa Hills CC
Riverside, California
William F. Bell
JDM CC (East Course)
Palm Beach Gardens, Florida
Dick Wilson, Joe Lee
JDM CC (North Course)
Palm Springs Gardens, Florida
Dick Wilson, Joe Lee
JDM CC (North Course) (A. 9)
Florida
Joe Lee
JDM CC (South Course)
Palm Springs Gardens, Florida
Dick Wilson, Joe Lee
JDM CC (South Course) (A. 9)
Florida
Joe Lee
JFK Memorial GC
Napa, California
Bob Baldock, Jack Fleming,Ben
Harmon
Kaanapali Kai GC NLE
Lahaina, Hawaii
Arthur Jack Snyder
Kah-nee-ta GC
Warm Springs, Oregon
Gene "Bunny" Mason
Kahkwa C
Erie, Pennsylvania
Donald Ross
Kalab Golf di Raja Darul Ehsan
Ampang Jay, Malaysia
Ronald Fream
Kalamazoo CC
Michigan
Tom Bendelow
Kalamazoo CC (R)
Michigan
William Newcomb
Kalamazoo Elks CC (R. 2)
Michigan
Bruce Matthews, Jerry Matthews
Kalispell G&CC
Montana
Gregor MacMillan
Kalona GC (R. 9)
Iowa
Charles Calhoun
Kalua Koi GC
Mauna Loa, Hawaii
Ted Robinson
Kalundborg GC
Denmark
Jan Sederholm
Kamirag GC
Cebu Island, Philippines
Ron Kirby, Denis Griffiths
**Kananaskis Country GC (Mount
Kidd)**
Alberta
Robert Trent Jones, Roger
Rulewich
**Kananaskis Country GC (Mount
Loretta)**
Alberta
Robert Trent Jones, Roger
Rulewich
Kanata GC
Ottawa, Ontario
Howard Watson

Kanawaki GC
Quebec
Charles Murray, Albert Murray
Kanawaki GC (R)
Quebec
Clinton E. Robinson
Kanawaki GC (R. 9)
Quebec
Howard Watson
Kanawaki GC (R. 3)
Quebec
Howard Watson, John Watson
Kanehoe Marine GC
Hawaii
William P. Bell
Kanehoe Marine GC ()
Hawaii
Jimmy Ukauka
Kankakee CC
Illinois
Tom Bendelow
Kankakee CC (R. 8)
Illinois
John Darrah
Kankakee CC (A.10)
Illinois
John Darrah
Kankakee Elks CC
St. Anne, Illinois
William B. Langford, Theodore J.
Moreau
Kannami Springs G&CC
Japan
Brad Benz, Mike Poellot
Kanon Valley CC
Oneida, New York
Hal Purdy
Kansas City CC
Shawnee Mission, Kansas
A.W. Tillinghast
Kansas City CC (R. 2)
Kansas
Floyd Farley
Kansas City CC (R)
Kansas
Bob Dunning
Kansas City CC (R)
Kansas
Rees Jones
Kansas City CC NLE
Missouri
Tom Bendelow
Kapalua GC (Bay Course)
Maui, Hawaii
Frank Duane, Arnold Palmer
Kapalua GC (Bay Course) (R)
Hawaii
Robin Nelson
Kapalua GC (Village Course)
Hawaii
Arnold Palmer, Ed Seay
Kapalua GC (Village Course) (R)
Hawaii
Robin Nelson
Karlovy Vary GC
Czechoslovakia
M.C. Noskowski
Karlskoga GC
Sweden
Jan Sederholm
Karlskrona GC (A. 7)
Sweden
Jan Sederholm
Karnataka GC
Bangalore, India
Peter Thomson, Michael
Wolveridge
Karori GC
Wellington, New Zealand
John Harris, Peter
Thomson,Michael Wolveridge
Kartner GC
Dellach, Austria
E. Leitner
Karuizawa GC
Japan
Yuji Kodera
Kass Inn & CC (A)
New York
Ernest E. Smith
Kassel-Wilhelmhohe GC
West Germany
Bernhard von Limburger

Kassel-Wilhelmhohe GC (A. 9)
West Germany
Donald Harradine, *Peter Harradine*
Kasugai CC (East Course)
Nagoya, Japan
Seichi Inouye
Kasugai CC (West Course)
Nagoya, Japan
Seichi Inouye
Kasumigaseki GC (East Course)
Saitama, Japan
Kinya Fujita
Kasumigaseki GC (East Course) (R)
Japan
C.H. Alison
Kasumigaseki GC (West Course)
Saitama, Japan
Kinya Fujita
Kasumigaseki GC (West Course) (R)
Japan
C.H. Alison
Katahdin CC
Milo, Maine
Larry H. Striley
Katke GC
Ferris State Univ., Michigan
Robert Beard
Katke-Cousins GC
Oakland Univ., Michigan
Robert Beard
Kauai Surf G&CC NLE
Kauai, Hawaii
Willard Wilkinson
Kauai Surf G&CC (A. 9)
Hawaii
Raymond F. Cain
Kaufman GC
Wyoming, Michigan
Bruce Matthews, Jerry Matthews
Kaufman GC
Texas
Leon Howard
Kawagoe CC
Japan
Pete Nakamura
Kawaguchi-ko GC
Mt. Fuji, Japan
Robert von Hagge, Bruce Devlin
Kawana GC (Fuji Course)
Shizuoka, Japan
C.H. Alison
Kawana GC (Fuji Course) (R)
Japan
Kinya Fujita
Kawana GC (Oshima Course)
Shizuoka, Japan
Komei Otani
Kawana GC (Oshima Course) (R)
Japan
C.H. Alison
Kawartha GC
Peterboro, Ontario
Stanley Thompson
Kayak Point GC
Stanwood, Washington
Peter Thomson, Michael
  Wolveridge,Ronald Fream, *Terry
  Storm*
Kazusa GC
Tokyo, Japan
Jack Nicklaus, Jay Morrish,Scott
  Miller
Kearney CC (R)
Nebraska
Harold Glissmann
Kearney CC (R. 9)
Nebraska
Leo Johnson
Kearney CC (A. 9)
Nebraska
Leo Johnson
**Kearsarge Valley CC now known
  as CC of New Hampshire**
Keauhou Kona CC
Kailua-Kona, Hawaii
William F. Bell
Keauhou Kona CC (R. 3)
Hawaii
Arthur Jack Snyder
Keauhou Kona CC (A. 9)
Hawaii
William F. Bell, Robin Nelson

Kebayoran GC (R)
Indonesia
Peter Thomson, Michael
  Wolveridge,Ronald Fream
Kebo Valley C
Bar Harbor, Maine
Herbert Leeds
Kebo Valley C (A. 9)
Maine
Andrew E. Liscombe
Kedleston Park GC
Derbyshire, England
J.S.F. Morrison, John R. Stutt
Keene CC (R)
New Hampshire
Manny Francis
Keerbergen GC
Belgium
Tom Simpson
Keerbergen GC (R)
Belgium
J.J.F. Pennink
Keesler AFB GC
Gulfport, Mississippi
Joseph S. Finger
Keighley GC (R)
England
Tom Simpson
Keith Hills CC
Buies Creek, North Carolina
Ellis Maples, Dan Maples
**Kelab Golf Diraja Terengganu
  (R. 9)**
Malaysia
Robin Nelson
Keller GC
St. Paul, Minnesota
Paul Coates
Keller GC (R. 1)
Minnesota
Don Herfort
Kelley Ridge G Links
California
Homer Flint
Kellogg GC
Peoria, Illinois
Edward Lawrence Packard,
  Roger Packard
Kelly Greens GC
Ft. Myers Beach, Florida
Gordon G. Lewis
Kelsey City GC NLE
West Palm Beach, Florida
William B. Langford, Theodore J.
  Moreau
Kelso Elks GC (R) NLE
Washington
Robert Muir Graves
Kelso GC
Roxboroughshire, Scotland
James Braid
Kemper Lakes GC
Hawthorne Woods, Illinois
Ken Killian, Dick Nugent
Kemper Lakes GC (R)
Illinois
Ken Killian
Kempsville Meadows G&CC
Norfolk, Virginia
Ellis Maples
Ken McDonald Muni
Tempe, Arizona
Arthur Jack Snyder
Ken-Wo G&CC (A. 9)
Newfoundland
Clinton E. Robinson
Kendale Lakes G&CC
Miami, Florida
Charles Mahannah
Kendale Lakes West CC
Miami, Florida
Charles Mahannah
Kendalville CC
Indiana
Tom Bendelow
Kendrick Muni
Sheridan, Wyoming
Edward A. Hunnicutt
Kendrick Muni (A. 9)
Wyoming
Frank Hummel
Keney Park GC
Hartford, Connecticut
Devereux Emmet, Alfred H. Tull

Keney Park GC (R. 3)
Connecticut
Geoffrey S. Cornish, William G.
  Robinson
Keney Park GC (R)
Connecticut
Everett Pyle
Keney Park GC (R)
Connecticut
Robert J. Ross
Kenilworth GC
Warwickshire, England
Roger Dyer
Kenilworth Lodge GC NLE
Sebring, Florida
Wayne Stiles, John Van Kleek
Kenloch G Links
Lombard, Illinois
David Gill
Kenmure GC
Flat Rocks, North Carolina
Joe Lee, Rocky Roquemore
Kennemer G&CC
Netherlands
H.S. Colt, C.H. Alison,J.S.F.
  Morrison
Kenogamisis GC
Geraldton, Ontario
Stanley Thompson
Kenora G&CC
Ontario
Stanley Thompson
Kenora G&CC (A.11)
Ontario
Robert Moote
Kenora G&CC (R. 7)
Ontario
Robert Moote
Kenosee Lakes GC (A. 9)
Saskatchewan
Clinton E. Robinson
Kenosha CC
Wisconsin
Donald Ross
Kensington GC
Milford, Michigan
H.A. Lemley
Kensington GC (R)
South Africa
Ron Kirby, Denis Griffiths
Kent CC
Grand Rapids, Michigan
E.C. Simonds
Kent CC (A. 9)
Michigan
Donald Ross
Kent CC (R. 9)
Michigan
Donald Ross
Kent CC (R. 9)
Michigan
James Foulis
Kent CC (R. 1)
Michigan
Jerry Matthews
Kent Fulton Estate GC
Connecticut
Devereux Emmet
Kentland GC
Indiana
Tom Bendelow
Kenton County CC (R. 9)
Kentucky
Jack Kidwell, Michael Hurdzan
Kenton County CC (A. 9)
Kentucky
Jack Kidwell, Michael Hurdzan
Kentuck GC
North Bend, Oregon
Don Houston, Wallace Wickett
Kentucky Dam Village GC
Gilbertsville, Kentucky
Hal Purdy
Kentville GC
Nova Scotia
Willie Park Jr
Kenwood CC (R)
Maryland
Edmund B. Ault
Kenwood CC (Kendale Course)
Cincinnati, Ohio
William H. Diddel

**Kenwood CC (Kendale Course)
  (R)**
Ohio
William H. Diddel
**Kenwood CC (Kendale Course)
  (R)**
Ohio
Jack Kidwell, Michael Hurdzan
Kenwood CC (Kenview Course)
Cincinnati, Ohio
William H. Diddel
**Kenwood CC (Kenview Course)
  (R)**
Ohio
William H. Diddel
**Kenwood CC (Kenview Course)
  (R)**
Ohio
Jack Kidwell, Michael Hurdzan
Keokuk CC
Iowa
Tom Bendelow
Keokuk CC (R)
Iowa
William B. Langford
Keowee Key CC
Seneca, South Carolina
George W. Cobb, John LaFoy
Keppel C (R.18)
Singapore
Ronald Fream
Kern City GC
Bakersfield, California
Arthur Jack Snyder
Kern River CC
Bakersfield, California
William F. Bell, William P. Bell
Kern Valley GC
California
William F. Bell
Kernwood CC
Salem, Massachusetts
Donald Ross
Kernwood CC (R)
Massachusetts
William F. Mitchell
Kerrville Hills CC
Texas
Donald Collett
Keswick C of Virginia
Virginia
Fred Findlay
Keswick C of Virginia (R)
Virginia
Arnold Palmer, Ed Seay
Keswick GC
Cumbria, England
Eric Brown
Kettenring CC
Defiance, Ohio
Tom Bendelow
Kettenring CC (A. 9)
Ohio
William J. Rockefeller
Key Biscayne GC
Florida
Robert von Hagge, Bruce Devlin
Key Biscayne Hotel GC
Miami Beach, Florida
Mark Mahannah
Key Colony Beach GC
Florida
John E. O'Connor
Key Colony GC NLE
Key Biscayne, Florida
Mark Mahannah
Key Royale GC
Holmes Beach, Florida
James C. Cochran
Key West GC NLE
Florida
William B. Langford, Theodore J.
  Moreau
Key West Resort GC
Key West, Florida
Rees Jones
Keystone G&CC
Florida
Donald Ross
Keystone G&CC (R)
Florida
R. Albert Anderson

Keystone Ranch GC
Dillon, Colorado
Robert Trent Jones Jr, Don Knott
Ki-8-EB GC
Three Rivers, Quebec
Stanley Thompson
Ki-8-EB GC (R)
Quebec
Clinton E. Robinson
Ki-8-EB GC (R. 2)
Quebec
Howard Watson
Ki-8-EB GC (R. 2)
Quebec
John Watson
Kiahuna Plantation GC
Poipu Beach, Hawaii
Robert Trent Jones Jr, Don Knott
Kickingbird GC
Edmond, Oklahoma
Floyd Farley
Kiel GC (R)
West Germany
Bernhard von Limburger
Kilbuck GC
Anderson, Indiana
William H. Diddel
Kilcock GC
Ireland
Bobby Browne
Kilkenny GC
County Kilkenny, Ireland
Tom Simpson
**Killarney G & Fishing C
  (Killeen)**
County Kerry, Ireland
Sir Guy Campbell
**Killarney G & Fishing C
  (Killeen) (A.12)**
Ireland
Fred W. Hawtree
**Killarney G & Fishing C
  (Killeen) (R. 6)**
Ireland
Fred W. Hawtree
**Killarney G & Fishing C
  (Mahony's Point)**
County Kerry, Ireland
Sir Guy Campbell
**Killarney G & Fishing C
  (Mahony's Point) (R.12)**
Ireland
Fred W. Hawtree
**Killarney G & Fishing C
  (Mahony's Point) (A. 6)**
Ireland
Fred W. Hawtree
Killarney GC NLE
County Kerry, Ireland
Willie Park
Killarney Racetrack GC
Ireland
Eddie Hackett
Killearn G&CC
Florida
Bill Amick
Killeen Muni
Texas
Jay Riviere
Killiney GC (R)
Ireland
Eddie Hackett
Killington GC
Vermont
Geoffrey S. Cornish
Killington GC (A. 9)
Vermont
Geoffrey S. Cornish, Brian Silva
Killymoon GC
County Tyrone, Northern Ireland
Fred W. Hawtree
Kilmarnock GC
Barassie, Scotland
John Allan
Kilmarnock GC (R)
Scotland
Theodore Moone
Kilspindle GC (R)
Scotland
Willie Park Jr
Kimberland Meadows GC
New Meadows, Idaho
Bob Baldock, Robert L. Baldock

Kimberley GC (A. 3)
Ontario
Ted Nagel
Kimberley GC (A. 9)
Ontario
Norman H. Woods
Kimberton GC
Pennsylvania
George Fazio
Kinchelo Memorial GC
Kinross, Michigan
Bob Baldock
Kinderton CC
Clarksville, Virginia
Dick Wilson
King City GC
California
Bob Baldock
King David CC
Cape Town, South Africa
Robert G. Grimsdell
King Emmanual Private Course
Italy
Seymour Dunn
King James VI GC
Perth, Scotland
Old Tom Morris
King Leopold Private Course
Belgium
Seymour Dunn
King's Lynn GC
England
Peter Alliss, David Thomas
Kingfisher GC
Oklahoma
Floyd Farley
Kinghorn GC
Fife, Scotland
Old Tom Morris
Kingman GC
Arizona
Milt Coggins
Kings Bay Naval Sub Base GC
St. Marys, Georgia
Arthur Hills, Steve Forrest
Kings Bay Y&CC
Miami, Florida
Mark Mahannah
Kings County CC (A. 9)
California
Bert Stamps
Kings Crossing G&CC
Corpus Christi, Texas
Bill Coore
Kings Grant GC
Charleston, South Carolina
Russell Breeden
Kings Mill GC
Waldo, Ohio
Jack Kidwell
Kings Norton GC
Worcestershire, England
Fred W. Hawtree, Martin
  Hawtree
Kings Point G&CC
Sun City Center, Florida
Robert Trent Jones, Rees Jones
Kings Point G&CC (Course No.
  1)
Delray Beach, Florida
Robert Trent Jones, Rees Jones
Kings Point G&CC (Course No.
  2)
Delray Beach, Florida
Robert Trent Jones, Rees Jones
Kings River G&CC
Kingsbury, California
Nick Lombardo
Kings River G&CC (R)
California
Bob Baldock
Kingsknowe GC
Edinburgh, Scotland
James Braid
Kingsmill GC (Plantation
  Course)
Williamsburg, Virginia
Arnold Palmer, Ed Seay
Kingsmill GC (River Course)
Williamsburg, Virginia
Pete Dye
Kingsmill GC (River Course) (R.
  5)
Virginia
Brian Ault, Tom Clark, Edmund
  B. Ault

Kingsport CC
Pennsylvania
Maurice McCarthy
Kingsport CC
Tennessee
A.W. Tillinghast
Kingsridge CC
Portchester, New York
Tom Winton
Kingsthorpe GC
England
H.S. Colt
Kingston Heath GC
Cheltenham, Australia
Des Soutar
Kingston Heath GC (R)
Australia
Peter Thomson, Michael
  Wolveridge
Kingston Heath GC (R)
Australia
Alister Mackenzie
Kingstree CC
South Carolina
Robert White
Kingsville GC (A. 9)
Ontario
Robert Moote, *David Moote*
Kingsway CC
Lake Suzy, Florida
Ron Garl
Kingsway GC
Massachusetts
Brian Silva, Geoffrey S. Cornish
Kingswood CC
Wolfeboro, New Hampshire
Donald Ross, Walter Hatch
Kingswood GC
Bella Vista, Arkansas
Edmund B. Ault
Kingswood GC
Surrey, England
James Braid, John R. Stutt
Kington GC
Herefordshire, England
C.K. Hutchison, Sir Guy
  Campbell, S.V. Hotchkin
Kingussie GC
Invernesshire, Scotland
Harry Vardon
Kingwood CC
Clayton, Georgia
Larry McClure
Kingwood CC (Forest Course)
Texas
Joseph S. Finger, Ken Dye
Kingwood CC (Island Course)
Texas
Joseph S. Finger
Kingwood CC (Lake Course)
Texas
Bruce Littell
Kinsdown GC
England
Tom Dunn
Kinston CC (R)
North Carolina
Ellis Maples
Kinston CC (R)
North Carolina
Russell Breeden, *Dan Breeden*
Kirbywood CC
Cleveland, Texas
Bruce Littell
Kirkbrae CC
Lincoln, Rhode Island
Geoffrey S. Cornish
Kirkbrae CC (R. 3)
Rhode Island
Samuel Mitchell
Kirkcaldy GC (R)
Scotland
J. Hamilton Stutt
Kirkistown Castle GC
Northern Ireland
James Braid
Kirriemuir GC
Perthshire, Scotland
James Braid
Kirtland CC
Willoughby, Ohio
C.H. Alison, H.S. Colt

Kirtland CC (R)
Ohio
Pete Dye
Kishwaukee CC
DeKalb, Illinois
Tom Bendelow
Kishwaukee CC (A. 9)
Illinois
David Gill
Kissena GC
Flushing, New York
John Van Kleek
Kissimmee GC NLE
Florida
John Hamilton Gillespie
Kissing Camels GC
Colorado Springs, Colorado
Press Maxwell
Kitsap G&CC (R)
Washington
William Teufel
Kittanning CC
Pennsylvania
Emil Loeffler, *John McGlynn*
Kittansett C
Marion, Massachusetts
Frederic C. Hood
Kittyhawk Muni (Eagle Course)
Dayton, Ohio
Robert Bruce Harris
Kittyhawk Muni (Hawk Course)
Dayton, Ohio
Robert Bruce Harris
Kittyhawk Muni (Kitty Course)
Dayton, Ohio
Robert Bruce Harris
Kitzenberg GC (R)
West Germany
Bernhard von Limburger
Kiwanis Muni
Little Rock, Arkansas
Herman Hackbarth
Kjekstad GC
Norway
Jan Sederholm
Kleberg County GC
Kingville, Texas
Dennis W. Arp
Kleiburg GC
Brielle, Netherlands
J.J.F. Pennink
Klingenburg-Gunzberg GC
West Germany
Donald Harradine
Klinger Lake CC
Michigan
William Newcomb
Klinger Lake CC
Michigan
Maurie Wells
Knebworth GC
Hertfordshire, England
Willie Park Jr
Knickerbocker CC NLE
Tenafly, New Jersey
Maurice McCarthy
Knickerbocker CC
Tenafly, New Jersey
Donald Ross
Knickerbocker CC (R)
New Jersey
Herbert Strong
Knickerbocker CC (R. 6)
New Jersey
Geoffrey S. Cornish, William G.
  Robinson
Knighton GC
Powys, Wales
Harry Vardon
Knighton Heath GC
Dorset, England
J. Hamilton Stutt
Knob Hill CC
New Jersey
James Gilmore Harrison,
  Ferdinand Garbin
Knole Park GC
Kent, England
Herbert Fowler, J.F. Abercromby
Knole Park GC (R)
England
Tom Simpson

Knoll East GC
Boonton, New Jersey
Hal Purdy
Knoll GC (A. 9)
Nebraska
William B. Kubly
Knoll GC
New Jersey
Charles Banks
Knolls GC
Lincoln, Nebraska
Floyd Farley
Knollwood C
Lake Forest, Illinois
C.H. Alison, H.S. Colt
Knollwood C (R)
Illinois
Edward Lawrence Packard,
  Roger Packard
Knollwood C (R)
Illinois
Roger Packard
Knollwood CC
Granada Hills, California
William F. Bell, William H.
  Johnson
Knollwood CC (R)
California
David W. Kent
Knollwood CC (R. 1)
Michigan
Bruce Matthews, Jerry Matthews
Knollwood CC (A. 1)
Michigan
Bruce Matthews, Jerry Matthews
Knollwood CC NLE
Elmsford, New York
Lawrence Van Etten
Knollwood CC
Elmsford, New York
Seth Raynor, Charles Banks
Knollwood CC (R)
New York
Charles Banks
Knollwood CC (R)
New York
Stephen Kay
Knollwood GC NLE
Irving, Texas
Perry Maxwell, Press Maxwell
Knowle GC
Gloucestershire, England
F.G. Hawtree, J.H. Taylor
Knowlton GC (A. 9)
Quebec
Howard Watson
Knowlton GC (R. 9)
Quebec
Howard Watson
Koganei CC
Tokyo, Japan
Walter Hagen
Kohlerhof GC
Bonn, West Germany
J.F. Dudok Van Heel
Kokanee Springs CC
Crawford Bay, British Columbia
Norman H. Woods
Kokkedal GC
Rungsted, Denmark
J.J.F. Pennink
Kokkedal GC (R)
Denmark
Jan Sederholm
Kokomo CC
Indiana
Tom Bendelow
Kokomo CC (A. 9)
Indiana
William H. Diddel
Kokomo CC (R. 9)
Indiana
William H. Diddel
Kolding GC (A. 9)
Denmark
Jan Sederholm
Kona International CC
Kailua-Kona, Hawaii
Robin Nelson
Koninklijke GC
Ostend, Belgium
Willie Park Jr

Konstaz GC
West Germany
Karl Hoffmann, Bernhard von
  Limburger
Kooralbyn Valley GC
Australia
Fred Bolton
Kooyonga GC (R)
Australia
Peter Thomson, Michael
  Wolveridge
Korakuen CC
Sapparo, Japan
Peter Thomson, Michael
  Wolveridge
Kornwestheim GC
West Germany
Bernhard von Limburger
Korsloet GC (A. 9)
Sweden
Jan Sederholm
Kountze Place GC NLE
Omaha, Nebraska
Harry Lawrie
Krefelder GC
Krefeld, West Germany
Karl Hoffmann, Bernhard von
  Limburger
Kronberg GC
West Germany
Herbert E. Gaertner
Kronberg GC (R)
West Germany
Bernhard von Limburger
Krueger Muni
Beloit, Wisconsin
Stanley Pelchar
Kuehn Park GC
Sioux Falls, South Dakota
Don Herfort
Kukuiolono GC NLE
Kauai, Hawaii
Walter Duncan McBryde
Kungsbacka GC
Sweden
J.J.F. Pennink
Kurabone GC
Japan
Robert Muir Graves
Kutshers Hotel GC
Monticello, New York
William F. Mitchell
Kwiniaska GC
Vermont
Paul J. O'Leary, Brad Caldwell
Kyushu Shima CC
Japan
Seichi Inouye
L & N GC
Brooks, Kentucky
Alex McKay
L.B. Houston Muni
Dallas, Texas
Leon Howard
L'Anse GC
Michigan
Edward Lawrence Packard
L'Isle d'Abeau GC
France
Robert Berthet
La Canada-Flintridge CC
California
Lawrence Hughes
La Ceiba GC
Yucatan, Mexico
Jaime Saenz, Felix Teran
La Cita G&CC
Titusville, Florida
Ron Garl
La Colina CC
Bogota, Colombia
Jeff Hardin, Greg Nash
La Contenta CC
Valley Springs, California
Richard Bigler
La Costa CC (Gold Course)
Carlsbad, California
Dick Wilson, Joe Lee
La Costa CC (Orange Course)
Carlsbad, California
Joe Lee
La Cumbre G&CC
Santa Barbara, California
Peter Cooper Bryce

La Cumbre G&CC (A. 9)
California
George C. Thomas Jr, William P.
Bell
La Cumbre G&CC (R. 9)
California
George C. Thomas Jr, William P.
Bell
La Cumbre G&CC (R)
California
William F. Bell
La Fontaine GC
Huntington, Indiana
Harry B. Smead
La Fontaine GC (R)
Indiana
Robert Bruce Harris
La Fontaine GC (A. 9)
Indiana
Gordon Ludwig, Robert Stoffel
La Fortune Park Muni
Tulsa, Oklahoma
Floyd Farley
La Fortune Park Muni (A.18)
Oklahoma
Floyd Farley
La Gorce CC
Miami, Florida
H.C.C. Tippetts
La Gorce CC (R)
Florida
Robert Trent Jones
La Grange CC NLE
Illinois
H.J. Tweedie
La Grange CC
Illinois
Tom Bendelow
La Grange CC (R)
Illinois
Edward B. Dearie Jr
La Grange CC (R)
Illinois
Edward Lawrence Packard
La Grange CC (R)
Illinois
Roger Packard
La Herliere CC
Arras, France
Fred W. Hawtree
La Jolla CC
California
William P. Bell
La Jolla CC (R. 3)
California
Arthur Jack Snyder
La Jolla CC (R. 3)
California
Ted Robinson
La Jolla CC (R)
California
Rees Jones
La Mandria GC
Turin, Italy
J.S.F. Morrison
La Mandria GC (A. 9)
Italy
John Harris
La Manga Campo de G (North
Course)
Costa Blanca, Spain
Robert Dean Putnam
La Manga Campo de G (South
Course)
Spain
Robert Dean Putnam
La Mantarraya GC
Las Hadras, Mexico
Roy Dye, Gary Grandstaff
La Mantarraya GC (A. 9)
Mexico
Roy Dye
La Mirada GC
California
William F. Bell
La Moraleja GC
Madrid, Spain
Desmond Muirhead, Jack
Nicklaus
La Moye GC
Channel Islands
George Boomer

La Moye GC (R)
Channel Islands
James Braid
La Moye GC (R)
Channel Islands
Henry Cotton
La Moye GC (R)
Channel Islands
David Melville
La Palma CC NLE
Arizona
Harry Collis
La Paloma GC
Tucson, Arizona
Jack Nicklaus, Scott Miller
La Penaza GC
Zaragoza, Spain
Fred W. Hawtree
La Pointe du Diamant GC
Martinique
Robert Moote, *David Moote*
La Porte CC
Pine Lake, Indiana
William B. Langford
La Purisima GC
Lompoc, California
Robert Muir Graves, Damian
Pascuzzo
La Quinta CC
California
Lawrence Hughes
La Quinta Hotel GC (Citrus
Course)
La Quinta, California
Pete Dye, *Lee Schmidt*
La Quinta Hotel GC (Dunes
Course)
La Quinta, California
Pete Dye, *Lee Schmidt*
La Quinta Hotel GC (Mountain
Course)
La Quinta, California
Pete Dye, *Lee Schmidt,Alice Dye*
La Rocca GC
Italy
M. Croze
La Tierra Bonita GC
Porter, Oklahoma
Art Lopez
La Tourette Muni
Staten Island, New York
David L. Rees
La Tourette Muni (A. 9)
New York
John Van Kleek
La Tourette Muni (R. 9)
New York
John Van Kleek
La Tourette Muni (R. 4)
New York
Frank Duane
La Tuque G & Curling C (A. 9)
Quebec
Howard Watson
La Tuque G & Curling C (R. 9)
Quebec
Howard Watson
La Vista G&CC
Wichita Falls, Texas
L. Wesley Flatt
Labour-in-Vain GC NLE
Ipswich, Massachusetts
Eugene "Skip" Wogan
Labuan
Malaysia
Robert Muir Graves
Lac Thomas GC
St. Didace, Quebec
Howard Watson
Lachute GC
Quebec
Stanley Thompson
Lachute GC (R. 9)
Quebec
Howard Watson
Lachute GC (A.18)
Quebec
Howard Watson
Lackland AFB GC (R)
Texas
Joseph S. Finger
Lacoma GC
East Dubuque, Illinois
Gordon Cunningham

Laconia CC
New Hampshire
Ralph Barton
Laconia CC (A. 9)
New Hampshire
Wayne Stiles
Laconia CC (R)
New Hampshire
Orrin Smith, William F. Mitchell
Lacrosse CC (R)
Wisconsin
Edward Lawrence Packard
Lacrosse CC (R)
Wisconsin
Dick Nugent
Lacuna CC
Lantana, Florida
Joe Lee
Ladbrook Park GC
Warwickshire, England
Tom Williamson
Ladera GC
Albuquerque, New Mexico
Dick Phelps, Brad Benz
Ladies GC of Toronto
Ontario
Stanley Thompson
Lady Bird Johnson Muni
Fredericksburg, Texas
George Hoffman
Ladybank GC
Fife, Scotland
Old Tom Morris
Lafayette C
Minnetonka Beach, Minnesota
Tom Bendelow
Lafayette City GC
Indiana
Bob Simmons
Lafayette CC
Indiana
Tom Bendelow
Lafayette CC (R. 9)
Indiana
William H. Diddel
Lafayette CC (R)
Louisiana
Ralph Plummer
Lafayette CC
Syracuse, New York
Seymour Dunn
Lafayette CC (A. 9)
New York
Augie Nordone
Lafayette CC (Battleground
Course)
Indiana
Bob Simmons
Lago Mar CC
Ft. Lauderdale, Florida
Bill Watts
Lago Vista CC
Lake Travis, Texas
Leon Howard
Lagoon Park GC
Montgomery, Alabama
Charles M. Graves
Laguna CC
California
William P. Bell
Laguna Hills GC
California
Harry Rainville, David Rainville
Laguna Hills GC (R)
California
Robert Muir Graves
Laguna Seca G Ranch
California
Robert Trent Jones, Robert Trent
Jones Jr
Lagunita CC
Caracas, Venezuela
Dick Wilson, Bob Simmons
Lahinch GC (Castle Course)
County Clare, Ireland
John Harris
Lahinch GC (Castle Course) (A.
9)
Ireland
D.M.A. Steel
Lahinch GC (Castle Course) (R)
Ireland
D.M.A. Steel

Lahinch GC (Old Course)
County Clare, Ireland
Old Tom Morris
Lahinch GC (Old Course) (R)
Ireland
Charles Gibson
Lahinch GC (Old Course) (A. 5)
Ireland
Charles Gibson
Lahinch GC (Old Course) (R)
Ireland
Alister Mackenzie
Lahinch GC (Old Course) (A.11)
Ireland
Alister Mackenzie
Lahinch GC (Old Course) (R)
Ireland
John Burke, Bill McCavery
Lai Lai International G&CC
Kaohsiung, Taiwan
Brad Benz, Mike Poellot
Lake of the Hills GC
Haslett, Michigan
Bruce Matthews, Jerry Matthews
Lake of the North GC
Mancelona, Michigan
Bruce Matthews, Jerry Matthews
Lake of the North GC (A.18)
Michigan
William Newcomb
Lake of the Woods GC
Mahomet, Illinois
Robert Bruce Harris
Lake of the Woods GC
Ypsilanti, Michigan
Leo J. Bishop
Lake Ajay GC
Florida
Ward Northrup
Lake Anna CC NLE
Palos Park, Illinois
Stanley Pelchar
Lake Anne CC
Monroe, New York
Alfred H. Tull
Lake Arbor GC
Arvada, Colorado
Clark Glasson
Lake Arlington GC
Arlington, Texas
Ralph Plummer
Lake Arrowhead CC NLE
California
William Watson
Lake Arrowhead CC
California
William F. Bell
Lake Arrowhead CC (R. 2)
California
Algie Pulley
Lake Arrowhead CC (R. 2)
California
William F. Bell
Lake Arrowhead GC
Nekoosa, Wisconsin
Ken Killian, Dick Nugent,Jeff
Brauer
Lake Barkley State Park GC
Kentucky
Edward Lawrence Packard
Lake Barrington Shores GC
Barrington, Illinois
Roger Packard
Lake Barton GC
Great Bend, Kansas
Harry Robb
Lake Bastrop GC
Texas
Leon Howard
Lake Bonaventure CC
St. Paul, Virginia
Alex McKay
Lake Buena Vista C
Florida
Joe Lee, Rocky Roquemore
Lake Chabot GC
Oakland, California
William Lock
Lake Chabot Vallejo GC
Vallejo, California
Jack Fleming
Lake Charles G&CC
Louisiana
Ralph Plummer

Lake Charles G&CC (R)
Louisiana
Jay Riviere
Lake City CC
Florida
Willard Byrd
Lake City CC
South Carolina
Ed Riccoboni
Lake Country Estates GC
Ft. Worth, Texas
Ralph Plummer
Lake Country Estates GC (A. 9)
Texas
Don January, Billy Martindale
Lake Creek CC
Storm Lake, Iowa
Homer Fieldhouse
Lake DeGray State Park GC
Bismarck, Arkansas
Leon Howard, *Charles Howard*
Lake Don Pedro GC
California
William F. Bell
Lake Doster GC
Plainwell, Michigan
Charles Darl Scott
Lake East GC
Sun City, Arizona
*James Winans, John W. Meeker,Jeff
Hardin*
Lake Elsinore GC NLE
California
John Duncan Dunn
Lake Estes GC
Estes Park, Colorado
Henry B. Hughes
Lake Fairfax GC
Virginia
Edmund B. Ault, Al Jamison
Lake Fairways GC
North Fort Myers, Florida
Ron Garl
Lake Forest CC (A. 9)
Alabama
Earl Stone
Lake Forest CC (R. 9)
Alabama
Earl Stone
Lake Forest CC
Hudson, Ohio
Herbert Strong
Lake Forest CC (R)
Ohio
James Gilmore Harrison
Lake Forest G&CC (R. 9)
Missouri
Gary Kern
Lake Forest G&CC (A. 9)
Missouri
Gary Kern
Lake Forest GC NLE
Kansas
Floyd Farley
Lake Garrett GC
Seattle, Washington
George S. "Pop" Merrit
Lake Geneva CC
Wisconsin
Robert Foulis
Lake George C
New York
Alex Findlay
Lake Guntersville State Park GC
Guntersville, Alabama
Earl Stone
Lake Hefner GC (North Course)
Oklahoma City, Oklahoma
Perry Maxwell, Press Maxwell
Lake Hefner GC (North Course)
(R)
Oklahoma
Floyd Farley
Lake Hefner GC (South Course)
Oklahoma City, Oklahoma
Floyd Farley
Lake Hickory CC
North Carolina
Willard Byrd
Lake Hills CC
Billings, Montana
George H. Schneiter

Lake Hills G&CC
St. John, Indiana
Charles Maddox, *Frank P. MacDonald*

Lake Hopatcong GC
New Jersey
Robert White

Lake Houston GC
Huffman, Texas
Jay Riviere

Lake Isabella GC
Weidman, Michigan
Bruce Matthews, Jerry Matthews

Lake James CC
Angola, Indiana
Robert Beard

Lake Jovita CC
Florida
Wayne Stiles, John Van Kleek

Lake Karrinyup CC
Perth, Australia
Alister Mackenzie, Alex Russell

Lake Karrinyup CC (R)
Australia
Peter Thomson, Michael Wolveridge

Lake Karrinyup CC (A. 9)
Australia
Peter Thomson, Michael Wolveridge

Lake Kezar C
Lovell, Maine
Donald Ross

Lake Lackawanna GC
Byram, New Jersey
William Gordon, David Gordon

Lake Lawn CC
Fort Myers, Florida
Ken Craig

Lake Lawn GC
Irwin, Pennsylvania
Ferdinand Garbin

Lake Lawn GC
Delaran, Wisconsin
Tom Bendelow

Lake Lindero GC
California
Ted Robinson

Lake Lorraine CC now known as Shalimar Pointe CC

Lake Lucerne GC
Cleveland, Ohio
Clyde W. Colby

Lake Lure Muni
North Carolina
John Van Kleek

Lake Marion GC
Santee, South Carolina
Ed Riccoboni

Lake Merced G&CC NLE
Daly City, California
Herbert Fowler

Lake Merced G&CC
Daly City, California
Robert Muir Graves

Lake Merced G&CC (R)
California
Alister Mackenzie

Lake Mohawk GC
New Jersey
Duer Irving Sewall

Lake Monticello GC
Palmyra, Virginia
Buddy Loving, Algie Pulley

Lake Morey Inn GC
Vermont
George Salling

Lake Nona GC
Orlando, Florida
Tom Fazio

Lake Norconian C NLE
California
John Duncan Dunn

Lake Oaks CC (Course No. 1)
Waco, Texas
Warren Cantrell

Lake Oaks CC (Course No. 2)
Waco, Texas
Warren Cantrell

Lake Oswego Muni
Oregon
Shirley Stone

Lake Padden Muni
Bellingham, Washington
Roy L. Goss, *Glen Proctor*

Lake Panorama National GC
Panora, Iowa
Richard Watson

Lake Panorama Par 3 GC
Panora, Iowa
Richard Watson

Lake Paoay GC
Ilocos Norte, Philippines
Ron Kirby, Denis Griffiths

Lake Park GC
Germantown, Wisconsin
James Jones

Lake Placid C NLE
Sebring, Florida
Seymour Dunn

Lake Placid C (Lower Course)
New York
Seymour Dunn

Lake Placid C (Practice Course)
New York
Seymour Dunn

Lake Placid C (Upper Course)
New York
Alex Findlay

Lake Placid C (Upper Course) (R)
New York
Alister Mackenzie

Lake Platte GC
Platte, South Dakota
Lee Tappe

Lake Quivira CC
Kansas City, Kansas
Eugene L. Williams

Lake Quivira CC (R)
Kansas
Floyd Farley

Lake Quivira CC (R)
Kansas
Chet Mendenhall

Lake Quivira CC (R. 4)
Kansas
Bill Love

Lake Region Y&CC
Winter Haven, Florida
David Wallace

Lake Region Y&CC (R)
Florida
Hugh Moore

Lake Region Y&CC (R)
Florida
Dean Refram

Lake Ridge GC
Seattle, Washington
Robert Johnstone

Lake Ross GC
Marulan, Australia
Peter Thomson, Michael Wolveridge

Lake Samanish State Park GC
Issaquah, Washington
Al Smith

Lake San Marcos Executive GC
California
David Rainville

Lake San Marcos G&CC
California
Harry Rainville, David Rainville

Lake Shastina G&CC
Weed, California
Robert Trent Jones, Robert Trent Jones Jr, Gary Roger Baird

Lake Shawnee GC
Topeka, Kansas
Larry W. Flatt

Lake Shore CC
Glencoe, Illinois
Tom Bendelow

Lake Shore CC (R)
Illinois
Ken Killian, Dick Nugent

Lake Shore CC
Burlington, Vermont
Herbert Strong

Lake Shore G&CC (R)
Ontario
Stanley Thompson

Lake Shore GC
Erie, Pennsylvania
Tom Bendelow

Lake Spanaway GC
Tacoma, Washington
Kenneth Tyson

Lake St Clair CC
Detroit, Michigan
William H. Diddel

Lake St. George G&CC (R. 9)
Ontario
Clinton E. Robinson

Lake St. George G&CC (A. 9)
Ontario
Clinton E. Robinson

Lake Success GC (R. 9)
New York
Orrin Smith, Al Zikorus

Lake Success GC (A. 9)
New York
Orrin Smith, Al Zikorus

Lake Sunapee CC
New London, New Hampshire
Donald Ross

Lake Sunapee CC (R)
New Hampshire
Orrin Smith, William F. Mitchell

Lake Surf CC now known as Woodlake CC

Lake Tahoe CC (A. 9)
California
William F. Bell

Lake Tarleton C NLE
Pike, New Hampshire
Donald Ross

Lake Texoma State Park GC
Kingston, Oklahoma
Floyd Farley

Lake Toxaway CC
North Carolina
R.D. Heinitsh

Lake Valley G&CC
Camdenton, Missouri
Floyd Farley

Lake Valley GC
Boulder, Colorado
Press Maxwell

Lake Venice CC
Venice, Florida
Mark Mahannah

Lake Venice CC (A. 9)
Florida
Carl Rohmann

Lake View GC
Johnson City, Tennessee
Alex McKay

Lake View Park GC
Rochester, Indiana
James Merdigh

Lake Wales CC
Florida
Donald Ross

Lake Wales CC (A. 9)
Florida
William L. Campbell

Lake Waneawega GC
Illinois
Tom Bendelow

Lake Wilderness CC
Maple Valley, Washington
Ray Coleman

Lake Wilderness CC (A. 9)
Washington
Norman H. Woods

Lake Wilderness CC (R)
Washington
Robert Muir Graves, Damian Pascuzzo

Lake Wildwood GC
Grass Valley, California
William F. Bell

Lake Windsor GC
Madison, Wisconsin
Marvin Busse

Lake Worth Muni
Florida
William B. Langford, Theodore J. Moreau

Lake Worth Muni (R)
Florida
Dick Wilson

Lake Worth Park GC
Florida
Karl Litten

Lake Wright GC
Norfolk, Virginia
Al Jamison

Lakeland Par 3 GC
Florida
Hans Schmeisser

Lakemont CC
Ohio
William J. Rockefeller

Lakeover CC
Bedford Village, New York
Al Zikorus

Lakepointe CC (A. 6) NLE
Michigan
Bruce Matthews, Jerry Matthews

Lakepointe State Park GC
Eufaula, Alabama
Thomas H. Nicol

Lakeport CC
New Hampshire
Ralph Barton

Lakeridge CC
Reno, Nevada
Robert Trent Jones, Robert Trent Jones Jr

Lakeridge G&CC
Lakeview, Oregon
Charles Sullivan

Lakes CC
Palm Desert, California
Ted Robinson

Lakes GC
Parrish, Florida
Ted McAnlis

Lakes GC
Sydney, Australia
Robert von Hagge, Bruce Devlin

Lakes West GC
Sun City, Arizona
Milt Coggins, *James Winans, John W. Meeker*, Jeff Hardin

Lakeshore CC (A. 9)
Iowa
David Gill

Lakeshore CC
Madisonville, Kentucky
Buck Blankenship

Lakeshore CC
Oradell, New Jersey
Al Zikorus

Lakeshore GC
Taylorsville, Illinois
William James Spear

Lakeside CC
Atlanta, Georgia
George W. Cobb

Lakeside CC
Houston, Texas
Ralph Plummer

Lakeside CC (R.14)
Texas
Joseph S. Finger

Lakeside CC
Manitowoc, Wisconsin
William H. Diddel

Lakeside CC
Fort Wayne, Indiana
Robert Beard

Lakeside CC
Miss. State Univ., Mississippi
Sonny Guy

Lakeside GC
Ohio
Edmund B. Ault

Lakeside GC
Moore, Oklahoma
Duffy Martin

Lakeside GC of Hollywood
North Hollywood, California
Max Behr

Lakeside GC of Hollywood (R)
California
Robert Muir Graves

Lakeside Hills GC
Olathe, Kansas
Charles Nash

Lakeside Memorial GC
Stillwater, Oklahoma
Labron Harris Sr

Lakeview CC
Lodi, Illinois
Charles Maddox

Lakeview CC NLE
Oklahoma
Leslie Brownlee

Lakeview CC
North East, Pennsylvania
James Gilmore Harrison, Ferdinand Garbin

Lakeview CC
Virginia
Fred Findlay, *Ben Loving*, Buddy Loving

Lakeview CC
Virginia
Russell Roberts

Lakeview G&CC
Toronto, Ontario
Herbert Strong

Lakeview GC
Delray Beach, Florida
Bill Dietsch

Lakeview GC
Ralston, Iowa
Harold Glissmann

Lakeview GC
Ralston, Nebraska
Harold Glissmann

Lakeview GC
Roanoke, Virginia
Fred Sappenfield

Lakeview Hills CC (R. 1)
Michigan
Jerry Matthews

Lakeview Inn & CC (North Course)
Morgantown, West Virginia
Brian Ault, Tom Clark

Lakeview Inn & CC (South Course)
Morgantown, West Virginia
James Gilmore Harrison, Ferdinand Garbin

Lakeview Motor Inn GC
Roanoke, Virginia
Buddy Loving

Lakeview Muni
Brandon, South Dakota
Richard Watson

Lakeville CC now known as Fresh Meadow CC

Lakeway GC (Live Oak Course)
Lake Travis, Texas
Leon Howard

Lakeway GC (Yaupon Course)
Lake Travis, Texas
Leon Howard

Lakewood on the Green GC
Cadillac, Michigan
Norman Smith, Pete Smith

Lakewood CC
Denver, Colorado
Tom Bendelow

Lakewood CC (R)
Colorado
Donald Ross

Lakewood CC (R)
Colorado
Press Maxwell

Lakewood CC
St. Petersburg, Florida
Herbert Strong

Lakewood CC (R)
Florida
Dick Wilson

Lakewood CC formerly known as Paganica CC
Hutchinson, Kansas
Leo Johnson

Lakewood CC
New Orleans, Louisiana
Robert Bruce Harris

Lakewood CC
Maryland
Edmund B. Ault, Al Jamison

Lakewood CC
Westlake, Ohio
A.W. Tillinghast

Lakewood CC (R. 1)
Ohio
Jack Kidwell, Michael Hurdzan

Lakewood CC
Tullahoma, Tennessee
Bubber Johnson, Pete Grandison

Lakewood CC (A. 9)
Tennessee
Kevin Tucker

309

Lakewood CC
Dallas, Texas
Tom Bendelow
Lakewood CC
Dallas, Texas
Ralph Plummer
Lakewood CC (R)
Texas
Leon Howard
Lakewood G&CC
Havana, Illinois
William James Spear
Lakewood GC
California
William P. Bell
Lakewood GC
Naples, Florida
Arthur Hills, Steve Forrest
Lakewood GC
New Jersey
Willie Dunn Jr
Lakewood GC (Azalea Course)
Point Clear, Alabama
Joe Lee
Lakewood GC (Azalea Course) (A. 9)
Alabama
Ron Garl
Lakewood GC (Dogwood Course)
Point Clear, Alabama
Perry Maxwell, Press Maxwell
Lakewood GC (Dogwood Course) (R)
Alabama
Robert Trent Jones
Lakewood GC (East Course)
Kanagawa, Japan
Ted Robinson
Lakewood GC (West Course)
Kanagawa, Japan
Ted Robinson
Lakewood Oaks GC
Lees Summit, Missouri
Jay Riviere
Lakewood Shores G&CC
Oscoda, Michigan
Bruce Matthews, Jerry Matthews
Lakewood Village GC
Texas
Leon Howard
Lakey Hill GC
Dorset, England
Brian Bramford, G.T. Holloway
Lakota Hills CC (R. 9)
Ohio
Jack Kidwell
Lakota Hills CC (A. 9)
Ohio
Jack Kidwell
Lamberhurst GC
England
C.K. Cotton, J.J.F. Pennink
Lambton G&CC (R)
Ontario
Clinton E. Robinson
Lambton G&CC (R)
Ontario
Stanley Thompson
Lamont Hill GC
Pomona, Kansas
Melvin Anderson
Lan-Yair GC
Spartanburg, South Carolina
Russell Breeden
Lanark GC
Lanarkshire, Scotland
Old Tom Morris
Lanark GC (R)
Scotland
John R. Stutt
Lancaster CC
New Hampshire
Ralph Barton
Lancaster CC
New York
Charles G. Nieman
Lancaster CC
Ohio
Donald Ross, J.B. McGovern
Lancaster CC (A. 9)
Ohio
William Gordon, David Gordon

Lancaster CC (R)
Ohio
Ken Killian
Lancaster CC
Pennsylvania
William S. Flynn
Lancaster CC (R.12)
Pennsylvania
William Gordon, David Gordon
Lancaster CC (A. 6)
Pennsylvania
William Gordon, David Gordon
Lancaster CC
South Carolina
Donald Ross
Lancaster CC (R)
South Carolina
Russell Breeden
Land und GC Dusseldorf (East Course)
Hubbelrath, West Germany
Fred W. Hawtree
Land und GC Dusseldorf (West Course)
Hubbelrath, West Germany
Fred W. Hawtree
Land Harbour GC
Blowing Rock, North Carolina
Tom Jackson
Land O'Golf GC
Miami, Florida
John E. O'Connor
Landa Park GC
New Braufels, Texas
Leon Howard
Lander Haven CC (A. 9)
Ohio
Ben W. Zink
Landings at Skidaway Island (Magnolia)
Georgia
Frank Duane, Arnold Palmer
Landings at Skidaway Island (Marshwood)
Georgia
Arnold Palmer, Ed Seay
Landings at Skidaway Island (Palmetto)
Georgia
Arthur Hills, Steve Forrest, Mike Dasher
Landings at Skidaway Island (Plantation)
Georgia
Willard Byrd, Clyde Johnston
Lands West GC
Douglasville, Georgia
Ward Northrup
Langhorne GC
Pennsylvania
Alex Findlay
Langhorne GC (R)
Pennsylvania
George Fazio
Langland Bay GC
West Glamorgan, Wales
J.J.F. Pennink
Langley AFB GC
Virginia
Edmund B. Ault
Langley AFB GC (A. 9)
Virginia
Al Zikorus
Langston GC (A. 9)
Washington, D.C.
William Gordon
Lansdown GC
England
Tom Dunn
Lansing Sportsman's C (A. 9)
Illinois
Ken Killian, Dick Nugent
Lanzo Intelvi GC
Italy
Donald Harradine
Laramie CC NLE
Chicago, Illinois
Harry Collis
Larch Tree CC
Trotwood, Ohio
Jack Kidwell
Larchmont Muni
Missoula, Montana
Richard Watson, *Keith Hellstrom*

Laredo CC
Texas
Joseph S. Finger, Baxter Spann
Larne GC
County Antrim, Northern Ireland
Willie Park
Larrimac GC (R. 9)
Ontario
Howard Watson
Larrimac GC (A. 3)
Ontario
John Watson
Larrimac GC (R. 3)
Quebec
John Watson
Larrimore CC
North Dakota
Charles Maddox
Larry Gannon Memorial GC
Lynn, Massachusetts
Wayne Stiles
Las Colinas CC
Dallas, Texas
Joseph S. Finger
Las Colinas Sports C
Irving, Texas
Robert Trent Jones Jr, Gary Roger Baird
Las Colinas Sports C (A. 9)
Texas
Jay Morrish
Las Colinas Sports C (TPC Course)
Irving, Texas
Jay Morrish
Las Huertas CC
Mexico
Percy Clifford
Las Lomas El Bosque GC
Madrid, Spain
Robert Dean Putnam
Las Posas CC
Camarillo, California
Lawrence Hughes
Las Positas Muni
Livermore, California
Robert Muir Graves
Las Praderas de Lujan GC
Argentina
Angel Reartes
Las Vegas CC
Nevada
Edmund B. Ault
Las Vegas CC (R)
Nevada
Ron Garl
Las Vegas GC
Nevada
William P. Bell
Las Vegas GC (A. 9)
Nevada
William F. Bell
Las Vegas GC (R)
Nevada
Jeff Brauer, *Jim Colbert*
Latrobe CC
Pennsylvania
Emil Loeffler, *John McGlynn*
Latrobe CC (A. 9)
Pennsylvania
James Gilmore Harrison, Ferdinand Garbin
Lauder GC
Berwickshire, Scotland
Willie Park, Willie Park Jr
Lauderdale Lakes CC
Ft. Lauderdale, Florida
Hans Schmeisser
Laughlin AFB GC
Texas
Joseph S. Finger
Launceston GC (A. 9)
England
J. Hamilton Stutt
Laurel CC
Maryland
George W. Cobb
Laurel G&RC
Montana
Theodore Wirth
Laurel G&RC (R)
Montana
Robert Muir Graves

Laurel Greens GC
Latrobe, Pennsylvania
X.G. Hassenplug
Laurel GC
Virginia
Fred Findlay
Laurel Hill GC
Gold Hill, Oregon
Harvey Granger
Laurel Oak CC
Gibbsboro, New Jersey
Gary Wren, C.H. Evans
Laurel Pines CC
Maryland
George W. Cobb
Laurel Ridge CC
Waynesville, North Carolina
Bob Cupp
Laurel Valley CC
Ligonier, Pennsylvania
Dick Wilson, Bob Simmons
Laurel Valley CC (R)
Pennsylvania
Paul E. Erath
Laurel View Muni
Hamden, Connecticut
Geoffrey S. Cornish, William G. Robinson
Laurelton GC (North Course) NLE
New York
Devereux Emmet
Laurelton GC (South Course) NLE
New York
Devereux Emmet
Laurelwood GC
Eugene, Oregon
Clarence Sutton
Lava Hills G&CC now known as Southgate GC
Lava Lava GC
American Samoa
Tolani Teleso
Laval sur le Lac GC
Quebec
Herbert Strong
Laval sur le Lac GC (R)
Quebec
Clinton E. Robinson
Laval sur le Lac GC (R. 9)
Quebec
Howard Watson
Laval sur le Lac GC (R. 3)
Quebec
John Watson
Lawrence CC
Kansas
Bob Peebles
Lawrence GC
New York
Devereux Emmet
Lawrence GC (R)
New York
Stephen Kay
Lawrence Harbour CC
New Jersey
Willie Dunn Jr
Lawrence Links
North Highland, California
Bert Stamps
Lawrence Park GC
Erie, Pennsylvania
Alfred H. Tull
Lawrence Park Village (R)
New York
Joseph S. Finger
Lawrence Welk Village GC
Escondido, California
David Rainville
Lawrenceburg CC (A. 9)
Tennessee
Arthur Davis
Lawrenceburg CC (R. 4)
Tennessee
Arthur Davis
Lawrenceville CC
Virginia
Fred Findlay, *Ben Loving*
Lawrenceville School GC
New Jersey
John Reid

Lawrenceville School GC (R)
New Jersey
William Gordon, David Gordon
Lawsonia Links
Green Lake, Wisconsin
William B. Langford, Theodore J. Moreau
Lawsonia Links (A. 9)
Wisconsin
Joe Lee, Rocky Roquemore
Lawton CC
Oklahoma
Perry Maxwell, Press Maxwell
Lawton CC (A. 9)
Oklahoma
Floyd Farley
Lazy H GC
California
Bob Baldock
Le Betulle GC
Biella, Italy
J.S.F. Morrison
Le Betulle GC (R)
Italy
John Harris
Le Chantecler GC
Quebec
Howard Watson
Le Chateau Montebello GC
Montebello, Quebec
Stanley Thompson
Le Chicciole GC (R)
Italy
M. Croze
Le Fronde GC
Avigliana, Italy
John Harris
Le G du Rhin
Mulhouse, France
Donald Harradine
Le Portage GC
Cheticamp, Nova Scotia
Robert Moote
Le Rovedine GC
Italy
M. Croze
Le Seigneurie de Vaudrevil GC
Louisville, Quebec
Howard Watson
Le Triomphe GC
Lafayette, Louisiana
Robert Trent Jones Jr, Gary Linn
Leamington and County GC
England
H.S. Colt
Leamington and County GC (R)
England
James Braid, John R. Stutt
Leaning Tree GC
West Richfield, Ohio
Richard W. LaConte, Ted McAnlis
Leathem Smith Lodge GC
Sturgeon Bay, Wisconsin
William B. Langford, Theodore J. Moreau
Leatherstocking CC
Cooperstown, New York
Devereux Emmet
Leavenworth CC
Kansas
Tom Bendelow
Leawood South CC
Leawood, Kansas
Bob Dunning
Lebanon CC (R)
New Hampshire
Orrin Smith, William F. Mitchell
Lebanon CC
Pennsylvania
Frank Murray, Russell Roberts
Lebanon CC NLE
Pennsylvania
Alex Findlay
Lebanon CC (R)
Pennsylvania
Ferdinand Garbin
Leckford GC
England
H.S. Colt, J.S.F. Morrison, C.H. Alison
Ledgemont CC
Seekonk, Massachusetts
Alfred H. Tull

Ledges CC
Roscoe, Illinois
Edward Lawrence Packard
Ledgeview G&CC
Abbotsford, British Columbia
Wally Shamenski
Lee Park GC (A. 9)
South Dakota
Clifford A. Anderson
Lee Park GC (R)
South Dakota
Gary L. Nelson
Lee Park GC
Liverpool, England
C.K. Cotton, J.J.F. Pennink
Lee Win GC
Salem, Ohio
Jack Kidwell
Lee-on-the-Solent GC
England
John Duncan Dunn
Lee-on-the-Solent GC (R)
England
J. Hamilton Stutt
Leeds Castle GC
England
Sir Guy Campbell, C.K.
 Hutchison, S.V. Hotchkin
Leek GC (R)
England
Tom Williamson
Lees Hall GC
Yorkshire, England
Sandy Herd
Lees Hall GC (R)
England
Tom Williamson
Leesburg G&CC
Virginia
Edmund B. Ault
Leewood GC
Eastchester, New York
Devereux Emmet
Legend Lake GC
Chardon, Ohio
Reece Alexander
Legion Memorial GC
Everett, Washington
H. Chandler Egan
Lehigh CC
Florida
R. Albert Anderson
Lehigh CC
Emmaus, Pennsylvania
William S. Flynn, Howard
 Toomey
Lehigh CC (R)
Pennsylvania
William Gordon, David Gordon
Leicester Hill CC (R)
Massachusetts
William F. Mitchell
Leisure Lakes G&CC
Lake Placid, Florida
J.R. "Buddy" Simpson
Leisure Town GC (R)
California
Robert Muir Graves
Leisure Village GC
Laguna Hills, California
Edward Lawrence Packard
Leisure Village GC
Woodlake, New Jersey
Edward Lawrence Packard
Leisure World GC
Mesa, Arizona
Johnny Bulla
Leisure World GC
Mesa, Arizona
Jeff Hardin, Greg Nash
Leland CC
Michigan
C.D. Wagstaff
Leland CC (R. 9)
Michigan
Rees Jones
Leland CC (A. 9)
Michigan
Rees Jones
Leland Meadows Par 3 GC
Long Bain, California
Bob Baldock

Lely Community GC
Florida
David Wallace
Lely G&CC
Naples, Florida
David Wallace
Lemontree GC
Belleville, Michigan
Clinton E. Robinson
Lemore Muni
California
Bob Baldock
Lenape Heights GC
Ford City, Pennsylvania
Ferdinand Garbin
Lennoxville GC
Quebec
Howard Watson
Lenoir CC
North Carolina
Donald Ross
Lenzerheide Valbella GC
Lenzerheide, Switzerland
James Gannon
Lenzerheide Valbella GC (A. 9)
Switzerland
Fred W. Hawtree
Leonard Litwin Private Course
New York
Stephen Kay
**Leonard Wheatley Private
 Course**
Hillhead, Quebec
Howard Watson
Leroy CC
Illinois
Tom Bendelow
Leroy King Private Course
Hesston, Kansas
Floyd Farley
Les Buttes Blanches GC (R)
Belgium
Fred W. Hawtree
Les Terrasses de Geneve G&CC
Bossey, France
Robert Trent Jones Jr, Don Knott
Les Vieux Chenes GC
Youngsville, Louisiana
Marvin Ferguson
Leslie Park GC
Ann Arbor, Michigan
Edward Lawrence Packard
Letchworth GC
Hertfordshire, England
Harry Vardon
Lethbridge GC
Alberta
Tom Bendelow
Lethbridge GC (A. 9)
Alberta
William G. Robinson
Lethbridge GC (R)
Alberta
William G. Robinson
Letterkenny GC
County Donegal, Ireland
Eddie Hackett
Levis GC (R)
Quebec
Howard Watson
Lew Galbraith Muni
Oakland, California
Bob Baldock
Lew Galbraith Muni (R)
California
Robert Muir Graves
Lew Wentz Memorial GC
Ponca City, Oklahoma
Arthur Jackson
Lew Wentz Memorial GC (R. 9)
Oklahoma
Floyd Farley
Lew Wentz Memorial GC (A. 9)
Oklahoma
Floyd Farley
Lewiston CC
Idaho
Bob Baldock, Robert L. Baldock
Lewiston Elks CC
Montana
William H. Diddel
Lewistown CC
Pennsylvania
Edmund B. Ault

Lexington CC
Kentucky
Tom Bendelow
Lexington CC (A. 5)
Kentucky
Benjamin Wihry
Lexington CC (R. 4)
Kentucky
Benjamin Wihry
Lexington GC
Virginia
Ellis Maples, Ed Seay
Lexington VA Hospital GC
Kentucky
Bob Baldock
Liberal CC
Kansas
Dewey Longworth
Liberty Hills CC
Liberty, Missouri
Ray Pettegrew
Liberty Lake GC
Spokane, Washington
Mel "Curley" Hueston
Liberty Lake GC (R. 1)
Washington
John Steidel
Libertyville CC
Illinois
Leonard Macomber
Lick Creek GC
Pekin, Illinois
Edward Lawrence Packard,
 Roger Packard
Lickey Hills GC
Birmingham, England
F.G. Hawtree, J.H. Taylor
Licking Springs G & Trout C
Newark, Ohio
Jack Kidwell
Lido Di Venezia GC (R)
Italy
Henry Cotton
Lido Golf Centre
Oakville, Ontario
Clinton E. Robinson
Lido GC NLE
Long Beach, New York
Charles Blair Macdonald, Seth
 Raynor
Lido Springs GC
Lido Beach, New York
William F. Mitchell
Lighthouse Sound GC
Maryland
Hal Purdy, Malcolm Purdy
Ligonier CC (R. 9)
Pennsylvania
X.G. Hassenplug
Lilleshall Hall GC
England
H.S. Colt, J.S.F. Morrison
Limburg GC
Hasselt, Belgium
Fred W. Hawtree
Limerick GC
Ireland
James Braid
Limerick GC (R)
Ireland
Eddie Hackett
Limerick GC (A. 9)
Ireland
James Braid
Limon GC
Colorado
Henry B. Hughes
Lincoln CC
Illinois
Tom Bendelow
Lincoln Greens GC
Springfield, Illinois
Robert Bruce Harris
Lincoln GC (A. 2)
Michigan
Jerry Matthews
Lincoln Hills CC
Riudoso, New Mexico
Ralph Plummer
Lincoln Hills CC
Marshfield, Wisconsin
Edward Lawrence Packard

Lincoln Hills GC
Birmingham, Michigan
Bruce Matthews, Jerry Matthews
Lincoln Hills GC (R. 1)
Michigan
Jerry Matthews
Lincoln Park GC (R)
California
Jack Fleming
Lincoln Park GC
Milwaukee, Wisconsin
Tom Bendelow
Lincoln Park Muni (East Course)
Oklahoma City, Oklahoma
Arthur Jackson
**Lincoln Park Muni (East Course)
 (R)**
Oklahoma
Perry Maxwell
**Lincoln Park Muni (East Course)
 (R)**
Oklahoma
Floyd Farley
**Lincoln Park Muni (West
 Course)**
Oklahoma City, Oklahoma
Arthur Jackson
**Lincoln Park Muni (West
 Course) (R)**
Oklahoma
Perry Maxwell
**Lincoln Park Muni (West
 Course) (R)**
Oklahoma
Floyd Farley
Lincolnshire CC (Course No. 1)
Crete, Illinois
Tom Bendelow
**Lincolnshire CC (Course No. 1)
 (R)**
Illinois
Ken Killian, Dick Nugent
Lincolnshire CC (Course No. 2)
Crete, Illinois
Tom Bendelow
**Lincolnshire CC (Course No. 2)
 (R)**
Illinois
Ken Killian, Dick Nugent
Lincolnshire Fields GC
Champaign, Illinois
Edward Lawrence Packard
Lindale Greens GC
Sacramento, California
Bob Baldock, Robert L. Baldock
Lindau-Bad Schachen GC
Lindau, West Germany
Bernhard von Limburger
Lindbook CC
Hope Valley, Rhode Island
Phil Wogan
Lindbrook CC (R)
Rhode Island
Phil Wogan
Lindeman Island GC
Queensland, Australia
Ted Ashby
Linden G&CC
Puyallup, Washington
William H. Tucker, Frank
 James, Gregor MacMillan
Linden GC
Alabama
Neil R. Bruce
Lindrick GC
England
Tom Dunn
Lindrick GC (R)
England
Fred W. Hawtree
Lindsay Muni
California
Bob Baldock
Lingan GC
Sydney, Nova Scotia
Stanley Thompson
Lingan GC (A. 9)
Nova Scotia
Clinton E. Robinson
Link Hills CC
Greenville, Tennessee
Robert Trent Jones

Linkopings GC
Sweden
Gunnar Bauer
Links at Monarch Beach
Laguna Niguel, California
Robert Trent Jones Jr, Gary Linn
Links at Nichols Park
Jacksonville, Illinois
David Gill, Garrett Gill
Links at Pinewood
Walled Lake, Michigan
Ernest Fuller
Links at Porto Carras
New Marmoras, Greece
Geoffrey S. Cornish, William G.
 Robinson
Links of Lake Bernadette
Zephyrhills, Florida
Dean Refram
Links GC
Highlands Ranch, Colorado
Dick Phelps
Links GC
Savannah, Georgia
P.B. Dye
Links GC NLE
Roslyn, New York
Charles Blair Macdonald, Seth
 Raynor
Links GC (R)
New York
Perry Maxwell
Links GC
Newmarket, England
S.V. Hotchkin
Links O'Tryon
Tryon, North Carolina
Tom Jackson
Linn CC
Missouri
Chet Mendenhall
Linrick GC
Columbia, South Carolina
Russell Breeden
Linville GC
North Carolina
Donald Ross
Linville GC (R)
North Carolina
Richard S. Tufts
Linville Ridge CC
Linville, North Carolina
George W. Cobb, John LaFoy
Linwood CC
New Jersey
Herbert Strong
Linz GC
Tillysburg, Austria
Donald Harradine
Lions Muni
Columbus, Georgia
Nolan Murrah
Liphook GC
England
A.C.M. Croome, J.F. Abercromby
Liphook GC (R)
England
Tom Simpson
Liphook GC (A. 2)
England
J.S.F. Morrison
Liphook GC (R)
England
J.S.F. Morrison
Lisbon Bissell GC (R. 9)
North Dakota
Don Herfort
Lisbon CC
Aroeira, Portugal
J.J.F. Pennink
Lisbon Sports C
Portugal
F.G. Hawtree
Lisbon Sports C (A. 9)
Portugal
Fred W. Hawtree
Lisburn GC
Belfast, Northern Ireland
Fred W. Hawtree
Lismore GC
County Waterford, Ireland
Eddie Hackett

Lismore GC (R)
Ireland
Eddie Hackett
Listowel GC (A.10)
Ontario
Robert Moote
Listowel GC (R. 8)
Ontario
Robert Moote
Litchfield CC
South Carolina
Willard Byrd
Lithia Springs CC
Georgia
Johnny Suggs
Little America GC
Cheyenne, Wyoming
William H. Neff
Little Aston GC
Staffordshire, England
Harry Vardon
Little Aston GC (R)
England
M.J. Lewis
Little Aston GC (R)
England
H.S. Colt
Little C
Delray Beach, Florida
Joe Lee
Little Chalfont GC
England
R. Garrad
Little Course
Norcross, Georgia
Ron Kirby
Little Crow CC
Spicer, Minnesota
Don Herfort
Little Cypress G&CC
Wauchulla, Florida
R. Albert Anderson
Little Harbor GC
Wareham, Massachusetts
Samuel Mitchell
Little Hay GC
Hertfordshire, England
Fred W. Hawtree, Martin
  Hawtree
Little Knoll GC
Napa, California
Clark Glasson
Little Lakes GC
Worcestershire, England
Michael Cooksey
Little Mill CC
Marlton, New Jersey
Garrett J. Renn
Little Mill CC (A. 9)
New Jersey
David Gordon
Little Mountain CC (R)
Georgia
Arthur Davis, Ron Kirby
Little Mountain State Park GC
Gunthersville, Alabama
Earl Stone
Little Sioux G&CC
Sioux Rapids, Iowa
Harold McCullough
Little St. Andrews GC
Springfield, Massachusetts
Geoffrey S. Cornish
Little Tam GC
Niles, Illinois
William James Spear
Little Turtle C
Columbus, Ohio
Pete Dye, Roy Dye
Littlehampton GC (R. 9)
England
F.G. Hawtree, J.H. Taylor
Littlehampton GC (A. 9)
England
F.G. Hawtree, J.H. Taylor
Littlestone GC
Kent, England
W. Laidlaw Purves
Littlestone GC (R)
England
James Braid
Littlestone GC (R)
England
Tom Dunn

Littlestone GC (R)
England
F.W. Maude
Lively GC (A. 9)
Ontario
Robert Moote
Lively GC (R. 9)
Ontario
Robert Moote
Liveoaks CC
Jackson, Mississippi
George C. Curtis
Livermore VA Hospital GC
California
Bob Baldock
Liverpool Muni
England
J. Large
Livingston G&CC
Edinburgh, Scotland
J.J.F. Pennink, C.D. Lawrie
Livingston GC
Alabama
Paul Hagen
Ljunghusens GC (R)
Sweden
Ronald Fream
Ljunghusens GC (R)
Sweden
Jan Sederholm
Llandrindod Wells GC
Powys, Wales
Harry Vardon
Llanerch CC
Havertown, Pennsylvania
Alex Findlay
Llanerch CC (R)
Pennsylvania
J.B. McGovern
Loch Ledge G&CC
Yorktown Heights, New York
Nat Squire
Loch March GC
Kanata, Ontario
Gordon Witteveen
Lochinvar GC
Houston, Texas
Jack Nicklaus, Jay Morrish, Bob
  Cupp
Lochland CC
Hastings, Nebraska
David Gill
Lochmere GC
Cary, North Carolina
Gene Hamm
Lochmoor C
Grosse Pointe Woods, Michigan
Walter J. Travis
Lochmoor C (R)
Michigan
C.H. Alison, H.S. Colt
Lochmoor C (R)
Michigan
Edward Lawrence Packard
Lochmoor C (R)
Michigan
Arthur Hills, Steve Forrest
Lockhaven CC
Alton, Illinois
Robert Bruce Harris
Lockmoor GC
North Ft. Myers, Florida
William F. Mitchell
Lockport CC (R)
New York
Stanley Thompson
Locust Grove GC
Rahway, New Jersey
Willard Wilkinson
Locust Hill CC
Rochester, New York
Seymour Dunn
Locust Hill CC (R)
New York
Robert Trent Jones
Locust Tree GC
New Paltz, New York
Hal Purdy
Locust Valley CC
Coopersburg, Pennsylvania
William Gordon, David Gordon
Lodge of the Four Seasons GC
Lake Ozark, Missouri
Homer Herpel

Log Cabin C
Clayton, Missouri
Robert Foulis
Log Cabin C (R)
Missouri
James Dalgleish
Log Cabin C (R)
Missouri
Robert Foulis
Logan G&CC
Utah
Mick Riley
Logansport CC
Indiana
Bob Simmons
Logo de Vita GC
Greensburg, Pennsylvania
Ferdinand Garbin
Lohersand GC
Rendsburg, West Germany
Bernhard von Limburger
Loholm GC
Sweden
Jan Sederholm
Loma Linda CC
Joplin, Missouri
Don Sechrest
Lomas Santa Fe Executive GC
Solana Beach, California
Ted Robinson
Lomas Santa Fe GC
Solana Beach, California
William F. Bell
London Bridge GC
Lake Havasu City, Arizona
Lawrence Hughes
London Bridge GC (A. 9)
Arizona
Arthur Jack Snyder
London GC
Kentucky
John Darrah
London Hunt & CC
London, Ontario
Robert Trent Jones, Frank Duane
London Scottish GC NLE
England
Willie Dunn
London Scottish GC (A. 9)
England
Tom Dunn
London Scottish GC (R)
England
Tom Dunn
Lone Oak CC
Nicholasville, Kentucky
Buck Blankenship
Lone Palm GC
Lakeland, Florida
Dick Wilson, Joe Lee
Lone Pine GC
West Palm Beach, Florida
Richard W. LaConte, Ted
  McAnlis
Lone Pine GC
New Jersey
Donald Ross
Lone Pine GC (R)
New Jersey
X.G. Hassenplug
Lone Pine GC
Washington, Pennsylvania
X.G. Hassenplug
Lone Tree GC
Littleton, Colorado
Arnold Palmer, Ed Seay
Long Bay C
North Myrtle Beach, South
  Carolina
Jack Nicklaus, *Tom Pearson*
Long Beach Hotel GC NLE
New York
John Duncan Dunn
Long Branch CC
New Jersey
Martin J. O'Loughlin
Long Cove C
Hilton Head Island, South
  Carolina
Pete Dye, P.B. Dye
Long Meadow GC
Lowell, Massachusetts
Alex Findlay

Long Meadows CC NLE
Jersey Village, Texas
Bob Simmons
Long Point GC
Amelia Island, Florida
Tom Fazio
Long Run GC
Anchorage, Kentucky
Benjamin Wihry
**Longboat Key C (Harborside
  Course)**
Sarasota, Florida
Willard Byrd, Clyde Johnston
**Longboat Key C (Islandside
  Course)**
Sarasota, Florida
William F. Mitchell
**Longboat Key C (Islandside
  Course) (R)**
Florida
Willard Byrd, Clyde Johnston
Longcliffe GC
Leicestershire, England
Tom Williamson
Longfellow House GC
Pascagoula, Mississippi
Earl Stone
Longmeadow CC
Springfield, Massachusetts
Donald Ross
Longmeadow CC (R)
Massachusetts
William F. Mitchell
Longmeadow CC (R. 1)
Massachusetts
Geoffrey S. Cornish
Longniddry GC
Scotland
H.S. Colt, C.H. Alison
Longniddry GC (R)
Scotland
P.M. Ross
Longshore C Park
Westport, Connecticut
Orrin Smith
Longue Vue C
Verona, Pennsylvania
Robert White
Longue Vue C (R)
Pennsylvania
Ferdinand Garbin
Longview Lake GC
Lee's Summit, Missouri
Brad Benz, Mike Poellot, Mark
  Rathert
Longview Muni (R. 3)
Maryland
Edmund B. Ault, Bill Love
Longwood CC
Dyer, Indiana
Harry Collis
**Lookout Mountain GC formerly
  known as Fairyland CC**
Georgia
Seth Raynor, Charles Banks
Lorain CC
Ohio
Tom Bendelow
Lord Mountbatten Estate GC
England
Herbert Fowler, Tom Simpson
Lords Valley CC
Hawley, Pennsylvania
Norman H. Woods
Lorette GC (R. 9)
Quebec
Howard Watson
Loring AFB GC
Limestone, Maine
William F. Mitchell
Los Alamitos GC (R)
California
William F. Bell
Los Alamitos GC (A.12)
California
William F. Bell
Los Altos G&CC
California
Tom Nicoll
Los Altos G&CC (R. 9)
California
Robert Muir Graves

Los Altos G&CC (R)
California
Clark Glasson
Los Altos Muni
Albuquerque, New Mexico
Bob Baldock
Los Andes GC
Lima, Peru
George Hardmann
Los Angeles CC (North Course)
California
George C. Thomas Jr
**Los Angeles CC (North Course)
  (R)**
California
William P. Bell
Los Angeles CC (South Course)
California
Herbert Fowler
**Los Angeles CC (South Course)
  (R)**
California
George C. Thomas Jr
Los Angeles National GC
California
William P. Bell
Los Banos CC
California
Bob Baldock
Los Caballeros GC
Wickenburg, Arizona
Jeff Hardin, Greg Nash
Los Coyotes CC
California
William F. Bell
Los Coyotes CC (R. 6)
California
Ted Robinson
Los Flamingos CC
Puerto Vallarta, Mexico
Percy Clifford
Los Gatos G&CC
San Jose, California
Clark Glasson
Los Lagos GC
Mijas, Spain
Robert Trent Jones, Cabell
  Robinson
Los Leones GC
Chile
A. Macdonald
Los Prados GC
Las Vegas, Nevada
Jeff Hardin
Los Rios CC
Plano, Texas
Don January, Billy Martindale
Los Robles Greens GC
Thousand Oaks, California
Bob Baldock
**Los Serranos Lakes CC (North
  Course)**
Chino, California
John Duncan Dunn
**Los Serranos Lakes CC (North
  Course) (R)**
California
Harry Rainville, David Rainville
**Los Serranos Lakes G&CC
  (South Course)**
Chino, California
Bill Eaton
**Los Serranos Lakes G&CC
  (South Course) (R)**
California
Harry Rainville, David Rainville
Los Verdes G&CC
California
William F. Bell
Losantiville CC
Cincinnati, Ohio
Tom Bendelow
Losantiville CC (R)
Ohio
Hal Purdy
Lost Brook GC
Norwood, Massachusetts
Samuel Mitchell
Lost Creek CC (R)
Ohio
Hal Purdy
Lost Creek GC
Texas
Dave Bennett

Lost Lake Woods GC (A. 9)
Michigan
Ken Killian, Dick Nugent
Lost Pines GC
Bastrop, Texas
Leon Howard
Lost Tree C
Singer Island, Florida
Mark Mahannah
Lost Tree C (R)
Florida
Bob Cupp, Jay Morrish
Loudoun G&CC
Virginia
Edmund B. Ault, Al Jamison
Loughrea GC (R)
Ireland
Eddie Hackett
Louis Stoner Private Course
West Hartford, Connecticut
Orrin Smith
Louisiana State Univ GC
Baton Rouge, Louisiana
E.E. Evans, Al Michael
Louisville CC
Kentucky
Robert White
Louisville CC (A. 9)
Kentucky
Walter J. Travis
Louisville CC (R. 9)
Kentucky
Walter J. Travis
Louisville CC (R)
Kentucky
William B. Langford, Theodore J. Moreau
Louisville CC (R)
Kentucky
William H. Diddel
Louisville CC (A. 1)
Kentucky
Benjamin Wihry
Louisville CC (R. 1)
Kentucky
Benjamin Wihry
Louth GC
Lincolnshire, England
Tom Williamson
Louth GC (R)
England
C.K. Cotton, J.J.F. Pennink
Loveland GC
Colorado
Henry B. Hughes
Loveland GC (R)
Colorado
Dick Phelps
Loveland GC (A. 9)
Colorado
Frank Hummel
Lovington Muni
New Mexico
Warren Cantrell
Lower Cascades GC
Virginia Hot Springs, Virginia
Robert Trent Jones
Lowestoft GC
England
J.J.F. Pennink
Lowry AFB GC
Colorado
Bob Baldock
Loxahatchee C
Jupiter, Florida
Jack Nicklaus, Bob Cupp, *Tom Pearson*
Lu Lu Temple CC
North Hills, Pennsylvania
Donald Ross
Lubbock CC (R)
Texas
Joseph S. Finger, Ken Dye
Lubbock CC (A. 9)
Texas
Warren Cantrell
Lubbock CC (R. 9)
Texas
Warren Cantrell
Lucan GC (R)
Ireland
Eddie Hackett

Lucaya Park G&CC
Freeport, Bahamas
Dick Wilson, Joe Lee, Bob Simmons
Lucerne GC
Winter Haven, Florida
David Wallace
Lucerne-in-Quebec GC
Montebello, Quebec
Stanley Thompson
Lucky Hills CC
Franklin, Pennsylvania
X.G. Hassenplug
Luden Riverside CC
Pennsylvania
Alex Findlay
Ludington Hills GC
Ludington, Michigan
Tom Bendelow
Ludington Hills GC (R. 4)
Michigan
Bruce Matthews, Jerry Matthews
Ludington Hills GC (A. 9)
Michigan
Bruce Matthews, Jerry Matthews
Ludlow CC
Massachusetts
Donald Ross
Ludlow Muni
Chicopee, Massachusetts
Orrin Smith, Al Zikorus
Luffenham Heath GC
England
James Braid
Luffness New GC
East Lothian, Scotland
Old Tom Morris
Luffness New GC (R)
Scotland
Tom Simpson
Luffness New GC (R)
Scotland
Willie Park Jr
Lugano GC (R)
Switzerland
Donald Harradine
Lugano GC (R. 3)
Switzerland
Pier Mancinelli
Luisita GC
Tarlac, Philippines
Robert Trent Jones
Lullingstone Park GC
Kent, England
Fred W. Hawtree
Lum International GC
Michigan
Joseph Hawald
Lumby GC
British Columbia
Reggie Betts
Luray Caverns CC
Luray, Virginia
Hal Purdy, Malcolm Purdy
Luray GC NLE
Virginia
Fred Findlay
Lurgan GC (R)
Netherlands
J.J.F. Pennink
Lusaka GC
Zambia
J.J.F. Pennink
Lusk GC
Wyoming
Frank Hummel
Lutterworth GC (A. 9)
England
Fred W. Hawtree
Lyford Cay C
New Providence, Bahamas
Dick Wilson, Joe Lee, Bob Simmons
Lyman Meadow GC
Middlefield, Connecticut
Robert Trent Jones, Roger Rulewich
Lyndhurst GC
Ohio
Sandy Alves
Lynn Haven CC
Norfolk, Virginia
Tom Winton

Lynnfield Center GC (R)
Massachusetts
William F. Mitchell
Lynwood G&CC
Martinsville, Virginia
Gene Hamm
Lynwood GC
London, Ontario
Robert Moote, *David Moote*
Lyon-Charbonniere GC
France
Pier Mancinelli
Lyons CC
Kansas
Dewey Longworth
Lyons Den GC
Akron, Ohio
Bill Lyons
Lyons VA Hospital GC
New Jersey
Robert Trent Jones
M & W GC
Winnsboro, Texas
Leon Howard
Macarena GC
Colombia
Mark Mahannah
Maccauvlei CC
Transvaal, South Africa
S.V. Hotchkin
Macdill AFB GC (New Course)
Tampa, Florida
Ron Garl
Macdill AFB GC (Old Course) (R)
Florida
Ron Garl
Macdonald Park Muni
Wichita, Kansas
James Dalgleish
Macdonald Park Muni (R)
Kansas
Orrin Smith
Macdonald Park Muni (R)
Kansas
William H. Diddel
Macdonald Park Muni (R)
Kansas
Bob Dunning
Mace Meadows GC
Jackson, California
Jack Fleming
Machrie Hotel GC
Scotland
Willie Campbell
Machrie Hotel GC (R)
Scotland
D.M.A. Steel
Machrihanish GC
Argyllshire, Scotland
Charles Hunter
Machrihanish GC (R)
Scotland
Sir Guy Campbell
Machrihanish GC (R)
Scotland
Old Tom Morris
Machrihanish GC (A. 6)
Scotland
Old Tom Morris
Machrihanish GC (R)
Scotland
J.H. Taylor
Machynlleth GC
Powys, Wales
James Braid
Mackenzie's GC
New Hampshire
Ralph Barton
Macktown GC
Rockton, Illinois
R. Welch
Macomb CC (R)
Illinois
Robert Bruce Harris
Mactaquac Provincial Park GC
New Brunswick
William F. Mitchell
MacDonald Estate GC
Bal Harbour, Florida
Robert Trent Jones
MacGregor Downs CC
Cary, North Carolina
Willard Byrd

Madeline Island G Links
Wisconsin
Robert Trent Jones, Robert Trent Jones Jr
Madera CC
California
Bob Baldock
Madge Lake GC (R)
Quebec
William F. Mitchell
Madge Lake GC (R. 9)
Saskatchewan
Clinton E. Robinson
Madge Lake GC (A. 9)
Saskatchewan
Clinton E. Robinson
Madison CC
Connecticut
Willie Park Jr
Madison CC (R)
Connecticut
Brian Silva, Geoffrey S. Cornish
Madison CC
Madison, Florida
Hans Schmeisser
Madison CC
Ohio
Sandy Alves
Madison Meadows GC
Ennis, Montana
Frank Hummel
Madison Park Muni
Illinois
Tom Bendelow
Madrona Links
Gig Harbor, Washington
Kenneth Tyson
Maggie Valley CC
North Carolina
William Prevost
Magnolia CC
Arkansas
Herman Hackbarth
Magnolia GC
Massachusetts
Ralph Barton
Magnolia Hills CC
Suncoast, Australia
Robert von Hagge, Bruce Devlin
Magnolia Point G&CC
Green Cove Springs, Florida
Mark McCumber
Magnolia Ridge CC
Liberty, Texas
Ralph Plummer
Magnolia Valley G&CC
New Port Richey, Florida
Phil Leckey
Magnolia Valley G&CC (R)
Florida
Bill Amick
Magnolia Valley G&CC (A. 4)
Florida
Bill Amick
Mahachia GC
Bangkok, Thailand
Greg Nash
Mahogany Run GC
St. Thomas, Virgin Islands
George Fazio, Tom Fazio
Mahon Muni
County Cork, Ireland
Eddie Hackett
Mahoney GC
Lincoln, Nebraska
Floyd Farley
Mahoning Valley CC NLE
Lansford, Pennsylvania
Maurice McCarthy
Mahoning Valley CC
Leighton, Pennsylvania
William Gordon, David Gordon
Mahopac GC
New York
Devereux Emmet
Mahopac GC NLE
Lake Mahopac, New York
Tom Bendelow
Maidenhead GC
England
Tom Dunn
Maidenhead GC (R)
England
Willie Park Jr

Maidstone C
East Hampton, New York
William H. Tucker
Maidstone C (R)
New York
Perry Maxwell
Maidstone C (A. 9)
New York
Willie Park Jr, *John A. Park*
Maidstone C (A. 9)
New York
C. Wheaton Vaughan
Maidstone C (R.11)
New York
Willie Park Jr, *John A. Park*
Maidstone C (R)
New York
Alfred H. Tull
Mainlands GC
Tamarac, Florida
William Boorman
Majestic Oaks CC
Blaine, Minnesota
Charles Maddox
Majestic Oaks CC
Salt Lake City, Utah
William H. Neff
Makaha Inn & CC (East Course)
Oahu, Hawaii
William F. Bell
Makaha Inn & CC (East Course) (R)
Hawaii
Robin Nelson
Makaha Inn & CC (West Course)
Oahu, Hawaii
William F. Bell
Makaha Inn & CC (West Course) (R)
Hawaii
Arthur Jack Snyder
Makena GC (New Course)
Maui, Hawaii
Robert Trent Jones Jr, Don Knott
Makena GC (Old Course)
Maui, Hawaii
Robert Trent Jones Jr, Don Knott
Malaga GC
Spain
Tom Simpson
Malahide GC
County Dublin, Ireland
N. Hone
Malahide GC (R)
Ireland
Eddie Hackett
Malden GC
Surrey, England
Sandy Herd, *H. Bailey*
Malkins Bank GC
Cheshire, England
Fred W. Hawtree, A.H.F. Jiggens
Mallard Head CC
Mooresville, North Carolina
J. Porter Gibson
Mallow GC (R. 9)
Ireland
John Harris
Mallow GC (A. 9)
Ireland
John Harris
Malmo GC
Sweden
Jan Sederholm
Malone GC
New York
Willard Wilkinson
Malone GC (A. 9)
New York
Albert Murray
Malone GC
Belfast, Northern Ireland
Fred W. Hawtree
Malton & Norton GC (A. 9)
England
Fred W. Hawtree, Martin Hawtree
Malvern GC (A. 9)
England
Fred W. Hawtree
Malvern Hills CC (R)
North Carolina
Ross Taylor

Manada GC
Lebanon, Pennsylvania
David Gordon
Manago CC
Japan
Arnold Palmer, Ed Seay
Manaki G&CC (R)
Ontario
Clinton E. Robinson
Manakiki G&CC
Willoughby, Ohio
Donald Ross
Manasquan River G&CC
Brielle, New Jersey
Robert White
Manatee County GC
Bradenton, Florida
Lane Marshall
Manchester CC
Connecticut
Tom Bendelow
Manchester CC
New Hampshire
Donald Ross
Manchester CC (R. 4)
New Hampshire
Phil Wogan
Manchester CC
Vermont
Geoffrey S. Cornish, William G.
   Robinson
Manchester GC
Lancashire, England
H.S. Colt
Manchester GC (R)
England
Alister Mackenzie
Manderly GC
North Gower, Ontario
Howard Watson
Mandurah Resort GC
Australia
Robert Trent Jones Jr, Don Knott
Mangrove Bay GC
St. Petersburg, Florida
Bill Amick
Manhattan CC NLE
Kansas
Mike Ahearn
Manhattan CC
Kansas
Smiley Bell
Manhattan CC (R. 1)
Kansas
Jeff Brauer
Manhattan CC
Freeport, New York
Devereux Emmet
Manila G&CC
Makati, Philippines
Bob Baldock
Manistee G&CC
Michigan
Tom Bendelow
Manistee G&CC (A. 9)
Michigan
Bruce Matthews
Manistee G&CC (R. 9)
Michigan
Bruce Matthews
Manito G&CC
Spokane, Washington
A. Vernon Macan
Manito G&CC (R)
Washington
Peter Thomson, Michael
   Wolveridge,Ronald Fream
Manitou Ridge GC (R)
Minnesota
Don Herfort
Manitouwadge GC
Ontario
Howard Watson
Manitowoc GC
Wisconsin
Tom Bendelow
Mankato GC
Minnesota
William B. Langford, Theodore J.
   Moreau
Mankato GC (A. 9)
Minnesota
William B. Langford

Mankato GC (R)
Minnesota
Donald G. Brauer, Emile Perret
Manley's GC
Albion, Michigan
Robert Beard
Mannheim-Viernheim GC
Mannheim, West Germany
Karl Hoffmann, Bernhard von
   Limburger
Manoir Richelieu GC
Murray Bay, Quebec
Herbert Strong
Manor CC
Rockville, Maryland
Harry Collis
Manor CC (R)
Maryland
Reuben Hines
Manor CC (R. 4)
Maryland
Edmund B. Ault, Brian Ault,Bill
   Love
Manor CC
Sinking Springs, Pennsylvania
Alex Findlay
Manor CC (R)
Pennsylvania
William S. Flynn
Manor House Hotel GC
England
J.F. Abercromby, Herbert Fowler
Manor House Hotel GC (R)
England
James Alexander
Manteca GC
California
Jack Fleming
Manufacturers G&CC
Oreland, Pennsylvania
William S. Flynn
Manufacturers G&CC (R. 1)
Pennsylvania
William Gordon
Manufacturers G&CC (A. 9)
Pennsylvania
William Gordon, David Gordon
Manwallimink GC
Shawnee-on Delaware,
   Pennsylvania
C.C. Worthington
Maple Bluff CC NLE
Madison, Wisconsin
H.J. Tweedie
Maple Bluff CC (R)
Wisconsin
George B. Ferry
Maple Bluff CC (R)
Wisconsin
Ken Killian, Dick Nugent
Maple City G&CC
Chatham, Ontario
Clinton E. Robinson, Robert
   Moote
Maple Crest CC
Kenosha, Wisconsin
Leonard Macomber
Maple Crest GC
LaGrange, Illinois
William B. Langford
Maple Downs G&CC
Ontario
William F. Mitchell
Maple Hill GC
Augusta, Michigan
Robert Beard
Maple Hill GC
Hemlock, Michigan
Carol O. Hegenauer
Maple Hill GC (R. 1)
Michigan
Jerry Matthews
Maple Hills GC
Grandville, Michigan
George Woolferd
Maple Lane GC (Course No. 2)
Warren, Michigan
Clarence Wolfrom
Maple Leaf Estates CC
Port Charlotte, Florida
Ward Northrup
Maple Ridge GC
Calgary, Alberta
Dick Phelps, *Claude Muret*

Maple River GC
West Fargo, North Dakota
Edward Lawrence Packard
Maple Village GC
Omaha, Nebraska
Harold Glissmann
Maplecrest CC (R)
Indiana
Gary Kern
Maplecrest GC NLE
Downers Grove, Illinois
Robert Bruce Harris
Mapledale CC
Dover, Delaware
Russell Roberts
Maplehurst CC
Frostburg, Maryland
James Gilmore Harrison
Maplemoor CC
White Plains, New York
Tom Winton, *Archie Capper*
Maplemoor CC (R)
New York
Tom Winton
Maples of Ballantrae GC
Whitchurch, Ontario
Robert Moote
Mapleview G&CC
Renton, Washington
Frank James
Maplewood CC
Bethlehem, New Hampshire
Donald Ross
Maplewood CC
Washington
Al Smith
Maplewood GC
New Hampshire
Alex Findlay
Mapperley GC
Nottinghamshire, England
Tom Williamson
Mar de Plata GC
Argentina
Juan Dentone
Mar de Plata GC (R)
Argentina
Alister Mackenzie
Maracaibo GC
Venezuela
James Baird Wilson
Maracay GC
Venezuela
C.H. Anderson
Maramarua GC
Pokeno, New Zealand
John Harris, Peter
   Thomson,Michael Wolveridge
Marayui G&CC (R)
Argentina
Ronald Fream
Marble Island G&YC
Essex Junction, Vermont
A.W. Tillinghast
Marble Island G&YC (R. 9)
Vermont
Frank Duane
Marceline CC
Missouri
Floyd Farley
Marco Island CC
Florida
David Wallace
Marco Island CC (R)
Florida
Pete Dye
Marco Shores CC
Marco Island, Florida
Robert von Hagge, Bruce Devlin
Mardon Lodge GC
Barrie, Ontario
Stanley Thompson
Marengo Ridge CC
Illinois
William James Spear
Margara GC
Allessandria, Italy
John Harris
Margate CC
Natal, South Africa
Arthur Lawrence Mandy
Mariah Hills Muni
Dodge City, Kansas
Frank Hummel

Marian Hills CC
Maltz, Montana
John Steidel
Marias Valley G&CC
Shelby, Montana
Norman H. Woods
Marias Valley G&CC (R)
Montana
Robert Muir Graves
Marienbad GC (R)
Czechoslovakia
Bernhard von Limburger
Marienburger GC
Cologne, West Germany
Bernhard von Limburger
Marietta CC
Ohio
Perl O. Hart
Marietta CC (R)
Ohio
Edmund B. Ault
Marigola GC
Italy
F. Pregazzi
Marin GC
Novato, California
Lawrence Hughes
Marina Del Ray GC
Venice, California
Harry Rainville
Marina GC
California
William F. Bell
Marina Vallarta GC
Puerto Vallarta, Mexico
Joseph S. Finger
Marina Velca GC
Italy
R. Russo
Marine Corps GC
Nebo, California
Lawrence Hughes
Marine Drive GC
Vancouver, British Columbia
A. Vernon Macan
Marine Memorial GC
Santa Ana, California
William P. Bell
Marine Memorial GC
Camp Pendleton, California
William P. Bell
Marine Memorial GC (R)
California
Peter Thomson, Michael
   Wolveridge,Ronald Fream
Marine Park GC
Brooklyn, New York
Robert Trent Jones
**Mariner Sands GC (Green
   Course)**
Stuart, Florida
Frank Duane, Arnold Palmer
**Mariner SandS CC (Gold
   Course)**
Stuart, Florida
Tom Fazio
Marion CC
Indiana
William H. Diddel
Marion CC (R)
Indiana
William H. Diddel
Marion CC (R)
Kansas
Mark Rathert
Marion CC (R)
Ohio
Jack Kidwell, Michael Hurdzan
Marion GC
Massachusetts
George C. Thomas Jr
Marion Oaks CC
Florida
John Denton
Mariposa Pines GC
California
Bob Baldock, Robert L. Baldock
Mark Twain GC
Elmira, New York
Donald Ross
Marks GC (A. 9)
Sweden
Jan Sederholm

Marland Estate GC NLE
Ponca City, Oklahoma
Arthur Jackson
**Marlboro CC formerly known as
   Duke of Marlborough GC**
Upper Marlboro, Maryland
Algie Pulley
Marlborough CC
Marlboro, Massachusetts
Wayne Stiles, John Van Kleek
Marlborough CC (A. 9)
Massachusetts
Geoffrey S. Cornish, William G.
   Robinson
Marlborough GC NLE
Montreal, Quebec
Stanley Thompson
Marlborough GC (R)
Quebec
Howard Watson
Marlborough GC (A. 9)
England
J. Hamilton Stutt
Marquette G&CC
Michigan
William B. Langford, Theodore J.
   Moreau
Marquette G&CC (A. 9)
Michigan
David Gill
Marquette Park GC
Chicago, Illinois
William B. Langford
Marrakesh CC
Palm Desert, California
Ted Robinson
Marriott Lincolnshire GC
Illinois
George Fazio, Tom Fazio
Marriott Lincolnshire GC (R. 2)
Illinois
Ken Killian, Dick Nugent
Marriott Orlando World GC
Orlando, Florida
Joe Lee
Marsden Park GC
Lancashire, England
C.K. Cotton
Marsden Park GC (A. 9)
England
Fred W. Hawtree
Marsh Harbour G Links
Calabash, North Carolina
Dan Maples
Marsh Landing CC
Ponte Vedra, Florida
Arnold Palmer, Ed Seay,Harrison
   Minchew
Marsh Point GC
Kiawah Island, South Carolina
Ron Kirby, Gary Player,Denis
   Griffiths
Marshall CC NLE
Michigan
Tom Bendelow
Marshall CC
Minnesota
J.W. Whitney
Marshall Lakeside CC (A. 9)
Texas
Lee Singletary
Marshall Muni
Missouri
Tom Talbot, Lloyd Thompson
Marshall Park GC
Moundsville, West Virginia
X.G. Hassenplug
Marshfield CC
Massachusetts
Wayne Stiles
Marshfield CC (A. 9)
Massachusetts
Wayne Stiles
Marston Green GC
England
Carl Bretherston
Marston Green Muni NLE
Birmingham, England
F.G. Hawtree, J.H. Taylor
Martin County G&CC (R. 9)
Florida
William B. Langford

Martin County G&CC (A. 9)
Florida
William B. Langford
Martin County G&CC (R)
Florida
Ernest E. Smith
Martin County G&CC (R.18)
Florida
Ron Garl
Martin Downs CC (Crane Creek Course)
Florida
Chuck Ankrom, Arthur Young
Martin Downs CC (Tower Course)
Florida
Chuck Ankrom
Martin Memorial GC
Weston, Massachusetts
William F. Mitchell
Martin Memorial GC (A. 9)
Massachusetts
Samuel Mitchell
Martindale CC
Auburn, Maine
Phil Wogan
Martingham G&TC
St. Michaels, Maryland
Pete Dye, Roy Dye
Martinsville CC
Indiana
William H. Diddel
Marvin Rupp GC
Stryker, Ohio
Robert Beard
Mary Calder GC
Savannah, Georgia
George W. Cobb
Maryland Bicycle C NLE
Maryland
David Ogilvie
Maryland G&CC
Belair, Maryland
Frank Murray, Russell Roberts
Marysville GC
Corvallis, Oregon
Fred Federspiel
Maryvale GC
Phoenix, Arizona
William F. Bell
Marywood CC
Battle Creek, Michigan
Maurice McCarthy
Mascoutin GC
Berlin, Wisconsin
Edward Lawrence Packard, Roger Packard
Mason City CC
Iowa
Tom Bendelow
Mason GC
Michigan
Henry Chisholm
Maspalomas GC (North Course)
Canary Islands
Ron Kirby, Gary Player, Denis Griffiths
Maspalomas GC (South Course)
Canary Islands
P.M. Ross
Massacre Canyon Inn & CC (River) NLE
Gilman Hot Springs, California
William H. Johnson
Massanuetten Mountain Greens GC
Harrisburg, Virginia
Richard Watson
Massawippi GC (R. 7)
Quebec
John Watson
Massena GC
New York
Albert Murray
Massereene GC (R)
Northern Ireland
Eddie Hackett
Massereene GC (A. 9)
Northern Ireland
Fred W. Hawtree
Matanzas Woods GC
Palm Coast, Florida
Arnold Palmer, Ed Seay, Bob Walker

Mather AFB GC
Sacramento, California
Jack Fleming
Matlock GC
Derbyshire, England
Tom Williamson
Mattoon G&CC (A. 9)
Illinois
Edward Lawrence Packard, Roger Packard
Mauh-Na-Tee-See CC
Rockford, Illinois
C.D. Wagstaff
Maui CC
Hawaii
Alex Bell, *William McEwan*
Maui Lu GC
Maui, Hawaii
J. Gordon Gibson
Maumelle G&CC
Arkansas
Edmund B. Ault
Mauna Kea Beach Hotel GC
Kameula, Hawaii
Robert Trent Jones
Mauna Kea Beach Hotel GC (R)
Hawaii
Robert Trent Jones Jr, Gary Roger Baird
Max Starcke Park GC
Seguin, Texas
Shelly Mayfield
Maxstoke Park GC
Birmingham, England
F.G. Hawtree, Fred W. Hawtree
Maxwell Muni (New Course)
Texas
Dave Bennett
Maxwelton Braes GC
Bailey Harbor, Wisconsin
George O'Neill, Joseph A. Roseman
Maxwelton GC
Syracuse, Indiana
William B. Langford
Mayacoo Lakes CC
West Palm Beach, Florida
Desmond Muirhead, Jack Nicklaus
Mayfair CC
Sanford, Florida
C.S. Butchart
Mayfair CC
Ohio
Edmund B. Ault
Mayfair G&CC
Alberta
J. Munro Hunter
Mayfield CC
South Euclid, Ohio
William "Bert" Way, Herbert Barker
Mayfield CC (R)
Ohio
William Newcomb
Mayfield CC
Clarion, Pennsylvania
X.G. Hassenplug
Mayflower GC NLE
New York, New York
Devereux Emmet, Alfred H. Tull
Mays Landing GC
Atlantic City, New Jersey
Hal Purdy
Maysville CC
Kentucky
William Newcomb
Maywood CC NLE
Hillside, Illinois
Tom Bendelow
McAlester CC NLE
Oklahoma
Arthur Jackson
McAlester CC
Oklahoma
Floyd Farley
McAlester CC (R. 9)
Oklahoma
Bob Dunning
McAllen CC
Texas
Jay Riviere

McCall Muni
Idaho
Robert Muir Graves
McCann Memorial GC
Poughkeepsie, New York
William F. Mitchell
McCleery GC
Vancouver, British Columbia
Ernest Brown
McCloskey Hospital GC
Fort Worth, Texas
John Bredemus
McConnell AFB GC
Wichita, Kansas
Floyd Farley
McCook CC
Salem, South Dakota
Emil Belzer
McCormick Ranch GC (Palm Course)
Scottsdale, Arizona
Desmond Muirhead
McCormick Ranch GC (Palm Course) (R)
Arizona
Tom Fazio
McCormick Ranch GC (Pine Course)
Scottsdale, Arizona
Desmond Muirhead
McCormick Ranch GC (Pine Course) (R)
Arizona
Tom Fazio
McFarland Park GC
Florence, Alabama
Earl Stone
McGregor GC
Saratoga Spa, New York
Devereux Emmet
McGuire AFB GC
New York
Edmund B. Ault
McGuires Evergreen GC
Cadillac, Michigan
Bruce Matthews
McHenry GC
Illinois
Harry Hall King
McHenry GC (R. 1)
Illinois
Ken Killian, Dick Nugent
McIntire Park GC
Charlottesville, Virginia
Fred Findlay, *Ben Loving*
McKellar GC
Memphis, Tennessee
Charles M. Graves
McKenzie River GC
Leaburg, Oregon
Ken Omlid, Earl Omlid, Lloyd Omlid
McKinney Muni GC
Texas
Ralph Plummer, Bob Dunning
McLaren Park GC
Daly City, California
Jack Fleming
McLaren Park GC (R)
California
Robert Muir Graves
McMillen Park GC
Ft. Wayne, Indiana
Hal Purdy
McMinnville CC
Tennessee
Edward Lawrence Packard
McNary GC
Salem, Oregon
Fred Federspiel, *Fred Sparks*
Meadia Heights CC (R)
Pennsylvania
Chester Ruby
Meadia Heights CC (R)
Pennsylvania
Ferdinand Garbin
Meadow Brook C NLE
Westbury, New York
Devereux Emmet
Meadow Brook C
Jericho, New York
Dick Wilson
Meadow Brook C (R) NLE
New York
A.W. Tillinghast

Meadow Brook CC NLE
St. Louis, Missouri
Robert Foulis
Meadow Brook GC
Reading, Massachusetts
Alex Findlay
Meadow Brook GC (R. 9)
Massachusetts
Geoffrey S. Cornish
Meadow C
Fairfax, California
Alister Mackenzie, Robert Hunter
Meadow C (R)
California
Robert Muir Graves
Meadow Greens CC
Eden, North Carolina
Ellis Maples
Meadow Heights CC
Jackson, Michigan
Tom Bendelow
Meadow Hills CC
Nogales, Arizona
Red Lawrence
Meadow Hills GC
Denver, Colorado
Henry B. Hughes
Meadow Hills GC (R)
Colorado
Dick Phelps, Brad Benz, Mike Poellot
Meadow Lake Acres CC
Missouri
Edmund B. Ault, Al Jamison
Meadow Lake CC NLE
Kansas City, Kansas
William B. Langford
Meadow Lake CC (A. 9)
Montana
Dick Phelps
Meadow Lake CC (R. 9)
Montana
Dick Phelps
Meadow Lark CC
Great Falls, Montana
William H. Diddel
Meadow Oaks G&CC
Hudson, Florida
Bill Amick
Meadow Springs GC
Richland, Washington
Jack Reimer
Meadow Springs GC (R. 9)
Washington
Robert Muir Graves
Meadow Springs GC (A. 9)
Washington
Robert Muir Graves
Meadow Valley GC
Caliente, Nevada
Richard Bigler
Meadowbrook CC
West Memphis, Arkansas
Joseph S. Finger
Meadowbrook CC (R)
Connecticut
William F. Mitchell
Meadowbrook CC
Gainesville, Florida
Steve Smyers
Meadowbrook CC (R)
Kansas
Bob Dunning
Meadowbrook CC
Detroit, Michigan
Willie Park Jr
Meadowbrook CC (R. 1)
Michigan
Bruce Matthews, Jerry Matthews
Meadowbrook CC (A.12)
Michigan
Harry Collis, Jack Daray
Meadowbrook CC (R. 6)
Michigan
Harry Collis, Jack Daray
Meadowbrook CC (R)
Michigan
Arthur Hills
Meadowbrook CC (R. 2)
Michigan
Jerry Matthews
Meadowbrook CC
Ballwin, Missouri
Robert Bruce Harris

Meadowbrook CC
Dayton, Ohio
William H. Diddel
Meadowbrook CC
Tulsa, Oklahoma
Press Maxwell
Meadowbrook CC (A. 9)
Oklahoma
Don Sechrest
Meadowbrook CC
Richmond, Virginia
Fred Findlay, *Ben Loving*
Meadowbrook CC (R)
Virginia
Edmund B. Ault
Meadowbrook CC
Charleston, West Virginia
Alex McKay
Meadowbrook GC
Hartley, Iowa
Everett Dunn
Meadowbrook GC
Hopkins, Minnesota
James Foulis
Meadowbrook GC (A. 9)
Minnesota
Ken Killian, Dick Nugent
Meadowbrook GC
Omaha, Nebraska
Floyd Farley
Meadowbrook GC
Pennsylvania
Leon Campbell
Meadowbrook GC
Rapid City, South Dakota
David Gill, Garrett Gill
Meadowbrook Muni
Ft. Worth, Texas
Ralph Plummer
Meadowbrook Muni (R.27)
Texas
Warren Cantrell
Meadowbrook Muni
Salt Lake City, Utah
Mick Riley
Meadowbrook Town & CC (R)
Wisconsin
David Gill
Meadowlakes G&CC NLE
Marble Falls, Texas
Leon Howard
Meadowlands CC (R)
Pennsylvania
William Gordon, David Gordon
Meadowlands GC
Willoughby, Ohio
Sandy Alves
Meadowlark CC
Huntington Beach, California
William P. Bell
Meadowmont G&CC
Arnold, California
Dick Fry
Meadowood G&RC
St. Helena, California
Norris M. Gaddis
Meadowood GC
Cascade, Michigan
Mark DeVries
Meadowood GC (A. 9)
Michigan
Mark DeVries
Meadows CC (Highlands Course)
Sarasota, Florida
Frank Duane
Meadows CC (Highlands Course) (A. 9)
Florida
Patrick Mulligan, Rod Robinson
Meadows CC (Meadows Course)
Sarasota, Florida
Frank Duane
Meadows CC (Meadows Course) (A. 9)
Florida
Patrick Mulligan, Rod Robinson
Meadows GC
Surfer's Paradise, Australia
Robin Nelson
Meadowview GC (R)
Tennessee
Rees Jones

315

Meadowwink GC
Murraysville, Pennsylvania
Ferdinand Garbin
Meadowwood CC
St. Helena, California
Jack Fleming
Meadville CC (R)
Pennsylvania
Ferdinand Garbin
Mechaneer GC
Fort Carson, Colorado
Dick Phelps
Medellin GC
Colombia
Stanley Thompson, Clinton E.
  Robinson
Medford Lakes CC
New Jersey
Alex Findlay
Medford Lakes CC (A. 9)
New Jersey
Hal Purdy
**Medford Village CC formerly
  known as Sunny Jim GC**
Medford, New Jersey
William Gordon, David Gordon
Medicine Hat GC
Alberta
Tom Bendelow
Medicine Lodge Muni (R. 9)
Kansas
Chet Mendenhall
Medina CC
Ohio
Ed Bowers, Larry Fink
Medina Public GC
Minnesota
Leo J. Feser
Medinah CC (Course No. 1)
Illinois
Tom Bendelow
Medinah CC (Course No. 1) (R)
Illinois
Edward Lawrence Packard
Medinah CC (Course No. 2)
Illinois
Tom Bendelow
Medinah CC (Course No. 3)
Illinois
Tom Bendelow
Medinah CC (Course No. 3) (R)
Illinois
Harry Collis
**Medinah CC (Course No. 3) (A.
  5)**
Illinois
Harry Collis
Medinah CC (Course No. 3) (R)
Illinois
Ken Killian, Dick Nugent
**Medinah CC (Course No. 3) (A.
  2)**
Illinois
Roger Packard
Meeker CC
Colorado
Henry B. Hughes
Megunticook GC
Rockport, Maine
Alex Findlay
Mehr Shahr GC
Iran
Pier Mancinelli
Meihan Kokusai CC
Sapparo, Japan
Peter Thomson
Mel's Executive GC
Arcata, California
Mel Babica
Melbourne CC
Arkansas
Orrin Smith
Melbourne G&CC
Florida
William H. Diddel
Melbourne G&CC (R)
Florida
Bill Amick
Mellody Farm CC NLE
Lake Forest, Illinois
George O'Neill, *Jack Croke,* Jack
  Daray

Melody Hill GC
Harmony, Rhode Island
Samuel Mitchell
Melody Hill GC (A. 9)
Rhode Island
Samuel Mitchell
Melreese GC
Miami, Florida
Dick Wilson, Joe Lee
Melreese GC (R)
Florida
Robert Trent Jones
Melreese GC (A. 4)
Florida
Robert Trent Jones
Melrose CC
Cheltenham, Pennsylvania
Perry Maxwell
Melrose CC (R)
Pennsylvania
Clinton E. Robinson
Melrose GC
Daufuskie Island, South Carolina
Jack Nicklaus, *Tom Pearson*
Melrose GC
Roxburghshire, Scotland
Willie Park
Melton Mowbray GC
Leicestershire, England
Tom Williamson
Memorial Muni NLE
Springfield, Massachusetts
Wayne Stiles, John Van Kleek
Memorial Park GC
Houston, Texas
John Bredemus
Memphis CC NLE
Tennessee
James Foulis
Memphis CC
Tennessee
Donald Ross
Memphis CC (A. 9) NLE
Tennessee
Tom Bendelow
Menaggio E. Cadenabbia GC
Milan, Italy
John Harris
**Menaggio E. Cadenabbia GC (A.
  5)**
Italy
J.J.F. Pennink
Menaggio E. Cadenabbia GC (R)
Italy
J.J.F. Pennink
Menard GC
Petersburg, Illinois
Charles Maddox
Mendham G&TC
New Jersey
Alfred H. Tull
Mendip GC
Avon, England
Harry Vardon
Mendip GC (A. 9)
England
C.K. Cotton, J.J.F. Pennink
Mendota Heights GC
Minnesota
Paul Coates
Mendota Heights GC (R)
Minnesota
Donald G. Brauer, Emile Perret
Menlo CC
Redwood City, California
Tom Nicoll
Menlo CC (R)
California
Robert Trent Jones, Robert Trent
  Jones Jr, Gary Roger Baird
Meon Valley CC
Hampshire, England
J. Hamilton Stutt
Merced G&CC
Slater, California
Bob Baldock
Merced G&CC (R)
California
Robert Muir Graves
Mercedes CC
Texas
John Bredemus

Mercer County Elks CC
Celina, Ohio
Harold Paddock
Mercer Island G&CC
Washington
Robert Johnstone
Mere G&CC
Surrey, England
James Braid, John R.
  Stutt, George Duncan
Meriden Park Muni
Connecticut
Robert D. Pryde
Meriden Park Muni (R)
Connecticut
Alfred H. Tull
Meridian GC
Englewood, Colorado
Jack Nicklaus, Bob Cupp, Scott
  Miller
Meridian GC
Oklahoma City, Oklahoma
Floyd Farley
Meridian Hills CC
Indianapolis, Indiana
William H. Diddel
Meridian Hills CC (R)
Indiana
George Fazio, Tom Fazio
Meridian Valley CC
Kent, California
Ted Robinson
Merion GC (East Course)
Ardmore, Pennsylvania
Hugh Wilson
Merion GC (East Course) (R)
Pennsylvania
Perry Maxwell
Merion GC (East Course) (R)
Pennsylvania
William S. Flynn, Howard
  Toomey
Merion GC (East Course) (R)
Pennsylvania
Dick Wilson
Merion GC (West Course)
Ardmore, Pennsylvania
Hugh Wilson
Merion GC (West Course) (R)
Pennsylvania
Perry Maxwell
Meriwether National GC
Hillsboro, Oregon
Fred Federspiel
Merrick Park GC
New York
Frank Duane
Merrill Hills CC (R)
Wisconsin
Edward Lawrence Packard
Merrimack GC
Methuen, Massachusetts
Eugene "Skip" Wogan
Merritt G&CC
British Columbia
Jack Reimer
Merry Hill G&CC
Ontario
Clinton E. Robinson
Meru GC
Kenya
E.B. Horne
Mesa CC
Arizona
William F. Bell, William P. Bell
Mesa CC (R)
Arizona
Arthur Jack Snyder
Mesa Del Sol CC (Blue Course)
Yuma, Arizona
Arnold Palmer, Ed Seay
Mesa Del Sol CC (White Course)
Yuma, Arizona
Arnold Palmer, Ed Seay
Mesa Verde CC
Costa Mesa, California
William F. Bell
Mesa Verde CC (R)
California
David Rainville
Mesa Verde GC
Mesa, Arizona
Greg Nash

Meshingomesia CC
Marion, Indiana
Clarence Lamboley
Mesquite CC
Palm Springs, California
Bert Stamps
Mesquite Muni
Texas
Leon Howard
Messalonkee GC
Waterville, Maine
Burton R. Anderson
Metacomet CC
East Providence, Rhode Island
Donald Ross
Metacomet CC (R. 2)
Rhode Island
Geoffrey S. Cornish
Metairie CC
Louisiana
Jack Daray
Metfield GC
Bella Vista, Arkansas
Tom Clark, Edmund B. Ault
Metro GC (R) NLE
Missouri
Floyd Farley
Metropolis CC
White Plains, New York
Herbert Strong
**Metropolitan G&TC formerly
  known as Fairington G&TC**
Decatur, Georgia
Rees Jones
Metropolitan GC
Australia
J. B. Mackenzie
Metropolitan GC (R)
Australia
Peter Thomson, Michael
  Wolveridge
Metropolitan GC (R.11)
Australia
Dick Wilson
Metropolitan GC (A. 8)
Australia
Dick Wilson
Mexicali G&CC
Mexico
Lawrence Hughes
Mexico City CC
Mexico
Willie Smith
Mexico City CC (R)
Mexico
John Bredemus
Meyrick Park GC
Hampshire, England
Tom Dunn
Meyrick Park GC (R)
England
John R. Stutt
Miacomet G Links
Nantucket, Massachusetts
Alex Findlay
Miami Beach Par 3 GC
Florida
Red Lawrence
Miami Beach Polo C (R) NLE
Florida
William S. Flynn
**Miami Biltmore GC (North
  Course) now known as Coral
  Gables Biltmore GC**
**Miami Biltmore GC (South
  Course) now known as Riviera
  CC**
Miami CC NLE
Florida
Donald Ross
Miami G Links NLE
Miami, Florida
Alex Findlay
Miami G&CC
Oklahoma
John Embry
Miami G&CC (A. 9)
Oklahoma
Don Sechrest
**Miami Lakes Inn & CC
  (Championship)**
Florida
Bill Watts

**Miami Lakes Inn & CC
  (Executive)**
Florida
John E. O'Connor
Miami Shores CC
Florida
Red Lawrence
Miami Shores GC
Troy, Ohio
Donald Ross
Miami Shores GC (R. 9)
Ohio
Jack Kidwell, Michael Hurdzan
Miami Springs GC
Florida
Thomas "Tubby" Palmer
Miami Springs GC (R.10)
Florida
Bill Dietsch
Miami Valley CC
Dayton, Ohio
Donald Ross
Miami Valley CC (R)
Ohio
Geoffrey S. Cornish, William G.
  Robinson
Miami Valley CC (R)
Ohio
Jack Kidwell, Michael Hurdzan
Miami View GC
Miamitown, Ohio
William H. Diddel
Michaywe Hills GC
Gaylord, Michigan
Robert W. Bills, Donald L. Childs
Michelbook CC
McMinnville, Oregon
Shirley Stone
Michelbook CC (A. 9)
Oregon
Robert Muir Graves, Damian
  Pascuzzo
Mick Riley GC
Murray, Utah
Mick Riley
Mid Carolina CC
Prosperity, South Carolina
Russell Breeden
Mid City GC NLE
Chicago, Illinois
William B. Langford, Theodore J.
  Moreau
Mid City GC (R) NLE
Illinois
William B. Langford, Theodore J.
  Moreau
Mid Kent GC
Gravesend, England
Willie Park Jr
Mid Pines CC
Southern Pines, North Carolina
Donald Ross
Mid-County GC
Arapahoe, Nebraska
Henry B. Hughes, Richard
  Watson
Mid-Ocean C
Tuckerstown, Bermuda
Charles Blair Macdonald, Seth
  Raynor, Charles Banks
Mid-Ocean C (R)
Bermuda
Robert Trent Jones
Mid-Pacific GC
Honolulu, Hawaii
Seth Raynor, Charles Banks
Mid-Pacific CC (R. 9)
Hawaii
Willard Wilkinson
Mid-Pacific CC (A. 9)
Hawaii
Willard Wilkinson
Mid-Pacific CC (R)
Hawaii
Bob Baldock, Robert L. Baldock
Mid-Rivers Y&CC
Stuart, Florida
Charles Prynne Martyn
Middle Bass Island GC
Sandusky, Ohio
Sandy Alves
Middle Bay CC (R)
New York
Alfred H. Tull

Middle Bay CC ()
New York
Hal Purdy
Middle Bay CC (R)
New York
Stephen Kay
Middleburg GC
Pennsylvania
Edmund B. Ault
Middlemarch GC
New Zealand
Charles H. Redhead
Middlemore GC (R)
Australia
Peter Thomson, Michael
    Wolveridge
Middlesborough GC
England
James Braid, John R. Stutt
Middlesborough GC (R)
England
J. Hamilton Stutt
Middlesbrough Muni
Yorkshire, England
J. Hamilton Stutt
Middleton GC
Massachusetts
Geoffrey S. Cornish, William G.
    Robinson
Middleton Park GC
Yorkshire, England
T.R. Trigg
Middletown GC (R)
Ohio
Hal Purdy
Midland CC
Kewanee, Illinois
Tom Bendelow
Midland CC
Kewanee, Illinois
William James Spear
Midland CC (R)
Michigan
Bruce Matthews, Jerry Matthews
Midland CC (R)
Michigan
Edward Lawrence Packard
Midland CC (R)
Michigan
Edward Lawrence Packard
Midland CC
Texas
Ralph Plummer
Midland CC (R)
Texas
Ron Kirby, Denis Griffiths
Midland CC (R)
Texas
Dick Nugent
Midland Farms CC
Pinehurst, North Carolina
Tom Jackson
Midland G&CC
Ontario
Nicol Thompson
Midland G&CC (A. 9)
Ontario
J. Ross Parrott
Midland Hills CC
St. Paul, Minnesota
Seth Raynor
Midland Hills CC (R)
Minnesota
Paul Coates
Midland Trail GC
Middletown, Kentucky
Edward Lawrence Packard
Midland Valley CC
St. Louis, Missouri
Robert Foulis
Midland Valley CC (R)
Missouri
William H. Diddel
Midland Valley CC
Aiken, South Carolina
Ellis Maples
Midlands GC
Victoria, Australia
Peter Thomson, Michael
    Wolveridge
Midlane GC
Wadsworth, Illinois
Robert Bruce Harris

Midlothian CC
Illinois
H.J. Tweedie
Midlothian CC (R)
Illinois
Ken Killian, Dick Nugent
Midvale G&CC
Penfield, New York
Robert Trent Jones, Stanley
    Thompson
Midway GC
Groton, Massachusetts
Geoffrey S. Cornish
Midway GC
Amherst, Ohio
Ted McAnlis
Midway GC
South Carolina
Edmund B. Ault, Bill Love
Midway GC
Greybull, Wyoming
Henry B. Hughes, Richard
    Watson
Midwest City Muni
Oklahoma
Floyd Farley
Midwest CC (East Course) (R)
Illinois
Robert Bruce Harris
Midwest CC (West Course) (R. 9)
Illinois
Robert Bruce Harris
Midwest CC (West Course) (A. 9)
Illinois
Robert Bruce Harris
Midwick CC NLE
Monterey Park, California
Norman Macbeth
Milan CC
Tennessee
George C. Curtis
Milano GC
Italy
Charles Blanchford
Milburn G&CC
Overland Park, Kansas
William B. Langford
Milburn G&CC (R)
Kansas
Orrin Smith, James Gilmore
    Harrison
Milburn G&CC (R)
Kansas
Floyd Farley
Milburn G&CC (R. 6)
Kansas
Bill Love
Milby GC (R. 3)
Quebec
John Watson
Mile Square GC
Fountain Valley, California
Harry Rainville, David Rainville
Miles City Town & CC (R)
Montana
Robert Muir Graves
Miles Grant CC
Stuart, Florida
Mark Mahannah, Charles
    Mahannah
Miles Grant CC (R)
Florida
Edmund B. Ault
Milford CC (R)
Connecticut
William F. Mitchell
Milford GC
Illinois
Edward Lawrence Packard
Milham Muni
Kalamazoo, Michigan
David T. Millar
Mililani GC
Hawaii
Bob Baldock, Robert L. Baldock
Mill Creek CC
Bothell, Washington
Ted Robinson
Mill Creek CC
Burlington, West Virginia
James Spencer
Mill Creek G&CC (R. 5)
Texas
Robert Trent Jones Jr

Mill Creek G&CC (A.13)
Texas
Robert Trent Jones Jr
Mill Creek GC
Nashville, Tennessee
Leon Howard
Mill Creek GC (North Course)
Youngstown, Ohio
Donald Ross
Mill Creek GC (South Course)
Youngstown, Ohio
Donald Ross
Mill Quarter Plantation GC
Virginia
Edmund B. Ault
Mill Race GC
Benton, Pennsylvania
Geoffrey S. Cornish, William G.
    Robinson
Mill Race GC (A. 9)
Pennsylvania
Geoffrey S. Cornish, William G.
    Robinson
Mill River CC
Stratford, Connecticut
Tom Winton
Mill River CC
New York
Gerald C. Roby
Mill River CC (R. 4)
New York
Frank Duane
Mill River GC
O'Leary, Prince Edward Island
Clinton E. Robinson
Mill Road Farm GC NLE
Lake Forest, Illinois
William S. Flynn, Howard
    Toomey
Millbrook C
Greenwich, Connecticut
Geoffrey S. Cornish
Millbrook C (R. 3)
Connecticut
Frank Duane
Millbrook C (R)
Connecticut
Stephen Kay
Millburn GC
New Jersey
Hal Purdy
Millcreek GC
Ostrander, Ohio
Dwight Black
Milledgeville CC
Georgia
George W. Cobb
Milligan Park GC (A. 9)
Indiana
Gary Kern
Millington NAS GC (R)
Tennessee
William H. Diddel
Millinocket Muni
Maine
Larry H. Striley
Millrace CC
Jonesville, Michigan
Arthur Hills
Millsaps GC
Mississippi
Ken Bottorf
Milltown GC (R)
Ireland
Eddie Hackett
Milne Memorial Park GC
Dysart, Iowa
Donald G. Brauer, Donald K. Rippel
Milngavie GC (R)
Scotland
Willie Auchterlonie
Milton-Freewater GC
Oregon
George McRae
Milton-Hoosic GC
Canton, Massachusetts
Willie Park Jr
Milwaukee CC NLE
Wisconsin
James Foulis
Milwaukee CC
Wisconsin
C.H. Alison, H.S. Colt

Milwaukee CC (A. 9) NLE
Wisconsin
Tom Bendelow
Milwaukee CC (R)
Wisconsin
Robert Trent Jones, Roger
    Rulewich
Mimosa Hills CC
Morganton, North Carolina
Donald Ross
**Minakami Kogen GC (Lower
    Course)**
Japan
Arnold Palmer, Ed Seay, Bob
    Walker
**Minakami Kogen GC (Upper
    Course)**
Japan
Arnold Palmer, Ed Seay, Bob
    Walker
Minaki Lodge GC
Minaki, Ontario
Stanley Thompson
Minchinhampton (Old Course)
Gloucestershire, England
R.B. Wilson
**Minchinhampton GC (New
    Course)**
Gloucestershire, England
Fred W. Hawtree
Mineral Springs GC
Martinsville, Indiana
William H. Diddel
Mingo Springs GC
Rangeley, Maine
Eugene "Skip" Wogan
Minikahda C
Minneapolis, Minnesota
Robert Foulis, William Watson
Minikahda C (A. 9)
Minnesota
Robert Taylor, C.T. Jaffray
Minikahda C (R. 9)
Minnesota
Robert Taylor, C.T. Jaffray
Minikahda C (R)
Minnesota
Donald Ross
Minikahda C (R)
Minnesota
Ralph Plummer
Minneapolis GC
Minnesota
Tom Bendelow
Minneapolis GC (R)
Minnesota
Donald G. Brauer, Emile Perret
Minneapolis GC (R)
Minnesota
Geoffrey S. Cornish, Brian Silva
Minnechaug GC
Glastonbury, Connecticut
Geoffrey S. Cornish
Minnechaug GC (R. 9)
Connecticut
William F. Mitchell, Al Zikorus
Minnechaug GC (Routing)
Connecticut
Graham Clark
Minnedosa G&CC
Manitoba
John A. Thompson
Minnehaha CC NLE
Sioux Falls, South Dakota
Tom Bendelow
Minnehaha CC
Sious Falls, South Dakota
William B. Langford, Theodore J.
    Moreau
Minnehaha CC (R)
South Dakota
Edward Lawrence Packard
Minnehaha CC (R. 6)
South Dakota
Ken Killian, Dick Nugent
Minnestrista GC
Muncie, Indiana
William H. Diddel
Minnetonka CC (R. 3)
Minnesota
Don Herfort
Minnreg GC
Minneapolis, Minnesota
Dick Phelps

Minocqua CC (A. 9)
Wisconsin
Edward Lawrence Packard
Minocqua CC (R. 9)
Wisconsin
Edward Lawrence Packard
Minor Park GC
Kansas City, Missouri
Larry W. Flatt
Minot CC
North Dakota
Tom Vardon
Minot CC (R)
North Dakota
John Steidel
Mint Valley Muni
Longview, Washington
Ronald Fream, *Terry Storm*
**Mira Vista G&CC formerly
    known as Berkeley CC**
Berkeley, California
William Watson, Robert Hunter
Mira Vista G&CC (R. 1)
California
Robert Muir Graves
Miracle Hill GC
Omaha, Nebraska
Floyd Farley
Miramar GC (R)
New Zealand
Peter Thomson, Michael
    Wolveridge
Miramar Memorial GC
San Diego, California
Kenneth Welton
Miramar Memorial GC (R)
California
Peter Thomson, Michael
    Wolveridge, Ronald Fream
Miramichi G&CC (A. 9)
New Brunswick
Clinton E. Robinson
Mirror Lake GC
Idaho
Edward A. Hunnicutt
Mirror Lakes CC
Lehigh Acres, Florida
Mark Mahannah
Mishawaka Muni
Indiana
Jack Jernigan
Misquemicut GC (R)
Rhode Island
Donald Ross
Mission Bay GC
San Diego, California
Ted Robinson
Mission Creek G&CC
Kelowna, British Columbia
Dan Kitsul, Vic Welder, Ruth Welder
Mission CC
Texas
Ralph Plummer
Mission CC
Odessa, Texas
Ken Killian, Dick Nugent, Jeff
    Brauer
Mission GC
British Columbia
Norman H. Woods
Mission Hills CC NLE
Northbrook, Illinois
Leonard Macomber
Mission Hills CC
Northbrook, Illinois
Edward Lawrence Packard,
    Roger Packard
Mission Hills CC (A)
Illinois
C.D. Wagstaff
Mission Hills CC
Fairway, Kansas
Tom Bendelow
Mission Hills CC (R)
Kansas
William H. Diddel
Mission Hills CC (R. 2)
Kansas
Floyd Farley
Mission Hills CC (R)
Kansas
Bob Dunning

Mission Hills CC (R. 7)
Kansas
Tom Clark
Mission Hills G&CC (New Course)
Rancho Mirage, California
Arnold Palmer, Ed Seay
Mission Hills G&CC (Old Course)
Rancho Mirage, California
Desmond Muirhead
Mission Hills G&CC (Resort Course)
Rancho Mirage, California
Pete Dye, *Lee Schmidt*
Mission Hills GC (A. 9)
Michigan
Jerry Matthews
Mission Inn & CC
Howey-in-Hills, Florida
Capt. Charles Clarke
Mission Inn & CC (R)
Florida
Tom Line
Mission Inn & CC (A. 3)
Florida
Tom Line
Mission Lakes CC
Desert Hot Springs, California
Ted Robinson
Mission Valley G&CC
Laurel, Florida
David Wallace
Mission Viejo CC
California
Robert Trent Jones
Mission Viejo CC (R. 2)
California
Jerry Martin
Mississauga G&CC
Port Credit, Ontario
George Cumming, *Percy Barrett*
Mississauga G&CC (R)
Ontario
Stanley Thompson
Mississauga G&CC (A. 9)
Ontario
Howard Watson
Mississauga G&CC (R. 3)
Ontario
Howard Watson
Mississinewa CC
Peru, Indiana
Tom Bendelow
Mississippi State Univ GC (R. 9)
Mississippi
Brian Ault
Mississippi Valley State Univ GC
Greenwood, Mississippi
Leon Howard
Missoula CC
Montana
Frank James
Missoula CC (R)
Montana
Robert Muir Graves
Missoula CC (R)
Montana
John Steidel
Misty Creek CC
Sarasota, Florida
Ted McAnlis
Mitchell Creek GC
Mitchell, Michigan
Bruce Matthews, Jerry Matthews
Mitchell CC
South Dakota
Richard Watson
Mitchelstown GC (R)
Ireland
Eddie Hackett
Mito International GC
Tokyo, Japan
Jack Nicklaus, Scott Miller
Mittelrheinscher GC
Bad Ems, West Germany
Karl Hoffmann
Moanalua GC
Honolulu, Hawaii
Donald MacIntyre
Mobray CC
Cape Province, South Africa
S.V. Hotchkin

Moccasin Bend GC (R)
Tennessee
Alex McKay
Moccasin Creek GC
Aberdeen, South Dakota
Charles Maddox
Modesto Muni
California
Ian MacDonald
Moffat GC
Scotland
Ben Sayers
Moffett Field GC
California
Bob Baldock
Moffett Field GC (A. 9)
California
Robert Muir Graves
Mohansic Park GC
Yorktown Heights, New York
Tom Winton
Mohawk CC
Tiffon, Ohio
William J. Rockefeller
Mohawk CC (A. 9)
Ohio
William J. Rockefeller
Mohawk CC (R.18)
Ohio
William J. Rockefeller
Mohawk GC
Schenectady, New York
Devereux Emmet
Mohawk GC NLE
Schenectady, New York
Tom Bendelow
Mohawk Hills GC
Carmel, Indiana
Gary Kern
Mohawk Park Muni (Pecan Valley Course)
Tulsa, Oklahoma
Floyd Farley
Mohawk Park Muni (Woodbine Course)
Tulsa, Oklahoma
William H. Diddel
Mohawk Park Muni (Woodbine Course) (R)
Oklahoma
Floyd Farley
Mohawk Park Muni (Woodbine Course) (R)
Oklahoma
Perry Maxwell
Mohawk Park Muni (Woodbine Course) (R)
Oklahoma
Floyd Farley
Mohican Hills GC
Wooster, Ohio
Jack Kidwell
Mohican Hills GC (A. 9)
Ohio
Jack Kidwell, Michael Hurdzan
Mojalaki CC
Franklin, New Hampshire
Wayne Stiles, John Van Kleek
Molndals GC
Goteborg, Sweden
Ronald Fream
Molyhills GC
Fraser Lake, British Columbia
Gerry Wreggitt
Momence CC
Illinois
William Watson
Monagh Lea GC
Portland, Oregon
Robert G. Duncan
Monarch CC
Florida
Arnold Palmer, Ed Seay, Harrison Minchew
Monastir International GC
Tunisia
Ronald Fream
Moncton G&CC
New Brunswick
Stanley Thompson
Moncton G&CC (A. 9)
New Brunswick
Clinton E. Robinson

Monifieth GC (R)
Scotland
Willie Park Jr
Monifieth GC (R)
Scotland
J. Hamilton Stutt
Monkstown GC (R)
Ireland
Eddie Hackett
Monmouth CC
Illinois
Tom Bendelow
Monmouthshire GC
Wales
James Braid
Monongahela Valley CC
Pennsylvania
Tom Bendelow
Monongahela Valley CC (A. 9)
Pennsylvania
Emil Loeffler, *John McGlynn*
Monongahela Valley CC (R. 9)
Pennsylvania
Emil Loeffler, *John McGlynn*
Monoosnock CC (R. 9)
Massachusetts
Wayne Stiles, John Van Kleek
Monroe County GC
Churchville, New York
Hal Purdy
Monroe Creek GC
Pennsylvania
Edmund B. Ault
Monroe CC
Georgia
Chic Adams
Monroe CC (A. 9)
Georgia
Bill Amick
Monroe CC
Pittsford, New York
Donald Ross
Monroe CC (R. 2)
New York
Geoffrey S. Cornish, William G. Robinson
Monroe CC (R)
New York
Arthur Hills, Steve Forrest
Monroe CC
North Carolina
Donald Ross
Monroe G&CC
Michigan
Donald Ross
Monroe G&CC (R)
Michigan
Clinton E. Robinson
Monsanto Employees GC
Pensacola, Florida
Bill Amick
Mont Adstock GC
Thetford Mines, Quebec
Howard Watson, John Watson
Mont Adstock GC (R. 9)
Quebec
John Watson
Mont D'Arbois GC
France
Henry Cotton
Mont St. Anne GC (Course No. 0
St. Anne de Beaupre, Quebec
Howard Watson, John Watson
Mont St. Anne GC (Course No.2)
St. Anne de Beaupre, Quebec
Howard Watson, John Watson
Mont St. Anne GC (Course No.2) (A. 9)
Quebec
John Watson
Mont St. Marie GC
St. Marie de Bauce, Quebec
Howard Watson
Mont St. Marie GC (R. 2)
Quebec
Howard Watson, John Watson
Mont St. Marie GC (A. 9)
Quebec
John Watson
Mont Tremblant GC (R. 9)
Quebec
Howard Watson

Montague GC (A. 3)
Vermont
Geoffrey S. Cornish, William G. Robinson
Montammy CC
Alpine, New Jersey
Frank Duane
Montammy CC (R. 4)
New Jersey
Joseph S. Finger
Montauk Downs GC NLE
Montauk, New York
H.C.C. Tippetts
Montauk Downs GC (R) NLE
New York
C.H. Anderson
Montauk G&RC
Montauk Point, New York
Robert Trent Jones, Rees Jones
Montaza Tabarka G Resort
Tabarka, Tunisia
Ronald Fream
Montclair CC
Chattanooga, Tennessee
Joe Lee
Montclair CC (A. 9)
Tennessee
Arthur Davis
Montclair CC (R. 9)
Tennessee
Arthur Davis
Montclair CC
Dumfries, Virginia
Algie Pulley
Montclair GC
Verona, New Jersey
Donald Ross
Montclair GC NLE
New Jersey
Tom Bendelow
Montclair GC (A. 9)
New Jersey
Charles Banks
Montclair GC (A. 9) NLE
New Jersey
Tom Anderson
Montclair GC (R)
New Jersey
Robert Trent Jones
Montclair GC (R)
New Jersey
Robert Trent Jones
Montclair GC (R)
New Jersey
Rees Jones
Monte Carlo CC
Monaco
Willie Park Jr
Monte Carlo CC (A. 2)
Monaco
Fred W. Hawtree
Monte Carlo CC (R)
Monaco
Fred W. Hawtree
Monte Carlo CC (R)
Monaco
F.G. Hawtree
Monte Cristo CC
Edinburg, Texas
Don Sechrest
Monte Gordo GC
Portugal
Henry Cotton
Montebello GC
California
Max Behr
Montebello GC (R. 5)
California
William F. Bell
Montecito CC
Santa Barbara, California
Max Behr
Monterey CC
Palm Desert, California
Ted Robinson
Monterey Hills GC
California
William F. Bell, William P. Bell
Monterey Peninsula CC (Dunes Course)
Pebble Beach, California
Seth Raynor, Charles Banks

Monterey Peninsula CC (Dunes Course) (R)
California
Alister Mackenzie, Robert Hunter
Monterey Peninsula CC (Shore Course)
Pebble Beach, California
Bob Baldock, Jack Neville
Monterey Peninsula CC (Shore Course) (R)
California
Robert Bruce Harris
Monterrey CC
Mexico
John Bredemus
Montgomery CC
Alabama
John M. "Jock" Inglis
Montgomery Village CC
Maryland
Edmund B. Ault
Monticello CC
Indiana
Pete Dye, Alice Dye
Monticello CC
Kentucky
Robert Thomason
Montour Heights CC
Coraopolis, Pennsylvania
Emil Loeffler, *John McGlynn*
Montour Heights CC
Pittsburgh, Pennsylvania
P.B. Dye
Montour Heights CC (A. 9)
Pennsylvania
James Gilmore Harrison, Ferdinand Garbin
Montour Heights CC (R. 9)
Pennsylvania
James Gilmore Harrison, Ferdinand Garbin
Montreal Muni (Yellow Course)
Quebec
Albert Murray
Montreux GC
France
Harry Vardon
Montreux GC (R)
France
Donald Harradine
Montrose GC
Colorado
Henry B. Hughes
Montrose GC (Bloomfield Course) (R)
Scotland
Willie Park Jr
Montrose GC (Medal Course) (R)
Scotland
Willie Park Jr
Moody AFB GC
Valdosta, Georgia
Joseph S. Finger
Moon Lake GC
Hoffman Estates, Illinois
Ken Killian, Dick Nugent
Moon Valley CC
Phoenix, Arizona
Dick Wilson, Bob Simmons
Moonbrook CC
Jamestown, New York
Willie Park Jr
Moonbrook CC (A. 9)
New York
William Harries
Moonbrook CC (R)
New York
William Gordon, David Gordon
Moonbrook CC (R)
New York
Robert Trent Jones, Frank Duane
Moor Allerton GC NLE
Yorkshire, England
Alister Mackenzie
Moor Allerton GC
Yorkshire, England
Robert Trent Jones, Cabell Robinson
Moor Park GC (High Course)
Hertfordshire, England
H.S. Colt
Moor Park GC (West Course)
Hertfordshire, England
H.S. Colt, C.H. Alison, Alister Mackenzie

Moore Estate GC
Roslyn, New York
Charles Blair Macdonald, Seth Raynor
Moore Place GC
Oxney, England
Harry Vardon
Moorefield Petersburg GC
West Virginia
Russell Roberts
Moorestown Field C
New Jersey
Alex Findlay
Mooresville GC
North Carolina
J. Porter Gibson
Moorings of Manatee GC
Rustin, Florida
Ward Northrup
Moorings GC
Vero Beach, Florida
Pete Dye
Moors of Portage GC
Portage, Michigan
Arthur Hills
Moortown GC
Yorkshire, England
Alister Mackenzie
Moraga CC
California
Robert Muir Graves
Moraine CC
Dayton, Ohio
Alex "Nipper" Campbell
Moraine CC (R)
Ohio
Dick Wilson
Moray GC (New Course)
Morayshire, Scotland
Henry Cotton
Moray GC (Old Course)
Morayshire, Scotland
Old Tom Morris
Morehead City CC
North Carolina
C.C. McCuiston, Phillip Ball
Morningside Hotel GC
Hurleyville, New York
Alfred H. Tull
Morpeth GC (R)
England
J. Hamilton Stutt
Morris County GC
Morristown, New Jersey
Tom Bendelow
Morris County GC
Morristown, New Jersey
Hal Purdy
Morris County GC (R) NLE
New Jersey
H.J. Whigham
Morris County GC (R. 6)
New Jersey
Seth Raynor
Morris County GC (A.12)
New Jersey
Seth Raynor
Morris CC NLE
Illinois
William B. Langford, Theodore J. Moreau
Morris CC
Illinois
John Darrah
Morris Park CC
South Bend, Indiana
Robert E. Dustin
Morris Williams Muni
Austin, Texas
Leon Howard
Morsum-Sylt GC
Sylt, West Germany
Bernhard von Limburger
Mortimer Singer Estate GC
England
Herbert Fowler
Morton Hall GC (R. 5)
Scotland
Fred W. Hawtree
Morton Hall GC (A. 9)
Scotland
Fred W. Hawtree

Morton Hall GC (R)
Scotland
J.H. Taylor
Moselem Springs CC
Fleetwood, Pennsylvania
George Fazio
Moseley GC (R)
England
H.S. Colt
Mosely GC (R)
California
H.S. Colt
Moses Lake GC
Washington
Mel "Curley" Hueston
Moss Creek Plantation GC (North Course)
Hilton Head Island, South Carolina
Tom Fazio
Moss Creek Plantation GC (South Course)
Hilton Head Island, South Carolina
George Fazio, Tom Fazio
Mosswood Meadows GC
Monroe City, Missouri
David Gill, Garrett Gill
Motala GC (A. 9)
Sweden
Jan Sederholm
Moulton Muni
Alabama
Earl Stone
Moundbuilders CC
Newark, Ohio
Tom Bendelow
Mount Airy Lodge & CC
Mt.Pocono, Pennsylvania
Hal Purdy, Malcolm Purdy,Chandler Purdy
Mount Bruno GC
Montreal, Quebec
Willie Park Jr
Mount Carroll GC
Illinois
Tom Bendelow
Mount Charron GC
Huntsville, Alabama
Luther O. "Luke" Morris
Mount Cobb Muni
Scranton, Pennsylvania
James Gilmore Harrison, Ferdinand Garbin
Mount Diablo CC
California
William Watson
Mount Dora GC (R. 9)
Florida
Harold Paddock
Mount Dora GC (A. 9)
Florida
Harold Paddock
Mount Hawley CC (R)
Illinois
Edward Lawrence Packard, Roger Packard
Mount Hope G&CC
Ontario
Clinton E. Robinson, Robert Moote
Mount Kinabalu GC
Kundasang, Malaysia
Robert Muir Graves
Mount Kineo GC
Kineo, Maine
Art Townley
Mount Kineo GC (R)
Maine
Orrin Smith, William F. Mitchell
Mount Kisco CC
New York
Tom Winton
Mount Kisco CC (R)
New York
A.W. Tillinghast
Mount Lebanon CC
Pennsylvania
James Gilmore Harrison
Mount Manor Inn & GC
Marshall's Creek, Pennsylvania
Russell Scott Jr

Mount Mitchell GC
Burnsville, North Carolina
Fred W. Hawtree
Mount Odin Muni (R. 9)
Pennsylvania
X.G. Hassenplug
Mount Ogden GC
Ogden, Utah
William Howard Neff
Mount Pleasant CC
Boylston, Massachusetts
William F. Mitchell
Mount Pleasant CC
Michigan
Mark DeVries
Mount Pleasant CC (A. 9)
Michigan
Bruce Matthews, Jerry Matthews
Mount Pleasant House GC
New Hampshire
Alex Findlay
Mount Pleasant Muni
Baltimore, Maryland
Gus Hook
Mount Snow GC
Vermont
Geoffrey S. Cornish, William G. Robinson
Mount St. Helena GC
Calistoga, California
Jack Fleming
Mount Vernon CC
Ohio
Tom Bendelow
Mount Vernon CC (R)
Ohio
Jack Kidwell, Michael Hurdzan
Mount Vernon GC (A. 9)
Illinois
Gary Kern
Mount Vernon GC
New Hampshire
Alex Findlay
Mount Whitney CC
Lone Pine, California
Bob Baldock
Mount. Crotched CC NLE
Francestown, New Hampshire
Donald Ross
Mountain Brook C
Birmingham, Alabama
Donald Ross
Mountain Brook C
Birmingham, Alabama
John LaFoy
Mountain Brook C (R)
Alabama
George W. Cobb
Mountain Brook C (R)
Alabama
John LaFoy
Mountain Dell GC
Salt Lake City, Utah
William F. Bell, William H. Neff
Mountain Gate CC
Los Angeles, California
Ted Robinson
Mountain Gate CC (A. 9)
California
Ted Robinson
Mountain Glen GC
Newland, North Carolina
George W. Cobb
Mountain Lake C
Lake Wales, Florida
Seth Raynor
Mountain Lake C (R)
Florida
William H. Diddel
Mountain Meadows G&CC NLE
California
William P. Bell
Mountain Meadows GC
Pomona, California
Ted Robinson
Mountain Meadows GC
Elkford, British Columbia
Reg Stone, Roy Stone
Mountain Ranch GC
Fairfield Bay, Arkansas
Brian Ault, Tom Clark,Edmund B. Ault

Mountain Ranches GC
Rigaud, Quebec
Howard Watson
Mountain Ridge CC
West Caldwell, New Jersey
A.W. Tillinghast
Mountain Ridge CC (R)
New Jersey
Herbert Strong
Mountain Shadows CC
Scottsdale, Arizona
Arthur Jack Snyder
Mountain Shadows GC (North Course)
Rohnert Park, California
Gary Roger Baird
Mountain Shadows GC (South Course)
Rohnert Park, California
Bob Baldock
Mountain Springs G&CC
Linville, North Carolina
Ellis Maples, Dan Maples
Mountain Valley GC
Waynesville, North Carolina
George W. Cobb
Mountain View CC
Thousand Palms, California
William F. Bell
Mountain View CC
Alamogordo, New Mexico
C. William Keith
Mountain View GC
New Hampshire
Ralph Barton
Mountain View GC
Boring, Oregon
Jack Beaudoin, Jack Waltmire
Mountain View GC
Pennsylvania
Edmund B. Ault, Brian Ault,Tom Clark
Mountain View GC
Jordan, Utah
William H. Neff
Mountain View GC
Sequim, Washington
Ray Coleman
Mountaindale CC NLE
California
Robert Johnstone
Mountrath GC (R)
Ireland
Eddie Hackett
Mountwood Park GC
West Virginia
George W. Cobb, John LaFoy
Mowbray CC (R)
South Africa
S.V. Hotchkin
Mowsbury Muni
Bedfordshire, England
Fred W. Hawtree, Martin Hawtree
Moyola Park GC
County Derry, Northern Ireland
Don Patterson
Mt. Lomond G&CC
Ogden, Utah
Mick Riley
Muirfield Golf Links NLE
New York
John Duncan Dunn
Muirfield GC
East Lothian, Scotland
Old Tom Morris
Muirfield GC (R)
Scotland
H.S. Colt, C.H. Alison
Muirfield GC (R)
Scotland
Tom Simpson
Muirfield Village GC
Dublin, Ohio
Desmond Muirhead, Jack Nicklaus
Mulberry Hill GC
East Huntington, Pennsylvania
Ferdinand Garbin
Mullet Bay GC
St. Marten
Joe Lee

Mullet Lake G&CC
Michigan
Tom Bendelow
Mullingar GC
County Westmeath, Ireland
James Braid, John R. Stutt
Mullingar GC (R)
Ireland
Eddie Hackett
Mullion GC (R)
England
Tom Williamson
Mullion GC (R)
England
J. Hamilton Stutt
Mulrany GC (R)
Ireland
Eddie Hackett
Multnomah GC NLE
Beavertown, Oregon
William Lock
Munchener GC
Munich, West Germany
Bernhard von Limburger
Muncie Elks GC
Indiana
William Barnes
Murcar GC
Aberdeen, Scotland
Archie Simpson
Murcar GC (R)
Scotland
James Braid
Murhof GC
Frohnleiten, Austria
Bernhard von Limburger
Murhof GC (A. 9)
Austria
J.F. Dudok Van Heel
Murhof GC (A. 9)
Austria
Bernhard von Limburger
Murray Muni
Utah
Robert Muir Graves
Murray Muni
Regina, Saskatchewan
Claude Muret
Murrayfield GC
Edinburgh, Scotland
Willie Park, Willie Park Jr
Murrayshall G&CC
Perthshire, Scotland
J. Hamilton Stutt
Murrieta GC
California
Robert Trent Jones, Robert Trent Jones Jr,Gary Roger Baird
Musashi CC (Sasai Course)
Saitama, Japan
Seichi Inouye
Musashi CC (Toyoka Course)
Saitama, Japan
Seichi Inouye
Musashino CC
Japan
Ichisuke Izumi
Muskego Lakes CC (R)
Wisconsin
Edward Lawrence Packard, Roger Packard
Muskegon CC
Michigan
Donald Ross
Muskegon CC (R. 3)
Michigan
Bruce Matthews, Jerry Matthews
Muskerry GC
County Cork, Ireland
Alister Mackenzie
Muskerry GC (R)
Ireland
Eddie Hackett
Muskogee CC NLE
Oklahoma
Leslie Brownlee
Muskogee CC
Oklahoma
Perry Maxwell
Muskogee CC (R)
Oklahoma
Don Sechrest

Muskoka Beach GC
Gravenhurst, Ontario
Stanley Thompson
Muskoka Lakes G&CC
Port Carling, Ontario
Stanley Thompson
Muskoka Lakes G&CC (A. 9)
Ontario
Clinton E. Robinson
Musqueam GC
Vancouver, British Columbia
Jack Ellis
Musselburgh GC
Scotland
James Braid, John R. Stutt
Muswell Hill GC
London, England
Willie Park
Muthaiga GC
Nairobi, Kenya
T.J. Anderson, Peter Whitelaw
Muttontown G&CC
East Norwich, New York
Alfred H. Tull
Muttontown G&CC (R. 1)
New York
Frank Duane
Muttontown G&CC (R)
New York
Robert Trent Jones, Rees Jones
Muttontown G&CC (R)
New York
Joseph S. Finger
Myakka Pines GC
Englewood, Florida
Lane Marshall
Myerlee CC
Fort Myers, Florida
Arthur Hills
Myers Park CC
Charlotte, North Carolina
A.W. Tillinghast
Myers Park CC (R)
North Carolina
Donald Ross
Myers Park CC (R)
North Carolina
Ellis Maples
Myers Park CC (R)
North Carolina
Rees Jones
Mylora GC
Richmond, British Columbia
Jack Reimer
Myopia Hunt C
Hamilton, Massachusetts
Herbert Leeds
Myopia Hunt C (A. 9)
Massachusetts
Herbert Leeds
Myopia Hunt C (R)
Massachusetts
Geoffrey S. Cornish
Myopia Hunt C (R. 1)
Massachusetts
Phil Wogan
Myopia Hunt C (R)
Massachusetts
Geoffrey S. Cornish, Brian Silva
Myosotis CC NLE
Eatontown, New Jersey
A.W. Tillinghast
Myrtle Beach National GC
(North Course)
South Carolina
Frank Duane, Arnold Palmer
Myrtle Beach National GC
(South Course)
South Carolina
Frank Duane, Arnold Palmer
Myrtle Beach National GC (West
Course)
South Carolina
Frank Duane, Arnold Palmer
Myrtlewood CC (Palmetto
Course)
Myrtle Beach, South Carolina
Edmund B. Ault
Myrtlewood GC (Pines Course)
Myrtle Beach, South Carolina
George W. Cobb
Mystery Valley CC
Lithonia, Georgia
Dick Wilson, Joe Lee

Nadi GC (A. 9)
Fiji
John Harris
Naga-Waukee Park GC
Pewaukee, Wisconsin
Edward Lawrence Packard
Naie GC
Sapporo, Japan
Peter Thomson, Michael
Wolveridge
Nairn Dunbar GC (A. 9)
Scotland
Fraser Middleton
Nairn GC
Nairnshire, Scotland
Archie Simpson
Nairn GC (R)
Scotland
Old Tom Morris
Nairn GC (R)
Scotland
James Braid
Naivasha Sporting C (R)
Kenya
*T.J. Anderson, S.J.O.
Armstrong,A.K. Gibson*
Nakoma CC
Madison, Wisconsin
Tom Bendelow
Nambu Fuji GC
Kwate, Japan
John Harris, Peter
Thomson,Michael Wolveridge
Nampa Muni
Idaho
Bob Baldock, Robert L. Baldock
Nanaimo G&CC
British Columbia
A. Vernon Macan
Nanticoke GC
Simcoe, Ontario
Renee Muylaert, *Charles Muylaert*
Napa Valley CC (A. 9)
California
Ronald Fream
Napa Valley CC (R. 9)
California
Ronald Fream
Naperville CC
Illinois
Tom Bendelow
Naperville CC (R. 5)
Illinois
David Gill
Naperville CC (R)
Illinois
Edward Lawrence Packard
Naples Beach Hotel GC (R)
Florida
Mark Mahannah
Naples Beach Hotel GC (R)
Florida
Ron Garl
Napoleon CC
Ohio
William J. Rockefeller
Nappanee Muni
Indiana
Gary Kern
Nara International GC
Hyogo, Japan
O. Ueda
Narashino CC (Kings Course)
Chiba, Japan
Kinya Fujita
Narashino CC (Queens Course)
Japan
Kinya Fujita
Narrowsburg GC
Syracuse, New York
Hal Purdy
Naruo CC
Japan
Rokuro Akaboshi, Shiro Akaboshi
Nashawtuc CC
Concord, Massachusetts
Geoffrey S. Cornish
Nashboro Village CC
Nashville, Tennessee
Benjamin Wihry
Nashua CC
New Hampshire
Wayne Stiles, John Van Kleek

Nashua CC (R)
New Hampshire
William F. Mitchell
Nashville G&AC formerly
known as Crockett Springs
National G&CC
Brentwood, Tennessee
Robert von Hagge, Bruce Devlin
Nassau CC
Glen Cove, New York
Devereux Emmet, Alfred H. Tull
Nassau CC (R. 1)
New York
Seth Raynor
Nassau CC (R. 9) NLE
New York
Tom Bendelow
Nassau CC (A. 9) NLE
New York
Tom Bendelow
Nassau CC (R)
New York
Herbert Strong, George Low Sr
Nassau CC (A. 3)
New York
Herbert Strong, George Low Sr
Nassau CC (R)
New York
Frank Duane
Nassau CC (R)
New York
Geoffrey S. Cornish, Brian Silva
Nassau G Links NLE
Bahamas
Alex Findlay
Nassawango CC
Snow Hill, Maryland
Russell Roberts
Nasu GC
Tochiga, Japan
Kinya Fujita
Natchez Trace CC
Sautillo, Mississippi
John W. Frazier
Natick CC (R. 4)
Massachusetts
Samuel Mitchell
Natick CC (A. 9)
Massachusetts
Samuel Mitchell
National City GC
California
Harry Rainville
National G Links of America
Southampton, New York
Charles Blair Macdonald
National G Links of America (R.
1)
New York
Perry Maxwell
National G Links of America (R)
New York
Robert Trent Jones
National G Links of America (R)
New York
Robert Trent Jones
National GC
Woodbridge, Ontario
George Fazio, Tom Fazio
National GC
Jakarta Pusat, Indonesia
Peter Thomson, Michael
Wolveridge,Ronald Fream
National GC of Australia
Australia
Robert Trent Jones Jr, Don Knott
National Town & CC NLE
Lake Wales, Florida
Leonard Macomber
National Town & CC NLE
Ohio
Leonard Macomber
Nautical Inn GC
Lake Havasu City, Arizona
Red Lawrence
Navajo Canyon CC
California
William P. Bell
Navajo Fields CC NLE
Worth, Illinois
Harry Collis
Navatanee CC
Thailand
Robert Trent Jones Jr, Gary
Roger Baird

Navesink CC
Red Bank, New Jersey
Hal Purdy
Navesink CC (R)
New Jersey
Geoffrey S. Cornish, Brian Silva
Navy GC (Cruiser Course)
Cypress, California
Ted Robinson
Navy GC (Destroyer Course)
Cypress, California
Joseph B. Williams
Navy GC (North Course)
San Diego, California
Jack Daray
Navy GC (North Course) (R. 6)
California
Ted Robinson
Navy Postgraduate School GC
Monterey, California
Robert Muir Graves
Navy Postgraduate School GC
(R. 4)
California
Robert Muir Graves
Navy Postgraduate School GC
(A. 9)
California
Robert Muir Graves
Navy-Marine GC
Pearl Harbor, Hawaii
William P. Bell
Neah-Kah-Nie GC
Manzanita, Oregon
Barney Lucas
Nealhurst GC NLE
Jacksonville, Florida
Stanley Thompson
Neckartal GC
Stuttgart, West Germany
Bernhard von Limburger
Needham GC NLE
Massachusetts
John Graham
Needham GC
Massachusetts
Wayne Stiles
Needham GC (A. 9)
Massachusetts
Eugene "Skip" Wogan
Needham GC (R)
Massachusetts
Orrin Smith, William F. Mitchell
Needles Muni
California
Harry Rainville, David Rainville
Needwood GC
Rockville, Maryland
Lindsay Ervin
Nefyn and District GC (R)
Wales
Fred W. Hawtree, A.H.F. Jiggens
Nehai Tonkayea GC
Marceline, Missouri
Richard Watson
Neipsic Par 3 GC
Glastonbury, Connecticut
Geoffrey S. Cornish, William G.
Robinson
Nelson GC (A. 9)
England
Fred W. Hawtree, A.H.F. Jiggens
Nelson GC (R)
New Zealand
John Harris, Peter
Thomson,Michael Wolveridge
Nelson Park GC
Decatur, Illinois
Tom Bendelow
Nemacolin CC
Beallsville, Pennsylvania
Emil Loeffler, *John McGlynn*
Nemacolin CC (R)
Pennsylvania
A.W. Tillinghast
Nemadji Muni (A. 9)
Wisconsin
Don Herfort
Nemaha G&CC NLE
Oklahoma
Floyd Farley
Nenagh GC (A. 9)
Ireland
Eddie Hackett

Neskowin Beach GC
Oregon
Ercel Kay
Neuchatel GC
Switzerland
Karl Hoffmann, Bernhard von
Limburger
Neumann Park GC (A. 9)
Ohio
Jack Kidwell, Michael Hurdzan
Neustadt GC
East Germany
Karl Hoffmann, Bernhard von
Limburger
Nevele GC
Ellenville, New York
Alfred H. Tull
Nevele GC (R)
New York
George Fazio, Tom Fazio
New Bern G&CC (R. 9)
North Carolina
Ellis Maples
New Bern G&CC (A. 9)
North Carolina
Ellis Maples
New Castle CC
Pennsylvania
A.W. Tillinghast
New CC
Versailles, Kentucky
Buck Blankenship
New Forest GC
England
Peter Swann
New Glasgow GC (R)
Quebec
Howard Watson
New GC
Deauville, France
Tom Simpson, P.M. Ross
New GC (A. 9)
France
Henry Cotton
New Haven CC
Connecticut
Willie Park Jr
New Haven CC NLE
Connecticut
Robert D. Pryde
New Haven CC (R. 1)
Connecticut
Al Zikorus
New London CC (R. 5)
Connecticut
Geoffrey S. Cornish, William G.
Robinson
New Meadows GC
Topsfield, Massachusetts
Phil Wogan
New Mexico Military Institute
GC
Roswell, New Mexico
Floyd Farley
New Mexico State Univ GC
Las Cruces, New Mexico
Floyd Farley
New Mexico Tech GC
Socorro, New Mexico
James E. Voss
New Orleans CC (R. 9)
Louisiana
Joe Lee
New Orleans CC (R)
Louisiana
Ron Kirby, Denis Griffiths
New Orleans NAS GC
Louisiana
Dick Metz
New Orleans VA Hospital GC
Louisiana
Ralph Plummer, Bob Dunning
New Prague GC (A. 9)
Minnesota
Don Herfort
New Quarter Park GC
Virginia
George W. Cobb, John LaFoy
New Richmond GC (R. 5)
Wisconsin
Don Herfort
New Richmond GC (A. 9)
Wisconsin
Don Herfort

New Ross GC (R)
Ireland
Eddie Hackett
New Smyrna GC
Florida
Donald Ross
New South Wales GC
Sydney, Australia
Alister Mackenzie
New St. Andrews GC
Ontawara City, Japan
Jack Nicklaus, Jay Morrish, Bob Cupp
New Ulm GC (A. 9)
Minnesota
Don Herfort
New York Hospital GC (R)
New York
Robert Trent Jones
New Zealand GC NLE
Surrey, England
S. Mure Ferguson
New Zealand GC
Surrey, England
Tom Simpson
Newark Athletic C NLE
New Jersey
Alex Findlay
Newark CC
Delaware
Wilfrid Reid
Newark CC (A. 9)
Delaware
Frank Murray, Russell Roberts
Newark GC
California
Jack Fleming
Newaukum Valley GC
Chehalis, Washington
John H. Date, Henry M. Date
Newbiggin-by-the-Sea GC
Northumberland, England
Willie Park
Newbold Cowyn GC
Warwickshire, England
Frederick Gibberd
Newbridge CC
Largo, Maryland
Russell Roberts
Newburgh CC (R. 9)
New York
Hal Purdy
Newcastle GC
Australia
Eric L. Apperly
Newcastle West GC (R)
Ireland
Eddie Hackett
Newcastle-under-Lyme GC
Staffordshire, England
Fred W. Hawtree, Martin Hawtree
Newlands G&RC
Langley, British Columbia
Clive Rogers
Newlands G&RC (R)
British Columbia
William L. Overdorf
Newlands GC
County Dublin, Ireland
James Braid
Newlands GC (R)
Ireland
Eddie Hackett
Newport Beach CC
California
William P. Bell, William F. Bell
Newport Beach CC (R)
California
Harry Rainville, David Rainville
Newport Beach CC (A. 9)
California
Harry Rainville, David Rainville
Newport CC (A. 9)
Arkansas
Edmund B. Ault
Newport CC
New Hampshire
Ralph Barton
Newport CC (R)
New Hampshire
Orrin Smith, William F. Mitchell

Newport CC
Rhode Island
William F. Davis
Newport CC (R. 9)
Rhode Island
A.W. Tillinghast
Newport CC (A. 9)
Rhode Island
A.W. Tillinghast
Newport CC (R)
Rhode Island
Donald Ross
Newport CC (R)
Rhode Island
Orrin Smith, William F. Mitchell
Newport CC
Texas
Gary Darling
Newport CC
Vermont
Ralph Barton
Newport GC
Michigan
Alex Lilac, Sam Lilac, Bill Lilac
Newporter Inn GC
Newport Beach, California
William F. Bell
Newquay GC
England
H.S. Colt
Newton Abbot GC NLE
Devonshire, England
Harold St. Maur
Newton Abbot GC
Devonshire, England
James Braid
Newton Commonwealth GC
Newton, Massachusetts
Wayne Stiles, John Van Kleek
Newton CC
Iowa
Harry Collis
Newton CC
Kansas
Harry Robb
Newton CC (A. 9)
Maryland
William Gordon, David Gordon
Newtonmore GC (R)
Scotland
Alister Mackenzie
Newtonmore GC (R)
Scotland
James Braid
Newtonmore GC (R)
Scotland
Old Tom Morris
Newtonstewart GC (R)
Northern Ireland
J.J.F. Pennink
Niagara Falls CC (R)
New York
William Newcomb
Niagara Falls CC (R)
New York
Robert Trent Jones
Niakwa G&CC
Winnipeg, Manitoba
Stanley Thompson
Nibley Park GC
Salt Lake City, Utah
Harold B. Lamb
Nibley Park GC (R)
Utah
Mick Riley
Niigata Forest GC
Toyoura Village, Japan
Ron Kirby, Denis Griffiths
Nile CC
Edmonds, Washington
Norman H. Woods
Nine Eagles GC (R. 9)
Florida
Ron Garl
Nine Eagles GC (A. 3)
Florida
Ron Garl
Niobrara GC
Wyoming
Frank Hummel
Nippersink Manor CC
Genoa City, Wisconsin
James Foulis

Niseko GC
Sapporo, Japan
Arnold Palmer, Ed Seay, Bob Walker
Niseko Kogen GC
Sapporo, Japan
Arnold Palmer, Ed Seay, Bob Walker
Nishi Biwako GC
Japan
Arnold Palmer, Ed Seay
Nishi Nihon GC
Nogata, Japan
Ron Kirby, Denis Griffiths
Nishinomiya CC
Hyogo, Japan
O. Ueda, K. Takeguchi
Nob North GC
Dalton, Georgia
Ron Kirby, Denis Griffiths
Nobleton Lakes GC
Ontario
Renee Muylaert
Nocona Hills CC
Texas
Leon Howard, *Charles Howard*
Nogales CC (R) NLE
Arizona
A.H. Jolly
Nolan River CC
Texas
Leon Howard
Nongsa Indah CC
Indonesia
Ronald Fream
Noord Nederlandse G&CC
Netherlands
John Duncan Dunn
Noordwijkse GC (R)
Netherlands
J.J.F. Pennink
Noranda Mines GC
Quebec
Stanley Thompson
Noranda Mines GC (R. 9)
Quebec
Howard Watson
Norbeck CC
Rockville, Maryland
Alfred H. Tull
Norbeck CC (R)
Maryland
Edmund B. Ault
Nordic Hills GC
Itasca, Illinois
Charles Maddox, *Frank P. MacDonald*
Norfolk CC (R.13)
Nebraska
Floyd Farley
Norfolk CC (A. 5)
Nebraska
Floyd Farley
Norfolk CC (R)
Virginia
William S. Flynn
Norfolk GC
England
J.H. Taylor
Norman GC
Oklahoma
Floyd Farley
Normanby Hall GC
Lincolnshire, England
Fred W. Hawtree, A.H.F. Jiggens
Normanby Park GC
Scunthorpe, England
Fred W. Hawtree, Martin Hawtree
Normandie GC
St. Louis, Missouri
Robert Foulis
Normandie GC
France
J. Hamilton Stutt
Normandy CC
Flossmoor, Illinois
Harry Collis
Normandy Shores GC
Miami Beach, Florida
William S. Flynn, Howard Toomey

Normandy Shores GC (R)
Florida
Mark Mahannah
Normanside CC
Elsmere, New York
William Harries
Norris Estate GC
St. Charles, Illinois
Robert Trent Jones
North Adams GC (R)
Massachusetts
Orrin Smith, William F. Mitchell
North Andover CC
Massachusetts
Donald Ross
North Andover CC (R)
Massachusetts
William F. Mitchell
North Bay G&CC
Ontario
Stanley Thompson
North Bay G&CC (R. 9)
Ontario
Howard Watson
North Bay G&CC (A. 9)
Ontario
Howard Watson
North Berwick GC (A. 9)
Scotland
David Strath
North Berwick GC (R. 9)
Scotland
David Strath
North Berwick GC (R)
Scotland
Tom Dunn
North Berwick GC (R)
Scotland
John Duncan Dunn
North Berwick GC (R)
Scotland
Sir Guy Campbell, C.K. Hutchison, S.V. Hotchkin
North Berwick Muni (Burgh Course) (R)
Scotland
P.M. Ross
North Castle CC
Armonk, New York
Gilman P. Tiffany
North Colvin GC
New York
A. Russell Tryon
North Conway CC
New Hampshire
Ralph Barton
North Conway CC (A. 9)
New Hampshire
Phil Wogan
North Downs GC (R)
England
J.J.F. Pennink
North Foreland GC
Kingsgate, England
Herbert Fowler, Tom Simpson
North Foreland GC (R)
England
J.S.F. Morrison
North Foreland GC (R)
England
Tom Simpson, J.S.F. Morrison
North Fork CC
Johnstown, Pennsylvania
James Gilmore Harrison
North Fulton Muni
Atlanta, Georgia
H. Chandler Egan
North Halton GC
Georgetown, Ontario
Robert Moote, *David Moote*
North Halton GC (R)
Ontario
Robert Moote
North Hants GC
Hampshire, England
James Braid
North Hants GC (R)
England
Tom Simpson
North Haven GC (R)
Maine
Wayne Stiles, John Van Kleek
North Hempstead CC (R)
New York
Ed Erickson

North Hempstead CC (R)
New York
Robert Trent Jones
North Hempstead GC
New York
A.W. Tillinghast
North Hill CC
Massachusetts
William F. Mitchell
North Hills CC (R)
Arkansas
Robert Trent Jones, Roger Rulewich
North Hills CC
Manhasset, New York
Robert Trent Jones, Frank Duane
North Hills CC (R. 1)
New York
Robert Bruce Harris
North Hills CC
Raleigh, North Carolina
George W. Cobb
North Hills Muni
Pennsylvania
Edmund B. Ault
North Hills Muni (R.10)
Pennsylvania
Bill Love
North Island GC (R)
California
Jack Daray Jr
North Jersey CC
Wayne, New Jersey
Walter J. Travis
North Jersey CC
New Jersey
Nicholas Psiahas
North Jersey CC (R)
New Jersey
Hal Purdy
North Jersey CC (R)
New Jersey
Robert Trent Jones, Roger Rulewich
North Kent GC
Rockford, Michigan
Warner Bowen
North Kern CC
California
William F. Bell
North Kingstown Muni
Rhode Island
Walter I. Johnson
North Lakes CC
Victoria, Australia
Peter Thomson, Michael Wolveridge
North Las Vegas GC
Nevada
Jack Walpole
North Middlesex GC
England
C.S. Butchart
North Oaks CC
St. Paul, Minnesota
Stanley Thompson
North Oxford GC
England
Tom Dunn
North Park Community GC
Coloma, Michigan
George B. Ferry
North Park GC (R)
Pennsylvania
X.G. Hassenplug
North Ranch CC
Westlake, California
Ted Robinson
North Redoubt C now known as Garrison GC
North Ridge CC
California
William F. Bell, William P. Bell
North Ridge CC (R)
California
Robert Muir Graves, Damian Pascuzzo
North Ridge CC (Lakes Course)
Raleigh, North Carolina
Gene Hamm
North Ridge CC (Oaks Course)
Raleigh, North Carolina
Gene Hamm

North River GC NLE
Tuscaloosa, Alabama
Ron Kirby, Gary Player, Denis
  Griffiths
North Salem Links NLE
Salem, Massachusetts
Robert White
North Shore Acres CC NLE
Kenosha, Wisconsin
William B. Langford
North Shore CC
Glenview, Illinois
C.H. Alison, H.S. Colt
North Shore CC (R)
Illinois
Ken Killian, Dick Nugent
North Shore CC (R)
Illinois
Edward Lawrence Packard
North Shore CC (R)
Illinois
Roger Packard
North Shore CC (R. 9)
Indiana
William H. Diddel
North Shore CC (A. 9)
Indiana
William H. Diddel
North Shore CC NLE
St. Louis, Missouri
Robert Foulis
North Shore CC
St. Louis, Missouri
Chic Adams, Homer Herpel
North Shore CC
Long Island, New York
A.W. Tillinghast
North Shore CC
Tacoma, Washington
Al Smith
North Shore CC
Mequon, Wisconsin
David Gill
North Shore CC (R)
Wisconsin
Dick Nugent
North Shore GC NLE
Kenilworth, Illinois
Tom Bendelow
North Shore GC
Menominee, Michigan
A.H. Jolly
North Shore GC
England
James Braid
North Shore GC (R)
New Zealand
John Harris, Peter
  Thomson, Michael Wolveridge
North Shore Towers GC
Little Neck, New York
Frank Duane
North West GC (A. 9)
Ireland
Eddie Hackett
North West GC (R)
Ireland
Eddie Hackett
North Woodmere GC
New York
David Gordon
North Worcestershire GC
England
James Braid
Northampton CC
Upper Marlboro, Maryland
Russell Roberts
Northampton GC (A. 6)
Pennsylvania
David Gordon
Northampton GC (R.12)
Pennsylvania
David Gordon
Northampton GC
Northamptonshire, England
Old Tom Morris
Northampton GC (R)
England
Willie Park Jr
Northampton Valley CC
Pennsylvania
Edmund B. Ault

Northamptonshire County GC
England
H.S. Colt
**Northamptonshire County GC
  (R)**
England
James Braid
Northdale G&CC
Tampa, Florida
Ron Garl
Northeast Park GC
Winnipeg, Manitoba
Claude Muret
Northern Hills CC
San Antonio, Texas
Joseph Beleau
Northernaire CC
Three Lakes, Wisconsin
Tom Bendelow
Northfield GC
East Northfield, Massachusetts
Alex Findlay
Northfield GC
Minnesota
Paul Coates
Northfield GC (A. 9)
Minnesota
Don Herfort
Northfield GC (R. 9)
Minnesota
Don Herfort
Northgate CC
Reno, Nevada
Brad Benz, Mike Poellot
Northgate CC
Houston, Texas
Robert von Hagge, Bruce Devlin
Northgreen Village GC
Rocky Mount, North Carolina
J. Porter Gibson
Northland CC NLE
Duluth, Minnesota
Ward Ames Jr.
Northland CC
Duluth, Minnesota
Donald Ross
Northland CC (A. 9) NLE
Minnesota
Tom Bendelow
Northland CC (R. 9) NLE
Minnesota
Tom Bendelow
Northland CC (R)
Minnesota
Don Herfort
Northmoor CC
Highland Park, Illinois
Donald Ross
Northmoor CC (R)
Illinois
Edward Lawrence Packard
Northport CC
New York
Devereux Emmet
Northport GC
Florida
LeRoy Phillips
Northport Point G&CC
Michigan
Tom Bendelow
Northshore CC
Portland, Texas
Robert von Hagge, Bruce Devlin
Northstar at Tahoe GC
Truckee, California
Robert Muir Graves
Northumberland G&CC
Pugwash, Nova Scotia
Clinton E. Robinson
Northumberland G&CC (A. 9)
Nova Scotia
William G. Robinson
Northumberland GC (R)
England
James Braid
Northumberland GC (R)
England
H.S. Colt, C.H. Alison, Alister
  Mackenzie
Northway Heights G&CC
Ballston Lake, New York
Pete Craig

**Northwest Mississippi Jr.
  College GC**
Mississippi
John W. Frazier
Northwest Park GC
Wheaton, Maryland
Edmund B. Ault
Northwest Park Muni NLE
Oklahoma City, Oklahoma
Arthur Jackson
Northwood C
Dallas, Texas
William H. Diddel
Northwood C (R)
Texas
Ralph Plummer
Northwood C (R. 5)
Texas
Marvin Ferguson
Northwood CC (A. 9)
Louisiana
Jeff Brauer
Northwood CC (R. 2)
Mississippi
Brian Ault
Northwood G&CC
Lawrenceville, Georgia
Willard Byrd
Northwood G&CC
Toronto, Ontario
Stanley Thompson
Northwood GC
Guernerville, California
Alister Mackenzie, Robert Hunter
Northwood GC
England
Tom Dunn
Nortonhall GC (A. 9)
Scotland
Fred W. Hawtree, Martin
  Hawtree
Nortonhall GC (R. 5)
Scotland
Fred W. Hawtree, Martin
  Hawtree
Norway CC
Maine
George Dunn Jr
Norway Point GC (R. 9)
Ontario
Stanley Thompson
Norwich Muni
Connecticut
Donald Ross
Norwich Muni
England
F.G. Hawtree, J.H. Taylor
Norwood CC
Massachusetts
Samuel Mitchell
Norwood CC NLE
Long Branch, New Jersey
A.W. Tillinghast
Norwood GC
Huntington, Indiana
Hal Purdy
Norwood Hills CC (East Course)
St. Louis, Missouri
Wayne Stiles
Norwood Hills CC (West Course)
St. Louis, Missouri
Wayne Stiles
Nottawasage Inn GC
Alliston, Ontario
Gordon Witteveen
Nottingham City GC
England
Tom Dunn
Nottingham City GC (R)
England
Willie Park Jr
Nottingham GC (R)
Pennsylvania
Edmund B. Ault
Notts GC (R)
Nottinghamshire, England
Willie Park Jr
Notts GC (R)
England
J.H. Taylor
Notts GC (R)
England
Tom Williamson

Noyac G&CC
Sag Harbor, New York
William F. Mitchell
Nubbins Ridge CC
Knoxville, Tennessee
Alex McKay
**Nueva Andalucia GC (Las Brisas
  Course)**
Marbella, Malaga, Spain
Robert Trent Jones
**Nueva Andalucia GC (Par 3
  Course)**
Marbella, Malaga, Spain
Robert Trent Jones
**Nueva Andulucia GC (Los
  Naranjos Course)**
Marbella, Malaga, Spain
Robert Trent Jones, Cabell
  Robinson
Nuevo Vallarta GC
Mexico
Arnold Palmer, Ed Seay, Bob
  Walker
Nun's Island GC
Montreal, Quebec
Howard Watson
Nuneaton GC
Warwickshire, England
Tom Williamson
Nuremore GC (R)
Ireland
Eddie Hackett
Nybro GC
Sweden
Jan Sederholm
Nyeri GC
Kenya
G. Sandbach Baker, Reggie McClure
NCR CC (North Course)
Dayton, Ohio
Dick Wilson
NCR CC (South Course)
Dayton, Ohio
Dick Wilson
O'Brien Estate GC
Plattsburg, New York
Howard Watson
O'Donnell GC
Palm Springs, California
Johnny Dawson
Oahu CC
Hawaii
Alex Bell
Oahu CC (R)
Hawaii
Robin Nelson
Oak n' Spruce GC
South Lee, Massachusetts
Geoffrey S. Cornish
Oak Brook GC
Illinois
Roger Packard
Oak Brook Hills CC
Oak Brook, Illinois
Dick Nugent, *Bruce Borland*
Oak Cliff CC
Dallas, Texas
Press Maxwell
Oak Forest CC
Longview, Texas
Billy Martindale
Oak Glen GC
Stillwater, Minnesota
Don Herfort
Oak Harbor GC
Baudette, Minnesota
Donald G. Brauer, Emile Perret
Oak Hill CC
Fitchburg, Massachusetts
Donald Ross
Oak Hill CC (A. 9)
Massachusetts
Wayne Stiles, John Van Kleek
Oak Hill CC (R)
Massachusetts
Orrin Smith, William F. Mitchell
Oak Hill CC (R. 5)
Massachusetts
Geoffrey S. Cornish, William G.
  Robinson
**Oak Hill CC formerly known as
  Alamo CC**
San Antonio, Texas
A.W. Tillinghast

Oak Hill CC (A. 3)
Texas
Joseph S. Finger
Oak Hill CC (R. 6)
Texas
Joseph S. Finger
Oak Hill CC (R. 2)
Texas
Ron Kirby, Denis Griffiths
Oak Hill CC (R)
Texas
Jay Morrish
Oak Hill CC (East Course)
Rochester, New York
Donald Ross
Oak Hill CC (East Course) (R)
New York
Robert Trent Jones
Oak Hill CC (East Course) (R)
New York
Robert Trent Jones
Oak Hill CC (East Course) (A. 3)
New York
George Fazio, Tom Fazio
Oak Hill CC (East Course) (R)
New York
George Fazio, Tom Fazio
Oak Hill CC (West Course)
Rochester, New York
Donald Ross
Oak Hill GC
Norwalk, Connecticut
Alfred H. Tull
Oak Hill GC
Middlebury, Indiana
William H. Diddel
Oak Hill GC
Milford, New Jersey
William Gordon, David Gordon
Oak Hill GC
Oak Creek, Wisconsin
R. Albert Anderson
Oak Hills CC NLE
Palos Heights, Illinois
David McIntosh
Oak Hills CC
Palos Heights, Illinois
Edward Lawrence Packard
Oak Hills CC
Omaha, Nebraska
Robert Popp
Oak Hills CC (R. 2)
Nebraska
Jeff Brauer
Oak Hills CC
Richmond, Virginia
Reuben Hines
Oak Hills CC
Japan
Robert Trent Jones Jr
Oak Hills G&CC (R)
Oklahoma
John Embry
Oak Hills GC
Spring Hill, Florida
Charles Almony
Oak Hills GC
Farmington, Missouri
John Ball
Oak Hollow GC
High Point, North Carolina
Pete Dye, David Pfaff
Oak Island CC
Southport, North Carolina
George W. Cobb
Oak Knoll GC
Independence, Oregon
Bill Ashby
Oak Knolls GC
Kent, Ohio
Howard Morette
Oak Lake GC (A. 9)
Pennsylvania
Ferdinand Garbin
Oak Lane CC
Woodbridge, Connecticut
Geoffrey S. Cornish
Oak Lawn GC
Elkhart, Indiana
William H. Diddel
Oak Leaf CC (R)
Iowa
Charles Calhoun

Oak Meadow G&TC
Evansville, Indiana
Ken Killian, Dick Nugent

Oak Meadows CC
Japan
Brad Benz, Mike Poellot

Oak Mountain State Park GC
Pelham, Alabama
Earl Stone

Oak Park CC
Illinois
Donald Ross

Oak Park CC (R)
Illinois
Edward B. Dearie Jr

Oak Park CC (R)
Illinois
William H. Diddel

Oak Ridge CC
Ft. Lauderdale, Florida
Hans Schmeisser

Oak Ridge CC
Hopkins, Minnesota
William D. Clark

Oak Ridge CC (A. 9)
Minnesota
William D. Clark

Oak Ridge CC
Madisonville, Texas
Leon Howard

Oak Ridge CC
Richardson, Texas
Jack Kidwell, Michael Hurdzan

Oak Ridge CC
San Jose, California
Bert Stamps

Oak Ridge GC
Agawam, Massachusetts
George Fazio, Tom Fazio

Oak Shore CC
Mississippi
Jack Daray

Oak Tree CC
Tehachapi, California
Ted Robinson

Oak Tree CC (R)
Ohio
Edmund B. Ault

Oak Tree CC (East Course)
Edmond, Oklahoma
Pete Dye

Oak Tree CC (West Course)
Edmond, Oklahoma
Pete Dye

Oak Tree GC
Edmond, Oklahoma
Pete Dye

Oak Tree GC
Pennsylvania
Edmund B. Ault

Oak Tree GC (R. 2)
Pennsylvania
Brian Ault, Bill Love

Oakbourne CC
Lafayette, Louisiana
Dick Wilson, Bob Simmons

Oakbourne CC (R)
Louisiana
Jay Riviere

Oakbourne CC (R)
Louisiana
Joseph S. Finger, Ken Dye

Oakcrest CC
Maryland
Edmund B. Ault, Al Jamison

Oakdale G&CC
California
Bob Baldock

Oakdale G&CC
Downsview, Ontario
Stanley Thompson

Oakdale G&CC (A. 9)
Ontario
Clinton E. Robinson, Robert Moote

Oakdale G&CC (R)
Ontario
Robert Moote

Oakdale GC
South Carolina
Roland "Robby" Robertson

Oakdale GC
Yorkshire, England
Alister Mackenzie

Oakdale GC (R. 7)
England
Fred W. Hawtree, A.H.F. Jiggens

Oakfield CC
Grand Lake, Nova Scotia
Clinton E. Robinson

Oakhurst CC
Grove City, Ohio
Jack Kidwell

Oakhurst G Links NLE
West Virginia
George Grant, Lionel Torrin

Oakland Acres CC
Grinnell, Iowa
Cliff Thompson

Oakland City GC
Indiana
William B. Langford

Oakland CC
Maryland
Edmund B. Ault

Oakland Greens GC (A. 9)
Ontario
Clinton E. Robinson

Oakland GC NLE
Bayside, New York
Seth Raynor

Oakland GC NLE
Bayside, New York
Tom Bendelow

Oakland Hills CC
Battle Creek, Michigan
George V. Nickolaou

Oakland Hills CC (North Course)
Birmingham, Michigan
Donald Ross

Oakland Hills CC (North Course) (R)
Michigan
Robert Trent Jones, Roger Rulewich

Oakland Hills CC (South Course)
Birmingham, Michigan
Donald Ross

Oakland Hills CC (South Course) (R)
Michigan
Robert Trent Jones

Oakland Hills CC (South Course) (R)
Michigan
Robert Trent Jones, Roger Rulewich

Oakland Hills CC (South Course) (R)
Michigan
Robert Trent Jones, Roger Rulewich

Oakland Hills GC
Portage, Michigan
Stuart Dustin, Lucien Axtell

Oaklawn GC
Chicago, Illinois
William B. Langford

Oakley CC NLE
Massachusetts
Willie Campbell

Oakley CC
Watertown, Massachusetts
Donald Ross

Oakmont CC
Glendale, California
Max Behr

Oakmont CC (R)
California
William P. Bell

Oakmont CC (R)
California
William F. Bell

Oakmont CC
Pennsylvania
Henry C. Fownes, William C. Fownes Jr

Oakmont CC (R)
Pennsylvania
William C. Fownes Jr, Emil Loeffler

Oakmont CC (R. 1)
Pennsylvania
Arthur Jack Snyder

Oakmont CC (R)
Pennsylvania
Robert Trent Jones

Oakmont CC (R)
Pennsylvania
Arnold Palmer, Ed Seay

Oakmont CC (R)
Pennsylvania
Ferdinand Garbin

Oakmont CC
Corinth, Texas
Roger Packard

Oakmont CC (East Course)
Santa Rosa, California
Ted Robinson

Oakmont CC (West Course)
Santa Rosa, California
Ted Robinson

Oakmont East GC
Oakmont, Pennsylvania
Emil Loeffler, *John McGlynn*

Oakmoore GC
Stockton, California
Donald A. Crump

Oakridge CC
Utah
William F. Bell, William H. Neff

Oaks CC
Tulsa, Oklahoma
A.W. Tillinghast

Oaks CC (R)
Oklahoma
Perry Maxwell

Oaks CC (Blue Heron Course)
Sarasota, Florida
Willard Byrd

Oaks CC (Eagle Course)
Sarasota, Florida
Willard Byrd

Oaks GC
Osage Beach, Missouri
Robert von Hagge, Bruce Devlin

Oaks North GC
Rancho Bernardo, California
Ted Robinson

Oakville GC (R)
Nova Scotia
Clinton E. Robinson

Oakway GC (R)
Oregon
John Zoller

Oakwood C
Cleveland, Ohio
Arthur Boggs

Oakwood C (A. 9)
Ohio
Tom Bendelow

Oakwood C (A. 6)
Ohio
Sandy Alves

Oakwood C (R. 2)
Ohio
Ted McAnlis

Oakwood CC
Coal Valley, Illinois
Pete Dye

Oakwood CC
Kansas City, Missouri
Tom Bendelow

Oakwood CC (A. 9)
Missouri
Orrin Smith, James Gilmore Harrison

Oakwood CC (R)
Missouri
William H. Diddel

Oakwood CC
Enid, Oklahoma
Perry Maxwell, Press Maxwell

Oakwood Park GC
Wisconsin
Edward Lawrence Packard

Oakwoods CC (R)
North Carolina
Tom Jackson

Oarai GC
Ibaraki, Japan
Kinya Fujita

Oasis CC
Palm Desert, California
David Rainville

Oasis GC
Plymouth, Michigan
William Newcomb

Oberau GC
Gut Buchwies, West Germany
Donald Harradine

Oberfranken GC
Bayreuth, West Germany
Bernhard von Limburger

Oberschwaben-Bad Waldsee GC
West Germany
Bernhard von Limburger

Oberschwaben-Bad Waldsee GC (R)
West Germany
Donald Harradine

Ocala GC NLE
Florida
John Duncan Dunn

Ocala Muni (Course No. 1)
Florida
William Gordon

Ocala Muni (Course No. 2)
Florida
Lou Bateman

Ocean Acres GC
Manahawkin, New Jersey
Hal Purdy

Ocean City CC NLE
New Jersey
Willie Park Jr

Ocean City G&YC
Berlin, Maryland
William Gordon, David Gordon

Ocean City G&YC (A. 9)
Maryland
Russell Roberts

Ocean Edge GC
Brewster, Massachusetts
Brian Silva, Geoffrey S. Cornish

Ocean G Links
Daytona Beach, Florida
Bill Amick

Ocean Isle Beach GC
North Carolina
Dan Breeden, Russell Breeden

Ocean Links
Newport, Rhode Island
Seth Raynor

Ocean Meadows GC
Goleta, California
Harry Rainville, David Rainville

Ocean Palm CC
Flagler Beach, Florida
Fred Bolton

Ocean Palm CC (R)
Florida
Lloyd Clifton

Ocean Pines G&CC
Ocean City, Maryland
Robert Trent Jones, Rees Jones

Ocean Reef C (Dolphin Course)
Key Largo, Florida
Mark Mahannah

Ocean Reef C (Dolphin Course) (R)
Florida
Robert von Hagge, Bruce Devlin

Ocean Reef C (Harbor Course)
North Key Largo, Florida
Robert von Hagge, Bruce Devlin

Ocean Shores GC
Brunswick, Australia
Robert von Hagge, Bruce Devlin

Oceana CC (R)
California
Robert Muir Graves

Oceanside G&CC
Ormond Beach, Florida
Alex Findlay

Oceanside G&CC (A. 9)
Florida
William H. Diddel

Oceanside G&CC (R. 9)
Florida
William H. Diddel

Oceanside GC
California
William H. Johnson

Oceanside Muni GC
California
Richard Bigler

Oconto GC
Wisconsin
A.H. Jolly

Ocotillo CC
Chandler, Arizona
Ted Robinson

Ocotillo Park GC
Hobbs, New Mexico
Warren Cantrell

Ocotillo Park GC (A. 9)
New Mexico
Marvin Ferguson

Odawara CC
Japan
Arthur Davis, Ron Kirby, Gary Player

Odense GC
Denmark
Jan Sederholm

Odsherred GC (R)
Denmark
Jan Sederholm

Oelwein CC
Iowa
Tom Bendelow

Ogden G&CC (R)
Utah
William Howard Neff

Oglebay Park GC
Wheeling, West Virginia
Devereux Emmet

Oglebay Park GC (A)
West Virginia
William Gordon, David Gordon

Ohio State Univ GC (Gray Course)
Columbus, Ohio
Alister Mackenzie, Perry Maxwell

Ohio State Univ GC (Scarlet Course)
Columbus, Ohio
Alister Mackenzie, Perry Maxwell

Ohio Univ GC (A. 9)
Ohio
Jack Kidwell

Ojai Valley Inn & CC
Ojai, California
George C. Thomas Jr, William P. Bell

Ojai Valley Inn & CC (R)
California
William F. Bell, William P. Bell

Okanagon Park GC
Kelowna, British Columbia
William G. Robinson

Okeechobee G&CC
Florida
Mark Mahannah

Okefenokee CC NLE
Waycross, Georgia
Bill Laffoon

Okefenokee GC
Waycross, Georgia
Joe Lee, Rocky Roquemore

Oklahoma City G&CC
Oklahoma
Perry Maxwell

Oklahoma City G&CC (R.10)
Oklahoma
Floyd Farley

Oklahoma City G&CC (R)
Oklahoma
Press Maxwell

Oklahoma City G&CC (R)
Oklahoma
Don Sechrest

Okoboji Vu GC
Spirit Lake, Iowa
E.G. McCoy

Olalla Valley GC
Toledo, Oregon
Vernon Warren

Olching GC
Munich, West Germany
J.F. Dudok Van Heel

Old Baldy C
Saratoga, Wyoming
Henry B. Hughes

Old Channel Trail GC
Montague, Michigan
Robert Bruce Harris

Old Channel Trail GC (A. 9)
Michigan
Bruce Matthews, Jerry Matthews

Old Channel Trail GC (R.11)
Michigan
Bruce Matthews, Jerry Matthews

Old Country Club NLE
Flushing, New York
Walter J. Travis
Old Country Club (R) NLE
New York
Devereux Emmet, Alfred H. Tull
Old Del Monte G&CC
Monterey, California
Charles Maud
Old Del Monte G&CC (R)
California
Jack Neville
Old Del Monte G&CC (A. 9)
California
Herbert Fowler
Old Del Monte G&CC (R. 9)
California
Herbert Fowler
Old Del Monte G&CC (R)
California
Nick Lombardo
Old Elm C
Fort Sheridan, Illinois
H.S. Colt, Donald Ross
Old Elm C (R)
Illinois
Ray Didier
Old Elm GC
Abilene, Texas
Warren Cantrell
Old Flatbush CC NLE
Brooklyn, New York
Maurice McCarthy
Old Fort CC
North Carolina
Alfred H. Tull
Old Hickory GC
Beaver Dam, Wisconsin
Tom Bendelow
Old Landing GC
Rehobeth, Delaware
Frank Murray, Russell Roberts
Old Lyme GC (R)
Connecticut
William F. Mitchell
Old Marsh GC
West Palm Beach, Florida
Pete Dye
Old Mill G&CC
Winton, North Carolina
Robert Thomason
Old Mill Pond GC
New Brunswick
William G. Robinson
Old Mission G&CC NLE
Kansas City, Kansas
Harry Robb
Old Oakland GC
Oaklandon, Indiana
Charles Maddox, William
  Maddox
Old Oaks CC
Purchase, New York
C.H. Alison, H.S. Colt
Old Oaks CC (R)
New York
William F. Mitchell
Old Oaks CC (R. 6)
New York
Frank Duane
Old Oaks CC (R)
New York
William Newcomb, Stephen Kay
Old Orchard Beach CC
Maine
George Dunn Jr
Old Ranch CC
Seal Beach, California
Ted Robinson
Old Ranfurly GC
Renfrewshire, Scotland
Willie Park Jr
Old Spanish Fort CC
Mobile, Alabama
Jack Daray
Old Tappan GC
New Jersey
Hal Purdy
Old Town C
Zebulon, Georgia
Arthur Davis
Old Town C
Winston-Salem, North Carolina
Perry Maxwell

Old Trail GC
Jupiter, Florida
Tom Fazio
Old Warson CC
Ladue, Missouri
Robert Trent Jones
Old Wayne GC
Chicago, Illinois
Charles Maddox
Old Westbury G&CC
New York
William F. Mitchell
Old Westbury G&CC (R. 2)
New York
Frank Duane
Old York Road CC (R) NLE
Pennsylvania
A.W. Tillinghast
Olde Hickory GC
Pennsylvania
Edmund B. Ault
Olde Mill GC
Hillsville, Virginia
Ellis Maples, Dan Maples
Olde Point CC
Hampstead, North Carolina
Jerry Turner
Oldenburgischer GC
West Germany
Bernhard von Limburger
Ole Monterey CC
Roanoke, Virginia
Fred Findlay
Olentangy CC
Columbus, Ohio
Charles Lorms
Olgiata CC
Italy
C.K. Cotton, J.J.F. Pennink
Olgiata CC (R)
Italy
Robert Trent Jones
Olhain GC
France
Robert Berthet
Olivas Park Muni
Ventura, California
William F. Bell
Olive Branch CC
Mississippi
Edward Creasey
Olive Glenn GC
Cody, Wyoming
Bob Baldock, Robert L. Baldock
Olmos Basin GC
San Antonio, Texas
George Hoffman
Olmstead AFB GC
Pennsylvania
Edmund B. Ault
Olney G&CC
Texas
Leon Howard
Olomana G Links
Waimanalo, Hawaii
Bob Baldock, Robert L. Baldock
Olympia Fields CC (Course No. 2) NLE
Illinois
Tom Bendelow
Olympia Fields CC (Course No. 3) NLE
Illinois
William Watson
Olympia Fields CC (North Course)
Illinois
Willie Park Jr
Olympia Fields CC (North Course) (R)
Illinois
Jack Daray
Olympia Fields CC (North Course) (R)
Illinois
Edward Lawrence Packard
Olympia Fields CC (North Course) (R. 3)
Illinois
Roger Packard
Olympia Fields CC (South Course)
Illinois
Tom Bendelow

Olympia Fields CC (South Course) (R)
Illinois
Jack Daray
Olympia Fields CC (South Course) (R)
Illinois
Edward Lawrence Packard
Olympia G&CC
Washington
William H. Tucker, Frank James
Olympia G&CC (A. 9)
Washington
Fred Federspiel
Olympia Spa & CC
Dothan, Alabama
Bob Simmons
Olympic C (Lake Course)
San Francisco, California
Wilfrid Reid, *Walter Fovargue*
Olympic C (Lake Course) (R)
California
Robert Trent Jones
Olympic C (Ocean Course)
San Francisco, California
William Watson, *Sam Whiting*
Olympic C (Ocean Course) (R)
California
Jack Fleming
Olympic G&CC
Arlington Heights, Illinois
C.D. Wagstaff
Olympic Hills GC
Eden Prairie, Minnesota
Charles Maddox
Omagh GC (R)
Northern Ireland
Eddie Hackett
Omaha CC
Nebraska
William B. Langford, Theodore J.
  Moreau
Omaha CC (R)
Nebraska
Perry Maxwell
Oneida G & Riding C
Green Bay, Wisconsin
Stanley Pelchar
Oneonta CC
New York
William Harries
Oneota CC
Decorah, Iowa
William B. Langford
Oneota CC (R. 9)
Iowa
Don Herfort
Oneota CC (A. 9)
Iowa
Don Herfort
Onion Creek CC
Austin, Texas
Jimmy Demaret
Onion Creek CC (R. 7)
Texas
Jay Morrish
Ono GC
Hyogo, Japan
O. Ueda
Onondaga G&CC
Fayetteville, New York
Stanley Thompson
Onondaga G&CC NLE
New York
Tom Bendelow
Onondaga G&CC (R)
New York
Hal Purdy
Onondaga G&CC (R. 2)
New York
Phil Wogan, Samuel Mitchell
Onotoyo GC
Hyogo, Japan
O. Ueda
Ontario GC
New York
George Swatt
Ontario Muni GC
Oregon
Bob Baldock, Robert L. Baldock
Ontario National GC (Course No. 1)
California
William H. Tucker Jr

Ontario National GC (Course No. 2)
California
William H. Tucker Jr
Ontonagon GC
Michigan
Harry E. Flora
Onwentsia C
Lake Forest, Illinois
James Foulis, Robert Foulis
Onwentsia C (A. 9)
Illinois
James Foulis, Robert Foulis, H.J.
  Tweedie, *H.J. Whigham*
Onwentsia C (R)
Illinois
Ken Killian, Dick Nugent
Oporto GC (R)
Portugal
P.M. Ross
Opperdorf Estate GC
Berlin, East Germany
C.S. Butchart
Oquirrah Hills Muni
Utah
Mick Riley
Orange Brook CC (East Course) (R)
Florida
Red Lawrence
Orange Brook CC (West Course) (R. 9)
Florida
Red Lawrence
Orange Brook CC (West Course) (A. 9)
Florida
Red Lawrence
Orange County CC (R. 3)
New York
Al Zikorus
Orange Hills GC (A. 9)
Connecticut
Geoffrey S. Cornish
Orange Lake CC
Kissimmee, Florida
Joe Lee
Orange Tree CC
Scottsdale, Arizona
Lawrence Hughes, Johnny Bulla
Orange Tree CC (R)
Arizona
Gary Panks
Orange Tree CC (R. 1)
Arizona
Arthur Jack Snyder
Orange Tree CC
Orlando, Florida
Bob Simmons
Orange Tree CC (R. 1)
Florida
Joe Lee
Orchard Beach G&CC
Lake Simcoe, Ontario
Stanley Thompson
Orchard Hills CC
Bryan, Ohio
R. Albert Anderson
Orchard Hills CC (A. 9)
Ohio
Arthur Hills
Orchard Hills CC (R. 9)
Ohio
Arthur Hills
Orchard Hills G&CC
Waukegan, Illinois
Robert Bruce Harris
Orchard Hills G&CC
Chesterland, Ohio
Gordon Alves
Orchard Hills G&CC
Washington
William Sander
Orchard Lake CC
Michigan
C.H. Alison, H.S. Colt
Orchard Lake CC (R)
Michigan
Wilfrid Reid, William Connellan
Orchard Lake CC (R)
Michigan
William H. Diddel

Orchard Lake CC (R)
Michigan
Arthur Hills, Steve Forrest, Mike
  Dasher
Orchard Park CC
Buffalo, New York
Walter J. Travis
Orchard Park CC (R)
New York
William Harries
Orchard Ridge CC (R)
Indiana
Charles Maddox, *Frank P.
  MacDonald*
Orchards GC
South Hadley, Massachusetts
Donald Ross
Oregon City GC
Oregon
George Junor
Oregon CC (R)
Illinois
C.D. Wagstaff
Orenco Woods GC
Oregon
Darrell Brown
Orillia GC
Ontario
Robert Moote, *David Moote*
Orinda CC
California
William Watson
Orinda CC (R)
California
Robert Muir Graves
Oriole G&TC
Margate, Florida
Bill Dietsch
**Oristo G&RC now known as
  Fairfield Ocean Ridge GC**
Orlando NTC GC
Orlando, Florida
Ward Northrup
Orleans GC
Vermont
Alex Reid
Ormond G&CC
Destrehan, Louisiana
Dick Biddle
Ormskirk GC
England
Harold Hilton
Oro Valley G&CC
Tucson, Arizona
Robert Bruce Harris
Oro Valley G&CC (R)
Arizona
Dave Bennett
Orono Public GC
Wayzata, Minnesota
Leo J. Feser
Oronoque Village GC
Stratford, Connecticut
Desmond Muirhead
Orsett GC
Essex, England
James Braid, John R. Stutt
Ortonville Muni
Minnesota
Joel Goldstrand
Osawatomie Muni (A. 9)
Kansas
Chet Mendenhall
Osceola Muni
Pensacola, Florida
Bill Melhorn
Oshawa GC (R)
Ontario
Stanley Thompson
Oshawa GC (R. 6)
Ontario
Clinton E. Robinson
Oshkosh CC
Wisconsin
Tom Bendelow
Osiris CC
Walden, New York
Frank Duane
Oskaloosa GC
Iowa
Tom Bendelow
Oso Beach GC
Corpus Christi, Texas
John Bredemus

Osprey Point G Links
Kiawah Island, South Carolina
Tom Fazio
Ostschweizischer GC
Niederburen, Switzerland
Donald Harradine
Ostwestfalen-Lippe GC
Bad Salzuflen, West Germany
Bernhard von Limburger
Oswego CC
New York
A.W. Tillinghast
Oswego CC NLE
New York
Tom Bendelow
Oswego CC (A. 9)
New York
Geoffrey S. Cornish, William G.
　Robinson
Oswego Lake CC
Lake Oswego, Oregon
H. Chandler Egan
Oswego Lake CC (R)
Oregon
Robert Muir Graves
Oswestry GC
Shropshire, England
James Braid, John R. Stutt
Othello G&CC
Washington
Mel "Curley" Hueston
Otis AFB GC
Massachusetts
Bob Baldock
Ottawa CC
Illinois
Tom Bendelow
Ottawa CC
Kansas
Harry Robb
Ottawa GC NLE
Ontario
William F. Davis
Ottawa Hunt & GC
Ontario
Willie Park Jr
Ottawa Park GC
Toledo, Ohio
Sylvanus Pierson Jermain
Ottawa Park GC (R)
Ohio
Arthur Hills
Otter Creek GC
Columbus, Indiana
Robert Trent Jones
Otterkill G&CC
Newburgh, New York
William F. Mitchell
Otto Kahn Estate GC NLE
Manhasset, New York
Charles Blair Macdonald, Seth
　Raynor
Ottumwa G&CC
Iowa
Tom Bendelow
Ottumwa G&CC (A. 9)
Iowa
Chic Adams
Oughterard GC (A. 9)
Ireland
Eddie Hackett
Ould Newberry CC (R)
Massachusetts
Orrin Smith, William F. Mitchell
Ould Newberry CC (R)
Massachusetts
Manny Francis
Ould Newbury GC
Massachusetts
James Lowe, Ben Pearson
Our CC
Salem, Wisconsin
William B. Langford, Theodore J.
　Moreau
Outdoor CC
Pennsylvania
Edmund B. Ault
Outdoor Recreation Par 3 GC
New York
George Swatt
Overbrook CC
Radnor, Pennsylvania
J.B. McGovern, X.G. Hassenplug

Overgaard GC
Arizona
Milt Coggins
Overlake G&CC
Medina, Washington
A. Vernon Macan
Overlake G&CC (R)
Washington
Desmond Muirhead
Overlake G&CC (R)
Washington
Robert Muir Graves, Damian
　Pascuzzo
Overland Park Muni
Denver, Colorado
William H. Tucker
Overland Park Muni (A. 9)
Colorado
William F. Bell
Overland Park Muni (R)
Colorado
Henry B. Hughes
Overland Park Muni
Kansas
Floyd Farley
Overoaks CC
Kissimmee, Florida
Karl Litten, Gary Player
Overpeck County GC
Teaneack, New Jersey
Nicholas Psiahas
Owen Sound GC
Ontario
Stanley Thompson
Owen Sound GC (A. 9)
Ontario
Robert Moote, *David Moote*
Owen Sound GC (R. 9)
Ontario
Robert Moote, *David Moote*
Owensboro CC (R)
Kentucky
Joe Lee
Owosso CC
Michigan
Tom Bendelow
Oxbow CC
Hickson, North Dakota
Robert Trent Jones Jr, Gary
　Roger Baird
Oxbow G&CC
Port LaBelle, Florida
LeRoy Phillips
Oxbow G&CC
Belpre, Ohio
Jack Kidwell, Michael Hurdzan
Oxford G&CC
Woodstock, Ontario
Clinton E. Robinson
Oxford G&RC
Massachusetts
Phil Wogan
Oxford Hills GC
Oxford, Michigan
Jim Hubbard
Oxon Run GC
Washington, D.C.
Reuben Hines
Oxton GC
Nottinghamshire, England
J.J.F. Pennink
Oyster Bay G Links
Sunset Beach, North Carolina
Dan Maples
Oyster Harbors C
Osterville, Massachusetts
Donald Ross
Oyster Reef GC
Hilton Head Island, South
　Carolina
Rees Jones
Ozark G&CC
Alabama
Ron Garl
Ozaukee CC
Mequon, Wisconsin
William B. Langford, Theodore J.
　Moreau
Ozaukee CC (R. 3)
Wisconsin
David Gill
Ozaukee CC (R)
Wisconsin
Bob Lohmann

P L Malibu CC
California
William F. Bell
P L CC
Japan
Tokuchika Miki
P L London CC
England
Fred W. Hawtree, Martin
　Hawtree
Pacific Grove G Links
California
H. Chandler Egan
Pacific Grove G Links (A. 9)
California
Jack Neville
Pacific Harbour G&CC
Fiji
Robert Trent Jones Jr, Gary
　Roger Baird
Pacific Palisades GC
Pearl City, Hawaii
Willard Wilkinson
Pacific Rim GC
California
Arnold Palmer, Ed Seay
Packachaug Hills CC
Worchester, Massachusetts
Orrin Smith
Packanack Lake CC (A. 9)
New Jersey
Geoffrey S. Cornish
Paddock CC
Florissant, Missouri
Homer Herpel
Padova GC
Italy
John Harris
Padre Isle GC
Texas
Bruce Littell
**Paganica CC now known as
　Lakewood CC**
Page Belcher GC (Course No. 2)
Tulsa, Oklahoma
Don Sechrest
**Page Belcher Muni (Course No.
　1)**
Tulsa, Oklahoma
Leon Howard
Pagosa Pines GC
Colorado
Johnny Bulla
Paint Branch GC
Maryland
Edmund B. Ault
Pajaro Valley CC (R)
California
Robert Muir Graves
Pala Mesa G&TC
Fallbrook, California
William H. Johnson
Pala Mesa G&TC (R)
California
Virgil C. "Dick" Rossen
Pala Mesa G&TC (R)
California
Ted Robinson
Palatine Hills GC
Illinois
Edward Lawrence Packard
Palembang GC
Sumatra, Indonesia
J.J.F. Pennink
Pali GC
Honolulu, Hawaii
Willard Wilkinson
Palisade Park GC
Manti, Utah
Gary Holman
Palisades Park GC NLE
Michigan
Tom Bendelow
Pallanza GC
Lake Maggiore, Italy
F.G. Hawtree
Palm Beach CC
Florida
Donald Ross
Palm Beach Lakes CC
West Palm Beach, Florida
William F. Mitchell

Palm Beach National G&CC
West Palm Beach, Florida
J. Porter Gibson
Palm Beach National G&CC (R)
Florida
Joe Lee
Palm Beach Par 3 GC
Florida
Dick Wilson, Bob Simmons
**Palm Beach Polo & CC (North
　Course)**
West Palm Beach, Florida
George Fazio, Tom Fazio
**Palm Beach Polo & CC (North
　Course) (R)**
Florida
Ted McAnlis
**Palm Beach Polo & CC (South
　Course)**
West Palm Beach, Florida
Ron Garl, *Jerry Pate*
Palm City CC
Palm Desert, California
William F. Bell
Palm Desert CC
California
William W. Mast
Palm Desert Greens CC
Palm Desert, California
Ted Robinson
Palm Desert Resort CC
Palm Desert, California
Joe Mulleneaux
Palm Gardens GC
Melbourne, Florida
Edward Ryder
Palm Harbor GC
Flager Beach, Florida
Bill Amick
Palm Lakes GC
Fresno, California
Richard Bigler
Palm Meadows GC
California
William F. Bell
Palm River CC
Naples, Florida
Ben W. Zink
Palm Springs CC
California
Paul J. Addessi
Palm Springs Riviera GC NLE
Palm Springs, California
Don Crabtree
Palm Valley CC (North Course)
Palm Desert, California
Ted Robinson
Palm Valley CC (South Course)
Palm Desert, California
Ted Robinson
Palm View Hills GC
Palmetto, Florida
Dick Hamilton
Palm View Muni
Texas
Ralph Plummer
Palm View Muni
McAllen, Texas
Ralph Plummer
Palm-Aire CC (Cypress Course)
Pompano Beach, Florida
George Fazio, Tom Fazio
Palm-Aire CC (Oaks Course)
Pompano Beach, Florida
George Fazio, Tom Fazio
Palm-Aire CC (Palms Course)
Pompano Beach, Florida
William F. Mitchell
Palm-Aire CC (Palms Course)
Pompano Beach, Florida
Robert von Hagge, Bruce Devlin
Palm-Aire CC (Sabals Course)
Pompano Beach, Florida
Robert von Hagge, Bruce Devlin
**Palm-Aire West CC (Champions
　Course) formerly known as
　DeSoto Lakes G&CC**
Sarasota, Florida
Dick Wilson
**Palm-Aire West CC (Champions
　Course) (R)**
Florida
R. Albert Anderson

**Palm-Aire West CC (Lakes
　Course)**
Sarasota, Florida
Joe Lee
Palma Ceia G&CC
Tampa, Florida
Tom Bendelow
Palma Ceia G&CC (R)
Florida
Donald Ross
Palma Ceia G&CC (R)
Florida
Mark Mahannah, Charles
　Mahannah
Palma Ceia G&CC (R. 4)
Florida
John LaFoy
Palma Real GC
Ixtapa, Mexico
Robert Trent Jones Jr, Gary
　Roger Baird
Palma Sola GC
Bradenton, Florida
Donald Ross, Walter I. Johnson
Palma Sola GC (R)
Florida
R. Albert Anderson
Palmares GC
Algarve, Portugal
J.J.F. Pennink
Palmas del Mar GC
Humacao, Puerto Rico
Arthur Davis, Ron Kirby, Gary
　Player
Palmbrook CC
Sun City, Arizona
James Winans, John W. Meeker, Jeff
　Hardin
Palmer Hills GC
Bettendorf, Iowa
William James Spear
Palmetto CC
Benton, Louisiana
Perry Maxwell, Press Maxwell
Palmetto CC
Aiken, South Carolina
Herbert Leeds
Palmetto CC (R)
South Carolina
Alister Mackenzie
**Palmetto Dunes CC (Fazio
　Course)**
Hilton Head Island, South
　Carolina
George Fazio, Tom Fazio
**Palmetto Dunes CC (Hills
　Course)**
Hilton Head Island, South
　Carolina
Arthur Hills, Steve Forrest, Mike
　Dasher
**Palmetto Dunes CC (Jones
　Course)**
Hilton Head Island, South
　Carolina
Robert Trent Jones
Palmetto G&CC
Florida
Wayne Stiles, John Van Kleek
Palmetto GC
South Miami, Florida
Dick Wilson, Bob Simmons
Palmetto Pine CC
Cape Coral, Florida
Arthur Hills
Palms of Terra Ceia GC
Palmetto, Florida
Ted McAnlis
Palo Alto Hills G&CC
Palo Alto, California
Clark Glasson
Palo Alto Hills G&CC (R. 5)
California
Robert Muir Graves
Palo Alto Hills G&CC (R)
California
Gary Roger Baird
Palo Alto Muni
California
William F. Bell, William P. Bell
Palo Alto Muni (R)
California
Robert Trent Jones Jr, Gary
　Roger Baird

Palo Alto VA Hospital GC
California
Bob Baldock
Palolo Muni NLE
Hawaii
Alex Bell
Palos CC
Palos Park, Illinois
Charles Maddox, *Frank P. MacDonald*
Palos Verdes CC
California
George C. Thomas Jr, William P. Bell
Palos Verdes CC (R)
California
David W. Kent
Palos Verdes CC (R)
California
Ted Robinson
Panama City Beach GC
Florida
Bill Amick
Panama CC
Lynn Haven, Florida
Donald Ross
Pannal GC
Yorkshire, England
Sandy Herd
Pannal GC (R)
England
Charles A. Mackenzie
Panorama CC
Conroe, Texas
Jack B. Miller
Panorama CC (R)
Texas
Joseph S. Finger, Ken Dye
Panorama Village GC
California
Harry Rainville, David Rainville
Panshanger GC
Hertfordshire, England
John Harris
Pantai Mentiri GC
Bandar Seri, Brunei
Ronald Fream
Panther Valley CC
Allamuchy, New Jersey
Robert Trent Jones, Rees Jones
Paola CC NLE
Kansas
James S. Watson
Papago Park GC
Phoenix, Arizona
William F. Bell
Papago Park GC (R)
Arizona
Arthur Jack Snyder
Par Mor GC
East Lansing, Michigan
Art Prior
Par Three GC
Daytona Beach, Florida
John T. Williamson
Par Three GC
Lakeland, Florida
Hans Schmeisser
Par Three GC
North Olmstead, Ohio
Harold Paddock
Paradise Hills G&CC
Albuquerque, New Mexico
Red Lawrence
Paradise Inn Ranch GC
Grants Pass, Oregon
Robert Muir Graves, Damian Pascuzzo
Paradise Island G&CC
Nassau, Bahamas
Dick Wilson, Joe Lee, Bob Simmons
Paradise Park GC (R)
Jamaica
Robert Moote, *David Moote*
Paradise Point GC (Gold Course)
Camp LeJeune, North Carolina
George W. Cobb
Paradise Point GC (Gold Course) (R. 7)
North Carolina
Brian Ault, Tom Clark

Paradise Point GC (Green Course)
Camp LeJeune, North Carolina
Fred Findlay
Paradise Pointe GC
Smithville, Missouri
Tom Clark, Brian Ault
Paradise Valley CC
Scottsdale, Arizona
Lawrence Hughes
Paradise Valley CC (R)
Arizona
Gary Panks, Geoffrey S. Cornish
Paradise Valley CC
Englewood, Colorado
Henry B. Hughes
Paradise Valley CC
Casper, Wyoming
Henry B. Hughes
Paradise Valley Park GC NLE
Phoenix, Arizona
Milt Coggins
Paradise Valley Park GC
Phoenix, Arizona
Jeff Hardin
Paraparaumu Beach GC
New Zealand
Alex Russell
Paris Landing State Park GC
Tennessee
Benjamin Wihry
Pariso Springs CC
Soledad, California
Bob Baldock
Park City GC
Utah
William H. Neff
Park City GC (A. 9)
Utah
Press Maxwell
Park City GC (R. 9)
Utah
Press Maxwell
Park City GC (R)
Utah
William Howard Neff
Park CC
Buffalo, New York
C.H. Alison, H.S. Colt
Park CC (R)
New York
Arthur Hills, Steve Forrest
Park District GC
Fallsburgh, New York
William F. Mitchell
Park Forest GC NLE
Illinois
Harry Collis
Park Hills CC (R)
Kansas
Smiley Bell
Park Hills CC
Altoona, Pennsylvania
James Gilmore Harrison
Park Hills GC (East Course)
Freeport, Illinois
C.D. Wagstaff
Park Hills GC (West Course)
Freeport, Illinois
C.D. Wagstaff
Park Lake GC
DesPlaines, Illinois
C.D. Wagstaff
Park Mammoth GC
Park City, Kentucky
Buck Blankenship
Park Meadows GC
Park City, Utah
Jack Nicklaus, Jay Morrish, Bob Cupp
Park Place GC
DeKalb, Illinois
William James Spear
Park Ridge CC
Illinois
H.J. Tweedie
Park Ridge CC (R)
Illinois
William B. Langford
Park Ridge CC (R. 4)
Illinois
David Gill

Park Ridge CC (R. 3)
Illinois
Ken Killian, Dick Nugent
Parkersburg CC (R)
West Virginia
Edmund B. Ault
Parkhurst CC NLE
Boynton Beach, Florida
William B. Langford, Theodore J. Moreau
Parknasilla GC (R)
Ireland
Eddie Hackett
Parkridge CC
California
John Duncan Dunn
Parkstone GC
Dorset, England
Willie Park Jr
Parkstone GC (R)
England
J. Hamilton Stutt
Parkstone GC (R)
England
James Braid, John R. Stutt
Parkview GC
Milliken, Ontario
Clinton E. Robinson
Parkview Heights GC
Mayfield Heights, Ohio
Richard W. LaConte
Parkview Manor GC
Hershey, Pennsylvania
Maurice McCarthy
Parkview Muni
Pekin, Illinois
Charles Maddox, *Frank P. MacDonald*
Parkview Muni (R. 9)
Illinois
Robert Bruce Harris
Parkview Muni (A. 9)
Illinois
Robert Bruce Harris
Parlor City CC (A. 9)
Indiana
Henry Culp
Parris Island GC
South Carolina
Fred Findlay
Partridge Point GC
Ludington, Michigan
William Newcomb, Stephen Kay
Pasadena Ellington GC
Texas
Jay Riviere
Pasadena GC NLE
California
Max Behr
Pasadena GC (R) NLE
California
George O'Neill, *Jack Croke*
Pasadena GC (R) NLE
California
William P. Bell
Pasadena GC
St. Petersburg, Florida
Wayne Stiles, John Van Kleek, Walter Hagen
Pasadena GC (R)
Florida
Bill Dietsch
Pasatiempo GC
Santa Cruz, California
Alister Mackenzie
Pasatiempo GC (R)
California
Clark Glasson
Pasatiempo GC (R)
California
Gary Roger Baird
Pasco Muni NLE
Washington
Bob Baldock
Pasco Muni
Washington
Robert Muir Graves
Paso Robles G&CC
California
Bert Stamps
Paso Robles GC NLE
California
Tom Bendelow

Pass Christian CC
Mississippi
Tom Bendelow
Pass Christian CC (R)
Mississippi
Alex Cunningham
Passaic County GC (A. 9)
New Jersey
Alfred H. Tull
Pastures GC
Derbyshire, England
J.J.F. Pennink
Patrick AFB GC
Cocoa Beach, Florida
Robert Trent Jones, Frank Duane
Patrick AFB GC (R)
Florida
Bill Amick
Patriots Point G Links
Charleston, South Carolina
Willard Byrd, Clyde Johnston
Patshull Park GC
Staffordshire, England
John Jacobs
Patterson C
Fairfield, Connecticut
Robert Trent Jones
Patterson C (R. 1)
Connecticut
Frank Duane
Patton Brook GC
Southington, Connecticut
Geoffrey S. Cornish, William G. Robinson
Patty Jewett GC
Colorado Springs, Colorado
James L. Haines
Patty Jewett GC (A.18)
Colorado
Press Maxwell
Patuxent NAS GC (R)
Virginia
Buddy Loving
Pau GC
France
Willie Dunn
Paul Block Private Course
Greenwich, Connecticut
Wayne Stiles, John Van Kleek
Paul Smith's Adirondack C
New York
Seymour Dunn
Pauls Valley G&CC
Oklahoma
Bob Dunning
Pauls Valley Muni GC
Oklahoma
Bob Dunning
Pauma Valley CC
California
Robert Trent Jones
Pauma Valley CC (R. 1)
California
Ted Robinson
Pautipaug CC
Norwich, Connecticut
Geoffrey S. Cornish
Pawnee Prairie Muni
Wichita, Kansas
Bob Dunning
Pawpaw CC
Bamberg, South Carolina
Russell Breeden
Pawtucket GC
Rhode Island
Willie Park Jr
Pawtuckett GC
Charlotte, North Carolina
Russell Breeden
Payson GC
Utah
William Howard Neff
Peace Pipe CC
Denville, New Jersey
Sidney C. Lee
Peace Portal GC (R)
British Columbia
Stan Leonard, *Philip Tattersfield*
Peaceful Valley CC
Colorado Springs, Colorado
Dave Bennett
Peach Tree CC
Marysville, California
Bob Baldock

Peachtree GC
Atlanta, Georgia
Robert Trent Jones, *Robert Tyre "Bobby" Jones Jr*
Peachtree GC (R)
Georgia
Joseph S. Finger
Peachtree Hills GC
Spring Hope, North Carolina
R.W. Renn
Pearl CC
Kaonohi, Hawaii
Akiro Sato
Pearl CC (R. 1)
Hawaii
Robin Nelson
Pearl GC
Sunset Beach, North Carolina
Dan Maples
Pearl Harbor GC NLE
Hawaii
Thomas O. Brandon
Pearl River Valley CC
Poplarville, Mississippi
W.W. Kilby
Pebble Beach G Links
California
Jack Neville, *Douglas S. Grant*
Pebble Beach G Links (R)
California
Alister Mackenzie, Robert Hunter
Pebble Beach G Links (R)
California
H. Chandler Egan
Pebble Brook GC
Manchester, Georgia
Arthur Davis, Ron Kirby
Pebble Brook CC
Cleveland, Ohio
Ben W. Zink
Pebble Brook GC
Noblesville, Indiana
James Dugan
Pebble Creek CC
Taylors, South Carolina
Tom Jackson
Pebble Creek GC
Lexington, Ohio
William F. Mitchell
Pebblebrook GC
Sun City West, Arizona
Jeff Hardin, Greg Nash, *John W. Meeker, Tom Ryan*
Pecan Grove CC
Texas
Bruce Belin
Pecan Hollow GC
Texas
Billy Martindale
Pecan Plantation GC
Granbury, Texas
Leon Howard
Pecan Valley CC
San Antonio, Texas
Press Maxwell
Pecan Valley Muni
Fort Worth, Texas
Ralph Plummer
Pecan Valley Muni (A. 9)
Texas
Dave Bennett
Peckets CC
New Hampshire
Ralph Barton
Pedernales CC
Spicewood, Texas
Leon Howard
Pedley Par 3 GC
Los Angeles, California
William H. Johnson
Peek 'n Peak GC
Clymer, New York
Ferdinand Garbin
Peel GC
Isle of Man
James Braid
Peel Village GC (R)
Ontario
Robert Moote
Pekin CC
Illinois
Edward Lawrence Packard

Pelham Bay Park GC (Pelham Course)
Bronx, New York
Lawrence Van Etten
Pelham Bay Park GC (Pelham Course) (R)
New York
John Van Kleek
Pelham Bay Park GC (Split Rock Course)
Bronx, New York
John Van Kleek
Pelham CC (R)
Georgia
Hugh Moore
Pelham CC NLE
New York
Lawrence Van Etten
Pelham CC
New York
Devereux Emmet
Pelham CC (R)
New York
Alfred H. Tull
Pelham CC (R)
New York
Robert Trent Jones, Roger Rulewich
Pelham Manor GC NLE
New York
Tom Bendelow
Pelican Bay G&CC
Daytona Beach, Florida
Bill Amick
Pelican GC
Clearwater, Florida
Donald Ross
Pelican's Nest GC
Bonita Springs, Florida
Tom Fazio
Pella G&CC (R)
Iowa
Charles Calhoun
Pembroke CC
Massachusetts
Phil Wogan
Pembroke Lakes G&CC
Hollywood, Florida
Howard Watson, John Watson
Pen Park GC
Charlottesville, Virginia
Buddy Loving
Penas Rojas GC
Alicante, Spain
John Harris
Pendaries G&CC
Rociada, New Mexico
Donald K. Burns
Pender Island G&CC
British Columbia
Sandy Crawford
Penderbrook GC
Virginia
Brian Ault, Edmund B. Ault
Pendleton CC
Oregon
Frank James
Penfield CC
New York
Pete Craig
Penina GC
Portugal
Henry Cotton
Penina GC (A. 9)
Portugal
Henry Cotton
Peninsula G&CC
San Mateo, California
Donald Ross
Peninsula G&CC (R)
California
Clark Glasson
Peninsula G&CC (R)
Australia
Peter Thomson, Michael Wolveridge
Peninsula GC
Amityville, New York
Maurice McCarthy
Peninsula GC
Marathon, Ontario
Stanley Thompson

Peninsula Park GC
Portage, Ontario
Stanley Thompson
Peninsula State Park GC
Fish Creek, Wisconsin
Edward Lawrence Packard
Penn Hills C (A. 9)
Pennsylvania
Dick Wilson
Penn Hills C (R. 9)
Pennsylvania
Dick Wilson
Penn Oaks CC
West Chester, Pennsylvania
Frank Murray, Russell Roberts
Penn State Univ GC (Blue Course)
State College, Pennsylvania
Willie Park Jr
Penn State Univ GC (Blue Course) (R)
Pennsylvania
James Gilmore Harrison, Ferdinand Garbin
Penn State Univ GC (White Course)
State College, Pennsylvania
James Gilmore Harrison, Ferdinand Garbin
Pennbrook GC
Basking Ridge, New Jersey
Alex Findlay
Pennbrook GC (R)
New Jersey
Arthur Hills, Steve Forrest
Pennhurst CC NLE
Turtle Creek, Pennsylvania
Orrin Smith
Pennsylvania National G&CC
Pennsylvania
Edmund B. Ault
Pennyrile Forest State Park GC
Dawson Springs, Kentucky
Edward Lawrence Packard
Penobscot Valley CC
Bangor, Maine
Donald Ross
Penrhos GC
Gwynedd, Wales
Fred W. Hawtree, Martin Hawtree
Penrose Park GC
Reidsville, North Carolina
Donald Ross
Penticton G&CC
British Columbia
A. Vernon Macan
Penticton G&CC (A. 9)
British Columbia
Norman H. Woods
Penwortham GC
England
Tom Dunn
Peoria North Shore CC NLE
Illinois
Tom Bendelow
Pepper Pike C
Ohio
William S. Flynn
Pequabuc CC (A. 3)
Connecticut
Geoffrey S. Cornish, William G. Robinson
Perdido Bay CC
Pensacola, Florida
Bill Amick
Perranporth GC
England
James Braid, John R. Stutt
Perrin AFB GC
Sherman, Texas
Joseph S. Finger
Perry CC
Georgia
Sid Clarke
Perry G&CC
Florida
Walter Ripley
Perry Park CC
Larkspur, Colorado
Dick Phelps
Persepolis GC
Iran
Jack Armitage

Persimmon Hill CC
Saluda, South Carolina
Fred Bolton
Perth GC
Perthshire, Scotland
Old Tom Morris
Petaluma G&CC (R)
California
Gary Roger Baird
Peter Hay GC
Pebble Beach, California
Leonard G. Feliciano
Peter Jans GC
Evanston, Illinois
Tom Bendelow
Peter Pan CC NLE
California
John Duncan Dunn
Peterborough G&CC (R)
Ontario
Stanley Thompson
Petersborough Milton GC
Northamptonshire, England
James Braid, John R. Stutt
Peterson Field GC
Colorado Springs, Colorado
Dick Phelps
Peterson Field GC (A. 9)
Colorado
Dick Phelps
Petrifying Springs GC
Kenosha, Wisconsin
Joseph A. Roseman
Pevero GC
Costa Smeralda, Sardinia
Robert Trent Jones, Cabell Robinson
Pfalz GC
Neustadt, West Germany
Bernhard von Limburger
Phalen Park GC (R)
Minnesota
Don Herfort
Pharoah's CC
Corpus Christi, Texas
Ralph Plummer
Pheasant Ridge GC
Cedar Falls, Iowa
Donald G. Brauer, Emile Perret, Paul S. Fjare
Pheasant Run CC
Newmarket, Ontario
Renee Muylaert, Charles Muylaert
Pheasant Run Lodge GC
St. Charles, Illinois
William Maddox
Pheasant Valley GC
Crown Point, Indiana
R. Albert Anderson
Phelps Manor GC
Teaneck, New Jersey
William H. Tucker
Phenix City Muni
Alabama
Lester Lawrence
Philadelphia Cricket C
Pennsylvania
Donald Ross
Philadelphia Cricket C (R)
Pennsylvania
A.W. Tillinghast
Philadelphia CC NLE
Pennsylvania
Willie Dunn Jr
Philadelphia CC
Gladwyne, Pennsylvania
William S. Flynn, Howard Toomey
Philadelphia CC (R) NLE
Pennsylvania
William H. Tucker
Philadelphia CC (R)
Pennsylvania
William S. Flynn, Perry Maxwell
Phillippines CC
Philippines
Bob Baldock
Phillips Park Muni
Aurora, Illinois
Spencer Meister
Phillipsburg CC
Pennsylvania
Alex Findlay

Philmont CC (North Course)
Philadelphia, Pennsylvania
William S. Flynn, Howard Toomey
Philmont CC (North Course) (R)
Pennsylvania
William Gordon, David Gordon
Philmont CC (South Course)
Philadelphia, Pennsylvania
Willie Park Jr
Phoenician G&RC
Phoenix, Arizona
Arthur Jack Snyder
Phoenix CC
Arizona
Harry Collis
Phoenix CC (R.14)
Arizona
Gary Panks
Piandiscole GC
Premeno, Italy
John Harris
Picacho Hills CC
Las Cruces, New Mexico
Joseph S. Finger
Picatinny GC
Dover, New Jersey
Eugene "Skip" Wogan
Pickaway CC
Circleville, Ohio
Jack Kidwell
Pickens County CC (R)
Georgia
Robert Renaud
Pico Rivera Muni
California
William F. Bell
Piedmont Crescent CC now known as Quarry Hills CC
Piencort CC
Normandy, France
J. Hamilton Stutt
Pierce Park Muni
Flint, Michigan
Frederick A. Ellis
Pierre Marques GC
Acapulco, Mexico
Percy Clifford
Pierre Marques GC (R)
Mexico
Robert Trent Jones
Pike Creek Valley GC
Delaware
Edmund B. Ault
Pike Run CC (R)
Pennsylvania
James Gilmore Harrison
Pikefold GC
Manchester, England
E.W. Phillips
Pilgrim's Harbor CC
Wallingford, Connecticut
Alfred H. Tull
Pilmoor Estate GC
Kaula Lumpur, Malaysia
Ronald Fream
Pilot Knob Park GC
Pilot Mountain, North Carolina
Gene Hamm
Piltdown GC (R)
England
G.M. Dodd
Pima GC
Scottsdale, Arizona
William F. Bell
Pin Oaks CC
Tuskegee, Alabama
Robert Leimbeck
Pinawa GC
Manitoba
Howard Watson
Pinch Brook GC
Florham Park, New Jersey
Rees Jones, Keith Evans
Pine Acres CC
Bradford, Pennsylvania
James Gilmore Harrison
Pine Beach East GC
Madden Beach, Minnesota
James Dalgleish
Pine Beach East GC (R)
Minnesota
Don Herfort

Pine Beach Par 3 GC
Minnesota
Jim Madden
Pine Beach West GC
Minnesota
Jim Madden
Pine Bluff CC
Arkansas
Herman Hackbarth
Pine Bluff CC (A. 9)
Arkansas
Joseph S. Finger
Pine Bluff CC (R. 9)
Arkansas
Joseph S. Finger
Pine Brook CC
Weston, Massachusetts
Wayne Stiles, John Van Kleek
Pine Brook CC (R)
Massachusetts
Brian Silva, Geoffrey S. Cornish
Pine Brook GC
Winston-Salem, North Carolina
Ellis Maples
Pine Burr CC
Wiggens, Mississippi
Earl Stone
Pine Creek CC
Colorado Springs, Colorado
Dick Phelps
Pine Creek GC
La Crescent, Minnesota
Sylvester Krajewski
Pine Crest CC
Gardendale, Alabama
Bancroft Timmons
Pine Forest CC NLE
Houston, Texas
John Bredemus
Pine Forest CC
Houston, Texas
Jay Riviere
Pine Forest CC (R. 9) NLE
Texas
Ralph Plummer
Pine Forest GC
Bastrop, Texas
Billy Martindale
Pine Grove CC (A. 9)
Michigan
Edward Lawrence Packard
Pine Grove CC (R)
Michigan
Don Herfort
Pine Harbor Champions G&CC
Pell City, Alabama
Harold Williams
Pine Hill GC NLE
Windsor, Connecticut
Everett Pyle
Pine Hill GC
Brutus, Michigan
Larry Holbert
Pine Hills CC
Calhoun City, Mississippi
George C. Curtis
Pine Hills G&CC
Pentiction, British Columbia
Norman H. Woods
Pine Hills GC
West Monroe, Louisiana
George C. Curtis
Pine Hills GC (R)
Louisiana
Jay Riviere
Pine Hills GC
Cleveland, Ohio
Harold Paddock
Pine Hills GC
Carrol, Ohio
Jack Kidwell
Pine Hollow CC
East Norwich, New York
William F. Mitchell
Pine Island GC
Ocean Springs, Mississippi
Pete Dye, David Pfaff
Pine Isle CC
Lake Lanier, Georgia
Arthur Davis, Ron Kirby, Gary Player
Pine Lake CC
Orchard Lake, Michigan
Willie Park Jr

Pine Lake CC (R. 1)
Michigan
Bruce Matthews, Jerry Matthews
Pine Lake CC (A. 2)
Michigan
Jerry Matthews
Pine Lake CC
Charlotte, North Carolina
Gene Hamm
Pine Lake CC (A. 9)
North Carolina
J. Porter Gibson
Pine Lake CC (R. 9)
North Carolina
J. Porter Gibson
Pine Lake CC (R)
North Carolina
John LaFoy
Pine Lake CC
Anderson, South Carolina
James T. Shirley
Pine Lake GC
Lincoln, Nebraska
Richard Watson
Pine Lake GC (A. 9)
Ontario
Clinton E. Robinson
Pine Lake GC
Japan
Robert Trent Jones Jr, Don
Knott,Gary Linn
Pine Lakes GC
Palm Coast, Florida
Arnold Palmer, Ed Seay,Bob
Walker
Pine Lakes International GC
Myrtle Beach, South Carolina
Robert White
Pine Meadow GC
Mundelein, Illinois
Joe Lee, Rocky Roquemore
Pine Mountain GC (A. 9)
Michigan
William Newcomb
Pine Mountain Lake CC
California
William F. Bell
Pine Needles CC
Fort Valley, Georgia
Sid Clarke
Pine Needles Lodge & CC
Southern Pines, North Carolina
Donald Ross
Pine Oaks GC
Easton, Massachusetts
Geoffrey S. Cornish, William G.
Robinson
Pine Oaks Muni
Johnson City, Tennessee
Alex McKay
Pine Orchards CC
Brantford, Connecticut
Robert D. Pryde
Pine Orchards CC (A. 4)
Connecticut
Al Zikorus
Pine Ridge CC
Newcastle, New York
Alfred H. Tull
Pine Ridge CC
Cleveland, Ohio
Harold Paddock
Pine Ridge CC
Edgefield, South Carolina
Russell Breeden
Pine Ridge G&CC
Roundup, Montana
Frank Hummel
Pine Ridge G&CC NLE
Manitoba
H.S. Colt
Pine Ridge G&CC
Winnipeg, Manitoba
Stanley Thompson
Pine Ridge G&CC (R)
Manitoba
Clinton E. Robinson
Pine Ridge GC
Florida
Charles Almony
Pine Ridge GC
Waterville, Maine
James Schoenthaler

Pine Ridge GC
Meadville, Pennsylvania
James Gilmore Harrison,
Ferdinand Garbin
Pine Ridge Muni
Lutherville, Maryland
Gus Hook
Pine River CC (A. 9)
Michigan
Bruce Matthews, Jerry Matthews
Pine Tree CC
Birmingham, Alabama
George W. Cobb
Pine Tree CC
Brooksville, Connecticut
Alfred H. Tull
Pine Tree CC
Delray Beach, Florida
Dick Wilson, Joe Lee,Robert von
Hagge
Pine Tree GC
Asheboro, North Carolina
Russell Breeden
Pine Tree GC
Kernersville, North Carolina
Gene Hamm
Pine Trees GC
Santa Ana, California
Harry Rainville
Pine Valley CC
Ft. Wayne, Indiana
Clyde Williams
Pine Valley GC (A. 9)
Kentucky
Bill Amick
Pine Valley GC
Southington, Maine
Orrin Smith
Pine Valley GC
Clementon, New Jersey
George Crump, H.S. Colt
Pine Valley GC (A. 4)
New Jersey
Hugh Wilson, *Alan Wilson*
Pine Valley GC (R)
New Jersey
William S. Flynn
Pine Valley GC (R)
New Jersey
Perry Maxwell
Pine Valley GC (A. 9)
Ohio
Ted McAnlis
Pine Valley GC (R. 9)
Ohio
Ted McAnlis
Pine Valley GC NLE
Woodbridge, Ontario
Howard Watson
Pine View GC (A.18)
Michigan
Ed Ruess
Pinecrest on Lotela GC
Avon Park, Florida
Donald Ross
Pinecrest CC (R. 9)
Texas
Press Maxwell
Pinecrest CC (A. 9)
Texas
Press Maxwell
Pinecrest CC (Course No. 2)
Fairfax, Virginia
Al Jamison
Pinecrest G&CC
Huntley, Illinois
Ted Lockie
Pinecrest G&CC (R)
Illinois
Ken Killian, Dick Nugent
Pinecrest G&CC (R)
Illinois
Bob Lohmann
Pinecrest G&CC
Winslow, New Jersey
Ralph Leopardi
Pinecrest GC
Trinity, Texas
Jay Riviere
Pinecrest Muni
Idaho Falls, Idaho
Frank James

Pinegrove G&CC
Montreal, Quebec
Howard Watson
Pinegrove G&CC (R. 3)
Quebec
John Watson
Pinehaven CC
Guilderland, New York
James Thomson, Armand Farina
Pinehurst CC
Denver, Colorado
Press Maxwell
Pinehurst CC
Orange, Texas
Donald Ross
Pinehurst CC (Course No. 1)
North Carolina
*James W. Tufts, Leonard Tufts,Dr. D.
Leroy Culver*
Pinehurst CC (Course No. 1) (A.
9)
North Carolina
Donald Ross
Pinehurst CC (Course No. 1) (R.
9)
North Carolina
Donald Ross
Pinehurst CC (Course No. 1) (R)
North Carolina
Donald Ross
Pinehurst CC (Course No. 2)
North Carolina
Donald Ross
Pinehurst CC (Course No. 2) (A.
9)
North Carolina
Donald Ross
Pinehurst CC (Course No. 2) (R)
North Carolina
Donald Ross
Pinehurst CC (Course No. 2) (R)
North Carolina
Donald Ross
Pinehurst CC (Course No. 2) (R)
North Carolina
Richard S. Tufts
Pinehurst CC (Course No. 2) (R)
North Carolina
Peter V. Tufts
Pinehurst CC (Course No. 3)
North Carolina
Donald Ross
Pinehurst CC (Course No. 3) (R)
North Carolina
Donald Ross
Pinehurst CC (Course No. 4)
NLE
North Carolina
Donald Ross
Pinehurst CC (Course No. 4)
North Carolina
Richard S. Tufts
Pinehurst CC (Course No. 4) (R)
North Carolina
Robert Trent Jones, Roger
Rulewich
Pinehurst CC (Course No. 4) (R)
North Carolina
Rees Jones
Pinehurst CC (Course No. 5)
NLE
North Carolina
Donald Ross
Pinehurst CC (Course No. 5)
North Carolina
Ellis Maples, *Richard S. Tufts*
Pinehurst CC (Course No. 5) (R)
North Carolina
Robert Trent Jones, Roger
Rulewich
Pinehurst CC (Course No. 6)
North Carolina
George Fazio, Tom Fazio
Pinehurst CC (Course No. 7)
North Carolina
Rees Jones, Keith Evans
Pineknoll CC
Sylvester, Georgia
Bill Amick
Pineland CC
Nichols, South Carolina
Gene Hamm

Pineland Plantation G&CC
Mayesville, South Carolina
Russell Breeden
Pinery GC
Parker, Colorado
David Bingaman
Pines CC
West Virginia
Edmund B. Ault
Pines GC
Hollywood, Florida
Hans Schmeisser
Pines GC
Wyoming, Michigan
George Woolferd
Pines GC
Emerson, New Jersey
Alec Ternyei
Pines GC
Pinebluff, North Carolina
Frank B. Hicks
Pines Hotel GC
South Fallsburg, New York
Robert Trent Jones, Frank Duane
Pinestone GC
Minden, Ontario
Jack Davison
Pinetop CC
Arizona
Milt Coggins
Pinetop CC (R)
Arizona
Gary Panks
Pinetop Lakes G&CC
Arizona
Milt Coggins
Pinetree CC
Marietta, Georgia
Chic Adams
Pineview G&CC
Florida
Bill Amick
Pineview GC (No. 1 Course)
Ottawa, Ontario
Howard Watson
Pineview GC (No. 2 Course)
Ottawa, Ontario
Howard Watson
Pineway GC
Lebanon, Oregon
Fred Federspiel
Pinewild CC (Holly Course)
Pinehurst, North Carolina
Gene Hamm
Pinewild CC (Magnolia Course)
Pinehurst, North Carolina
Gene Hamm
Pinewood Camps GC
Canton, Maine
George Dunn Jr
Pinewood CC
Munds Park, Arizona
Lawrence Hughes
Pinewood CC (R)
Arizona
Arthur Jack Snyder
Pinewood CC
North Carolina
Russell Breeden
Pinewood GC
Beaumont, Texas
Leon Howard
Piney Branch G&CC
Maryland
Edmund B. Ault
Piney Point CC
Norwood, North Carolina
J. Porter Gibson
Piney Point GC
Houston, Texas
Joseph S. Finger
Piney Woods CC
Nacagdoches, Texas
Karl Litten
Pinnacle Peak CC
Scottsdale, Arizona
Dick Turner
Pinnacle Peak CC (R)
Arizona
Gary Grandstaff
Pinner Hill GC
Middlesex, England
F.G. Hawtree, J.H. Taylor

Pioneer Park GC
Lincoln, Nebraska
William H. Tucker, Gregor
MacMillan
Pipe O'Peace GC
Blue Island, Illinois
James Foulis
Pipe O'Peace GC (R)
Illinois
Dick Nugent
Piper's Landing G&CC
Stuart, Florida
Joe Lee
Pipestem State Park GC
West Virginia
Geoffrey S. Cornish, William G.
Robinson
Piping Rock C
Locust Valley, New York
Charles Blair Macdonald, Seth
Raynor
Piping Rock C (R)
New York
Pete Dye
Piqua CC
Ohio
Donald Ross
Piqua CC (A. 9)
Ohio
Jack Kidwell
Pistakee Hills CC
McHenry, Illinois
Harry Collis
Pit G Links
Aberdeen, North Carolina
Dan Maples
Pitcheroak GC
Worchestershire, England
D.M.A. Steel
Pitlochry GC
Perthshire, Scotland
Willie Fernie
Pitlochry GC (R)
Scotland
C.K. Hutchison
Pitman GC
New Jersey
Alex Findlay
Pitreavie GC
Fife, Scotland
Alister Mackenzie
Pittsburg GC
California
Alister Mackenzie, Robert Hunter
Pittsburgh Field C
Pennsylvania
Donald Ross
Pittsburgh Field C (R)
Pennsylvania
Emil Loeffler
Pittsburgh Field C (R. 5) NLE
Pennsylvania
Alex Findlay
Pittsburgh Field C (R)
Pennsylvania
A.W. Tillinghast
Pittsburgh Field C (R) NLE
Pennsylvania
Willie Park Jr
Pittsburgh Field C (A. 2) NLE
Pennsylvania
Willie Park Jr
Pittsburgh Field C (R)
Pennsylvania
Robert Trent Jones
Pittsburgh Field C (R)
Pennsylvania
X.G. Hassenplug
Pittsburgh Field C (R)
Pennsylvania
X.G. Hassenplug
Pla-Mor GC
Fort Smith, Arkansas
Herman Hackbarth
Placid Lakes Inn & CC
Lake Placid, Florida
Frank Murray
Plainfield CC
New Jersey
Donald Ross
Plainfield CC (R)
New Jersey
Donald Ross

328

Plainfield CC (A. 3)
New Jersey
Donald Ross
Plainfield Elks GC
Illinois
Pete Dye
Plainfield GC NLE
New Jersey
Tom Bendelow
Plainfield West GC
New Jersey
Martin J. O'Loughlin
Plandome CC
New York
Orrin Smith
Plandome CC (R)
New York
Frank Duane
Plano Muni
Texas
Don January, Billy Martindale
Plano Muni (R)
Texas
Jeff Brauer, *Jim Colbert*
Plantation at Ponte Vedra GC
Florida
Arnold Palmer, Ed Seay,Harrison
   Minchew
Plantation Bay GC
Florida
Lloyd Clifton
Plantation G&CC (East Course)
Venice, Florida
Ron Garl
Plantation G&CC (West Course)
Venice, Florida
Ron Garl
Plantation GC
Ft. Lauderdale, Florida
Red Lawrence
Plantation GC (R)
Idaho
Robert Muir Graves
Plantation Hotel GC
Crystal River, Florida
Mark Mahannah
Platteview CC
Omaha, Nebraska
Edward Lawrence Packard
Plattsburgh AFB GC
New York
Al Zikorus
Plausawa Valley CC
Concord, New Hampshire
William F. Mitchell
Playa Dorada GC
Playa Dorado, Dominican
   Republic
Robert Trent Jones, Roger
   Rulewich
Playa Granada GC
Granada, Spain
John Harris
Playland Park G Center
South Bend, Indiana
William James Spear
Pleasant Hill GC
Monroe, Ohio
Jack Kidwell
Pleasant Hills GC
San Jose, California
Henry Duino
Pleasant Point Plantation CC
Beaufort, South Carolina
Russell Breeden
Pleasant Valley CC
Little Rock, Arkansas
Joseph S. Finger
Pleasant Valley CC
Sutton, Massachusetts
Donald Hoenig
Pleasant Valley CC (R. 3)
Massachusetts
Brian Ault, Tom Clark
Pleasant Valley CC
Mt. Pleasant, Pennsylvania
Emil Loeffler, *John McGlynn*
Pleasant Valley CC (R. 9)
Pennsylvania
X.G. Hassenplug
Pleasant Valley CC
West Virginia
Horace W. Smith

Pleasant Valley GC
Medina, Ohio
Jack Kidwell
Pleasant Valley GC
Clackamas, Oregon
Barney Lucas, Shirley Stone
Pleasant View CC
Norvelt, Pennsylvania
Paul E. Erath
Pleasant View GC
Independence, Kansas
Gene Schmidt
Pleasant View GC
Pennsylvania
Edmund B. Ault, Al Jamison
Pleasant View Lodge GC
Freehold, New York
Frank Duane
Pleasant View Lodge GC (A. 9)
New York
Frank Duane
Pleasant Vue GC
Paris, Ohio
James Gilmore Harrison,
   Ferdinand Garbin
Pleasant Vue GC (A. 9)
Ohio
Ferdinand Garbin
Pleasure Park GC
Concord, Ontario
Robert Moote
Plettenberg Bay CC
Cape Province, South Africa
Fred W. Hawtree
Plum Brook GC
Sandusky, Ohio
Tom Bendelow
Plum Hollow G&CC
Southfield, Michigan
Wilfrid Reid, William Connellan
Plum Hollow G&CC (R)
Michigan
William Newcomb
Plum Hollow G&CC (R. 1)
Michigan
Bruce Matthews, Jerry Matthews
Plum Hollow G&CC (R)
Michigan
Arthur Hills, Steve Forrest
Plum Tree National GC
Harvard, Illinois
Joe Lee
Plumas Lake G&CC
Marysville, California
Donald McKee
Plumas Lake G&CC (A. 9)
California
Bob Baldock
Plumas Lake G&CC (R. 9)
California
Bob Baldock
Plymouth CC (R)
Indiana
Gary Kern
Plymouth CC
Massachusetts
Donald Ross
Plymouth CC
New Hampshire
Ralph Barton
Plymouth CC
North Carolina
William S. Flynn
Plymouth CC (R)
Pennsylvania
William S. Flynn
Plymouth Park GC
Niles, Michigan
Tom Bendelow
Pocalla Spring CC
Sumter, South Carolina
Ed Riccoboni
Pocantico Hills GC
Tarrytown, New York
William S. Flynn
Pocasset GC
Massachusetts
Donald Ross
Poco Diablo GC
Sedona, Arizona
Arthur Jack Snyder
Pocono Farms CC
Tobyhanna, New York
Art Wall

Pocono Manor GC (East Course)
Pennsylvania
Donald Ross
Pocono Manor GC (West Course)
Pennsylvania
George Fazio
Pohick Bay GC
Virginia
George W. Cobb, John LaFoy
Poinciana G&RC
Kissimmee, Florida
Robert von Hagge, Bruce Devlin
Point Aquarius CC
Conroe, Texas
Jay Riviere
Point Grey G&CC (R)
British Columbia
Geoffrey S. Cornish, William G.
   Robinson
Point Judith CC (A. 9)
Rhode Island
Donald Ross
Point Judith CC (R. 9)
Rhode Island
Donald Ross
Point Judith CC (R. 9)
Rhode Island
Geoffrey S. Cornish, William G.
   Robinson
Point Loma GC
California
Tom Bendelow
Point Mallard Park GC
Decatur, Alabama
Charles M. Graves
Point North GC
Billings, Montana
Theodore Wirth, Dave Bennett
Point O'Woods G&CC
Benton Harbor, Michigan
Robert Trent Jones, Frank Duane
Point Pleasant GC
New Jersey
Tom Bendelow
Point Pleasant GC (. 9)
New Jersey
William F. Bell
Point Venture Y&CC
Jonestown, Texas
Bruce Littell
Point Venture Y&CC (A. 9)
Texas
Leon Howard, *Charles Howard*
Pointe CC
Lake Monroe, Indiana
Bob Simmons
Pointe Royale G&CC
Missouri
Tom Clark, Edmund B. Ault
Pok-Ta-Pok GC
Cancun, Mexico
Robert Trent Jones Jr, Gary
   Roger Baird
Pokemouche GC
Caraquet, New Brunswick
Howard Watson, John Watson
Pokemouche GC (R. 9)
New Brunswick
John Watson
Pokemouche GC (A. 9)
New Brunswick
John Watson
Poland CC
Youngstown, Ohio
Leonard Macomber
Poland Springs GC
Maine
Arthur H. Fenn
Poland Springs GC (R)
Maine
Donald Ross
Pole Creek GC
Tabernash, Colorado
Ron Kirby, Denis Griffiths
Polo C
Boca Raton, Florida
Karl Litten
Polson G&CC
Montana
Gregor MacMillan
Polvadero CC (R. 9)
California
Bob Baldock

Pomonok CC NLE
Flushing, New York
Devereux Emmet
**Pompano Beach CC (Palms
   Course)**
Florida
Red Lawrence
**Pompano Beach CC (Palms
   Course) (R)**
Florida
Robert von Hagge
**Pompano Beach CC (Pines
   Course)**
Florida
Robert von Hagge
Pompano Park GC
Pompano Beach, Florida
Frank Murray
Pompey Hills
Syracuse, New York
Hal Purdy
Ponca City CC
Oklahoma
Perry Maxwell
Ponca City CC (A. 9)
Oklahoma
Perry Maxwell
Ponca City CC (R)
Oklahoma
Don Sechrest
**Ponce de Leon CC formerly
   known as St. Augustine Links
   (North Course)**
St. Augustine, Florida
Donald Ross
Ponce de Leon CC (R)
Florida
William H. Diddel
Ponce de Leon CC (R. 2)
Florida
Willard Byrd, Clyde Johnston
Ponce de Leon CC (A. 2)
Florida
Willard Byrd, Clyde Johnston
Ponce GC
Puerto Rico
Alfred H. Tull
Pond A River GC
Woodburn, Indiana
Robert Beard
Pond View GC
Westerly, Rhode Island
Phil Wogan
Ponderosa CC
Warren, Ohio
Homer Fieldhouse
Ponderosa Muni
California
Bob Baldock
Ponderosa Par 3 GC
Burley, Idaho
Ernest Schneiter
Pondok Indah GC
Indonesia
Robert Trent Jones Jr, Gary
   Roger Baird
Ponkapoag GC
Canton, Massachusetts
Donald Ross
Ponkapoag GC (A. 9)
Massachusetts
William F. Mitchell
Ponoka Community GC
Alberta
William G. Robinson
Pont St. Maxence GC
France
Wilfrid Reid
Ponte Vedra C (Lagoon Course)
Ponte Vedra Beach, Florida
Robert Trent Jones, Frank Duane
**Ponte Vedra C (Lagoon Course)
   (A. 9)**
Florida
Joe Lee
Ponte Vedra C (Ocean Course)
Ponte Vedra Beach, Florida
Herbert Strong
**Ponte Vedra C (Ocean Course)
   (R)**
Florida
Robert Trent Jones

Pontiac CC
Michigan
Ernest Way
Pontiac Elks GC (A. 9)
Illinois
Edward Lawrence Packard
Poolesville GC
Maryland
Edmund B. Ault, Al Jamison
Pope AFB GC
Fayetteville, North Carolina
George W. Cobb
Pope AFB GC (A. 9)
North Carolina
George W. Cobb, John LaFoy
Poplar Bluff Muni
Missouri
Brian Ault, Tom Clark,Edmund
   B. Ault
Poplar Forest GC
Lynchberg, Virginia
Ken Killian, Dick Nugent
Poplar Hills G&CC
Fort Nelson, British Columbia
William G. Robinson
Poppy Hills GC
Pebble Beach, California
Robert Trent Jones Jr, Don Knott
Poquoy Brook GC
Lakeville, Massachusetts
Geoffrey S. Cornish
Port Allegre G&CC
Brazil
Jose Gonzales, J.E. Millender
Port Armor CC
Lake Oconee, Georgia
Bob Cupp
Port Arthur CC
Texas
Ralph Plummer
Port Charlotte CC
Florida
David Wallace
Port Charlotte CC (A. 9)
Florida
Mark Mahannah
Port Charlotte CC (R. 9)
Florida
Mark Mahannah
Port Charlotte CC (R)
Florida
Chuck Ankrom
Port Cherry Hills CC
McDonald, Pennsylvania
Paul E. Erath
Port Colbourne GC (R)
Ontario
Robert Moote, *David Moote*
Port Colbourne GC (R)
Ontario
Robert Moote
Port Columbus GC
Columbus, Ohio
Jack Kidwell
Port Elizabeth GC
South Africa
S.V. Hotchkin
Port Huron CC
Michigan
Wilfrid Reid, William Connellan
Port Huron CC (R)
Michigan
William Newcomb, Stephen Kay
Port Jervis CC
New York
A.W. Tillinghast
Port Ludlow GC
Washington
Robert Muir Graves
Port Malabar CC
Florida
Chuck Ankrom
Port Royal GC
Southampton, Bermuda
Robert Trent Jones, Roger
   Rulewich
Port Royal GC (Barony Course)
Hilton Head Island, South
   Carolina
George W. Cobb
**Port Royal GC (Barony Course)
   (R)**
South Carolina
Willard Byrd, Clyde Johnston

Port Royal GC (Planters Row Course)
Hilton Head Island, South Carolina
Willard Byrd, Clyde Johnston
Port Royal GC (Robbers Row Course)
Hilton Head Island, South Carolina
George W. Cobb
Port Royal GC (Robbers Row Course) (A. 9)
South Carolina
George W. Cobb, John LaFoy
Port Royal GC (Robbers Row Course) (R)
South Carolina
Willard Byrd, Clyde Johnston
Port Sunlight GC
England
Fred W. Hawtree
Port-Au-Peck GC
New York
Mungo Park II
Portage CC
Akron, Ohio
William B. Langford
Portage CC (R)
Ohio
Geoffrey S. Cornish, William G. Robinson
Portage La Prairie GC (R. 9)
Manitoba
Clinton E. Robinson
Portage La Prairie GC (A. 9)
Manitoba
Clinton E. Robinson
Portage Lake GC
Houghton, Michigan
William Newcomb
Portage Park GC NLE
Houghton, Michigan
William B. Langford
Portage Y&CC
Treasure Lake, Florida
Chic Adams
Portales CC
New Mexico
William H. Tucker
Porter Valley CC
North Ridge, California
Ted Robinson
Porters Park GC
Hertfordshire, England
C.S. Butchart
Portland CC
Falmouth, Maine
Donald Ross
Portland CC (R)
Maine
Orrin Smith, William F. Mitchell
Portland CC (R)
Maine
Robert Trent Jones
Portland CC
Connecticut
Geoffrey S. Cornish, William G. Robinson
Portland GC
Oregon
William Dickson, Donald Junor
Portland GC (R)
Oregon
Robert Trent Jones
Portland GC (R)
Oregon
Robert Muir Graves
Portland Meadows GC
Portland, Oregon
Eddie Hogan, Stan Terry
Portmadoc GC
Wales
James Braid
Portmarnock GC
Dublin, Ireland
George Ross, W.C. Pickeman
Portmarnock GC (R. 1)
Ireland
Eddie Hackett
Portmarnock GC (R)
Ireland
H.M. Cairnes

Portmarnock GC (R)
Ireland
Fred W. Hawtree
Portmarnock GC (A. 9)
Ireland
Fred W. Hawtree
Porto D'Orra GC
Cantanzaro Lido, Italy
M. Croze
Portsdown Hill GC
England
Fred W. Hawtree
Portsmouth AFB GC
New Hampshire
Al Zikorus
Portsmouth CC
Ohio
Donald Ross
Portsmouth G&CC
New Hampshire
Robert Trent Jones, Frank Duane
Portstewart GC
County Londonderry, Northern Ireland
Willie Park
Portumna GC (R)
Ireland
Eddie Hackett
Possum Trot GC
North Myrtle Beach, South Carolina
Russell Breeden
Potomac C
Keyser, West Virginia
Algie Pulley
Potowatomi CC
Michigan City, Indiana
Tom Bendelow
Potowatomi Tribal GC
Shawnee, Oklahoma
Don Sechrest
Potowomat CC (A. 9)
Rhode Island
Walter I. Johnson
Potrero G&CC NLE
Inglewood, California
Robert Johnstone
Pottawatomie Park GC
St. Charles, Illinois
Robert Trent Jones
Poughkeepsie Muni (R)
New York
William F. Mitchell
Poult Wood GC
Kent, England
Fred W. Hawtree
Powder Horn GC
Lexington, Massachusetts
Geoffrey S. Cornish
Powder River CC
Broadus, Montana
Frank Hummel
Powell Muni
Wyoming
Theodore Wirth
Powelton C
Newburgh, New York
J. Taylor
Powelton C (R. 6)
New York
Devereux Emmet
Powelton C (A.12)
New York
Devereux Emmet
Powelton C (R)
New York
Robert Trent Jones
Powelton C (R. 4)
New York
Geoffrey S. Cornish, Brian Silva
Powfoot GC
Scotland
James Braid
Poxebogue GC
Bridgehampton, New York
Alfred H. Tull
Prairie Creek GC
DeWitt, Michigan
William Newcomb
Prairie Dog GC
Norton, Kansas
Frank Hummel

Prairie Dunes CC
Hutchinson, Kansas
Perry Maxwell
Prairie Dunes CC (A. 9)
Kansas
Press Maxwell
Prairie Hill GC NLE
Maple Hill, Kansas
L.J. "Dutch" McClellan
Prairie Oaks G&CC
Sebring, Florida
Ron Garl
Prairie View GC
Cheyenne, Wyoming
Jim Church
Prairiewood GC
Fargo, North Dakota
Dick Phelps, Brad Benz
Pratt Estate GC
Glen Cove, New York
Tom Bendelow
Preakness Hills CC
Paterson, New Jersey
William H. Tucker
Preakness Hills CC (R)
New Jersey
Geoffrey S. Cornish, Brian Silva
Preakness Valley Park GC
New Jersey
Frank Duane
Prenton GC (R)
England
Fred W. Hawtree
Prescott CC
Arizona
Milt Coggins
Prescott Hills GC
Plainfield, New Jersey
Willard Wilkinson
President CC (North Course)
West Palm Beach, Florida
William F. Mitchell
President CC (South Course)
West Palm Beach, Florida
William F. Mitchell
Presidential CC
North Miami Beach, Florida
Mark Mahannah
Presidents GC
North Quincy, Massachusetts
George Fazio, Tom Fazio
Presidio GC
San Francisco, California
Robert Johnstone
Presidio GC (R)
California
William McEwan
Presidio GC (R)
California
Robert Muir Graves
Presidio GC (R)
California
Desmond Muirhead
Prestbury GC
England
H.S. Colt, J.S.F. Morrison
Preston CC
West Virginia
Edmund B. Ault
Preston Trail GC
Dallas, Texas
Ralph Plummer
Preston Trail GC (R. 1)
Texas
Pete Dye, *David Postlethwaite*
Preston Trail GC (R)
Texas
Jay Morrish, Bob Cupp
Preston Trail GC (R)
Texas
Joseph S. Finger, Ken Dye
Prestonwood CC (Creek Course)
Dallas, Texas
Ralph Plummer
Prestonwood CC (Creek Course) (R)
Texas
Joseph S. Finger, Ken Dye
Prestonwood CC (Hills Course)
Dallas, Texas
Dave Bennett
Prestwick CC NLE
Orland Park, Illinois
Charles Maddox, *Frank P. MacDonald*

Prestwick CC
Frankfort, Illinois
Edward Lawrence Packard
Prestwick GC
Ayrshire, Scotland
Old Tom Morris
Prestwick GC (A. 6)
Scotland
Old Tom Morris
Prestwick GC (R)
Scotland
Charles Hunter
Prestwick GC (R)
Scotland
James Braid
Prestwick GC (A. 4)
Scotland
James Braid
Prestwick GC (R)
Scotland
Harold Hilton
Prestwick GC (R)
Scotland
James Braid, John R. Stutt
Prestwick GC (R)
Scotland
J. Hamilton Stutt
Prestwick St. Cuthbert GC (R)
Scotland
J. Hamilton Stutt
Prestwick St. Nicholas GC
Ayrshire, Scotland
Charles Hunter
Pretoria CC
South Africa
Clarrie Moore
Pretoria GC (R)
South Africa
Robert G. Grimsdell
Pretty Acres GC
New Orleans, Louisiana
Louis Prima
Prince George CC
British Columbia
Ernest Brown
Prince Georges G&CC NLE
Landover, Maryland
Donald Ross
Prince Georges G&CC
Mitchellville, Maryland
Arnold Palmer, Ed Seay, Bob Walker
Prince Rupert GC
Edmonton, Alberta
William Brinkworth
Prince's GC (Blue Course)
Kent, England
Charles Hutchings, Percy Montagu Lucas
Prince's GC (Blue Course) (R)
England
C.K. Hutchison
Prince's GC (Blue Course) (R)
England
Sir Guy Campbell, J.S.F. Morrison
Prince's GC (Red Course)
Kent, England
Sir Guy Campbell, J.S.F. Morrison
Princeton CC
Minnesota
Willie Kidd
Princeton CC
New Jersey
William Gordon, David Gordon
Princeton Hills Golf Academy
Princeton, New Jersey
Alec Ternyei
Princeville Makai GC
Kauai, Hawaii
Robert Trent Jones Jr, Gary Roger Baird
Princeville Makai GC (A.18)
Hawaii
Robert Trent Jones Jr, Don Knott
Prineville G&CC
Oregon
Eddie Hogan, Bob Hogan
Profile C
New Hampshire
Ralph Barton

Progress Downs GC
Progress, Oregon
Ervin Thoresen
Prospect Bay CC
Graysonville, Maryland
Lindsay Ervin
Prospect CC
Connecticut
Al Zikorus
Prospect Hill CC
Bowie, Maryland
George W. Cobb
Prouts Neck GC (A. 9)
Maine
Wayne Stiles, John Van Kleek
Prouts Neck GC (R. 9)
Maine
Wayne Stiles, John Van Kleek
Prouts Neck GC (R)
Maine
Geoffrey S. Cornish
Province Lake CC (A. 9)
New Hampshire
Brian Silva, Geoffrey S. Cornish
Pruneridge Farms GC
Santa Clara, California
Jack Fleming
Pruneridge Farms GC (R)
California
Robert Trent Jones Jr
Pryor Muni
Oklahoma
Hugh Bancroft
Puckerbrush GC
Willoughby, Ohio
R. Albert Anderson
Pueblo CC (R. 9)
Colorado
Henry B. Hughes
Pueblo CC (A. 9)
Colorado
Henry B. Hughes
Pueblo El Mirage CC
El Mirage, Arizona
Ken Killian
Pueblo West G&CC
Colorado
Clyde B. Young
Puerto del Sol GC
Albuquerque, New Mexico
Arthur Jack Snyder
Puerto Azul GC
Pasay City, Philippines
Ron Kirby, Denis Griffiths
Pukalani CC
Hawaii
Bob Baldock, Robert L. Baldock
Pulgas Pandas GC
Aguacaliente, Mexico
Joseph S. Finger
Punderson Lake GC
Cleveland, Ohio
Jack Kidwell
Punta del Este GC
Canteril, Uruguay
Alister Mackenzie
Punta Ala GC
Italy
G. Cavalsani
Punta Borinquen CC
Puerto Rico
Ferdinand Garbin
Punta Gorda CC
Florida
Donald Ross
Punta Gorda CC (R)
Florida
R. Albert Anderson
Punxsutawney CC
Pennsylvania
James Gilmore Harrison
Purdue Univ GC (North Course)
West Lafayette, Indiana
Kenneth Welton
Purdue University GC (South Course)
West Lafayette, Indiana
William H. Diddel
Purdue University GC (South Course) (R)
Indiana
Edward Lawrence Packard

Purley Chase GC
Warwickshire, England
J.B. Tomlinson
Purley Downs GC
Surrey, England
S.V. Hotchkin
Purple Hawk CC
Cambridge, Minnesota
Don Herfort
Purple Sage GC
Wyoming
Mick Riley
Purple Sage Muni
Caldwell, Idaho
A. Vernon Macan
Purpoodock C (R. 2)
Maine
Brian Silva, Geoffrey S. Cornish
Puslinch Lake GC (R)
Ontario
Robert Moote
Put-In-Bay GC NLE
Pennsylvania
Frederick Stafford
Putnam CC
Lake Mahopac, New York
William F. Mitchell
Putterham Meadows Muni
Brookline, Massachusetts
Wayne Stiles, John Van Kleek
Putterham Meadows Muni (R. 2)
Massachusetts
Phil Wogan
Pwllheli GC
Wales
Old Tom Morris
Pwllheli GC (A. 9)
Wales
James Braid
Pwllheli GC (R. 9)
Wales
James Braid
Pyecombe GC (R. 4)
England
Fred W. Hawtree, Martin Hawtree
Pyle and Kenfig GC
Wales
H.S. Colt, C.H. Alison
Pyle and Kenfig GC (A. 9)
Wales
P.M. Ross
Pyle and Kenfig GC (R)
Wales
J. Hamilton Stutt
Pyma Valley GC
Andover, Ohio
J. Thomas Francis
Pype Hayes Muni
Warwickshire, England
F.G. Hawtree, J.H. Taylor
Pyrmonter GC
Bad Byrmont, West Germany
Donald Harradine
PGA National GC (Champion Course)
Palm Beach Gardens, Florida
Tom Fazio
PGA National GC (Haig Course)
Palm Beach Gardens, Florida
Tom Fazio
PGA National GC (Squire Course)
Palm Beach Gardens, Florida
Tom Fazio
PGA National GC (The General Course)
Palm Beach Gardens, Florida
Arnold Palmer, Ed Seay
PGA West GC (Palmer Course)
La Quinta, California
Arnold Palmer, Ed Seay, Harrison Minchew
PGA West GC (Stadium Course)
La Quinta, California
Pete Dye, Alice Dye, *Lee Schmidt*
Quabog GC (R. 2)
Massachusetts
Geoffrey S. Cornish, William G. Robinson
Quail Brook Park GC
New Jersey
Brian Ault, Tom Clark, Edmund B. Ault

Quail Creek CC (Creek Course)
Naples, Florida
Arthur Hills, Steve Forrest
Quail Creek CC (Quail Course)
Naples, Florida
Arthur Hills, Steve Forrest
Quail Creek G&CC
Oklahoma, Oklahoma
Floyd Farley
Quail Creek GC
North Liberty, Iowa
Leo Johnson
Quail Creek GC
Myrtle Beach, South Carolina
Gene Hamm
Quail Heights CC
Lake City, Florida
Jerry Cooper
Quail Hollow CC
Charlotte, North Carolina
George W. Cobb
Quail Hollow CC (R)
North Carolina
Tom Jackson
Quail Hollow CC (R)
North Carolina
Arnold Palmer, Ed Seay
Quail Hollow G&CC
Zephyrhills, Florida
Charles E. Griffin
Quail Hollow Inn & CC
Painesville, Ohio
Robert von Hagge, Bruce Devlin
Quail Lake CC
Moreno, California
Desmond Muirhead
Quail Ridge CC
Spring Hill, Florida
Lee Duxstad
Quail Ridge CC (North Course)
Delray Beach, Florida
Joe Lee
Quail Ridge CC (South Course)
Delray Beach, Florida
Joe Lee
Quail Ridge G&TC
Bloomington, Indiana
Bob Simmons
Quail Ridge GC
Sanford, North Carolina
Mike Souchak, Sidney Davis
Quail Run GC
Sun City, Arizona
Jeff Hardin, Greg Nash
Quail Run GC
Santa Fe, New Mexico
Arthur Jack Snyder
Quail Valley GC
Missouri City, Texas
Jack B. Miller
Quail Valley CC (A.27)
Texas
Jay Riviere
Quaker Hill GC
Pawling, New York
Robert Trent Jones
Quaker Ridge CC
Scarsdale, New York
John Duncan Dunn
Quaker Ridge CC (R. 9)
New York
A.W. Tillinghast
Quaker Ridge CC (A. 9)
New York
A.W. Tillinghast
Quaker Ridge CC (R)
New York
Robert Trent Jones
Quaker Ridge CC (R)
New York
Frank Duane
Quarry Hill GC
Vermont
Walter Barcomb
Quarry Hills CC formerly known as Piedmont Crescent CC
Burlington, North Carolina
Ellis Maples, Ed Seay
Quashnet Valley CC
Massachusetts
Geoffrey S. Cornish, William G. Robinson

Quechee Lakes CC (Highland Course)
Vermont
Geoffrey S. Cornish, William G. Robinson
Quechee Lakes CC (Lakeland Course)
Vermont
Geoffrey S. Cornish, William G. Robinson
Queens Park GC
Bermuda
David Gordon
Queens Park GC
Bournemouth, England
J.H. Taylor
Queens Park GC (R)
England
James Braid
Queensboro Links
Astoria, New York
Devereux Emmet
Queretaro CC
Mexico
Percy Clifford
Quidnesset CC
East Greenwich, Rhode Island
Geoffrey S. Cornish
Quidnesset CC (A. 9)
Rhode Island
Geoffrey S. Cornish, William G. Robinson
Quilchena G&CC
British Columbia, British Columbia
Desmond Muirhead
Quilchena G&CC (R. 6)
British Columbia
Geoffrey S. Cornish, William G. Robinson
Quincy CC (R)
Massachusetts
Orrin Smith, Al Zikorus
Quincy G&CC
Washington
William Teufel
Quinnatisset CC (A. 9)
Connecticut
Geoffrey S. Cornish, William G. Robinson
Quinta da Marinha GC
Faro, Portugal
Robert Trent Jones, Cabell Robinson
Quinta de Arambepe GC
Bahia, Brazil
Pier Mancinelli
Quintado de Lago GC (Course No. 1)
Algarve, Portugal
William F. Mitchell
Quintado de Lago GC (Course No. 2)
Faro, Portugal
Joe Lee, Rocky Roquemore
Quit-Qui-Oc GC
Elkhart Lake, Wisconsin
Tom Bendelow
Quoque Field C
New York
James Hepburn
Quoque Field C (R. 2)
New York
Stephen Kay
R.H. Storrer Estate GC
Woodbridge, Ontario
Howard Watson
Rabbit Creek GC
Louisburg, Kansas
Leon Andrews
Raccoon Creek GC
Littleton, Colorado
Dick Phelps, Brad Benz, Mike Poellot
Raccoon Run GC
Myrtle Beach, South Carolina
Gene Hamm
Racebrook CC
Orange, Connecticut
Robert D. Pryde
Racebrook CC (R)
Connecticut
Orrin Smith, William F. Mitchell

Racebrook CC (R. 2)
Connecticut
Al Zikorus
Raceway GC
Thompson, Connecticut
Donald Hoenig
Racine CC
Wisconsin
Joseph A. Roseman
Racine CC
Wisconsin
Tom Bendelow
Racine CC (R)
Wisconsin
David Gill
Racine CC (R)
Wisconsin
Edward Lawrence Packard, Roger Packard
Racing C de France (Valley)
La Boulie, France
Wilfrid Reid
Racing C de France (Valley) (R)
France
Seymour Dunn
Racing C de France (Valley) (R)
France
Willie Park Jr
Rackham Park Muni
Huntington, Michigan
Donald Ross
Rackham Park Muni (R. 9)
Michigan
Jerry Matthews
Radcliffe on Trent GC
Nottinghamshire, England
Tom Williamson
Radcliffe on Trent GC (R)
England
Tom Williamson
Radcliffe on Trent GC (R)
England
J.J.F. Pennink
Radisson Greens GC
Baldwinsville, New York
Robert Trent Jones, Roger Rulewich
Radium CC
Albany, Georgia
Wayne Stiles, John Van Kleek
Radium CC (R)
Georgia
Hugh Moore
Radium Hot Springs GC
British Columbia
Doug McIntosh, Bruce McIntosh
Radley College GC
England
D.M.A. Steel
Radley Run CC
West Chester, Pennsylvania
Alfred H. Tull
Radnor Valley CC
Villanova, Pennsylvania
Dick Wilson, X.G. Hassenplug
Radnor Valley CC (A.14)
Pennsylvania
William Gordon, David Gordon
Radnor Valley CC (R. 4)
Pennsylvania
William Gordon, David Gordon
Radrick Farms GC
Ann Arbor, Michigan
Pete Dye
Rail GC
Springfield, Illinois
Robert Trent Jones, Rees Jones
Rainbow Bay GC formerly known as Edgewater GC
Biloxi, Mississippi
Jack Daray, Harry Collis
Rainbow Bay GC (R.12)
Mississippi
Earl Stone
Rainbow Bay GC (A. 6)
Mississippi
Earl Stone
Rainbow Canyon GC
Temecula, California
Virgil C. "Dick" Rossen
Rainbow Lake GC
Geneva, Indiana
Henry Culp

Rainbow's End G&CC
Dunellon, Florida
Joe Lee
Rainelle CC (R)
West Virginia
George W. Cobb, John LaFoy
Rainey Estate GC
Huntington, New York
A.W. Tillinghast
Raintree CC (North Course)
Charlotte, North Carolina
Russell Breeden
Raintree CC (South Course)
Charlotte, North Carolina
Russell Breeden
Raintree GC
Pembroke Pines, Florida
Charles Mahannah
Raisin River CC
Monroe, Michigan
Charles Maddox
Ralara GC
Canary Islands
Tom Dunn
Raleigh CC
North Carolina
Donald Ross
Raleigh Golf Assoc GC
North Carolina
George W. Cobb
Ralph G. Cover Estate GC
Maryland
Edmund B. Ault
Ralston GC NLE
Nebraska
Henry C. Glissmann, Harold Glissmann
Ramapo GC
Haverstraw, New York
Duncan Fountaine
Ramblewood CC
New Jersey
Edmund B. Ault
Rams Hill CC
Borrego Springs, California
Ted Robinson
Ramsey G&CC
New Jersey
Hal Purdy
Ramsey GC
Cambridgeshire, England
J. Hamilton Stutt
Ramsey GC
Cambridgeshire, Isle of Man
James Braid, John R. Stutt
Ramsgate GC
Inman, South Carolina
Russell Breeden, *Dan Breeden*
Ramshorn CC
Fremont, Michigan
Max Dietz
Ramshorn CC (A. 9)
Michigan
Jerry Matthews
Ranch at Roaring Fork GC
Carbondale, Colorado
Milt Coggins
Ranch CC
Palm Springs, California
Joseph Calwell
Ranch CC
Westminster, Colorado
Dick Phelps
Ranch Hills GC
Mulino, Oregon
Bob Blaine
Ranchland Hills GC
Midland, Texas
Ralph Plummer
Ranchland Hills GC (R)
Texas
Robert von Hagge, Bruce Devlin
Rancho del Ray GC
California
Bob Baldock
Rancho Bernardo Inn & CC (West Course)
California
William F. Bell
Rancho Bernardo Inn & CC (West Course) (R. 3)
California
Ted Robinson

Rancho Canada GC (East Course)
Carmel, California
Robert Dean Putnam

Rancho Canada GC (West Course)
Carmel, California
Robert Dean Putnam

Rancho CC NLE
Los Angeles, California
Max Behr

Rancho Duarte GC
California
William F. Bell

Rancho Las Palmas CC
Rancho Mirage, California
Ted Robinson

Rancho Los Penasquitos GC
Poway, California
William F. Bell

Rancho Mirage CC
California
Harold Heers

Rancho Murieta CC (South Course)
Sloughhouse, California
Ted Robinson

Rancho Murieta GC (North Course)
Sloughhouse, California
Bert Stamps

Rancho Park GC
Los Angeles, California
William P. Bell, William H. Johnson

Rancho San Joaquin CC
Irvine, California
William F. Bell

Rancho San Joaquin CC (R)
California
Robert Muir Graves

Rancho Santa Fe CC
California
Max Behr

Rancho Santa Fe CC (R)
California
Harry Rainville

Rancho Santa Ynez CC
Solvang, California
Ted Robinson

Rancho Viejo CC (El Angel Course)
Brownsville, Texas
Dennis W. Arp

Rancho Viejo CC (El Diablo Course)
Brownsville, Texas
Dennis W. Arp

Randall Oaks GC
Dundee, Illinois
William James Spear

Randers GC
Denmark
C.K. Cotton

Randolph Field GC
San Antonio, Texas
Perry Maxwell, Press Maxwell

Randolph Field GC (A. 9)
Texas
Joseph S. Finger

Randolph Field GC (R. 3)
Texas
Joseph S. Finger

Randolph Park GC (North Course)
Tucson, Arizona
William P. Bell

Randolph Park GC (North Course) (R. 4)
Arizona
Pete Dye, *David Postlethwaite*

Randolph Park GC (South Course)
Tucson, Arizona
William F. Bell

Range End GC
Dillsburgh, Pennsylvania
James Gilmore Harrison

Rank Estate GC
Sussex, England
Tom Simpson

Ransom Oaks CC
Amherst, New York
Robert Trent Jones, Rees Jones

Rantau Petronas GC (Links Course)
Kertah, Malaysia
Ronald Fream

Raquette Lake CC
New York
Seymour Dunn

Raritan Arsenal CC (R)
New Jersey
David Gordon

Raritan Arsenal CC (R. 9)
New Jersey
Hal Purdy

Rarotonga GC (A. 9)
New Zealand
Peter Thomson, Michael Wolveridge

Rathfarnham GC (R)
Ireland
Eddie Hackett

Ratho Park GC
Edinburgh, Scotland
James Braid, John R. Stutt

Rattle Run G&TC
St. Clair, Michigan
Lou Powers

Ravelston GC
Scotland
James Braid

Raveneaux CC (Gold Course)
Spring, Texas
Robert von Hagge, Bruce Devlin

Raveneaux CC (Orange Course)
Spring, Texas
Robert von Hagge, Bruce Devlin

Ravenna CC
Ohio
Edmund B. Ault

Ravenstein GC
Belgium
George Pannall

Ravenwood C
Tennessee
L.N. Adwell

Ravines GC
Middleburg, Florida
Mark McCumber

Ravinia Green CC
Deerfield, Illinois
Edward Lawrence Packard

Ravinia Green CC (R)
Illinois
Ken Killian, Dick Nugent

Ravisloe CC (R)
Illinois
William B. Langford, Theodore J. Moreau

Ravisloe CC (R)
Illinois
Donald Ross

Ravisloe CC (R)
Illinois
Robert White

Rawiga CC
Seville, Ohio
Edward Lawrence Packard

Rayburn G&CC (Blue Nine)
Jasper, Texas
Rees Jones

Rayburn G&CC (Gold Nine)
Jasper, Texas
Jay Riviere

Rayburn G&CC (Green Nine)
Jasper, Texas
Robert von Hagge, Bruce Devlin

Reading CC
Pennsylvania
Alex Findlay

Real Automovil C de Espana
Spain
Javier Arana

Real C de la Puerto de Hierro (New)
Madrid, Spain
John Harris

Real C de la Puerto de Hierro (New) (R)
Spain
Henry Cotton

Real C de la Puerto de Hierro (Old)
Madrid, Spain
J.S.F. Morrison, H.S. Colt,C.H. Alison

Real C de la Puerto de Hierro (Old) (R)
Spain
Tom Simpson

Real C de la Puerto de Hierro (Old) (R)
Spain
John Harris

Real C de G de Menorca
Shangri-La, Spain
John Harris

Real C de G El Prat
Spain
Javier Arana

Real C de San Sebastian
Spain
Tom Simpson

Real G de Pedrena
Spain
J.S.F. Morrison, H.S. Colt,C.H. Alison

Real Sociedad de G Neguri La Galea
Spain
Javier Arana

Real Sociedad Hipica Espanola
Spain
Javier Arana

Real Sociedad Hipica Espanola (R)
Spain
John Harris, Michael Wolveridge

Reames G&CC
Klamath Falls, Oregon
H. Chandler Egan

Reames G&CC (A. 9)
Oregon
Bob Baldock, Robert L. Baldock

Rebelstoke GC (A. 9)
British Columbia
Norman H. Woods

Rebsamen Park Muni
Little Rock, Arkansas
Herman Hackbarth

Recreation GC
Healdton, Oklahoma
Floyd Farley

Recreation Park GC
Long Beach, California
William F. Bell

Red Apple Inn GC
Heber Springs, Arkansas
Leon Howard

Red Apple Inn GC (A. 9)
Arkansas
Gary Panks

Red Apple Inn GC (R. 9)
Arkansas
Gary Panks

Red Bank G&CC (R)
New Jersey
Seymour Dunn

Red Butte CC
Gillette, Wyoming
Frank Hummel

Red Cloud GC
Nebraska
Harry Obitz

Red Deer G&CC (R)
Alberta
William G. Robinson

Red Fox CC
Tryon, North Carolina
Ellis Maples, Ed Seay

Red Hill CC
Cucamonga, California
George C. Thomas Jr

Red Hill CC (R)
California
Harry Rainville, David Rainville

Red Hill CC (A. 9)
California
William P. Bell

Red Hill CC (R. 9)
Massachusetts
William F. Mitchell, Al Zikorus

Red Hill CC (A. 9)
Massachusetts
William F. Mitchell, Al Zikorus

Red Hook GC (R)
New York
Alfred H. Tull

Red Lake CC
Venice, Florida
R. Albert Anderson

Red Lodge CC
Montana
Bob Baldock, Robert L. Baldock

Red Mountain Ranch GC
Mesa, Arizona
Perry Dye

Red Oaks GC
Michigan
Robert W. Bills, Donald L. Childs

Red Oaks GC
Texas
Leon Howard

Red Run GC
Royal Oak, Michigan
Willie Park Jr

Red Run GC (R)
Michigan
Clinton E. Robinson

Red Run GC (R)
Michigan
Emil Loeffler, *John McGlynn*

Red Wing CC (R. 9)
Minnesota
Don Herfort

Red Wing Lake GC
Virginia Beach, Virginia
George W. Cobb

Red Wood Meadows GC
Bragg Creek, Alberta
Stan Leonard, *Philip Tattersfield*

Redbourn GC
Hertfordshire, England
John Day

Redding CC
Connecticut
Edward Ryder

Redding CC (A. 9)
Connecticut
Rees Jones

Reddish Vale GC
Cheshire, England
Alister Mackenzie

Redford Muni
Detroit, Michigan
Donald Ross

Redland G&CC
Homestead, Florida
Red Lawrence

Redlands CC (R)
California
Alister Mackenzie

Redmond G Links
Washington
Al Smith

Redondo Beach GC
California
Tom Bendelow

Redwoods G&CC
Virginia
Dale Nolte

Reedsburg CC (A. 9)
Wisconsin
Ken Killian, Dick Nugent,Bob Lohmann

Reeves GC
Cincinnati, Ohio
Jack Kidwell

Reeves Memorial GC
Cincinnati, Ohio
William H. Diddel

Reflections GC
La Quinta, California
Ted Robinson

Regensburg G und Land C
West Germany
Donald Harradine

Regina GC
Saskatchewan
William Brinkworth

Regina GC (R)
Saskatchewan
Clinton E. Robinson

Rehobeth Beach CC NLE
Delaware
Francis B. Warner

Rehobeth Beach CC
Delaware
Frank Murray, Russell Roberts

Rehoboth GC
Massachusetts
Geoffrey S. Cornish, William G. Robinson

Reichswald GC
Nuremburg, West Germany
Bernhard von Limburger

Reid Park GC (North Course)
Springfield, Ohio
Jack Kidwell

Reid Park GC (South Course)
Springfield, Ohio
Jack Kidwell

Reina Cristina GC
Spain
Javier Arana

Remuera GC
Auckland, New Zealand
H.G. Bobbagr

Rend Lake GC
Benton, Illinois
Edward Lawrence Packard, Roger Packard

Renfrew GC
Renfrewshire, Scotland
John Harris

Renishaw GC (R)
England
Tom Williamson

Reno CC
Nevada
Lawrence Hughes

Reno GC NLE
Nevada
May Dunn Hupfel

Renwood CC
Gray's Lake, Illinois
William James Spear

Reservation GC formerly known as Jekyll-Hyde GC
Lakeland, Florida
Warner Bowen

Reserve G&CC
Fort Pierce, Florida
George Fazio, *Jim Fazio*

Restigouche G&CC (A. 9)
New Brunswick
Clinton E. Robinson

Reston South GC
Virginia
Edmund B. Ault

Retford GC
Nottinghamshire, England
Tom Williamson

Retreat G&CC
Berryville, Virginia
Buddy Loving

Reynolds Park GC
Winston Salem, North Carolina
Perry Maxwell

Reynolds Park GC (R)
North Carolina
Ellis Maples, Ed Seay

Rhinelander CC
Wisconsin
Charles Maddox, *Frank P. MacDonald*

Rhinelander CC (A. 9)
Wisconsin
Harry Collis

Rhode Island CC
West Barrington, Rhode Island
Donald Ross

Rhode Island CC (R)
Rhode Island
Geoffrey S. Cornish

Rhodo Dunes GC
Florence, Oregon
Fred Federspiel

Rhos-on-Sea GC (R)
Wales
Tom Simpson, Tom Simpson

Rhuddlan GC
Clwyd, Wales
F.G. Hawtree, J.H. Taylor

Rhyl GC
Wales
James Braid

Rib Mountain Lodge GC
Wausau, Wisconsin
Edward Lawrence Packard

Ribault GC
Jacksonville, Florida
Luther O. "Luke" Morris

Rice Lake CC
Minnesota
Donald G. Brauer, Emile Perret

Rice Lake CC (A. 9)
Minnesota
Donald G. Brauer, Emile Perret
Rich Acres GC
Richfield, Minnesota
Donald G. Brauer, Paul S. Fjare
Richard C. Jones Memorial GC
Cedar Rapids, Iowa
Robert Everly
Richard Nixon Estate GC
San Clemente, California
Joseph B. Williams
**Richelieu Valley CC (Blue
  Course)**
Montreal, Quebec
William Gordon, David Gordon
**Richelieu Valley CC (Red
  Course)**
Montreal, Quebec
William Gordon, David Gordon
Richfield Muni
Minnesota
Dick Schwarz, Neil Weber
Richland CC
Nashville, Tennessee
Donald Ross
Richland CC (R. 9)
Tennessee
Joseph S. Finger
Richmond County CC
Staten Island, New York
Robert White
Richmond County CC (R. 4)
New York
Frank Duane
Richmond CC
British Columbia
A. Vernon Macan
Richmond GC
Maine
Arnold Smith, Bernard Smith
Richmond GC
England
Tom Dunn
Richmond GC (R)
England
Willie Park Jr
Richmond Hill G&CC
Richmond, Ontario
Clinton E. Robinson, Robert
  Moote
Richmond Park GC NLE
London, England
Willie Park Jr
**Richmond Park GC (Dukes
  Course)**
London, England
F.G. Hawtree, J.H. Taylor
**Richmond Park GC (Princes
  Course)**
London, England
F.G. Hawtree, J.H. Taylor
Richmond Pines GC
Rockingham, North Carolina
Donald Ross
Richter Park GC
Danbury, Connecticut
Edward Ryder
Richton Park GC
Illinois
Harry Collis
Richview G&CC
Oakville, Ontario
Clinton E. Robinson
Rickmansworth GC
Hertfordshire, England
F.G. Hawtree, J.H. Taylor
Riddell's Bay G&CC
Warwick, Bermuda
Devereux Emmet
Ridder Farm GC
East Bridgewater, Massachusetts
Henry Homan
Ridder's GC (A. 9)
Massachusetts
Geoffrey S. Cornish
Rideau View CC
Manotick, Ontario
Howard Watson
Rideau View CC (A. 9)
Ontario
Clinton E. Robinson

Ridenoor Park GC
Gahanna, Ohio
Jack Kidwell, Michael Hurdzan
Ridge CC
Chicago, Illinois
H.J. Tweedie
Ridge CC (R)
Illinois
Ken Killian, Dick Nugent
Ridge GC
Sedona, Arizona
Gary Panks
Ridgefield GC NLE
Connecticut
Tom Bendelow
Ridgefield Muni
Connecticut
George Fazio, Tom Fazio
Ridgefields CC
Kingsport, Tennessee
Donald Ross
Ridgefields CC (R)
Tennessee
John LaFoy
Ridgemark G&CC
Hollister, California
Richard Bigler
Ridgemont CC (R. 2)
New York
Brian Ault
Ridgemoor CC
Harwood Heights, Illinois
William B. Langford
Ridgemoor CC (R)
Illinois
William B. Langford, Theodore J.
  Moreau
Ridgemoor CC (R)
Illinois
Edward B. Dearie Jr
Ridgemoor CC (R)
Illinois
Edward Lawrence Packard
Ridgemoor CC (R)
Illinois
Edward Lawrence Packard,
  Roger Packard
Ridges Inn & CC
Wisconsin Rapids, Wisconsin
John Murgatroyd
Ridgeway CC (R. 9)
New York
Frank Duane
Ridgeway CC NLE
Memphis, Tennessee
William B. Langford
Ridgeway CC
Collierville, Tennessee
Ellis Maples, Ed Seay
Ridgeway CC (A. 9) NLE
Tennessee
William B. Langford
Ridgewood CC (R)
Connecticut
C.H. Anderson
Ridgewood CC (R)
Connecticut
Robert Trent Jones, Frank Duane
Ridgewood CC
New Jersey
A.W. Tillinghast
Ridgewood CC (R) NLE
New Jersey
Donald Ross
Ridgewood CC (R)
New Jersey
Rees Jones, Keith Evans
Ridgewood CC (R)
Texas
Ralph Plummer
Ridgewood Muni
Cleveland, Ohio
Sandy Alves
**Ridglea CC (Championship
  Course)**
Ft. Worth, Texas
Ralph Plummer
Ridglea CC (North Course)
Fort Worth, Texas
John Bredemus
**Ridglea CC (North Course) (R.
  6)**
Texas
Ralph Plummer

Riding Mountain GC (R. 9)
Manitoba
A.W. Creed
Riding Mountain GC (A. 9)
Manitoba
A.W. Creed
Rifle Creek GC
Colorado
Dick Phelps, Brad Benz,Mike
  Poellot
Rio del Mar GC (R)
California
Clark Glasson
Rio del Mar GC (R)
California
Bert Stamps
Rio Bravo GC
Bakersfield, California
Robert Muir Graves
Rio Grande Valley GC
Texas
Ralph Plummer
Rio Hondo CC
Downey, California
John Duncan Dunn
Rio Mar CC
Vero Beach, Florida
Herbert Strong
Rio Mar CC (A. 9)
Florida
Ernest E. Smith
Rio Mar GC
Palmer, Puerto Rico
George Fazio, Tom Fazio
Rio Pinar CC
Orlando, Florida
Mark Mahannah
Rio Rancho G&CC
Albuquerque, New Mexico
Desmond Muirhead
Rio Rico G&CC
Arizona
Robert Trent Jones Jr, Gary
  Roger Baird
**Rio Verde CC (Quail Run
  Course)**
Scottsdale, Arizona
Fred Bolton, Milt Coggins
**Rio Verde CC (Quail Run
  Course) (A. 9)**
Arizona
Jeff Hardin, Greg Nash
**Rio Verde CC (White Wing
  Course)**
Arizona
Fred Bolton, Milt Coggins
**Rio Verde CC (White Wing
  Course) (A. 9)**
Arizona
Jeff Hardin, Greg Nash
Rio Vista GC
Bridgeburg, Ontario
Stanley Thompson
Rip Van Winkle GC
Palenville, New York
Donald Ross
Ripon City GC
Yorkshire, England
George Lowe
Risebridge GC
Essex, England
Fred W. Hawtree
Rittwood CC
Butler, Pennsylvania
James Gilmore Harrison
Riva Dei Tessali GC
Taranto, Italy
M. Croze
**River Bend G&CC formerly
  known as Forest Lake CC**
Virginia
Edmund B. Ault, Al Jamison
River Bend GC
Story City, Iowa
Charles Calhoun
River Bend GC
New Bern, North Carolina
Gene Hamm
River Bend Muni
Red Deer, Alberta
William G. Robinson
River C
Pawley's Island, South Carolina
Tom Jackson

River Crest CC
Fort Worth, Texas
Tom Bendelow
River Crest CC (R)
Texas
Ralph Plummer
River Forest CC
Elmhurst, Illinois
Charles Maddox, *Frank P.
  MacDonald*
River Forest CC (R)
Illinois
Edward Lawrence Packard
River Greens GC
Avon Park, Florida
Jack Kidwell
River Greens GC
West Lafayette, Ohio
Jack Kidwell
River Hills CC
Lake Wylie, South Carolina
Willard Byrd
River Hills CC
Robstown, Texas
Leon Howard
River Island GC
Porterville, California
Bob Baldock
River Island GC (R)
California
Robert Muir Graves
River Island GC
Oconto Falls, Wisconsin
Edward Lawrence Packard
River North G&CC
Macon, Georgia
Arthur Davis, Ron Kirby,Gary
  Player
River Oaks CC
Grand Island, New York
Desmond Muirhead
River Oaks GC
Houston, Texas
Donald Ross
River Oaks CC (R)
Texas
Ralph Plummer
River Oaks CC (R)
Texas
Joseph S. Finger
River Oaks GC
Calumet City, Illinois
Ken Killian, Dick Nugent
River Oaks GC
Grandview, Missouri
Larry Runyon, Michael H. Malyn
River Oaks
Myrtle Beach, South Carolina
Gene Hamm
River Place CC
Austin, Texas
Jay Morrish, *Tom Kite*
River Plantation G&CC
Conroe, Texas
Jay Riviere
River Ranch GC
Lake Wales, Florida
Joe Lee
River Ridge CC
Bradley, Virginia
Jerry Turner
River Ridge GC
Oxnard, California
William F. Bell
River Run G Links
Bradenton, Florida
Ward Northrup
River Run GC
Kohler, Wisconsin
Pete Dye
River Vale CC
New Jersey
Orrin Smith
River Vale CC (R)
New Jersey
Hal Purdy
River Valley CC
Canton, Missouri
William Klinger
River Valley CC
Westfield, Pennsylvania
Geoffrey S. Cornish

River Wilderness Y&CC
Parrish, Florida
Ted McAnlis
River's Edge Y&CC
Fort Myers, Florida
Ron Garl
Riverbend CC
Tequesta, Florida
George Fazio, Tom Fazio
Riverbend CC
Sugarland, Texas
Press Maxwell
Riverbend CC (R)
Texas
Jay Riviere
Riverbend G&CC
Broderick, California
Jack Fleming
Riverbend G&CC (R)
North Dakota
Robert Bruce Harris
Riverbend G&CC
Miamiburg, Ohio
Robert Bruce Harris
Riverchase CC
Birmingham, Alabama
Joe Lee
Rivercliff GC
Bull Shoals, Arkansas
Earl Stone
Riverdale GC
Little Rock, Arkansas
Herman Hackbarth
Riverdale GC
Montana
George H. Schneiter
Riverdale GC (Dunes Course)
Brighton, Colorado
Perry Dye
Riverdale GC (Knolls Course)
Brighton, Colorado
Henry B. Hughes
Riverforest CC
Freeport, Pennsylvania
Wynn Tredway
Rivergreens GC
Gladstone, Oregon
John Junor
Riverhill C
Kerrville, Texas
Joseph S. Finger, Byron Nelson
Riverlands G&CC
LaPlace, Louisiana
John Schneider, Henry Thomas
Rivermont G&CC
Alpharetta, Georgia
Joe Lee, Rocky Roquemore
Rivermont G&CC (R)
Georgia
Bill Amick
Rivers Bend GC
Everett, Pennsylvania
X.G. Hassenplug
Rivers Bend GC
Germantown, Wisconsin
Roger Packard
Rivershore GC
Kamloops, British Columbia
Robert Trent Jones, Roger
  Rulewich
Riverside C
Grand Prairie, Texas
Roger Packard
Riverside CC
Menominee, Michigan
Tom Bendelow
Riverside CC
Menominee, Michigan
A.H. Jolly
Riverside CC
Battle Creek, Michigan
Bruce Matthews, Jerry Matthews
Riverside CC (R. 9)
Michigan
Roger Packard
Riverside CC (A. 9)
Michigan
Roger Packard
Riverside CC
Bozeman, Montana
Herbert J. Hasch
Riverside CC (A. 9)
Montana
Dick Phelps, Brad Benz

Riverside CC
Carlsbad, New Mexico
William H. Tucker, William H.
Tucker Jr
Riverside CC (A. 9)
New Mexico
Brad Benz, Mike Poellot,Mark
Rathert
Riverside CC (R. 9)
New Mexico
Brad Benz, Mike Poellot,Mark
Rathert
Riverside CC
Syracuse, New York
Edward Lawrence Packard
Riverside CC
Robbins, North Carolina
J. Porter Gibson
Riverside CC
Lake Jackson, Texas
Ralph Plummer
Riverside CC
Provo, Utah
William F. Bell, William H. Neff
Riverside G&CC
Coyote, California
Jack Fleming
Riverside G&CC (A. 9)
California
William F. Bell
Riverside G&CC
Macon, Georgia
Chic Adams
Riverside G&CC
Swea City, Iowa
George Morton
Riverside G&CC
Portland, Oregon
H. Chandler Egan
Riverside G&CC (R)
Oregon
William F. Bell
Riverside G&CC (R)
New Brunswick
Clinton E. Robinson
Riverside G&CC (R)
New Brunswick
Donald Ross
Riverside G&CC
Saskatoon, Saskatchewan
William Kinnear
Riverside G&CC (R)
Saskatchewan
William G. Robinson
Riverside GC
Riverside, California
Edward Newkirk
Riverside GC (R. 9)
California
William P. Bell
Riverside GC (A. 9)
California
William P. Bell
Riverside GC
North Riverside, Illinois
William B. Langford
Riverside GC (R)
Illinois
William B. Langford
Riverside GC (R)
Illinois
Edward Lawrence Packard
Riverside GC
St. Francis, Kansas
Herman R. Johnson
Riverside GC
Bozeman, Montana
Theodore Wirth
**Riverside GC formerly known as
CC of Austin**
Austin, Texas
Perry Maxwell, Press Maxwell
Riverside GC
San Antonio, Texas
George Hoffman
Riverside GC
Ogden, Utah
Ernest Schneiter
Riverside Inn & CC
Pennsylvania
William Baird
Riverside Muni
Indianapolis, Indiana
William H. Diddel

Riverside Muni
Portland, Maine
Wayne Stiles
Riverside Muni (R)
Maine
William F. Mitchell
Riverside Muni (A. 9)
Maine
Geoffrey S. Cornish, William G.
Robinson
Riverside Muni
Jackson, Mississippi
Earl Stone
Riverside Muni
Victoria, Texas
Ralph Plummer
Riverside Muni (R)
Texas
Jay Riviere
Riverside Muni
Janesville, Wisconsin
Robert Bruce Harris
Riverside Park NLE
San Antonio, Texas
George Hoffman
Riverton CC
New Jersey
Donald Ross
Riverton CC
Wyoming
Richard Watson
Riverton CC (A. 9)
Wyoming
Dick Phelps, Brad Benz,Mike
Poellot
Riverton CC (R. 9)
Wyoming
Dick Phelps, Brad Benz,Mike
Poellot
Riverton GC
Henrietta, New York
Edmund B. Ault
Riverview CC
Milford, Connecticut
Al Zikorus
Riverview CC
Missouri
Robert Foulis
Riverview CC
Cleburne, Texas
Leon Howard
Riverview GC
Mesa, Arizona
Gary Panks
Riverview GC
Sun City, Arizona
*James Winans, John W. Meeker,*Jeff
Hardin
Riverview GC
Pennsylvania
Royce Hewitt
Riverview Highlands GC
Riverview, Michigan
William Newcomb
Riverview Highlands GC (A. 9)
Michigan
Arthur Hills, Steve Forrest
Riverview Muni
Sterling, Colorado
Frank Hummel
Riverwood GC
Dundee, Oregon
George Junor
Riverwood GC
Port Arthur, Texas
John Barlow
Riverwood Muni
Bismarck, North Dakota
Leo Johnson
Riviera Africaine GC
Ivory Coast
Arthur Davis, Ron Kirby,Gary
Player
Riviera CC
California
George C. Thomas Jr, William P.
Bell
**Riviera CC formerly known as
Miami Biltmore GC (South
Course)**
Coral Gables, Florida
Donald Ross

Riviera CC (R)
Florida
Lloyd Clifton
Riviera CC (R)
Florida
Mark Mahannah
Riviera CC (R)
Florida
Dick Wilson
Riviera CC (A. 9)
Florida
David Wallace
Riviera CC (A. 9)
West Virginia
Buck Blankenship
Riviera Marin GC
San Rafael, California
William F. Bell
Riviere Du Loup GC (A. 9)
Quebec
Howard Watson, John Watson
Riviere Du Loup GC (R. 9)
Quebec
Howard Watson, John Watson
Roadhaven GC
Bullhead City, Arizona
Greg Nash
Roadrunner Dunes GC
Borrego Springs, California
Lawrence Hughes
Roan Valley CC
Mountain City, Tennessee
Ellis Maples, Dan Maples
Roanoke CC
Williamston, North Carolina
Ellis Maples
Roanoke CC NLE
Virginia
Alex Findlay
Roanoke CC (R)
Virginia
A.W. Tillinghast
Roanoke CC (R. 5)
Virginia
Tom Clark
Roaring Gap G&CC
North Carolina
Donald Ross
Rob Roy GC
Illinois
Edward B. Dearie Jr
Robber's Roost GC
North Myrtle Beach, South
Carolina
Russell Breeden
Robbinhead Lakes GC
Brandon, Mississippi
Sonny Guy
Robert A. Black GC
Chicago, Illinois
Ken Killian, Dick Nugent,Jeff
Brauer
Robert Van Patten GC
New York
Armand Farina
Robin Hood CC NLE
Illinois
George O'Neill
Robin Hood GC (R)
England
H.S. Colt
Robstown CC
Texas
Warren Cantrell
Roca Llisa GC
Ibiza, Spain
Fred W. Hawtree
Rochdale GC (R)
England
J.J.F. Pennink
Roche Harbor GC
San Juan, Washington
William H. Tucker, Frank
James,Gregor MacMillan
Rochelle CC
Illinois
Perry Maxwell
Rochelle CC (A. 9)
Illinois
David Gill
Rochelle CC (R. 9)
Illinois
David Gill

Rochester City GC
Indiana
James R. Neidigh
Rochester CC (R)
New Hampshire
Manny Francis
Rochester CC (R)
New Hampshire
Orrin Smith, William F. Mitchell
Rochester CC (A. 9)
New Hampshire
Phil Wogan
Rochester G&CC (R. 9)
Minnesota
A.W. Tillinghast
Rochester G&CC (A. 9)
Minnesota
A.W. Tillinghast
Rochester GC
Michigan
Tom Bendelow
Rochford Hundred GC (R)
England
F.G. Hawtree
Rock Barn GC
Conover, North Carolina
Russell Breeden
Rock Creek G&CC
Jacksonville, North Carolina
Jerry Turner
Rock Creek G&CC
Oregon
William Sander
Rock Creek Park GC (R)
Washington, D.C.
William S. Flynn
Rock Hill CC
South Carolina
A.W. Tillinghast
Rock Hill CC (A. 9)
South Carolina
J. Porter Gibson
Rock Hill G&CC
Manorville, New York
Frank Duane
Rock Island Arsenal C (R)
Illinois
David Gill
Rock Island CC NLE
Blue Island, Illinois
Tom Bendelow
Rock Island State Park GC
Tennessee
Benjamin Wihry
Rock River CC
Sterling, Illinois
William James Spear
Rock River Hills GC
Horizon, Wisconsin
Homer Fieldhouse
Rock River Hills GC (A. 9)
Wisconsin
Bob Lohmann
Rock Spring CC
New Jersey
Charles Banks
Rock Spring CC (R)
New Jersey
Hal Purdy
Rock Springs CC
Alton, Illinois
Tom Bendelow
Rockaway Hunting C NLE
Cedarhurst, New York
Willie Dunn Jr
Rockaway Hunting C
Cedarhurst, New York
Devereux Emmet
Rockaway Hunting C (A. 9) NLE
New York
Tom Bendelow
Rockaway Hunting C (R)
New York
A.W. Tillinghast
Rockaway Hunting C (A. 7)
New York
A.W. Tillinghast
Rockaway Hunting C (R)
New York
Perry Maxwell
Rockaway Hunting C (R)
New York
Press Maxwell

Rockaway Hunting C (R)
New York
Brian Silva, Geoffrey S. Cornish
Rockaway River CC (R)
New Jersey
Hal Purdy, Malcolm Purdy
Rockaway River CC (A. 9)
New Jersey
George Low Sr
Rockdale CC
Texas
Leon Howard
Rockfish CC
Hope Mills, North Carolina
C.C. McCuiston
Rockford CC
Illinois
H.J. Tweedie
Rockford CC (R)
Illinois
C.D. Wagstaff
Rockford G&CC
Iowa
Beryl Taylor
Rockland CC
Massachusetts
Phil Wogan
Rockland CC (R)
New York
Robert Trent Jones
Rockland CC (R. 9)
New York
Robert White
Rockland CC (R)
New York
Alfred H. Tull
**Rockland Lake GC (North
Course)**
Congers, New York
David Gordon
**Rockland Lake GC (South
Course)**
Congers, New York
David Gordon
Rockledge CC (R)
Connecticut
William F. Mitchell
Rockledge CC (R. 9)
Connecticut
Orrin Smith, Al Zikorus
Rockledge CC (A. 9)
Connecticut
Orrin Smith
Rockleigh GC (Bergen Course)
Hackensack, New Jersey
William Gordon, David Gordon
**Rockleigh GC (Bergen Course)
(R)**
New Jersey
Robert Trent Jones
**Rockleigh GC (Rockleigh
Course)**
Hackensack, New Jersey
Alfred H. Tull
**Rockleigh GC (Rockleigh
Course) (R)**
New Jersey
William Gordon, David Gordon
Rockport CC
Texas
Bill Coore
Rockport GC (R. 2)
Massachusetts
Phil Wogan
Rockrimmon CC
Stamford, Connecticut
Robert Trent Jones
Rockrimmon CC (A. 9)
Connecticut
Orrin Smith, Al Zikorus
Rockville CC
New York
Devereux Emmet
Rockville CC (R. 1)
New York
Frank Duane
Rockville Lake GC
Indiana
William H. Diddel
Rockwell College GC
Ireland
Eddie Hackett

Rockwood CC
Independence, Missouri
John S. Davis
Rockwood CC (A. 9)
Missouri
Charles Dupree
Rockwood Hall CC
Tarrytown, New York
Devereux Emmet, Alfred H. Tull
Rockwood Hall CC (R)
New York
A.W. Tillinghast
Rockwood Hall CC (A. 5)
New York
A.W. Tillinghast
Rockwood Muni
Fort Worth, Texas
John Bredemus
Rockwood Muni (A. 9)
Texas
Ralph Plummer
Rockwood Muni (R.18)
Texas
Ralph Plummer
Rockwood Park GC (A. 3)
New Brunswick
William G. Robinson, John F. Robinson
Rocky Bayou CC
Niceville, Florida
Bill Amick
Rocky Point GC
Tampa, Florida
Willie Black
Rocky Point GC
Tampa, Florida
Ron Garl
Rocky Point GC (R)
Florida
Hans Schmeisser
Rocky Point GC (A. 9)
Florida
David Wallace
Rocky Point GC
Essex, Maryland
Russell Roberts
Rocky Point GC (R)
Maryland
Orrin Smith, William F. Mitchell
Rocky Ridge CC
Vermont
Walter Barcomb
Rodgers Forge CC
Baltimore, Maryland
Herbert Strong, George Low Sr
Roehampton GC
London, England
Tom Simpson
Rogers Park GC
Tampa, Florida
Willie Black
Rogers Park GC (R)
Florida
Ron Garl
Rogue River GC
Sparta, Michigan
Warner Bowen
Rogue Valley CC
Medford, Oregon
H. Chandler Egan
Rogue Valley CC (R. 9)
Oregon
William F. Bell, William P. Bell
Rogue Valley CC (A. 9)
Oregon
William F. Bell, William P. Bell
Rokko International GC
Hyogo, Japan
F. Kato
Rolling Acres CC
Beaver Falls, Pennsylvania
James Gilmore Harrison, Ferdinand Garbin
Rolling Acres CC (A. 9)
Pennsylvania
Ferdinand Garbin
Rolling Green CC
Prattville, Alabama
R. Albert Anderson
Rolling Green CC
Arlington Heights, Illinois
William H. Diddel

Rolling Green CC (R. 6)
Illinois
David Gill
Rolling Green CC
Hamel, Minnesota
Charles Maddox
Rolling Green CC
Springfield, Pennsylvania
William S. Flynn, Howard Toomey
Rolling Green CC
Green River, Wyoming
Henry B. Hughes
Rolling Green G&CC
Sarasota, Florida
R. Albert Anderson
Rolling Green G&CC (A. 9)
Florida
Bill Dietsch
Rolling Green GC
Huntsburg, Ohio
Richard W. LaConte
Rolling Greens GC
Newton, New Jersey
Nicholas Psiahas
Rolling Hills CC
Tucson, Arizona
William F. Bell
Rolling Hills CC
Rolling Hills Estate, California
Ted Robinson
Rolling Hills CC
Golden, Colorado
Press Maxwell
Rolling Hills CC
Wilton, Connecticut
Alfred H. Tull
Rolling Hills CC (R. 5)
Connecticut
Brian Ault, Tom Clark
Rolling Hills CC
Ft. Lauderdale, Florida
William F. Mitchell
Rolling Hills CC (A. 9)
Florida
Bill Dietsch
Rolling Hills CC
Newburgh, Indiana
William H. Diddel
Rolling Hills CC
Wichita, Kansas
Walter Angle
Rolling Hills CC (R)
Kansas
Floyd Farley
Rolling Hills CC
Crystal Springs, Mississippi
George C. Curtis
Rolling Hills CC
Monroe, North Carolina
George W. Cobb
Rolling Hills CC (A)
North Carolina
George W. Cobb, John LaFoy
Rolling Hills CC (R)
North Carolina
John LaFoy
Rolling Hills CC
Tulsa, Oklahoma
Perry Maxwell
Rolling Hills CC (R)
Oklahoma
Floyd Farley
Rolling Hills CC
Pittsburgh, Pennsylvania
James Gilmore Harrison, Ferdinand Garbin
Rolling Hills CC
Moody, Texas
Leon Howard
Rolling Hills CC
Arlington, Texas
C.M. Mimms
Rolling Hills GC NLE
Tempe, Arizona
Milt Coggins
Rolling Hills GC
Tempe, Arizona
Gary Panks
Rolling Hills GC (A. 9)
Arizona
Gary Panks

Rolling Hills GC
California
William F. Bell, William P. Bell
Rolling Hills GC
Weisner, Idaho
Frank James
Rolling Hills GC (R)
Illinois
Gary Kern
Rolling Hills GC
Ionia, Michigan
Warner Bowen
Rolling Hills GC
Washington
Donald A. Hogan
Rolling Hills Par 3 GC NLE
Massachusetts
Rowland Armacost
Rolling Meadows GC
Junction City, Kansas
Richard Watson, Keith Evans
Rolling Road GC
Baltimore, Maryland
Willie Park Jr
Rolling Rock GC
Ligonier, Pennsylvania
Donald Ross
Roman Hills GC
Splendora, Texas
Jay Riviere
Roman Nose State Park GC
Watonga, Oklahoma
Floyd Farley
Romford GC
England
James Braid
Romsey GC (R)
England
J.J.F. Pennink, C.D. Lawrie
Rondout GC
Accord, New York
Hal Purdy
Roodepoort Muni
South Africa
Ron Kirby, Gary Player, Denis Griffiths
Rookery Park GC
Suffolk, England
J.J.F. Pennink, C.D. Lawrie
Roosevelt Muni
Utah
Joseph B. Williams
Rosapenna GC
County Donegal, Ireland
Old Tom Morris
Rosapenna GC (R)
Ireland
James Braid
Rosapenna GC (R)
Ireland
H.S. Colt
Roscommon GC (R)
Ireland
Eddie Hackett
Roscrea GC (R)
Ireland
Eddie Hackett
Rose City GC
Portland, Oregon
George Otten
Rose Hill GC
Hilton Head Island, South Carolina
Gene Hamm
Rose Hill GC
Birmingham, England
Carl Bretherston
Rose Park GC
Salt Lake City, Utah
Mick Riley
Rose Park GC (A. 9)
Utah
William F. Bell, William H. Neff
Rose Park GC (R. 5)
Utah
Arthur Jack Snyder
Roseburg CC
Oregon
George Junor
Roseburg CC (A. 9)
Oregon
Gary Roger Baird

Roseburg CC (R. 9)
Oregon
Gary Roger Baird
Rosedale CC (R)
Ontario
Clinton E. Robinson
Rosedale CC (R)
Ontario
Donald Ross
Rosedale CC (R)
Ontario
Howard Watson
Roseland G&CC
Windsor, Ontario
Donald Ross
Roselawn GC
Danville, Illinois
Tom Bendelow
Roselle CC
New Jersey
Seth Raynor
Rosemere G&CC (R. 3)
Quebec
John Watson
Rosemont G&CC
Winter Park, Florida
Lloyd Clifton
Rosemont GC
Akron, Ohio
Tom Bendelow
Rosemont GC (A. 9)
Ohio
Edward Lawrence Packard
Rosendaelsche GC
Arnhem, Netherlands
John Duncan Dunn
Rosendaelsche GC (A. 9)
Netherlands
J.J.F. Pennink
Rosendaelsche GC (R. 9)
Netherlands
J.J.F. Pennink
Roseneath Farms GC
Pennsylvania
Alex Findlay
Roseville Rolling Green GC
California
Jack Fleming
Roskilde GC
Denmark
Jan Sederholm
Ross on Wye GC
England
C.K. Cotton, J.J.F. Pennink
Ross Hill Muni
Annadale, Virginia
Leon Howard
Ross Rogers Muni NLE
Amarillo, Texas
William A. McConnell
Ross Rogers Muni (Course No. 1)
Amarillo, Texas
Leon Howard
Ross Rogers Muni (Course No. 2)
Amarillo, Texas
Leon Howard, *Charles Howard*
Rossland Trail CC (Birchbank Course)
Trail, British Columbia
Reg Stone
Rosslare GC (R)
Ireland
J. Hamilton Stutt
Rossmere G&CC
Winnipeg, Manitoba
Norman H. Woods
Rossmoor CC (North Course)
Walnut Creek, California
Robert Muir Graves
Rossmoor CC (South Course)
Walnut Creek, California
Harry Rainville, David Rainville
Rossmoor GC
Jamesburg, New Jersey
Desmond Muirhead
Rossmoor Leisure World GC
Rossmoor, California
Desmond Muirhead
Rossmoor Leisure World GC
Silver Spring, Maryland
Desmond Muirhead

Rossmore GC (R)
Ireland
Eddie Hackett
Rosswood CC
Pine Bluff, Arkansas
Alfred H. Tull
Rothesay GC
Island of Bute, Scotland
James Braid
Rothley Park GC
Leicestershire, England
Tom Williamson
Rothschild Estate GC
France
Seymour Dunn
Rotorua GC
New Zealand
Charles H. Redhead
Rotterdamsche GC (R)
Netherlands
John Harris
Rough River State Park GC
Falls of Rough, Kentucky
Benjamin Wihry
Round Hill C
Greenwich, Connecticut
Walter J. Travis
Round Hill C (R)
Connecticut
Robert Trent Jones
Round Hill CC
East Sandwich, Massachusetts
Sam Volpe
Round Hill G&CC
Alamo, California
Lawrence Hughes
Round Hill G&CC (R)
California
Robert Muir Graves
Round Meadow CC
Christiansburg, Virginia
J. Porter Gibson
Round Valley CC
Utah
Mark Dixon Ballif
Routenburn GC
Ayrshire, Scotland
James Braid
Rowlands Castle GC
England
H.S. Colt
Rowley CC
Massachusetts
Phil Wogan
Roxboro CC (A. 9)
North Carolina
Ellis Maples, Ed Seay
Roxbury Run GC
Denver, New York
Hal Purdy, Malcolm Purdy
Roxiticus CC
Mendham, New Jersey
Hal Purdy
Roy Rogers GC
Chatsworth, California
William H. Johnson
Royal Aberdeen GC
Scotland
Archie Simpson
Royal Aberdeen GC (R)
Scotland
Tom Simpson
Royal Aberdeen GC (Ladies Course)
Scotland
J.J.F. Pennink
Royal Adelaide GC (R)
Australia
Peter Thomson, Michael Wolveridge
Royal Adelaide GC (R)
Australia
Des Soutar
Royal Adelaide GC (A. 4)
Australia
Des Soutar
Royal Adelaide GC (R)
Australia
Alister Mackenzie
Royal Antwerp GC
Kapellenbos, Belgium
Willie Park Jr

Royal Antwerp GC (R.18)
Belgium
P.M. Ross
Royal Antwerp GC (A. 9)
Belgium
Tom Simpson, P.M. Ross
Royal Ascot GC
Berkshire, England
J.H. Taylor
Royal Ashdown Forest GC (Blue Course)
Sussex, England
A.T. Scott
Royal Ashdown Forest GC (Red Course)
Sussex, England
A.T. Scott
Royal Belfast GC
Northern Ireland
H.S. Colt
Royal Belgique GC (R)
Belgium
Wilfrid Reid
Royal Bhutan GC
Thimphu, Bhutan
Stephen Kay
Royal Birkdale GC
Southport, England
George Lowe, Charles Hawtree
Royal Birkdale GC (R)
England
F.G. Hawtree, J.H. Taylor
Royal Birkdale GC (R)
England
Fred W. Hawtree
Royal Birkdale GC (R)
England
Fred W. Hawtree
Royal Blackheath GC
England
James Braid, John R. Stutt
Royal Blackheath GC (R) NLE
England
Willie Dunn
Royal Brunei Polo C
Jerudong Park, Brunei
Ronald Fream
Royal Burgess G Society of Edinburgh
Scotland
Old Tom Morris
Royal Burgess G Society of Edinburgh (R)
Scotland
Willie Park Jr
Royal Burgess G Society of Edinburgh (R)
Scotland
James Braid
Royal Calcutta GC (R)
India
Peter Thomson, Michael Wolveridge
Royal Canberra GC
Yarralumia, Australia
John Harris
Royal Canberra GC (R)
Australia
Peter Thomson, Michael Wolveridge
Royal Cinque Ports GC
Deal, England
Tom Dunn
Royal Cinque Ports GC (R)
England
Sir Guy Campbell, Henry Cotton
Royal Colwood G&CC
Victoria, British Columbia
A. Vernon Macan
Royal County Down GC
Newcastle, Northern Ireland
Old Tom Morris
Royal County Down GC (R)
Northern Ireland
C.S. Butchart
Royal County Down GC (R)
Northern Ireland
Seymour Dunn
Royal County Down GC (R)
Northern Ireland
Harry Vardon
Royal County Down GC (R)
Northern Ireland
Harry Vardon

Royal County Down GC (Course No. 2)
Newcastle, Northern Ireland
C.S. Butchart
Royal Cromer GC
Norfolk, England
James Braid
Royal CC de Tangier
Morocco
J.J.F. Pennink
Royal Dornoch GC
Sutherland, Scotland
Old Tom Morris
Royal Dornoch GC (R. 9)
Scotland
John Sutherland
Royal Dornoch GC (A. 9)
Scotland
John Sutherland
Royal Dornoch GC (R)
Scotland
J.H. Taylor
Royal Dornoch GC (A. 2)
Scotland
Donald Ross
Royal Dornoch GC (R)
Scotland
Donald Ross
Royal Dornoch GC (A. 4)
Scotland
George Duncan
Royal Dornoch GC (R)
Scotland
George Duncan
Royal Downs GC
Thornhill, Ontario
Renee Muylaert
Royal Dublin GC (R)
Ireland
Sir Guy Campbell
Royal Dublin GC (R)
Ireland
H.S. Colt, C.H. Alison
Royal Dublin GC (R. 2)
Ireland
Eddie Hackett
Royal Eastbourne GC
Sussex, England
Horace Hutchinson, Charles Mayhewe
Royal Eastbourne GC (R)
England
J. Hamilton Stutt
Royal G d'Evian
Evian, France
Willie Park Jr
Royal G d'Evian (R)
France
Robert Berthet
Royal G Dar Es Salaam (Blue Course)
Rabat, Morocco
Robert Trent Jones, Cabell Robinson
Royal G Dar Es Salaam (Green Course)
Rabat, Morocco
Robert Trent Jones, Cabell Robinson
Royal G Dar Es Salaam (Red Course)
Rabat, Morocco
Robert Trent Jones, Cabell Robinson
Royal Green GC
Utah
Keith Downs
Royal Guernsey GC
Channel Islands
P.M. Ross
Royal GC de Belgique
Brussels, Belgium
Seymour Dunn
Royal GC de Belgique (R)
Belgium
Tom Simpson
Royal GC du Sart Tilman
Liege, Belgium
Tom Simpson
Royal GC Des Fagnes
Balmoral Spa, Belgium
Tom Simpson, P.M. Ross
Royal GC Les Buttes Blanches (R. 3)
Belgium
Fred W. Hawtree

Royal Hong Kong GC (Eden Course)
Fanling, Hong Kong
John Harris, Peter Thomson,Michael Wolveridge
Royal Hong Kong GC (New Course)
Hong Kong
L.S. Greenhill
Royal Hong Kong GC (New Course) (R)
Hong Kong
Peter Thomson, Michael Wolveridge
Royal Hong Kong GC (Old Course)
Hong Kong
Capt. H.N. Dumbleton
Royal Hong Kong GC (Old Course) (R)
Hong Kong
Peter Thomson, Michael Wolveridge
Royal Hylands GC
Knightstown, Indiana
Gary Kern
Royal Johannesburg CC (East Course)
South Africa
Robert G. Grimsdell
Royal Johannesburg GC (West Course)
South Africa
Laurie Waters
Royal Johannesburg GC (West Course) (R)
South Africa
Ron Kirby, Denis Griffiths
Royal Kaanapali GC (North Course)
Maui, Hawaii
Robert Trent Jones
Royal Kaanapali GC (South Course)
Maui, Hawaii
Arthur Jack Snyder
Royal Liverpool GC
Hoylake, England
Robert Chambers Jr, George Morris
Royal Liverpool GC (R)
England
H.S. Colt
Royal Liverpool GC (R)
England
J.J.F. Pennink
Royal Liverpool GC (R)
England
Fred W. Hawtree
Royal Lytham & St. Annes GC
Lancashire, England
George Lowe
Royal Lytham & St. Annes GC (R)
England
Tom Simpson
Royal Lytham & St. Annes GC (R)
England
Herbert Fowler
Royal Lytham & St. Annes GC (R. 2)
England
Thomas Simpson
Royal Lytham & St. Annes GC (R)
England
H.S. Colt, C.H. Alison
Royal Lytham & St. Annes GC (R)
England
H.S. Colt, J.S.F. Morrison,J.S.F. Morrison
Royal Lytham & St. Annes GC (R)
England
C.K. Cotton, J.J.F. Pennink
Royal Lytham & St. Annes GC (Short Crs)
Lancashire, England
J.J.F. Pennink, C.D. Lawrie
Royal Melbourne GC (East Course)
Black Rock, Australia
Alex Russell

Royal Melbourne GC (East Course) (R)
Australia
Dick Wilson
Royal Melbourne GC (West Course)
Black Rock, Australia
Alister Mackenzie, Alex Russell
Royal Melbourne GC (West Course) (R)
Australia
Dick Wilson
Royal Mid-Surrey GC
Surrey, England
Tom Dunn
Royal Mid-Surrey GC (R)
England
Reginald Beale
Royal Mid-Surrey GC (R)
England
J.H. Taylor
Royal Mid-Surrey GC (R. 3)
England
Fred W. Hawtree, Martin Hawtree
Royal Mid-Surrey GC (Ladies Course)
England
J.H. Taylor
Royal Montreal GC (Black Course)
Ile Bizard, Quebec
Dick Wilson, Bob Simmons
Royal Montreal GC (Blue Course)
Ile Bizard, Quebec
Dick Wilson, Bob Simmons
Royal Montreal GC (North Course) NLE
Dixie, Quebec
Willie Park Jr
Royal Montreal GC (Red Course)
Ile Bizard, Quebec
Dick Wilson, Bob Simmons
Royal Montreal GC (South Course)
Dixie, Quebec
Willie Dunn Jr
Royal Montreal GC (South Course) (R)
Quebec
H.S. Colt
Royal Montreal GC (South Course) (R) NLE
Quebec
Willie Park Jr
Royal Musselburgh GC
East Lothian, Scotland
James Braid, John R. Stutt
Royal Musselburgh GC (R)
Scotland
Mungo Park II
Royal North Devon GC
Westward Ho!, England
Old Tom Morris
Royal North Devon GC (R)
England
Herbert Fowler
Royal Oak G&CC
Titusville, Florida
Dick Wilson, Robert von Hagge
Royal Oak GC
Michigan
Bruce Matthews, Jerry Matthews
Royal Oak Inn GC
Victoria, British Columbia
James P. Izatt
Royal Oaks CC
Chapel Hill, North Carolina
Gene Hamm
Royal Oaks CC
Dallas, Texas
Don January, Billy Martindale
Royal Oaks CC (R)
Texas
Arthur Davis
Royal Oaks CC
Vancouver, Washington
Fred Federspiel
Royal Oaks CC (R. 2)
Washington
Ted Robinson

Royal Oaks CC (R)
Washington
Robert Muir Graves
Royal Oaks GC NLE
Clayton, California
Robert Muir Graves
Royal Oaks GC
Cartersville, Georgia
Arthur Davis, Ron Kirby,Gary Player
Royal Ottawa GC
Hull, Quebec
Tom Bendelow
Royal Ottawa GC (R)
Quebec
Clinton E. Robinson
Royal Ottawa GC (R.27)
Quebec
Howard Watson
Royal Ottawa GC (A. 9)
Quebec
Howard Watson
Royal Ottawa GC (R. 4)
Quebec
John Watson
Royal Ottawa GC (A. 2)
Quebec
John Watson
Royal Palm Beach G&CC
Palm Beach, Florida
Mark Mahannah
Royal Palm Hotel GC NLE
Fort Myers, Florida
John M. "Jock" Inglis
Royal Palm Y&CC
Boca Raton, Florida
Robert Trent Jones, Frank Duane
Royal Palms Inn & C
Mesa, Arizona
David Gill
Royal Park G&CC NLE
Vero Beach, Florida
Herbert Strong
Royal Perth GC
Australia
S. Cohen
Royal Perth GC (R)
Australia
Peter Thomson, Michael Wolveridge
Royal Pine G&CC
Pinewald, New Jersey
Conrad Schupkagel
Royal Pines CC (Marsh Course)
South Carolina
Walter I. Rodgers
Royal Pines CC (Pines Course)
South Carolina
Walter I. Rodgers
Royal Poinciana GC (Cypress Course)
Naples, Florida
David Wallace
Royal Poinciana GC (Pines Course)
Naples, Florida
David Wallace
Royal Port Alfred GC (R)
South Africa
S.V. Hotchkin
Royal Porthcawl GC
Mid Glamorgan, Wales
Charles Gibson
Royal Porthcawl GC (R)
Wales
James Braid
Royal Porthcawl GC (R)
Wales
H.S. Colt
Royal Porthcawl GC (A. 4)
Wales
F.G. Hawtree, J.H. Taylor
Royal Porthcawl GC (R)
Wales
F.G. Hawtree, J.H. Taylor
Royal Porthcawl GC (R)
Wales
Tom Simpson
Royal Porthcawl GC (R)
Wales
C.K. Cotton
Royal Portrush GC (Dunluce Course) (R)
Northern Ireland
H.S. Colt

Royal Portrush GC (Dunluce Course) (R)
Northern Ireland
J.S.F. Morrison, H.S. Colt
Royal Portrush GC (Valley Course) (R)
Northern Ireland
H.S. Colt
Royal Portrush GC (Valley Course) (R)
Northern Ireland
J.S.F. Morrison, H.S. Colt
Royal Quebec CC (Kent Course) NLE
Montgomery Falls, Quebec
Albert Murray
Royal Quebec CC (Kent Course) NLE
Quebec
Herbert Strong
Royal Quebec CC (Quebec Course)
Boischatel, Quebec
Howard Watson
Royal Quebec CC (Quebec Course) (R. 9)
Quebec
Howard Watson, John Watson
Royal Quebec CC (Royal Course)
Boischatel, Quebec
Willie Park Jr
Royal Quebec CC (Royal Course) (A. 2)
Quebec
Howard Watson, John Watson
Royal Queensland GC (R)
Australia
Alister Mackenzie
Royal Salisbury GC
Zimbabwe
Laurie Waters
Royal Salisbury GC (R)
Zimbabwe
Fred W. Hawtree
Royal Salisbury GC (A. 2)
Zimbabwe
Fred W. Hawtree
Royal Scot CC
Green Bay, Wisconsin
Don Herfort
Royal Selangor GC (New Course)
Kuala Lumpur, Malaysia
J.J.F. Pennink
Royal Selangor GC (New Course) (R)
Malaysia
Ronald Fream
Royal Selangor GC (Old Course) (R)
Malaysia
C.H. Alison, H.S. Colt
Royal Selangor GC (Old Course) (R)
Malaysia
Ronald Fream
Royal St. Davids GC
Harlech, Wales
Harold Finch-Hatton
Royal St. Davids GC (R)
Wales
Fred W. Hawtree
Royal St. George's GC
Kent, England
W. Laidlaw Purves
Royal St. George's GC (R)
England
Alister Mackenzie
Royal St. George's GC (R)
England
J.J.F. Pennink
Royal St. Kitts GC
St. Kitts
John Harris, Peter Thomson,Michael Wolveridge, Ronald Fream
Royal Swan CC
Betterton, Maryland
Alex Findlay
Royal Sydney GC
Australia
S.R. Robbie
Royal Sydney GC (R)
Australia
Peter Thomson, Michael Wolveridge

Royal Sydney GC (R)
Australia
Alister Mackenzie
Royal Tara GC (R)
Ireland
Eddie Hackett
Royal Tara GC (R. 9)
Ireland
John Harris
Royal Tara GC (A. 9)
Ireland
John Harris
Royal Tee CC
Cape Coral, Florida
Gordon G. Lewis
Royal Troon GC formerly known as Troon GC
Ayrshire, Scotland
Charles Hunter
Royal Troon GC (R)
Scotland
Alister Mackenzie
Royal Troon GC (R)
Scotland
Willie Fernie
Royal Troon GC (R)
Scotland
James Braid
Royal Waterloo GC NLE
Belgium
H.S. Colt, C.H. Alison
Royal Waterloo GC (Course No. 1)
Ohain, Belgium
Fred W. Hawtree
Royal Waterloo GC (Course No. 2)
Ohain, Belgium
Fred W. Hawtree
Royal West Norfolk GC
Norfolk, England
Horace Hutchinson, Holcombe Ingleby
Royal West Norfolk GC (R)
England
C.K. Hutchison, Sir Guy Campbell,S.V. Hotchkin
Royal Wimbledon GC
Surrey, England
H.S. Colt
Royal Wimbledon GC (R)
England
J.J.F. Pennink, C.D. Lawrie
Royal Worlington and Newmarket GC
Suffolk, England
Tom Dunn
Royal Worlington and Newmarket GC (R. 9)
England
H.S. Colt
Royal Zoute GC
Belgium
Seymour Dunn
Royale Green GC
Coldspring, Texas
Bruce Littell
Royan GC
France
Robert Berthet
Royston GC
England
Tom Dunn
Rozella Ford GC
Warsaw, Indiana
William H. Diddel
Ruby View Muni NLE
Elko, Nevada
Pete Marich
Ruby View Muni
Elko, Nevada
Arthur Jack Snyder
Ruislip GC
Middlesex, England
F.G. Hawtree, J.H. Taylor
Ruislip GC (A. 9)
England
John R. Stutt
Ruma CC
Zimbabwe
Laurie Waters, *George Waterman*
Runaway Bay CC
St. Annes, Jamaica
John Harris

Rungsted GC
Kyst, Denmark
Charles A. Mackenzie
Rungsted GC (R)
Denmark
Jan Sederholm
Running Fox GC
Chillicothe, Ohio
Lawrence T. Cox
Running Hills CC
Frye Island, Maine
Geoffrey S. Cornish, William G. Robinson
Rush GC
Dublin, Ireland
John Temple
Rush GC (R)
Ireland
Eddie Hackett
Rush Lake GC
Pinckney, Michigan
Robert Herndon
Rushcliffe GC
Nottinghamshire, England
Tom Williamson
Rushcliffe GC (R)
England
J.J.F. Pennink
Rushden & District GC
North Hants, England
C. Catlow
Rushden & District GC (R)
England
Tom Williamson
Rushville CC
Illinois
Jack Keywood
Rushville Elks CC
Indiana
William H. Diddel
Rushyford GC
Aycliffe, Durham, England
J. Hamilton Stutt
Russell Cottage GC
Kearsarge, New Hampshire
Alex Findlay
Russley GC (R)
New Zealand
John Harris, Peter Thomson,Michael Wolveridge
Rutgers University (R. 9)
New Jersey
Hal Purdy
Rutgers University (A. 9)
New Jersey
Hal Purdy
Ruth Lake CC
Hinsdale, Illinois
William B. Langford, Theodore J. Moreau
Ruth Lake CC (R)
Illinois
Edward Lawrence Packard
Ruth Lake CC (R)
Illinois
Edward Lawrence Packard, Roger Packard
Ruth Lake CC (R)
Illinois
Ken Killian, Dick Nugent
Ruth Lake CC (R. 1)
Illinois
Dick Nugent
Ruth Park GC
University City, Missouri
Robert Bruce Harris
Rutland CC
Vermont
George Low Sr
Rutland CC (A. 9)
Vermont
Wayne Stiles, John Van Kleek
Rutland CC (R. 9)
Vermont
Wayne Stiles, John Van Kleek
Ruttgers Resort GC
Richfield, Minnesota
Donald G. Brauer, Paul S. Fjare
Ryan Hill GC
Osceola, Nebraska
Harold Glissmann
Ryde GC (R)
England
J. Hamilton Stutt

Rye GC (R)
New York
Rees Jones
Rye GC
Deal, England
Douglas Rolland, H.S. Colt
Rye GC (R)
England
Sir Guy Campbell
Rye GC (A. 9)
England
J.J.F. Pennink
Rye GC (R)
England
Tom Simpson
RAF Cranwell GC
England
S.V. Hotchkin
Saarbrucken GC
West Germany
Bernhard von Limburger
Sabah G&CC
Kota Kinbalu, Malaysia
Robert Muir Graves
Sabal Palm CC
Tamarac, Florida
Frank Murray
Sabal Point CC
Longwood, Florida
Ward Northrup
Sadaquada GC (R)
New York
William F. Mitchell
Saddle Hill CC
Hopkinton, Massachusetts
William F. Mitchell
Saddlebrook G&TC (Palmer Course)
Florida
Arnold Palmer, Ed Seay,Bob Walker
Saddlebrook G&TC (Refram Course)
Florida
Dean Refram
Safari Inn GC
Miami, Florida
C.H. Anderson
Safari Pines CC
Vero Beach, Florida
Dick Bird
Saffron Walden GC
Cambridgeshire, England
Harry Vardon
Sagamihara GC (East Course)
Kanagawa, Japan
Yuji Kodera
Sagamihara GC (West Course)
Kanagawa, Japan
Y. Murakami
Sagamore GC
Bolton Landing, New York
Donald Ross
Saginaw CC
Michigan
Tom Bendelow
Saginaw CC (R)
Michigan
William Newcomb
Saginaw CC (R. 2)
Michigan
Bruce Matthews, Jerry Matthews
Saginaw CC (R. 2)
Michigan
Jerry Matthews
Saguenay CC
Arvida, Quebec
Stanley Thompson
Sahalee CC
Redmond, Washington
Ted Robinson
Sahalee CC (R)
Washington
Robert Muir Graves
Sahara CC
Las Vegas, Nevada
Bert Stamps
Sail Ho GC
San Diego, California
Jack Daray
Sailfish Point CC
Stuart, Florida
Jack Nicklaus, Jay Morrish,Bob Cupp

Sakonnet GC
Little Compton, Rhode Island
Donald Ross
Salem CC
Peabody, Massachusetts
Donald Ross
Salem G&CC
Missouri
Floyd Farley
Salem GC
North Salem, New York
Edward Ryder, *Val Carlson*
Salem GC (A. 9)
Ohio
Bob Simmons
Salem GC (R)
Ohio
Geoffrey S. Cornish
Salem GC
Oregon
Ercel Kay
Salem Hills GC
Michigan
Bruce Matthews, Jerry Matthews
Salemtowne GC
Salem, Oregon
Bill Schaefer
Salina CC
Kansas
John J. Eberhardt
Salina Muni
Kansas
Floyd Farley
Salinas Fairways GC
California
Jack Fleming
Salisbury & South Wilts GC
Wiltshire, England
J.H. Taylor
Salisbury & South Wilts GC (R. 6)
England
Fred W. Hawtree, Martin Hawtree
Salisbury CC (R)
Virginia
Edmund B. Ault
Salisbury CC (R)
Virginia
Rees Jones
Salishan G Links
Gleneden Beach, Oregon
Fred Federspiel
Salishan G Links (R)
Oregon
Robert Muir Graves
Sallandsche GC (R)
Netherlands
J.J.F. Pennink
Sallandsche GC "De Hock"
Netherlands
J.J.F. Pennink
Salmon Brook CC (R) NLE
Connecticut
Orrin Smith
Salmon Creek CC
Rochester, New York
Pete Craig
Salt Fork State Park GC
Cambridge, Ohio
Jack Kidwell
Saltcoats GC (R)
Scotland
Old Tom Morris
Salton City CC
California
William F. Bell
Salzborg GC
Morin Heights, Quebec
Howard Watson
San Andres GC
San Martin, Argentina
Mungo Park II
San Andres GC
Bogota, Colombia
Stanley Thompson
San Angelo CC
Texas
Warren Cantrell
San Antonio CC
Texas
Alex Findlay

San Antonio CC (R)
Texas
A.W. Tillinghast
San Antonio CC (R.15)
Texas
Joseph S. Finger
San Antonio Shores GC
Mexico
Bob Baldock, Robert L. Baldock
San Bernardino CC (R. 5)
California
Algie Pulley
San Bernardino CC (A. 1)
California
Jeff Brauer, *Jim Colbert*
San Carlos G&CC
Sonora, Mexico
Roy Dye, Gary Grandstaff
San Carlos Park G&CC
Florida
John E. O'Connor
San Clemente Muni
California
William P. Bell
San Clemente Muni (R. 9)
California
William F. Bell
San Clemente Muni (A. 9)
California
William F. Bell
San Dar Acres GC
Bellville, Ohio
Jack Kidwell, Michael Hurdzan
San Diego CC
Chula Vista, California
William P. Bell
San Diego CC (R. 1)
California
Harry Rainville
San Felipe CC
Del Rio, Texas
Joseph S. Finger
San Fernando VA Hospital GC
California
William H. Johnson
San Francisco GC
California
A.W. Tillinghast
San Francisco GC (R)
California
William P. Bell
San Gabriel CC
California
Norman Macbeth
San Gabriel CC (R)
California
William F. Bell
San Gabriel CC (R)
California
Robert Trent Jones, Robert Trent
    Jones Jr
San Geronimo National GC
California
A. Vernon Macan
San Gil GC
San Juan El Rio, Mexico
Roy Dye
San Gorgonio GC
Banning, California
William H. Johnson
San Isidro GC (R. 3)
Argentina
Ronaldo Fream
San Joaquin CC (R)
California
Bob Baldock
San Joaquin CC (R)
California
Robert Dean Putnam
San Jose CC
California
Tom Nicoll
San Jose CC (R)
California
Robert Muir Graves
San Jose CC (R)
California
Ed Seay
San Jose CC
Jacksonville, Florida
Donald Ross
San Jose Muni
California
Robert Muir Graves

San Juan GC
Monticello, Utah
Arthur Jack Snyder
San Juan Hills CC
San Juan Capistrano, California
Harry Rainville, David Rainville
San Juan Hills CC (R)
California
Peter Thomson, Michael
    Wolveridge, Ronald Fream
San Luis Bay Inn & CC
Avila Beach, California
Desmond Muirhead
San Luis Bay Inn & CC (A. 9)
California
Olin A. Dutra
San Luis Bay Inn & CC (R)
California
Robert Muir Graves
San Luis Obispo CC
California
Bert Stamps
San Luis Rey GC
California
William F. Bell
San Marcos Hotel & C
Chandler, Arizona
Harry Collis
San Marcos Hotel & C (R)
Arizona
Red Lawrence
San Marino GC
Farmington, Michigan
Bruce Matthews, Jerry Matthews
San Mateo Muni (R)
California
Robert Muir Graves
San Michele GC
Italy
R. Conti, C. Siniscalchi
San Miguel GC
Azores Islands
P.M. Ross
San Pedro Community Hotel GC
California
William P. Bell
San Pedro CC
California
William P. Bell
San Pedro GC
Mexico
Willie Smith
San Ramon CC
California
Clark Glasson
San Vicente CC
Ramona, California
Ted Robinson
San Vito de Normanni GC
Brindisi, Italy
Pier Mancinelli
Sand Creek C
Chesterton, Indiana
Ken Killian, Dick Nugent, Bob
    Lohmann
Sand Creek Muni
Idaho Falls, Idaho
William F. Bell
Sand Springs Muni
Oklahoma
Floyd Farley
Sandalfoot Cove G&CC
Margate, Florida
Robert von Hagge, Bruce Devlin
Sandelie GC
West Linn, Oregon
Harvey Junor
Sandelie GC (A. 9)
Oregon
William Kaiser
Sandestin GC (Baytowne Course)
Destin, Florida
Tom Jackson
Sandestin GC (Links Course)
Destin, Florida
Tom Jackson
Sandia Mountain GC
Albuquerque, New Mexico
Robert Dean Putnam
Sandilands GC
Sutton-on-Sea, England
S.V. Hotchkin

Sandilands GC (R)
England
Tom Williamson
Sandiway GC
Cheshire, England
S. Collins, Ted Ray
Sandiway GC (R)
England
H.S. Colt
Sandiway GC (R. 3)
England
Fred W. Hawtree
Sandmoor GC
Leeds, England
Henry Barran
Sandmoor GC (R)
England
Alister Mackenzie
Sandown Park GC
Surrey, England
John Jacobs, John Corby
**Sandpiper Bay CC (Saints
    Course)**
Port St. Lucie, Florida
David Wallace
**Sandpiper Bay CC (Sinners
    Course)**
Port St. lucie, Florida
Mark Mahannah
**Sandpiper Bay CC (Sinners
    Course) (R)**
Florida
Chuck Ankrom
**Sandpiper Bay GC (Family
    Course)**
Florida
Chuck Ankrom
**Sandpiper CC (Wilderness
    Course)**
Port St. Lucie, Florida
LeRoy Phillips
Sandpiper G Links
Goleta, California
William F. Bell
Sandpiper G Links (R)
California
Robert Muir Graves, Damian
    Pascuzzo
Sandringham GC
Melbourne, Australia
Alister Mackenzie
Sandringham GC (A. 9)
Australia
Peter Thomson, Michael
    Wolveridge
Sands Point CC (A. 9)
New York
A.W. Tillinghast
Sands Point CC (R. 9)
New York
A.W. Tillinghast
Sands Point CC (R)
New York
Robert Trent Jones, Frank Duane
Sands Point CC (R)
New York
Frank Duane
Sands Point CC
Seattle, Washington
William H. Tucker, Frank James
Sands Point CC (R)
Washington
Robert Muir Graves
Sandy Brae G&CC
West Virginia
Edmund B. Ault
Sandy Burr CC
Wayland, Massachusetts
Donald Ross
Sandy Hollow Muni
Rockford, Illinois
C.D. Wagstaff
Sandy Hollow Muni (R)
Illinois
David Gill
Sandy Lane Hotel & GC
Barbados
Robertson Ward
Sandy Lodge GC
England
H.S. Colt, Harry Vardon
Sandy Ridge GC
Midland, Michigan
Bruce Matthews, Jerry Matthews

Sandy Run CC
Oreland, Pennsylvania
J. Franklyn Meehan
Sandy Run GC (R)
Georgia
Arthur Davis, Ron Kirby
Sankaty Head GC
Nantucket, Massachusetts
Eugene "Skip" Wogan
Sanlando G&CC (R) NLE
Florida
Robert Bruce Harris
Sanpete County GC
Manti, Utah
Keith Downs
Sanremo GC
Italy
James Gannon
Sanrizuka GC
Japan
Kinya Fujita
Santa Ana CC
California
John Duncan Dunn
Santa Ana CC (R)
California
Desmond Muirhead
Santa Ana CC (R)
California
Harry Rainville, David Rainville
Santa Ana CC (R)
California
Ronald Fream
Santa Barbara Community GC
California
Lawrence Hughes
Santa Barbara CC NLE
California
Tom Bendelow
Santa Barbara CC (R) NLE
California
Walter Fovargue
Santa Clara Muni
California
Robert Muir Graves, Damian
    Pascuzzo
Santa Cruz CC
Nogales, Arizona
Red Lawrence
Santa Cruz G&CC
California
Tom Bendelow
Santa Fe CC
New Mexico
Tom Bendelow
Santa Maria GC (R)
California
Bob Baldock, Robert L. Baldock
Santa Maria GC
Baton Rouge, Louisiana
Robert Trent Jones, Roger
    Rulewich
Santa Marta GC
Colombia
Mark Mahannah
Santa Martretta GC
Italy
P.L. Ariotti
Santa Monica Shores GC
California
George S. "Pop" Merrit
Santa Ponsa GC
Majorca, Spain
Pepe Gancedo
Santa Rosa G&BC
Santa Rosa Beach, Florida
James Root
Santa Rosa G&CC
California
Jack Fleming, Ben Harmon
Santa Rosa G&CC (R)
California
Robert Trent Jones Jr
Santa Rosa G&CC
Brandenton, Florida
R. Albert Anderson
Santa Susana CC
California
William P. Bell
**Santa Teresa CC (Spanish Dagger
    Course)**
Sunland Park, New Mexico
Dave Bennett

Santa Teresa CC (Yucca Course)
Sunland Park, New Mexico
Dave Bennett
Santa Teresa GC
San Jose, California
George E. Santana
Santee-Cooper CC
South Carolina
George W. Cobb
Santiago GC
California
Ed Burns
Santiam GC
Salem, Oregon
Fred Federspiel
Santiam GC (R)
Oregon
Robert Muir Graves
Santo da Serra GC
Madeira Islands
Henry Cotton
Sao Fernando GC (R)
Brazil
Alberto Serra
Sao Paulo GC (R)
Brazil
Stanley Thompson
Sapona CC
Lexington, North Carolina
Ellis Maples, Ed Seay
Sapphire Lakes CC
Sapphire, North Carolina
Russell Breeden, *Dan Breeden*
Sapphire Lakes CC (A. 9)
North Carolina
Tom Jackson
Sapporo CC
Japan
Robert Trent Jones Jr
Sapulpa City GC (R. 9)
Oklahoma
Joe Aycock
Sara Bay CC
Sarasota, Florida
Donald Ross
Sara Bay CC (R)
Florida
Joe Lee
Sarah Shank Muni (A. 9)
Indiana
William H. Diddel
Sarah Shank Muni (R. 9)
Indiana
William H. Diddel
Saranac GC
Stahistown, Pennsylvania
Paul E. Erath
Saranac Inn G&CC
New York
Seymour Dunn
Saranac Lake GC
New York
Alex Findlay
Sarasota GC
Florida
Wynn Tredway
Saratoga GC (R)
California
Robert Muir Graves
Saratoga Spa GC (R)
New York
William F. Mitchell
Saratoga Spa GC (A. 9)
New York
William F. Mitchell
Sarnia GC
Ontario
George Cumming
Sarnia GC (R)
Ontario
Clinton E. Robinson
Sarvik GC
Finland
Jan Sederholm
Saskatoon CC
Saskatchewan
William Kinnear
Saskatoon GC
Alto, Michigan
Mark DeVries
Saticoy CC
California
William F. Bell

338

Saticoy Public Links
Saticoy, California
George C. Thomas Jr
Saucon Valley CC (Grace Course)
Bethlehem, Pennsylvania
William Gordon, David Gordon
Saucon Valley CC (Junior Course)
Bethlehem, Pennsylvania
William Gordon, David Gordon
Saucon Valley CC (Saucon Course)
Bethlehem, Pennsylvania
Herbert Strong
Saucon Valley CC (Saucon Course) (R)
Pennsylvania
Perry Maxwell
Saucon Valley CC (Saucon Course) (R)
Pennsylvania
William Gordon
Saucon Valley CC (Saucon Course) (R)
Pennsylvania
William Gordon, David Gordon
Saucon Valley CC (Weyhill Course)
Bethlehem, Pennsylvania
William Gordon, David Gordon
Sauerland GC
Neheim-Husten, West Germany
Bernhard von Limburger
Saugahatchee CC
Opelika, Alabama
Ward Northrup
Saugatuck CC
Michigan
George B. Ferry
Saujana G&CC (Orchid Course)
Subang, Malaysia
Ronald Fream
Saujana G&CC (Palm Course)
Subang, Malaysia
Ronald Fream
Sault St. Marie CC (R)
Ontario
Stanley Thompson
Sault St. Marie Muni (A. 9) NLE
Michigan
Jerry Matthews
Saunton GC
England
Tom Dunn
Saunton GC (East Course) (R)
England
C.K. Cotton, J.J.F. Pennink
Saunton GC (New Course) NLE
Devonshire, England
Herbert Fowler
Saunton GC (West Course)
Devon, England
J.J.F. Pennink
Savana C
Port St. Lucie, Florida
Chuck Ankrom
Savannah GC
Georgia
Donald Ross
Savannah GC (R)
Georgia
George W. Cobb
Savannah GC (A. 9)
Georgia
Ron Kirby, Denis Griffiths
Savannah GC (Course No. 2) NLE
Georgia
Donald Ross
Savannah Inn & CC
Georgia
Donald Ross
Savannah Inn & CC (R)
Georgia
Willard Byrd
Sawgrass GC (Oakbridge Course)
Ponte Vedra Beach, Florida
Bill Amick
Sawgrass GC (Oakbridge Course) (R)
Florida
Ed Seay

Sawgrass GC (Oceanside Course)
Ponte Vedra Beach, Florida
Ed Seay
Sawgrass GC (Oceanside Course) (R)
Florida
Gardner Dickinson
Sawgrass GC (Oceanside Course) (R)
Florida
Ed Seay
Sawgrass GC (Oceanside Course) (R)
Florida
Edmund B. Ault
Sawgrass GC (Oceanside Course) (A. 9)
Florida
Arnold Palmer, Ed Seay,Bob Walker, Harrison Minchew
Sawmill Creek GC
Huron, Ohio
George Fazio, Tom Fazio
Sawmill GC
Fenwick, Ontario
Gordon Witteveen
Sawyer AFB GC
Michigan
Bob Baldock
Sawyerkill GC
Saugerties, New York
Hal Purdy
Saxon Woods GC
Mamaroneck, New York
Tom Winton
Scarboro G&CC (R)
Ontario
A.W. Tillinghast
Scarboro G&CC (R)
Ontario
Stanley Thompson
Scarborough North Cliff GC
Yorkshire, England
James Braid, John R. Stutt
Scarborough Southcliff GC
England
Alister Mackenzie
Scarlett Woods GC
Toronto, Ontario
Howard Watson
Scarlett Woods GC (A. 9)
Ontario
Howard Watson, John Watson
Scarsdale GC
Hartsdale, New York
Willie Dunn Jr
Scarsdale GC (A. 6)
New York
A.W. Tillinghast
Scarsdale GC (R)
New York
A.W. Tillinghast
Scarsdale GC (R)
New York
Dick Wilson
Scarsdale GC (R)
New York
Robert Trent Jones
Scarsdale GC (R. 4)
New York
Frank Duane
Scenic Hills G&CC
Pensacola, Florida
Chic Adams
Schenectady CC
New York
Devereux Emmet
Schenectady Muni
New York
Arthur F. Knight
Schilling AFB GC NLE
Salina, Kansas
Leon Howard
Schloss Anholt GC
West Germany
Bernhard von Limburger
Schloss Braunfels GC
West Germany
Bernhard von Limburger
Schloss Fuschl G&CC
Austria
Bernhard von Limburger

Schloss Mittersill GC
Austria
Tom Simpson, *Molly Gourlay*
Schloss Myllendonk GC
Monchengladbach, West Germany
Bernhard von Limburger
Schloss Myllendonk GC (A. 9)
West Germany
Donald Harradine
Schloss Pichlarn GC
Irdning, Austria
Bernhard von Limburger
Schloss Pichlarn GC (A. 9)
Austria
Donald Harradine
Schloss Rheden GC
West Germany
Bernhard von Limburger
Schoenenberg G&CC
Switzerland
Donald Harradine
Schroon Lake GC
New York
Seymour Dunn
Schuss Mountain GC
Mancelona, Michigan
Warner Bowen
Schuss Mountain GC (R)
Michigan
William Newcomb, Stephen Kay
Schuyler Meadows C
Loudonville, New York
Devereux Emmet, Alfred H. Tull
Schuyler Meadows C (R)
New York
Geoffrey S. Cornish, Brian Silva
Scioto CC
Columbus, Ohio
Donald Ross
Scioto CC (R)
Ohio
Dick Wilson, Joe Lee,Robert von Hagge
Scioto CC (R)
Ohio
Bob Cupp
Scona Lodge GC
Alcoa, Tennessee
Robert Trent Jones, Frank Duane
Scotch Meadows CC
Morganton, North Carolina
Russell Breeden
Scotch Pines GC
Payette, Idaho
William Graham
Scotch Settlement GC
Bradford, Ontario
Robert Moote
Scotch Valley GC
Holidaysburg, Pennsylvania
James Gilmore Harrison
Scotfield CC (R)
North Carolina
Clement B. "Johnny" Johnston, Clyde Johnston
Scothurst CC
Lumber Bridge, North Carolina
A.F. "Bud" Nash
Scotsdale GC
Bella Vista, Arkansas
Tom Clark, Edmund B. Ault
Scotsland GC
Oconomowoc, Wisconsin
Tom Burrows
Scott County GC
Scott City, Kansas
Henry B. Hughes, Richard Watson
Scott Lake CC
Comstock Park, Michigan
Bruce Matthews, Jerry Matthews
Scott Park Muni
Silver City, New Mexico
Arthur Jack Snyder
Scott Schreiner Muni
Kerrville, Texas
Donald Collett
Scottburgh GC (R)
South Africa
Robert G. Grimsdell
Scottsbluff CC
Nebraska
Frank Hummel

Scottsdale CC
Arizona
Lawrence Hughes
Scottsdale CC (R. 4)
Arizona
Arthur Jack Snyder
Scottsdale CC (R)
Arizona
Arnold Palmer, Ed Seay,Bob Walker
Scottsdale CC (A. 9)
Arizona
Arnold Palmer
Scraptoft GC
Leicestershire, England
Tom Williamson
Scunthorpe GC
Lincolnshire, England
Fred W. Hawtree, A.H.F. Jiggens
Sea 'N Air GC
California
Jack Daray
Sea Gull GC
Pawley's Island, South Carolina
Gene Hamm
Sea Island GC (Marshside 9)
St. Simons Island, Georgia
Joe Lee, Rocky Roquemore
Sea Island GC (Plantation 9)
St. Simons Island, Georgia
Walter J. Travis
Sea Island GC (Plantation 9) (R)
Georgia
C.H. Alison, H.S. Colt
Sea Island GC (Plantation 9) (R. 9)
Georgia
Robert Trent Jones
Sea Island GC (Retreat 9)
Georgia
Dick Wilson, Joe Lee
Sea Island GC (Seaside 9)
St. Simons Island, Georgia
C.H. Alison, H.S. Colt
Sea Island GC (Seaside 9) (R)
Georgia
Robert Trent Jones
Sea Palms G&CC
St. Simons Island, Georgia
George W. Cobb
Sea Palms G&CC (A. 9)
Georgia
Tom Jackson
Sea Pines Plantation GC (Club Course)
Hilton Head Island, South Carolina
Frank Duane, Arnold Palmer
Sea Pines Plantation GC (Ocean Course)
Hilton Head Island, South Carolina
George W. Cobb
Sea Pines Plantation GC (Sea Marsh Crs)
Hilton Head Island, South Carolina
George W. Cobb
Sea Ranch GC
California
Robert Muir Graves
Sea Trail G Links
Sunset Beach, North Carolina
Dan Maples
Sea View Village GC
Massachusetts
Geoffrey S. Cornish
Seabrook Island GC (Crooked Oaks Course)
South Carolina
Robert Trent Jones, Roger Rulewich
Seabrook Island GC (Ocean Winds Course)
South Carolina
Willard Byrd
Seacliff CC formerly known as Huntington Seacliff CC
Huntington Beach, California
Press Maxwell
Seacliff CC (R)
California
Ronald Fream

Seacroft GC
Lincolnshire, England
Tom Dunn
Seacroft GC (R)
England
Sir Guy Campbell
Seacroft GC (R. 9)
England
Wilfrid Reid
Seafield GC
Scotland
James Braid, John R. Stutt
Seaford CC
Delaware
Alfred H. Tull
Seaford GC NLE
Sussex, England
Tom Dunn
Seaford GC
Sussex, England
J.H. Taylor
Seaford GC (R)
England
J.S.F. Morrison
Seaford GC (R)
England
Willie Park Jr
Seaforth GC
Ontario
Howard Watson
Seamountain GC
Ka'u, Hawaii
Arthur Jack Snyder
Seascale GC
England
Willie Campbell
Seascale GC
Cumbria, England
Sir Guy Campbell
Seascale GC (A. 9)
England
George Lowe
Seascape G Links
Kitty Hawk, North Carolina
Art Wall
Seascape G&RC
Destin, Florida
Robert Logan
Seascape G&RC (A. 4)
Florida
Joe Lee
Seascape G&RC (R)
Florida
Joe Lee
Seaside CC
Oregon
H. Chandler Egan
Seattle GC
Washington
Robert Johnstone
Seattle GC (R)
Washington
A. Vernon Macan
Seattle GC (R)
Washington
Ted Robinson
Seattle GC (R. 2)
Washington
Peter Thomson, Michael Wolveridge,Ronald Fream
Seaview GC (R. 9)
Nova Scotia
Clinton E. Robinson
Seaview GC (A. 9)
Nova Scotia
Clinton E. Robinson
Seaview GC (A. 9)
Nova Scotia
Robert Moote
Seaview GC (Bay Course)
Absecon, New Jersey
Donald Ross
Seaview GC (Bay Course) (R)
New Jersey
A.W. Tillinghast
Seaview GC (Bay Course) (R)
New Jersey
William Gordon, David Gordon
Seaview GC (Pines Course)
Absecon, New Jersey
William S. Flynn, Howard Toomey

339

Seaview GC (Pines Course) (A. 9)
New Jersey
William Gordon, David Gordon
Seawane C
Hewlitt Harbor, New York
Devereux Emmet, Alfred H. Tull
Seawane C (R)
New York
Frank Duane
Seawane C (R)
New York
Stephen Kay
SeaBees GC
Port Hueneme, California
Jack Daray
Sebastian Muni
Florida
Chuck Ankrom
Sebring GC
Ohio
Ray Henry
Sebring Shores GC
Florida
Hans Schmeisser
Secession GC
Beaufort, South Carolina
P.B. Dye
Sedalia CC
Missouri
Floyd Farley
Sedgefield CC
Greensboro, North Carolina
Donald Ross
Sedgefield CC (R)
North Carolina
Gene Hamm
Sedgefield CC (R)
North Carolina
Willard Byrd
Sedgefield CC (Red Course) NLE
Greensboro, North Carolina
Donald Ross
Seefeld-Wildmoos GC
Seefeld, Austria
Donald Harradine
Segregansett CC (A. 9)
Massachusetts
Geoffrey S. Cornish, William G. Robinson
Seguin CC
Texas
John Bredemus
Seguin CC (A. 9)
Texas
Ralph Plummer
Sehoy Plantation GC
Huntsboro, Alabama
Ellis Maples, Dan Maples
Selkirk GC
Selkirkshire, Scotland
Willie Park
Selma Valley CC
California
Bob Baldock
Selsdon Park Hotel GC
Surrey, England
F.G. Hawtree, J.H. Taylor
Selva Marina CC
Atlantic Beach, Florida
Ernest E. Smith
Semiahmoo GC
Everett, Washington
Arnold Palmer, Ed Seay, Harrison Minchew
Seminole GC
North Palm Beach, Florida
Donald Ross
Seminole GC
Tallahassee, Florida
R. Albert Anderson
Seminole GC (R)
Florida
Dick Wilson
Seminole GC (A. 9)
Florida
Bill Amick
Seminole Lake G&CC
Florida
Chic Adams
Seminole Valley GC
Chattahoochee, Florida
Bill Amick

Sene Valley, Folkstone and Hythe GC
England
Henry Cotton
Seneca Muni
Louisville, Kentucky
Alex McKay
Seneca Muni (R)
Kentucky
Edward Lawrence Packard
Seneca Muni (R. 8)
Kentucky
Benjamin Wihry
Senior Estates G&CC
Woodburn, Oregon
William Graham
Senneville CC
Montreal, Quebec
Willie Park Jr
Sentosa Island GC (Sentosa Course)
Singapore
J.J.F. Pennink
Sentosa Island GC (Serapong Course)
Singapore
Peter Thomson, Michael Wolveridge, Ronald Fream
SentryWorld GC
Stevens Point, Wisconsin
Robert Trent Jones Jr
Sepulveda GC (Balboa Course)
California
William F. Bell, William P. Bell, William H. Johnson
Sepulveda GC (Encino Course)
California
William F. Bell, William P. Bell, William H. Johnson
Sepulveda VA Hospital GC
Encino, California
William H. Johnson
Sequoyah CC (R.13)
California
Robert Muir Graves
Sequoyah State Park GC
Hulbert, Oklahoma
Floyd Farley
Serlby Park GC
Yorkshire, England
Tom Williamson
Serrento Valley CC
Laurel, Florida
Bill Amick
Seth Hughes GC NLE
Tulsa, Oklahoma
Floyd Farley
Seven Devils GC
Boone, North Carolina
George Brownlow
Seven Hills CC
Hemet, California
Harry Rainville, David Rainville
Seven Hills G&CC
Port Hardy, British Columbia
William L. Overdorf
Seven Hills GC
Hartville, Ohio
William Newcomb
Seven Lakes CC
Palm Springs, California
Ted Robinson
Seven Lakes CC
Fort Myers, Florida
Ernest E. Smith
Seven Lakes CC (R)
Florida
Edward Lawrence Packard
Seven Lakes GC
West End, North Carolina
Peter V. Tufts
Seven Lakes West GC
West End, North Carolina
Dan Maples
Seven Oaks GC
Colgage Univ., New York
Robert Trent Jones, Frank Duane
Seven Oaks GC (A. 9)
New York
Robert Trent Jones
Seven Oaks GC
Beaver, Pennsylvania
X.G. Hassenplug

Seven Rivers CC
Crystal River, Florida
Bill Amick
Seven Springs G&CC
New Port Richey, Florida
James King
Seven Springs G&CC (A.18)
Florida
Ron Garl
Seven Springs G&CC (R.18)
Florida
Ron Garl
Seven Springs GC
Champion, Pennsylvania
X.G. Hassenplug
Seven Springs GC (R. 9)
Pennsylvania
Ferdinand Garbin
Seventy Six Falls CC
Albany, Kentucky
Harold England
Seward CC
Nebraska
Harold Glissmann
Sewells Point GC (R)
Virginia
Tom Clark
Sewickley Heights CC
Sewickley, Pennsylvania
James Gilmore Harrison, Ferdinand Garbin
Sewickley Heights CC (R)
Pennsylvania
Ferdinand Garbin
Seymour CC
Indiana
Victor George
Seymour G&CC
North Vancouver, British Columbia
James P. Izatt
Shackamaxon G&CC
Westfield, New Jersey
A.W. Tillinghast
Shades Valley CC
Alabama
Bancroft Timmons
Shadow Brook CC
Tunkhannock, Pennsylvania
Karl Schmidt
Shadow Hills CC
Junction City, Oregon
Alex Kindsfather
Shadow Lake G&RC
Rochester, New York
Pete Craig
Shadow Mountain GC
Palm Desert, California
George Von Elm
Shadow Mountain GC (R)
California
Ronald Fream
Shadowmoss G&TC
Charleston, South Carolina
Russell Breeden
Shadowridge CC
Vista, California
David Rainville
Shady Acres GC
Springfield, Missouri
Herman Siler
Shady Hills GC
Marion, Indiana
William H. Diddel
Shady Hollow CC
Massillon, Ohio
William F. Mitchell
Shady Lawn GC
Beecher, Illinois
R. Albert Anderson
Shady Lawn GC (R)
Illinois
Roger Packard
Shady Oaks CC
Fort Worth, Texas
Robert Trent Jones, Lawrence Hughes, Ralph Plummer
Shady Oaks GC
Baird, Texas
Leon Howard
Shaftsbury GC
Fairfield Glade, Tennessee
Gary Roger Baird

Shaganappi Muni
Calgary, Alberta
Neil Little
Shaker Farms CC
Westfield, Massachusetts
Geoffrey S. Cornish
Shaker Heights CC
Ohio
Donald Ross
Shaker Heights CC (R)
Ohio
Geoffrey S. Cornish
Shaker Ridge CC
New York
James Thomson
Shaker Run GC
Middletown, Ohio
Arthur Hills
Shalimar Pointe CC formerly known as Lake Lorraine CC
Shalimar, Florida
Bill Amick
Shalimar Pointe CC (R)
Florida
Joseph S. Finger, Ken Dye
Sham-Na-Pum GC
Richland, Washington
Mel "Curley" Hueston
Shamanah GC
Boise, Idaho
Robert von Hagge, Bruce Devlin
Shambolee GC
Petersburg, Illinois
Charles Maddox
Shamokin Valley CC
Pennsylvania
Alex Findlay
Shamrock GC
Ligonier, Pennsylvania
Ferdinand Garbin
Shamrock Hills GC
Lee's Summit, Missouri
Jim Weaver
Shandin Hills GC
San Bernardino, California
Cary Bickler
Shangri-La CC (Blue Course)
Afton, Oklahoma
Don Sechrest
Shangri-La CC (Gold Course)
Afton, Oklahoma
Don Sechrest
Shanklin & Sandown GC
Isle of Man
J. Cowper
Shanklin & Sandown GC (R)
Isle of Man
J. Hamilton Stutt
Shannon G&CC
Freeport, Bahamas
Joe Lee
Shannon Green GC
Fredericksburg, Virginia
Edmund B. Ault
Shannon GC
County Clare, Ireland
John Harris
Shannon Lake GC
Westbank, British Columbia
John Moore
Shannopin CC
Ben Avon Heights, Pennsylvania
Emil Loeffler, *John McGlynn*
Shannopin CC (R)
Pennsylvania
Ferdinand Garbin
Shanty Creek GC (Deskin course)
Bellaire, Michigan
William H. Diddel
Shanty Creek GC (Legend Course)
Michigan
Arnold Palmer, Ed Seay, Bob Walker
Sharon C
Sharon Center, Ohio
George W. Cobb
Sharon C (R)
Ohio
Geoffrey S. Cornish, Brian Silva
Sharon CC (R. 9)
Massachusetts
Wayne Stiles

Sharon CC
Pennsylvania
Tom Bendelow
Sharon Heights G&CC
Menlo Park, California
Jack Fleming
Sharon Woods CC
Sharon Center, Ohio
William H. Diddel
Sharp Park GC
Pacifica, California
Alister Mackenzie
Sharpstown CC
Houston, Texas
Ralph Plummer
Sharpstown CC (R)
Texas
Jay Riviere
Shasta Valley CC
Montague, California
Clark Glasson
Shattuck GC
Oklahoma
Floyd Farley
Shaughnessy G&CC
Vancouver, British Columbia
A. Vernon Macan
Shaughnessy G&CC (R)
British Columbia
Norman H. Woods
Shaughnessy Heights C NLE
Vancouver, British Columbia
A. Vernon Macan
Shaw AFB GC
Sumter, South Carolina
Ed Riccoboni
Shaw Hill G&CC
Lancashire, England
T.J.A. McAuley
Shawinigan G&CC
Quebec
Howard Watson
Shawnee CC
Delaware
Edmund B. Ault
Shawnee CC (A. 9)
Delaware
Edmund B. Ault, Al Jamison
Shawnee CC (A. 9)
Delaware
Edmund B. Ault, Bill Love
Shawnee CC
Topeka, Kansas
Donald Ross
Shawnee CC (R)
Kansas
Chet Mendenhall
Shawnee CC
Lima, Ohio
Tom Bendelow
Shawnee CC (R)
Ohio
Jack Kidwell, Michael Hurdzan
Shawnee CC
Shawnee-on-Delaware, Pennsylvania
A.W. Tillinghast
Shawnee CC (R)
Pennsylvania
J. Franklyn Meehan
Shawnee CC (R)
Pennsylvania
William H. Diddel
Shawnee CC (R.18)
Pennsylvania
William H. Diddel
Shawnee CC (A. 9)
Pennsylvania
William H. Diddel
Shawnee Elks CC
Shawnee, Oklahoma
Perry Maxwell
Shawnee GC
Institute, West Virginia
Ron Kirby, Denis Griffiths
Shawnee Hills GC
Cleveland, Ohio
Ben W. Zink
Shawnee Lookout GC
Cincinnati, Ohio
Jack Kidwell, Michael Hurdzan
Shawnee Muni
Louisville, Kentucky
Alex McKay

Shawnee Slopes GC
Alberta
Peter Olynyk, Ernie Tate
Shawnee Slopes GC (R)
Alberta
Robert Moote
Shawnee State Park GC
Portsmouth, Ohio
Jack Kidwell, Michael Hurdzan
Sheaffer Memorial Park GC
Fort Madison, Iowa
C.D. Wagstaff
Sheboygan Town & CC
Wisconsin
Tom Bendelow
Sheboygan Town & CC (A. 9)
Wisconsin
Harry B. Smead
Sheerness GC
Kent, England
Willie Park Jr
Shelby CC
Ohio
Ben W. Zink
Shelby Oaks GC
Sidney, Ohio
Ken Killian, Dick Nugent
Shelbyville CC (A. 2)
Kentucky
Benjamin Wihry
Shelbyville CC
Tennessee
R. Albert Anderson
Shelbyville Elks CC
Indiana
William H. Diddel
Shelbyville GC
Michigan
Arthur Young
Shelbyville GC (A. 9)
Michigan
Arthur Young
Shelridge CC
Medina, New York
X.G. Hassenplug
Shenandoah CC
Virginia
Fred Findlay
Shenandoah G&CC
Walled Lake, Michigan
Bruce Matthews, Jerry Matthews
Shenandoah Valley CC
Middleburg, Virginia
Buddy Loving
Shenandoah Valley CC (R)
Virginia
Rees Jones
Shennecossett GC
Groton, Connecticut
Donald Ross
Shenvallee Lodge & GC (A. 9)
Virginia
Edmund B. Ault
Shenvallee Lodge & GC (R. 9)
Virginia
Edmund B. Ault
Shepard Hill CC (A. 9)
New York
Geoffrey S. Cornish, William G.
  Robinson
Sheraton Inn GC
Greensburg, Pennsylvania
X.G. Hassenplug
Sherborne GC
England
James Braid
Sherbrooke G&CC
Lake Worth, Florida
Robert von Hagge, Bruce Devlin
Sheridan Park GC
Kenmore, New York
William Harries
Sheridan Park GC (R)
New York
A. Russell Tryon
Sherill Park Muni (East Course)
Richardson, Texas
Leon Howard
Sherill Park Muni (West Course)
Richardson, Texas
Leon Howard, *Charles Howard*
Sheringham GC
England
Tom Dunn

Sherman GC
Texas
Tom Bendelow
Sherwood Forest CC
Baton Rouge, Louisiana
Ralph Plummer
Sherwood Forest GC
Sanger, California
Bob Baldock, Robert L. Baldock
Sherwood Forest GC
Annapolis, Maryland
Herbert Strong
Sherwood Forest GC (R. 4)
Maryland
Brian Ault
Sherwood Forest GC
Nottinghamshire, England
Tom Dunn
Sherwood Forest GC (R)
England
Tom Williamson
Sherwood Forest GC (R)
England
James Braid, John R. Stutt
Sherwood G&CC
Titusville, Florida
Bill Amick
Sherwood G&CC (A. 9)
Florida
Lloyd Clifton
Sherwood GC
Salisbury, Zimbabwe
Robert G. Grimsdell
Sherwood Hills GC
Sardine Canyon, Utah
Mark Dixon Ballif
Sherwood Park GC
Edmonton, Alberta
William Brinkworth
Shewani CC
Watseka, Illinois
Dick Nugent
Shifferdecker CC (A. 9)
Missouri
Smiley Bell
Shifferdecker CC (R. 9)
Missouri
Smiley Bell
Shifnal GC (R)
England
J.J.F. Pennink
Shiloh Park GC
Zion, Illinois
Edward Lawrence Packard
Shimotsuke CC
Japan
Arnold Palmer, Ed Seay
Shinnecock Hills GC NLE
New York
William F. Davis
Shinnecock Hills GC
Southampton, New York
William S. Flynn, Howard
  Toomey
**Shinnecock Hills GC (R.12)
NLE**
New York
Willie Dunn Jr
Shinnecock Hills GC (A. 8) NLE
New York
Willie Dunn Jr
Shinnecock Hills GC (R)
New York
William F. Mitchell
**Shinnecock Hills GC (Ladies
Course) NLE**
New York
Willie Dunn Jr
Shipyard GC (Brigantine Nine)
Hilton Head Island, South
  Carolina
Willard Byrd, Clyde Johnston
**Shipyard GC (Clipper and
Galleon Nines)**
Hilton Head Island, South
  Carolina
George W. Cobb
Shirehampton Park GC
Bristol, England
A.N. Andrews
Shirkey GC
Richmond, Missouri
Chet Mendenhall

**Shishido Kokusai GC (Shizu
Course)**
Ibaraki, Japan
Gary Roger Baird
Shiskine GC
Isle of Arran, Scotland
Willie Park
Shiun CC
Nugata, Japan
Kinya Fujita
Shizukuishi GC
Japan
Robert Trent Jones Jr, Don Knott
Shizuoka CC
Japan
Kinya Fujita
Shoaff Park GC
Ft. Wayne, Indiana
Hal Purdy
Shoal Canyon GC
Glendale, California
William F. Bell
Shoal Creek
Birmingham, Alabama
Jack Nicklaus, Jay Morrish, Bob
  Cupp
Shooter's Hill GC
London, England
Willie Park Jr
Shoreacres
Lake Bluff, Illinois
Seth Raynor
Shoreacres GC
Ontario
Stanley Thompson
Shorecliffs CC
San Clemente, California
Joseph B. Williams
Shorecliffs CC (R)
California
Bob Baldock, Robert L. Baldock
Shoreham GC
Southdown, England
Sir Guy Campbell, C.K.
  Hutchison, S.V. Hotchkin
Shorehaven GC
Norwalk, Connecticut
Robert White
Shoreline Park Muni GC
California
Robert Trent Jones Jr, Gary Linn
Shores CC
Lake Hubbard, Texas
Ralph Plummer
Shorewood CC
Dunkirk, New York
William Harries
Short Hills CC
East Moline, Illinois
Ted Lockie
Short Hills CC (R)
Illinois
Roger Packard
Show Low CC
Arizona
Arthur Jack Snyder
Showboat CC
Las Vegas, Nevada
Clark Glasson
Shreveport CC (R. 9)
Louisiana
Leon Howard
Shreveport CC (A. 3)
Louisiana
Joseph S. Finger
Shreveport CC (R.15)
Louisiana
Joseph S. Finger
Shrewsbury GC (R)
England
J.J.F. Pennink
Shuswap Lake Estates G&CC
Blind Bay, British Columbia
Ernest Brown
Shuswap Lake Estates G&CC (R)
British Columbia
Norman H. Woods
Shuttle Meadow CC
New Britain, Connecticut
Willie Park Jr
Siasconset GC
Nantucket, Massachusetts
Alex Findlay

Sibu GC
Sarawak, Malaysia
J.J.F. Pennink
Sickleholme GC (R)
England
Tom Williamson
Siderurgia GC
Argentina
Angel Reartes
Sidmouth GC
Devon, England
Charles Gibson
Sidmouth GC (R)
England
J.H. Taylor
Sidmouth GC (A. 9)
England
J.H. Taylor
Sidney G&CC
Ohio
Hal Purdy
Siegen-Olpe GC
Seigen, West Germany
Bernhard von Limburger
Sierra Blanca CC
Texas
William Cantrell
Sierra Estrella GC
Goodyear, Arizona
Red Lawrence
Sierra Estrella GC (A. 9)
Arizona
Red Lawrence
Sierra Sky Ranch GC
Oakhurst, California
Bob Baldock
Sierra View CC
Visalia, California
Jack Fleming
Sierra View CC (A. 9)
California
Bob Baldock, Robert L. Baldock
Sierra Vista GC
White Sands, New Mexico
Leon Howard
Signal Hill CC
Armonk, New York
Orrin Smith
Signal Point C
Niles, Michigan
Robert Bruce Harris
Signal Point CC
Fort Benton, Montana
Norman H. Woods
Sigwick G&CC
Virginia
Edmund B. Ault
Siler City CC
North Carolina
Ellis Maples
Silloth-on-Solway GC
Cumbria, England
Willie Park, Willie Park Jr
Silver Creek GC
White Mountain Lakes, Arizona
Gary Panks
Silver Creek GC
San Bernardino, California
William H. Johnson
Silver K GC
Oxnard, California
William F. Bell
Silver Lake CC
Akron, Ohio
Edward Lawrence Packard, Brent
  Wadsworth
Silver Lake G&CC
Leesburg, Florida
Ernest E. Smith
Silver Lake GC
Pomona, Kansas
Ted Haworth
**Silver Lake GC (North Course)
  formerly known as Euclid Hill
  CC**
Orland Park, Illinois
Leonard Macomber
**Silver Lake GC (North Course)
  (R. 1)**
Illinois
Ken Killian, Dick Nugent
Silver Lake GC (South Course)
Orland Park, Illinois
Charles Maddox, *Frank P.
  MacDonald*

Silver Lake School GC
Pittsburg, Pennsylvania
Ferdinand Garbin
Silver Lakes CC
Helendale, California
Ted Robinson
Silver Pines GC NLE
Florida
Lloyd Clifton
Silver Sage GC
Mountain Home, Idaho
Bob Baldock
Silver Spring CC
Ridgefield, Connecticut
Robert White
Silver Spring CC (R)
Connecticut
Alfred H. Tull
Silver Spring GC NLE
Ocala, Florida
Seymour Dunn
Silver Spring GC
Mechanicsburg, Pennsylvania
George Fazio
Silver Spring Shores G&CC
Ocala, Florida
Desmond Muirhead
Silver Springs G&CC
Calgary, Alberta
Dick Phelps, *Claude Muret*
Silver Springs GC
Maryland
Donald Ross
Silver Springs GC (R)
Maryland
Edmund B. Ault, Al Jamison
Silver Springs Resort GC
Pennsylvania
X.G. Hassenplug
Silverado CC (North Course)
Napa, California
Ben Harmon, *Johnny Dawson*
Silverado CC (North Course) (R)
California
Robert Trent Jones, Robert Trent
  Jones Jr
Silverado CC (South Course)
Napa, California
Robert Trent Jones, Robert Trent
  Jones Jr
Silverbell Muni
Tucson, Arizona
Arthur Jack Snyder
Silvercrest G&CC (R)
Iowa
Charles Calhoun
Silvermine CC
Connecticut
John E. Warner Jr
Silvermine CC (R)
Connecticut
Alfred H. Tull
Sim Park Muni
Wichita, Kansas
Harry Heimple, Jack Shearman
Sim Park Muni (R)
Kansas
Bob Dunning
Simsbury Farms Muni
Connecticut
Geoffrey S. Cornish, William G.
  Robinson
**Singapore Island CC (Island
  Course) (R)**
Singapore
C.K. Cotton, J.J.F. Pennink
**Singapore Island GC (Bukit
  Course)**
Singapore
James Braid
**Singapore Island GC (Bukit
  Course) (R)**
Singapore
J.J.F. Pennink
**Singapore Island GC (New
  Course)**
Singapore
John Harris, J.J.F. Pennink
**Singapore Island GC (Sime
  Course)**
Singapore
J.J.F. Pennink

Singapore Island GC (Sime
Course) (R)
Singapore
Ronald Fream
Singing Hills CC (Oak Glen
Course)
El Cajon, California
Cecil B. Hollingsworth
Singing Hills CC (Oak Glen
Course) (R)
California
Ted Robinson
Singing Hills CC (Pine Glen
Course)
El Cajon, California
Cecil B. Hollingsworth
Singing Hills CC (Pine Glen
Course) (R)
California
Ted Robinson
Singing Hills CC (Willow Glen
Course)
El Cajon, California
William F. Bell, William P.
Bell, William H. Johnson
Singing Hills CC (Willow Glen
Course) (R)
California
Ted Robinson
Singletree GC
Edwards, Colorado
Jay Morrish, Bob Cupp
Sinking Valley CC
Pennsylvania
Edmund B. Ault
Sinnissippi Park GC NLE
Rockford, Illinois
Tom Bendelow
Sinton Muni
Texas
Leon Howard
Sioux City CC
Iowa
Tom Bendelow
Sippihaw CC
Fuquay-Varina, North Carolina
C.D. Wagstaff
Sippihaw CC (A. 9)
North Carolina
Gene Hamm
Sir Archibald Birkmyre Estate
GC
England
Tom Simpson
Sir Harry Oakes Private Course
Niagara Falls, Ontario
Stanley Thompson
Sir Mortimer Singer Estate GC
England
Tom Simpson
Sir Phillip Sassoon Estate GC
England
Tom Simpson
Sitwell Park GC
Yorkshire, England
Alister Mackenzie
Siwanoy CC
Bronxville, New York
Donald Ross
Siwanoy CC (R)
New York
Tom Winton
Siwanoy CC (R)
New York
Geoffrey S. Cornish, William G.
Robinson
Siwanoy CC (R)
New York
Robert Trent Jones
Skaneatelas CC
New York
Hal Purdy
Skelleftea GC (R)
Sweden
Ronald Fream
Skenandoa C
New York
Russell D. Bailey
Skerries GC (A. 9)
Ireland
Eddie Hackett
Skibo Castle GC
Scotland
John Sutherland

Sklo Bohemia Podebrady GC
Czechoslovakia
J.J.F. Pennink
Skokie CC
Glencoe, Illinois
Tom Bendelow
Skokie CC (R)
Illinois
Donald Ross
Skokie CC (R)
Illinois
William B. Langford, Theodore J.
Moreau
Skokie CC (R)
Illinois
Ken Killian, Dick Nugent
Skokie CC (R)
Illinois
Rees Jones, Keith Evans
Skokie Playfield GC NLE
Winnetka, Illinois
William B. Langford, Theodore J.
Moreau
Sky Meadow GC
Nashua, New Hampshire
Bill Amick
Sky Valley CC
Dillard, Georgia
Bill Watts
Sky Valley GC
Hillsboro, Indiana
Gary Kern
Skycenter GC
Huntsville, Alabama
Bob Baldock, Robert L. Baldock
Skyland GC
Crested Butte, Colorado
Robert Trent Jones Jr, Gary Linn
Skyline CC
Mobile,
Chic Adams
Skyline CC (A. 9)
Alabama
Earl Stone
Skyline CC
Tucson, Arizona
Guy S. Greene
Skyline GC
Pittsville, Massachusetts
Rowland Armacost
Skyline GC (A. 9)
West Virginia
Ferdinand Garbin
Skyline GC (R)
West Virginia
Ferdinand Garbin
Skyline Woods CC
Elkhorn, Nebraska
Frank Ervin
Skylinks GC
Long Beach, California
William F. Bell
Skytop C
Pennsylvania
Robert White
Skywest Public GC
Hayward, California
Bob Baldock
Slade Valley GC
County Dublin, Ireland
D. O'Brien, W. Sullivan
Slade Valley GC (R)
Ireland
Eddie Hackett
Sleaford GC
Lincolnshire, England
Tom Williamson
Sleeping Giant GC
Connecticut
Ralph Barton
Sleeping Giant GC (R)
Connecticut
William F. Mitchell
Sleepy Hole Muni
Portsmouth, Virginia
Russell Breeden
Sleepy Hollow G&CC (Lake
Course)
Dallas, Texas
Press Maxwell
Sleepy Hollow G&CC (Lake
Course) (R)
Texas
Karl Litten

Sleepy Hollow G&CC (River
Course)
Dallas, Texas
Press Maxwell
Sleepy Hollow G&CC (River
Course) (R)
Texas
Karl Litten
Sleepy Hollow GC
Prospect, Kentucky
Harold England
Sleepy Hollow GC
Scarboro-on-Hudson, New York
Charles Blair Macdonald, Seth
Raynor
Sleepy Hollow GC (R)
New York
Tom Winton
Sleepy Hollow GC (A. 5)
New York
A.W. Tillinghast
Sleepy Hollow GC (R)
New York
A.W. Tillinghast
Sleepy Hollow GC (R)
New York
Robert Trent Jones
Sleepy Hollow GC
Cleveland, Ohio
Stanley Thompson
Sleepy Hollow GC
Hurricane, West Virginia
James Gilmore Harrison
Sligo Park GC
Maryland
Edmund B. Ault, Al Jamison
Slocan Lake GC
New Denver, British Columbia
James Greer, Neil Tatrie
Sluispolder GC
Netherlands
J.F. Dudok Van Heel
Smiley's Sportland GC NLE
Kansas City, Kansas
Smiley Bell
Smiley's Sportland GC
Overland Park, Kansas
Everett Tull
Smithfield CC (A. 9)
North Carolina
Ellis Maples
Smithfield CC (R. 9)
North Carolina
Ellis Maples
Smoky Hill CC
Hays, Kansas
Dick Phelps
Smoky Hill CC (A. 9)
Kansas
Greg Nash
Smoky Mountain CC
Newport, Tennessee
Alex McKay
Snapfinger Woods GC
Decatur, Georgia
Joe Lee, Rocky Roquemore
Snee Farm CC
Charleston, South Carolina
George W. Cobb
Snowmass GC
Snowmass-at-Aspen, Colorado
Press Maxwell
Snowmass GC (A. 9)
Colorado
John Cochran
Snowmass GC (R)
Colorado
Arnold Palmer, Ed Seay
Snyder Park CC (R. 4)
Ohio
Jack Kidwell
Soangetaha CC
Galesburg, Illinois
Tom Bendelow
Sobhu CC (R)
Japan
Robert Trent Jones
Soboba Springs CC
San Jacinto, California
Desmond Muirhead
Sodegaura GC
Japan
Ichisuke Izumi

Soderkoping GC
Sweden
Ronald Fream
Sodus Point GC
New York
Robert Trent Jones
Sodus Point GC (R. 9)
New York
Geoffrey S. Cornish
Sodus Point GC (A. 9)
New York
Geoffrey S. Cornish, William G.
Robinson
Soldiers Field GC (R)
Minnesota
Donald G. Brauer, Emile Perret
Sombrero CC
Marathon, Florida
C.H. Anderson
Somers CC (R. 9)
New York
Al Zikorus
Somers CC (A. 9)
New York
Al Zikorus
Somerset CC (R)
Minnesota
Stanley Thompson
Somerset CC (R)
Minnesota
Robert Bruce Harris
Somerset CC (R)
Minnesota
George W. Cobb, John LaFoy
Somerset CC (R)
Minnesota
Geoffrey S. Cornish, William G.
Robinson
Somerset CC (A. 9)
Pennsylvania
Ferdinand Garbin
Somerset Hills CC NLE
Bernardsville, New Jersey
Tom Bendelow
Somerset Hills CC
Bernardsville, New Jersey
A.W. Tillinghast
Son Servera GC
Mallorca, Spain
John Harris
Son Vida GC
Mallorca, Spain
Fred W. Hawtree
Sonderjyllands GC (A. 9)
Denmark
Jan Sederholm
Sonning GC (R. 9)
England
F.G. Hawtree, J.H. Taylor
Sonning GC (A. 9)
England
F.G. Hawtree, J.H. Taylor
Sonny Guy Muni
Jackson, Mississippi
Sonny Guy
Sonoma National GC
California
William Watson, Sam Whiting
Sorrento GC (R)
Australia
Peter Thomson, Michael
Wolveridge
Sorrento Par 3 GC
Florida
R. Albert Anderson
Sorrento Valley CC
Laurel, Florida
Bill Amick
Sotogrande G&TC
Fort Worth, Texas
Leon Howard
Sotogrande GC (New Course)
Cadiz, Spain
Robert Trent Jones, Cabell
Robinson
Sotogrande GC (Old Course)
Cadiz, Spain
Robert Trent Jones
Sotogrande GC (Short Course)
Cadiz, Spain
Robert Trent Jones
Soule Park GC
Ojai, California
Carl Dwire

Soule Park GC (A. 9)
California
Bob Baldock, Robert L. Baldock
Sound Shore GC
Greenport, New York
Frank Duane
Sourabia GC
Indonesia
Tom Simpson
Souris Valley GC
Minot, North Dakota
William James Spear
South Bend CC
Indiana
George O'Neill
South Bluff CC
Peru, Illinois
William B. Langford
South Boston CC (New Course)
Virginia
Gene Hamm
South Boston CC (Old Course)
Virginia
Fred Findlay
South Boston CC (Old Course)
(R. 9)
Virginia
Gene Hamm
South County GC
St. Louis, Missouri
Gary Kern
South Fork CC (R. 3)
New York
Frank Duane
South Gate GC
California
William H. Johnson
South Haven GC
Michigan
Tom Bendelow
South Herts GC
London, England
Willie Park Jr
South Herts GC (R)
England
J. Hamilton Stutt
South Herts GC (R)
England
Harry Vardon
South Highland CC
Mayfield, Kentucky
Scott Nall
South Hill CC
Virginia
Fred Findlay
South Hills CC
West Covina, California
William F. Bell, William P. Bell
South Hills CC (R)
California
Desmond Muirhead
South Hills GC
Hanover, Pennsylvania
William Gordon, David Gordon
South Hills GC
Pennsylvania
Edmund B. Ault
South Hills GC (R)
Pennsylvania
X.G. Hassenplug
South Muskoka Curling & GC
Bracebridge, Ontario
Clinton E. Robinson
South Ocean Beach Hotel GC
New Providence Is., Bahamas
Joe Lee
South Park GC (R)
Pennsylvania
X.G. Hassenplug
South Pine Creek GC
Fairfield, Connecticut
Geoffrey S. Cornish, William G.
Robinson
South Ridge Greens GC
Fort Collins, Colorado
Frank Hummel
South Seas Plantation GC
Captiva Island, Florida
Ernest E. Smith
South Shore CC
Chicago, Illinois
Tom Bendelow

342

South Shore CC
Hingham, Massachusetts
Wayne Stiles
South Shore Harbour GC
League City, Texas
Jay Riviere, *Dave Marr*
South Side CC (R)
Illinois
Robert Bruce Harris
South Suburban GC
Littleton, Colorado
Dick Phelps
South Wales G&RC
Virginia
Edmund B. Ault
Southampton GC
New York
Seth Raynor, Charles Banks
Southampton GC (R)
New York
William F. Mitchell
Southampton GC
Hampshire, England
F.G. Hawtree, J.H. Taylor
Southampton GC (R)
England
J. Hamilton Stutt
Southampton Princess GC
Bermuda
Alfred H. Tull
Southampton Princess GC (R)
Bermuda
Ted Robinson
Southcliffe and Canwick GC
Lincolnshire, England
F.G. Hawtree, J.H. Taylor
Southern GC (R)
Australia
Peter Thomson, Michael
  Wolveridge
Southern GC (A. 9)
Australia
Peter Thomson, Michael
  Wolveridge
Southern Hills CC
Bowden, Indiana
James R. Neidigh
Southern Hills CC
Hastings, Nebraska
Reuben Schneider
Southern Hills CC
Tulsa, Oklahoma
Perry Maxwell
Southern Hills CC (R)
Oklahoma
Robert Trent Jones
Southern Hills CC (R)
Oklahoma
George Fazio, Tom Fazio
Southern Hills CC
Hot Springs, South Dakota
Dick Phelps, Brad Benz
Southern Hills CC
Murfreesboro, Tennessee
Karl Litten
Southern Hills GC
Youngstown, Ohio
R. Albert Anderson
Southern Manor CC NLE
Boca Raton, Florida
William F. Mitchell
Southern Pines CC
North Carolina
Donald Ross
Southern Pines CC (R)
North Carolina
William F. Mitchell
Southern Trace CC
Shreveport, Louisiana
Arthur Hills, Steve Forrest,Mike
  Dasher
Southerndown GC
Glamorgan, Wales
Willie Fernie
Southerndown GC (R)
Wales
Herbert Fowler
Southerndown GC (R)
Wales
Willie Park Jr
Southerndown GC (R)
Wales
H.S. Colt

Southerness GC
Dumfrieshire, Scotland
P.M. Ross
Southfield GC
England
H.S. Colt
**Southgate GC formerly known as
  Lava Hills G&CC**
St. George, Utah
John V. Lagant
Southgate GC (R)
Utah
William Howard Neff
Southmoor GC
Flint, Michigan
Bruce Matthews, Jerry Matthews
Southmore CC (R)
West Virginia
William Gordon
Southport and Ainsdale GC
England
James Braid
Southport GC
Queensland, Australia
John Harris
Southridge GC
Delano, Florida
David Wallace
Southview CC (R)
Minnesota
Donald G. Brauer, Emile Perret
Southview CC (R. 7)
Minnesota
Dick Phelps
Southview GC
Belton, Missouri
John Nash
Southward Ho! CC
Bayshore, New York
A.W. Tillinghast
Southwell GC NLE
Nottinghamshire, England
Tom Williamson
Southwest Park Muni NLE
Oklahoma City, Oklahoma
Arthur Jackson
Southwest Point G&CC
Kingston, Tennessee
Alex McKay
**Southwick Park GC (HMS
  Dryad)**
Hampshire, England
J.J.F. Pennink, C.D. Lawrie
Southwind CC
Garden City, Kansas
Don Sechrest
Southwood G&CC
Winnipeg, Manitoba
Stanley Thompson
Southwood G&CC (R)
Manitoba
John A. Thompson
Southwood GC
Hampshire, England
John Harris, Michael Wolveridge
Spa GC
Ballynahinch, Northern Ireland
R.R. Bell, A. Mathers
Spaarwoude GC
Velsen, Netherlands
J.J.F. Pennink
Spallumcheen G&TC
Vernon, British Columbia
Bill Simms, Cyril Foster
Spangdahlem GC
West Germany
Bernhard von Limburger
Spanish Bay G Links
Pebble Beach, California
Robert Trent Jones Jr, Don
  Knott,*Frank "Sandy" Tatum, Tom
  Watson*
Spanish Oaks GC
Ogden, Utah
Donald Collett, Gary Darling
Spanish Trail G&CC
Las Vegas, Nevada
Robert Trent Jones Jr, Don Knott
Spanish Wells CC
Bonita Springs, Florida
Gordon G. Lewis
Spanish Wells CC
Hilton Head Island, South
  Carolina
George W. Cobb

Sparrow Hawk GC
Jackson, Michigan
Floyd Hammond
Sparrows Point CC
Baltimore, Maryland
William Gordon, David Gordon
Spartan Meadows GC
Elgin, Illinois
Edward Lawrence Packard
Spartanburg GC
Roebuck, South Carolina
Tom Jackson
Sparwood GC
British Columbia
Ernest Brown
Speedlinks GC
Shoemakersville, Pennsylvania
Luther O. "Luke" Morris
Speedway 500 GC
Indianapolis, Indiana
William H. Diddel
Speedway 500 GC (A. 9)
Indiana
William H. Diddel
Speidel GC
Wheeling, West Virginia
Robert Trent Jones, Roger
  Rulewich
Spencer G&CC
Iowa
David Gill
Spessard Holland GC
Melbourne, Florida
Arnold Palmer, Ed Seay,Bob
  Walker
Spokane County GC
Spokane, Washington
Robert Muir Graves, Damian
  Pascuzzo
Spokane CC
Washington
Jim Barnes
Spokane CC (R)
Washington
Joe Novak
Spook Rock GC
Ramapo, New York
Frank Duane
Spooky Brook GC
New Jersey
Edmund B. Ault
Spooncreek GC
Stuart, Virginia
Gene Hamm
Sporting C de Beauvallon
France
Pier Mancinelli
Sports Center GC
North Hollywood, California
Joe Kirkwood Jr.
Sportsman G&CC
Northbrook, Illinois
Tom Bendelow
Sportsman G&CC (R)
Illinois
Ken Killian, Dick Nugent
Sportsman's GC
Harrisburg, Pennsylvania
James Gilmore Harrison,
  Ferdinand Garbin
Spotswood CC NLE
Harrisonburg, Virginia
Fred Findlay
Spotswood CC
Harrisburg, Virginia
Edmund B. Ault
Spotswood CC (A. 9)
Virginia
Edmund B. Ault
Spotswood CC (A. 9)
Virginia
Alex McKay
Sprain Brook GC
Yonkers, New York
Tom Winton
Spring Brook GC
New Jersey
Thomas Hucknall
Spring Brook CC
Antigo, Wisconsin
Charles Maddox, *Frank P.
  MacDonald*

Spring Creek G&CC
Ripon, California
Jack Fleming
Spring Creek GC (A. 9)
Illinois
Ken Killian, Dick Nugent
Spring Creek GC (R. 9)
Illinois
Ken Killian, Dick Nugent
Spring Creek GC
Hershey, Pennsylvania
Maurice McCarthy
Spring Haven GC
Rhode Island
Phil Wogan
Spring Hill CC
Tifton, Georgia
Willard Byrd
Spring Hill GC
Richmond, Ohio
James Gilmore Harrison,
  Ferdinand Garbin
Spring Hill CC
Albany, Oregon
Fred Federspiel
Spring Hill G&CC
Florida
David Wallace
Spring Lake CC (A. 9)
Illinois
Edward Lawrence Packard
Spring Lake CC
Lexington, Kentucky
Buck Blankenship
Spring Lake CC
York, South Carolina
Fred Bolton
Spring Lake CC (A. 9)
South Carolina
Robert Renaud
Spring Lake CC
Rosebud, Texas
Leon Howard
Spring Lake G&CC
Sebring, Florida
Frank Duane
Spring Lake G&CC
Michigan
Tom Bendelow
Spring Lake G&CC (R)
Michigan
William Newcomb
Spring Lake G&CC (R. 1)
Michigan
Bruce Matthews, Jerry Matthews
Spring Lake G&CC (R. 2)
Michigan
Jerry Matthews
Spring Lake G&CC
New Jersey
George C. Thomas Jr
Spring Lake G&CC (R)
New Jersey
A.W. Tillinghast
Spring Lake GC
Columbia, South Carolina
Fred Bolton
Spring Lakes GC (Course No. 1)
Stouffville, Ontario
Renee Muylaert, *Charles Muylaert*
Spring Lakes GC (Course No. 2)
Stouffville, Ontario
Renee Muylaert, *Charles Muylaert*
Spring Meadows CC
Linden, Michigan
Edward Lawrence Packard, Brent
  Wadsworth
Spring Rock CC
Central Valley, New York
Orrin Smith
Spring Valley CC
Sharon, Massachusetts
Geoffrey S. Cornish, Samuel
  Mitchell
Spring Valley CC
Elyria, Ohio
Harold Paddock
Spring Valley CC
Columbia, South Carolina
George W. Cobb
Spring Valley CC
Salem, Wisconsin
William B. Langford, Theodore J.
  Moreau

Spring Valley GC
Milpitas, California
Brad Benz, Mike Poellot
Spring Valley GC
Reed City, Michigan
Warner Bowen
Spring Valley GC
Union Center, Wisconsin
R. Albert Anderson
Spring Valley Lake CC
Victorville, California
Robert Trent Jones, Robert Trent
  Jones Jr,Gary Roger Baird
Springbrook CC
Lawrenceville, Georgia
Perrin Walker
Springbrook GC
Naperville, Illinois
Edward Lawrence Packard,
  Roger Packard
Springdale CC
Princeton, New Jersey
William S. Flynn, Howard
  Toomey
Springdale CC (R)
New Jersey
William S. Flynn
Springdale GC
Canton, North Carolina
Joseph Holmes
Springfield CC (R)
Massachusetts
William F. Mitchell
Springfield CC (A. 7)
Massachusetts
Brian Silva, Geoffrey S. Cornish
Springfield CC
Ohio
Donald Ross, Walter Hatch
Springfield CC
Oregon
Sid Milligan
Springfield CC (R)
Oregon
Robert Muir Graves
Springfield G&CC
Virginia
Edmund B. Ault, Al Jamison
Springfield GC
Japan
Robert Trent Jones Jr, Don
  Knott,Gary Linn
Springfield Oaks GC
Davisburg, Michigan
Mark DeVries
Springhaven C (R)
Pennsylvania
William S. Flynn
Springhill GC
Aurora, Colorado
Dick Phelps, Brad Benz
Springs C
Rancho Mirage, California
Desmond Muirhead
Springs GC
Spring Green, Wisconsin
Robert Trent Jones, Rees Jones
Springs Mill CC
Fort Mill, South Carolina
Donald Ross
Springs Mill CC (A. 9)
South Carolina
George W. Cobb
Springtree GC
Sunrise, Florida
Bill Dietsch
Springvale CC
North Olmstead, Ohio
James Gilmore Harrison
Spruce Creek GC
Daytona Beach, Florida
Bill Amick
Spruce Grove GC
Edmonton, Alberta
William G. Robinson
Spruce Needles GC
Timmins, Ontario
Howard Watson
Spruce Needles GC (A. 9)
Ontario
Clinton E. Robinson
Spruce Needles GC (R. 9)
Ontario
Clinton E. Robinson

Spruce Pine CC
North Carolina
Ross Taylor
Spyglass Hill G Links
Pebble Beach, California
Robert Trent Jones
Squaw Creek CC
Vienna, Ohio
Stanley Thompson
Squaw Creek CC
Ft. Worth, Texas
Ralph Plummer
Squaw Creek GC
Marion, Iowa
Herman Thompson
Squaw Mountain Inn GC (R)
Maine
John S. Parsons
Squaw Mountain Inn GC (R)
Maine
John A. Shirley
Squires GC
Fallbrook, California
William H. Johnson
Squires GC
Ambler, Pennsylvania
George Fazio
Squirrel Run GC
New Iberia, Louisiana
Joe Lee
St Eurach Land und GC
Iffeldorf, West Germany
Donald Harradine
St. Albans CC
New York
Willie Park Jr
St. Albans CC (R)
New York
A.W. Tillinghast
St. Andrew CC
Saint-Andre, Quebec
Herbert Strong
St. Andrews (Eden Course)
Fife, Scotland
H.S. Colt, Alister Mackenzie
St. Andrews (Jubilee Course)
Fife, Scotland
Willie Auchterlonie
St. Andrews (New Course)
Fife, Scotland
Old Tom Morris
St. Andrews (Old Course) (R)
Scotland
Alister Mackenzie
St. Andrews (Old Course) (R)
Scotland
Old Tom Morris
St. Andrews (Old Course) (R)
Scotland
Allan Robertson
St. Andrews CC
Mobile, Alabama
Earl Stone
St. Andrews CC (East Course)
Boca Raton, Florida
Ted McAnlis
St. Andrews CC (West Course)
Boca Raton, Florida
Ted McAnlis
St. Andrews G&CC
Ocean Springs, Mississippi
James Thompson
St. Andrews G&CC (Course No. 1)
West Chicago, Illinois
Edward B. Dearie Jr
St. Andrews G&CC (Course No. 1) (R)
Illinois
Joe Lee
St. Andrews G&CC (Course No. 2)
West Chicago, Illinois
Edward B. Dearie Jr
St. Andrews G&CC (Course No. 2) (R)
Illinois
Joe Lee
St. Andrews GC NLE
Laguna Niguel, California
Norman Macbeth
St. Andrews GC
Overland Park, Kansas
John Nash, Charles Nash

St. Andrews GC NLE
Kansas City, Missouri
James Dalgleish
St. Andrews GC
Hastings-on-Hudson, New York
William H. Tucker
St. Andrews GC (R)
New York
James Braid
St. Andrews GC (R)
New York
Jack Nicklaus, Bob Cupp
St. Andrews GC NLE
Memphis, Tennessee
David Patrick
St. Andrews GC
Calgary, Alberta
Willie Park Jr
St. Andrews GC NLE
Toronto, Ontario
Stanley Thompson
St. Andrews GC (R. 3)
Ontario
John Watson
St. Andrews GC NLE
Moka, Trinidad and Tobago
J.S.F. Morrison, H.S. Colt
St. Andrews GC
Maraval, Trinidad and Tobago
John Harris, Peter Thomson,Michael Wolveridge, Ronald Fream
St. Andrews South GC
Punta Gorda, Florida
Ron Garl
St. Ann GC
St. Louis, Missouri
Al Linkogel
St. Anne's GC (R. 9)
Ireland
Eddie Hackett
St. Anne's GC (A. 9)
Ireland
Eddie Hackett
St. Augustine CC NLE
Florida
Alex Findlay
St. Augustine Links (North Course) now known as Ponce de Leon CC
St. Augustine Links (South Course) NLE
Florida
Donald Ross
St. Augustine Shores CC
Florida
John Denton
St. Austell GC
England
James Braid
St. Bernard CC
Ohio
Earl F. Yesberger
St. Boswells GC
Roxburghshire, Scotland
Willie Park
St. Catharines G&CC
Ontario
Stanley Thompson
St. Catharines G&CC (R)
Ontario
Clinton E. Robinson, Robert Moote
St. Catherines Muni
Ontario
Renee Muylaert
St. Charles CC
Illinois
Tom Bendelow
St. Charles CC (R)
Illinois
Robert Trent Jones
St. Charles CC (R)
Illinois
David Gill
St. Charles CC (North Nine)
Winnipeg, Manitoba
Alister Mackenzie
St. Charles CC (North Nine) (R)
Manitoba
Geoffrey S. Cornish, William G. Robinson

St. Charles CC (North Nine) (R)
Manitoba
Clinton E. Robinson
St. Charles CC (South Nine)
Winnipeg, Manitoba
Donald Ross
St. Charles CC (West Nine) NLE
Winnipeg, Manitoba
Tom Bendelow
St. Charles CC (West Nine)
Winnipeg, Manitoba
Norman H. Woods
St. Charles CC (West Nine) (R)
Manitoba
Geoffrey S. Cornish, William G. Robinson
St. Charles CC (West Nine) (R)
Manitoba
Geoffrey S. Cornish, William G. Robinson
St. Charles GC
Missouri
Al Linkogel
St. Clair CC
Belleville, Illinois
William B. Langford, Theodore J. Moreau
St. Clair CC
Michigan
Donald Ross
St. Clair CC
Pittsburgh, Pennsylvania
Tom Bendelow
St. Clair CC
Pittsburgh, Pennsylvania
William Gordon, David Gordon
St. Clair CC (R)
Pennsylvania
James Gilmore Harrison, Ferdinand Garbin
St. Clair CC (A. 9)
Pennsylvania
Joe Lee
St. Clair CC (A. 1)
Pennsylvania
Dominic Palombo
St. Clair CC (R)
Pennsylvania
Dominic Palombo
St. Clair Shores CC
Michigan
Bruce Matthews, Jerry Matthews
St. Cloud CC
Minnesota
Tim Murphy
St. Cyprien GC
Perpignan, France
J.B. Tomlinson
St. Davids GC
Philadelphia, Pennsylvania
Donald Ross
St. Davids GC (R)
Pennsylvania
A.W. Tillinghast
St. Deiniol GC
Wales
James Braid
St. Elmo GC
Illinois
William James Spear
St. Enodoc GC
Cornwall, England
James Braid
St. George Hotel GC (R)
Bermuda
Devereux Emmet, Alfred H. Tull
St. George's G&CC
Stony Brook, New York
Devereux Emmet
St. George's G&CC NLE
Islington, Ontario
H.S. Colt
St. George's G&CC (R)
Islington, Ontario
Stanley Thompson
St. George's G&CC (R. 4)
Ontario
Clinton E. Robinson
St. George's GC
Bermuda
Robert Trent Jones, Roger Rulewich

St. George's Hill GC
Surrey, England
H.S. Colt
St. George's Hill GC (R)
England
J. Hamilton Stutt
St. Georges GC
St. Georges de Beauc, Quebec
Howard Watson
St. Helens GC
Warren, Oregon
Clarence Johnson, Gordon Johnson
St. James GC NLE
Montego Bay, Jamaica
William B. Langford
St. James Muni
Missouri
Chic Adams
St. Johnsbury CC
Vermont
Willie Park Jr
St. Joseph CC (R. 1)
Missouri
Bob Dunning
St. Joseph CC (R)
Missouri
Don Sechrest
St. Joseph's Bay CC
Florida
Bill Amick
St. Jude CC
Chicora, Pennsylvania
Emil Loeffler, *John McGlynn*
St. Jude CC (A. 4)
Pennsylvania
Ferdinand Garbin
St. Knuds GC
Denmark
C.K. Cotton, J.J.F. Pennink
St. Laurent GC
I'le D'Orleans, Quebec
Howard Watson, John Watson
St. Lawrence Univ
Canton, New York
Devereux Emmet
St. Lawrence Univ (A.12)
New York
Geoffrey S. Cornish, William G. Robinson
St. Leonard's School for Girls GC
Fife, Scotland
Old Tom Morris
St. Louis CC NLE
Missouri
James Foulis
St. Louis CC
Clayton, Missouri
Charles Blair Macdonald, Seth Raynor
St. Louis CC (R)
Missouri
Robert Trent Jones
St. Luc GC
Quebec
Howard Watson
St. Luc GC (A. 9)
Quebec
John Watson
St. Lucie River CC NLE
Port Sewall, Florida
William B. Langford, Theodore J. Moreau
St. Marys CC
Ohio
Tom Bendelow
St. Marys GC
West Virginia
X.G. Hassenplug
St. Mellion G&CC
Cornwall, England
J. Hamilton Stutt
St. Mellons GC
Wales
H.S. Colt, J.S.F. Morrison,Henry Cotton
St. Michael GC
Sydney, Australia
Clement Glancey
St. Michael Jubilee GC
England
Fred W. Hawtree

St. Michaels G Links
Fife, Scotland
Old Tom Morris
St. Michaels GC (R)
South Africa
Jock Brews
St. Nom La Breteche GC (Blue Course)
France
Fred W. Hawtree
St. Nom La Breteche GC (Blue Course) (R)
France
Pier Mancinelli
St. Nom La Breteche GC (Red Course)
France
Fred W. Hawtree
St. Nom La Breteche GC (Red Course) (R)
France
Pier Mancinelli
St. Pierre G&CC (New Course)
Gwent, Wales
William Cox
St. Pierre G&CC (Old Course)
Gwent, Wales
C.K. Cotton, J.J.F. Pennink
St. Queen Hotel GC
Channel Islands
Tony Jacklin
St. Thomas G&CC
Ontario
Stanley Thompson
St. Thomas G&CC (A. 9)
Ontario
Clinton E. Robinson
Stadium CC
Schenectady, New York
James Thomson
Stafford CC
New York
Walter J. Travis
Stafford CC (R)
New York
Stanley Thompson, Robert Trent Jones
Stag Island GC
Port Huron, Michigan
Tom Bendelow
Stagg Hill GC
Manhattan, Kansas
Ray B. Weisenburger, Richard H. Morse
Stan Peschel Estate GC
Boston Corners, New York
Stephen Kay
Standard C NLE
Atlanta, Georgia
Robert Trent Jones
Standard C
Norcross, Georgia
Arthur Hills, Steve Forrest,Mike Dasher
Standard C (R. 1) NLE
Georgia
Arthur Davis, Ron Kirby,Gary Player
Standard C (A. 1) NLE
Georgia
Ron Kirby
Standard CC
Louisville, Kentucky
Robert Bruce Harris
Standard CC (A. 9)
Kentucky
Edward Lawrence Packard
Standing Stone GC
Huntingdon, Pennsylvania
Geoffrey S. Cornish, William G. Robinson
Stanford University GC
Palo Alto, California
William P. Bell
Stanford University GC (R)
California
Robert Trent Jones, Robert Trent Jones Jr
Stanhope G&CC
Prince Edward Island
Clinton E. Robinson
Stanislaus CC
Modesto, California
William Lock

Stanley GC
New Britain, Connecticut
Robert J. Ross
Stanley GC (A. 9)
Connecticut
Orrin Smith, Al Zikorus
Stanley GC (R.27)
Connecticut
Geoffrey S. Cornish, William G.
  Robinson
Stanly County CC (R)
North Carolina
Ellis Maples, Ed Seay
Stannum GC
Grabo, Sweden
J.J.F. Pennink
Stansbury Park CC
Tooele, Utah
William H. Neff
Stanton Heights CC
Pittsburgh, Pennsylvania
Tom Bendelow
Stanton-on-the-Wolds GC
Nottinghamshire, England
Tom Williamson
Stanwich C
Greenwich, Connecticut
William Gordon, David Gordon
Stanwich C (R. 3)
Connecticut
Brian Silva, Geoffrey S. Cornish
Star Fort National GC
Ninety-Six, South Carolina
George W. Cobb
Star Hill G&CC
Cape Carteret, North Carolina
Russell T. Burney
Stardust CC
San Diego, California
Lawrence Hughes
Stardust CC (R. 6)
California
Ted Robinson
Stardust GC
Sun City West, Arizona
Jeff Hardin, Greg Nash, *Tom Ryan*
Starhaven GC
Keokuk, Iowa
C.D. Wagstaff
Starke G&CC
Florida
R. Albert Anderson
Starmount Forest CC
Greensboro, North Carolina
Perry Maxwell
Starmount Forest CC (R)
North Carolina
George W. Cobb
Starr Hollow GC
Fort Worth, Texas
Joseph S. Finger
State Line GC
Texarkana, Texas
William B. Langford, Theodore J.
  Moreau
States GC
Vicksburg, Michigan
Elmer Travis
Statesville CC
North Carolina
Alex McKay
Statham's Landing GC
Georgia
Tom Clark, Bill Love
Staunton CC (R)
Virginia
Buddy Loving
Stavanger GC
Norway
Fred Smith
Staverton Park GC
Northamptonshire, England
John Harris
Stayton Meadows GC
Kansas City, Missouri
Charles Stayton
Ste. Marguerite GC
Sept Isles, Quebec
Howard Watson
Stead AFB GC
Nevada
Bob Baldock

Steamboat Village CC
Steamboat Springs, Colorado
Robert Trent Jones Jr, Gary
  Roger Baird
Steed and Evans GC
Fonthill, Ontario
Renee Muylaert
Steinback Fly Inn GC
Manitoba
Clinton E. Robinson
Steinback Fly Inn GC (A. 9)
Manitoba
John A. Thompson
Stepaside GC
Dublin, Ireland
Eddie Hackett
Stephen F. Austin GC (R)
Texas
Jay Riviere
Sterling CC
Colorado
Henry B. Hughes
Sterling CC
Kansas
Dewey Longworth
Sterling Farms Muni
Stamford, Connecticut
Geoffrey S. Cornish, William G.
  Robinson
Sterling Park GC
Virginia
Edmund B. Ault
Steubenville CC (A. 9)
Ohio
Ferdinand Garbin
Steubenville CC (R. 9)
Ohio
Ferdinand Garbin
Stevenage GC
Hertfordshire, England
John Jacobs
Stevens Park GC (R)
Texas
Arthur Davis
Stevens Point CC
Wisconsin
Edward Lawrence Packard
Stevens Point CC (R)
Wisconsin
Edward Lawrence Packard
Stevensville Lake G&CC
Swan Lake, New York
William F. Mitchell
Still Meadow CC (R)
Ohio
William H. Diddel
Still Waters CC
Dadeville, Alabama
George W. Cobb
Stillwater CC
Minnesota
Paul Coates
Stillwater G&CC
Oklahoma
Don Sechrest
Stinchcombe Hill GC
England
James Braid
Stirling GC
Stirlingshire, Scotland
Old Tom Morris
Stirling GC (R)
Scotland
Henry Cotton
Stockbridge GC (R)
Massachusetts
Joseph Franz
Stockdale CC
Bakersfield, California
Lloyd Tevis
Stockdale CC (A. 9)
California
Robert Muir Graves
Stockdale CC (R. 9)
California
Robert Muir Graves
Stockgrove GC
England
Fred W. Hawtree
Stockholm GC
Sweden
H.S. Colt, C.H. Alison, J.S.F.
  Morrison

Stocksfield GC (R)
England
J.J.F. Pennink
Stockton G&CC
California
Alister Mackenzie
Stockton G&CC (R)
California
Robert Muir Graves
Stockwood Park GC
Bedfordshire, England
J.J.F. Pennink
Stoke Poges GC
England
H.S. Colt
Stoke Rochford GC
Lincolnshire, England
S.V. Hotchkin
Stone Creek Cove GC
Anderson, South Carolina
J. Porter Gibson
Stone Mountain GC
Georgia
Robert Trent Jones, Roger
  Rulewich
Stone Mountain GC (R. 9)
Georgia
John LaFoy
Stonebriar CC
Dallas, Texas
Joseph S. Finger, Ken Dye
Stonebridge CC
Blanchard, Idaho
James R. Kraus
Stonebridge G&CC
Boca Raton, Florida
Karl Litten
Stonebridge GC
Memphis, Tennessee
George W. Cobb
Stoneham GC
Hampshire, England
Willie Park Jr
Stonehaven GC
Scotland
George Duncan
Stonehenge GC
Barrington, Illinois
Charles Maddox
Stonehenge GC
Fairfield Glade, Tennessee
Joe Lee, Rocky Roquemore
Stonehenge GC
Bon Air, Virginia
Edmund B. Ault
Stoneridge CC
Poway, California
David W. Kent
Stoneridge CC (A. 9)
California
Ted Robinson
Stoneridge CC (R. 9)
California
Ted Robinson
Stones River CC (R. 9)
Tennessee
Arthur Davis
Stonewal CC
Lake Park, Florida
Karl Litten
Stoney Brook GC
Hopewell, New Jersey
Robert H. Kraeger
Stoney Creek GC
Wintergreen, Virginia
Rees Jones, Keith Evans
Stoney Plain GC
Alberta
Norman H. Woods
Stoneyholme GC
Cumbria, England
J.J.F. Pennink
Stony Brae GC
Quincy, Massachusetts
Wayne Stiles
Stony Brook CC
Litchfield, Connecticut
Al Zikorus
Stony Creek GC
Rochester, Michigan
Robert Beard
Stony Ford GC
Goshen, New York
Hal Purdy

Stonybrook GC
Litchfield, Connecticut
Tom Bendelow
Stonycroft Hills CC (R. 5)
Michigan
Bruce Matthews, Jerry Matthews
Stornoway GC
Isle of Lewis, Scotland
John R. Stutt
Stornoway GC (R)
Scotland
J.J.F. Pennink
Stow Acres CC (North Course)
Stow, Massachusetts
Geoffrey S. Cornish, William G.
  Robinson
**Stow Acres CC (South Course)
(R. 9)**
Massachusetts
Geoffrey S. Cornish, William G.
  Robinson
**Stow Acres CC (South Course)
(A. 9)**
Massachusetts
Geoffrey S. Cornish, William G.
  Robinson
Stowe CC
Vermont
William F. Mitchell
Stowe School GC
England
J.J.F. Pennink
Strabane GC (A. 9)
Northern Ireland
Eddie Hackett
Straengnaes GC (R. 9)
Sweden
Jan Sederholm
Strandhill GC (R)
Ireland
Eddie Hackett
Stranraer GC
Wigtownshire, Scotland
James Braid
Stranraer GC (R)
Scotland
John R. Stutt
Stratford-On-Avon GC
Warwickshire, England
J.H. Taylor
Strathaven GC (A. 9)
Scotland
Fraser Middleton
Strathaven GC (R)
Scotland
J. Hamilton Stutt
Strathcona GC
Huntsville, Ontario
Clinton E. Robinson
Strathcona GC (R.13)
Ontario
John Watson
Strathlene GC
Aberdeen, Scotland
George E. Smith
Strathroy CC
Ontario
Renee Muylaert
Stratton Mountain Golf Academy
Vermont
Geoffrey S. Cornish, William G.
  Robinson
Stratton Mountain GC
Vermont
Geoffrey S. Cornish, William G.
  Robinson
Stratton Mountain GC (A. 9)
Vermont
Geoffrey S. Cornish, Brian Silva
Streetsville Glen GC
Ontario
Robert Moote, *David Moote*
Stressholme GC
England
C.K. Cotton, J.J.F. Pennink
Stumpy Lake GC
Norfolk, Virginia
Robert Trent Jones, Frank Duane
Sturgeon Point GC
Ontario
Clinton E. Robinson
Sturgeon Valley G&CC (A.12)
Alberta
William G. Robinson

Stuttgarter GC
Monsheim, West Germany
Karl Hoffmann, Bernhard von
  Limburger
Subic Bay GC
Philippines
Willard Wilkinson
Suburban CC
Waukegan, Illinois
Joseph A. Roseman
Suburban CC (R)
Maryland
Robert Trent Jones
Suburban CC (R)
Maryland
Edmund B. Ault
Suburban CC (R. 4)
Maryland
Edmund B. Ault, Bill Love
Suburban GC NLE
Elizabeth, New Jersey
Tom Bendelow
Suburban GC (R)
New Jersey
A.W. Tillinghast
Sudbury GC
Middlesex, England
Willie Park Jr
Sudden Valley G&CC
Bellingham, Washington
Ted Robinson
Suffield CC
Connecticut
Orrin Smith
Suffolk County CC NLE
East Islip, New York
Seth Raynor
Suffolk CC
Virginia
Russell Breeden
Sugar Creek CC
Sugarland, Texas
Robert Trent Jones, Rees Jones
Sugar Creek G&CC
Ohio
Ken Killian, Dick Nugent
Sugar Hill CC
New Hampshire
Ralph Barton
Sugar Hollow GC
Banner Elk, North Carolina
Frank Duane
Sugar Isle GC
New Carlisle, Ohio
Jack Kidwell
Sugar Mill CC
New Smyrna Beach, Florida
Joe Lee
Sugar Mill CC (A. 9)
Florida
Joe Lee, Rocky Roquemore
Sugar Springs GC
Gladwin, Michigan
Bruce Matthews, Jerry Matthews
Sugarbush CC
Garrettsville, Ohio
Harold Paddock
Sugarbush GC
Warren, Vermont
Robert Trent Jones, Frank Duane
Sugarloaf GC
Carrabassett Valley, Maine
Robert Trent Jones Jr, Don Knott
Sugarloaf GC
Pennsylvania
Geoffrey S. Cornish, William G.
  Robinson
Sugarloaf Mountain GC
Cedar, Michigan
C.D. Wagstaff
Sugarmill Woods G&CC
Homosassa, Florida
Ron Garl
Sullivan CC
Illinois
Robert Bruce Harris
Sulphur Hills CC
Oklahoma
Floyd Farley
Summerfield G&CC
Tigard, Oregon
Ted Robinson

Summerlea G&CC (Cascades
  Course)
Montreal, Quebec
Geoffrey S. Cornish
Summerlea G&CC (Dorion
  Course)
Montreal, Quebec
Geoffrey S. Cornish
Summerlea GC NLE
Montreal, Quebec
Willie Park Jr
Summersett CC (R)
South Carolina
Tom Jackson
Summertree GC
New Port Richey, Florida
Arthur Davis
Summertree GC
Crown Point, Indiana
Bruce Matthews, Jerry Matthews
Summit Chase G&CC
Snellville, Georgia
Ward Northrup
Summit CC
Pennsylvania
Edmund B. Ault
Summit GC
New Jersey
Hal Purdy
Summit GC
Virginia
Tom Clark, Edmund B. Ault
Summit GC at Lake Holiday
Winchester, Virginia
Richard Watson
Summit Hills CC (A. 1)
Kentucky
Jack Kidwell, Michael Hurdzan
Summit Hills CC (R.10)
Kentucky
Jack Kidwell, Michael Hurdzan
Summit Hills CC (R)
Kentucky
Arthur Hills, Steve Forrest, Mike
  Dasher
Summit Springs GC
Poland, Maine
Alex Findlay
Sumner Heights GC
Cornwall, Ontario
Howard Watson
Sumner Hills GC
North Carolina
Clement B. "Johnny" Johnston,
  Clyde Johnston
Sun 'n Lake CC
Lake Placid, Florida
Bill Watts
Sun 'n Sky CC
Barstow, California
Ted Robinson
Sun 'N Lake GC
Sebring, Florida
Donald Dyer
Sun 'N' Surf GC
Boca Raton, Florida
Joe Kirkwood Jr.
Sun and Fun Par 3 GC
Illinois
Charles Maddox
Sun Blest GC
Noblesville, Indiana
William H. Diddel
Sun City Center G&CC (North
  Course)
Florida
Milt Coggins
Sun City Center G&CC (North
  Course) (A. 9)
Florida
Mark Mahannah, Charles
  Mahannah
Sun City Center G&CC (South
  Course)
Florida
Mark Mahannah
Sun City CC
Arizona
Milt Coggins, Jeff Hardin, Greg
  Nash
Sun City CC
Arizona
James Winans, John W. Meeker, Jeff
  Hardin

Sun City Lakes West GC
Arizona
Milt Coggins, James Winans
Sun City North GC
Arizona
Milt Coggins
Sun City South GC
Arizona
Milt Coggins
Sun City Vistoso GC
Tucson, Arizona
Greg Nash
Sun Country Resort GC
Lake Whitney, Texas
Leon Howard
Sun Lake CC
Utsunomiya, Japan
Ron Kirby, Denis Griffiths
Sun Lakes GC
Arizona
James Winans, Jeff Hardin, Greg
  Nash
Sun Lakes GC (A. 9)
Arizona
Jeff Hardin, Greg Nash
Sun Meadow CC
Houston, Texas
Jay Riviere
Sun Valley CC
Sioux City, Iowa
Leo Johnson
Sun Valley GC
Idaho
William P. Bell
Sun Valley GC (A. 9)
Idaho
William P. Bell
Sun Valley GC (R)
Idaho
George Von Elm
Sun Valley GC (A. 4)
Idaho
Robert Trent Jones Jr, Don Knott
Sun Valley GC (R)
Idaho
Robert Trent Jones Jr, Don Knott
Sun Valley GC
Louisville, Kentucky
Benjamin Wihry
Sun Valley GC
Rehobeth, Massachusetts
Geoffrey S. Cornish
Sun Valley GC (Routing)
Massachusetts
Walter I. Johnson
Sunbird GC
Chandler, Arizona
Gary Panks
Suncrest CC
Palm Desert, California
Richard Watson
Suncrest GC
Butler, Pennsylvania
James Gilmore Harrison
Suncrest GC (R)
Pennsylvania
Ferdinand Garbin
Suncrest GC (A. 9)
Pennsylvania
James Gilmore Harrison
Sundance GC
Washington
Dale Knott
Sundown GC
Burlington, Iowa
Tom Clark, Brian Ault, Edmund
  B. Ault
Sundown Muni
Sweetwater, Texas
William Cantrell
Sundowner GC
Ashland, Kentucky
William "Bert" Way
Sundridge Park GC (East
  Course)
Kent, England
Willie Park, Willie Park Jr
Sundridge Park GC (East
  Course) (R)
England
Sir Guy Campbell, C.K.
  Hutchison

Sundridge Park GC (West
  Course)
Kent, England
Willie Park, Willie Park Jr
Sunflower Hills GC
Bonner Springs, Kansas
Roger Packard
Sunken Gardens Muni
Sunnyvale, California
Clark Glasson
Sunken Meadow Park GC
Northport, New York
Alfred H. Tull
Sunkist CC
Biloxi, Mississippi
Roland "Robby" Robertson
Sunland CC
Sequim, Washington
A. Vernon Macan
Sunland Village GC
Mesa, Arizona
Milt Coggins, Jeff Hardin, Greg
  Nash
Sunnehanna CC
Johnstown, Pennsylvania
A.W. Tillinghast
Sunnehanna CC (R)
Pennsylvania
Ferdinand Garbin
Sunnehanna CC (R. 1)
Pennsylvania
Jerry Matthews
Sunningdale CC (R)
New York
A.W. Tillinghast
Sunningdale CC (New Course)
London, Ontario
Clinton E. Robinson
Sunningdale CC (Old Course)
London, Ontario
Stanley Thompson
Sunningdale GC
Dover, New Hampshire
Geoffrey S. Cornish
Sunningdale GC (New Course)
Berkshire, England
H.S. Colt, C.H. Alison
Sunningdale GC (New Course)
  (R)
England
J.S.F. Morrison
Sunningdale GC (New Course)
  (R)
England
Tom Simpson
Sunningdale GC (Old Course)
Berkshire, England
Willie Park Jr
Sunningdale GC (Old Course)
  (R)
England
H.S. Colt, C.H. Alison
Sunny Acres CC
Roseville, Michigan
Lou Powers
Sunny Brae CC
Osage, Iowa
William H. Livie
Sunny Hill GC
Greenville, New York
Hal Purdy
Sunny Jim GC now known as
  Medford Village CC
Sunnybreeze Palms GC
Florida
R. Albert Anderson
Sunnybrook CC
Grandville, Michigan
Bruce Matthews
Sunnybrook CC
Plymouth Meeting, Pennsylvania
William Gordon, David Gordon
Sunnycrest CC
Rochester, New York
Pete Craig
Sunnyfield GC
Gozenyama, Japan
Jack Nicklaus, Jay Morrish, Scott
  Miller
Sunnyhill GC (R)
Ohio
Ferdinand Garbin

Sunnyhill GC (A. 9)
Ohio
Ferdinand Garbin
Sunnylands GC
Rancho Mirage, California
Dick Wilson, Joe Lee
Sunnyside CC
Fresno, California
William P. Bell
Sunnyside CC (R)
California
Robert Dean Putnam
Sunnyside CC NLE
Waterloo, Iowa
Tom Bendelow
Sunnyside CC
Waterloo, Iowa
Edward Lawrence Packard
Sunnyside CC (R) NLE
Iowa
Robert Bruce Harris
Sunnyside CC
Texas
Bruce Littell
Sunnyside GC
Decatur, Illinois
Tom Bendelow
Sunnyvale Muni
California
Clark Glasson
Sunol Valley GC (Cypress
  Course)
Sunol, California
Clark Glasson
Sunol Valley GC (Palm Course)
Sunol, California
Clark Glasson
Sunport CC
Albuquerque, New Mexico
Red Lawrence
Sunrise CC
Rancho Mirage, California
Ted Robinson
Sunrise CC
Ft. Lauderdale, Florida
Bill Watts
Sunrise GC
Las Vegas, Nevada
Ted Robinson
Sunrise GC (A. 9)
Nevada
Ted Robinson
Sunrise Lakes Phase 3 GC
Sunrise, Florida
Bill Dietsch
Sunrise National CC
Sarasota, Florida
R. Albert Anderson
Sunriver CC (South Course)
Oregon
Fred Federspiel
Sunriver CC (South Course) (R)
Oregon
Peter Thomson, Michael
  Wolveridge, Ronald Fream
Sunriver GC (North Course)
Oregon
Robert Trent Jones Jr, Don Knott
Sunset Canyon GC NLE
Burbank, California
William Watson
Sunset CC
Moultrie, Georgia
Hugh Moore
Sunset CC (R. 4)
Illinois
David Gill
Sunset CC
St. Louis, Missouri
Robert Foulis, James Foulis
Sunset CC (R)
Missouri
Edward Lawrence Packard
Sunset CC
Bartesville, Oklahoma
Bob Dunning
Sunset Dunes GC
Colton, California
Robert Trent Jones
Sunset Fields GC NLE
California
William P. Bell

Sunset G Centre
Fort Erie, Ontario
Renee Muylaert
Sunset G&CC
St. Petersburg, Florida
William H. Diddel
Sunset G&CC (R)
Florida
Hans Schmeisser
Sunset GC
Hollywood, Florida
Red Lawrence
Sunset Hill GC (R)
New York
Tom Winton
Sunset Hills CC
Thousand Oaks, California
Ted Robinson
Sunset Hills CC
Tarpon Springs, Florida
William H. Diddel
Sunset Hills CC
Carrollton, Georgia
Robert Trent Jones
Sunset Hills CC (A. 9)
Georgia
Ward Northrup
Sunset Hills CC (A. 2)
Illinois
Gary Kern
Sunset Hills CC (R)
Illinois
Gary Kern
Sunset Hills CC (A. 9)
Illinois
Edward Lawrence Packard
Sunset Hills CC (A. 9)
Illinois
Edward Lawrence Packard, Brent
  Wadsworth
Sunset Hills GC
Guymon, Oklahoma
Bob Dunning
Sunset Oaks CC
Rocklin, California
William F. Bell
Sunset Park GC NLE
New York
Tom Bendelow
Sunset Ridge CC
Northbrook, Illinois
William H. Diddel
Sunset Ridge CC (R)
Illinois
C.D. Wagstaff
Sunset Valley GC (R)
Illinois
Ken Killian, Dick Nugent
Sunset Valley GC
Pequannock, New Jersey
Hal Purdy, Malcolm Purdy
Sunshine Coast G&CC
Roberts Creek, British Columbia
Ernest Brown, Roy Taylor
Sunshore GC
Chase, British Columbia
Ernest Brown
Suntree CC (North Course)
Melbourne, Florida
Richard W. LaConte
Suntree CC (South Course)
Melbourne, Florida
Arnold Palmer, Ed Seay
Surbiton GC
England
Tom Dunn
Surf GC
Myrtle Beach, South Carolina
George W. Cobb
Surfer's Paradise GC
Queensland, Australia
Sloan Morpeth
Surprise Park GC
Cedar Lake, Indiana
Stanley Pelchar
Surrey Public GC
British Columbia
Heinz Knoedler
Susquehanna Valley CC (R)
Pennsylvania
William Gordon, David Gordon
Sussex GC
New Brunswick
Clinton E. Robinson

Sussex Pines CC
Delaware
Edmund B. Ault
Sutherland Knolls GC
Oregon
Vernon Warren
Sutton Park GC
Yorkshire, England
L. Herrington
Suwanee CC (R)
Florida
Walter Ripley
Suwannee River Valley CC
Jasper, Florida
Joe Lee
Swaim Fields GC
Cincinnati, Ohio
William H. Diddel
Swaim Fields GC (A. 9)
Ohio
William H. Diddel
Swakopmund GC
Namibia
Rees Jones
Swallow's Nest GC
Sacremento, California
Bob Baldock
Swallow's Nest GC
Clarkston, Washington
Bob Baldock
Swan Creek CC
Belair, Maryland
Frank Murray, Russell Roberts
Swan Creek CC (R. 9)
Maryland
Tom Clark
Swan Hills GC
Avon, Illinois
William James Spear
Swan Lake CC
Clarksville, Tennessee
Benjamin Wihry
Swan Point GC
Issue, Maryland
Arthur Davis
Swan Valley GC
Saginaw, Michigan
Carl Mueller
Swannanoa GC
Waynesboro, Virginia
Fred Findlay
Swansea Bay GC (R. 6)
Wales
Fred W. Hawtree, Martin
  Hawtree
Swansea GC
Massachusetts
Geoffrey S. Cornish
Swartkop CC
Pretoria, South Africa
Robert G. Grimsdell
Swartz Creek Muni
Flint, Michigan
Frederick A. Ellis
Sweetwater CC
Sugarland, Texas
Roger Packard
Sweetwater GC
Bear Lake, Utah
William H. Neff, William Howard
  Neff
Sweetwater Oaks CC
Longwood, Florida
Lloyd Clifton
Swenson Park Muni
Stockton, California
Jack Fleming
Swenson Park Muni (A. 9)
California
Robert Muir Graves
Swinford GC (R)
Ireland
Eddie Hackett
Swinley Forest GC
England
H.S. Colt
Swinton Park GC
Lancashire, England
F.G. Hawtree, J.H. Taylor
Swope Park GC
Kansas City, Missouri
James Dalgleish

Swope Park GC (R)
Missouri
A.W. Tillinghast
Sycamore Creek CC
Ohio
Jack Ortman
Sycamore Creek CC (R)
Ohio
Arthur Hills
Sycamore GC
Rarenna, New York
Frank Duane
Sycamore Hills CC (A.10)
Illinois
Gary Kern
Sycamore Hills CC (R. 8)
Illinois
Gary Kern
Sydney GC (R)
Nova Scotia
Stanley Thompson
Sylvania CC
Toledo, Ohio
Willie Park Jr
Sylvania CC (R. 6)
Ohio
Sandy Alves
Sylvania CC (R)
Ohio
Arthur Hills, Steve Forrest
Table Mountain GC
Oroville, California
Louis Bertolone
Table Rock GC
Centerburg, Ohio
Jack Kidwell
Table Rock GC (A. 9)
Ohio
Jack Kidwell, Michael Hurdzan
Table Rock GC (A. 9)
Ohio
Jack Kidwell
Taboada GC
Mexico
Dave Bennett
Tacoma C&GC
Washington
Stanley Thompson
Taconic GC
Williamstown, Massachusetts
Wayne Stiles, John Van Kleek
Tadmarton Heath GC
Banbury, England
Harry Vardon
Tadmarton Heath GC (A. 9)
England
C.K. Hutchison
Tagus VA Hospital GC
Maine
Bob Baldock
Tahoe Donner GC
Truckee, California
Joseph B. Williams
Tahoe Paradise GC
Lake Tahoe, California
Fred R. Blanchard
Tahoe Tavern GC NLE
Tahoe, Nevada
May Dunn Hupfel
Taieri GC
Mosgiel, New Zealand
John Harris, Peter
  Thomson,Michael Wolveridge
Tain GC
Rossshire, Scotland
Old Tom Morris
Tain GC (R)
Scotland
John Sutherland
Taiwan G&CC
Taipei, Taiwan
Rokuro Akaboshi, Shiro Akaboshi
Takaha Royal CC
Fukuoka, Japan
Peter Thomson, Michael
  Wolveridge
Takanodai CC
Chiba, Japan
Seichi Inouye
Takarazuka GC (New Course)
Hyogo, Japan
G. Ohashi

Takarazuka GC (Old Course)
Hyogo, Japan
K. Hiroka, K. Fukui
Tall Pines at River Ridge GC
New Port Richey, Florida
Ron Garl
Tall Pines GC
California
Bob Baldock, Robert L. Baldock
Tall Pines GC
Sewell, New Jersey
William Gordon, David Gordon
Tall Timber GC
Langley, British Columbia
Wayne Lindberg, Stan
  Leonard,*Philip Tattersfield*
Tall Timbers CC
Slingerlands, New York
Frank Duane
Tall Wood CC
Connecticut
Michael Ovian
Tallgrass C
Wichita, Kansas
Arthur Hills
Tallulah GC
Louisiana
Winnie Cole
Tally Ho GC
Vernon Hills, Illinois
Ken Killian, Dick Nugent
Tally Mountain C
Tallapoosa, Georgia
Joe Lee
Tam O'Shanter CC NLE
Niles, Illinois
C.D. Wagstaff
Tam O'Shanter CC (R) NLE
Illinois
Joseph A. Roseman
Tam O'Shanter CC (R) NLE
Illinois
William B. Langford
Tam O'Shanter CC
Orchard Lake, Michigan
Wilfrid Reid, William Connellan
Tam O'Shanter CC
Bellevue, Washington
William Teufel
Tam O'Shanter CC (Dales Course)
Canton, Ohio
Leonard Macomber
Tam O'Shanter CC (Hills Course)
Canton, Ohio
Leonard Macomber
Tam O'Shanter GC (R)
New York
Robert Trent Jones, Rees Jones
Tam O'Shanter Muni
Toronto, Ontario
Howard Watson, John Watson
Taman Tun Abdul Razak GC
Ampangjaya, Malaysia
Ronald Fream
Tamarac CC
Ft. Lauderdale, Florida
Dick Wilson, Robert von Hagge
Tamarac GC
Reidville, North Carolina
Clement B. "Johnny" Johnston
Tamarack CC
Portchester, New York
Charles Banks
Tamarack CC
Mt. Lebanon, Pennsylvania
James Gilmore Harrison
Tamarack GC
New Brunswick, New Jersey
Hal Purdy, Malcolm Purdy
Tamarisk CC
Rancho Mirage, California
William F. Bell, William P. Bell
Tamarisk CC (R)
California
Ted Robinson
Tamarisk CC (R)
California
Ronald Fream
Tamarron CC
Durango, Colorado
Arthur Hills

Tamcrest CC
Alpine, New Jersey
Frank Duane
Tamcrest CC (R)
New Jersey
Stephen Kay
Tamiment CC
Pennsylvania
Robert Trent Jones
Tammy Brook CC
Cresskill, New Jersey
Robert Trent Jones, Frank Duane
Tampa Bay Hotel GC NLE
Florida
Seymour Dunn
Tampa Palms CC
Tampa, Florida
Arthur Hills, Steve Forrest,Mike
  Dasher
Tampico CC
Mexico
John Bredemus
Tampico CC (A. 9)
Mexico
Enrico Robles
Tamworth Muni
Staffordshire, England
Fred W. Hawtree, Martin
  Hawtree,A.H.F. Jiggens
Tan-Tara CC
North Tonawanda, New York
Dennis Schreckengost
Tanah Merah CC
Singapore
Ronald Fream
Tandragee GC (A. 9)
Northern Ireland
Fred W. Hawtree, Martin
  Hawtree
Tandridge GC
England
H.S. Colt
Tanforan GC
California
Jack Fleming
Tanglewood CC
Chagrin Falls, Ohio
William F. Mitchell
Tanglewood GC
Downling, Ohio
Richard Wyckoff
Tanglewood GC
Delaware, Ohio
Jack Kidwell
Tanglewood GC
Stroudsburg, Pennsylvania
George Fazio
Tanglewood GC (East Course)
Clemmons, North Carolina
Robert Trent Jones
Tanglewood GC (East Course) (A. 9)
North Carolina
Robert Trent Jones, Roger
  Rulewich
Tanglewood GC (West Course)
Clemmons, North Carolina
Robert Trent Jones, Frank Duane
Tanglewood GC (West Course) (R)
North Carolina
Robert Trent Jones
Tanglewood Manor GC
Pennsylvania
Chester Ruby
Tanglewood-on-the Texoma GC
Pottsboro, Texas
Ralph Plummer
Tannenhauf GC
Alliance, Ohio
James Gilmore Harrison,
  Ferdinand Garbin
Tanoan GC
Albuquerque, New Mexico
Robert von Hagge, Bruce Devlin
Tansi Resort GC
Crossville, Tennessee
Robert Renaud
Tantallon CC
Maryland
Ted Robinson
Tapatio Springs CC
Boerne, Texas
William Johnston

Tapps Island GC
Sumner, Washington
Ronald Fream, Peter
  Thomson,Michael Wolveridge
Tapton Park GC
Derby, England
George Duncan
Tara Ferncroft CC
Danvers, Massachusetts
Robert Trent Jones, Rees Jones
Tara Hills GC
Papillion, Nebraska
Richard Watson, Keith Evans
Tarbat GC
Scotland
John Sutherland
Targhee CC
Utah
Mark Dixon Ballif
Tarkio CC
Missouri
Chet Mendenhall
Tarpon Lake Village GC
Palm Harbor, Florida
Lane Marshall
Tarpon Springs CC
Florida
Wayne Stiles, John Van Kleek
Tarpon Springs CC (R)
Florida
Mark Mahannah
Tarpon Woods GC
Palm Harbor, Florida
Lane Marshall
Tarratine C of Dark Harbor
Islesboro, Maine
Alex Findlay
Tarry Brae GC
South Fallsburgh, New York
William F. Mitchell
Tartan Park GC
St. Paul, Minnesota
Don Herfort
Tartan Park GC (R.16)
Minnesota
Dick Nugent
Tascosa CC
Amarillo, Texas
Warren Cantrell
Tashua Knolls G&RC
Trumbull, Connecticut
Al Zikorus
Tasmania GC
Australia
Al Howard
Tasmanian Casino CC
Launceston, Australia
Peter Thomson, Michael
  Wolveridge
Tate Springs GC
Kentucky
Donald Ross
Tate Springs GC
Tennessee
Alex Findlay
Tatnuck CC
Worcester, Massachusetts
Donald Ross
Tatnuck CC NLE
Worcester, Massachusetts
Willie Campbell
Tatnuck CC (R. 5)
Massachusetts
Geoffrey S. Cornish, William G.
  Robinson
Taughannock G&CC
New York
Wester White
Tavares Cove GC
West Palm Beach, Florida
William F. Mitchell
Tavistock CC
Haddonfield, New Jersey
Alex Findlay
Tavistock CC (R)
New Jersey
James Gilmore Harrison,
  Ferdinand Garbin
Tavistock CC (R)
New Jersey
Robert Trent Jones
Taylorsville Lake GC
Kentucky
Buck Blankenship

Tazewell County CC
Pounding Mill, Virginia
Ellis Maples, Dan Maples
Tchefuncta GC
Covington, Louisiana
Jack Daray
Tchefuncta GC (A. 9)
Louisiana
Joe Lee
Teaford Lake GC
Bass Lake, California
Bob Baldock
Teamsters GC
Missouri
Homer Herpel
Tecolote Canyon GC
San Diego, California
Robert Trent Jones
Tecumseh CC
Michigan
Leo J. Bishop
Ted Makalena GC
Waipahu, Hawaii
Bob Baldock, Robert L. Baldock
Tedesco CC (R)
Massachusetts
Eugene "Skip" Wogan
Teeside GC
England
C. Robertson
Tega Cay CC (Cross Keys Course)
Fort Mill, South Carolina
William B. Lewis
Tega Cay CC (South Winds Course)
Fort Mill, South Carolina
William B. Lewis
Tegernseer GC
Bad Wiessee, West Germany
Donald Harradine
Teignmouth GC
England
H.S. Colt, C.H. Alison, Alister Mackenzie
Tejas GC
Houston, Texas
Joseph S. Finger
Telemark GC
Cable, Wisconsin
Arthur Johnson
Telford Hotel G&CC
Great Hay, England
John Harris, Peter Thomson, Michael Wolveridge
Temple CC
Texas
Ralph Plummer
Temple CC (R. 9)
Texas
Jay Riviere
Temple CC (A. 9)
Texas
Jay Riviere
Temple GC
Berkshire, England
Willie Park Jr, *J. Hepburn*
Temple GC (R)
England
Henry Cotton
Temple Hills CC
Columbia, Tennessee
Leon Howard
Temple Terrace G&CC
Florida
Tom Bendelow
Temple Terrace G&CC (R)
Florida
Hans Schmeisser
Tenby GC
Dyfed, Wales
C.K. Cotton
Tenison Muni (East Course)
Dallas, Texas
Ralph Plummer
Tenison Muni (East Course) (R)
Texas
Arthur Davis
Tenison Muni (West Course)
Dallas, Texas
John Bredemus
Tenison Muni (West Course) (R)
Texas
Ralph Plummer

Tenison Muni (West Course) (R)
Texas
Arthur Davis
Tennanah Lake House GC
Roscoe, New York
Alfred H. Tull
Tennwood C
Hockley, Texas
Ralph Plummer
Tennwood C (R.18)
Texas
Tom Fazio
Tequesta CC
Jupiter, Florida
Dick Wilson, Joe Lee
Teresopolis GC
Brazil
Stanley Thompson
Terra Nova National Park GC
Newfoundland
Clinton E. Robinson
Terrace Hills GC
Algonquin, Illinois
Charles Maddox
Terrace Lakes GC
Garden Valley, Idaho
Edward A. Hunnicutt
Terrace Park CC (R)
Ohio
Arthur Hills
Terrace Park CC (R)
Ohio
Arthur Hills, Mike Dasher
Terradyne CC
Andover, Kansas
Don Sechrest
Terrapin Hills GC
Ft. Payne, Alabama
Harold Williams
Terre du Lac CC
Bonne Terre, Missouri
R. Albert Anderson
Terrell CC
Texas
Ralph Plummer
Terri Pines CC
Culman, Alabama
Tom Jackson
Terry Walker G&CC
Leeds, Alabama
Bancroft Timmons
Teton Pines GC
Wyoming
Arnold Palmer, Ed Seay
Teugega CC
Rome, New York
Donald Ross
Teugega CC (R)
New York
William F. Mitchell
Tewkesbury Park GC
Gloucestershire, England
J.J.F. Pennink
Texarkana CC
Arkansas
William B. Langford, Theodore J. Moreau
Texarkana CC (R)
Arkansas
Leon Howard
Texas A&M Univ GC
College Station, Texas
Ralph Plummer
Texas A&M Univ GC (R)
Texas
Bruce Littell
Texas National GC
Huntsville, Texas
Jack B. Miller
The Country Club
Reform, Alabama
Harold Williams
The Country Club
Brookline, Massachusetts
Willie Campbell
The Country Club (A. 3)
Massachusetts
Willie Campbell
The Country Club (A. 9)
Massachusetts
William S. Flynn, Howard Toomey

The Country Club (R. 2)
Massachusetts
Geoffrey S. Cornish
The Country Club (R. 2)
Massachusetts
Geoffrey S. Cornish, William G. Robinson
The Country Club (R)
Massachusetts
Rees Jones
The Country Club
Cleveland, Ohio
William S. Flynn, Howard Toomey
The Country Club
Donora, Pennsylvania
Tom Bendelow
The Country Club
Salt Lake City, Utah
Harold B. Lamb
The Country Club (R)
Utah
William F. Bell, William P. Bell
The Country Club (R. 9)
Utah
William H. Neff
The Country Club (R)
Utah
Ralph Plummer
The Country Club
Johannesburg, South Africa
Fred W. Hawtree
The Golf Club
New Albany, Ohio
Pete Dye
The Golf Links
Frostproof, Florida
Henry C. Higginbotham
Thendara CC
Old Forge, New York
Donald Ross
Thendara CC (A. 9)
New York
William Harries, *A. Russell Tryon*
Thendara CC (R. 1)
New York
Geoffrey S. Cornish, William G. Robinson
Theodore Wirth GC
Minneapolis, Minnesota
Charles Erickson
Theodore Wirth GC (A. 9)
Minnesota
Edward Lawrence Packard
Thetford GC
England
Charles H. Mayo
Thetford GC (R)
England
James Braid
Thetford GC (R)
England
P.M. Ross
Thetford Mines G & Curling C (R. 9)
Quebec
Howard Watson, John Watson
Thetford Mines G & Curling C (A. 9)
Quebec
Howard Watson, John Watson
Theydon Bois GC
Essex, England
James Braid
Theydon Bois GC (A. 2)
England
Fred W. Hawtree, Martin Hawtree
Thistledown GC
Owen Sound, Ontario
Renee Muylaert
Thomas County GC
Thomasville, Georgia
Willard Byrd
Thomas Memorial GC
Turners Falls, Massachusetts
Walter Hatch
Thomaston CC
Georgia
Willard Byrd
Thomson C
North Reading, Massachusetts
Geoffrey S. Cornish

Thomson CC
Georgia
Walter Ripley
Thomson CC (R. 9)
Georgia
Robert Renaud
Thornapple Creek GC
Kalamazoo, Michigan
Mike Shields
Thornapple CC
Columbus, Ohio
Jack Kidwell
Thorngate CC
Deerfield, Illinois
Jack Croke
Thorngate CC (R)
Illinois
Robert Bruce Harris
Thornhill GC (R)
Ontario
Clinton E. Robinson
Thornhill GC (R)
Ontario
Stanley Thompson
Thornhill GC (R)
Ontario
Howard Watson
Thornhill GC (R)
Ontario
Robert Moote
Thorny Lea GC
Brockton, Massachusetts
Wayne Stiles, John Van Kleek
Thorpe Wood GC
England
Peter Alliss, David Thomas
Thorpeness GC
Suffolk, England
James Braid
Thousand Islands C
Alexandria Bay, New York
Seth Raynor
Thousand Islands C (A. 9)
New York
J. Webb
Three Lakes CC
Kuwana, Japan
Peter Thomson, Michael Wolveridge
Three Pines CC
Woodruff, South Carolina
Bill Amick
Three Rivers GC
Kelso, Washington
Robert Muir Graves
Thunder Bay CC
Ontario
Tom Bendelow
Thunder Bay G&CC
Ontario
Stanley Thompson
Thunder Bay G&CC (R)
Ontario
Clinton E. Robinson
Thunder Hill CC
South Madison, Ohio
Fred Slagle
Thunder Hills GC
Dubuque, Iowa
Gordon Cunningham
Thunder Ridge CC
Rush, New York
Pete Craig, *Joseph Demino*
Thunderbird CC
Phoenix, Arizona
Johnny Bulla, *Clarence Suggs*
Thunderbird CC
Cathedral City, California
Lawrence Hughes
Thunderbird CC (R)
California
Harry Rainville, David Rainville
Thunderbird CC (R)
California
Hal Purdy
Thunderbird CC (R)
California
Ted Robinson
Thunderbird GC
Tyngsboro, Massachusetts
Geoffrey S. Cornish
Thurgoona GC
Albury, Australia
Peter Thomson, Michael Wolveridge

Thurles GC (R)
Ireland
Eddie Hackett
Tiara Rado GC
Grand Junction, Colorado
Tom Kolacny
Tiara Rado GC (R)
Colorado
Dick Phelps
Ticonderoga CC
New York
Seymour Dunn
Tides GC
St. Petersburg, Florida
David Gill
Tides Inn & CC (Golden Eagle Course)
Irvington, Virginia
George W. Cobb, John LaFoy
Tides Inn & CC (Golden Eagle Course) (R)
Virginia
Buddy Loving
Tides Inn & CC (Short Nine)
Irvington, Virginia
Fred Findlay
Tides Inn & CC (Tartan Course)
Irvington, Virginia
Sir Guy Campbell
Tides Inn & CC (Tartan Course) (A. 9)
Virginia
George W. Cobb
Tides Inn & CC (Tartan Course) (A. 3)
Virginia
John LaFoy
Tides Inn & CC (Tartan Course) (R)
Virginia
John LaFoy
Tidewater Beach GC
Destin, Florida
Chuck Ankrom
Tidewater GC
Trenton, Maine
Phil Wogan
Tierra del Sol GC
New Mexico
Gary Panks
Tierra Del Sol GC
California City, California
Robert von Hagge, Bruce Devlin
Tierra Grande GC
Casa Grande, Arizona
Arthur Jack Snyder
Tierras De San Jose GC
Brazil
Frederico E. Bauer
Tierre Verde GC
Tierre Verde Island, Florida
Frank Murray
Tifton GC
Darlington, South Carolina
Roland "Robby" Robertson
Tiger Point G&CC (East Course)
Gulf Breeze, Florida
Bill Amick
Tiger Point G&CC (East Course) (A. 9)
Florida
Ron Garl, *Jerry Pate*
Tiger Point G&CC (East Course) (R. 9)
Florida
Ron Garl, *Jerry Pate*
Tiger Point G&CC (West Course)
Gulf Breeze, Florida
Bill Amick
Tijeras Arroyo GC
Kirkland, New Mexico
Robert Dean Putnam
Tijuana CC formerly known as Aqua Caliente GC
Mexico
William P. Bell
Tilden Park GC
Berkeley, California
William P. Bell
Tilgate Forest GC
Crawley, England
Brian Huggett, Neil Coles, *Roger Dyer*

Timaru GC (R)
New Zealand
John Harris, Peter
 Thomson,Michael Wolveridge
Timber Pines GC
New Port Richey, Florida
Ron Garl
Timber Point GC
Great River, New York
C.H. Alison, H.S. Colt
Timber Ridge CC
Minocquo, Wisconsin
Roger Packard
Timber Trails CC
LaGrange, Illinois
Robert Bruce Harris
Timber Trails CC (R)
Illinois
Robert Bruce Harris
Timberlake GC
Sullivan, Illinois
Robert Bruce Harris
Timberlane CC
Gretna, Louisiana
Robert Trent Jones, Frank Duane
Timberlin GC
Berlin, Connecticut
Al Zikorus
Timberlink GC
Ligonier, Pennsylvania
X.G. Hassenplug
Timberwild GC
Augusta, Maine
Robert L. Elder
Timmendorfer Strand GC
 (Course No. 1)
West Germany
Bernhard von Limburger
Timmendorfer Strand GC
 (Course No. 2)
West Germany
Bernhard von Limburger
Timpanogas Muni
Provo, Utah
Mick Riley
Timuquana CC
Jacksonville, Florida
Donald Ross
Timuquana CC (R)
Florida
George W. Cobb
Timuquana CC (R)
Florida
David Gordon
Tinker AFB GC
Oklahoma
Floyd Farley
Tinsley Park GC
Yorkshire, England
F.G. Hawtree, J.H. Taylor
Tioga GC
Nichols, New York
Hal Purdy
Tippecanoe CC
Monticello, Indiana
Joseph A. Roseman
Tippecanoe CC
Canfield, Ohio
Allen A. Mackenzie, Denny Shute
Tippecanoe CC (R)
Ohio
Geoffrey S. Cornish
Tippecanoe Lake CC (R)
Indiana
Gary Kern
Tipsinah Mounds GC
Grant, Minnesota
Joel Goldstrand
Tipton Muni
Indiana
William H. Diddel
Tipton Muni (A. 9)
Indiana
William H. Diddel
Tipworth GC
England
Tom Williamson
Tirrenia CC
Italy
Henry Cotton
Titirangi GC
New Zealand
F.G. Hood, Gilbert Martin

Titirangi GC (R)
New Zealand
Alister Mackenzie
Titusville CC
Pennsylvania
Emil Loeffler, *John McGlynn*
Tiverton GC
Devon, England
James Braid, John R. Stutt
Tobago GC
Mount Irvine, Trinidad and
 Tobago
John Harris
Toccoa G&CC
Toccoa, Georgia
J. Porter Gibson
Toftrees GC
State College, Pennsylvania
Edmund B. Ault
Tokatee GC
Blue River, Oregon
Ted Robinson
Tokuyama CC
Japan
Peter Thomson, Michael
 Wolveridge
Tokyo CC
Japan
C.H. Alison
Toledo CC
Ohio
Willie Park Jr
Toledo CC (R)
Ohio
Robert Bruce Harris
Toledo CC (R)
Ohio
Arthur Hills
Tolliston GC
Gary, Indiana
Tom Bendelow
Tom O'Leary GC
Bismarck, North Dakota
David Gill, Garrett Gill
Tomac Woods GC
Albion, Michigan
Robert Beard
Tomahawk CC
Welshfield, Ohio
Ben W. Zink
Tomahawk Hills GC
Jamestown, Indiana
Gary Kern
Tomahawk Hills GC
Kansas
Harry Robb
Tomahawk Hills GC (R)
Kansas
*William V. Leonard, L.J. "Dutch"
 McClellan*
Tomahawk Hollow GC
Gambier, Ohio
R.C. Rowley
**Tomahawk Lake GC formerly
 known as Homestead Mine GC**
Deadwood, South Dakota
Lawrence Hughes
Tomoka Oaks G&CC
Ormand Beach, Florida
J. Porter Gibson
Toms River CC
New Jersey
Paul Losi
Tonga GC
Tonga
Peter Thomson, Michael
 Wolveridge
Tonto Vista CC
Rio Verde, Arizona
Gary Panks
Tony Lema Memorial GC
San Leandro, California
William F. Bell
Tooele GC
Utah
Mick Riley
Tooting Bec C
England
Tom Dunn
Tooting Bec C (R)
England
Willie Park Jr

Top of the World GC
Clearwater, Florida
Chic Adams
Topeka CC
Kansas
Tom Bendelow
Topeka CC (R. 1)
Kansas
Chet Mendenhall
Topeka CC (A. 9)
Kansas
Perry Maxwell
Topeka CC (R. 9)
Kansas
Perry Maxwell
Topeka Public GC
Kansas
*William V. Leonard, L.J. "Dutch"
 McClellan*
Topsail Greens GC
Hampstead, North Carolina
Russell T. Burney
Toqua GC
Tennessee
Tom Clark, Edmund B. Ault
Tor Hill GC
Regina, Saskatchewan
John A. Thompson
Torey Pines Resort GC
Francetown, New Hampshire
Dick Tremblay
Torino GC
Turin, Italy
John Harris, Henry Cotton
Toronto GC
Ontario
H.S. Colt
Toronto GC (R. 9)
Ontario
Howard Watson
Toronto GC (A. 5)
Ontario
Howard Watson
Toronto Hunt C
Ontario
Willie Park Jr
Torquay GC
Devonshire, England
James Braid, John R. Stutt
Torrance House GC
Lanarkshire, Scotland
Fred W. Hawtree, Martin
 Hawtree
Torreon GC
Mexico
Percy Clifford
Torrequebrada GC
Malaga, Spain
Pepe Gancedo
Torresdale-Frankford CC
Philadelphia, Pennsylvania
Willie Campbell
Torresdale-Frankford CC (R. 9)
Pennsylvania
Donald Ross
Torresdale-Frankford CC (A. 9)
Pennsylvania
Donald Ross
**Torrey Pines Muni (North
 Course)**
La Jolla, California
William F. Bell
**Torrey Pines Muni (North
 Course) (R)**
California
David Rainville
**Torrey Pines Muni (South
 Course)**
La Jolla, California
William F. Bell
**Torrey Pines Muni (South
 Course) (R)**
California
David Rainville
Torrington CC
Connecticut
Orrin Smith
Torwoodlee GC
Selkirkshire, Scotland
Willie Park, Willie Park Jr
Totem Par Four GC
Penticton, British Columbia
James P. Izatt

Totsuka CC (East Course)
Kanagawa, Japan
S. Manno
Totsuka CC (West Course)
Kanagawa, Japan
Seichi Inouye
Totteridge GC
Scotland
Willie Park Jr
Tower Hill GC
Somerset, England
Samuel Chisholm
Tower Tee GC
St. Louis, Missouri
R. Albert Anderson
Tower Vue CC
Pittsburgh, Pennsylvania
Edward Holowka
Town & Country C
St. Paul, Minnesota
George McRee
Town & Country C (R)
Minnesota
Robert Foulis
Town & Country C (R)
Minnesota
Dick Nugent
Town & Country C
Devil's Lake, North Dakota
William B. Langford, Theodore J.
 Moreau
Town & Country C
Fond du Lac, Wisconsin
Tom Bendelow
Town & Country GC
Ohio
Edmund B. Ault
Town'N Country GC
Chattanooga, Tennessee
Dick Wilson, Bob Simmons
Towson G&CC
Maryland
Geoffrey S. Cornish, William G.
 Robinson
Toy Town Tavern GC NLE
Winchendon, Massachusetts
Donald Ross, Walter Hatch
Trabolgan GC
Ireland
Eddie Hackett
Tracy CC
California
Bob Baldock
Tracy Park G&CC
England
Grant Aitken
Trafalgar G&CC
Milton, Ontario
Clinton E. Robinson, Robert
 Moote
Trails GC
Moore, Oklahoma
Leon Howard, *Charles Howard*
Tralee GC
County Kerry, Ireland
Arnold Palmer, Ed Seay
Tralee GC (R) NLE
Ireland
Eddie Hackett
Tramark GC
Gulfport, Mississippi
Floyd Trehern
Tramore GC
County Waterford, Ireland
Willie Park, Willie Park Jr
Tramore GC (R)
Ireland
John Harris
Travelodge GC
Papeete, Tahiti
Robert von Hagge, Bruce Devlin
Traverse City CC
Michigan
Tom Bendelow
Traverse City CC (R)
Michigan
Bruce Matthews, Jerry Matthews
Traverse City CC (R)
Michigan
William Newcomb, Stephen Kay
Travis Pointe CC
Ann Arbor, Michigan
William Newcomb, *Jim Lipe*

Treadway-Samoset GC
Rockport, Maine
*Thurman D. Donovan, Robert L.
 Elder*
Treadway-Samoset GC (R)
Maine
Geoffrey S. Cornish, William G.
 Robinson
Treasure Cay GC
Abaco, Bahamas
Dick Wilson, Joe Lee
Treasure Hills CC
Texas
Richard Watson
Treasure Island GC
Lubbock, Texas
Warren Cantrell
Treasure Lake CC
DuBois, Pennsylvania
Dominic Palombo
Tredyffrin CC
Paoli, Pennsylvania
Alex Findlay
Tree Top GC
Manheim, Pennsylvania
*Robert Hummer, Ken Brown,Tom
 Brown*
Treetops GC
Gaylord, Michigan
Robert Trent Jones, Roger
 Rulewich
Trehaven GC (R)
Ontario
Robert Moote
Trent GC
Bolsouer, Ontario
Renee Muylaert
Trentham Park GC
Staffordshire, England
Tom Williamson
**Tres Vidas en la Playa (East
 Course) NLE**
Mexico
Robert Trent Jones
**Tres Vidas en la Playa (West
 Course) NLE**
Mexico
Robert Trent Jones
Trevose G&CC
England
H.S. Colt, C.H. Alison,J.S.F.
 Morrison
Trevose G&CC (R)
England
Sir Guy Campbell
Trevose G&CC (A. 9)
England
Sir Guy Campbell
Tri-way GC
Republic, Missouri
Press Maxwell
Tri-City GC
American Fork, Utah
Joseph B. Williams
Tri-County GC
Muncie, Indiana
Robert Beard
Tri-County GC (R. 9)
Kentucky
Robert Thomason
Tri-County GC
Batesburg, South Carolina
Mike Serino, David Todd
Tri-Palm GC
Thousand Palms, California
Jim Petrides
Trim GC (R)
Ireland
Eddie Hackett
Triple A CC (R)
Missouri
Robert Foulis
Tripoli CC
Milwaukee, Wisconsin
Tom Bendelow
Tripoli GC
Libya
J.J.F. Pennink
Troia GC
Setubal, Portugal
Robert Trent Jones, Cabell
 Robinson

Troon G&CC
Scottsdale, Arizona
Jay Morrish, *Tom Weiskopf*
Troon GC now known as Royal Troon GC
Troon Portland GC
Ayshire, Scotland
Willie Fernie
Trophy C (Creek Course)
Roanoke, Texas
Arthur Hills, Steve Forrest
Trophy C (Oaks Course)
Roanoke, Texas
Joe Lee, *Ben Hogan*
Tropicana CC
Las Vegas, Nevada
Bert Stamps
Tropicana CC (R)
Nevada
Tom Clark, Brian Ault
Trosper Park GC
Oklahoma City, Oklahoma
Arthur Jackson
Trout Lake CC
Wisconsin
Charles Maddox, *Frank P. MacDonald*
Troy CC (R. 9)
New York
Jack Kidwell, Michael Hurdzan
Troy CC (A. 9)
New York
Jack Kidwell, Michael Hurdzan
Trull Brook GC
North Tewksbury, Massachusetts
Geoffrey S. Cornish
Trumbull CC
Warren, Ohio
Stanley Thompson
Trumbull CC (R)
Ohio
William Newcomb
Truro GC (R)
Nova Scotia
Stanley Thompson
Truro GC (A. 9)
Nova Scotia
Clinton E. Robinson
Truro GC (R. 9)
Nova Scotia
Clinton E. Robinson
Truro GC
Cornwall, England
James Braid, John R. Stutt
Tryall G & Beach C
Jamaica
Ralph Plummer
Tryon CC
North Carolina
Tom Bendelow
Tsawwassen G&CC
British Columbia
Norman H. Woods, *Jack Reimer*
Tsugaru Kogen GC
Amori, Japan
Arnold Palmer, Ed Seay,Bob Walker
Tsumeb GC (R. 9)
South Africa
Harry Hickson
Tsumeb GC (A. 9)
South Africa
Harry Hickson
Tualatin CC
Oregon
H. Chandler Egan, *George Junor*
Tuam GC
County Galway, Ireland
Eddie Hackett
Tuas GC
Singapore
Robert Trent Jones Jr, Don Knott
Tubac Valley CC
Arizona
Red Lawrence
Tuckaway CC
Franklin, Wisconsin
Ken Killian, Dick Nugent
Tucson CC
Arizona
William F. Bell, William P. Bell
Tucson CC (R. 3)
Arizona
Red Lawrence

Tucson CC (R)
Arizona
Arthur Jack Snyder
Tucson Estates GC (East Course)
Arizona
Red Lawrence
Tucson Estates GC (West Course)
Arizona
Red Lawrence
Tucson National GC
Tucson, Arizona
Robert Bruce Harris
Tucson National GC (R. 6)
Arizona
Red Lawrence
Tucson National GC (A. 9)
Arizona
Robert von Hagge, Bruce Devlin
Tucson National GC (R)
Arizona
Robert von Hagge, Bruce Devlin
Tulare CC
California
Bob Baldock
Tullamore GC
County Offaly, Ireland
Lionel Hewson
Tullamore GC (R)
Ireland
Eddie Hackett
Tullamore GC (R)
Ireland
James Braid
Tulsa CC
Oklahoma
A.W. Tillinghast
Tulsa CC (R)
Oklahoma
Floyd Farley
Tulsa CC (A. 3)
Oklahoma
Floyd Farley
Tulsa CC (R. 2)
Oklahoma
James L. Holmes
Tulsa CC (R. 5)
Oklahoma
Jay Morrish
Tumble Brook CC
Bloomfield, Connecticut
Willie Park Jr
Tumble Brook CC (A. 9)
Connecticut
Orrin Smith, William F. Mitchell
Tumble Brook CC (A. 9)
Connecticut
George Fazio, Tom Fazio
Tumblebrook CC
Bloomfield, Connecticut
Orrin Smith, William F. Mitchell
Tumblebrook GC
Pewaukee, Wisconsin
Edward Lawrence Packard
Tumwater Valley GC
Olympia, Washington
Roy L. Goss, *Glen Proctor*
Tunbridge Wells GC
England
C.K. Cotton
Tunxis Plantation CC
Farmington, Connecticut
Al Zikorus
Tupelo CC
Mississippi
John W. Frazier
Tupper Lake GC
New York
Donald Ross
Tura Beach CC
Merimbula, Australia
Peter Thomson, Michael Wolveridge
Turf and Surf GC
Florida
Chic Adams
Turf Valley CC (North Course)
Maryland
Edmund B. Ault, Al Jamison
Turf Valley CC (South Course)
Maryland
Edmund B. Ault
Turin Highlands GC
Turin, New York
William Harries

Turkey Creek CC
Gary, Indiana
Charles Maddox, *Frank P. MacDonald*
Turkey Creek G&RC
Alachua, Florida
Ward Northrup
Turkey Run GC
Waveland, Indiana
Gary Kern
Turlock G&CC
California
Bob Baldock, Jack Fleming
Turnberry CC
Crystal Lake, Illinois
Edward Lawrence Packard, Roger Packard
Turnberry GC (Ailsa Course)
Ayrshire, Scotland
Willie Fernie
Turnberry GC (Ailsa Course) (R)
Scotland
C.K. Hutchison
Turnberry GC (Ailsa Course) (R)
Scotland
P.M. Ross, *James Alexander*
Turnberry GC (Ailsa Course) (R)
Scotland
Peter Alliss, David Thomas
Turnberry GC (Arran Course)
Ayrshire, Scotland
Willie Fernie
Turnberry GC (Arran Course) (R)
Scotland
James Alexander
Turnberry Isle G&CC (North Course)
North Miami, Florida
Robert Trent Jones, Rees Jones
Turnberry Isle G&CC (South Course)
North Miami, Florida
Robert Trent Jones, Rees Jones
Turner AFB GC
Albany, Georgia
Hugh Moore
Turnhouse GC
Edinburgh, Scotland
James Braid
Turnhouse GC (R)
Scotland
Willie Park Jr
Turtle Bay GC (New Course)
Kahuku, Oahu, Hawaii
Arnold Palmer, Ed Seay
Turtle Bay GC (Old Course)
Oahu, Hawaii
George Fazio, Tom Fazio,*James Winans, John W. Meeker*
Turtle Bay GC (Old Course) (R)
Hawaii
Robert Trent Jones Jr
Turtle Cove GC
Atlanta, Georgia
William James Spear
Turtle Creek C
Jupiter, Florida
Joe Lee
Turtle Lake GC
Winchester, Wisconsin
Stanley Pelchar
Turtle Point G Links
Kiawah Island, South Carolina
Jack Nicklaus, Jay Morrish,Bob Cupp
Turtle Point Y&CC
Florence, Alabama
Robert Trent Jones, Frank Duane
Tuscarora CC
New York
Seymour Dunn
Tuscarora CC
Danville, Virginia
Gene Hamm
Tuscawilla CC
Winter Springs, Florida
Joe Lee
Tuscumbia CC
Green Lake, Wisconsin
Tom Bendelow
Tuxedo Muni
Manitoba
A.W. Creed

Tuxedo Park C NLE
New York
Henry Hewett
Tuxedo Park C
Tuxedo Park, New York
Robert Trent Jones, Frank Duane
Tuxedo Park C (R) NLE
New York
William S. Flynn
Twain Harte GC
California
Clark Glasson
Twenty Greens GC
Catoosa, Oklahoma
Richard Audrain
Twenty Valley G&CC
Beamsville, Ontario
Clinton E. Robinson, Robert Moote
Twentynine Palms Muni
California
Lawrence Hughes
Twickenham GC
Middlesex, England
J.J.F. Pennink, C.D. Lawrie
Twiggs Muni
Providence, Rhode Island
Donald Ross
Twilight GC
Denver, Colorado
Henry B. Hughes
Twin Creek CC
Dahlonega, Georgia
Arthur Davis
Twin Falls State Park GC
Mullens, West Virginia
Geoffrey S. Cornish, William G. Robinson
Twin Falls State Park GC (A. 9)
West Virginia
George W. Cobb, John LaFoy
Twin Hills CC
Massachusetts
Al Zikorus
Twin Hills CC
Joplin, Missouri
Smiley Bell
Twin Hills G&CC
Oklahoma City, Oklahoma
Perry Maxwell
Twin Hills G&CC (R. 1)
Oklahoma
Floyd Farley
Twin Hills G&CC (R)
Oklahoma
Don Sechrest
Twin Hills GC
Spencerport, New York
Pete Craig
Twin Hills GC (A)
New York
Geoffrey S. Cornish, William G. Robinson
Twin Lakes CC
Rathdrum, Idaho
Edward A. Hunnicutt
Twin Lakes CC
Kent, Ohio
Sandy Alves
Twin Lakes CC
Tacoma, Washington
Al Smith
Twin Lakes G&CC
Federal Way, Washington
William Teufel
Twin Lakes GC
Mountain Home, Arkansas
Cecil B. Hollingsworth
Twin Lakes GC
El Monte, California
William H. Johnson
Twin Lakes GC (R)
California
Robert Muir Graves, Damian Pascuzzo
Twin Lakes GC
Mansfield, Ohio
Jack Kidwell
Twin Lakes GC
Mainland, Pennsylvania
Charles Bunton
Twin Lakes GC (A. 9)
Pennsylvania
David Gordon

Twin Lakes GC (A. 9)
Pennsylvania
David Gordon
Twin Lakes GC
Centerville, Virginia
Charles B. Schalestock
Twin Mountain GC
New Hampshire
Alex Findlay
Twin Oaks CC
Springfield, Missouri
Floyd Farley, *Horton Smith*
Twin Oaks GC
St. John, Michigan
Warner Bowen
Twin Oaks CC
Greensboro, North Carolina
Ellis Maples
Twin Orchard CC NLE
Bensenville, Illinois
William B. Langford, Theodore J. Moreau
Twin Orchards CC (Red Course)
Long Grove, Illinois
C.D. Wagstaff
Twin Orchards CC (Red Course) (R)
Illinois
Ken Killian, Dick Nugent
Twin Orchards CC (White Course)
Long Grove, Illinois
C.D. Wagstaff
Twin Orchards CC (White Course) (R)
Illinois
Edward Lawrence Packard
Twin Peaks Muni
Longmont, Colorado
Frank Hummel
Twin Pines G&CC
Missouri
Dewitt "Maury" Bell
Twin Ponds GC
Crystal Lake, Illinois
C.D. Wagstaff
Twin Run GC
Cincinnati, Ohio
William H. Diddel
Twin Shields CC
Maryland
Ray Shields, Roy Shields
Twin Valley CC
Wadesboro, North Carolina
Ron Kirby, Denis Griffiths
Two Bridges CC
Lincoln Park, New Jersey
Nicholas Psiahas
Two Rivers Muni
Nashville, Tennessee
Leon Howard, *Charles Howard*
Tyandaca Muni
Burlington, Ontario
Clinton E. Robinson
Tygarts Valley CC (R)
West Virginia
James Gilmore Harrison, Ferdinand Garbin
Tyler's Creek GC
Alto, Michigan
Mark DeVries
Tyndall AFB GC
Panama City Beach, Florida
Bob Baldock
Tyndall AFB GC (A. 9)
Florida
Joe Lee, Rocky Roquemore
Tynemouth GC
Northumberland, England
Willie Park Jr
Tyneside GC
England
H.S. Colt
Tynley Park GC
England
W. Wiltshire
Tyoga CC
Wellsboro, Pennsylvania
Edmund B. Ault
Tyoga CC (A. 9)
Pennsylvania
Tom Clark

Tyrone CC
Pennsylvania
Edmund B. Ault
Tyrone CC
Pennsylvania
Alex Findlay
Tyrone Hills CC
Livingston, Michigan
Bruce Matthews
Tyrrells Wood GC
England
James Braid
TPC at Avenel
Potomac, Maryland
Edmund B. Ault, Brian Ault, Tom
Clark, Bill Love
TPC at Canyon Springs
San Antonio, Texas
Ron Prichard
TPC at Eagle Trace
Coral Springs, Florida
Arthur Hills, Steve Forrest, Mike
Dasher
TPC at Monte Carlo
Fort Pierce, Florida
Chuck Ankrom
TPC at Monte Carlo (R)
Florida
Arnold Palmer, Ed Seay
TPC at Piper Glen
Charlotte, North Carolina
Arnold Palmer, Ed Seay, Harrison
Minchew
TPC at Plum Creek
Castle Rock, Colorado
Pete Dye, Perry Dye
TPC at Prestancia (Course No.
1) formerly known as CC of
Sarasota
Sarasota, Florida
Robert von Hagge, Bruce Devlin
TPC at Prestancia (Course No.
2)
Sarasota, Florida
Ron Garl
TPC at Sawgrass
Ponte Vedra Beach, Florida
Pete Dye, Alice Dye
TPC at Sawgrass (R)
Florida
Pete Dye
TPC at Star Pass
Tuscon, Arizona
Bob Cupp
TPC at The Woodlands formerly
known as Woodlands Inn &
CC (East Course)
Texas
Robert von Hagge, Bruce Devlin
TPC of Connecticut formerly
known as Edgewood GC
Cromwell, Connecticut
Robert J. Ross, Maurice Kearney
TPC of Connecticut (R)
Connecticut
Orrin Smith
TPC of Connecticut (R)
Connecticut
Pete Dye, David Postlethwaite
TPC of Memphis
Tennessee
Ron Prichard
TPC of Scottsdale
Arizona
Jay Morrish, Tom Weiskopf
TRW GC
Chesterfield, Ohio
Pete Dye, Roy Dye
U.S. Navy Medical Center GC
(R)
Maryland
Edmund B. Ault
Udine GC
Italy
M. Croze
Ugolino GC
Florence, Italy
Seymour Dunn
Ugolino GC (R)
Italy
Pier Mancinelli
Ukiah Muni
California
Paul Underwood

Ulen CC
Lebanon, Indiana
William H. Diddel
Ulm GC
West Germany
Bernhard von Limburger
Ulm-Do GC
West Germany
Bernhard von Limburger
Ulverston GC
Cumbria, England
Sandy Herd
Ulverston GC (R)
England
H.S. Colt
Undermountain GC
Boston Corners, New York
John Shakshober
Unicorn CC
Stoneham, Massachusetts
Wayne Stiles, John Van Kleek
Unicorn CC (R)
Massachusetts
Orrin Smith, William F. Mitchell
Union City GC
Pennsylvania
Tom Bendelow
Union CC NLE
Dover, Ohio
Tom Bendelow
Union CC
New Philadelphia, Ohio
William Newcomb
Union Hills CC
Sun City, Arizona
Jeff Hardin, Greg Nash
Uniontown CC
Pennsylvania
Emil Loeffler, John McGlynn
Unionville Fairways
Ontario
Renee Muylaert
Univ of Iowa GC NLE
Iowa City, Iowa
Charles Kennett
Univ of New Mexico GC (North
Crs.)
Albuquerque, New Mexico
William H. Tucker
Univ of New Mexico GC (North
Crs.) (A. 9) NLE
New Mexico
William H. Tucker
University of the Phillipines GC
Philippines
Francisco D. Santana
University of Alabama GC
Tuscaloosa, Alabama
Harold Williams, Thomas H. Nicol
University of Florida GC
Gainesville, Florida
Donald Ross
University of Florida GC (R)
Florida
Ron Garl
University of Georgia GC
Athens, Georgia
Robert Trent Jones, Roger
Rulewich
University of Idaho GC
Moscow, Idaho
Frank James
University of Idaho GC (A. 9)
Idaho
Bob Baldock
University of Idaho GC (R. 9)
Idaho
Bob Baldock
University of Illinois GC (Blue
Course)
Champaign, Illinois
C.D. Wagstaff
University of Illinois GC
(Orange Crs.)
Champaign, Illinois
C.D. Wagstaff
University of Maryland GC
College Park, Maryland
George W. Cobb
University of Michigan GC
Ann Arbor, Michigan
Alister Mackenzie, Perry Maxwell

University of Minnesota GC
St. Paul, Minnesota
Seth Raynor
University of Minnesota GC (R)
Minnesota
Donald G. Brauer, Emile Perret
University of Mississippi GC
Oxford, Mississippi
Sonny Guy
University of Montana GC
Missoula, Montana
Gregor MacMillan
University of New Mexico GC
(South Crs.)
Albuquerque, New Mexico
Red Lawrence
University of Oklahoma GC
Norman, Oklahoma
Perry Maxwell, Press Maxwell
University of South Florida GC
Tampa, Florida
William F. Mitchell
University of Southern
Mississippi GC
Hattiesburg, Mississippi
Sonny Guy
University City GC
Missouri
Samuel Lyle
University GC
Vancouver, British Columbia
Davey Black
University GC (R)
British Columbia
Clinton E. Robinson
University Heights GC
Cleveland, Ohio
Sandy Alves
University Park CC
Boca Raton, Florida
Frank Murray
University Park GC
Muskegon, Michigan
Bruce Matthews, Jerry Matthews
Upland Hills GC
Upland, California
David Rainville
Uplands G&CC
Ontario
Stanley Thompson
Upper Canada CC
Oakville, Ontario
Howard Watson
Upper Canada CC
Morrisburg, Ontario
Clinton E. Robinson
Upper Landsdowne CC
Asheville, Ohio
Jack Kidwell
Upper Main Line CC
Philadelphia, Pennsylvania
William Gordon, David Gordon
Upper Montclair CC
Clifton, New Jersey
Robert Trent Jones
Upper Montclair CC (R) NLE
New Jersey
A.W. Tillinghast
Upton By Chester GC
Cheshire, England
J.W. Davies
Upton G&CC
Jamaica
John S. Collier
Upton G&CC (R. 9)
Jamaica
Howard Watson
Urban GC
Chicago Heights, Illinois
Edward Lawrence Packard
Urban Hills CC
Richton Park, Illinois
Edward Lawrence Packard
Urbana CC
Illinois
Tom Bendelow
Useless Bay G&CC
Whidbey Island, Washington
William Teufel
Useless Bay G&CC (R)
Washington
William Teufel

Utrecht GC
Netherlands
H.S. Colt, C.H. Alison, J.S.F.
Morrison
Utrecht GC (R)
Netherlands
J.J.F. Pennink
US Naval Academy GC (R)
Maryland
William S. Flynn
Vache Grasse CC
Arkansas
William M. Martin
Vail GC
Colorado
Press Maxwell
Val Halla CC
Cumberland, Maine
Phil Wogan
Val Halla CC (A. 9)
Maine
Phil Wogan
Val Morin GC
Quebec
Howard Watson, John Watson
Val Morin GC (R)
Quebec
Howard Watson
Val Niegette GC
Rimouski, Quebec
John Watson
Valdosta CC
Georgia
Joe Lee, Rocky Roquemore
Vale do Lobo GC
Portugal
Henry Cotton
Vale do Lobo GC (A. 9)
Portugal
Henry Cotton
Valencia GC
California
Robert Trent Jones
Valhalla CC
Louisville, Kentucky
Jack Nicklaus, Tom Pearson
Valle Alto GC
Monterrey, Mexico
Lawrence Hughes
Valle Arriba GC
Venezuela
James Baird Wilson
Valle Grande GC
Bakersfield, California
William P. Bell, William F. Bell
Valle Grande GC (A. 9)
California
William F. Bell
Valle Oaks GC
Zephyr Hills, Florida
Ron Garl
Valle Verde CC
Kingman, Arizona
Alex McLaren, Jock McLaren
Valle Vista CC
Kingman, Arizona
Fred Bolton
Valle Vista CC
Greenwood, Indiana
Bob Simmons
Valleaire GC
Hinckley, Ohio
Harold Paddock
Valley Brook CC
McMurray, Pennsylvania
Ferdinand Garbin
Valley Brook CC (R)
Pennsylvania
Robert Trent Jones, Roger
Rulewich
Valley C of Montecito
Santa Barbara, California
Alister Mackenzie, Robert Hunter
Valley C of Montecito (R)
California
William P. Bell
Valley CC NLE
Scottsdale, Arizona
David Gill
Valley CC
Aurora, Colorado
William F. Bell

Valley CC (R)
Colorado
Dick Phelps
Valley CC
Nebraska
William B. Kubly
Valley CC (R)
Pennsylvania
A.W. Tillinghast
Valley CC
Rizal, Philippines
Fred Smith, James D. Scott
Valley Forge V.A. Hospital GC
Pennsylvania
Alfred H. Tull
Valley Gardens CC
Santa Cruz, California
Bob Baldock, Robert L. Baldock
Valley Green CC
Aurora, Illinois
Robert Bruce Harris
Valley Green GC
Greensburg, Pennsylvania
X.G. Hassenplug
Valley GC
Hines, Oregon
Shelby McCool
Valley Heights CC (R)
Pennsylvania
James Gilmore Harrison,
Ferdinand Garbin
Valley Hi CC
Sacramento, California
William F. Bell
Valley Hi GC
Colorado Springs, Colorado
Henry B. Hughes
Valley Hi GC (R. 9)
Colorado
Dick Phelps
Valley High GC
Houston, Minnesota
Homer Fieldhouse
Valley Hill CC (R.27)
Alabama
John LaFoy
Valley International CC
Brownsville, Texas
Joseph S. Finger
Valley International CC (R)
Texas
Dennis W. Arp
Valley International CC (Par 3
Course)
Brownsville, Texas
Dennis W. Arp
Valley Ledgemont CC (A. 9)
Rhode Island
Geoffrey S. Cornish
Valley Oaks GC
Clinton, Iowa
Robert Bruce Harris
Valley Pines CC
North Carolina
Leo Green
Valley Springs GC
Oxen Hill, Maryland
Russell Roberts
Valley View CC
White Sulphur Spgs, West
Virginia
Russell Roberts
Valley View GC
New Albany, Indiana
William H. Diddel
Valley View GC (A. 9)
Indiana
Buck Blankenship
Valley View GC
Bozeman, Montana
Theodore Wirth
Valley View GC (R. 9)
Montana
William G. Robinson
Valley View GC (A. 9)
Montana
William G. Robinson
Valley View GC
Fremont, Nebraska
Harold Glissmann
Valley View GC
Central City, Nebraska
Harold Glissmann

Valley View GC NLE
Omaha, Nebraska
James Dalgleish
Valley View GC (R)
New York
Robert Trent Jones
Valley View GC
Lancaster, Ohio
Harold Paddock
Valley View GC
Layton, Utah
Joseph B. Williams
Valley View Muni (R)
New York
Robert Trent Jones
Valleybrook G&CC
Hixson, Tennessee
Chic Adams
Vallromanas GC
Barcelona, Spain
Fred W. Hawtree
Valparaiso CC NLE
Florida
William B. Langford, Theodore J. Moreau
Valparaiso CC (R. 9)
Indiana
John Darrah
Valparaiso CC (A. 9)
Indiana
John Darrah
Valparaiso GC
Argentina
John "Jock" Anderson
Van Buren GC
Keosauqua, Iowa
Leo Johnson
Van Buskirk Muni (A. 9)
California
Robert Muir Graves
Van Cortlandt Park GC
Bronx, New York
T. McClure Peters
Van Cortlandt Park GC (A. 9)
New York
Tom Bendelow
Van Cortlandt Park GC (R)
New York
William F. Mitchell
Van Nuys GC (North Course)
California
Joe Novak
Van Patten GC
New York
James Thomson
Van Zandt CC
Canton, Texas
Leon Howard
Vancouver GC (R)
British Columbia
William G. Robinson
Vancouver GC (R)
British Columbia
Clinton E. Robinson
Vancouver GC (R)
British Columbia
James P. Izatt
Vandenberg Village CC
California
Ted Robinson
Vanderbilt Estate GC NLE
Manhasset, New York
Devereux Emmet, Alfred H. Tull
Varese GC
Italy
Charles Blanchford
Varese GC (R)
Italy
Donald Harradine
Vasatorp GC
Helsingborg, Sweden
Ture Bruce
Vashon Island G&CC
Washington
H.D. Williams
Vashon Island G&CC (R)
Washington
William Teufel
Vassar G&CC
Michigan
William Newcomb
Vaughan Valley GC
Ontario
Renee Muylaert

Veenker Memorial GC
Iowa State Univ., Iowa
Perry Maxwell
Veenker Memorial GC (R)
Iowa
Beryl Taylor
Veenker Memorial GC (A. 4)
Iowa
Beryl Taylor
Vejle GC (R)
Denmark
Jan Sederholm
Venango Trails GC
Pittsburgh, Pennsylvania
James Gilmore Harrison
Venango Valley GC
Venango, Pennsylvania
Paul E. Erath
Venice CC NLE
Florida
C.H. Anderson
Venice East GC
Florida
R. Albert Anderson
Venice GC (A. 9)
Italy
C.K. Cotton
Ventana Canyon G&RC
Tucson, Arizona
Tom Fazio
Ventnor GC
England
Tom Dunn
Ventnor GC (R)
England
J. Hamilton Stutt
Ventura CC
Orlando, Florida
Mark Mahannah, Charles Mahannah
Ventura Muni
Montalvo, California
William P. Bell
Ver Hoven CC
Memphis, Michigan
Emil Beck
Veradera Beach CC
Havana, Cuba
Herbert Strong
Vereeniging CC
Transvaal, South Africa
C.H. Alison
Vermillion Hills CC
Danville, Illinois
Edward Lawrence Packard, Brent Wadsworth
Vernal CC
Utah
William Johnston
Vernal CC (A. 9)
Utah
Mark Dixon Ballif
Vernon G&CC
British Columbia
Tom Bendelow
Vernon G&CC (R. 5)
British Columbia
Ernest Brown
Vernon Hills CC
Mt. Vernon, New York
Devereux Emmet, Alfred H. Tull
Vernonia CC
Oregon
George Junor
Vero Beach CC
Florida
Herbert Strong
Verona GC
Italy
John Harris
Verulam GC (R)
England
James Braid
Vesper CC
Tyngsboro, Massachusetts
Alex Findlay
Vesper CC (R. 9)
Massachusetts
Donald Ross
Vesper CC (A. 9)
Massachusetts
Donald Ross

Vesper CC (R)
Massachusetts
Manny Francis
Vesper CC (R)
Massachusetts
Orrin Smith, William F. Mitchell
Vesper Hills CC
Otisco, New York
Geoffrey S. Cornish, William G. Robinson
Vestal Hills CC
Binghampton, New York
Geoffrey S. Cornish
Vestal Hills CC (R) NLE
New York
Robert Trent Jones
Vestavia CC (R)
Alabama
George W. Cobb
Vestischer GC
Recklinghausen, West Germany
Donald Harradine
Veterans Memorial GC
Springfield, Massachusetts
Geoffrey S. Cornish
Veterans Memorial GC
Walla Walla, Washington
Frank James
Via Verde CC
San Dimas, California
Lawrence Hughes
Viborg GC
Denmark
Jan Sederholm
Victor Hills GC
New York
Pete Craig
Victoria CC
Texas
George Hoffman
Victoria CC (R)
Texas
Joseph S. Finger, Baxter Spann
Victoria GC
Riverside, California
Charles Maud, *Col. W.E. Pedley*
Victoria GC (R)
California
Walter Fovargue
Victoria GC (A. 9)
California
Max Behr
Victoria GC (R. 9)
California
Max Behr
Victoria GC (R)
California
William P. Bell
Victoria GC (R. 3)
California
William H. Johnson
Victoria GC
Oak Bay, British Columbia
Harvey Coombe
Victoria GC (R)
British Columbia
A. Vernon Macan
Victoria GC (R)
British Columbia
Gary Panks
Victoria GC
Cheltenham, Australia
Alister Mackenzie
Victoria GC (R)
Australia
Peter Thomson, Michael Wolveridge
Victoria Muni
Carson, California
William F. Bell
Victoria Park GC (Course No. 1)
Guelph, Ontario
Renee Muylaert
Victoria Park GC (Course No. 2)
Guelph, Ontario
Renee Muylaert
Victory Hills CC
Kansas City, Kansas
James Dalgleish
Vienna GC
Austria
Willie Park Jr

Vilamoura GC
Portugal
J.J.F. Pennink
Villa de Paz CC
Phoenix, Arizona
Jeff Hardin, Greg Nash
Villa de Paz CC (A. 9)
Arizona
Jeff Hardin, Greg Nash
Villa Condulmer GC
Italy
John Harris, *M. Croze*
Villa D'este GC
Como, Italy
James Gannon
Villa D'este GC (R)
Italy
John Harris
Villa Delray CC
Delray Beach, Florida
Frank Batto
Villa Du Parc CC
Mequon, Wisconsin
David Gill
Villa Du Parc CC (A. 9)
Wisconsin
Robert Chamberlain
Villa Monterey CC NLE
Scottsdale, Arizona
Milt Coggins
Villa Monterey CC
Scottsdale, Arizona
Arthur Jack Snyder
Villa Olivia CC
Bartlett, Illinois
Tom Bendelow
Villa Olivia CC (R)
Illinois
Bob Lohmann
Villa Olivia CC (R)
Illinois
Ken Killian, Dick Nugent
Villa Real GC
Havana, Cuba
Dick Wilson, Joe Lee
Villa Roma CC
Calakoon, New York
Lindsay Ervin
Village of Oak Creek CC
Arizona
Robert Trent Jones, Robert Trent Jones Jr
Village CC
Lompoc, California
Ted Robinson
Village CC
Dallas, Texas
Press Maxwell
Village Green CC
Mundelein, Illinois
William B. Langford
Village Green GC
Sarasota, Florida
William B. Lewis
Village Green GC
Bradenton, Florida
William B. Lewis
Village Green GC
Tavares, Florida
William B. Lewis
Village Green GC
Newaygo, Michigan
Bob Frain
Village Green GC (A. 9)
Michigan
Bob Frain
Village Green GC
Moorhead, Minnesota
Donald G. Brauer, Paul S. Fjare
Village Green GC
Syracuse, New York
Hal Purdy, Malcolm Purdy
Village Green GC
North Kingsville, Ohio
J. Thomas Francis
Village Green GC
Green Bay, Wisconsin
Robert Bruce Harris
Village Greens of Woodridge
Illinois
Robert Bruce Harris
Village Greens CC
South Carolina
Russell Breeden, *Dan Breeden*

Village Greens GC
Ozaukie, Kansas
Buck Blankenship
Village Greens GC (A. 9)
Kansas
L.J. "Dutch" McClellan
Village Inn GC
McHenry, Maryland
Dominic Palombo
Village Links of Glen Ellyn
Illinois
David Gill
Villages G&CC
San Jose, California
Robert Muir Graves
Villars GC (R. 9)
Switzerland
Donald Harradine
Vincennes GC
Indiana
Charles Maddox
Vineyards GC
St. Helena, California
Robert L. Baldock
Vineyards GC
Naples, Florida
Bill Amick
Vineyards GC
Cininnati, Ohio
Michael Hurdzan, Jack Kidwell
Vinoy Park C
St. Petersburg, Florida
David Gill
Vintage C (Desert Course)
Indian Wells, California
Tom Fazio
Vintage C (Mountain Course)
Indian Wells, California
Tom Fazio
Vintage G&CC
Fort Myers, Florida
Gordon G. Lewis
Virginia CC
California
William P. Bell
Virginia CC
Illinois
Robert Bruce Harris
Virginia GC
County Caren, Ireland
Tom Travers
Virginia Tech GC
Blacksburg, Virginia
Buddy Loving
Visalia CC (R)
California
Desmond Muirhead
Visalia Plaza GC
California
Robert Dean Putnam
Visalia Plaza GC (R)
California
Richard Bigler
Vista Chica GC
Valencia, California
Terry E. Van Gorder
Vista Hermosa GC
Cadiz, Spain
John Harris
Vista Hills CC
El Paso, Texas
Robert von Hagge, Bruce Devlin
Vista Plantation GC
Vero Beach, Florida
Arthur Hills, Steve Forrest, Mike Dasher
Vista Royale GC
Vero Beach, Florida
Arthur Hills
Vista Royale GC (A. 9)
Florida
Arthur Hills, Steve Forrest, Mike Dasher
Vista Valencia GC
Valencia, California
Terry E. Van Gorder
Vista Valley CC
Vista, California
Ted Robinson
Vista View Village GC
Zanesville, Ohio
Jack Kidwell

Vivary GC
England
J. Hamilton Stutt
Vizcaya CC
Miami, Florida
Frank Murray
Volcano G&CC (R. 9)
Hawaii
Arthur Jack Snyder
Volcano G&CC (A. 9)
Hawaii
Arthur Jack Snyder
Voyager Village GC
Danbury, Wisconsin
William James Spear
Vulpera GC
Switzerland
Gordon Spencer
VFW GC
Indiana, Pennsylvania
James Gilmore Harrison
VFW GC (A. 9)
Pennsylvania
Edmund B. Ault
W G Young CC
Gaastra, Michigan
W.G. Young
Wabeek CC
Bloomfield Hills, Michigan
Pete Dye, Roy Dye, Jack Nicklaus
Waccabuc CC
New York
George Gullen
Waccabuc CC (R)
New York
Alfred H. Tull
Wachesaw Plantation GC
Pawley's Island, South Carolina
Tom Fazio
Wachusett CC
West Boylston, Massachusetts
Donald Ross
Wack Wack G&CC (East Course)
Manila, Philippines
James Black
Wack Wack G&CC (East Course) (R)
Philippines
Ron Kirby, Denis Griffiths
Wack Wack G&CC (West Course)
Philippines
James Black
Waco Muni
Texas
Ralph Plummer
Wade Hampton GC
Cashiers, North Carolina
Tom Fazio
Wadena GC (R. 9)
Minnesota
Don Herfort
Wadesboro CC NLE
North Carolina
Arthur Ham
Wagon Wheel GC
Rockton, Illinois
Edward Lawrence Packard
Wahconah CC
Dalton, Massachusetts
Wayne Stiles
Wahconah CC (A. 9)
Massachusetts
Geoffrey S. Cornish, *Rowland Armacost*
Waialae CC
Honolulu, Hawaii
Seth Raynor, Charles Banks
Waialae CC (R)
Hawaii
Bob Baldock
Waialae CC (R. 3)
Hawaii
Arthur Jack Snyder
Waialae CC (R)
Hawaii
Robin Nelson
Waiehu Muni (R. 3)
Hawaii
Arthur Jack Snyder
Waikoloa Beach GC
Kamuela, Hawaii
Robert Trent Jones Jr

Waikoloa Village GC
Kamuela, Hawaii
Robert Trent Jones Jr, Gary Roger Baird
Waikoloa Village GC (R)
Hawaii
Robert Trent Jones Jr
Wailea GC (Blue Course)
Maui, Hawaii
Arthur Jack Snyder
Wailea GC (Orange Course)
Maui, Hawaii
Arthur Jack Snyder
Wailua Muni
Hawaii
Toyo Shirai
Wairakei International GC
Taupo, New Zealand
John Harris, Peter Thomson, Michael Wolveridge
Waitikiri GC
New Zealand
A.R. Blank
Wake Forest CC
North Carolina
Gene Hamm
Wakefield GC
England
Sandy Herd
Wakonda C
Des Moines, Iowa
William B. Langford, Theodore J. Moreau
Wakonda C (R)
Iowa
Dick Nugent, *Bruce Borland*
Waldemere Hotel GC
Livingston Manor, New York
William F. Mitchell
Walden on Lake Conroe CC
Montgomery, Texas
Robert von Hagge, Bruce Devlin
Walden on Lake Houston GC
Texas
Robert von Hagge, Bruce Devlin
Walden G&TC
Aurora, Ohio
William F. Mitchell
Walden Lake CC
Plant City, Florida
Bob Cupp, Jay Morrish
Walden Lake CC (A. 9)
Florida
Ron Garl
Walla Walla CC
Washington
W.W. Baker
Walla Walla CC (A. 9)
Washington
Frank James
Walla Walla CC (R)
Washington
John Steidel
Wallasey GC
Cheshire, England
Old Tom Morris
Wallasey GC (R)
England
Harold Hilton
Wallasey GC (R)
England
James Braid, John R. Stutt
Wallasey GC (R)
England
W.H. Davies
Walled Lake CC NLE
Michigan
Harry Collis
Wallingford CC
Connecticut
Al Zikorus
Walnut Creek CC
Goldsboro, North Carolina
Ellis Maples, Ed Seay
Walnut Creek CC
Oklahoma City, Oklahoma
Don January, Billy Martindale
Walnut Creek CC (R. 9)
Oklahoma
Tom Clark
Walnut Creek GC
Mansfield, Texas
Don January, Billy Martindale

Walnut Creek Muni
California
Robert Muir Graves
Walnut Grove CC
Dayton, Ohio
William H. Diddel
Walnut Grove GC
New Albany, Indiana
William H. Diddel
Walnut Hill CC
Columbus, Ohio
James Gilmore Harrison
Walnut Hills CC
East Lansing, Michigan
Joseph A. Roseman
Walnut Hills CC (R. 2)
Michigan
Bruce Matthews, Jerry Matthews
Walnut Hills CC (R. 4)
Michigan
Jerry Matthews
Walnut Hills CC
Oklahoma City, Oklahoma
Floyd Farley
Walnut Hills CC (R)
Oklahoma
Alfred H. Tull
Walnut Hills CC NLE
Ft. Worth, Texas
Perry Maxwell
Walnut Hills GC
Chicago, Illinois
Stanley Pelchar
Walnut Lane GC
Philadelphia, Pennsylvania
Alex Findlay
Walnut Woods CC
Michigan
Warner Bowen
Walnut Woods GC (A. 9)
Michigan
Ray Sudekis
Walpole CC NLE
Massachusetts
Eugene "Skip" Wogan
Walpole CC
Massachusetts
Al Zikorus
Walsall GC
Staffordshire, England
Alister Mackenzie
Walter Peak Resort GC
New Zealand
Arnold Palmer, Ed Seay
Walton Hall GC
Cheshire, England
J.J.F. Pennink
Walton Heath GC (New Course)
Surrey, England
Herbert Fowler
Walton Heath GC (Old Course)
Surrey, England
Herbert Fowler
Wampanoag CC
West Hartford, Connecticut
Donald Ross, Walter Hatch
Wampanoag CC (R)
Connecticut
William F. Mitchell
Wampatuck CC
Canton, Massachusetts
Geoffrey S. Cornish
Wanakah CC (R)
New York
Bob Cupp, Jay Morrish
Wanango CC
Reno, Pennsylvania
Tom Bendelow
Wanango CC (R)
Pennsylvania
A.W. Tillinghast
Wanango CC (R)
Pennsylvania
Ferdinand Garbin
Wannamoisett CC NLE
Rumford, Rhode Island
Willie Campbell
Wannamoisett CC
Rumford, Rhode Island
Donald Ross
Wantage G Center
New Jersey
Nicholas Psiahas

Wanumetonomy CC
Middletown, Rhode Island
Seth Raynor
Wapsipinicon GC
Independence, Iowa
Tom Bendelow
Wareham GC
Massachusetts
Geoffrey S. Cornish
Warkworth GC
Ontario
Gordon Witteveen
Warkworth GC (A. 9)
Ontario
Gordon Witteveen
Warley Park GC
Essex, England
R. Plumbridge
Warm Springs GC
Fremont, California
Jack Fleming
Warm Springs GC
Georgia
Donald Ross
Warner Robins AFB GC
Macon, Georgia
Hugh Moore
Warner Robins AFB GC (R)
Georgia
Arthur Davis, Ron Kirby
Warner Springs G Resort
California
Harry Rainville, David Rainville
Warren C (A.12)
Singapore
Ronald Fream
Warren C (R. 6)
Singapore
Ronald Fream
Warren GC
Pennsylvania
Clinton E. Robinson
Warren GC
Cheshire, England
F.G. Hawtree, J.H. Taylor
Warren Hills GC
Salisbury, Zimbabwe
Robert G. Grimsdell
Warren Meadows CC
Bowling Green, Kentucky
Bob Baldock, Robert L. Baldock
Warren Park GC
Illinois
Ken Killian, Dick Nugent
Warren Valley CC (East Course)
Wayne, Michigan
Donald Ross
Warren Valley CC (West Course)
Wayne, Michigan
Donald Ross
Warrenbrook CC
Plainfield, New Jersey
Hal Purdy
Warrentown CC
Virginia
Reuben Hines
Warrington CC
Pennsylvania
William Gordon, David Gordon
Warrington GC
Cheshire, England
J.J.F. Pennink
Warrington GC (R)
England
J.J.F. Pennink
Warriors Path State Park GC
Kingsport, Tennessee
George W. Cobb
Warsash GC
England
Sir Guy Campbell, C.K. Hutchison, S.V. Hotchkin
Warwick CC
Rhode Island
Donald Ross, Walter Hatch
Warwick CC (A. 9)
Rhode Island
Geoffrey S. Cornish
Warwick CC
Virginia
William Gordon, David Gordon
Warwick GC
Warwickshire, England
D.G. Dunkley

Warwick Hills G&CC
Grand Blanc, Michigan
James Gilmore Harrison, Ferdinand Garbin
Warwick Hills G&CC (R)
Michigan
Joe Lee
Warwick Neck GC
Rhode Island
Geoffrey S. Cornish
Wasatch Mountain GC
Midway, Utah
William H. Neff
Wasatch Mountain GC (A. 9)
Utah
William H. Neff, William Howard Neff
Wascana G&CC
Saskatchewan
William Brinkworth
Wascana G&CC (R)
Saskatchewan
Clinton E. Robinson
Washington CC
Connecticut
Al Zikorus
Washington CC
Ohio
George Sargent
Washington G&CC
Arlington, Virginia
Donald Ross
Washington G&CC (R)
Virginia
Fred Findlay
Washington G&CC (R)
Virginia
Al Jamison
Washington G&CC (R)
Virginia
William S. Flynn
Washington G&CC (R. 5)
Virginia
Buddy Loving, Algie Pulley
Washington GC (R. 9)
Georgia
Walter Ripley
Washington GC
Dunham, England
John Harris, Michael Wolveridge
Washington Park CC NLE
Chicago, Illinois
H.J. Tweedie
Washington Park Muni
Racine, Wisconsin
Tom Bendelow
Washington State Univ GC
Pullman, Washington
Robert Muir Graves
Washington Y&CC (A. 9)
North Carolina
Gene Hamm
Washingtonian CC (Country Club Course)
Gaithersburg, Maryland
Frank Murray, Russell Roberts
Washingtonian CC (National Course)
Gaithersburg, Maryland
Frank Murray, Russell Roberts
Washtenaw CC (R. 1)
Michigan
Bruce Matthews, Jerry Matthews
Waskesiu Lake GC
Saskatchewan
Stanley Thompson
Waskesiu Lake GC (R)
Saskatchewan
Clinton E. Robinson
Water Gap CC
Delaware Watergap, Pennsylvania
Robert White
Water Oak GC
Leesburg, Florida
Mel Bishop
Waterford GC
County Waterford, Ireland
Willie Park Jr
Waterford GC (A. 9)
Ireland
Cecil Barcroft
Waterford GC (R)
Ireland
Eddie Hackett

Waterford GC (A. 9)
Ireland
James Braid, John R. Stutt
Waterford GC (R. 9)
Ireland
James Braid, John R. Stutt
Waterford Park GC
Chester, West Virginia
X.G. Hassenplug
Waters Edge GC
Penhook, Virginia
Buddy Loving
Waterton National Park GC
Alberta
Stanley Thompson
Watertown CC (R)
Connecticut
William F. Mitchell
Watertown CC (A. 9)
Connecticut
Geoffrey S. Cornish, William G.
  Robinson
Watertown CC (A. 9)
Wisconsin
Edward Lawrence Packard, Brent
  Wadsworth
Waterville CC
Maine
Orrin Smith
Waterville CC (A. 9)
Maine
Geoffrey S. Cornish, William G.
  Robinson
Waterville G Links
County Kerry, Ireland
Eddie Hackett
Waterway Hills GC
Myrtle Beach, South Carolina
Rees Jones
Waterwood GC
Ocean City, Delaware
Reginauld Giddings
Waterwood National GC
Huntsville, Texas
Roy Dye
Waterwood National GC (R)
Texas
Bill Coore
Watsonville CC
California
Ben Harmon
Waubeeka Springs G Links
Williamstown, Massachusetts
Rowland Armacost
Waukegan GC
Illinois
Charles Maddox, *Frank P.
  MacDonald*
Waukegan Willow GC NLE
Techny, Illinois
Leonard Macomber
Waukon G&CC
Iowa
Charles Calhoun
Waumbek Village GC
New Hampshire
Ralph Barton
Wausau GC
Wisconsin
Edward Lawrence Packard
Wave Oak CC
Waverly, Pennsylvania
James Gilmore Harrison
Waveland GC
Chicago, Illinois
Joseph A. Roseman
Waveland GC (R. 9)
Illinois
Edward B. Dearie Jr
Waveland GC
Des Moines, Iowa
Tom Bendelow
Waveland GC (R)
Iowa
Paul Coates
Waveland GC (R)
Iowa
Edward Lawrence Packard
Waverley CC
Portland, Oregon
Jack Moffett
Waverley CC (R)
Oregon
A. Vernon Macan

Waverley CC (R)
Oregon
H. Chandler Egan
Waverley CC (R. 1)
Oregon
Robert Muir Graves
Waverley GC (A. 9)
Iowa
Dick Phelps
Waverley GC (R. 9)
Iowa
Dick Phelps
Wawasee GC
Syracuse, Indiana
Tom Bendelow
Wawasee GC (R. 9)
Indiana
William H. Diddel
Wawasee GC (A. 9)
Indiana
William H. Diddel
Wawashkamo GC
Mackinac Island, Michigan
Alex Smith
Wawashkamo GC (R)
Michigan
Frank Dufina
Wawenock GC
Damariscotta, Maine
Wayne Stiles, John Van Kleek
Wawona Hotel GC
Yosemite, California
Harold Sampson
Wawonowin GC
Ishpeming, Michigan
Tom Bendelow
Wayland CC (R)
Massachusetts
William F. Mitchell
Wayne CC
Nebraska
Henry B. Hughes, Richard
  Watson
Wayne CC NLE
New Jersey
Robert Trent Jones
Wayne CC
Lyons, New York
Edward Lawrence Packard, Brent
  Wadsworth
Wayne CC (A. 9)
New York
Edward Lawrence Packard
Wayne G Centre
New Jersey
Nicholas Psiahas
Wayne Public GC
Bothel, Washington
Al Smith
Waynesboro CC
Georgia
George W. Cobb
Waynesboro CC (A. 9)
Georgia
George W. Cobb, John LaFoy
Waynesboro CC
Mississippi
Earl Stone
Waynesboro CC
Pennsylvania
Edmund B. Ault
Waynesborough CC
Paoli, Pennsylvania
George Fazio
Waynesville CC
North Carolina
John Drake
Waynesville CC (R)
North Carolina
Ross Taylor
Wayzata CC
Minnesota
Robert Bruce Harris
Wayzata CC (R)
Minnesota
Geoffrey S. Cornish, Brian Silva
Weatherford GC
Oklahoma
Labron Harris Sr
Weatherwax GC
Middletown, Ohio
Arthur Hills

Webb Brook GC
Burlington, Massachusetts
William F. Mitchell
Webb Hill CC
Wolfe City, Texas
Leon Howard
Weber Park GC
Skokie, Illinois
Ken Killian, Dick Nugent
Webhannett GC
Kennebunkport, Maine
Eugene "Skip" Wogan
Webhannett GC (R. 4)
Maine
Geoffrey S. Cornish, William G.
  Robinson
Wedgefield Plantation GC
North Georgetown, South
  Carolina
J. Porter Gibson
Wedgewood CC
Missouri
Floyd Farley
Wedgewood CC
North Carolina
Edmund B. Ault
Wedgewood CC
Texas
Ron Prichard
Wedgewood G&CC (R)
Florida
Ron Garl
Wedgewood GC
Joliet, Illinois
Edward Lawrence Packard
Wedgewood GC
Allentown, Pennsylvania
William Gordon, David Gordon
Wee Burn CC
Darien, Connecticut
Devereux Emmet
Wee Burn CC (R. 4)
Connecticut
Geoffrey S. Cornish, William G.
  Robinson
Wee-Ma-Tuk Hills CC
Cuba, Illinois
Robert L. Jordan
Weeks Park GC (R.10)
Texas
Jeff Brauer
Weequahic GC
Newark, New Jersey
George Low Sr
Weequahic GC (A. 9)
New Jersey
Hal Purdy
Weidenbruck - Gutersloh GC
West Germany
Bernhard von Limburger
Weir Park GC
Devonshire, England
James Braid
Wekiva GC
Longwood, Florida
Ward Northrup
Welcombe Hotel GC
Stratford-on-Avon, England
T.J.A. McAuley
Weld GC
Massachusetts
Wayne Stiles, John Van Kleek
Welkom Muni
South Africa
Ron Kirby, Gary Player,Denis
  Griffiths
Welland CC
Ontario, Ontario
Walter J. Travis
Wellesley CC
Massachusetts
Donald Ross
Wellesley CC (R. 9)
Massachusetts
Wayne Stiles
Wellesley CC (A. 9)
Massachusetts
Geoffrey S. Cornish
Wellingborough GC
Northhamptonshire, England
Fred W. Hawtree, A.H.F. Jiggens
Wellingborough GC (A. 9)
England
Fred W. Hawtree, Martin
  Hawtree

Wellingborough GC (R)
England
Tom Williamson
Wellingborough GC (R)
England
Fred W. Hawtree, A.H.F. Jiggens
Wellington GC
West Palm Beach, Florida
Ted McAnlis
Wellington GC
New Zealand
J.S. Watson
Wellington Hills GC
Gaylord, Michigan
Bruce Matthews, Jerry Matthews
Wellman CC
Johnsonville, South Carolina
Ellis Maples, Ed Seay
Wells GC
Gloucestershire, England
F.G. Hawtree
Wells Muni
Nevada
Arthur Jack Snyder
Wells-by-the-Sea GC
England
F.G. Hawtree, J.H. Taylor
Wellshire GC
Englewood, Colorado
Donald Ross, Walter Hatch
Welshpool GC
Powys, Wales
James Braid, John R. Stutt
Welwyn Garden City GC
Hertfordshire, England
F.G. Hawtree, J.H. Taylor
Welwyn Garden City GC (R)
England
Fred W. Hawtree, Martin
  Hawtree
Wembley GC
England
Willie Park Jr
Wenawatchee CC (A. 9)
Washington
A. Vernon Macan
Wenham GC (R)
Massachusetts
Orrin Smith, William F. Mitchell
Wentworth GC
Ile Perrot, Quebec
Howard Watson
Wentworth GC (East Course)
Surrey, England
H.S. Colt, C.H. Alison,J.S.F.
  Morrison
Wentworth GC (Short Nine)
Surrey, England
C.K. Cotton, J.J.F. Pennink
Wentworth GC (West Course)
Surrey, England
H.S. Colt, C.H. Alison,J.S.F.
  Morrison
Wentworth Hall GC
Jackson, New Hampshire
Wayne Stiles
Wentworth-by-the-Sea GC
Portsmouth, New Hampshire
Donald Ross
Wentworth-by-the-Sea GC (A. 9)
New Hampshire
Geoffrey S. Cornish, William G.
  Robinson
Wentworth-by-the-Sea GC (R)
New Hampshire
Bill Amick
Wepaug CC (R.13)
Connecticut
Al Zikorus
Wesselman Park GC
Indiana
Edmund B. Ault
West Baden GC (R. 9)
Indiana
Tom Bendelow
West Baden GC (A.18)
Indiana
Tom Bendelow
West Beach GC
Hawaii
Ted Robinson
West Bend CC
Wisconsin
William B. Langford, Theodore J.
  Moreau

West Bend CC (A. 9)
Wisconsin
David Gill
West Bend CC (R)
Wisconsin
Roger Packard
West Boggs Muni
Lakeview, Indiana
Brian Ault, Edmund B. Ault
West Branch GC
Michigan
William Newcomb
West Delta Park GC
Portland, Oregon
Robert Trent Jones, Robert Trent
  Jones Jr,Gary Roger Baird
West End CC
New Orleans, Louisiana
Tom Bendelow
West End GC
Gainesville, Florida
John E. O'Connor
West Herts GC
Hertfordshire, England
Old Tom Morris
West Herts GC (R)
England
Harry Vardon
West Herts GC (R)
England
Alister Mackenzie
West Hill CC
Camillus, New York
Hal Purdy
West Hills CC
Canton, Ohio
Leonard Macomber
West Hills Muni NLE
Portland, Oregon
H. Chandler Egan
West Hove GC
Sussex, England
James Braid
West Kent GC
Kent, England
Herbert Fowler, J.F. Abercromby
West Lake CC
Augusta, Georgia
Ellis Maples, Ed Seay
West Lakes GC
Boca Raton, Florida
Frank Batto
West Lancashire GC (R)
England
Fred W. Hawtree
West Lancashire GC (R)
England
C.K. Cotton
West Lothian GC
Bo'ness, Scotland
Willie Park
West Lothian GC (A. 9)
Scotland
Fraser Middleton
West Malling GC
Kent, England
Max Faulkner
West Meadows GC
Englewood, Colorado
Dick Phelps, Brad Benz,Mike
  Poellot
West Meadows GC
Jacksonville, Florida
Sam Caruso
West Middlesex GC
Middlesex, England
Willie Park
West Middlesex GC (A. 9)
England
F.G. Hawtree, J.H. Taylor
West Oak GC
Marietta, Georgia
Arthur Davis
West Orange CC NLE
Oakland, Florida
Tom Bendelow
West Orange GC
Florida
Lloyd Clifton
West Orange Muni NLE
West Caldwell, New Jersey
David S. Hunter

West Ottawa GC
Holland, Michigan
Bruce Matthews, Jerry Matthews

West Palm Beach CC NLE
Florida
William B. Langford, Theodore J. Moreau

West Palm Beach CC
Florida
Dick Wilson

West Plains CC
Missouri
Marvin Ferguson

West Point GC
US Military Academy, New York
Robert Trent Jones

West Potomac Park GC
Washington, D.C.
Walter J. Travis, Dr. Walter S. Harban

West Runton GC (R) NLE
England
Tom Williamson

West Sayville GC
New York
William F. Mitchell

West Seattle GC
Seattle, Washington
H. Chandler Egan

West Seattle GC (R)
Washington
Peter Thomson, Michael Wolveridge,Ronald Fream

West Shore CC
Camp Hill, Pennsylvania
George Morris

West Shore CC (A. 9)
Pennsylvania
Jack Norrie, Earl Moyer

West Shore G&CC
Grosse Ile, Michigan
George B. Ferry

West Surrey GC NLE
Surrey, England
Herbert Fowler

West Sussex GC
Sussex, England
Sir Guy Campbell, C.K. Hutchison,S.V. Hotchkin

West Village GC
Aurora, Illinois
Dave Bennett

West Wilmette Illuminated GC
Wilmette, Illinois
Joseph A. Roseman

West Wiltshire GC (R)
England
J.H. Taylor

West Wiltshire GC (R)
England
Brian Huggett, Neil Coles,*Roger Dyer*

West Winds GC
George AFB, California
Bob Baldock

Westborough CC
Kirkwood, Missouri
Tom Bendelow

Westbrook CC
Great River, New York
Willie Dunn Jr

Westbrook Village CC
Peoria, Arizona
Ted Robinson

Westchester CC (South Course)
Rye, New York
Walter J. Travis

Westchester CC (South Course) (R)
New York
William S. Flynn

Westchester CC (South Course) (R)
New York
Perry Maxwell

Westchester CC (South Course) (R)
New York
Tom Winton

Westchester CC (South Course) (R)
New York
Rees Jones, Keith Evans

Westchester CC (West Course)
Rye, New York
Walter J. Travis

Westchester CC (West Course) (R)
New York
William S. Flynn

Westchester CC (West Course) (R)
New York
Alfred H. Tull

Westchester CC (West Course) (R)
New York
Joseph S. Finger

Westchester CC (West Course) (R)
New York
Rees Jones, Keith Evans

Western Avenue GC
Los Angeles, California
William P. Bell

Western G&CC
Redford, Michigan
Donald Ross

Western G&CC (R)
Michigan
Edward Lawrence Packard

Western G&CC (R)
Michigan
Arthur Hills, Steve Forrest

Western Gailes GC
Ayrshire, Scotland
Willie Park, Willie Park Jr

Western Gailes GC (R. 4)
Scotland
Fred W. Hawtree

Western Greens GC
Wright, Michigan
Mark DeVries

Western Hills CC
Little Rock, Arkansas
Herman Hackbarth

Western Hills G&CC
Chino, California
Harry Rainville

Western Hills GC
Waterbury, Connecticut
William Gordon, David Gordon

Western Hills GC
Cincinnati, Ohio
Tom Bendelow

Western Hills GC (R)
Ohio
William H. Diddel

Western Hills GC
Ft. Worth, Texas
Leon Howard

Western Hills Muni
Hopkinsville, Kentucky
Earl Stone

Western Illinois Univ GC NLE
Macomb, Illinois
Robert Bruce Harris

Western Illinois Univ GC
Macomb, Illinois
Ken Killian, Dick Nugent

Western Maryland GC
Maryland
Edmund B. Ault

Western Michigan Univ GC
Kalamazoo, Michigan
David T. Millar

Western Park GC
Leicester, England
Fred W. Hawtree

Western Row GC
Mason, Ohio
William H. Diddel

Western Turnpike GC
New York
James Thomson

Western Village GC NLE
Tulsa, Oklahoma
Floyd Farley

Western Woods GC
Michigan
Warner Bowen

Westfaelischer GC
Gutersloh, West Germany
Bernhard von Limburger

Westfield CC (R)
Minnesota
Edward Lawrence Packard, Brent Wadsworth

Westfield CC (North Course)
Ohio
Geoffrey S. Cornish, William G. Robinson

Westfield CC (South Course)
Ohio
Nelson Monical

Westfield CC (South Course) (R. 9)
Ohio
Geoffrey S. Cornish, William G. Robinson

Westfield CC (South Course) (A. 9)
Ohio
Geoffrey S. Cornish, William G. Robinson

Westfield G&CC (A. 9)
New Brunswick
Clinton E. Robinson

Westfield G&CC (R. 9)
New Brunswick
Clinton E. Robinson

Westhampton CC
New York
Seth Raynor

Westhampton CC (Oneck Course) NLE
New York
Charles Banks

Westhill GC
Aberdeenshire, Scotland
J.J.F. Pennink, C.D. Lawrie

Westlake Village GC
California
Ted Robinson

Westland Hills GC
Jordan, Utah
William H. Neff

Westland Muni
Michigan
William Newcomb

Westminster GC
Fitchburg, Massachusetts
Manny Francis

Westmoor GC (R. 5)
Wisconsin
William B. Langford

Westmoor GC (R. 9)
Wisconsin
David Gill

Westmoreland CC
Wilmette, Illinois
Joseph A. Roseman

Westmoreland CC (R)
Illinois
Ken Killian, Dick Nugent

Westmoreland CC (R)
Illinois
William B. Langford

Westmoreland CC (R)
Illinois
A.W. Tillinghast

Westmoreland CC (R)
Illinois
William H. Diddel

Westmoreland CC NLE
Verona, Pennsylvania
Emil Loeffler, *John McGlynn*

Westmoreland CC
Export, Pennsylvania
Dick Wilson, X.G. Hassenplug

Westmoreland CC (R)
Pennsylvania
Robert Trent Jones, Frank Duane

Westmoreland CC (A.12)
Pennsylvania
Joseph S. Finger

Westmoreland CC (R)
Pennsylvania
Joseph S. Finger

Westmoreland G&CC
Sedalia, Missouri
Edward Lawrence Packard

Westmount GC (A. 4)
Ontario
Clinton E. Robinson, Robert Moote

Westmount GC (R)
Ontario
Clinton E. Robinson, Robert Moote

Westmount GC (R. 3)
Ontario
Robert Moote, *David Moote*

Weston G&CC
Toronto, Ontario
Willie Park Jr

Weston GC
Massachusetts
Donald Ross

Weston GC (R. 2)
Massachusetts
Geoffrey S. Cornish

Weston GC (R)
Massachusetts
Bob Cupp

Weston-Super-Mare GC
Somerset, England
Tom Dunn

Weston-Super-Mare GC (R)
England
Alister Mackenzie

Westonbirt GC
Gloucestershire, England
Monty Hearn

Westport GC
New York
Tom Winton

Westport GC
Denver, North Carolina
J. Porter Gibson

Westport GC
County Mayo, Ireland
Fred W. Hawtree, Martin Hawtree,A.H.F. Jiggens

Westport GC (R)
Ireland
Eddie Hackett

Westside GC
Firebaugh, California
Bob Baldock

Westview CC
Miami, Florida
Dick Wilson

Westview CC (A. 9)
Florida
Mark Mahannah

Westview CC
Marshfield, Wisconsin
Edward Lawrence Packard

Westview GC (R. 9)
Ontario
Robert Moote, *David Moote*

Westview GC (A. 9)
Ontario
Robert Moote, *David Moote*

Westview GC (R)
Ontario
Robert Moote

Westview Park GC
DuBois, Wyoming
Frank Hummel

Westward Ho CC NLE
Oak Park, Illinois
H.J. Tweedie

Westward Ho CC
Sioux Falls, South Dakota
Edward Lawrence Packard

Westward Ho CC (R. 1)
South Dakota
Dick Nugent, *Bruce Borland*

Westwood CC
St. Louis, Missouri
Harold Paddock

Westwood CC (R)
Missouri
William H. Diddel

Westwood CC (R. 1)
Missouri
Marvin Ferguson

Westwood CC
New Jersey
Horace W. Smith

Westwood CC
Williamsville, New York
William Harries

Westwood CC (R)
New York
Geoffrey S. Cornish

Westwood CC (R)
New York
Robert Moote

Westwood CC
Rocky River, Ohio
C.H. Alison, H.S. Colt

Westwood CC (R)
Ohio
Michael Hurdzan

Westwood CC
Houston, Texas
Ralph Plummer

Westwood CC (A.15)
Texas
Joseph S. Finger

Westwood CC (R. 3)
Texas
Joseph S. Finger

Westwood CC
Vienna, Virginia
Alfred H. Tull

Westwood CC (R)
Virginia
Edmund B. Ault, Brian Ault

Westwood GC
Marietta, Georgia
Charles M. Graves

Westwood GC (A. 9)
Iowa
David Gill

Westwood GC
Staffordshire, England
J. Hamilton Stutt

Westwood Heights GC
Omaha, Nebraska
Harold Glissmann

Westwood Muni
Oklahoma
Floyd Farley

Westwood Park Muni
Norman, Oklahoma
Floyd Farley

Westwood Shores GC
Trinity, Texas
Carlton E. Gipson

Westwoods CC
Farmington, Connecticut
Geoffrey S. Cornish

Wethersfield CC
Connecticut
Robert D. Pryde

Wethersfield CC (R. 9)
Connecticut
Robert J. Ross

Wethersfield CC (A. 9)
Connecticut
Robert J. Ross

Wethersfield CC (R. 1)
Connecticut
Geoffrey S. Cornish, William G. Robinson

Wethersfield CC (R)
Connecticut
Geoffrey S. Cornish, Brian Silva

Wewoka Muni
Oklahoma
Floyd Farley

Wexford GC
Hilton Head Island, South Carolina
Willard Byrd, Clyde Johnston

Wexford GC
County Wexford, Ireland
J. Hamilton Stutt

Wexford GC (A. 9)
Ireland
J. Hamilton Stutt

Wexham Park GC
Berkshire, England
Emil Lawrence

Whaling City CC
New Bedford, Massachusetts
Donald Ross

Whaling City CC (R. 9)
Massachusetts
William F. Mitchell

Whaling City CC (A. 9)
Massachusetts
Samuel Mitchell

Wheatland CC
Wyoming
Frank Hummel

Wheatley GC
Yorkshire, England
Alister Mackenzie

Wheatley GC (R)
England
George Duncan

Wheatley Hills CC (R)
New York
Alfred H. Tull
Wheatley Hills CC (A. 9)
New York
Howard Watson
Wheatley Hills GC (R)
New York
Ted West
Wheatley Hills GC (R)
New York
Devereux Emmet, Alfred H. Tull
Wheeling GC
Illinois
C.D. Wagstaff
Whetstone CC
Marion, Ohio
William F. Mitchell, Richard W.
  LaConte
Whickham GC
England
Tom Dunn
Whiffletree Hill GC
Concord, Michigan
Arthur Young
Whip-poor-will CC
Hudson, New Hampshire
Manny Francis
Whippoorwill CC
Armonk, New York
Donald Ross
Whippoorwill CC (R)
New York
Charles Banks
Whippoorwill CC (R)
New York
Geoffrey S. Cornish, Brian Silva
Whirlpool GC
Niagara Falls, Ontario
Stanley Thompson
Whirlpool GC (R)
Ontario
Clinton E. Robinson
Whiskey Creek GC
Ft. Myers, Florida
William B. Lewis
Whispering Firs GC
McChord AFB, Washington
Bob Baldock
Whispering Hills GC
Conesis, New York
Pete Craig
Whispering Lakes GC
Pompano Beach, Florida
Pat Pattison
Whispering Oaks CC
Ridge Manor, Florida
Hans Schmeisser
Whispering Oaks CC (R. 9)
Florida
Willie Ogg
Whispering Oaks CC (A. 9)
Florida
Willie Ogg
Whispering Palms CC
Rancho Santa Fe, California
Harry Rainville
Whispering Palms CC (A. 9)
California
Harry Rainville, David Rainville
Whispering Willows GC
Livonia, Michigan
Mark DeVries
Whistler Village GC
British Columbia
Arnold Palmer, Ed Seay,Bob
  Walker
Whitby GC (R)
England
J. Hamilton Stutt
White Barn GC
Pleasant View, Utah
Keith Downs
White Bear G&YC
Minnesota
Donald Ross
White Bear G&YC (R. 1)
Minnesota
Don Herfort
White Beeches G&CC
Haworth, New Jersey
Walter J. Travis

White Beeches G&CC (R)
New Jersey
Maurice McCarthy
White Beeches G&CC (R)
New Jersey
Alfred H. Tull
White Beeches G&CC (R)
New Jersey
William F. Mitchell
White Birch Hills GC
Bay City, Michigan
Bruce Matthews
White City VA Hospital GC
Oregon
Bob Baldock
White Cliffs of Plymouth GC
Massachusetts
Karl Litten, Gary Player
White Cliffs GC NLE
Plymouth, Massachusetts
Geoffrey S. Cornish
White Deer CC
Pennsylvania
Kenneth J. Polakowski
White Lake GC
Whitehall, Michigan
E.E. Roberts
White Lake GC (R)
Michigan
Bruce Matthews, Jerry Matthews
White Lakes GC NLE
Topeka, Kansas
Harry Robb
White Manor CC
Malvern, Pennsylvania
William Gordon, David Gordon
White Mountain CC
Pinetop, Arizona
Arthur A. Snyder
White Mountain CC (A. 9)
Arizona
Arthur Jack Snyder
White Mountain Muni
Wyoming
*Donald G. Brauer, Paul S.
  Fjare,Emile Perret*
White Oak GC
Newnan, Georgia
Joe Lee, Rocky Roquemore
White Path CC
Ellijay, Georgia
Willard Byrd
White Pines CC (East Course)
Bensonville, Illinois
Jack Daray
**White Pines CC (East Course)
  (R)**
Illinois
Ken Killian, Dick Nugent
White Pines CC (West Course)
Bensonville, Illinois
Jack Daray
**White Pines CC (West Course)
  (R)**
Illinois
Ken Killian, Dick Nugent
White Pines GC
Ely, Nevada
Bob Baldock
White Plains GC
LaPlata, Maryland
J. Porter Gibson
White Point Beach GC
Hunts Point, Nova Scotia
Donald Ross, Walter Hatch
White Rock CC
Mooresville, Indiana
Henry Culp
White Tract GC
Maryland
Robert L. Elder
White Webbs Muni
Enfield, Middlesex, England
F.G. Hawtree, J.H. Taylor
Whitecraigs GC
Glasgow, Scotland
Willie Fernie
Whiteface Inn & GC
Lake Placid, New York
John Van Kleek
Whitefish GC (A. 9)
Minnesota
Don Herfort

Whitefish Lake GC
Montana
Gregor MacMillan
Whitefish Lake GC (R. 9)
Montana
Gregor MacMillan
Whitefish Lake GC (A. 9)
Montana
Gregor MacMillan
Whitefish Lake GC (A. 9)
Montana
Keith Hellstrom
Whitehaven CC
Tennessee
John W. Frazier
Whitehead GC
County Antrim, Northern Ireland
C.S. Butchart
Whiteman AFB GC
Sedalia, Missouri
Edward Lawrence Packard, Brent
  Wadsworth
Whitemarsh Valley CC
Chestnut Hill, Pennsylvania
George C. Thomas Jr
Whitemarsh Valley CC (R)
Pennsylvania
William S. Flynn
Whitemarsh Valley CC (R)
Pennsylvania
Donald Ross
Whitewater Creek CC
Georgia
Arnold Palmer, Ed Seay
Whitford CC
Downington, Pennsylvania
William Gordon, David Gordon
Whitinsville CC
Massachusetts
Donald Ross, Walter Hatch
Whitlock G&CC
Hudson Heights, Quebec
Willie Park Jr
Whitlock G&CC (A. 9)
Quebec
Howard Watson
Whitlock G&CC (R)
Quebec
Howard Watson
Whitnall GC
Hales Corner, Wisconsin
George Hansen
Whitney Farms CC
Monroe, Connecticut
Hal Purdy, Malcolm Purdy
Whitsand Bay Hotel GC
Cornwall, England
Willie Fernie
Whittier Narrows GC
California
William F. Bell
Wianno CC
Massachusetts
Leonard Biles
Wianno CC (R)
Massachusetts
Donald Ross
Wichita CC
Kansas
William H. Diddel
Wichita Falls CC (R)
Texas
Ralph Plummer
Wichita Falls CC (R. 2)
Texas
Jeff Brauer
Wickenburg CC
Arizona
William F. Bell, William P. Bell
Wickenburg CC (R)
Arizona
Arthur Jack Snyder
Wicker Park GC
Hammond, Indiana
Tom Bendelow
Wicklow GC
County Wicklow, Ireland
Michael Moran
Wicklow GC (R)
Ireland
Eddie Hackett
Widnes Muni
Lancashire, England
Fred W. Hawtree, A.H.F. Jiggens

Widow Maker GC
Spartanburg, South Carolina
Russell Breeden, *Dan Breeden*
Wien GC
Austria
M.C. Noskowski
Wien GC
Vienna, Austria
Willie Park Jr
Wigan GC (R)
England
J.J.F. Pennink
Wigwam CC (R. 9) NLE
Arizona
Arthur Jack Snyder
Wigwam CC (A. 9) NLE
Arizona
Arthur Jack Snyder
Wikiup G&TC
Santa Rosa, California
Clark Glasson
Wilbraham CC
Massachusetts
Willie Ogg
Wilcox Oaks CC
Red Bluff, California
Ben Harmon
Wild Coast Holiday Inn GC
South Africa
Robert Trent Jones Jr, Don Knott
**Wild Dunes G Links (Links
  Course)**
Isle of Palms, South Carolina
Tom Fazio
**Wild Dunes G Links (Yacht
  Harbor Course)**
Isle of Palms, South Carolina
Tom Fazio
Wildcat Cliffs CC
Highlands, North Carolina
George W. Cobb
Wildcat Run CC
Estero, Florida
Arnold Palmer, Ed Seay
Wildcat Run GC
Cobourg, Ontario
Robert Moote
Wildcreek GC
Sparks, Nevada
Dick Phelps, Brad Benz
Wilderness CC
Naples, Florida
Arthur Hills
Wilderness GC
Carp Lake, Michigan
Elmer Dankert
Wilderness GC
Kent, England
James Braid
Wilderness Valley GC
Gaylord, Michigan
Bruce Matthews, Jerry Matthews
Wildewood CC
Columbia, South Carolina
Russell Breeden
Wildflower CC
Grove City, Florida
Lane Marshall
Wildflower CC
Temple, Texas
Leon Howard, *Charles Howard*
Wildwood CC
Louisville, Kentucky
William H. Diddel
Wildwood CC
Riverhead, New York
Frank Duane
Wildwood CC
Raleigh, North Carolina
Gene Hamm
Wildwood CC
Fairfield, Ohio
Ted McAnlis
Wildwood CC (R)
Ohio
Arthur Hills
Wildwood CC
Beaumont, Texas
Leon Howard
Wildwood G&CC
Cape May Court House, New
  Jersey
Wayne Stiles, John Van Kleek

Wildwood GC
Rush, New York
Pete Craig
Wildwood GC (R)
New York
Geoffrey S. Cornish, Brian Silva
Wildwood GC (R. 3)
Ohio
Jack Kidwell, Michael Hurdzan
Wildwood GC
Allison Park, Pennsylvania
Emil Loeffler, *John McGlynn*
Wildwood GC (R)
Pennsylvania
William Gordon, David Gordon
Wildwood Muni
Nebraska
Robert Popp
Wildwood Muni GC (R)
Iowa
Charles Calhoun
Wildwood Park GC
Decatur, Illinois
Edward Lawrence Packard
Wilkes-Barre Muni
Pennsylvania
Geoffrey S. Cornish, William G.
  Robinson
Willamette Valley CC
Canby, Oregon
Shirley Stone
Willard CC
Ohio
Harold Paddock
Willard CC (A. 9)
Ohio
Richard W. LaConte, Ted
  McAnlis
William S. Sahm Muni
Indianapolis, Indiana
Pete Dye, Alice Dye
Williamsburg Colony Inn GC
Virginia
Buddy Loving
Williamsburg CC NLE
Virginia
Fred Findlay
Williamsburg CC
Virginia
William Gordon, David Gordon
Williamsburg G&CC
Kentucky
Robert Thomason
Williamsburg Inn GC NLE
Virginia
Fred Findlay
Williamsport CC (R)
Pennsylvania
A.W. Tillinghast
Williamsport CC (R)
Pennsylvania
David Gordon
Williamston CC
North Carolina
Gene Hamm
Williamwood GC
Glasgow, Scotland
James Braid
Williamwood GC (R)
Scotland
F.G. Hawtree, J.H. Taylor
Willingboro CC
New Jersey
Robert Trent Jones
Willingdon GC (R)
England
J.H. Taylor
Willingdon GC (R)
England
Alister Mackenzie
Williston Muni
North Dakota
Lane Marshall, *Carl Thuesen*
Willow Brook CC (R. 9)
Texas
Joseph S. Finger
Willow Brook CC (A. 9)
Texas
Ralph Plummer
Willow Brook CC (R. 9)
Texas
Ralph Plummer

Willow Brook CC (R)
Texas
Joseph S. Finger
Willow Brook GC
Winter Haven, Florida
David Wallace
Willow Brook GC
Moorestown, Maryland
William Gordon, David Gordon
Willow Creek CC
High Point, North Carolina
Willard Byrd
Willow Creek CC
Sandy, Utah
Henry B. Hughes
Willow Creek CC (R)
Utah
William Howard Neff
Willow Creek CC
Virginia
Charles B. Schalestock
Willow Creek GC (A. 9)
Iowa
Dick Phelps
Willow Creek GC
Rochester, Minnesota
William James Spear
Willow Creek GC
Blowing Rock, North Carolina
Tom Jackson
Willow Creek GC
Spring, Texas
Robert von Hagge, Bruce Devlin
Willow Grove GC
Solon, Ohio
George B. Ferry
Willow Haven CC
Durham, North Carolina
George W. Cobb
Willow Lakes G&CC (Lakewood Course)
Jacksonville, Florida
Fred Bolton
Willow Lakes G&CC (Troon Course)
Jacksonville, Florida
Lloyd Clifton
Willow Lakes GC
Miami, Florida
Charles Mascaro
Willow Metro GC
New Boston, Michigan
William Newcomb
Willow Oaks CC
Richmond, Virginia
William Gordon, David Gordon
Willow Park CC
Calgary, Alberta
Norman H. Woods
Willow Park GC
Castro Valley, California
Bob Baldock, Robert L. Baldock
Willow Point G&CC
Alexander City, Alabama
Thomas H. Nicol
Willow Ridge CC formerly known as Green Meadow CC
Port Chester, New York
Maurice McCarthy
Willow Run CC
Denver, Iowa
Gordon Cunningham
Willow Run GC
Alexander, Ohio
Jack Kidwell
Willow Run GC
Boardman, Oregon
Marty Leptich, Dallas Wilson
Willow Springs CC
Morrison, Colorado
Stanley A. Harwood
Willow Springs CC
Missouri
Floyd Farley
Willow Springs CC
Texas
LaVerne Schmidt
Willow Springs G&CC
Roswell, Georgia
Randy Nichols
Willowbend GC
Wichita, Kansas
Jay Morrish, *Tom Weiskopf*

Willowbrook CC
Huntsville, Alabama
Leon Howard
Willowbrook CC
Lakeside, California
Al Pilon
Willowbrook CC
Belle Vernon, Pennsylvania
James Gilmore Harrison
Willowbrook CC
Sun City, Arizona
George Fazio, Tom Fazio, *James Winans, John W. Meeker*
Willowcreek GC
Sun City, Arizona
George Fazio, Tom Fazio, *John W. Meeker*, Greg Nash
Willowdale GC
Scarborough, Maine
Eugene "Skip" Wogan
Willowick CC (R)
Ohio
Donald Ross
Willowick GC
Santa Ana, California
William P. Bell
Willowood CC
Flint, Michigan
Bruce Matthews
Willows GC
Rexford, New York
William F. Mitchell
Willows GC
British Columbia
Bill Maxwell, Bill Mathers, Marge Mathers
Willunga GC (R. 3)
New Zealand
Ronald Fream
Wilmar CC (A. 9)
Minnesota
R. Albert Anderson
Wilmette GC
Illinois
Joseph A. Roseman
Wilmette Park GC
Glenview, Illinois
Joseph A. Roseman
Wilmette Park GC (R)
Illinois
Ken Killian, Dick Nugent
Wilmington CC NLE
Vermont
Ralph Barton
Wilmington CC (North Course)
Greenville, Delaware
Dick Wilson
Wilmington CC (South Course)
Greenville, Delaware
Robert Trent Jones
Wilmington Muni
North Carolina
Donald Ross
Wilmslow GC (R)
England
Tom Simpson
Wilshire CC
Los Angeles, California
Norman Macbeth
Wilson CC
Georgia
Willard Byrd
Wilson GC
Columbus, Ohio
Jack Kidwell
Wilson Lake CC
Maine
Wayne Stiles, John Van Kleek
Wilton Grove CC
New Jersey
A.W. Tillinghast
Wiltwyck CC
Kingston, New York
Robert Trent Jones
Wimbledon Common GC
London, England
Willie Park Jr
Winberie GC
Port Clinton, Ohio
Arnold Palmer, Ed Seay
Winchester CC
Massachusetts
Donald Ross

Winchester CC (R)
Massachusetts
Donald Ross
Winchester G&CC
Virginia
Fred Findlay, *Ben Loving*
Winchester G&CC (R)
Virginia
Edmund B. Ault
Windance G&CC
Gulfport, Mississippi
Mark McCumber
Windber CC
Pennsylvania
James Gilmore Harrison, Ferdinand Garbin
Windbrook GC
Parkville, Missouri
Buss Peele
Windbrook GC (A. 9)
Missouri
Dick Phelps
Windbrook GC (R. 7)
Missouri
Dick Phelps
Windcrest GC
San Antonio, Texas
George Hoffman
Windemere House GC
Ontario
George Cumming
Windermere CC
Florida
Ward Northrup
Windermere G&CC
Edmonton, Alberta
Clinton E. Robinson
Windermere GC
Cumbria, England
George Lowe
Windham CC
New York
Hal Purdy
Winding Brook CC
Valatie, New York
Paul Roth
Winding Creek GC
Zeeland, Michigan
Bruce Matthews, Jerry Matthews
Winding Hollow CC
Columbus, Ohio
Robert Trent Jones
Windmill Hill GC
England
Henry Cotton
Windmill Lakes GC
Cleveland, Ohio
Edmund B. Ault
Windsor Forest CC
Savannah, Georgia
George W. Cobb
Windsor Gardens GC
Denver, Colorado
Henry B. Hughes
Windsor GC
New Zealand
A.R. Blank
Windstar C
Naples, Florida
Tom Fazio
Windward CC
Atlanta, Georgia
Arthur Hills, Steve Forrest, Mike Dasher
Windward Hills G&CC
Guam
William F. Bell
Windyhill GC
Scotland
Henry Cotton
Windyke CC (East Course)
Germantown, Tennessee
John W. Frazier
Windyke CC (West Course)
Germantown, Tennessee
Bill Amick
Winfield CC (R. 9)
Kansas
Dick Metz
Winfield CC (A. 9)
Kansas
Dick Metz

Winfield Dunn GC
Tennessee
Benjamin Wihry
Wing Point G&CC
Bainbridge Island, Washington
William Teufel
Wingate Park CC
Pretoria, South Africa
Arthur Frank Tomsett
Winged Foot GC (East Course)
Mamaroneck, New York
A.W. Tillinghast
Winged Foot GC (West Course)
Mamaroneck, New York
A.W. Tillinghast
Winged Foot GC (West Course) (R)
New York
Robert Trent Jones
Winged Foot GC (West Course) (R. 3)
New York
Dick Wilson
Winged Foot GC (West Course) (R)
New York
George Fazio, Tom Fazio
Winged Pheasant GC
Farmington, New York
Pete Craig
Wingfield Pines GC
Upper St. Clair, Pennsylvania
Dominic Palombo
Winnapaug GC
Westerly, Rhode Island
Donald Ross
Winnapaug GC (A. 9)
Rhode Island
Donald Ross
Winnemucca Muni
Nevada
Bob Baldock
Winnepeg GC
Manitoba
Willie Park Jr
Winnepeg Hunt C
Manitoba
Willie Park Jr
Winnetka Park GC
Illinois
C.D. Wagstaff
Winnetka Park GC (A. 9)
Illinois
William B. Langford
Winnetka Park GC (A.18)
Illinois
C.D. Wagstaff
Winona CC
Minnesota
Ben Knight
Winona CC (A. 9)
Minnesota
Donald G. Brauer, Emile Perret
Winston Lake Park GC
Winston-Salem, North Carolina
Ellis Maples
Winter Hill GC
Berkshire, England
J.J.F. Pennink, C.D. Lawrie
Winter Park GC NLE
Florida
John Duncan Dunn
Winter Pines GC
Winter Park, Florida
Lloyd Clifton
Winter Springs GC formerly known as Big Cypress GC
Florida
Robert von Hagge, Bruce Devlin
Winters Creek GC (R. 9)
Michigan
Bruce Matthews, Jerry Matthews
Winters Run GC
Bel Air, Maryland
Buddy Loving
Winthrop GC (R)
Massachusetts
William F. Mitchell, Al Zikorus
Winton CC
Virginia
Edmund B. Ault
Wiscasset GC
Pennsylvania
Robert White

Wishaw GC
Lanarkshire, Scotland
James Braid
Wittem G&CC
Netherlands
Fred W. Hawtree
Wittenberg GC
East Germany
Karl Hoffmann, Bernhard von Limburger
Woburn G&CC (Duchess Course)
Buckinghamshire, England
J.J.F. Pennink, C.D. Lawrie, D.M.A. Steel
Woburn G&CC (Duke Course)
Buckinghamshire, England
J.J.F. Pennink, C.D. Lawrie
Woking GC
England
Tom Dunn
Wolf Creek CC
Eden, Utah
Mark Dixon Ballif
Wolf Creek G Resort
Ponoka, Alberta
Rod Whitman
Wolf Creek GC
Olathe, Kansas
Marvin Ferguson
Wolf Creek GC
Bluefield, Virginia
Maurice Brackett
Wolf Laurel GC
Mars Hill, North Carolina
William B. Lewis
Wolferts Roost CC
Albany, New York
H.F. Andrews
Wolferts Roost CC (R)
New York
A.W. Tillinghast
Wollaston CC NLE
Massachusetts
George Wright
Wollaston CC
Milton, Massachusetts
George Fazio, Tom Fazio
Wollaston CC (R)
Massachusetts
Wayne Stiles
Wollaston CC (R)
Massachusetts
William F. Mitchell
Wollaton Park GC
Nottinghamshire, England
Tom Williamson
Wolverine GC
Mt. Clemens, Michigan
Bruce Matthews, Jerry Matthews
Wolverine GC (A.27)
Michigan
Jerry Matthews
Women's CC NLE
Waukegan, Illinois
Stanley Pelchar
Women's National G&CC now known as Glen Head CC
Wood Ranch CC
Simi Valley, California
Ted Robinson
Woodbine Downs GC
Toronto, Ontario
Howard Watson
Woodbridge CC
Connecticut
Orrin Smith
Woodbridge CC (R. 1)
Connecticut
Brian Ault
Woodbridge CC
Kings Mountain, North Carolina
J. Porter Gibson
Woodbridge G&CC
Lodi, California
Harold Sampson
Woodbridge G&CC (R)
California
Bert Stamps
Woodbridge G&CC (R)
California
Robert Muir Graves, Damian Pascuzzo

Woodbridge GC
Suffolk, England
Fred W. Hawtree
Woodbridge GC (A. 9)
England
Fred W. Hawtree
Woodbrook GC (A. 2)
Ireland
Fred W. Hawtree, A.H.F.
Jiggens,Martin Hawtree
Woodbrook GC (R)
Ireland
Fred W. Hawtree, Martin
Hawtree,A.H.F. Jiggens
Woodbury CC
New Jersey
Alex Findlay
Woodcote Park GC
Surrey, England
Herbert Fowler
**Woodcreek CC (Brook Hollow
Course)**
Wimberly, Texas
Bruce Littell
**Woodcreek CC (Cypress Creek
Course) NLE**
Wimberley, Texas
Leon Howard
Woodcrest C
Syosset, New York
William F. Mitchell
Woodcrest CC
Cherry Hill, New Jersey
William S. Flynn, Howard
Toomey
Woodcrest CC (R. 1)
New Jersey
Rees Jones
Woodcrest CC (R)
New York
Frank Duane
Woodcrest CC
Grand Prairie, Texas
Don January, Billy Martindale
Woodcrest Par 3 GC
Sarasota, Florida
R. Albert Anderson
Woodenbridge GC (R)
Ireland
Tom Travers
Woodhall Spa GC
Lincolnshire, England
Harry Vardon
Woodhall Spa GC (R)
England
H.S. Colt
Woodhall Spa GC (R)
England
S.V. Hotchkin
Woodhall Spa GC (R)
England
Sir Guy Campbell, C.K.
Hutchison,S.V. Hotchkin
Woodhaven CC
Palm Desert, California
Harold Heers
Woodhaven CC
Bethany, Connecticut
Al Zikorus
Woodhaven CC
Ft. Worth, Texas
Leon Howard
Woodhill CC
Wayzata, Minnesota
Donald Ross
Woodhill CC
Wayzata, Minnesota
Donald Ross
Woodhill CC (R)
Minnesota
Geoffrey S. Cornish, William G.
Robinson
Woodholme CC
Pikesville, Maryland
Herbert Strong
Woodholme CC (R)
Maryland
Edmund B. Ault
Woodlake CC
Lakewood, New Jersey
Edward Lawrence Packard
**Woodlake CC formerly known as
Lake Surf CC**
Vass, North Carolina
Ellis Maples, Ed Seay

Woodlake CC (A. 9)
North Carolina
Dan Maples
Woodlake CC
San Antonio, Texas
Desmond Muirhead
Woodland CC
Newton, Massachusetts
Wayne Stiles
Woodland CC (R)
Massachusetts
Donald Ross
Woodland CC (R)
Massachusetts
Geoffrey S. Cornish
Woodland CC
North Kingston, Rhode Island
Geoffrey S. Cornish
Woodland CC (R)
West Virginia
James Gilmore Harrison
Woodland GC
Carmel, Indiana
William H. Diddel
Woodland GC (R)
Indiana
Gary Kern
Woodland GC (A. 9)
Ohio
Jack Kidwell
Woodland Hills CC
California
William P. Bell
Woodland Hills GC
Nacogdoches, Texas
Don January, Billy Martindale
Woodland Terrace GC
Maine
Burton R. Anderson
Woodlands CC
South Carolina
George W. Cobb, John LaFoy
Woodlands CC (R)
South Carolina
Russell Breeden, *Dan Breeden*
Woodlands CC (East Course)
Tamarac, Florida
Robert von Hagge, Bruce Devlin
Woodlands CC (West Course)
Tamarac, Florida
Robert von Hagge, Bruce Devlin
**Woodlands Inn & CC (East
Course) now known as TPC at
The Woodlands**
**Woodlands Inn & CC (South
Course)**
Texas
Robert von Hagge, Bruce Devlin
**Woodlands Inn & CC (West
Course)**
Texas
Joe Lee
**Woodlands Inn & CC (West
Course) (R)**
Texas
Carlton E. Gipson
Woodlands Manor GC
Sevenoaks, England
F.G. Hawtree, J.H. Taylor
Woodlawn CC
Farmer City, Illinois
Tom Bendelow
Woodlawn CC
Mt. Vernon, Virginia
Russell Roberts
Woodlawn GC
Fort Smith, Arkansas
Larry Campbell
Woodlawn GC
Oklahoma City, Oklahoma
Floyd Farley
Woodley Muni
Los Angeles, California
Ray Goates
Woodmar CC
Hammond, Indiana
Ken Killian, Dick Nugent
Woodmar CC (R. 9)
Indiana
William H. Diddel
Woodmere C
Great Neck, New York
Jack Pirie

Woodmere C (R)
New York
Gil Nicholls
Woodmere C (R)
New York
Robert Trent Jones
Woodmont CC NLE
Bethesda, Maryland
Alfred H. Tull
Woodmont CC
Rockville, Maryland
Alfred H. Tull
Woodmont CC (R)
Maryland
William S. Flynn
Woodmont CC (A. 9)
Maryland
Alfred H. Tull
Woodmont CC (A. 9)
Tennessee
Brian Ault, Edmund B. Ault
Woodmont CC
Milwaukee, Wisconsin
Alex Pirie
Woodmont CC (Cypress Course)
Tamarac, Florida
Robert von Hagge, Bruce Devlin
Woodmont CC (Pines Course)
Tamarac, Florida
Robert von Hagge, Bruce Devlin
Woodmoor CC
Monument, Colorado
Press Maxwell
Woodridge CC (R)
Illinois
Edward Lawrence Packard
Woodruff GC (R)
Illinois
Edward Lawrence Packard
Woods Hole GC
Falmouth, Massachusetts
Tom Winton
Woods Hole GC (R)
Massachusetts
Wayne Stiles
Woodson Bend CC
Burnside, Kentucky
Dave Bennett, John F. Robinson
Woodson Park GC NLE
Oklahoma City, Oklahoma
Arthur Jackson
Woodstock CC
New York
Wayne Stiles
Woodstock CC NLE
Vermont
William H. Tucker
Woodstock CC
Vermont
Robert Trent Jones
Woodstock CC (R)
Vermont
Donald Ross
Woodstock CC (R. 9)
Vermont
Wayne Stiles, John Van Kleek
Woodstock CC (. 9)
Vermont
Wayne Stiles, John Van Kleek
Woodstock CC (R)
Vermont
Robert Trent Jones
Woodstock CC (R)
Vermont
Robert Trent Jones, Roger
Rulewich
Woodstock GC
Indianapolis, Illinois
Tom Bendelow
Woodward Muni
Oklahoma
Bob Dunning
Woodway CC
Darien, Connecticut
Willie Park Jr
Woodway CC (R. 4)
Connecticut
Geoffrey S. Cornish, William G.
Robinson
Woodway CC (R)
Connecticut
Maurice McCarthy

Woodway CC (R. 1)
Connecticut
Al Zikorus
Woolacombe Bay Hotel GC
England
F.G. Hawtree, J.H. Taylor
Woonsocket CC (A. 9)
Rhode Island
Geoffrey S. Cornish, Samuel
Mitchell
Wooster CC (A. 9)
Ohio
William Newcomb
Worcester CC
Massachusetts
Donald Ross
Worcester CC (R. 2)
Massachusetts
Geoffrey S. Cornish
Worcester G&CC (R)
England
Alister Mackenzie
Worcestershire GC (A. 9)
England
Fred W. Hawtree, A.H.F. Jiggens
Worcestershire GC (R)
England
Alister Mackenzie
Workington GC
Cumbria, England
James Braid
Worksop GC
Nottinghamshire, England
Tom Williamson
World of Golf (R)
Kentucky
Jack Kidwell, Michael Hurdzan
World of Golf (A.10)
Kentucky
Jack Kidwell, Michael Hurdzan
World of Resorts GC
Lago Vista, Texas
Leon Howard, *Charles Howard*
World Houston GC
Texas
Joseph S. Finger
Worplesdon GC
Surrey, England
J.F. Abercromby
Worplesdon GC (R)
England
Willie Park Jr, J.F. Abercromby
Worplesdon GC (R)
England
H.S. Colt
Worsley GC
Lancashire, England
Fred W. Hawtree, A.H.F. Jiggens
Worsley GC (A. 9)
England
Fred W. Hawtree, A.H.F. Jiggens
Worthing GC (Lower Course)
England
H.S. Colt
Worthing GC (Upper Course)
England
H.S. Colt
Worthington CC
Minnesota
Leo Johnson
Worthington Estate GC NLE
Irvington-on-Hudson, New York
C.C. Worthington
Worthington Hills CC
Ohio
Charles Lorms
Worthington Hills CC (R. 2)
Ohio
Brian Silva, Geoffrey S. Cornish
Wray CC
Colorado
Frank Hummel
Wright-Patterson AFB GC
Dayton, Ohio
William H. Diddel
Wright-Patterson AFB GC (A. 9)
Ohio
Edward Lawrence Packard, Brent
Wadsworth
Wright-Patterson AFB GC (R. 9)
Ohio
Edward Lawrence Packard, Brent
Wadsworth

Wright-Patterson AFB GC (R. 9)
Ohio
Alex McKay
Wright-Patterson AFB GC (A. 9)
Ohio
Alex McKay
Wright-Patterson AFB GC (R. 4)
Ohio
Jack Kidwell
Wrigley Estate GC
Lake Geneva, Wisconsin
William P. Bell
Wuppertal GC
West Germany
Bernhard von Limburger
Wyandot Muni
Worthington, Ohio
Donald Ross
Wyandotte Hills GC
Toivola, Michigan
Wilbert Poyhonen
Wyantenuck GC
Great Barrington, Massachusetts
Robert D. Pryde
Wyantenuck GC (R. 3)
Massachusetts
Charles Banks
Wyaton Hills GC
Illinois
John Darrah
Wyckoff Park GC
Holyoke, Massachusetts
Donald Ross
Wyckoff Park GC
Holyoke, Massachusetts
Al Zikorus
Wykagyl CC
New Rochelle, New York
Lawrence Van Etten
Wykagyl CC (R)
New York
Donald Ross
Wykagyl CC (R)
New York
Robert White
Wykagyl CC (R)
New York
A.W. Tillinghast
Wykagyl CC (R)
New York
Hal Purdy
Wyke Green GC
Middlesex, England
F.G. Hawtree, J.H. Taylor
Wyndemere G&CC
Naples, Florida
Arthur Hills, Steve Forrest
Wyndham Rose Hall GC
Montego Bay, Jamaica
Hal Smedley
Wyndhurst C
Lenox, Massachusetts
Wayne Stiles
Wynding Brook CC (A. 9)
Pennsylvania
Alec Ternyei
Wyndwyck CC
St. Joseph, Michigan
Arthur Hills
Wynlakes CC
Montgomery, Alabama
Joe Lee, Rocky Roquemore
Wyoming CC
Cincinnati, Ohio
Tom Bendelow
Wyoming Valley CC
Wilkes Barre, Pennsylvania
A.W. Tillinghast
Wytheville CC
Virginia
Fred Findlay
Xenia GC (A. 9)
Ohio
Jack Kidwell, Michael Hurdzan
Yacht GC
Florida
Chic Adams
Yadkin CC
Yadkinville, North Carolina
Gene Hamm
Yahata CC
Japan
Kinya Fujita

Yahnundasis GC NLE
Utica, New York
Tom Bendelow
Yahnundasis GC
Utica, New York
Walter J. Travis
Yahnundasis GC (R. 5)
New York
William Gordon, David Gordon
Yakima CC
Washington
A. Vernon Macan
Yakima CC (R. 5)
Washington
Ted Robinson
Yale University GC
New Haven, Connecticut
Charles Blair Macdonald, Seth
  Raynor,Charles Banks
Yamoussoukro GC
Ivory Coast
Pier Mancinelli
Yampa Valley GC
Craig, Colorado
William H. Neff, William Howard
  Neff
Yani GC (R)
Indonesia
Peter Thomson, Michael
  Wolveridge
Yankee Run GC
Ohio
William McMullin, Ben McMullin
Yardley CC
Pennsylvania
Fred Findlay
Yarra Yarra GC
Melbourne, Australia
Alister Mackenzie, Alex Russell
Yarrawonga GC (A. 9)
Australia
Peter Thomson, Michael
  Wolveridge

Yeaman's Hall C
Hanrahah, South Carolina
Seth Raynor
Yellowstone G&CC
Billings, Montana
Robert Trent Jones, Frank Duane
Yellowstone G&CC (R)
Montana
Robert Muir Graves
Yelverton GC
Devon, England
Herbert Fowler
Yolo Fliers C
Woodland, California
Bob Baldock
Yolo Fliers C (A. 9)
California
Michael J. McDonagh
Yomiuri CC
Tokyo, Japan
Seichi Inouye
Yomiuri CC (Blue Course)
Osaka, Japan
Seichi Inouye
Yomiuri CC (Red Course)
Osaka, Japan
Seichi Inouye
Yorba Linda CC
California
Harry Rainville
York Downs CC NLE
Toronto, Ontario
C.H. Alison, H.S. Colt
York Downs CC (R) NLE
Ontario
Stanley Thompson
York Downs G&CC
Toronto, Ontario
Geoffrey S. Cornish, William G.
  Robinson
York G&CC
Maine
Donald Ross

York GC (R)
England
J.H. Taylor
York Temple CC (R. 1)
Ohio
Jack Kidwell, Michael Hurdzan
Yorktown CC (R)
Virginia
William S. Flynn
Yorktown GC
Belleville, Illinois
Pete Dye
Yoro CC
Nagoya, Japan
Peter Thomson, Michael
  Wolveridge
Yosemite Lakes GC
Coarse Gold, California
Bob Baldock, Robert L. Baldock
Youche CC (A. 9)
Indiana
John Darrah
Youche CC (R. 9)
Indiana
John Darrah
Youghal GC (A. 9)
Ireland
John Harris
Youghal GC (R. 9)
Ireland
John Harris
Youghiogheny CC
McKeesport, Pennsylvania
Willie Park Jr
Youghiogheny CC (R. 3)
Pennsylvania
Ferdinand Garbin
Youngstown CC
Ohio
Walter J. Travis
Youngstown CC (R)
Ohio
Donald Ross

Youngstown CC (R)
Ohio
Geoffrey S. Cornish
Yountakah CC NLE
Delawanna, New Jersey
Tom Bendelow
Yountakah CC
Delawanna, New Jersey
Arthur Lockwood
Yowani CC
Australia
Al Howard
Yuma East GC
Arizona
Warner Bowen
Yuma G&CC
Arizona
William F. Bell, William P. Bell
Z. Boaz GC
Fort Worth, Texas
John Bredemus
Z. Boaz GC (R)
Texas
Ralph Plummer
Zahram CC
Lebanon
John Arnold
Zahram GC
Lebanon
John Arnold
Zanesville CC (R)
Ohio
Orrin Smith
Zanesville CC (R. 5)
Ohio
Jack Kidwell, Michael Hurdzan
Zellwood Station CC
Zephyrhills, Florida
William Maddox
Zen CC
Himeji, Japan
Peter Thomson, Michael
  Wolveridge

Zoar Village GC
Ohio
Geoffrey S. Cornish, William G.
  Robinson
Zoate GC
Italy
F. Marmori
Zollner GC
Tri-State University, Indiana
Robert Beard
Zumikon G&CC
Zurich-Zumikon, Switzerland
Tom Simpson
Zumikon G&CC (R)
Switzerland
Donald Harradine
Zumikon G&CC (R)
Switzerland
Tom Williamson
Zuni Mountain GC
Grants, New Mexico
Warren Cantrell
Zur Vahr GC (Garlstedt Course)
Bremen, West Germany
Bernhard von Limburger
Zurich G&CC
Switzerland
Tom Simpson
Zurich-Hittnau G&CC
Switzerland
Bernhard von Limburger
1001 Ranch GC (R)
California
Bob Baldock, Robert L. Baldock
108 Mile Resort GC
Cariboo, British Columbia
Stan Leonard, *Philip Tattersfield*

ARCHITECTS' ASSOCIATIONS

The American Society of Golf Course Architects, founded by thirteen men in 1947, was the first professional organization of course designers in America. Robert Bruce Harris was elected the first president while Donald Ross served as honorary president. An earlier organization, the International Society of Golf Architects, had existed in Great Britain in the 1920s but disbanded during World War II.

Qualifications for membership in the ASGCA included experience (six years on the job) and accomplishment (responsibility for five finished designs). Consequently membership grew slowly. But over the years, the majority of prominent course architects in North America became members.

Critics of the ASGCA claimed it perpetuated only its own membership, not the art or practice of design. Perhaps, like any professional organization, the ASGCA in the beginning did concentrate on membership affairs, and its first few annual meetings were get-togethers at golf resorts for a few days of camaraderie and golf. But by the early 1950's the group was undertaking serious discussions of issues pertinent to course design and issuing public policy statements on some issues.

For example, in 1953 the ASGCA resolved some basic standards for course architecture, favoring strategic design, the placement of hazards to provide minimum interference to high handicap golfers and green bunkering that didn't sacrifice the need for accuracy in the name of easy maintenance. The next year it publicized the membership's opposition to a federal tax on club memberships.

In 1956 the ASGCA stated its opposition to the rapid rise in use of motorized golf carts, feeling they damaged courses, compromised design and maintenance and diminished much of the charm of the game by reducing exercise and companionship. The Society urged the use of golf carts only by those with a medical need. It was a parting shot on a controversy that would last many more years.

Still, despite public positions and promotion of the profession through articles, advertisements, and appearances, the Society remained a once-a-year activity for most members until 1970, the year of E. Lawrence Packard's presidency.

The public relations firm of Selz, Seabolt Inc. of Chicago was retained to conduct fulltime relations for the Society, and one of its staff members was named executive director of the ASGCA. He was Paul Fullmer, a Notre Dame graduate in journalism who happened to be married to the daughter of course architect Percy Clifford. Fullmer, who remained as executive director of the ASGCA throughout the Seventies assisted in the institution of a number of dynamic changes under the direction of Packard and subsequent presidents.

Committees were formed to address the problems and challenges of course design:

• The Foundation Committee under chairman E. L. Packard collected funds to establish a research project directed by Dr. Albert E. Dudek of the University of Florida on the effect of heavy metals in waste water used for irrigation. In 1978 this committee also co-sponsored the first conference on the use of waste water for turfgrass irrigation.

• The Environmental Committee, chaired by Philip Wogan, a graduate biologist, prepared a widely circulated White Paper on the impact of golf courses and their construction on the environment.

• The Design Committee, chaired by Edmund Ault, prepared comprehensive design standards for consideration by members.

• The Professional Development Committee, co-chaired by David Gill and Dr. Michael Hurdzan, organized seminars at annual meetings and devised a limited form of certification for course architects.

• The Hall of Fame Committee, chaired by Roger Rulewich, established a display showing the history of course architecture at the World Golf Hall of Fame in Pinehurst, North Carolina.

• The Awards Committee, chaired by Rees Jones, initiated an annual Donald Ross Award for outstanding contributions to golf and its architecture. Recipients subsequently included Robert Trent Jones, a founding member of the Society; Herbert Warren Wind, noted writer; Herb and Joe Graffis, founders of the National Golf Foundation; Joe Dey, former director of the USGA and PGA tour commissioner; and Gerald H. Micklem, former captain of the Royal and Ancient, president of the English Golf Union and chairman of the Rules Committee of the Royal and Ancient. The award to Micklem was presented at Gleneagles, Scotland, during the Society's pilgrimage in 1980 to Dornoch, the home of Donald Ross. Later recipients included former Ohio Governor James Rhodes; Geoffrey Cornish; USGA agronomist Alexander Radko; entertainer Dinah Shore; golf writer Peter Dobereiner; and PGA Tour Commissioner Deane Beman.

Photograph and Drawing Credits

The photographs of the renowned Brian Morgan, official photographer for a host of British Opens and the 1981 United States Open, and the drawings of the talented course architect and artist William G. Robinson of Vancouver, British Columbia, were a boundless help in illustrating the authors' thoughts. Special thanks are also due to the photographers listed below.

The authors are not unmindful that a number of persons generously provided wonderful illustrations that could not be used because of lack of space. Among these were Janet Seagle of the U.S.G.A., golf architects Robert Muir Graves and Richard Phelps and course superintendents Bruce Cadenelli, Edward Horton, John O'Connell, Tom Rader and Charles Tadge.

Photo Credits

ex-excluding   b-bottom
t-top   l-left
c-center   r-right

ASGCA (Paul Fullmer); 153
Cornish, Carol Burr; 42-43, 50 (t), 51, 54-55, 58-59 (ex bl), 78 (b), 82, 84 (tr), 91 (t), 94, 103 (tr,cr), 106-107 (ex cl, bl), 115 (b), 118 (t), 126-127, 136-137
deGarmo, John; 25 (t,b), 85 (b), 90, 91 (b)
Dickinson, Lawrence S.; 84-85 (t)
Dunn, Mrs. Gordon; 46 (cr)
Hemmer, John (Givens Memorial Library); 58 (bl), 70-71
Hawtree, Fred W.; 114-115 (ex br)
Jones, R. T. (Jones, Rulewich, Hoffman); 22, 96-97, 110-111 (bl)
Kelsey Airviews (Richard C. Kelsey); 34-35
Loft, Mara; 40 (bl), 56-57, 134-135
Mahoney, James; Title Page
Morgan, Brian (Golf Photography Int.); Dust jacket, 6-7, 9, 10-11, 14-15, 17, 18, 23, 24, 26-27, 30-31, 37, 40 (ex bl), 52-53, 62-63, 65, 68-69, 72-73, 75 (t), 80-81, 98-99, 102-103 (ex tr, cr), 110-111 (tc & tr), 118 (b), 122-123, 148-149, 154-155
Robinson, William; 20, 21 (c,b), 29 (t), 83 (tr, r, br), 128-133, 138-147
St. Pierre, Leon; 75 (b)
Silva, Brian; 78 (t), 86-87, 151
Steel, Donald; 19 (b)
Whitten, Ronald; 19 (t), 21 (t), 29 (b), 33, 45, 46 (ex cr), 48, 50 (b), 84 (b), 89, 93, 95, 106 (bl, cl), 109, 110-111 (br), 112-113, 119, 120-121, 124-125

BIBLIOGRAPHY

Bibliography 1

Several are out of print but are obtainable at libraries or through a search.

Allen, Peter. *Play the Best Courses: Great Golf in the British Isles.* London: Stanley Paul, 1973.

Baron, Harry. *Golf Resorts of the U.S.A..* New York: The New American Library, 1967.

Bartlett, Michael, and Roberts, Tony. *The Golf Book.* New York, Arbor House, 1980.

Bauer, Aleck, *Hazards, Those Essential Elements in a Golf Course Without Which the Game Would be Tame and Uninteresting.* Chicago: Toby Rubovitis, 1913.

Braid, James. *Advanced Golf.* London: Methuen, 1908.

Browning, Robert. *A History of Golf.* New York: E. P. Dutton, 1955.

Clark, Robert. *Golf: A Royal and Ancient Game.* London: Macmillan, 1899.

Colt, H. S. and Alison, C. H. *Some Essays on Golf Course Architecture.* New York: Charles Scribner's Sons, 1920.

Colville, George M. *Five Open Champions and the Musselburgh Golf Story.* Musselburgh, Scotland: Colville Books, 1980.

Cornish, G.S., and Robinson, W.G. *Golf Course Design, An Introduction.* Amherst: Cornish-Robinson. Distributed by National Golf Foundation, North Palm Beach, Florida. 1975, Reprinted 1979.

Cotton, Henry. *Henry Cotton's Guide to Golf in the British Isles.* Manchester: Cliveden Press, 1959.

Cousins, Geoffrey. *Golf in Britain.* London: Routledge and Kegan Paul, 1975.

Darwin, Bernard. *James Braid.* London: Hodder and Stoughton, 1952.

Darwin, Bernard. *The Golf Courses of the British Isles.* London: Duckworth & Co., 1910.

Darwin, Bernard; Campbell, Sir Guy; and others. *A History of Golf in Britain.* London: Cassel and Co. Ltd., 1952.

Davis, William H., and Editors of *Golf Digest. Great Golf Courses of the World.* Norwalk, Conn.: Golf Digest, 1974.

Davis, William H. and Editors of *Golf Digest. 100 Greatest Golf Courses And Then Some,* Norwalk, Conn.: Golf Digest, 1982, 1983 (2nd ed.), 1986 (3rd ed.).

Dawe, Alan. *The Golf Courses of British Columbia.* British Columbia: A & J Publishing, 1985.

Dawson, Taylor. *St. Andrews, Cradle of Golf.* London: A. S. Barnes & Co., 1976.

Dobereiner, Peter. *The Glorious World of Golf.* New York: McGraw-Hill,1973.

Evan, Webster. *Encyclopedia of Golf.* New York: St. Martin's Press, 1971.

Everard, H.S.C. *A History of the Royal and Ancient Golf Club, St. Andrews from 1754-1900.* Edinburgh: William Blackwood, 1907.

Ferguson, Dr. Marvin H. *Building Golf Holes for Good Turf Management.* New York: USGA, 1968.

Finger, Joseph S. *The Business End of Building or Rebuilding a Golf Course.* Houston: Joseph S. Finger Assoc., 1972. Distributed by National Golf Foundation, North Palm Beach, Florida.

Gallup, Don & Jim. *Golf Courses of Colorado.* Colorado: Colorado Leisure Sports, 1984.

Gill, Garrett D. *Golf Course Design and Construction Standards.* College Station, Texas: Texas A & M University, 1977.

Graffis, Herb. *Esquire's World of Golf -- What Every Golfer Must Know.* New York: Esquire, Inc. in association with Trident Press, 1933, revised 1965.

Graffis, Herb. *The P.G.A..* New York: Thomas Y. Crowell, 1975.

Grant, Donald. *Donald Ross of Pinehurst and Royal Dornoch.* Golspie, Scotland: The Sutherland Press, 1973.

Grimsley, Will. *Golf—Its History, People & Events.* Englewood Cliffs, N.J.: Prentice-Hall, 1966.

Hamilton, E. A., Preston C., and Laney, A. *Golfing America.* Garden City, New York: Doubleday and Co., Inc., 1958.

Hawtree, Frederick W. *The Golf Course: Planning, Design, Construction & Maintenance.* London: E. & F. N. Spon, 1983.

Henderson, I. T., and Stirk, D. I. *Golf in the Making.* London: Henderson and Stirk, Ltd., 1979.

Huggins, Percy, ed. *The Golfer's Handbook 1971.* Glasgow: The Golfer's Handbook, 1971. Printed annually.

Hunter, Robert. *The Links.* New York, London: Charles Scribner's Sons, 1926.

Hutchinson, Horace G. *Fifty Years of Golf.* New York: Charles Scribner's Sons, 1919.

Hutchinson, Horace G. *Golf.* Badminton Series. London: Longmans, Green & Co., 1895 and other years.

Hutchinson, Horace G. *Golf Greens and Greenkeeping.* London: George Newnes and Country Life, 1906.

Jenkins, Dan. *The Best 18 Golf Holes in America.* New York: Delacorte Press, 1966.

Jones, Rees L., and Rando, Guy L. *Golf Course Developments.* Washington, D.C.: Urban Land Institute Technical Bulletin 70, 1974.

Jones, Robert Tyre. *Golf Is My Game.* Garden City, New York: Doubleday and Co., Inc., 1960.

Kavanagh, L. V. *History of Golf in Canada.* Ontario: Fitzhenry & Whiteside Ltd., 1973.

Low, John L. *Concerning Golf.* London: Hodder and Stoughton Ltd., 1903.

Lyle, Sandy and Ferrier, Bob. *The Championship Courses of Scotland.* Tadworth, Surrey: World's Work Ltd., 1982.

Macdonald, Charles Blair. *Scotland's Gift—Golf.* New York, London: Charles Scribner's Sons, 1928.

Mackenzie, Dr. Alister. *Golf Architecture.* London: Simpkin, Marshall, Hamilton, Kent & Co., Ltd., 1920. Reprinted as *Dr. Mackenzie's Golf Architecture.* Victoria Square, Worchestershire: Grant Books Ltd., 1982.

Mahoney, Jack. *The Golf History of New England.* Farmingham, Mass.: New England Golf, Wellesly Press, Inc., 1973.

Martin, H. B. *Fifty Years of American Golf.* 2nd ed. New York: Argosty- Antiquarian Ltd., 1966.

McCormack, Mark H. *The Wonderful World of Professional Golf.* New York: Atheneum, 1973.

Miller, Dick. *America's Greatest Golfing Resorts.* Indianapolis, N.Y.: Bobbs-Merrill, 1977.

Montague, W.K. *The Golf of Our Fathers.* Grand Rapids, Minnesota: Grand Rapids Herald Review, 1952.

Morris, John and Cobb, Leonard. *Great Golf Holes of New Zealand.* New Zealand: Morris/Cobb Publications, 1971.

Mulvoy, Mark, and Spander, Art. *Golf: The Passion and the Challenge.* New York: Rutledge Books for Prentice Hall, 1977.

Myers, Kent C. *Golf in Oregon.* Portland: Ryder Press, 1977.

Park, William Jr. *The Art of Putting.* Edinburgh: James J. Gray, 1920.

Park, William Jr. *The Game of Golf.* London: Longmans, Green & Co., 1896.

Peper, George. *Golf Courses of the PGA* Tour. New York, Harry F. Abrams, Inc., 1986.

Pennink, J. J. F. *Frank Pennink's Choice of Golf Courses.* London: Adam & Charles Black, 1976.

Pennink, J. J. F. *Golfer's Companion.* London: Cassell, 1962.Pollard, Frank C. *Golf on the Peninsula.* California: Courses & Links, Inc., 1972.

Price, Charles, ed. *The American Golfer.* New York: Random House, 1964.

Price, Charles. *The World of Golf.* New York: Random House, 1962.

Robertson, James K. *St. Andrews -- Home of Golf.* St. Andrews, Fife, Scotland: J. & G Innes, Ltd., 1967.

Robinson, Robby. *Golf Guide to the Caribbean.* Denver: Shannon Golf Publications, 1984.

Ryde, P.; Steel, D. M. A.; and Wind, H. W. *Encyclopedia of Golf*. New York: Viking Press, 1975.

Scharff, Robert, and Editors of Golf Magazine. *Encyclopedia of Golf*. New York: Harper & Row, 1970.

Scharff, Robert and Editors of Golf Magazine. *Great Golf Courses You Can Play*. New York: Charles Scribner's Sons, 1973.

Scott, Tom. *The Concise Dictionary of Golf*. New York: Mayflower Books, 1978.

Scott, Tom, ed. *A. A. Guide to Golf in Great Britain*. London: Octopus Books, 1977.

Simpson, Tom. *The Game of Golf*. Vol. IX. The Lonsdale Library, New York: A. S. Barnes, revised 1952.

Sorenson, Gary L. *The Architecture of Golf*. College Station, Texas: By the Author, Department of Environmental Design, Texas A & M, 1976.

Steel, Donald. *Golf Facts and Feats*. London: Guinnes Superlatives Ltd., 1980.

Steel, Donald. *The Golf Course Guide*. Glasgow, London: Collins with Daily Telegraph, revised 1980.

Steel, Donald; Ryde, Peter; and Wind, Herbert Warren. *The Shell International Encyclopedia of Golf*. London: E. Bury Press and Pelham Books, 1975.

Sutton, Martin H. F., ed. *The Book of the Links*. London: W.H. Smith & Sons, 1912.

Sutton, Martin H. F., ed. *Golf Course Design, Construction and Upkeep*. Reading, England: Sutton and Sons, Ltd., 1950.

Thomas, George C., Jr. *Golf Architecture in America — Its Strategy and Construction*. Los Angeles: The Times-Mirror Press, 1927.

Tufts, Richard S. *The Scottish Invasion*. North Carolina: Pinehurst Publishers, 1962.

Ward-Thomas, Pat. *The Royal and Ancient*. Edinburgh Scottish Academic Press, 1980.

Ward-Thomas, Pat, and others. *The World Atlas of Golf*. New York: Random House, 1976.

Wethered, H. N., and Simpson, T. *The Architectural Side of Golf*. London: Longmans, Green & Co., 1929. (2nd edition, *Design for Golf*, 1952)

Wild, Roland. *Golf, The Loneliest Game*. Vancouver: Mitchell Press, Ltd., 1969.

Wind, Herbert Warren, ed. *The Complete Golfer*. New York: Simon & Schuster, 1954.

Wind, Herbert Warren. *Following Through*. New York: Tickner & Fields, 1985.

Wind, Herbert Warren. *Herbert Warren Wind's Golf Book*. New York: Simon & Schuster, 1971.

Wind, Herbert Warren. *The Story of American Golf*. New York: Alfred A. Knopf, 1948 (1st ed.), 1956 (2nd ed.), 1975 (3rd ed.).

Bibliography 2
Selected Articles in Periodicals

Barkow, Al. "The Course Builders." *Golf*. December, 1970.

Bartlett, Michael. "A Short Look at a Lot of Golf History." *Golf Journal*. January/February, 1977.

Bartlett, Michael. "A Tradition in the Balance." *Golf Journal*. March, 1977.

Brown, Cal. "How to be an Armchair Golf Architect." *Golf Digest*. November/December, 1972.

Brown, Gwilyn S. "Golf's Battling Architects" (Dick Wilson and R. T. Jones). *Sports Illustrated*. July 2, 1962.

Cornish, Geoffrey S. "Golf at the Town Dump." *Parks and Recreation*. May, 1977.

Dann, Mike. "Donald Ross, Giant in Golf." *Golf World*. November 29 and December 6, 1974.

Dunn, Tom. "Random Notes by Tom Dunn." *Professional Golfer*. (Two-part series) April and May, 1969.

Dye, Alice. "Today's Courses are Too Long." *Golf Digest*. May, 1985.

Edmonson, Jolee. "Short Course, Long Future." *Golf Magazine*. February, 1977.

English, John P. "Dorset's Claim as Oldest Club." *Golf Journal*. September, 1965.

Finegan, James. "Emerald Golf — Golf In Ireland." *Golf Journal*. January/February, 1977.

Goodner, Ross. "Joe Lee's Course Designs are Challenging But Fun." *Golf Digest*. February, 1981.

Hannigan, Frank. "Golf's Forgotten Genius" (A. W. Tillinghast). *Golf Journal*. May, 1974.

Harris, Robert Bruce. "The Course Architect." *Golfing*. June, 1962.

Hawtree, Frederick W. "British Golf Course Architecture." *Golf Superintendent*. January, 1975.

Hurdzan, Dr. Michael J. "Defending the Golf Course: It's More Than Just a Game." *Weeds, Trees & Turf*. February, 1986.

Hurdzan, Dr. Michael J. "Designers Forum." *Golf Business*. (Monthly column) 1979, 1980.

Hurdzan, Dr. Michael J. "Evolution of the Modern Green." *PGA Magazine*. (Four-part series) January - April, 1985.

Hurdzan, Dr. Michael J. "So You Want to be a Golf Course Architect." *Golf Business*. March, 1980.

Jenkins, Dan. "The Course that Jack Built." *Sports Illustrated*. October 14, 1974.

Jonah, Kathy. "Is Your Course Designed for Women?" *Golf Digest*. May, 1976.

Jones, Rees. "Hazards." *Golf Magazine*. November, 1978.

Jones, Robert Trent. "The Rise and Fall of Penal Architecture." *Golf Journal*. April, 1974.

Lacerda, John. "He Drives Golfers Crazy on Purpose" (Stanley Thompson). *Saturday Evening Post*. June 8, 1946.

Levy, Joseph. "A Recreation Renaissance." *Parks and Recreation*. December, 1977.

Littler, Frank. "The Sun Never Sets — Golf Around the World." *Golf Journal*. March, 1977.

Packard, E. Lawrence. "Golf Course Design Principles." *Golf Superintendent*. August, 1970.

Palmer, Arnold. "A Good Golf Course Should Challenge the Mind" *Golf Magazine*. May, 1976.

Pearson, David. "You Aren't Playing the Course, You're Playing the Designer." *Esquire*. April, 1969.

Peper, George. "Jack's Other Career." (Jack Nicklaus) *Golf Magazine*. March, 1981.

"Robert Trent Jones." *Golf Magazine*. February, 1976.

Saltzstein, Rob. "Letting Nature Make a Course" (Alister Mackenzie). *Golf Journal*. April, 1977.

Seay, Edwin B. "Master Planning for Golf Course Construction." *Golf Journal*. July, 1977.

Seitz, Nick. "The Changing State of

the Game." *Golf Digest*. June, 1979.

Shecter, Leonard. "The Jones Idea of a Golf Course." (Robert Trent Jones) *The New York Times Magazine*. July 7, 1968.

Silva, Brian. "Donald Ross: A Man of Discovery." *Golf Journal*. May/June, 1985.

Simpson, Tom. "John's Principles of Golf Architecture Stand Up." *Golfdom*. May, 1955. Reprinted from *Golf Monthly*. Edinburgh. Sommers, Robert. "Charles Blair Macdonald." *Golf Journal*. June, 1975.

Tatum, Frank D. Jr. "The Decline of Design." *Golf Journal*. May, 1976.

Weiss, Don. "In the Beginning." *Golf Journal*. March, 1977.

Whitten, Ronald E. "Bringing the Game Down to Earth." *Golf Course Management*. November, 1984.

Whitten, Ronald E. "Design (Courtesy of Mother Nature)." *Golf Course Management*. June, 1985.

Whitten, Ronald E. "Jack Kidwell — Once a Superintendent." *Golf Course Management*. June, 1983.

Whitten, Ronald E. "Minimal Maintenance: Illusion or Vision." (Pete Dye) *Golf Course Management*. September, 1983.

Whitten, Ronald E. "Of Inspiration and Winged Foot." (A. W. Tillinghast) *Golf Course Management*. June, 1984.

Whitten, Ronald E. "The Place of Trees on American Courses Today." *GolfCourse Management*. November, 1985.

Whitten, Ronald E. "Retouching a Masterpiece." (Augusta National) *Golf Course Management*. March, 1983.

Whitten, Ronald E. "Tom Bendelow: A Victim of History." *Golf Journal*. January/February, 1985.

Whitten, Ronald E. "Will the Real Architect Please Stand Up?" (William S. Flynn) *Golf Digest*. June, 1986.

Wind, Herbert Warren. "A Calling for Correct Proportions." *Golf Journal*. July, 1977.

Wind, Herbert Warren. "Austin and Augusta." *The New Yorker*. June 10, 1985.

Wind, Herbert W. "Changing Golf Scene." *Golf Digest*. (Three-part series) March, April and May, 1972.

Wind, Herbert W. "Linksland and Meadowland." *The New Yorker*. August 4, 1951.

Wind, Herbert W. "North to the Links of Dornoch." *The New Yorker*. June 6, 1964.

Wind, Herbert W. "Pete Dye: Improving on Mother Nature." *Golf Digest*. (Two-part series) May and June, 1978.

Wind, Herbert W. "The Masters." *Sports Illustrated*. April 4, 1955.

Wind, Herbert W. "Understanding Golf Course Architecture." *Golf Digest*. (Two-part series) November and December, 1966.

Wind, Herbert W. "Watson, Weather and Muirfield." *The New Yorker*. August 11, 1980.

Bibliography 3
Sources of Related Publications

1. Two periodicals no longer in circulation with which golf architects Max Behr, Walter Travis and A. W. Tillinghast were associated contain articles on course design and can be found in libraries. They are:

American Golfer
Golf Illustrated

2. *National Golf Foundation Publications*. National Golf Foundation, Inc., 200 Castlewood Drive, North Palm Beach, Florida 33408, is the nation's clearinghouse for golf information. The Foundation has many publications on course development, several of which contain historical material.

3. *Golf Development Course*, 3 The Quadrant, Richmond, Surrey England T.W. 91BY, offers services in Great Britain similar to those of the NGF in the United States.

4. *American Society of Golf Course Architects*, 221 North LaSalle Street, Chicago, Illinois 60601, Paul Fullmer, Executive Secretary, distributes publications on golf course development.

5. Bibliographies:

Murdoch, Joseph F. *The Library of Golf* 1743-1966. Detroit: Gale Research Co., 1968. Supplement 1978.

Murdoch, Joseph F., and Seagle, Janet. *Golf, A Guide to Information Sources*. Detroit: Gale Research Co., 1979.

6. *Turfgrass Science*:

Beard, James B. *Turf Management for Golf Courses*. Minneapolis:Burgess Publishing Co., 1982.

Beard, James B. *Turfgrass Science and Culture*. Englewood Cliffs, N.J.: Prentice-Hall, 1973.

Daniel, W. H. and Freeborg, R. P. *Turf Managers Handbook*. Cleveland, Ohio: The Harvest Publishing Co., 1979.

Hanson, A. A. and Juska, F. W., ed. *Turfgrass Science*. Madison, Wisc.: American Society of Agronomy, 1969.

Madison, John H. *Practical Turfgrass Management*. New York: Van Nostrand-Reinhold Co., 1971.

Madison, John H. *Principles of Turfgrass Culture*. New York: Van Nostrand-Reinhold Co., 1971. Musser, Burton H. *Turf Management*. McGraw-Hill, 1950,1962 (2nd ed.).

Piper, C. V. and Oakley, R. A. *Turf for Golf Courses*. New York: The Macmillan Co., 1917, 1929 (2nd ed.).

Turgeon, A. J. *Turfgrass Management*. Reston, Virginia: Reston Publishing Co., 1980.

ACKNOWLEDGMENTS

The authors are gratified by the immense assistance so many persons gave them. It seems almost as though the world of golf yearned to contribute to a history of course architecture, a subject never written on at length before.

Nearly every course architect in North America responded to our requests for information about themselves, as did every colleague we reached in Great Britain, Ireland and on the continent of Europe. Descendants of architects now deceased also responded, as did friends and strangers, golf course superintendents, professional golfers and others in the business world of golf.

Five names stand out as links to the publisher: William G. Robinson, course architect and associate of Cornish for many years, who prepared several of the sketches and urged that the manuscript be prepared; Naomi H. Gillison of West Vancouver, Canada, who persuaded us to persevere; Dr. T. T. Kozlowski of the University of Wisconsin, who persuaded us to find a publisher; Kathryn R. Buckheit of Amherst, Massachusetts, who rearranged many passages and typed the manuscript; and Richard Bartholomae of Manchester, Vermont, who instructed us in the methods of finding a publisher.

We must also remark on the help Cameron Dunn, retired professional of the Carlisle Country Club, Pennsylvania, gave us in providing otherwise unavailable information concerning his ancestors, the Dunns of Musselburgh and Royal Blackheath, who were pioneer designers on both sides of the Atlantic.

Here is a partial list of those whose help we should acknowledge. Included with the list are those members of the ASGCA and the BAGCA who researched material and checked innumerable points for us in addition to furnishing the information on themselves that appears in the biographies and appendix:

J. W. L. Adams, Henley on Thames, England (author of "Willie Park, Jr. and His Family," unpublished paper)
Robert Alves, North Olmstead, Ohio (brother of Grange Alves) William W. Amick, ASGCA
Don B. Austin, Texas A & M University Charles J. Backus, Springfield, Massachusetts
Paul Barratt, CC of New Bedford, Massachusetts
Ted M. Bishop, Phil Harris GC, Indiana
Norman Blackburn, Burbank, California
Richard C. Blake, Woodstock CC, Vermont
Elmer C. Border, El Caballero CC, California
Jean Bryant, director Ralph W. Miller Golf Library, City of Industry, California
Orin E. Burley, Wharton School of Business, Pennsylvania
John Campbell, Foxhill GC, Surrey, England
Elmer O. Cappers, The Country Club, Massachusetts
William P. Carey, Florida State Golf Association
Steven Carlson, San Jose CC, California (the late) Percy Clifford, ASGCA
George M. Colville, Musselburgh, Scotland (author of *5 Open Champions and the Musselburgh Golf Story*)
Martin J. Connelly, Wykagyl CC, New York
Henry Cotton, Penina, Portugal
Sidney T. Cox, Ives Hill CC, New York
John Cronin, Cocheco GC, New Hampshire
Allan J. Cumps, Amherst, Massachusetts
Jack Daray, Jr., El Cajon, California (son of Jack Daray)
J. B. Devany Jr., Allen Park, Michigan
James Diorio, Manchester CC, New Hampshire
Mrs. Gordon Dunn, Lake Placid, New York (daughter-in-law of Seymour Dunn)
Harry C. Eckhoff, National Golf Foundation
Ashton G. Eldredge, Huntington CC, Long Island, New York
William Emerson, Chevy Chase Club, Maryland
Peter Engelhart, Berkeley, California (grandson of Max Behr)
Daniel England, Pittsfield CC, Massachusetts
John English, Eastward Ho! CC, Massachusetts
Gerald Faubel, Saginaw CC, Michigan
David Fearis, CC of Peoria, Illinois G. Ward Fenley, *The Albuquerque* (New Mexico) *Journal*
John Fleming, Olympic CC, California (son of Jack Fleming)
Ronald J. Foulis, Washington, D.C. (son of Robert Foulis)
Paul Fullmer, ASGCA
Mrs. F. Paul Gardner, Indian Wells, California (daughter of George C. Thomas)
Miss Holly Gleason, Shaker Heights, Ohio
David W. Gordon, ASGCA (the late) William F. Gordon, ASGCA
David Gourlay, Thornhill G&CC, Ontario, Canada
Herb Graffis, golf writer and former editor *Golfdom*, Florida (the late) Donald Grant, Royal Dornoch GC, Scotland
Robert Grant, Braeburn CC, Massachusetts
Dr. Fred V. Grau, turfgrass scientist, Maryland
Robert Muir Graves, ASGCA
Bryan G. Griffiths, Great Britain
Harland C. Hackbarth, Ft. Worth, Texas (son of Herman C. Hackbarth)
Joseph Hadwick, CC of Lincoln, Nebraska
Brinley M. Hall, Myopia Hunt Club, Massachusetts
J. Kennedy Hamill, Adventures in Golf, New Hampshire
Robert E. Hanna, Northern California Golf Association
William Harding, Kittansett Club, Massachusetts
John C. Harper II, Pennsylvania State University
Frederick W. Hawtree, BAGCA
Martin Hawtree, BAGCA
C. Thomas Herbert, Riviera CC, California
Bruce Herd, Ft. Myers, Florida
Aimee L. Herpel, University City, Missouri (widow of Homer Herpel)

Cyril Hewertson, O.B.E., Walton Health GC, England
Dr. Thomas K. Hitch, Waialae CC, Hawaii
Arthur R. "Red" Hoffman of R. T. Jones Inc.
Donald Hogan, Seattle, Washington
Edward Horton, Westchester CC, New York
Howard C. Hosmer, Locust Hill CC, New York
Neil S. Hotchkin, Woodhall Spa GC, England (son of S. V. Hotchkin)
Henry B. Hughes, Denver, Colorado
W. D. Hughes, Golf Development Council, England
Dr. Michael Hurdzan, ASGCA (the late) Arthur Jackson, Oklahoma City, Oklahoma
William Johnson, Hanover CC, New Hampshire
A. H. Jolly Jr., San Diego, California
Harvey Junor, Portland GC, Oregon
Jack Kidwell, ASGCA
Ms. M. S. Kinney, Flossmoor CC, Illinois
Mrs. Joseph M. Lagerman, Jr., Pennsylvania (daughter of architect William Flynn)
Thomas Langford, Chicago, Illinois (son of William B. Langford)
William Lansdowne, CC of Scranton, Pennsylvania
John P. LaPoint, National Golf Foundation
Joseph L. Lee, Boynton Beach, Florida
James R. Lefevre, Capilano G&CC, West Vancouver, British Columbia
James Lipe, Ann Arbor, Michigan Bertram Lippincott, Jamestown, Rhode Island
Karl Litten, Miami, Florida
R. F. Loving, ASGCA
Melvin B. Lucas, Piping Rock Club, Long Island, New York
Norman Macbeth Jr., Spring Valley, New York (son of Norman Macbeth)
Neil C. H. Mackenzie, Town Clerk, St. Andrews, Fife, Scotland
H. G. MacPherson, Secretary, Royal Liverpool GC, England
Ted R. Maddock, CC of Pittsfield, Massachusetts
Edward D. Magee Jr., manager, Pine Valley GC, New Jersey
Dan Maples, ASGCA
Palmer Maples, formerly GCSAA
Charles Martineau, Whippoorwill Club, New York
Frank McGuiness, formerly Lake Placid Club, New York
John C. McHose, Esq., Wilshire CC, California
Eleanora F. Miller, Colorado Springs, Colorado (daughter of Robert Foulis)
Robert Miller, Interlachen CC, Minnesota
Philip Mitchell, Edison Club, New York
Harvey Moelter, St. Paul, Minnesota
Hugh Moore Jr., professional, Brunswick CC, Georgia (son of Hugh Moore)
Sherwood Moore, Captains GC, Massachusetts
Rodney A. Morgan, Dartmouth College
George Morris, formerly Colonial CC, Pennsylvania (grandson of George Morris, brother of "Old Tom")
Harold Nathanson, Plymouth CC, Massachusetts
W. H. Neale, Connecticut Golf Association
Gary L. Nelson, Lee Park GC, North Dakota (the late) Jack Neville
Paul J. O'Leary, Ekwanok GC, Vermont
Albert William Olsen, Jr., Hotchkiss School, Connecticut
Warren Orlick, professional, Tam O'Shanter GC, Michigan
A. W. Patterson, Gulph Mills CC, Pennsylvania
David Patterson, Adventures in Golf, England (the late) Ralph Plummer, ASGCA
Tom Rader, formerly Sup't, Shoreacres, Illinois
Alexander M. Radko, USGA Green Section
Fred Reese, Hot Springs G&TC, Virginia
W. H. Richardson, Royal Melbourne GC, Australia
David A. Root, Gary CC, Indiana
Warren Roseman, Glenview, Illinois (Son of Joseph Roseman)
Roger G. Rulewich, ASGCA
Leon St. Pierre, Longmeadow CC, Massachusetts
Chester Sawtelle, Sawtelle Brothers, Massachusetts
Janet Seagle, USGA
Charles H. Seaver, Pebble Beach, California
Edwin B. Seay, ASGCA
Brian Silva, ASGCA
Arthur A. Snyder, retired superintendent Arizona
Jack Snyder, ASGCA
Frank Socash, Elmira CC, New York
D.M.A. Steel, BAGCA (the late) Leonard Strong (brother of Herbert Strong)
Mrs. Leonard Strong, Center Valley, Pennsylvania
J. Hamilton Stutt, BAGCA
E. Clinton Swift Jr., Golf Photography Internation
Frederick Swochuck, Lake Placid Club, New York
George Thompson, Columbia CC, Maryland (the late) Alfred Tull, ASGCA
Lee Tyler, Burlingame, California
Mrs. C. D. Wagstaff, Boca Raton, Florida (widow of C. D. Wagstaff)
Edward Weeks, Myopia Hunt Club, Massachusetts
Gordon Whitaker, British Transport Hotels
Roland Wild, Vancouver Daily Province, British Columbia
Robert Williams, Bob-O-Link GC, Illinois
Katherine Cameron Winton, Bronxville, New York (daughter of Tom Winton)
Philip Wogan, ASGCA
Richard Wynn, Wildwood Park GC, Iowa
Joan Zmistowski, West Palm Beach, Florida (daughter of Wilfrid Reid)

INDEX TO PART I

*(Numbers in Italics Indicate
Illustrations of the Named Subject)*

THE
GOLF
COURSE